Women's Studies

A Recommended Bibliography

THIRD EDITION

Linda A. Krikos and Cindy Ingold

LIBRARIES
UNLIMITED
A Member of the Greenwood Publishing Group

Westport, Connecticut • London

Library of Congress Cataloging-in-Publication Data

Krikos, Linda A.
   Women's studies : a recommended bibliography / Linda A. Krikos and Cindy Ingold.—
3rd ed.
      p. cm.
   Updates: Women's studies : a recommended core bibliography, 1980–1985 / Catherine R.
Loeb, Susan E. Searing, Esther F. Stineman. 1987.
   Includes indexes.
   ISBN 1-56308-566-6
   1. Feminism—Bibliography.   2. Women's studies—Bibliography.   3.
Women—Bibliography.   I. Ingold, Cindy.   II. Loeb, Catherine. Women's studies.   III. Title.
Z7963.F44K75   2004
[HQ1180]
016.30542—   2004040918
British Library Cataloguing in Publication Data is available.

Library of Congress Catalog Card Number: 2004040918
ISBN: 1–56308–566–6

First published in 2004

Libraries Unlimited, 88 Post Road West, Westport, CT 06881
A Member of the Greenwood Publishing Group, Inc.
www.lu.com

Printed in the United States of America

The paper used in this book complies with the
Permanent Paper Standard issued by the National
Information Standards Organization (Z39.48–1984).

10 9 8 7 6 5 4 3 2 1

Contents

PERIODICALS

Foreword

In 1979, Libraries Unlimited published a groundbreaking reference work, *Women's Studies: A Recommended Core Bibliography* by Esther F. Stineman. Stineman, with the assistance of Catherine R. Loeb, compiled a core listing of books and periodicals in women's studies. The bibliography was 670 pages long, with 1,763 entries. At that early stage in the growth of women's studies as an academic field, a mere list of the best titles would have been invaluable to librarians who sought to fill gaps in their collections, but Stineman and Loeb went further. Their insightful annotations charted the impact of feminist thought on the major disciplines and illuminated the exciting intersections of academic and activist perspectives. The bibliography covered English-language titles through mid-1979, including classic and rediscovered works as well as new publications.

Later I collaborated with Esther and Cathy to produce the next bibliographical installment: *Women's Studies: A Recommended Core Bibliography, 1980–1985* (Libraries Unlimited, 1987). Covering a mere five years, that volume was nonetheless a hefty 538 pages long and contained 1,211 annotated entries. We explained in our introduction that scholarly output in women's studies had mushroomed, and we had in fact been "ruthlessly selective."

Imagine, then, the challenge that Linda Krikos and Cindy Ingold faced in compiling the present volume, which covers 1986 to 1999—a time period three times as long as that of the second volume, encompassing years in which women's studies publishing grew to unprecedented proportions and moved from the margins to the mainstream of academia. These wise editors did not undertake the task alone, but instead commissioned chapters by other librarians with knowledge of various facets of women's studies.

Together, these experts have winnowed and described the best printed and Web-based information sources on women and gender. Most helpfully, "best" is broadly defined to include not only well-known works by prominent scholars, but also pathbreaking and provocative titles that push the boundaries of feminist theory and pedagogy.

This bibliography faithfully reflects the shape that the literature of women's studies has assumed since the 1980–1985 installment. In addition to nurturing the new academic fields of women's studies, gender studies, and queer studies, feminist perspectives have infused new ways of thinking into all the disciplines. The placement of subject-specific reference works within the topical chapters, instead of lumping them in the "Reference" chapter as the earlier bibliographies did, recognizes the importance of discipline-grounded research. Complementing this new approach, the "Reference" chapter stands on its own as a thorough guide to overarching, interdisciplinary works.

The inclusion of selected Web sites in each chapter is an important new feature, and the choices emphasize stable, reputable information sources. Within chapters, the selection of titles is admirably balanced. Each chapter illustrates the breadth and depth of the field(s) it covers. Studies of women in many regions and cultures are conscientiously included throughout, as are works that shed light on minority women's lives in the United States. Although core bibliographies inevitably favor wide-ranging surveys and anthologies that present multiple viewpoints, the authors of these chapters do not shy away from recommending worthy books on specialized topics. There are no glaring biases or blind spots, yet each chapter retains the mark of its individual author.

The annotations are, by and large, gems—thorough, readable, appropriately (but not overly) critical. The annotators often suggest the best use for a particular book (e.g., as a course text), note its likely audience, establish the author's credentials, and situate the title within contemporary intellectual debates. Content descriptions are concise and informative. The editors' introduction to the volume does an excellent job of synthesizing a decade and a half of feminist scholarship and summarizing the progress made during the period. Likewise, the brief introductions to each chapter point out the key topics, perspectives, and omissions in specialty areas within women's studies.

I am thrilled to see what a fine successor this volume is to the earlier two. Guided by Linda and Cindy, the contributors have accomplished the Herculean task of sifting the best and most important titles from a mountain of publications. For generations to come, this volume will stand as a lasting and truthful record of the intellectual achievements of women's studies scholars and writers at the end of the twentieth century.

Susan E. Searing
Library and Information Science Librarian
Associate Professor of Library Administration
University of Illinois, Urbana-Champaign

Preface and Acknowledgments

The first volume of *Women's Studies: A Recommended Core Bibliography*, by Esther Stineman with the assistance of Catherine Loeb, appeared in 1979 with much support from the University of Wisconsin. The second volume, published in 1987 with the support of the university and a grant from the National Endowment for the Humanities, added editor Susan Searing, the women's studies librarian for the University of Wisconsin System at the time. The third volume involved two editor/authors, Linda Krikos, head of the Women's Studies Library, Ohio State University, and Cindy Ingold, women and gender resources librarian, University of Illinois at Urbana-Champaign, who collaborated with fourteen librarians and faculty from universities across the United States. Without the variety of subject and interdisciplinary expertise and familiarity with the women's studies literature represented by the contributors and support from their institutions, the project would never have come to fruition.

First, we thank Susan E. Searing, Esther F. Stineman, and Catherine R. Loeb, the pioneers who showed us the way. We thank our representative from Libraries Unlimited, Barbara Ittner, for her patience and continuing belief in the project. The unwavering support and encouragement from our colleagues in the Women's Studies Section of the Association of College and Research Libraries of the American Library Association sustained us throughout the project. We thank them from our hearts.

Linda Krikos thanks Dr. William J. Studer and Ohio State University Libraries' Advisory Committee on Research for granting special research leaves and funds for this project; the Department of Women's Studies for very generous support in the form of graduate research assistants (GRAs); student Ami Chitwood for compiling the appendix; GRAs Sangita Eknath Koparde for gathering reviews and Chrissy Fowler, Jen Kiper and Min Sook Heo for compiling indexes; Linda Bernhard in the Department of Women's Studies and Nursing for reading and making suggestions for the "Medicine and Health" chapter; and colleagues Marti Alt, Lisa Pillow, David Lincove, Cheryl Mason-Middleton, and Akua Bandele for their concern and encouragement. Also warmest thanks to James K. Bracken for his mentorship and to Virginia Reynolds, the extraordinary bibliographic associate of the Women's Studies Library, for her steadfast confidence and myriad contributions to the project. Special, loving thanks go to friends and to Helen and Ted Krikos for their patience, support, and faith. Cindy Ingold thanks all her colleagues and friends at the Pennsylvania State University Libraries who supported her through the long years of this project, especially the people in the Social Sciences Library. Special thanks go to Jane Charles, who provided numerous hours of proofreading and editing, and Doris Herr, who helped format several chapters. At the University of Illinois, special thanks go to Hyon Joo Kim, library technical assistant of the Women and Gender Resources Library; Jenny Shaw, student assistant; and Sue Searing, library and information science librarian. I too give special loving thanks to friends and to Fred and Genie Ingold for their patience, support, and faith.

Introduction

Since the publication of the second volume of *Women's Studies: A Recommended Core Bibliography, 1980–1985* by Catherine Loeb, Susan Searing, and Esther Stineman, the field of women's studies has continued to evolve and change dramatically. The field has expanded beyond the social sciences and humanities to the sciences, mathematics, and technologies, which include information technology, reproductive and other medical technologies, and cyberspace. Women's studies continues to ask new questions, revisit old ones using multiple methodologies borrowed across disciplines to uncover gaps in discipline-based research, and question existing taxonomies, hierarchies, and dichotomies as well as the so-called objectivity of knowledge and the existence of universal, generic experiences. In short, women's studies endeavors to uncover more inclusive, complex, and insightful knowledge(s).

Women's studies programs and courses proliferated during the period covered by this project, a reflection of the desire to develop a separate discipline. By the end of the 1990s at least 700 women's studies programs existed worldwide, including numerous stand-alone master's and a growing number of stand-alone Ph.D. programs. Many programs in the United States achieved full departmental status, giving them independence as tenure-initiating units and more clout in academic politics. As a result of debates around women versus gender, several programs changed their name from women's studies to gender studies to reflect the importance of including men and gender analysis, especially in terms of differences, in women's studies research or to help undermine the women/men binary. Other programs made the same adjustments in their research and curricula but retained the name "women's studies" to highlight their continuing focus on women's lived experiences.

The move toward mainstreaming women's studies within curricula made progress as well. Despite the growth of women's studies programs, many feminist scholars still find themselves attached to other departments, thereby extending women-centered scholarship throughout the academy. Additionally, many colleges and universities integrated gender and race components into their undergraduate curricula both as separate areas of study and within traditional disciplines.

Many women's studies scholars believe that research serves as a form of activism, but nevertheless have renewed their commitment to establishing or improving sometimes strained ties to their communities. Ties with community activism add important perspectives to women's studies research and make research relevant beyond the academy. Internships in community agencies provide excellent opportunities for women's studies students to translate theory to real situations and gain practical work experience. In some instances women's studies programs even developed strategies for introducing gender-related issues to K–12 teachers and students. Other scholars believe that the academic and intellectual components should be separate from the social and political activist movement.

The 1980s and 1990s also witnessed the graduation of the first generation of women's studies students. Many graduates cite the critical thinking, collaborative learning, and especially the connections between course content and debates and issues taking place in the real world as the characteristics that most attracted them to the field. Some even contend that a third wave of feminism started to evolve in the late 1980s. Young women began criticizing some stances of second-wave feminism as too exclusive, impractical, and rigid. They focused attention on issues facing adolescent girls and young women and were concerned with both personal aspirations and broad cultural and social changes. They consider feminism to be a pragmatic and flexible effort and believe that by producing culture through independent music, writing, and art they in fact are changing it. This criticism reflected a change in focus already taking place in the field from women's victimization and oppression to women's agency and power.

This period unfortunately also witnessed what has been termed a backlash against women's studies and feminism both within and outside of the academy. Conservative elements attacked the need for academic programs and roundly criticized feminist social and political agendas. The media spotlighted women scholars who wrote about negative aspects they believe exist in some women's studies programs. Sadly, some programs faced challenges originating in their own universities that questioned the very existence of their programs and dismissed women's studies research and pedagogical techniques.

Backlash has been linked to postfeminism. Critics of postfeminism believe that its concentration on examining cultural forms and language, rather than structural analysis, implies that women's struggles for basic rights are no longer necessary and ignores effects of very real economic, social, sexual, and political constraints on women's lives. Proponents of postfeminism counter that it can be used to correct limitations of the more liberal and modernist perspectives of feminist analysis and that it provides new directions for feminist thought and practice.

In response to criticism from women of color that women's studies and feminism dealt with white, middle-class women's issues, the field became more reflexive and self-critical. Research and curricula began to focus on differences in women's lives resulting from intersections of gender, race, ethnicity, sexuality, class, age, ability, religion, geographic location, and other categories. Many African American women's studies scholars embraced the term "womanism," coined by author Alice Walker, to distinguish and give voice to black feminisms. Critical race feminists examine how and why American society perpetuates racism in its political, legal, and social systems. Using various critical epistemological strategies, they ground their research in material and social realms, thereby challenging the abstract and universal thinking prevalent in Eurocentric discourse. Women of color in various institutions established their own programs, most notably African American women's studies (or womanist studies) and Chicana/Latina studies.

Women in formerly colonized countries in Africa, Asia, and the Caribbean have adapted postcolonial theory to women's concerns. They address questions of "otherness" based on sex as well as race in their research, examining issues such as women's self-representation, nationalism, cultural identity, and language in ways that displace Western knowledge, methods of production, and white feminist assumptions. Scholars around the world have become concerned with the material effects of economic structural adjustment programs and global capitalism on women and children, especially in developing countries. They point out that many programs ignore unequal power relationships between men and women, do not consider women's unpaid labor, and sometimes even undermine indigenous women's rights. Many women's studies programs have responded to international scholarship by incorporating global concerns into their undergraduate and graduate curricula.

Since Western male scholars traditionally have identified women with nature and an immutable, universal, and inferior body, many women's studies scholars have turned their attention to the body, corporeality, and embodiment. They challenge the mind/body binary and question prevailing beliefs about women's relationships with their bodies and the roles assigned to their bodies. In contrast, they theorize a fluid, embodied subjectivity and assert that knowledge cannot be disembodied. Other scholars specifically examine the criminalization or medicalization of women's bodies, women's disability issues, or the ramifications of virtual bodies and multiple identities for women on the Internet.

The development of the Internet revolutionized communication and opened new avenues of research for women's studies scholars. Many cyberfeminists are concerned with issues of access along gender, race, and economic lines. They also examine to what extent the Internet reproduces negative stereotypes found in society. Although researchers find that many stereotypes and much negative behavior toward women do occur, they also point to the potential of the Internet to transform women's lives. Additionally, girls and young women utilize the Internet to create discourse and as a means for wider distribution of their zines and other creative projects.

Other developments, notably poststructuralism, postmodernism, deconstruction, and social constructivism, also challenge value-laden universal, essentialist assumptions of traditional knowledge. Many women's studies scholars working in a variety of disciplines have appropriated, adapted, and contested these developments. They utilize poststructuralism to uncover the important roles that language and representation play in creating sexual differences, and critically explore relationships between power and discourse. They utilize postmodernism to question the usefulness of the category "women" and to examine social relations between the sexes. They use deconstruction to challenge categories, foundational theories, the uncritical acceptance of unexamined experience as objective evidence, and the notion of context-free knowledge. They utilize social constructivism to assert that reality is socially produced, not a reflection of universal givens, and varies across historical settings and cultural locations.

Many women's studies scholars in science studies use one or more of these developments to challenge biological determinism's assumptions about women that ignore pluralities of women's experiences. Some even question the two-sex and two-gender dichotomies, as do activists in the transgender and transsexual movements. Other scholars have contributed concepts, such as situated knowledges and cyborgs, to the field or have experimented with feminist standpoint theory to challenge the so-called objectivity of empiricism.

In the early 1990s queer theory, a political, artistic, intellectual, and interdisciplinary movement, began to evolve. Proponents strove to represent a range of sexualities across gender, race, class, and cultural lines, overcome exclusions connected with the terms "lesbian," "gay," or "les/bi/gay," and separate questions of sexuality from questions of gender. While some feminists and lesbians find queer theory a useful tool, others reject it because it erases lesbian and lesbian feminist agendas dependent upon the notion that sexuality is derived from gender identity. Despite the "disarray" caused by queer theory, institutions established programs in lesbian studies, gay, lesbian, bisexual, transsexual, and transgender studies, or sexuality studies.

The preceding paragraphs provide a very basic and simplified outline of several developments within women's studies. Many titles throughout this bibliography address these issues from various perspectives. For more in-depth information about developments in women's studies, see Marilyn Boxer's *When Women Ask the Questions: Creating Women's Studies in America* (Johns Hopkins University Press, 1998), (see entry 390) Patrice McDermott's *Politics and Scholarship: Feminist Academic Journals and the Production of Knowledge* (University of Illinois Press, 1994), (see entry 401) both annotated in the "Education and Pedagogy" chapter, and the special issue of the journal *Feminist Studies* entitled *Disciplining Feminism? The Future of Women's Studies* (vol. 24, no. 2, Summer 1998).

Scholarship and teaching in the field have influenced every traditional discipline. Discipline-based journals regularly publish women's studies research, and research within other fields seems incomplete if it does not include perspectives that consider gender, race, and ethnicity. We look forward to further development of topics that include transnational feminisms, indigenous women's studies, visual and textual representation and self-representation of women, the state, nationalism, and citizenship, sexuality studies, and more insights and initiatives from women of color within the United States and around the world.

Because of the phenomenal growth in women's studies research, many academic and mainstream publishers embraced the field. Many have developed book series pertaining to various aspects of women, feminism, gender, or lesbianism. They also support interdisciplinary and discipline-based scholarly journals in the field, both in print and online. During the 1990s the number and variety of women's studies reference sources, in print and a variety of electronic formats, increased dramatically, with multivolume encyclopedias and discipline-based or issue-based handbooks and dictionaries becoming more common. Additionally, microform companies began digitizing some of their products or developed new products for the World Wide Web. The number of small feminist presses decreased, but those remaining still often provide forums for new areas of interest, political issues, and alternative perspectives.

The Internet and electronic developments greatly affected women's studies librarianship. The Women's Studies Section of the Association of College and Research Libraries of the American Library Association (ALA) has developed collaborative projects, such as the Core List of Women's Studies Books, Electronic Resources Information and Assessment, Collection Development Resources, and WSSLINKS: Women and Gender Studies Web Sites, designed to serve as resources for those in the field. Listservs enable consultation and discussion with other librarians, and several universities host timesaving metasites leading to extensive information pertinent to women's studies and women's studies librarianship.

This guide provides a survey of titles pertinent to women's studies published between 1986 and 1998, with lists of core titles published in 1999. It is, in essence, a third volume of the bibliographies created by Esther Stineman, Catherine Loeb, and Susan Searing, published in 1979 and 1987. A reference for faculty and students in academic women's studies programs and scholars working in the field, this guide may also be used as a collection development tool in academic and public libraries. Please note that the word "core" has been dropped from the volume's title. As with many other terms the seemingly firm definition of the word has become nebulous, as universal applications of the word have been questioned. Some would argue that definitions of "core" vary by location, context, and time.

Because this edition extends coverage from 1986 into 1998, a span nearly triple that covered by previous editions, and a period in which publishing in this area mushroomed, we faced an overwhelming task in choosing titles to include. According to *New Books on Women and Feminism*, published twice a year by the University of Wisconsin Women's Studies Librarian's Office, more than 35,000 books fall into the pertinent time period.

We realized that three people could not possibly complete a project of this size. We decided that two coeditors would coordinate the work of numerous contributors who agreed to write chapters. Since we did not consider it feasible to examine every title, we started by searching for reviews in women's studies sources, using *Women Studies Abstracts*, also available in the database *Women's Resources International* (now renamed *Women's Studies International*), and the databases *Contemporary Women's Issues* and *GenderWatch*, supplemented by general review sources, such as *Periodicals Abstracts* and *Academic Search Premier*, as well as discipline-based databases such as *America: History and Life* and *Art Abstracts*. This provided us with an idea of the breadth, depth, and shape of the literature as a whole and within each discipline, helping us identify the best-written and the most controversial, groundbreaking, and important titles.

We thoroughly examined each work to determine to what extent it advanced knowledge of women, gender, or feminism; represented women from various races, classes, ethnicities, abilities, sexualities, ages, geographic locations, and the like; and considered various viewpoints, especially about contested or sensitive issues. We also examined bibliographies in each title and in pertinent women's studies reference sources to determine titles that have been consistently cited. In short, we endeavored to select works that represented the multiple developments in the field.

As in the second volume of the bibliography, with a few exceptions, we omitted government documents, reports of organizations, associations, and like bodies, reprints of books, and juvenile and young adult titles, nor did we include every title by prolific authors or every title on major issues. We exclude annotations for special issues of journals but offer an appendix listing special issues published by new and still published older journals from 1986 through 1999 to highlight their often groundbreaking treatments of new topics. Due to the size of the project, we reluctantly decided to also omit poetry, fiction, plays, literary anthologies, titles discussing individuals (with some exceptions), and titles influential in the field that do not specifically address women, gender, or feminism. Highly specialized or narrowly focused titles are excluded as well. Although this volume includes titles published by small women's presses, academic publishers, and mainstream publishers, it contains fewer popular titles than the previous two volumes.

We made several changes in the organization of the bibliography. Instead of arranging chapters in an alphabetical sequence, we moved the "Reference" and "Feminist Theories and Women's Movements" chapters to the front of the book. "Periodicals" remains the final chapter. Other chapters are grouped into three broad areas, social sciences, humanities, and science and technology, to mirror academic divisions. We eliminated the "Language and Linguistic" chapter, incorporating materials on these topics into the new "Communications, Mass Medias, and Language" chapter. The "Communications" chapter also covers film criticism, formerly included in the "Art and Material Culture" chapter (now named "Art, Architecture, Music, and Dance"), mass media and television, formerly included in the "Sociology" chapter, and journalism, formerly included in the "Literature" chapter. Recognizing that sexuality consists of more than the merely physical, we moved titles addressing social aspects of the topic from the "Medicine and Health" chapter to the newly named "Sociology, Social Lives, and Social Issues" chapter.

Titles classed under P (Literature) in the Library of Congress Classification System that examine specific subjects, such as women and war or Chicana identity, and that contain more than literary treatments of the subject will be found in pertinent subject chapters. It is important to note that some contributors disagreed with this decision, but nevertheless complied. Numerous other titles appropriately fit into more than one chapter. We attempted to place titles by the subject content rather than the perspective so that various aspects of the subject would be covered in the same chapter. In many cases, however, titles did not fall neatly into one subject category, and the decision came down to the pragmatics of which chapter could most easily absorb them. We strove for consistency in making these decisions but did not always succeed. It is important to mention that we did not always follow the Library of Congress Classification System (LCCS) because, in our opinion, LCCS does not suit the interdisciplinary nature of women's studies research and sometimes results in inconsistent and occasionally inaccurate classifications.

We also made some adjustments in chapter contents. Since the number of discipline-based reference titles has greatly increased since the last edition was published, each chapter begins with a reference section. Although the book still contains a "Reference" chapter, for the most part it discusses general women's studies sources. "Monographs" sections follow reference sections. We often subdivided "Monographs," especially in longer chapters, to enhance access. To reflect the electronic publishing phenomenon, each chapter concludes with a highly selected annotated list of pertinent electronic/Web sources.

We began this project in 1997 with the intent to produce a lasting record of the best and most influential publications in the field. This necessarily requires some distance in time from the date of publications. After examining well over a decade's worth of titles, we selected those we deemed best and most useful to the discipline. Thus this volume extends coverage of the important work of the previous two editions to the end of the twentieth century.

Notes on Using This Bibliography

ANNOTATIONS

Annotations are based on thorough examinations of each title as well as consideration of its critical reception. We wanted annotations to provide an idea of each book's specific content, its importance or contribution to women's studies, and its relationship to other titles on the subject. Most annotations mention other titles by the same author or on the same subject. The author and title indexes contain entries for all works in the bibliography. Titles published in 1999 are indexed by author and title only. Although scholars and specialists may take issue with our choices and comments, we have, as generalist librarians, done our best to select the core titles for general academic readers. In addition to annotated titles, in each chapter we have included lists of titles published in 1999 to further map coverage and to bridge the guide to works published in the new millennium.

BIBLIOGRAPHIC INFORMATION

The authority for all bibliographic information for print materials is Library of Congress cataloging. We verified entries using OCLC's *WorldCat*. Unlike the previous two volumes, this volume does not include biographical dates for authors.

IN-PRINT, OUT-OF-PRINT, AND REPRINTED WORKS

The print status for each title was verified using *Books in Print*.

We identify out-of-print titles by the abbreviation (OP) at the end of the entry head (or, if applicable, placed to indicate that a hardcover or paperback edition is out of print).

We checked only the edition of the main entry titles that we examined for this project. Subsequent editions or editions published by other companies may well exist and be available for purchase.

Since we intend this bibliography to serve as a reference guide as well as a tool for evaluating and developing library collections, we include out-of-print titles. Because of their historical value, we also include titles, such as statistical sources and directories, that tend to go out of date quickly. Additionally, many online out-of-print dealers that include women's studies titles are easily accessible on the Web, and many titles are readily available in libraries. We generally do not include reprinted titles in this bibliography, but a few are present.

PRICING, ISBN, AND LC NUMBERS

We list ISBNs for both hardback and paperback editions of main entries still in print, using Cataloging-in-Publication or *WorldCat*. We note paperback editions with a "pa" immediately following the ISBN. Due to the time lag involved in compiling the bibliography and the rapid changes in print status, we decided to omit prices. Because the profession no longer relies on LC numbers as search keys, we have also omitted these.

INDEXING

All works included in this supplement are indexed by author, title, and broad subject. The author index uses names as established by the Library of Congress. The title index includes full titles and subtitles.

1 Reference

Linda Friend

In contrast to previous editions, core reference titles will be found throughout this bibliography rather than compiled in a single chapter. Therefore, this chapter has become an interesting collection of general reference sources and worthwhile core and/or significant reference works not covered elsewhere. The most useful secondary sources in the preparation of this chapter included *Women's Studies International*, Sarah Carter and Maureen Ritchie's *Women's Studies: A Guide To Information Sources* (McFarland, 1990), and "Recent Reference Sources in Women's Studies" by Linda Krikos (*Reference Services Review*, Spring 1993, pp. 19–36). The period covered by this bibliography saw the substantial publishing output of a maturing scholarly discipline that also has elements of popular culture interest and attention. The first true gender-based encyclopedias and almanacs appeared. Particularly strong are the areas of language, women's quotations, statistics, chronologies, and almanacs. Refer to the individual topical chapters for more coverage of the significant reference resources, particularly in history, biography, the arts, health, and literature.

Although the large majority of the titles can be considered "core" and have enduring value, other resources have been included occasionally, particularly in cases where this item is the only one available on the topic in this time frame or fits a unique niche. With the advent of the Web, many of the directories are coming to have counterparts or "born-digital" versions of information that was formerly only in print and often difficult to locate. Some of the core titles are currently not in print. Fortunately, Amazon.com and other Web-based sources can now bring libraries and individuals together with out-of-print but still valuable reference titles. Titles in this chapter are organized by reference type into the following categories: "Encyclopedias and Handbooks"; "Indexes and Catalogs"; "Dictionaries and Language Studies"; "Desk Reference and Resource Guides"; "Bibliographies"; "Timelines and Chronologies"; "Almanacs and Related Reference Serials"; "Atlases"; "Statistics, Demography, and Fact Books"; "Directories and Resource Guides" (including subcategories for "Groups and Associations"; "Education/Women's Studies in Higher Education"; and "Financial Opportunities"); and "Periodical Reference Works."

ENCYCLOPEDIAS AND HANDBOOKS

1. Adler, Leonore Loeb, ed. *International Handbook on Gender Roles*. Westport, CT: Greenwood Press, 1993. 525p. bibliog. index. ISBN 0313283362.

This handbook is a good starting point for those unfamiliar with the topic or who want a contemporary overview of another country's gender-role expectations. Thirty-one different nations are included, focusing primarily on Africa, Asia, and Latin America, with chapters on Canada, Mexico and the United States. As in many multiauthored works, the scope and scholarship are uneven, but all the chapters are well written, and many include statistical information. Each chapter is organized around gender roles in infancy/early childhood, school years, young adulthood, adulthood, and old age. Most of the chapters stress the overall philosophies and cultural mores relating to gender of the peoples inhabiting the country, and most include information about childrearing practices, courtship and marriage, schooling, rites of passage, work, relevant legislation, care of the aging, and the like. A very selective bibliography is provided, and each chapter has its own references. Serious students of gender will need to draw on the extensive literature in their areas of study, but this is a good volume for the reference collection in school, public, and academic libraries.

2. Conner, Randy P., David Hatfield Sparks, and Mariya Sparks. *Cassell's Encyclopedia of Queer Myth, Symbol, and Spirit: Gay, Lesbian, Bisexual, and Transgender Lore.* Herndon, VA: Cassell, 1997. 382p. bibliog. index. (OP)

This attractive encyclopedia brings together information in one place that was formerly available only in more general encyclopedias of mythology and spiritual symbolism. The work opens with bibliographic essays, generally of several pages, about each spiritual tradition and its queer aspects: African, ancient Near Eastern, Christian, Islamic, Judaic, Buddhist, Goddess reverence, "Queer Spirit," Wicca, women's spirituality, and so on. Included are a lengthy bibliography and a thematic index. Although illustrations would have added to the work, the text is engaging and the research is generally sound. What other encyclopedic work will have, within a few pages of each other, the poet Adrienne Rich, *The Rocky Horror Picture Show* movie, the Rapunzel fairy tale, and a discussion of female characters in literature named Raven? This volume is recommended as background reading for women's studies courses in spirituality and for libraries that want to provide balanced viewpoints on mythology and symbolism.

3. Hogan, Steve, and Lee Hudson. *Completely Queer: The Gay and Lesbian Encyclopedia.* New York: Henry Holt, 1998. 704p. ISBN 0805036296pa.

In their introduction, the authors report that this reference work grew out of their desire to use the original meaning of "encyclopedia" as a means to "encircle the learning amassed to date on a group of men and women who have chosen, mostly in the West and mostly in the last three decades of the twentieth century, to think of themselves as gay and lesbian" (p. xi). Included are suggestions of how to use the encyclopedia and a fairly extensive index (although subheads for major topics like AIDS, "Out," and lesbian feminism, which have extensive page references, would have added considerably to its usefulness). Entries are wide-ranging and include musicians, authors, photographers, politicians, places, media, sports and leisure, and historical and contemporary events and issues. The volume is enhanced with well-chosen black-and-white photos and includes an annotated historical chronology from 12,000 B.C. to November 1996. The volume was nominated for the 1998 ALA Gay and Lesbian Book Award.

4. McFadden, Margaret, ed. *Women's Issues.* Pasadena, CA: Salem Press, 1997. 3v. 1041p. (Ready Reference). ISBN 0893567655.

The introduction states that the goal of this reference work is to "create an encyclopedia that would address the changing, dynamic nature of women's lives in America" (p. v). Several hundred experts nationwide contributed essays that cover the gamut from breast implants and bra burning to sex stereotypes, witchcraft, and women at war in almost 700 entries. Topics range from reviews in historical context (e.g., *The Silent Scream*, an influential antiabortion film from the 1980s) to thorough coverage of relevant legislation (Title IX). Potentially controversial issues are given highly balanced coverage. There is a good chapter describing women's studies programs in the United States, and the set would be a fine starting point to assist students in choosing research topics. Each of the more lengthy signed articles includes a brief bibliography. Excellent features are the list of keywords ("relevant issues") assigned to each entry (reproductive rights, crime, arts and entertainment) as well as the thorough cross-references. Occasional photos, graphs, charts, and other illustrations enliven the text. The set includes five appendices: chronology of events, selective bibliography, filmography, and indexes both topical and alphabetical. This set is very highly recommended for all levels and types of libraries as a scholarly and readable overview of the major issues for women.

5. Tierney, Helen, ed. *Women's Studies Encyclopedia*. New York: Greenwood Press, 1989–1991. 3v. index. ISBN 0313246467 (set); 0313267251 (v. 1); 031327357X (v. 2); 0313273588 (v. 3). Also available in CD-ROM and online.

In three volumes, Tierney and a large list of contributors deliver a collaborative scholarly approach to the field of women's studies. Volume 1 covers the sciences (including social sciences), volume 2 deals with literature, arts, and learning, and volume 3 develops concepts within history, philosophy, and religion. Locations of articles sometimes seem random; for example, the Equal Rights Amendment appears in the science volume, while the civil rights movement is in history. The work focuses on the American experience almost exclusively and incorporates a variety of feminist perspectives; authors were given the opportunity to express their viewpoints without any overall editorial expectations. Tierney, a professor of history at the University of Wisconsin at Platteville, notes in the introduction that "the articles are meant to convey information to an educated audience without expertise in the subject area of the individual entry. They are not intended for use in research" (p. xvi). As such, the three volumes provide a good introduction to the breadth of women's studies and leave it to other resources to provide the depth. More than one reviewer of this work (as the volumes appeared) noted that the depth of coverage is uneven, but as one of the first works to attempt to provide a broad-based introduction and reference for the entire field of women's studies, it fulfills that purpose. In 1999 a revised and expanded edition was released that contains articles on new subjects, updates old articles, and expands coverage of deserving topics. *Women's Movements of the World: An International Directory and Reference Guide*, edited by Sally Shreir (Longman, 1988), and Lisa Tuttle's *Encyclopedia of Feminism* (Facts on File, 1986) can still be used (although in some areas they are dated) for their information on historical aspects of the feminist movement. The latter title is particularly good for biographical information and its extensive bibliography of titles up to about 1985.

INDEXES AND CATALOGS

6. Brownmiller, Sara, and Ruth Dickstein. *An Index to Women's Studies Anthologies: Research across the Disciplines, 1980–1984*. Boston: G. K. Hall, 1994. 494p. index. ISBN 0816105898.

Much of the richness of women's studies scholarship, research, and contemporary thinking has been published over the years in anthologies and proceedings. Recognizing that a means of easier access to this somewhat "fugitive" literature is important, the authors have accomplished a comprehensive search of the literature for 1980 through 1984. This work indexes almost 500 anthologies in all aspects of women's studies, which they gathered primarily from *New Books on Women and Feminism* (1979–), *Essay and General Literature Index*, and available online catalogs. The work includes author, subject, editor, and keyword indexes and provides the tables of contents and page references from the 474 anthologies. Their volume serves as a complement to the pioneering work of Susan Cardinale, who published an index to women's anthologies of the late 1960s and 1970s as *Anthologies by and about Women: An Analytical Index* (1982). Brownmiller and Dickstein also compiled *An Index to Women's Studies Anthologies: Research Across the Disciplines, 1985–1989* (G. K. Hall, 1996), which completes coverage through the 1980s and mirrors the arrangement and features of the first volume.

7. *Interdisciplinary Bibliographic Guide to Women's Studies, 1997–* . New York: G. K. Hall, 1998. 2v. 1456p. ISBN 0783802781 (set).
   This is one of many similar spin-offs in G. K. Hall's series of bibliographic guides. This one has full bibliographic information for the collected topical holdings, cataloged during a particular year, in the New York Public Library and the Library of Congress, presented in a single alphabetical list of author/title/subject. While this compilation is not an essential item for other than major research collections, access to it will be valuable for individuals developing women's studies collections and for the serious researcher who prefers paper copy to electronic access.

8. Potter, Clare, ed. *The Lesbian Periodicals Index*. Tallahassee, FL: Naiad, 1986. 413p. (OP)
   Starting coverage with the 1947 publication *Vice Versa*, the first known politically oriented lesbian magazine, Potter's index provides who, what, where, and when information for lesbian periodicals ignored by mainstream indexes. The preface, written by Joan Nestle and Deborah Edel, presents a decade-by-decade overview of general trends in lesbian magazine publishing. They also consider this source as "a public communal diary" (p. vi) that traces lesbians' conscious attempts to address issues important to them. The first section provides indexing by author and subjects, such as astrology, blackmail, dancers and dance companies, Japanese lesbians, and rural living. The second section indexes writings (diary and journal entries, humor and satire, stories, and poems), while the third section indexes visual art (cartoons, drawings, photographs, and other work), usually excluded from indexes. Potter notes the number of issues published for each magazine along with standard citation information and provides a directory of libraries and archives that contain lesbian magazines. This index contains valuable information not easily found elsewhere and serves as an important historical and cultural document about lesbian life in the United States from the 1940s into the 1980s.

9. *Women's Studies Index, 1989–* . Boston: G. K. Hall, 1991. 502p. ISBN 0816105103.
   Another spin-off from G. K. Hall that provides in one volume a record of journal articles in this area of study, this work includes indexing of 78 publications, but there is no indication if it is cover-to-cover or selective. *Women Studies Abstracts* indexes the majority of the scholarly journals, and others can be found in other standard periodical indexes, but it can be convenient to find this mix of popular and scholarly coverage in a single place. In 1995 G. K. Hall began producing an alternative electronic format in a five-year accumulation titled *Women's Studies on Disc*.

DICTIONARIES AND LANGUAGE STUDIES

10. Capek, Mary Ellen S., ed. *A Women's Thesaurus: An Index of Language Used to Describe and Locate Information by and about Women*. New York: Harper & Row, 1987. 1052p. bibliog. (OP)
   A Women's Thesaurus was a project of the National Council for Research on Women and contains more than 5,000 individual terms in eleven subject areas. Each entry includes broader,

narrower, and related terms wherever appropriate, as well as the subject group(s) to which it has been assigned. The scope is very broad and the aim is to be inclusive, from "flowers" and "folk music" to "surrogate families" and "sexually transmitted diseases." The volume also includes the marks of a well-constructed thesaurus: a rotated display and a hierarchical display to further explicate the terminology. *Women in LC's Terms: A Thesaurus of Library of Congress Subject Headings Relating to Women* by Ruth Dickstein and others (Oryx Press, 1988) is a complementary work that, in conjunction with *A Women's Thesaurus*, is designed to "complete the identification of women's studies terminology" by gathering all the applicable LC Subject Headings used for women and topics relevant to their lives. The Dickstein volume follows the same subject groupings as *A Women's Thesaurus* and collects subject headings that meet one of the following criteria: gender-specific; issues of interest to women; all medical, health, and sexual terms dealing primarily or exclusively with women; or terms for groups that include women. *Women in LC's Terms* includes an appendix of call numbers assigned to women and related topics.

11. Kerschen, Lois. *American Proverbs about Women: A Reference Guide*. Westport, CT: Greenwood Press, 1998. 200p. bibliog. index. ISBN 0313304424.

Proverbs, defined as the "wisdom of many and the wit of one," are a powerful means of shorthand communication by metaphor, and as part of the world's folklore, the author sees them as an expression of a group's culture and beliefs. She believes that the scholarly study of the folklore of women has been minimal and that many of the proverbs she has identified prove a historically unflattering view of women overall. In her research, the author searched standard and foreign collections to find the origin of American proverbs, and if a country of origin was discovered, she lists it in the category and alphabetical indexes. The book is organized by general topics such as women as property, widows, a women in her house, bad women/virtuous women, and so on. Proverbs cited range from the well known ("Men seldom make passes at girls who wear glasses") to the obscure ("A woman remembers a kiss long after a man has forgotten"). This is a valuable and unique scholarly contribution to the literature of women and language/ communication theory.

12. Maggio, Rosalie, ed. *The New Beacon Book of Quotations by Women*. Boston: Beacon Press, 1998. 844p. bibliog. indexes. ISBN 0807067830.

Maggio, also the author of *The Nonsexist Word Finder*, has created a valuable compendium of quotations organized by topics from ability to zucchini. There are indexes by name, subject, and key line. According to her introduction, about 80 percent of the quotations are unique to this book and appear in no other collection. In her notes, she suggests ways to use the quotations and, of course, not rewrite but adapt or explain the ones that today could be considered sexist or inaccurate. An earlier compilation, Carolyn Warner's *The Last Word: A Treasury of Women's Quotes* (Prentice Hall, 1992), is a useful volume aimed at the public speaker who needs something quick and pithy. She includes historical quotations, but the majority are from contemporary women such as Margaret Thatcher ("I'm extraordinarily patient provided I get my own way in the end") and Sally Ride ("All adventures, especially into new territory, are scary"). *Wit and Wisdom of Famous American Women* (Peter Pauper, 1998), edited by Evelyn Beilenson and Ann L. Tenenbaum, provides similar well-chosen and interesting quotations from various historical periods.

13. Partnow, Elaine, ed. and comp. *The New Quotable Woman*. New York: Facts on File, 1992. 714p. indexes. ISBN 0816021341.

The first *Quotable Woman, 1800–1975* (Corwin Books), was published in 1977. This volume updates and expands Partnow's 1982 work *The Quotable Woman, 1800–1981* (Facts or File, 1982) and its companion publication, *The Quotable Woman: From Eve to 1799* (Facts on File, 1985). In her preface, Partnow describes beginning this work on index cards and the subsequent growth of the volume over sixteen years. Her approach is scholarly and includes references and footnotes where appropriate to identify the context or meaning. Through all the editions, her criteria are: (1) does the quotation have an emotional, spiritual, or intellectual impact? and (2) does it possess either timelessness or pertinent timeliness? The arrangement is chronological, and the coverage of topics is broad and international in scope, not limited to a particular area of feminist thought or women's content. The two-column format makes for easy browsing and reference checking, and the indexes by person, topic, occupation, and ethnicity/nationality are well done and useful.

14. Stibbs, Anne. *Like a Fish Needs a Bicycle*. London: Bloomsbury, 1992. 307p. index. (OP)

This is an interesting and worthwhile book of quotations in that it attempts to chronicle prevailing attitudes toward women through the centuries. The topical chronological section begins with the Book of Genesis and continues through the early 1990s with provocative chapter titles such as "Let Us Have Our Liberty" (p. 14) and "Not Born a Woman" (p. 52). The second section is a single alphabetic index of personal names and topics with quotations relevant to many topics, including abortion, feminism, subjection, and prostitution. This work is international in coverage, and the women quoted include Harriet Beecher Stowe, Naomi Wolfe, Anne Boleyn, Mae West, and Sylvia Plath. It contains keyword and biographical indexes.

DESK REFERENCE AND RESOURCE GUIDES

15. Brennan, Shawn, Julie Winklepleck, Gina Renee Misiroglu, and Marie J. MacNee. *Resourceful Woman*. Detroit: Visible Ink, 1994. 833p. index. (OP)

Resourceful Woman is intended for use as both a reference tool and a browsing item and intersperses excerpts from relevant books and journal articles with photos, sidebar quotations, poetry, and lists of relevant organizations, videos, educational institutions, and other information. The index is fairly thorough in identifying groups and individuals, but considerably less useful for topics (for example, "Abuse" leads to a single page reference even though there is an entire chapter on "Violence against Women"; Under "Violence," again one is directed to a single page). Chapters include aging, the arts, community, education, global issues, health, history, kinship, politics, sexuality, spirituality, sports, violence against women, work, and youth. The choices of material are sound, juxtapositions are graceful, and this volume works very well as an "idea book" and a unique contribution to women's resources literature.

16. Franck, Irene M., and David Brownstone. *The Women's Desk Reference*. New York: Viking/Penguin, 1993. 840p. (OP)

The premise of this reference title is to provide an alphabetical compendium to the entire spectrum of women's concerns, including health, political, psychological, and societal issues. The stated goal is a balanced review of a topic, including any controversial aspects, and emphasis on providing relevance to women of any age or background. Entries are well done but vary greatly in length and complexity; pregnancy has an entry of more than forty pages and genetics has about ten pages of information, while depression rates two pages and marital property is covered in about a page. This volume has a wealth of cross-references that somewhat make up for the lack of an index. For example, looking at "antenuptial agreement" leads one to "prenuptial," where there are additional extended references to cohabitation, divorce and separation, inheritance rights, insurance, and other related entries. This is a recommended reference resource for its breadth and accuracy of information.

17. Rosoff, Ilene. *The WomanSource Catalog and Review: Tools for Connecting the Community of Women*. Berkeley, CA: Celestial Arts, 1996. 504p. ISBN 0890878315pa.

   This volume has the "look" of a counterculture compendium, and indeed a chance-found copy of the old *Whole Earth Catalog* was its inspiration. (An older equivalent for women can be found in the *Women's Almanac*, originally published in 1973 and sporadically since.) Many of the resources Rosoff discusses are found in other bibliographies and reference books, but this volume is valuable for its browsability, chatty reviews and different perspectives, and positive messages for women. Rosoff has unearthed and compiled valuable reference sources such as newsletters for women travelers, information on ecological home design, sexuality, political involvement, the women's Web, and many other topics.

BIBLIOGRAPHIES

18. Amico, Eleanor, ed. *Reader's Guide to Women's Studies*. Chicago and London: Fitzroy Dearborn, 1998. 732p. bibliog. indexes. ISBN 188496477X.

   The editor's goal was to develop bibliographic essays identifying and describing the best books available in English published on more than 500 topics and individuals in women's studies, a discipline she dates from the late 1960s. The majority of the references are relatively current and easily available, but each topic author includes "the best" in her opinion. Contributors, whose credentials are included, were limited to fourteen sources, so this is obviously a selective rather than a comprehensive work. For example, the entry on Cleopatra includes resources from 1914 through 1997, with an explanation of each author's scholarly perspective and the place of the work in the literature available on this individual. The author notes that a number of influential women, such as Jane Addams, Martina Navratilova, Lucretia Mott, and Sandra Day O'Connor, could not be included with their own individual chapters because of the lack of books about them, but they are mentioned in the appropriate topical areas. This is a well-researched encyclopedic reference work and will be especially valuable in undergraduate collections and public libraries.

19. Ashcraft, Donna Musialowski, ed. *Women's Work: A Survey of Scholarship by and about Women*. New York: Haworth Press, 1998. 373p. (Haworth Innovations in Feminist Studies). bibliog. index. ISBN 0789002337.

   This volume was compiled to function as an overview text for a women's studies course but is also valuable for the undergraduate who needs to understand the key concepts of women's studies. Rather than the more common topical approach, it takes its context from women's studies approached through the focus of the disciplines: sociology, geography, business, health, biology, science, psychology, communication, literature, art, anthropology, religion, philosophy, and education. The chapters on gender and communication, women and anthropology, and feminist research are particularly strong. The text includes background sections on women's studies research and theory, and each chapter includes a glossary, discussion questions, and a bibliography.

20. Carter, Sarah, and Maureen Ritchie. *Women's Studies: A Guide to Information Sources*. New York: Mansell; Jefferson, NC: McFarland, 1990. 278p. bibliog. index. (OP)

   This volume is international in scope and could serve as an update and complement to Sue

Searing's *Introduction to Library Research in Women's Studies* (Westview Press, 1985) and Joan Ariel's publication in cooperation with the Association of College and Research Libraries, *Building Women's Studies Collections: A Resource Guide* (Choice, 1987). Brief annotated entries lead the scholar to international information sources, primarily from 1978 through 1988, organized (1) by region (Europe, Asia/the Pacific, North America, and so on), (2) by general resources, and (3) by topical chapters. Some of the sources are also annotated in *Women's Studies: A Recommended Core Bibliography* (Libraries Unlimited, 1987), while others offer unique information such as research reports and collections (e.g., the Women Artists Slide Library in photography). Most of the chapters that are organized by study of a geographic area include general guides, periodicals, organizations, and information about particular countries in the region (Africa includes Botswana, Egypt, Cameroon, Sudan, and so on). The topical chapters cover similar formats and are organized by discipline; "Mind and Body" deals with health and health occupations, reproduction, disability, prostitution, psychology, sexuality, aging, and related subjects. This is an important work in the bibliography of women's studies and is recommended for all research collections. In addition to this attempt at a comprehensive resource on English-language materials for the stated period, a number of guides have been published with information about specific countries. Some of the more noteworthy ones include *Guide to Women's Studies in China* by Gail Hershatter (University of California Press, 1998); *Women's Studies International: Nairobi and Beyond* by Aruno Rao (Feminist Press, 1991), a follow-up to the Women's Studies International meetings in Nairobi in 1985; and *Women's Studies in Western Europe: a Resource Guide* by Stephen Lehmann and Eva Martin Sartori (Association of College and Research Libraries, 1986).

21. Gillon, Margaret. *Lesbians in Print: A Bibliography of 1,500 Books with Synopses.* Irvine, CA: Bluestocking Books, 1995. 478p. indexes. (OP)

    The publisher and editor intend this book as a general guide "that will reflect, nurture, educate, and entertain the Lesbian community" (p. 4). The source is arranged by title (including "a" and "an" but not "the") and includes fiction, nonfiction, and titles aimed at young readers. Citations provide names of author or editor, publisher, price, subject category, date of publication, and ISBN for each title, for the most part accompanied by a brief 25- to 100-word description of the contents. Author, subject (category), and publisher indexes and a directory of feminist, lesbian, and gay bookstores complete the source. The publishers' index provides address, phone, and fax information. The bibliography focuses on books reflecting positive and diverse perspectives and can serve as a useful tool for building or evaluating library collections about lesbians.

22. Loeb, Catherine, Susan E. Searing, and Esther F. Stineman. *Women's Studies: A Recommended Core Bibliography, 1980–1985.* Littleton, CO: Libraries Unlimited, 1987. 538p. index. ISBN 08728747.

    Loeb, Searing, and Stineman provided the next chronological core bibliography for women's studies in 1987, following a similar methodology and approach to Stineman's original work (1979). They note in their introduction that women's studies had changed radically since the first edition, particularly in "its base of scholars . . . and range of inquiry," and observe that women's studies is being both mainstreamed and recognized as a separate discipline (p. xi). In a departure from Stineman's challenge of finding enough books to fill a core collection in 1979, the current editors grappled with an exponential increase in publications and the challenge of selecting a key percentage of them for the volume. The result was more than 1,200 entries in all fields pertaining to women's studies. The volume contains author, title, and subject indexes, including a subject index that expands on Stineman's 1979 original edition, and excellent cross-references. It ultimately presents more than 2,000 reviews from relevant subject areas as well as a brief review of women's studies as a scholarly discipline. This reference resource, which also appeared in an abridged version (1987) of 645 titles designed for use by smaller libraries, will assist in identifying core collections for both public and academic libraries and serves as an annotated record of key works in women's studies for the period. For the 1990s, the American Library Association's Association of College and Research Libraries compiled all the relevant reviews from its review publication, *Choice*, into *Choice Reviews in Women's Studies, 1990–96*, edited by Helen MacLam (1996, Association of College and Research Libraries).

23. Miller, Connie, with Corinne Treitel. *Feminist Research Methods: An Annotated Bibliography*. Westport, CT: Greenwood Press, 1991. 279p. indexes. ISBN 031326029X.

This work is a thoughtful, well-annotated selection of information. Miller notes that her work is somewhat inconsistent with feminist scholarship, which recognizes the interdisciplinary and gray areas over rigid topics, but she chose to organize the work in a way that she felt would make sense to the average user, hence the topical organization into anthropology, psychology, communication, science, and other fields. Each section includes an introduction to the area, and all the citations are extensively annotated. This is a useful volume for understanding faculty research methodology and expectations and has been a significant contribution to the bibliography of research in women's studies. It is recommended for any collections serving researchers in women's studies. A related but older volume is Maggie Humm's *An Annotated Critical Bibliography of Feminist Criticism* (G. K. Hall, 1987).

24. Mumford, Laura Stempel. *Women's Issues: An Annotated Bibliography*. Pasadena, CA: Salem Press, 1989. 163p. (Magill Bibliographies). index. ISBN 0893566543.

This highly selective bibliography, with references mostly from 1982 through 1988, might be useful in small libraries or undergraduate collections where a few selected items on a topic are desirable. Annotations are well done and insightful, and the source includes all the major areas of women's studies and contains a name index. Patricia K. Ballou's second edition of *Women: A Bibliography of Bibliographies* (G. K. Hall, 1986) consists of new titles plus a selective inclusion of still relevant items from the first edition (that have not been superseded) for a total of around 900 sources. She attempts to include mostly in-print items and bases her selections on organization, content, length, scope, and commentary, choosing those with annotations whenever possible. Besides monographs, she references ERIC documents and National Technical Information Services (NTIS) reports, with some additional information from other available databases. Ballou also provides name, title, and subject indexes.

25. Seeley, Charlotte Palmer, comp. *American Women and the U.S. Armed Forces: A Guide to the Records of Military Agencies in the National Archives Relating to American Women*. Rev. by Virginia C. Purdy and Robert Gruber. Washington, DC: National Archives and Records Administration, 1992. 355p. index. ISBN 0911333908.

This is a well-done compilation of records in the National Archives relating to women's roles and activities from the eighteenth through the twentieth centuries, including the families of military personnel. The bulk of the book is an annotated listing of federal records, arranged chronologically, supplemented by material from seven presidential libraries. It contains a thorough index and a list of acronyms. The volume can be used in conjunction with Jonathan Heller's *War & Conflict: Selected Images from the National Archives, 1765–1970* (National Archives Trust Fund Board, 1989), which contains archival photos and other representations from the Revolution to the war in Vietnam.

TIMELINES AND CHRONOLOGIES

26. Brakeman, Lynne, ed. *Chronology of Women Worldwide: People, Places, and Events That Shaped Women's History*. Detroit: Gale Research, 1997. 605p. bibliog. indexes. ISBN 0787601543.

A team of thirty scholars contributed to this textual chronology, which is accented by photos and line drawings. It emphasizes culture, the media, and politics, with some international events. Entries range from a few sentences to a page. The volume includes some interesting appendices, the one on "Myths and Legends" being the most unexpected addition. There is also a forty-page "Documents of History." The selections are interesting and include Abigail Adams's 1776 correspondence promoting the rights of women to her husband, works from Sojourner Truth and Elizabeth Cady Stanton, and the proposed Equal Rights Amendment of 1923 (but nothing from more recent attempts at an amendment to the Constitution). The book's bibliography is too brief to be useful, but there are indexes by name and by day and month and a well-constructed and thorough subject index.

27. Greenspan, Karen. *The Timetables of Women's History: A Chronology of the Most Important People and Events in Women's History*. New York: Simon & Schuster, 1994. 459p. index. ISBN 0671671502.

Greenspan covers much of the same ground as Olsen and Trager (see the next entry), perhaps with a bit more emphasis on cultural matters. The format is different, however. A volume in the publisher's Timetables series, Greenspan's work will be useful to those who prefer their information in a column or table arrangement. A unique feature of this chronology is the approximately 50 brief topical paragraphs (for example, foot binding, women's roles in early modern Europe, and women's roles in modern Islam), albeit unsigned and with no bibliographies. The coverage is international in scope. Many black-and-white photos enliven the text, including a female Russian cosmonaut from the early 1960s, a photo of Helen Keller, and a classic photo of a speakers' panel that included Gloria Steinem, Bella Abzug, Shirley Chisholm, and Betty Friedan.

28. Olsen, Kirstin. *Chronology of Women's History*. Westport, CT: Greenwood Press, 1994. 506p. bibliog. index. ISBN 0313288038.

All chronologies are necessarily selective, but Olsen has managed in approximately 400 pages to provide a viable capsule of important landmarks in international women's history. The volume is refreshingly easy to use and browsable because of the subheads in each time period (up to ten categories, including athletics, performing arts, literature, activism, science, government, religion, and so on) that indicate the place of the event in historical context. It provides a selective bibliography of major reference resources and an extensive index with many cross-references and subheadings. Olsen's *Chronology* is recommended as a core item over James Trager's *The Women's Chronology: A Year by Year Record, from Prehistory to the Present* (Henry Holt, 1994). Trager, uses a series of symbols as his content indicators, but this is the only way a user attempting to work through a topic can find items, and this work is obviously a spin-off of his previous general publication. Irene M. Franck and David M. Brownstone have published two worthwhile reference chronologies, including a recent one, *The Wilson Chronology of Women's Achievements* (H. W. Wilson, 1998), and *Women's World: A Timeline of Women in History* (Harper Perennial, 1995). Both of the latter are particularly appropriate for school and public libraries.

ALMANACS AND RELATED REFERENCE SERIALS

29. *The American Woman*. New York: Norton, 1987– (annual).

This volume contains essays that develop a portrait in time of American women in the context of economics, family, the military, science, media, sports, and reproduction, as well as populations such as black, Latina, and immigrant women. Illustrative tables and figures are included. Each edition is somewhat different in scope and coverage; 1999–2000, published in 1998, includes more up-to-date names for representative groups (Hispanic women, African American women) and chapters on the law, demographics, employment, and elected office. These volumes are always well indexed and include bibliographic references. This series is recommended for all libraries, particularly when used in conjunction with other statistical and contemporary events sources.

30. Schlager, Neil, ed. *St. James Press Gay and Lesbian Almanac*. Detroit: St. James Press, 1998. 680p. bibliog. index. ISBN 1558623582.

The years 1995 and 1996 saw a spike in publishing in the areas of gay/lesbian almanacs and related information. Schlager's volume is significantly superior to others available as a core reference resource in that it is a substantive scholarly reference work with contributors and an advisory board. Unfortunately, this is not the place for a "quick lookup"; the index is less than adequate for the wealth of material contained within the covers and is stronger on individuals than topics. It shares some features with other almanacs in that it is selective rather than comprehensive, but rather than lists and brief entries, we are treated to well-written text. Even the chapter on organizations is textual in its content, discussing the history and founders of each group, including community centers, activist groups, family organizations, and educational/archival organizations nationwide. The "Chronology" chapter is a series of short historical essays beginning with the late 1940s and highlighting selective significant events in politics, the law, health, the military, people of color, and other areas. The concluding bibliography is extremely selective, but each major section has its own list of references. Nevertheless, this volume is recommended for the quality, depth, and breadth of its content and is especially pertinent for undergraduates and public libraries. Occasional black-and-white photos enliven the text.

One of the earliest almanacs specifically for the gay lifestyle was *The Alyson Almanac* (Alyson Publications, 1989, 1993), which resembles *The People's Almanac* in its mixing of trivia and browsing items with truly practical information. A similar but more authoritative work is *The Lesbian Almanac* (Berkley, 1996) compiled by The National Museum and Archive of Lesbian and Gay History in New York City (along with a complementary volume, *The Gay Almanac*, with identical chapter headers and much identical text). While the health information will become dated, many of the organizations and certainly the issues are still valid. Another representative recommended title is *Out in All Directions: The Almanac of Gay and Lesbian America* (Warner Books, 1995). Primarily a browsing item rich with photos and sidebars, it both informs and celebrates. Each item ranges from a paragraph to a few pages and includes interesting trivia (clothing preferences) as well as information with enduring reference value, fortunately accessible via an adequate index (how the rainbow flag came to be, lesbian/gay award winners, a brief history of political activism).

31. Snyder, Paula, ed. *The European Women's Almanac*. New York: Columbia University Press, 1992. 399p. ISBN 0231080646.

This volume provides well-researched, basic statistics and related information on twenty-six European nations, from Iceland in the west to Finland, Romania, and Bulgaria to the east. Each chapter is fifteen to twenty pages in length and includes information on the country's politics, population, size, and culture and a discussion of women's rights and benefits. Unfortunately, some of the textual information is cumulated, with the sources at the end of the section, so it is impossible to know where certain facts came from without consulting all the originals; for example, there is a sidebar in the chapter on Finland indicating that "prostitution is not a crime, though pimping is" (p. 104). Some chapters include relevant excerpts from letters contributed by European women. This is an interesting, eclectic approach to statistics and could be used in conjunction with *Statistical Record of Women Worldwide*, annotated in the "Statistics, Demography, and Fact Books" section later.

32. Zilboorg, Caroline, ed. *Women's Firsts*. Detroit: Gale Research, 1997. 564p. bibliog. indexes. ISBN 0787601519.

This volume is an international collection of information on women who "went first," although more Western women, British, French, and American in particular, are covered than any other nationalities. To access subjects, users must browse the fifteen chapter divisions, which include sports, the military, education, science, religion, and other broad topics. An index by subject would have enhanced the work. Each chapter is chronological, and some of the chapters, such as literature, include women from ancient Greece, twelfth-century France, and 1970s South Africa. "Firsts" range from the political (the first woman prime minister of Turkey, Tansu Ciller, was elected in 1993) (p. 193) to the scientific (Mary Ann Mantell was the first person to discover the tooth of a dinosaur, in 1820) (p. 394). Many black-and-white photos, a brief chronology, a calendar of firsts by day and month, and an alphabetical index that includes place and organization names enhance the volume. Individuals are listed again under the country of origin (for example, 11 Norwegians, 1 Bulgarian, 38 Italians, 4 Nigerians). A complementary work is Phyllis J. Read and Bernard L. Witlieb's *The Book of Women's Firsts: Break-Through Achievements of Almost 100 American Women* (Random House, 1992). As the title indicates, this work limits itself to achievements of women from the United States. Organized alphabetically by name, it also includes photos and supplies a more chatty tone. Entries range from a few sentences to half a page and are very eclectic. One representative page includes the first woman intern, Sarah Dolley (1851), the first woman to be editor in chief of a law review, Mary Donlon (1919), and the first woman executive in major league baseball, Margaret Donahue of the Chicago Cubs (1926) (p. 124). Both resources are difficult to put down as browsing items and can serve inspirational as well as informational needs in reference collections of all types of libraries.

ATLASES

33. Gibson, Anne, and Timothy Fast. *The Women's Atlas of the United States*. New York: Facts on File, 1986. 246p. bibliog. index. ISBN 0816029709.

This atlas and Barbara Gimla Shortridge's *Atlas of American Women* (Macmillan, 1987) cover approximately the same time period and topics and can be alternatives to compilations such as Cynthia Taeuber's *Statistical Handbook on Women in America*, discussed in the next section, for users who prefer their statistics presented graphically. Shortridge has divided her volume into eleven sections, including demography, education, occupations, relationships, family, and politics. Gibson and Fast add more subsections to their table of contents, and the main chapter headings are "Demographics," "Education," "Employment," "Family," "Health," "Crime," and "Politics." Shortridge's maps are more "flat" and scholarly in appearance, while Gibson and Fast's maps often include symbols and are more colorfully presented. Both have brief indexes and selected bibliographies. Shortridge provides a full chapter on sports (high school, college, Olympians, and lifelong sports), while Gibson and Fast do not cover sports or exercise in any detail. Gibson and Fast spend some time discussing data and types of maps, while Shortridge merely includes a brief preface. Gibson and Fast are more creative in their mapping presentation: one fascinating map truncates the United States to show how few states have more men than women (p. 12), and another overlays symbols for men's suicide rates, showing the same statistic for women but using color. Overall, Shortridge provides more textual commentary. While there is inevitable overlap in the coverage of women's statistics, each has merit and uniqueness and stands on its own. If feasible, libraries should include both in their collections. Fast, with Cathy Carroll Fast, compiled a revised edition in 1995 (Facts on File) that adds a chapter covering women's involvement in politics, provides a brief list of suggested readings, and updates statistics from the previous edition. It also contains more maps reflecting race and ethnicity.

34. Seager, Joni, and Ann Olson. *Women in the World: An International Atlas*. New York: Simon & Schuster, 1986. 128p. index. (OP)

Seager and Olson cover forty topical areas and include several pages of colorful maps and charts with brief illuminating text. The authors note their frustration with finding adequate and accessible international data on women, but despite that have developed an absorbing sampling that creates a strong picture of women internationally. Use of multiple resources in developing each chapter provides a check on reliability and accuracy of the data. Information within each individual map page is more extensive than one would expect since there are also overlays of small subcharts or information "snapshots" on each (for example, the legal age for a woman to marry in India is eighteen, but the most common marriage age was nine). The creative map titles provide colorful phrasing for critical women's issues internationally, including "Time Budgets" (do women work longer hours than men?), "Job Ghettoes" (the common jobs women hold), "Bread and Water" (access to nourishment), and so on. Appendices include a table of information by country, several paragraphs of notes on each map topic, and a bibliography. Seager and Olson's slim but informative volume has a second edition titled *The State of Women in the World Atlas* (Penguin, 1997). Both the new and older versions should be retained if the time period covered is appropriate since some data appear in one volume but not in the other, or appear in order to illustrate a different point. A map and concept page relating to lesbians is new to the 1997 edition, and the "Seats of Power" map in the new edition has been considerably strengthened. This atlas is recommended for all types of users from public and K–12 through undergraduates.

STATISTICS, DEMOGRAPHY, AND FACT BOOKS

35. *American Women: Who They Are and How They Live*. Ithaca, NY: New Strategist Publications, 1997. 400p. bibliog. index. ISBN 188507008X.

Compiled by the editors of New Strategist Publications, this volume is a good option for the undergraduate student who wants some basic statistics pertaining to women in America circa 1995. Written to identify aspects of women's lives as a significant consumer group, the book consists chiefly of tables introduced by a provocative or descriptive phrase: "women marry educational equals," "women's occupations differ from men's," "more than one in three births is to a Black, Hispanic, or Asian." Each table identifies the originator and date of the statistics, generally a federal source. This is a nice compendium of basic statistics covering aspects of income, health, family and living status, work life, money, attitudes, and education. For more in-depth information, but still in a compilation, Cynthia Taeuber's *Statistical Handbook on Women in America* (annotated later in this section) can be consulted.

36. Schmittroth, Linda, comp. and ed. *Statistical Record of Women Worldwide*. Detroit: Gale Research, 1991. 763p. ISBN 0810383497.

Although it may be consulted for many of the same statistical trends as Cynthia Taeuber's *Statistical Handbook on Women in America*, this publication is noteworthy for its impressive collection of sources consulted and its emphasis on historical and comparative international statistics where available. There is information on radio listening preferences for women and men from *Mediamark Research Multimedia Audiences Report, Spring 1990* (p. 665), elderly lesbian sexual activity from a *Journal of Homosexuality* article (p. 638), crime rates worldwide by type from *International Crime Statistics, 1981–82* (pp. 66–67), and numbers of women clergy by denomination from *Yearbook of American and Canadian Churches, 1989* (p. 627). The index is reasonably useful, containing entries for specific countries and racial and ethnic groups in the United States, and there is a complete list of sources of the statistics. Schmittroth compiled a second edition in 1995, consisting of 1047 pages, which contains more information gleaned from international opinion polls and statistics, expands coverage of several topics, and adds new subtopics, such as sexual harassment and the economics of sports. Although necessarily selective in content, Schmittroth's volume provides a rich resource of varied statistical data, and her work is recommended for libraries of all types.

37. Taeuber, Cynthia Murray, comp. and ed. *Statistical Handbook on Women in America*. Phoenix: Oryx Press, 1991. 385p. bibliog. index. (OP)

This volume of more than 400 charts and tables is a convenient collection of statistics drawn from U.S. government publications (census data, *Current Population Survey, Vital Statistics*, and others). The origin of the data is referenced on each table, with a convenient accumulation of specific sources, tables, and figures as an appendix. This source contains statistics in all relevant topical areas and covers demography, employment, health, and social characteristics. The author also provides a short glossary of terms. If users take the time to discover it, a particularly nice feature is the introduction to each section, where trends and explanations of the tables appear. A second edition appeared in 1996 with the same title containing about 260 tables and 80 charts. According to the preface (1996), the author indicates that the new edition "is more of a companion than a replacement to the first edition. It updates some tables and charts from the first edition and includes new topics" (p. xxv). This is a true statement. For example, the general statistics on population and immigration drop from eighteen to seven tables in the second edition, while other sections are considerably expanded, for example, a new reproductive health section and more information in the section on health and disability status. The introductions to the sections in the second edition are longer and provide enhanced information on trends. Although the title makes it seem otherwise, Taeuber's compilations of statistics do include some international data as comparators. However, the international information is not very easy to locate in toto since many references in the index say, "See also names of specific countries."

38. *The World's Women, 1995: Trends and Statistics*. New York: United Nations, 1995. 188p. (Social Statistics and Indicators. Series K, no. 12). bibliog. ISBN 9211613728pa.

The 1995 title and *The World's Women, 1970–1990: Trends and Statistics* (United Nations, 1991) are a nice complement to the source documents contained in *The United Nations and the Advancement of Women, 1945–1996* (see entry 543). The format is attractive and is composed of textual content supplemented by appropriate tables in two colors. The usual areas of population, family, health, education, and work appear, with coverage of more than 170 nations. An interesting final chapter in the 1995 title, "Power and Influence," provides information about women's government and political leadership opportunities, women in the media, and violence against women. The second edition also serves as one of the official documents from the Fourth World Conference on Women.

DIRECTORIES AND RESOURCE GUIDES

Groups and Associations

39. Barrett, Jacqueline K., and Jane A. Malonis, eds. *Encyclopedia of Women's Associations Worldwide: A Guide to over 3,400 National and Multinational Nonprofit Women's and Women-Related Organizations*. Detroit: Gale Research, 1993. 471p. index. ISBN 1873477252.

This reference resource can be used as an international companion to Shawn Brennan's *Women's Information Directory* for the United States. It includes an alphabetical index by name of group and a very general topical breakdown that is not nearly as useful as the full subject indexing provided in Brennan's work. Prefaces appear in English, French, German, and Spanish, with the rest of the text in English. The directory is recommended for comprehensive women's studies collections.

40. Brennan, Shawn, ed. *Women's Information Directory: A Guide to Organizations, Agencies, Institutions, Programs, Publications, Services, and Other Resources Concerned with Women in the United States*. Detroit: Gale Research, 1993. 795p. index. ISBN 0810384221.

Brennan had the extensive databases of Gale Research to draw on in compiling this useful directory of women's organizations and related information. The introduction states that Brennan also consulted government publications and local and national organization lists, as well as gathering information by telephone. Twenty-six chapters totaling almost 11,000 entries include ten topical divisions that include national organizations, battered women's services, museums and galleries, and women's studies programs, followed by chapters on scholarships, government agencies, journals, newspapers and newsletters, publishers and booksellers, videos, and electronic resources. (A somewhat comparable publication for the United Kingdom listing about 5,000 women's organizations is Loulou Brown's *The She National Women's Directory* [Cassell, 1998].) Data include at least an address, phone, and other contact information. Almost all of the organizations have a descriptive paragraph, and the indexing is very thorough. A complementary work is the National Council for Research on Women's *NWO: A Directory of National Women's Organization* (1992). This almost-700-page compilation contains contact information for national, regional, and local women's groups and organizations in the United States, but the information is not as extensive as that in the Gale publication and is almost all duplicated there. Brennan's work is recommended for all libraries with the need for a reasonably comprehensive directory specific to women's organizations and other related information.

41. Slavin, Sarah, ed. *U.S. Women's Interest Groups: Institutional Profiles*. Westport, CT: Greenwood Press, 1995. 645p. (Greenwood Reference Volumes on American Policy Formation). bibliog. index. ISBN 0313250731.

Slavin supplies a well-written, in-depth survey of women's issues through the systematic study of a sampling of about 200 women's interest groups, with a particular focus on each group's development through time. The introductory material includes a good overview of women's issues, with the preface mentioning the wide variety of women's issues group types, including civic, social, union, and professional. Also included are several businesses, government agencies, partisan groups, and research groups. Entries provide the history of an interest group, along with its stated policy areas of concern and tactics (advocacy, lobbying, and so on) and any relevant publications or newsletters. Through survey data, the author has ascertained that women's issues groups were most concerned with health and safety issues, with interests also in abortion, aging, children, economics, education, the First Amendment, health, housing, free speech, international relations, minority women, and politics. The alphabetical index includes persons and organizations as well as some topics (nuclear weapons, lesbians, and welfare), but does not provide entries listing organizations by race and ethnicity. This volume is recommended to larger collections for its in-depth coverage of major women's issues groups in the United States.

Education/Women's Studies in Higher Education

42. Brown, Loulou, Helen Collins, Pat Green, Maggie Humm, and Mel Landells, eds. *W.I.S.H: The International Handbook of Women's Studies*. New York: Harvester Wheatsheaf, 1993. 464p. bibliog. ISBN 0133022099.

This worthwhile international directory lists opportunities for training and study on women's issues in more than 100 countries. Besides formal degree programs, it also includes information about work-study possibilities and lists of bookstores, libraries, and women's resource centers in each country. This is an important and valuable addition to women's studies collections.

43. Schult, Linda, ed. *WAVE: Women's Audio-Visuals in English: A Guide to Nonprint Resources in Women's Studies: Coverage of Selected Titles, 1985–1990*. Madison, WI: Women's Studies Librarian, University of Wisconsin System, 1993. 88p. bibliog. index. ISBN n.g.

Alternative media have often been fugitive and difficult to locate and are even more subject to obsolescence than print materials. This reference resource from the University of Wisconsin Library provides a selective print list of English-language films, videos, filmstrips, slide shows, and audiocassettes for the stated period. The list was developed by examining distributors' catalogs, filmographies, and reviews, but the items listed were not personally examined by the compilers. This is a "slice in time" for areas of concern in women's studies and is included as an example of the video resources of the late 1980s. With the advent of the Web and ready access to national and international bibliographic databases, this type of secondary printed compilation becomes much less necessary, and indeed WAVE is to be developed as a resource available from the Web site of the University of Wisconsin Women's Studies Librarian. The 1993 edition is included in the database *Women's Resources International* (National Information Services Corporation, 1997–   ), now called *Women's Studies International*.

44. *WIP: A Directory of Work-in-Progress and Recent Publications*. New York: National Council for Research on Women, 1992. 439p. ISBN 1880547106.

This is a print version of a primary source database (RIPD) developed in collaboration with the Research Libraries Group and Radcliffe College and is international in scope. Representing a creative approach to information dissemination for its time, this directory provided an outlet for women's studies scholars to share information even prior to publication. The print volume has been expanded and updated with additional information, including more than 1,000 projects and more than 1,000 individuals and providing information about papers, books, questionnaires, artworks, research, dissertations, and archives. The directory contains indexes by name, keyword, funding source, and genre.

Financial Opportunities

45. Littman, Barbara. *The Women's Business Resource Guide: A National Directory of over 600 Programs, Resources, and Organizations to Help Women Start or Expand a Business.* 2nd ed. Chicago: Contemporary Books, 1996. 302p. index. ISBN 0809231662.

The first edition of this source was a brief (131 pages) self-published guide coauthored by Littman and Michael Ray that outlined basic information sources for women in business. The 1996 edition found a commercial publisher and more than doubled in size. Topics covered are federal, state, and private resources for information, training, and financial assistance and a chapter on selling to the government. While most of this information is readily available elsewhere and women can obviously benefit equally from any general business guide for entrepreneurs, this guide has looked specifically at programs available nationally and membership organizations that will have particular applicability to women. A complementary guide written specifically for women, with chapters on startups, marketing, financing, banking, regulatory compliance, and networking, but no resource list, is Vickie L. Montgomery's *The Smart Woman's Guide to Starting a Business* (Career Press, 1994; 2nd ed., 1998). Another worthwhile related handbook is Emily Card and Adam Miller's *Business Capital for Women: An Essential Handbook for Entrepreneurs* (Macmillan, 1996), which introduces the concepts of capital and investment and potential sources and contains several useful appendices.

46. *National Guide to Funding for Women and Girls.* New York: Foundation Center, 1991– . ISBN 0879543930.

This publication is a spin-off from the Foundation Center's database and does an excellent job of identifying funding sources, both nonprofit and corporate, in all fifty states. Brief entries include contact information, type of foundation, types of support, areas of interest, limitations, a summary of their financial data, and application information. A caveat is that the title may lead women to think that unlimited opportunities for individual grants exist in the source, but many sources fund "programs serving women or girls" (p. vii, 1995) and will only work with organizations. Between the 1991 and 1995 editions, it grew in size from 258 to more than 400 pages.

PERIODICAL REFERENCE WORKS

47. Clardy, Andrea Fleck. *Words to the Wise: A Writer's Guide to Feminist and Lesbian Periodicals and Publishers.* 2nd ed. Ithaca, NY: Firebrand Books, 1987. 48p. ISBN 0932379168.

The focus of this slim, regularly updated pamphlet is to give writers a list of explicitly feminist and lesbian publishers, periodicals, and related resources. A brief introduction may assist fledgling writers with initial ideas for contacting potential publishers and making submissions. Each entry includes complete addresses, phone numbers, names of editorial staff if available, and a brief annotation describing the types of materials the company or journal publishes and its "philosophy."

48. Endres, Kathleen, and Therese L. Lueck, eds. *Women's Periodicals in the United States: Social and Political Issues.* Westport, CT: Greenwood Press, 1996. 509p. (Historical Guides to the World's Periodicals and Newspapers). bibliog. index. ISBN 0313286329.

To accompany available article bibliographies, this volume provides chapters on what the authors consider the primary periodicals important to women's political and social issues in the United States. Interestingly, few could achieve momentum, and only about one-third had a publishing life span of more than ten years. Each chapter is extensively annotated with notes and other sources of information. A simple alphabetical list of the journals covered in the chapters would have been a convenience. Appendices include a chronology, a thorough bibliography, and an extensive index. Endres and Lueck edited a companion volume titled *Women's Periodicals in the United States: Consumer Magazines* (Greenwood Press, 1995), published just prior to *Women's Periodicals in the United States: Social and Political Issues.* The editors profile a variety of influential and representative magazines ranging from *Twins, Playgirl,* and *Prevention* to *Seventeen* and *WB,* "the oldest continuously published women's sports magazine" (p. 428), which covers bowling. The chapters are extremely well written, and this could serve as a browsing item in American women's collections as well as a significant research tool.

49. Zuckerman, Mary Ellen, comp. *Sources on the History of Women's Magazines, 1792–1960: An Annotated Bibliography.* New York: Greenwood Press, 1991. 297p. (Bibliographies and Indexes in Women's Studies, 12). index. ISBN 0313263787.

In this annotated, evaluative work, Zuckerman covers the title's topic from the late eighteenth century (the publication of the first American magazine especially for women) until 1960 (when the women's movement was beginning to take shape). The author includes primarily books and journal articles and focuses more on the "business" of publishing in this area, with much information on advertising, market surveys, and the like. Unique features include a chapter on people involved in women's magazines and an individual chapter with primary and secondary sources on ten significant women's magazines, including *Vogue, Good Housekeeping, Harper's Bazaar, Family Circle,* and *Woman's Day.* There is much interesting information here, such as the fact that the novelist Theodore Dreiser edited three of the Butterick publications for several years. A basic index is available but becomes difficult to navigate when it lists many entries under a topic (British women's magazines have more than thirty entries) without subheads. This reference work is thorough, meticulously researched, and highly recommended. Nancy K. Humphreys covers some of the same ground as Zuckerman but in a more selective way in *American Women's Magazines: An Annotated Historical Guide* (Garland, 1989). All the magazines included here are or were published in the United States, with the exception of *The Lady's Magazine* (England) and *Elle* (France). The scholarship ranges from "Romance/Confession" magazines from as far back as the 1920s to mainstream publications such as *American Heritage.* Part 1 includes alternative publications (early women's rights and feminist magazines), while part 2 covers mainstream periodicals, with both sections arranged chronologically. Extensive annotations add to the value of this work, which is recommended for reference collections in women's studies and for anyone researching media history.

1999 CORE TITLES

Quinn, Tracy. *Quotable Women of the Twentieth Century*. New York: William Morrow & Co., 1999. 268p. ISBN 0688159915.

Scanlon, Jennifer. *Significant Contemporary American Feminists: A Biographical Sourcebook*. Westport, CT: Greenwood Press, 1999. 384p. bibliog. index. ISBN 0313301255.

Schaefer, Christina K. *The Hidden Half of the Family: A Sourcebook for Women's Genealogy*. Baltimore: Genealogical Publishing Company, 1999. 298p. bibliog. index. ISBN 0806315822.

WORLD WIDE WEB/INTERNET SITES

50. *Association of College and Research Libraries [American Library Association]. Women's Studies Section (WSS)*. http://libr.org/wss.

WSS "was formed to discuss, support, and promote women's studies collections and services in academic and research libraries." Its Web page provides useful information, usually updated annually, for core lists of women's studies books in a variety of disciplines, core journals, and Web sites pertaining to women and gender issues in health, music, philosophy, politics, and other subjects as well as international and lesbian sites. Particularly useful is the section titled "Electronic Resources Information and Assessment" (http://www.libr.org/wss/projects/electronic.html) that provides invaluable information for full-text and citation databases, digital archives, and other electronic sources, including *Women's Studies on Disc, Women's Resources International, Contemporary Women's* Issues, and *GenderWatch* (see entry in the next section). The page also provides information about WSS and related organizations.

51. *Women's Studies Librarian's Office at the University of Wisconsin*. http://www.library.wisc.edu/libraries/WomensStudies.

Maintained by women's studies librarian Phyllis Holman Weisbard, this metasite offers a wide range of information, including links to the office's publication *Feminist Collections* and *WAVE: Women's Videos Database*. It also provides links to periodical home pages, books, bibliographies, publishers, video distributors, and reference sources as well as extensive links to resources such as virtual women's studies course handouts, women's organizations, listings for programs, research centers, libraries, and archives, sites for international and culturally diverse women, including Jewish women, and women and gender issues arranged by subject.

52. *Women's Studies: UMBC and Beyond at the University of Maryland Baltimore County*. http://www-unix.umbc.edu/~korenman/wmst/.

Developed and maintained by Joan Korenman, this award-winning, frequently updated site offers local information about women's studies at the University of Maryland Baltimore County and beyond. It contains links, many of them annotated, to a wealth of information in the field, including syllabi on gender-related courses, links to electronic forums for women's issues, comprehensive women's Web sites, and sites pertaining to such areas as activism, information technology, women's studies programs around the world, film, financial aid, health, international women, periodicals, sexuality, science and technology, women of color, and work. This metasite also serves as the archive for the academic women's studies discussion group WMST-L. A related site, *Women's Studies Resources at the University of Maryland* (http://www.inform.umd.edu/EdRes/Topics/WomensStudies) was created in 1992. It lists conference and internship announcements, calls for papers, grants, and employment opportunities as well as bibliographies, syllabi, film reviews, gender issues in computing, and links to organizations and sites dealing with a variety of gender and women's issues. A picture gallery and listings of government documents are two of the site's more notable features.

ONLINE DATABASES

53. *Contemporary Women's Issues (CWI).* Gale Group, 1992– . Subscription. http://www.galegroup.com/tlist/cwi.htm.

CWI contains more than 65,000 full-text items covering a broad range of topics pertaining to women, such as human rights, health and reproductive issues, human rights, violence, work, development, feminism, and legal information. It contains articles from more than 600 sources worldwide, including periodicals, newsletters, reports, fact sheets, and pamphlets. Coverage is international, with a focus on English-language materials, and the database is updated weekly. For several major women's studies journals, *CWI* provides only abstracts of articles (but full-text book reviews) and does not always include cover-to-cover contents. It is, however, an excellent source for ephemera not always readily available in libraries and for background and factual information.

54. *GenderWatch (GW).* ProQuest, 1978– . Subscription. http://www.il.proquest.com.

GenderWatch, updated quarterly, contains more than 80,000 full-text items from academic and scholarly journals, magazines, newspapers, newsletters, regional publications, books, booklets and pamphlets, conference proceedings, government publications, and nongovernmental organization (NGO) and special reports. It also includes archival material, in some cases as far back as the 1970s, with new archival material added as it becomes available. The database supports programs in gender and women's studies, public policy, political science, sociology and contemporary culture, education, literature and the arts, health sciences, history, business, and more. Like *CWI, GW* is interdisciplinary and international in scope, with a focus on English-language materials, and provides only abstracts for articles in scholarly journals. Unlike *CWI, GW* provides cover-to-cover contents. The database was originally produced by Softline Information and called *Women "R."*

55. *Women's Studies International.* Baltimore: National Information Services Corp. (NISC), 1997– . Subscription. http://biblioline.nisc.com/.

Because Women's Studies International begins coverage of the women's studies literature in 1972, it is the essential choice for libraries supporting large women's studies programs, especially graduate programs. It provides interdisciplinary, international coverage and is updated in April and October. The database combines two important indexes, Women's Studies Database (1972–present) and *Women Studies Abstracts* (1984–present), with several bibliographic databases, including *New Books on Women and Feminism* (1987–), *WAVE, Women, Race, and Ethnicity:*

A Bibliography (1970–1990), and *The History of Women and Science, Health, and Technology: A Bibliographic Guide to the Professions and Disciplines* (1970–1995), produced by the University of Wisconsin's Women's Studies Librarian's Office, as well as *Women of Color and Southern Women* (1975–1995) from the Center for Research on Women at Memphis State University, *Women's Health and Development: An Annotated Bibliography* (1995) from the World Health Organization, and other databases. Although this resource contains abstracts on many of its records, it does not provide full text of articles. NISC plans to add new databases as they become available and extend coverage of *Women Studies Abstracts* back to 1972.

2 Feminist Theories and Women's Movements

Joan Ariel

Simultaneously a theory (or set of theories) and a social movement, feminism is increasingly both prominent and contested in the contemporary world. Indeed, one of the most fundamental yet perennially challenging goals of feminism has been to link women's movements and feminist theory so that they are mutually reflective, constitutive, and supportive. This chapter thus combines the literatures addressing these two major strands of thought and action, theory and practice, arguably the tapestry through which all other threads of feminism and women's studies are woven. The books discussed in this chapter not only cover a broad range of women's movements and theoretical perspectives, but also underscore feminist challenges to conventional definitions of theory and knowledge as well as of politics and activism. In addition, these titles reflect the tensions and debates between competing visions of "feminism," theory and practice.

The continued growth of feminist theory since the late 1980s has been nothing short of astonishing, stretching over an expansive terrain of critical analysis, dialogue, and debate. The dichotomy/tension between (1) feminism as a set of theoretical concepts and practices and (2) activist women's movements has in some ways been exacerbated during this period as certain forms of academic feminist theory have moved into closer alignment with postmodernism, discourse analysis, and queer theory. This has unleashed charges of elitism, inaccessibility, and irrelevance to women's daily and material lives. More recent work in postcolonial theory, cultural studies, and transnational feminist practices perhaps holds greater promise in bridging these divides.

A veritable explosion in publishing mirrors this astonishing growth of interest in feminist theories/theorizing. Few subjects fall outside the scope of the feminist theoretical lens, but some clearly have more resonance than others. Among the most frequently interrogated topics are the body; sexualities; identities, their social construction and fluidity; space from bounded geographical to virtual cyber; gender and class formation; work and political economy; Western imperialism, colonialism, and transnational feminist practices; globalization; and information and communication technologies. Add to this list feminist contributions to and interventions in other significant theoretical arguments of the last twenty-five years, and one uncovers a wealth of materials spanning disciplines throughout the humanities and the social and natural sciences.

At the same time, the momentum of women's organizing around the world has expanded to encompass the far reaches of the globe and many dimensions of existence, from the political and economic to the social and cultural. The selections in this chapter move away to some extent from literature defined as core by standard criteria (e.g., widely read, reviewed, assigned in the classroom) in an attempt to provide the breadth of geographical, ideological, and theoretical scope essential to an adequate exploration of women's movements and feminist theorizing at the end of the twentieth century. While ideally theory and practice coexist in synergistic relationship to each other, the challenges remain as to how to negotiate the differences and divides so that they are mutually informative and transformative.

Debates about the accessibility and uses of theory remain contentious, both within and outside of academic circles, and community activists often ask how theory informs and improves women's daily lives. Confronting frequent charges of elitism, many theorists today would argue, however, that discursive practices in fact not only represent but also construct material realities, while others also advocate theory that is empirically grounded and politically engaged. The authors and works represented in this chapter reflect multiple facets of these vibrant and necessary debates. In spite of dynamic connections between theory and practice, the monographs section consists of two parts, "Feminist Thought and Theories" and "Women's Movements and Activism."

REFERENCE SOURCES

56. Andermahr, Sonya, Terry Lovell, and Carol Wolkowitz. *A Glossary of Feminist Theory.* New York: St. Martin's Press, 1997. 351p. bibliog. ISBN 0340596627; 0340762799pa.

This dictionary, available also in a paper student edition that "omits some of the more general entries and abridges certain others" (p. 6), provides a useful and well-organized introduction to feminist theories in circulation since the late 1960s. It successfully documents critical theoretical concepts and their origins and traces their movement and transformation through critique, contestation, and appropriation. While Maggie Humm's *The Dictionary of Feminist Theory* (annotated later in this section) is broader in scope and includes biographical entries, this volume attempts to engage more deeply with the complexity of many of the terms and concepts included here. Nonetheless, the entries are generally readable and thoroughly cross-referenced, using small capitals within entries to point to related entries and bracketed references to direct readers to the extensive bibliography of all references cited.

57. Boles, Janet. *Historical Dictionary of Feminism.* Lanham, MD: Scarecrow Press, 1996. 429p. (Historical Dictionaries of Religions, Philosophies, and Movements). bibliog. ISBN 0810830426.

This alphabetical handbook aims to compile short introductions to important events, people, organizations, court cases, campaigns, achievements, and concepts in the history of the feminist movement. A chronology of feminism from 1405 through 1995 offers a unique timeline that incorporates an international perspective, and a bibliography and a listing of feminist journals add utility.

58. Carabillo, Toni, Judith Meuli, and June Bundy Csida. *Feminist Chronicles, 1953–1993.* Los Angeles: Women's Graphics, 1993. 306p. bibliog. index. ISBN 0963491202.

This work provides a selective chronology of the modern feminist movement, dating its beginning from 1953, the year Simone de Beauvoir's *The Second Sex* was first published in the United States, and extending through 1993. The information is organized in a visual timeline of events and people in the women's movement. Each year is arranged in a three-column format outlining events, issues, and backlash and listing achievements by individuals, significant births, deaths, legislation passed, and other important events. If disproportional emphasis is placed on information and dates related to the National Organization for Women (NOW)—one full section of the volume is devoted to "The Early Documents," comprising reports, position papers, and minutes from NOW meetings—the volume nevertheless provides a useful, albeit narrow, perspective on abortion rights and other feminist issues and history of particular concern to NOW.

59. Harlan, Judith. *Feminism: A Reference Handbook.* Santa Barbara, CA: ABC-CLIO, 1998. bibliog. index. ISBN 0874368944.

This handbook offers a multifaceted introduction to modern feminism, emphasizing the United States but also incorporating global issues perspectives in most chapters. It provides a wide range of types of information, including history and chronology, biographical sketches of twenty-five American and British feminists, and feminist organizations. Topical chapters address issues of concern to many feminists such as affirmative action, reproductive freedom, and education as well as economics and politics. Annotated bibliographies of both print and nonprint resources, including Web sites as well as videos, while highly selective, nonetheless enhance the usefulness of the volume for initial reference and research.

60. Humm, Maggie. *The Dictionary of Feminist Theory.* Columbus: Ohio State University Press, 1990. 278p. bibliog. ISBN 0814205062; 0814205070pa.

In one of the earliest feminist dictionaries (a second, longer edition was issued in 1995), Humm provides thoughtful if personally idiosyncratic definitions of and commentary on terms, concepts, and persons central to an understanding of Anglo-American and French feminist theory. The scope of the more than 400 words included ranges from the expected (e.g., abortion, essentialism, marriage) to the less common (e.g., binary, womanculture). Numerous feminist theorists, well-known and lesser figures, are included, but the work generally omits the political realm, including such key public figures as Gloria Steinem. The entries, typically one to three paragraphs in length, provide citations to sourcebooks or articles identified by publication date, referring the reader to full citations in the bibliography. Despite obvious bias in the treatment, Humm provides a useful if somewhat uneven resource. Readers or researchers seeking another feminist lexicography will find Jane Mill's earlier *Womanwords: A Vocabulary of Culture and Patriarchal Society* (Longman, 1989) a welcome companion to Humm. Mills takes a distinctive historical approach, presenting some 300 words relating to women selected for their "rich semantic history" and using these to analyze patriarchal society and "to explore the history of changing (and sometimes relentlessly unchanging) attitudes towards women" (p. viii). Slang and insults thus are included along with more "neutral" terms, making for a fascinating range of "womanwords" not found in other feminist dictionaries.

61. Jaggar, Alison M., and Iris Marion Young, eds. *Companion to Feminist Philosophy.* Malden, MA: Blackwell, 1998. 703p. bibliog. index. ISBN 1557866597; 0631220674pa.

Jagger and Young, both noted feminist scholars, provide an invaluable introduction to feminist philosophy and philosophies of feminism. Comprehensive in scope, the volume is organized into ten sections reflecting the many dimensions of feminist philosophy and theorizing: "The Western Canonical Tradition"; "Africa, Asia, Latin America, and Eastern Europe"; "Language and Knowledge"; "Nature"; "Religion"; "Subjectivity and Embodiment"; "Art"; "Ethics"; "Society"; and "Politics." The second section is particularly welcome in its much-needed coverage of non-Western perspectives. Contributors offer knowledgeable articles that demonstrate a clarity and depth at once accessible to students and informative for scholars. An extensive bibliography adds to the book's utility as a guide to the voluminous literature of the field. This excellent compendium stands as one of the best introductions to the broad scope of feminist theory and an essential resource for reference and consultation.

62. Nordquist, Joan. *Queer Theory: A Bibliography.* Santa Cruz, CA: Reference and Research Services Press, 1997. 64p. (Social Theory). ISBN 0937855952pa.

————. *Feminism and Postmodernism: A Bibliography*. Santa Cruz, CA: Reference and Research Services, 1996. 60p. (Social Theory). ISBN 0937855812pa.

————. *Feminism Worldwide: A Bibliography*. Santa Cruz, CA: Reference and Research Services, 1996. 64p. (Contemporary Social Issues). ISBN 0937855863pa.

————. *French Feminist Theory (III): Luce Irigaray and Helene Cixous: A Bibliography*. Santa Cruz, CA: Reference and Research Services, 1996. 72p. (Social Theory). ISBN 0937855871pa.

————. *Women of Color: Feminist Theory: A Bibliography*. Santa Cruz, CA: Reference and Research Services, 1995. 76p. (Social Theory). ISBN 0937855790pa.

————. *The Feminist Movement: A Bibliography*. Santa Cruz, CA: Reference and Research Services, 1992. 68p. (Contemporary Social Issues). ISBN 0937855464pa.

————. *Feminist Theory: A Bibliography*. Santa Cruz, CA: Reference and Research Services, 1992. 76p. (Social Theory). ISBN 0937855553pa. (Note: 2nd edition published in 2000).

Joan Nordquist, a virtual cottage industry of bibliographies, diligently compiles numerous useful titles in her series on contemporary social issues and theories. The titles listed here are those related to feminist theory and women's movements. Most are less than 100 pages in length. Although they are unannotated, they nonetheless may serve as a useful starting point for student research and investigation.

63. Ryan, Barbara. *The Women's Movement: References and Resources*. New York: G. K. Hall, 1996. (Reference Publications on American Social Movements). 339p. index. ISBN 0816172544.

Ryan provides an excellent annotated bibliography of books and articles that traces the development of the women's movement in the United States from the early nineteenth century into the past decade. Entries are carefully selected and provide brief but informative descriptions of each work arranged in a thoughtful organizational scheme. Ryan covers first- and second-wave feminism subdivided by topics relevant to the particular era (e.g., suffrage in the first and violence against women in the second), biographical and autobiographical works on women's activism, and feminist discourse, including feminist thought, feminist theory, and methodology. The distinction between feminist thought and theory is particularly interesting in its divide between feminism as a worldview with gender as a category of analysis and theories of feminism such as Marxist, socialist, radical, liberal, and separatist theoretical perspectives. Ryan examines discourse from multiple angles and addresses social movement theories, identity politics, multiculturalism, and black feminist and black women's activism. She identifies works that address issues prevalent in the contemporary women's movement, including race, class, and gender; work, welfare, and trade unionism; sex and pornography; feminist critique and contributions (literature, arts, science, family); politics, the law, and policy; sexism and discrimination; and finally, religion and spirituality. A concluding "Guide to Sources" describes various types of reference works, library collections and archives, and other sources for those seeking additional information. Subject, author, and title indexes augment Ryan's well-considered section headings.

Readers interested in lesbian movements will find another volume in this series, Robert B.

Marks Ridinger's *The Gay and Lesbian Movement: References and Resources* (New York: G. K. Hall, 1996), particularly useful. Robin Morgan's 1996 edition of *Sisterhood Is Global: The International Women's Movement Anthology* (Feminist Press at the City University of New York, 1996), originally published in 1984 and an important resource for women's movements around the globe, documents the status of women across more than eighty countries with revealing data and informed perspectives.

MONOGRAPHS

Feminist Thought and Theories

64. Ahmed, Sara. *Differences That Matter: Feminist Theory and Postmodernism.* New York: Cambridge University Press, 1998. 222p. bibliog. index. ISBN 0521592259; 0521597617pa.

Ahmed's dense and challenging text contributes to the ongoing debates around feminism and postmodernism. She takes up the question of how feminism and postmodernism "speak to each other" (p. 1) and "under what conditions is feminism included within, and excluded from, postmodernism?" (p. 3). She structures her engagement with the debate through a cross-disciplinary reading of postmodern texts (Lyotard, Derrida, Barthes, Foucault, and others) in which she "speaks back" to and challenges postmodernism for its failure to acknowledge feminist theorizing. Topical chapters on rights, ethics, woman, subjects, authorship, literature, and film frame her analysis of the differences that matter: the differences between postmodernism and feminism and differences within feminist theory. It is their different relation to "difference" that is fundamental, she argues, asserting that postmodernism reifies "difference" as such, while feminist theory and practice ask "which differences?" and "demand that we analyze differences in relation to the structuring of social relations" (p. 192).

65. Alexander, M. Jacqui, and Chandra Talpade Mohanty, eds. *Feminist Genealogies, Colonial Legacies, Democratic Futures.* New York: Routledge, 1997. 422p. bibliog. index. ISBN 0415912113; 0415912121pa.

This pioneering, highly regarded collection of essays by fifteen scholars and activists traces the historical legacies of colonialism and global capitalism within the context of transnational women's lives, practices, and collective actions. Several key essays tackle international economic and cultural institutions, for instance, the World Bank, the International Monetary Fund (IMF), the General Agreement on Tariffs and Trade (GATT), media, and tourism, and their effects on Third World women. Others explore the genealogy of feminist organizing and focus on such women's movements/organizations as the Jamaican group Sistren, Stree Shakti Sanghatana (SSS) in Hyderabad, India, and Women in Nigeria (WIN). Incisive challenges to Western notions of freedom, equality, ownership, citizenship, immigration, the self and the social, the nation-state, colonization, and democracy reverberate throughout the volume. In sharp contrast to liberal feminism's focus on self-advancement and "maintenance of the first-world status quo," Alexander and Mohanty compellingly argue that a "world increasingly refigured by global economic and political processes" demands nothing less than a transnational "feminist democracy . . . based on anticolonialist, socialist principles" (p. xli). An extensive index and the thorough documentation provided in chapter notes further enhance this essential and, in many ways, exemplary text of feminist theory and practice.

66. Anzaldúa, Gloria. *Borderlands: The New Mestiza = La Frontera*. San Francisco: Aunt Lute Books, 1987. 203p. bibliog. ISBN 1879960125pa.

In a groundbreaking work at once deeply analytical and poetic, Anzaldúa draws upon her geographical home in the Texas-Mexico borderland and her life as a mestiza, a woman of mixed Indian and Spanish ancestry. She traces the metaphorical borderlands of her multiple, intersecting identities as woman, writer, "queer," and Chicana in their full complexity, contradiction, and creativity. "The new mestiza copes by developing a tolerance for contradictions, a tolerance for ambiguity.... She learns to juggle cultures" (p. 79). The mestiza consciousness at the frontera shapes a new ethnic and sexual identity. The new mestiza consciousness rejects dualisms, accepts ambiguity, and celebrates the borderlands of race, gender, and sexualities that surround and sustain us. Combining ethnographic essays, history, cultural criticism, autobiography, and poetry, this hybrid text weaves the personal, political, and poetic into the fabric of Anzaldúa's analysis. She offers a probing exploration of her internalized borderlands, rooted in material reality, and creates in the process feminist theory at its most vital and illuminating. (A second edition was issued in 1999.) Anzaldúa also edited *Making Face, Making Soul/Haciendo Caras: Creative and Critical Perspectives by Women of Color* (Aunt Lute Foundation Books, 1990). The volume similarly blends poetry and prose, fiction, autobiography, and essays to give voice to women frequently silenced by the dominant culture. Organized thematically, the collection addresses ways in which racism wounds and degrades, ways to combat racism and sexism, growth strategies, silence and learning to speak, identities as artists and intellectuals, alliances, and theories of identity and consciousness. This challenging and inspiring anthology won the Lambda Literary Award for 1990.

67. Barrett, Michele, and Anne Phillips, eds. *Destabilizing Theory: Contemporary Feminist Debates*. Stanford, CA: Stanford University Press, 1992. 224p. bibliog. index. ISBN 0804720304; 0804720312pa.

Barrett and Phillips have amassed a collection of chapters from British, Australian, and American feminists specially commissioned to explore feminism's relationship to theory and to scrutinize the differences between early feminist theory of the 1970s and more heterogeneous and contentious theories of the 1990s. The editors point to profound differences between the founding assumptions of the two periods, between discourses centered on causes of oppression subject to the dangers of abstraction and generalization and those that critique universalistic and modernist thought. This possibly paradigmatic shift is reflected in the critique of dichotomies and dualisms and efforts to destabilize pervasive binary structures, most particularly here the equality difference/ opposition. Women's experiences and articulations of difference have fragmented a unitary conception of "woman." At the same time poststructuralist and postmodernist theories have challenged conceptions of causation and raised new insights and implications for feminism. In addition to the editors, eight contributors, including such well-known theorists as Chandra Mohanty and Gayatri Spivak, tackle these questions in essays ranging from social and political theory to examinations of sexual identity and the body and of meaning and representation in painting and in literary texts. The anthology serves as a succinct, stimulating, and generally accessible introduction to complex issues and debates.

68. Beemyn, Brett, and Mickey Eliason, eds. *Queer Studies: A Lesbian, Gay, Bisexual, and Transgender Anthology*. New York: New York University Press, 1996. 318p. bibliog. index. ISBN 0814712576; 0814712584pa.

Born of their own frustrations with finding suitable texts to use in undergraduate courses in queer studies, editors Beemyn and Eliason set themselves the task of bringing together in one volume essays that cover a range of topics in queer theory/studies, are accessible to an undergraduate audience, and center on racial, ethnic, and sexual diversity. Drawn from expanded versions of papers presented at the 1994 Sixth North American Lesbian, Gay, and Bisexual Studies Conference, titled "InQueery/InTheory/InDeed," the volume is divided into two broad sections of sixteen essays each, "Issues of Identity" and "Queer Theory in Practice." The editors have provided clear and concise introductions to each part, helping the reader contextualize the material and drawing out the connections among the contributions included. Essays in the first section cover such diverse forms or expressions of identity as Sherrie A. Inness and Michele E. Lloyd's work on "G.I. Joes in Barbie Land: Recontextualizing Butch in Twentieth-Century Lesbian Culture" and Gregory Conerly's "The Politics of Black Lesbian, Gay, and Bisexual Identity." Section 2, the more traditionally theoretical of the two, includes essays on MTV (Lynda Goldstein's contribution "Revamping MTV: Passing for Queer Culture in the Video Closet"), transgender subjectivity as explored in Ki Namaste's contribution "Tragic Misreadings: Queer Theory's Erasure of Transgender Subjectivity," and the often contentious issue of bisexuality as explored in Christopher James's piece "Denying Complexity: The Dismissal and Appropriation of Bisexuality in Queer, Lesbian, and Gay Theory." Annamarie Jagose's *Queer Theory: An Introduction* (New York University Press, 1996) provides a useful complement, placing queer theory in its historical context and examining arguments both for and against the concept and terminology of queer.

69. Bell, Diane, and Renate Klein, eds. *Radically Speaking: Feminism Reclaimed.* North Melbourne, Victoria: Spinifex Press, 1996. 624p. bibliog. index. ISBN 1875559388pa.

Sixty-six articles by radical feminists tackle the past misrepresentations of radical feminism and argue for the power of radical feminist analysis to create a better world for women. They counter the attacks on radical feminist theory and praxis through analyses of the intersections of race, class, and (hetero)sexism in the oppression of women under patriarchy. The global reach of radical feminism emerges in articles focusing on Russia, South Africa, Taiwan, Chile, and the former Yugoslavia as well as Western countries like Norway, the United Kingdom, and the United States. The contributors reject postmodernist notions of feminism (humorously concluding their volume with "A Po-Mo Quiz") as well as liberal individualism and point to the diversity of standpoints and issues among radical feminists. The selections gathered here describe the multiplicity of initiatives and projects spearheaded by radical feminists, from rape crisis centers, women's shelters, and health centers to organizing against pornography and developing courses in women's studies. Catharine MacKinnon reflects the philosophical premise of the volume in her emphasis on the politics of women's everyday lives and theory derived from lived experience. She joins many of the contributors here in seeking to articulate "the theory of women's practice—women's resistance, visions, consciousness, injuries, notions of community, experience of inequality" (p. 46) and in so doing to reclaim radical feminism, which, in their view, has been silenced too long.

70. Butler, Judith P. *Bodies That Matter: On the Discursive Limits of "Sex."* New York: Routledge, 1993. 288p. bibliog. index. ISBN 0415903653; 0415903661pa.

Butler draws on Foucault and psychoanalysis to rearticulate and further develop her theories of the body and the denaturalization of gender presented in her 1990 innovative and provocative text *Gender Trouble*. She engages with critics of the earlier work who faulted her analysis for its disregard of the "materiality" of the body. Taking up the task of correcting misconceptions about her theory of gender, sex, and sexuality as forms of reiterative cultural performance, she expands and deepens her attempt to rethink the body, identity, and the constructedness of sex, seen as a regulatory/cultural norm. She draws critical distinctions between performance and performativity, the latter seen as citation, not a singular "act," but "a reiteration of a norm or a set of norms"

(p. 12). She further applies citationality to materialization, "the acquisition of being through the citation of power" (p. 15), and seeks to "think through the matter of bodies as a kind of materialization governed by regulatory norms," including regimes of power like normative heterosexuality or racializing interpellations. She asks: which bodies are culturally intelligible, which ones matter? In extending her analysis more directly here to questions of race and homosexuality, she discusses these abjected or delegitimated bodies that fail to count as "bodies" (p. 15) or bodies that matter. In the course of her exploration, she provides trenchant and often oppositional readings of Jennie Livingston's film *Paris Is Burning*, Willa Cather's fiction, and Nella Larsen's novella *Passing*. Butler concludes this rigorous text with an exploration of the "contentious practices of 'queerness' " and its "reworking of abjection into political agency," claiming that "the public assertion of 'queerness' enacts performativity as citationality for the purposes of resignifying the abjection of homosexuality into defiance and legitimacy" (p. 21).

71. Butler, Judith P. *Gender Trouble: Feminism and the Subversion of Identity.* New York: Routledge, 1990. 172p. (Thinking Gender). bibliog. ISBN 0415900425; 0415900433pa.

A preeminent feminist philosopher and theorist, Butler irrevocably reshaped feminist theory and set the direction for the emerging field of queer theory. In this ambitious work that fast became a classic if controversial text, Butler broke new theoretical ground in her postmodern analysis of the body, sex, gender, and identity and their relation to feminist politics. In developing her argument, she builds upon and critiques the work of Freud, Lacan, Beauvoir, Irigaray, Kristeva, Wittig, and Foucault. She takes issue with much of feminist theory and the notion of woman as subject prevalent at the time, positing an enormously influential new theory of gender performance. Confounding prevailing feminist assumptions "that the term *women* denotes a common identity," Butler asserts that "rather than a stable signifier that commands the assent of those whom it purports to describe and represent, *women*, even in the plural, has become a troublesome term, a site of contest, a cause for anxiety" (p. 3). It is this trouble, this anxiety that she analyzes here, dismantling any unitary, essentialist notion of *woman* or *women* and developing important theoretical models as she does so.

Butler further complicates conventional conceptions and pushes beyond feminist theories that draw distinctions between sex and gender, that regard gender as the social and cultural construction of "natural," biologically sexed bodies. Arguing that the "natural" is a "dangerous illusion," she deconstructs sex and identity along with gender, demonstrating their fluidity and embeddedness within discursive practices that make them culturally intelligible. Gender, she asserts, is a performance, based in part on sex and bodies that are themselves, following the "linguistic turn," a function of language and discourse, constructed through metaphors. Critiquing compulsory heterosexuality within feminism, she convincingly challenges dominant ideologies that presume fixed gender identities based in bodies, or sex, or heterosexuality as well as the binaries of male/female or heterosexual/homosexual. The instability of these categories brings into question "the very terms through which identity is articulated . . . [and] the foundationalist frame in which feminism as an identity politics has been articulated" (p. 148). Indeed, Butler argues that identity is inherently oppressive and that feminists must seek a new configuration of politics in liberation from identity. This is an essential, if theoretically and linguistically challenging, text (the second edition was published in 1999).

72. Caraway, Nancie. *Segregated Sisterhood: Racism and the Politics of American Feminism.* Knoxville: University of Tennessee Press, 1991. 282p. bibliog. index. ISBN 0870497197; 0870497200pa.

Written from the standpoint of an antiracist white feminist, a working-class woman (from Alabama) who acknowledges her current position of privilege as a white woman within the academy, *Segregated Sisterhood* is both a critical analysis of racism within the (white) women's movement and a call for a new, more powerful and inclusive feminism. As Caraway describes her project in the introduction, she seeks to understand and discuss how "Black feminist discourse shatters white feminist illusions of inclusion, making way for new paradigms and political alternatives" (p. 6). While avoiding the pitfalls of universalizing and homogenizing rhetoric, Caraway draws connections between postcolonial discourse and black feminism. She points to and underscores the significant contributions of black feminist theory to issues of political economy, social creation, and subjectivity, not as add-ons to some preexisting white position but as core theoretical constructs upon which other theories have rested. Caraway cogently discusses significant trends in black feminist thought and analyzes black feminist theory as informing and informed by postcolonial theory, Afrocentric feminism, and postmodernism.

Caraway later turns her attention to historical and symbolic investigations of the less-than-stellar relations between white feminists and black women, both in the nineteenth and early twentieth centuries as well as in the contemporary period. She ends the book with what she labels "a playful and politically valuable metaphor . . . crossover multicultural feminism" (p. 12). Caraway makes powerful arguments for both a fuller and more nuanced brand of feminism and a principled articulation of racism within white feminism, historically and in the present moment. Critics, however, have noted the fact that although she acknowledges the contributions of other women of color to feminism and antiracism, her book focuses on a black/white dichotomy and thereby falls short of its goal to be truly multicultural.

73. Chow, Esther Ngan-ling, Doris Wilkinson, and Maxine Baca Zinn, eds. *Race, Class, and Gender: Common Bonds, Different Voices*. Thousand Oaks, CA: Sage Publications, 1996. 406p. (Gender and Society Readers). bibliog. ISBN 0803970560; 0803970579pa.

Initially published in the journal *Gender and Society*, the nineteen articles collected here offer a multifaceted introduction to the powerful intersections and simultaneity of race, class, and gender. The editors aim to promote inclusive feminist scholarship through analysis of the ways in which race, ethnicity, class, and gender and, to some extent, sexual orientation are "structurally interconnected in major social institutions and in daily interaction" (p. xxv). The essays review recent work in sociology and economics, examining such widely divergent topics as eating disorders, masculinities and athletic careers, women's employment, occupational mobility of immigrant women, intergenerational relations, community activism, political legislation, and social policy. Additional selections examine theory construction and methodological strategizing in the context of these multiple, interlocking dimensions of identity and social organization. Although grounded in sociology, the volume represents a broad and provocative scope of inquiry and interdisciplinary emphasis that makes it highly suitable for classroom use.

74. Collins, Patricia Hill. *Black Feminist Thought: Knowledge, Consciousness, and the Politics of Empowerment*. Boston: Unwin Hyman, 1990. 265p. (Perspectives on Gender). bibliog. index. ISBN 0044451377; 0044451385pa.

In this pathbreaking volume, Patricia Hill Collins documents the long-standing intellectual community of African American women and the theoretical power of black women's experiences and ideas. Tracing the social construction of black feminist thought from Maria Stewart, Sojourner Truth, Ellen Frances Watkins Harper, Anna Julia Cooper, and Ida B. Wells in the nineteenth century, Collins irrefutably demonstrates its origins, development, and integrity independent of white feminisms. She acknowledges the current historical and political necessity to present black feminist thought as "overly coherent," deemphasizing contradictions and inconsistencies in an effort to demonstrate its undeniable existence and authenticity. Shying away from any single theoretical tradition, her analysis probes the interconnections of race, gender, and social class in the lives of black women in the United States and the complexity of ideas in scholarly and daily life that emerge from these. She argues for a particular black feminist standpoint in which any analysis of oppression must account for these inextricable intersections and then presents supporting evidence through the core themes of work and family, controlling images and stereotypes of black women, motherhood, politics and activism, sexuality, and sexual politics. Concluding the volume, Collins articulates her conceptual work toward an "Afrocentric feminist epistemology" rooted in the everyday experiences of African American women, concrete experience as a criterion of meaning, dialogue as a way to assess knowledge claims, and an ethic of caring and accountability to community. *Black Feminist Thought* fast became and remains an invaluable synthesis and an indispensable classic. A revised tenth-anniversary edition was published in 2000.

Collins expands this theoretical work in her 1998 interdisciplinary book *Fighting Words: Black Women and the Search for Justice* (University of Minnesota Press). Aiming to produce oppositional knowledge in the service of social and economic justice, she further develops the "outsider within" perspective of the earlier work in the investigation of the relationship of black feminist thought to critical social theory in terms of issues confronted, issues raised, and contributions made.

75. Curthoys, Jean. *Feminist Amnesia: The Wake of Women's Liberation*. New York: Routledge, 1997. 200p. bibliog. index. ISBN 0415148065; 0415148073pa.

A former "radical" who taught one of the first courses in feminist theory in an Australian university, Jean Curthoys has lately joined the ranks of more conservative commentators on women's liberation and feminist/women's studies. In this analysis of the "mediocrity" of current feminist thinking, she joins a growing number of studies that purport to show the intellectual and, on occasion, moral poverty of the women's liberation movement and the feminist analysis that informs and drives it. Curthoys clearly stands at the more academic end of the spectrum, using sophisticated philosophical and political arguments to indicate ways in which feminist thinkers have failed to engage with and carry forward what was most special about the women's liberation movement, "the fact that it was a social movement, engaged in a search for a personal and individual ethic of a Socratic nature" (p. 157). Corrupted by the appeal of power and authority, especially in academia, feminism turned away from its founding principles, which resulted in unclear thinking and, as Curthoys's title implies, amnesia. In a similar philosophical vein, Ellen R. Klein's *Feminism under Fire* (Prometheus Books, 1996) takes feminism to task for confusing and conflating a social and political movement with an intellectual/academic undertaking. She clearly states in her preface that she was "moved to expose feminism to the philosophical method of critical analysis and put feminism to the test" (p. 11) and not, incidentally, refute feminist critics of her earlier work.

76. Digby, Tom, ed. *Men Doing Feminism*. New York: Routledge, 1998. 359p. bibliog. ISBN 0415916259; 0415916267pa.

The eighteen writers whose works appear in Digby's anthology represent a broad spectrum of voices and perspectives that includes straight white men, gay men, and transsexuals. Many of their essays tackle the contested question of whether men can be feminists, and what such feminism might mean in theory and practice. Responses to male feminism from several prominent feminist theorists such as Susan Bordo, Sandra Harding, Joy James, and Judith Kegan Gardiner explore topics like fatherhood, epistemologies, and coalition politics and enhance the dialogue.

In contrast to Digby's collection, *Men in Feminism* (Methuen, 1987), edited by Alice Jardine and Paul Smith, includes contributors who are primarily white, straight, literary academics (a limitation that the editors acknowledge). This still worthwhile collection emerged out of discussions at the 1984 Modern Language Association conference around the thorny debates about the appropriation of feminist theory by male intellectuals in the humanities. It contains wide-ranging and provocative essays by several notable scholars like Rosi Braidotti, Jacques Derrida, Robert Scholes, and Elizabeth Weed and reflects the conviction of the editors that "thinking about 'men in feminism' brings up questions and problems which go right to the heart of feminist theory" (p. viii). Readers investigating the viewpoints and analyses of profeminist men engaging with the paradoxes of men's power and hegemonic masculinities will also want to examine *Theorizing Masculinities* (Sage Publications, 1994), edited by Harry Brod and Michael Kaufman.

77. Elam, Diane, and Robyn Wiegman, eds. *Feminism beside Itself.* New York: Routledge, 1995. 334p. bibliog. index. ISBN 0415910404; 0415910412pa.

This important collection of fifteen essays presents thought-provoking and challenging conversations about feminist theory and analyses of the way feminism constructs, represents, and questions its history and identity. Elam and Wiegman seek to highlight "how feminism had become increasingly anxious about itself" in the midst of vigorous contemporary debates surrounding its own "political and philosophical assumptions, omissions, and oppressive complicities" (p. 2). Their volume asks questions about feminism as history and narrative, its audience and political purpose, and explores the ways in which feminism is in conflict with itself, looking at issues such as political correctness, feminist misogyny, and the ways in which feminism can be itself "against women" through its own exclusionary and oppressive dimensions. The last section, titled simply "Besides . . . ," posits that feminism always stands besides something else, be it other theories, movements, or "things," for instance, as included here, nationalism, personal narrative, or contemporary popular culture. The self-reflective anxiety and self-critical reflection are modeled in the volume itself as it takes up disparate issues, emphasizes divergent directions, and foregrounds disagreement, undermining any unity and singular identity of feminism while locating its political force, the editors assert, in its very lack of coherence and homogeneity, its contingent "unknowability."

78. England, Paula, ed. *Theory on Gender/Feminism on Theory.* New York: Aldine de Gruyter, 1993. 377p. (Social Institutions and Social Change). bibliog. index. ISBN 020230437X; 0202304388pa.

This collection embodies some of the best qualities of feminist theory, providing clear articulations and an inclusive space for dialogue and debate within its very pages. Abundant material for discussion is presented, sparked by two key questions: "How do various sociological theories understand gender differentiation and gender inequality? Are these theories infused with masculinist bias that needs to be redressed with insights from feminist theory?" (p. 3). Sociologist England, seeking to deepen her own understanding of social theories, commissioned essays from proponents of a remarkable range of theoretical perspectives, including Marxism, world system theory, macrostructural theories, rational choice theory, neofunctionalism, psychoanalysis, ethnomethodology, expectation states theory, poststructuralist symbolic interactionism, and network theory. Following England's contextual introduction, these ten chapters each aim to outline the theory, describe its incorporation and/or explanation of gender, review associated empirical research, and assess the power and limitations of the theory from a feminist perspective. In the third section of the volume, England structures dialogue and debate in a unique and engaging fashion. Under four thematic rubrics, scholars from different vantage points scrutinize the essays: philosopher Nancy Tuana, sociologist Linda Molm, economist Nancy Folbre, and Marxist sociologist John Wilson. Their commentaries not only critique the essays but also attempt to bring them into dialogue with each other. Following these selections and advancing the dialogue, the essay authors reply to the commentators. Although limited attention is paid to diversity and none to sexuality, as a whole, the collection offers a dynamic introduction to multiple intersections between feminist and sociological theories, calling for their mutually informed elaboration and enrichment.

79. Evans, Judith. *Feminist Theory Today: An Introduction to Second-Wave Feminism.* Thousand Oaks, CA: Sage Publications, 1995. 183p. bibliog. index. ISBN 0803984782; 0803984790pa.

In an ambitious attempt to synthesize modern feminist theory in a concise and readable format, suitable for the classroom, Evans, a British political scientist, draws upon the writings of second-wave feminism from the 1963 publication of Betty Friedan's *The Feminine Mystique* through the 1990s works of Catharine MacKinnon focused on the law. Her sources include Shulamit Firestone, Susan Okin, Alice Rossi, Adrienne Rich, Mary Daly, Carol Gilligan, Joan Scott, and Judith Butler, among other theorists. She classifies this work (and the organization of the volume) into the "conventional schools" of liberal, radical, cultural, socialist, postmodernist, and legal thought. Structuring her examination through the conceptual framework of equality, sameness, and difference, she seeks not so much to resolve the shifting debates but rather to illuminate the dynamics and tensions between and within the theoretical "schools" through these concepts.

Readers will find a comparable, if less rigidly structured, survey of second-wave feminist thought in Imelda Whelehan's *Modern Feminist Thought* (Edinburgh University Press, 1995). Whelehan begins by tracing the genealogies of the second wave through constructs similar to those of Evans—liberal, Marxist/socialist, and radical—but also diversifies her scope through the inclusion of lesbian feminism and black feminism. Further, she productively complicates this history in the second part of the volume, which addresses "crises," debates, and rifts as well as "post-feminism." If she clarifies the impossibility of any unitary definition of feminism or even its division into neat, discrete strands, she also "offers reasons why detractors of feminism must be ceaselessly challenged" and underscores her "conviction that feminism remains an exciting and enabling political and philosophical standpoint in the '90s" (p. 3).

80. Evans, Mary. *Introducing Contemporary Feminist Thought.* Malden, MA: Polity Press, 1997. 170p. bibliog. index. ISBN 0745614752; 0745614760pa.

Evans, a professor of women's studies in Britain, offers a survey of contemporary academic feminism and women's studies. She sets as her purpose "to suggest some of the main ways in which a feminist understanding of the world can disturb and disrupt conventional assumptions," especially the assumption that there is a firm division between the academic/theoretical and the "real" world (p. 3). Intended for students, this book draws upon both historical and recent examples to present a broad sweep of feminist thinking focusing on central themes such as distinctions between the public and the private, relationships between women and the state, engendering knowledge, representation, and the body. It concludes with an exploration of feminism and the academy and questions of difference, both difference among women and the difference women can make in the world.

81. Flax, Jane. *Thinking Fragments: Psychoanalysis, Feminism, and Postmodernism in the Contemporary West.* Berkeley: University of California Press, 1990. 277p. bibliog. ISBN 0520065867; 0520073053pa.

In this highly influential work, Flax takes up the question "How is it possible to theorize in the contemporary West?" especially within current understandings of the fragmented and fluid nature of knowledge, truth, power, self, and gender. She trenchantly examines and critiques "three modes of contemporary Western thought": psychoanalysis, feminism, and postmodern philosophy. Using an engaging mode of "conversation" among the three, she analyzes each in turn and uses the tools of each to scrutinize the others, revealing strengths and limitations. Flax thus uncovers the blind spots in each theory and concludes that while each mode of theorizing offers useful insights and analytical tools, none of the three provides sufficient explanatory power alone. Indeed, she titles her last chapter "No Conclusions" and, far from seeking to resolve inherent conflicts, argues against the possibility of a single fully adequate, unified theory. In the course of her analysis, Flax evaluates the ideas of Freud and Lacan as well as object relations theorists like Winnicott, engages the feminist work of Chodorow and Irigaray, and extends her discussion to postmodernist theorists, including Derrida, Rorty, Lyotard, and Foucault. Her multitextured treatment, at once both appreciative and critical, provides a comprehensive, balanced, and stimulating overview that serves to bridge the divide among these theoretical perspectives.

82. Fox-Genovese, Elizabeth. *Feminism without Illusions: A Critique of Individualism.* Chapel Hill: University of North Carolina Press, 1991. 347p. bibliog. index. ISBN 0807819409; 0807843725pa.

Noted historian Fox-Genovese intends, she says, to provide a feminist critique of individualism in this wide-ranging, dense, and scholarly work. Yet *Feminism without Illusions* has been highly contested, with many critics regarding the work as a critique of feminism itself rife with sweeping generalizations. In a fairly reductionist mode, Fox-Genovese casts contemporary feminism as bourgeois individualism concerned primarily with equality and opportunity for the few at the expense of the many. She argues that feminism's deep and uncritical commitment to individualism only fosters competition among women and works against interdependent social obligation and community. In her view, the issue of abortion exemplifies the "chasm between feminist principles and politics . . . [pitting] American women against one another in passionate combat" (p. 81). She supports women's right to control their own bodies and sexuality but opposes sexual individualism and "the defense of abortion on the grounds of absolute individual right" (p. 86). Taking up the question of pornography, she extends her position that collectivity should be privileged over individual rights, emphasizing pornography's degradation of women and demanding its regulation if not suppression. This approach to feminism, equating it with individual ambition and achievement, often fails to account for its multifaceted and radical history that also works collectively to broaden the base of opportunity and privilege for all women. Fox-Genovese ultimately urges feminists to critique the excesses of unbridled individualism toward the goal of "a new conception of community—of the relation between freedom of individuals and the needs of society" (p. 256).

Fox-Genovese continues some of these same themes in her later, more popularized work *Feminism Is Not the Story of My Life: How Today's Feminist Elite Has Lost Touch with the Real Concerns of Women* (Nan A. Talese, 1996). Here she presents the viewpoints of women who claim that feminism does not address their experience and primary concerns, especially the centrality of marriage, motherhood, and family in women's lives. While admitting that she has not constructed a scientific sample, she draws from interviews, polling data from the 1960s through the early 1990s, and her own research. Opposing both conservatives and "elitist" feminists alike, she argues that the conflation of feminism with the sexual revolution and abortion on demand, ultimately separating sex from morality, has had pernicious and tragic social and economic consequences.

83. Fraser, Nancy. *Unruly Practices: Power, Discourse, and Gender in Contemporary Social Theory*. Minneapolis: University of Minnesota Press, 1989. 201p. bibliog. ISBN 0816617775; 0816617783pa.

Nancy Fraser locates herself as a social theorist trained as a philosopher, a democratic socialist, and a feminist. From this vantage point, she attempts to straddle the divide between academia and activism. Albeit highly theoretical, the eight essays collected here, first published between 1981 and 1988, grew out of "problems generated in, and solvable only through, political practice" (p. 3) and wrestle with "the links between left academics and social movements" (p. 7). Throughout the volume she engages critically with the work of prominent social theorists, including Foucault, Derrida, Rorty, and Habermas, and addresses the implications of social theory in public policy in the capitalist welfare state. Building on this foundation, she moves to the articulation of her own theory, examining the structure of the U.S. welfare system and women's greater dependence on it.

84. Fraser, Nancy, and Sandra Lee Bartky, eds. *Revaluing French Feminism: Critical Essays on Difference, Agency, and Culture*. Bloomington: Indiana University Press, 1992. 201p. bibliog. index. ISBN 025332436X; 0253206820pa.

After a decade of American feminists' engagement with French feminism, editors Fraser and Bartky gather contributions from leading feminist scholars, including Diana Fuss and Judith Butler, for a critical reappraisal of French feminist theory. The introduction by Nancy Fraser informatively frames the volume, contextualizing the production and American reception of key French feminist texts. Two interviews with Simone de Beauvoir and writings by French theorists Luce Irigaray and Sarah Kofman join writings from U.S. feminist philosophers in addressing themes of identity, difference, and femininity as well as the feminist debates around essentialism. If they are forcefully divergent in many respects, the writers share a common rejection of compulsory motherhood, a theme that weaves through most of the selections. Further, the essays examine the problems of male dominance and women's agency, "French feminist insights about the formative force of language in social life" (p. 19), and the question of the usefulness of French feminist theory for feminist practice. Suggestions for further reading on French feminist theory can be found in Joan Nordquist's *French Feminist Theory (III): Luce Irigaray and Helene Cixous: A Bibliography* (Reference and Research Services, 1996) (see entry 62).

85. Friedman, Susan Stanford. *Mappings: Feminism and the Cultural Geographies of Encounter*. Princeton, NJ: Princeton University Press, 1998. 314p. bibliog. index. ISBN 0691058032; 0691058040pa.

Spurred by "the urgent debates and conflicts taking place in the academy about the future of academic feminism" (p. xi), Friedman "maps the engagements of feminist theory with multiculturalism, postcolonial studies, cultural studies, and poststructuralism" (p. 4) in the face of the increasing permeability of national and personal borders during the past twenty years. In her timely and cogent work, she interweaves feminism/multiculturalism, feminism/globalism, and feminism/poststructuralism, organized around narratives of encounter. Rejecting false notions of a universal feminism and reductionist identity politics and borrowing from Edward Said's "traveling theory," Friedman compellingly argues for a "locational feminism" that develops out of transcultural interaction, requires a fundamental geopolitical literacy, and "encourages the study of difference in all its manifestations without being limited to it" (p. 5). Locational feminism recognizes the interlocking dimensions of global cultures and gender relations and complicates simplistic binaries like First World/Third World, which mask differentiation and difference across locations and time periods. Particularly concerned about the "Culture Wars" of the 1980s and

1990s, Friedman stresses the importance of academic feminism and its impact on the production and dissemination of knowledge.

86. Frye, Marilyn. *Willful Virgin: Essays in Feminism, 1976–1992*. Freedom, CA: Crossing Press, 1992. 169p. bibliog. (OP)

Frye, author of the widely read earlier collection *The Politics of Reality* (Crossing Press, 1983), writes from the vantage point of a lesbian engaged in identity politics who is also a professor of philosophy. The essays gathered here extend her reflections on lesbian identity and agency in contention with the totalizing "Patriarchal Universe of Discourse (PUD)" that conflates culture with phallocentric culture and meaning with the male symbolic (p. 7). If her earlier work focused more on male dominance and oppression, these essays, reflective of the evolution of feminism during the decade, are particularly concerned about relations among women, separations—accomplished by the institutions of female heterosexuality, racism, and economic stratification—and potential connections based in self-knowledge and bridging differences. In the title essay, Frye reclaims the original meaning of the word "virgin" as a free woman unbound to any man, sexually and socially her own person, untouched by patriarchy. Provocatively, if controversially, Frye rejects assimilation in any form and incites women to "virginity" through the creation of new meanings and realities outside of PUD. Other essays take up the equally charged questions of lesbian community, heterosexual bias in women's studies, political correctness, and the need for feminists to resist "whiteliness," the socially constructed sense of authority and entitlement.

87. Fuss, Diana. *Essentially Speaking: Feminism, Nature, and Difference*. New York: Routledge, 1989. 144p. bibliog. ISBN 0415901324; 0415901332pa.

Diana Fuss, one of the most articulate theorists to engage in the debate between essentialism and constructionism, provides a lucid introduction complete with definitions. Fuss explains, "Essentialism is most commonly understood as a belief in the real, true essence of things, the invariable and fixed properties which define the 'whatness' of a given entity" (p. xi). She outlines the most significant features of the debate and describes instances in which "essence operates as a privileged signifier" (p. xiii). Her ultimate project in the book, however, is to illustrate those situations in which the dichotomy breaks down and essentialism and constructionism or antiessentialism actually exist in more fluid relationship to each other, each borrowing from the other. She unpacks the complicated relationship between these two theoretical views, with particular attention to Monique Wittig (antiessentialist) and Luce Irigaray (essentialist). Finally, she examines specific social and theoretical issues strongly influenced by essentialist and antiessentialist schools, including race, homosexuality, and pedagogy.

Fuss also edited *Inside/Out: Lesbian Theories, Gay Theories* (Routledge, 1991) in which eighteen scholars contribute their ideas to the ongoing arguments on the utility of queer theory to "call into question the stability and ineradicability of the hetero/homo hierarchy" (p. 1). Divided into five sections, "Decking Out: Performing Identities," "Cutting Up: Specters, Spectators, Authors," "Zoning In: Body Parts," "Acting Up: AIDS, Allegory, Activism," and "Speaking Out: Teaching In," the essays address a broad range of contemporary concerns, with significant focus on lesbian as well as gay male theory.

88. García, Alma, ed. *Chicana Feminist Thought: The Basic Historical Writings*. New York: Routledge, 1997. 324p. bibliog. index. ISBN 0415918006; 0415918014pa.

This exceptional collection documents the development and evolution of Chicana feminism dually contextualized within white Anglo-American feminism and the Chicano movement yet independent and distinct from each. Eighty-two essays, interviews, poetry, and photographs chronicle the struggles of Chicanas to develop feminist activism and theorizing that preserves their culture and heritage while also challenging the gender contradictions and sexual politics frequently embedded in cultural nationalism. Organized chronologically and thematically, the volume provides a solid historical overview of activism in the areas of education, child care, health care, employment, abortion rights, and sexuality. It also includes selections that analyze Chicana oppression, interrogate relationships between Chicana feminists and white feminists, and map a Chicana feminist agenda in an "evolving future." Concluding with selections from contemporary Chicana literature, including work from Anzaldúa, Castillo, Mora, and Moraga, and an interview with Sandra Cisneros, the anthology further illustrates the theoretical power of cultural expressive forms. The variety of genres, scholarly, literary, and visual, and the interweaving of history, politics, sociology, and literature into one volume effectively mirror the multiple dimensions of daily life and theorizing. This breadth and depth, enhanced by a well-constructed index, particularly recommend this collection for the classroom.

89. Gardiner, Judith Kegan, ed. *Provoking Agents: Gender and Agency in Theory and Practice.* Urbana: University of Illinois Press, 1995. 342p. bibliog. index. ISBN 0252021320; 0252064186pa.

Gardiner's engaging anthology focuses on the concept and implications of agency as a central problem in feminist theory. Ambitious in scope, it "ranges across and between the fields of philosophy, literary criticism, history, political science, sociology, psychology, anthropology, legal theory, film, cultural, African, women's and lesbian-gay-bisexual studies" (p. 17). Among multiple definitions of agency, bell hooks describes it as "the ability to act in one's best interest" (p. 6), but, as many of the contributors here assert, it must be understood to encompass both action and representation as well as the interaction between individual and political agency. The fifteen essays apply the theory and practice of agency contextualized within a wide variety of activities from consciousness-raising to reproductive technologies and abortion, the performance art of Annie Sprinkle to AIDS activism, family photographs to literature, and U.S. Third World feminist criticism to women's political and cultural resistance in patriarchal-capitalist postcolonial Kenya. Throughout, the salient, bottom-line question "Who benefits?" implicitly or explicitly recurs in an effort to counter feminist factionalism and further progressive social change.

90. Grant, Judith. *Fundamental Feminism: Contesting the Core Concepts of Feminist Theory.* New York: Routledge, 1993. 226p. bibliog. index. ISBN 0415908256; 0415908264pa.

Grant, a political scientist, critiques many current Anglo-American feminist theories, especially those grounded in essentializing concepts of women and female experience. She seeks to disclose and discuss an underlying, "fundamental feminism" manifested in three "fetishized" core concepts: "woman," experience, and personal politics. These concepts, developed by radical feminists in the late 1960s and early 1970s, provide the conceptual and, Grant argues, highly problematic basis for subsequent varieties of feminism, including socialist feminism, identity theories, and standpoint theory. She argues that feminism must more inclusively "entail a reconstruction of both woman and man" and cast itself as "a new version of humanism" (p. 184). She rejects the "fruitless quest for the authentic female experience" (p. 191) and advocates an alternative focus on "the idea of an ideological structure of gender from which we seek liberation" (p. 189). Pauline Johnson's *Feminism as Radical Humanism* (Westview Press, 1994) similarly calls for a reassessment and revitalization of feminism through its shared commitments and values with contemporary humanism.

91. Grewal, Inderpal, and Caren Kaplan, eds. *Scattered Hegemonies: Postmodernity and Transitional Feminist Practices*. Minneapolis: University of Minnesota Press, 1994. bibliog. index. ISBN 0816621373; 0816621381pa.

In this important work, Grewal and Kaplan aim to counter the homogeneity of much feminist theory in the United States and Europe and to deepen the analysis of gender through transnational "work across differences in culture, discipline and profession" (p. 2) within the context of contemporary global cultures and relations. Quite distinct from the "Western cultural imperialism" of "global feminism" grounded in individuality, modernity, and notions of a unitary world of women, they argue for the conceptual power of postmodernity to foster comparative, gendered analyses of transnational "scattered hegemonies such as global economic structures, patriarchal nationalisms, 'authentic' forms of tradition, local structures of domination, and legal-juridical oppression on multiple levels" (p. 17). The section "Gender, Nation, and Critiques of Modernity" gathers writings by Lydia Liu, May Layoun, Nalini Natarajan, Kamala Visweswaran, and Norma Alarcon that examine symbolic relationships between women and nation from different geographic, historical, and cultural locations, including the Chinese state, contemporary India, and Chicana feminism. In "Global-Colonial Limits," essays by Kaplan, Robert Carr, Tani Barlow, Fred Pfeil, and Grewal explore the possibilities and limitations of the politics of location, drawing upon new readings of the work of such writers as Adrienne Rich, Teresa de Lauretis, bell hooks, Bharati Mukherjee, Sara Suleri, and Gloria Anzaldúa.

92. Grieve, Norma, and Alisa Burns, eds. *Australian Women: Contemporary Feminist Thought*. New York: Oxford University Press, 1994. 356p. bibliog. index. ISBN 0195535030.

Grieve and Burns extend the Oxford University Press series on Australian feminism, building on the companion volumes *Australian Women: Feminist Perspectives* (1981) and *Australian Women: New Feminist Perspectives* (1986). This third volume collects writings from the early 1990s selected to represent Australian feminist scholarship across a range of disciplines, focusing on "topics which have emerged as important theoretical and political issues, and/or that appear especially important for the 1990s" (p. 1). Within the context of feminism's firmly embedded place in Australian culture, distinguished scholars offer trenchant perspectives on Australian feminist discourse and debates, relationships with Australian nationalism, and questions of theory salient in Australian feminism since 1970. Ann Curthoys traces the evolution of various theoretical frameworks and the emergence and impact of postmodern and postcolonial critiques. She tackles the thorny debates concerning universality versus difference with particular clarity, vexing questions also addressed by other contributors to this volume. Three essays from historians Jackie Higgins, Patricia Grimshaw, and Marilyn Lake interrogate the complex relationships between white feminists and Australian Aboriginal women who often reject antimasculinist analyses of subordination and critiques of the family. Comparisons with feminisms in Europe and North America offered by social scientist Gisela Kaplan and former "femocrat" Ann Summers further illuminate the distinctive character of Australian feminism and its flexible and pragmatic integration into the political mainstream. This volume is an eclectic and excellent introduction to contemporary feminist thought in Australia.

93. Grosz, E.A. *Volatile Bodies: Toward a Corporeal Feminism*. Bloomington: Indiana University Press, 1994. 250p. bibliog. index. ISBN 0253326869; 0253208629pa.

A formidable feminist philosopher, Grosz joins Judith Butler and other theorists in asserting the critical importance of bodies to understandings of sexual difference, gender, and relations of power. She argues for the superiority of corporeality as a theoretical framework for understanding subjectivity. Adroitly employing the metaphorical model of the Möbius strip, she presents complex arguments to subvert the dualistic, inside-outside dichotomy of mind and body, reconceptualizing the relationship as "the inflection of mind into body and body into mind . . . [where] one side becomes another" (p. xii). She rejects Cartesian notions of the body as given or "naturally" complete to explore the mutually constitutive and reconstitutive processes of corporeality, psyche, and subjectivity through social and cultural networks of meaning. Regarding the body as a historically specific "sociocultural artifact," she examines and builds on the theories of Freud, Lacan, Schilder, Nietzsche, Foucault, and others but contests their universalizing of the masculine body. She insists on the sexual specificity of bodies and the need to theorize bodies as sexed in order to analyze sexual difference not as biologically fixed but as volatile, "an open materiality, a set of (possibly infinite) tendencies and potentialities which may be developed" (p. 191). Through the course of her work, Grosz provides insightful investigations of such topics as anorexia and body image as well as women's bodies and bodily fluids, drawing on the work of Mary Douglas, Julia Kristeva, and Luce Irigaray.

Grosz extends her analysis of corporeality in her subsequent work *Space, Time, and Perversion: Essays on the Politics of Bodies* (Routledge, 1995). Here she gathers essays written during the previous decade that examine the epistemological implications of bodily differences and sexual specificity, problematize conventional conceptions of the relations between knowledge and power, and critique "tokenistic feminism that is assured of its own certainty and correctness, that refuses to rethink, to reconsider the possibility or even likelihood of its own transformation" (p. 4). Subsequent essays deal with space, spatiality, and related arts, including architecture, urban planning, and geography, exploring their relation to subjectivity, corporeality, and thought. Grosz ultimately takes up questions of sexuality and sexual desire, challenging privileged discourses of sexuality (psychoanalytic, Foucauldian, feminist, and queer theory) and rejecting totalizing theories in her concern "with how thought might accommodate a positive, joyous understanding of sexual pleasure in all its strange permutations, raising a series of questions rather than offering solutions, proclamations, or manifestos" (p. 5). She provides trenchant arguments that "sexual differences, like those of class and race, *are* bodily differences, but in order to acknowledge their fundamentally social and cultural 'nature,' the body must be reconceived, not in opposition to culture but as its preeminent object" (p. 32).

94. Gunew, Sneja, ed. *Feminist Knowledge: Critique and Construct.* New York: Routledge, 1990. 357p. bibliog. index. (OP)

Gunew's eclectic collection of writings by Australian feminists explores the relationships among academic feminist knowledge, theory, and political change and further interrogates the "paradoxical interaction of feminist theory and women's experience" (p. 13). The text grew out of a women's studies course and takes a pedagogical approach to a range of debates. It provides a lucid and balanced discussion of critical theory, emphasizing critiques of classic poststructuralist texts while offering summaries of key feminist works. An examination of the relationship of feminism to women's movements and to the academic discipline of women's studies probes the tensions among education, research, and cultural politics. Disciplinary essays covering philosophy, psychoanalysis, biology, and religion further explore the contours of feminist knowledge production, followed by political perspectives on radical, socialist, and poststructuralist feminisms. A companion volume, *A Reader in Feminist Knowledge* (Routledge, 1991), further develops the information and perspectives covered here.

Gunew also subsequently expands the range of her inquiry in *Feminism and the Politics of Difference*, edited with Anna Yeatman (Allen & Unwin, 1993), which gives voice to women often silenced in postcolonial societies. Informed by poststructuralist theory, contributors from many different geographical (Australia, New Zealand, Sri Lanka, Canada, Japan) and subject (Chinese, Vietnamese, Maori) locations address the politics of difference, focusing primarily on discursive and cultural forms. Included are readings of film, analyses of literature (Anzaldúa's *Borderlands*) and of erotically subversive Japanese girls' comics, a description of racism and power relations in women's book publishing, and a critique of feminist ethnography as complicitous with conventional masculinist and even imperialist methods. If only two essays address difference in terms of power and the politics of social movements and feminist practice, the anthology nonetheless provides a critical space for articulating difference from marginalized locations too seldom present in feminist theorizing.

95. Guy-Sheftall, Beverly, ed. *Words of Fire: An Anthology of African-American Feminist Thought*. New York: New Press/Norton, 1995. 577p. bibliog. index. ISBN 1565842561pa.

This groundbreaking collection traces the evolution of more than 150 years of black feminist thought from the 1830s to contemporary "discourses of resistance" by Alice Walker and others. Guy-Sheftall provides a much-needed corrective to histories and narratives centered almost exclusively on white women, documenting the "continuous feminist intellectual tradition in the nonfictional prose of African American women" (p. xiii) and including the writings of activists and academics, community organizers and artists. Organized both chronologically and thematically, this extensive and well-indexed volume spans the writings of nineteenth-century "race women" to black feminist theorizing in the 1970s and 1980s. Headnotes introduce each selection, providing information about the author and highlighting the significance of the text. Necessarily selective, this anthology nonetheless covers an astonishing range of issues, including "the moral integrity of black women, lynching, poverty, institutionalized racism and sexism, the racism of white women, the sexism of black men, education, black families, male/female relationships, economics, reproductive freedom, sexual and family violence, sexuality, heterosexism, the Civil Rights movement, black nationalism, women's liberation struggles nationally and internationally, and female genital mutilation" (p. xv). This volume is an important contribution to the literature of feminist history and theory suitable for classroom use.

96. Hartsock, Nancy C.M. *The Feminist Standpoint Revisited and Other Essays*. Boulder, CO: Westview Press, 1998. 262p. bibliog. index. ISBN 0813315573; 0813315581pa.

The essays collected here span twenty years of theorizing by Marxist feminist Hartsock as she probes and juxtaposes interlocking themes of power and epistemology. Organized into three parts—"Political Movements and Political Theories"; "Reoccupying Marxism as Feminism"; and "Structuralism, Poststructuralism, and Politics"—the volume engages debates around the feminist standpoint, examining the work of Lukacs, Althusser, Lévi-Strauss, Gayle Rubin, and Foucault, among other theorists. Hartsock argues that theory plays a critical role in political organizing for social change and that "political theorists must respond to and concentrate their energies on problems of political action" (p. 7). She draws direct connections between labor, power relations, and epistemology: "Our work produces both our material existence and our consciousness" (p. 47). The centrality of work leads not only to investigations of the sexual division of labor and the gendered nature of production, but also necessarily to the structure and dynamics of family life in which women's labor is undervalued and uncompensated in a commodity-based economy. Hartsock's concluding essay, "The Feminist Standpoint Revisited," presents an important expansion of and corrective to her earlier work, often criticized as essentialist. She engages her critics, summarizing their arguments and acknowledging that she "did not give proper attention to differences among women" (p. 235), and builds on the work of Michelle Cliff, Frederic Jameson, and Gloria Anzaldúa to rethink the nature of a standpoint and reformulate her theory.

97. Heller, Dana, ed. *Cross-Purposes: Lesbians, Feminists, and the Limits of Alliance.* Bloomington: Indiana University Press, 1997. 238p. bibliog. index. ISBN 025333246X; 0253210844pa.

In this timely anthology, Heller has compiled fourteen multidisciplinary essays to "stage a long-overdue critical intervention into the history, current condition, and evolving shape of lesbian alliances with feminisms in the United States" (p. 1). Contributors from the interrelated fields of lesbian and gay studies, women's studies, and queer theory interrogate the kaleidoscopic relationships of lesbians to feminism and, more recently, to queer theory, how lesbians are now, in Carolyn Dever's words, "caught between the feminist and the queer" (p. 39), often subordinate and discounted if not invisible. Through the exploration of such wide-ranging topics as Sandra Bernhard, film, HIV and AIDS as women's health issues, lesbian chic, the neglect of transgender and transsexual identities, women's music, and butch-femme, these theorists and cultural critics offer a stimulating mix of perspectives that illuminate crucial issues of language, gender and sexuality, politics, identity, and generation. The collection calls for a revitalization of lesbian feminism while also providing cogent arguments for a recognition and elaboration of independent lesbian realities and a distinct lesbian theory.

98. Hennessy, Rosemary, and Chrys Ingraham, eds. *Materialist Feminism: A Reader in Class, Difference, and Women's Lives.* New York: Routledge, 1997. bibliog. ISBN 041591633X; 0415916348pa.

Documenting the development of materialist feminist analyses from 1969 to 1996, the editors of this volume aim to reclaim historical materialism and anticapitalist feminism and to counter the assimilation of feminism into the mainstream, which they view as happening through identity politics, postmodernism, and post-Marxism. They tackle the "problem of how historical materialism might be used to explain and change women's oppression and exploitation under capitalism" (p. 10) and probe the differences between women and the ways in which race, gender, and sexuality are interlinked in capitalism as a global system. Essays by younger scholars address "more recent social developments—reproductive engineering, the Green Revolution, and ecofeminism—as well as longstanding issues often ignored by socialist feminists—heterosexuality and prostitution" (p. 13). Contributors include such notable writers as Barbara Ehrenreich, Hazel Carby, Gloria Joseph, Margaret Benston, Gayle Rubin, Lillian Robinson, Nellie Wong, and Norma Chinchilla, among others, representing a variety of backgrounds, ethnicities, and standpoints. The volume incorporates both theoretical and more pragmatic texts as well as a broad range of perspectives, often in disagreement with each other, especially as regards concepts of patriarchy and specific strategies of Marxism as useful analytical and political tools. Taken together, however, these essays challenge postmodern cultural politics, arguing for material and social change to meet women's collective needs. Exploitation rather than discrimination must be the primary target of feminism and feminist theory, and activism must aim not only to explain the world but also to transform it. This excellent introduction to a broad sweep of important feminist work builds on an earlier body of literature, including Hennessy's own *Materialist Feminism and the Politics of Discourse* (Routledge, 1993) and Donna Landry and Gerald MacLean's *Materialist Feminisms* (Blackwell, 1993). The extensive bibliography of references used by the authors and key works on materialist feminism provides an additional useful resource.

99. Herrmann, Anne C., and Abigail J. Stewart, eds. *Theorizing Feminism: Parallel Trends in the Humanities and Social Sciences*. Boulder, CO: Westview Press, 1994. 483p. bibliog. ISBN 0813387051; 0813367883pa.

This volume ambitiously strives to bring together twenty years' worth of significant work on feminism from the perspectives of both the humanities and the social sciences. As the title suggests, the essays selected for inclusion focus on theory and the ways in which the disciplines within the humanities and the social sciences complement, inform, and occasionally clash with one another. The editors make quite clear their objective to promote interdisciplinary analysis and, wherever possible, team teaching. The introductory essay, "Reading Feminist Theories: Collaborating across Disciplines," not only presents and contextualizes the contributions that follow but serves as a guide to teachers and students in their efforts to incorporate a range of feminist theorizing into their teaching and reading. The editors have included well-known as well as somewhat less familiar selections from the wide corpus of women on feminist theory, including, for example, the deservedly famous 1983 articulation of black feminist theory "The Combahee River Collective Statement" as well as Rosalind Delmar's less often cited essay "What Is Feminism?" The editors place the previously published essays in relation to each other in ways that further the project of encouraging interdisciplinary dialogue and add value to the book. Theorists represented in the collection include poet and playwright Cherrie Moraga, art critic and historian Linda Nochlin, critical legal theory scholar Patricia J. Williams, and historians of science and culture Donna Haraway and Sandra Harding, among other noteworthy contributors. A second edition was published in 2001.

100. Hirsch, Marianne, and Evelyn Fox Keller, eds. *Conflicts in Feminism*. New York: Routledge, 1990. 397p. bibliog. index. ISBN 0415901774; 0415901782pa.

During the decade of the 1980s, North American feminism and feminist theory not only were confronted by a hostile social and political climate, they were, even more significantly, marked by internal conflicts and intense divisiveness—over race, ethnicity, class, and sexual preference; pornography and "the sex wars"; meanings of "motherhood" and "fatherhood"; and the Sears and Baby M legal cases, to cite just a few of the flash points. Hirsch and Keller commissioned this collection of illuminating and provocative essays from twenty-three noted feminists and scholars in an urgent attempt to restore dialogue, counter the potential paralysis of intractable debate, and sustain the progressive momentum of feminism in multiple, differing, and even contradictory forms. Indeed, several of the chapters exemplify dialogic practice in themselves, most notably the exchange between Peggy Kamuf and Nancy K. Miller, "Parisian Letters: Between Feminism and Deconstruction," and the cross-race "Conversation about Race and Class" between Mary Childers and bell hooks. If the disciplinary emphasis tilts toward literary criticism, the reach of this highly influential anthology also encompasses contentious debates farther afield in science and law and fulfills its objective to "examine several of the most critically divisive issues in contemporary U.S. feminist theory" (p. 4). Hirsch and Keller set their sights on the larger goal to spawn "new models for a discourse of difference—models that would preserve the dynamic possibilities but defuse the explosive potential of enduring disagreements" (p. 5). Despite the acknowledged absence of contemporary women's activism and an analysis of power structures beyond the academy, the volume provides a pathbreaking antidote to all unitary approaches and successfully creates a framework for the productive practice of conflict in feminism.

101. hooks, bell. *Talking Back: Thinking Feminist, Thinking Black*. Boston: South End Press, 1989. 184p. bibliog. ISBN 0896083535; 0896083527pa.

No bibliography of works on feminist theory would be complete without the inclusion of bell hooks. As a thinker who challenges accepted "wisdom," even the accepted wisdom of something as new as second-wave feminism, hooks has few peers. The strength of hooks's work, however, lies in her positive articulation of a different, more highly nuanced feminism. *Talking Back* offers a uniquely personal, highly political rendering of the importance of words, both in the context of hooks's community of origin and in the often unwelcoming and challenging worlds of graduate school ("on being black at yale: education as the practice of freedom") and in the feminist movement. Covering topics ranging from violence against women to her decision to adopt a pseudonym, this work is a singular contribution to feminist theory that, a decade after its initial publication, still offers critical food for thought. One of the more prolific feminist writers, hooks expanded the breadth and depth of her theorizing in subsequent years through the publication of *Yearning: Race, Class, Gender, and Cultural Politics* (South End Press, 1990), *Black Looks: Race and Representation* (South End Press, 1992), *Outlaw Culture: Resisting Representations* (see entry 690) (Routledge, 1994), and *Killing Rage: Ending Racism* (Henry Holt and Co., 1995), among other titles. Throughout, she grounds her theory in her own experiences and works diligently to unite theory and practice.

102. Jackson, Stevi, and Jackie Jones, eds. *Contemporary Feminist Theories*. New York: New York University Press, 1998. 271p. bibliog. index. ISBN 0814742483; 0814742491pa.

Feminist theory is nothing if not a dynamic and reflexive phenomenon now impossible to capture within traditional liberal, Marxist, or radical classifications. During the past three decades, it has developed into an immense, heterogeneous field marked by multiple directions and forms. This introductory collection, intended as a classroom text, covers the growth of feminist theory since 1970, reflecting the diversity and shifting currents within it. British-based contributors, incorporating American and European theorizing and explicitly acknowledging the need to question and move beyond white Western perspectives, describe the historic evolution of feminist thought and chart future directions and possibilities in specific areas. Discipline-based chapters emphasize the humanities (literature, media, and film) and social sciences (economics, politics, law, anthropology, and linguistics) along with women's studies. Others take a more conceptual approach and offer lucid explorations of particular paradigms, including postcolonial, lesbian, and psychoanalytic theories as well as black feminisms and postmodernism. If the absence of science, technology, and medicine is lamentable, the collection nevertheless serves as a multidisciplinary guide to a broad range of feminist theories. An alternative textbook, *Contemporary Feminist Theory: A Text/Reader*, edited by Mary F. Rogers (McGraw-Hill, 1998), offers diverse and accessible readings from twenty-nine prominent theorists, including Judith Lorber, Chela Sandoval, Sandra Harding, Patricia Williams, Judith Butler, and bell hooks, organized under thematic rubrics, each framed by Rogers's orientation to the theory and its objectives.

103. Jaggar, Alison M., ed. *Living with Contradictions: Controversies in Feminist Social Ethics*. Boulder, CO: Westview Press, 1994. 698p. bibliog. ISBN 0813317754; 0813317762pa.

Jaggar's substantial and impressive volume compiles some 100 selections to illustrate the wide range of ethical concerns facing feminists. It does not focus on conflicts between feminists and antifeminists, but rather takes up the challenge of exploring issues that divide feminists themselves and of probing the question of what makes a moral or public policy issue, beyond the conventionally defined "women's issues," an issue for feminism. The broad sweep of topics that come under scrutiny and analysis here includes sexual difference, feminist jurisprudence, affirmative action, comparable worth, prostitution and other sex work, pornography, fashion and beauty, abortion, reproductive technologies, alternative families, sexual practices, vegetarianism, animal rights, militarism, and environmentalism. The multiple and often contradictory approaches taken by feminists to these issues in the essays and excerpts gathered here represent a key strength of the collection and particularly recommend it for classroom use.

The imperative connections between feminist ethics and politics also are a central theme of Janet R. Jakobsen's *Working Alliances and the Politics of Difference: Diversity and Feminist Ethics* (Indiana University Press, 1998). Using case studies of the intersections of gender, race, class, and sexuality in the nineteenth-century abolition movement and in the feminist movement of the late twentieth century, she argues for alliance rather than coalition politics, organizing that recognizes and incorporates diversity and complexity. One of the more thought-provoking aspects of the volume is her reading of the right-wing video *Gay Rights, Special Rights*.

104. Jagose, Annamarie. *Lesbian Utopics*. New York: Routledge, 1994. 214p. bibliog. index. ISBN 0415910188; 0415910196pa.

Jagose takes feminist and lesbian feminist scholars and theorists to task for failing to problematize "lesbian" and for using the term (and the concept of the lesbian body) in universalizing, essentializing, and, in certain instances, phobic ways. Jagose argues that Monique Wittig, Bonnie Zimmerman, and other lesbian writers and theorists fail in their political projects because they attempt to "theorize a perfect lesbian space, system, or economy that is altogether elsewhere" (p. 2) and further essentialize the lesbian subject as transgressive in ways that paradoxically bolster dominant systems of power. Jagose interrogates five different texts published between 1985 and 1989, critiquing their "various formations of 'lesbian' as constituting a space beyond the symbolic order, beyond the economy of the closet . . . and patriarchal nomination" (p. 23). Like the texts she selects—writings by Irigaray, Brossard, Hacker, Fallon, and Anzaldúa—her arguments are richly textured and theoretically challenging.

105. James, Stanie M., and Abena P.A. Busia, eds. *Theorizing Black Feminisms: The Visionary Pragmatism of Black Women*. New York: Routledge, 1993. 300p. bibliog. index. ISBN 0415073367; 0415073375pa.

The essays in this volume developed out of two interdisciplinary conferences on black feminist theory, first at the University of Wisconsin at Madison in 1990, then at Spelman College in Atlanta in 1991. The participants sought to articulate black feminist theorizing as a form of agency, developing "out of Black women's experience of multiple interrelated oppressions including (but not limited to) racism/ethnocentrism, sexism/homophobia and classism" and reflecting a "proactive/reactive stance of pragmatic activism" (p. 2). The essays frequently draw upon the work of theorists Deborah King and Patricia Hill Collins and address a broad range of issues, among them political activism, mothering, academic feminism and theory, labor and employment, health, literature and visual art, and questions of identity and difference. Roundly rejecting any "megatheory about the Black woman" (p. 291), Busia and the other contributors strive to complicate all such categories and articulate different voices and practices. The inclusion of essays in each section dealing with issues in the United States and Africa further reflects this pluralistic approach, cross-cultural theoretical perspectives, and the interplay of differences critical to contemporary black feminism.

106. Joeres, Ruth-Ellen B., and Barbara Laslett, eds. *The Second Signs Reader: Feminist Scholarship, 1983–1996*. Chicago: University of Chicago Press, 1996. 424p. bibliog. index. ISBN 0226400603; 0226400611pa.

Arguably the leading feminist journal since its inception in 1975, *Signs: A Journal of Women in Culture and Society* often represents academic feminism at its best. Following the first *Signs Reader: Women, Gender, and Scholarship*, published in 1983, this second reader traces the scope and variety of scholarship in the intervening decade and beyond. New scholarly work takes increasingly multidisciplinary and international directions and investigates ever more complex questions of gender and its intersections with other analytical categories. Editors Joeres and Laslett have selected work primarily published since 1990 from literary scholars, historians, philosophers, sociologists, political scientists, and psychologists. The disciplinary boundaries, however, are increasingly breached, and new interdisciplinary areas of interest like cultural studies, identity, and diversity are addressed. The thirteen essays compiled here include Evelyn Brooks Higginbotham's "African-American Women's History and the Metalanguage of Race"; Gayle Greene's "Feminist Fiction and the Uses of Memory"; Nancy Chodorow's "Gender as a Personal and Cultural Construction"; Iris Marion Young's "Gender as Seriality: Thinking about Women as a Social Collective"; and Wendy Luttrell's " 'The Teachers, They All Had Their Pets': Concepts of Gender, Knowledge, and Power." Other writers represented include Evelyn Nakano Glenn, Ann DuCille, Susan Stanford Friedman, Maureen A. Mahoney and Barbara Yngvesson, Maria Lugones, Trisha Franzen, Marilyn Frye, and Lisa Disch and Mary Jo Kane. If necessarily highly selective, the volume nonetheless stands as a thought-provoking overview of the widening reach of feminist scholarship and the multiple valences within it. A subsequent collection from *Signs* issued the following year, *History and Theory: Feminist Research, Debates, Contestations*, edited by Laslett and others (University of Chicago Press, 1997), illustrates "the uses of theory in recent historical research and the often contentious debates that surround them" (p. 4).

107. Kauffman, Linda S., ed. *American Feminist Thought at Century's End: A Reader.* Cambridge, MA: Blackwell, 1993. 477p. bibliog. ISBN 1557863466; 1557863474pa.

Kauffman has gathered an anthology of highly regarded feminist writings from Gayle Rubin's "Thinking Sex . . . ," published in 1984, to Joan Wallach Scott's 1992 essay "Women's History." The seventeen essays are organized into five sections addressing sexuality, race, and gender; theories of difference; science, technology, and the academic disciplines; feminist activism on AIDS, reproductive politics, and pornography; and finally, American feminism within an international framework. Suitable as a classroom text, this thought-provoking collection highlights the intersection of theory with contemporary social issues and provides a multifaceted introduction to the influential works of such well-known theorists as bell hooks, Tania Modleski, Sandra Harding, Donna Haraway, Evelyn Fox Keller, Angela Davis, Catharine MacKinnon, Gloria Anzaldúa, and Cynthia Enloe.

108. Kemp, Sandra, and Paola Bono, eds. *The Lonely Mirror: Italian Perspectives on Feminist Theory.* New York: Routledge, 1993. 251p. bibliog. index. (OP)

The publication of *Liberazione della Donna: Feminism in Italy* by the Italian American historian Lucia Chiavola Birnbaum (Wesleyan University Press, 1986), followed by Judith Adler Hellman's *Journeys among Women: Feminism in Five Italian Cities* (Polity Press, 1987), marked a welcome beginning to materials in English on contemporary Italian feminism. Editors Kemp and Bono subsequently expanded the availability of this work, focusing on feminist theory in Italy. *The Lonely Mirror* is the second volume in their two-book project. The first, *Italian Feminist Thought* (Blackwell, 1991), surveyed a range of theoretical positions and then further documented Italian feminist debates from 1966 to 1989 through essays, newspaper articles, manifestos, and book extracts. The editors attempted to provide a full intellectual and political history of Italian feminism, examining a variety of social issues: sexuality, abortion and rape-law reform, trade unions, "lesbofemminismo," feminist publishing, salaries for housewives, and even terrorism, military service, and Chernobyl. Further documentation of this period included a table of women's centres, a 1965–1986 chronology of events in Italy within an international context, an annotated list of Italian feminist periodicals, and a chronological bibliography.

The Lonely Mirror deepens the scope of the project by focusing on complete scholarly articles published in the decade 1979–1989, a time of significant change in the Italian feminist movement and contested and renegotiated meanings in theorizing. Drawn from literature, linguistics, semiotics, history, psychoanalysis, and philosophy, thirteen essays depict multifaceted attempts "to recover the female subject who cannot identify herself in the mirrors of history and of philosophical thought" (p. 18) and multiple visions of the ways in which "women have started being mirrors for one another" (p. 10). Topical emphases include sexual difference, the body, and sexuality encompassing both women as the subject of pornography and women as writers of erotica.

Italian feminist theory is examined from a different angle in *Feminine Feminists: Cultural Practices in Italy*, edited by Giovanna Miceli Jeffries (University of Minnesota Press, 1994). Here, researchers in Italian studies based in the United States explore the dynamics of relations between feminism and femininity in Italian culture through the lens of history (fascism and futurism), feminist writing, cinema, fashion, ethics, and transcultural dialogues between Italian and American feminisms and theories.

109. Kemp, Sandra, and Judith Squires, eds. *Feminisms*. New York: Oxford University Press, 1997. 599p. (Oxford Readers). bibliog. index. ISBN 0192892703pa.

One of a series of readers designed to compile primary and secondary sources on contemporary interdisciplinary issues, *Feminisms* provides a rich and engaging selection of readings. More theoretical than other classroom anthologies, this collection takes up debates in American, British, and French feminist theory and criticism dating from 1980 through the mid-1990s. Eighty-six abridged extracts from a diverse group of authors are arranged chronologically within six sections: "Academies," "Epistemologies," "Subjectivities," "Sexualities," "Visualities," and "Technologies." In selecting such innovative and thought-provoking categorization, the editors effectively cross-cut disciplinary boundaries and jettison conventional taxonomies of feminisms to focus on key debates within current feminist discourse. Introductions to each section provide lucid thematic frameworks to and foster critical thinking about the articles that follow.

Similarly titled and also theoretically oriented, Maggie Humm's earlier *Feminisms: A Reader* (Harvester Wheatsheaf, 1992) represents a more conventional organizational schema, with articles grouped under historical rubrics (first- and second-wave feminism) and types of feminism (socialist/Marxist, lesbian, liberal, and so on) followed by chapters on "Difference," "Nature," "Sexuality and Reproduction," "Philosophy and the Sciences," "History," "Culture," "Language and Writing," and "Feminism and Education." Both anthologies encourage students and other readers to see the world and personal experience in new ways and demonstrate the range and vitality of feminist knowledge production.

110. King, Katie. *Theory in Its Feminist Travels: Conversations in U.S. Women's Movements*. Bloomington: Indiana University Press, 1994. 190p. bibliog. index. ISBN 0253331382; 0253209056pa.

Drawing upon resources from a variety of fields, including "postcolonial theory, transnational cultural studies, antiracist cultural theory, sex radical approaches to lesbian and gay studies," King offers a guided tour to the "production and reception of theory in U.S. feminism" (p. xi). She posits the question "What counts as theory?" to frame her explorations, then, countering any unitary formulation, presents theory as "conversations" in feminist thinking, traveling across a shifting terrain of contingent and contested meanings. Along the way, she engages critically with the work of Echols, Hartsock, Jaggar, Collins, and Sandoval as well as Gallop, Hirsch, and Miller. Turning to the production of feminist culture and identity politics, she uses such diverse "texts" as the music of Sweet Honey and the Rock and Holly Near and the 1981 feminist film *Mitsuye and Nellie*. Of particular interest is her use of "writing technologies" relating to the politics of oral and written knowledge production and distribution, publication systems, and "the investments of feminism in specific ethnic/racial/sexual/national literacies" (p. xii). In the final chapter, written in 1992, on AIDS activism and feminist theory, she takes up questions of "global gay formations and local homosexualities." King's multitextured narrative and relatively inaccessible language may make the trip, while worthwhile, a bit grueling for the uninitiated reader.

111. Landes, Joan, ed. *Feminism: The Public and the Private*. New York: Oxford University Press, 1998. 507p. (Oxford Readings in Feminism). bibliog. index. ISBN 0198752032; 0198752024pa.

The concepts of public and private have often been central to feminist theory and practice and have themselves been developed and transformed through feminist scholarship. Historian Landes brings together an excellent collection of essays dating from 1974 (Sherry Ortner's early classic "Is Female to Male as Nature Is to Culture?") and traversing wide intellectual and political ground. Issues of gender identity and feminist politics are examined in the context of the public/private distinction in four parts. "The Public/Private Distinction in Feminist Theory" includes pieces by Mary Dietz, Seyla Benhabib, and Bonnie Honig in addition to Ortner. "Gender in the Modern Liberal Sphere" takes a historical approach, with writings by Mary Ryan and Carole Pateman along with Landes and others. The selections in part 3, "Gendered Sites in the Late Modern Public Sphere," examine the "intersections between art, media, commerce, and publicity" and "feminist perspectives on representation—of bodies, sexuality, and feminism" (p. 10), including not only work by Lauren Berlant, Nancy Fraser, and Jennifer Wicke but also, perhaps surprisingly, an article by Erica Jong about Hillary Clinton. In the final section, "Public and Private Identity: Questions for a Feminist Public Sphere," Iris Marion Young, Wendy Brown, and Anne Phillips "relate the demand for the representation of gender, race, ethnicity and sexuality in the cultural/symbolic sphere to the problem of political representation" (p. 14). This diverse range of perspectives on the gendered nature of public and private life provides a stimulating overview for research or classroom use.

112. Landry, Donna, and Gerald MacLean, eds. *The Spivak Reader: Selected Works of Gayatri Chakravorty Spivak*. New York: Routledge, 1996. 334p. bibliog. index. ISBN 0415910005; 0415910013pa.

Gayatri Spivak is one of the best-known, most widely respected, and most frequently quoted theorists. Whether focusing her attention on feminism, cultural studies, colonization and decolonization, or the question of the subaltern, Spivak has made major contributions to the study of topics ranging from analyses of Jacques Derrida to the challenges of creating a new, more culturally inclusive pedagogy. In this volume, Landry and MacLean have taken on the task of introducing Spivak to an audience either unfamiliar with or completely baffled by her work. This is a challenging undertaking, as Spivak's writing often requires of the reader both tremendous patience and a solid grounding in Marxism and deconstruction. Landry and MacLean begin this collection of Spivak's essays with an introduction, "Reading Spivak," that provides biographical data about Spivak, sets an intellectual, academic, and political frame for her work, and, most important, offers guidance to the reader about to encounter Spivak for the first time. Using what they label as "slogans" (p. 4), the editors approach Spivak through explication of major themes in her work, referring to selections in this volume as well as to other examples of her writings and presentations. In addition to the biographical data and explication of the slogans, the editors use the introduction to explain the organization of the reader and the rationale for the choices they made of what to include from the corpus of Spivak's published writings, talks, and interviews. Arranged thematically rather than strictly chronologically, the first five essays cover Spivak's influential critique of deconstruction, while the final four "sharpen, extend, and broaden that project by examining the politics of translation and multiculturalism" (p. 8). Included as well are two interviews with Spivak, one conducted in 1993 by poet and Chicano literary scholar Alfred Arteaga and another, focusing one of Spivak's most important lectures, "Can the Subaltern Speak?" with the editors of the *Reader*. The volume concludes with a checklist of Spivak's publications from 1965 to 1995.

113. Lovell, Terry, ed. *British Feminist Thought: A Reader*. Cambridge, MA: Basil Blackwell, 1990. 385p. bibliog. index. ISBN 0631169148; 0631169156pa.

This anthology provides a wide-ranging introduction to British feminist thought prevalent at the beginning of the 1990s and is organized into four sections with selections focusing on history, the politics of difference (race, class, and gender), psychoanalysis, and finally, feminist criticism and cultural studies. Contributions from Ann Oakley, Michele Barrett, Juliet Mitchell, and Toril Moi, among others, are compiled to convey distinctive characteristics of British feminist thought contextualized in intellectual and political life. Lowell acknowledges the impossibility of representing the full spectrum of British feminism and in particular notes the absence of the women's peace movement. Within these inevitable constraints, "a critical engagement with socialist theory and practice" (p. 4) is her primary criterion of selection for the collection.

114. Malson, Micheline R., Jean F. O'Barr, Susan Westphal-Wihl, and Mary Wyer, eds. *Feminist Theory in Practice and Process*. Chicago: University of Chicago Press, 1989. 368p. bibliog. index. ISBN 0226502937; 0226502945pa.

First published in *Signs: Journal of Women in Culture and Society*, the articles collected here represent the emergence in the 1980s of a more self-reflective feminist theorizing grounded in a process of multiplicity, interconnections, temporalities, and reconfigurations. The fourteen essays engage the contradictions in feminist theory, many of them examining literary representations or autobiographical narratives, and reject totalities while addressing such topics as black feminist ideology, sexual violence and literary history, the lesbian literary imagination, women's social practices, and cultural feminism versus poststructuralism.

115. Mann, Patricia S. *Micro-politics: Agency in a Postfeminist Era*. Minneapolis: University of Minnesota Press, 1994. 253p. bibliog. index. (OP)

In this ambitious work, Mann asserts that our "postmodern, postfeminist era" (p. 25) demands new feminist theories of social and political agency. She points to the enfranchisement of women, the demise of the patriarchal family and its embedded forms of identity, and, perhaps most especially, the dismantling of liberal ideologies of free and autonomous individualism to underscore her call for a more flexible, interactive, and egalitarian theory of agency that incorporates the "relations between two or more individuals" (p. 14). If her emphasis on "micro-political" interpersonal relations pays insufficient attention to the importance of collective forms of agency and political mobilizing, Mann nonetheless provides a stimulating and suggestive consideration of the failings of liberalism in the face of feminism's challenge to patriarchal notions of sexual difference ("the most significant social phenomenon of our time," p. 2) and its transformation of contemporary gender relations.

116. Marshall, Barbara. *Engendering Modernity: Feminism, Social Theory, and Social Change*. Boston: Northeastern University Press, 1994. 197p. bibliog. index. ISBN 1555532128; 1555532136pa.

Marshall aims to offer "a revised account of modernity" (p. 3) that completes its emancipatory project by incorporating gender and feminist theory while also employing insights from poststructuralist and postmodern critiques. Her wide-ranging survey of social and critical theory (Jürgen Habermas, Anthony Giddens, Michel Foucault, Cornel West) is followed by several chapters that examine the legacies of modernist thought in current theories of the division of labor, reproduction, identity, and rights and the state. Countering feminist critiques of modernism, she acknowledges the shortcomings of Enlightenment thought while also arguing to retain its emancipatory principles. She calls for a "theoretical eclecticism" (p. 161) that incorporates discourse analysis into a feminist theory that is at once a critique and a defense of modernity (p. 148).

117. Martin, Biddy. *Femininity Played Straight: The Significance of Being Lesbian*. New York: Routledge, 1996. 252p. bibliog. index. ISBN 0415916801; 041591681Xpa.

Written between 1978 and 1993, the articles collected here trace Martin's ongoing concerns around issues of feminism, gender, and lesbian sexuality and point to intersections between lesbian-feminist and queer theorizing. The essays cover a broad spectrum, including critiques of Marxist and radical feminist thought, tensions between Foucault and psychoanalysis, feminist politics (written with Chandra Talpade Mohanty), and feminist metaphysics through a critique of Mary Daly's *Gyn/Ecology*. Most important, "All the essays try to make 'lesbianism' a significant part of ongoing intellectual debates" (p. 1) and reflect Martin's "belief in the importance of something as simple and basic as attachment, investment, even love" as she resists and counters "theories that elevate radical detachment, anti-societalization, and transgression to the level of the reactive sublime" (p. 2).

118. Mellor, Mary. *Feminism and Ecology*. Washington Square, NY: New York University Press, 1997. 220p. bibliog. index. ISBN 081475600X; 0814756018pa.

In this wide-ranging work, Mellor traces the multiple dimensions of and debates within and around ecofeminism. Seeking to counter negative stereotypes of ecofeminism as naïve and essentialist, she develops her arguments for a materialist ecofeminism, grounded in the materiality of human existence, physical bodies that need to be developed and nurtured and are themselves embedded within a natural environment. She rejects claims that women are essentially closer to nature, but persuasively links women's subordination and ecological degradation, illuminating the gendered nature of the "destructive relations between humanity and the non-human natural world" (p. viii). The eight chapters provide a useful overview of ecofeminism, its connections to women's participation in environmental movements, the theoretical debates within it, and its relation to feminist theory, with particular attention to questions around women and nature and women and knowledge and to feminist critiques of epistemology and science. Relationships between ecofeminism and deep ecology, ecoanarchism, ecosocialism, and Marxism are outlined in the later chapters as Mellor works toward a historical materialist position reformulated within an ecofeminist framework. She demonstrates that the close relations between women and the natural world are not based in biologistic or spiritual connections, but rather in the social and economic circumstances of their lives, in their work of producing the means of life and of survival. Taking a critical realist standpoint based on "women's experience" as an analytical concept, she interrogates the position of women in sex/gender systems and the structural power relations underlying the "fact that the majority of those who benefit from the exploitation of the planet and its peoples are men" (p. 193). In building her case for structures of responsibility and reciprocity in place of dualistic and exploitative structures of mediation and parasitism, Mellor marshals compelling arguments for cooperative, egalitarian, and ecologically sustainable relationships that she names "a feminist, green socialism" (p. 196).

119. Miles, Angela R. *Integrative Feminisms: Building Global Visions, 1960s–1990s.* New York: Routledge, 1996. 187p. (Perspectives on Gender). bibliog. ISBN 041590756X; 0415907578pa.

A departure from the many books on global feminism that take an empirical approach, *Integrative Feminisms* presents "a theoretical analysis of the politics of feminist radicalism in a global context" (p. ix). Miles distinguishes between what she labels assimilationist or equality-frame feminisms and integrative or transformative feminisms. She roundly rejects the former as binary and reductionist, focusing narrowly on equality and rights within a given social and political structure. Rather, she presents strong arguments for and evidence of the latter, feminisms that reject dualistic approaches and "challenge not just women's exclusion from social structures and rewards but the very nature of these structures and rewards" (p. xi). The somewhat unfocused first section of the book traces the history of Western feminist theory within this construct, while the more successful second half focuses on multiple examples of integrative feminisms in the "Two-Thirds World." Miles argues that many differing types of feminism hold integrative principles in common, claiming both women's equality and women's specificity as mutually constitutive and recognizing the creative tensions in the contradictions between them. The feminisms she advocates reach beyond assimilationist goals of women's equality to center the historically marginalized life-oriented work and concerns of women as organizing principles of society. This fundamental challenge to existing social relations demands the dismantling of exploitative hierarchical relations and militarized economies and cultures; redistributions of power and resources; and redefinitions of the very concepts of power, wealth, human rights, work, and progress. The vigorous resistance of North American feminists to the "colonizing global processes of 'modernization' and 'development' " (p. 145) reinforces, in Miles's view, the feminist frame for global solidarity and transformation.

120. Mohanty, Chandra Talpade, Ann Russo, and Lourdes Torres, eds. *Third World Women and the Politics of Feminism.* Bloomington: Indiana University Press, 1991. 338p. bibliog. index. ISBN 0253338735; 0253206324pa.

One of the most searing critiques of Western feminism has been, in Chandra Mohanty's words, its "production of the 'third world woman' as a singular monolithic subject" (p. 51). This pathbreaking and highly regarded collection stands in strong opposition to such myopia. From differing backgrounds and sometimes contradictory positions, the contributors offer highly nuanced analyses of oppression and resistance that contradict the false notions of gender and patriarchy as necessarily primary or equally oppressive to all women and incorporate the critical ideological and material forces of colonialism, imperialism, and world capitalism. Charting "third world women's engagements with feminism" (p. 40), the anthology contains essays by Mohanty, Rey Chow, and Barbara Smith that address questions centering around representations of Third World women in scholarly texts, popular media, and fiction; essays that analyze racialized womanhood within relations of ruling and the role of the state through case studies on Trinidad and Tobago, Brazil, Jamaica, and the United States; divergent perspectives on nationalism and sexuality within different contexts, including Islamic fundamentalism; and examinations of feminist struggles around questions of racism, identity, and feminist praxis.

121. Moi, Toril, ed. *French Feminist Thought: A Reader.* New York: Blackwell, 1987. 260p. bibliog. index. (OP)

This interdisciplinary work seeks to introduce English-speaking readers to key works by French feminists, most translated here for the first time. It includes contributions from noted theorists such as Julia Kristeva and Luce Irigaray complemented by other texts illustrating the diversity of French feminist thought since the 1970s. Particularly salient relationships between the political and the intellectual emerge in the exploration of such topics as the women's movement, sexual difference, creativity and art, and femininity. Clare Duchen's *Feminism in France* (Routledge & Kegan Paul, 1986) also provides useful information on the development of French feminist theory and the women's movement between 1968 and 1981, while her edited and translated collection *French Connections: Voices from the Women's Movement in France* (Hutchinson, 1987) moves away from an emphasis on theory to introduce readers to the MLF (mouvement de libération des femmes) and the key debates within it, as well as to outline similarities between British and French feminisms. The more recent *French Feminisms: Gender and Violence in Contemporary Theory* by Gill Allwood (UCL Press, 1998) explores French feminist theory in relation to the study of masculinity.

122. Nicholson, Linda, ed. *The Second Wave: A Reader in Feminist Theory*. New York: Routledge, 1997. 414p. bibliog. ISBN 0415917603; 0415917611pa.

Tracing the development of feminist theory during the past fifty years, Nicholson provides an excellent selection of influential texts from Simone de Beauvoir's *The Second Sex* to Radicalesbians *The Woman Identified Woman* to the Combahee River Collective's *A Black Feminist Statement*. Writings by such diverse feminist theorists as Heidi Hartmann, Carol Gilligan, Catharine MacKinnon, Patricia Hill Collins, Norma Alarcon, Judith Butler, Monique Wittig, Luce Irigaray, and Gayatri Spivak are represented here. Organized historically, the volume highlights major debates and turning points in feminist theorizing across five thematic sections: "Early Statements"; "With and against Marx"; "Gynocentrism: Women's Oppression, Women's Identity, and Women's Standpoint"; "Theorizing Difference/Deconstructing Identity"; and finally, "The Question of Essentialism." Issues addressed include the problematizing of the concept of woman, the essentialist debate, feminist standpoint theories, poststructuralist critiques of liberal and radical feminism, social constructions of sexuality, and differences among women, westernization, and Third World feminism. The result is an engaging survey of critical analyses and debates framed within their historical context for fuller understanding of the evolution of feminist theory in the last half of the twentieth century.

Judith Evans's *Feminist Theory Today: An Introduction to Second-Wave Feminism* (see entry 79) (Sage Publications, 1995) and Rosemarie Tong's *Feminist Thought: A More Comprehensive Introduction* (Westview Press, 1998) survey feminist theory during this same time period, addressing from different angles liberal, radical, cultural, socialist, and postmodern feminism. Evans adds a discussion of "the legal challenge," taking up the work of Carol Bacchi on feminism and sexual difference and of Catharine MacKinnon, both of whom Evans terms "equality feminists." Tong offers chapters on ecofeminism and multicultural and global feminism. Further, Tong presents the premises of each position with supportive but also opposing views, serving to foster critical thinking and evaluation by the reader.

123. Nicholson, Linda J., ed. *Feminism/Postmodernism*. New York: Routledge, 1990. 348p. (Thinking Gender). bibliog. index. ISBN 0415900581; 041590059Xpa.

By 1990, feminist theorists were coming under increasing attack for their tendency to universalize female experience from the standpoint of white North American and Western European women. This collection, the second volume in the Thinking Gender series, represents a conscious effort to expand that frame of reference while at the same time drawing attention to the fact that "feminists were not used to acknowledging that the premises from which they were working possessed a specific location" (p. 2). Editor Linda Nicholson sets the tone and direction for this compilation, comprised of essays reprinted here as well as materials appearing for the first time, first in an informative introduction that explains the parameters of the work while at the same time posing many of the questions and philosophical quandaries the contributors tackle in the rest of the book. She further defines the terms of the argument in the first essay in the work, "Social Criticism without Philosophy: An Encounter between Feminism and Postmodernism," written with Nancy Fraser. The essays offer a range of viewpoints on the relationship between postmodernism and feminism, with such leading scholars as Sandra Harding and Seyla Benhabib positing alternatives to both a feminist embrace of postmodernism and the limits of feminist theoretical writings of the 1970s and 1980s. Other selections articulate concerns about the intersection of feminism and postmodernism, asking "whether the category of gender can survive the postmodern critique" and "if postmodernism entails the abandonment of all generalizations, would not the end result be a nominalist ontology and an individualist politics?" (p. 8). Under the theme "Identity and Differentiation," arguments by such scholars as Judith Butler and Iris Young posit the possibilities of an affinity between feminism and postmodernism, provided the more problematic aspects of each are kept firmly in mind.

Four years later, Margaret Ferguson and Jennifer Wicke published a collection with a very similar title, *Feminism and Postmodernism* (Duke University Press, 1994). The "and" that replaced the "/" in Nicholson's title is telling because it indicates both a greater degree of acceptance of as well as comfort with the intersections and, in some instances, the convergence of the two theoretical positions, as reflected in the title of the first essay in the volume, Ferguson's and Wicke's "Introduction: Feminism and Postmodernism; or, The Way We Live Now."

124. Nnaemeka, Obioma, ed. *Sisterhood, Feminisms, and Power: From Africa to the Diaspora*. Trenton, NJ: Africa World Press, 1998. 513p. bibliog. index. ISBN 0865434387; 0865434395pa.

This unique work gathers papers presented at an international conference on "Women in Africa and the African Diaspora (WAAD)" held in July 1992 in Nigeria. Scholars, creative writers, and activists from the African continent, Australia, Canada, Jamaica, Finland, and the United States are represented here. Through theoretical arguments and personal reflections, they address questions of politics, economics, and religion as well as debates around feminism and womanism, elite and grassroots relationships, urban and rural conflicts, and the tensions between indigenous African feminisms and some Western feminist notions of sexuality and motherhood. Demonstrating a far-reaching scope of interest, contributors explore the problems of research and documentation on women in Uganda and also describe women organizing for change from South Africa to Egypt, developing sisterhood in Memphis, Tennessee, and resisting colonialism in Nigeria. The varied selections collected here and the divergent experiences and views they represent together begin important dialogues across geographic and ethnic lines to foster understandings of the differences between African and Western feminisms and to recognize and honor feminisms uniquely "rooted in the African environment" (p. 9).

125. Pateman, Carole, and Elizabeth Gross, eds. *Feminist Challenges: Social and Political Theory*. Boston: Northeastern University Press, 1986. 215p. bibliog. ISBN 1555530036; 1555530044pa.

Pateman and Gross provide a valuable critique of mainstream academic theory and liberal as well as socialist approaches to integrating women into existing theoretical models and categories. Eleven contributors raise provocative questions about the assumptions and methods of most contemporary social and political theory, scrutinizing in the process such concepts as consent, power, equality, and justice. The essays gathered here seek to "develop a theory in which women and femininity have an autonomous place" (p. 9). They argue for a reconceptualization of theory, asserting that it must begin with women and their material realities and challenge conventional, male-centered notions of public and private, social and political. Gross, for instance, calls for a "new discursive space . . . where women can write, read, and think as women" (p. 204). She resists deconstructionism in her claim that "the dissolution of female identity does not have the same strategic or subversive effect as the subversion of male identity" (p. 133), especially at this historical moment when women are struggling for self-representation.

126. Penelope, Julia. *Call Me Lesbian: Lesbian Lives, Lesbian Theory*. Freedom, CA: Crossing Press, 1992. 155p. bibliog. (OP)

Lesbian feminist writer Julia Penelope offers a sampling of nine of her essays exploring lesbian lives and perspectives. She tackles questions of lesbian history, identities, sexuality, and politics in provocative ways that acknowledge inherent ambiguities, complexities, and contradictions. Along the way, she provides insights into such issues as role playing in lesbian relationships, lesbian separatism, sadomasochism, incest, lesbian femininity, and the necessity, in her view, of a radical feminist framework. She challenges notions of a unitary lesbian identity, rejecting even reductionist sexual definitions. Rather, lesbian identities are multiple, deriving from the varied backgrounds and lives of individuals. It is this lived experience, she argues, that must be shared and communicated, breaking silence and isolation, to build community. Reflecting back on the sources of her own life, she attempts to understand and theorize broader lesbian existence and asserts that lesbian perspectives, originating through resistance and a profound sense of difference, challenge conventional interpretations of the world and ways of knowing and seeing. Key to this process, she maintains, is language and the power of words not only to reflect but also to shape values, experience, and possibilities.

127. Phelan, Shane. *Getting Specific: Postmodern Lesbian Politics*. Minneapolis: University of Minnesota Press, 1994. 190p. bibliog. index. ISBN 0816621098; 0816621101pa.

Phelan's first book, *Identity Politics: Lesbian Feminism and the Limits of Community* (Temple University Press, 1989), explored the related themes of identity and community among lesbian feminist theorists and argued that a monolithic view of identity as homogeneity leads to a profound failure to account for the plurality and diversity of lesbian experience and, consequently, to totalizing theories. Extending her analysis here, she wrestles with the potentials and pitfalls of lesbian identity and lesbian political theory, seeking a "politics that might foster different, more resilient, and potentially coalitional identities" (p. ix). She assertively employs and builds upon the story of her own life and often grounds her narrative in specific historical and political events. Emphasizing the local, she ultimately proposes "getting specific" as a new kind of theorizing that "turning social science and theory on its head . . . works out from the centers of our lives to seeing the connections and contradictions in them" (p. 32). She does not call for a rejection of identity categories but rather a recognition, informed by postmodern and poststructuralist theories, that they are fluid, provisional, and contingent. Within this frame, she examines questions of citizenship, justice, and democracy, engaging a multivalent identity politics "arising out of the specific oppressions faced by each of us" (p. 156). These differences and the productive tensions among them, she argues, form the basis for effective transformative coalitions and alliances.

128. Phelan, Shane, ed. *Playing with Fire: Queer Politics, Queer Theories*. New York: Routledge, 1997. 291p. bibliog. ISBN 0415914167; 0415914175pa.

Three decades after the Stonewall rebellion ushered in the modern lesbian and gay rights movement(s), academics who choose to concentrate on LGBT (lesbian, gay, bisexual, transgender) or queer topics are still "playing with fire." In an increasingly conservative political environment, the risks to careers are still great. This has not, however, silenced the voices of scholars who continue to argue for new and challenging ways to use theory to understand and explicate experience. The eleven essays in this volume address and complicate questions of identity by issuing a "challenge to the ontological and political status of sexuality, race, and gender" (p. 2). In three sections, "Queer Identities," "Queer Critiques," and "Queer Agendas," the authors tackle such thorny topics as the erasure of bisexuality in lesbian/gay and even queer narratives, the *Bowers v. Hardwick* decision, lesbian and gay marriage, and problem of "official recognition." Through an overview of the organization of the book, Phelan provides an accessible introduction to the complex themes the various essayists cover.

129. Richardson, Laurel, Verta Taylor, and Nancy Whittier, eds. *Feminist Frontiers.* Vol. 4. New York: McGraw-Hill, 1997. 561p. bibliog. ISBN 0070523797pa.

One of the most widely used readers in women's studies, this collection presents a wide selection of essays carefully chosen to frame an analysis of women's status and to explore the multiple ways in which gender intersects with culture, class, race, ethnicity, and sexuality. The editors, all sociologists, provide introductory conceptualizations of gender, including pieces on diversity and difference and a section on feminist theoretical perspectives. Essays address the ways in which gender is learned, focusing on language, images, and culture as well as socialization. The social organization of gender is examined in readings on work, families, intimacy and sexuality, bodies and medicine, and violence against women. The sweeping topic of social change is taken up with articles on politics and the state and on social protest and the feminist movement. The readings are scholarly yet accessible and generally engaging. Further, the editors conscientiously revise each edition of the anthology, adding articles that address new research areas and expanding their focus to reflect current emphases in feminist theory and teaching. (*Feminist Frontiers V* was published in 2001.) Richardson and Diane Robinson's *Introducing Women's Studies: Feminist Theory and Practice* (New York University Press, 1997) covers some of the same ground from a British perspective.

130. Sawicki, Jana. *Disciplining Foucault: Feminism, Power, and the Body.* New York: Routledge, 1991. 130p. bibliog. index. ISBN 0415901871; 041590188Xpa.

Sawicki seeks to introduce Foucault to feminists and "to lay out the basic features of a Foucauldian feminism that is compatible with feminism as a pluralistic and *emancipatory* radical politics" (p. 8). She draws upon Foucault's *Discipline and Punish, Power/Knowledge*, and volume 1 of *The History of Sexuality* to argue for the use of his analysis of power and subjectivity to support feminist struggles for sexual and reproductive freedom. Through this, she envisions a "radically pluralist feminism" that "recognizes plurality both within and between subjects" and not only "politicizes social and personal relationships" but also politicizes theory, described as "practices that serve as instruments of domination as well as liberation" (pp. 8–9). Sawicki uses Foucault to engage with such charged feminist issues as identity and difference, sexual desire, mothering theory, and reproductive technologies and politics. If she presents feminism through Foucault, she also thinks beyond him where she finds that his theory "might subvert feminism and other oppositional movements" (p. 15) while also acknowledging that resistance to dogmatic impositions of theory is itself Foucauldian.

131. Schor, Naomi, and Elizabeth Weed, eds. *The Essential Difference: Another Look at Essentialism.* Bloomington: Indiana University Press, 1994. 196p. (Books from Differences). bibliog. index. ISBN 0253350921; 025335093Xpa.

This volume began its life as a special issue of the journal *Differences* and is, in fact, a volume in the series Books from Differences. Naomi Schor, one of the editors of both the special issue and this monograph, uses the introduction to explain the genesis of both publications, the debate between essentialism and antiessentialism, its history, root causes, and reasons for its longevity. Tracing part of its history back to arguments between Simone de Beauvoir and "Beauvoirean 'equality feminists' and the newer French 'difference feminists' " (p. x), the essays in this collection situate and complicate the debate within the context of larger critical feminist discussions about the usefulness of "essentialism" as a philosophical construct. In challenges to received wisdom about essentialism as a negative, indeed, a conservative theoretical position, essays by Teresa de Lauretis and Leslie Wahl Rabine provide examples of essentialism in the service of women's political activism. Other contributions by such renowned and venerated feminist thinkers as Luce Irigaray, Diana Fuss, and Gayatri Spivak offering various positions on the debate round out this significant yet extremely challenging and highly theoretical collection.

132. Spelman, Elizabeth V. *Inessential Woman: Problems of Exclusion in Feminist Thought.* Boston: Beacon Press, 1988. 221p. bibliog. index. ISBN 080706744X; 0807067458pa.

Although Spelman's groundbreaking book was published in 1988, it continues to hold a significant place among works on feminist theory. As one of the first and most successful efforts to bring to the fore issues of exclusion in the theories and writings of middle-class white feminists, *Inessential Woman* reminds us both of how far we have come and how much further we need to go. Spelman explains on the very first page of the preface that she has adopted the term "inessential" to cover two critical aspects of late-twentieth-century feminist theory. In the first instance, "inessential" refers to the idea, held by many Western philosophers, that "women . . . lack what is essentially human" (p. ix). She then goes on to elucidate what it is about essentialism that is equally problematic. Her use of the term is "meant to point to and undermine a tendency in dominant Western feminist thought to posit an essential "womanness" (p. ix) shared by all women, regardless of race, class, ethnicity, or other characteristics. Spelman's book serves as both a cogent argument against this essentializing tendency and an excellent introduction to the ways in which Western philosophers, starting with Plato and Aristotle, treated women and what we might learn from them. It is written in a lively and readable manner (the chapter on Plato is entitled "Hairy Cobblers and Philosopher Queens," while she calls the next one, which deals with Aristotle, "Who's Who in the Polis"). After laying the groundwork for feminist reaction against traditional philosophy's constructions of women, she turns to feminist theory itself, starting with Beauvoir, and examines examples of views that are "as deeply inegalitarian as the views of Plato and Aristotle" (p. 6). She ends with an argument for the vitality of feminist theory, especially when faced with the absolute necessity of ceasing to homogenize or essentialize "woman."

133. Trujillo, Carla, ed. *Living Chicana Theory.* Berkeley, CA: Third Woman Press, 1998. 444p. bibliog. ISBN 0943219159pa.

This collection of essays and performance pieces gathers leading voices of Chicana feminism into one landmark volume. The critical and creative works of scholars and writers cover a remarkable variety of disciplines and subjects: philosophy and psychology, religion and spirituality, photography and poetry, politics and history, and literature and sexuality. Editor Trujillo frames the anthology to rethink Chicana consciousness, theory, and practice and to redefine and reconstruct theory in new ways that encompass the complex negotiations of daily consciousness and practice. This overarching theme is reflected in the selection by historian Deena Gonzalez, "Speaking Secrets: Living Chicana Theory," which also provides the collection's evocative title. The additional twenty contributors include Anzaldúa, Cisneros, and Moraga, as well as Emma Perez, Alicia Gaspar de Alba, Lara Medina, Yvonne Yarbro-Bejarano, Monica Palacios, Chela Sandoval, Norma Alarcon, and Aída Hurtado, among others. Together their work stands as a powerful corrective to stereotypes and silencing of Chicana feminists and a compelling challenge to the sexism, racism, and homophobia they often encounter. The diversity of voices, topics, and perspectives represented here particularly recommends this collection for the classroom. Trujillo's earlier award-winning anthology *Chicana Lesbians: The Girls Our Mothers Warned Us About* (Third Woman Press, 1991) provides a valuable companion work (see entry 729).

134. Vicinus, Martha, ed. *Lesbian Subjects: A Feminist Studies Reader.* Bloomington: Indiana University Press, 1996. 273p. bibliog. index. ISBN 0253330602; 0253210380pa.

Vicinus gathers essays that appeared over a fifteen-year period, 1980 to 1995, in the journal *Feminist Studies* as well as one essay originally published in *Gender and History* to provide "both a historical document . . . and a summation of work to date" (p. 1). All the essays draw upon the wide variety of ways, across historical epochs and disciplinary frames, that one may define, map, or explore the lesbian as subject. At the same time, Vicinus adds a cautionary note, pointing out that there is no easy or facile way to determine what set of specific practices (or discourses) holds true throughout the lesbian past and present. Divided into two main parts, "Explorations" and "Affirmations," each beginning with Vicinus's contextualizing comments, the essays in *Lesbian Subjects* approach different historical moments and illuminate different historical actors, some obvious, others far harder to detect and label. The selections in part 1 draw attention to "forgotten, unnoticed, or neglected lesbian figures in literature, history, and literary theory" (p. 13). The six essays reprinted here range from Akasha (Gloria) Hull's examination of Alice Dunbar-Nelson to interrogations of subjects as diverse as women's sports figures in the United States, romantic friendships in nineteenth-century England, and depictions of cross-dressing women in contemporary fiction. Subsequent essays "explicitly or implicitly address the political importance of claiming a lesbian identity" (p. 137). From an examination of an erotic friendship between two nineteenth-century African American women to Vicinus's own contribution, " 'They Wonder to Which Sex I Belong': The Historical Roots of the Modern Lesbian Identity," these selections affirm the existence of the lesbian subject. To serve as a bridge between the two text-based essay sections, Vicinus has inserted a part titled "Intermission" that contains photos originally published in the British anthology *Stolen Glances* as well as a selection of Tee A. Corinne's photomontages of female genitalia.

135. Vogel, Lise. *Woman Questions: Essays for a Materialist Feminism.* New York: Routledge, 1995. 162p. bibliog. index. ISBN 0415915791; 0415915805pa.

A historical account of materialist feminism emerges through Vogel's selection of previously published essays, each contextualized with commentary and framed overall by an introductory account of her own intellectual and political genealogy. She counters revisionist histories of second-wave feminism that have too frequently erased the contributions of socialist feminists to feminist theory and activism, especially as regards their efforts to theorize class and race and to build political coalitions. Vogel argues for the value of a particular focus on the material conditions of women's oppression, "human labor and material processes—most especially those carried out primarily by women and previously invisible to theory" (p. xii). The collection is organized thematically into three sections addressing the relationship between feminism and socialism, the significance of the Marxist theoretical tradition for women's liberation, and issues of difference, diversity, and equality. Vogel examines issues of public policy, as exemplified by her last chapter, in which she analyzes the Family and Medical Leave Act, and she tackles the dilemmas of difference/equality, suggesting the application of "differential consideration." This volume is a useful corrective and engaging overview of the work of an influential theorist.

136. Walters, Suzanna Danuta. *Material Girls: Making Sense of Feminist Cultural Theory.* Berkeley: University of California Press, 1995. 221p. bibliog. index. ISBN 0520089774; 0520089782pa.

With the now-famous Madonna song "Material Girl" as her point of departure, Walters provides an overview of the increasingly prolific field of feminist cultural studies. She is particularly concerned with issues of representation of women and how different and frequently competing theories within cultural studies frame their arguments. Writing about complex theoretical matters in a clear and accessible style, Walters organizes her book around four central themes: the images perspective, the signification perspective, central concepts and theories of feminist cultural studies, and the Centre for Contemporary Culture in Birmingham, England, the acknowledged birthplace of cultural studies. The book consists of Walters's elaboration of each of these themes and/or concepts. In addition to her analysis of historical antecedents and current trends, Walters, in a chapter on backlash that she says could be subtitled "Whose Life Is It Anyway? Fatal Retractions in the Backlash 1980s," tackles the particularly thorny issues around postfeminism, concentrating both on its manifestations in the popular press and its presence in the academy alongside poststructuralism and postmodernism. She concludes, however, on a positive note. In the final chapter, "Material Girls: Toward a Feminist Cultural Theory," she offers concrete models of how different critical perspectives might come together to form a persuasive theoretical framework for feminists to "demystify dominant cultural products and to help construct a liberatory and expressive feminist culture" (p. 160). Published the same year, *Feminist Cultural Theory: Process and Production* (Manchester University Press), edited by Beverley Skeggs, covers some of the same conceptual ground. The work is divided into two parts, "Texts and Responses" and "Responses and Texts." All but two of the eleven essays on topics ranging from the American sitcom *Roseanne* to issues in feminist ethnography are written by scholars from British universities, the undisputed original home of cultural studies.

137. Weed, Elizabeth, ed. *Coming to Terms: Feminism, Theory, Politics.* New York: Routledge, 1989. 294p. bibliog. ISBN 0415900670; 0415900689pa.

This edited volume offers critical and thought-provoking perspectives on the relationships between feminism and poststructuralist theory. Concentrating on questions of identity, difference, and agency, contributors seek to "come to terms" with such contested categories as "woman," "women," and "Third World women." In the treatment of politics, some contributors take a discursive approach, privileging language as the source of meaning and of domination and resistance. Others, including Donna Haraway and Gayatri Spivak, engage with the power relations inherent in a global political economy.

Weed joined with Naomi Schor to edit *Feminism Meets Queer Theory* (Indiana University Press, 1997), another collection first published as an issue of the journal *Differences* and especially important in its examination of the tensions between feminism and queer theory. Contributions from Judith Butler, Rosi Braidotti, Biddy Martin, Elizabeth Grosz, and Teresa de Lauretis, among other prominent theorists, draw from literary criticism, psychoanalytic theory, and poststructuralism in their interrogations of intersections and divergences. They tackle the assertion of queer theory that "considerations of sex and sexuality cannot be contained by the category of gender"

(p. viii) and the resultant arbitrary separation and relegation of gender to feminist theorizing and sexuality to queer theory. Weed argues in her introduction that despite the fact that they have common roots, queer theory caricatures feminism as "bound to a regressive and monotonous binary opposition," but she also urges feminists to use the insights and challenges of queer theory to reinvigorate debates about gender, sex, and sexuality within feminism (pp. viii–ix). Butler, for instance, challenges the heterosexism of feminism as well as queer theory's splitting of sex from sexuality, while Evelyn Hammond interrogates the racism of queer theory. In two of the more accessible and engaging selections in this fairly difficult text, Butler first interviews European scholar Rosi Braidotti on naming feminism and the "intellectual reasons for preferring the term Feminist Studies over Gender or Women's Studies" (p. 40), then Gayle Rubin on "Sexual Traffic."

138. Weedon, Chris. *Feminist Practice and Poststructuralist Theory*, 2nd edition. New York: Basil Blackwell, 1997. 195p. bibliog. index. ISBN 0631198253.

For many feminists, especially those outside the rarified atmosphere of certain academic institutions, poststructuralism appears as an alien imposition on otherwise seemingly straightforward assessments of women's condition under patriarchy. Weedon's work is an attempt to introduce challenging theoretical concepts in an accessible manner and to explain how these theories might prove useful, perhaps even invaluable, to feminism. In the 1987 edition of the book, Weedon concentrated on delineating the meaning and utility of psychoanalytic and poststructural theory, offering readers clear, concise interpretations of Derrida, Foucault, and Lacan. She also introduced the pantheon of early second-wave feminist theorists, Irigaray, Chodorow, Kristeva, and Cixous, who brought their own unique interpretations to questions of language, identity, and subjectivity. In chapters on feminism and theory, principles of poststructuralism, and language and subjectivity, she invites the reader to enter the realm of high theory and see its applicability to feminist discourse. In the second edition, ten years later, she adds an entirely new chapter on feminism and postmodernism that underscores the continued integration of poststructuralism into feminist theory. Weedon presents this as a maturing of feminist theoretical practice, but it is left to the reader to determine whether this is indeed a mark of greater sophistication or of theoretical usurpation.

Ann Brooks's 1997 work *Postfeminisms: Feminism, Cultural Theory, and Cultural Forms* (Routledge) offers a more sophisticated reading of the intersections of feminist theory and poststructuralism. The same thinkers, male and female, figure in Brooks's work, with the addition of the concept of "postfeminism." Brooks strives to recuperate this term from its negative antifeminist connotations and treat it as "a useful frame of reference encompassing the intersections of other anti-foundationalist movements including post-modernism, post-structuralism and post-colonialism" (p. 1).

139. Weeks, Kathi. *Constituting Feminist Subjects*. Ithaca, NY: Cornell University Press, 1998. 196p. bibliog. index. ISBN 0801434270; 0801484472pa.

The postmodern critiques of the 1980s incited many feminists to develop nonessentialist theories of subjectivity that account for multiplicity and difference in the lives, experiences, and perspectives of women. In this work, Weeks, a Marxist theorist, strives to clear a space and provide tools for building an alternative conception of subjectivity that is "adequate to a feminist politics" (p. 1), actively acknowledging and cultivating feminism's antagonistic force and subversive potential, particularly the "antagonistic potential of women's laboring practices" (p. 15). She provides a lively discussion of the modernist-postmodernist debate, contesting the accepted notion that a linear progression links Nietzsche, Foucault, and postmodernism and highlighting both continuities and distinctions among these discourses. She proceeds to interrogate and adapt the concepts of totality and labor, then excavates productive elements from socialist feminist theorists (Mariarosa Dalla Costa, Heidi Hartmann, and Iris Young) as well as other Marxist theorists (Georg Lukacs, Louis Althusser, and Antonio Negri). While recognizing the importance of the differences and disputes between Marxist and poststructuralist frameworks, Weeks argues that the modernist-postmodernist paradigm debate, no longer timely or effective, inhibits productive engagements between the two. She urges feminist theorists to go beyond these formulas in order to rethink the categories of the economic and the cultural, consider the complexities of their intersections, and create more nuanced theoretical options. This is a dense text suitable for graduate students and advanced undergraduates.

140. Weisser, Susan Ostrov, and Jennifer Fleischner, eds. *Feminist Nightmares: Women at Odds: Feminism and the Problem of Sisterhood*. New York: New York University Press, 1994. 405p. bibliog. index. ISBN 0814726194; 0814726208pa.

This collection of eighteen essays tackles the thorny question of "sisterhood," its definitions and uses in feminism. Topical chapters range from feminist literary criticism (*The Color Purple* and *Mansfield Park* as well as the novels of Louise Erdrich and Leslie Silko) to French history, Harlequin novels, the cult of women's suffering in Russia, and the tensions between women in East and West Germany. Throughout, the contributors scrutinize any unquestioned definitions of sisterhood to uncover the complexities, problems, and promise of women's relations with each other as well as fundamental inequalities among women of various classes and races. Bravely broaching the discussion of conflicts between and among women, including the ways in which they reproduce power relations and oppress other women, the collection spans conflict in a variety of forms: theoretical, behavioral, and representational.

141. Wiegman, Robyn. *American Anatomies: Theorizing Race and Gender*. Durham, NC: Duke University Press, 1995. 267p. bibliog. index. ISBN 0822315769; 0822315912pa.

Wiegman makes a key contribution to feminist theory and cultural studies in her study of whiteness and masculinity that maps the "categorical constructs of race and gender" (p. 17) and the entangled relationship between patriarchy and white supremacy in nineteenth- and twentieth-century America. Organized into three sections—"Economies of Visibility," "The Ends of 'Man,' " and "White Mythologies"—the volume probes racialized and gendered visual economies, effectively employing an impressive array of evidence and sources from anatomy and phrenology of the eighteenth and nineteenth centuries to post-Reconstruction lynchings and from Harriet Beecher Stowe's *Uncle Tom's Cabin* to the novels of Richard Wright and Toni Morrison to 1980s Hollywood "male bonding narratives" like *Lethal Weapon*. Wiegman is highly critical of white feminists who subordinate race to gender. From the perspective of her "feminist disloyalty," she provides a theoretical critique of contemporary debates about difference and multiculturalism, revealing the problematics and perils of identity politics. She unflinchingly demonstrates how race and gender are interlocked and mutually constitutive, their dynamics and meanings always historically contingent.

142. Wing, Adrien Katherine, ed. *Critical Race Feminism: A Reader*. New York: New York University Press, 1997. 431p. (Critical America). bibliog. index. ISBN 0814792936; 0814793096pa.

This groundbreaking anthology of legal writings by women of color explores the intellectual, social, and political dimensions of critical race feminism (CRF). Antiessentialist at its core, this new genre extends the radical analyses of critical legal studies (CLS) and critical race theory

(CRT), both of which contest the inviolability and objectivity of laws, racial orthodoxies, monocultural norms, and dominant legal theories. CRF joins the evolving and powerful criticism of "the ability of conventional legal strategies to deliver social and economic justice" (p. 2), expanding and strengthening the critique through the multileveled identities and perspectives of women of color. The collection thus "focuses on the lives of those who face multiple discrimination on the basis of race, gender, and class, revealing how all these factors interact within a system of white male patriarchy and racist oppression" (p. 3). It gathers the work of an ethnically diverse group of forty-one contributors, including nationally known Anita Hill and Lani Guinier, as well as recognized scholars in legal academia such as Regina Austin, Linda S. Greene, and Patricia J. Williams, who explore a wide range of topics and arenas such as higher education, pregnancy and motherhood, sexual harassment, criminality and law-breaking, employment and discrimination, and issues of international and comparative law that affect women of color in a global context. Many selections draw upon the narrative or storytelling techniques of critical race theory; others explore what makes critical race feminism distinctive from both CRT and other strands of feminism. Wing later published *Global Critical Race Feminism: An International Reader* (New York University Press, 2000).

143. Wittig, Monique. *The Straight Mind and Other Essays*. Boston: Beacon Press, 1992. 110p. bibliog. ISBN 0807079162; 0807079170pa.

Wittig, a preeminent lesbian French theorist, is renowned for *Les Guérilleres* (1969) and *The Lesbian Body* (1973). This collection of nine essays spanning the more recent fourteen years includes "The Straight Mind," with its provocative and influential assertion that "lesbians are not women" (p. 32). In this spirit of distinguishing "lesbian" from "woman" that "has meaning only in heterosexual systems of thought and heterosexual economic systems" (p. 32), the first half of the anthology reflects her "materialist lesbianism." Unlike many French theorists, Wittig consistently works at the intersection of theory and political struggle, asserting a political and philosophical approach fundamentally critical of heterosexuality as "a political regime, which rests on the submission and appropriation of women" (p. xiii). Following this first section, which also explores "sex" as a political category, the second half of the volume addresses her concerns about writing, language as social contract, and gender as "the linguistic index of women's material oppression" (p. xvii). Throughout, Wittig argues strenuously against biological determinism and essentialism, positing a lesbian perspective outside of the gender dichotomy. Further, she defines "the individual subject in materialist terms" and insists that "without class and class consciousness there are no real subjects, only alienated individuals" (p. 19).

Countering the prevailing identification of French feminist theory with psychoanalytic discourse and literary criticism, Wittig shares her materialist feminist perspective with other French feminists whose work is collected in *Sex in Question: French Materialist Feminism*, edited by Diana Leonard and Lisa Adkins (Taylor & Francis, 1996). Five key members of the group that established the influential journal *Questions féministes* with Simone de Beauvoir, including Wittig, offer a distinctive analysis in the theoretical debates around "the construction and inter-relationship of gender, sex and sexuality" (p. 1). As this volume attests, they unequivocally demonstrate the existence and vitality of French feminist theory grounded in the "significance of social relations and the economy in understanding the relations of the sexes and the construction of individual consciousness" (p. 8).

144. Wolff, Janet. *Feminine Sentences: Essays on Women and Culture*. Berkeley: University of California Press, 1990. 146p. bibliog. index. (OP)

Wolff takes a social-historical approach to cultural (including feminist) theory and analysis.

She builds on the premise that culture and cultural politics are fundamental to gender formation and gender-based social arrangements, that cultural politics is a "vital enterprise, located at the heart of the complex order which (re)produces sexual divisions in society" (p. 1). In combining both sociological and textual analysis, she challenges the "inhibiting dichotomy" (p. 4) and, in her view, dangerous limitations inherent in their conventional separation. "Feminine Sentences," evoking Virginia Woolf and debates about modernism, explores the possibilities and problematics of feminine writing (or artistic production) but also interrogates the sentencing of women in patriarchal culture to containment and silence. An exploration of women's relationships to modern and postmodern culture draws distinctions between modernity and modernism as reflected, for instance, in women's work in art and literature. Wolff acknowledges the benefits of postmodernism for feminist artists and critics, yet questions its "radical relativism and skepticism," asserting that it is "more usefully seen as a renewal and continuation of the project of modernism" (p. 99). The final essay, "Reinstating Corporeality," turns to the art form of dance and demonstrates the possibilities of a feminist cultural politics of the body. Here again, Wolff emphasizes both social and discursive construction as well as material existence. The work presents a cogent argument that sexual and textual politics cannot be separated from social analysis and that feminist cultural analysis must reach beyond the text itself to encompass the sociological dimensions of production and reception.

Women's Movements and Activism

145. Adamson, Nancy, Linda Briskin, and Margaret McPhail. *Feminist Organizing for Change: The Contemporary Women's Movement in Canada.* Toronto: Oxford University Press, 1988. 332p. bibliog. index. (OP)

Adamson, Briskin, and McPhail document the history, development, and heterogeneity of the Canadian women's movement, emphasizing grassroots, socialist feminism. Divided into three parts, the book provides a historical overview, a theoretical grounding and elaboration of the politics of social change, and finally, analyses of the women's movement focusing on feminist practice, ideology, and organizations. Useful appendices include key primary documents, a chronology, and a list of member groups of the National Action Committee on the Status of Women.

Similar grassroots approaches are further developed within a context of diverse community struggles in *And Still We Rise: Feminist Political Mobilizing in Contemporary Canada*, edited by Linda Carty (Women's Press, 1993). This multitextured collection counters the perceived insularity of academic feminism and feminist theorizing that marginalizes "racial-ethnic women" through widely variant essays organized into five sections: "Identity, Race, and Feminist Politics"; "Politicizing Sex and Sexuality"; "Recovering Women's Histories"; "The State, Women's Labour, and Feminist Struggle"; and "Voice, Empowerment, and Change."

146. Afshar, Haleh. *Women in the Middle East: Perceptions, Realities, and Struggles for Liberation.* Houndmills, Basingstoke, Hampshire: Macmillan, 1993. 250p. bibliog. index. (OP)

Home to vibrant and thriving women's communities and women's movements, rich in history and tradition, the Middle East has been depicted in the West as anything but vibrant and thriving, especially for women. Whether they have been exoticized and portrayed as mysterious or seen as suffering under the oppressive rule of Islam, the realities of daily life and the political struggles of women in the Arab world, Iran, and Turkey have been ignored in favor of constructed and outwardly imposed images. Edited by Haleh Afshar, who, along with Mary Maynard, is the general editor of the Women's Studies at York/Macmillan series, this collection of essays brings the perspectives of Middle Eastern women to bear on topics as diverse as attitudes toward female employment in four Middle Eastern countries and discussions of marriage in postrevolutionary Iran. Selections on Islam in women's lives tackle both Western misperceptions about and constructions of women in the Middle East as well as offer critical analysis of women's lives from positions within the culture and traditions of the Islamic world. Additional essays focus on struggles for liberation. Nawal El Sawaadi's overview piece on "Women's Resistance in the Arab World and Egypt" provides a short but powerful historical overview of the history of women's activism in this part of the Muslim world. Other contributions are more specific and touch on such extraordinarily timely topics as the development of a joint Israeli-Palestinian peace movement during the first Intifada and women's struggles against the rising tide of fundamentalism within Islam.

Five other titles on women in the Middle East, three covering a specific country and a particular historical or sociopolitical moment, complement Afshar's overview collection. Margot Badran's *Feminists, Islam, and Nation: Gender and the Making of Modern Egypt* (Princeton University Press, 1995) (see entry 1106) is a history of the role of the nineteenth- and early- to mid-twentieth-century women's movement and feminism as Egypt emerged from the position of a vassal state of the Ottoman Empire to a modern and modernizing nation. Moving the story further, Azza Karam's *Women, Islamisms, and the State: Contemporary Feminisms in Egypt* (Macmillan, 1998) (see entry 245) provides an analysis of women's activism in the modern Egyptian state. Other North African countries have a rich history of women's activism, both in nationalist and feminist struggles. Marnia Lazreg's *The Eloquence of Silence: Algerian Women in Question* (Routledge, 1994) is another fine example of the history of women's participation in anticolonialist struggles and in the forging of postcolonial societies. Finally, *Organizing Women: Formal and Informal Women's Groups in the Middle East*, edited by Dawn Chatty and Annika Rabo (Berg, 1997), and *Remaking Women: Feminism and Modernity in the Middle East*, edited by Lila Abu-Lughod (Princeton University Press, 1998), offer fine collections of more current perspectives on gender, feminism, and modernity in the Middle East.

147. Albrecht, Lisa, and Rose M. Brewer, eds. *Bridges of Power: Women's Multicultural Alliances*. Philadelphia: New Society Publishers, 1990. 244p. bibliog. (OP)
    After enduring several years of searing criticism for racism and the absence of an international perspective, in June 1988 the National Women's Studies Association held its tenth annual conference at the University of Minnesota. With the theme "Leadership and Power: Women's Alliances for Social Change," the association determined to reconstruct its focus and work on a foundation of inclusive feminism. Drawing from 1988 conference papers, this volume elaborates the multifaceted issues associated with coalition building examined through inevitable matrices of multiple and intersecting identities: gender, race, ethnicity, class, sexual orientation, and age. From a wide variety of experiences and perspectives, the contributors seek to bridge the divide between and among diverse groups of feminists and between feminist theory and praxis. The collective goal is to move beyond coalitions to alliances for social change founded upon alternative conceptions of leadership and power that account for differences. Useful case studies include feminist organizing in Latin America and Hong Kong, Palestinian women's expanded roles during the Intifada, and cross-class and cross-race cooperation among women in the U.S. welfare rights movement. Women's alliances in cultural domains are covered as well in chapters focusing on music (the International Sweethearts of Rhythm and the Bay Area Women's Philharmonic) and literature. Importantly in the mix with inspiring examples, several chapters also raise challenging questions about power dynamics and other problems that threaten effective cross-cultural alliances.

A short appendix on "Global Networking in Women's Studies" provides resources in four categories: international meetings, periodicals with an interdisciplinary perspective, multinational research centers, and women's studies programs with an international operation or clientele.

148. Baker, Alison. *Voices of Resistance: Oral Histories of Moroccan Women.* Albany: State University of New York Press, 1998. 341p. bibliog. index. ISBN 0791436217; 0791436225pa.

Baker presents the compelling stories of remarkable Muslim women who participated in the anticolonialist struggles against the French in Morocco, a history largely unwritten to this time. Two oral history chapters form the core of the book, with multiple voices of nationalist women in the first and the narratives of women of the armed resistance in the second. Notes on family background and personal history introduce each selection, and photographs of many of the women amply included throughout bring a vivid dimension to the storytelling. In an introductory section, Baker discusses oral history in Morocco and provides historical and cultural context for the interviews in a chapter on "Nationalism and Feminism in Moroccan History" and another on "Colonialism, Conflict, and Independence." Further enhancing the utility of the volume, appendices offer notes on methodology, a chronology of events mentioned in the oral histories, and a glossary of Moroccan Arabic and French terms.

Published a decade earlier, *Both Right and Left Handed: Arab Women Talk about Their Lives* by Bouthaina Shaaban (Women's Press, 1988) also offers illuminating personal accounts, here from Algerian, Palestinian, Lebanese, and Syrian women. Shaaban, a Syrian feminist and professor of literature, interviewed educators, peasants, feminists, refugees, poets, and nomad matriarchs, engaging with their lives, their family relationships, and their views of social, political, and religious issues. She does not attempt a sociological study here, but rather interweaves the women's stories with her own personal narrative, reflections, and feminist passions in order to both portray and provoke the agency of Arab women.

149. Basu, Amrita, ed. *The Challenge of Local Feminisms: Women's Movements in Global Perspective.* Boulder, CO: Westview Press, 1995. 493p. (Social Change in Global Perspective). bibliog. index. ISBN 0813326273; 0813326281pa.

This pioneering collection offers an impressive and insightful overview of women's movements worldwide. Looking toward the 1995 United Nations Fourth World Conference on Women in Beijing, the Ford Foundation Women's Program Forum commissioned the seventeen essays collected here, the reflections of scholar-activists most of whom have both studied and participated in the movements they describe. In her excellent introduction, editor Basu traces the development of the international women's movement during the past two decades, marked midway by the publication of *Sisterhood Is Global* in 1984. She posits the pivotal question "Is there such a thing as global feminism?" and, while acknowledging the inherent tensions, emphasizes the "productive interplay between global and local feminism." Through brief histories and case studies of local feminisms and women's activism, the contributions examine the nature and strategies of national women's movements in Asia, Africa and the Middle East, Latin America, the former Soviet Union, Europe, and the United States. The essays illustrate Basu's contention that while women's movements may address a range of common issues (women's legal and political rights, employment opportunities and discrimination, reproductive choice and abortion, sexual freedom, violence against women, political participation and representation), they do so in distinctive ways, operate in differing arenas, and assume culturally variant forms of expression. The remarkable diversity of perspectives, goals, and agendas serves to underscore the theoretical and practical complexity of the intersections of patriarchy, nationality, gender, class, and identity. Taken as a whole, the collection documents the profound impact of feminist activism and scholarship (however it may be described or labeled) on local politics and social structures, national policies, and international debates. Highlighting both achievements and persistent challenges, this essential work provides a solid basis for comparative analyses among countries and regions and points to the imperative of alliances across controversy and difference.

150. Blackhouse, Constance, and David H. Flaherty, eds. *Challenging Times: The Women's Movement in Canada and the United States.* Buffalo: McGill–Queen's University Press, 1992. 335p. bibliog. index. ISBN 0773509100; 0773509194pa.

A joint project of the University of Western Ontario's Centre for Women's Studies and Feminist Research and the Centre for American Studies, this collection of twenty-one chapters seeks to foster greater communication between academic feminists in North America and to assess the similarities and differences between the women's movements in Canada and the United States. The authors grapple with fundamentally important questions of how one defines "the contemporary women's movement," exploring myriad factors that shape its origins, directions, and goals in each country as well as in subregions such as Quebec. Thought-provoking comparisons extend from the analysis of political campaigns (the U.S. Equal Rights Amendment contrasted with the equality provisions in the Canadian Charter of Rights and Freedoms) to the growth of women's studies and its actual and potential interrelationships of academic and activist feminism. Several contributors scrutinize the thorny issues of racism, a major issue in the women's movements of both countries; others focus on sexual assault, economic issues, the imperatives of reproductive freedoms, or the inherent dangers of reproductive technologies. Perhaps not surprisingly, given the relative dominance of American culture, throughout the work the Canadian writers strive more consistently and successfully to employ a comparative analysis. This lively and accessible anthology provides an excellent introduction to contemporary Canadian feminism and its shared agendas and marked divisions with its North American neighbor.

151. Buckley, Sandra. *Broken Silence: Voices of Japanese Feminism.* Berkeley: University of California Press, 1997. 382p. bibliog. index. ISBN 0520085132; 0520085140pa.

Buckley sets out to disprove a colleague's claim that there is no feminism in Japan, "at least no serious feminist theorists" (p. xi). This volume not only demonstrates the existence of Japanese feminism but also illuminates its origins and character distinct from feminism in Western contexts. Aiming to "create a space in English translation where Japanese feminists could speak in their own voices," she has gathered a unique and informative collection of first-person accounts. While the voices represented include those of professors and writers, lawyers and business owners also offer their reflections, mirroring the primary development of Japanese feminism outside of academic institutions. Between 1988 and 1991, Buckley interviewed the ten women represented here, then worked collaboratively with each respondent in the further development and editing of her chapter. The issues and ideas explored across the pieces span a broad range, including ecofeminism, reproductive technologies, marriage, family, law, medicine, and relationships of Japanese to Western feminisms as well as feminist critiques of Japan's role in the Third World. A chronology of recent events in the history of Japanese feminism provides useful contextualization for the individual stories. In addition, Buckley provides a glossary to assist readers unfamiliar with Japan and a directory of women's organizations in Japan to encourage further contacts with Japanese feminists. The range of perspectives presented here is further broadened through the earlier anthology of twenty-six essays *Voices from the Japanese Women's Movement* (M.E. Sharpe, 1996, edited by AMPO Japan-Asia Quarterly Review). It spans generations of women and includes trade unionists and other activists, a rural farmer, and a lesbian translator in addition to writers, artists, and filmmakers, covering such topics as politics, child care, the sex industry, comfort women, employment, sexuality, women's spaces, and the women's movement.

152. Bulbeck, Chilla. *Re-orienting Western Feminisms: Women's Diversity in a Post-colonial World.* New York: Cambridge University Press, 1998. 270p. bibliog. index. ISBN 0521580307; 0521589754pa.

In an earlier inquiry into the "possibility of global feminism," *One World Women's Movement* (Unwin Hyman, 1988), Australian feminist scholar Bulbeck analyzed debates between white Western feminists and other feminists during the United Nations Decade for Women (1975–1985) around the multiple intersections of global patriarchy, race and gender, and colonialism, imperialism, and development. In *Re-orienting Western Feminism*, written a decade later, she provides a more complex, nuanced, and substantive investigation of similarities and differences, tensions and connections among women in a postcolonial world. Addressed explicitly to white Western women, the book aims not only to challenge stereotypes of "other" women, but also to demonstrate how these stereotypes are "so integral to white western women's construction of themselves" (p. 1). By looking at Western Feminism through the lens of the scholarship of "Third World" women like Gayatri Spivak and Chandra Mohanty, Bulbeck seeks to "re-orient" it, to challenge its theoretical and empirical preoccupations. She builds on a brief historical overview of Western feminisms to offer critical examinations of debates around colonialism, tradition, and modernity; law and human rights; individual and community; motherhood and marriage; sexual identities; and trade, labor, and the traffic in women. Contesting ethnocentric Western notions and assumptions, she puts each issue into perspective, highlighting meanings and positions contingent upon location and culture, economics, and politics in Africa, Asia, Latin America, and the Pacific Islands. Both books provide fairly comprehensive and useful bibliographies.

153. Caine, Barbara, ed. *Australian Feminism: A Companion.* New York: Oxford University Press, 1998. 607p. bibliog. index. ISBN 0195538188.

Australian feminism is distinguished by its diversity, its engagement with the state, and its wide-ranging integration into many facets of society, culture, and daily life. Drawing on the work of some 100 contributors, this comprehensive reference guide comprises two major parts: interpretive essays and encyclopedia entries. The forty-nine substantive essays explore the many dimensions of Australian feminism, its historical development, and issues, debates, and struggles within it. Topics range from "Aboriginal Women and Economic Ingenuity" to "International Links" to "Women's Studies." Cross-references to related essays in the volume and suggestions for further reading augment each selection. The alphabetical entries in part 2 include organizational, issue, and biographical entries. A useful chronology attempts "to place Australian feminist developments in a national and international context," outlining historical events, Australian feminist milestones, and lives and publications from 1791 through 1998. Fully indexed, the companion also provides a lengthy bibliography of feminist writings.

154. Calman, Leslie J. *Toward Empowerment: Women and Movement Politics in India.* Boulder, CO: Westview Press, 1992. 230p. bibliog. index. (OP)

This widely reviewed and recommended work documents the vitality and impact of the contemporary women's movement in India. It is organized into two parts. The first examines the development of the movement, the political opportunities and structural context from which it emerged, and the resources that fueled it. Part 2 assesses the achievements and failures of the movement, projects its promises and obstacles for the future, and contextualizes it within theories of new social movements. Calman classifies the movement into two categories: the rights wing, which emphasizes legal and constitutional reforms, and the empowerment wing, which "aims at the personal and community empowerment of poor women in both urban and rural areas" (p. 15). Notably, the leadership of educated, middle-class activists sustains both wings. Using personal interviews and unpublished documents as well as secondary sources, Calman informatively locates the Indian women's movement not only within Indian state politics but also within the wider frames of international feminism.

Women's organizations and feminist collective action in India also are described in Nandita Gandhi and Nandita Shah's *The Issues at Stake: Theory and Practice in the Contemporary Women's Movement in India* (Kali for Women, 1992). Grounded in action research, this work builds on interviews with some thirty-five social change organizations that taken collectively constitute much of the Indian women's movement (IWM). It assesses the phases and dimensions of the IWM, centered on thematic issues "described wherever possible chronologically, along with the various methods of action and campaigns and with the numerous theoretical explanations used by different groups and political tendencies" (p. 33). The salient issues addressed across four distinct chapters include violence against women (rape, dowry murder, wife battering, sexual harassment, and demeaning media representations); work, "its absence, nature and conditions"; health; and legal campaigns. A succeeding chapter takes up dilemmas faced by activists, including the restructuring and foreign funding of organizations. Further analyses of specific women's organizations can be found in *The Empowerment of Women in India: Grassroots Women's Networks and the State* by Sangeetha Purushothaman (Sage, 1998). *Women of Pakistan: Two Steps Forward, One Step Back?*, edited by Khawar Mumtaz and Farida Shaheed (Zed Books, 1987), remains one of the few works to address the Pakistani women's movement and focuses on its founding organization, the Women's Action Forum (WAF), formed in 1981 to resist the antiwomen legislation and actions taken as part of the Zia government's program of Islamicization.

155. Chafetz, Janet Saltzman, Anthony Gary Dworkin, with the assistance of Stephanie Swanson. *Female Revolt: Women's Movements in World and Historical Perspective.* Totowa, NJ: Rowman & Allanheld, 1986. 260p. bibliog. index. (OP)

This ambitious work combines comparative historical investigation and quantitative analysis in an effort to develop a theory for the emergence and ideology of women's movements, defined as coordinated activities of groups whose "first and essentially only priority is to rectify female disadvantage" (p. 1). Following an introductory description of previous forms of female revolt, including witchcraft and food riots, the authors take up the challenge of developing an explanatory theory for both the lack and emergence of women's movements "across time and space" (p. ix). The core of the book presents data on thirty-two first-wave and sixteen second-wave movements covering not only Western countries but also Russia, China, Japan, Persia/Iran, and India, among others. The authors then apply their theory on the size and ideological scope of women's movements based on these forty-eight cases to support the claim that, as opposed to many varieties of female revolt over the years, "women's movements have been rare in history, and have occurred only in the last century" (p. 1).

156. Davis, Flora. *Moving the Mountain: The Women's Movement in America since 1960.* Urbana: University of Illinois Press, 1991. 604p. bibliog. index. ISBN 0671602071.

Davis offers a sweeping account of the contemporary U.S. women's movement, covering a vast array of topics, feminist groups, and activities while also tracing the impacts of feminism on public policy. If the debates among feminists, such as the tensions between "equality" and "difference," find thoughtful examination here, Davis nevertheless emphasizes activism and policy over theoretical discourse. As a journalist, she draws upon press reports, personal and organizational files, interviews, and anecdotes to chronicle the gritty excitement, frustrating obstacles, and often chaotic creativity that have marked the reinvention of feminism since the 1960s. Her passionate and informative "activists' history" (p. 9) includes excellent chapters on abortion and the women's health movement as well as lively essays on politics, education, family issues, lesbian feminism, the loss of the Equal Rights Amendment (ERA), and the New Right's war on feminism. Davis engages the increased organizing among women of color in the 1980s and their demands that the women's movement address issues of direct relevance to them. She attempts to tackle the "whiteness problem," but the problem persists in Davis's own understatement of the roles and importance of women of color in the modern women's movement. Still, her work is one of the most encyclopedic and highly recommended books on the challenges, struggles, and accomplishments of feminism during the recent decades. A second edition published in 1999 includes a revised and expanded chapter on the 1990s as well as additional references added to the bibliography. Readers seeking additional information and perspectives on the critical decade of the 1970s will also want to consult Winifred D. Wandersee's *On the Move: American Women in the 1970s* (Twayne, 1988), part of a decade-by-decade series on American Women in the Twentieth Century. A revised edition with a new introduction and last chapter was published in 1999.

157. DuPlessis, Rachel Blau, and Ann Snitow, eds. *The Feminist Memoir Project: Voices from Women's Liberation.* New York: Three Rivers Press, 1998. 531p. bibliog. (OP)

Personal memoirs from some thirty feminists give passionate voice to the history of the women's liberation movement in the United States. The diverse contributors, including such notable writers as Joan Nestle, Paula Gunn Allen, Michele Wallace, and Shirley Geok-lin Lim, mine their individual and collective memory to reflect upon the seemingly all-encompassing social transformation brought about by the feminist activism of the past three decades. The feminism(s) that they sparked and nurtured took many political and cultural forms that are described here with intensity, wit, and, at times, astute critical hindsight. Concluding the volume, Barbara Smith, Ellen Willis, Beverly Guy-Sheftall, and three other activists offer "responses" to the collected memoirs, "adding memories, talking back, thinking through" (p. 468). Editors DuPlessis and Snitow have succeeded in gathering invaluable first-person accounts that vividly capture the experiences, ideas, and fervor that fueled the movement as well as the controversies and conflicts that challenged its existence from within. Through the "responses," they also make critical space for "second thoughts, controversies, feelings, and counterinterpretations" that embody the continuing dynamism of feminism(s).

In the Company of Women: Voices from the Women's Movement, edited by Bonnie Watkins and Nina Rothchild (Minnesota Historical Society Press, 1996), also captures the impact of feminism on diverse women's lives, drawing from seventy-six interviews with women living in Minnesota in the mid-1990s. Readers seeking more comprehensive memoirs will welcome Sheila Tobias's *Faces of Feminism: An Activist's Reflections on the Women's Movement* (Westview Press, 1997), a multifaceted book that extends beyond autobiography to provide informative historical and political context and analysis of the contemporary women's movement.

158. Echols, Alice. *Daring to Be Bad: Radical Feminism in America, 1967–1975.* Minneapolis: University of Minnesota Press, 1989. 416p. bibliog. index. ISBN 0816617864; 0816617872pa.

In this groundbreaking book, Echols astutely combines intellectual and social history with collective biography to thoroughly document the history of radical feminism for the first time.

She contextualizes the movement and its intellectual roots within 1960s civil rights and other social struggles, then traces its contentious evolution until, by 1975, it was eclipsed by cultural feminism. Drawing extensively from interviews and early feminist publications, she describes the formative thinkers and organizations (especially Redstockings, Cell 16, the Feminists, and New York Radical Feminists) and charts internal dynamics, shifting ideologies, and political strategies in enormous and dramatic detail. If the movement became rife with factionalism and the deadly denial of class and sexual preference differences among women, it also established the preconditions for future feminisms in its terminology (e.g., "sexism"), tactics, and conceptual tools. Echols unabashedly writes "as a partisan of radical feminism" (p. 19) who seeks to illuminate reasons for the movement's demise in hopes of its revitalization.

Love and Politics: Radical Feminist and Lesbian Theories by Carol Anne Douglas (ism press, 1990) presents another view of radical feminism. Finding her sources in the writings of Simone de Beauvoir, Shulamith Firestone, Mary Daly, Ti-Grace Atkinson, Andrea Dworkin, Adrienne Rich, and bell hooks, among others, Douglas brings clarity to the variant configurations of radical and lesbian feminist theories, lucidly exploring their assumptions, central ideas, disjunctures, and interconnections. More recently, in their edited collection *All the Rage: Reasserting Radical Lesbian Feminism* (Teachers College Press, 1996), British lesbian feminists Lynne Harne and Elaine Miller intervened in debates around queer theory and other "currently fashionable representations and practices of lesbianism" that, in their view, undermine feminism.

159. Eisenstein, Hester. *Gender Shock: Practicing Feminism on Two Continents.* Boston: Beacon Press, 1991. 138p. bibliog. index. (OP)

Evoking Alvin Toffler's "future shock," Eisenstein coined the term "gender shock" to describe "the shock that has been produced in society and in individuals by the successful introduction of feminist ideas" (p. 4). In this readable collection of nine short essays, she compares feminist practice and its cultural impact in Australia and the United States, informed by her experiences as an American feminist academic who migrated to Australia in 1980 and worked until 1988 as a government affirmative action officer. In the relationship of feminist activism to the state, the most significant differences emerge, she argues, documenting the development of the "femocrat," feminists working within government to advance women's issues. Three essays focus on this singular phenomenon that reflects the focus of Australian feminism on "socialist-feminist praxis linked to the politics of the welfare state" (p. 42). The final sections offer an eclectic exploration of "issues raised by the successful reception of feminist ideas culturally and politically in the past twenty years" (p. 5), including postmodernism and feminist theory, feminist concepts of the family, and an investigation of the use of the concept of gender as a category of analysis in law (Catharine MacKinnon), film (Teresa de Lauretis), and political economy and Malaysian factory workers (Aihwa Ong). Eisenstein furthers her analysis of feminism and the state, developing it through interviews with other femocrats and offering a more complex and critical perspective, in her later work *Inside Agitators: Australian Femocrats and the State* (Temple University Press, 1996).

160. Faludi, Susan. *Backlash: The Undeclared War against American Women.* New York: Crown, 1991. 552p. bibliog. index. ISBN 0517576988; 0385425074pa.

Faludi, a Pulitzer Prize–winning journalist, launched the 1990s with a powerful investigation of the insidious and pervasive antifeminist forces at work in the previous decade, "the undeclared war against American women." In her popular critique, she examines the multiple sites in society and popular culture complicit in promoting the message that feminism is women's worst enemy. She takes aim at the antifeminist agendas of the New Right and the Reagan-Bush era, but also targets books, movies, television, and newspapers in addition to the fashion and beauty industries. She forcefully attacks media claims that equality has been achieved and, further, that this new "equality" has only made women unhappy and deprived them of the joys of family life. If media manipulations of social science research misrepresent the impacts of feminism's hard-won gains, that research itself in many instances is also to blame, according to Faludi, for its reluctance to confirm dubious results through follow-up studies or deeper statistical analyses. Arguing with clarity and wit, she dismantles the rampant, media-hyped myths—the miserable career women, the "man shortage" and "spinster boom," the negative effects of day care, the "infertility epidemic," the return of women to the home—and fixes her critical sights not only on neoconservative male writers like Allan Bloom, but also, more problematically, on "neofem" members of the "backlash brain trust," including Betty Friedan and Carol Gilligan. Widely read and reviewed, *Backlash* sparked both great acclaim and furious debate and fast became a most unusual phenomenon: a profeminist best-seller. If this popularized account demonstrates troubling class and race biases, it also provides a thought-provoking topography, however partial, of the barriers to women's equality, then sketches a map to negotiate the obstacle course and persuasively documents feminism's absolute necessity and enduring vitality.

161. Ferree, Myra Marx, and Patricia Yancey Martin, eds. *Feminist Organizations: Harvest of the New Women's Movement*. Philadelphia: Temple University Press, 1995. 474p. bibliog. index. ISBN 1566392284; 1566392292pa.

This well-crafted collection is particularly noteworthy for its unique focus on the institutionalization of feminism in its organizations, the "intersection of feminism as a social movement with organizations as entities that mobilize and coordinate collective action" (p. 13). Twenty-five essays from a variety of disciplinary perspectives investigate the expression and impact of feminism through a remarkably diverse group of organizations from local rape crisis centers and battered women's shelters to "discursive politics" within the Catholic Church to the Women's Electoral Lobby of Australia. Arranged in sections "to represent the particular challenges that feminist organizational practice poses to established social theory and to the political status quo" (p. 18), the essays probe a breadth of issues, notably including the internal dynamics of feminist organizations and the emotional aspects of work within them. Despite the acknowledged shortcoming of a predominant focus on U.S. organizations staffed largely by white middle-class women, this volume makes significant progress toward redressing the lack of research on feminist organizations and sets a foundation for future studies. The volume includes an extensive bibliography and detailed index.

162. Friedlander, Eva, ed. *Look at the World through Women's Eyes: Plenary Speeches from the NGO Forum on Women, Beijing 1995*. New York: NGO Forum on Women, Beijing 1995; distributed by Women's Ink, 1996. 289p. ISBN 0965155609; 0614173191pa.

The NGO Forum on Women, Beijing 1995, represented the largest gathering of women in history. It brought together more than 30,000 participants from all parts of the world who shared a common determination to work for justice, peace, and improved conditions for women and girls around the globe. This compilation of plenary speeches from this historic event provides an excellent overview of the gains achieved since the first United Nations World Conference on Women in 1975 as well as persistent problems, work still to be done, and action plans for the future. The volume is organized into three parts: "Overview of Global Forces," "Strategies and Mechanisms," and finally, "Commitment to the Future: Accountability and Action." Some of the speeches were written; others are transcriptions from tape recordings. Salient themes that emerged include the rise of conservatism, politics of identity and difference, women's rights as human rights, collective rights of indigenous peoples, roles, responsibilities, and accountability of governments and nongovernmental organizations, and the need to transform institutions, "educational, professional, governmental, nongovernmental, and all others . . . at all levels, from the local to the international" (p. xxvii), to combat structures of inequality and oppression and achieve women's equal access and representation. The plenaries were organized to foster cross-regional analysis of such powerful forces as the globalization of the economy and of the media, culture, and communication. Looking to the future, hopes are pinned on intergenerational dialogue and growing commitments to common interests strengthened through networks of diversity and difference. This volume offers a unique and compelling compendium of the voices of global feminism.

163. Gottfried, Heidi, ed. *Feminism and Social Change: Bridging Theory and Practice.* Urbana: University of Illinois Press, 1996. 286p. bibliog. index. ISBN 0252021983; 025206495Xpa.

This thought-provoking collection addresses the relationships between academic work and the advancement of women, probing the problems and possibilities of activist research. Gottfried gathers twelve essays by well-known feminist social scientists, including Heidi Hartmann, Nancy Naples, Dorothy Smith, and Verta Taylor. Contributors probe the questions raised by their efforts to develop a social science in the service of social change. The more theoretical essays explore the dilemmas and contradictions of doing feminist research, including Judith Stacey's "Can There Be a Feminist Ethnography?" Others describe participatory research projects that engage different women's communities from immigrant women to lesbian existence to survivors of childhood sexual abuse or examine strategies for advocacy research in support of feminist policy objectives and coalition building. This is an important work in the literature of feminist methodology and praxis.

164. Hansen, Karen V., and Ilene J. Philipson, eds. *Women, Class, and the Feminist Imagination: A Socialist-Feminist Reader.* Philadelphia: Temple University Press, 1990. 624p. bibliog. ISBN 087722630X; 0877226547pa.

This anthology surveys socialist feminism in the United States, tracing its development in the 1960s and 1970s and its demise as an autonomous movement a decade later. Hansen and Philipson, editors of *Socialist Review* in the 1980s, have compiled key texts, some of which appeared in their journal series titled "Socialist Feminism Today." The essays illustrate the influences of radical feminism and demonstrate the shared agendas around such issues as comparable worth, day care, and reproductive rights. At the same time, socialist feminists distinguished themselves in their opposition to separatist politics and their commitment to maintaining ties with the Left. They further sought to identify a distinctive critique, to engage in unique, independent projects, and to frame these within Marxist theory. Both theoretically ambitious and contentious, these efforts at independence and theorizing too often inhibited their effectiveness and ultimately contributed to the demise of socialist feminism as an activist movement. Nonetheless, as this volume documents, socialist feminists expanded feminist debates and progress in critical areas, including sexual freedom and reproductive rights. The latter area is cogently addressed, for example, in the essay on "Class, Race, and Reproductive Rights" by Adele Clarke and Alice Wolfson, which rejects the narrow focus on choice in favor of more inclusive struggles for reproductive and sexual freedom that include access to health care as well as opposition to sterilization abuse and to compulsory heterosexuality.

165. Howard, Angela, and Sasha Ranae Adams Tarrant, eds. *Opposition to the Women's Movement in the United States, 1848–1929.* New York: Garland Publishing,

1997. 379p. (Antifeminism in America; 1). bibliog. ISBN 0815327137 (Vol. 1). *Redefining the New Woman, 1920–1963*. New York: Garland Publishing, 1997. 329p. (Antifeminism in America; 2). bibliog. ISBN 0815327145 (Vol. 2). *Reaction to the Modern Women's Movement, 1963 to the Present*. New York: Garland Publishing, 1997. 335p. (Antifeminism in America; 3). bibliog. ISBN 0815327153 (Vol. 3). ISBN 0815327129 (3 Vol. set).

This three-volume set of primary sources documents the social and political context of feminism and movements for women's rights in the United States from 1848 to the 1990s. It gathers diverse and representative examples of public discourse in opposition to feminist goals of gender equality and social justice in order to provide students and other readers "the opportunity to encounter directly the opinions of those who resisted and criticized the goals as well as the tactics of feminism in all its forms" (p. viii). Drawn from both academic and popular sources, the selections are grouped within three major chronological periods, one per volume in the series, in order to foster understanding and evaluation in their own historical context. Volume 1, *Opposition to the Women's Movement in the United States, 1848–1929*, extends from the antebellum period through the suffrage movement and covers issues such as the cult of domesticity and the emergence of scientific theories on physical gender differences. The second volume, *Redefining the New Woman, 1920–1963*, traces reactions from the Roaring Twenties to the rise of the civil rights movement and includes applications of new Freudian theories, claims that "biology is destiny," and pressures for social conformity. The final volume, *Reaction to the Modern Women's Movement, 1963 to the Present*, spans contemporary American feminism from the publication of *The Feminine Mystique* by Betty Friedan to the mid-1990s and covers a multiplicity of topics, including the women's liberation movement (1968–1972), *Roe v. Wade* (1973), the development and flourishing of women's studies, and postmodernist feminism. While analysis and evaluation of each selection are left to the reader, this series serves as an invaluable chronicle of the trends and arguments of antifeminism.

Additional resources can be located through Cynthia Kinnard's *Antifeminism in American Thought: An Annotated Bibliography* (G. K. Hall, 1986), which lists books, periodical articles from a wide spectrum of sources, and pamphlets. Kinnard divides the work into eight topical chapters, including women's bodies, women's rights and feminism, women's intellect and character, domesticity, and femininity and motherhood. She includes a brief name index; however, the topical chapters provide the only subject access to the material. The bibliography is useful for tracing the history of attitudes toward women in the United States.

166. Jaquette, Jane, ed. *The Women's Movement in Latin America: Feminism and the Transition to Democracy*. New York: Routledge, 1989. 215p. bibliog. index. ISBN 0044451865; 0044451857pa.

Jaquette is one of the foremost scholars of women in politics in Latin America and women and democratization worldwide. Essays in this collection focus on gender and democratic movements in a range of countries in Latin America, including Brazil, Chile, Argentina, Uruguay, and Peru. A second edition (Westview Press, 1994) incorporates new perspectives informed by the democratic transitions in Latin America during the ensuing years and the role of women. It also includes new articles on Mexico by Carmen Ramos Escandon and on Nicaragua by Norma Stoltz Chinchilla.

In *The Costa Rican Women's Movement: A Reader* (University of Pittsburgh Press, 1997), Ilse Leitinger builds on Jaquette's work to focus more specifically on the social-historical development of the women's movement and feminism in Costa Rica. This collection of thirty-four articles addresses a variety of topics, including contemporary politics, promoting the visibility of women in Costa Rican history, women's organizations, feminism and the arts, and the evolution of women's studies. For Argentina, Marifran Carlson's chronological narrative *Feminismo! The Women's Movement in Argentina from Its Beginnings to Eva Perón* provides a historical assessment of women's issues and organizing in the Argentinean context up to the fall of Juan and Eva Perón.

167. Kahn, Karen, ed. *Frontline Feminism, 1975–1995: Essays from Sojourner's First 20 Years*. San Francisco: Aunt Lute Books, 1995. 494p. ISBN 1879960435; 1879960427pa.

Sojourner holds the distinctive position of being one of the oldest and largest women's newspapers in the United States. It was begun in 1975 as "the New England women's journal of news, opinions, and the arts," but its audience and impact reached far beyond the Northeast. The articles collected here represent two decades of reporting and debates around key feminist issues of the time: identity politics, economic justice, politics of the family, reproductive freedom, women's health, sex and sexuality, violence against women, and building coalitions toward an inclusive movement. At the beginning of each of these thematic chapters, editor Kahn offers introductory reflections on the articles, interviews, reviews, and letters selected to provide varied perspectives on the issue or complex of issues addressed. Readers will recognize familiar names like Audre Lorde, Paula Gunn Allen, and Adrienne Rich among the more than 100 writers included here. This lively anthology constitutes a valuable grassroots intellectual history, reflecting the commitment, anger, humor, and passion of the times.

168. Kaplan, Gisela T. *Contemporary Western European Feminism*. New York: New York University Press, 1992. 340p. bibliog. index. ISBN 0814746225; 0814746233pa.

Kaplan's compendium presents an overview of feminism and women's movements in non-English-speaking countries of Western Europe intended to inform English-speaking readers. Emphasizing breadth of coverage and general trends rather than in-depth analyses, Kaplan describes the kaleidoscope of European women's movements explored within the political, social, economic, and cultural contexts in which they developed. A comparative overview introduces and frames her work, focusing first on postwar movements and then examining women's status and employment, using, in addition to economic variables, such indicators as abortion, domestic violence, political participation, and technology. From this base, she goes on to offer fourteen case studies grouped according to "the theoretical paradigms of individual countries" (p. 59) labeled progressive (Scandinavia), conservative (the Germanic countries), marginal (France and the Netherlands), and revolutionary (the postdictatorial countries of southern Europe, Portugal, Spain, Greece, and Italy). Employing a wide variety of historical and statistical sources, she surveys social conditions, chronologies and events, and political strategies and accomplishments in each country while also wrestling with salient theoretical debates and differing outcomes and accomplishments. She hypothesizes a "seesaw effect" that "when and where women have achieved visible success in one or two or three areas (political, economic or personal) one or two areas will show marked signs of regression or maintenance of traditional gender divisions" (p. 58). Her cautionary conclusion alerts feminists, women's organizations, and international groups to the necessity to defend and extend the hard-won gains she so ably describes here. She provides an impressive bibliography of English-language materials that also includes useful references to significant texts in German, French, and Italian.

169. Kaplan, Gisela T. *The Meagre Harvest: The Australian Women's Movement, 1950s–1990s*. St. Leonards, New South Wales, Australia: Allen & Unwin, 1996. 242p. bibliog. index. ISBN 1864480629.

Sociologist Kaplan offers the first book-length overview of the second-wave women's movement in Australia. Framing her survey within a wide-ranging historical and social context (1950s–1990s), she measures achievements and political gains such as the notable emergence of "femocrats," women working within government and bureaucracy to advance a feminist agenda. She notes that most women are more independent, healthier, and better educated, yet in the final analysis, "the changes are ambiguous and, if anything, there have been too few unequivocal gains for women" (p. 192). Particularly attentive to "minority issues," Kaplan also critiques the movement's ambivalence toward working-class, immigrant, lesbian, and Aboriginal women and describes its "meagre harvest" for too many women. She not only cogently argues that much remains to be done, but also warns against tokenism, the advancement of the few at the expense of many, and the dangers of "a contraction of feminism into ever smaller and tighter circles defined by self-interest and prejudice" (p. 197).

Chilla Bulbeck offers a more optimistic assessment of Australian feminism during this same time period in *Living Feminism: The Impact of the Women's Movement on Three Generations of Australian Women* (Cambridge University Press, 1997). Based on the accounts of sixty women of diverse ethnic backgrounds, ages, and geographic regions, this book documents the transformative power of feminism even for those who reject the label and the movement. Readers interested in a more theoretical perspective on Australian feminism will find *Transitions: New Australian Feminism* (St. Martin's Press, 1995) especially useful. The fifteen essays assembled by editors Barbara Caine and Rosemary Pringle represent multiple dimensions of Australian feminist scholarship in the humanities and social sciences. They address a remarkable diversity of topics and concepts, including the meanings of "woman" and "women's studies," technology, prostitution, women artists, the "new" musicology informed by feminist, poststructural, and queer theories, and postnational feminism.

170. Katzenstein, Mary Fainsod, and Carol Mueller, eds. *The Women's Movements of the United States and Western Europe: Consciousness, Political Opportunity, and Public Policy*. Philadelphia: Temple University Press, 1987. 321p. (Women in the Political Economy). bibliog. index. ISBN 0877224633; 1566390125pa.

This collection explores the feminist movement in seven Western democracies: the United States, Great Britain, France, West Germany, Italy, Sweden, and the Netherlands. Thirteen essays from political scientists and sociologists probe feminism's challenges to gendered social hierarchies and the intersections between feminist goals and consciousness and political parties and institutions. Cross-national comparisons investigate the links between feminist organizations and other political groups and seek to illuminate complexities of these relationships as well as their impact on policy and other reforms. Thematic organization highlights the dissemination of feminist consciousness, political parties and opportunities, and state action and public policy. The chapters often demystify formal political processes and attempt to trace the influence of feminism on political outcomes, yet focus almost exclusively on mainstream politics. The editors argue for the value of comparative assessments of feminist movements to spur the imagining of "what is possible in a more feminist world" (p. 17). At the same time, useful descriptions and further analysis of feminist movements in Europe can be found in studies that focus on a single country. These include *Against the Grain: The Contemporary Women's Movement in Northern Ireland* (Attic Press, 1991) by Eileen Evason; *Is There a Nordic Feminism?* (UCL Press, 1998) edited by Drude van der Fehr, Bente Rosenbeck, and Anna G. Jonasdottir; *Out of the Shadows: Contemporary German Feminism* (Melbourne University Press, 1996) by Silke Beinssen and Kate Rigby; and *Sharing the Difference: Feminist Debates in Holland* (Routledge, 1991) edited by Joke J. Hermsen and Alkeline van Lenning.

171. Kumar, Radha. *The History of Doing: An Illustrated Account of Movements for Women's Rights and Feminism in India, 1800–1990.* New York: Verso, 1993. 203p. bibliog. index. ISBN 0860914550; 0860916650pa.

Kumar largely succeeds in her ambitious project to provide a descriptive and interpretive history of some 200 years of women's movements in India. She organizes her account into two main periods, pre- and postindependence (1947) feminisms, marked first by colonial rule and the symbolism of motherhood, then by democratic experiments and the principles of equality and opposition to the sexual division of labor and other gendered systems of subordination. Characteristic of feminism in India, as in many other countries, she claims, is this tension "between the desire for equality which opposed sex-based differentiation, and the sex or gender-based celebrations of the feminine" (p. 3). Drawing upon speeches, memoirs, and autobiographies, the first part highlights individual women who were important in the nationalist movement against the British as well as women's use of their status as wives and mothers to mobilize against such customs as child marriage and sati and for female education and the betterment of women's social condition. The second part, however, reflects the more contemporary focus on collective action and movements as opposed to individual achievement and examines women's struggles for employment rights and economic independence as well as legal representation and legislative reforms. Many illustrations, photographs, short biographies and case studies, and excerpts from primary sources enhance this multifaceted introduction to Indian feminism.

172. Lycklama à Nijeholt, Geertje, Virginia Vargas, and Saskia Wieringa, eds. *Women's Movements and Public Policy in Europe, Latin America, and the Caribbean.* New York: Garland Publishers, 1998. 189p. (Gender, Culture, and Global Politics). bibliog. ISBN 0815324790.

The second volume of a pathbreaking series edited by Chandra Talpade Mohanty, this book attempts to provide a systematic analysis of the "processes of interaction underlying national policies on women" (p. xv). The editors propose an analytic framework of the "triangle of empowerment" to examine the connections between feminist activism and public policy. The triangular and synergistic relationships between the women's movement, feminist politicians, and feminist civil servants or "femocrats" illuminate the national and transnational struggles of women seeking to transform politics and government and the multiple and gendered meanings of rebellion, justice, citizenship, and democracy. The Fourth International Conference on Women in Beijing and the interactions between national women's movements and international nongovernmental organizations (NGOs) receive substantial attention and assessment. Case studies on Jamaica, Peru, Brazil, Mexico, Chile, the Netherlands, and Norway analyze women's political histories and strategies and offer useful comparisons between European and Latin American contexts. Given the divergent political and socioeconomic conditions among these countries, a concluding chapter synthesizing commonalities and drawing out implications for transnational and global strategies would have strengthened the arguments and new theoretical model presented here.

173. Miller, Francesca. *Latin American Women and the Search for Social Justice.* Hanover, NH: University Press of New England, 1991. 324p. bibliog. index. ISBN 0874515572; 0874515580pa.

Miller offers a comprehensive account of the mobilization of women in Latin America in the twentieth century. Examining the intersections of feminism and politics, she assesses the roles and accomplishments of women's organizations in promoting economic and social change. Issues and agendas ranged from suffrage in the 1930s to socioeconomic and social justice concerns in the latter half of the century. She traces the development of hard-won recognition and legitimacy of organizations as well as the inevitable divisions and ideological differences between and within Latin American women's movements. The volume is particularly noteworthy in the range and sophistication of Miller's analysis. At one level, she details the intersections between local, regional, national, and global events as well as urban and rural issues and struggles; at another, she reviews the emergence of feminist ideologies through scholarship in feminist journals and forums. Throughout, she captures the distinctive passion and perspective of Latin American feminism with a rare combination of complexity and clarity.

A later focused investigation of Latin American feminism in the early years can be found in Asunción Lavrin's 1995 study *Women, Feminism, and Social Change in Argentina, Chile, and Uruguay, 1890–1940* (Lincoln: University of Nebraska Press). This work, highlighting these three more urbanized and industrialized nations, also provides regional, national, and international comparisons in addition to useful analyses of institutional and legislative reforms toward gender inclusion and equity. Issues taken up along the way include employment, education, divorce, and reproductive freedom, as well as campaigns for women's suffrage in each country.

174. Naples, Nancy, ed. *Community Activism and Feminist Politics: Organizing across Race, Class, and Gender.* New York: Routledge, 1998. 411p. (Perspectives on Gender). bibliog. index. ISBN 0415916291; 0415916305pa.

Motivated and informed by her own working-class background, Naples has compiled a groundbreaking collection of ethnographic case studies and analyses by scholar-activists committed to progressive change and social justice through community-based political action. Naples determines to redress the invisibility of "the women-centered activism of many women of color as well as working class and poor women of all racial-ethnic backgrounds" (p. ix) in histories of the U.S. women's movement. The array of U.S. women's community activism presented here dates from the 1960s to the 1990s and reflects "varying constructions of community and social identities" (p. 344). Many projects focus on efforts to organize across differences of race and class, often illustrating the challenges of joining theory with practice. Most of the organizers are poor or working class; many are also mothers, immigrants, and/or women of color. Their compelling accounts describe oppositional consciousness and activism across a broad sweep of issues encompassing domestic violence, toxic waste, and paid domestic work along with schooling and educational equity, economic development, immigrant's rights, homophobia, and racism. Most draw upon qualitative methodologies of differing types but commonly characterized by participatory design and dialogic analysis. Not all the projects described can be counted as successful; some portray effective cross-race and cross-class coalitions, while others contain cautionary tales of failures to negotiate across differences. Naples introduces and concludes the collection with two excellent chapters, conceptually framing the issues and raising salient and important questions for future work. She argues for an inclusive activist scholarship, focusing on the perspectives and experiences of women "usually left out of the historical record." Through the lens of multidimensional standpoint analysis, the diverse strategies and lessons of women's political activism can be most clearly discerned and understood and community activist and feminist identities reconciled. Naples's work offers useful models for inclusive feminist activism and scholarship and provides an excellent classroom resource in the bargain.

175. Oakley, Ann, and Juliet Mitchell, eds. *Who's Afraid of Feminism? Seeing through the Backlash.* New York: New Press, 1997. 291p. bibliog. ISBN 1565843843; 1565843851pa.

Noted feminist scholars Oakley and Mitchell have compiled a weighty collection from an international group of prominent feminists to counter the backlash of the 1990s. With a self-critical eye, contributors look within as well as outside of the American and European feminist movements to lucidly assess the gains and shortcomings of feminist activism in recent decades. This internal scrutiny distinguishes this volume from examinations of the backlash as it boldly questions whether feminists have lost touch with basic issues like reproductive freedom, struggles for economic parity, and the needs of working-class and poor women; whether there is, in fact, misogyny within feminism (e.g., Margaret Walters on Camille Paglia and Catharine MacKinnon); and whether white, mainstream feminists persistently impose a demeaning and disempowering victimology on women of color (Parmindu Bhachu's essay "Dangerous Design"). Nira Yuval-Davis's "Women, Ethnicity, and Empowerment" and Oakley's own "Brief History of Gender" are among this diverse group of essays, whose authors also include Carol Gilligan, Patrizia Romito, Susan Heath, Joanna Ryan, and Carolyn Heilbrun, tackling topics from psychoanalysis and lesbian motherhood to masculinist academia. This multifaceted and groundbreaking volume underscores the fact that feminism has indeed unsettled and transformed our political, social, and personal relations, but also that feminism is itself unsettled, and much yet remains to be done to move beyond the backlash in ways that benefit all. It will serve as an excellent and thought-provoking text for courses in women's studies, politics, and sociology.

176. Racioppi, Linda, and Katherine O'Sullivan See. *Women's Activism in Contemporary Russia*. Philadelphia: Temple University Press, 1997. 277p. bibliog. index. ISBN 1566395208; 1566395216pa.

Focusing on Russian women activists and their organizations in Moscow and St. Petersburg in the late 1980s and early 1990s, this work traces the vicissitudes, challenges, and accomplishments of the emerging women's movement in Russia. Racioppi and See briefly outline the historical context for women's activism from tsarist autocracy through the revolutionary period and the Soviet order, then explore the perestroika and glasnost' periods "that undermined the hegemony of Soviet ideology about women and allowed the emergence of organizations independent of the state" (p. 9). Such organizations provide the focal point of the body of the work, a multifaceted investigation of the movement through the work of the Union of the Women of Russia, the Independent Women's Forum, and the Women's League as well as business and economic development organizations. Woven throughout are the narratives of nine individual activists engaged in these organizations who present their life stories and their understandings of the movement, thereby augmenting standard historical accounts of this period as well as contesting official Soviet versions of women's emancipation and equality. *Ana's Land: Sisterhood in Eastern Europe*, edited by Tanya Renne (Westview Press, 1997), offers a corollary cross-section of women activists in Poland, Slovakia and the Czech Republic, Hungary, Romania, Bulgaria, and Serbia, Croatia, and Slovenia.

177. Reinfelder, Monika, ed. *Amazon to Zami: Towards a Global Lesbian Feminism*. New York: Cassell, 1996. 171p. bibliog. index. ISBN 0304331937; 0304332038pa.

Reinfelder, a German-born working-class instructor of women's studies and politics at the University of London, presents strong testimony to counteract the prevailing myth that lesbianism is an exclusively Western phenomenon. She draws together accounts from lesbian feminist activists from a diversity of regions around the globe, including Latin America, Asia and the Pacific Islands, and southern Africa, specifically, Argentina, Malaysia, and Namibia, among other countries. The thirteen contributors reflect a variety of occupational backgrounds and political perspectives. None claims to represent all lesbians in her country; indeed, the various descriptions of the status of lesbians and lesbian feminism divulge commonalities of oppression but also significant divergences of analysis, objectives, and strategies. Organized lesbian groups exist in

Chile and other regions, while in others, like Africa, where race and class issues still undermine solidarity, lesbians still must rely on more informal networks. The collection gathers reflections on issues from the relationship of lesbianism to economic development in India to the influence of fundamentalist Catholicism on the lives of lesbians in the Philippines. This pioneering documentation of lesbian lives and struggles represents a significant beginning in filling the gaps of information about global lesbian feminism. It includes an index and a short list of autonomous lesbian feminist groups arranged by region.

178. Rowbotham, Sheila. *Women in Movement: Feminism and Social Action*. New York: Routledge, 1992. 370p. (Revolutionary Thought/Radical Movements). bibliog. index. (OP)

Rowbotham, a noted socialist feminist historian, provides a useful teaching resource through this comparative study of the history of the feminist social movement. She marks its emergence in the French Revolution, then charts its development and impact through economic, social, and political movements not only in the Western world but also in Russia, China, and India. She highlights its distinctive geographical forms, noting the diversity of feminisms as well as similarities through such themes as definitions of needs, rights and equality, personal and political transformations, collective action, identity, and difference. The organization of the volume facilitates both historical and theoretical readings, highlights themes for discussion, and provides short bibliographies for further reading. Rowbotham's earlier work *The Past Is before Us: Feminism in Action since the 1960s* (Pandora Press, 1989) traces the activities, issues, and ideas of the British women's movement from the late 1960s through the mid-1980s, examining consciousness-raising groups, reproductive rights, the family and housework, and new possibilities for women's work and for relations with children and partners. Throughout, she incorporates the experiences of Asian, Afro-Caribbean, and working-class women and advocates new forms of strategic organizing to address broad social needs.

179. Rupp, Leila J. *Worlds of Women: The Making of an International Women's Movement*. Princeton, NJ: Princeton University Press, 1997. 325p. bibliog. index. ISBN 0691016763; 0691016755pa.

Rupp presents an engaging and authoritative history of international women's movements working transnationally for peace and human rights. She focuses on the period from the 1880s to 1945, challenging conventional notions of periodization and presenting original analyses in political and institutional history. Framing her investigation conceptually around "social movement communities," she compares three different women's organizations—the International Council of Women (ICW), the International Alliance of Women, and the Women's International League for Peace and Freedom—in terms of their origins and development, their membership (primarily Anglophone, white, bourgeois, and Christian), their political issues, tactics, and strategies of representation and activism. Rupp explores key issues of international feminist concern, including education, protective labor legislation, laws around marriage, custody, and citizenship, sexual violence and "the traffic in women," and pacifism. She reveals both points of consensus and division and further uncovers generational differences between suffragette and international feminists. Rupp demonstrates the continuing force of feminist movements during the interwar period leading up to the second wave and the subsequent United Nations International Decade for Women beginning in 1975.

Complementing and extending Rupp's book, Georgina Ashworth's edited volume *A Diplomacy of the Oppressed: New Directions in International Feminism* (Zed Books, 1995) charts the more recent history of the international feminist movement since the 1970s. She credits the Decade for Women for stimulating global feminism and the emphasis on human rights for providing a powerful basis for women's activism and claims worldwide to equality and justice. Women have a new recognition that their condition transnationally is interconnected and structural, Ashworth asserts, and she offers examples of their "active insistence" on social change exerted in a wide variety of forms and locales. The diplomacy of the oppressed emerges in women's "force of ideas, invention and commitment rather than economic resources, of courage, morality and justice instead of technology and tanks" (p. 2).

180. Rupp, Leila J., and Verta Taylor. *Survival in the Doldrums: The American Women's Rights Movement, 1945 to the 1960s.* New York: Oxford University Press, 1987. 284p. bibliog. index. (OP)

Rupp and Taylor's unique history counters prevailing assumptions of the death of feminism after the "first wave." Drawing upon archival materials, interviews, and other sources to document women's activism during the postwar years, focusing on the 1950s, Rupp and Taylor argue that even in "the doldrums," a women's movement persisted, albeit an elite one represented primarily by the National Women's Party (NWP), centered on its charismatic founder Alice Paul and generally isolated from other social movements. They describe the NWP's continuing struggle for the Equal Rights Amendment, including their early infiltration of the nascent National Organization for Women in an attempt to assure the primacy of efforts to pass the Equal Rights Amendment. The strategies they used and the intersections of the members' political and personal lives also give added dimension to the story of how a small group of privileged women could have a significant impact even in a hostile postwar environment. At the same time, the significance of this work derives as well from its depiction of the dangers of a single-minded advocacy for women in isolation from other progressive causes, resulting in an elitist feminism that succumbed to the prevailing racism, anti-Semitism, and anti-Communism of the day. Such painful lessons underscored the complexities of feminism and its legacies and served to inform the later resurgence of a broader, more inclusive feminist movement.

181. Ryan, Barbara. *Feminism and the Women's Movement: Dynamics of Change in Social Movement Ideology and Activism.* New York: Routledge, 1992. 203p. (Perspectives on Gender). bibliog. index. ISBN 0415905982; 0415905990pa.

Using a framework of social movement and resource mobilization theory, Ryan tracks the changes in feminist activism and thought from the mid-nineteenth century through the 1980s. Based on research grounded in primary documents, oral histories with longtime activists, documentation from organizations, and participant observation, the book analyzes the vicissitudes and transformation of the women's movement. Introduced by two chapters that provide historical background, the work consists primarily of a sociological study of contemporary feminism since 1970. The National Organization for Women (NOW) takes center stage here, both as a focus in itself and as a marker of difference from other branches of the movement like radical, socialist, and cultural feminism. Ryan argues, however, against the categorization of feminist groups into "reform" and "radical," proposing an alternative conceptualization of "mass movement sector" and "small group sector" that favors structural characteristics over ideological ones. She showcases the campaign for the Equal Rights Amendment, claiming it as a "unifying issue" that prompted a convergence of feminist purpose and mobilization between 1975 and 1982. She suggests that subsequent divisiveness around race, pornography, and sexuality, for example, can be traced to the defeat of the ERA and consequent disarray in the movement. In her quest for unifying goals and her defense of NOW, Ryan controversially asserts that identity politics weakened feminism and neglects the contributions of small groups in such areas as labor, health, and violence against women.

182. Schneir, Miriam, ed. *Feminism in Our Time: The Essential Writings, World War II to the Present*. New York: Vintage Books, 1994. 503p. bibliog. index. ISBN 0679745084pa.

Schneir's anthology, updating her 1972 volume *Feminism: The Essential Historical Writings*, maps the development of modern feminism through its major writings and documents from Simone de Beauvoir in 1949 to Anita Hill and Ruth Bader Ginsburg in the early 1990s. The diverse selections are arranged chronologically within sections that attempt to trace the trajectories of the modern women's movement by reflecting such themes as sisterhood, ideological challenges, women's bodies, and working for change. Primarily nonfiction with the exception of an excerpt from Doris Lessing's highly influential *The Golden Notebook* and several poems, these readings, framed by Schneir's brief but informative introductions, provide an excellent and thought-provoking portrait of the second-wave women's movement.

Robin Morgan, editor of *Ms.*, offers another view into the latter years of this critical period in *The Word of a Woman: Feminist Dispatches, 1968–1992* (Norton, 1992). These essays—polemical, theoretical, and reflective—span the evolution of feminism from a white, middle-class movement to one that has a more global agenda addressing such topics as Palestinian women in Israel's Occupied Territories as well as feminist perspectives on the Gulf War. Many of the themes addressed in these collections also are taken up in *Feminism: Opposing Viewpoints*, part of the series that seeks to provide perspectives on current issues in a pro/con format. While somewhat uneven in its treatment, this volume gathers provocative and contrary perspectives on the historical debates on women's rights, how feminism affects women and society, whether feminism is obsolete, and what the goals of feminism should be.

183. Simon, Rita James, and Gloria Danzinger. *Women's Movements in America: Their Successes, Disappointments, and Aspirations*. New York: Greenwood Press, 1991. 171p. bibliog. index. ISBN 0275939480; 0275939499pa.

The use of the plural "women's movements" in the title of this work heralds its focus less on the evolution of feminism as a unified social movement than on the advances of women in the realms of suffrage and politics, education and the workplace, and marriage and family. Divided into three sections reflecting women's efforts to achieve equality in these areas, the book contextualizes each historically and provides data and documentation "that includes legal statutes and judicial decisions, census and demographic information, public opinion polls, biographical excerpts, and narrative accounts of the changes in women's place in American society from the nation's founding to 1990" (p. 5). The chapters examine both successes and failures and issues that divided women as well as goals that were shared as the status of women changed in American society between 1790 and 1990.

Steven Buechler's *Women's Movements in the United States: Women's Suffrage, Equal Rights, and Beyond* (Rutgers University Press, 1990) addresses some of the same key issues, but takes a sociological approach, analyzing the women's movement as a social movement. His organizational scheme centers around comparisons of the women's suffrage movement to the contemporary feminist movement within each of six conceptual frameworks: roots and origins; organizations and communities; ideologies and visions; classes and races; oppositions and countermovements; and endings and futures. Using this topical approach over a chronological one, he is able to elicit patterns, similarities, and differences in women's organizing over time. Throughout, he employs social movement theory, more specifically the "newly dominant paradigm of resource mobilization," to "illuminate the dynamics of feminist mobilization," while also using women's movements "to critically evaluate the utility of resource mobilization theory" (p. x). In the final analysis, he demonstrates the limitations of the theoretical models and the "richness of women's movements" (p. 228).

184. Sommers, Christina Hoff. *Who Stole Feminism? How Women Have Betrayed Women*. New York: Simon & Schuster, 1994. 320p. bibliog. index. ISBN 0671794248; 0684801566pa.

In 1994 Christina Hoff Sommers launched her salvo against women's liberation and, most especially, academic feminism in this work. Her arguments range from accusations of feminist victimology to attacks on the intellectual weaknesses of women's studies programs and concerns about the wholesale abduction of women's liberation by women who think that patriarchy lives and thrives. In her estimation, there is good feminism and bad or "gender feminism" (pp. 19–22). Gender feminists are marked by their insistence that women remain oppressed in patriarchal society. A frequently cited portion of her surprisingly well reviewed book concentrates on correcting "facts" gathered and used by feminists (and others) to illustrate the condition of women in the modern world. In chapters titled "Noble Lies," "Rape Research," and "The Backlash Myth," Sommers uses statistics against statistics to demolish arguments about male violence against women. She reserves some of her harshest criticism for academic women's studies programs, which, in her view, are populated by fanatic ideologues who prevent others from voicing contrary views. Sommers's book is important more for the controversy it generated than for the quality of either its tone or scholarship. Many of her most provocative assertions have been successfully challenged, and since some reviewers have called attention to the sources of her funding (including the conservative John M. Olin Foundation), Sommers's book hardly passes the test of objectivity, a criticism she readily levels at feminism.

185. Stephen, Lynn. *Women and Social Movements in Latin America: Power from Below*. Austin: University of Texas Press, 1997. 332p. bibliog. index. ISBN 0292777159; 0292777167pa.

Based on collaborative research with grassroots activists that Stephen conducted between 1989 and 1995, this work presents six case studies of women's activism in Latin American political movements. Each provides description and historical background, enhanced by the addition of excerpts from interviews with a woman active in the particular movement(s) or organization under discussion. The geographical coverage spans El Salvador, Mexico, Brazil, and Chile and usefully includes examples of organizing in both urban and rural contexts. Some activist work focuses on collective economic strategies, such as the creation of soup kitchens and economic workshops in Mexico, whereas others more directly challenge dominant gender ideologies and hierarchies in labor organizing. Stephen's analysis is informed by her own extensive education and political activism as well as poststructuralist and Gramscian theories of multiple subjectivities and identities, dominance, power, and hegemony. She concludes the volume with a comparative analysis of the case studies, focusing on recurrent themes of "gender relations, economic development, political mobilization, identity, and power relations between researchers and 'the researched' " (p. 25).

Women and Social Change in Latin America, edited by Elizabeth Jelin (Zed Books, 1990), also seeks to highlight women's influential participation in the public sphere, albeit in social movements often organized outside of mainstream political parties. Like Stephen, Jelin includes case studies that demonstrate women's collective political and economic activism in addressing concerns once relegated to the domestic, private realm. Women mobilize around multiple issues, including housing, education, health care, transportation, and food shortages. While these women generally retain their traditional identification as housewives, mothers, and grandmothers, their collective mobilization around common problems extends their domestic role and responsibilities into the political, as exemplified by the new identity of "political mother." Innovative forms of activism are described, from a housewives' movement against price hikes and the well-known Madres de Plaza de Mayo in Argentina to mutual-aid networks among neighborhood women in Peru and Brazil. Jelin argues and the collection demonstrates that despite the persistence of the sexual division of labor, Latin American women have succeeded in transforming their traditional roles as they seek collective solutions to shared problems, which, as Teresa Caldeira argues in her essay on neighborhood movements in São Paulo, "can have complex, subversive implications" (p. 190).

Women, Culture, and Politics in Latin America, a collective work produced by the Seminar on Feminism and Culture in Latin America of the University of California–Stanford University (Berkeley: University of California Press, 1990) addresses related questions from the multidisciplinary perspective of history and literature.

186. Stienstra, Deborah. *Women's Movements and International Organizations*. New York: St. Martin's Press, 1994. 201p. (International Political Economy Series). bibliog. index. (OP)

This work exemplifies the recent growth and importance of feminist international relations theory. Stienstra, a political scientist, "explores how international women's movements have been involved in constructing, supporting and challenging specific gender relations within the League of Nations and the United Nations" (p. xii). Three theoretical themes—nonstate actors, change, and gender relations—structure her investigation. Nonstate actors include formally organized nongovernmental organizations (NGOs) or more informal social movements, both important to the study of world order because they "embody responses to changes in social relations within that order" (p. xii). The theme of change within and of world orders is developed through the text, with particular scrutiny of changes in programs directed to women in the United Nations and League of Nations in terms of their "material capabilities, discourses, or institutional practices" (p. xiii). Finally, Stienstra addresses the impact of international women's movements on gender relations in international practices and organizations. She employs these rubrics as her framework for analysis through chapters highlighting three main chronological periods: 1840–1920, 1920–1970, and 1970–1990. From 1880 until 1970, the first international women's organizations were established, working through the League of Nations and the United Nations "to attain political and civil reforms based on the principle of equal rights" (p. xiii). After 1970, alternative international feminist networks emerged that, although separate from the United Nations, also influenced changes in gender relations within it.

187. Tétreault, Mary Ann, ed. *Women and Revolution in Africa, Asia, and the New World*. Columbia: University of South Carolina Press, 1994. 456p. bibliog. index. ISBN 1570030162; 1570030316pa.

Covering twentieth-century revolutions in sixteen countries, this eclectic collection of both theoretical and descriptive essays examines nationalist, socialist, religious, and capitalist/modernizing movements in light of gains for women and the expansion of political agendas to include issues that impact women, such as domestic violence or unpaid labor. Revolution here is broadly defined and encompasses the Zimbabwe war of independence and socialist revolutions in China, Cuba, Mozambique, and Angola, as well as the "liberation" of Kuwait. In the geographical organization of the volume, other countries covered in the case studies include Vietnam, South and

North Korea, Indonesia, Afghanistan, Yugoslavia, Iran, Israel, Bolivia, Mexico, and Chile. Of particular interest are the essays addressing revolutionary and postrevolutionary negotiations of the meanings of women's activities and gender relations. This work was named one of *Choice*'s Outstanding Academic Books for 1995 in political science for its scholarship and relevance to undergraduate students.

188. Threlfall, Monica, ed. *Mapping the Women's Movement: Feminist Politics and Social Transformation in the North*. New York: Verso, 1996. 312p. (Mapping). bibliog. index. ISBN 1859849539; 1859841201pa.

Focusing on the Northern Hemisphere, this collection traces the development of the women's movement in nine developed countries, including Great Britain, the United States, France, Spain, Italy, Ireland, Japan, and the post-Communist societies of Eastern Europe. Taken from articles published in the *New Left Review* in the 1980s, the chapters map the salient political, economic, and cultural factors that shaped feminism in each of the countries, from grassroots mobilizing to mainstream politics.

189. Walker, Rebecca, ed. *To Be Real: Telling the Truth and Changing the Face of Feminism*. New York: Anchor Books, 1995. 292p. ISBN 0385472617; 0385472625pa.

One of the most important developments in feminism in the 1990s was the emergence of the "third wave" of youthful, independently minded activists and theorists. Two pioneering collections of essays appeared in 1995: Walker's title and *Listen Up: Voices from the Next Feminist Generation* (Seal Press), edited by Barbara Findlen, giving voice to the challenging perspectives of these young feminists. Born in the 1960s and 1970s, the editors and contributors to these books represent part of the "first generation for whom feminism has been entwined in the fabric of our lives" (Findlen, p. xii). As such, they bring a refreshing sense of entitlement to their experience along with provocative challenges to unexamined assumptions or orthodoxy of any kind, including those embedded in legacies from the second wave. Many of the contributors acknowledge the activism and writings of their feminist "mothers" as crucial in shaping their own thinking and experience, thus demonstrating historical continuities. However, in their inclusive and determined efforts to bust open confining parameters of "the feminist community," they embrace complexities, contradictions, and ambiguity, even taboos (violence and misogynistic hip-hop music, to mention but two). Both volumes present personal testimonies, using the authors' lived experience as a basis for moving reflections and innovative theorizing. Together they document the ongoing renewal and reinvention of feminism, earlier taken up in Paula Kamen's *Feminist Fatale: Voices from the "Twentysomething" Generation Explore the Future of the "Women's Movement"* (Donald I. Fine, 1991), further elaborated in Rene Denfeld's *The New Victorians: A Young Woman's Challenge to the Old Feminist Order* (Warner Books, 1995), and most recently examined in *Third Wave Agenda: Being Feminist, Doing Feminism* (University of Minnesota Press, 1997), edited by Leslie Heywood and Jennifer Drake. Natasha Walter provides a British slant on the status of contemporary feminism in *The New Feminism* (Little, Brown, and Company, 1998). Phyllis Chesler offers an engaging and thought-provoking companion to these volumes; her *Letters to a Young Feminist* (Four Walls Eight Windows, 1997) speaks to these emerging feminist generations, including her son and other young men, with clarity and wisdom.

190. Weise, Elizabeth Reba, ed. *Closer to Home: Bisexuality and Feminism*. Seattle: Seal Press, 1992. 330p. bibliog. index. ISBN 1878067176pa.

"Bisexuality is about choice. About living out the consequences of loving and desiring people of either sex." So Weise begins her introduction to this early anthology of the essays of bisexual women. Organizing, networking, and visibility of bisexuals as a movement of their own emerged in the 1970s, grew through the 1980s, and were marked in 1990 by the first National Bisexual Conference. While recognizing their political and social debt to the feminist and gay liberation movements, bisexuals often felt invisible, excluded, and silenced within these struggles. The essays presented here give voice to twenty-one women who, in diverse and differing ways, "address the unique situation of bisexual women caught between heterosexual sexism and the ideological purity of the lesbian community" (p. xiv). Both longtime activists and newer voices offer personal narratives and reflections that address bisexuality with a seriousness of purpose, probing issues around the fluidity of sexual expression and politics. In their expansive exploration of the implications of their choices, the contributors collectively trace the political, social, emotional, and intellectual contours of a bisexuality grounded in feminism. Intended to be controversial, the collection encourages readers to question assumptions about sexuality and anticipates the later development of queer theory and politics and the move beyond rigid constructs of gender and sexuality.

191. Whittier, Nancy. *Feminist Generations: The Persistence of the Radical Women's Movement*. Philadelphia: Temple University Press, 1995. 309p. bibliog. index. ISBN 1566392810; 1566392829pa.

Giving the lie to the postfeminist myth, this ethnographic history traces the rise and multi-faceted evolution of radical feminism in the university town of Columbus, Ohio, from the late 1960s through the early 1990s. Whittier employs a range of sources, including primary documents from feminist organizations and interviews with thirty-four feminists who entered the movement before 1977 and were active during its early heyday. These women ranged in age from thirty-three to eighty-four years and were highly educated and predominantly middle class. Only 26 percent identified as heterosexual, yet, reflecting the homogeneity of this 1960s and 1970s women's movement, all but one were white. Bringing her study into the 1980s and 1990s, Whittier draws upon the reflections of recent participants in ten women's movement organizations, three of whom were African American. If she demonstrates the central role played by lesbians in sustaining radical feminism, she also gives short shrift to socialist feminists and the critical issues of race and class they articulated. Whittier extends her analysis beyond national or centralized political organizations and argues that the vitality of radical feminism must be discerned in more informal networks and communities of women who share a collective identity and history "and in the diaspora of feminist individuals who carry the concerns of the movement into other settings" (p. 23). Indeed, she asserts, it is this very informality and loosely organized, grassroots character that has made the survival of radical feminism largely invisible to scholars. In the microcosm of Columbus, she documents this survival through sequential political generations, shifting notions and definitions of feminism, and internal debates and conflicts shaped by changing contexts, values, goals, ideologies, strategies, and behaviors.

192. Wine, Jeri Dawn, and Janice L. Ristock. *Women and Social Change: Feminist Activism in Canada*. Toronto: J. Lorimer, 1991. 395p. bibliog. (OP)

In part a response to the relative dearth of materials documenting Canadian feminism, this collection ambitiously attempts to provide "useful learning and teaching materials on the Canadian women's movement" (p. ix) while also strengthening ties between academic and nonacademic feminists. The editors gather experiential and analytical articles from feminists active in the movement, organizing the volume into three parts that reflect these multiple goals. Part 1 sets a framework through the examination of feminist strategies in the Canadian political environment working toward social change over two decades. It traces shifts in consciousness as well as significant legislative, constitutional, and judicial reforms. The second part provides further elaboration by focusing on specific organizing efforts and forms from the unique National Action Committee on the Status of Women to local community action projects addressing Ontario farmwomen, immigrant women in New Brunswick, or lesbians in Toronto. The final portion of the anthology takes up questions of theory and practice, describing collaborative organizational forms and promoting links while also exploring inherent tensions between academic feminists and those whose activism is located primarily in the community. The text is supported by an extensive list of references. In particular, additional information on Canadian feminism can be found in the earlier historical overview by Nancy Adamson, Linda Briskin, and Margaret McPhail, *Feminist Organizing for Change: The Contemporary Women's Movement in Canada* (1988) (see entry 145).

193. Wolf, Naomi. *Fire with Fire: The New Female Power and How It Will Change the 21st Century.* New York: Random House, 1993. 373p. bibliog. index. ISBN 0394223683.

Difficult to classify as either profeminist or anti, this book alternates between impassioned pleas for women to take and assert power and an equally strong denunciation of women as the major obstacle to this assertion of power. Written in an upbeat tone and full of punchy sound bites, this is a work aimed at an audience supposedly put off by stereotypical images of the women's movement, women who would never call themselves feminists. Wolf, already well known for an earlier work, *The Beauty Myth*, heaps scorn on academic and radical feminists. These women practice what Wolf has labeled "insider feminism," which has as its hallmark "litmus tests" (p. 126) on such core feminist issues as reproductive freedom, antimilitarism, and gay rights. "Feminism should not be the property of the left or of the Democrats" (p. 126), she asserts. Insider feminism has sapped strength from the movement for women's liberation through its anticapitalist, pro-choice, prolesbian rhetoric. Although she positions herself ideologically on the left (stating her pro-choice, antihomophobic credentials), she argues throughout the book for power feminism, a feminism based on the power of the purse and the ballot. Wolf is also outraged by "victim feminism" (p. 180) and uses stories ripped from the headlines (e.g., convicted murderer Jean Harris) to illustrate the misguided efforts to create heroines out of profoundly undeserving women. The last chapter, "What Do We Do Now? Power Feminism in Action," offers Wolf's strategy for moving away from both insider/radical feminism and victim feminism. Through the electoral process (sending money to PACs rather than the MS Foundation), consumer power, charitable donations, technology, and so on, women will realize the subtitle of this book: *The New Female Power and How It Will Change the 21st Century.*

194. Young, Stacey. *Changing the Wor(l)d: Discourse, Politics, and the Feminist Movement.* New York: Routledge, 1997. 249p. bibliog. index. ISBN 0415913764; 0415913772pa.

Young asserts that changing the word changes the world. She examines the myopia and limitations of liberal feminism and conventional social science research, seeking to challenge assumptions about the methods and subjects of study and to scrutinize the embedded values that marginalize radical critiques within and beyond the women's movement. In her concern with the "discursive aspects of direct-action activism" (p. 3), she sets a unique focus of her study: feminist small press publishing, their networks, and the ways in which they redefine political activity, reflect new economic and ideological models, and effect social change. Young calls for creative visions of what counts as politics, extending beyond liberal notions of legislation and social policy to encompass what she calls "autotheoretical texts." These critical, theoretical texts grounded in autobiography trace their roots to the 1981 publication of *This Bridge Called My Back: Writings by Radical Women of Color*, edited by Cherríe Moraga and Gloria Anzaldúa. They include the work of such writers as Patricia Williams, Rosario Morales, Minnie Bruce Pratt, and Cherríe Moraga that complicate the category "women," analyzing individual lives within complex political contexts of race, ethnicity, class, religion, and sexuality.

1999 CORE TITLES

Allen, Amy. *The Power of Feminist Theory: Domination, Resistance, Solidarity*. Boulder, CO: Westview Press, 1999. 150p. bibliog. index. ISBN 0813390729; 0813365554pa.

Beasley, Chris. *What Is Feminism? An Introduction to Feminist Theory*. Thousand Oaks, CA: Sage Publications, 1999. 171p. bibliog. index. ISBN 0761963340; 0761963359pa.

Bell, Vikki. *Feminist Imagination: Genealogies in Feminist Theory*. Thousand Oaks, CA: Sage, 1999. 168p. bibliog. index. ISBN 0803979703; 0803979711pa.

Berkeley, Kathleen C. *The Women's Liberation Movement in America*. Westport, CT: Greenwood Press, 1999. 225p. (Greenwood Press "Guides to Historic Events of the Twentieth Century"). bibliog. index. ISBN 0313298750.

Bystydzienski, Jill M., and Joti Sekhon, eds. *Democratization and Women's Grassroots Movements*. Bloomington: Indiana University Press, 1999. 397p. bibliog. ISBN 0253334454; 0253212790pa.

D'Itri, Patricia Ward. *Cross Currents in the International Women's Movement, 1848–1948*. Bowling Green, OH: Bowling Green State University Popular Press, 1999. 267p. bibliog. index. ISBN 0879727810; 0879727829pa.

Heitlinger, Alena, ed. *Émigré Feminism: Transnational Perspectives*. Buffalo, NY: University of Toronto Press, 1999. 333p. bibliog. index. ISBN 0802009298; 0802078990pa.

Hekman, Susan J. *The Future of Differences: Truth and Method in Feminist Theory*. Malden, MA: Blackwell Publishers, 1999. 173p. bibliog. index. ISBN 0745623786; 0745623794pa.

Moi, Toril. *What Is a Woman? and Other Essays*. New York: Oxford University Press, 1999. 517p. bibliog. index. ISBN 019812242X.

Nicholson, Linda J. *The Play of Reason: From the Modern to the Postmodern*. Ithaca, NY: Cornell University Press, 1999. 179p. bibliog. index. ISBN 080143517X; 0801485169pa.

Nussbaum, Martha Craven. *Sex and Social Justice*. New York: Oxford University Press, 1999. 476p. bibliog. index. ISBN 0195110323.

O'Farrell, Mary Ann, and Lynne Vallone, eds. *Virtual Gender: Fantasies of Subjectivity and Embodiment*. Ann Arbor: University of Michigan Press, 1999. 255p. bibliog. index. ISBN 0472097083; 0472067087pa.

Price, Janet, and Margrit Shildrick, eds. *Feminist Theory and the Body: A Reader*. New York: Routledge, 1999. 487p. bibliog. index. ISBN 0415925657; 0415925665pa.

Ramet, Sabrina P., ed. *Gender Politics in the Western Balkans: Women and Society in Yugoslavia and the Yugoslav Successor States*. University Park: Pennsylvania State University Press, 1999. 343p. bibliog. index. ISBN 0271018011; 027101802Xpa.

Ray, Raka. *Fields of Protest: Women's Movements in India*. Minneapolis: University of Minnesota Press, 1999. 217p. bibliog. index. ISBN 081663131X; 0816631328pa.

Shiach, Morag, ed. *Feminism and Cultural Studies*. 597p. bibliog. index. New York: Oxford University Press, 1999. ISBN 0198752350; 0198752369pa.

Spivak, Gayatri Chakravorty. *A Critique of Postcolonial Reason: Toward a History of the Vanishing Present*. Cambridge, MA: Harvard University Press, 1999. 449p. bibliog. index. ISBN 0674177630; 0674177649pa.

Tanesini, Alessandra. *An Introduction to Feminist Epistemologies*. Malden, MA: Blackwell, 1999. 288p. (Introducing Philosophy). bibliog. index. ISBN 0631200126; 0631200134pa.

Teske, Robin L., and Mary Ann Tétreault, eds. *Conscious Acts and the Politics of Social Change*. Columbia: University of South Carolina Press, 1999. (Feminist Approaches to Social Movements, Community, and Power). 308p. bibliog. index. ISBN 1570033315.

Weedon, Chris. *Feminism, Theory, and the Politics of Difference*. Malden, MA: Blackwell, 1999. 220p. bibliog. index. ISBN 0631198237; 0631198245pa.

Yang, Mayfair Mei-hui, ed. *Spaces of Their Own: Women's Public Sphere in Transnational China*. Minneapolis: University of Minnesota Press, 1999. 375p. bibliog. index. ISBN 081663145X; 0816631468pa.

WORLD WIDE WEB/INTERNET SITES

195. Drew, Allison. *Women's Movements: Internet Resources*. http://www-users.york .ac.uk/~ad15/Women'sMovementsInternetResources.htm.

Developed for the York University MA in History and Politics: Popular Movements program, this site provides links to some twenty sites with information on women's movements around the world.

196. Dublin, Thomas, and Kathryn Kish Sklar, SUNY Binghamton Center for the Historical Study of Women and Gender. *Women and Social Movements in the United States, 1775–2000.* http://womhist.binghamton.edu/.

A gold mine of primary resources on women's movements in the United States, this site includes more than 750 documents, more than 200 images, and 300 links to other useful Web sites for students, teachers, and scholars. "Teacher's Corner" lesson plans focus primarily on women's history, but document collections extend up to the Guerrilla Girls in 2001. Since September 2003, a significantly expanded and enhanced version of this Web site has been published jointly with Alexander Street Press. Half of the site remains freely available; the other half, supplemented by a rich array of additional online resources, is available only by subscription.

197. Duke University, Special Collections Library. *Documents from the Women's Liberation Movement.* http://scriptorium.lib.duke.edu/wlm/.

Duke's online archival collection of documents on the U.S. women's liberation movement is a treasure. It focuses on feminist radicalism of the late 1960s and early 1970s, ranging from "radical theoretical writings to humorous plays to the minutes of an actual grassroots group." Subject categories include organizations and activism, medical and reproductive rights, music, sexuality and lesbian feminism, socialist feminism, women of color, and women's work and roles, among others. The site provides search and browse features.

198. *Feminist Majority Foundation Online.* http://www.feminist.org/.

Produced by this nonprofit advocacy organization founded in 1987 to utilize "research and action to empower women economically, socially, and politically," this site includes sections on student activism, global feminism, and feminist, research as well as daily updates of news and links.

199. Institute for Global Communications (IGC). *WomensNet.* http://www.igc.org/index.html.

IGC supports progressive online networking, also including *PeaceNet* and the recently added *Anti-racism Net.* Launched in 1995, *WomensNet,* an online community of individuals and organizations, works to support women's interests worldwide. Site categories include "Access to Technology," "Activism for Women," "Development," "Economics," "Health Rights," "Human Rights," and "Feminist Directories."

200. Korenman, Joan. *Activist Websites for Women's Issues.* http://www.research.umbc.edu/~korenman/wmst/links_actv.html.

Korenman produces the highly acclaimed *Women's Studies Online Resources* site, one of the best on the Web. Like the overall site, the section on activism gathers numerous yet selective links, annotated and faithfully updated. While many focus on the United States and Europe, others highlight activism in other countries.

201. Liu, Alan. *Voice of the Shuttle: Women's Studies and Feminist Theory.* http://vos.ucsb.edu/browse-netscape.asp?id=2711#id2828.

Liu is justifiably celebrated for his wide-ranging metasite that includes especially useful links for feminist theory. Well organized not only by topic (e.g., ecofeminism) but also by individual theorist (Beauvoir, Butler, Irigaray, and others), this site also provides selected links related to women's movements and activism.

202. Osted, Denise. *Global List of Women's Organizations*. http://www.euronet.nl/%7Efullmoon/womlist/womlist.html.

Osted provides a useful list of women's organizations around the world arranged by country or territory.

203. Polk, Danne. *Queer Theory*. http://www.queertheory.com/.

Produced in association with Philosophy Research Base, this site provides online resources integrated with recommended visual and textual resources in queer culture, queer theory, queer studies, gender studies, and related fields. It features well-organized access to such relevant topics as gender, feminism, difference, and essentialism, among many others.

204. *Sisterhood Is Global Institute* (SIGI). http://www.sigi.org/.

An international nongovernmental and nonprofit organization, SIGI promotes women's rights education and leadership at local, regional, national, and global levels. This site includes sections for resources, human rights education, publications, newsletters, action alerts, and events and milestones.

205. Switala, Kristin. *Feminist Theory Website*. http://www.cddc.vt.edu/feminism/.

Available in English, Spanish, and French, this site has a dual focus and audience: feminist theory and women's movements for activists and scholars. It aims to encourage a wide range of research into feminist theory, and dialogue between women (and men) from different countries around the world. The site is organized into three parts: (1) various fields within feminist theory, (2) different national and ethnic feminisms, and (3) individual feminists.

206. Tonella, Karla. *Women's Studies Resources: Activism and Feminist Theory*. http://bailiwick.lib.uiowa.edu/wstudies/general.html.

Tonella's collection of women's studies resources includes sections on activism and on feminist theory. It contains information on organizations and on French feminists, book reviews, and images of women philosophers and theorists.

SOCIAL SCIENCES

3 Anthropology, Cross-Cultural Studies, and International Studies

Hope Yelich

In the innovative collection *Women Writing Culture*, coeditor Ruth Behar writes, "If there is a single thing, a common land that all of us are seeking, it is an anthropology without exiles" (p. 8). This commitment to inclusiveness summarizes the third wave of feminist anthropology. No longer content merely to document women's roles in ethnographic writings, the goal of the first wave (c. 1850–1920), or to concentrate on gender and the universality of women's experiences, the preoccupation of the second wave (c. 1920–1980), scholars since 1980 have recognized the need to consider race, class, sexual orientation, and other factors. What has emerged is revolutionary work by and about indigenous women, immigrants, women of color, and nonheterosexual women and the worlds in which they live.

This concern for diversity extends to cross-cultural and international studies as well. For instance, scholarly work written in English about women in the Third World has increased tremendously since 1980. Reflecting such changes, this chapter includes works not only on the traditional areas of anthropology and culture, but also on women in archaeology and prehistory; geography; international women; ecofeminism and ecology; beauty, reproduction and sexual rites of passage; folklore; and development.

The "Monographs" section in this chapter is arranged topically in the following categories: "Anthropology and Social Conditions of Women"; "Archaeology and Prehistory"; and "Geography." Within these groupings are fieldwork studies, ethnologies, works of literature, memoirs, folktales, polemics, archaeological site reports, and oral histories, in addition to traditional scholarly monographs and collections of essays. Not included are books on history (except those on archaeology and prehistory) or international studies if their thematic focus clearly belongs in another chapter (such as those on politics or sociology).

REFERENCE SOURCES

207. Acosta-Belen, Edna, and Christine E. Bose, eds. *Researching Women in Latin America and the Caribbean*. Boulder, CO: Westview Press, 1993. 201p. bibliog. index. ISBN 0813384656.

The bibliographic essays in this work not only summarize recent trends in scholarship on Latin American and Caribbean women, but also point to areas for further research. The editors approach the work from a multidisciplinary perspective, including ideas from scholars of history, anthropology, and literature. Moreover, as a testament to the multidisciplinary nature of gender research, contributors extend the boundaries of traditional disciplines to include pertinent issues such as development, politics, and migration. In the last essay, Acosta-Belen calls for a better theoretical integration of women's, ethnic, and area studies. Each chapter features research notes and an extensive bibliography. Concise name and subject indexes conclude the volume.

208. Bacus, Elisabeth, and Kurt F. Anschuetz, eds. *A Gendered Past: A Critical Bibliography of Gender in Archaeology*. Ann Arbor: University of Michigan Museum of Anthropology, 1993. 172p. (Technical Report no. 25). ISBN 0915703319.

Bacus and Anschuetz based this annotated bibliography on a seminar about gender and archaeology that graduate students from the Archaeology Department at the University of Michigan organized. Fifteen contributors evaluate 197 journal articles, books, book chapters, and conference proceedings published as of September 1992. Contributors cite works in anthropological, historical, and classical archaeology and ethnoarchaeology that deal with gender. The editors arrange the entries according to the last names of the authors and include an author and subject index to facilitate access to particular topics. The entries feature extensive annotations. In the forward, Alison Wylie, a feminist scholar engaged in the philosophy of archaeology, laments that scholars have neglected to research feminist archaeology, and that only a few archaeological studies of women prior to the late 1980s exist. This compilation, which contains citations to more conference proceedings and "special issues" of journals than mainstream publications, aptly begins to fill the scholarly gaps of this gender in archaeology.

209. Gacs, Ute, Aisha Khan, Jerrie McIntyre, and Ruth Weinberg, eds. *Women Anthropologists: A Biographical Dictionary*. New York: Greenwood Press, 1988. 428p. bibliog. index. ISBN 0313244146.

The women's movement of the 1970s, which greatly influenced the editors of this book while they attended undergraduate school, revealed that scholars traditionally overlooked early female contributions to anthropology. The editors of this reference work thus highlight the lives and careers of fifty-eight women born between 1836 and 1934. Contributors profile women who hail from the following countries and regions: America, New Zealand, Latin America, South Africa, and the Soviet Union. The entries are six to eight pages long, feature a list of resources about the anthropologist, and include a bibliography of her major works. The following enhance the work: a reflective introduction, two appendices that include a list of places where the women conducted fieldwork and a chronology of birth dates, a general bibliography, and a subject index.

210. Huber, Kristina Ruth. *Women in Japanese Society: An Annotated Bibliography of Selected English Language Materials*. Westport, CT: Greenwood Press, 1992. 484p. (Bibliographies and Indexes in Women's Studies, v. 16). index. ISBN 0313252963.

Using her skills as a librarian, Huber attempts to comprehensively cover every aspect of Japanese women's lives in the public, private, and professional spheres from prehistory to the present. According to the author, "Japanese women" include both Japanese and non-Japanese women living in Japan and excludes women of Japanese descent living in other countries. Books and journal articles published between 1841 and 1990, as well as translations of original sources, primarily compose the 2,311 entries that Huber features in this work. She cites most of the work from mainstream publications, which should tremendously benefit undergraduates. Huber includes wide-ranging subject areas, such as marriage and domestic life, health, religion, fashion, labor, legal status, education, political and social activism, and women in the arts and literature. She also includes highly useful overviews of the scholarship on women in Japan. Huber arranges the brief annotations into topical chapters, which makes for easy access. In addition to a detailed table of contents, Huber includes three indexes: author/editor/translator/interviewee, title/phrase/series/ proceedings, and subject. Two additional bibliographies in this series are Parvin Ghorayshi's *Women and Work in Developing Countries: An Annotated Bibliography* (1994) (see entry 304) and Anna Brady's *Women in Ireland: An Annotated Bibliography* (1988).

211. Kimball, Michelle R., and Barbara R. von Schlegell. *Muslim Women throughout the World: A Bibliography.* Boulder, CO: Lynne Rienner Publishers, 1997. 309p. index. ISBN 1555876803.

Kimball and von Schlegell, scholars in the field of Islamic studies, have compiled almost 3,000 fiction and nonfiction books, book chapters, and journal articles about Muslim women who live across the globe. The authors mostly cite English-language resources and do not annotate the sources. Central topics include social and legal status, education, gender and feminist issues, religion, development, marriage and family life, employment, and politics. The authors also feature entries on art, dress and veiling, history, female circumcision, mysticism, literature, music, mass media, and social change. They alphabetically arrange the bibliography according to author's name. The fine index features geographical and topical listings, making the book easy to use. An annotated list of the fifty most important books and articles on Muslim women based on a specialists' survey should prove particularly valuable for students and collection development librarians. This work is also available in electronic form on NetLibrary.

212. Kinnear, Karen L. *Women in the Third World: A Reference Handbook.* Santa Barbara, CA: ABC-CLIO, 1997. 348p. (Contemporary World Issues). bibliog. index. ISBN 0874369223.

This resource provides very basic information about an extremely complex and wide-ranging subject. Kinnear presents an overview that focuses on issues such as gender roles, violence against women, education, health care, women's rights, family relations, and women's roles in economics and politics. She then chronicles the status and rights of women from 1919 to 1996 and includes biographical sketches of prominent twentieth-century women. The "Facts and Statistics" section features basic statistics in textual form, including the text of eighteen international agreements, perhaps the most valuable part of the book. Kinnear brings several organizations together in a directory that contains the following information: a description, address, phone and fax numbers, and e-mail and Web sites, if applicable. Most sections conclude with a short list of secondary sources. The author also includes an annotated bibliography of both print and nonprint resources, such as videos and Web sites, at the end of the volume. In *Women in the Third World: A Directory of Resources* (Orbis Books, 1987), Thomas Fenton and Mary Heffron identify organizations, books, periodicals, pamphlets, and audiovisual materials that support the notion that improving the lives of women in "the Third World" requires fundamental change. The carefully selected annotated entries in this directory of alternative resources make it highly useful.

213. Neft, Naomi, and Ann D. Levine. *Where Women Stand: An International Report on the Status of Women in 140 Countries, 1997–1998.* New York: Random House, 1997. 534p. bibliog. index. ISBN 0679780157pa.

To summarize the improvements and reversals made in women's lives at the end of the twentieth century, Neft and Levine analyze a set of data in three divergent ways. The authors cover the following topics: women's rights, population, politics, education and literacy, employment, marriage and divorce, reproduction, health, and violence against women. The first section functions as a sort of global status report on these issues, while the authors explore the topics in twenty-one countries in the second section. In the third section, Neft and Levine arrange the same data into statistical tables according to country. The authors largely base their findings on an assortment of U.S. and international sources, such as United Nations reports and publications, especially the *Demographic Yearbook* and the *Statistical Yearbook*, as well as documents from the World Health Organization, the World Bank, the U.S. and International Olympic Committees, and various federal agencies.

214. Stoner, K. Lynn, ed. *Latinas of the Americas: A Source Book*. New York: Garland, 1989. 692p. (Garland Reference Library of Social Science, v. 363). bibliog. index. ISBN 0824083361; 0824085361pa.

This work updates Meri Knaster's *Women in Spanish America: An Annotated Bibliography from Pre-conquest to Contemporary Times* (G. K. Hall, 1977). Stoner, a history professor at Arizona State University, and several eminent scholars arranged more than 3,000 bibliographic citations into fifteen sections that represent traditional fields of study, such as history, literature, and education, along with interdisciplinary fields, including health, family studies, and rural and urban development. Each section begins with an excellent review essay that not only summarizes the status of that particular topic but also indicates new directions for further research. The non-annotated list of citations that follows reflects research on women from Latin America who speak Spanish, Portuguese, and French, as well as Hispanic American women in the United States. Stoner features published and unpublished resources, mostly consisting of books, book chapters, journal articles, dissertations, conference papers, and United Nations and aid agency material. Although the majority of the materials are published in the United States and Latin America in the English language, Stoner includes works written in Spanish, Portuguese, French, and other languages. Three indexes arranged by author, country, and subject enhance the work.

215. Stromquist, Nelly P., and Karen Monkman, eds. *Women in the Third World: An Encyclopedia of Contemporary Issues*. New York: Garland, 1998. 683p. (Garland Reference Library of Social Science, v. 760). bibliog. index. ISBN 0815301502.

Under the leadership of Nelly Stromquist, professor of international development education at the University of Southern California, an impressive group of feminist scholars and activists from both industrialized and "developing" countries have produced an excellent introduction to the issues facing women who live in Third World countries at the end of the twentieth century. The editors organized the sixty-eight essays, which consist of roughly ten pages each, according to the following themes: conceptual and theoretical issues, political and legal contexts, sex-role ideologies, demographics and health, marriage and the family, women and production, women and the environment, and conditions and movements for change. The final section critiques the status of women in fourteen geographical regions. Each deftly organized chapter includes an introduction, a conclusion, and a list of references that frame the text. The editors include an annotated bibliography that details the most recent and important scholarship, as well as appendices that reproduce five major proclamations on the rights of women. Readers interested in earlier research on women in developing countries should consult *Women in the Third World: A Historical Bibliography*, edited by Pamela R. Byrne and Suzanne R. Ontiveros (ABC-CLIO, 1986). The editors culled 600 annotated citations to journal articles published between 1970 and 1985 from ABC-CLIO's databases *Historical Abstracts* and *America: History and Life*. Most of the citations refer to topics in modern history.

216. United Nations. Economic and Social Commission for Asia and the Pacific. *Women in . . .: A Country Profile*. New York: United Nations. (Statistical Profiles).

This series of sixteen books, all published during the 1990s and averaging 100 pages in length, provides an overview of the economic, public, and social status of both women and men in several countries in the Asian and Pacific region. Contributors surveyed the following countries: Bangladesh, China, Fiji, India, Iran, Japan, Nepal, Pakistan, the Philippines, Korea, Samoa, the Solomon Islands, Sri Lanka, Thailand, Tonga, and Vanuatu. The Economic and Social Commission for Asia and the Pacific initiated this project not only to help governments integrate women into the development process, but to improve their lives as well. Realizing the need for accurate and current statistical data, the commission enlisted experts in the countries to compile information from various agencies, research studies, and other sources. The resulting surveys include both statistics and text that provide an informative, up-to-date introduction to the status of women in the profiled countries.

MONOGRAPHS

Anthropology and Social Conditions of Women

217. Abu-Lughod, Lila. *Writing Women's Worlds: Bedouin Stories*. Berkeley: University of California Press, 1993. 266p. bibliog. ISBN 0520079469; 0520083040pa.

Abu-Lughod, an associate professor of anthropology and Middle Eastern studies at New York University, attempts to develop "a new ethnographic style" (p. xvi) in her work *Writing Women's Worlds: Bedouin Stories*. She decontextualizes stories written by and about women and girls who form part of an extended family spanning four generations, living in a small town on the coast of northwestern Egypt. Abu-Lughod spent time with these women during the late 1970s and 1980s, becoming very familiar with their lifeways. *Writing Women's Worlds* is a companion volume to an earlier work by the author titled *Veiled Sentiments: Honor and Poetry in a Bedouin Society* (University of California Press, 1986), which concentrated on social life and gender relations in the community. Her new work, however, focuses on the "richness in people's conversations and complexity in their lives" (p. 1), in which she cautions against making anthropological generalizations and forming stereotypes of Islamic Arab societies. Moreover, Abu-Lughod asserts that the lives of these women, whose families recently became wealthy through various business ventures, highly contrast with those of the majority of Middle Eastern women. The author organizes the revealing conversations, stories, songs, poems, and recollections around five anthropological themes associated with the study of women in the Arab world: patrilineality, polygamy, reproduction, patrilateral parallel-cousin marriage, and honor and shame.

218. Adler, Leonore Loeb, ed. *Women in Cross-Cultural Perspective*. New York: Praeger, 1991. 270p. bibliog. index. ISBN 0275936589.

Women in Cross-Cultural Perspective provides a brief introduction to the lives of women from various societies. The authors represent several disciplines, most notably psychology. Chapters focus on women in the following countries and regions: the United States, Canada, Latin America, Great Britain, Poland, the USSR, Israel, Egypt and the Sudan, Nigeria, India, Thailand, China, Japan, Western Samoa, and Australia. Adler presents short historical background sketches of each country or region and organizes the chapters according to the life cycle, from childhood through old age. The contributors address issues such as education, economic development, female circumcision, progress toward gender equality, and culture, readily supplying the means for comparing and contrasting how women live their lives in various societies. The authors, however, regrettably generalize the female population; they do not take into account ethnicity, religion, social and economic status, or type of society ("tribal" versus urban). *Women in Cross-Cultural Transitions*, edited by Jill Bystydzienski and Estelle P. Resnik (Phi Delta Kappa Educational Foundation, 1994), relies on personal stories by women who have moved between cultures. Despite the diversity of place and experience, common themes and issues emerge from these individual narratives.

219. Afshar, Haleh. *Women and Empowerment: Illustrations from the Third World.* New York: St. Martin's Press, 1998. 214p. (Women's Studies at York). bibliog. index. ISBN 0312176465; 0333719743pa.

Academics and development practitioners have come together in this eleven-chapter volume to advance a clearer understanding of what empowerment is and how exactly one can measure it. Jo Rowlands analyzes the term "empowerment" and looks at it in light of recent history in chapter 1. To set the stage for the case studies that follow, she asks these questions: "How do we construct a definition of empowerment that can serve a useful purpose in analyzing and debating issues of the empowerment of women?" (p. 11), and "Where does this fit with the development discourse and theories of women's development?" (p. 15). Women who primarily work in the fields of economics, politics, health, and peace studies cover the following issues in their case studies: agribusiness, temporary workers, rural-urban migration, credit organizations, political involvement, civil liberties, and intimate relationships. Geographic areas include Chile, China, Bangladesh, Brazil, Syria, Iran, and India. A consensus emerges regarding the inability to measure empowerment in general terms. Contributors determine that empowerment represents a process that depends on the specific needs of differing groups (and on specific individuals) in different places and at different times.

220. Barber, Elizabeth Wayland. *Women's Work: The First 20,000 Years: Women, Cloth, and Society in Early Times.* New York: Norton, 1994. 334p. bibliog. index. ISBN 0393035069.

In 1991 Elizabeth Barber published *Prehistoric Textiles: The Development of Cloth in the Neolithic and Bronze Ages with Special Reference to the Aegean* (Princeton University Press). In the course of her research, Barber, a weaver herself, became intrigued by what the textile record could reveal about the creators of the cloth. This curiosity resulted in *Women's Work*, which covers the period 20,000–500 B.C. and focuses on textiles found in Greece, Egypt, the Balkans, Crete, Anatolia, and Mesopotamia. Since few textiles have survived, evidence from archaeological and geologic records, ancient texts and linguistic analysis, and especially Greek, Roman, and Slavic mythology became especially significant tools in her research. One surviving textile, a small string skirt found on a figure dating to 20,000 B.C., exemplifies what Barber calls the "String Revolution." That women learned to twist fibers together into a string, thus allowing for more sophisticated products to emerge, represents "the unseen weapon that allowed the human race to conquer the earth" (p. 45). Barber argues that spinning and weaving were so integral to society that the famous statue Venus de Milo, if still intact, would be spinning. Barber enhances her lively text, aimed at the nonspecialist, with simple black-and-white illustrations and photographs.

221. Behar, Ruth. *Translated Woman: Crossing the Border with Esperanza's Story.* Boston: Beacon Press, 1993. 372p. bibliog. ISBN 0807070521.

Esperanza Hernandez (a pseudonym) is an intriguing woman: she is a Mexican street peddler of Indian (Tlaxcalan) descent whom many people generally think of as a witch for "causing" her abusive husband's blindness after he left her for another woman. Hernandez believes that the rages she felt at the hands of her husband soured her milk, causing her to lose the first six of her twelve children to malnutrition. Instead of allowing these and other difficulties to break her, however, Hernandez emerges as a strong, even belligerent woman who finds some peace in a cult centered on Pancho Villa. A feminist ethnographer and professor at the University of Michigan, Ruth Behar met fifty-five-year-old Hernandez in 1985 in Mexquitic, which lies 500 miles south of the U.S. border. They eventually developed a respectful, trusting friendship known as *comadrazgo*, in which members of different social classes engage in a mutually beneficial relationship.

Behar financially helped Hernandez and her family, and Hernandez recounted her life story, a story she believed was full of suffering, rage, and redemption, a story worthy to take over the border. Behar does not attempt to maintain professional distance, constructing her work in a personal, conversational, and often compelling style. Behar reflects about her own background as a Jewish Cuban émigré and the similarities she shares with her *comadre* at the end of her work.

222. Behar, Ruth, and Deborah A. Gordon, eds. *Women Writing Culture*. Berkeley: University of California Press, 1995. 457p. bibliog. index. ISBN 0520202074; 0520202082pa.

Acknowledging the work of early women writers of anthropology such as Elsie Clews Parsons and Ruth Benedict, as well as the various debates among feminist anthropologists regarding sex and gender issues, the editors assert that "this book will make it impossible to ever again think about the predicaments of cultural representation without seeing the central role of women in its theory and practice. With chutzpah and pathos, we mean to push anthropology over the edge" (p. xii). Behar, a feminist ethnographer at the University of Michigan, and Gordon, a professor of women's studies at Wichita State University, offer a variety of feminist visions in this important anthology, which focuses on the difficulties inherent in writing about culture in the twentieth century. Many of the twenty-three contributions exemplify the "new ethnography": personal memoirs, poetry, drama, and prose. The editors even challenge readers to accept women's theoretical and literary contributions as legitimate ethnographic writings in and of themselves. Contributors devote chapters to Mourning Dove (the first Native American woman to publish a novel), Zora Neale Hurston, and Alice Walker, among other writers. Nearly half of the book's subject matter is more traditional and includes insights into the roles of male/female anthropological practitioners and their subjects, and the experiences of international women. This work is both well documented and highly readable.

223. Bell, Diane, Pat Caplan, and Wazir-Jahan Begum Karim, eds. *Gendered Fields: Women, Men, and Ethnography*. New York: Routledge, 1993. 260p. bibliog. index. ISBN 0415062519; 0415062527pa.

Ethnographers "do fieldwork by establishing relationships, and by learning to see, think and be in another culture, and we do this as persons of a particular age, sexual orientation, belief, educational background, ethnic identity, and class . . . we also do it as women and men" (pp. 1–2). The editors and the anthropologists who contribute to this volume reflect on how their sex affects fieldwork experiences. The twelve female and three male contributors discuss power, inequality, relationships (sexual and otherwise), and particularly, the similarities and differences between themselves and the people they study. They find that their sex—male or female—is merely one variable involved in the complexities of fieldwork. Most of the essayists geographically focus on Asia; however, they also concentrate on Africa, Europe, and Latin America. *Self, Sex, and Gender in Cross-Cultural Fieldwork*, edited by Tony Larry Whitehead and Mary Ellen Conaway (University of Illinois Press, 1986), is an earlier publication with similar findings. The ten contributors to the European Association of Social Anthropologists' *Gendered Anthropology*, edited by Basque anthropologist Teresa del Valle (Routledge, 1993), provide a good overview of the concerns and debates within European gender studies. The authors decry the absence of gender studies in mainstream anthropology, which they attribute to the notion within academia that gender studies represents a biased form of knowledge based on women only. Addressing familiar themes of power and difference, the authors discuss varied topics, including kinship in Samoa and Nepal, home decorating in Norway, and women doing fieldwork in Turkey.

224. Beyene, Yewoubdar. *From Menarche to Menopause: Reproductive Lives of Peasant Women in Two Cultures*. Albany: State University of New York Press, 1989. 169p. (SUNY Series in Medical Anthropology). bibliog. index. ISBN 0887068669; 0887068677pa.

Until fairly recently, most literature on menopause relied upon a Western model that constructed menopause as a disease. After conducting fieldwork among Greek and Mayan peasant women in the early 1980s, however, Beyene found that these women did not view this reproductive rite of passage as a disease; they saw it as a very liberating event. According to taboos and rituals associated with menstruation in these societies, the end of the menses signifies increased status. Beyene found that the Mayan women particularly did not experience any menopausal symptoms, suggesting that such symptoms are culturally rather than physiologically induced. Figures, tables, and photographs enhance the text. Another work in this series by Brian M. Du Troit, titled *Aging and Menopause among Indian South African Women* (State University of New York Press, 1990), concentrates on the climacteric, the phase of the life cycle that encompasses the premenopausal, perimenopausal, and postmenopausal stages, roughly twenty-five years in a woman's life. Du Toit places his study within the cultural and geographic confines of Indian women living in southern Africa. The title is somewhat misleading, however, since the author not only considers the aging Indian woman, but her entire adult life as well. Du Toit discusses the history of southern Africa, the social position of Indians within this region, and women's roles and their perspectives on health, sexuality, menstruation, and menopause. This very thorough study includes maps, tables, and an extensive list of references.

225. Brydon, Lynne, and Sylvia H. Chant. *Women in the Third World: Gender Issues in Rural and Urban Areas*. New Brunswick, NJ: Rutgers University Press, 1989. 327p. bibliog. index. ISBN 0813514703; 0813514711pa.

Although now somewhat dated, *Women in the Third World* remains a solid work of scholarship that provides a fine overview of women's lives (and, more specifically, of gender relations) in the Third World toward the end of the twentieth century. The authors constructed the work as a college text and accordingly rely more on comparisons and generalizations than on specific analysis. Brydon, a social anthropologist affiliated with the Centre for West African Studies at the University of Birmingham, and Chant, a geography professor at the London School of Economics, divide their book into two sections. The first section examines women in rural areas, and the second section deals with women in towns and cities; in both cases, the authors concentrate on low-income women. Within this framework, Brydon and Chant introduce five major topics: the household, reproduction, production, policy, and migration between urban and rural areas. They cover the following geographic regions: Latin America, the Caribbean, sub-Saharan Africa, South and Southeast Asia, the Middle East, and North Africa. The work includes an extensive bibliography, as well as author, place name, and subject indexes.

226. Buckley, Thomas, and Alma Gottlieb, eds. *Blood Magic: The Anthropology of Menstruation*. Berkeley: University of California Press, 1988. 326p. bibliog. index. ISBN 0520060857; 0520063503pa.

The pioneering *Blood Magic* is the first work about menstruation published by a major university press. The editors divide the book into four parts that explore the symbolism of menstruation across many cultures and from different perspectives. The introduction provides a good overview of the anthropological literature on menstruation, with the editors taking a revisionist position that menstrual taboos are not universal, and menstrual customs do not necessarily subjugate women. In part 2, three contributors present studies of the different beliefs among the Beng of the Ivory Coast, the Rungus of Borneo, and the inhabitants of a Muslim village in Turkey. Part 3 deals with some social implications of menses in Portugal, Wales, and the United States, while part 4 examines the question of menstrual synchrony. Although this work clearly represents the anthropological camp, its interdisciplinary approach (drawing on folklore, symbolic analysis, sociology, and biology) lends it relevance for researchers in many fields.

227. Cohen, Colleen B., Richard Wilk, and Beverly Stoeltje, eds. *Beauty Queens on the Global Stage: Gender, Contests, and Power.* New York: Routledge, 1996. 256p. bibliog. index. ISBN 0415911524; 0415911532pa.

Contributors overturn the notion of beauty pageants as either superficial exercises in narcissism or commercial exploitation of women in this collection of essays that describe beauty contests in fourteen cultures. The editors point out that beauty pageants occur all over the world and involve various ages and groups, yet they remain remarkably similar in what takes place. They reflect, through the crowning of an individual, the standards and values of a particular culture. These standards closely connect with nationalistic concerns, as many contests are linked to class, ethnic, and political struggles. Through implication of a "beauty standard," which is objective and separate from the individual, promoters of these rituals exercise powerful cultural control. Although the imposition of Western ideals of beauty represents one major result of the globalization of beauty pageants, such as the Miss Universe pageant, contributors analyze multifarious pageants and their queens, including the Snake Charmer Queen in Texas, Miss Gay Super Model of the World in the Philippines, the Maya Queen in Guatemala, and Miss Heilala in Tonga. These case studies provide an alternative perspective on the formation of national identity.

Editor Nicole Sault's *Many Mirrors: Body Image and Social Relations* (Rutgers University Press, 1994) considers many different body types. Contributors—anthropologists, sociologists, and human service workers—explore issues of power, control, self-awareness, and the presentation of self in widely different contexts. They look at Bedouin women, godparents in Mexico, American teenagers with eating disorders, "fat" men and women in rural Jamaica, women recovering from rape, and professional women experiencing pregnancy. The volume is divided into four sections: the first deals with makeup, tattooing, and body building; the second examines the meaning of fatness, thinness, and age; the third studies the mind/body split inherent in eating disorders or pregnancy; and the fourth analyzes self-image after cosmetic surgery, rape, and parenthood. Using a more quantitative approach, Linda Jackson examines how gender affects one's perception of attractiveness and why it is important in *Physical Appearance and Gender* (State University of New York Press, 1992). Jackson draws on sociobiological perspectives, that sexual selection is tied to reproductive health, as well as on sociocultural perspectives, that people in the United States, where she focuses her study, value physical attractiveness in women more than in men.

228. Dandekar, Hemalata C., ed. *Shelter, Women, and Development: First and Third World Perspectives.* Ann Arbor, MI: George Wahr Publishing Co., 1993. 447p. bibliog. ISBN 0911586962.

The fifty essays in *Shelter, Women, and Development* emerged from a conference of the same name held in 1992 at the College of Architecture and Urban Planning at the University of Michigan. Dandekar organizes the work according to nine "themes": shelter policy and the implications for women's development, legal interventions, shelter and women in crisis, women's participation in the production of shelter, shelter and income, women and shelter-related services, nontraditional living arrangements, design and creation of shelters, and shelter opportunities for elderly women. Although the editor includes case studies from Third World countries such as

Bangladesh, India, Zimbabwe, Botswana, Nigeria, and Ghana, the essayists tend to make general comparisons, relying upon examples from many sources. An index would have enhanced the work. *Women, Human Settlements, and Housing*, edited by Caroline Moser and Linda Peake (Tavistock Publications, 1987), also emphasizes the importance of housing for women. The authors describe women in their roles as mothers, housekeepers, laborers, and members of the community in seven case studies from Central and South America, Africa, and Asia.

229. Davis-Floyd, Robbie E., and Carolyn F. Sargent, eds. *Childbirth and Authoritative Knowledge: Cross-Cultural Perspectives.* Berkeley: University of California Press, 1997. 510p. index. ISBN 0520206258; 0520207858pa.

This philosophical continuation of Brigitte Jordan's *Birth in Four Cultures: A Crosscultural Investigation of Childbirth in Yucatan, Holland, Sweden, and the United States* (4th ed., Waveland Press, 1993) defines the childbirth process as significant for its own sake, and not as part of a larger construct. Contributors to *Childbirth and Authoritative Knowledge* assert that childbirth practices are culturally bound. Contributors present sixteen case studies based upon what Jordan calls authoritative knowledge: "the knowledge that counts, on the basis of which decisions are made and actions taken" (p. 4). Contributors describe childbirth practices in Greece, the United States, Japan, Nepal, Eastern Europe, Italy, Mexico, Sierra Leone, the Inuits of Canada, and the Ju/'hoan women of Botswana and Namibia. They find that women, particularly in the West, transfer authoritative knowledge to obstetricians and medical staff. Moreover, Western medical practitioners are attempting to replace indigenous low-cost birthing systems with modern biomedical practices on an international scale. Davis-Floyd and Sargent's introduction provides a good review of the literature.

230. Di Leonardo, Micaela, ed. *Gender at the Crossroads of Knowledge: Feminist Anthropology in the Postmodern Era.* Berkeley: University of California Press, 1991. 422p. bibliog. index. ISBN 0520070925; 0520070933pa.

According to Louise Lamphere, "Anthropology has the potential of taking feminist thinking about gender differences out of a white, middle-class, and Western milieu, to expand our perspectives . . . and to provide multiple models for gender relations that go beyond our accepted Western dualisms" (p. ix). Contributors to this work, whose influences include Marxism and political economy, challenge the conventional ways of thinking and doing anthropology with a poststructuralist approach to the anthropology of gender, the construction of knowledge, and social theory. Authors of each of the twelve chapters highlight new debates and propose alternative theories within the subfields of anthropology: archaeology, physical or biological anthropology, linguistics, and cultural anthropology. Contributors urge readers to look beyond the cultural, racial, and class prejudices of "white" feminism and instead acknowledge the variety of worldwide gender relations. The diverse approaches within this work, coupled with Micaela di Leonardo's excellent summary of the history of feminist ethnography through the early 1990s, makes it a useful classroom text. In *Exotics at Home: Anthropologies, Others, American Modernity* (University of Chicago Press, 1998), di Leonardo traces how the public and the media have perceived American anthropologists, such as Margaret Mead, during the past 100 years.

Firmly committed to the intrinsic value of ethnography, Margery Wolf embarks on a "personal exploration" of postmodernism in *A Thrice-Told Tale: Feminism, Postmodernism, and Ethnographic Responsibility* (Stanford University Press, 1992). Around 1960, Wolf, now a professor of anthropology and women's studies at the University of Iowa, conducted fieldwork while she was living in Taiwan with her anthropologist husband. She wrote a semifictional story, "The Hot Spell," about a peasant woman whose neighbors thought she was crazy. Wolf reproduces this tale with two variants: rough field notes that she took during the incident, and a scholarly article, "The Woman Who Didn't Become a Shaman," published in 1990. After each version, the author includes a commentary critiquing postmodern ethnography from a feminist perspective. Wolf also addresses central issues of the self, the "other," power relations between the two, and contradictions between fieldwork and fieldwork accounts.

231. Diamond, Irene, and Gloria Feman Orenstein, eds. *Reweaving the World: The Emergence of Ecofeminism*. San Francisco: Sierra Club Books, 1990. 320p. bibliog. ISBN 087156694X; 0871566230pa.

Based on the proceedings of a 1987 conference on ecofeminist perspectives, *Reweaving the World* is one of the earliest works on ecofeminism and signals the convergence of the ecology, feminist, and women's spirituality movements into a social movement rooted in the belief that the fate of human beings is intertwined because of our dependence on the earth's natural resources, which have intrinsic value. Diamond, an associate professor of political science at the University of Oregon, and Orenstein, a professor of comparative literature at the University of Southern California, have assembled a diverse group of academics, writers, and activists who ask political and philosophical questions about what the editors call "a new term for an ancient wisdom" (p. xv). Contributors include Susan Griffin, Riane Eisler, Carol Christ, Vandana Shiva, Charlene Spretnak, Carolyn Merchant, Michael E. Zimmerman, Starhawk, and Paula Gunn Allen. Diamond and Orenstein divide the anthology into three parts. Part 1 introduces ecofeminism and analyzes topics such as the Gaia tradition, ancient nature religion, and the importance of interpreting scientific facts with an ecofeminist consciousness. Part 2 connects politics and ethics and explores issues including deep ecology, bioregionalism, and the politics of resistance. The final part identifies specific contemporary ecological concerns and offers creative solutions. This sourcebook, with its variety of readable essays, provides an excellent introduction to ecofeminist thinking in the late 1980s.

232. Dorkenoo, Efua. *Cutting the Rose: Female Genital Mutilation: The Practice and Its Prevention*. London: Minority Rights Group, 1994. 196p. bibliog. index. ISBN 1873194609; 1873194951pa.

Dorkenoo, a Ghanian nurse based in London, serves as director for FORWARD (the Foundation for Women's Health, Research, and Development), located in the Africa Centre in London. She is a pioneer lobbyist in the fight against female genital mutilation (FGM). In this slim volume, Dorkenoo defines female circumcision, explains the act of circumcising a woman, and recounts the physical and psychological implications of female genital mutilation. In two of the seven chapters, Dorkenoo places FGM in its cultural context across cultures, including the West, as immigrants bring their traditions with them. In another chapter, the author focuses on case studies in Africa. Dorkenoo ends with a discussion of efforts of various organizations and individuals to end FGM. *Cutting the Rose* is a clear and comprehensive work that includes numerous maps, charts, statistical tables, graphic photographs, and illustrations.

Esther K. Hicks discusses the most extreme form of female circumcision in *Infibulation: Female Mutilation in Islamic Northeastern Africa* (2nd ed. rev. and exp., Transaction Publishers, 1996). Hicks places the practice of infibulation in northeastern Africa, particularly the Horn of Africa and northern Sudan, in its historical, geographical, and cultural contexts. She determines that infibulation occurs traditionally among pastoral, often nomadic people who value family and kinship groups. Hicks argues that infibulation is a normal activity within these closed societies, and that scholars should not examine the practice without considering its cultural context.

233. Eisler, Riane Tennenhaus. *The Chalice and the Blade: Our History, Our Future.* San Francisco: HarperSanFrancisco, 1987. 261p. bibliog. index. ISBN (OP); 0062502891pa.

This groundbreaking book defies easy categorization. Eisler, an activist and futurist, presents a reenvisioning of history from a gender-holistic perspective. Eisler proposes a theory called cultural transformation theory, which includes two models for structuring society: the dominator model and the partnership model. The chalice in the book title represents the life-giving, nurturing powers reflected in a partnership model of society, while the blade represents the lethal power reflected in a dominator model. Relying on evidence from art, archaeology, religion, the social sciences, history, and the sciences, the author argues that humans were evolving toward a partnership model thousands of years ago, but that a period of chaos and cultural disruption shifted the emphasis to the dominator model: "The root of the problem lies in a social system in which the power of the Blade is idealized—in which both men and women are taught to equate true masculinity with violence and dominance and to see men who do not conform to this ideal as 'too soft' or 'effeminate' " (p. xviii). Beginning in the Paleolithic era and moving to the present, *The Chalice and the Blade* provides a revolutionary restructuring of politics, economics, science, and spirituality and envisions a society where men and women share power equally. *Sacred Pleasure: Sex, Myth, and the Politics of the Body* (HarperSanFrancisco, 1995), a follow-up to the previous title, "explores the past, present, and potential future of sex" (p. 1). Focusing primarily on Western heterosexual culture, Eisler draws upon biology, psychology, sexology, sociology, economics, archaeology, history, literature, art, and mythology to illustrate how culture moved from a partnership to a dominator model. The author argues that the dominator model is no longer functioning, and that in order for culture to survive, we must move back to a partnership model, a model where sex and spirituality are intertwined, where "sex can be a form of sacrament" (p. 7). Eisler's synthesis of a wide range of scholarship from a variety of disciplines written in a clear and appealing manner offers fascinating reading about the potential for human society.

234. Estes, Clarissa Pinkola. *Women Who Run with the Wolves: Myths and Stories of the Wild Woman Archetype.* New York: Ballantine Books, 1992. 520p. bibliog. index. ISBN 0345377443; 0345409876pa.

This first book by now-prolific author Clarissa Pinkola Estes remained on the *New York Times* nonfiction best-seller list for one year. *Women Who Run with the Wolves* continues to enjoy popularity, and scholars have translated it into German, Spanish, Swedish, and Hebrew. A Jungian psychoanalyst, Estes received her Ph.D. in psychology from the Union Institute in Cincinnati in 1981 and considers herself a "cantadora": a collector and teller of stories. In *Women Who Run with the Wolves*, she argues that women and wolves share certain key characteristics: they are strongly intuitive, have a playful nature, and possess a great capacity for devotion, creativity, endurance, bravery, and strength. Moreover, women and wolves frequently must adapt to changing circumstances. According to Estes, both have been "hounded, harassed, and falsely imputed to be devouring and devious. . . . The predation of wolves and women by those who misunderstand them is strikingly similar" (p. 2). Estes developed the concept of the Wild Woman archetype— wild, meaning living in nature—while studying wolves. In this book, she seeks to help women reclaim their instinctual Wild Woman heritage. She features fairy tales, myths, and stories from many cultures and analyzes them to learn about female behavior. Some of these stories are well known, including "The Little Match Girl," "The Ugly Duckling," and "The Red Shoes." Despite its popular appeal, *Women Who Run with the Wolves* includes extensive notes and a bibliography on women and the psyche.

235. Flueckiger, Joyce Burkhalter. *Gender and Genre in the Folklore of Middle India.* Ithaca, NY: Cornell University Press, 1996. 351p. (Myth and Poetics). bibliog. index. ISBN 0801432065.

According to one reviewer, *Gender and Genre in the Folklore of Middle India* is "one of the most wide-ranging, meticulous, and insightful monographs on Indian folklore ever published" (Gloria G. Raheja, *American Ethnologist*, vol. 25, no. 1, February 1998, p. 84). Flueckiger, an associate professor of religion at Emory University, conducted fieldwork for more than fifteen years in the Chhattisgarh region of Madhya Pradesh. She examines six folklore genres that the people of Chhattisgarh consider typical. Women traditionally perform three of them, called *bhojali, dalkhai,* and *sua nac,* and men traditionally perform the other three, called *kathani kuha, candaini,* and *pandvani.* They all involve singing, storytelling, and dancing. Flueckiger examines each ritual in depth and discerns common themes, including the power of women, either as heroines of epics or as performers; inevitable change as traditions evolve and new actors and audiences alter the context of the performance; and the realities inherent in living performance traditions. The volume concludes with translations of several performance texts and a glossary.

Much like the symbolic heron who acts as the narrator in North Indian women's songs, Gloria Raheja and Ann Gold, authors of *Listen to the Heron's Words* (University of California Press, 1994), invite readers to share in the experiences of women of the Uttar Pradesh and Rajasthan regions of northern India, where Raheja and Gold conducted their fieldwork. They use stories, ritual songs, individual narratives, and everyday conversations to analyze women's oral traditions and use of language. The authors discovered that these rural women exercise resistance to patrilinear authority with a sense of fun, bawdiness, and irony not acknowledged in the accepted scholarship on women of South Asia.

236. Fujimura-Fanselow, Kumiko, and Atsuko Kameda, eds. *Japanese Women: New Feminist Perspectives on the Past, Present, and Future.* New York: Feminist Press at the City University of New York, 1995. 422p. bibliog. ISBN 1558610936; 1558610944pa.

To many, Japanese women teeter between traditional and modern worlds, representing a combination of East and West, submission and resistance, and oppression and fulfillment. Contributors to *Japanese Women* explore the status of women and gender relations in contemporary Japanese society. Japanese feminist scholars produced most of the twenty-seven essays, written in English or translated from Japanese to make their research accessible to Western audiences. Because they believe that Westerners frequently distort and/or stereotype Japanese women, the authors provide an overview of current scholarship. While acknowledging the special restrictions of Japanese culture, contributors not only assert that Japanese women confront the same issues and problems that other women encounter, but also argue that international communication would prove mutually beneficial. Part 1 provides historical, cultural, and social contexts for women's lives since the Meiji restoration (1868). Part 2 looks at sexism in education; part 3 examines changing values and practices within marriage and the family; and part 4 studies women and work. The final section addresses women's efforts to attain equality and includes essays on a variety of topics, including women's place in Japanese Buddhism, women and television, the changing portrait of Japanese men, and Japan's sex industry. The editors unfortunately do not provide an index.

Anne Imamura's collection *Re-imaging Japanese Women* (University of California Press, 1996) updates Gail L. Bernstein's *Recreating Japanese Women, 1600–1945* (University of California Press, 1991) by focusing on Japanese women from the end of World War II to the mid-1990s. Imamura and contributors challenge the traditional portrayal of Japanese women as "good wife, wise mother" (*ryosai-kenbo*) by examining numerous female images in modern-day Japan, the sources of these images, and the examples that they set for Japanese women as they make decisions throughout their lives. Despite changes that indicate that women's options increasingly have become varied, a picture of two types of Japanese women emerges: those who pursue careers and postpone or refuse marriage, and those who marry, have a family, and settle for low-paying, part-time, or no outside employment.

237. Gilmartin, Christina K., ed. *Engendering China: Women, Culture, and the State.* Cambridge, MA: Harvard University Press, 1994. 454p. (Harvard Contemporary China Series, no. 10). bibliog. index. ISBN 0674253310; 0674253329pa.

The sixteen essays in *Engendering China* evolved from a conference held in Boston in 1992. The authors represent a multitude of disciplines and have various associations with China. Their common goal is to "decenter" Western women as the norm for analyzing other women's lives, as well as to debunk universal theories of femininity and masculinity. They argue that because Chinese women represent a diverse group, no single category exists for them. The editors divide the essays into four parts, encompassing subjects from the sixteenth century to the present. The first part demonstrates how, instead of being passive victims, Chinese women have acted with agency against powerful social forces in various ways. Part 2 addresses issues of sexuality and reproduction, while part 3 posits gender as a vital factor in matters of state formation and policy making in the twentieth century. The final part, "Becoming Women in the Post-Mao Era," includes writings by and about women as creative attempts to define "woman" outside of state representation. This important work is clearly written, accessible to undergraduates, and essential for anyone interested in modern China.

Ellen R. Rudd analyzes one issue in *Gender and Power in Rural North China* (Stanford University Press, 1994): the political-economic position of contemporary women in three Shandong Province villages in rural northern China. Judd, a professor of anthropology at the University of Manitoba, uses the principles of practice theory to consider change from the perspective of ordinary women. She determines that women have enjoyed greater respect and autonomy in household-based enterprises, since men traditionally have not marginalized women in the domestic sphere, than outside the home, which remains a male-dominated sphere.

238. Göçek, Fatma Müge, and Shiva Balaghi, eds. *Reconstructing Gender in the Middle East: Tradition, Identity, and Power.* New York: Columbia University Press, 1994. 233p. bibliog. index. ISBN 0231101228; 0231101236pa.

Most of the essays in this collection began as papers delivered at the conference "Gender and Society in the Middle East," held at the University of Michigan in 1991. The resulting publication, *Reconstructing Gender in the Middle East*, is wide-ranging in terms of geographic coverage; subject matter, including literary analysis, personal narratives, and field studies; and the contributors' interdisciplinary backgrounds: history, anthropology, sociology, political science, and literature. The editors organized the work according to three themes commonly associated with women in the Middle East: tradition, identity, and power. Historian Juan Cole introduces the first part, which analyzes women as both followers and agents in the creation of tradition in Iran, Morocco, and Turkey. Anthropologist Ruth Behar introduces part 2, which examines the complex forces that converge to form identity in various contexts in Iran, Turkey, Israel, and Palestine. Literary scholar Anne Herrmann introduces the third part, which details the gendered implications of power negotiations both at home and in society in Lebanon, Israel, Egypt, and Morocco. Due to the variety and richness of material, *Reconstructing Gender* would serve as an excellent introduction to gender and the Middle East.

Haya Mughni examines upper-class women's organizations in Kuwait in *Women in Kuwait: The Politics of Gender* (Saqi, 1993). She finds that Kuwaiti women of the elite and merchant classes are primarily loyal to their families and class and behave in ways that reinforce their secondary position in society. Mughni faults the exclusionary organizations, most formed in the 1960s and dependent on volunteers, for failing to address issues that affect all Kuwaiti women. In contrast, Marxist-feminist scholar Valentine Moghadam challenges the traditional notion that Islamic theology and law force women into an inferior status in Muslim countries in *Modernizing Women: Gender and Social Change in the Middle East* (Lynne Rienner, 1993). She instead emphasizes the centrality of gender to the upheavals that social and political change caused in this region, specifically in the Middle East, North Africa, and Afghanistan, and maintains that limited industrialization and high fertility rates restrict women's participation in the labor force. In *World of Difference: Islam and Gender Hierarchy in Turkey* (Zed Books, 1992), Julie Marcus, an Australian professor of social anthropology, also struggles with theoretical issues involving the scope and character of women's power in an Islamic, patriarchal society. Taking a strongly structuralist approach to examining Turkish society and gender hierarchies, Marcus argues that the Orient is essentially a Western invention. She critiques images of the East ("orientalism") in Western literature and draws upon her fieldwork in western Turkey to reveal evidence of a prevalent female worldview that is woman centered and egalitarian within the context of an Islamic cosmology.

239. Greenhalgh, Susan, ed. *Situating Fertility: Anthropology and Demographic Inquiry*. New York: Cambridge University Press, 1995. 304p. ill. bibliog. index. ISBN 0521470447; 0521469996pa.

In this collection of essays drawn from a session at the 1990 annual meeting of the American Anthropological Association ten anthropologists and two historians integrate culture, history, and politics into a cross-cultural analysis of reproduction, traditionally a subject for demographers. Issues such as marriage, contraception, abortion, and reproduction figure in the case studies, which cover various places and times. One contributor examines poor women's networks in nineteenth-century Paris; another looks at the status of children of previous conjugal unions in modern-day Sierra Leone; while another focuses on fertility changes in the Balkans from 1700 to 1900. Contributors reach three conclusions: gender, the culturally bound study of men and women, pervades all aspects of life, including reproduction; as opposed to accepting the position of passive victim, women in oppressed and/or patriarchal societies have used covert strategies to improve their situations; and women's lives are not necessarily improving despite socioeconomic gains. Statistical charts, a subject index, and a thirty-page bibliography supplement this volume. Beverly Winikoff and contributors examine mothers' feeding decisions in *Feeding Infants in Four Societies: Causes and Consequences of Mothers' Choices* (Greenwood Press, 1988). Responding to the debate on whether the advertising of breast milk substitutes caused a decline in breast-feeding in developing countries, this study focuses on urban centers in Thailand, Colombia, Kenya, and Indonesia. This work, which includes numerous tables and figures, is written in the style of a technical report.

240. Harcourt, Wendy, ed. *Feminist Perspectives on Sustainable Development*. Atlantic Highlands, NJ: Zed Books, in association with the Society for International Development, Rome, 1994. 255p. bibliog. index. ISBN 1856492435; 1856492443pa.

Australian Wendy Harcourt, director of programmes for the Society for International Development in Rome and the editor of its journal, *Development*, has brought gender awareness to this international, forty-five-year-old nongovernmental organization. Harcourt also worked with the Institute of Social Studies in The Hague to bring together women from all over the world to debate sustainable development at a meeting held there in 1993, which resulted in *Feminist Perspectives on Sustainable Development*. Contributors include academics and activists, both women and men. The authors look at women not as victims, but as agents of change, and advocate stronger alliances among feminists, economists, policy makers, scientists, and others involved in the dialogue on power and knowledge within the new global context. As development scholar Lourdes Arizpe writes in the preface, "There is a consensus in this book that development should mean gender equity, secure livelihoods, ecological sustainability and political participation. . . . we must go forward into a world that *articulates diversity yet builds a global commonality that will hold us together.*" (p. xiii; Anizpe's emphasis). Harcourt divides the volume into four parts. The first provides a valuable overview of the feminist position on sustainable development; the second enumerates theoretical challenges to the major theories on development; and the third examines politics and resistance. The final part focuses on the interrelationships among population, women, and the environment. This work is a useful contribution for both advanced students and scholars. The anthology *The Women, Gender, and Development Reader*, edited by Nalini Visvanathan and others (Zed Books, 1997), is the first work to explicitly acknowledge the vital role that Third World women play in international development processes. The editors organize its thirty-five chapters according to five themes: key theoretical debates in the field, women's roles within households and families, women's work, women and social transformation, and women organizing for change.

241. Iwao, Sumiko. *Japanese Woman: Traditional Change and Changing Reality*. New York: Free Press, 1993. 304p. bibliog. index. ISBN 0029323150.

In *Japanese Woman*, Iwao argues that the traditional woman of Japan is "rapidly becoming but one of several breeds of women in a society that is growing increasingly pluralistic" (p. 1). Acknowledging that American and Japanese women view the central issue of gender equality differently, Iwao, a professor of psychology in Tokyo, asserts that women enjoy more choices than men in Japan today. In what she calls a "quiet revolution," she contends that women in her country experience more freedom and independence despite the absence of a well-organized and clearly defined feminist movement. She conversely argues that men, the "worker bees" of Japanese society, feel constrained. Iwao mostly depicts the lives of urban, educated, middle class, and married women. Using numerous case studies and anecdotes, the author discusses the women in the context of family, work, education, and politics.

In *Contemporary Portraits of Japanese Women* (Praeger, 1995), journalist Yukiko Tanaka uses her own experiences to comment on contemporary Japanese society. Although she grew up in Japan, she eventually relocated to the United States. She now looks upon herself as American and thus has become an outsider to Japanese culture. Tanaka attributes both the negative and positive changes in lifestyle that have affected Japanese men, women, and children to the economic shift from agriculture to industry. She devotes three chapters to the decrease in arranged marriages, the role of women in modern marriage, and the increasing divorce rate. She considers the mother-child relationship and the current lifestyle of young women in two additional chapters. In the final four chapters, Tanaka analyzes women in the labor market, growing old, gaining political power, and the status of the women's movement in Japan. She draws her examples from her own life, acquaintances, and a thorough knowledge of the literature.

242. Jones, David E. *Women Warriors: A History*. Washington, DC: Brassey's, 1997. 279p. bibliog. index. ISBN 157488106X.

In this entertaining study, David E. Jones, a cultural anthropology professor at the University of Central Florida and an instructor in Japanese martial art, contends that although society has culturally conditioned women to avoid combat, many women warriors have taken to the battlefield over time. Jones organizes his chapters according to geographic regions: Arabia, Asia, India, the British Isles, Africa, Latin America, Egypt, the Middle East, Eastern Europe, Western Europe, and North America. The author provides a chronological accounting of female martial history not only to highlight recurring patterns, but also to suggest the prevalence of female warriors in a particular region. He includes several names and exploits of individuals, such as "Black Queen Candace of Ethiopia," who repelled Alexander the Great; sixteenth-century pirate Grace O'Malley, who vexed Queen Elizabeth I; and Confederate lieutenant Loreta Velazquez, who shot Yankees. Jones also focuses on modern women in the military: young women training at the U.S. Military Academy, female recruits in the Israeli army, and women soldiers in the Gulf War.

243. Kabeer, Naila. *Reversed Realities: Gender Hierarchies in Development Thought.* New York: Verso, 1994. 346p. bibliog. index. ISBN 0860913848; 0860915840pa.

This comprehensive synthesis of contemporary feminist economists' thought and work, as one reviewer wrote, is "an important landmark in gender and development scholarship, an essential resource for students and scholars alike" (*Journal of Development Studies*, vol. 32, no. 4, April 1996, p. 639). Kabeer, an economist and fellow at the Institute of Development Studies at the University of Sussex, outlines two main themes in her preface: first, the exclusion or misinterpretation of feminist perspectives in mainstream development; second, the connection between "ways of thinking and ways of doing," especially regarding gender issues. Kabeer believes that concentrating on women alone has proven unproductive, and that scholars should instead focus on the relations between women and men. She divides the book into three sections. Chapters 1 through 4 primarily cover theoretical debates about the appearance of women as a constituency in development and the changing conceptualizations of women as mothers, housewives, dependents, neglected producers, and victims of patriarchy. Chapters 5 through 7 provide a critique of liberal economic concepts that many development planners favor. Kabeer focuses on research methodology and specifically looks at three developmental theory analytical tools: household economies, measurement of poverty, and social cost-benefit analysis. In the final section, chapters 8 through 10, the author examines the interaction between ideas and practice and chronicles the evolution of three areas of development in relation to women: population policy, female empowerment through grassroots programs, and gender training.

244. Kapadia, Karin. *Siva and Her Sisters: Gender, Caste, and Class in Rural India.* Boulder, CO: Westview Press, 1995. (Studies in Ethnographic Imagination). 269p. bibliog. index. ISBN 0813381584.

Kapadia, an anthropology professor in England formerly affiliated with the Christian Michelsen Institute in Norway, a private research foundation that deals with issues of development and human rights, currently works with the World Bank on social development issues in South Asia, serving as the gender coordinator. Kapadia thus analyzes both men and women of five castes in the village of Aruloor in Tamilnadu, South India. She concentrates on the "untouchable" caste of Pallar women, not only because earlier studies generally have excluded them, but also because their experiences clearly illustrate the intersection of gender, class, and caste in South India. Through an examination of the Pallars' rituals, values, and everyday life, Kapadia determines that they do not share the cultural values of the Brahmin elites, even though the Brahmins enjoy economic and political power. Instead, Pallar women reject the elites' values in subtle ways. Kapadia argues that one must analyze gender to understand class dynamics. Moreover, she asserts that women's status is actually higher among poor agricultural workers than among the highest castes. *Siva and Her Sisters* (Siva is the name Kapadia gives to her Pallar research assistant) is both scholarly and well documented and includes tables, figures, and photographs of life among the Pallars. The author subdivides each chapter in the table of contents, which allows for easy pinpointing of specific interests.

245. Karam, Azza M. *Women, Islamisms, and the State: Contemporary Feminisms in Egypt.* New York: St. Martin's Press, 1998. 284p. bibliog. index. ISBN 0312175019.

According to the author of *Women, Islamisms, and the State*, three "contemporary feminisms" exist in Egypt: secular feminism, Muslim feminism, and Islamist feminism. Although both Muslims and Christians compose secular feminists, this group prefers to separate religion from politics. Islamist feminists take the opposite view: women's rights must exist within an Islamic state and under Muslim law. The Muslim feminists, however, argue that men and women can achieve equality within Islam. Karam, a young Egyptian scholar and professor in the School of Politics at the Queen's University of Belfast, analyzes the power dynamics that govern the relationships among the Islamists, the state, and these feminist groups. Since she based this work upon her dissertation, which she completed at the University of Amsterdam, she includes her methodology, a literature review, a brief history of Egypt in the twentieth century, and other trappings of this genre. Her fieldwork, which resulted in numerous interviews with both men and women, lends a freshness and immediacy to the book.

Khalida Messaoudi's *Unbowed: An Algerian Woman Confronts Islamic Fundamentalism* (University of Pennsylvania Press, 1998) chronicles one woman's fight against the Islamic regime in Algeria. In 1995, French journalist Elisabeth Schemla extensively interviewed women's rights activist Messaoudi, who has lived under a fatwa, or death sentence, that Islamic fundamentalists have imposed since 1993. Messaoudi, whose story is translated from French by Anne C. Vila, recounts her efforts to secure constitutional democracy in Algeria, eliminate the antiwomen Family Code, suppress Islamic fundamentalism, and promote the French language rather than Arabic as a way to highlight her country's uniqueness and diversity.

246. Knight, Chris. *Blood Relations: Menstruation and the Origins of Culture.* New Haven, CT: Yale University Press, 1991. 448p. bibliog. index. ISBN 0300049110; 0300063083pa.

In this controversial work, Knight, an anthropologist, proposes a parallel between the Marx-Engels model of the workers' struggle against rulers and the relatively recent biological origins of man. He claims that "virtually everything primatologists and palaeo-anthropologists have been saying about human origins since twentieth-century science began addressing this topic is wrong—and not just wrong in detail, but utterly wrong!" (p. 3). According to Knight, humankind's evolution is based on the struggle of women (the workers) against men (the rulers). He argues that women initially made certain that their hunter-men returned to them and their children with meat through sex strikes and synchronous menstrual periods. Over time, not only did these patterns become ritualized, but taboos became established as well, thus forming the basis for human culture. Knight uses a cross-disciplinary approach and draws upon the work of many others, making use of work done in sociology, biology, archaeology, and anthropology. Generous with his citations, the author provides a valuable review of evolutionary theory. He includes an author and subject index, as well as a thirty-one-page bibliography. This work would prove useful for upper-level undergraduates and graduate students.

Taking an opposing yet equally controversial approach, lesbian poet and author Judy Grahn asserts that women are responsible for the development of society and that the rhythmic cycle of menstruation has regulated all human discoveries in *Blood, Bread, and Roses: How Menstruation*

Created the World (Beacon Press, 1993). Grahn studied creation stories, menstrual rituals across cultures, archaeological evidence, religious beliefs, and her own experience in the modern world to develop this provocative theory. Her personal observations, which she italicizes, heighten the intimacy of the text. *Blood, Bread, and Roses*, which Grahn wrote over the course of twenty years, is well researched and heavily annotated and includes an index and extensive bibliography.

247. Kulick, Don, and Margaret Wilson, eds. *Taboo: Sex, Identity, and Erotic Subjectivity in Anthropological Fieldwork*. New York: Routledge, 1995. 283p. bibliog. index. ISBN 0415088186; 0415088194pa.

Fieldwork studies traditionally have avoided mention of sexual attraction, let alone sexual intercourse, between anthropologists and members of the society under study. Scholars generally assumed that anthropologists sacrificed objectivity if they permitted sexual relations. Although sexual activities undoubtedly existed, "going public" or disclosing sexual encounters represents an outgrowth of both the feminist and gay rights movements, which have emerged during the last thirty years. The editors of *Taboo: Sex, Identity, and Erotic Subjectivity in Anthropological Fieldwork* maintain that erotic subjectivity provides fieldworkers with insights that they otherwise would not have obtained. Contributors confront issues from love to rape while exploring anthropologist/informant relations among gays and straights, men and women, in Greece, Indonesia, Korea, the United States, Belgium, Tonga, St. Vincent, and Ethiopia in the eight chapters of this work. The stories are highly personal. In *Out in the Field: Reflections of Lesbian and Gay Anthropologists*, edited by Ellen Lewin and William Leap (University of Illinois Press, 1996), fifteen lesbian and gay anthropologists share personal stories as well. However, these anthropologists more deeply explore their place within the profession, their choices to hide or disclose their gender identities, and their relationships with informants of similar sexual orientation. The authors of these well-written works pose questions and raise issues that are relevant for all fieldworkers, regardless of sexual orientation.

248. Lamphere, Louise, Helena Ragoné, and Patricia Zavella, eds. *Situated Lives: Gender and Culture in Everyday Life*. New York: Routledge, 1997. 493p. bibliog. index. ISBN 0415918065; 0415918073pa.

The editors of this collection of twenty-seven essays emphasize the daily life of ordinary men and women in the United States, as well as in developing countries such as Malaysia, Mexico, Liberia, and Jamaica. Modernist anthropologist Louise Lamphere and editors Ragone and Zavella have amassed essays that are firmly grounded in fieldwork and not only underscore the variety of women's experiences, but also recognize the complex interrelationships among culture, politics, economics, and history. The editors divide the work into five sections. Contributors cover topics including theoretical issues of gendered ethnography, reproduction, abortion, sterilization and other agents of change to women's bodies, family life, resistance in the workplace, and explorations of gender in colonial and postcolonial political economies. Since this clearly written work incorporates a variety of topics, *Situated Lives* would serve as a useful text in introductory courses on women's issues.

249. Lock, Margaret M. *Encounters with Aging: Mythologies of Menopause in Japan and North America*. Berkeley: University of California Press, 1993. 439p. bibliog. index. ISBN 0520082214.

In *Encounters with Aging*, Lock asks: "Why should menopause, an ostensibly private experience that is painless and presents no obvious threat to life, command so much attention?" (p. xviii). She then suggests that menopause is "a concept with boundaries and meanings that shift depending upon the viewpoint and interests of speaker and listener" (p. xviii). Lock, a medical anthropologist, interviewed more than 1,000 Japanese women during a twelve-year period to glean their viewpoints of menopause and to learn what symptoms they experienced. The author includes many quotations and excerpts from conversations to enhance her portrait of women confronting social change in twentieth-century Japan. How culture affects a woman's natural biological journey through life serves as a key theme of the book. Lock, who relies upon information about North American women for comparison purposes, determines that the meaning of menopause differs in Japan and North America. She argues that Japanese women seemingly experience menopause more easily. In fact, no term for menopause exists in Japanese. The closest term to menopause is the word *konenki*, or "change of life," which is characterized by a myriad of social, personal, emotional, and physiological changes. Moreover, Japanese women look upon *konenki* as an overall and natural transition. Lock argues that in the United States menopause only signifies the end of menstruation, and that women tend to focus on physical symptoms, such as hot flashes, for which they seek medical intervention. This significant work would prove beneficial for readers interested in either women or aging.

250. Lopez Springfield, Consuelo, ed. *Daughters of Caliban: Caribbean Women in the Twentieth Century*. Bloomington: Indiana University Press, 1997. 316p. bibliog. index. ISBN 0253332494; 0253210925pa.

In Shakespeare's *The Tempest*, the mute and deformed half-beast Caliban solely inhabits an island until Prospero, who eventually enslaves Caliban, and his daughter are washed ashore. According to the feminist scholars of anthropology, sociology, literature, law, health, and culture studies who wrote *Daughters of Caliban*, Caliban's descendants also have contended with newcomers: white merchants and entrepreneurs, African slaves, and Asian laborers. This mingling of races, languages, traditions, and a history of colonial oppression against regional resistance has bred a fluid population that constantly redefines itself. How women deal with this heritage today is the focus of this five-part work. Contributors examine the differences between European American and Caribbean feminisms in the first part. The second part deals with the nature of women's work, both paid and unpaid, and the third part focuses on health issues. Contributors analyze law and political change in the fourth part and look at women and popular culture in the fifth part. According to Lopez Springfield, the essays "contribute to the overall task of shattering the myth of the West Indian matriarch and the passive Hispanic Caribbean woman" (p. xviii). *Women of the Caribbean*, edited by Patricia Ellis (Zed Books, 1986), is an older work that deals with the same topic. In *Women of Belize: Gender and Change in Central America* (Rutgers University Press, 1996) Irma McClaurin, an African American anthropologist, examines the life histories of three women, a Creole, a Garifuna, and an East Indian woman, in Belize to demonstrate how they have made changes in their own lives. McClaurin argues that an individual's changes in thinking and behavior eventually can effect changes in society. The author describes the following successful changes: the minimum-wage campaign that the Belize Organization for Women and Development launched in 1992, the passage of the Domestic Violence Bill in 1993, women obtaining child support, and Women Against Violence's introduction of a sexual harassment bill.

251. Lutkehaus, Nancy C., and Paul B. Roscoe, eds. *Gender Rituals: Female Initiation in Melanesia*. New York: Routledge, 1995. 265p. bibliog. index. ISBN 0415911060; 0415911079pa.

This study features descriptions and analyses of female initiation rites in eight diverse societies in Papua New Guinea, a country in the western Pacific region known as Melanesia. Anthropology professor Lutkehaus argues that Melanesian ethnography has advanced feminist anthropology and theory in several ways, although most ethnographic studies of this region have concentrated on male, rather than female, initiation rites. Advances include cultural construction of human sexuality, fertility, reproduction, the individual, and the relationship between the individual and gender identity. Contributors contend that more elaborate rituals appear in communities in which women are important members of its politico-ritual life. Women perform certain rites to achieve full personhood. Moreover, the female body becomes a metaphor for the social body through rituals surrounding menarche, marriage, and widowhood. *Gender Rituals*, produced under the auspices of the Association for Social Anthropology in Oceana, would benefit a wide audience.

In *Affecting Performance: Meaning, Movement, and Experience in Okiek Women's Initiation* (Smithsonian Institution Press, 1994), which reviewers hailed as an "ethnographic tour de force," Corinne Ann Kratz not only examines how female initiation rites transform girls into young women, but also what initiation rites reveal about conceptions of gender and cultural identity. Kratz draws upon her extensive fieldwork with the Okiek people of southwestern Kenya, a forest-dwelling hunting and honey-gathering people. She bases her conclusions on observations of the ceremonies, discussions with Okiek men and women, and a careful analysis of the native language, in which she became fluent. The text alternates between scholarly interpretation and first-person account, which includes a richly detailed description of one "journey to adulthood." She includes numerous quotations from women and other community members, as well as a photo essay that demonstrates the various stages of ceremonies.

252. Marsh, Rosalind J., ed. *Women in Russia and Ukraine*. New York: Cambridge University Press, 1996. 350p. bibliog. index. ISBN 0521495229; 0521498724pa.

An excellent essay about the status of women's studies in present-day Russia, Ukraine, and the former Soviet states introduces this compilation of twenty-one essays that emerged from a conference held at the University of Bath in 1993. Marsh divides the volume into four sections: women from the seventeenth to the twentieth century, sexuality and health, women and labor, and the impact of feminism on politics. Contributors examine diverse topics, including a cultural analysis of Peter the Great's two weddings, Russian merchant women at the turn of the twentieth century, venereal disease during the Soviet era, young women's lifestyles today, the impact of economic reform, and maternity in post-Communist Russia. The writers approach this interdisciplinary work from a feminist perspective. *Women in Russia and Ukraine* is a well-documented and scholarly overview of the topic, best suited for undergraduates. A companion volume, *Women's Voices in Russia Today*, edited by Anna Rotkirch and Elina Haavio-Mannila (Dartmouth, 1996), is composed of interviews with well-educated urban Russian women who discuss professional identities, gender ideals, everyday life, and social and political activities. *Women in the Face of Change: The Soviet Union, Eastern Europe, and China*, edited by Shirin Rai and others (Routledge, 1992), addresses the political and economic changes affecting women in the countries previously known as the "Communist bloc." The authors, mostly Western academics, discuss how the disintegration of the socialist regimes has affected women in the following ways: social status, gender identity, and the evolution of state-sponsored women's organizations.

253. Merchant, Carolyn. *Earthcare: Women and the Environment*. New York: Routledge, 1996. 280p. bibliog. index. ISBN 0415908876; 0415908884pa.

Merchant, professor of environmental history, philosophy, and ethics at the University of California at Berkeley, writes extensively on ecological history, women, and the environment in Western culture. She provides a personal history of her ecofeminist intellectual travels in *Earthcare*. Two-thirds of the book is a compendium of selections from earlier works; the remaining one-third consists of new essays with a more global perspective. She includes an essay from her groundbreaking work *The Death of Nature: Ecology and the Scientific Revolution* (Harper & Row, 1980) in which she links the domination of women and nature since the rise of capitalism in the seventeenth century. Merchant includes chapters on female symbols of nature, such as the Greek Gaia, the Christian Eve, and the Egyptian Isis; history, including women and ecology in the scientific revolution, ecological history in New England to 1860, and the conservation crusade in the early 1900s; and practice, such as the environmental movements in Sweden and the United States. She also recounts her experiences in 1991 as a visiting scholar to Australia, where she studied women's role in repairing environmental damage.

254. Mies, Maria, and Vandana Shiva. *Ecofeminism*. Atlantic Highlands, NJ: Zed Books, 1993. 328p. bibliog. index. ISBN 1856491552; 1856491560pa.

Mies, a feminist social scientist living in Germany, and Shiva, an ecologist trained in theoretical physics living in India, represent the dichotomy of the North (Western and industrial) versus the South (oppressed and agrarian). They believe that the shared concerns and perspectives of women worldwide override the differences of history, language, culture, and place. In twenty essays, Mies and Shiva attack the prevailing capitalist and patriarchal economic system, which they contend is causing a self-destructive cycle of expansion and exploitation. The authors thus argue for a "subsistence perspective," or a democratic, self-sufficient way of life based upon an alternative relationship to nature that still satisfies basic human needs. In *Close to Home: Women Reconnect Ecology, Health, and Development* (New Society Publishers, 1994), Shiva, editor and activist, argues that a separation between mind and body and between human and nature does not exist. Using material presented at a seminar on women, ecology, and health held in southern India in 1991, contributors to this text explore topics such as women fighting toxic waste in the United States, victims of the Union Carbide disaster in Bhopal, the ecological and political consequences of ethnic conflict in Sri Lanka, and the dangers of biotechnology. Shiva also wrote *Staying Alive: Women, Ecology, and Development* (Zed Books, 1988), in which she compares the violation of nature to the violation and marginalization of women, especially women who live in developing countries.

255. Momsen, Janet. *Women and Change in the Caribbean: A Pan-Caribbean Perspective*. Bloomington: Indiana University Press, 1993. 308p. bibliog. index. ISBN 0852554036; 0852554044pa.

The nineteen interdisciplinary essays in this collection signal the direction that much of the research on Caribbean women took in the 1990s. A key area in the development of world capitalism and the oldest area of European colonization, the Caribbean experienced changes in population, language, class, and religion during hundreds of years. Contributors examine many aspects of contemporary women's lives in the region, specifically in Jamaica, Curaçao, Montserrat, Barbuda, Dominica, Guadeloupe, Guyana, Suriname, Nevis, Puerto Rico, Barbados, Grenada, Trinidad, and Cuba, to demonstrate how the changes that colonialism brought about have affected gender roles and relations. Momsen, a geography professor, emphasizes the paradoxical nature of gender relations: although traditionally patriarchic, Caribbean women enjoy a certain amount of autonomy in the "domestic domain," with female-headed households, and a domestic ideology that allows political activity as well as economic independence. Momsen organizes the material into two sections: first, the social interactions among women, family, and society, and second, women's roles in the economy. This work would serve as an excellent regional overview.

Oliver Senior's *Working Miracles: Women's Lives in the English-Speaking Caribbean* (Indiana University Press, 1991) focuses on women in the English-speaking Caribbean. *Gender: A Caribbean Multi-disciplinary Perspective*, edited by Elsa Leo-Rhynie and others (Ian Randle Publishers, 1997), emerged from a series of seminars held at the Centre for Gender and Development Studies of the University of the West Indies in Jamaica between 1986 and 1994 and is the first publication of that institution. This compact volume details the following issues that Caribbean women face: research and policy, law, education, language and literature, health, and agriculture.

256. Moore, Henrietta L. *A Passion for Difference: Essays in Anthropology and Gender.* Bloomington: Indiana University Press, 1994. 177p. bibliog. index. ISBN 0253338581; 025320951Xpa.

Moore, who is an anthropology professor at the London School of Economics and served as director of the Gender Institute at LSE from 1994 to 1999, examines the relationships among feminism, anthropology, and contemporary theory in this collection of essays. The writings reflect the author's "struggle to develop a specifically anthropological approach to feminist post-structuralist theory" (p. 7). Each chapter focuses on contemporary theoretical issues and revolves around three themes: bodies and identities, the individual and the social, and language and the imagination. Most of the essays were published previously. Moore's complex writing style and the intricacies of these issues make this volume best suited for those already well versed in the study of gender in anthropology. Moore's earlier work *Feminism and Anthropology* (University of Minnesota Press, 1988) is an overview of feminist anthropology to the late 1980s. She mainly relies upon examples from Third World countries, tackling subjects such as women's labor, both within and outside the home; marriage and family; the effects of capitalism on women; and women's organizations.

257. Morgen, Sandra, ed. *Gender and Anthropology: Critical Reviews for Research and Teaching.* Washington, DC: American Anthropological Association, 1989. 462p. bibliog. ISBN 0913167339pa.

A group of scholars affiliated with the American Anthropological Association accepted a mandate from the U.S. Department of Education to institute change in introductory college anthropology courses. As a result, these scholars, all of whom had taught undergraduate anthropology courses, spent three years working with feminist anthropologists in each subfield of anthropology to compile this anthology. Although the chapters cover a variety of analytical topics, geographic areas, and cultures, each follows a similar format. Contributors craft conceptual essays that contextualize a particular topic; they make suggestions for teachers; and they include a valuable list of resources for classroom use. The authors' key goal consisted of helping teachers mainstream feminist research into the entire course and not separate it out. Unfortunately, however, no one has updated this classic curriculum guide. Editors and anthropology professors Mari Womack and Judith Marti created *The Other Fifty Percent: Multicultural Perspectives on Gender Relations* (Waveland Press, 1993) as a text for introductory classes in anthropology to specifically focus on women's roles in society. Contributors discuss global balance, the use of case studies, and a broad representation of key conceptual categories in anthropology. The editors divide the text into six sections: biological differences between women and men, the neglect of women as subjects and as researchers, marriage and sexuality, economics and power, religion and spirituality, and the impact of modernization on gender roles. Although the majority of the essays appeared in other publications during the 1980s and early 1990s, the editors also include seminal essays by Simone de Beauvoir, Margaret Mead, and Hortense Powdermaker.

258. Okely, Judith. *Own or Other Culture.* New York: Routledge, 1996. 244p. bibliog. index. ISBN 0415115124; 0415115132pa.

Okely's work, a collection of ten papers that she crafted during a twenty-year period, constitutes a history of anthropological thought on women and gender from the early 1970s to the 1990s. Okely, a professor of social anthropology at the University of Edinburgh, bemoans the increasing compartmentalization of anthropology, calling instead for an interconnectedness of areas and issues. Okely relies upon her fieldwork among Gypsies to argue that one can encounter "the exotic" not only among non-Western peoples, but also in Western societies. She mainly uses examples from fieldwork conducted in England and France, which includes discussions of life at an English girls' boarding school, thoughts on feminism in Paris, and a brief history of the women's liberation movement in Europe. Although *Naturalizing Power: Essays in Feminist Cultural Analysis*, edited by Sylvia Yanagisako and Carol Delaney (Routledge, 1995), covers a variety of subjects, the work centers on anthropologist David Schneider's revolutionary theory that kinship is based on culture, not blood ties. Feminist scholars have extended this theory to include gender inequality and the ways in which power is embedded in culture. The essays examine North America, except two that focus on Turkey and New Guinea. Essayists consider American kinship, classification schemes, relations between humans and animals, nationalism, and the American Dream.

259. Ong, Aihwa, and Michael G. Peletz, eds. *Bewitching Women, Pious Men: Gender and Body Politics in Southeast Asia*. Berkeley: University of California Press, 1995. 309p. bibliog. index. ISBN 0520088603; 0520088611pa.

Contributors presented most of the nine essays of this compilation at a conference on gender held in Southeast Asia in 1992. The scholars share an interdisciplinary approach to contemporary gender and power issues and write from a postmodern perspective. Essayists analyze how citizens face economic restructuring and social change at the local level, which entails the negotiation of femininity and masculinity. Contributors write about women in Indonesia, Malaysia, the Philippines, Singapore, and Thailand. Topics include Filipina feminists' writings, Thai stories of widow ghosts, eyewitness accounts of beheadings, narratives about state fatherhood and model mothers, middle-class Islamic revivalists, recalcitrant husbands, promiscuous market women, and " 'hard' and 'soft' societies" (p. 11). *Power and Difference: Gender in Island Southeast Asia*, edited by Jane Atkinson and Shelly Errington (Stanford University Press, 1990), examines many of the same issues.

260. Ortner, Sherry B. *Making Gender: The Politics and Erotics of Culture*. Boston: Beacon Press, 1996. 262p. bibliog. index. ISBN 0807046329.

Ortner, an anthropology professor at Columbia University known for her work in gender theory, includes eight essays that she wrote during a twenty-year period in *Making Gender*. The first chapter introduces the essays and briefly reviews the literature on "practice theory," which involves examining what people actually do versus what they say they do. Power, especially in relation to women, is a key concept in Ortner's work. In her classic essay "Is Female to Male as Nature Is to Culture?" (1972), she examines the culturally subordinate status of women, whom people universally view as closer to nature than men. Ortner analyzes egalitarian societies in "Gender Hegemonies" and relates examples of ways in which women have used the power within their accepted societal norms in the other six essays. She uses studies from Polynesia, the Andaman Islands in the Bay of Bengal, the traditional societies of Hawaii, and the Sherpas of Nepal.

261. Radner, Joan Newlon, ed. *Feminist Messages: Coding in Women's Folk Culture*. Urbana: University of Illinois Press, 1993. 309p. (Publications of the American Folklore Society). bibliog. ISBN 0252019571; 0252062671pa.

In *Feminist Messages* contributors focus on coding: messages that women use to communicate through disguised forms of expression, particularly in their stories, crafts, and songs. Radner divides the essays into four sections demonstrating how women code messages within male-dominated households, among themselves, in the larger community, and through interpretations of their own stories. The introductory chapter places women's communication within individual communities and cultures. Examples of coding include indirection/distancing in the context of the child ballads of England and Scotland and the appropriation, or women adapting activities associated with men, of Indian Pueblo women and their reclamation of storytelling traditions from their male peers. *Feminist Messages* and Susan Hollis, Linda Pershing, and M. Jane Young's *Feminist Theory and the Study of Folklore* (University of Illinois Press, 1993) emerged from meetings held at the American Folklore Society during the 1980s that caused these scholars to realize that they needed new paradigms to integrate feminist theory into the study of folklore. In part 1 of *Feminist Theory and the Study of Folklore*, the authors challenge the canon through an examination of traditional models and patriarchal assumptions inherent in the discipline. The final two parts cover girls' games, quilting and other needlework, the Finnish folk text *Kalevala*, tall tales among the Gascon in southwestern France, ancient Egyptian women, reproduction among the western Puebloan people, women Pentecostal preachers, everyday housework, birth, and political cartoons. Literary scholar Barbara Fass Leavy examines two story groups, the supernatural swan maiden domesticated by a human man and the supernatural demon lover paired with a human woman, in *In Search of the Swan Maiden: A Narrative on Folklore and Gender* (New York University Press, 1994). Leavy argues that one can encounter versions of swan maiden–demon lover stories that resonate with the tiresome domestic existence of most women all over the world.

262. Rajan, Rajeswari Sunder. *Real and Imagined Women: Gender, Culture, and Postcolonialism.* New York: Routledge, 1993. 153p. index. ISBN 0415085039; 0415085047pa.

A self-described feminist academic and English professor, Rajan has gathered six essays that explore the distinctions between perceptions of "real" and "imagined" women in postcolonial India. She analyzes gendered subjectivities through an examination of various cultural representations of Indian women. Five chapters focus on sati, or suttee, the traditional Hindu custom in which a widow "voluntarily" throws herself upon her husband's funeral pyre to indicate her devotion to him; rape; wife murder, called dowry deaths; and Indira Gandhi. Rajan begins each chapter with a summary of current debates on the particular topic and discusses potential scholarly subjects to explore. In the final chapter, she examines the representation of the "new," modern Indian woman, whom the media depict as drastically different from traditional Indian women. Rajan selects cross-cultural texts; for example, she draws on E. M. Forster, Maya Angelou, Alice Walker, and Samuel Richardson, as well as on Indian literature and films.

263. Saadawi, Nawal. *The Nawal El Saadawi Reader.* New York: Zed Books, 1997. 292p. bibliog. index. ISBN 1856495132; 1856495140pa.

Born in 1931, Nawal El Saadawi, a well-known Egyptian feminist, psychiatrist, and prolific writer on Arab women's issues, previously has served as Egypt's director of public health. However, her leftist political views landed her in prison during 1981 and 1982, under the Anwar Sadat administration. She also served as chief editor of a health journal, the assistant general secretary of the Egyptian Medical Association, the United Nations advisor for the Women's Program in Africa and the Middle East, the founder of the Arab Women's Solidarity Association, and a visiting professor at Duke University (1993–1996) and at Washington State University. *The Nawal*

El Saadawi Reader is a collection of her nonfiction writing since the publication of *The Hidden Face of Eve: Women in the Arab World* (Zed Books, 1980). Both works explore Arab women's sexuality and legal status and women's roles in fundamentalist societies, what Saadawi calls "the taboos (sex, politics, religion)" (p. 2). These translated twenty-three essays testify to women's collective power of resistance. Saadawi's other recent books include *Searching* (Zed Books, 1991), *The Innocence of the Devil* (University of California Press, 1994), and *Memoirs from the Women's Prison* (University of California Press, 1994).

264. Sachs, Carolyn E. *Gendered Fields: Rural Women, Agriculture, and Environment.* Boulder, CO: Westview Press, 1996. (Rural Studies Series of the Rural Sociological Society). 205p. bibliog. index. ISBN 0813325196; 081332520Xpa.

Sachs, director of the women's studies program and professor of rural sociology and women's studies at the Pennsylvania State University, delivers a clearly written examination of the relationship between feminist theory and the lives of agrarian women. Proposing that the experiences and viewpoints of rural women differ from those of urban women, Sachs seeks to answer the following questions: What are women's relationships to the natural environment? What forms do patriarchal relations take in the countryside? How does global economic restructuring affect rural women? What strategies do rural women utilize to shape their lives? The first two chapters deal with theory, and the remaining chapters describe rural women's relationships with the natural environment, land, crops, animals, family farms, and global restructuring. Sachs incorporates a variety of examples into her study from different countries, including India, Africa, Latin America, and the United States, to provide depth to this overview of an important topic.

265. Seager, Joni. *Earth Follies: Coming to Terms with the Global Environmental Crisis.* New York: Routledge, 1993. 332p. bibliog. index. ISBN 0415907209.

In *Earth Follies*, Seager, an associate professor of geography at the University of Vermont, passionately argues that "the *real* story of the environmental crisis is a story of power and profit and political wrangling; it is a story of the institutional arrangements and settings, the bureaucratic arrangements and the cultural conventions that *create* conditions of environmental destruction" (p. 3). She focuses on the question of agency, proposing that powerful people in institutions, such as militaries, corporations, governments, and environmental organizations, have the greatest bearing on the state of our environment. Seager contends that they must take responsibility for maintaining the environment. Applying feminist theory, she determines that these institutions are imbued with a "masculinist" institutional culture. The author devotes a chapter to each of these "environmental vandals," citing several examples from newspapers, interviews, advertisements, and other data that record environmental destruction. Seager also includes chapters criticizing the environmental movement, the "eco-establishment," and fringe groups. Seager discusses women-led grassroots movements in her final chapter, "Hysterical Housewives, Treehuggers, and Other Mad Women." *Earth Follies* is a clearly written, engaging, and thought-provoking work.

266. Sears, Laurie J., ed. *Fantasizing the Feminine in Indonesia.* Durham, NC: Duke University Press, 1996. 349p. bibliog. index. ISBN 0822316846; 082231696Xpa.

Sears, a professor of Southeast Asian history at the University of Washington, compiles essays that discuss "circumscribed feminine behavior in nineteenth- and twentieth-century Indonesia by revealing the shifting and illusive margins of feminine identities in Indonesian historical and narrative traditions" (p. 4) in this work. Scholars from Europe, North America, and Southeast Asia contribute the fourteen articles of this work, which Sears divides into two parts: "Structures of Control" and "Contested Representations." In the first part, contributors analyze state-imposed definitions of women's roles. Since men view women as "on the margin" and therefore see them as dangerous, they encourage women to become wives, mothers, and servants of the New (post-colonial) Order. Essayists continue this theme in part 2, which looks at nineteenth- and twentieth-century literary works, as well as Indonesian television, whose producers tend to withhold state funding from programs that do not feature the "ideal woman" image. Contributors also analyze cultural tolerance toward the reversibility and flexibility of gender roles, including transsexuals, homosexuals, and men belonging to an androgynous "third sex" called *banci*.

267. Smith, Lois M., and Alfred Padula. *Sex and Revolution: Women in Socialist Cuba.* New York: Oxford University Press, 1996. 247p. bibliog. index. ISBN 0195094905; 0195094913pa.

Lois Smith, a social scientist, and Alfred Padula, a history professor at the University of Southern Maine, have written what they consider the first comprehensive history of women in revolutionary Cuba. Padula asks: "How did three decades of socialist revolution change the lives of Cuban women?" Smith counters: "What lessons did the Cuban experience offer regarding the revolutionary model and sexual equality?" (p. vii). The first two chapters describe the lives of women during the years prior to Fidel Castro's overthrow of dictator Fulgencio Batista's regime in 1959. Castro subsequently set about a Marxist program of women's liberation. The authors chronologically arrange the following chapters according to broad themes: the Federation of Cuban Women, health, reproduction, education, employment, day care, family, and sexuality. The authors trace the economic and social reforms of Cuban socialism, looking at how they both positively and negatively have affected women. *Sex and Revolution*, which contains statistical and factual information, is a descriptive, as opposed to an analytical, study of this complex issue.

268. Tarlo, Emma. *Clothing Matters: Dress and Identity in India.* Chicago: University of Chicago Press, 1996. bibliog. index. ISBN 0226789756; 0226789764pa.

An adaptation of Tarlo's Ph.D. thesis, *Clothing Matters* traces the development of dress for each caste in Indian public life, specifically in a rural northwestern village, from the early colonial period, with its British sartorial influence, to the mid-1990s. Tarlo provides incidents involving "real" people in her fieldwork, which gives her book a very personal feeling. She examines the influence of Mohandas Gandhi's use of the homespun cloth, *khadi*, on both rich and poor. Today, Indians have gone from "ethnic chic," a combination of Western fashion and peasant dress and "Artwear," one-of-a-kind garments, to more diversified styles. Editor Hildi Hendrickson explores "treatments of the body surface" (p. 1) in *Clothing and Difference: Embodied Identities in Co-lonial and Post-Colonial Africa* (Duke University Press, 1996). The eight essays in this anthology describe the various ways that people express and change their personal and social identities through clothing. Contributors discuss virginity cloths in Nigeria, the dress of women performers in Lesotho, and the identity of spirits as revealed through their mediums' clothing in southern Niger. Contributors also analyze the relationship between power and clothing, as well as foreign influence on local dress and personal hygiene. Black-and-white photographs and cartoons enhance both works. For an excellent introduction to how dress reflects and interacts with Western culture and identity, see Fred Davis, *Fashion, Culture, and Identity* (University of Chicago Press, 1992).

269. Tucker, Judith E., ed. *Arab Women: Old Boundaries, New Frontiers.* Bloomington: Indiana University Press, 1993. 264p. (Indiana Series in Arab and Islamic Studies). bibliog. index. ISBN 025336096X; 0253207762pa.

In this collection of essays, "old boundaries," or the "Arab world," refers to geographic regions in which people primarily speak Arabic. "New frontiers" entails the ways in which ideas about gender and the realities of women's lives are changing. Tucker argues that despite diversity, certain commonalities bring various Arabic peoples together, such as the importance of Islam, men prohibiting women from directly accessing power, and the emphasis on female domesticity. Tucker centers the work on four key issues: how people treat gender issues in the region, women's work and economic activities, power in the political arena, and women's roles in the family and community. The contributors, all trained in the West in various social sciences and languages, cover a wide range of topics. Historical discussions include economic change in nineteenth-century Syria, feminism in Egypt, and the Arab family. Other essays detail women's issues in modern Islamic thought, Palestinian women under Israeli occupation, politics in Lebanon, and Arab women's contributions to literature. Editor Ebba Augustin provides a social history, through the lens of gender, of Palestinian occupation in *Palestinian Women: Identity and Experience* (Zed Books, 1993). This collection of fifteen essays and two poems describes, the changes that have occurred in women's roles since 1967.

270. Visweswaran, Kamala. *Fictions of Feminist Ethnography*. Minneapolis: University of Minnesota Press, 1994. 204p. index. ISBN 0816623368; 0816623376pa.

Visweswaran, an associate professor of anthropology at the University of Texas at Austin, explores the intersection of feminist theory, ethnographic practices, and the difficulties that women face when writing about other women in nine essays that she wrote between 1984 and 1993. The "Asian-American" author, who refers to herself as a "hyphenated anthropologist," reflects on how her own identity influenced both where and what she chose to study. Visweswaran interviewed Tamil women who supported India's nationalist movement during the late 1980s. The author's experiences during these interviews, which she describes as refusals, betrayals, and failures, affected her professional outlook. Visweswaran examines the anthropological writings of Laura Bohannon, Marjorie Shostak, Ella Deloria, and Zora Neale Hurston to explore the relationship between ethnography and literature, specifically fiction and autobiography. The author argues that a feminist ethnography should concentrate on women's relations with other women, as opposed to gender issues. Nita Kumar, along with six other authors, uses a different approach to determine how women should conceptualize and write about other women in *Women as Subjects: South Asian Histories* (University Press of Virginia, 1994). Contributors employ theory, method, data, and analysis to document how "women exercise their agency even while outwardly part of a repressive normative order" (p. 4). The theme of resistance figures prominently as the authors examine songs, proverbs, myths, autobiographical writings, and other forms of verbal expression.

271. Walker, Alice, and Pratibha Parmar. *Warrior Marks: Female Genital Mutilation and the Sexual Blinding of Women*. New York: Harcourt Brace & Company, 1993. 373p. bibliog. ISBN 0151000611.

In 1993 writer Alice Walker and Indian filmmaker Pratibha Parmar collaborated on *Warrior Marks*, a documentary film that details the practice of female circumcision in Africa. This tradition is still practiced in Africa, the Middle East, and Asia. In the book, the authors personalize their experience in creating the documentary through correspondence, photographs, and poems. The volume is composed of three parts. The first, "Alice's Journey," contains Walker's diary entries, which include her reflections on making the film. The second part, "Pratibha's Journey," parallels the first. A series of seventeen interviews with and by Alice Walker and Pratibha Parmar comprises the third part. The authors interview various activists, including Efua Dorkenoo, Aminata Diop, and Awa Thiam. They also convene with circumcisers, victims of the practice, and the mother of a circumcised child. The book concludes with descriptions of female genitalia, types of circumcision, a list of contact organizations, and a bibliography.

272. Warren, Karen J., ed. *Ecofeminism: Women, Culture, Nature.* Bloomington: Indiana University Press, 1997. 454p. bibliog. index. ISBN 0253330319; 0253210577pa.

Warren, a philosophy professor at Macalester College in St. Paul, Minnesota, takes a multidisciplinary, multicultural, and comprehensive approach to ecological feminism in this work. Warren enlists the expertise of academics in various disciplines, along with activists and writers, to "provide a balanced cross-cultural lens through which to begin to access the potential strengths and weaknesses of ecofeminism as a political movement and theoretical position" (p. xi). She organizes the work into three sections. The eight essays in "Taking Empirical Data Seriously," the first section, discuss the importance of observational data. The second section, "Interdisciplinary Perspectives," consists of ten essays on ecofeminism by scholars from a variety of disciplines, such as chemical engineering, biology, anthropology, education, and literary studies. Six philosophers contribute to the third section, "Philosophical Perspectives." They examine the following topics: androcentrism/anthropocentrism, environmental ethics, Kant, and Wittgenstein. Warren also edited *Ecological Feminism* (Routledge, 1994), which includes eleven essays by Western environmental philosophers who argue that the oppression of women and the degeneration of the natural environment are linked. They differently account for the link using tools of philosophical discourse, such as conceptual analysis, argumentative support, and the examination of key areas of philosophy, including ethics, epistemology, metaphysics, politics, and the history of philosophy.

273. White, Sarah C. *Arguing with the Crocodile: Gender and Class in Bangladesh.* Atlantic Highlands, NJ: Zed Books, 1992. 186p. bibliog. index. ISBN 1856490858; 1856490866pa.

Although striving to become autonomous, the poverty-stricken people of Bangladesh largely depend on substantial amounts of foreign aid, mostly from the West, thus allowing agencies that supply aid and nongovernmental organizations to play a major role in the economic, ideological, and sociological development of Bangladesh. Development studies typically conclude that women form a homogeneous, passive, and one-dimensional group with set gender roles. White asserts that this is not true. She argues that gender relations are dynamic instead of static, which gives women and men the power to construct identity to suit their needs. White's book, a revision of her doctoral dissertation completed at Bath University, stems from observations she made while living in the village of Kumirpur during 1985 and 1986. The eight chapters include case studies and interviews that reveal that women engaged in small business, agricultural labor, and household work, among other endeavors.

274. Wolf, Diane L., ed. *Feminist Dilemmas in Fieldwork.* Boulder, CO: Westview Press, 1996. 226p. bibliog. ISBN 0813384966; 0813384990pa.

Wolf, who teaches sociology at the University of California at Davis, examines researchers' ethical and political dilemmas when researching a particular subject. She contends that such dilemmas become especially acute when dealing with oppressed or poor subjects. According to Wolf, Western researchers, who typically are white and affluent, intrude upon another person's life, making them both an insider and outsider. Wolf argues that women in the field question their own motives, both personal and professional, and the power relations between their subjects and themselves. The contributors, primarily sociologists and anthropologists, call upon feminists to face these identity crises, reexamine what constitutes quality research, and continue to promote meaningful projects. Nine of the ten chapters detail the personal fieldwork experiences of researchers among working-class and rural women in the United States and the Third World. Most conclude with extensive notes and references.

Editors Sally Cole and Lynne Phillips highlight Western feminist biases applied to other cultures and seek to develop cross-cultural understandings of the "paths women choose in their struggles to make better lives for themselves" (p. 37) in *Ethnographic Feminisms: Essays in Anthropology* (Carleton University Press, 1995). The three sections of the book examine teachings of the academy that contradict women's actual experiences in the field, new ways of interpreting women's roles in domestic and economic spheres within Western capitalist societies, and experimental ethnographic writing. *Confronting the Margaret Mead Legacy: Scholarship, Empire, and the South Pacific* (Temple University Press, 1992), edited by cultural historian Lenora Foerstel and anthropologist Angela Gilliam, includes analyses of Mead's impact on Western anthropology, addressing the relationship between colonialism and anthropology, and Western stereotypes of Pacific peoples and cultures.

Archaeology and Prehistory

275. Claassen, Cheryl, ed. *Women in Archaeology*. Philadelphia: University of Pennsylvania Press, 1994. 252p. bibliog. index. ISBN 0812232771; 0812215095pa.

In her introduction, Claassen, a professor of anthropology at Appalachian State University, observes that life experiences influence one's choices, including the choice and management of a career. The essayists of *Women in Archaeology*, who acknowledge that one's gender directly affects such choices, examine the contributions that forty-one women archaeologists made, primarily before 1940, and the state of the profession for women, especially in North America, since the early 1990s. The biographies generally reveal that the professionalization of archaeology did not involve women. In fact, most women who participated in archaeological endeavors did not have academic appointments; instead, they either were affiliated with museums or held positions as research associates. By the late 1960s, more women entered graduate programs in archaeology; however, the number of women who have attained senior academic status has proven highly disappointing.

Nancy Parezo and other authors focus on women anthropologists of the American Southwest in *Hidden Scholars: Women Anthropologists and the Native Southwest* (University of New Mexico Press, 1993). The contributors parallel Claassen's observations, arguing that people in the field have slighted women and have not acknowledged their contributions. The authors consider the lives and careers of fifty women anthropologists, some well known, including Ruth Benedict, Elsie Clews, and Esther Goldfrank, and others who are less well known, such as Dorothy Keur and Jane Holden Kelley. Parezo's excellent introduction chronicling the history of women's participation in anthropology, the "welcoming science," is highly readable for both students and general readers. The book emerged from a larger project that included a conference in 1986, an exhibition and accompanying catalog, *Daughters of the Desert: Women Anthropologists and the Native American Southwest, 1880–1980: An Illustrated Catalogue*, by Barbara Babcock and Nancy Parezo (University of New Mexico Press, 1988), a video documentary, and a collection of oral histories.

276. Diaz-Andreu, Margarita, and Marie Louise Stig Sorensen, eds. *Excavating Women: A History of Women in European Archaeology*. New York: Routledge, 1998. 320p. bibliog. index. ISBN 0415157609.

This collection of essays, which emerged from a session held at the Theoretical Archaeology Group Annual Meeting in Durham, England, in December 1993, provides a historiography of European women archaeologists who paved the way for today's feminist archaeologists. The editors introduce the volume with two background chapters. The first chapter not only chronicles the stages of the professionalization of archaeology in Europe, but also examines women's evolving role within it. The second chapter includes a theoretical discussion regarding why scholars should examine women's role in archaeology, which traditionally has proven nearly invisible. By "excavating" the lives of individual women in the twelve case studies that follow, the contributors demonstrate how cultural, regional, and historical factors have led to discrimination against women archaeologists and their work. Contributors describe women archaeologists from the nineteenth century to the present, including women from France, Poland, Norway, Spain, Germany, Great Britain, Crete, Denmark, and Greece. This work is scholarly and highly readable and includes extensive lists of references that conclude most of the chapters. Personal biographies and telling photographs balance statistics and other quantitative information.

Turning attention toward subjects as opposed to scholars, *Invisible People and Processes: Writing Gender and Childhood into European Archaeology*, edited by Jenny Moore and Eleanor Scott (Leicester University Press, 1997), is the first work on gendered archaeology to focus solely on Europe. Twenty-three scholars contributed to this work, which the editors divided into three sections: a discussion of engendered archaeology as a remedy to the incompleteness of archaeological narratives, a presentation of case studies, and an examination of children and women. Contributors cover the following geographic areas: Britain, Hungary, the Aegean, Italy, and the Ukraine. Time periods represented span the Mesolithic era to the European Middle Ages. An extensive list of references concludes most of the chapters.

277. Gero, Joan M., and Margaret W. Conkey, eds. *Engendering Archaeology: Women and Prehistory*. Cambridge, MA: Basil Blackwell, 1991. 418p. (Social Archaeology). bibliog. index. ISBN 0631165053; 0631175016pa.

Based on papers presented at a conference in 1988, this classic collection synthesizes much of the pioneering work done in the field of archaeology. The fourteen essays, written by well-known scholars in this field, including Cheryl Claassen, Henrietta Moore, Janet Spector, and Rita Wright, center on two themes: women in prehistoric societies and the concept of gender in archaeological inquiry. Androcentric bias traditionally has plagued both themes. Two chapters discuss theory and serve as an introduction, while additional chapters explore topics such as women's role during the Magdalenian era, domestic architecture in the Late Neolithic Vinca culture, women's participation in stone tool and pottery production, women's role in the development of horticulture and shell fishing in the eastern United States, and art at a Yugoslavian Mesolithic site. In the epilogue, Moore argues that a feminist archaeology, in which gender is a structuring principle in the archaeological record, will substantially alter the development of archaeological theory and practice. *Archaeology of Gender: Proceedings of the Twenty-second Annual Conference of the Archaeological Association of the University of Calgary*, edited by Dale Walde and Noreen D. Willows (Archaeological Association, University of Calgary, 1991), and *Exploring Gender through Archaeology: Selected Papers from the Boone Conference*, edited by Cheryl Claassen and Mary C. Beaudry (Prehistory Press, 1992), are two other collections culled from conferences around the same time. The 1989 Calgary conference, known informally as the "Chacmool" conference, "qualifies as the first truly public meeting on the topic of gender and archaeology anywhere in the world" (Cheryl Claassen, *Exploring Gender Through Archaeology*, p. 1). Sixty-nine articles reflect the burgeoning interest in gender archaeology during the late 1980s and include topics such as the status of women in archaeology, theoretical issues regarding gender in the archaeological record, the evolution of sex differences from prehistory on, and the effect of gender roles on the division of labor. *Archaeology of Gender* remains an important work in that it is one of the first collections to deal with gender in archaeology. *Exploring Gender through Archaeology* consists of fourteen essays that emerged from a 1991 conference held at Appalachian

State University. It tackles topics such as mothering in prehistoric societies, Mayan stone carving, physical differences between male and female skeletons, early pottery use, and the underrepresentation of women among professional archaeologists.

278. Hager, Lori D., ed. *Women in Human Evolution*. New York: Routledge, 1997. 214p. bibliog. index. ISBN 0415108330; 0415108349pa.

What did prehistoric women do aside from birthing and raising children? How have women paleoanthropologists altered traditional male assumptions, and are these new assumptions objective? The women contributors, including anthropologists, a biologist, and a philosopher, of this collection of nine essays focus on these important questions. Recent feminist scholarship and new discoveries of prehistoric human bones indicate that the earliest women took on highly active roles and were neither "invisible nonparticipants" nor "handmaidens" to men (p. 91). Although more women paleoanthropologists are entering the field, men still primarily analyze the fossil remains, such as those of the famous early hominid "Lucy," whose femaleness is questionable. By examining previously neglected topics in human evolution and depositing them squarely in the middle of contemporary scholarship, contributors to this book have made an important contribution to the literature.

In *Women in Prehistory* (University of Oklahoma Press, 1989), the first modern work on prehistoric women, archaeologist and author Margaret R. Ehrenberg clearly explains the use of archaeological evidence to those interested in women but unfamiliar with archaeology and examines the challenges of interpreting this evidence in feminist terms. She begins with a section on methodology and follows with chapters in which she chronologically examines the Paleolithic and Mesolithic eras (the "stone ages"), the Neolithic period (the "first farmers"), the Bronze Age, and the Iron Age. Ehrenberg mostly focuses on Europe, with some Southeast Asia examples. *Women in Prehistory: North America and Mesoamerica* (University of Pennsylvania Press, 1997) is a collection of conference papers that address the need to identify women as participants in the archaeological record of early America. In the introduction, editor Cheryl Claassen argues that most of the archaeological work done on women thus far has proven "womanist," concerned with the presence of women, as opposed to "feminist," concerned with the relationships between genders. She groups the chapters into four sections: "Women in the Archaeological Record," "Prehistoric Women as Social Agents," "The Symbolic Construction of Gender," and "The Material Construction of Gender." Contributors examine geographic areas from the Arctic to Central America, as well as eras from the Paleo-Indian into the nineteenth century A.D./C.E.

279. Hays-Gilpin, Kelley, and David S. Whitley, eds. *Reader in Gender Archaeology*. New York: Routledge, 1998. 383p. (Routledge Readers in Archaeology). bibliog. index. ISBN 0415173590; 0415173604pa.

This highly readable volume, which emphasizes Anglo-American archaeology, succeeds as an introduction to the history and literature on sex and gender in prehistory. Hays-Gilpin and Whitley compile important articles from several journals and anthologies and excerpts from books to present an overview of the various opinions, issues, and controversies surrounding this relatively recent discipline. The editors divide the twenty essays, mostly written in the 1990s, although one reaches back to 1978, into seven thematic sections: "Sex, Gender, and Archaeology," "Human Origins," "Identifying 'Sexual' Divisions of Labor," "From Sexual Divisions to Gender Dynamics," "Gender Iconography and Ideology," "Power and Social Hierarchies," and "New Narratives, New Visions." Each section begins with a one- to two-page introduction, a brief list of books for further reading, and a list of references. *Reader in Gender Archaeology* would serve as an excellent textbook or an essential addition to a small library's collection, since it brings together fundamental essays in the field.

280. Kent, Susan, ed. *Gender in African Prehistory.* Walnut Hills, CA: AltaMira Press, 1998. 352p. bibliog. index. ISBN 0761989676; 0761989684pa.

According to Kent, the study of gender in archaeology is a recent undertaking in comparison to its appearance in cultural anthropology and other social sciences. She seeks to redress this imbalance via demonstrating how scholars incorporate gender in the African archaeological record and examining why patterns have changed through time. *Gender in African Prehistory* is the first treatment of gender in prehistory in the African continent. Kent and sixteen contributors examine a broad range of sites, including ones in Egypt, South Africa, Ghana, and Tanzania, with time periods ranging from the Stone Age to the period just before European colonization (one chapter focuses on craft production in Ghana to the present). Although the contributors write from varying theoretical orientations, they all concentrate on the role that gender plays in cultural change. In the last chapter, "Reflections on Gender Studies in African and Asian Archaeology," Sarah Milledge Nelson deftly summarizes and evaluates the preceding twelve case studies. She concludes that "the studies in this book demonstrate that seeking gender creates better archaeology" (p. 294).

In *Discovering Eve: Ancient Israelite Women in Context* (Oxford University Press, 1988), Carol L. Meyers examines the Holy Land and Israeli prehistory to determine how village-based Israeli women lived at the time of the Hebrew Bible (1200–1000 B.C.E.). Meyers draws upon biblical texts, particularly the story of Micah in Judges 17–18 and the story of Adam and Eve in Genesis 2–3; archaeological remains; and feminist anthropological scholarship. Meyers, a professor of religion at Duke University, argues that these women enjoyed more status and power than previously thought.

281. Scott, Elizabeth M. *Those of Little Note: Gender, Race, and Class in Historical Archaeology.* Tucson: University of Arizona Press, 1994. 215p. bibliog. index. ISBN 0816514119; 0816514992pa.

Those of Little Note, one of the first attempts to address gender in historical archaeology, consists of nine essays that scholars initially presented at the annual meeting of the Society for Historical and Underwater Archaeology in Kingston, Jamaica, in 1992. Contributors draw upon case studies from colonial and postcolonial North America to shed light upon those of "little note": Native Americans, African Americans, and Euro-Americans who lived on the geographical or cultural margins of society. Diverse topics include Aleut women in the cloth industry in Russian Alaska, Western Apaches' labor at the Roosevelt Dam site, African Americans in Great Barrington, Massachusetts, members of an all-male religious community in Baltimore, women at military forts and encampments in upstate New York and New Hampshire, men and women in mining towns out west, prostitutes in Washington, D.C., and social reformers, primarily in Boston. Despite the range of examples, essayists, using recent feminist scholarship, address similar themes: resistance to and innovative use of power, the interrelatedness of gender, race, and class, and sexual relations within various groups. Extensive use of documentary, pictorial, and oral sources, as well as a close examination of artifacts, makes the essays both lively and accessible.

In *Archaeology of Gender: Separating the Spheres in Urban America* (Plenum Press, 1994), Diana Wall studies middle- and upper-class men and women's roles in New York City between 1790 and 1840 to determine when and why the home and workplace separated into separate spheres for men and women. Through an examination of the changing structure and ritualization of daily meals, the evolving composition of the household as men moved out into the workplace and women domestic servants moved in, and the symbolism behind choice of architecture for new buildings, Wall proposes that both men and women actively participated in the creation of the ideological and actual spheres that separated them.

282. Spector, Janet. *What This Awl Means: Feminist Archaeology at a Wahpeton Dakota Village*. St. Paul: Minnesota Historical Society Press, 1993. 161p. bibliog. index. ISBN 0873512774; 0873512782pa.

Cheryl Claassen, a highly respected anthropologist and author, called this slim volume "a landmark" and "the first explicitly feminist site report" (*American Antiquity*, vol. 59, no. 4, October 1994, p. 791). This highly personal account details Spector's use of traditional archaeological fieldwork combined with nineteenth-century documentary evidence to explore the roles of men, and especially women, of a particular village. She excavated a site at the Wahpeton Dakota planting village, which was active until the 1850s, in Little Rapids, Minnesota. In the first and final chapters, Spector recounts how as a child she wanted to become an archaeologist to connect emotionally with people from the past, yet her professors in college taught her a male-centered, objective, and dispassionate archaeology. In 1980, the first year of her three-year dig, her team discovered a small awl handle. This find inspired her to write *What This Awl Means*, a beautifully illustrated short story that describes how a Dakota woman, Mazaokiyewin, might have lived and used the awl. In the remainder of the work, she details the excavation, in which Spector and her team worked closely with the descendants of the Wahpeton Dakota. This lively, fluid narrative incorporates both empathy and keen observation.

283. Wright, Rita P., ed. *Gender and Archaeology*. Philadelphia: University of Pennsylvania Press, 1996. 296p. bibliog. index. ISBN 0812233395; 0812215745pa.

Gender and Archaeology consists of ten essays that focus on archaeology in terms of research, teaching, and practice. Contributors examine ways in which complex or state-level societies have organized men and women according to gender systems. The authors chose to analyze complex societies because they typically yield more data to work with, including ethnohistories, artwork, surviving oral traditions, period texts, mortuary material, and other artifacts. Contributors employ varying methodologies in this diverse volume, which encompasses several geographic and cultural areas, in order to demonstrate the many "archaeolog*ies* of gender" (p. 3). Following an introduction by Wright, an associate professor of anthropology at New York University, the first two chapters look at prehistoric reproduction and the history of feminine technologies. The next four chapters rely upon excavation data to examine how the Incas and people of Mesopotamia used textiles, the impact of the Aztecs on gender roles in Mexico, and the ways in which Mayans depicted gender on classic Maya sculpture. The final three chapters explore how an archaeologist's gender ideology influences his or her research. These essays incorporate gender into traditional archaeology, ask new questions of archaeological data, and show how archaeologists are integrating gender into fieldwork and teaching. Wright includes black-and-white maps, illustrations, and photographs.

Sarah M. Nelson argues that the assumptions and models that scientists traditionally used to explain the past exclude an understanding of gender in *Gender in Archaeology: Analyzing Power and Prestige* (AltaMira Press, 1997). Nelson advocates gendered archaeology because it includes the roles of both women and men in society. Using case studies from the prehistoric past, Nelson examines activities including gathering and hunting, food preparation, pottery making, the creation and use of tools, kinship roles, leadership within the larger community, and women and ideology.

Geography

284. Blunt, Alison, and Gillian Rose, eds. *Writing Women and Space: Colonial and Postcolonial Geographies.* New York: Guilford Press, 1994. 256p. (Mappings: Society/Theory/Space). bibliog. index. ISBN 0898624975; 0898623983pa.

Acknowledging that "the remaking of spaces is central . . . to much feminist and postcolonial work" (p. 19), the authors of this anthology contribute ten essays that delve into the mapping of space and difference—especially race, class, and gender—and the roles of women who inhabit these spaces. The editors provide an excellent introduction that outlines the history of feminist poststructural theory in relation to geography. The table of contents includes chapter subsections, which allows readers to easily scan topics without using the index. The editors organize the essays around two major themes: how location influences identity, representation, and power, and ways in which one can change the traditional hegemonic mapping of transparent space. The authors, most of whom are geographers or historians, focus on specific examples from the heyday of British imperialism, travel writings of white women from late-nineteenth-century West Africa, a captivity narrative from Australia during the 1830s, and the experiences of American women during World War II. Contributors argue that cartography determines the worldview of those mapped. They also consider contemporary ways of displacing traditional maps with innovative uses of art and other media. This work would serve as a stimulating and accessible introduction to the myriad of ways to redefine space.

285. Duncan, Nancy, ed. *BodySpace: Destabilising Geographies of Gender and Sexuality.* New York: Routledge, 1996. 278p. bibliog. index. ISBN 0415144418; 0415144426pa.

BodySpace includes fifteen essays by feminist geographer Nancy Duncan and other scholars, representing the fields of geography and women's studies, that together provide an excellent scholarly introduction to current thinking about feminist geography. Duncan divides the work into three sections according to theory ("Re-readings"), case studies ("Re-negotiations"), and methodology ("Re-searchings"). In each section, the authors question and reassess dualities, such as public and private, self and other, straight and queer, real and imagined, and power and weakness. Kathleen Kirby focuses on cartography and the technologies developed to conceptualize space; Gill Valentine discusses the public assumptions that create the "heterosexual street"; Joanne Sharp analyzes nationalism in post-Communist Eastern Europe; and Matthew Sparke critiques fieldwork and masculinist power. Contributors argue that scholars must take issues of race, sexuality, disability, nationalism, and class, which all contribute to oppression, into account. Despite the engaging subject matter and variety of topics addressed, the abundance of nomenclature and dissections of theoretical principles makes this work challenging.

286. Katz, Cindi, and Janice Monk, eds. *Full Circles: Geographies of Women over the Life Course.* New York: Routledge, 1993. (International Studies of Women and Place). 317p. bibliog. index. ISBN 0415075521; 0415075629pa.

Katz and Monk begin *Full Circles* with personal reflections: Monk recounts how the lives of her great-grandmother, grandmother, and mother all differed from her own and from one another, while Katz considers how physical place, class, and culture, as opposed to time, resulted in contrasting choices for the women in the Sudan with whom she lived, as well as for herself. Individual values and social status, time and place, race and nationality, and cultural and economic settings all figure prominently not only in terms of how women lead their lives, but also in terms of why they make the choices that they make. Noting that much recent feminist work has focused on women during their childbearing years, the editors examine women's entire lives in both postindustrial and developing nations. Their approach is cross-cultural, with chapters chronicling the lives of women in the United States, the Sudan, the eastern Caribbean, Colombia, Montreal, Australia, and France. The contributors, most of whom are trained geographers, argue that women differently experience their daily lives as a result of the spaces and places in which they live and the stages of their life course, such as daughter, mother, student, wife, and wage earner. Each of the thirteen chapters begins with a short introduction, which contextualizes the subject, and ends with a conclusion. Graphs, maps, statistical tables, photographs, and an excellent index expand the text. This collection is personal and anecdotal, thus establishing a sort of intimacy between author and reader.

287. Massey, Doreen B. *Space, Place, and Gender*. Minneapolis: University of Minnesota Press, 1994. 280p. bibliog. index. ISBN 0816626162; 0816626170pa.

Doreen Massey, senior professor of geography at the Open University, brings together eleven articles that she wrote between 1978 and 1992 that explicate her theories about the relationships among space, place, and gender. Key themes include the connection among local, national, and international developments, the relationship between family and economic roles for women, and the links between capitalism and patriarchy. She groups the essays into three sections, with an introduction for each. The first section, "Space and Social Relations," includes early writings that advance her theories on the social constitution of space within the context of industrial restructuring and regional development in England. In "Place and Identity," she discusses social space in terms of social relations at home, within the community, and across the world. In section 3, "Space, Place, and Gender," she examines the intersections of gender and geography and space and place, citing examples to demonstrate not only how gender relations can vary greatly within local communities, but also how the diversity among women, as well as men, causes women to think and act differently. *Space, Place, and Gender* provides a good synthesis of the work that this influential feminist geographer has contributed.

288. Momsen, Janet H., and Vivian Kinnaird, eds. *Different Places, Different Voices: Gender and Development in Africa, Asia, and Latin America*. New York: Routledge, 1993. 322p. (International Studies of Women and Place). bibliog. index. ISBN 0415075386; 0415075637pa.

The first conference on gender and development for geographers, the Commonwealth Geographical Bureau Workshop, was held at the University of Newcastle-upon-Tyne in 1989. Nearly 100 scholars and students from forty countries participated. In twenty-one essays, contributors report on their field research, which focuses on gender issues in four developing areas: Africa, South Asia, Southeast Asia and Oceania, and Latin America. As a resident of the British Commonwealth, each author is aware of the impact of colonialism on development and interprets his or her findings accordingly. Essayists use women's everyday experiences to give regional perspectives on urban/factory life, rural/farm life, reproduction, household responsibilities, and community organization. Key essays evaluate women's labor and argue against the way in which the customary divisions of domestic and "production-related" work affect the status and empowerment of women. Following their introduction, "Geography, Gender, and Development," the editors contextualize each geographically arranged group of chapters with an overview of the gender issues and geography particular to a specific region. Numerous figures and tables enhance the text. Janet Momsen and Janice Monk edited the important series International Studies of Women and Place, which explores the diversity and complexity of women's experiences. *Feminist Political Ecology: Global Issues and Local Experience*, edited by Dianne Rocheleau and others (Routledge,

1996), and Janet Townsend's *Women's Voices from the Rainforest* (Routledge, 1995) are two notable volumes of the series.

289. Momsen, Janet, and Janet Townsend, eds. *Geography of Gender in the Third World.* Albany: State University of New York Press, 1987. 424p. bibliog. index. ISBN 0887064418; 088706440Xpa.

Geography professors and prolific authors Janet Momsen and Janet Townsend's *Geography of Gender in the Third World* is the first work that focuses on gender issues in the Third World from a geographical perspective. The editors, along with several contributors, include case studies from Egypt, Bangladesh, Bolivia, Thailand, and Sri Lanka, as well as other developing countries, to illustrate how the roles "male" and "female" vary significantly from place to place. Yet the heaviest burden of Third World poverty uniformly falls upon women. The volume begins with an excellent introduction and ends with a section on proposed directions for research. Thirteen chapters about survival, agriculture, labor, and industrialization compose the heart of this work.

290. Rose, Gillian. *Feminism and Geography: The Limits of Geographical Knowledge.* Minneapolis: University of Minnesota Press, 1993. 205p. bibliog. index. ISBN 0816624178; 0816624186pa.

According to leading British geographer Gillian Rose, white, bourgeois, and heterosexual men historically have dominated the discipline of geography, "perhaps more so than any other human science" (p. 1). Rose explores how scholars conceptualize the connections among masculinity, knowledge, and power, why those who represent contemporary human geography still resist work about and by women, and the implications for feminist critiques. She uses deconstruction and psychoanalysis to scrutinize the methods and assumptions of geography, discussing women and everyday spaces, both public and private; time-geography (how women spend their time); humanistic geography, or the emotional responses of people to places; masculinist concepts of space and place, and erosions of such concepts; and the relationship between the natural environment and human society. The last chapters delineate her model for an alternative geography based on the acknowledgment of differences between women and men, differences of race, class, sexuality, place, identity, and space, and other defining differences.

1999 CORE TITLES

Banet-Weiser, Sarah. *The Most Beautiful Girl in the World: Beauty Pageants and National Identity.* Berkeley: University of California Press, 1999. 277p. bibliog. index. ISBN 0520217896; 0520217918pa.

Bruhns, Karen Olsen, and Karen E. Stothert. *Women in Ancient America.* Norman: University of Oklahoma Press, 1999. 343p. bibliog. index. ISBN 0806131691.

El Guindi, Fadwa. *Veil: Modesty, Privacy, and Resistance.* New York: Berg, 1999. 242p. bibliog. index. ISBN 1859739245; 1859739296pa.

El-Shamy, Hasan M., collector and translator. *Tales Arab Women Tell and the Behavioral Patterns They Portray.* Bloomington: Indiana University Press, 1999. 560p. bibliog. index. ISBN 0253335299.

Fenster, Tovi, ed. *Gender, Planning, and Human Rights*. New York: Routledge, 1999. 182p. (International Studies of Women and Place). 182p. bibliog. index. ISBN 0415154952; 0415154944pa.

Hahn, Robert A., and Kate W. Harris, eds. *Anthropology in Public Health: Bridging Differences in Culture and Society*. New York: Oxford University Press, 1999. 384p. bibliog. index. ISBN 0195129024; 019511955Xpa.

Hendry, Joy. *An Anthropologist in Japan: Glimpses of Life in the Field*. New York: Routledge, 1999. 167p. (ASA Research Methods in Social Anthropology). bibliog. index. ISBN 041519573X; 0415195748pa.

Houppert, Karen. *The Curse: Confronting the Last Unmentionable Taboo: Menstruation*. New York: Farrar, Straus and Giroux, 1999. bibliog. index. ISBN 0374273669.

Lapsley, Hilary. *Margaret Mead and Ruth Benedict: The Kinship of Women*. Amherst: University of Massachusetts Press, 1999. 351p. bibliog. index. ISBN 1558491813.

Markowitz, Fran, and Michael Ashkenazi, eds. *Sex, Sexuality, and the Anthropologist*. Urbana: University of Illinois Press, 1999. 230p. bibliog. index. ISBN 0252024370; 0252067479pa.

Matsui, Yayori. *Women in the New Asia: From Pain to Power*. New York: Zed Books, 1999. 194p. index. ISBN 1856496252; 1856496260pa.

McDowell, Linda, and Joanne P. Sharp, eds. *A Feminist Glossary of Human Geography*. New York: Arnold, 1999. 372p. bibliog. ISBN 0340706597pa.

Meriwether, Margaret L. and Judith E. Tucker, eds. *Social History of Women and Gender in the Modern Middle East*. Boulder, CO: Westview Press, 1999. 220p. bibliog. index. ISBN (OP); 0813321018pa.

Mohanram, Radhika. *Black Body: Women, Colonialism, and Space*. Minneapolis: University of Minnesota Press, 1999. 250p. (Public Worlds, v. 6). bibliog. index. ISBN 0816635420; 0816635439pa.

Morley, Patricia A. *The Mountain Is Moving: Japanese Women's Lives*. New York: New York University Press, 1999. 226p. bibliog. index. ISBN 0814756263.

Okin, Susan Moller. *Is Multiculturalism Bad for Women?* Princeton, NJ: Princeton University Press, 1999. 146p. ISBN 0691004315; 0691004323pa.

Seymour, Susan C. *Women, Family, and Child Care in India: A World in Transition*. New York: Cambridge University Press, 1999. 323p. bibliog. index. ISBN 0521591279; 0521598842pa.

Silliman, Jael M., and Ynestra King, eds. *Dangerous Intersections: Feminist Perspectives on Population, Environment, and Development: A Project of the Committee on Women, Population, and the Environment.* Cambridge, MA: South End Press, 1999. 283p. bibliog. index. ISBN 0896085988; 089608597Xpa.

Sperling, Valerie. *Organizing Women in Contemporary Russia: Engendering Transition.* New York: Cambridge University Press, 1999. 303p. bibliog. index. ISBN 0521660173; 0521609634pa.

Sweely, Tracy L., ed. *Manifesting Power: Gender and the Interpretation of Power in Archaeology.* New York: Routledge, 1999. 210p. bibliog. index. ISBN 0415171792; 0415197449pa.

White, Nancy Marie, Lynne P. Sullivan, and Rochelle A. Marrinan, eds. *Grit Tempered: Early Women Archaeologists in the Southeastern United States.* Gainesville: University Press of Florida, 1999. 392p. bibliog. index. ISBN 081301686X.

WORLD WIDE WEB/INTERNET SITES

General Sites

291. *Association for Feminist Anthropology.* http://ssci.berkeley.edu/~afaweb.
A subsection of the American Anthropological Association, the Association for Feminist Anthropology (AFA) has several goals, which include to "1. Improve the outreach of AFA to feminists from all four fields of Anthropology; 2. To include U.S. women of color in all our activities, but especially to utilize our travel grants to assist women of color in attending the AAA meetings; 3. To increase outreach and mentoring to students at all levels." This site also contains book reviews, job listings, and links to Web sites pertaining to the field of anthropology. It also features articles from the AFA's newsletter, called *Anthropology Newsletter*, as well as its yearly publication, *Voices*, which features articles about important issues, including feminism and antiracism in anthropology. The *Commission on the Anthropology of Women* (http://ruls01.fsw. leidenuniv.nl/~nas/06-18.htm), a section of the International Union of Anthropological and Ethnological Sciences (IUAES), lists current officers and publications and provides links to other commission sites.

292. *Celebrating Women Anthropologists.* http://www.cas.usf.edu/anthropology/women/.
Students at the University of South Florida created this Web site to profile several pioneering women anthropologists who have significantly influenced the field. The profiles include brief descriptions of each anthropologist, a list of her published works, and links of interest.

293. *Feminist Anthropology.* http://www.indiana.edu/~wanthro/fem.htm.
An Indiana University anthropology graduate student, Angela Bratton, created this Web site to discuss the history and theory of feminist anthropology. She provides a substantial bibliography of relevant sources. She also aptly summarizes the current state of feminist anthropology under the organizations and resources section. In addition, she includes a diagram that delineates the

development of the "three waves" of feminist anthropology, placing them within larger theoretical movements in anthropology and social theory.

Ecofeminism

294. *Women's Environmental Network.* http://www.wen.org.uk/.
The slogan for this group reads, "Educating, empowering, and informing women and men who care about the environment." For ten years, the Women's Environmental Network (WEN) has campaigned and raised awareness on environmental and health issues. Created by a small group of women, WEN has a history of successful action and public information campaigns.

295. *WWW.Ecofem.Org.* http://www.ecofem.org/.
This site is intended primarily as an educational resource for the philosophy and social movement that since the 1970s has come to be known as ecofeminism. It contains the "Ecofeminism Web Ring," in which all the major Web resources are linked together, and also has links to listservs, groups devoted to ecofeminism, a bibliography, and current news.

International Women

296. *Sisterhood Is Global Institute.* http://www.sigi.org/.
The goal of the Sisterhood Is Global Institute (SIGI), which was established in 1984, is twofold: first, to further the understanding of women's rights at the local, regional, national, and global levels; and second, to strengthen women's capacity to exercise these rights. SIGI currently has members in seventy countries and maintains a network of more than 1,300 individuals and organizations. Its Web site features action alerts for urgent human rights issues, information on the Sisterhood Is Global Institute's Human Rights Education program, upcoming events and conferences, SIGI's newsletter, and a detailed list of publications.

297. *Womankind Worldwide.* http://www.womankind.org.uk/.
Womankind Worldwide, a nonprofit United Kingdom organization, is dedicated to women's development and women's human rights. Believing that the best people to help women are women themselves, Womankind Worldwide works with local groups, assisting the efforts of women who live in Third World countries to overcome poverty and ill health, gain access to education, and generally obtain greater control over their lives. Womankind provides funding and information to developing communities worldwide. Its Web site includes statistics about women and poverty, violence, education, and health. It also includes a list of relevant publications and links to other useful Web sites. Another site dedicated to women's rights is *Human Rights Watch: Women's Rights Division* (http://www.hrw.org/women/). This site provides news releases concerning recent activities relating to women's rights around the world.

298. *WomenWatch.* http://www.un.org/womenwatch/.
WomenWatch is a joint initiative of three United Nations entities: the Division for the Advancement of Women (DAW), the United Nations Development Fund for Women (UNIFEM), and the International Research and Training Institute for Women (INSTRAW). This site serves as a gateway to UN information and data about women across the globe. It also provides a continually changing forum on international women's issues, as well as a place to exchange

information and ideas concerning women's issues. This site includes information on the UN's work on behalf of women all over the world, the global agenda for improving the status of women, UN committees and conferences, and activities of the Commission on the Status of Women. The site includes a news archive, publications, and statistics pertaining to women of all ethnic groups.

299. *World Bank: GenderNet.* http://www.worldbank.org/gender/.

This informative site provides gender profiles by country, statistics, a list of publications, news, links to other pertinent sites, and links to the World Bank project for women. The World Bank project focuses on the following: developing strategies to define and implement gender policies, spreading the knowledge and tools necessary to achieve such policies, and strengthening partnerships and dialogue with other organizations about gender.

Development

300. *GenderReach.* http://www.genderreach.com/.

GenderReach is the official Web site for the Office of Women in Development (WID), which was established in 1974 to ensure that women participate fully in and benefit equally from U.S. development assistance programs. The WID office assists the U.S. Agency for International Development (USAID) with the integration of gender concerns into USAID programs and identifies gender as a key concern in relevant emerging issues. The four major objectives of the office include enhancing the economic status of women, expanding educational opportunities for girls and women, improving women's legal rights and increasing their participation in society, and incorporating gender concerns into USAID programs. The Web site features Office of Women in Development publications, including bulletins, newsletters, fact sheets, and reports. These publications focus on international women's issues, such as trafficking, economics, war, education, and violence. This Web site provides detailed descriptions of various projects under the "activities" link.

301. *United Nations Development Program: Gender in Development.* http://www.undp.org/gender/.

The United Nations Development Program (UNDP) is the world's largest multilateral source of grant funding for development cooperation. Major goals of the UNDP include ending poverty, improving the environment, creating jobs, and advancing the status of women. The site contains press releases (in English, French, and Spanish), UN documents, publications, and videos, reports, news about conferences, a list of WWW servers worldwide, and an online forum.

4 Business, Economics, and Labor

Jill Morstad and Tracy Bicknell-Holmes

Since the publication of the second edition of this bibliography in 1987, the focus of writing and research on women in business, labor, and economics has remained faithful to several constants: the documentation and analysis of occupational sex segregation, equal employment, and the important work of recovering the histories of working women in blue-collar as well as professional jobs. One category—the needs of working mothers—has arguably been expanded to include the notion of working families even as the research shows that women still do most of the housework and child care in addition to any paid job they may have outside the home, and that divorced women and single mothers still suffer economically. *Women's work* and *women working* remain cultural referents in need of further definition. Subjects represented in this section include women and work (including international aspects and race/ethnicity), feminist economic theory, sexual harassment in the workplace, comparable worth, glass ceilings, nontraditional careers, unions and the labor movement, economic and labor histories, unpaid household labor, sex segregation in careers/professions, independent wage earners, women/gender (race/ethnicity) in specific careers/professions, international economic development/conditions, technology in the workplace, and blue-collar workers. The "Monographs" section is subdivided into three categories: "Economics, Development, and Globalization"; "Business, Entrepreneurship, and Labor"; and "Workplace Issues, Unions, and Activism."

In addition to its research capabilities, the World Wide Web has emerged as a terrific networking resource for women. We have included representative noncommercial sites (national and international) providing timely information about work-related issues, business directories, government policy, nonprofits, and professional and trade organizations.

REFERENCE SOURCES

302. Dubeck, Paula J., and Kathryn Borman, eds. *Women and Work: A Handbook.* New York: Garland, 1996. 550p. bibliog. index. ISBN 0824076478.

Women and Work is an encyclopedia containing 150 entries focusing on the status of women and work in the United States. Cross-national research that places U.S. women in a broader context and compares them with women in other countries is also mentioned. The entries are grouped into eight categories: labor-force participation patterns, approaches to analyzing women's work, occupations, factors influencing career and occupation choice, legal factors impacting work and opportunities, work experiences and the organizational context of work, work/family issues, and cross-cultural and international studies. Each signed entry consists of a two- to three-page summary of the topic, supplemented with statistics and historical context, where appropriate, and includes a set of references pointing users to further sources for more in-depth research. The volume provides author and subject indexes.

303. Ferber, Marianne A. *Women and Work, Paid and Unpaid: A Selected Annotated Bibliography.* New York: Garland, 1987. 408p. (Garland Reference Library of Social Science, v. 315). index. ISBN 0824086902.

Ferber focuses on economics literature from 1960 through the mid-1980s, with references to related fields that made particularly important contributions to economics. The bibliography contains mainly original, scholarly works and primary sources and includes worldwide information where available. Ferber usefully notes argumentative, speculative titles, titles where the content raises questions about the intent of the publication, whether the title focuses on theory, methodology, empirical evidence, or policy issues, and whether more technical titles require a background in mathematics or economics. *Women and Work* contains 1,031 annotated entries divided into nine major sections, each arranged alphabetically by author, covering topics such as occupations, earnings, discrimination, unemployment, labor-force participation, family issues, and general works. The volume includes a list of journal name abbreviations and subject and author indexes.

304. Ghorayshi, Parvin. *Women and Work in Developing Countries: An Annotated Bibliography.* Westport, CT: Greenwood Press, 1994. 223p. index. ISBN 0313288348.

Ghorayshi's critical bibliography focuses on the nature of women's work in developing countries "in all its variations and permutations" (p. xii). A section on general works outlines essential, overall themes such as theory, methodology, and economic, social, and political theory. Sections that follow examine the themes in more detail by region: Africa, Asia, Latin America and the Caribbean, and the Middle East. The book also contains a section of audiovisual resources, an appendix of women's organizations and resource centers, and indexes by subject, author, country, and region.

305. Marman, Marie, and Thelma H. Tate. *Women in Agriculture: A Guide to Research.* New York: Garland, 1996. 298p. (Women's History and Culture, 11). bibliog. index. ISBN 0815313543.

This bibliography strives to synthesize widely dispersed information on many topics addressing women working in the field of agriculture. Books included address the ways in which women have contributed to agriculture, the efforts of scholars to articulate these contributions, and the impact of gender in agricultural policy and economic development. Additionally, annotated titles reference the status of gender equity in the division of farm labor and in agricultural education. The first part of the book, organized under broad topics, lists annotations alphabetically by author. The second part of the book consists of the research guide and includes a list of studies in French, a chapter on other bibliographies, bibliographic articles in journals, book chapters, and journals that publish materials on topics related to women farmers or women in agriculture. A final section lists electronic resources and print indexes.

306. Schneider, Dorothy, and Carl J. Schneider. *The ABC-CLIO Companion to Women in the Workplace.* Santa Barbara, CA: ABC-CLIO, 1993. 371p. (ABC-CLIO Companions to Key Issues in American History and Life). bibliog. index. ISBN 0874366941.

The authors present an interesting and valuable text filled with definitions of terminology unique or significant to women's work history, such as "Harvey Girls" and "boarding." They focus on paid work and the impact of household labor on our understanding of paid work in the United States. In addition to entries on terminology, the book contains brief biographical statements on key figures in women's labor history, summaries of important legal cases relevant to women's labor, discussions of women's issues such as "academic women" and "dress for success," and histories of organizations. All entries conclude with a brief list of references, and many supplement text with photographs and illustrations. The book begins with a brief but informative look at women's labor history in North America from colonial times to the 1990s and contains an extremely useful chronology of women's employment history.

307. Wilkinson, Carroll Wetzel. *Women Working in Nontraditional Fields: References and Resources, 1963–1988*. Boston: G. K. Hall, 1991. 213p. index. ISBN 081618934X.

This reference text cites and categorizes jobs in American society still considered unusual and sometimes exceptional for women to hold. It is intended as a sourcebook of qualitative, bibliographic analysis of a significant portion of the twenty-five years of literature on women in nontraditional jobs and occupations. Reference sources used to construct this research include four major bibliographic studies on the subject of women in nontraditional occupations, as well as the work of scholars whose own efforts made extensive use of bibliographic analysis.

MONOGRAPHS

Economics, Development, and Globalization

308. Albelda, Randy Pearl. *Economics and Feminism: Disturbances in the Field*. New York: Twayne, 1997. 222p. bibliog. index. ISBN 0805797599.

Despite an introductory acknowledgment that feminism has had little historical influence in the field of economics, this survey text identifies feminism's impact on American economic thought, practice, and policy. Part 1 examines the history of women in the field and in the profession, presenting relevant data compiled over thirty years. Part 2 outlines and categorizes the responses of a random sample of American Economic Association (AEA) members surveyed in 1992, empirically documenting "for the first time ever" feminism's marginal impact on economics. Part 3 looks at economic methodology and the reproduction of ideas in economics as they intersect with gender and feminist theory, suggestive of the potential for feminism to redefine economics as a discipline and as a profession. Illustrated with tables and figures throughout, this title contains useful, accessible information for feminists unfamiliar with economics and economists unfamiliar with feminism.

Women of Value: Feminist Essays on the History of Women in Economics (Edward Elgar, 1995), edited by Mary Ann Dimond, Robert W. Dimond, and Evelyn L. Forget, provides historical background on the topic and recovers accomplishments of women economists in the United States and Great Britain. The book contains analysis of women economists' doctoral dissertations and research specialties between 1900 and 1940, mentoring practices, and networking efforts. Several chapters review the work and contributions of specific economists such as Harriet Taylor, Barbara Bodichon, and Charlotte Perkins Gilman.

309. Amott, Teresa L. *Caught in the Crisis: Women and the US Economy Today*. New York: Monthly Review Press, 1993. 160p. (Cornerstone Books). bibliog. index. ISBN 0853458456; 0853458464pa.

Amott explores both positive and negative impacts of an economic slowdown on women. She evaluates how class, race, ethnicity, sexual orientation, age, and family status shape women's choices and opportunities, and ways in which women resist the economic crisis. The book begins with a brief history of the development of women's economic roles and the economic and social hierarchies that create similarities and differences among women of various racial/ethnic groups and classes. It continues with an exploration of the nature and causes of the economic crisis, the impact on women's wages, working conditions and opportunities for advancement, the increasing burden of unpaid work in the home, and the impact of conservative legislative, health, job safety, child care, and welfare policies. The book is readable and peppered with quotes; however, readers should keep in mind that Amott's focus on radical feminist economics puts a definite bias into her arguments.

Bette Woody's extensively researched *Black Women in the Workplace: Impacts of Structural Change in the Economy* (Greenwood Press, 1992) traces black women's labor participation from 1930 through the 1980s. Woody compares black women with white women, white men, and black men in terms of wages/benefits, work sites, and educational and occupational statuses as the U.S. economy transitioned from industry to service. The author examines social and political factors that affect the rate and quality of work experiences of women, particularly African American women.

310. Aslanbeigu, Nahid, Steven Pressman, and Gale Summerfield, eds. *Women in the Age of Economic Transformation: Gender Impact of Reforms in Post-socialist and Developing Countries.* New York: Routledge, 1994. 232p. bibliog. index. ISBN (OP); 0415104238pa.

Chapters in this exceptional collection explore economic transitions in countries in Eastern Europe, Africa, Asia, and South America. Several of the well-designed case studies investigate country transitions using a framework of gender equity in terms of employment, child care, maternity leave, health, and entrepreneurial opportunities. Others examine economic consequences for women in countries undergoing privatization and other economic structural changes. Unfortunately, most findings indicate that conditions for women deteriorate no matter what kind of transition takes place.

Barbara Lobodzinska chooses to focus on women in transitional European economies in *Family, Women, and Employment in Central-Eastern Europe* (Greenwood Press, 1995). She examines the political, economic, and social transitions that altered life, family, and gender relationships after the events of 1989 in several countries, including Bulgaria, the Czech and Slovak Republics, the former German Democratic Republic within united Germany, Hungary, Lithuania, Poland, Romania, Slovenia, and Serbia. The book presents views generated by two ways of life and two types of research experience, capitalist and socialist. Consequently, it evolves into a discourse between domestic experts and Western specialists. Throughout, contributors analyze aspects of family and women's life that differ from those in Western democracies: legislation, the economy, social services, political participation, employment, income, educational priorities, agriculture, health care, and attendant changes in attitudes. The conclusion takes a closer look at technology and its impact on the changing economy (and women's lives) of the region.

311. Aymer, Paula. *Uprooted Women: Migrant Domestics in the Caribbean.* Westport, CT: Praeger, 1997. 172p. bibliog. index. ISBN 0275958833.

This close and intimate look at the lives and work of twenty-six women—migrant domestics on the island of Aruba—examines the phenomenon of poor women who leave their homes in search of waged labor and a better life. Early chapters establish the economic basis for migrant work and the contributions of women to the regional economies. The middle sections examine migration patterns and the mobilization of workers. In later chapters the women tell their own stories, and the author recontextualizes the labor of migrant women within the history of the Caribbean and contemporary transnational relations with the United States.

Muchachas No More: Household Workers in Latin America and the Caribbean (Temple University Press, 1989), edited by Elsa M. Chaney and Mary Garcia Castro, also explores central issues pertaining to domestic workers in the region. Chapters analyze the work domestics do, why this work is undervalued, and the recruitment of domestics from poor, uneducated, or indigenous women who are socially isolated and denied the means to organize. The collection is notable for including a multiplicity of voices, from scholars to the workers themselves, and its extensive historical context. *Maid in the U.S.A.* (Routledge, 1992) by Mary Romero concentrates on employers of Latina and, to a lesser extent, African American domestic workers in the United States. The author divides employers into six categories: bosses, utopian feminists, dodgers and duckers, victims, maternalists, and contractors. More important, she scrutinizes the daily activities of the workers, incorporating historical and twentieth-century perspectives into her analysis.

312. Beneria, Lourdes, and Shelley Feldman, eds. *Unequal Burden: Economic Crises, Persistent Poverty, and Women's Work.* Boulder, CO: Westview Press, 1992. 278p. bibliog. index. ISBN 0813382297; 0813382300pa.

Unequal Burden collects essays about the debt crisis of the 1980s and its impact on women worldwide. Beneria and Feldman's work stems from the pioneering work of UNICEF, *Adjustment with a Human Face* (1987), and a UNICEF workshop, "Economic Crisis, Household Strategies, and Women's Work," held in September 1988. The editors argue that the International Monetary Fund (IMF) model of structural adjustment policies did not succeed in promoting growth, but indeed created unequal, polarized distribution of income, placing the burden of foreign debt on poor people, mostly women. The remaining chapters present original work from the workshop and discuss the debt crisis and its impact on women in various world regions.

Development, Crises, and Alternative Visions: Third World Women's Perspectives (Monthly Review Press, 1987) by Gita Sen and Caren Grown serves as an excellent introduction to the topic. Writing the book for the organization Development Alternatives with Women for a New Era (DAWN), the authors present feminist perspectives of broad trends in structural adjustment policies and make concrete, practical suggestions for changes at international, national, regional, and organizational levels. In *Bringing Women In: Women's Issues in International Development Programs* (Lynne Rienner, 1991), Nuket Kardam evaluates responses by the United Nations Development Program, the World Bank, and the Ford Foundation to attempts by international women's groups to influence their definitions, policies, and programs. *Women and Adjustment Policies in the Third World* (St. Martin's Press, 1992), edited by Haleh Afshar and Carolyne Dennis, collects critical examinations of IMF and World Bank policies. In *Mortgaging Women's Lives: Feminist Critiques of Structural Adjustments* (Zed Books, 1994), Pamela Sparr offers another critique of World Bank policies.

313. Boris, Eileen, and Elisabeth Prügl, eds. *Homeworkers in Global Perspective: Invisible No More.* New York: Routledge, 1996. 327p. bibliog. index. (OP)

Chapters in this intriguing collection situate homework as a strategy within the global economy. Contributors relate homework to women's reproductive work and the socially constructed idea of women as "housewives," who do not do "real work." They conclude that home-based labor counts as work and that increasing activities in the informal sector affects gendered division of labor within families and households. *Living Rooms as Factories: Class, Gender, and the Satellite Factory System in Taiwan* (Temple University Press, 1996) by Ping-Chun Hsiung and *The Crossroads of Class and Gender: Industrial Homework, Subcontracting, and Household Dynamics in Mexico City* (University of Chicago Press, 1987) by Lourdes Beneria and Martha Roldan provide perspectives from specific countries on the topic. Ping-Chun Hsiung combines macro data analysis and feminist ethnography in her examination of married women, home workers, government policy, kinship, and international capital. The author concludes that a repressive labor policy, a patriarchal culture, kinship's role in discouraging collective action, and international economic forces combine to exploit women's productive and reproductive work and reinforce gender divisions of labor. Beneria and Roldan connect gender with the segmentation of both the labor market and production to argue that development plans must consider ideological constraints about women as well as raise income. The authors also explore the impact of homework on urban economies, examine the role women's homework plays in increasing their status within the household, and describe women's collective actions.

314. Dignard, Louise, and José Havet, eds. *Women in Micro- and Small-Scale Enterprise Development.* Boulder, CO: Westview Press, 1995. 282p. bibliog. index. (OP)

This important collection of studies begins with an introduction exploring the many difficulties in defining the term "women's micro- and small-scale enterprises" (WMSEs) and discussing major issues and the importance of social context. The heart of the book consists of case studies on WMSEs in various Asian, Caribbean/Latin American, and African countries and discussions recommending strategies for overcoming cultural, behavioral, and social constraints such as lack of family support and poor access to credit, information, appropriate technologies, and training. This title contributes to the WMSE literature, raises new questions, and identifies specific areas needing more research.

The studies collected in *Money-Go-Rounds: The Importance of Rotating Savings and Credit Associations for Women* (Berg, 1995), edited by Shirley Ardner and Sandra Burman, apply an inductive methodology, based on comparisons of different kinds of ROSCAs operating in different socioeconomic contexts. This method enables contributors to focus on both disadvantages and strengths of women and elicits practical information with important ramifications for policy and action. *Women at the Center: Grameen Bank Borrowers after One Decade* (Westview Press, 1996) by Helen Todd follows the lives of women in two villages for a period of two years as they create self-employment opportunities or buy land to ensure their own and their families' survival. Todd, a journalist, documents the slow increases in women's empowerment, self-esteem, and family status. She also suggests that a secure land title system and the bank's belief in the resourcefulness and family loyalty of poor women helped create an entrepreneurial culture that was key to the bank's success.

315. Ferber, Marianne A., and Julie A. Nelson, eds. *Beyond Economic Man: Feminist Theory and Economics.* Chicago: University of Chicago Press, 1993. 178p. bibliog. index. ISBN 0226242005; 0226242013pa.

Ferber and Nelson collect essays that explore possible implications of feminist theories to reframe science with particular applications to economics. The editors point out that men dominate the profession of economics and that most economic studies ignore women and female-dominated professions. Furthermore, they assert that simply adding women to the analysis may not be sufficient and question the tools of analysis and popular theories of economics. For example, most models do not adequately consider issues of dependence, interdependence, tradition, and power. Contributors investigate topics such as masculine biases embedded in mathematical models of individual choice, the neoclassical premise of economic agent as a separate economic self, differences in men's and women's economic lives and cognitive styles and how these might impact economic theory, the interplay of socialism and feminism in economics, and feminist institutional approaches to economics. Nelson, in *Feminism, Objectivity, and Economics* (Routledge, 1996), proposes a "gender value compass" designed to reveal how gender relationships influence male-biased economic theory and methods. She then applies her framework to economics history, feminist theories of the family, household equivalence scales, federal taxation of the family unit (and the "marriage tax"), and welfare. Finally, she answers various criticisms of feminist economics and provides an extensive bibliography.

Chris Beasley also points to limitations of existing analyses of women in economic theories in *Sexual Economyths: Conceiving a Feminist Economics* (St. Martin's Press, 1994). She presents an overview of feminist economic analysis, Marxist thought, and household work studies in terms of women's unpaid labor in the home to develop a feminist materialist economic theory and sexual epistemology of economics. *Feminism and Anti-feminism in Early Economic Thought* (Elgar Publications, 1992) by Michele A. Pujol stands as one of the first critical evaluations of neoclassical economics in terms of its treatment of women and their work. Pujol traces the development of this school of thought, exposing male biases in methodologies and assumptions that helped determine its approach toward women. The author argues that the discipline of economics has been socially constructed and that neoclassical theory still contains nineteenth-century stereotypes of women and their roles.

316. Folbre, Nancy. *Who Pays for the Kids? Gender and the Structure of Constraint.* New York: Routledge, 1994. 335p. (Economics and Social Theory). bibliog. index. ISBN (OP); 0415075653pa.

Informed by feminist perspectives, Folbre critiques traditional theories of economics, notably classical liberalism and Marxism, in terms of how they explain costs of social reproduction. She believes that preoccupation with market forces obscures the importance of power relationships between men and women and between parents and children and results in the devaluation of family labor. The author counters with a framework she calls structures of constraint, asserting that these sometimes conflicting constraints (such as gender, age, sexual orientation, class, race, and nation) profoundly affect individual economic status. Folbre applies her framework to historical analysis of the northwestern European welfare state, economic development in the United States, and colonial development in Latin America and the Caribbean and succeeds in providing more complex, fuller understandings of economic development, social welfare, and politics.

Like Folbre, Antonella Picchio, in *Social Reproduction: The Political Economy and the Labour Market* (Cambridge University Press, 1992), provides a feminist analysis of tensions in the relationship between commodity production and social reproduction. Picchio, however, restores the concept of the natural price of labor as a cost of social reproduction, determined by social and cultural norms, institutions, and processes, to the central place it held in classical surplus frameworks. She argues that prevailing neoclassical economic theories view the price of labor as mechanistically determined by market forces, which exclude traditional women's work, thereby offering only a limited understanding of the realities of the labor market. Using historical cases, such as the British Poor Laws, the author points out problems, especially for women, that result when the needs of capitalistic accumulation drive social policies. Picchio closes with a framework that views labor supply as based on social processes of reproduction. Both titles provide provocative, feminist challenges to the so-called objectivity and gender neutrality of neoclassical economic thought.

317. French, John D., and Daniel James, eds. *The Gendered Worlds of Latin American Women Workers: From Household and Factory to the Union Hall and Ballot Box.* Durham, NC: Duke University Press, 1997. 320p. (Comparative and International Working-Class History). bibliog. index. ISBN (OP); 0822319969pa.

Editors French and James write first and last chapters that provide a coherent theoretical context for the chapters collected in this volume. The collection seeks to analyze male and female relationships at work in terms of both gender and class in order to present fuller representations of all aspects of working women's material lives. To this end, most contributors incorporate oral histories and testimonies into the statistical, historical, and other factual information presented in their chapters. Striving for depth of coverage, the editors devote two chapters to Argentina, three to Brazil, two to Chile, and one chapter apiece to Colombia and Guatemala. This excellent collection uses complementary theoretical and methodological approaches that uncover numerous levels of oppression in working women's lives.

Additional titles examining various aspects of women, work, and economics in Latin America include Florence E. Babb's *Between Field and Cooking Pot: The Political Economy of Marketwomen in Peru* (University of Texas Press, 1989; rev. ed., 1998) and *Women's Ventures: Assistance to the Informal Sector in Latin America* (Kumarian, 1989), edited by Marguerite Berger and Mayra Buvinic. Babb presents an analysis of the diverse products, political participation, competition, and generational conflicts among women street vendors in the informal economies in a highland town. In *Women's Ventures* several contributors present case studies examining women's work in the informal sector, especially microenterprise and credit programs. Others explore the effects of training and assistance programs in terms of gender. This important book discusses key issues concerning women's employment and enhances the visibility and importance of microenterprise for women.

318. Ghorayshi, Parvin, and Claire Belanger, eds. *Women, Work, and Gender Relations in Developing Countries: A Global Perspective.* Westport, CT: Greenwood Press, 1996. 246p. (Contributions in Sociology, no. 118). bibliog. index. ISBN 0313297975.

Chapters in this informative collection explore interactions between the sexual division of labor, production site, gender, and power. The first section articulates theoretical and methodology considerations, including a dialogue with Nawal El Saadawi, an Egyptian feminist scholar, psychiatrist, and novelist. The next section presents case studies illustrating the many ways women contribute to family, community, national, and global economies. The two final sections consist of studies highlighting empowerment strategies that challenge assumptions of capitalism and stress the importance of self-organization. This excellent title includes some English translations of materials originally published in French, German, and Spanish and contains a useful, wide-ranging bibliography.

Contributors to *Engendering Wealth and Well-Being: Empowerment for Global Change* (Westview Press, 1995), edited by Rae Lesser Blumberg, Cathy Rakowski, Irene Tinker, and Michael Monteon, also focus on women's contributions to economies in studies of countries such as Guatemala, Turkey, Kenya, and Taiwan. They particularly examine interconnections between the economy and the household, linking women's economic contributions to empowerment of themselves, their families, and their communities. The book also serves as a useful history of women in development since the 1970s. Both collections underscore the importance of cross-national research recognizing that various outcomes of economic development affect women very differently from men.

319. Gonzalez de la Rocha, Mercedes. *The Resources of Poverty: Women and Survival in a Mexican City.* Cambridge, MA: Blackwell, 1994. 311p. bibliog. index. ISBN 0631192239.

This important English-language study places poor women at the center of inquiry linking household organization to labor participation. The author recognizes the important relationship between structural constraints and individual choices, highlighting the importance of such "private" issues as violence, male alcoholism, and family decision-making and budgeting processes to household survival. Gonzalez de la Rocha helps break stereotypes of low-income women in developing regions. Patricia Zavella studies the connections between household structures and Mexican women's participation in the workforce in the United States in *Women's Work and Chicano Families: Cannery Workers of the Santa Clara Valley* (Cornell University Press, 1987). The author combines ethnographic and historical approaches in her examination of the influence of work culture and experience on Chicana women's roles and expectations within the family. This study is particularly notable for its attention to inter- and intraethnic divisions of the workers. Fiona Wilson, more interested in employment settings than the previous authors, considers economic arrangements in a small-scale rural knitwear factory in *Sweaters: Gender, Class, and Workshop-Based Industry in Mexico* (St. Martin's Press, 1991). The author uses gender (as well as class and ethnicity) as her theoretical framework to explore women workers' interpretations of gender relations and how they changed as the factory grew.

320. Hijab, Nadia. *Womanpower: The Arab Debate on Women at Work.* New York: Cambridge University Press, 1988. 176p. (Cambridge Middle East Library). bibliog. index. ISBN (OP); 052126992pa.

Hijab draws on observations and interviews in the Arab world, as well as Arab and Western writing on Arab society, politics, and economy as seen through an examination of the debate on Arab women at work. Selected chapters provide in-depth explorations of Arab family law, cultural loyalty (both conservative and liberal), Arab women working, and economic conditions in Jordan and the Arab Gulf States. Hijab correlates factors apart from gender, such as religion, national independence, colonization, and cultural power, with the relative rate of economic development in the Arab states and believes that equal rights and empowerment for women are connected to the struggle for an Arab identity in the region.

Women in Arab Society: Work Patterns and Gender Relations in Egypt, Jordan, and Sudan (Berg, 1990), edited by Shami Seteney, Lucine Taminian, Soheir A. Morsy, Zeinab B. El Bakri, and El-Wathig M. Kameir, provides a social science perspective of the continuing efforts of UNESCO to work with scholars in the study of gender relations and of constraints to women's equality in the social and economic life in their societies. The studies document the differing forms and types of women's work in both rural and urban contexts, where the status and roles of women in the public and private sphere remain disadvantaged compared to those of men. This collection also reveals the ways in which women do wield power and influence, and how they work out both daily and longer-term economic and survival strategies for their families, kin, and communities.

321. Mies, Maria. *Patriarchy and Accumulation on a World Scale: Women in the International Division of Labor.* Atlantic Highlands, NJ: Zed Books, 1986. 251p. bibliog. index. ISBN 086232341X. New ed. with preface, Zed Books, 1998. 251p.

In this key text, Mies traces the history of the sexual division of labor in an effort to determine how nonwage labor affected unequal wages in the twentieth century. The author believes that capitalist patriarchy serves as the modern manifestation of a 5,000-year-old exploitive system whereby nonproductive men depended on and appropriated women's productive work, setting up a hierarchy of consumers and producers that still underpins capitalism's relentless cycle of expansion and accumulation. The author also contends that this led to an ideology she calls "housewifization," which naturalized women's dependent role and rendered their work invisible. Over time housewifization, combined with capitalism, allowed European countries to justify colonization and the destruction of nature. Mies insightfully analyzes gender divisions, class dynamics, and North-South hierarchies historically and globally.

Another theorist concerned with patriarchy and capitalism, Sylvia Walby, answers the criticism from feminists, most notably postmodernists, who dismiss patriarchy as an outmoded, ahistorical, and universalizing concept. In her books *Patriarchy at Work: Patriarchal and Capitalist Relations in Employment* (University of Minnesota Press, 1986) and *Theorizing Patriarchy* (Blackwell, 1990), Walby counters by claiming that postmodernism ignores changing social contexts of power relations and fails to recognize systemic oppressions of gender, race, and class. She also maintains that examining the intersections of racism, capitalism, and patriarchy in the context of the international division of labor helps explain persistent economic and social inequalities. Sharon Stichter and Jane L. Parpart, editors of *Women, Employment, and the Family in the International Division of Labor* (Temple University Press, 1990), claim that previous studies slight the importance of household structure as a factor influencing patterns of women's labor-force participation in developing countries. Contributors, using different methodologies and representing a variety of disciplines, find that the structure of households often mirrors patriarchal employment structures and state policies even though these vary by cultural and economic context. They also demonstrate the importance of recognizing women's productive and reproductive contributions to both economy and household and of understanding the many interactions between them.

322. Moghadam, Valentine. *Women, Work, and Economic Reform in the Middle East and Northern Africa.* Boulder, CO: Lynne Rienner, 1998. 259p. bibliog. index. ISBN 1555877850.

Basing her work on extensive fieldwork as well as a synthesis of world survey data for the region, Moghadam uses a gender contract framework to evaluate women's labor participation during the 1990s structural adjustments in Turkey, Jordan, Syria, Iran, Egypt, Morocco, Tunisia, and Algeria. She believes that understanding connections between women, work, and education provides a critical basis for developing more effective adjustment policies that could eventually empower women by expediting their economic participation and transforming patriarchal gender contracts. She also supplies a useful survey of women's nongovernmental organizations in the region. This important book provides solid information about globalization, gender constraints in employment, education, and training, labor legislation, and the informal sector in each country and contains practical suggestions for their improvement.

Titles providing research on women's labor in specific countries in the region include *Accommodating Protest: Working Women, the New Veiling, and Change in Cairo* (Columbia University Press, 1991) by Arlene Elowe Macleod and *Money Makes Us Relatives: Women's Labor in Urban Turkey* (University of Texas Press, 1994) by Jenny B. White. Macleod's ethnographic study depicts the dilemmas of lower-class women who must juggle their belief in traditional values with the necessity for wage work in a rapidly changing society. The "new veiling" is symbolic of women's acquiescence and resistance to this struggle. White focuses on changes to traditional social networks caused by women who do piecework in their homes. This situation causes households to become more flexible but has created new forms of "kinship" that increase women's obligations and duties to neighbors and community.

323. Robb, Carol S. *Equal Value: An Ethical Approach to Economics and Sex.* Boston: Beacon Press, 1995. 198p. bibliog. index. (OP)

Robb articulates a theory of social and sexual justice in economic terms, completely informed by her work as a theologian. This text collapses economies of gender, economies of state, and economies of social structure into an overarching construct of ethical principles and practices that could lead to true equality. Robb's introduction reviews the legal and sacred literature and defines her concept of justice, the moral principle centering her argument. The introduction also develops a working definition of economics and economies, so that chapters examining topics such as sexual harassment, violence, and childbearing can delineate the ways in which sex (gender) compromises women's experiences and their continued and continuing access to the public forum.

In *Women and Ethics in the Workplace* (Praeger, 1997), editors Candice Frederick and Camille Atkinson, with backgrounds in religion and philosophy, respectively, collect chapters critically analyzing gendered assumptions embedded in capitalism and consequent impacts of these assumptions at work. Contributors combine theory with statistical data, personal narratives, and case studies about issues such as sexual harassment, comparable worth, advertising, leadership, and working-class concerns. Designed as a textbook, this title does a very good job of defining terms, providing concrete examples, and revealing the complexities involved in the issues, but could have included more race analysis.

324. Rowbotham, Sheila, and Swasti Mitter, eds. *Dignity and Daily Bread: New Forms of Economic Organising in the Third World and the First.* New York: Routledge, 1994. 233p. bibliog. index. ISBN 0415095859; 0415095867pa.

An outgrowth of the Women's Programme of the World Institute for Development Economics Research (WIDER), this collection of historical and twentieth-century case studies examines women's grassroots efforts to overcome poverty. Contributors call into question prevailing separations between market processes, state policies, and poor women's lives. They focus on women's resourceful organizing, cooperative, and networking initiatives in a variety of contexts and locations, including the garment industry in Mexico, free trade zones in Malaysia, the Philippines, and Sri Lanka, sweat work in Great Britain, and the Self Employed Women's Association (SEWA) in India. The chapters suggest that women's responses to economic vulnerability can indeed influence economic and social processes and that gender relations, work, family, the state, and international economic contexts must be examined in order to develop appropriate, effective long-term development policies and processes. In *Where Women Are Leaders: The SEWA Movement in India* (Zed Books, 1992), author Kalima Rose presents an informative history of this movement. The author bases her narrative on eighteen months of interviews with SEWA members and executive committee activists. She concludes that SEWA's efforts to sustain old members while attracting new ones and its flexibility in response to changing circumstances and locations help make the association successful and provide a basis for similar projects elsewhere in the world.

325. Safa, Helen Icken. *Myth of the Male Breadwinner: Women and Industrialization in the Caribbean.* Boulder, CO: Westview Press, 1995. 208p. (Conflict and Social Change Series). bibliog. index. ISBN 0813312116; 0813312124pa.

Safa compares women's paid industrial employment in Puerto Rico, the Dominican Republic, and Cuba in terms of how women's labor participation influences household structures. She challenges several myths associated with the region, among them that men are the primary earners. Her findings also reveal that both state and work policies, particularly in the Dominican Republic, reinforce traditional patriarchal family structures and allow occupational segregation and wage differentials favoring men to remain in place.

In *Puerto Rican Women and Work: Bridges in Transnational Labor* (Temple University Press, 1996), edited by Altagracia Ortiz, contributors make intriguing comparisons of women in Puerto Rico and the United States that suggest a link between U.S. economic structural changes and the feminization of poverty. Other excellent titles that illustrate interactions between work, gender, class, race, and ethnicity in the region include *Producing Power: Ethnicity, Gender, and*

Class in a Caribbean Workplace (Temple University Press, 1995) by Kevin A. Yelvington and *Women, Labour, and Politics in Trinidad and Tobago: A History* (Zed Books, 1994) by Rhoda Reddock. Yelvington studies power interactions between (mostly male) white and East Indian supervisors and (mostly female) black and East Indian shop workers. He concludes that power relations help construct ideas about gender, race, and ethnicity that are re-created in work situations. Reddock finds that women's work varies by class, ethnicity, and color and encourages a new conceptualization of work activities, particularly women's. She also connects feminist grassroots activism with the labor movement and the struggle toward democracy.

326. Stichter, Sharon B., and Jane L. Parpart, eds. *Patriarchy and Class: African Women in the Home and Workforce.* Boulder, CO: Westview Press, 1988. 233p. (OP)

The contributors to this volume take steps toward theorizing the relations between production and reproduction and tracing their historical interconnections. The essays draw from eastern, western, central, and southern Africa, exploring such topics as women's position in agricultural production, women's position in wage labor, and women both within and outside of marriage and the household. All the essays use a materialist approach to patriarchy, discuss Marxism, and acknowledge that Western feminists need to understand and support the efforts of African women to set priorities for economic and social change.

Titles representing research on other perspectives of women, work, the economy, and Africa include Claire C. Robertson's *Trouble Showed the Way: Women, Men, and Trade in Nairobi, 1890–1990* (Indiana University Press, 1997), a well-researched and thoughtful study that reveals the historical importance of women traders to the East African economy and powerfully documents survival strategies of women with few resources, and Ingrid Palmer's *Gender and Population in the Adjustment of African Economies* (International Labour Office, 1991), in which the author explores the huge gap between women's economic responsibilities and their access to resources (landownership, credit, markets, education), especially in sub-Saharan areas, that renders adjustment policies inefficient and ineffective.

327. Waring, Marilyn. *If Women Counted: A New Feminist Economics.* New York: Harper & Row, 1989. 386p. bibliog. index. ISBN 0062509330.

In this very important work, Waring condemns the United Nations System of National Accounts (UNSNA), the system used by most countries as well as the World Bank and the International Monetary Fund for measuring and rewarding economic value, as inherently flawed and sexist. The author, an economist who chaired the Public Expenditure Select Committee as a member of Parliament in New Zealand from 1975 to 1984, reveals how the UNSNA's dependence on quantitative statistical analysis makes women's work completely invisible by not counting unpaid labor and distorts the economic value of surplus production. She clearly explains economic processes and definitions, using diverse examples from many cultures and countries to illustrate her arguments. Believing that reproduction is the most basic form of production, Waring concludes by offering an alternative system that incorporates qualitative assessments for measuring a nation's economic value, assigns monetary value to women's unpaid labor, and includes environmental indicators that calculate pollution and destruction. In a second edition titled *Counting for Nothing: What Men Value and What Women Are Worth* (University of Toronto Press, 1999), Waring updates various arguments in a lengthy introduction.

Women's unpaid labor is also the subject of *Work without Wages: Domestic Labor and Self-Employment within Capitalism* (State University of New York Press, 1990), edited by Jane L. Collins and Martha Gimenez. Contributors present Marxist analysis of women's unwaged domestic labor in industrialized nations and unwaged productive labor, such as farming, informal economies, and the like, in developing countries. All contributors place their studies within the context of market processes and class relations of capitalism. Although the chapters examine diverse settings, all reveal that the reproduction of social relations (gender, class, family, and community) essentially depends on women's unwaged labor.

Business, Entrepreneurship, and Labor

328. Adler, Nancy J., and Dafna N. Izraeli, eds. *Competitive Frontiers: Women Managers in a Global Economy.* Cambridge, MA: Blackwell, 1993. 414p. bibliog. index. ISBN (OP); 1557865108pa.

Expanding on the work in their previous collection, *Women in Management Worldwide* (M.E. Sharpe, 1988), an attempt to explain the small number of women in top management positions, the editors collect chapters exploring the changing nature of world business and its impact on women managers in twenty-one countries on four continents. They view women managers via a broader social context in order to find international commonalities of success and exclusion from four perspectives that, they believe, combine to limit the upward mobility of women: individual difference between woman and man, organizational context, institutional discrimination, and powers of influence within organizations. The volume includes a chapter by Adler outlining research that attempts to dispel three myths of women expatriates: that women do not want to be international managers, that companies refuse to send women abroad, and that foreigners' prejudice renders women ineffective.

Other volumes that examine the subject in various countries include Morgan Tanton's *Women in Management: A Developing Presence* (Routledge, 1994), which discusses future directions for women managers with essays aimed at particular issues such as emotions at work, the white male management heritage, motherhood, and reasons women leave senior management positions, and *European Women in Business and Management* (P. Chapman, 1993), edited by Marilyn J. Davidson and Cary L. Cooper, an overview of women's employment issues in the European Economic Union, with detailed country profiles that provide insight on the diverse, complex historical and cultural factors involved in women and work.

329. Allen, Sheila, and Carole Truman, eds. *Women in Business: Perspectives on Women Entrepreneurs.* London: Routledge, 1993. 180p. bibliog. index. ISBN 0415063116; 0415063124pa.

Allen and Truman state that a broader understanding of the process and practices of how gender relations facilitate or obstruct business activity is crucial to understanding the development and prospects for success and failure of small business enterprises. Chapters discuss small business in Great Britain and its role in the economy, with a focus on the relationship of human agency to social process and structure. The book itself originated from a series of papers presented during a 1989 conference at the University of Bradford titled "Women Entrepreneurs." It groups the chapters into three categories: classifying business enterprises, analyzing social and economic change, and themes and issues related to researching women's enterprise. While this collection points out the absence of gender in studies on entrepreneurship, *Enterprising Women: Ethnicity, Economy, and Gender Relations* (Routledge, 1988), edited by Sallie Westwood and Parminder Bhachu, connects ethnicity as well as gender to the British economy during the 1980s in its examination of relationships between formal labor-force participation, the informal sector (paid but unregulated work), homework, and housework. Discussions with Chinese, Greek Cypriot, Sikh, and Afro-Caribbean women reveal that ethnic and sex-role stereotypes and traditional family expectations present difficulties for women in terms of both work and entrepreneurship.

330. Amott, Teresa L., and Julie Matthaei. *Race, Gender, and Work: A Multicultural Economic History of Women in the United States.* Boston: South End Press, 1991. 433p. bibliog. index. (OP)

Amott and Matthaei use a method of "capitalist development" to trace women's work lives in this volume about the historical economic status of women from various cultures and races in the United States. This method explores immigration as a profit-motivated production for the market based on wage labor. The book covers colonial times to the 1990s. After the authors explain their methodology and gender, race/ethnicity, and class conceptual framework, they trace economic histories of women in each racial/ethnic group. The remainder of the book explore similarities and differences between women's work experiences across groups. This illuminating history succeeds in elucidating the complexities involved in women's paid and unpaid work and their effects on women's work as capitalist economic expansion developed historically. A second edition of this title came out in 1996 (South End Press).

Angel Kwolek-Folland's *Incorporating Women: A History of Women and Business in the United States* (Twayne, 1998) provides a unique survey of women's business ventures, beginning with seventeenth-century Native American fur traders. This title is notable for its extensive coverage of minority women's activities and its consideration of the effects of race, class, and ethnicity on women's economic opportunities. It includes appendices of U.S. census sources, definitions of occupational categories, and data on labor-force participation. *Women and Work: Exploring Race, Ethnicity, and Class* (Sage, 1997) edited by Elizabeth Higginbotham and Mary Romero, provides both historical and late-twentieth-century economic perspectives to examinations of women working within several broad job categories such as manufacturing, domestic work, the professions and management, and unpaid or volunteer work. All of these titles reinforce the importance of comparing experiences of women from various racial and ethnic backgrounds for more complex and insightful understandings of economic issues.

331. Barthel, Diane. *Putting On Appearances: Gender and Advertising.* Philadelphia: Temple University Press, 1988. 220p. (Women in the Political Economy). bibliog. index. (OP)

A somewhat problematic and, at times, troubling history and analysis of gender and gendered images in advertising, this title reflects Barthel's reliance on gender categories and behaviors drawn from essential and traditional constructions of women and men that emphasize appearances. Her central argument is that people influence advertising (and culture) as much as advertising (and culture) influence people. Her metaphors of surface and appearance become an investigative liability. Even though Barthel's analysis begins to investigate advertising's prescriptions for social behaviors and classical myth and iconography as a source for advertising's insidious presence and influence, her examinations remain only surface-level ones. Nevertheless, this book, influential at its time of publication, would be a useful text for introducing discussions of advertising's power to create desire and alter social behaviors. A supplement title is Carol Moog's *Are They Selling Her Lips? Advertising and Identity* (Morrow, 1990), an intriguing and entertaining examination of stereotypes, sex, and aggression using recognizable examples with illustrations.

332. Bartos, Rena. *Marketing to Women around the World.* Boston: Harvard Business School Press, 1989. 320p. bibliog. index. (OP)

Historically, conventional definitions of women consumers classed them as housewives or girls. Bartos has produced a groundbreaking qualitative and quantitative study of women consumers in ten countries on four continents. She bases her data on census figures, supplemented with survey data where authoritative government data were not available. In order to make a meaningful cross-national comparison, Bartos covers a consistent set of topics and issues that include demographic trends, attitudes, and marketing behavior and grounds her depiction of women consumers by occupation, education, marital status, the presence of children, and husband's occupation. She also explores marketing and advertising implications of the role of women in each country. After a discussion of why women work or do not work, which compares working women, nonworking women, and housewives, the volume examines marriage and children, lifestyle differences, and attitudes of working women and housewives toward work. The remainder of the book discusses traditional women's products, changing markets, and changing audiences.

Additional studies on the topic that focus on the United States include E. Janice Leeming and Cynthia Tripp's *Segmenting the Women's Market: Using Niche Marketing to Understand and Meet the Diverse Needs of Today's Most Dynamic Consumer Market* (Probus, 1994), a detailed discussion of segments in the women's market by age, race, income, and other significant categories such as homemakers, mothers, and singles, and Carol Nelson's *Women's Market Handbook: Understanding and Reaching Today's Most Powerful Consumer Group* (Gale, 1994), which argues that the "women's market" really consists of numerous separate niches targeting each stage of women's lives.

333. Berry, Mary Frances. *The Politics of Parenthood: Child Care, Women's Rights, and the Myth of the Good Mother.* New York: Viking, 1993. 303p. bibliog. index. ISBN 0670837059.

An exhaustive examination of the cultural construction and economics of late-twentieth-century child care in America, this text reveals how the care, education, and well-being of children of employed parents, especially mothers, is a continuing political issue. In chapters that trace the history of father care, mother care, and "other" care for children, Berry surveys various cultural histories and identifies a wide variety of approaches to family structures, work, both inside and outside the home, and raising children. She suggests that the government does not allocate funding "providing for the general welfare" because of societal ambivalence toward nonparental child care, and that societal allegiance to the idea of traditional heterosexual families allows workplaces to ignore any other definitions of family or work.

In *Balancing Act: Motherhood, Marriage, and Employment among American Women* (Sage, 1996), authors Daphne Spain and Suzanne M. Bianchi provide a comprehensive statistical snapshot of working women's lives during the 1990s. The authors combine analysis of data from sources such as the census and the Bureau of Labor Statistics, theoretical explorations, and policy discussions to examine childbearing, education, occupational attainment, earnings, and other areas. They take care to contrast conditions between women in various racial and ethnic groups and often include data from other countries to place American trends in broader perspective. Jean L. Potuchek analyzes the connection between married women's paid work and meanings given to it by husbands and wives in *Who Supports the Family? Gender and Breadwinning in Dual-Career Marriages* (Stanford University Press, 1997). Based on statistical analysis, interviews, and questionnaires from 153 dual-earner families, the author finds that women's self-perceptions as breadwinners depend on interactions between changing employment situations, external economic factors, family situations, and each spouse's beliefs about child care, domestic work, and paid work.

334. Blossfeld, Hans-Peter, and Catherine Hakim, eds. *Between Equalization and Marginalization: Women Working Part-Time in Europe and the United States of America.* New York: Oxford University Press, 1997. 333p. bibliog. index. ISBN 0198280866.

Blossfeld and Hakim present findings from their study comparing the historical development of women's part-time work in European countries and the United States, beginning after World War II. They evaluate labor-force data from three viewpoints: increased labor participation of women and decreased dependence on men affords women greater equality; increased part-time work of women marginalizes women and puts them at a disadvantage; and part-time jobs can be advantageous for dependent women and secondary wage earners within the context of the sexual division of labor in the family. The volume begins with evaluations of part-time work from comparative and sociological perspectives and follows with chapters analyzing specific regions and countries. The volume liberally illustrates text with tables and figures, provides bibliographic references after each chapter, and includes both name and subject indexes.

Part-Time Work in Europe: Gender, Jobs, and Opportunities (Campus Verlag, 1997), edited by Martina Klein, collects chapters focusing on gendered employment situations in sixteen countries, most of them European Union members. Contributors find that some countries boost employment statistics by creating part-time jobs with low pay, poor working conditions, few opportunities for advancement, and little stability; most of the workers in these jobs are women; no country shows equal participation of men and women in the workforce; and unemployment rates are higher for women than men in all countries. *Just a Temp* (Temple University Press, 1996) by Kevin D. Henson provides insight into this segment of the workforce in the United States through detailed portraits of people in temporary employment and debunks several myths, among them, that employees, especially women, prefer temp and part-time work. *Gender, Time, and Reduced Work* (State University of New York Press, 1993) by Cynthia Negrey differentiates four forms of reduced work: conventional part-time work, temporary employment, job sharing, and work sharing. Using qualitative analysis, the author shows that reduced work does not affect all employees the same way, but reinforces gender inequities found in full-time work.

335. Boris, Eileen. *Home to Work: Motherhood and the Politics of Industrial Homework in the United States.* New York: Cambridge University Press, 1994. 383p. bibliog. index. ISBN 0521443709; 0521455480pa.

In this groundbreaking work, Boris illustrates the bifurcation of public paid labor and private-domain labor and how the growth of industrial capitalism during the nineteenth century contributed to the devaluation and invisibility of women's work. Her analysis of homework regulations reveals embedded concepts of womanhood and manhood, visions of proper home life and childhood, and a persistent ideology of the separation of home from work through state policy. It also traces the evolution of the state's role in shaping labor conditions and women's position in the labor market. Boris describes her work as a reinterpretation of history that illuminates the gendering of the welfare state. Boris, with Cynthia R. Daniels, in *Homework: Historical and Contemporary Perspectives on Paid Labor at Home* (University of Illinois Press, 1989), presents chapters, using a variety of methodologies, data sources, and approaches, that examine whether homework is a terrific option, the best of several evils, or an exploitative system of work in terms of race, class, and gender.

In *Hidden in the Home: The Role of Waged Homework in the Modern World Economy* (State University of New York Press, 1994), author Jamie Faricellia Dangler interviews female home workers in electronics to illustrate their lives and the conditions under which homework became a viable option. She asserts that homework production processes in capitalistic countries guarantee an available female labor force and reinforce gender segregation. Dangler then explores ways in which state actions affect and are affected by capital and labor and critiques homework policies, particularly limitations stemming from conflicts between the political right's belief in conventional women's roles and liberals' claim that homework exploits women.

336. Brinton, Mary C. *Women and the Economic Miracle: Gender and Work in Postwar Japan*. Berkeley: University of California Press, 1993. 299p. bibliog. index. ISBN (OP); 0520089200pa.

In both capitalist and socialist Western industrial nations, high female labor-force participation does not necessarily mean the rapid extinction of sharply delineated sex roles in the economy or the disappearance of the wage gap. This book examines how Japan demonstrates this phenomenon more clearly than perhaps any other industrial society. Sociologist Brinton's closely comparative study argues that the Japanese educational and labor market systems developed in ways that economically disadvantage women. Methodologically eclectic, the author concentrates on ways in which these systems structure the opportunities and constraints of the economic roles of Japanese men and women. Her conclusion both charts and analyzes a high level of gender differentiation and stratification in the Japanese economy.

In *Office Ladies and Salaried Men: Power, Gender, and Work in Japanese Companies* (University of California Press, 1998), author Yuko Ogasawara provides an insightful ethnographic analysis of the complex gendered social structure commonly found in Japanese companies between upwardly mobile men and low-paid office ladies (OLs), who are expected to work only until marriage. In *Japanese Women Working* (Routledge, 1993), edited by Janet Hunter, several contributors historically examine women's lives as paid laborers in the textile and coal-mining industries and in occupations such as domestic service and shell diving. Other contributors explore twentieth-century gender and work issues such as motherhood protection and equal opportunity.

337. Clark-Lewis, Elizabeth. *Living In, Living Out: African American Domestics in Washington, DC, 1910–1940*. Washington, DC: Smithsonian Institution Press, 1994. 242p. bibliog. index. ISBN 1560983620.

Clark-Lewis presents oral histories of family members and other elderly women who migrated from the rural South to the urban North, specifically Washington, D.C., to work as domestic servants during the early decades of the twentieth century. The first chapters examine African American family life in post-Reconstruction farming communities and explore migration patterns that resulted from dwindling social and economic options. In later chapters the women discuss adjustments required by life in the city and describe their daily lives. Ultimately, the live-in workers became live-out workers, thereby expanding control over their lives.

Bonnie Dill also uses stories of twenty-six domestic workers and their employers to illustrate the nature and structure of domestic work, especially in terms of family relationships, race, ethnicity, culture, and immigration, in *Across the Boundaries of Race and Class: An Exploration of Work and Family among Black Female Domestic Servants* (Garland, 1994). Dill's theoretical and creative approaches to analyzing life histories help reveal more complex worker subjectivities. In *Domesticity and Dirt: Housewives and Domestic Servants in the United States, 1920–1945* (Temple University Press, 1989), author Phyllis Palmer examines the class relations and social sensibilities of white American middle-class women who relied on the efforts of other (hired) women, usually women of color, to get "their" housework done. This title serves as a fine theoretical and practical text that explores Marxist, capitalist, and feminist "explanations" for the devaluation of women's labor and cultural prescriptions for who gets it done and who makes sure it gets done right.

338. Cohen, Miriam. *Workshop to Office: Two Generations of Italian Women in New York City, 1900–1950*. Ithaca, NY: Cornell University Press, 1993. 237p. bibliog. index. ISBN 0801427223; 0801480051pa.

Cohen uses census data, government reports, and the Julia Richman High School yearbook for her study of Italian women that illustrates the significant changes in family roles, work lives, and educational patterns of two generations of women. The book begins with a description of work and family roles in southern Italy, then discusses women's work patterns as they evolved in New York City from 1900 to the early depression. It continues with an analysis of the poor school attendance of Italians in the early twentieth century and the social and economic changes toward the end of the depression that encouraged women to attend high school. Cohen argues that shifts in education and occupations for Italian women were the result of pragmatic family decisions to increase economic resources in households, adapt to changes in family structure, and take advantage of new opportunities. The volume concludes by summarizing changes in work and family life over fifty years.

Susan Glenn's *Daughters of the Shtetl: Life and Labor in the Immigrant Generation* (Cornell University Press, 1991) offers another analysis of women immigrants and work but focuses on young eastern European Jewish women in the garment industry from 1880 to World War I. The author's analysis is notable for examining interactions between religion, gender, ethnicity, class, technology, and geography. Louise Lamphere's *From Working Daughters to Working Mothers: Immigrant Women in a New England Industrial Community* (Cornell University Press, 1987) is an anthropological and historical case study of women immigrants from a variety of countries employed in the textile industry in Central Falls, Rhode Island, from 1915 to 1980. Lamphere particularly examines working-class women as active agents who developed a range of tactics and behaviors to deal with wage work and help families cope with the "industrial order."

339. Dex, Shirley. *Women's Occupational Mobility: A Lifetime Perspective*. London: Macmillan, 1987. 157p. bibliog. index. (OP)

In this crucial study of women's occupational mobility, Dex uses the Women and Employment Survey (WES), the first systematic, large-scale survey of women's employment histories in Britain, to study the occupational, industrial, and class distribution of women and identify patterns of employment and occupation choices, occupational mobility, and industrial employment. Dex points out that women's occupations, crucially important to the lifetime rewards received via employment, help determine their unequal status and play a key role in affecting their standard of living. Women's occupational mobility also provides critical insight to understanding women's role in class structures, theories of labor markets, and industrial structures. In spite of the importance of this topic, few studies have been completed that identify patterns of women's occupations over time, or that consider whether women become segregated into the same occupation over a lifetime, create strategies of occupation choice, or experience forced downward mobility with childbirth. Dex concludes the book with an analysis of how the emerging patterns could impact labor market theory and industrial policy. The volume includes several appendices: a copy of the WES survey, aggregates of occupational and industrial mobility, and supplementary tables. *The Social Mobility of Women* (Falmer Press, 1990), edited by Geoff Payne and Pamela Abbott, contributes to the debate in Britain, collecting chapters that argue for the inclusion of women in class theory and examines changing patterns of occupational mobility.

340. Dublin, Thomas. *Transforming Women's Work: New England Lives in the Industrial Revolution*. Ithaca, NY: Cornell University Press, 1994. 324p. bibliog. index. ISBN 0801428440.

Over the years, social theorists and historians have focused questions about women's wage work during and after the industrial revolution on the relative significance and consequences of both the liberating and exploitative elements involved in women's paid employment in capitalist societies. Here Dublin places the factory and the farm side by side to better examine these elements and changes in work and family life in New England. He explores a wide variety of wage work available to women and adds considerably to our understanding of women's labor and the ways in which industrialization affected women and men quite differently. This title is suitable as a text for undergraduate courses in the history of women and work.

Mary H. Blewett's *We Will Rise in Our Might: Workingwomen's Voices from Nineteenth-Century New England* (Cornell University Press, 1991) presents a detailed study of the history of boot and shoe manufacturing in Essex County, Massachusetts. Blewett describes the slow transformation of shoemaking from individual households to male-dominated workshops, then examines the increasing industrialization of shoe manufacturing from after the Civil War to 1910. Throughout the book, Blewett analyzes changes in experiences of work, concepts of womanhood, manhood, and family, and effects of labor organization and politics on women. In *Hard Times Cotton Mill Girls: Personal Histories of Womanhood and Poverty in the South* (ILR Press, 1986), Victoria Morris Byerly explores the later industrialization of another region of America. Based on interviews with twenty-one women in a North Carolina community, the book provides insight into working-class women's strategies for dealing with hardship, struggle, and crushing family responsibilities and demonstrates how gender, race, and class affect the material lives of poor women and their families.

341. Farmer, Helen S., and associates. *Diversity and Women's Career Development: From Adolescence to Adulthood.* Thousand Oaks, CA: Sage, 1997. 344p. (Women's Mental Health and Development, v. 2). bibliog. index. ISBN 0761904892; 0761904905pa.

Farmer's long-term study contains both qualitative and empirical elements, designed to determine what encouragement and obstacles girls and women face in planning their careers, particularly in the sciences and technology. In 1980, the author and her associates interviewed diverse high-school students in rural, inner-city, and suburban areas about their career aspirations. Follow-up interviews, conducted in 1990 and 1993, enabled them to discern variations in patterns of career development between males and females; determine the effects of race, ethnicity, and class on career planning and development; and explore interconnections between work and family life. This insightful study suggests directions for further research and practical strategies for strengthening career counseling and development programs for girls and women.

Career Counseling for Women (L. Erlbaum, 1994), edited by W. Bruce Walsh and Samuel H. Osipow, also discusses many significant issues on the topic from a feminist perspective. The first chapter reviews basic feminist theories and their importance to career counseling for women. Subsequent chapters examine psychological factors such as self-esteem and self-confidence, external cultural constraints, gender stereotypes, and discriminatory practices. Additionally, the book devotes chapters to ethnic and racial minority women, gifted women, women wanting careers in science and technology, and women wanting careers in management. Incorporating race and ethnicity in every chapter would have strengthened the collection. However, it contains clearly written and thoroughly researched chapters that point toward a comprehensive growth orientation in career counseling for women and girls.

342. Harris, Roma M. *Librarianship: The Erosion of a Woman's Profession.* Norwood, NJ: Ablex, 1992. 186p. (Information Management, Policy, and Services). bibliog. index. (OP)

Harris evaluates strategies used by librarians to professionalize librarianship, a traditionally female field. She asserts that librarians did this by mimicking higher-status male professions, focusing on the scientific basis of the field, and changing the field's name to library science. She notes, however, that the profession rewards traditionally "masculine" aspects of library science that relate to management and technology, but ignores more "feminine" aspects of the field such as children's librarianship and cataloging. The first and longest part of the book discusses the nature and value attributed to the work, the methods of "status climbing" used to reframe the field, the efforts made to control entry into the field via education and licensing, attempts to manage occupational image, and successes of library unions and associations. The second part of the book explores the impact of external factors like the rapid advance of computer technology and the commodification of information.

343. McCaffrey, Edward J. *Taxing Women*. Chicago: University of Chicago Press, 1997. 310p. bibliog. index. ISBN 0226555577; 0226555585pa.

Written in a style accessible to general readers, McCaffrey clearly explains gender biases embedded in the U.S. tax code. He demonstrates that the code taxes middle-income married women at a higher rate than middle-income married men, but rewards poor women for single parenthood and affluent women for staying out of the labor force. He also provides historical, social, and political context behind tax rules, thereby revealing unfair gender assumptions, such as considering working wives "secondary earners." Finally, McCaffrey makes concrete, but unrealistic, proposals for tax reform and supplements conceptual and mathematical points with useful charts and anecdotal examples.

Another title including analysis of tax policies in the United States, *Working Wives and Dual-Earner Families* (Praeger, 1994) by Rose Rubin and Bobye J. Riney, stands as one of the first studies to focus on the impact of married women's labor-force participation on the economic status of households. It uses empirical findings to analyze the effects of public policies (such as taxation and Social Security), costs and benefits of two-earner families, and the inequality of income distribution between husbands and wives. Not surprisingly, Rubin and Riney, both economists, find that government policies still assume husband (only) as breadwinner and claim that dual-earner families end up subsidizing one-earner married-couple families. They further claim that income disparities between one- and two-earner families will increase, and recommend policy changes to offset disparities.

344. Moore, Dorothy P., and E. Holly Buttner. *Women Entrepreneurs: Moving beyond the Glass Ceiling*. Thousand Oaks, CA: Sage Publications, 1997. 262p. bibliog. index. ISBN 0761904638; 0761904646pa.

Moore and Buttner examine the growth in women's entrepreneurship, including the role of glass ceilings. The concept of the glass ceiling, which Ann Morrison, Randall P. White, and Ellen Van Velsor helped introduce in their book *Breaking the Glass Ceiling: Can Women Reach the Top of America's Corporations?* (Addison-Wesley, 1987; updated ed., 1992), refers to invisible barriers and obstacles that prevent women and minorities from advancing to the highest positions in their fields. The authors incorporate a review of the literature as they present findings gleaned from focus groups and structured questionnaires. They divide respondents into two groups of women business owners: corporate climbers who "hit" glass ceilings and intentional entrepreneurs who entered corporate workplaces to learn a set of specific skills before starting their own businesses. The authors compare the two groups on a number of issues, including career transitions, networking, leadership styles, conflicts between work and family, and measures of success. The book contains both qualitative and quantitative information, providing useful "how-to" suggestions and uncovering similar behaviors, attitudes, and paths that help develop a profile of successful women.

345. Neth, Mary C. *Preserving the Family Farm: Women, Community, and the Foundations of Agribusiness in the Midwest, 1900–1940*. Baltimore: Johns Hopkins University Press, 1995. 347p. (Revisiting Rural America). bibliog. index. (OP)

Arguing against the hierarchy depicted in the child's rhyme "The Farmer in the Dell," Neth focuses on the Midwest—Wisconsin, Illinois, Missouri, Iowa, Minnesota, Kansas, Nebraska, and the Dakotas—to better reexamine the "golden age of agriculture" and the evolving role(s) of women on the farm and in farming communities. Divided into three sections, this well-researched, in-depth study considers the connections between patriarchal family structures and capitalist development. The first section defines and outlines the development and challenges of a rural "neighborhood." The second section explores the understanding of community and the role of emergent technology in making a distinct notion of *modern* farming. The third section questions ideologies of progress and prosperity, asking and answering an especially relevant question these days: "How you gonna keep 'em down on the farm?" The bibliographic notes at the end of this book also provides an exhaustive set of resources for researchers interested in everything from the literary image of farmers to transitions to capitalism and from gender in rural settings to a history of labor.

In Katherine Jellison's *Entitled to Power: Farm Women and Technology, 1913–1963* (University of North Carolina Press, 1993), the idea of farm women entitled to power begins where women themselves claim a title traditionally reserved for men, namely, that of *farmer*. The book also acknowledges what more traditional histories of farming fail to acknowledge: the presence and influence of women in rural communities. Jellison identifies relevant governmental policies before, during, and after the war years and provides a feminist reading of how these policies and their attendant cultural consequences both affected and were affected by women in the rural Midwest.

346. Rose, Nancy E. *Workfare or Fair Work: Women, Welfare, and Government Work Programs*. New Brunswick, NJ: Rutgers University Press, 1995. 263p. bibliog. index. ISBN 0813522323; 0813522331pa.

Rose examines the history of welfare in the United States, beginning with colonial poorhouses and continuing through reforms such as the Aid to Families with Dependent Children program (abolished by Congress in 1996), proposed in the 1990s. She thoroughly evaluates the history of government job creation and work programs in terms of their inadequacy for women who receive welfare. She contrasts "workfare," the requirement that people work in order to receive welfare, with "fair work," the voluntary participation in jobs created by the government, to reveal how gender assumptions embedded in capitalism and patriarchy shape and limit the effectiveness of job creation policies for women. She proposes that fair work replace welfare, and that the Earned Income Tax Credit should expand to include unpaid work in the home.

Kathryn Enid and Laura Lein base their title *Making Ends Meet: How Single Mothers Survive Welfare and Low-Wage Jobs* (Russell Sage Foundation, 1997) on 379 interviews with both low-wage and welfare-dependent women in Chicago, Boston, Charleston, and San Antonio. They find that women in both groups must constantly adjust strategies as situations change, and that they often survive by accepting additional support from boyfriends or family members. The authors also show that neither welfare nor low-wage work allow women to meet even basic needs of their children. The authors effectively combine qualitative research with statistical data and provide insight into poor women's financial decision-making processes. *Glass Ceilings and Bottomless Pits: Women's Work, Women's Poverty* (South End Press, 1997) by Randy Pearl Albelda and Chris Tilly explores contradictions between traditional beliefs and actual realities about motherhood, work, and families, especially motherhood. The authors assert that these contradictions help explain government failure to devise effective policies that could end patterns of poverty for women and children. Despite the title, Albelda and Tilly focus on "bottomless pits," critically analyzing 1990s welfare reform, which they consider punitive. They also make detailed proposals, based on social realities, for new policies for poverty relief. The latter two titles would make excellent supplementary texts in women (or gender) and economic courses.

347. Rosener, Judy B. *America's Competitive Secret: Utilizing Women as a Management Strategy*. New York: Oxford University Press, 1995. 230p. bibliog. index. ISBN 0195080793.

In order to connect organizational effectiveness with the full utilization of professional women, this descriptive and prescriptive managerial overview reinscribes gender lines more horizontally than vertically. Rejecting the idea of the glass ceiling, Rosener outlines an enlightened management strategy and defines an interactive leadership style that she believes would better identify and reclassify how the corporation thinks about gender(ed) work. Early chapters review models of leadership and statistical studies pursuant to defining utilization as a management term and strategy. Later chapters take on gender issues more directly, outline the rethinking necessary to reform organizations, and specify processes for change.

Sally Helgesen's *The Female Advantage: Women's Ways of Leadership* (Doubleday Currency, 1990; revised, 1995) examines successful women managers in action and illustrates their effective leadership techniques. Part 1 of the volume contrasts traditionally male and female leadership strategies, that is, hierarchical versus web management structures. Part 2 presents diary studies of five women managers. Part 3 discusses particular principles and their impact on management vision, efficiency, and humanity in the workplace. *When the Canary Stops Singing: Women's Perspectives on Transforming Business* (Berrett-Koehler, 1993), edited by Pat Barrentine and Riane Tennenhaus Eisler, uses organic metaphors to discuss humanizing the workplace and facilitating the shift from control and conquest models of leadership to partnership models in business. Margaret Foegen Karsten's *Management and Gender: Issues and Attitudes* (Quorum Books, 1994) applies a feminist perspective to the history of managerial women, women's contributions to the evolution of management, and issues such as diversity, stereotypes, career planning, and mentoring pertinent to both women and minorities in management positions.

348. Rury, John L. *Education and Women's Work: Female Schooling and the Division of Labor in Urban America, 1870–1930*. Albany: State University of New York Press, 1991. 277p. (SUNY Series on Women and Work). bibliog. index. ISBN 0791406172; (OP) pa.

In this thoroughly researched book, Rury traces the relationship between education and the labor market during a period of rapid urbanization and industrialization. He examines data from the U.S. census, the commissioner of education, and contemporary statistical studies and descriptive narratives, as well as work by social scientists and historians on women and labor. He suggests that the changing job market encouraged schools to move toward vocational education and that this resulted in the development of sex-specific curricula. Looking at who went to school, who did not, and why they did or did not offers important insights into the history of class, women, work, and education. Focusing on the situation later in the twentieth century, the conference papers in *Women, Work, and School: Occupational Segregation and the Role of Education* (Westview

Press, 1991), edited by Leslie R. Wolfe, describe the crucial role education plays in perpetuating the segregation of women, particularly African American women, in the workplace. They use statistical information to examine specific inequities in areas such as job training and make policy recommendations based on successful programs.

349. Shelton, Beth Anne. *Women, Men, and Time: Gender Difference in Paid Work, Housework, and Leisure.* New York: Greenwood Press, 1992. 182p. bibliog. index. ISBN 0313265127.

Uncomfortable with essentialized cultural assumptions about women and domestic devotion, sociologist Shelton examines gender roles by assessing men's and women's time investments relative to household labor, paid labor, and leisure. Believing that time use reveals priorities of individuals as well as their society, she examines national samples of individuals over a period of years, enabling her to discern and map patterns that could establish which (if any) personal characteristics determine the use of time. Shelton's data suggest that although changes in gender roles and time-use patterns have taken place, significant differences still exist. Predictably, women continue to juggle paid labor and household chores, sometimes hiring help for the latter, while men still spend significantly less time doing housework and do not face the dilemma of balancing work and family responsibilities.

Arlie Russell Hochschild investigates ways that working mothers (and fathers) allocate their increasingly scarce time in *The Time Bind: When Work Becomes Home and Home Becomes Work* (Metropolitan Books, 1997). The author analyzed work and family lives in an unidentified Fortune 500 corporation that had established a variety of programs, including paid maternity leave. Hochschild found that employees used programs, for instance, child care, that freed them from family distractions, but generally did not use programs, for instance, flextime, that shortened work hours. Part of the reason for the latter was employees' perception that their supervisors would interpret shorter hours options as lack of commitment. More disturbing, however, was the discovery that many women and men did not want to spend more time at home because they found it a site of conflict, disagreement, and even violence. Also, both men and women found work a better source of self-esteem than home. The popular media unfortunately focused on Hochschild's concern for the time bind's effect on children and used the situation to blame working mothers. Hochschild in reality urges building a society with increased concern for children and gender equality and developing corporate cultures more conducive to family life.

350. Stockman, Norman, Norman Bonney, and Sheng Xuewen. *Women's Work in East and West: The Dual Burden of Employment and Family Life.* London: UCL Press, 1995. 232p. (Cambridge Series in Work and Social Inequality, 3). bibliog. index. ISBN 1857283074.

Making a distinction between private household and public enterprise, this work compares gendered activities and social roles for men and women in China and Japan and in Britain and the United States. It focuses mainly on experiences of women with young children, statistically less likely to be engaged in paid work, and relies on data from two large-scale surveys in which the authors were involved. Early chapters provide historical and institutional background on the four societies and present material on the paid work of women, labor-force participation, occupations, earnings, and work hours. Later chapters move into the household, examine the division of domestic labor, and explore norms governing gender roles in the four societies. The conclusion attempts to discern trends of stability and change in gender roles and reconsiders the convergence theory in light of globalization.

Dual-Earner Families: International Perspectives (Sage, 1992), edited by Suzan Lewis,

Dafna N. Izraeli, and Helen Hootsmans, examines several postindustrial countries to see whether the prevalence of dual-earner families has led to reconstructions of gender roles in the home. Despite examining a variety of social, political, religious, and cultural contexts, the chapters find that women in dual-earner families still shoulder most of the domestic labor and that governments help women enter the workforce, but do not consider policies that would help men spend more time at home. *The Second Shift: Working Parents and the Revolution at Home* (Viking, 1989) by Arlie Hochschild studies strategies of couples in the United States for rationalizing inequality between wives and husbands in the distribution of housework and child care. Based on in-depth interviews conducted over eight years, this study is notable for Hochschild's interactions with all family members (even babysitters) and its discussion of how strategies differed by class. Harriet Fraad, Stephen Resnick, and Richard Wolff propose applying Marxist-feminist class analysis to relationships within American households in *Bringing It All Back Home: Class, Gender, and Power in the Modern Household* (Pluto Press, 1994). The reactions of prominent theorists, such as Heidi Hartmann, Zillah Eisenstein, and Nancy Folbre, and an introduction by Gayatri Spivak provide possible future directions for refining the initial analysis.

351. Szockyj, Elizabeth, and James G. Fox, eds. *Corporate Victimization of Women.* Boston: Northeastern University Press, 1996. 289p. bibliog. index. ISBN 1555532594, 1555532608pa.

Using a modified socialist feminist analytical framework, the thoroughly referenced papers in this collection examine women, both as consumers and employees, to question why unfair practices, such as unequal pay, job exclusions, pricing practices, and health/reproduction practices, are not considered criminal. After a clear discussion of various theoretical perspectives, chapters provide detailed explanations of the issues, supplemented with specific examples, case studies, and statistics. The book includes both historical and late-twentieth-century examples and concludes with wide-ranging suggestions and strategies for remedying the situation aimed at courts, governments, corporations, and, of course, women.

Nicole J. Grant's *The Selling of Contraception: The Dalkon Shield Case, Sexuality, and Women's Autonomy* (Ohio State University Press, 1992) serves as a detailed analysis of unfair practices in the area of health and reproduction. Grant presents a sociological study of the Dalkon Shield case based on seventeen oral history interviews, thorough research of the medical literature, Food and Drug Administration (FDA) and congressional investigations, popular magazines, and family-planning literature. The book begins with histories of birth control, the health care system, and the Dalkon Shield. It focuses, however, on the complexity of relationships that impact women's health and sexuality, especially social conditions that limit women's choices. The volume concludes by illustrating that the Dalkon Shield represents a typical case of the health care and FDA approval systems within a specific context.

352. Tsurumi, E. Patricia. *Factory Girls: Women in the Thread Mills of Meiji, Japan.* Princeton, NJ: Princeton University Press, 1990. 209p. bibliog. index. ISBN 069103138X.

The "Meiji miracle" refers to the nation building taking place in modern Japan from 1868 to 1912, a time when women and girls working in the silk and cotton-thread factories produced the profit that drove the country's industrial and military revolution. Called kojo, the textile workers included the samurai daughters of the ruling class as well as girls from poor, rural homes, workers with different goals and loyalties. Taken separately and together, their stories reveal that each kojo increasingly considered herself a member of a distinct group with a distinct identity. The kojo experience parallels that of many factory girls around the world who worked long hours in dangerous and brutal conditions for low pay. Final chapters reproduce the contracts and agreements made between parents of girls and those who "employed" the girls in mills and in brothels. Tsurumi concludes in part that girls and women working in the mills and brothels were caught between competing traditions and, like women in other countries at other times in history, paid dearly for the contributions they made to their family's welfare and to the rise of the new industrial state.

Based on interviews, oral histories, and contemporary documents from the 1930s and 1940s, *Sisters and Strangers: Women in the Shanghai Cotton Mills, 1919–1949* (Stanford University Press, 1986) by Emily Honig examines labor politics in mills as women entered the workforce in increasing numbers within the context of urbanization and industrialization. Honig finds that differences in class, place of origin, and dialect divided women workers. Women from the same area, however, formed sisterhoods for protection and social support and used them as a basis for union activities.

353. Valenze, Deborah. *The First Industrial Woman.* New York: Oxford University Press, 1995. 245p. bibliog. index. ISBN 0195089812.

Valenze searches for the first factory girl, tracing the appearance and disappearance of this particular female archetype through the nineteenth century and the industrial revolution in England. The author shows that even though few options existed during the eighteenth century for the "female poor," who were considered economic dependents in a largely agricultural society, women developed strategies to find work. As industrialization increased, so did options for women's economic survival. At the same time, however, the industrial notion of the male breadwinner helped limit women's roles. Coming full circle, Valenze documents the return of the working-class woman to the domestic sphere in a phenomenon she terms the "feminization of the female worker," where "The Other Victorian Woman" refers to the unskilled domestic servant. The presence of tables, graphs, and charts in the introduction gives this book a firm foundation in locating women and work. In spite of its chronological telling of history, the book's gendered perspectives enable a greater understanding of nonlinear processes by which women left the work of their own homes to find work in the homes of other women. Jane Rendall's *Women in an Industrializing Society: England, 1750–1850* (Blackwell, 1991) examines connections between households and industrial economies, with a focus on the forces shaping women's lives and redefining gender roles. The author considers factors from this period still in effect and possible implications for developing countries.

354. Wise, Nancy Baker, and Christy Wise, eds. *A Mouthful of Rivets: Women at Work in World War II.* San Francisco: Jossey-Bass, 1994. 282p. bibliog. index. ISBN 1555427030.

Filled with inspiring stories and examples of women's participation in the workforce during World War II, this title examines the experiences of women working in manufacturing, white-collar jobs, and other professions. The editors organize the study thematically into eleven categories, including transience, training programs, and working conditions. The book's emphasis on oral history enables contributors to preserve valuable frontline stories that provide a more intimate dimension to women's lived experiences than is generally found in other histories.

Rosie the Riveter Revisited: Women, the War, and Social Change (Twayne, 1987) by Sherna Berger Gluck also collects oral histories of women already working at the advent of World War II, new young workers, homemakers turned war workers, and women counselors who referred workers to community services. The stories illustrate how defense work affected women's lives by increasing interactions between races and changing concepts of themselves and their abilities.

In the conclusion, Gluck pulls together common themes from the stories and discusses the collective impact of the experience on women's lives. *Gender at Work: The Dynamics of Job Segregation by Sex during World War II* (University of Illinois Press, 1987) by Ruth Milkman analyzes the automobile and electronic manufacturing industries in the United States for insights into sex segregation of jobs. Milkman examines changes in job assignments, with attention to how jobs become labeled "male" or "female" as the industries developed historically. The author finds that after the war, women's participation in these industries returned to what it had been before the war.

Workplace Issues, Unions, and Activism

355. Baron, Ava, ed. *Work Engendered: Toward a New History of American Labor.* Ithaca, NY: Cornell University Press, 1991. 385p. bibliog. index. ISBN 0801422566; ISBN 0801495431pa.

Work Engendered consists of a series of essays seeking to reinterpret North American working-class history through a "lens of gender" (p. i). Papers explore how gender-role socialization influences ways men and women respond to unfair practices and unsafe conditions at work. Baron introduces the volume by discussing the background and history of women's involvement in labor movements, which she claims previous labor histories ignore. Subsequent chapters, written by innovative scholars, such as Nancy Gabin (please see the Gabin annotation later in this section), Mary Blewett, and Angel Kwolek-Folland (please see the Kwolek-Folland annotation later in this section), discuss specific occupations, such as printing, textiles, life insurance, and food service, labor movements in Minneapolis and Seattle, or topics such as the United Auto Workers' response to mandatory overtime.

Dorothy Cobble, in *Dishing It Out: Waitresses and Their Unions in the Twentieth Century* (University of Illinois Press, 1991), examines factors that promoted or inhibited union success, the impact of unionism in the workplace, the craftlike traits of waitress unions, differing perspectives of women's and men's unions on various issues, and strategies women used to enhance their power. In *Community of Suffering and Struggle: Women, Men, and the Labor Movement in Minneapolis, 1915–1945* (University of North Carolina Press, 1991), Elizabeth Faue contends that various conditions during the 1930s depression caused unions to shift from a relatively inclusive community focus to a more bureaucratic, centralized, and male-oriented workplace focus that marginalized women's involvement in them. Most intriguing is Faue's analysis of union iconography and language, which she argues became more masculine as the 1930s progressed.

356. Blum, Linda M. *Between Feminism and Labor: The Significance of the Comparable Worth Movement.* Berkeley: University of California Press, 1991. 249p. bibliog. index. ISBN (OP); 0520072596pa.

Blum believes that the comparable worth movement stalled because neither the labor movement nor the feminist movement saw the potential for comparable worth to broaden its discourse. She uses two California case studies to illustrate the complex relationship between gender and class and to explore the potential of comparable worth to organize low-paid women. The author especially examines problems that result when comparable worth policies leave sex segregation in place and discusses various aspects of comparable worth as a progressive strategy. Paula England's *Comparable Worth: Theories and Evidence* (Aldine de Gruyter, 1992) provides a thorough overview of the economic theories, labor-force structures, and policy processes needed to fully understand complexities of the issues. England also develops an intriguing feedback model, designed to reveal discriminatory effects policies might inadvertently create, and tests it against statistical data. Elaine Sorensen's *Comparable Worth: Is It a Worthy Policy?* (Princeton University Press, 1994) serves as an informative and accessible introduction to the subject that is a worthy update to *Women, Work, and Wages: Equal Pay for Jobs of Equal Value* (National Academy Press, 1981) by Donald Treiman and Heidi Hartmann. Sorensen's book is notable for the author's clear explanation of problems within technical aspects of job evaluations and her discussion of discrimination that suggests new strategies for claiming the illegality of prevailing wage systems.

In *Rights at Work: Pay Equity Reform and the Politics of Legal Mobilization* (University of Chicago Press, 1994), Michael W. McCann challenges the traditional view that litigation has had little positive impact on pay equity by claiming that in fact "legal tactics provided movement activists an important resource for advancing their cause" (p. 4). To prove his case, McCann provides an empirically supported and intriguing examination of legal mobilization and the implementation of pay equity reform law within the historical and cultural contexts of the activists and their movement.

357. Clark, Claudia. *Radium Girls: Women and Industrial Health Reform, 1910–1935.* Chapel Hill: University of North Carolina Press, 1997. 289p. bibliog. index. ISBN 0807823317; 0807846406pa.

Clark uses the history of the radium dial painters from 1917 through World War II to illustrate the political process through which a society came to agree on an explanation for the various illnesses among the radium-exposed workers, recognize radium exposure as an industrial disease, compensate workers, and prevent further illness. The book begins with a discussion of the New Jersey dial painters and their first suspicious illnesses and traces historical uses of radium and early studies on its effects, carefully outlining the financial stake many scientists and inventors had in radium. Subsequent chapters analyze the dial painters' alliance with the Consumers' League, compare Connecticut's and New Jersey's demands for compensation, and examine federal government responses to radium as a medicine and worker exposure to radium. Clark concludes with a chapter on the Illinois dial painters and a discussion of the wide impact the Radium Girls had on business, law, government, medical practice, science, and insurance. The author makes creative use of contemporary newspaper interviews, court records, and autobiographical information to study the dial painters' attitudes and efforts to help themselves by forging political and social power. Clark sees little improvement in worker safety from chemicals in the 1990s, urging more stringent evaluations of current workplace safety.

An additional title on the topic of women and workplace hazards, *Toxic Work: Women Workers at GTE Lenkurt* (Temple University Press, 1991) by Steve Fox, provides a powerful, detailed account of a class-action suit filed by women high-tech workers, for the most part Latinas, in Albuquerque. Although the author does not focus specifically on gender and ethnicity, he exposes the dangers in this type of work and briefly critiques medical and legal responses to the suit.

358. Clayton, Susan D., and Faye J. Crosby. *Justice, Gender, and Affirmative Action.* Ann Arbor: University of Michigan Press, 1992. 152p. bibliog. index. ISBN (OP); 0472064649pa.

Clayton and Crosby attempt to dispel the myths and misunderstandings surrounding affirmative action in the United States by describing its original purpose: to adjust pervasive and subtle biases in social systems. They operationally define and describe affirmative action and detail the genesis of the law and points of legal agreement and disagreement. Additionally, the authors outline the relative deprivation theory, its gradual evolution, and its relevance to issues of equality for women. They use public surveys to document that while women agree that sex discrimination generally pervades the workplace, they overwhelmingly do not admit any personal disadvantage. Because of this, Clayton and Crosby declare the need for proactive policies. Barbara Bergmann's *In Defense of Affirmative Action* (Basic Books, 1996) examines existing and newly collected data to investigate the extent of wage gaps and job segregation by race and sex. Bergmann questions the definition of "merit" used by opponents of affirmative action, calling it subjective and ambiguous, and includes an insightful discussion of quotas versus merit-based hiring, salary, and promotion decisions. The author convincingly asserts that sex and race discrimination remains pervasive in the United States and urges stricter enforcement of laws.

Barbara F. Reskin, in *The Realities of Affirmative Action in Employment* (American Sociological Association, 1998), explores both positive and negative effects of affirmative action, using empirical research across several disciplines on employees, employers, organizations, firms, the economy, and the public, from the policy's beginnings in the 1960s. In *The Politics of Affirmative Action: "Women," Equality, and Category Politics* (Sage, 1996), author Carol Bacchi believes that the affirmative action debate must focus on social and historical contexts that exclude women and minorities from labor-force participation and policy formation. The author argues that identity categories not only place "women" in a less advantageous position relative to other minority groups, but also render African American women completely invisible.

359. Cook, Alice Hanson, with Val R. Lorwin and Arlene Kaplan Daniels. *The Most Difficult Revolution: Women and Trade Unions*. Ithaca, NY: Cornell University Press, 1992. 300p. bibliog. index. (OP)

Using a comparative, sociological framework, the authors examine how well unions represent the concerns of women working in Austria, Great Britain, Sweden, and the United States. They particularly examine the unions' internal structures, bargaining, and education programs in terms of pay equity, vocational training, labor market policy, part-time work, and health and safety. The authors find that the United States lags behind European countries in several of these areas. They also encourage wage solidarity strategies, rather than pay equity based on gender, to close the wage gap and conclude that women's double shift is "the basic source of injustice" (p. 267).

Dorothy Cobble, editor of *Women and Unions: Forging a Partnership* (ILR Press, 1993), describes in her introduction the social and economic shifts in the United States that could encourage a new evaluation of both historical and future relationships between organized labor and women. In the remainder of the book, essayists explore broad themes such as the wage gap, family needs, temporary and part-time work, homework, and women's potential for reshaping labor unions. Support, commentaries, and critiques of the author's work accompany each essay and provide additional insights into the topics.

Women in Trade Unions: Organizing the Unorganized (International Labour Office, 1994), edited by Margaret Hosmer Martens and Swasti Mitter, collects case studies that explore both successful and unsuccessful attempts to organize women workers in several industrialized and developing countries. The studies examine a variety of situations, but all reveal how technological changes often decentralize production and scatter workers, thereby making unionization extremely difficult. The studies also reveal the importance of considering the needs and desires of the women in each particular situation.

360. Fried, Mindy. *Taking Time: Parental Leave Policy and Corporate Culture*. Philadelphia: Temple University Press, 1998. 207p. (Women in the Political Economy). bibliog. index. ISBN 1566396468; 1566396476pa.

Feminist sociologist and organizational analyst Fried uses an ethnographic, participant-observer methodology for her investigation of a large American corporation she calls Premium, Inc. She specifically looks at the correspondence between the corporation's reputation as a family-friendly company and internal experiences and perspectives of its employees with respect to parental leave, gendered double standards, corporate hierarchies, and job expectations (such as overtime). Fried, in her conclusion, demonstrates that while family- and child-friendly policies in the workplace exist, they are complex and challenging to enact, often serving merely to reinscribe old gender roles in slightly different ways.

Mothers on the Job: Maternity Policy in the U.S. Workplace (Rutgers University Press, 1993) by Lise Vogel provides an excellent summary and analysis of American debates surrounding pregnancy discrimination and maternity leave policy in the workplace. Vogel deftly dissects the "difference" versus "equality" debates and supports policies that "encase female specificity within a larger gender-neutral context to effectively transcend the equality/difference dichotomy in practice" (p. 157). The six chapters collected in *Gender and Family Issues in the Workplace* (Russell Sage Foundation, 1997), edited by Francine D. Blau and Ronald G. Ehrenberg, examine family leave policies in the United States and European countries, particularly their impact on women's economic status. The collection is notable for including insightful critical commentaries with each essay. Contributors to *The Work-Family Challenge: Rethinking Employment* (Sage, 1996), edited by Suzan Lewis and Jeremy Lewis, use an organizational culture framework to investigate factors that serve as barriers toward or that enhance the effectiveness of "family-friendly" initiatives.

361. Fudge, Judy, and Patricia McDermott, eds. *Just Wages: A Feminist Assessment of Pay Equity.* Toronto: University of Toronto Press, 1991. 307p. bibliog. index. ISBN 0802059376; 0802068782pa.

The editors collect essays that use differing political considerations, theoretical perspectives, evaluative standards, and methodologies to discuss the efficacy of pay equity policies and legislation in Canada, the United States, and other Western countries. Contributors share a belief in the radical potential of the pay equity movement to influence larger social changes, especially if it addresses the unacknowledged politics and unequal power relations involved in existing policy development and implementation. Papers in *Pay Equity: Empirical Inquiries* (National Academy Press, 1989), edited by Robert T. Michael, Heidi I. Hartmann, and Brigid O'Farrell, present research about labor market functions, wage-setting practices, hiring, promotion, wage structures, and related topics. Most of the studies reveal the importance of sex job segregation in maintaining pay inequities. Several also claim that comparable worth policies in various locations, including Iowa, Minnesota, Great Britain, and Australia, resulted in mostly positive and few negative effects for either women or men.

Equal Value/Comparable Worth in the UK and the USA (St. Martin's Press, 1992), edited by Peggy Kahn and Elizabeth Meehan, consists of chapters exploring developments in pay equity issues in each country. Several chapters relate movement strategies to those used in unions and feminism. Others discuss technical problems in job evaluation processes or present case studies. As a whole, the collection concludes that pay equity must be one part of an overall plan to improve conditions for women workers. Steven Rhoads provides a negative view of pay equity in *Incomparable Worth: Pay Equity Meets the Market* (Cambridge University Press, 1993). He applies a market analysis framework to policies in Australia, the United Kingdom, European Union countries, and Minnesota to argue that the policies cause problems, do not reduce sex discrimination, and create market distortions.

362. Gabin, Nancy F. *Feminism in the Labor Movement: Women and the United Auto Workers, 1935–1975.* Ithaca, NY: Cornell University Press, 1990. 257p. bibliog. index. ISBN (OP); 0801497256pa.

In this title, Gabin illustrates women's relationship to, and experience of, unionism. Using the United Auto Workers (UAW) as a case study, the author demonstrates strategies women employed in the UAW to create better conditions, such as establishing the Women's Department in 1944, the first of its kind. Gabin also illustrates the relationship of women to the traditionally male-dominated and male-oriented labor movement and discusses the significance of feminism for women in blue-collar occupations. She arranges this carefully referenced book by time period, beginning with the 1930s and ending in 1975.

Melinda Chateauvert's *Marching Together: Women of the Brotherhood of Sleeping Car Porters* (University of Illinois Press, 1998) relates the story of women's role in forming what became the most powerful African American union in the country, from its organizing activities in the 1920s to its disbandment in 1957. Through the International Ladies' Auxiliary, African American women (wives, mothers, and sisters of Brotherhood members as well as Pullman maids) asserted their power to fight for respectability in a society that reduced them to mere stereotypes. Chateauvert also provides insight into gender conventions in African American communities during this period, especially conflicts between manhood rights and equality for women. In *Sisterhood and Solidarity: Feminism and Labor in Modern Times* (South End Press, 1987), author Diane Balser provides an excellent analysis of the organizing activities of three feminist groups: the Working Women's Association, established in 1868; Union WAGE, established in 1971; and the Coalition of Labor Union Women (CLUW), established in 1972. The author provides historical and social context to her study and believes that these groups helped create stronger, larger women's organizations and contributed to a resurgence in unionization.

363. Hacker, Sally. *Pleasure, Power, and Technology: Some Tales of Gender, Engineering, and the Cooperative Workplace.* Boston: Unwin Hyman, 1989. 188p. (Perspectives on Gender, v. 1). bibliog. ISBN 0044450966; (OP) pa.

Hacker, a sociologist known for her analysis of the affirmative action plan at American Telephone and Telegraph (AT&T), was one of the first researchers to show that links between technology, gender, and power often appear when the workplace introduces new technologies. She was also one of the first to study the link between masculine eroticism and power as expressed through technology. The first part of the book reflects these interests in its examination of the histories of technology and engineering. The author then discusses cooperative systems generally, and specifically examines the industrial Mondragon system, located in the Basque region of Spain, with particular attention to gender. Finding that conditions of women workers in the cooperative still exhibit patriarchal, hierarchical elements, Hacker concludes with suggestions, aimed mainly at working women, that she hopes will lead to a more egalitarian society. *In Doing It the Hard Way: Investigations of Gender and Technology* (Unwin Hyman, 1990), editors Dorothy E. Smith and Susan M. Turner intersperse excerpts from interviews conducted with Hacker shortly before her death with several representative writings that reflect the development of Hacker's activist methodology.

364. Jacobs, Jerry A., ed. *Gender Inequality at Work.* Thousand Oaks, CA: Sage, 1995. 438p. bibliog. index. ISBN (OP); 0803956977pa.

In the introduction, Jacobs outlines how sex segregation came to be recognized as the main culprit of gender inequality at work. He then reviews economic and social approaches to gender inequality that concentrate on four areas: the gap in earnings; managerial authority in the workplace; career paths, processes, and trends; and occupational feminization and resegregation. Jacobs's previous title on the topic, *Revolving Doors: Sex Segregation and Women's Careers* (Stanford University Press, 1989), uses extensive empirical data to provide a comprehensive outline of economic and social factors that help sustain sex job segregation in the United States. The author places job segregation within historical and comparative contexts, finding that significant mobility occurs for individual women between male, sex-neutral, and female occupations, but that general and persistent social controls and discriminatory practices constrain women's career opportunities throughout their lives.

Economist Barbara Bergmann, like Jacobs, links sex job segregation and women's disadvantaged position in labor markets to institutionalized discriminatory practices in her thorough investigation of changing gender roles in the American economy titled *The Economic Emergence of Women* (Basic Books, 1986). *Gender and Jobs: Sex Segregation and Occupations of the World* (International Labour Office, 1998) by Richard Anker provides an international perspective on the subject. The author conducts a very extensive statistical analysis of 150 occupations in forty-one countries, allowing rare cross-national comparisons that reveal significant differences between jobs "assigned" to women and men.

365. Kessler-Harris, Alice. *A Woman's Wage: Historical Meanings and Social Consequences.* Lexington: University Press of Kentucky, 1990. 168p. (Balzer Lectures, 1988). bibliog. index. ISBN 081310551X.

Any investigation of women's role and status in the fields of business, labor, and economics must include the work of Kessler-Harris, author of the award-winning title *Out to Work: A History of Wage-Earning Women in the United States* (Oxford University Press, 1982). In *A Woman's Wage*, Kessler-Harris explores the idea of wage in twentieth-century United States and ways in which hegemonic structures of patriarchy in the supposedly "neutral" world of (paid and unpaid) work determine and influence this idea. Her research reveals that the idea of wage and wages themselves prove to be "neither neutral nor natural." Taken independently, each essay examines wages from distinct perspectives and can stand on its own. Read in sequence, however, the essays chart the movement of women from economic dependence to various degrees of independence and from strictly domestic (family) to more individual lives. The text also reviews what Kessler-Harris calls the "major wage strategies of this century: family wage, living wage, minimum wage, equal pay and comparable worth" (p. 5).

Vivien Hart's excellent *Bound by Our Constitution: Women, Workers, and the Minimum Wage* (Princeton University Press, 1994) presents a clearly written, very thorough discussion of the dynamic history of minimum-wage laws and their impact on women in the United States, beginning with the late nineteenth century. Claudia Dale Goldin's *Understanding the Gender Gap: An Economic History of American Women* (Oxford University Press, 1990) is a complex, comprehensive statistical portrait of women's participation in the labor force, beginning with the early nineteenth century and examining such topics as the origins of wage discrimination and the wage gap, prohibitions on hiring married women, and occupational segregation by gender. Jeanne Boydston's *Home and Work: Housework Wages and the Ideology of Labor in the Early Republic* (Oxford University Press, 1990) provides insight into relationships between gender roles, households, and labor systems during the period leading up to the country's move toward industrialization.

366. Kwolek-Folland, Angel. *Engendering Business: Men and Women in the Corporate Office, 1870–1930.* Baltimore: Johns Hopkins University Press, 1994. 256p. (Gender Relations in the American Experience). bibliog. index. ISBN 0801848601.

Engendering Business makes a truly interdisciplinary contribution to the history of women in business, labor, and economics. Instead of adhering to chronology as persuasive strategy, Kwolek-Folland uses the historicization of "conversational" topics about men and women at work to support her central argument that in the history of financial industries many used gender to explain and justify office work. Other chapters explore womanhood and the ideal office worker, manhood, salesmanship, management, the gender of office architectures, and gendered perspectives on work, family, and leisure as defined and determined by the corporation. The conclusion establishes the efforts of workers to create business environments more suited to their own purposes. Illustrated with photographs, blueprints, and postcards, as well as charts and tables, this book should prove especially useful to students of popular or corporate culture.

In *Beyond the Typewriter: Gender, Class, and the Origins of Modern American Office Work, 1900–1930* (University of Illinois Press, 1992), author Sharon Hartman Strom also explores origins of gendered hierarchies in office work and office work culture. She believes that changing cultural images of masculinity and femininity influenced the development of scientific management theories, which resulted in gender segregation of job specialties, especially the feminization of clerical work. Strom's race and class analysis of women office workers illustrates the importance of power relationships in multifaceted business cultures.

367. Norwood, Stephen H. *Labor's Flaming Youth: Telephone Operators and Worker Militancy, 1878–1923.* Urbana: University of Illinois Press, 1990. 340p. (Working Class in American History). bibliog. index. ISBN 0252016335.

Told chronologically, this social history begins with the emergence of the Bell system and the establishment of a work hierarchy that installed women as operators in a monotonous and standardized job with poor wages, no benefits, and long hours in substandard facilities. The gender gap and relief from these conditions resulted in the formation of the Telephone Operators' Union, a separate women's union within the International Brotherhood of Electrical Workers (IBEW). Under the leadership of department president Julia O'Connor, the union established training and educational programs, and as their rosters swelled, the trade-union woman emerged as an increasingly recognizable cultural figure. At the intersection of gender politics, organized labor movements, youth culture, American feminism, and the workplace, this history provides insight into understandings of women and work in the first decade of the twentieth century and chronicles the challenges to the telephone worker that brought women squarely into the center of the organized labor movement.

Author Carole Turbin creatively examines statistical data to consider intersections of gender, race, class, ethnicity, religion, and political consciousness in her lucidly written chronicle of the evolution and struggles of the Collar Laundry Union, *Working Women of Collar City: Gender, Class, and Community in Troy, New York, 1864–86* (University of Illinois Press, 1992). This enables her to highlight variations among women's work lives, household arrangements, and labor activism and to provide a more complex picture of interactions between gender, the union, and the community. *Cannery Women, Cannery Lives: Mexican Women, Unionization, and the California Food Processing Industry, 1930–1950* (University of New Mexico Press, 1987) by Vicki Ruiz is an important historical account of Mexican and Chicana women's roles in unionization. Ruiz demonstrates that despite cultural traditions encouraging female passiveness, women played active, leading roles in the United Cannery, Agricultural, Packing, and Allied Workers of America. She believes that this was possible because workers combined elements of Mexican and American cultures: Mexican kinship networks among workers allowed women to become involved in union activities out of family loyalty rather than individualized need.

368. Probert, Belinda, and Bruce W. Wilson, eds. *Pink Collar Blues: Work, Gender, and Technology*. Carlton, Vic.: Melbourne University Press, 1993. 173p. bibliog. index. ISBN 0522845207.

The editors present an informative, thoroughly researched collection that assesses the effects of technology on women workers in Australia, Great Britain and other European countries, and the United States. Focusing on benefits of technological changes for women workers and their wages, contributors examine the influences of gender and gender relations in the historical constructions of jobs, the development of technology, limited career paths for women, and the lack of recognition for women's work skills. Many contributors refer to international statistical studies, compare results of similar research in industrial countries, and apply a variety of perspectives to their studies. The collection as a whole calls for reorganizing workplaces toward increased efficiency and higher quality.

In *Women Workers and Technological Change in Europe in the Nineteenth and Twentieth Centuries* (Taylor & Francis, 1995), edited by Gertjen de Groot and Marlou Schrover, contributors critically analyze the concepts "technology," "skill," and "deskilling" in historical case studies representing a variety of settings and contexts. Since they consider these concepts socially constructed, the researchers uncover more complex relationships between women, work, and technology than many studies and help trace the origins of gender job segregation and wage differentials. Taking up the challenge of documenting the changing position of women in developing areas, *Women Encounter Technology: Changing Patterns of Employment in the Third World* (Routledge, 1995), edited by Swasti Mitter and Sheila Rowbotham, examines the impact of information technology (IT) on the working lives of women in various countries. Contributors raise questions about women's autonomy and agency and try to articulate women's needs and demands as they convey empirical observations. The challenges women face in adjusting to the demands of IT serve as the focal point of each essay, and women's responses and organizing strategies when confronted with such challenges equally permeate the arguments and analyses. Contributors also examine the roles that family, ideology, state policies, and trade-union structures play in distributing IT-related employment between women and men.

369. Reskin, Barbara F., and Patricia A. Roos. *Job Queues, Gender Queues: Explaining Women's Inroads into Male Occupations*. Philadelphia: Temple University Press, 1990. 388p. (Women in the Political Economy). bibliog. index. ISBN 0877227438; 0877227446pa.

Reskin and Roos attempt to discover factors associated with sex composition changes in occupations by presenting fourteen case studies that consider the same five areas: the nature and characteristics of changes in the occupation; the expansion, contraction, or increased accessibility of training required; changes in the labor market that might affect entry barriers; the characteristics of occupational incumbents; and occupational rewards. The authors visited work sites and used a wide variety of statistical sources and interview styles. They discuss their methodology in selecting specific occupations for study and provide an overview of previous studies about desegregation in male fields. They go on to examine the forms and consequences of desegregation, discuss their discovery that little true integration has occurred, and present the case studies. Reskin and Roos conclude by discussing queuing theory, exploring the implications of using the theory to explain sex inequality, and summarizing the common factors that emerge from the case studies.

Susan Eisenberg's *We'll Call You If We Need You: Experiences of Women Working Construction* (ILR Press, 1998) is a powerful narrative based on interviews with thirty women members of local unions that highlights the appalling racist, sexist, and even dangerous treatment women carpenters, iron workers, painters, and electricians faced on a daily basis. Marat Moore, a former coal miner, collects oral histories of twenty-four other women minors who worked during the 1970s and 1980s in *Women in the Mines: Stories of Life and Work* (Twayne, 1996). Like the women in construction, the miners, especially women of color, endured an environment filled with harassment, hostility, and danger. They also shared the same motive for working in mines: the sometimes desperate need for money to support a family. Dorothy Moses Schultz, in *From Social Worker to Crimefighter: Women in United States Municipal Policing* (Praeger, 1995), documents women's entry and evolving roles in policing, beginning in the 1800s, and compares women and men in the profession in terms of economic and social backgrounds.

370. Samuels, Suzanne Uttaro. *Fetal Rights, Women's Rights: Gender Equality in the Workplace*. Madison: University of Wisconsin Press, 1995. 221p. bibliog. index. ISBN 0299145409; 0299145441pa.

The central argument presented here—that governmental and privately held fetal protection policies significantly alter both gender and the gender politics of the workplace—will be useful to anyone interested in the individual rights of women, men, and fetuses. Part 1 provides an analysis that examines whether equality means sameness and connects biology to American culture by looking at protective laws, the Equal Rights Amendment, and the male-only draft. Part 2 specifically zeroes in on protective laws, beginning with Congress and Title VII, and features a history of fetal rights under the law. Samuels's conclusions are that some "employers bar susceptible workers instead of cleaning up dirty workplaces" (p. 165), protection policies successfully segregate the workforce, and the policies themselves reflect a particular view of gender that regards women first as potentially pregnant employees. She also asserts that media manipulations of cultural images thoroughly essentialize women for particular ends, and that the question of fetal rights goes to the heart of the abortion debate as it seeks to determine the role of reproduction, or reproductive capacity, in society at large.

Fetal Protection in the Workplace: Women's Rights, Business Interests, and the Unborn (Columbia University Press, 1993) by Robert Blank clearly explains the complex legal, moral, economic, and political controversies that result when fetal protection, increased maternal responsibility, women's reproductive control, workers' health, and business interests all intersect. *Protecting Women: Labor Legislation in Europe, the US, and Australia, 1880–1920* (University of Illinois Press, 1995) by Ulla Wikander, Alice Kessler-Harris, and Jane Lewis provides an excellent historical examination of the conflict over protective labor legislation in Europe, the United States, and Australia during the nineteenth and early twentieth centuries. The authors examine explicitly gendered laws, gender-neutral laws, and legislation that appears gender neutral, but in reality affects only women.

371. Sokoloff, Natalie J. *Black Women and White Women in the Professions: Occupational Segregation by Race and Gender, 1960–1980*. New York: Routledge, 1992. 175p. bibliog. index. ISBN (OP); 0415906091pa.

Nearly ten years in the writing, Sokoloff's thoroughly researched study builds on her earlier research in *Between Money and Love: The Dialectics of Women's Home and Market Work* (Praeger, 1980). The current text further explores the presence of women in the job hierarchy and their segregation by race, class, and age. After a discussion of the 1960s and 1970s, when partial integration in the professions occurred, Sokoloff focuses more closely on black men, white women, and black women in the professions themselves. The study concludes with a discussion of the paradox of partial change—groups may experience upward mobility in the professions precisely as the professions themselves are being downgraded in some way (p. 131)—and some strategies for building coalitions. Appendices contain extensive census data and detailed worker and occupational profiles.

Gender and Racial Inequality at Work: The Sources and Consequences of Job Segregation (ILR Press, 1993) by Donald Tomaskovic-Devey stands as one of the first examinations of sex and race segregation at the job level rather than the occupational level. Tomaskovic-Devey skillfully combines theory and empirical data to document the extraordinary persistence of race and sex job segregation and highlights the inadequacy of neoclassical economic models to account for labor market processes, particularly in regard to gender. Stephanie J. Shaw's excellent book *What a Woman Ought to Be and to Do: Black Professional Women Workers during the Jim Crow Era* (University of Chicago Press, 1996) provides a richly detailed analysis of African American middle-class women during an earlier time period. Based on interviews, the book reveals that many families hoped that higher education and appropriate behavior instilled in daughters would prevent their economic and sexual exploitation, and prepare them to make a difference in their own lives, their families, and their communities.

372. Webb, Susan L. *Shockwaves: The Global Impact of Sexual Harassment*. New York: MasterMedia, 1994. 434p. bibliog. ISBN 0942361911; 0942361903pa.

Webb, author of *Step Forward: Sexual Harassment in the Workplace* (MasterMedia, 1991), evaluates the impact of sexual harassment on organizations worldwide. She begins with an analysis of the global impact of the U.S. Senate's confirmation hearings for Clarence Thomas, in which Anita Hill testified against him, citing sexual harassment. After discussing the term, as defined by such entities as the Equal Employment Opportunity Commission (EEOC) and the Supreme Court, Webb examines American Civil Liberties Union policies and insurance liability coverage. She continues with a look at sexual harassment in twenty countries and completes the book with suggestions for global actions that could curb harassment. The volume includes extensive lists of fair employment practices agencies, offices of the EEOC, and policy organizations worldwide. *Sexual Harassment on the Job* (3rd ed., Nolo Press, 1998) by William Petrocelli and Barbara Kate Repa examines legal protection from sexual harassment in the United States and serves as an excellent, clearly presented overview of the subject. Kerry Segrave, in *The Sexual Harassment of Women in the Workplace, 1600–1993* (McFarland, 1994), painstakingly gathers scattered information from sources such as slave narratives and labor histories that document how prevalent the sexual harassment of working women is and has been in a variety of occupations in a number of cultures over 400 years. The author finds that "blaming the victim" also has had a long history.

373. Zandy, Janet, ed. *Calling Home: Working-Class Women's Writings: An Anthology*. New Brunswick, NJ: Rutgers University Press, 1990. 366p. bibliog. index. ISBN (OP); 0813515289pa.

Zandy compiled this title to show that personal writings can be a powerful tool for understanding class differences. She begins by situating working-class women in relation to the managerial class and the poverty stricken. Zandy then arranges the stories into three sections: telling stories, bearing witness, and celebrating solidarity, preceding each section with a brief overview of its social and economic context. The writings themselves represent a diversity of working-class experience in a variety of forms, such as letters, diary entries, and poems, and reveal common struggles to determine identity, resist oppression, find economic security, and control labor.

The revised edition of the groundbreaking 1976 title *America's Working Women: A Documentary History, 1600 to the Present* (Norton, 1995), edited by Rosalyn Baxandall and Linda

Gordon, replaces more than half the material contained in the first edition, includes more selections by minority women and women settlers in the West, provides completely new introductions to each historical section, and addresses work issues, such as disability, sexual harassment, and sex work, from the 1980s and 1990s. Priscilla Murolo's *The Common Ground of Womanhood: Class, Gender, and Working Girls' Clubs, 1884–1928* (University of Illinois Press, 1997) examines internal documents of major clubs to trace changes in club ideologies, goals, and activities to shed light on class differences between club members and sponsors, club connections with the labor movement, race relations, and extra responsibilities of working women. Robin Miller Jacoby also focuses on class and gender in *The British and American Women's Trade Union Leagues, 1890–1925* (Carlson, 1994), her investigation of the similar goals but different paths of each league as influenced by interactions between feminism, the labor movement, and politics in each country.

374. Zuckerman, Amy J., and George F. Simons. *Sexual Orientation in the Workplace: Gay Men, Lesbians, Bisexuals, and Heterosexuals Working Together.* Thousand Oaks, CA: Sage, 1996. 114p. bibliog. ISBN 0761901191pa.

Formatted as a workbook, this title serves as an excellent primer on sexual orientation and workplace issues. Part 1 discusses the costs of discriminating against gays and the impact of discrimination on the work productivity of both gay and straight workers. Part 2 consists of exercises designed to raise consciousness about gender stereotypes and case studies about work situations that explore the consequences of various possible responses. Part 3 makes practical suggestions for developing nondiscrimination policies. The book contains an extensive directory of resources, listing specific companies and labor unions with nondiscrimination policies and companies, agencies, colleges and universities, organizations, cities, and states offering domestic partner benefits. Brian McNaught, in *Gay Issues in the Workplace* (St. Martin's Press, 1993), and Liz Winfield and Susan Spielman, in *Straight Talk about Gays in the Workplace: Creating an Inclusive, Productive Environment for Everyone in Your Organization* (Amacom, 1995), provide outlines for sexual orientation training sessions and straightforward information about topics such as homophobia, heterosexism, and costs of discrimination. Although Winfield and Spielman present sexual orientation as genetic and do not include references, they include very useful information concerning domestic partner benefits.

More interested in the perspectives of gay and lesbian employees, Annette Friskopp and Sharon Silverstein, authors of *Straight Jobs, Gay Lives: Gay and Lesbian Professionals, Harvard Business School, and the American Workplace* (Scribner, 1995), uncover both positive and negative effects of being open or not open about sexual orientation at work, based on a survey and interviews with gay and lesbian graduates of Harvard Business School. While none of these titles presents rigorous scholarship, they all point to areas needing more research and provide practical information for both employers and employees.

1999 CORE TITLES

August, Andrew. *Poor Women's Lives: Gender, Work, and Poverty in Late-Victorian London.* Madison, NJ: Fairleigh Dickinson University Press, 1999. 218p. bibliog. index. ISBN 0838638074.

Bradley, Harriet. *Gender and Power in the Workplace: Analyzing the Impact of Economic Change.* New York: St. Martin's Press, 1999. 250p. bibliog. index. ISBN 0312218877; 0333681770pa.

Browne, Irene, ed. *Latinas and African American Women at Work: Race, Gender, and Economic Inequality.* New York: Russell Sage Foundation, 1999. 441p. bibliog. index. ISBN 0871541475.

Catalyst. *Creating Women's Networks: A How-to Guide for Women and Companies.* San Francisco: Jossey-Bass, 1999. 208p. (Business and Management). index. ISBN 0787940143.

Cortese, Anthony. *Provocateur: Images of Women and Minorities in Advertising.* Lanham, MD: Rowman & Littlefield, 1999. 161p. (Postmodern Social Futures). bibliog. index. ISBN 0847691748; 0847691756pa.

Enstad, Nan. *Ladies of Labor, Girls of Adventure: Working Women, Popular Culture, and Labor Politics at the Turn of the Twentieth Century.* New York: Columbia University Press, 1999. 266p. (Popular Cultures, Everyday Lives). bibliog. index. ISBN 0231111029; 0231111037pa.

Garey, Anita Ilta. *Weaving Work and Motherhood.* Philadelphia: Temple University Press, 1999. 239p. (Women in the Political Economy). bibliog. index. ISBN 1566397006.

Gilligan, Maureen Carroll. *Female Corporate Culture and the New South: Women in Business between the World Wars.* New York: Garland, 1999. 200p. (Garland Studies in the History of American Labor). bibliog. index. ISBN 0815331843.

Gregory, Jeanne, Rosemary Sales, and Ariane Hegewisch, eds. *Women, Work, and Inequality: The Challenge of Equal Pay in a Deregulated Labour Market.* New York: St. Martin's Press, 1999. 220p. bibliog. index. ISBN 033372141X.

Handler, Joel F., Lucie White, and Daniel J.B. Mitchell, eds. *Hard Labor: Women and Work in the Post-Welfare Era.* Armonk, NY: M.E. Sharpe, 1999. 264p. (Issues in Work and Human Resources). bibliog. index. ISBN 0765603330.

Hewitson, Gillian J. *Feminist Economics: Interrogating the Masculinity of Rational Economic Man.* Northampton, MA: Edward Elgar, 1999. 277p. bibliog. index. ISBN 1858989469.

Hunt, Gerald, ed. *Laboring for Rights: Unions and Sexual Diversity across Nations.* Philadelphia: Temple University Press, 1999. 302p. (Queer Politics, Queer Theories). bibliog. ISBN 1566397170; 1566397189pa.

Ilic, Melanie. *Women Workers in the Soviet Interwar Economy: From "Protection" to "Equality."* New York: St. Martin's Press, 1999. 304p. (Studies in Russian and East European History and Society). bibliog. index. ISBN 0312217803.

Kilbourne, Jean. *Deadly Persuasion: Why Women and Girls Must Fight the Addictive Power of Advertising.* New York: Free Press, 1999. 366p. bibliog. index. ISBN 0684865998.

Mills, Mary Beth. *Thai Women in the Global Labor Force: Consuming Desires, Contested Selves*. New Brunswick, NJ: Rutgers University Press, 1999. 240p. bibliog. index. ISBN 0813526531; 081352654Xpa.

Nelson, Robert L., and William P. Bridges. *Legalizing Gender Inequality: Courts, Markets, and Unequal Pay for Women in America*. New York: Cambridge University Press, 1999. 393p. (Structural Analysis in the Social Sciences, 16). bibliog. index. ISBN 0521627508.

Peterson, Janice, and Margaret Lewis, eds. *The Elgar Companion to Feminist Economics*. Northampton, MA: Edward Elgar, 1999. 811p. ISBN 185898453X; 1840647833pa.

Powell, Gary, ed. *Handbook of Gender and Work*. Thousand Oaks, CA: Sage, 1999. 651p. bibliog. index. ISBN 0761913556.

Prügl, Elisabeth. *The Global Construction of Gender: Home-Based Work in the Political Economy of the 20th Century*. New York: Columbia University Press, 1999. 231p. bibliog. index. ISBN 0231115601; 023111561Xpa.

Rao, Aruna, Rieky Stuart, and David Kelleher. *Gender at Work: Organizational Change for Equality*. West Hartford, CT: Kumarian, 1999. 272p. bibliog. index. ISBN 1565491033; 1565491025pa.

Reese, Laura A., and Karen E. Lindenberg. *Implementing Sexual Harassment Policy: Challenges for the Public Sector Workplace*. Thousand Oaks, CA: Sage, 1999. 213p. bibliog. index. ISBN 0761911448; 0761911456pa.

Renshaw, Jean R. *Kimono in the Boardroom: The Invisible Evolution of Japanese Women Managers*. New York: Oxford University Press, 1999. 291p. bibliog. index. ISBN 0195117654.

Tanner, Bonnie O. *The Entrepreneurial Characteristics of Farm Women*. New York: Garland, 1999. 252p. (Garland Studies in Entrepreneurship). bibliog. index. ISBN 0815329989.

WORLD WIDE WEB/INTERNET SITES

375. *Catalyst*. http://www.catalystwomen.org/.
    Celebrating forty years of existence, Catalyst is a nonprofit research and advisory organization that helps women make the most of their talents and helps companies develop effective programs for advancing women. The site provides overviews of the organization's research, publications, and services, including an Information Center, which provides information about issues affecting working women, and a Speakers Bureau.

376. *The Glass Ceiling Commission*. http://www.ilr.cornell.edu.
    This site is maintained by the Catherwood Library School of Industrial and Labor Relations at Cornell University. The electronic archive—*The Glass Ceiling Commission*—holds the com-

mission's news releases, fact-finding reports, and recommendations, as well as additional papers that form part of the commission's advancement study containing current assessments of various aspects of the glass ceiling. Each paper includes policy and research recommendations and an annotated bibliography.

377. *Women-Related Business/Work Web Sites.* http://www-unix.umbc.edu/~korenman/ wmst/links_bus.htm.
   Another of Joan Korenman's excellent sites, this page provides an annotated list covering a wide variety of interests: entrepreneurship, statistics, research, money management, working women, job searches, minority women, career information, and workplace issues.

378. *Women's Bureau. United States Department of Labor.* http://www.dol.gov/dol/wb.
   This site contains relevant press releases, fact sheets, statistics, news, programs, and special reports. It provides many useful links for researchers needing government information.

379. *Women's Professional Organizations.* http://www.feminist.org/gateway/women .org.html.
   Sponsored by the Feminist Majority Foundation, this site provides an exhaustive listing of business organizations by, for, and about women, including women in business, education, law, medicine, and politics.

380. *WSSLINKS: Women and Business.* http://www.csulb.edu/%7Esbsluss/Women _and_Business.htm
   This annotated site lists associations, biographies, directories, electronic discussion forums, newsletters, journals, small business resources, statistical sources, and metasites. Several links cover women of color and international women.

5   Education and Pedagogy

Linda D. Tietjen

Gathering material, researching, and writing this chapter have proven daunting tasks. I felt enormous responsibility in having to choose relatively few titles from the hundreds of truly excellent books written about women's education and feminist pedagogy under consideration in the last decade. My thanks and congratulations go to all the authors of these books. I truly believe that as girls and women become more thoughtfully educated, the lives of girls and women, as well as boys and men, can only become more fulfilling.

The "Monographs" section in this chapter is arranged topically in the following categories: "Pedagogy, Teaching, and Curriculum Transformation in the Academy," "Women Faculty, Students, and Academic Climates," "K–12 Education in the United States," and "Global Perspectives on the Education of Women and Girls." Historical treatments are included in the appropriate categories.

The chapter generally focuses on the United States, with some international coverage. Many of the books in this chapter are edited works: collections of essays addressing a particular topic area. Several works were written by and for women of color, and one even deals with working-class women.

Areas for further and more in-depth analysis include an emerging literature on the education of girls, kindergarten through grade 12, with particular attention needed for the critical adolescent years. Books and articles about students, teachers, and administrators in academic settings also warrant monitoring. The intersection of gender, race, sexual preference, and class are also exciting areas for further inquiry. Curriculum development at all levels, international educational trends, legislative issues, sex equity and discrimination, feminist activism, and sociological, epistemological, and psychological studies round out some of the other areas to monitor. The topics of education and pedagogy have truly come a long way since the birth of women's studies in the early 1970s.

REFERENCE SOURCES

381. Eisenmann, Linda, ed. *Historical Dictionary of Women's Education in the United States*. Westport, CT: Greenwood Press, 1998. 552p. index. ISBN 0313293236.

This historical reference work about women's education contains 245 original entries contributed by 104 American and international scholars. This collaborative effort, given the knowledge and expertise of the contributors about their topics, greatly benefits readers in terms of the scope and depth of the entries. The introduction provides a nine-page chronological overview of women's education from the colonial and republican eras (1600s to early 1800s) through the modern era (from the 1940s into the 1990s). Each entry consists of two or more pages and ends with a three- or four-item "bibliography," and most include cross-references to related articles. The dictionary provides more extensive information in some areas than others. For example, the entry for African American women is longer than the one for Asian American women, reflecting the amount of scholarship in these areas, not worthiness of coverage. Entries also focus on the geographic, historical, and demographic aspects of women's educational history rather than biographical information.

382. Grant, Carl A., and Gloria Ladson-Billings, eds. *Dictionary of Multicultural Education*. Phoenix: Oryx Press, 1997. 308p. bibliog. index. ISBN 0897747984.

The editors and a list of distinguished scholars, four pages long, contributed to this excellent dictionary. They have created a worthwhile reference tool that should prove beneficial for teachers as well as students of both general ethnic and women's studies classes. The editors collect more than 150 signed entries covering pedagogical and philosophical concepts (such as Neo-Marxism and hegemony), various concentrations within multicultural studies (such as Latino studies, Chicano and Chicana studies, and gay, lesbian, and bisexual studies), issues (such as hyphenated Americans and marginalization), and court cases (such as *Brown v. Board of Education*). They specifically exclude biographical information. The editors' commitment to "the spirit of multicultural education; that is, we included both supporters and critics of the field to demonstrate our commitment to including multiple perspectives" (p. xviii) separates this work from standard reference works. This dictionary should become part of reference collections in academic and public libraries, as well as women's studies and ethnic studies libraries. Another excellent reference work devoted to one specific ethnic group is the 575-page *Encyclopedia of African-American Education* (Greenwood Press, 1996) edited by Faustine C. Jones-Wilson and others. Unlike Grant and Ladson-Billings, the editors include biographical entries for educators such as Horace Mann Bond, an educator and historian of African American education, and Johnnetta B. Cole, a feminist, educator, and college president.

383. Kelly, David, Gail P. Kelly, Chen Shu-Ching, Junko Kanamura, Machiko Matsui and Wu Yen-Bo. *Women's Education in the Third World: An Annotated Bibliography*. New York: Garland, 1989. 478p. (Garland Reference Library of Social Science, v. 544; Reference Books in International Education, v. 6). indexes. (OP)

Concentrating on women's education in countries in Asia, Africa, Latin America and the Caribbean, and the Middle East, the authors gather approximately 1,200 journal articles, books, and book chapters published in English, French, German, Portuguese, and Spanish but exclude dissertations, unpublished reports and conference papers, and polemical works. They arrange entries topically with geographic subdivisions: bibliographies, general titles, and history; educational processes; women teachers and administrators; higher education; nonformal education; adult development; workforce fertility; politics; family; and women's studies. The book, notable for including titles in a variety of languages, also contains author and geographic indexes.

384. Seller, Maxine Schwartz, ed. *Women Educators in the United States, 1820–1993: A Biobibliographical Sourcebook*. Westport, CT: Greenwood Press, 1994. 603p. bibliog. index. ISBN 0313279373.

The editor and contributors profile sixty-six women chosen to reflect the broad range of contributions in various fields of education. Arranged alphabetically by name, each signed entry begins with a paragraph summarizing the educator's accomplishments and concludes with bibliographies of works by and about the entrant. The body of each entry averages six to ten pages in length and provides information about family background, education, career, people and events that influenced the educator, and the impact of gender on her career. An appendix lists the educators in four chronological sections: "Pioneers (1820–1870)," "Expanders and Reformers (1870–

1920)," "Gains and Losses (1920–1960)," and "Equality and Excellence (1960–1993)." The sourcebook includes educators who represent all geographical areas of the United States, immigrants, slaves, and social classes. The index contains entries for various races and ethnicities as well as names, subjects, organizations, schools, and publications.

385. Stafford, Beth, ed. *Directory of Women's Studies Programs and Library Resources.* Phoenix: Oryx Press, 1990. 154p. indexes. (OP)

Stafford, former longtime women's studies librarian at the University of Illinois at Urbana-Champaign and compiler of annual directories of women's studies programs for the National Women's Studies Association during the 1980s, provides information about programs, individuals, and library collections in the United States. She arranges entries in the two main sections, "Programs" and "Courses," geographically by state and city. Entries in both sections list individual faculty and affiliate faculty, course titles, credentials offered (certificate, concentration, degree[s], minor), library collections, support services, and contact person. Stafford provides multiple points of access to information in the entries by including four indexes: by institution, credentials, discipline and orientation (criminal justice, lesbian studies, ethnic studies, labor, urban planning, women in development, and so on), and subject strength of library collections (feminist theory, education, fine arts, and so on). This directory is unique in compiling information about both women's studies programs and library collections.

386. Stitt, Beverly A. *Gender Equity in Education: An Annotated Bibliography.* Carbondale: Southern Illinois University Press, 1994. 168p. index. ISBN 0809319373.

The staff of the Illinois Building Fairness Resource Center began compiling this bibliography in 1985 to fulfill one of the center's objectives: to suggest specific sources that would help administrators, teachers, and counselors overcome sex bias and gender stereotypes in schools. Stitt, the former director of the center, continued compiling the bibliography until early 1993. She examined hundreds of books, videos, articles, curriculum guides, workshop guides, and suggestions for classroom activities and includes only those materials she considers "worthy" (not outdated or poorly designed). She arranges more than 700 entries into twenty-three chapters that cover subjects such as agriculture and industry, math and science, nontraditional careers, pregnant and parenting teens, and vocational training. Stitt provides full citations, sometimes including ordering information, and brief, descriptive annotations. An index helps locate materials that fit into more than one category.

387. Touchton, Judith G., Lynne Davis, and Vivian Parker Makosky, comps. *Fact Book on Women in Higher Education.* New York: American Council on Education, Macmillan, 1991. 289p. (American Council on Education/Macmillan Series on Higher Education). bibliog. index. ISBN 0029009510.

Touchton, Davis, and Makosky collect the fullest information possible pertaining to women and higher education. They present charts, graphs, tables, and other visual formats on such topics as enrollment patterns, earned degrees, salaries, administration and leadership, and promotion and tenure. The editors frequently include historical statistics often dating back to the 1960s, and occasionally the 1950s, to trace important changes for women in higher education. The book gathers information, some of it compiled specifically for this source and available for the first time, from a wide variety of federal and state government agencies, private research centers, educational organizations, and professional associations, listed in the detailed data source section. Although the editors include information pertaining to race and ethnicity, differences in definitions and methodologies among data sources hamper statistical comparison. Touchton, with Carol S.

Pearson and Donna L. Shavlik, also edited *Educating the Majority: Women Challenge Tradition in Higher Education* (American Council of Education, Macmillan, 1989), a collection of chapters that provides a clear and very diverse picture of both theoretical and practical issues concerning women's education during the 1980s.

MONOGRAPHS

Pedagogy, Teaching, and Curriculum Transformation in the Academy

388. Adams, Maurianne, Lee Anne Bell, and Pat Griffin, eds. *Teaching for Diversity and Social Justice.* New York: Routledge, 1997. 374p. bibliog. index. ISBN 0415910560; 0415910579pa.

The editors, collaborators for more than two decades on researching, experimenting with, and designing curricula, strive to combat a variety of isms, including racism, sexism, and classism, still present in curricula of all levels of education. Adams has proven particularly prolific: she has written books on racism, sexism, "gay lesbianism," and anti-Semitism. The contributors of this sourcebook seek to "address both theoretical and practical issues that confront faculty who introduce diversity and social justice content in their classrooms" (p. xv). The authors of the seven chapters presented in part 1 address "Theoretical Foundations and Frameworks" via analysis of a particular problem and placing it into historical context, often using the seminal work of Paolo Freire, especially *Pedagogy of the Oppressed* (Seabury Press, 1970; revised ed., Continuum, 1993). Some of the authors of the six chapters in part 2 address a particular ism: racism, sexism, heterosexism, anti-Semitism, ableism, and classism. Other authors suggest ways to design a class for multiple issues and present some of their own curricula designed to raise awareness of various isms. The authors of chapters in part 3, "Issues for Teachers and Trainers," encourage self-analysis so teachers can identify their own biases. The writers warn educators of potential pitfalls in student/teacher relationships and classroom settings. The work concludes with bibliographic references, a video resource list, and an index. This valuable sourcebook combines a thorough theoretical framework with specific course design suggestions. It is highly recommended for education, women's studies, and ethnic studies classes at the undergraduate level.

389. Antler, Joyce, and Sari Knopp Biklen, eds. *Changing Education: Women as Radicals and Conservators.* Albany: State University of New York Press, 1990. 388p. (Feminist Theory in Education) bibliog. index. ISBN 0791402339; 0791402347pa.

This work is a compilation of papers that the authors presented at a 1985 special interest group called "Research on Women and Education" of the American Educational Research Association. Despite the 1985 conference date, this book, published in 1990, contains an informative selection of historical papers that delve into previously ignored or infrequently researched areas of study. Historians and women's studies educators examine topics such as "Losing Birth: The Erosion of Women's Control over and Knowledge about Birth, 1650–1990" by Janet Carlisle Bogdan, a sociologist, and "Weeding Women out of 'Women's True Profession': The Effects of the Reforms on Teaching and Teachers" by Sara Freedman, a former public school teacher. The authors also address topics such as the education of southern black women from 1865 to 1940 and the informal information-dissemination channels that a group of Jewish immigrant women used through a daily ethnic newspaper in 1919. This excellent collection is a culmination of women scholars' forays into manuscript collections and libraries as well as research conducted with more formal methodologies, such as surveys and interviews. The authors contribute to a developing body of historical research on women's education that provides background information vis-à-vis current educational theory and pedagogy.

390. Boxer, Marilyn Jacoby. *When Women Ask the Questions: Creating Women's Studies in America.* Baltimore: Johns Hopkins University Press, 1998. 344p. bibliog. index. ISBN 0801858348.

Boxer, the first chair of the oldest women's studies program in the United States, at San Diego State University, presents a comprehensive, engaging account of academic feminism from its birth in the late 1960s onward. The author discusses early dilemmas such as whether or not to create a separate discipline, what to call this discipline, joint appointments, and so on as she documents the development of key feminist journals, publishers, and organizations, such as the National Women's Studies Association (NWSA), and the roles they played in the development of the discipline. Boxer also provides an intriguing analysis of the content of early women's studies textbooks and traces changes in content over time. Most notable, however, is the author's succinct, coherent, and accessible account of scholars' ongoing struggle to develop feminist theory. Earlier important accounts of the history and growth of women's studies as a discipline include *Women's Studies in the United States* (Ford Foundation, 1986) by Catherine Stimpson, a shorter version of the author's consultant report to the foundation, and *Women's Studies: A Retrospective* (Ford Foundation, 1995) by Beverly Guy-Sheftall, in which the author updates and expands upon Stimpson's report, describes mainstream curricular changes in American universities, and identifies global developments in women's studies. For an overview of the development of women's studies programs and debates about theory, difference, and pedagogy in universities, colleges, polytechnics, and adult education in Great Britain, see *Out of the Margins: Women's Studies in the Nineties* (Falmer Press, 1991), edited by Jane Aaron and Sylvia Walby.

391. Butler, Johnnella, and John C. Walter, eds. *Transforming the Curriculum: Ethnic Studies and Women's Studies.* Albany: State University of New York Press, 1991. 341p. bibliog. index. ISBN 0791405869; 0791405877pa.

Johnnella Butler and John C. Walter, two experts in the study of curriculum transformation through collaboration/cooperation between ethnic studies and women's studies programs, present a collection of thoughtful, incisive chapters that address the complex issues implicit in ethnic and women's studies. Butler's introduction reveals her vision: "The experience of the woman of color is the bridge that joins us all—white male, men of color, white women, and women of color. She is the link between Ethnic Studies and Women's Studies content, and as such occupies a pivotal place in curricular change" (pp. xix–xx). The editors interlace chapters with interpretive narrative, introducing five major topics. Contributors define and analyze interrelationships between ethnic studies and women's studies, and several also examine pedagogy, theory building, and curriculum development and include class syllabi. Representative chapter titles include "Gender and the Transformation of a Survey Course in Afro-American History," a case study by John C. Walker, and "Jewish Invisibility in Women's Studies" by Evelyn Torton Beck, a women's studies and Jewish studies scholar. Johnnella Butler produces the capstone chapter, "Praxis and the Prospect of Curriculum Transformation," in which she revisits the questions, complexities, and challenges examined throughout the book. The authors urge readers to transcend their tendency to view women's and/or ethnic studies solely through the "lens of gender," and to strive toward a pluralistic worldview.

392. Deats, Sara Munson, and Lagretta Tallent Lenker, eds. *Gender and Academe: Feminist Pedagogy and Politics*. Lanham, MD: Rowman & Littlefield, 1994. 343p. bibliog. index. ISBN 0847679691; 0847679705pa.

The essays in this book emerged from work that educators presented at the University of South Florida's first two "Gender in Academe" conferences held in 1989 and 1991. Gerda Lerner, a historian instrumental in both recovering women's history and creating what would become a discipline known as women's studies, served as the keynote speaker for the 1989 conference. Given this propitious beginning, the caliber of this anthology's individual chapters is excellent. The essays, penned by scholars from many disciplines, especially literature, examine the impact of feminist ideology on classroom curricula. One section of the book consists of five essays that consider the question "How does a feminist perspective influence how we teach in the classroom?" Another section, consisting of seven essays, critiques how educators teach outside the classroom via authored or edited books, journal articles, conference presentations, and general philosophies. A suggested reading section guides readers to further resources. This title is recommended as required or supplemental reading for classes in feminist theory and pedagogy, women's studies, and general education classes. Five authors (Janice Jipson, Karen Froude Jones, Gretchen Freed-Rowland, Petra Munro, and Susan Victor), members of a research and writing support group, discuss their extraordinary collaborative project in *Repositioning Feminism and Education: Perspectives on Educating for Social Change* (Bergin & Garvey, 1995). They particularly examine tensions between collaboration, difference, and imposition outside traditional classrooms by exploring the integration of pedagogical theory with political work in educational settings such as summer camps and community-based classes for teenage mothers.

393. Fiol-Matta, Liza, and Miriam K. Chamberlain, eds. *Women of Color and the Multicultural Curriculum: Transforming the College Classroom*. New York: Feminist Press at the City University of New York, 1994. 390p. bibliog. ISBN 1558610820; 1558610839pa.

This work, largely supported by the Ford Foundation, expands on the groundwork that women's and ethnic studies scholars created during the 1970s and 1980s. The foundation's 1988 "Mainstreaming Minority Women" grant "forced Women's Studies to look within its own course offerings, programs, and research to address its white-privileged structures" (p. 3). The thirteen research centers that received grant monies to conduct research for this work produced some groundbreaking research aimed at transforming the curriculum, with particular emphasis on addressing the "ampersand problem" of being both "black & female." The resulting research evolved into this tightly edited volume of chapters by authors who examine curriculum transformation in various disciplines, including art history, theology, and the social sciences. Editors Fiol-Matta and Chamberlain divide the book into three major topics: "Faculty Development," including faculty seminar models and a variety of class syllabi, "Model Undergraduate Curriculum," and "Focus on Puerto Rican Studies," a stand-alone interdisciplinary guide for research and curriculum that focuses on Puerto Rican women. This invaluable collection of essays largely fulfills its goal of transforming women's studies curricula so that "women of color" may feel "neither marginal nor irrelevant" in the future (p. 3).

394. Garber, Linda, ed. *Tilting the Tower: Lesbians, Teaching, Queer Subjects*. New York: Routledge, 1994. 280p. bibliog. ISBN (OP); 0415908418pa.

Linda Garber, a professor at California State University at Fresno, gathers a series of essays that collectively endeavor to define a place for lesbian studies in academic curricula. She arranges the essays into three sections: "Classrooms: College/University" (thirteen chapters), "Classrooms:

High Schools" (four chapters), and "Institutions" (twelve chapters). The classroom chapters reveal personal experiences and observations about the status of lesbian teachers, the issue of whether and/or when to "come out," and the fears and subtle, or not-so-subtle, pressure these women face in traditional classrooms. The "Institutions" section discusses the place of lesbian, gay, and queer studies in classrooms, using a contextual viewpoint that explores how and when teachers should develop a curriculum that addresses issues of sexual orientation and sexual preference. How can one protect lesbian and gay teachers from the overt and subtle sexism so ingrained in our schools' curricula? Where do lesbian studies fit into the curriculum, and how do these women differ from women of color, white women, and other women? Garber reminds readers: "While Lesbian Studies grew out of Women's Studies and feminist activism, it is now in danger of being subsumed under the banner of Queer Studies" (p. ix). The contributors, through personal narratives, coming-out stories, and pedagogical essays, pose as many questions as they attempt to answer. A variety of voices successfully present clear, multifaceted discussions about a variety of complex issues, making this book a fine text for women's studies and queer studies classes.

395. hooks, bell. *Teaching to Transgress: Education as the Practice of Freedom*. New York: Routledge, 1994. 216p. index. ISBN (OP); 0415908086pa.

bell hooks is a college professor, public speaker, philosopher, educational innovator, and writer. Born Gloria Watkins, this black feminist scholar, a proponent of "liberatory pedagogy," took her grandmother's name as her "writing voice." Her belief centers on the concept of teachers as healers, a demanding proposition that requires teachers to work constantly on their own self-actualization processes and to continuously engage in active listening and self-examination in order to self-correct their own flawed assumptions. She devotes one of her fourteen essays to Paolo Freire, in which she discusses Freire's philosophy, its sometimes sexist flaws, and its over-riding revolutionary and valuable contributions to her growth as a teacher. In another essay, hooks constructs a dialogue between her name identities—Gloria Watkins "interviewing" bell hooks—that enables her to ask herself questions about her philosophy and teaching methodology most interviewers do not think to ask. *Teaching to Transgress*, although relentlessly antipatriarchal, is written in an intriguing and passionate style that interweaves the scholarly with the personal in an accessible and never boring manner. Scholars should consider this work or any other work by bell hooks as required reading for pedagogical methods classes in academic disciplines such as political science, women's studies, ethnic studies, and general education. As the author in her irrepressible style writes: "I celebrate teaching that enables transgressions—a movement against and beyond boundaries" (p. 12).

396. Kramarae, Cheris, and Dale Spender, eds. *The Knowledge Explosion: Generations of Feminist Scholarship*. New York: Teachers College Press, 1992. 533p. (Athene Series). bibliog. index. ISBN 080776258X; 0807762571pa.

This celebratory anthology from Columbia University's venerable Athene Series focuses on the discipline created in the early 1970s that scholars would call "women's studies." The forty-four essays address the multivariate methodologies scholars are developing to construct and evaluate knowledge that better accommodate the research needs of the world's women and other subordinated, invisible groups. To provide structure for the book, the editors provided each author with ten questions geared toward either "Disciplines" or "Debates," the titles of the two sections comprising this work. The twenty-eight contributors in "Disciplines" examine epistemological changes within their subject areas, including nursing, geography, architecture, economics, and library science. In the "Debates" section sixteen contributors explore complex and gnarly issues such as sexual violence, ecofeminism, pornography, and patriarchy unearthed during the feminist knowledge explosion. Every academic library should own a copy of this book, one of the most important and comprehensive texts available on feminist epistemologies, and every women's studies and feminist pedagogy program should include it as required reading. Editor Liz Stanley, in *Knowing Feminisms: On Academic Borders, Territories, and Tribes* (Sage Publications, 1997), collects essays that study the actual practice of feminisms in academe and consider internal political factions and other areas of contention that developed as feminism formed, grew, and diverged.

397. Lather, Patricia Ann (Patti Lather). *Getting Smart: Feminist Research and Pedagogy with/in the Postmodern*. New York: Routledge, 1991. 212p. (Critical Social Thought). bibliog. index. ISBN (OP); 0415903785pa.

Patti Lather tackles the theoretical underpinnings of feminist research in what some scholars claim is a post-Marxist, poststructuralist, postmodern world. The concepts are difficult and fraught with implications about the insufficiency of any one research methodology to serve the various strands of feminism that have developed since the late 1960s. Lather treats the difficult conundrum postmodernism poses: that any research problem is, by definition, situational, and without contextual information, no learning or knowledge is possible. The author states, "My hope is to create a text open enough, evocative enough on multiple levels, that it will work in ways I cannot even anticipate" (p. xx). She discusses concepts within the context of her studies examining student resistance to liberatory curriculum. Student journals, diaries, and interviews comprise part of what Lather calls her "data base." She describes the connections between herself and the graduate students and asserts that everyone learned from each other as they interpreted and developed her initial methodology. It seems appropriate that a work about postmodernism closes with a series of "open endings": a postscript, an epilogue, an afterword, and a coda.

398. Lewis, Magda Gere. *Without a Word: Teaching beyond Women's Silence*. New York: Routledge, 1993. 207p. bibliog. index. ISBN 0415905931; 041590594Xpa.

Canadian professor Lewis exemplifies the depth of this beautiful book in the statement regarding her own silences that she claims are "grown . . . not out of inadequacy and deficiency, but of a deeply felt rage at those who live their unexamined privilege as entitlement" (p. 3). The author warns that her book, while highly academic and theoretical, is also quite personal, even intimate. She decries the historical precedent of repressing personal experiences as a means of contributing to androcentric epistemologies and explores "the potential of a feminist pedagogy as a transformative practice in the context of institutional settings" (p. 4). Basing her study on observations of classrooms in Canada, Lewis speaks of a political feminism, an evolving understanding of how to transform women's experiences into a legitimate contribution to the body of knowledge that institutions of higher education prize and perpetuate. The author's courage and ability to articulate the oppressions and social constructs that cause women to remain silent make this work a pivotal choice for inclusion in any women's studies library. *Feminisms in Education: An Introduction* (Open University Press, 1994) by Gaby Weiner also discusses the transformative potential of feminism, especially when it is informed by poststructuralist perspectives. The author uses the British school system to consider the relationships between pedagogy and curriculum and ways in which both contribute to educational inequalities. She also provides a fine overview of feminist theories and their influence on education from the mid-1960s through the early 1990s and an important chapter that develops a feminist praxis in pedagogy and research that addresses connections between power and knowledge.

399. Luke, Carmen, and Jennifer Gore, eds. *Feminisms and Critical Pedagogy*. New York: Routledge, 1992. 224p. bibliog. index. ISBN (OP); 0415905346pa.

Editors Carmen Luke and Jennifer Gore, education professors at the University of Newcastle, Australia, and the University of Queensland, Australia, respectively, gather chapters that examine the use of various critical pedagogies espoused by scholars such as Paulo Freire and Henry Giroux. The introduction describes the evolution of an ever-widening gap between critical pedagogy and feminist critical pedagogy as feminists attempted to integrate, however unsuccessfully, these theories into their classrooms. Concerned that the original theories do not thoroughly address gender issues, contributors explore the history of critical pedagogy by addressing ways in which such theories help disempower women. Many contributors also believe it vitally important to consider class, race, age, and other variables that might alienate individuals from a body of knowledge or classroom experience. Jennifer Gore continues her examination of postmodern and poststructural theories, including the sometimes obtuse theory of Michel Foucault, in *The Struggle for Pedagogies: Critical and Feminist Discourses as Regimes of Truth* (Routledge, 1993). Carmen Luke examines the concepts of "feminisms" and of "pedagogies" outside the classroom by addressing gender stereotypes in toys, mass-media games, and other day-to-day activities in her fascinating work *Feminisms and Pedagogies of Everyday Life* (State University of New York Press, 1996).

400. Maher, Frances A., and Mary Kay Thompson Tetreault. *The Feminist Classroom: An Inside Look at How Professors and Students Are Transforming Higher Education for a Diverse Society.* New York: Basic Books, 1994. 303p. bibliog. index. ISBN 0465033024.

One of the most influential titles written about women's education in the last several decades of the twentieth century, this work documents the authors' ethnographic study of feminist classrooms involving seventeen professors at three institutions. Maher and Tetreault spent three weeks at each institution observing and videotaping classes and interviewing students and teachers. They begin with a brief historical overview of feminist pedagogical theory, then provide profiles for the participating institutions. After explaining the context of the study, the authors present the results of the study in four chapters corresponding with the study's main premises and findings: mastery, voice, authority, and positionality. The authors interweave theory and praxis with the words of teachers and students, which results in a title that reads like a scholarly diary or journal, complete with lapses in chronology and rethinking/restating of conclusions. Maher and Tetreault, however, do not sacrifice scholarly rigor and provide thirty-eight pages of notes and bibliographic citations that support the theoretical underpinning of their work. This widely reviewed title is a collaborative effort that becomes, in one sense, its own argument—a pedagogical work about pedagogy in which previous theory becomes current, evolving praxis. This work would make an excellent textbook in any education or women's studies curriculum, and all women's studies or feminist libraries should own it.

401. McDermott, Patrice. *Politics and Scholarship: Feminist Academic Journals and the Production of Knowledge.* Urbana: University of Illinois Press, 1994. 197p. bibliog. index. ISBN 0252020782; 0252063694pa.

McDermott traces the development of three key interdisciplinary women's studies journals, *Feminist Studies* (1972–), *Signs* (1972–), and *Frontiers* (1972–), to provide a thoughtful history of the intellectual debates, tensions, and controversies that emerged as the discipline developed. She argues that one of women's studies' core assumptions, that research should be politically relevant, differs from other disciplines and underlies much of the struggle for academic legitimacy that the journals, the discipline, and faculty have faced and continue to face. McDermott presents insightful, sophisticated theoretical discussion in accessible language and asserts that diverse research subjects and methodologies can form a cohesive body of knowledge. This important book is recommended for research methods classes in education and women's studies curricula. Extensive notes and references and author and subject indexes add further value to the book

402. Middleton, Sue. *Educating Feminists: Life Histories and Pedagogy.* New York: Teachers College Press, Teachers College, Columbia University, 1993. 209p. bibliog. index. ISBN 0807732346; 0807732338pa.

How does one become a feminist? Middleton attempts to answer this question as she explores and analyzes a matrix of complex interwoven issues. This personal journey about the making of a feminist teacher speaks eloquently of the soul-searching, the existential struggle, and the ultimate rewards of choosing such an often difficult path. Middleton, a New Zealander, began teaching women's studies classes while she remained at a personal loss to understand her subject. "I could not see myself in what I was reading or teaching. . . . feminist knowledge was from elsewhere" (p. 61). She also realized that other women, regardless of geographic locale, might also struggle with the problem of seeing themselves as not positioned or valued in their respective academies. Middleton documents a search for legitimizing the feminist viewpoint within (and outside of) the body of knowledge that academicians teach in colleges and universities worldwide. She interweaves theoretical concepts from the writings of Foucault and the literature of feminist critical pedagogy with her own personal development as a feminist professor. Middleton uses excerpts from various interviews, conversations, and journals of women students and teachers to support her contention that research must always consider "lived lives" in its quest to develop an epistemology that both challenges and enriches women, yet possesses the scholarly rigor that enables legitimization within or at the side of "traditional knowledge." Her impressive and thorough bibliography attests to the theoretical underpinnings to this seemingly nonchalant book. *Changing Our Lives: Doing Women's Studies* (Pluto Press, 1994), edited by Gabriele Griffin, collects personal experiences of British pioneers in the field who discuss learning how to teach women's studies courses, even though such courses did not exist when they were undergraduates.

403. Minnich, Elizabeth Kamarck. *Transforming Knowledge.* Philadelphia: Temple University Press, 1990. 240p. ISBN 0877226954; 0877228809pa.

Minnich, trained as a philosopher, brings the tools of that discipline to bear on the topic of transforming knowledge vis-à-vis women. Her book analyzes ways of thinking or epistemology— how and what we can know, as well as how knowledge can be transmitted to others, including future generations. An extremely personal work, *Transforming Knowledge* results from years of Minnich's questioning of herself and others and her voracious reading and study of the philosophical and historical repertoire. She supplements her somewhat informal, but elegant text with quotes from other works that both support and augment her arguments, thereby creating a kind of dialogue.

Minnich stresses the importance of inclusive language by providing historical context to her analysis of language use and enumerating how the exclusion of women's ways of speaking and knowing became perpetuated and reinforced over time. She examines textbooks and ponders the implications of art books that cover only four women artists and music history texts that do not cover even a single woman composer. She cautions that "we need to go to the root (*radix*) of the tradition that is premised on our exclusion, or we will watch helplessly as the tree of knowledge continues to grow exactly as it did before" (p. 14) and believes that our language must be "transformed, not just corrected or supplemented" (p. 31). Minnich raises questions and proposes possible answers critical for women scholars to consider as they attempt to construct a voice and a language that no longer exclude women from their worldview and body of knowledge. This groundbreaking, complex philosophical work is recommended for all scholars, especially feminist and women's studies scholars, across the disciplines. For one of the pioneer works on feminist epistemology, see *Feminist Thought and the Structure of Knowledge* (New York University Press, 1988) edited by Mary M. Gergen, a collection of essays that is an outgrowth of a 1986 conference of the same name held at the Pennsylvania State University.

404. Paludi, Michele, and Gertrude A. Steuernagel, eds. *Foundations for a Feminist Restructuring of the Academic Disciplines*. New York: Haworth Press, 1990. 276p. (Haworth Series on Women). bibliog. index. ISBN 0866568786; 0918393647pa.

Editors Paludi and Steuernagel give partial "credit" to Allan Bloom, author of the best-selling *Closing of the American Mind* (Simon & Schuster, 1987), for inspiring this collection of discipline-integrated essays. Where Bloom decries the integration of women's studies classes across the curriculum, Paludi and Steuernagel celebrate it. Uncharacteristically for a feminist treatise, this work does not target those involved solely in women's studies as a separate discipline. Rather, it concentrates on curricula in disciplines that persistently remain male oriented despite well over three decades of women-inclusive research and activism. Chapters written by historians, economists, political scientists, and behavioral scientists address the historical place of women within various academic disciplines. Barbara Evans Clements's history chapter, for example, mentions a 900-page U.S. history survey text written in 1967 that contained only two pages about women in history, specifically, women's suffrage. Another chapter explores the history of medicine, focusing on ways in which male physicians have perceived and treated women both as objects of research and as patients. This fine collection of essays makes for a fascinating scholarly read.

Editors Donna Stanton and Abigail Stewart showcase essays written by scholars in women's studies and other disciplines that examine women as outsiders in academe and explore why some disciplines, such as literature and archaeology, incorporate women's theory more readily than others in *Feminisms in the Academy* (University of Michigan Press, 1995). For various perspectives about K–12 curricula, see *Gender In/forms Curriculum: From Enrichment to Transformation* (Teachers College Press, 1995), edited by Jane Gaskell and John Willinsky, a collection of papers originally presented at a Canadian conference, initially considered somewhat of a failure, that later yielded a variety of rich, discipline-based curricular research.

405. Patai, Daphne, and Noretta Koertge. *Professing Feminism: Cautionary Tales from the Strange World of Women's Studies*. New York: Basic Books, 1994. 235p. bibliog. index. (OP)

The authors interviewed thirty women (some of whom volunteered) who represent disenfranchised professors and students associated with academic women's studies programs for the basis of this book. Some of the topics addressed in the interviews include feminist pedagogy and politics, the place of women's studies in higher-education curricula, and philosophical underpinnings, such as women's ways of knowing. The book's publication created a furor: critics of women's studies almost instantly endorsed it as the definitive exposé of "radical feminism," while many feminists, stung by the book's strident tone, reviled it as a treasonous act of betrayal. Patai and Koertge, however, point out some legitimate criticisms, and their well-written historical, philosophical, and political contextual narrative does not warrant dismissal as antifeminist carping. Interviewees report experiencing hostility in women's studies classrooms and feeling pressured to embrace a specific feminist stance or new form of "political correctness" lest colleagues label them "the wrong kind of feminist." Feminists cannot deny that some teachers commit reprehensible acts in women's studies classrooms in the name of feminism. Nevertheless, Patai and Koertge helped damage the discipline by choosing to give voice to women who suffered from the excessive zeal and the pent-up anger sometimes unleashed in feminist classrooms and to ignore the life-enriching, worldview-altering aspects of women's studies programs. In the end, the authors advise that "feminists need to recover their senses and *smell* the roses, rather than worry so much about what to call them" (p. 134). This sometimes maddeningly critical book nonetheless can ultimately prove helpful in identifying and rectifying excesses in current and future women's studies curricula.

406. Statham, Anne, Laurel Richardson, and Judith A. Cook. *Gender and University Teaching: A Negotiated Difference.* Albany: State University of New York Press, 1991. 202p. (SUNY Series in Gender and Society). bibliog. index. ISBN (OP); 0791407047pa.

Much like previous women researchers, Statham, Richardson, and Cook experiment with accepted methodology via incorporating additional data-gathering and interpretation criteria into it. In order to determine ways in which the teaching styles of men and women college professors differ, the authors use a three-step "triangulation approach" that they believe combines the best of both quantitative and qualitative tools and produces a more finely granulated data set. Their methodology involved in-depth interviews with thirty professors using semistructured and open-ended questions; observation of 167 professors and their students in their classrooms using the Hough and Duncan time-unit method to calculate time expenditure on various classroom activities; and surveying the students' reactions to the professors. After crunching the numbers, the authors conclude that differences definitely exist between the instructional styles and classroom management techniques of women and men. For example, male professors tend to use more negative reinforcement techniques than do female professors. Additionally, men do not provide as much face-saving behavior to inattentive or disruptive students as women. On the other hand, female professors tend to use more supportive, participatory classroom management techniques than do male professors. Women in academia receive a certain amount of status and authority by virtue of their positions; however, universities remain largely male centered and often expect women "to demonstrate both female and male sex-typed behaviors—to be simultaneously 'warm' and 'logical' " (p. 4). The closely detailed methodologies contained in the appendices make replication of this important study possible for other researchers investigating the validation and refutation of supposed "truths" about women (and men) in academe. Extensive notes and references and author and subject indexes add further value to the book. This work is recommended for research methods classes in education and women's studies curricula.

407. Torre, Adela de la, and Beatríz M. Pesquera, eds. *Building with Our Hands: New Directions in Chicana Studies.* Berkeley: University of California Press, 1993. 246p. bibliog. index. ISBN 0520070895; 0520070909pa.

Before the introduction to this collection of essays, the editors include a "Note on Ethnic Labels" explaining popular and scholarly usage of such terms as "Chicana," "Mexicana," "Latino," and "Hispanic." The social sciences use the term "Chicana" to refer to women of Mexican descent residing in the United States, the term "Mexicana" refers to Mexican immigrant women, and the term "Latina", to refer to women from Latin America. That the editors felt compelled to begin their book by clarifying these terms clues readers to the lack of societal knowledge about these "women of color," yet another nomenclature some women use to describe themselves. The editors contend, "Our voices have gone largely unnoticed and undocumented" (p. 1). *Building with Our Hands* begins with various perspectives on the historical and intellectual roots of Chicana studies and its emergence as a discipline that intersects, somewhat problematically, with parts of women's studies, ethnic studies, and Chicano (used "generically") studies but somehow needs space for its own separate discipline. Contributors include sociologists, historians, and professors of Chicana, ethnic, and women's studies. Four sections comprise the body of the work. The first, tellingly titled "Acts of Domination/Acts of Resistance," deals with historical aspects of the topic. Part 2 deals with cultural aspects, and part 3 addresses economic and family aspects of Chicana experience. Part 4 consists of two essays, one about Chicana studies by Denise A. Segura, a sociologist at the University of California at Santa Barbara, the other a study of Chicana elderly by sociologist Elisa Facio from the University of Colorado at Boulder. The editors collaborate with their contributors to write a concluding chapter. This seminal work is highly recommended as a textbook for introductory women's studies classes; it is one of the best available resources for giving voice and visibility to a group of women who have felt unheard and unacknowledged for many years.

408. Zimmerman, Bonnie, and Toni McNaron, eds. *The New Lesbian Studies: Into the Twenty-First Century.* New York: Feminist Press at the City University of New York, 1996. 295p. bibliog. index. ISBN (OP); 1558611363pa.

Zimmerman and McNaron collect 40 brief chapters that address lesbians in the classroom and other areas of the academy, survey the state of lesbian studies within a number of disciplines in the humanities and social sciences, and discuss the impact of queer theory on the field. The introduction describes both positive changes and the subsequent backlash in the field since the publication of Margaret Cruikshank's groundbreaking title *Lesbian Studies* (Feminist Press, 1982). They also assert the importance of lesbian feminism's focus on lesbians as women rather than as queers. The first section reprints nine chapters from the 1982 publication that effectively summarize the historical roots of lesbian studies. Chapters in other sections discuss the importance of analyzing lesbian individual and social identities, pedagogy, lesbian studies within specific disciplines, issues for lesbians and lesbian studies within institutions, and theoretical debates. Contributors represent a variety of ages, races, ethnicities, and national locations (United States, United Kingdom, Sweden, and Aotearoa/New Zealand). The collection is accessibly written and should be useful to readers not very familiar with feminist theory. *Straight Studies Modified: Lesbian Interventions in the Academy* (Cassell, 1997), edited by Gabriele Griffin and Sonya Andermahr, is also concerned with the influences of lesbian feminism and queer theory on lesbian studies and reviews the field for the most part in Great Britain but to some extent in Canada, Australia, and the United States. Like the previous title, this one contains chapters that discuss lesbian studies within specific disciplines but notably includes cultural studies, biology, computing, geography, health, and linguistics in addition to humanities and social science disciplines.

Women Faculty, Students, and Academic Climates

409. Aisenberg, Nadya, and Mona Harrington. *Women of Academe: Outsiders in the Sacred Grove.* Amherst: University of Massachusetts Press, 1988. 207p. bibliog. ISBN (OP); 0870236075pa.

The idea for this book took root in a Massachusetts women's group, the Alliance of Independent Scholars, initially formed to discuss women's failures to obtain tenure and the consequent loss of their academic appointments. Editors Aisenberg and Harrington developed a formal study based on two sets of interviews: thirty-seven two-hour interviews conducted in 1980 with women described as "off the normal academic career track" and twenty-five interviews with women who received tenure at their institutions. As a result, they accumulated more than 1,500 pages of transcripts during the course of the project that they developed into this seminal work, now considered a classic in the field of women's studies. The authors were "astonished to find less difference than commonality in the stories of tenured and deflected women" (p. xii). Women in both groups spoke of marginality and isolation on a male-dominated playing field and emphasized the influence of the "unspoken rules" underpinning academic politics of retention, promotion, and tenure. Lack of mentoring, perceptions of noncollegiality, and feelings of aloneness represent some of the recurring themes in this seminal work. A prescriptive final chapter outlines strategies to help women successfully negotiate the tenure process that include dispelling "naïve" beliefs such as "the merit dream," especially when their research centers on "soft" subjects such as women's studies. This book suggests that if women are educated in the ways of the academic world, they can gain a toehold in the male bastion and initiate change themselves once they are on the inside and safely tenured. Books such as this, rife with case studies, particulars, and postmortems regarding tenure experiences, provide ammunition for the continuing battle for gender equity in institutions of higher education.

410. Bannerji, Himani, Linda Carty, Kari Dehli, Susan Heald, and Kate McKenna. *Unsettling Relations: The University as a Site of Feminist Struggles.* Boston: South End Press, 1992. 159p. bibliog. ISBN 0896084531; 0896084523pa.

In a thoughtful and hard-hitting introduction, the five authors acknowledge the influence of Marx and Marxist feminists on their thought and state their intention to describe their explicit experiences with feminism. These women, members of races and ethnic groups that are not empowered, write about the consequences of their status as "outsiders within," how this affected both their careers and their private lives. They strive admirably to make the personal political, often at tremendous psychological risk. As Kate McKenna articulates in her chapter "Subjects of Discourse: Learning the Language That Counts," "I did not want to be thought of as self-indulgent, egocentric, emotional—all of which are, of course, used to discredit women's ability to think and know" (p. 127). Each author acknowledges her essay as social discourse, a piece of work that continued to evolve for her, and that benefited from dialogue with the other authors. All the authors suffered disenfranchisement over the years, feeling silenced and ignored. All struggled with the concept of feminism, especially when white feminist colleagues insisted that women's efforts to gain a foothold in patriarchal universities mattered more than class and race. The lives and experiences of these women suggest much room for improvement before the word "feminist" can include more than just a small, presumably white, minority of the world's women. This rich collection provides glimpses into the lives of feminists just beginning to articulate their own experiences as legitimate and valued expressions of discourse. This work would prove useful to any self-proclaimed feminist or activist who believes that equity and equality battles in academia already have been won.

411. Caplan, Paula J. *Lifting a Ton of Feathers: A Woman's Guide to Surviving in the Academic World.* Toronto: University of Toronto Press, 1993. 273p. bibliog. ISBN 0802029035; 0802074111pa.

One of the most heavily reviewed books in the field of women's studies education, *Lifting a Ton of Feathers* exposes many embedded forms of gender bias still ensconced in institutions of higher education in North America. Caplan, a Canadian professor and psychologist, targets any woman involved in academia, from graduate student to professor, administrator, and job seeker. She devotes a chapter to a detailed listing of the many unwritten rules upon which women in higher education may unknowingly stumble, such as the "myth of collegiality," and a discussion of various possible manifestations of "subtle sexism" that prove more difficult to recognize and combat. Another chapter deals with what the author refers to as "Catch-22s," such as "a woman who speaks up is aggressive and doesn't know when to quit; but a woman who remains silent is passive and incompetent and has nothing worth saying" (pp. 69–70). In the remainder of the work, Caplan analyzes the politics of higher education and suggests possible strategies for sidestepping common land mines that women encounter in academia. Checklists, three appendices, and a thirty-seven-page bibliography, divided into topics, such as "grievances and legal proceedings" and "older women," provide a real "tool kit" for any woman thinking of going into academia. Many scholars consider this work the classic "self-defense" handbook for women academics. Later entries in the women's-survival-in-academia subgenre include the much more irreverent *Ms. Mentor's Impeccable Advice for Women in Academia* (University of Pennsylvania Press, 1997) by Emily Toth, in which the author dispenses serious advice for academic women in a deceptively lighthearted manner, and *Career Strategies for Women in Academe: Arming Athena* (Sage Publications, 1998) by Lynn Collins, in which the author acknowledges her indebtedness to Caplan, then analyzes the current academic climate for women, stressing the need for women to continuously strategize the development of their own careers.

412. Clark, VèVè, Shirley Nelson Garner, Margaret Higonnet, and Ketu H. Katrak, eds. *Antifeminism in the Academy.* New York: Routledge, 1996. 288p. bibliog. index. ISBN (OP); 0415910714pa.

The idea for this collection originated in the Modern Language Association's Committee on the Status of Women in the Profession. Antifeminism, defined by the editors as a backlash against all things and individuals perceived as feminist, serves as the subject of the work, whose purpose "was to name the problem, gather documentation, and examine antifeminist intellectual harassment in three related areas: the history of feminist activisms; campus politics; academic sites of power" (p. x). The editors organize the essays under three topics: (antifeminist) intellectual harassment, multiple jeopardy, and feminist resistance in the academy. An especially compelling chapter on scholarship and culture by Elaine Ginsberg and Sara Lennox points out that many popular press antifeminist books receive much more media attention than scholarly, academic feminist works, which results in members of the general public recognizing names such as Camille Paglia, Christina Hoff Sommers, and Katie Roiphe, but not recognizing names such as Patti Lather, Mary Belenky, or Frances Maher. Law professor Patricia Williams writes a chapter titled "Talking about Race, Talking about Gender, Talking about How We Talk" that addresses the importance of semantics and examines ways in which some people use language to silence dissident voices. The essays in this collection caution that the progress achieved by women, particularly feminists, and people of color can never be taken for granted and must be protected by eternal vigilance. *Antifeminism in the Academy* would make a fine textbook or supplemental reading for both women's studies and education classes at undergraduate and graduate levels alike. For perspectives on the topic from Great Britain, see *Feminist Academics: Creative Agents for Change* (Taylor & Francis, 1995), edited by Louise Morley and Val Walsh, in which contributors examine the distribution of power and influence within the academy, especially in terms of gender, race, and class, and discuss feminist interventions within academic structures and cultures.

413. Gordon, Lynn D. *Gender and Higher Education in the Progressive Era.* New Haven, CT: Yale University Press, 1990. 258p. bibliog. index. ISBN 0300045506.

Lynn D. Gordon, a scholar who has written extensively about the history of women's education, gathers cultural, historical, and educational information about women college students during the Progressive Era in the United States, from 1890 to 1920, a period that represents a second generation of women in higher education. Gordon carefully and thoroughly researched primary documents, such as diaries, student newspapers, alumnae memoirs, scrapbooks, photographs, letters, and papers, enabling her to expand upon previous, narrowly focused research about this critical period and add both depth and a more incisive historical framework for understanding women in higher education. She included private and coeducational institutions in her study, specifically, the University of California at Berkeley, the University of Chicago, Vassar, H. Sophie Newcomb Memorial College, and Agnes Scott College. Gordon concludes, "Women students of the Progressive Era found no ivory towers on their campuses" (p. 189). Male students and administrators at coed colleges felt threatened by what they called the "effeminization" of their institutions. At the same time, all-female institutions tended to adhere to and reinforce traditional gender roles. The women in this bridge generation made substantial contributions in spite of all the obstacles they faced and embraced the radical concept that women could have both a marriage and an education. Although the post-1920s backlash returned male dominance to the nation's campuses, these women had planted the seeds that would blossom into the activism of college women throughout the United States during the 1970s.

414. Holland, Dorothy C., and Margaret A. Eisenhart. *Educated in Romance: Women, Achievement, and College Culture.* Chicago: University of Chicago Press, 1990. 273p. bibliog. index. ISBN 0226349438; 0226349446pa.

This book documents an intriguing ethnographic study conducted over a period of ten years in the lives of twenty-three young women entering college at the study's inception. The women attended one of two pseudonymous colleges, "Bradford," a traditionally black school, and "Southern University" ("SU"), a traditionally white school. The authors chose women who aspired to enter careers in science or mathematics (a nonrandom sample). They conducted monthly interviews with each participant (nine interviews over three semesters) during the first two years, using both standardized and open-ended questions. They conducted follow-up interviews at the anticipated time of graduation and followed four years later with even more in-depth interviews. Although the sample was small, the results of the study prove compelling; scholars reviewed this work in at least seventeen scholarly journals. The authors, both anthropologists, remained open minded in terms of both tweaking their intended methodology and interpreting their results. They conclude that career paths for these women did not form a clear trajectory toward their initial goals of successful science careers. Rather, a majority of these promising young women compromised their plans by dropping out of school and/or becoming underemployed. The authors also learned, to their surprise, that participants' social activities took precedence over academic concerns and that the pervasive atmosphere of male privilege in the two universities seemed to contribute heavily to the women's disenchantment with high-pressure academic subjects in settings where attractiveness to men counted most. The women, however, often stated that they left academia in the name of "romance." The authors suggest topics for future study and provide appendices that document the study's methodology and contain extensive notes.

415. James, Joy, and Ruth Farmer, eds. *Spirit, Space, and Survival: African American Women in (White) Academe.* New York: Routledge, 1993. 293p. bibliog. ISBN (OP); 0415906377pa.

Angela Y. Davis provides a short foreword in this book of very personal and often polemical essays. The editors refer to their work as "an anthology by the least institutionally empowered in academe: African American women working as untenured assistant professors, lower-echelon administrators, and artist-in-residence instructors" (p. 1). The book's title refers to its three sections: "Spirit" consists of three essays by authors who strongly feel that spirituality and ancestral rituals need to claim a place in the college curriculum; "Space" includes nine essays by authors who examine where African American women "fit" into traditional university programs and curricula; and "Survival" includes particularly hard-hitting, sometimes painful chapters by authors who discuss inequities that prevent transformative change in white male-dominated institutions. Ruth Farmer's essay "Place but Not Importance: The Race for Inclusion in Academe," in which the author refers to American higher education as "a lopsided, narrow system which has miseducated and undereducated people of all races for centuries" (p. 198), represents the thoughtful, frank analyses in this collection. The authors, dissatisfied with superficial initiatives universities and colleges hold up as proof of change, call for the inclusion of African American women in all decision-making processes that affect "acceptable scholarship" and curriculum development. The book also contains syllabi and proposals, garnered from classes and workshops the authors have taught, and a comprehensive bibliography. *Spirit, Space, and Survival* is highly recommended as a text or supplementary reading for women's studies, black/African American/Africana studies, multicultural, or general American history classes for students in both high school and college.

Another excellent title, *Black Women in the Academy: The Secrets to Success and Achievement* by Sheila T. Gregory (University Press of America, 1995) presents the results of the author's national study that collected and analyzed educators decisions to stay, leave, or return to academia. Gregory also supplies a literature review and an outline for attracting and retaining black women faculty.

416. Luebke, Barbara F., and Mary Ellen Reilly. *Women's Studies Graduates: The First Generation.* New York: Teachers College Press, Columbia University, 1995. 207p. (Athene Series). bibliog. ISBN 080776275X; 0807762741pa.

Luebke and Reilly gather information documenting the influence of women's studies courses on a group of pioneer students from across the United States. How have these students used their women's studies degrees to begin and advance their careers in fields such as law or business or to enhance their other roles as wives, partners, mothers, and friends? The authors describe their approach as follows: "From the beginning, we agreed that the graduates were the experts and it was their voices we wanted readers to hear" (p. x). Chapter 1 provides a demographic overview of the eighty-nine graduates (eighty-eight women and one man) involved in the project. The next chapter discusses the project's significance for women's studies as a discipline, pointing out the need to educate both administrators who control university budgets and members of the general public, who either do not know what women's studies is or have preconceived, often hostile notions that women's studies programs serve as training grounds for "radical, man-hating feminists." Chapters 3 through 6 present one- or two-page profiles that include information about the participants both before and after earning their degrees, organized by broad occupational categories, such as law and government, education and library services, and health, social, and human services. Most participants generally gave quite positive, certainly very thoughtful responses, with very few negative comments. In the final chapters, Luebke and Reilly usefully summarize the graduates' advice to women's studies majors and potential majors, as well as to faculty and administrators, and discuss recurring themes, such as empowerment and thinking critically, in participants' responses, but make no sweeping generalizations. Instructors should require this well-constructed book as reading at some point in the career of any women's studies major and can use it as a vocational guidance tool for students considering women's studies.

417. Maschke, Karen, ed. *Educational Equity.* New York: Garland, 1997. 322p. (Gender and American Law Series; The Impact of the Law on the Lives of Women, 4). ISBN 0815325185pa.

Known as a scholar who examines important and engaging topics, Karen Maschke, an attorney and an assistant professor of political science at Oakland University in Rochester, Michigan, previously edited seven books in the Gender and American Law Series. In this volume, Maschke collects essays by contributors who address the many facets of educational equity, including educational inequities for both girls and women. The chapters span the nineteenth and twentieth centuries and include a variety of exciting and pertinent topics, as reflected in chapter titles such as "An Interview on Title IX (of the Educational Amendments of 1972)" by Shirley Chisholm and others, "Sex Discrimination in Athletics," "Biases in LSAT," "The Fear of Feminization: Los Angeles High Schools in the Progressive Era," and "*U.S. vs. Virginia*: The Case of Coeducation at Virginia Military Institute," devoted to the Citadel case. This collection provides readers with a solid base for understanding the types of legislation enacted to assist women, as well as the litigation that interprets those laws. It yields an excellent overview of inequities that women have endured in educational institutions in the United States during the past century and a half. It is recommended for education and law classes, particularly at the graduate level, as well as for women and education courses.

418. McNaron, Toni A.H. *Poisoned Ivy: Lesbian and Gay Academics Confronting Homophobia*. Philadelphia: Temple University Press, 1997. 234p. bibliog. ISBN 1566394872; 1566394880pa.

McNaron queried more than 300 gay and lesbian teachers with at least fifteen years' experience in academe about their encounters in various universities and colleges. In 1994, the author distributed 865 survey instruments she considered so sensitive that she promised to keep completed copies under lock and key and initially promised to destroy them at the end of the study. (Her lawyer advised her to rescind that decision.) McNaron, a recipient of several teaching awards, uses her own thirty years as a professor of English and women's studies at the University of Minnesota as a backdrop to her skillful analysis, organization, and presentation of narratives from colleagues throughout the United States. Areas needing further research and ideas for follow-up studies surface and point to the paucity of information available about real-life experiences of longtime gay and lesbian professors, many of whom have remained "in the closet" as a result of harassment and very justified fears of retribution or irrational homophobic acts. *Poisoned Ivy* would make an excellent textbook or supplementary reading for lesbian, women's studies, and general education classes.

419. O'Barr, Jean, and Mary Wyer, eds. *Engaging Feminism: Students Speak Up and Out*. Charlottesville: University Press of Virginia, 1992. 168p. (Feminist Issues). bibliog. ISBN (OP); 081391387Xpa.

O'Barr and Wyer present one of the first books to collect student writings documenting both personal and intellectual effects that occurred as a result of taking a women's studies course. The editors organize the writings into nine chapters that reflect the learning trajectory characteristic within the discipline. The first chapters reveal students' individual, emotional connections to course content. In later chapters, students move toward collective action and development of a politics of knowledge. The work provides a fine contrast to Katie Roiphe's title, annotated later in this section, offers insight into student criticisms and criticisms about higher education generally, and serves as an assessment of the women's studies program at Duke University. Caryn McTighe Musil also incorporates students' voices into her report titled *The Courage to Question* (National Women's Studies Association, 1992). This report evaluates a three-year project, funded by the Fund for the Improvement of Postsecondary Education (FIPSE), that explored students' personal and intellectual transformations set in motion by their course work in women's studies. Musil also offers a theoretical framework for interpreting student evaluations that explicitly links women's studies to the assessment movement and positions women's studies to play a central role in changing higher education. In a companion report, *Students at the Center: Feminist As-sessment* (National Women's Studies Association, 1992), Musil presents detailed designs and methodologies that should prove useful for assessment efforts.

420. Pagano, Jo Anne. *Exiles and Communities: Teaching in the Patriarchal Wilderness.* Albany: State University of New York Press, 1990. 165p. (Feminist Theory in Educa-tion). bibliog. ISBN 0791402738; 0791402746pa.

Pagano presents what is essentially a thought-provoking, Socratic venture into her vision of education and educators as framed by her own life as a woman. She shares insights that are saddening, are often tinged with anger and resignation, and at times border on the voyeuristic, so intimate is her writing style. Toward the end of this slim volume, Pagano asks poignantly whether there "was ever a life more riddled with self-doubt than that of the female professor" (p. 39) and touches upon tender areas of her own vulnerability as she makes her way around the "patriarchal wilderness" of higher education. In another plaintive question she wonders whether "women students' and teachers' anger comes from their sense of being always wrong, always other" (p. 37). Yet her writing does not take on any air of stridency. Rather, her tone is gentle and pensive while simultaneously demanding so that the reader engages with her impeccably constructed thought poem.

421. Roiphe, Katie. *The Morning After: Sex, Fear, and Feminism on Campus.* Boston: Little, Brown, and Company, 1993. 180p. bibliog. ISBN 0316754323pa.

The publication of this book created a frenzy in the media. Roiphe, the daughter of noted feminist author Anne Roiphe, brashly chronicles what she considers the oversensitivity of female students to such topics as "date rape" and "sexual harassment" on the Princeton University campus during the early 1990s. She contends that the "overreaction" of her college administration to these concepts, in part to avoid overzealous feminists' potential lawsuits, reduced the campus to pro-viding mandatory, if inane, sexual harassment orientation sessions and a particularly ridiculous, according to Roiphe, annual "Take Back the Night" rally. This author's pop psychology writing style is full of sound bites, such as "A new bedroom politics had entered the university" (p. 6), and provides a fast, if sometimes rather annoying, read. Her tone is youthfully self-righteous: "It is out of the deep belief that some feminisms are better than others that I have written this book" (p. 7). The entire premise of this slim volume rests precariously upon Roiphe's personal, rather narrow experiences at Princeton, supplemented with anecdotal tales from a few other students. It hardly represents a cross section of the women on U.S. college campuses, who still fight legitimate and often difficult battles against sexual harassment and "real" date rape. Sounding like a Gen-X Camille Paglia, Roiphe has written a book that on one hand amounts to little more than an interesting memoir. On the other hand, due to its subject, the book received an inordinate amount of media coverage; scholars and critics reviewed it in more than thirty major publications. Roi-phe's work obviously struck a chord with the American public, and feminists should not ignore it. It ultimately serves as a prominent example of what some consider "antifeminist backlash."

422. Sandler, Bernice Resnick, Lisa A. Silverberg, and Roberta M. Hall. *The Chilly Classroom Climate: A Guide to Improve the Education of Women.* Washington, DC: National Association for Women's Education, 1996. 123p. bibliog. (OP)

The authors review research findings about women in higher education since the publication of Sandler and Hall's *The Campus Climate Revisited: Chilly for Women Faculty, Administrators, and Graduate Students* (Project on the Status and Education of Women, Association of American Colleges, 1986). The introduction defines terms, explains methodology, and articulates the assumptions underpinning the guide. Sections that follow discuss gender behaviors in the classroom, race, pedagogy, curriculum, classroom structure, faculty evaluation processes, and strategies that institutions, administrators, and individual faculty can use to improve conditions for women. The authors also provide guidelines for faculty to evaluate course content in terms of women, questions designed to expose inadvertent faculty bias in classroom situations, and a list of resources.

423. Tokarczyk, Michelle M., and Elizabeth A. Fay, eds. *Working-Class Women in the Academy: Laborers in the Knowledge Factory.* Amherst: University of Massachusetts Press, 1993. 335p. bibliog. index. ISBN (OP); 0870238353pa.

Although defining the term "working-class" women vis-à-vis the academy remains problematic, Tokarczyk and Fay define it using two criteria: the person's parents hold jobs of a nonprofessional nature, usually characterized by close supervision, for example, waitress or factory worker; and the person represents the first generation of her family to attend college. This fascinating collection of essays addresses the topic from both theoretical and practical perspectives. A recurring theme throughout the book focuses on how a lower-class upbringing confers the status of perennial "outsider" in the halls of academe. In a lengthy and thoughtful introduction, the editors observe, "The chances that a woman from the working class will become an academic are slim, and those women who do are highly aware of their new privileged status" (pp. 16–17). Most working-class women academics have a solid, enduring work ethic. This work ethic can backfire, however, leading to a tendency for the fledgling academic to work too hard on the "wrong" things, such as committee work, to the detriment of potential research accomplishments or to feel too much obligation to "pay back," resulting in the tendency to invest too much energy in activities, such as mentoring and advising students, that will not help her attain tenure. Sample chapter titles include "Keeping Close to Home" by bell hooks, "Telling Tales in School: A Redneck Daughter in the Academy" by Hephzibah Roskelly, and "A Farmer's Daughter in Academia" by Jacqueline Burnside. The voices in this collection present many compelling ideas that deserve incorporation into general feminist theory. This work is worthwhile reading for women's studies, feminist theory, sociology, and education classes.

K–12 Education in the United States

424. AAUW Educational Foundation and the Wellesley College Center for Research on Women. *How Schools Shortchange Girls: The AAUW Report: A Study of Major Findings on Girls and Education.* New York: Marlowe and Company, 1995. 116p. bibliog. ISBN 1569248214.

Twenty years after Title IX of the 1972 Educational Amendments, the American Association of University Women (AAUW) commissioned the Wellesley College Center for Research on Women to produce a report assessing the impact of the legislation. People have quoted and misquoted the report ever since the AAUW Educational Foundation originally published it in 1992. For example, Judith Kleinfeld, author of several articles arguing that boys face worse problems than girls do, accused the AAUW of producing "junk science." A plethora of negative articles, written largely by men, disturbingly miss the larger point: that the education of both girls and boys is in a pathetic state. Yet *How Schools Shortchange Girls* cites thirty-five educational reform documents as well as the abysmally low percentage of women who serve on committees that produce the very documents supposedly representing girls' welfare. Problems enumerated in the report include the perpetuation of sexist language in textbooks, the "evaded curriculum" (avoided subjects, such as sex education), self-esteem issues, and poverty prevention. Solutions for the problems uncovered in this report include stronger enforcement of Title IX, improved teacher education, encouragement of girls in math and science, and meaningful inclusions of girls and women in history and literature texts that teachers incorporate into their curricula.

A follow-up report, *Gender Gaps: Where Schools Still Fail Our Children* (AAUW Educational Foundation, 1998), provides a five-year pulse check on educational reform and recommends further remedies for lingering problems. Contrary to what some critics dismiss as the work of "radical feminists," the liberal use of sidebars, extensive notes, citations, charts, and graphs validates the thoroughly researched AAUW reports. These works are recommended for anyone interested in the education of girls and women, especially those involved in college-level education and women's studies programs. Carrie Paechter presents an important analysis of girls' subordination in British schools that she believes can be used to investigate other marginalized groups in *Educating the Other: Gender, Power, and Schooling* (Falmer Press, 1998).

425. Bank, Barbara J., and Peter M. Hall, eds. *Gender, Equity, and Schooling: Policy and Practice*. New York: Garland, 1997. 252p. (Missouri Symposium on Research and Educational Policy Series). bibliog. indexes. ISBN 0815325347; 0815325355pa.

This important work, a product of the Missouri Symposium on Research and Educational Policy held in Columbia, Missouri, in March 1995, consists of chapters that strive to "provide readers with an understanding of the gendered nature of schooling and educational policy at multiple levels" (p. vii). The editors target academic researchers as well as public policy makers and politicians, who often propose "educational reform" based on political expediency. Several contributors present multidisciplinary perspectives in which they provide in-depth analysis of both positive and negative processes involved in understanding and initiating change in public policy. These chapters provide an excellent starting point for those wishing to find real solutions to deeply ingrained problems of gender bias that have virtually solidified into conventional "wisdom" over the years.

426. Casey, Kathleen. *I Answer with My Life: Life Histories of Women Teachers Working for Social Change*. New York: Routledge, 1993. 196p. (Critical Social Thought Series). ISBN (OP); 041590403Xpa.

In the introduction, Michael Apple, series editor, expresses concern that documents systematically produced by educational policy makers tend to silence teachers' voices. In this title, author Casey sets out to explore means of making the voices of teachers heard and describes her project as follows: "Using the work of both the Popular Memory Group and Mikhail Bakhtin as theoretical justification of my own group biographies, I have tried to create more dynamic and dialogic patterns" (p. 25). Choosing teachers from three distinct groups, Catholic nuns, Jewish women, and African American women, Casey charges her thirty-three subjects with one task: to tell "the story of your life" in one interview with her and with an optional follow-up interview. After analyzing the interviews, Casey concedes that her write-up of the life stories did not match her proposed interactive methodology. Instead, she weaves a tapestry of life vignettes of teachers who take "activist" stands on one or more issues. Casey's first and last chapters deal with the study's theoretical underpinnings and suggest that this method points to exciting possibilities that will further expand educational research without resorting to the quantitative, often nonrevealing methods currently prevalent in much of academia.

427. Dunlap, Diane M., and Patricia A. Schmuck, eds. *Women Leading in Education*. Albany: State University of New York Press, 1995. 444p. bibliog. index. ISBN 0791422151; 079142216Xpa.

A special-interest group, Research on Women in Education of the AERA (American Educational Research Association) serves as the locus of the book's beginnings. This work collects a patchwork quilt of essays, research studies, and personal narratives written by female administrators, teachers, and other leaders in education, for the most part K–12. In the introduction, Dunlap and Schmuck state, "The chapters document the day-to-day drama of how women lead, how they envision their roles, how they are socialized, what inspired them to go forward—or not" (p. 3). Chapter titles include "Learning Leadership through Mentorships," "Mom and Pop Model of School Administration: A Case Study," "Women Principals—Leading with Power," and "Ten Years Later: Too Little, Too Late?" Dunlap, dean of the Graduate School at Hamline University in Minnesota, skillfully pulls together the themes woven throughout the work into a concluding chapter titled "Women Leading: An Agenda for a New Century." A stimulating variety of women's voices make this work an ideal textbook for undergraduate and graduate teachers-in-training, as well as women's studies courses.

428. Grumet, Madeleine R. *Bitter Milk: Women and Teaching*. Amherst: University of Massachusetts Press, 1988. 225p. ISBN (OP); 087023613Xpa.

Madeleine R. Grumet, an editor of the State University of New York's Feminist Theory in Education Series and former dean of education at Brooklyn College, titles her work based on her and other women's ambivalence toward teaching. Her stated goal involves the exploration of her own "contradictions" and attempts to understand what teaching means to women, who comprise the majority of public school teachers. She contends that the dearth of writing about women's experience as teachers represents a kind of denial or perhaps even an unspoken prohibition against speaking about it. Grumet points out that the ten chapters in her book "go back and forth between the experience of domesticity and the experience of teaching, between being with one's own children and being with the children of others" (p. xv). The author, who wrote the essays for various occasions, ties them together in the first and last chapters. The core chapters are more autobiographical and represent expository writing at its most eloquent. Extensive notes, a bibliography, and an index, however, remind the reader that this is a scholarly work, based on pedagogical principles spelled out in feminist, psychoanalytic, and other epistemological theory. Scholars repeatedly cite Grumet's book in the women's studies and feminist literature. This profound work is highly recommended as supplementary reading for education, literature, and advanced women's studies and feminist pedagogy courses.

429. Hauser, Mary, and Janice Jipson, eds. *Intersections: Feminisms/Early Childhoods*. New York: Peter Lang, 1998. 424p. (Rethinking Childhood Series). ISBN 0820430684pa.

The editors of this volume collect chapters by contributors who pose questions, but do not force answers in their analysis of "intersections" between feminism and early childhood education on many levels. The editors loosely weave together philosophy, theory, and practice of childhood education via introductions, conclusions, and dialogues, attributing discrete paragraphs or sections to either "Mary" or "Jan." Authors (and editors) represent a variety of viewpoints in a variety of styles and do not attempt to meld styles into one seamless voice or imply facile agreement where none exists. Thus the editors incorporate letters, diaries, and a play as well as more conventional and "scholarly" essays into their collection. Women educators from many walks of life, searching for and finding their voices, explore both personal and powerful ways to learn, teach, and write. The contributions represent women learning to become better teachers, who share the ambiguities they face when attempting to reconcile their various personal and academic roles and who reveal what the editors call "the collaborative nature of teaching and learning" (p. 208). This book is recommended for women's studies and education classes in critical pedagogy because of its emphasis on the search for ways to legitimize women's and girls' ways of knowing and the importance of teachers finding their own authentic voices.

430. Johnson, Louanne. *Girls in the Back of the Class*. New York: St. Martin's Press, 1995. 256p. ISBN (OP); 0312958803pa.

Johnson, a white teacher who wanted to make a difference, documents her experiences teaching African American and Hispanic youth in a Los Angeles barrio high school. Although she often succeeds in connecting with her students, the power and influence she wields as a teacher cannot touch upon every aspect of their often violent and loveless worlds, even though she opens up her home to several of them. Johnson's autobiographical journal successfully conveys a sense of what teachers in "nontraditional" settings may confront on a daily basis and serves as an antidote for all the literature and scholarly writings about teaching middle-class and non-ethnic sectors. The author also provides a much-needed glimpse into a dark, often hopeless environment and contemplates both problems and possible solutions for these "forgotten" children of the barrio and other urban "jungles" in the world. Johnson suggests that schools reflect girls' upbringing in impoverished, blatantly sexist environments and that this causes most girls to perceive themselves as second-class citizens. Thus they sit "in the back of the class," remaining quiet, silenced, and resigned to a world they feel powerless to change. This work is recommended for women's studies, social studies, political science, and education classes at the high-school and college levels.

431. Marshall, Catherine, ed. *Feminist Critical Policy Analysis*. Washington, DC: Falmer Press, 1997. (Education Policy Perspectives). v. 1: *A Perspective from Primary and Secondary Schooling*. 224p. ISBN 0750706341; 075070635Xpa. v. 2: *A Perspective from Post-secondary Education*. 272p. ISBN 0750706546; 0750706554pa.

Compiled to fill a gap in the literature caused by scholars' relative neglect toward educational policy analysis, these volumes collect chapters, written by scholars from various countries, that address a range of topics, such as school organization, social influences on education, and teacher evaluation and training. The volumes include reprints of important articles and chapters by well-known authors, such as bell hooks, Carmen Luke, and Sandra Acker, as well as many new chapters. Basically the contributors seek political means to influence the implementation of policy that considers routinely ignored feminist and women's concerns.

432. Prentice, Alison, and Marjorie R. Theobald, eds. *Women Who Taught: Perspectives on the History of Women and Teaching*. Toronto: University of Toronto Press, 1991. 301p. bibliog. ISBN (OP); 0802067859pa.

Prentice and Theobald collect ten essays, originally published between 1975 and 1990, considered key to the development of the historiography of women teachers. Essays examine women teaching in public and private schools and higher education during the mid-nineteenth century and early twentieth century in Great Britain, Canada, Australia, and the United States. Most contributors provide wider historical contexts; however, more information about the educational system and social history of each country would have been useful. Contributors show that women teachers garnered respect in the classroom and community and were among the first to organize in professional organizations and unions. They also helped shape gender inequities in education systems. The introduction serves as a quite useful historiography on women teachers, at least white teachers in English-speaking countries, and contains an impressive bibliography. The collection provides insight into the complexities, contradictions, and difficulties involved in historical research. Geraldine J. Clifford provides more personal perspectives of women teaching in higher education during the same time period in *Lone Voyagers: Academic Women in Coeducational Universities, 1870–1937* (Feminist Press, 1989). She focuses on autobiographical writings of individual women to shed light on the challenges women who wanted academic careers faced in carving out a place for themselves.

433. Sadker, Myra and David Sadker. *Failing at Fairness: How America's Schools Cheat Girls*. New York: Macmillan Library Reference, 1994; Simon & Schuster Trade, 1995pa. 347p. bibliog. index. ISBN 0684195410pa.

Myra and David Sadker, dedicated researchers of gender bias in education for two decades, authored this groundbreaking work, one of the most reviewed books in the field. The Sadkers and their research teams spent thousands of hours observing the behavior of male and female students and teachers in elementary, high-school, and college classrooms. Some educators and media criticized *Failing at Fairness* for its supposed lack of scholarly rigor. The research studies, however, solidly document that schools in the United States are filled with "well-intentioned professionals . . . who inadvertently teach boys better than girls" (p. 3). Early in the book, the Sadkers point out that the sexism so ingrained in American culture carries over to schools and negatively affects both boys and girls. The Sadkers reveal the many ways in which teachers reinforce gender stereotypes in the classroom: calling on boys more often than girls, responding more fully to boys, coaching boys more than girls, and even criticizing and punishing boys more often. Boys thus obtain more teacher attention, both positive and negative, and "girls grow quieter as they grow older" (p. 10). The Sadkers also present their intriguing analysis of gender bias in textbooks. They found texts filled with womanless history (including an 819-page world history text, published in 1991, that devoted exactly one page to American women), womanless math, and womanless science. In a chapter titled "The Miseducation of Boys," however, the authors suggest that school systems do not educate boys much better than girls. The book contains an extensive notes section, a nine-page recommended reading list, and a ten-page index. Scholars should include this landmark study as required reading in college-level education and women's studies curricula. The Myra Sadker Associates Web site (http://www.sadker.org/index.htm) provides information about research David Sadker continues to conduct after Myra Sadker's death.

434. Shmurak, Carole. *Voices of Hope: Adolescent Girls at Single Sex and Coeducational Schools*. New York: Peter Lang, 1998. 220p. (Adolescent Cultures, School, and Society). bibliog. index. ISBN 0820438340pa.

Shmurak sets out to test a much-repeated assertion: that girls fare better at same-sex schools and in same-sex classes. She presents her analyses and findings throughout this book. Her first chapter contains a thorough literature review of studies and reports produced in the United States, supplemented with research conducted in Great Britain, Canada, and Australia. Shmurak augments the literature review with charts she created using data collected in the studies. The next chapter describes the methodology and reasoning behind her five-year longitudinal study. Beginning in 1992, Shmurak collected and compared data from two same-sex and two coeducational high schools. She conducted lengthy annual interviews with selected girls, starting with their freshman year of high school, "to trace the development of the participants' thinking about school, career, and women's roles while also tracking their grades, standardized test scores, and college admission data" (p. 23). A significant portion of this ambitious book consists of transcribed interviews, and each chapter concludes with a section called "Reflections," in which Shmurak provides thoughtful summaries of her findings. She tabulates and interprets the data collected in her study, again accompanied by charts, and the last chapter, "Reconsiderations," summarizes the study and poses questions for scholars to consider in future research. Shmurak's highly readable book is recommended for vocational guidance counselors as well as general education and women's studies classes. Trudy J. Hanmer, an educator who strongly suggests that parents consider same-sex schools for their daughters, bemoans the slow progress of girls' education in American coeducational settings, citing many studies that document differences in girls' and boys' learning preferences and capabilities, in *The Gender Gap in Schools: Girls Losing Out* (Enslow Publishers, 1996).

435. Thorne, Barrie. *Gender Play: Girls and Boys in School.* New Brunswick, NJ: Rutgers University Press, 1993. 237p. bibliog. index. ISBN (OP); 0813519233pa.

Barrie Thorne, a sociologist and college professor, has studied the play patterns of children for many years. In *Gender Play*, she documents two ethnographic studies she conducted, one in the mid-1970s and the other in 1980. Thorne spent many hours in classrooms and playgrounds at two elementary schools, one in California and one in Michigan, observing and recording the behavior of girls and boys while simultaneously recording raw data. She uses these data as the basis for her analysis of gender behaviors she encountered, with particular attention to power plays between genders. Thorne reveals ways in which teachers unintentionally contribute to gender segregation: pitting girls against boys in learning exercises, for instance. Although Thorne generally agrees with the feminist theory that gender roles are social constructs, she concludes that a true explanation is more complex than even she originally thought. In the final chapter, "Lessons for Adults," Thorne states, "A more complex understanding of the dynamics of gender, of tensions and contradictions, and of the hopeful moments that lie within present arrangements can help broaden our sense of the possible" (p. 173). A careful researcher, Thorne provides detailed citations for the work of other researchers across disciplines, particularly those in sociology, feminist pedagogy, and women's studies, in thirty-seven pages of notes. This work is recommended for elementary education teachers and students, as well as courses in women's studies and feminist pedagogy.

436. Tyack, David, and Elisabeth Hansot. *Learning Together: A History of Coeducation in American Public Schools.* New Haven, CT: Yale University Press for the Russell Sage Foundation, 1990. 369p. bibliog. index. ISBN (OP); 0871548887pa.

Perhaps appropriately, both a female and a male scholar collaborated to write this history of coeducation in the United States. Tyack, a historian, and Hansot, a political scientist, contend that "historians have largely ignored gender policies and practices in education" (p. 3). They seek to remedy this oversight by examining the historical roles of each gender and the relationships between them as they trace education's evolution since the birth of the United States. Although the authors focus on schools as institutions, they enrich their text with details of individual lives and perceptions, often accompanied by a number of photographs. Sample chapter titles include "Why Educate Girls?" "Differentiating the High School: The 'Boy Problem,' " "Differentiating the High School: The 'Woman Question,' " and "Feminists Discover the Hidden Injuries of Coeducation." Tyack and Hansot provide extensive notes and an interesting appendix titled "Using Photographs as Evidence of Gender Practices in Schools." This widely reviewed work provides valuable historical information and influenced later research about the education of girls and women in the United States. Catherine Hobbs's fascinating book *Nineteenth-Century Women Learn to Write* (University Press of Virginia, 1995) examines historical gaps that Tyack and Hansot pointed out in *Learning Together*, using women's essays, diaries, and other primary sources.

Global Perspectives on the Education of Women and Girls

437. Arnot, Madeleine, and Kathleen Weiler, eds. *Feminism and Social Justice in Education: International Perspectives.* New York: Falmer Press, 1993. 235p. bibliog. index. ISBN 0750701013; 0750701021pa.

The contributors to this volume, all from industrial, white-dominant, Anglophone settings, examine feminist theory, politics, and practices within their own countries (Australia, New Zealand, the United States, and Great Britain). Each evaluates the impact of twenty years of feminist research and policy development on education, using what the editors term critical feminism, an examination of gender equality and power relations within specific material conditions and locations. Topics covered include the promotion of Maori culture in a predominantly white education system, school desegregation in the United States, the politics of teaching history in Great Britain, black feminist education philosophies, feminist education policy in Australia, and African Caribbean women in the British education system. This volume addresses feminist educators' struggle with theory and the importance of constant reassessment so that meaningful practices for all students can be developed. Another title, *Anti-racism, Feminism, and Critical Approaches to Education* (Bergin & Garvey, 1995), edited by Roxana Ng, Pat Staton, and Joyce Skane, collects chapters, also written by contributors from Anglophone countries, that provide in-depth analysis of intersecting oppressions in education due to ethnicity, race, gender, and class. Contributors presented their chapters to the other contributors and made revisions based on the feedback they received from them. This process helps provide coherence across chapters and enables thorough discussions of theoretical debates.

438. Bloch, Marianne N., Josephine A. Beoku-Betts, and B. Robert Tabachnick, eds. *Women and Education in Sub-Saharan Africa: Power, Opportunities, and Constraints.* Boulder, CO: Lynne Rienner, 1998. 320p. (Women and Change in the Developing World). bibliog. index. ISBN 1555877044.

A conference held at the University of Wisconsin served as the impetus for this collection of fourteen heavily referenced essays by scholars who represent a wide variety of disciplines and philosophies and address issues of women's education in sub-Saharan Africa from feminist, postmodern, Marxist, and more traditional perspectives. Deconstruction of the terms "African women," "sub-Saharan," and even "women's education" reveals the complexity of the topic. This book provides both introductory information and detailed analysis of topics, such as traditional education for girls and boys, the importance of long-standing oral traditions, and the emphasis in certain geographical areas upon spirituality, religion, ritual, and folktales. Thirty-five charts and graphs supplement the text. This collection is an excellent example of a single-volume introduction to the educational issues facing women and children in a particular region of the world. It adds depth to general women's studies curricula, as well as to ethnic studies programs dealing with women of color.

439. Committee on Women's Studies in Asia, ed. *Changing Lives: Life Stories of Asian Pioneers in Women's Studies.* New York: Feminist Press at the City University of New York, 1995. 225p. bibliog. ISBN (OP); 1558611096pa.

Thirteen writers from eleven Asian countries, including India, Japan, China, and the Philippines, relay stories of their involvement with women's studies in this edited collection. It documents both inner and outer struggles women faced as they tried to reconcile their own lives with their countries of birth, where society expected women to play subservient roles. Fanny M. Cheung attended school in the United States between 1966 and 1975 and found the feminist approach "too simplistic, rhetorical, antagonistic, and militant" (p. 65). Yet she wanted to transcend her prescribed mission in life as a woman who married, then realized that her heightened expectations for herself indeed made her feminist. Thanh-Dam Truong, born in South Vietnam and sent to the United States at the age of eighteen to attend college, contributes a particularly moving essay in which she recalls questioning herself, her parents, her religion, and her country as she adjusted to the turbulent 1960s in the United States, when America waged war against her birth country. *Changing Lives* is an excellent introduction to exceptional women who belie any rigid definitions of what it means to be a woman. In another recommended title, *Women, Education, and Development in Asia: Cross-National Perspectives* (Garland, 1996), edited by Grace C. L. Mak, contributors examine educational gains, and the lack thereof, for women in ten countries in East, South, and Southeast Asia since the end of World War II. Both books address the political and economic ramifications of educating women in the countries or regions covered, and both would prove worthwhile for international women's studies, political science, and education classes.

440. Conway, Jill Ker, and Susan C. Bourque, eds. *The Politics of Women's Education: Perspectives from Asia, Africa, and Latin America.* Ann Arbor: University of Michigan Press, 1993. 261p. (Women and Culture Series). (OP)

This book, a product of the 1987 Mount Holyoke College Sesquicentennial Conference on World Wide Education for Women, consists of four sections. Contributors of chapters in the first three sections consider women's educational and economic situations in Asia, Africa, and Latin America. Contributors of the two chapters in the fourth section discuss methodology and comparison. The editors collect pieces that reveal the numerous, often dissimilar struggles that international women experience to gain economic power and fulfill their desire for better educational systems. Women in some countries have made strides, but these strides do not always benefit them. In-ho Lee, for example, in her chapter "Work, Education, and Women's Gains: The Korean Experience," points out that "there is an inverse relationship between a woman's level of education and her participation in the labor force, and this is because education for women encourages them to accept traditional roles" (p. 77). Several contributors discuss the inevitable connection between prevailing educational policy and political conditions, especially in countries where political leaders view education as a powerful tool they can use to indoctrinate people. Jill Ker Conway's final chapter questions the prevailing assumption that better access to education necessarily increases women's economic opportunities. This very worthwhile collection of writings articulates international educational policies and their impact on women.

An excellent companion volume, *Gender in Popular Education: Methods for Empowerment* (Zed Books, 1996), edited by Shirley Walters and Linzi Manicom, investigates informal education in six countries, including South Africa, India, Australia, and the Philippines, and discusses a variety of subjects, such as global restructuring, educational projects with women factory workers in Malaysia, and women in Appalachian grassroots educational organizations. This work reinforces the idea of education as a tool of empowerment as articulated by Paulo Freire, the Brazilian activist educator whose work frequently serves as a point of departure for feminists engaging in educational activism.

441. Kelly, David H., ed. *International Feminist Perspectives on Educational Reform: The Work of Gail Paradise Kelly.* New York: Garland, 1996. 247p. (Garland Reference Library on Social Science). bibliog. index. ISBN 0815320051.

David Kelly collects twenty years of groundbreaking essays authored by his wife, Gail Paradise Kelly, a long-term professor at the State University of New York at Buffalo and a pioneer in international comparative education, who died in 1991. Her doctoral dissertation, titled "Franco-Vietnamese Schools, 1918–1938," marked the start of a career that would take her to Vietnam, Nigeria, and South Africa, where she continuously searched for more effective means to assess international educational systems. Educators still use Paradise Kelly's feminist framework that incorporated women's issues into research in comparative international education. Scholars and teachers must include this work about one of the foremothers of feminist education in women's history collections and curricula. Paradise Kelly also edited the *International Handbook on Women's Education* (Greenwood Press, 1989), in which she collects information about women's education from representative countries in all world regions. Each chapter profiles a country, presents difficult-to-find statistical information, and addresses schooling history (ideological, religious, political, and cultural aspects), education status in the 1980s (enrollment patterns, content), and outcomes (labor-force and political participation, government policies). This work, more descriptive and analytical than theoretical, is notable for its assertion that educational systems contribute to women's subordination in other areas of life.

442. King, Elizabeth M., and Anne M. Hill, eds. *Women's Education in Developing Countries: Barriers, Benefits, and Policies*. Baltimore: published for the World Bank by Johns Hopkins University Press, 1993. 337p. bibliog. index. ISBN 0801845343; 0801858283pa.

This book's unique approach to the topic of women's education worldwide makes it an important read. The editors and contributors emphasize socioeconomic, demographic, and other quantifiable information and provide surveys and studies that correlate economic indicators with variables related to the welfare of and economic impact on women. Researchers collected raw data from various geographic locations within the following regions: sub-Saharan Africa, the Middle East and North Africa, Latin America and the Caribbean, South Asia, and East Asia. The final chapter, written by Rosemary T. Bellew and editor Elizabeth M. King, titled "Educating Women: Lessons from Experience," summarizes specific educational problems that women experience in various countries. Extensive notes at the end of each chapter assist the reader in locating further information. This work should prove helpful for classes that deal with international women and ethnic studies classes since its political perspective adds a dimension sorely lacking in some of the more general research books on women's education.

443. Moseley, Eva Steiner, ed. *Women, Information, and the Future: Collecting and Sharing Resources Worldwide*. Fort Atkinson, WI: Highsmith Press, 1995. 296p. index. ISBN 0917846672pa.

This important collection consists of forty-six short essays originally presented in workshops at a conference at Radcliffe College in 1994. Before the 200 international women dispersed, they drafted an "Information Statement" that encouraged participants at the 1995 United Nations Fourth World Conference on Women held in Beijing to urge their governments to make education and information sources available to their countries' women. Librarians, archivists, information workers, and teachers from around the world provide evidence that much remains to be done to ensure that women's history, health information, labor statistics, and other usable and timely data will be collected and made available in accessible formats and technologies. This historic and significant book is recommended for every women's studies and feminist library or archive.

444. Stromquist, Nelly P., ed. *Women and Education in Latin America: Knowledge, Power, and Change*. Boulder, CO: Lynne Rienner, 1992. 309p. (Women and Change in the Developing World). bibliog. index. ISBN 1555872867.

This title collects case studies conducted in countries such as Peru, Brazil, and Costa Rica that examine the role education plays in the lives of women and girls. Editor Stromquist points out in her fine introduction that education as socializing agent has been relatively ignored in Latin America and that education is "a gendered experience with its own dynamics and consequences" (p. ix). Contributors from various disciplines address political and economic aspects of education, girls and women in both formal education systems and popular education, and strategies that can lead to improvements in education at all levels. Although the studies reveal many regional differences affecting women's education, all of them find that discrimination toward women and girls in educational systems is persistent and perpetuates gender stereotypes. Furthermore, they also show, like Paradise Kelly, that education systems greatly contribute to women's inequality in other areas of society. Each chapter concludes with notes and a list of references in English, Spanish, and Portuguese. Most chapters also contain useful statistics, many of them not readily available. This collection publishes the work of several contributors in English for the first time and is recommended for development, education, and women's studies collections. Another title, *Pedagogy, Democracy, and Feminism: Rethinking the Public Sphere* (State University of New York Press, 1996) by Adriana Hernández, explores critical pedagogy in the streets and chronicles activism as practiced by the Mothers of Argentina against that nation's various dictatorships from 1976 to 1983.

1999 CORE TITLES

Alvine, Lynne B., and Linda E. Cullum, eds. *Breaking the Cycle: Gender, Literacy, and Learning*. Portsmouth, NH: Boynton/Cook, Heinemann, 1999. 184p. bibliog. ISBN 0867094907.

Arnot, Madeleine, Miriam David, and Gaby Weiner. *Closing the Gender Gap: Postwar Education and Social Change*. Malden, MA: Blackwell, 1999. 191p. bibliog. index. ISBN 0745618839; 0745618847pa.

Bethune, Mary McLeod, Audrey Thomas McCluskey, and Elaine M. Smith, eds. *Mary McLeod Bethune: Building a Better World: Essays and Selected Documents*. Bloomington: Indiana University Press, 1999. 317p. bibliog. index. ISBN 0253336260.

Blackmore, Jill. *Troubling Women: Feminism, Leadership, and Educational Change*. Philadelphia: Open University Press, 1999. 242p. (Feminist Educational Thinking). bibliog. index. ISBN 033519480X; 0335194796pa. .

Boler, Megan. *Feeling Power: Emotions and Education*. New York: Routledge, 1999. 235p. bibliog. index. ISBN 0415921031; 041592104Xpa.

Crocco, Margaret, Petra Munro, and Kathleen Weiler. *Pedagogies of Resistance: Women Educator Activists, 1880–1960*. New York: Teachers College Press, 1999. 132p. (Athene Series). bibliog. index. ISBN 0807762989; 0807762970pa.

Davis, Sara N., Mary Crawford, and Jadwiga Sebrechts, eds. *Coming into Her Own: Educational Success in Girls and Women*. San Francisco: Jossey-Bass, 1999. 361p. bibliog. index. ISBN 0787944904.

Erskine, Sheena, and Maggie Wilson, eds. *Gender Issues in International Education: Beyond Policy and Practice*. New York: Falmer Press, 1999. 182p. (Garland Reference Library of Social Science, v. 1162; Reference Books in International Education, v. 43). bibliog. index. ISBN 0815328613.

Glazer-Raymo, Judith. *Shattering the Myths: Women in Academe*. Baltimore: Johns Hopkins University Press, 1999. 237p. bibliog. index. ISBN 0801861209.

Lingard, Bob, and Peter Douglas. *Men Engaging Feminisms: Pro-Feminism, Backlashes, and Schooling*. Philadelphia: Open University Press, 1999. 192p. (Feminist Educational Thinking). bibliog. index. ISBN 033519818X; 0335198171pa.

Mayberry, Maralee, and Ellen Cronan Rose, eds. *Meeting the Challenge: Innovative Feminist Pedagogies in Action*. New York: Routledge, 1999. 354p. bibliog. index. ISBN 0415922488.

Merrill, Barbara. *Gender, Change, and Identity: Mature Women Students in Universities*. Brookfield, VT: Ashgate, 1999. bibliog. index. ISBN 1840149930.

Morley, Louise. *Organising Feminisms: The Micropolitics of the Academy*. New York: St. Martin's Press, 1999. 215p. (Women's Studies at York). bibliog. index. ISBN 0312216769; 0312216785pa.

Shapiro, Sherry B. *Pedagogy and the Politics of the Body: A Critical Praxis*. New York: Garland, 1999. 176p. (Garland Reference Library of Social Science, v. 1153: Critical Education Practice, v. 16). bibliog. index. ISBN 0815327811.

Streitmatter, Janice. *For Girls Only: Making a Case for Single-Sex Schooling*. Albany: State University of New York Press, 1999. bibliog. index. ISBN 0791440931; 079144094Xpa.

Tidball, M. Elizabeth, Daryl G. Smith, Charles S. Tidball, and Lisa E. Wolf-Wendel, eds. *Taking Women Seriously: Lessons and Legacies for Educating the Majority*. Phoenix: Oryx Press, 1999. 228p. (American Council on Education/Oryx Press Series on Higher Education). bibliog. index. ISBN 1573560928.

Weiler, Kathleen, and Sue Middleton, eds. *Telling Women's Lives: Narrative Inquiries in the History of Women's Education*. Philadelphia: Open University Press, 1999. 166p. (Feminist Educational Thinking). bibliog. index. ISBN 0335201741; 0335201733pa.

WORLD WIDE WEB/INTERNET SITES

445. *The American Association of University Women (AAUW).* http://www.aauw.org.

The AAUW promotes quality education for all women and girls and is comprised of three corporations: the Association, the AAUW Educational Foundation, and the AAUW Legal Advocacy Fund. The site contains fact sheets and position papers, research findings, and public policy principles and priorities and encourages activism by providing links to members of Congress, monitoring congressional voting records, and maintaining *Get the Facts*, a voter education fax and e-mail network, and *Action Alert*, a monthly newsletter. For a historical study of this highly effective organization, see Susan Levine's *Degrees of Equality: The American Association of University Women and the Challenge of Twentieth-Century Feminism* (Temple University Press, 1995). The National Association for Women in Education (NAWE), an organization devoted to advancing women in higher education, also maintains a useful site (http://www.nawe.org) that identifies professional development, networking, and employment opportunities. It includes information about conferences, publications, and other resources and provides a list of links to sites of related professional associations and organizations and sites that provide information about scholarships and funding, listservs and discussion groups, and employment opportunities.

446. Freyd, Jennifer, and J.Q. Johnson. *References on Chilly Climate for Women Faculty in Academe.* http://dynamic.uoregon.edu/~jjf/chillyclimate.html.

Freyd and Johnson of the Psychology Department and the Library of the University of Oregon, respectively, compile a thorough online bibliography of sources for women faculty in academe. The Web site's introduction cites two studies, one from 1986 and the other from 1997, that suggest that the academy consistently rates female faculty substantially lower than males in terms of both quality and quantity of research, as well as other academic work. The authors of this site indicate several erroneous assumptions regarding gender bias, such as the notion "that gender bias and discrimination require a conscious sexist ideology or a conscious attempt to discriminate against women." In fact, instances of gender bias and discrimination are so ingrained in academe that they manifest themselves in unintended ways through even the best-meaning colleagues. The site contains more than fifty books and journal articles that address the general chilly climate, bias in student evaluations, bias in hiring and evaluation, tenure inequity, and the difficulties involved in balancing academic and personal responsibilities. The authors supplement the list with online and print sources on pay inequity statistics and studies. Freyd and Johnson do not appear to update the site very often and heavily favor print materials. Still, the authors collect much valuable information, incorporate it into one convenient Web site, and successfully combine a traditional bibliography with some hypertext links to other Web sites.

447. Korenman, Joan. *Syllabi on the Web for Women- and Gender-Related Courses.* http://www.umbc.edu/cwit/syllabi.html.

Approximately 600 discipline-related syllabi for women- and gender-related courses comprise this Web site. As with all of Joan Korenman's excellent Web sites, this one is well constructed, resource filled, and frequently updated. The site contains hypertext links to sites for disciplines including education, sexuality/sexual orientation, women of color, and women's studies/gender studies, with each link providing the date of its last revision. Course links to syllabi indicate whether or not they require substantial Internet use. Additionally, Korenman provides links to other academic sites, such as that of Northern Arizona University, that contain women-related courses. Other valuable sites authored and maintained by Korenman include *Women's Studies Programs, Departments, and Research Centers* (http://research.umbc.edu/~korenman/

wmst/programs.html), a directory of links to approximately 500 women and gender studies programs, departments, and research centers' Web sites worldwide, *Women-Related Higher Education Web Sites* (http://www-unix.umbc.edu/~korenman/wmst/links_edu.html), and *Internet Resources on Women: Using Electronic Media in Curriculum Transformation* (http://www .umbc.edu/wmst/updates.html), which updates Korenman's 1997 manual of the same title published by the National Center for Curriculum Transformation Resources on Women.

448. *National Women's Studies Association (NWSA).* http://www.nwsa.org/.

Another excellent Web site sponsored and maintained by the University of Maryland, the NWSA page contains available up-to-date interdisciplinary, multicultural feminist scholarship in order to link feminist theory and praxis. NWSA, a research organization that strives to "support and promote feminist/womanist teaching, learning, research, and professional and community service," maintains this metasite of resources related to NWSA activities and research nationwide. The site includes short descriptions and buying information about NWSA publications, such as *Liberal Learning and the Women's Studies Major* (1991) by Johnnella Butler and others, *Selected Syllabi of Women's Studies Courses* (1995) by Wendy Kolmar and Patricia Voight, *The NWSA Backlash Report: Problems, Investigations, and Strategies* (1997) by Diana Scully and Danielle Currier, and *Guide to Graduate Work in Women's Studies* (1990, 1995, 2000).

449. Vanfossen, Beth. *The Institute for Teaching and Research on Women, Towson University.* http://www.towson.edu/itrow.

Founded in 1990, the Institute for Teaching and Research on Women (ITROW) promotes both research on women and the integration of women into the curriculum. The Web site provides information about research projects, funding sources, grant writing, curriculum integration activities, and feminist pedagogy. It also contains bibliographies on various pertinent topics, links to other sites on the Internet, and ITROW newsletters. A related Web site, the National Center for Curriculum Transformation Resources on Women (NCCTRW) (http://www.towson.edu/ncctrw), collects and maintains comprehensive information about curriculum transformation projects in secondary and higher education in the United States.

450. Weisbard, Phyllis Holman, with the Women's Study Section of the Association of College and Research Libraries. *WSSLINKS: Women, Girls, and Education.* http:// www.library.wisc.edu/libraries/WomensStudies/womened.htm.

Weisbard, the women's studies librarian at the University of Wisconsin, and Joan Korenman, mentioned earlier, are two true Web site pioneers in the area of women's studies. If one could chose only two Web sites for daily use, the Korenman and Weisbard sites would prove most useful. The University of Wisconsin site, actually a metasite, can connect researchers to hundreds of other women-related Web sites through its collection of fully annotated hypertext links covering topics like curriculum, pedagogy, research, funding, issues, periodicals, and discussion lists. Examples of the carefully selected, content-rich sites include the *AskERIC Lesson Plans Database* (http://askeric.org/Virtual/Lessons/) and *Research Sponsored by the American Association of University Women* (http://www.aauw.org/2000/research.htm).

6 Law

Cindy Ingold

Feminists have continued to critique the legal system for its injustices toward women in the past fifteen years. Since the publication of the previous edition of this bibliography, the field of feminist jurisprudence, the philosophy of law based on the political, economic, and social equality of the sexes, has continued to grow. Important voices in this debate include Drucilla Cornell, Cynthia Daniels, Catharine MacKinnon, and others. Globalization, a transnational economy, and ongoing political unrest in several regions of the world have forced human rights violations and issues of inequity, including gender inequity, into the public eye. While individuals and organizations continue to address these issues from an activist stand, scholars too have begun to focus more on the legal rights of women and children worldwide, including the rights of refugee and immigrant women. Several ongoing legal challenges for women remain, however, including the low number of women serving in governmental bodies or as heads of state, the gradual erosion of a woman's right to a legal abortion in the United States, and the continuing struggle to create just laws for victims of domestic violence, rape, or sexual harassment. These challenges indicate that women still have a long way to go before achieving "legal" equality.

This chapter includes books on the philosophy and theory of law, along with titles focused on key legal issues for women, such as abortion, reproductive rights, domestic violence, rape, sexual harassment, and the body. A few titles in the chapter expose the challenges female students face in law schools and the challenges practicing female lawyers face in the still male-dominated world of law. Several books deal with legal and civil rights concerns of lesbians and gay men. Additionally, significant titles focusing on women's legal issues in other countries are included, although this is an area where further research needs to be done.

For the most part, self-help books, guides for the layperson, and popular literature have been excluded. Readers should note that many books dealing with sexual harassment, domestic violence, rape, and divorce fall into these categories. Because of the overwhelming number of titles published on certain topics, including abortion or rape, only selected, representative titles have been included. Readers should check Frances Holland's excellent source *Feminist Jurisprudence: Emerging from Plato's Cave: A Research Guide* (Scarecrow Press, 1996) (see entry 454) for additional sources. Government documents are not included.

The "Politics and Political Theory" chapter lists books on women in government as well as books on women's human rights issues, although some human rights sources are listed in this chapter. The "Feminist Theories and Women's Movements" chapter includes books on women's movements from around the world.

Readers should consult the Web sites listed in this chapter for up-to-date information on the status of pending laws and initiatives. Many of the Web sites also provide access to excellent reports, white papers, newsletters, and other publications.

REFERENCE SOURCES

451. DeCoste, F.C., K.M. Munro, and Lillian MacPherson, comps. *Feminist Legal Literature: A Selective Annotated Bibliography*. New York: Garland Publishing, 1991. 499p. (Garland Reference Library of Social Science, v. 671). indexes. ISBN 0824071174.

This annotated bibliography of journal articles covering the decade of the 1980s includes "multi-disciplinary materials dealing with issues of interest to feminists, written from a feminist perspective, and of relevance to law" (p. vii). Articles from legal periodicals as well as alternative press titles, social science journals, and international human rights literature are included. The authors searched several online databases, including legal databases, *PAIS, Humanities Index*, and *Sociological Abstracts*, as well as print resources, including *Women Studies Abstracts* and *Alternative Press Index*. The bibliography includes mostly English-language articles, but articles in French are also included from French Canadian periodicals. Divided into seventeen topical chapters, the bibliography includes chapters on legal issues such as constitutional law, criminal law, and legal practice. Additional chapters cover such topics as abortion and reproduction, race, lesbianism and sexual orientation, pornography, and prostitution. Three indexes by author, journal title, and topic will help users locate relevant works.

452. Feinberg, Renee. *The Equal Rights Amendment: An Annotated Bibliography of the Issues, 1976–1985*. New York: Greenwood Press, 1986. 151p. indexes. ISBN 0313247625.

This is a sequel to *The Equal Rights Amendment: A Bibliographic Study* by Anita Miller and Hazel Greenberg (Greenwood Press, 1976). Feinberg includes 380 citations to newspaper articles from the *New York Times*, the *Washington Post*, and the *Wall Street Journal*, 250 citations to journal articles, and a very select number of government documents. Approximately one-third of the references are annotated. No monographs are included. The bibliography is organized into eleven chapters. The first six chapters are topical, including employment, education, and public opinion. The remaining chapters cover the chronology of the Equal Rights Amendment from ratification efforts to after 1982. One chapter includes citations to television news broadcasts. An introduction provides a historical overview of the fight for the ERA. One author index and one subject index are included.

453. Hartel, Lynda Jones, and Helena M. VonVille. *Sexual Harassment: A Selected, Annotated Bibliography*. Westport, CT: Greenwood Press, 1995. 158p. (Bibliographies and Indexes in Women's Studies, no. 23). index. (OP)

Hartel and VonVille's title picks up from *Sexual Harassment: A Guide to Resources* by M. Dawn McCaghy (G. K. Hall, 1985), which covered the period from 1974 to 1984. This resource includes 535 references covering the period from January 1984 through 1994. Designed for students, researchers, librarians, legal professionals, and personnel officers, the bibliography includes articles, books, and dissertations selected because of "their scholarly, original, or creative contribution to sexual harassment literature" (p. ix). The focus is on the United States. The authors excluded the following types of materials: editorials and letters, generic works, materials not readily available in the United States, newspaper articles, and popular titles. The authors retrieved citations from a variety of databases and indexes, including *Books in Print, Business Periodicals Index, Cumulative Index to Nursing and Allied Health Literature, Dissertation Abstracts International, ERIC, FirstSearch, Legal Resources Index, LegalTrac, MEDLINE, PsycLIT, Social Sciences Index*, and *SocioFile*. Every source, except for dissertations, includes a brief descriptive annotation. Entries are listed in eighteen chapters, organized under four broad categories, although it is difficult to discern where each new section begins: history and theory, sexual harassment in workplace settings, sexual harassment in academic and social settings, and legal aspects. An appendix provides a chronology of significant legislation and publications relating to sexual harassment. An author index and a subject index are included.

454. Holland, Frances Schmid. *Feminist Jurisprudence: Emerging from Plato's Cave: A Research Guide*. Lanham, MD: Scarecrow Press, 1996. indexes. ISBN 0810831414.

This exceptional source was created to provide researchers with a selective list of monographs and to develop library collections to meet the needs of students in law school and women's studies. The focus is the U.S. legal system. Entries are arranged under main topics, then alphabetically by author or editor. Annotations include a description of contents, depth of coverage of a topic, scope, and date ranges. Because titles could easily fall under more than one topic, entries are cross-referenced. Chapter 1 discusses research strategies, providing keywords for in-depth searching, leading authors, databases, types of sources such as case law, articles, annotated law reports, and government documents. Chapter 2 offers an introduction to feminist jurisprudence, and chapter 3 lists general sources, including books on feminist theory, philosophy, and politics, as well as newsletters, bibliographies, dictionaries, and other reference sources. The remaining chapters are topical, covering a variety of areas, including religion, international sources, reproductive rights, pornography and rape, and the workplace. This title includes an author index and a topic index. *Feminist Jurisprudence* is an essential source for libraries with law and women's studies collections. Another key bibliography is the *Women's Annotated Legal Bibliography*, published annually by the Benjamin N. Cardozo School of Law at Yeshiva University from 1983 through 1992 in seven volumes. The bibliography included an annotated listing of cases, statutes, and law review articles listed under topical sections. In the early years, the sections included such topics as the Equal Rights Amendment or employment discrimination or abuse. Over the years, topics changed and became more specific so that in volume 7 topics included gay rights or child abuse. In 1993, the scope and coverage of this source changed to become the *Cardozo Women's Law Journal*. The journal, published annually, includes scholarly articles, notes, and the "Women's Annotated Legal Bibliography."

455. Jones, Constance. *Sexual Harassment*. New York: Facts on File, 1996. 280p. (Library in a Book). index. (OP)

Although currently out of print, this title is indispensable for reference collections, as well as women's studies and feminist libraries. The book begins with an overview of sexual harassment: Jones both defines it and discusses related issues. One entire chapter presents a chronology of sexual harassment in the United States. Another short chapter contains biographical listings of key players such as Catharine MacKinnon, Anita Hill, and Sandra Day O'Connor. Most of the book consists of a guide to researching information on sexual harassment and a topically arranged bibliography more than 100 pages long. A comprehensive listing of organizations that help in filing complaints or provide general information about sexual harassment concludes the work. Although the series title may seem pretentious, Jones manages to present a fairly thorough treatment of the topic, providing a fine starting point to research, identify, and deal with sexual harassment, even suspected sexual harassment.

456. Salokar, Rebecca M., and Mary L. Volcansek, eds. *Women in Law: A Bio-Bibliographical Sourcebook*. Westport, CT: Greenwood Press, 1996. bibliog. index. 392p. ISBN 0313294100.

Women in Law presents short contributed biographies of forty-three women "who chose the vehicle of law to achieve" (p. 8). The alphabetically arranged work includes women from nations trained in the Western legal tradition. It does not include women from nations with a Marxist tradition, certain parts of Asia, and most of the Islamic world. Some of the women listed in the biobibliography were trained in law, but many were not. Many of the women worked for a variety of causes, including divorce reform, family and adoption law, abortion, gender equity, ethnic reconciliation, the environment, and the poor. An editorial advisory board of eight scholars from the United States, Canada, and Europe nominated women for inclusion in this source. The biographies do not include photographs, but they do include notes and references. An appendix lists women by their professional contribution to law.

457. Sellen, Betty-Carol, and Patricia A. Young. *Feminists, Pornography, and the Law: An Annotated Bibliography of Conflict, 1970–1986*. Hamden, CT: Library Professional Publications, 1987. 204p. index. (OP)

This bibliography provides annotated citations of books, articles, unpublished reports, nonprint materials, and organizations on the antipornography debate, covering the years 1970 to 1986. It does not include legal citations, or sources on the "link between viewing pornography and committing acts of violence" (p. 3). The authors relied on computer databases and print bibliographies to identify sources. The bibliography is organized by type of source, including books; magazine articles; newspapers; nonprint media, which includes television broadcasts, documentaries, sound recordings, and slides; unpublished material, which includes papers from conferences and transcripts of hearings; and organizations. Within each section, references are listed alphabetically by author or editor. One appendix provides a short list of periodicals with frequent references to the feminist antipornography movement. A subject index is included.

MONOGRAPHS

458. Arjava, Antti. *Women and Law in Late Antiquity*. New York: Oxford University Press, 1996. 304p. bibliog. index. (OP)

Focusing on the period between the second and seventh centuries A.D., Arjava analyzes the evolution of legal changes for women during the decline of the Roman Empire. Arjava concludes that very little changed for women during this period, even with the influence of Christianity and the onslaught of invasions from Germanic tribes beginning in the third century. As the author writes, "The central theme of this study is change—or the lack of it. How did the legal and social position of Roman women change during the period which is called late antiquity?" (p. 3). Arjava relies mainly on surviving legal codes from the period for this study. In six chapters, the author examines several topics: mothers and children, fathers' relationships with children, married women's rights, single women, sexual relations outside marriage, and finally, women's roles in male society. While legal changes did occur for women during this period, the author suggests that such changes had little effect on the daily lives of families. The rule of the father over all members of the family remained absolute; married women continued to be able to inherit property; divorce laws did not seem to have been influenced by Christian moral doctrines; and while women had strong legal rights in the Roman world, their role in society was quite restricted. Well researched and well argued, *Women and Law in Late Antiquity* provides a clear picture of the legal lives of women during the decline of the Roman Empire and the beginnings of the early Middle Ages. Writing as a social anthropologist, Roger Just attempts to present the Athenian conception of women in the fifth and fourth centuries B.C. in *Women in Athenian Law and Life* (Routledge,

1991). Just employs existing legal texts as well as literature of the period to offer a coherent depiction of Athenian women.

459. Cornell, Drucilla. *At the Heart of Freedom: Feminism, Sex, and Equality*. Princeton, NJ: Princeton University Press, 1998. 253p. bibliog. index. ISBN 0691028974; 0691028966pa.

In the opening pages of her book, Drucilla Cornell writes: "Where does women's freedom begin? It should begin with the demand that we free ourselves from the use of gender comparisons as the ideal of equality" (p. 3). For Cornell, professor of law, political science, and women's studies at Rutgers University, women should not strive to be equal to men, because this does not allow women to achieve true freedom. Using Kantian political philosophy, Cornell argues that "we should privilege the freedom of every member of society simply as a human being.... Second, we should demand the equivalent evaluation of our sexual difference, a demand clearly mandated by any *fair* theory of distributive justice" (p. 11). How to overcome the so-called differences of "sexed" beings is a problem for Cornell that must be addressed: "it demands that we explicitly recognize the moral space necessary for equivalent evaluation of our sexual difference as free and equal persons.... It is this moral space that I have named 'the imaginary domain' " (pp. 14–15). Cornell discusses several issues, including the regulation of prostitution, the rights of birth mothers and adopted children, family law, the fathers' movement, and international human rights.

In *The Imaginary Domain: Abortion, Pornography, and Sexual Harassment* (Routledge, 1995), Cornell writes that she "will develop a view of equality that provides us with a new perspective on the relationship of sexual difference to equality and of equality to freedom in the hotly contested issues of abortion, pornography, and sexual harassment" (p. 4). Cornell argues that there are three conditions necessary for all of us, but especially women, to "transform ourselves into individuated beings who can participate in public and political life as equal citizens" (p. 4): "1.) bodily integrity, 2.) access to symbolic forms sufficient to achieve linguistic skills permitting the differentiation of oneself from others, and 3.) the protection of the imaginary domain itself" (p. 4).

In *Beyond Accommodation: Ethical Feminism, Deconstruction, and the Law* (Routledge, 1991), Cornell deliberates over a central issue of feminist theory, what Cornell labels the essentialist and the naturalist arguments to construct Woman: "If there is to be a feminism at all, we must rely on a feminine 'voice' and a feminine 'reality' that can be identified as such and correlated with the lives of actual women; and yet at the same time, all accounts of the feminine seem to reset the trap of rigid gender identities, deny the real differences between women . . . and reflect the history of oppression and discrimination rather than an ideal or an ethical positioning to the Other to which we can aspire" (p. 3). Cornell asserts that we need to deconstruct essentialism and free feminine writing, stating that "we will then be able to distinguish the attempts to elaborate the specificity of Women or women as constructed by a particular context—my focus will be the law—from either essentialist or naturalist contexts" (p. 4). Cornell's writings are highly theoretical and difficult to read, and her ideas are perhaps too utopian for some. However, because she raises important questions concerning the nature of true equality for men and women, her writings are essential to all academic library collections.

Postmodern Legal Feminism (Routledge, 1992) collects the writings of Mary Joe Frug, and was published posthumously after Frug's murder in 1991. *Postmodern Legal Feminism* "rereads legal texts in resistance to the standard discursive assertions that law is neither constructed by gender dichotomies nor constitutive of gender" (p. xxiii). In rereading these texts, especially contract casebooks, Frug asks "how our understandings of gender affect our understandings of the law" (p. xxiii).

460. Craig, Barbara Hinkson, and David M. O'Brien. *Abortion and American Politics.* Chatham, NJ: Chatham House, 1993. 382p. bibliog. index. ISBN (OP); 0934540896pa.

Abortion and American Politics uses "the abortion controversy as an illustrative portrait, even if in some ways a disappointing reflection, of the American governmental and political process" (p. xv). The initial five chapters analyze abortion politics from the 1973 *Roe v. Wade* decision to the 1989 *Webster v. Reproductive Health Services* ruling, with each chapter focusing on a different political actor: the courts, interest groups, states, Congress, and the executive branch. Additional chapters explore public opinion and abortion and how polls can be used and misused, as well as abortion politics after *Webster* at both the federal and state levels, "showing how the strategies and apparent political advantages of interest groups were altered by that ruling" (p. xvi). This book includes illustrations, plus several tables and figures.

Karen O'Connor's *No Neutral Ground? Abortion Politics in an Age of Absolutes* (Westview Press, 1996) presents the abortion issue in a broad social and political context and focuses on many of the same actors and issues as the previous title, including interest groups, Congress, the courts, and the executive branch. O'Connor divides the book into seven sections, beginning with an overview of the issues, moving through the history of the abortion debate, and ending with the politics of abortion from 1980 through the Clinton administration. *No Neutral Ground?* includes discussion questions, a glossary, a timeline, and a table of cases. Both titles could be used as textbooks in classes on women and government.

Abortion Law in the United States, edited by Jenni Parrish (Garland Publishing, 1995), includes relevant cases, statutes, and legal and popular articles in three volumes. Volume 1 provides an introduction and covers the years 1973 to 1994; volume 2 includes laws and readings from the nineteenth century; and volume 3 consists of recent articles from a variety of perspectives. This source would be an excellent supplement to the previous two titles. Finally, *Abortion Politics: Public Policy in Cross-Cultural Perspective*, edited by Marianne Githens and Dorothy McBride Stetson (Routledge, 1996), contains essays discussing abortion politics and policies in several modern industrialized countries, including the United States, Canada, Western and Eastern Europe, and Japan.

461. Daniels, Cynthia R. *At Women's Expense: State Power and the Politics of Fetal Rights.* Cambridge, MA: Harvard University Press, 1993. 183p. bibliog. index. ISBN 0674050436; 0674050444pa.

In her introduction, Daniels writes, "The notion that the fetus has rights as a patient and a citizen, separate from the pregnant woman's, has generated a deep crisis in reproductive relations in the United States" (p. 1). Exploring this concept of fetal rights, Daniels employs three case studies to explore three emerging dimensions within the debate over fetal rights. Daniels defines the first dimension, the power of self-sovereignty, as the right to bodily integrity and claims that it is more fundamental than the right to vote or to earn a living. This dimension is illustrated by the forced medical treatment of a pregnant woman. Dimension two, the power of political agency, is the "ability to transform public structures . . . to reflect one's needs, interests, and concerns" (p. 5). Ironically, as women have brought into the public light the special concerns of reproductive health and family concerns, public structures have often responded with forced controls. Dimension three, perhaps the most compelling, is the power of moral discourse or the power of the state to legitimize "shared moral norms and cultural beliefs which under girdpower relations" (p. 6). The case analyzed here involves the prosecution of a pregnant woman for addiction, and as Daniels argues, it raises important questions about the mythology of motherhood and how society views women in the public culture. Daniels analyzes these dimensions in three chapters; in her conclusion, she argues that we must begin to have a new, more complex view of body politics.

Human Reproduction, Emerging Technologies, and Conflicting Rights by Robert Blank and Janna C. Merrick (CQ Press, 1995) explores several issues relating to human reproduction, including surrogate mothers, embryo research, preselection of sexual preference for children, and neonatal care for critically ill infants. Synthesizing a great deal of medical and policy information within each chapter and providing supporting data in tables and charts, Blank and Merrick assert that medical advances, changing social values, and emerging legal cases are challenging the traditional views of reproductive rights and creating complex policy dilemmas.

In *Misconceiving Mothers: Legislators, Prosecutors, and the Politics of Prenatal Drug Exposure* (Temple University Press, 1997), Laura E. Gómez writes, "In this book, we see how prenatal drug exposure moved from widespread popular recognition to institutionalization in the state apparatus that responds to social problems" (p. 4). Focusing on California during the period from 1983 to 1996, Gomez documents the evolution of the "problem" of prenatal drug exposure from a social concern to a political issue.

462. Downs, Donald Alexander. *More Than Victims: Battered Women, the Syndrome Society, and the Law*. Chicago: University of Chicago Press, 1996. 309p. (Morality and Society). bibliog. index. ISBN 0226161595.

Donald Downs critiques the syndrome excuses that "have gripped criminal law and justice for better than a decade" (p. 3). Focusing specifically on battered woman syndrome (BWS), Downs believes that the criminal justice system must envision a new approach when dealing with women who kill abusive partners. For Downs, the focus on BWS in legal cases is a political issue because it portrays women as weak and helpless. By concentrating on battered woman syndrome, Downs hopes to show not only the legal but the political inequities women face in American society: "The multiple themes of violence, abuse, power and powerlessness, citizenship, justice, and political and legal constructions of the self emerge most prominently in the consideration of this syndrome" (p. 14).

Patricia Gagné's *Battered Women's Justice: The Movement for Clemency and the Politics of Self-Defense* (Twayne Publishers, 1998) explores the battered women's movement and its role in changing law. Gagne draws upon the Ohio battered women's movement as a case study, but also analyzes events in six other states to document the history "of the battered women's movement and the role it played in creating legal defense strategies for women who killed or assaulted abusive partners and in securing large-scale clemency reviews for women incarcerated for such crimes" (p. 6).

463. Drachman, Virginia G. *Sisters in Law: Women Lawyers in Modern American History*. Cambridge, MA: Harvard University Press, 1998. 334p. bibliog. index. ISBN 0674809912.

Drachman provides a history of female lawyers in the United States from the late 1860s to the 1930s. The author, who also has written a history of female doctors, contends that during the nineteenth and early twentieth centuries, the legal profession strove to keep women out of its ranks more than any other profession, and that the women who did fight to become lawyers had to overcome a patriarchal dominance that was inherent in the profession. In other words, women who wanted to practice law had to defend laws that discriminated against them: "The very act of gaining admission to practice law demanded that women change the law of the land" (p. 2). Drachman chronicles women's struggles to gain entrance into law schools, to integrate state bars, to establish female legal associations and organizations, and to balance family and career. The author shows that women did make some strides to integrate the profession early on, but by the 1930s, women could claim only moderate successes in this field, a situation that barely changed until the 1970s. Drachman employs a wide array of sources, including manuscript collections of women lawyers, law schools, and legal organizations; newspapers and magazines; judicial decisions, statutes, and legal periodicals; and the letters of the Equity Club, a correspondence club of women lawyers in the late 1880s. This work also includes illustrations, as well as a variety of tables with such data as the marital status of women lawyers, specializations of female lawyers, and the decennial growth of women lawyers from 1870 to 1960. This is a compelling social history providing an excellent overview on the sexism within the legal profession and the women who fought to challenge this sexism.

464. Eisenstein, Zillah R. *The Female Body and the Law*. Berkeley: University of California Press, 1988. 235p. bibliog. index. (OP)

This highly theoretical text aims to create a new understanding of the meanings of sameness and difference between men and women by focusing on the body: "I intend to reconceptualize the meaning of equality and, with it, the meaning of difference. In particular, my focus reintroduces the pregnant body in order to decenter the privileged position of the male body" (p. 1). The problem, as the author sees it, is that for women, gender is regarded as biologically determined: "Gender is a mix of both woman's unique biological potential and its cultural reduction to her determined function" (p. 3). The pregnant body is especially problematic because in our society, it becomes "conflated with the 'idea' of the mother, [and] we are left with the *en*gendered meaning of sex 'difference' which attributes the hierarchal opposition of 'woman' and 'man' to nature" (p. 3). Eisenstein views the law, at least in the Western world, "as an authorized discourse—as a language constituted by a series of symbols that is located in not merely the realm of the 'ideal' or the 'real' but a place somewhere in between" (p. 4). The author is especially interested in this place in between because she sees it as a mix of diversity rather than "dualistic oppositions" (p. 5). She assesses the legacy of the Reagan administration on the politics of inequality, focusing especially on pornography, affirmative action, and abortion.

In *Hatreds: Racialized and Sexualized Conflicts in the 21st Century* (Routledge, 1996), Eisenstein considers hatreds, including genocide; gender and transnational feminisms; nationalisms; and the morass of the new world/old world order. The works of this compelling, forward-looking social critic and vigorous theorist are highly recommended for all types of libraries.

465. Erickson, Amy Louise. *Women and Property in Early Modern England*. New York: Routledge, 1993. 306p. bibliog. index. (OP)

Erickson examines the lives of ordinary English women from 1580 to 1720, "comparing laws of property transmission with women's everyday experience of inheritance, marriage, and widowhood" (p. 4). She examines a wealth of legal documents, including wills, inventories of property, and probate records from four counties, Lincolnshire, Cambridgeshire, the southern half of Northamptonshire, and West Sussex. Part 1 of the book provides an introduction and overview of English law, as well as describing the sources Erickson consulted. The remaining three sections discuss women and property during three periods of women's lives: as unmarried women, as wives, and as widows. Contending that common law provided the strictest interpretation of property settlements for women, Erickson believes that common law was balanced with other types of laws, such as equity, manorial, and ecclesiastical law, all of which were fairer to women. Erickson concludes that daughters inherited property on a scale equal to sons, and that wives had a great deal of influence over their husband's property decisions. Nonetheless, Erickson cautions that the legal system and the men who controlled it worked to keep women firmly subordinate. By the beginning of the nineteenth century, social and political forces conspired to resolve "conflicting legal practices, usually in the favor of common law" (p. 6), which had an even more harmful effect on women's legal rights.

Married Women's Separate Property in England, 1660–1833 (Harvard University Press, 1990) by Susan Staves presents similar ideas while examining several aspects of married women's property rights in England from 1660 to 1833; Staves, however, concentrates on the lives of upper-class women, showing again how the plurality of laws and different courts worked in favor of property settlements for women. She too concludes that by the early 1800s, an ideological and political shift occurred so that women's property rights became more restricted during the nineteenth century.

Feminism, Marriage, and the Law in Victorian England, 1850–1895 (Princeton University Press, 1989) explores how Victorian feminists worked to reform marriage laws. Mary Lynn Shanley discusses Victorian feminists who believed in nothing less than full equality for men and women and sought to persuade Parliament to pass new laws governing divorce, married women's property rights, child abuse, and conjugal rights. While these remarkable women were successful on some issues, their quest for full legal equality between men and women did not succeed.

466. Fairstein, Linda A. *Sexual Violence: Our War against Rape*. New York: William Morrow and Co., 1993. 288p. index. (OP)

Sexual Violence: Our War against Rape is both a compelling memoir of Linda Fairstein's twenty-year career in the Manhatten District Attorney's Office Sex Crimes Unit and a social history of the profound changes that have occurred regarding rape law in the past twenty-five years. Fairstein writes that the book was "written as feminist attention to these issues was finally beginning to help revolutionize the way these crimes were treated in our courts" and to show how "we have started to make great progress in removing the veil of secrecy from these crimes and in attacking them vigorously and creatively in the courtroom" (p. 9). In her introduction, Fairstein cites a *New York Times* article from 1969 reporting "that although more than one thousand arrests were made in New York City for rape that year, only *eighteen* men were convicted of the crime" (p. 14). The author discusses several causes for the slow evolution of changes in rape law, including a criminal justice system that labored "under archaic and unjust laws inherited from the British centuries ago" (p. 7) and the often misleading and sensationalized stories of rape in the media. The majority of the book provides a view of the daily life of a prosecutor, including discussion of the case of the "midtown rapist," date and acquaintance rape, and the tools used in legal cases, including DNA identification. While Fairstein admits that "we have made little progress in the effort to eradicate the crime of rape" (p. 17), she does believe that we have made great strides in rape law. *Date Rape: Feminism, Philosophy, and the Law* (Pennsylvania State University Press, 1996), edited by Leslie Francis, centers around the chapter "Date Rape: A Feminist Analysis" by Lois Pineau. Pineau argues "for the criminalization of nonconsensual sex among acquaintances by developing a model of communicative sexuality" (p. xii). Two lawyers and two philosophers respond to this article, debating and critiquing definitions of acquaintance rape, consent, and legal issues.

467. Fineman, Martha Albertson. *The Neutered Mother, the Sexual Family, and Other Twentieth Century Tragedies*. New York: Routledge, 1995. 239p. ISBN (OP); 0415910277pa.

In this powerful book, Fineman explores how gendered notions of the family, that is, the sexual-intimate connection between husband and wife, have limited family law policy and practice. Beginning with the assumption that ideological beliefs about the family have remained unchanged even as new structural forms of the family have emerged, Fineman writes, "It [this book] reflects my conviction that legal regulation is grounded on societal beliefs and expectations that continue to reflect unexamined gendered politics, policies, and practices" (p. 6). Claiming that "the ideological components of patriarchy and their role in the construction of gender as reflected in law and policy" (p. 6) have a tenacious hold on societal views, Fineman asserts that real change can occur only if we begin to view notions of family apart from sexual connections. The first of four parts provides a historical overview of the development of ideas about family, looks at the many ways our lives are gendered, and discusses the evolution of feminist legal theory. Part 2 explores the construction of motherhood in law, including two contrasting symbolic views: the virtuous mother and the deviant mother. Chapters in part 3 explicate how prevailing views of the sexual family limit new discourse and thus real change in family law. In the final part, Fineman argues for an end to marriage as a legal category and proposes a new "family" model based on the caretaking metaphor of mother/child. In presenting this dyad, Fineman hopes to expand upon the positive aspects of mothers as caretakers and extend the view of caretaking beyond the nuclear family.

In *The Illusion of Equality: The Rhetoric and Reality of Divorce Reform* (University of Chicago Press, 1991), Fineman critiques the legal reforms inherent in divorce and child custody laws during the past two decades, reforms that have argued for the equal treatment of men and women in such cases. She claims that equality reforms "have actually reinforced men's control within the family before and after divorce" (p. 3) and argues that women and children "will fare better under legal rules which reference their material and emotional circumstances, not grand theoretical abstractions" (p. 11).

Fineman and Nancy Sweet Thomadsen edited *At the Boundaries of Law: Feminism and Legal Theory* (Routledge, 1991), which includes selected papers presented over four years at the Feminism and Legal Theory Conference at the University of Wisconsin. Six sections present topics ranging from the construction of the body in law to discussions of pleasure and pain to feminist strategies within legal institutions. Here, as in the previous two works, Fineman continues her argument that feminist theory and criticism "must continue to be the subject of discourses located outside of law" (p. xv). As a feminist legal scholar, Fineman is one of the most powerful voices speaking today.

468. Glendon, Mary Ann. *Abortion and Divorce in Western Law*. Cambridge, MA: Harvard University Press, 1987. 197p. bibliog. index. ISBN (OP); 0674001613pa.

This short text presents a comparison of abortion and divorce law from twenty countries and then considers how such a comparative analysis could affect legal changes regarding these two issues. Glendon suggests that American law differs on these topics primarily because of a different way of "thinking about law that gained greater predominance in the Anglo-American world than elsewhere," and because of different types of "linkages that were made between law and political theory in the common law and civil law systems" (p. 3). Glendon also considers the rhetoric of law, including how it tells a story, how and why there might be a distinctly American story, and the types of meaning family law is creating. Throughout the work, the author stresses the importance of comparative legal analysis to help resolve many social issues, and the idea that law should be educational and not just prescriptive.

469. Griffiths, Anne M.O. *In the Shadow of Marriage: Gender and Justice in an African Community*. Chicago: University of Chicago Press, 1997. 310p. bibliog. index. ISBN 0226308731; 0226308758pa.

Griffith examines the rules and laws on family, procreation, marriage, and divorce within a small African community, basing her work on her ethnographic study carried out over a period of seven years. Griffiths writes, "This book addresses the question of women's procreative relationships with men and their access to family law in Botswana" (p. 11). The study, drawing from detailed life histories and case studies, analyzes "the impact that these social contexts have on an individual's (especially a woman's) ability to access and manipulate a legal system which incorporates Tswana customary and European law. This raises issues about legal identity which revolve around the colonial/postcolonial dimension of law and how it is played out in terms of national, regional and local domains" (p. 11). By focusing on the law within a broader social context, Griffiths aims to show the links between legal, social, and political identities. Griffiths also examines power structures within kinship, family, and the community and the types of discourse people use to make legal claims. The eight chapters discuss the gendered dynamics of households, procreation, pregnancy and marriage, divorce, and legal claims to property. Various charts and photographs enhance this study, while specific hearings on legal disputes are included in appendices. While focusing on one small community in Africa, *In the Shadow of Marriage* nonetheless reveals the intricate relationships between legal, political, and social systems.

470. Guinier, Lani, Michelle Fine, and Jane Balin. *Becoming Gentlemen: Women, Law School, and Institutional Change*. Boston: Beacon Press, 1997. 175p. bibliog. index. ISBN (OP); 0807044059pa.

This provocative work presents an important message for the twenty-first century of how a truly fair and egalitarian society will benefit all involved. Focusing on the education of women in law schools, the authors present powerful new ways of thinking about how we educate, train, and employ women and other outsiders not only in the legal profession but in other male-dominated professions as well. At the center of this work is a study of the experiences of law students at the University of Pennsylvania enrolled between 1987 and 1992. The authors examined the academic performance of 981 students, surveyed 366 students, extracted essays from 104 students, and interviewed groups from 80 female and male students. They learned that the experiences of women law students differ markedly from those of men. Asserting that the single one-size-fits-all means of admitting and educating students in law schools needs to change, the authors argue that a more broad-minded set of criteria needs to be established for the changing dynamics of what lawyers will do in the coming years. They are not advocating lowering standards, but "adapting standards to fit a changing and changed work environment" (p. 18). The final chapter by Guinier, using autobiographical material, attempts to answer this question: What can we learn from women of color in law school? This important book presents a model of rethinking conventional institutional practices and policies, which do not benefit all members of society.

Mona Harrington takes this picture one step further by presenting a view of practicing female lawyers in *Women Lawyers: Rewriting the Rules* (Knopf, 1994). Harrington interviewed more than 100 women lawyers, all graduates of Harvard Law School, from cities all over the country under diverse circumstances. Harrington analyzes how female lawyers may be changing the landscape of the law and thus "of the larger, society-wide upheaval that is reshaping all our lives" (p. 9). She examines two questions to provide answers: "What stands in the way of equal professional authority for women lawyers? And second, How are women lawyers using the authority they have to advance the equality of women generally?" (p. 10). While the author admits that many gains have been made, she also acknowledges that women still have a long way to go to gain equality in society.

Rebels in Law: Voices in History of Black Women Lawyers, edited by J. Clay Smith Jr. (University of Michigan Press, 1998), includes sixty-two articles focusing on the history of black women in the law. The essays, which include theory, philosophy, personal reflections, and stories, cover the topics of law and its call to black women; legal education and the legal profession;

presidents and judges; race, equality, justice, and freedom; crime and criminal justice; and international concerns.

471. Hoff, Joan. *Law, Gender, and Injustice: A Legal History of U.S. Women.* New York: New York University Press, 1991. 525p. (Feminist Crosscurrents). bibliog. index. ISBN 0814734677.

This dense text argues that the history of women's legal rights in the United States has always settled for too little, too late. Hoff writes: "The Second Women's movement, like the First Women's movement, may also end up settling for too little, too late and hence, in retrospect, may also reflect no more than the sum of its achievements in behalf of individual female rights. . . . [This book] calls for a revolutionary reform of the U.S. legal system through a feminist demystification and reinterpretation of legal texts and the reassertion of the relevance of history in that process" (p. 2). The author believes that women have made legal gains only when the power brokers of society have moved on to more important political and economic issues. She argues that true legal rights for women will come only with emancipation, which she defines to mean "equitable treatment that is not grounded, as equal treatment is, in dominant male values of any time period and that does not violate women's sense of community, commonality, and/or culture by demanding assimilation or acceptance of stereotypic 'feminine' roles as the price for full participation in U.S. society" (p. 9). The book presents a chronological history of women's legal rights in the United States from the American Revolution to 1990. Six appendices contain primary documents focusing on women's legal rights, including the 1848 Declaration of Sentiments, constitutional amendments, and a summary of litigation and legislation from 1963 to 1990. This powerful work, which calls for a revolutionary change in legal rights for women, should be required reading in all law schools.

In *Caring for Justice* (New York University Press, 1997), Robin West proposes that legal institutions and common laws have failed women. She argues "that if it is true, as relational feminists claim, that the act of caring for others to whom we are connected in some way is central to our moral lives, then our capacity for care should be at the center of our virtues, and specifically that it should be central to the meaning of legal justice" (p. 9).

472. Hoskyns, Catherine. *Integrating Gender: Women, Law, and Politics in the European Union.* New York: Verso, 1996. 248p. bibliog. index. ISBN (OP); 1859840787pa.

Hoskyns's intention in writing her book is "to subject the operations of the European Union to a feminist scrutiny, and in so doing to open up hitherto ignored spaces and ask new questions" (p. 1). Her analysis adds an important dimension to EU activities and works to connect the fields of European studies and women's studies. Hoskyns traces the development of the European Union's policy on women's rights from its origins in "Article 119 of the Treaty of Rome on equal pay, through to its current spread of policy initiatives, legislative provisions and funding programmes" (p. 1). Writing that the women's policy is the most developed of social program policies within the European Union and the one where political constituencies have influenced legislative decisions for several years, Hoskyns is interested in the interactions between governments, institutions, and policy groups. Hoskyns utilizes primary documents, secondary sources, interviews, and archives from the Council of Ministers in Brussels to reconstruct her history of women's rights and the European Union from the 1950s to December 1992, when the Treaty on the European Union was signed. Three threads run throughout this work: "the substantive content of the EU women's policy and its implications and effects," "the impact of different kinds of organization and mobilization among women on EU policy making," and "the structural development of the EU itself" (p. 2). The first thread concerns the merits of equal and special treatment for women and "how polarization can be transcended" (p. 3). The second thread concerns women's activism and how it has influenced policy over time. The final thread evaluates the role of the European Court of Justice, EU law and structure, and how these have influenced women's issues. Hoskyns writes, "Paradoxically, as this book shows, the integration of states (and of markets) has the effect of destabilising existing patterns of social integration, including those relating to gender" (p. 4).

Sexual Politics and the European Union: The New Feminist Challenge (Berghahn Books, 1996), edited by R. Amy Elman, includes ten essays that provide "a unique exploration of the ways in which EU policies and actions affect more than just the realm of employment—they significantly influence the everyday lives of women" (p. 2). The essays discuss sexual harassment policy, pornography, sexual trafficking of women, reproductive technology, abortion, and violence.

473. Itzin, Catherine, ed. *Pornography: Women, Violence, and Civil Liberties*. Oxford: Oxford University Press, 1992. 645p. bibliog. index. (OP)

The thread connecting the articles in this lengthy collection is that pornography results in harm to women. The purpose of the book is clearly to show, as Itzin writes, that we should be concerned about pornography because it "plays an important part in contributing to sexual violence against women and to sex discrimination and sexual inequality" (p. 1). Itzin continues by stating, "Our case against pornography is based on what it means and what it does to women: the part played by pornography in contributing to sexual inequality, sex discrimination and to sexual violence" (p. 3). Contributors to the volume include activists, academics, writers, and journalists. The collection begins with a chapter about the pornography industry in both the United States and the United Kingdom, explaining "what this 'entertainment for men' actually does to and communicates about women" (p. 3). Part 2 presents a series of essays on pornography and power, including essays on the racist and homophobic political elements of pornography. Part 3 includes chapters on pornography and the evidence of harm. Chapters in part 4 focus on legal issues related to pornography, and the chapters in part 5 discuss pornography, censorship, and civil liberties.

In contrast to this volume, *Dirty Looks: Women, Pornography, Power* (BFI Publications, 1993), edited by Pamela Church Gibson and Roma Gibson, "stands on the anti-censorship side of the fence" (p. 1). This eclectic volume includes a variety of chapters concerned with the representation and reading of the meanings of pornography. Gibson writes, "The essays in this volume vary greatly in what they have to say about pornography, but they are all animated by the spirit of dissent, and they all refuse a scheme that discounts dissenters as complicit with male domination" (p. 1). *Blue Politics: Pornography and the Law in the Age of Feminism* by Dany Lacombe (University of Toronto Press, 1994) explores on the one hand "the production of pornography as an object of knowledge and of institutional practices, and on the other the production of new collective identities as they were both deployed in the feminist campaign to reform obscenity legislation in Canada during the 1980s" (p. 3).

474. Kapur, Ratna, and Brenda Cossman. *Subversive Sites: Feminist Engagements with Law in India*. Thousand Oaks, CA: Sage Publications, 1996. 352p. bibliog. index. ISBN 0803993153.

This work attempts to answer several questions about whether law can be a subversive site, including the following: Is law inherently conservative? Does the law work to sustain unequal power relations? Has law outlived its usefulness, or have we not exploited it enough? The authors "seek to strengthen feminist engagements with law by revealing the complex and contradictory nature of law" (p. 11). Drawing on developments in poststructuralism and cultural studies, *Sub-

versive Sites goes beyond law as a means of oppression for women in India and explores its many complexities and contradictions. Kapur and Cossman examine legal issues relating to women and the family, asking what is "the extent to which the legal regulation of women is informed by and serves to reinscribe familial ideology" (p. 13). Chapter 1 explores the role of law in feminist legal struggles for social change. Following chapters deal with how familial ideology has subverted women's legal rights, constitutional challenges, how "legal discourse is being used to advance the political agenda of the Hindu Right" (p. 17), and finally, what role law can play in advancing women's cause.

Enslaved Daughters: Colonialism, Law, and Women's Rights by Sudhir Chandra (Oxford University Press, 1998) follows the case of Rukhmabai, who at the age of twenty-two refused to recognize her arranged marriage at the age of eleven. The case, which ran from 1884 to 1888, embodied several areas of contestation, not only between differing groups in Indian society, but also between the British colonial rulers and the colonized. Chandra clearly demonstrates the ambiguities the case brought up among the Hindu conservatives and the British courts.

475. Kerber, Linda K. *No Constitutional Right to Be Ladies: Women and the Obligations of Citizenship*. New York: Hill and Wang, 1998. 405p. bibliog. index. ISBN 0809073838; 0809073846pa.

Kerber examines the meaning of citizenship for both women and men in U.S. history: "But from the beginning American women's relationship to the state has been different in substantial and important respects from that of men" (p. xxi). The author distinguishes between rights of citizens, claiming that women have always had the same rights as men, and obligations, stating, "That there is a history of gendered *obligation* is less well understood" (p. xxi). Using obligation in its "primary sense—to be bound, to be constrained, to be under compulsion" (p. xxi), Kerber considers five obligations that invite state punishment if not performed: the obligation to pay taxes, the obligation to avoid vagrancy, the obligation to serve on juries, the obligation to serve in the military, and the obligation to refrain from treason. In five chapters, Kerber explores these obligations, recounting the stories of individual women and their families who challenged each of these obligations, from the period of the Revolution up to the 1990s. The author pays particular attention to the differences in legal standing between single women and married women and between white and black women. Part complex legal treatise, part narrative, part a history of women's rights, *No Constitutional Right to Be Ladies* is an essential book. It should be in the collections of all academic and large public libraries.

476. Lawson, Annette, and Deborah L. Rhode, eds. *The Politics of Pregnancy: Adolescent Sexuality and Public Policy*. New Haven, CT: Yale University Press, 1993. 348p. bibliog. index. ISBN (OP); 0300065485pa.

Scholars from the United States and Great Britain, working in psychology, sociology, history, philosophy, economics, medicine, and law, debate public policy issues concerning teenage pregnancy. Essays in part 1 place the "problem" of teenage pregnancy in broader historical, social, and political contexts, looking at such topics as the history of adolescent pregnancy, the view from the United Kingdom, and the dynamics of race. The editors note that the "problem" is not really a crisis, but appears to be because of "the socioeconomic context in which those births occur and the cultural ideology they challenge" (p. 3). Essays in part 2 focus on the choices and decisions adolescents face regarding sex and pregnancy, while part 3 discusses the role of fathers. The final part concentrates on social policy centered around two themes: increased access to birth control for teenagers and altering the social conditions that "simultaneously promote and punish early childbearing" (p. 11). *The Politics of Pregnancy* presents compelling arguments and clear evidence that the current public policy debate concerning the issue of adolescent sexuality must change.

Rhode also wrote *Justice and Gender: Sex Discrimination and the Law* (Harvard University Press, 1989), an ambitious work that approaches unequal protection under the law by turning the discussion from gender difference to gender disadvantage. Rhode writes, "American equal-protection doctrine has drawn heavily on Aristotelian traditions, which define equality as similar treatment for those similarly situated" (p. 3). However, Rhode claims that a "determination that the sexes are not 'similarly situated' only begins the discussion" (p. 3). The author hopes to present a new dialogue around the issues of women's rights, reproductive freedom, and sex and violence.

477. Lockwood, Carol Elizabeth, Daniel Barstow Magraw, Margaret Faith Spring, and S.I. Strong, eds. *The International Human Rights of Women: Instruments of Change*. Washington, DC: American Bar Association, Section of International Law and Practice, 1998. 607p. bibliog. index. ISBN 1570736103.

This excellent sourcebook reprints fifty documents outlining the evolution of women's human rights from 1791 through 1995. The editors note that the book was conceived amid discussions on how the American Bar Association should follow up on the United Nations Fourth World Conference on Women, which was held in Beijing in September 1995. It was not until the Beijing Conference that women's rights were fully recognized as human rights within the international community. Participants at the Beijing Conference emphasized "the absence of knowledge by women of their legal rights" (p. xii). The editors write that "this book is designed to increase the legal literacy with respect to women's human rights by compiling the most important international instruments on women's human rights, up to and including the Beijing Conference's recognition of the full dimensions of women's rights and its declaration that women's rights are human rights" (p. xii). An introductory note providing background information and historical context precedes each document. Felice D. Gaer, who was a public member of the U.S. delegations to both the World Conference on Women held in Vienna in 1993 and the Beijing Conference, provides a lengthy, well-researched introductory chapter to the book tracing the evolution of women's human rights from 1945 to the present. Among the instruments included in this sourcebook are the Declaration of the Rights of Woman and the Female Citizen (1791) by Olympe de Gouges, the League of Nations' Resolution on the Nationality of Women (1931), the Convention on the Political Rights of Women (1953), Nairobi Forward-Looking Strategies for the Advancement of Women (1985), the Convention of the Rights of the Child (1989), and, of course, the Beijing Declaration and Platform for Action of the United Nations Fourth World Conference on Women (1995). A list of abbreviations and a short select Internet bibliography are included.

From Basic Needs to Basic Rights: Women's Claim to Human Rights (Women, Law, and Development International, 1995), edited by Margaret A. Schuler, contains essays grouped in the following categories: "Gender and Hierarchy in Human Rights," "Social and Economic Rights," "Religious, Cultural, and Ethnic Identity and Human Rights," "Sexual and Reproductive Rights," and "Activism to Advance Women's Human Rights." Written by international scholars and activists, the essays cover broad theoretical issues, including the implications for women of international human rights law and practice, women in conditions of war and peace, and a global overview of reproductive rights and technologies. Several essays also present case studies of such topics as the rhetoric of welfare reform within the United States, female circumcision in the Sudan, and sex education in Costa Rica.

478. MacKinnon, Catharine A. *Toward a Feminist Theory of the State*. Cambridge, MA: Harvard University Press, 1989. 330p. bibliog. (OP)

Toward a Feminist Theory of the State brings together essays written by MacKinnon during an eighteen-year period concerning her arguments on Marxism and feminism, critiques of these theories, and her visions of a "feminist theory of the state." Part 1, on feminism and Marxism, uses Marxist and feminist theory to analyze inequality. Admitting that these chapters seem "groping," that is, "Is it sex or is it class?" (p. x), MacKinnon moves on to explore methodology in part 2. In the final part, on the state, MacKinnon critiques laws of rape, abortion, and pornography and explores issues of sex equality: "In a very real sense, the project went from marxism to feminism through method to analyze congealed power in its legal form, and state power emerged as male power" (p. xi). While claiming that "this book is not a moral tract" (p. xii) nor "an idealist argument that law can solve the problems of the world or that if legal arguments are better made, courts will see the error of their ways" (p. xiii), MacKinnon nonetheless clearly believes that male dominance accounts for the inequalities and subordination of women.

Feminism Unmodified: Discourses on Life and Law (Harvard University Press, 1987) includes texts of speeches MacKinnon gave between 1981 and 1986. Three themes connect the speeches: "the social relation between the sexes is organized so that men may dominate and women must submit, and this relation is sexual"; "a critique of the notion that gender is basically a difference rather than a hierarchy"; and finally, a look at pornography in America "as a key means of actualizing these two dynamics in life" (p. 3).

In late 1983, MacKinnon and Andrea Dworkin wrote a law for the city of Minneapolis that "conceived of pornography as a human rights violation" (p. 4). Other places followed suit, including Indianapolis, Los Angeles County, and Massachusetts. Hearings resulting from the introduction of such legislation are presented in *In Harm's Way: The Pornography Civil Rights Hearings* (Harvard University Press, 1997), edited by MacKinnon and Dworkin. MacKinnon and Dworkin also wrote *Pornography and Civil Rights: A New Day for Women's Equality* (Organizing against Pornography, 1988), which discusses the Minneapolis ordinance along with philosophical examinations of law and civil rights in society.

479. Mansbridge, Jane J. *Why We Lost the ERA*. Chicago: University of Chicago Press, 1986. 327p. bibliog. index. ISBN (OP); 0226503585pa.

The Equal Rights Amendment (ERA) failed to win ratification in 1982, having received the support of only thirty-five of the required thirty-eight states. Jane Mansbridge details the fight for the passage of the ERA from 1972 to 1982, arguing that both the proponents and the opponents of the ERA had a stake in believing that it would produce profound societal changes, and thus both groups exaggerated the effects of passage of the amendment. While Mansbridge herself acknowledges that the ERA would have had minimal immediate effects, she still believes that its defeat was a major setback for equality between men and women. The book reveals the struggle of ERA activists to convince the populace of the importance of this amendment alongside that of the ERA opponents to convince the populace how damaging passage of the ERA would be for society. Mansbridge contends that the death of the ERA was also related to two broader changes in American political beliefs. The first was "the growing legislative skepticism about the consequences of giving the U.S. Supreme Court authority to review legislation" (p. 4), citing a legislative backlash against progressive Court decisions ever since the 1954 *Brown v. Board of Education* decision on school desegregation. The second change in political attitudes was the growth of the New Right. Mansbridge argues that for many conservative Americans, the personal became political during the fight over the ERA because the amendment dealt with questions of family, children, sexual behavior, and women's roles. When the ERA lost the "aura of benefiting all women" and pitted women against each other, it could never have won. This title includes several tables citing statistics of the U.S. population who supported or were opposed to the passage of the Equal Rights Amendment.

Rights of Passage: The Past and Future of the ERA (Indiana University Press, 1986), edited by Joan Hoff-Wilson, includes essays, many of which first appeared in the newsletter of the Organization of American Historians. The essays are grouped into three categories: the origins of and disagreements over the ERA; the reasons for defeat of the ERA; and the significance of the defeat of the ERA. The introduction by Hoff-Wilson presents a brief history of the struggle for equal rights for women in the United States, in which she writes, "The ERA's defeat in 1982 perpetuates the condition of unequal constitutional status which generations of women have experienced because of their being omitted from the federal Constitution and the Bill of Rights" (p. xi). In *Sex, Gender, and the Politics of ERA: A State and the Nation* (Oxford University Press, 1990), Donald G. Mathews and Jane Sherron De Hart focus their study of the ERA on North Carolina, which "provides an excellent opportunity to analyze the ratification process in depth" (p. ix). All three of these books provide excellent analysis of one of the most important events in American political history.

480. Miller, Diane Helene. *Freedom to Differ: The Shaping of the Gay and Lesbian Struggle for Civil Rights*. New York: New York University Press, 1998. 195p. bibliog. index. ISBN 081475595X; 0814755968.

Diane Miller explores two high-profile cases of discrimination against lesbians to illustrate how public discourse helps shape identity and to highlight the ongoing struggle for lesbian civil rights in this country: Roberta Achtenberg, who was nominated for the position of assistant director of housing and urban development by President Clinton in 1993, and Colonel Margarethe Cammermeyer, who applied for the position of chief nurse of the National Guard in 1989. Miller is especially interested in the ways public discourse shapes identity, specifically, sexual identity: "More broadly, this book points to the ways in which all categories of sexuality are shaped and delimited by language and in which sexual and other minority classifications may be produced by the very discourses that seek to regulate or protect them" (p. 6). By focusing on cases of discrimination within politics and the military, Miller also shows how institutional discourse seeks to control identities. This study aims to answer two broad questions: "First, what kinds of lesbian representations emerge from the competing discourse in each of these case studies?" and "How do the strategies of supporters and opponents broaden the possibilities for lesbian self-definition and enable a wider range of lesbian identities and politics?" (p. 13). *Freedom to Differ* is an essential source that reveals the lack of civil rights and the limitations of the legal system for lesbians in this country.

Lesbians, Gay Men, and the Law (New Press, distributed by Norton, 1993), edited by William B. Rubenstein, is a comprehensive work that would be suitable for use as a casebook in law classes. Chapter 1 presents basic documents on sexuality, identity, sin, and sickness and provides an introduction to concepts surrounding sexual orientation. The remaining five chapters include articles, essays, cases, and statutes on the following topics: the regulation of lesbian and gay sexuality, the regulation of lesbian and gay identity, lesbians and gays in the workplace, legal recognition of gay relationships, and lesbian and gay parenting.

481. Morrison, Toni, ed. *Race-ing Justice, En-gendering Power: Essays on Anita Hill, Clarence Thomas, and the Construction of Social Reality*. New York: Pantheon Books, 1992. 475p. ISBN 0679741453pa.

Eighteen contributors, including legal scholars, historians, political scientists, and literary theorists, present provocative discussions surrounding the confirmation hearings of Clarence Thomas to the Supreme Court. Such esteemed scholars as Cornel West, Paula Giddings, and Nell Irvin Painter debate topics including African American leadership, racial stereotypes, feminism's stance on the hearings, and the political process of appointing Supreme Court justices. *Race-ing Justice* opens with the actual letter A. Leon Higginbotham Jr., chief judge emeritus of the U.S. Court of Appeals for the Third Circuit, sent to Thomas in which Higginbotham stated his apprehensions about Thomas, apprehensions that Morrison clearly articulates in the introduction. For Morrison, the confirmation hearings brought into clear focus the issues of racial injustice and gender inequity. In a powerful, articulate essay, Morrison writes how black people are rarely individualized, and that "without individuation, without nonracial perception, black people as a group are used to signify the polar opposites of love and repulsion. On the one hand, they signify benevolence, harmless and servile guardianship, and endless love. On the other hand, they have come to represent insanity, illicit sexuality, and chaos. In the confirmation hearings, the two fictions were at war and on display" (p. xv).

Race, Gender, and Power in America: The Legacy of the Hill-Thomas Hearings (Oxford University Press, 1995), edited by Anita Faye Hill and Emma Coleman Jordan, grew out of a conference held at Georgetown University Law Center on the first anniversary of the hearings. The essays explore a variety of topics, including the compromised status of African American women, viewing the hearings in the context of popular culture, ways to stop sexual harassment, and Hill's own essay on marriage as an empowering act for women.

Speaking Truth to Power (Doubleday, 1997) imparts Hill's own story of the hearings and their impact on her life. It is not a dispassionate chronicle, but as Hill says, "I write to offer my own perspective" (p. 7) and to not be silenced by fear. Finally, in *African American Women Speak Out on Anita Hill–Clarence Thomas*, edited by Geneva Smitherman (Wayne State University Press, 1995), twenty African-American women write on the significance of the hearings and Thomas' subsequent confirmation as a Supreme Court Justice. Among the contributors are Margaret Walker Alexander, Harriette Pipes McAdoo, Barbara Ransby, Darlene Clark Hine, Angela Davis, and Toi Derricote. Libraries without U.S. government documents collections will also want to consider *The Complete Transcripts of the Clarence Thomas–Anita Hill Hearings, October 11, 12, 13, 1991*, edited by Anita Miller and reprinted by Academy Chicago Publishers (1994).

482. Okin, Susan Moller. *Justice, Gender, and the Family.* New York: Basic Books, 1989. 216p. bibliog. index. (OP)

Susan Okin states, "The injustice that results from the division of labor between the sexes affects virtually all women in our society, though not in all the same ways" (p. vii). Okin argues that this unequal division of labor within families, along with the disdain our society has for families headed by single working women and the value placed on men's work, creates grave injustices within the family system. The author asserts that until justice exists within the family, women will make few gains not only in the workplace but also in politics. Chapter 1 introduces both past and contemporary theories of justice, defines terms, and clearly shows why gender must become an issue of justice. The remaining chapters set out to prove how family injustice carries over into the larger social context. In several chapters, Okin questions various political theories, including traditional and libertarian ones, and highlights the inadequacies inherent in each of them. In one chapter, Okin discusses the public/private dichotomy, an idea developed in the nineteenth century. Okin argues that this idea is still strong and is ingrained in our approach to family life. In another chapter, the author contends that marriage is an inequitable institution for women. The final chapter presents Okin's ideas on public policy changes that could begin to alleviate gender injustice.

483. Robson, Ruthann. *Sappho Goes to Law School: Fragments in Lesbian Legal Theory.* New York: Columbia University Press, 1998. 303p. (Between Men—Between Women: Lesbian and Gay Studies). bibliog. index. ISBN 0231105606; 0231104614pa.

In her preface, law professor Ruthann Robson invokes the essence of Sappho, saying that if Sappho were alive today, she would be enrolled in law school, fighting for social justice. Robson's essays consider the complexity of lesbian identity and especially how law conceives of lesbianism. Other essays explore the interconnections of feminism, postmodernism, queer theory, and legal theory and how these theories affect policies toward lesbians. Finally, Robson interweaves her own experiences as a "dyke law professor at a progressive law school [City University of New York School of Law]" (p. xv) throughout the essays. Her ultimate goal is to provide a safe and welcoming space for any Sappho entering law school, as well as to "ensure that the law protects and nourishes Sappho rather than silencing, distorting, and appropriating her talents" (p. xv). This is an important text for feminist, legal, and queer theory classes.

In *Lesbian (Out)Law: Survival under the Rule of Law* (Firebrand Books, 1992), Robson is concerned with "how the rule of men and law impacts upon lesbian survival" (p. 11). For Robson, survival means both daily survival and survival as lesbians. The author argues for no less than a specific lesbian legal theory "that allows us to assimilate our lesbianism to law. In doing so, we can make the law responsive to our survival needs" (p. 12). Finally, Robson presents a clear, concise overview of legal issues in *Gay Men, Lesbians, and the Law* (Chelsea House Publishers, 1997). The author touches on everything from educational issues to criminal justice to health, citing cases and statutes along the way.

Lesbians and Child Custody: A Casebook (Garland, 1992), edited by Dolores J. Maggiore, includes chapters dealing with various aspects of lesbian mothers and child custody. The final section presents the perspective of the legal profession.

484. Rosenfeld, Michel. *Affirmative Action and Justice: A Philosophical and Constitutional Inquiry.* New Haven, CT: Yale University Press, 1991. 373p. bibliog. index. ISBN 0300047819.

Between 1978 and 1990, the Supreme Court ruled on ten affirmative action cases. Rosenfeld examines these ten cases, focusing on both the philosophical or moral arguments and the constitutional or legal arguments. The author cogently speculates on the meaning of equality, arguing that both opponents and proponents agree, at least in the abstract, on equality: "Both the most ardent advocates of affirmative action and its most vehement foes loudly proclaim their allegiance to the ideal of equality" (p. 2). Furthermore, Rosenfeld contends that the debate over affirmative action is influenced by two broad propositions "over which there is widespread agreement (at least in the context of public discourse)" (p. 4). The first proposition is that "first-order discrimination is morally wrong" (p. 5). This is discrimination against women and African Americans because they are different. The second idea is that "it is widely accepted in the United States that the individual rather than the group is the subject of equality" (p. 4). Within this framework, Rosenfeld seeks to answer the following question: "What consistent set of assumptions, conditions, and arguments operating at the various levels of abstraction would lend support to the claim that affirmative action is legitimate in terms of both a suitable philosophical conception of justice and a suitable constitutional conception of equal protection?" (p. 5).

In part 1, Rosenfeld assesses the key philosophical arguments for and against affirmative action. Part 2 explores the relationship between the constitutional idea of equality and equal protection. The final part seeks integration: "In Part Three I attempt to construct an integrated philosophical and constitutional conception of the justice of affirmative action, based on an understanding of the dynamic relationship between identity and difference, and on the implementation of a dilogical conception of justice" (p. 7). *Affirmative Action and Justice* is a thought-provoking, well-argued book that belongs in all libraries.

485. Schulhofer, Stephen J. *Unwanted Sex: The Culture of Intimidation and the Failure of Law*. Cambridge, MA: Harvard University Press, 1998. 318p. bibliog. index. ISBN 0674576489.

Unwanted sex and harassment occur everywhere in our society: in the workplace, in relationships with professionals such as doctors and lawyers, with strangers and acquaintances, and in dating relationships. Schulhofer, a law professor, believes that laws against rape and sexual harassment have failed to protect women "from sexual overreaching and abuse" (p. ix), and that "sex can be coerced in a multitude of ways that the law tolerates and sometimes tacitly encourages" (p. x). The author argues that what is missing from essential protected rights in this society is the right to sexual autonomy: "In the pages that follow, I undertake to show how our laws and our social practices devalue what should be every person's unambiguous right: the right to choose—or refuse—sexual contact and to do so freely without undue pressure or constraint" (p. x). Opening chapters outline the evolution of current rape law, providing the context for Schulhofer's argument for the protection of sexual autonomy. Several chapters then detail the author's ideas within the context of specific situations, including power relationships such as those between supervisors and workers, psychologists and clients, and doctors and patients, and within dating relationships. Schulhofer even provides a "Model Criminal Statute for Sexual Offenses." *Unwanted Sex* provides a clearly articulated case for the evolution of rape law and sexual harassment.

486. Smart, Carol. *Law, Crime, and Sexuality: Essays in Feminism*. Thousand Oaks, CA: Sage Publications, 1995. 250p. bibliog. index. ISBN 0803989598; 0803989601pa.

In this collection of previously published articles, Carol Smart aims to provide access to theories about law, criminology, and feminism for students. She wants students to understand the deeply textured concept of law, to "become aware of the extent to which law is implicated in our daily lives" (p. 3), and to begin to think about the relationship between knowledge and power. The introduction provides an accessible overview of feminist empiricism, standpoint feminism, and postmodern feminism and of Smart's own evolving use of these theories in her writings over the years. Smart's discussion of poststructuralism and postmodernism in particular provides a challenging rethinking of law as an unquestionable block of knowledge and "its power to subjugate other discourses" (p. 8) of knowledge, particularly women's discourses.

The book is divided into three sections, criminology, sexuality, and feminist theory and law, each of which begins with an introduction that outlines the ideas of feminist epistemology, poststructuralism, and postmodernism. The final chapter, titled "Postscript for the 1990s, or Still Angry after All These Years," reminds us how law still casts women into the following categories: the criminal woman, the prostitute, the raped woman, the sexed woman, and the unruly mother. Smart discusses how the theories remain in flux, and the ongoing need to address more research on women and to think about ways to incorporate a concern with difference into our theorizing. This work would be a valuable text for undergraduate courses in criminology and law.

In an earlier work, *Feminism and the Power of Law* (Routledge, 1989), Smart investigates "why law is so resistant to the challenge of feminist knowledge and critique" (p. 2). Once again, Smart is particularly concerned about how the absolutism of law as knowledge and knowledge as a form of the exercise of power can disqualify other forms of knowledge such as feminism.

487. Solinger, Rickie, ed. *Abortion Wars: A Half Century of Struggle, 1950–2000*. Berkeley: University of California Press, 1998. 413p. bibliog. index. ISBN (OP); 0520209524pa.

In the introduction to this collection, Solinger discusses the basis for placing the abortion debate in a historical context. First, she claims that it "becomes unsettlingly impossible to think about the subject in a fixed, static way or to claim universalized, decontextualized meanings for abortion and its satellite issues" (p. 2). A historical framework demonstrates that the meanings of the most fundamental terms associated with abortion, including life, choice, fetal viability, and even mother, have shifted over time, and that when foundational terms "have fluid and mutable meanings over time, their usage is easily manipulated or distorted and politicized" (p. 2).

A second benefit of looking at abortion in a historical framework is that it helps challenge and demolish myths that have surrounded the political discussion in recent years. The collection begins with the year 1950, a period when women began to enter the workforce in great numbers, and also, Solinger contends, a time when powerful social and political authorities began arguing for a weaker status for women. The authors of the eighteen essays, including Faye Ginsburg, Alison M. Jaggar, Laura Kaplan, and Amy Kesselman, represent the fields of medicine, journalism, law, and philosophy, among others. Writing on a central theme that abortion rights really refers to a "broad array of entitlements, services, and resources constituting *reproductive rights* that *all* women must possess in order to be full members of society" (p. 7), *Abortion Wars* presents a broad-ranging critique of the challenges and controversies surrounding abortion rights.

When Abortion Was a Crime: Women, Medicine, and Law in the United States, 1867–1973 (University of California Press, 1997) by Leslie J. Reagan is the first study of the "entire era of illegal abortion in the United States" (p. 2). Reagan presents a finely nuanced study of the changing practices and politics of abortion during the 100 years when abortion was illegal in the United States, focusing closely on the complex, competing views toward abortion within the medical establishment as well as the enforcement of laws at the state and local levels. Using Chicago as a case study, Reagan contends that individual women helped sway opinion and public policy toward abortion.

In *Breaking the Abortion Deadlock: From Choice to Consent* (Oxford University Press, 1996), author Eileen L. McDonagh turns the abortion debate upside down by arguing that the fetus is an intrusion on a woman's body. McDonagh's arguments are well articulated, citing specific cases and examples of inconsistencies in arguments against abortion. All three books should be considered essential for large public and academic library collections.

488. Stone, Lawrence. *Uncertain Unions: Marriage in England, 1660–1753.* New York: Oxford University Press, 1992. 281p. bibliog. index. (OP)

Lawrence Stone presents a detailed study of marriage in early modern England derived from ecclesiastical court records from the Court of Arches in London, which covered all of southern England and Wales. Presenting case studies from the depositions of these records, Stone writes that "the central questions of concern in this volume are first to illustrate the significant changes in how marriages were made in the late seventeenth and early eighteenth centuries; and second to tease out from recorded behaviour the moral attitudes both towards courtship, including the display of female physical attraction, and towards irregular marriages or types of concubinage based on no more than vague verbal promises" (pp. 6–7). The lengthy introduction provides background for the case studies. Here Stone discusses at some length courtship; marriage, property, and common law; customary unions and concubinage; contract marriage; and clandestine marriage. The second section of the book presents actual case studies grouped by topic, such as clandestine marriage, and then arranged chronologically. Many of the words of the participants in these cases are presented verbatim. Stone concludes "that the marriage law as it operated in practice in England from the fourteenth to the nineteenth century was a mess. The root cause of the trouble was that there was no consensus within the society at large about how a legally binding marriage should be carried out" (p. 31). *Broken Lives: Separation and Divorce in England, 1660–1857* also by Stone (Oxford University Press, 1993), which is organized like the preceding title, presents case studies about how and why marriages ended during the period 1660 to 1857, when the first Divorce Act was passed. Together, both titles give a thorough picture of the legal complexities and social ramifications of marriage and divorce in early modern England.

Laura Gowing's *Domestic Dangers: Women, Words, and Sex in Early Modern London* (Oxford University Press, 1996) "takes the language of sexual insult as a starting point for an examination of the workings of sex, gender, and honour in language, law, and popular practice" (p. 8). Studying the ecclesiastical records of early modern London (1570–1640) for cases involving sexual disputes, slander, and marital discord, Gowing argues that a double standard of morality and behavior existed for men and women, and that the boundaries of these practices were constantly being reshaped within the church courts.

489. Yamani, Mai, ed. *Feminism and Islam: Legal and Literary Perspectives.* New York: New York University Press, 1996. 385p. bibliog. index. ISBN 081479680X; 0814796818pa.

Academics from history, law, political science, sociology, anthropology, and literature examine "the phenomenon of feminism within the Islamic cultural framework" (p. 1). While Yamani notes that as a field, Islamic feminism includes a variety of approaches, she states, "For all these thinkers, however, there is a common concern with the empowerment of their gender within a rethought Islam" (p. 1). Essays in part 1 provide the historical context for the study of women and Islam. Part 2 includes two chapters focusing on the treatment of women's issues in recent Arabic literature. Part 3 includes studies focusing on women's political struggles within the Islamic world, and the final grouping offers essays looking at the confines of law.

Jamal J. Nasir's *The Status of Women under Islamic Law and under Modern Islamic Legislation* (Graham and Trotman, 1990; 2nd ed., 1994) provides a detailed accounting of the "legal rights and obligations of women under the Sharia [Islamic law] and under modern Arab Islamic legislation" (Preface p. xi). Nasir, a lawyer, discusses marriage, the dower, the dissolution of marriage, parenting, and custody. *Women, the Family, and Divorce Laws in Islamic History* (Syracuse University Press, 1996), edited by Amira El Azhary Sonbol, offers essays by a group of international scholars, mostly historians, who reexamine women's status in the Muslim world, focusing especially on the period from the seventeenth century to the early nineteenth century. The essays examine Muslim women and the courts, children and family law, and women and violence.

Women, Property, and Islam: Palestinian Experiences, 1920–1990 (Cambridge University Press, 1995) by Annelies Moors is an anthropological study of property rights of Palestinian women from the Jabal Nablus region of the West Bank. The stories and experiences of poor and wealthy, urban and rural women demonstrate that women's access to property varies a great deal. In *In the House of the Law: Gender and Islamic Law in Ottoman Syria and Palestine* (University of California Press, 1998), Judith Tucker explores "the ways in which intellectuals and the general population . . . posed questions about gender and devised answers that suited their sense of their inherited tradition as well as their immediate needs" (p. 4). Focusing on the urban worlds of Syria and Palestine in the seventeenth and eighteenth centuries, Tucker is concerned with how one Muslim society "understood the law and the gender system it ordained" (p. 4).

1999 CORE TITLES

Askin, Kelly D., and Dorean M. Koenig, eds. *Women and International Human Rights Law.* Ardsley, NY: Transnational, 1999–2001. 3v. bibliog. index. ISBN 1571050647 (v. 1, published 1999); (OP) (v. 2); 1571050930 (v. 3; published 2000).

Baer, Judith A. *Our Lives before the Law: Constructing a Feminist Jurisprudence.* Princeton, NJ: Princeton University Press, 1999. 276p. bibliog. index. ISBN 0691033161; 0691019452pa.

Cook, Sandy, and Susanne Davies, eds. *Harsh Punishment: International Experiences of Women's Imprisonment.* Boston: Northeastern University Press, 1999. 326p. (Northeastern Series on Gender, Crime, and Law). bibliog. index. ISBN 1555534120; 1555534112pa.

Cornell, Drucilla. *Beyond Accommodation: Ethical Feminism, Deconstruction, and the Law.* Second Edition. Lanham, MD: Rowman & Littlefield, 1999. 239p. bibliog. index. ISBN 084769268X; 0847692698pa.

Eskridge, William N. *Gaylaw: Challenging the Apartheid of the Closet.* Cambridge, MA: Harvard University Press, 1999. 470p. bibliog. index. ISBN 0674341619.

Gerstmann, Evan. *The Constitutional Underclass: Gays, Lesbians, and the Failure of Class-Based Equal Protection.* Chicago: University of Chicago Press, 1999. 195p. bibliog. index. ISBN 0226288595; 0226288609pa.

Hirshman, Linda R. *A Woman's Guide to Law School.* New York: Penguin Books, 1999. 290p. index. ISBN 014026437X.

Lawyers Committee for Human Rights. *Islam and Equality: Debating the Future of Women's and Minority Rights in the Middle East and North Africa.* New York: Lawyers Committee for Human Rights, 1999. 207p. ISBN 0934143919.

Muraskin, Roslyn, ed. *Women and Justice: Development of International Policy.* Amsterdam: Gordon & Breach, 1999. 229p. (Women and the Law). bibliog. index. ISBN 9057005506; 9057005514pa.

Pillai, Vijayan K., and Guang-zhen Wang. *Women's Reproductive Rights in Developing Countries.* Brookfield, VT: Ashgate, 1999. 194p. bibliog. index. ISBN 1840149086.

Ptacek, James. *Battered Women in the Courtroom: The Power of Judicial Responses.* Boston: Northeastern University Press, 1999. 240p. (Northeastern Series on Gender, Crime, and Law). bibliog. index. ISBN 1555533914; 1555533906pa.

Taslitz, Andrew E. *Rape and the Culture of the Courtroom.* New York: New York University Press, 1999. 210p. bibliog. index. ISBN (OP); 0814782302.

WORLD WIDE WEB/INTERNET SITES

490. *American Bar Association: Commission on Women in the Profession.* http://www.abanet.org/women/.

The Commission on Women is a small group of twelve members appointed by the president of the American Bar Association to "assess the status of women in the legal profession and to identify barriers to advancement" (commission home page). Created in 1987, the commission seeks to create changes in the legal workplace and address issues related to women lawyers. The Web site includes statistics on women in the law, a link to publications by the commission, a listing of commission activities, press releases, information on initiatives undertaken by the commission, and links to other sites. The National Association of Women Lawyers (http://www.abanet.org/nawl/home.html) is a voluntary legal organization dedicated to the interests of women lawyers and their families. The NAWL Web site includes information on the organization, employment listings, and a link to the National Directory of Women-Owned Law Firms and Women Lawyers. The Multicultural Women Attorneys' Network (http://www.abanet.org/women/mwan.html), a joint project of the Commission on Women and the ABA Commission on Racial and Ethnic Diversity in the Profession, "addresses issues of special concern to multicultural women lawyers. It produces programs, roundtables and publications to identify the impact of race/ethnicity and gender on the professional development of multicultural women lawyers" (commission home page).

491. *American Civil Liberties Union: Women's Rights Issues.* http://www.aclu.org/WomensRights/WomensRightsMain.cfm.

The *Women's Rights Issues* page of the ACLU presents current information on a variety of issues regarding women's rights, including criminal justice, discrimination, violence against women, education, employment, poverty/welfare, and pregnancy and parenting. Under each topic, users will find press releases, court cases, and other documents pertaining to each issue. The page includes a timeline of major Supreme Court decisions on women's rights.

492. *Center for Reproductive Rights.* http://www.crlp.org/.

Formerly known as the Center for Reproductive Law and Policy, the Center for Reproductive Rights is "a non-profit legal advocacy organization dedicated to promoting and defending women's reproductive rights worldwide" (center home page). This well-organized site offers information on the following topics: legal advocacy, human rights, equality, adolescents, safe pregnancy, contraception, and abortion. Linking to each subject provides access to the latest information on the topic, with cross-references to additional publications, cases, legislative policy, statutes, and press releases. Users can also search the Web site under the following categories: on the Hill, in the states, in the courts, worldwide, publications, and press. The site is available in Spanish and French and includes an index.

493. *National Women's Law Center.* http://www.nwlc.org.

The mission of the National Women's Law Center is "to protect and advance the progress of women and girls at work, in school, and in virtually every aspect of their lives." The Web site provides current information on several issues relating to women's legal rights, including athletics, Social Security, and women in the military, to name just a few. A "Take Action" center allows users to stay informed about current legislation and offers users a convenient way to contact politicians. The "Information" center includes links to the history of the organization, the newsletter, and other publications from NWLC. A link titled "If You Need Legal Assistance" includes a list of web sites of organizations offering assistance and counseling.

494. *Women's Human Rights Resources.* http://www.law-lib.utoronto.ca/diana/main page.htm.

This first-rate Web site, which is maintained by the Bora Laskin Law Library, University of Toronto, provides a wealth of information. Dedicated to providing "reliable and diverse information on international women's human rights via the Internet" (main home page), *Women's Human Rights Resources* is organized under several broad categories: "Special Features," "Advocacy Guides," the "Women's Human Rights Database," "Research Guides," "Graduate Fellowships," and "Sister Sites." The "Special Features" section includes "Hot Topics," fact sheets, and "Case Collections," listing decisions and judgments by international/regional tribunals and domestic courts. "Research Guides" includes outlines on several legal issues that provide background information, define terms, and suggest sources for further research. An excellent feature of this site is the "Women's Human Rights Database," which includes annotated references to articles, books, book chapters, and documents. Full text is included when available. Another site to consider is *Women, Law, and Development International* (http://www.wld.org). WLDI is a nonprofit, nongovernmental organization committed to the promotion and defense of women's rights globally. WLDI conducts research and provides training and advocacy to women's rights groups in developing countries, identifies and publicizes violations of women's human rights, networks with women's rights leaders and organizations to develop common strategies for action, and trains women to become women's rights advocates.

495. *Women's Law Initiative.* http//www.womenslaw.org.

Women's Law Initiative was founded in February 2000 by a group of lawyers, teachers, and activists who wanted to use the power of the Internet to work for more disadvantaged people, specifically for survivors of domestic violence. This site provides legal information for the layperson on domestic violence. It includes state-specific legal information on domestic violence as well as providing information on getting help in one's local community.

7 Politics and Political Theory

Linda D. Tietjen

The disciplines of politics and political theory have proven particularly resistant to the ideas and thoughts of more than half of the world's population throughout the years. Because women traditionally occupied marginalized roles in society, they could only hope to grasp onto the fringes of the political arena. However, during the past several decades, women have begun to make their voices heard, not only as activists in the political arena, but also as policy makers, philosophers, political scientists, and instructors of women's studies curricula and through taking on a myriad of other vital roles.

Subtopics within this chapter represent the literature on women and politics that scholars are currently creating. The chapter is organized around a small group of reference works, followed by monographs divided into the following subtopics: "Political Theory," "Women and Politics Worldwide" (including women's rights as human rights and ecofeminism), "Women in the Third World," "Women in Europe," and "Women in North America" (including women in local, regional, state, and national politics). An addendum list of 1999 titles representing various subtopics follows the monographs. The chapter concludes with three excellent Web sites, each of which contains hypertext links to many other valuable women's political sites, both in the United States and worldwide.

The books annotated in this chapter represent a small percentage of the important work scholars are currently creating at an unprecedented rate on behalf of and, more significantly, by women. Because so much exciting research is finally being done on the topic of women in the political arena, I am in the unenviable position of having to choose only a small number of the available books.

I will end this introduction by pointing out what I consider to be an ironic historical turn of events in terms of women's political and human rights, namely, that while so much of the political literature about and by women is being written in the United States, as of the end of the twentieth century, among more than 160 nations, the United States and Afghanistan were the only major countries who had not ratified the United Nations Convention on the Elimination of All Forms of Discrimination against Women (CEDAW). The United Nations General Assembly adopted CEDAW, which is essentially an international bill of rights for women, in 1979. Its preamble and thirty articles define discrimination against women and set an agenda for national action to end such discrimination. Between U.S. ratification of CEDAW and passage of the Equal Rights Amendment (ERA), I would say that there is still much work to be done by and for women in the political arena, even in the presumably "enlightened" United States of America.

I wish to thank Janni Aragon of the University of California at Riverside Political Science Department for her invaluable assistance in poring through the titles of many possible books for this chapter. I also thank Marilyn Grotzky, my friend and colleague, of the Auraria Library, for all her assistance. Finally, thanks to Jana Everett, University of Colorado at Denver, Political Science Department, and Jodi Wetzel, director of the Women's Studies Institute at Metropolitan State College in Denver, Colorado, for sharing their expertise.

REFERENCE SOURCES

496. Cox, Elizabeth M. *Women in Modern American Politics: A Bibliography, 1900–1995*. Washington, DC: Congressional Quarterly, 1997. 414p. indexes. ISBN 156802133X.

This thorough bibliography documents women in politics during most of the twentieth century in the United States. The extensive research of Jo Freeman, who served as editorial advisor for this comprehensive work, comprises approximately one-third of the almost 6,000 entries included in this work. During the first two decades of the twentieth century, most women could not yet vote, and their presence in the political arena remained negligible. Yet a vociferous group of women who engaged in a flurry of political activity on behalf of women emerged by the early 1920s. Cox imposes order upon the vast amount of material included in this bibliography through the use of standard political science topics, which she chronologically categorizes according to time period and geography (by state). She includes entries that identify books, magazine and journal articles, theses, and papers delivered at professional conferences. Topics include movement and advocacy, social reform, the Equal Rights Amendment (ERA), lesbian rights, public policy, and running for elective office. Subject and author indexes provide extra access points. This well-organized bibliography is indispensable to any women's studies or political science reference collection. Since Cox does not cover government publications, Mary Ellen Huls's two-volume work *United States Government Documents on Women, 1800–1990: A Comprehensive Bibliography* (Greenwood Press, 1993) would be an excellent companion work.

497. Hardy, Gayle J. *American Women Civil Rights Activists: Biobibliographies of 68 Leaders, 1825–1992*. Jefferson, NC: McFarland, 1993. 497p. index. ISBN 0899507735.

Librarian Gayle J. Hardy's prototypical information-packed volume contains sixty-eight "biobibliographies" about women civil rights activists in the United States. Each entry consists of a biography that provides a year-by-year chronology of the individual's life, including information about her family background, as well as a bibliography that lists relevant books, journal and newspaper articles, theses and dissertations, and works within special collections by and about fellow civil rights activists, such as Shirley Chisholm, Rosa Parks, and Angela Davis. Hardy alphabetically arranges the entries, which she supplements with a timeline (1820–1990) to chronologically situate each woman's contributions. She also includes ten appendices that list information such as the occupations, fields of activity, and religious affiliation of each individual, as well as an index. Hardy broadly uses the term "civil rights" to include African American and Native American rights, birth control, child welfare, older adult rights, and temperance. She collects and organizes a vast amount of information that not only was previously widely dispersed, but also had proven difficult to access. Thirteen scholars who contributed twenty entries assisted Hardy in this work, which is a highly recommended addition to all women's studies and political science reference collections.

498. Nelson, Barbara J., and Najma Chowdhury, eds. *Women and Politics Worldwide*. New Haven, CT: Yale University Press, 1994. 818p. bibliog. index. ISBN (OP); 0300054084pa.

Although the editors assert that they did not attempt to create a handbook or encyclopedia, this major work is clearly encyclopedic in scope. It took nine years to prepare and involved sixty-one scholars writing about forty-three countries. Nelson and Chowdhury chronicle the early 1960s to the early 1990s, depending on the political activities of the women of the particular country in question. Although chapters vary in terms of coverage, each chapter begins with a chart of political, demographic, and economic information and ends with extensive bibliographic notes. The book's introductory chapters, which outline research and methodological procedures, are especially valuable. A twenty-two-page index provides quick access to this reference book's rich contents. This excellent work belongs in every political science and women's studies collection.

499. U.S. House of Representatives. *Women in Congress, 1917–1990.* Prepared under direction of the Commission on the Bicentenary of the U.S. House of Representatives by the Office of the Historian, U.S. House of Representatives. Washington, DC: U.S. GPO, 1991. not paginated. (House Document [U.S. Congress] 101–238, 101/2)

Jeannette Rankin was the first woman to serve in the U.S. House of Representatives. She was elected in 1916 and began her term in 1917. Between 1917 and 1990, 129 women were elected or appointed to Congress; this figure includes 115 representatives and 16 senators. This reference work contains biographical and political sketches of each of these women, several of whom were appointed to Congress upon the deaths of their husbands. Entries include a large portrait of the featured woman and consist of dates of service and party affiliation. Various governmental agencies, in collaboration with the Commission on the Bicentenary of the U.S. House of Representatives, chaired by Lindy (Mrs. Hale) Boggs, created this excellent reference source. Lindy Boggs wrote a brief introduction to the book. Newt Gingrich served as one of the six members of the commission.

MONOGRAPHS

Political Theory

500. Bryson, Valerie. *Feminist Political Theory.* New York: Marlowe and Co., 1994. 304p. ISBN (OP); 1569249733pa.

This book, which would make an excellent overview text for women's studies and political science classes, traces the development of feminist political theory from the seventeenth century's Mary Astell, whom some scholars believe was the first English feminist, to the early 1990s. Bryson examines various types of feminisms, from the socialist feminism of Britain and America to the Marxist feminism of Germany and Russia. Bryson also discusses the political writings of John Stuart Mill, Karl Marx and Friedrich Engels, Simone de Beauvoir, Betty Friedan, and Kate Millet. Despite the large number of topics and theories treated, Bryson's style makes the work accessible, and she never trivializes or dilutes her topics. Wendy Brown's *Manhood and Politics: A Feminist Reading in Political Thought* (Rowman & Littlefield, 1988) is another fine study of feminist political theory. Brown's book provides in-depth analysis of the writings of four major classical political theorists: Aristotle, Machiavelli, Max Weber, and Hannah Arendt. This feminist work transcends the traditional bounds of feminism to examine a "post-masculinist politics" in which gender issues involve both men and women.

501. Butler, Judith, and Joan W. Scott, eds. *Feminists Theorize the Political.* New York: Routledge, 1992. 485p. index. ISBN 0415902738; 0415902746pa.

The twenty-two chapters of this eclectic work present the writings of prominent feminists in the academic disciplines of English, law, the humanities, government, and political science. The editors forwarded a set of fifteen formidable questions to contributing scholars for them to consider when writing their chapters. As a beacon or reference point for readers, the editors state that in each essay "the value of poststructuralist theories is confirmed or contested in particular contexts" (p. xiii). Each essay is a study of the language, the epistemology, and the methodology of a discrete (if somewhat arbitrary) topic such as George Sand's feminism, Hannah Arendt and the politics of identity, rape prevention, and postcolonial pedagogy. Another heavily reviewed political theory book is Joan Cocks's *The Oppositional Imagination: Feminism, Critique, and Political Theory* (Routledge, 1989) which begins with analyses of cultural power differentials in the works of Antonio Gramsci and Michael Foucault and continues with later feminist viewpoints. These books are recommended for graduate-level political science, philosophy, English, and women's studies classes. Neither is particularly easy reading; instead, they are well-reasoned philosophical critiques that demand careful study.

502. Cohen, Cathy J., Kathleen B. Jones, and Joan C. Tronto, eds. *Women Transforming Politics: An Alternative Reader*. New York: New York University Press, 1997. 602p. index. ISBN 0814715575; 0814715583pa.

To broaden the scope of the meaning of politics, the editors refuse to define political activity in traditional ways. Thus the variety of topics in the thirty-three essays that compose this collection reflect the editors' goal of decentralizing traditional politics by "foregrounding" marginalized groups such as lesbians, disabled women, and Native American, African American, Latina, and Pan-Asian women. Several chapters blur the distinction between the public and private domain, thus stretching the boundaries of the term "politics." Editors do not rely upon the traditional male-centric political theory that limits the political realm to public-sector activities, as contributors interpret the political implications of the music of 2 Live Crew, examine the saga of Vanessa Williams, the first "Black Miss America," and investigate Chinese American sweatshops in New York's garment district. Its eclectic topics and inclusion of numerous, all-too-often-subdued voices of a variety of women make this work highly engaging and innovative. This fine work would make an excellent undergraduate textbook for women's studies and political science classes.

503. Costain, Anne N. *Inviting Women's Rebellion: A Political Process Interpretation of the Women's Movement*. Baltimore: Johns Hopkins University Press, 1992. 188p. index. ISBN (OP); 0801848741pa.

Professor Anne Costain presents an extensively researched political history of the women's movement from 1945 to the early 1990s. She includes interviews with lobbyists for women's causes, archives of women's groups, and a year-by-year-analysis of the *New York Times Annual Index* from 1950 to 1986 to identify articles on women's rights activism. Costain also scrutinized several decades of the *Congressional Record* and the *United States Statutes at Large* to locate women's rights legislation. She innovatively uses "political process theory" to reinterpret the political impact of the women's movement and posits that the general political climate, in addition to belonging to a broadly based social movement, reinforced the initial strength of the women's movement during the 1960s and 1970s. According to Costain, the 1980s saw "women's issues" largely subsumed under more general political rhetoric, which placed increasing emphasis on "the family." Despite what she views as the decline of the women's movement in the 1980s, however, Costain argues that activists can leverage future social upheavals to build upon the significant political gains that women have achieved during the past four decades.

504. Daley, Caroline, and Melanie Nolan, eds. *Suffrage and Beyond: International Feminist Perspectives*. New York: New York University Press, 1994. 369p. bibliog. index. ISBN 0814718701; 081471871Xpa.

To honor the 100th anniversary of women's suffrage in New Zealand, celebrants held an international conference in Wellington in 1993. Although the authors of the sixteen conference papers included in this work are scholars from New Zealand and Australia, *Suffrage and Beyond* is international in scope, featuring the work of several British, American, and Japanese scholars. Women's suffrage is a complex topic; each country eventually enfranchised women according to its own timetable as a result of varying circumstances. Contributors thus examine how long it took to achieve suffrage in the various countries, why women sometimes organized against their own enfranchisement, the "gift" versus "struggle" interpretations of suffrage, race, and class problems, and each country's postsuffrage history. A comprehensive timeline of women's suffrage and an excellent bibliography arranged by geographic region conclude the work. This book is recommended for undergraduate women's history and political science classes.

505. Duerst-Lahti, Georgia, and Rita Mae Kelly, eds. *Gender Power, Leadership, and Governance*. Ann Arbor: University of Michigan Press, 1995. 305p. bibliog. index. ISBN (OP); 0472066102pa.

American political science scholars familiar with feminist scholarship wrote the eleven essays about gender power differentials in the United States that are featured in this work, which explores "gender power in explicitly political institutions, settings, symbolism, and behaviors" (p. 3). The editors emphasize the analysis of leadership and governance, areas wherein women have experienced a disadvantage throughout most of history. The essays address pragmatic topics such as the dynamics of men working on legislative committees chaired by women and the politics involved in Hillary Clinton's health care plan and include a chapter titled "Making Something of Absence: The 'Year of the Woman' and Women's Representation" and a chapter dealing with sex-role identity and decision styles as a means to explain the "paucity of women at the top."

Women, the State, and Development (State University of New York Press, 1989), edited by Sue Ellen M. Charlton, Jana Everett, and Kathleen Staudt, provides an excellent international perspective on women and the state. Contributors examine the following areas of the world: Eastern and Western Europe, colonial Africa, Islamic West Africa, Latin America, Chile, and India. Both books are not only well organized and researched, but also accessible, making them good choices for undergraduate women's studies, political science, and government studies curricula.

506. Eisenstein, Zillah R. *The Color of Gender: Reimaging Democracy*. Berkeley: University of California Press, 1994. 277p. index. ISBN (OP); 0520084225pa.

Eisenstein analyzes court cases, the Clarence Thomas Supreme Court confirmation hearings in the Senate, and legislation and policies from the Reagan-Bush years and beyond in this fine work. Her conclusions indicate that discrimination based upon race, class, and gender has become simultaneously subtle and insidious. A self-described middle-class, white woman, Eisenstein suggests that pregnant women of color should become the standard against which policy makers measure legislation to gauge women's political gains and losses in the United States. Eisenstein argues that using this standard would graphically illustrate some of the race, class, and gender issues that people routinely ignore, to the detriment of women and children. She dislikes using the oft-maligned term "feminism," yet argues that she "needs" it because "we are better off radicalizing and specifying feminism than speaking only from our differences" (p. 10). Eisenstein deconstructs terms such as "PC" (political correctness) and "family values," identifying them not only as a means to silence the dissent of feminists, ethnic minorities, and gays and lesbians, but also as exclusionary rhetoric to perpetuate the inherent racism and sexism in American society. The author concludes that "the individual (neoconservative politicians) have in mind is always a white male" (p. 3).

For the perspective of a white woman who realizes and admits racial privilege and seeks to create a more inclusive political system based upon her realizations, read *White Political Women: Paths from Privilege to Empowerment* (University of Tennessee Press, 1992) by Diane L. Fowlkes. Both of these thought-provoking works should be required reading for undergraduate political science, women's studies, and ethnic studies classes.

507. Elshtain, Jean Bethke. *Real Politics: At the Center of Everyday Life.* Baltimore: Johns Hopkins University Press, 1997. 375p. index. ISBN (OP); 0801856000pa.

Prolific political science writer Jean Bethke Elshtain can find politics anywhere she looks (as in the personal is political). She writes with great scholarly acumen and a highly developed sense of humor. *Real Politics* contains twenty-three essays, some previously published, and is arranged into five sections: real politics, political languages and political realities, families and children, victims/oppressors, and media. The essays themselves, along with Elshtain's narrative comments before each section, account for the seeming eclecticism of this volume. The author's phrase "the drama of democracy" characterizes the book's tone. Another of Elshtain's works, *Power Trips and Other Journeys: Essays in Feminism as a Civic Discourse* (University of Wisconsin Press, 1990), would make a fine companion volume. She writes across a broad terrain of topics and, as always, poses many more questions and quandaries to the reader than she answers in her essays. She makes suggestions and presents pros and cons, but never gives pat, definitive answers. Finally, anyone in the field of political science or women's studies must read Elshtain's landmark work *Public Man, Private Woman: Women in Social and Political Thought* (2nd ed., Princeton University Press, 1993), an update of the 1981 edition. She provides a historical analysis, beginning with Plato and Aristotle, of the ubiquitous, practically universal political assumption, which has become a legacy, that men's "natural" place in the world is in the public sphere where much of the world's policy making happens, while women should remain in the "less important" private sphere, that of hearth, home, and childbearing.

508. Flamming, Janet A. *Women's Political Voice: How Women Are Transforming the Practice and Study of Politics.* Philadelphia: Temple University Press, 1997. 419p. index. ISBN 156639533X; 1566395348pa.

The academic discipline of political science began as a male-dominated field in the late nineteenth century; it remained within the male domain until the early 1970s. According to Janet Flamming, however, at this time several women conducted feminist research that appeared in specialized journals, but was absent from the *American Political Science Review.* This book presents a very thorough review of the literature of political science, describing ways in which the research has privileged the interests as well as the epistemological and methodological techniques that male researchers use. Flamming divides feminist researchers into "accommodationists," who believe that marginal adjustments to current research methodology will suffice, and "transformationalists," who want fundamental changes in the discipline to fully accommodate the political needs of women. Throughout the book, the author uses San Jose, Santa Clara County, as an example of what transformationalist politics can accomplish. *Women's Political Voice* covers three major areas: mass politics, including political mobilization and participation; elite politics, including recruitment, policy preferences, and political styles; and elite-mass interaction, including agenda setting and coalition building. This work would make an excellent textbook for undergraduate political science and women's studies classes.

509. Gelb, Joyce, and Marian Lief Palley. *Women and Public Policies: Reassessing Gender Politics.* Rev. and expanded ed. Charlottesville: University Press of Virginia, 1996. 268p. bibliog. index. ISBN (OP); 081391695Xpa.

Two seasoned policy analysts and professors of political science have written a useful book for activists and lobbyists on women's issues. The 1996 "revised and expanded edition" updates the second edition (Princeton University Press, 1987). This newest edition reflects increasing pressure from right-leaning factions seeking to undermine legislative gains made by women during the past four decades. Chapters are dedicated to in-depth analysis of equal credit opportunities for women, Title IX education issues, pregnancy disability, abortion, and the Retirement Equity Act of 1983. Concluding paragraphs of each chapter sum up the success (or lack thereof) in enacting legislation. The authors recommend that women lobbyists emphasize role equity issues rather than role changes (by which "comparable worth" becomes "pay equity"). This book is recommended for political science and women's studies curricula as well as for grassroots organizers. Another title by Joyce Gelb, *Feminism and Politics: A Comparative Perspective* (University of California Press, 1989), compares and contrasts three countries, the United States, the United Kingdom, and Sweden. She concludes that autonomous movements, those that are separate from institutional interests (political parties, unions, and so on), have a greater chance for long-term success.

510. Hawkesworth, M.E. *Beyond Oppression: Feminist Theory and Political Strategy.* New York: Continuum, 1990. 283p. bibliog. index. (OP)

Hawkesworth begins this landmark study with a thorough overview and analysis of how "feminist theorists have revealed substantive defects in traditional philosophical and religious claims about women" (p. 13). She devotes her first chapter to an examination of the writings of Plato, Aristotle, St. Augustine, Thomas Aquinas, John Locke, Immanuel Kant, and others. After outlining what modern readers would perceive as shockingly "sexist" statements by these great Western thinkers, philosophers, and writers, Hawkesworth argues that these thinkers have not discovered gender differences in their arguments, but have created them. She outlines the social consequences of gender misconceptions in chapter 2 and then continues to delineate the theoretical constructs and consequences of male oppression in the several exquisitely reasoned chapters that follow. Hawkesworth brings her theory to bear on our modern world in chapter 6, "Feminist Theory Confronts the Polis," and concludes her groundbreaking, well-reasoned critique with a proposal to amend constitutions to mandate that women hold 50 percent of all elective, appointive, and bureaucratic offices in government. This mandate would ensure transcendence of the myriad religious, political, racial, and other constraints that have precluded women from winning their legitimate place as full players in the political arena.

511. Hirschmann, Nancy J., and Christine Di Stefano, eds. *Revisioning the Political: Feminist Reconstructions of Traditional Concepts in Western Political Theory.* Boulder, CO: Westview Press, 1996. 281p. (Feminist Theory and Politics). index. ISBN 0813386403; 081338639X.

Editors Hirschmann and Di Stefano present the ideas of thirteen of the most prestigious contemporary political scientists and academicians in the area of feminist political theory in this volume. The editors asked these scholars to construct a workable vision of a particular aspect, such as justice, freedom, autonomy, and even "care" (a feminist contribution to political theory), of political theory that has developed in accordance with feminist research during the past three decades. Since much of women's writing about political theory is a critique of what does not work, Hirschmann and Di Stefano attempted to "put forth feminist 'blueprints' for constructing 'positive' feminist theories and for shaping a feminist world" (p. xiii). One of Hirschmann's chapters is an excerpt from a previous book that she wrote, titled *Rethinking Obligation: A Feminist Method for Political Theory* (Cornell University Press, 1992), in which she uses feminist psychoanalysis and standpoint theory to identify the gender bias of early social contract theory. She contends that social contract theory is circular and is inappropriately applied to the political situation of women. The essays in both works would provide excellent reading material for graduate-level women's studies, political science, and philosophy classes. Kathleen B. Jones, who contributed a chapter to *Revisioning the Political*, has herself written an important book that should be considered required reading. *Compassionate Authority: Democracy and the Representation of Women* (Routledge, 1993) provides valuable new insights into the gendered nature of governments and how women might revision conventional democratic theory.

512. McClintock, Anne, Aamir Mufti, and Ella Shohat, eds. *Dangerous Liaisons: Gender, Nation, and Postcolonial Perspectives*. Minneapolis: University of Minnesota Press, 1997. 551p. (Cultural Politics). index. ISBN (OP); 0816626499pa.

This 551-page "guidebook" on postcolonialism assembles twenty-eight essays by several prominent scholars, including Chandra Mohanty, Audre Lorde, bell hooks, and Judith Butler. The editors divide the work into four parts: "Contesting Nations," which includes two chapters on Zionism, one on ethnic cleansing in the Balkans, and one on British educational and cultural policy in India; "Multiculturalism and Diasporic Identities"; "Gender and the Politics of Race," which consists of eight chapters that collectively dismiss the idea of "Third World women" as a singular, monolithic subject and includes a chapter by bell hooks that dispels the notion of "bonding over shared victimization" (p. 398); and "Postcolonial Theory," which is comprised of chapters that deal with postcolonialism in African and Indian cultures. The collection emphasizes multiculturalism as opposed to "Eurocentrism," which scholars commonly examine. *Gender and Imperialism* (Manchester University Press, 1998; distributed by St. Martin's Press, 1998), edited by Clare Midgley, provides a British perspective on postcolonialism. Midgley aims to incorporate writings about women and gender within the scholarship on British imperialism and colonialism. These two works provide an excellent overview of postcolonialism from the vantage point of various international scholars; they would complement undergraduate political science and women's studies curricula.

513. Phillips, Anne. *Democracy and Difference*. University Park: Pennsylvania State University Press, 1993. 175p. index. ISBN 0271010967; 0271010975pa.

Anne Phillips, the author of several excellent political science books, analyzes the concept of "democracy" via delineating the various characteristics of the democracy of a particular culture in *Democracy and Difference*. She devotes chapters to fraternity, a concept that she believes "has a richly archaic ring" (p. 25), the concept of the individual, and the promise of democracy. Phillips explores and seeks to debunk what she calls "universal pretensions in political thought." She asserts that one must openly define the democracy that she envisions in order to accommodate differences in gender, class, race, and other characteristics. Phillips's compelling writing style and her fine scholarship, which is rich in historical and contemporary references, make this a worthwhile work. Another of her works, *Engendering Democracy* (Pennsylvania State University Press, 1991), received the American Political Science Association's Victoria Schuck Award for the Best Book on Women in Politics in 1992. In this work, Phillips urges people to reconceptualize politics via creating a political framework that does not incorporate the construct of gender. She articulately argues her case in chapters that outline classic debates, such as the age-old dilemma of "public versus private." All of Anne Phillips's works would make excellent textbooks or supplementary reading for women's studies and political science undergraduate curricula.

514. Sapiro, Virginia. *A Vindication of Political Virtue: The Political Theory of Mary Wollstonecraft*. Chicago: University of Chicago Press, 1992. 366p. bibliog. index. ISBN 0226734900; 0226734919pa.

Virginia Sapiro marked the bicentennial of the publication of Mary Wollstonecraft's most famous work, *A Vindication of the Rights of Woman* (1792), with a tribute to the early "feminist." Sapiro, who has a background in women's studies and political science, employs both disciplines to examine her topic. The author thematically approaches this biography to analyze Wollstone-craft's many essays, fiction, and the ubiquitous *Vindication*. Sapiro painstakingly frames her richly comprehensive interpretation in a historical context, describing her early chapters as a "Wollstone-craft lexicon" (p. xviii), and effectively examines Mary Wollstonecraft and her oeuvre, which consists of approximately seven volumes and includes personal letters, in light of feminist theory, carving out new interpretations based upon the political aspects of the early feminist's work. *Feminist Interpretations of Mary Wollstonecraft* (Pennsylvania State University Press, 1996), ed-ited by Maria J. Falco, is a companion volume that features a chapter by Virginia Sapiro. The essays included in this work respond to Sapiro's 1992 challenge to broaden the traditional view of Wollstonecraft, an often misinterpreted writer whom scholars continue to read two centuries after her heyday. Both books would make worthwhile texts or supplementary reading in women's studies and undergraduate political science and political theory classes.

515. Shanley, Mary L., and Carole Pateman, eds. *Feminist Interpretations and Political Theory*. University Park: Pennsylvania State University Press, 1991. 288p. index. ISBN 0271007362; 0271007427pa.

The editors of this fourteen-essay work present interpretations of several key feminist polit-ical science scholars in the field who examine one or more of the classics of Western political thought. Although males mostly have crafted these classics, Shanley and Pateman include the writings of Mary Wollstonecraft, Simone de Beauvoir, and Hannah Arendt in their work. Con-tributors reexamine the works of early philosophers, such as Plato, Aristotle, Hobbes, Locke, and Rousseau, as well as later writers, including Marx, John Rawls, Foucault, and Jürgen Habermas, in light of feminist theories that have developed during the past thirty years. Pateman, who also wrote *The Sexual Contract* (Stanford University Press, 1988) and *The Disorder of Women: De-mocracy, Feminism, and Political Theory* (Stanford University Press, 1989), contributes a chapter on the political writings of Thomas Hobbes. Among Mary Shanley's other books is *Reconstructing Political Theory: Feminist Perspectives* (Pennsylvania State University Press, 1997), which she coedited with Uma Narayan, a noted scholar on Third World women. *Feminist Interpretations and Political Theory* and Pateman's previous philosophical/political science works would make fine texts for undergraduate- and graduate-level philosophy, political science, and women's studies classes.

516. Staudt, Kathleen A., and William G. Weaver. *Political Science and Feminisms: Integration or Transformation?* New York: Twayne, 1997. 193p. (Impact of Feminism on the Arts and Sciences). bibliog. index. ISBN 0805745297.

According to Staudt and Weaver, even by the 1990s, scholars of U.S. political science had made few strides in integrating women, gender, and feminism into their discipline. The authors address this phenomenon through an examination of political science syllabi at the college level, political science journals, major professional organizations in the field, and a supplemental ques-tionnaire that they sent to various political science departments. Staudt and Weaver analyze the six major political science subfields: political theory, American politics, comparative politics, international relations, public law, and public administration. In their concluding chapter, the authors present valuable ideas for better integration of women and feminism into the various subfields. Suggestions include mainstreaming women's political writings and titling them so their feminist slant is not so obvious, promoting more academic rewards for cross-disciplinary publishing, and elevating theory and comparative politics to the central prominence that they once held. They emphasize that all of the political science subfields require transformation. This title would make excellent reading for undergraduate political science and women's studies classes.

517. Young, Iris M. *Intersecting Voices: Dilemmas of Gender, Political Philosophy, and Policy*. Princeton, NJ: Princeton University Press, 1997. 195p. index. ISBN 0691012016; 0691012008pa.

Award-winning political scientist and professor Iris M. Young explores the inherent complexities and seeming contradictions in developing a feminist theory of politics in this collection of seven essays. Young examines the theoretical writings of philosophers such as Jean-Paul Sartre, Luce Irigaray, Simone de Beauvoir, and Susan Okin and weaves some of their insights and conclusions into her own ideas about how to apply various feminist theories of politics to the "real world." The author provides social critiques as well as alternative ways of thinking in each of her essays. One of the most cumbersome problems that she addresses involves how to develop a feminist politics that functions as a collective without marginalizing some types of women while simultaneously empowering others. Young uses Sartre's phenomenon of "serial collectivity" to respect the differences in individual women while still allowing for the possibility of collective action. Despite the philosophical rigor of her writing, Young cogently defines her concepts, making them socially relevant to marginalized and, in some cases, stigmatized groups such as pregnant, drug-addicted women, as well as women who do not wish to adhere to socially restricted "traditional family values."

Iris Young's earlier work *Justice and the Politics of Difference* (Princeton University Press, 1990) is an excellent social critique that reexamines traditional concepts of justice into which former oppressed groups have been factored. These and other Young titles should be required reading for aspiring philosophers and political scientists alike.

Women and Politics Worldwide

518. Alonso, Harriet Hyman. *Peace as a Women's Issue: A History of the U.S. Movement for World Peace and Women's Rights*. Syracuse, NY: Syracuse University Press, 1993. 340p. bibliog. index. ISBN (OP); 0815602693pa.

History professor Harriet Alonso chronicles women's peace movements in the United States from the 1820s through the early 1990s. Her comprehensive bibliography reveals extensive use of primary source material such as manuscript collections, oral histories, and interviews, as well as numerous secondary sources. Photographs, posters, and illustrations also complement the text. Alonso covers nearly two centuries of women organizing protests against various wars, including the Civil War, World Wars I and II, and the Vietnam War. She also examines how women collectively opposed nuclear testing, slavery, and sexual inequality. *Peace as a Women's Issue* provides a historical context for women activists to learn how to effectively organize future peace politics initiatives. Two appendices contain valuable timelines and details of events. This richly historical work would complement both women's studies and political history collections.

519. Beckman, Peter R., and Francine D'Amico, eds. *Women, Gender, and World Politics: Perspectives, Policies, and Prospects*. Westport, CT: Greenwood Press, 1994. 250p. bibliog. index. ISBN 0897893050; 0897893069pa.

An important question raised by editors Beckman and D'Amico and their collaborators, all noted political science scholars, is "why women's role in world politics and the effect of world politics on women have been obscured" (p. x). Their goal is to address this quandary in a new and substantive way. Chapters analyze gender issues from various perspectives, including Marxist and postmodernist. A particularly incisive essay by Hamideh Sedghi, "Third World Feminist Perspectives on World Politics," warns that the phrase "Third World women" is not to be considered a monolithic concept. She analyzes four international conflicts, the Turkish national movement, the Algerian national liberation struggle, the Iran-Iraq regional war, and the Persian Gulf War, and compares and contrasts the effects upon each country's women. Several chapters outline women's progress since creation of the United Nations in 1945.

D'Amico and Beckman edited a companion volume, *Women in World Politics: An Introduction* (Bergin & Garvey, 1995), which devotes chapters to such women heads of state as Margaret Thatcher, Corazon Aquino, and Indira Gandhi. Other chapters address women in the United Nations, the global green movement, and women revolutionaries in Cuba and Nicaragua. These volumes offer a rich introduction to the topic of women in international politics and are recommended, in tandem, as textbooks for undergraduate women's studies and political science curricula.

520. Biehl, Janet. *Rethinking Ecofeminist Politics*. Boston: South End Press, 1991. 181p. index. ISBN 0896083926; 0896083918pa.

Janet Biehl was an early proponent of the environmental movement of social ecology. She is also a disciple of Murray Bookchin, social ecology's founder. Biehl, an environmental activist, assembles and examines various strands of the loosely constructed concepts of ecofeminism. She argues that ecofeminism is not a cohesive discipline, nor has a definitive theory been developed around it. Rather, "ecofeminist theory defines itself largely by a plethora of short, often self-contradictory essays on the subject" (p. 2). Biehl's goal in this groundbreaking work is to "open up a serious debate about ecofeminism in the ecology and feminist movements, on questions that have gone unaddressed for far too long" (p. 7).

Noël Sturgeon has taken up this challenge in *Ecofeminist Natures: Race, Gender, Feminist Theory, and Political Action* (Routledge, 1997). Sturgeon's copious endnotes and extensive bibliography attest to the scholarly acumen brought to bear on the historical (approximately 1980 to 1996) and theoretical frameworks of ecofeminism. Completing a triumvirate of theoretical books on the topic is Ariel Salleh's *Ecofeminism as Politics: Nature, Marx, and the Postmodern* (Zed Books, 1997; distributed in the United States by St. Martin's Press). Salleh also took up Biehl's challenge to rethink ecofeminism as a feminist tool of activism. These three books could be used as texts or supplementary reading for undergraduate classes in ecology, women's studies, or international politics.

521. Brill, Alida, ed. *A Rising Public Voice: Women in Politics Worldwide*. New York: Feminist Press at the City University of New York, 1995. 284p. ISBN 155861110X; 1558611118.

Gertrude Mongella, secretary-general of the 1995 United Nations Fourth World Conference on Women held in Beijing, wrote the foreword to this anthology. Editor Brill collected twenty-one essays written by women from various countries, including Chile, Nicaragua, Australia, New Zealand, India, Germany, and Norway. Nine of the essays are profiles of political luminaries such as Mary Robinson, the first woman elected president of Ireland (1990), Senator Carol Moseley Braun, the first African American woman elected to the U.S. Senate, and Vigdís Finnbogadóttir, the first woman elected president of Iceland (1980). The remaining brief essays consist of biographical portraits and personal narratives that provide an overview of the lives of an eclectic group of politically active women. Brill also includes an interview with Hanan Ashrawi, the official spokesperson for the Palestinian delegation to the Middle East peace talks in 1992, and an essay by Maria de Lourdes Pintasilgo, onetime prime minister of Portugal.

In a similar work, titled *Women as National Leaders* (Sage Publications, 1993), Michael A. Genovese provides in-depth biographical treatment of seven of the foremost women politicians in the world: Corazon Aquino, Benazir Bhutto, Indira Gandhi, Golda Meir, Isabel Perón, Margaret Thatcher, and Violeta Chamorro. He frames each case study with questions that prominent political science scholars posed to the women politicians. Genovese wrote introductory and concluding chapters positioning the studies politically and summarizing what has been learned from these influential women leaders.

522. Bunch, Charlotte, and Niamh Reilly. *Demanding Accountability: The Global Campaign and Tribunal for Women's Human Rights.* New York: UNIFEM, 1994. 169p. ISBN (OP); 0912917296pa.

Charlotte Bunch, founding director of the Center for Women's Global Leadership, and Niamh Reilly, coordinator of the Vienna Tribunal for Women's Human Rights, compiled this book to document testimony and chronicle events associated with the 1993 Tribunal. The Tribunal encompassed five thematic sessions: human rights abuse in the family, war crimes against women, violations of women's bodily integrity, socioeconomic violation of women's human rights, and gender-based political persecution and discrimination. Thirty-three women from twenty-five countries presented ten-minute prepared statements to five internationally prominent judges during this one-day Tribunal, which formed part of the United Nations World Conference on Human Rights. Each judge responded to testimony on one area in a written statement; the five judges collaborated on a final statement. Women throughout the world worked strategically for many years to ensure that women's human rights became an integral component of the proceedings, emphasizing the near invisibility of the violence routinely perpetrated against women worldwide: "Abuses of women have too long been dismissed as private, family, cultural or religious matters. Today, we demand that they be seen for what they are: fundamental violations of the 'right to life, liberty and security of person,' as guaranteed by the Universal Declaration of Human Rights" (p. 131). The Tribunal paved the way for the 1995 Fourth World Conference on Women in Beijing. A comprehensive resource list concludes this important history of the struggle for recognition of women's rights as human rights. All college-level political science and women's studies collections should include this work.

523. Cook, Rebecca J., ed. *Human Rights of Women: National and International Perspectives.* Philadelphia: University of Pennsylvania Press, 1994. 634p. (Pennsylvania Studies in Human Rights). index. ISBN (OP); 0812215389pa.

The International Human Rights Programme of the University of Toronto hosted a conference in 1992, "a consultation on Women's International Human Rights Law." This book of more than 600 pages, funded in part by the Ford Foundation, contains papers and summaries of discussions from that conference. Rebecca J. Cook edited the writings of twenty-two international lawyers and legal scholars. The result is a heavily and favorably reviewed work that analyzes legal rights, women's rights, and human rights of women worldwide. Several of the well-documented chapters emphasize that the United Nations Convention on the Elimination of All Forms of Discrimination against Women (CEDAW) notwithstanding, the rights of women are not interpreted uniformly throughout the world. One of the problems is the weighing of international law against national law and of national/state laws versus "personal laws," those that may be interpreted to govern marriage and the family, which some consider beyond the purview of government. The role of ethnic, religious, and cultural norms and traditions can also clash with women's human rights, for example, the ancient practice of sati in some sects of Hinduism, a tradition whereby a widow was burned alive on the funeral pyre of her deceased husband. Case studies and documentation of court judgments highlight areas of contention. For biographical studies of seventeen women activists who have dedicated themselves to human rights reform, *Women Reshaping Human Rights* (Scholarly Resources, 1996), by Marguerite Guzmán Bouvard, is an excellent choice. In it, activists such as Gertrude Mongella, onetime assistant secretary-general of the United Nations, describe women's struggles to obtain these rights, which were mandated as early as the 1948 United Nations Universal Declaration of Human Rights.

524. Elshtain, Jean Bethke. *Women and War*. New York: Basic Books, 1987. 301p. bibliog. index. ISBN (OP); 0226206262pa.

Jean Bethke Elshtain is one of the most prolific and important scholars in the area of feminist political theory. Her works add dimension, depth, and gender balance to the literature. In *Women and War*, Elshtain draws from the philosophical works of key thinkers such as Hegel, Rousseau, Mary Wollstonecraft, and Machiavelli, as well as popular portrayals of war and stereotypical depictions of gender roles in movies such as *An Officer and a Gentleman, Joan of Arc*, and *Private Benjamin*. The author uncovers historical oversimplifications and misrepresentations perpetuated over many centuries, exploring numerous philosophical and cultural examples without offering any pat answers to the many questions that she raises.

Her later work *Women, Militarism, and War: Essays in History, Politics, and Social Theory* (Rowman & Littlefield, 1990), edited with Sheila Tobias, consists of essays by some of the most important feminist political theorists, including Amy Swerdlow, Linda K. Kerber, and Sara Ruddick. The editors provide insightful comments before each chapter. All women's studies and political science collections would benefit from acquisition of several Elshtain titles.

525. Enloe, Cynthia. *The Morning After: Sexual Politics at the End of the Cold War*. Berkeley: University of California Press, 1993. 326p. bibliog. index. ISBN 0520083350; 0520083369pa.

Cynthia Enloe is another of the premiere feminist interpreters of international military and political theory. *The Morning After* is a must-read for anyone interested in answering the question "where are the women?" in military actions or wars. Enloe, professor of government and director of the women's studies program at Clark University in Massachusetts, also wrote the scholarly and provocative (and perhaps better-known) *Bananas, Beaches, and Bases: Making Feminist Sense of International Politics* (University of California Press, 1990). The author uses numerous primary and secondary resources for her research. In *The Morning After*, she explores post–Cold War politics around the world. She does not downplay the complexity of her topic. War is traditionally considered a man's concern even though wars could not be financed without the complicity and support of women. The military-industrial complex is most often supported by the labor of low-paid women workers. In addition, women have been "educated" and socialized to provide emotional and sexual nurturing for soldiers during and after a war. She also wonders why military budgets continue to increase even in times of "peace." Enloe concludes, "We are living in a new postwar period without having resolved the questions of earlier postwar periods" (p. 261). Enloe's works have cut a wide swath across previously little-examined political terrain and deserve a spot in all women's studies, political science, and military studies curricula and collections.

526. Harris, Adrienne, and Ynestra King, eds. *Rocking the Ship of State: Toward a Feminist Peace Politics.* Boulder, CO: Westview Press, 1989. 301p. (Feminist Theory and Politics Series). ISBN 0813307104.

The fourteen chapters that comprise this work provide a well-rounded overview of issues involved in shaping a peace politics, or a politics by, about, and for women. Following several theoretical chapters, the book devotes itself to three women's peace encampments or rallies: the Greenham Common Women's Peace Camp in England; the 1961 Women Strike for Peace (WSP) groups in Washington, D.C., formed to oppose nuclear testing; and the Seneca Women's Peace Camp in New York, formed to protest the cruise and Pershing II missiles. Sara Ruddick and Amy Swerdlow each contribute a chapter.

Sasha Roseneil's *Disarming Patriarchy: Feminism and Political Action at Greenham Common* (Taylor & Francis, 1995) offers more detailed information about the Greenham Common experience, which began in 1981 and withstood many years of the British government's concerted efforts to evict, harass, and jail the women protesters, all to little avail. Roseneil lived at Greenham Common for ten months and interviewed women who were encamped there. In addition, Jill Liddington's *The Road to Greenham Common: Feminism and Anti-militarism in Britain since 1820* (Syracuse University Press, 1991) provides historical background gleaned from diaries, interviews, and other primary source materials. For an in-depth analysis of the Seneca Women's Peace Encampment, see Louise Krasniewicz's *Nuclear Summer: The Clash of Communities at the Seneca Women's Peace Encampment* (Cornell University Press, 1992). Krasniewicz, an anthropologist, spent time at the encampment and conducted an ethnographic study about the politics and relational dynamics of its women.

527. Lovenduski, Joni, and Pippa Norris, eds. *Gender and Party Politics.* Thousand Oaks, CA: Sage Publications, 1993. 358p. bibliog. index. ISBN 0803986599; 0803986602pa.

Joni Lovenduski and Pippa Norris, eminent scholars of women's studies and politics, edited this collection of thirteen essays by prominent political scientists from the United States, Europe, Canada, and Australia. Contributors describe the political parties and processes in place in various countries and analyze why 30 to 40 percent of women in countries like Sweden and Norway consistently get elected to national offices, whereas the United States, Great Britain, and Italy continue to yield abject single-digit percentages. Lovenduski contextualizes the eleven essays that compose the body of the work in her excellent introduction. Norris examines the role of gate-keeping within political parties and the mechanics of how candidates get recruited into the political machinery in her insightful conclusion. Norris posits that women face more difficulties in attempting to establish themselves as political players in a country like the United States, which has only two major political parties. Lovenduski and Norris fortify some chapters with tables and graphs and contribute a joint chapter titled "Gender and Party Politics in Britain" to the work.

528. MacDonald, Eileen. *Shoot the Women First: Inside the Secret World of Female Terrorists.* New York: Random House, 1991. 241p. (OP)

Many scholars refer to women who commit acts of violence and are willing to maim and kill to advance their own causes as enigmas and perhaps even biological contradictions. But are they? MacDonald, a British journalist, interviews some of the world's notorious twentieth-century terrorists, including women from Palestine, Northern Ireland, Germany, Italy and Basque women, in this work. The book's title comes from a directive, perhaps apocryphal, to West German antiterrorist squads to shoot women first in a terrorist incident, ostensibly because women are seen as more treacherous. MacDonald interviewed many women, including Leila Khaled, a

Palestinian refugee who almost single-handedly hijacked a commercial airliner, evacuated the passengers, and then blew up the plane, and Kim Hyou Hui of North Korea, who planted a bomb in a commercial airliner, which subsequently crashed, killing all 115 passengers. These women saw their terrorist activities as acts of war, and all but two of them notably referred to themselves as feminists. Robin Morgan also wrote a book about women terrorists at the urging of feminist friends Mary Daly, Andrea Dworkin, and Gloria Steinem. *The Demon Lover: On the Sexuality of Terrorism* (Norton, 1989) is one of the first works on women terrorists. Both books help dispel the prevailing myth that all women are nurturing pacifists.

529. Peterson, V. Spike, and Anne Sisson Runyan. *Global Gender Issues*. Boulder, CO: Westview Press, 1993. 202p. (Dilemmas in World Politics). bibliog. index. (OP)

Written as a textbook for undergraduate college classes in world politics, this work carefully defines terms and lays out assumptions for readers who may not have a sophisticated understanding of either international relations or feminist theory. In the introduction to world politics "viewed through a gender-sensitive lens" (p. 1), the authors admit that while using such a lens simplifies the arguments and makes them more easily understandable, it has the consequence of obscuring differences within categories; for example, in analyzing such concepts as "women" and "men" in isolation, we sacrifice other significant variables such as race, age, class, and ethnicity. According to the authors, "World politics has long been practiced and studied as if it were 'ungendered' " (p. 149). This book reveals historical and political traditions that have rendered women next to invisible in the arena of international politics.

V. Spike Peterson also edited *Gendered States: Feminist (Re)visions of International Relations Theory* (Lynne Rienner, 1992), which could serve as a text for more advanced political science and women's studies students. It is based upon a two-day conference, "Gender and International Relations," held at Wellesley College's Center for Research on Women in 1990. Eight essays by prominent feminist political scientists examine gendered aspects of international relations, discuss terminology, and examine the implications for all women.

Another text in this vein is Georgina Waylen's *Gender in Third World Politics* (Lynne Rienner, 1996). It devotes two chapters to a discussion of the meanings of the phrase "Third World women" and continues with a thematic approach to women in four political contexts: colonialism, revolution, authoritarianism, and democratization.

530. Pettman, Jan Jindy. *Worlding Women: A Feminist International Politics*. New York: Routledge, 1996. 272p. bibliog. index. ISBN 0415152011; 041515202Xpa.

This excellent book provides a broad overview of a huge topic, international relations (IR), an area of inquiry that the author asserts has been particularly resistant to feminist scholarship. Pettman's ambitious goal is to analyze previous approaches to IR, including feminist attempts to insert women into the equation of this male-dominated discipline. She divides her book into three parts. The first is an analysis of the gendered constructions of states, nations, and citizenship. "Traditional" theory as well as feminism, critical theory, and postmodernism are compared and contrasted. The second part addresses women vis-à-vis war and peace. Pettman considers whether men are perceived to be more aggressive and women more "peaceful" due to nature or nurture—and then ponders whether this is even the right question. The final section deals with sexual division of labor where "work is primarily associated with the man and home with the woman" (p. 165). Relegating women to the home has led to violence against women, whether in a domestic situation as their husbands' "property" or as civilian victims of rape by military personnel (United Nations sanctions notwithstanding). Pettman emphasizes that women's experiences need to be validated in order to restructure what she describes as "a dangerously masculinist world" (p. 214).

Another well-received book that dissects the socially constructed boundaries of IR theory and covers some of the same theoretical ground is Christine Sylvester's *Feminist Theory and International Relations in a Postmodern Era* (Cambridge University Press, 1994). These fine scholarly treatises are a must for all feminists, political scientists, and graduate students in women's studies.

531. Pietilä, Hilkka, and Jeanne Vickers. *Making Women Matter: The Role of the United Nations*. 3rd ed. Atlantic Highlands, NJ: Zed Books, 1996. 198p. index. ISBN (OP); 1856494586pa.

The third edition of this important book contains an introduction highlighting the accomplishments of the 1995 Fourth World Conference on Women held in Beijing. The authors devote the remainder of the book to a history of the United Nations' efforts on behalf of women, with particular emphasis on developments during and after the First World Conference on Women held in Mexico City in 1975. Pietila and Vickers, who have worked for the United Nations for decades, delineate the feats and outcomes of various United Nations agencies and nongovernmental organizations (NGOs). The authors' combined expertise and dedication to advancing the cause of international women contribute highly to the book's power and integrity. The last chapter, aptly titled "Promises and Doubts," analyzes numerous accomplishments during the last three decades and projects what remains to be done. The "Annexes," or appendices, include the text of the Convention on the Elimination of All Forms of Discrimination against Women (CEDAW). *Human Rights Are Women's Rights* (Amnesty International, 1995) details the atrocities suffered by women worldwide, in peace and in war, as well as proposing how governments can protect women's human rights. Students of international political studies and women's studies should read both works.

532. Reardon, Betty. *Women and Peace: Feminist Visions of Global Security*. Albany: State University of New York Press, 1993. 209p. (SUNY Series in Global Conflict and Peace Education). bibliog. index. ISBN 0791413993; 0791414000pa.

Betty Reardon, director of the Peace Education program at Teachers College, Columbia University, has compiled a valuable educational guide. This book grew out of a study kit published by the United Nations in 1989 and would make an ideal text on the topic of women and peace. Each chapter ends with a discussion section and a brief bibliography for further study. Five appendices include the text of the Universal Declaration of Human Rights as well as excerpts from the United Nations Convention on the Elimination of All Forms of Discrimination against Women, commonly referred to as CEDAW. Reardon proclaims, "Peace will ultimately depend on the abolition of war, the negation of armed conflict" (p. 39). This way of thinking is a definite departure from previous, for the most part male-dominated, works that assert that war is inevitable, part of *la condition humaine*, a nonnegotiable fact of life. Another offshoot from the United Nations peace kit is *Women and War* (Zed Books, 1993) by Jeanne Vickers, who collaborated with Reardon on the original United Nations peace kit. Vickers's book examines the causes of war, the impact of war on women, and the economics of war. She proposes a feminist approach to problem solving aimed at avoiding future wars. For readers wishing more information about the actual violence perpetrated against women and children in the name of "just wars," see Ronit Lentin's *Gender and Catastrophe* (Zed Books, 1997). Although Lentin's edited collection, which reveals atrocities committed upon women and children in Northern Ireland, Iran, the former Yugoslavia, Bangladesh, Guatemala, Japan, Brazil, and Tibet, is painful to read, it collects previously unavailable information into one volume.

533. Ruddick, Sara. *Maternal Thinking: Toward a Politics of Peace*. Boston: Beacon Press, 1989. 291p. index. ISBN (OP); 0807014095pa.

Sara Ruddick provides a thorough reexamination of the concept of peace in this landmark work. Her early chapters create a philosophical framework for a theory and methodology of "peace politics." Ruddick brings her skills as a philosopher to the task of creating a new model for world peace. She is not content with a facile, even, she contends, erroneous explanation that women are inherently more peaceful and men more violent. "Just because mothering and peace have been so long and so sentimentally married, a critical understanding of mothering and maternal nonviolence will itself contribute to the reconception of 'peace' " (p. 137). Ruddick proposes that maternal thinking can (and should) be appropriately used by men as well as women since it is not tied to the physical act of giving birth, but rather the nurturing approach to educating and protecting young minds and bodies. This book underscores the violence prevalent in today's world and presents a rigorous new philosophical construct that could make the world safer, less violent, and, since women's wisdom is factored into the politics, a much more inclusive place. Mandatory for women's studies and political theory collections, it is one of the most important books of the twentieth century.

A recommended companion volume is Amy Swerdlow's *Women Strike for Peace: Traditional Motherhood and Radical Politics in the 1960s* (University of Chicago Press, 1993). Swerdlow has painstakingly chronicled the 1961 gathering of approximately 50,000 women who protested in Washington, D.C., demanding a nuclear test ban and seeing their demands met just two years later. This example of "motherist politics" applied many of Sara Ruddick's theories more than twenty-five years before the publication of *Maternal Thinking*.

534. Staudt, Kathleen, ed. *Women, International Development, and Politics: The Bureaucratic Mire*. Philadelphia: Temple University Press, 1990. 320p. (Women in the Political Economy Series). ISBN (OP); 1566395461pa.

Editor Kathleen Staudt draws upon a worldwide tableau for her research on international development programs. She maintains that bureaucracies, which she characterizes as closed institutions, are more insidious than they may appear or than is revealed (obfuscated?) in their official policies, since these very policies are often selectively ignored. Case studies of organizations from such diverse countries as Brazil, Cameroon, and Nicaragua, as well as the World Bank and various nongovernmental organizations (NGOs), are presented. These studies indicate that bureaucracies have, for the most part, been created based upon "essentialist" stereotypes that characterize men as breadwinners and women as homemakers. The book's final chapter suggests ways to work from within and outside bureaucracies to change development policies so that more than single-digit percentages of money can make their way into the households of the world's women.

A 1997 edition (Temple University Press, 1997) includes outcomes of the 1995 Beijing Fourth World Conference on Women and the tireless efforts of several United Nations bureaus. NGOs are seen to be making some progress toward correcting the devastating economic inequities that have plagued women worldwide for far too long. This would make a useful textbook for political science classes as well as for the personal collections of political activists in search of more effective lobbying strategies.

535. Tickner, J. Ann. *Gender in International Relations: Feminist Perspectives on Achieving Global Security*. New York: Columbia University Press, 1992. 180p. (New Directions in World Politics). bibliog. index. ISBN (OP); 0231075391pa.

Only during the last decade have significant numbers of scholarly books been written about women in international relations (IR). IR, particularly the subfields of national and international security, which author J. Ann Tickner calls "the privileged core of the field" (p. x) has been almost an exclusively male domain. Tickner, a student of IR since the early 1960s, addresses gendered perspectives in national security, global economic security, and ecological security. For coverage of gender in international institutions, including the International Planned Parenthood Federation (IPPF), Sandra Whitworth's *Feminism and International Relations: Towards a Political Economy of Gender in Interstate and Non-governmental Institutions* (St. Martin's Press, 1994) is recommended. Whitworth's book is part of the International Political Economy Series.

Another excellent book, Jill Stean's *Gender and International Relations: An Introduction* (Rutgers University Press, 1998), first published in Great Britain, begins by outlining various feminisms: liberal, radical, postmodern, and Marxist. Steans does not attempt to construct a single feminist theory of IR, but rather compares and contrasts prevailing methodologies, with some suggestions for nudging IR in a more gender-inclusive direction. *The "Man" Question in International Relations* (Westview Press, 1998), edited by Marysia Zalewski and Jane Parpart, proffers a 180-degree turnabout. Chapters reframe the "woman question" (women as the problem) by posing instead the "man question" as a locus for their research. Significantly, five of the contributing scholars are men. Any or all of these books could be used as texts or supplementary reading for international politics and women's studies classes at the undergraduate or graduate level.

536. Yuval-Davis, Nira. *Gender and Nation*. Thousand Oaks, CA: Sage. 1997. 157p. (Politics and Culture). bibliog. index. ISBN 0803986637; 0803986645pa.

Nira Yuval-Davis's book reads like an extensively annotated bibliographic essay. She brings together previous scholarly writing and conceptualizations of such terms as "woman," "state," "nation," and "citizen," which might seem to be so common and universally understood as to need no definition. The author intertwines these necessary definitions with her own insightful commentary in such a way that the book's topics, complex at best, should be accessible to graduate and perhaps even upper-division undergraduate students of women's studies and political science. One of Yuval-Davis's goals is to answer the question "why . . . are women usually 'hidden' in the various theorizations of the nationalist phenomena?" (p. 2). Her analysis is deconstructionist in the sense that she puts a magnifying glass upon many assumed and unexamined "truths." Her scope is broad, and she brings in examples from around the world: Bosnia, Zimbabwe, the United States, Yemen, China, and Brazil. She digs deeply into the subterranean underpinnings of essentialism, which assumes a simplistic, biological basis for the terms "man" and "woman," and exposes areas where even sophisticated thinkers can get caught in arguments that privilege some people and situations above others: men/women, public/private, and nature/civilization, as well as class, gender, race, religion, culture, and age. This book, if read with the care it deserves, will question much of our knowledge about the world and shift our sense of what we can genuinely "know" about how women live as gendered beings in their gendered worlds. This book encourages the intellectual rigor that will be demanded if women are to continue to redefine themselves and their worlds in the search for lasting gender equity.

Women in the Third World

537. Emmett, Ayala H. *Our Sisters' Promised Land: Women, Politics, and Israeli-Palestinian Coexistence*. Ann Arbor: University of Michigan Press, 1996. 278p. (Women and Culture Series). bibliog. index. ISBN 047210733X.

Emmett, an anthropologist at the University of Rochester, conducted an ethnographic study in Israel between 1990 and 1993. The author initially intended to recount stories of individual Israeli women peace activists; however, the women invariably turned Emmett's questions into a conversation about groups of women, changing the "I" into "we." The interviewees invited Emmett to attend several weekly Friday afternoon "Women in Black" rallies that women of various backgrounds, religions, and ethnicities held in public squares. She rounded out her research by attending five conferences in addition to scouring popular literature and official public documents. This book reflects the author's change in focus from individual women to a more finely textured study of Israeli politics seen from the perspective of women who have formed alliances to protect themselves and their loved ones. According to Emmett, "When we pay attention to the simmerings on the margins, we should assume that we will find out more about the center" (p. 240).

Gender in Crisis: Women and the Palestinian Resistance Movement (Columbia University Press, 1991) by anthropologist Julie M. Peteet is a similar ethnographic study. Peteet interviewed Palestinian women in refugee camps and in Lebanon between 1980 and 1982. In addition, she provides historical background beginning with the early twentieth century. Instructors would benefit from using these complementary works in tandem as textbooks for political science, women's studies, and Middle East studies curricula.

538. Fisher, Jo. *Out of the Shadows: Women, Resistance, and Politics in South America.* New York: Latin America Bureau, distributed in North America by Monthly Review Press, 1993. 228p. ISBN (OP); 0853458731pa.

Fisher's accessible writing style and the book's logical organization make *Out of the Shadows* an excellent choice for women's studies and political science classes and library collections. In the introductory chapter, Fisher defines important cultural terms like "machismo," which she describes as "an ideology which owes much to Spanish colonial ideas about women (they were classified in colonial legal codes as 'imbeciles by nature') and the teachings of the Roman Catholic Church" (p. 3). The author examines four countries: Uruguay, Chile, Paraguay, and Argentina. Chapters begin with a chronological chart and include interviews with local, politically active women. Fisher describes how grassroots organizations of women in the four countries developed in response to local cultural and geographical factors.

In-depth analysis of a single country can be found in *Engendering Democracy in Brazil: Women's Movements in Transition Politics* (Princeton University Press, 1990). Sonia E. Alvarez examines Brazilian politics over a decade and reformulates that history with recognition of the contributions of women. Editors Sarah A. Radcliffe and Sallie Westwood similarly explore the complexity of analyzing the disparate countries of Latin America, especially considering how variables such as race and class interact, in *"Viva": Women and Popular Protest in Latin America* (Routledge, 1993), a collection of nine essays by international scholars. The editors explicitly assert that they attempt to dispense once and for all with the idea of a monolithic definition of "feminism" in this work.

539. Jaquette, Jane S., and Sharon L. Wolchik, eds. *Women and Democracy: Latin America and Central and Eastern Europe.* Baltimore: Johns Hopkins University Press, 1998. 250p. index. ISBN 0801858372; 0801858380pa.

This volume focuses on political changes in Latin American countries after the fall of military dictatorships and in post-Communist Central and Eastern Europe. The editors maintain that women's roles in political transitions have been little examined until quite recently. Jaquette and Wolchik have been researching Latin America and post-Communist Europe since their initial idea for such a book in 1990, based upon their belief that transition politics "provide a rare window on how social structures underlie political structures and practices, and they lend themselves well to a comparative approach that includes gender" (p. 4). Each chapter is a case study of the political environment for women in a particular country. An initial chapter by the editors provides a context to understand the differences and the similarities faced by the women from each country before, during, and after the political events through which they lived. A final chapter, "Contemporary Democratization: The Prospects for Women," by Philippe C. Schmitter, glimpses how the future could play out in these countries vis-à-vis the inclusion of women as fully participating (political) citizens. Jaquette and Wolchik's book should be required reading for undergraduate women's studies and international political science classes.

540. Jeffery, Patricia, and Amrita Basu, eds. *Appropriating Gender: Women's Agency: The State and Politicized Religion in South Asia.* New York: Routledge, 1998. 276p. bibliog. index. ISBN 0415918650; 0415918669pa.

Four countries are covered in this book: India, Pakistan, Bangladesh, and Sri Lanka. The chapters, written by scholars who either are from or have done extensive fieldwork in these countries, not only provide in-depth analysis of the complex intersections of politics and religion in these women's lives, but also introduce class, economics, and other variables into the equation. The result is a work of rich scholarship that considers global gender issues while paying keen attention to the fabric of daily life within a particular geographic locale and within the context of a religion, most often Hindu or Muslim. It becomes apparent why westernized feminisms have not taken deep root in these countries when the reader considers the complexity of religious, political, and social-class issues facing individual women in individual regions of individual countries. Patricia Jeffery's concluding chapter thankfully does not resort to easy answers. Instead, she presents more questions for future research about the women in South Asia as they endeavor to define for themselves what it means to be a woman in these countries, and how they can participate in their own empowerment. The book ends with a comprehensive bibliography.

541. Moghadam, Valentine M., ed. *Gender and National Identity: Women and Politics in Muslim Societies.* Atlantic Highlands, NJ: published for the United National University World Institute for Development Economics Research (UNU/WIDER) by Zed Books; Oxford University Press, 1994. 180p. bibliog. index. ISBN 1856492451; 185649246Xpa.

An eclectic group of contributors who all hail from or currently teach outside of the United States examine gender and national identity in the following countries: Algeria, Bangladesh, Iran, Afghanistan, and Occupied Palestine. Editor Moghadam contextualizes the ideas of feminism, nationalism, and religion, in this case Islam, in her introductory chapter, asserting that the alliance between nationalism and feminism essentially has dissolved in these countries. Contributors write about the "domestication of women" and about women who took on new, participatory roles during their countries' revolutions in support of new governmental regimes trying to solve their countries' political and economic crises. Authors argue that when fundamentalist sects of Islam secure a country, especially if they become allies with the existing government, those in power tend to order women to return to traditional, prerevolutionary roles. A number of women are refusing to comply.

Haleh Esfandiari, in *Reconstructed Lives: Women and Iran's Islamic Revolution* (Johns Hopkins University Press, 1997), interviews a group of thirty-two such Iranians, middle- to upper-class professional women who do not wish to lose the ground gained after the 1979 Iranian Revolution. Mahnaz Afkhami, executive director of the Sisterhood Is Global Institute and the Foundation for Iranian Studies, edited a similar work, part of the Gender, Culture, and Politics in the Middle East series, titled *Faith and Freedom: Women's Human Rights in the Muslim World* (Syracuse University Press, 1995). This work features important activists and writers, such as Afkhami, Deniz Kandiyoti, Fareeda Shaheed, and Fatima Mernissi, an outspoken feminist and preeminent Koranic scholar. In addition, Afkhami and Erika Friedl coedited *Muslim Women and the Politics of Participation: Implementing the Beijing Platform* (Syracuse University Press, 1997), a series of essays by noted Muslim scholars, most of which were presented at a 1996 follow-up conference to the Beijing Fourth World Conference on Women. Both works are recommended for undergraduate and graduate political science, women's studies, and Middle Eastern collections.

542. Randall, Margaret. *Gathering Rage: The Failure of Twentieth Century Revolutions to Develop a Feminist Agenda.* New York: Monthly Review Press, 1992. 192p. ISBN 085345860X; 0853458618pa.

Margaret Randall spent several years living in Nicaragua and Cuba around the time of their respective revolutions and has written several books about her experiences. She uses a literary style that blends journalism, diary entries, and a comparative political science treatise in this extensive essay. The socialisms she supported as a pro-Sandinista in Nicaragua after the overthrow of Anastasio Somoza and in Fidel Castro's Cuba did not develop in the way she and her revolutionary sisters had hoped. Although women comprised almost a third of the combatants during the Nicaraguan revolution following the Sandinistas' victory in 1979, women returned to their "traditional," prerevolutionary status; the equal footing promised to them hence quickly eroded. Randall argues that if the revolutionaries had incorporated feminist thought and concerns into their new regimes and policy-making bodies, they might have retained the ground that they fought side by side with women to gain. Moreover, if women had not felt so disenfranchised in 1990, the "contras" or counterrevolutionaries, whom capitalist countries, including the United States, heavily financed, might not have been elected in Nicaragua. The author symbolically connects the problems of Nicaragua and Cuba with what occurred in other socialist countries, wherein men excluded women, who comprise more than half the population, from the true bases of power, thus preventing women from contributing their unique ways of knowing to help shape postrevolutionary governments.

Randall's *Sandino's Daughters Revisited: Feminism in Nicaragua* (Rutgers University Press, 1994) contains interviews with twelve female Sandinistas. Randall's compelling and provocative works on the topic of feminism in Nicaragua and Cuba are highly recommended for women's studies and political science classes.

543. Sharoni, Simona. *Gender and the Israeli-Palestinian Conflict: The Politics of Women's Resistance.* Syracuse, NY: Syracuse University Press, 1995. 199p. (Peace and Conflict Resolution Series). bibliog. index. ISBN 0815626436; 0815602995pa.

In spite of a growing literature on Palestinian and Israeli-Jewish women, it is difficult for outsiders to understand the complexities involved in their political lives. Sharoni, who describes herself as both insider (she was born and grew up in Israel and was involved in both the women's and the peace movements) and outsider (she earned her Ph.D. and teaches in the United States), here seeks to "challenge the presumed symmetry between Israelis and Palestinians" (p. 5). She describes the multifaceted struggles of the women in this contentious, even violent, political arena. Following a powerful introduction, her first chapter provides an overview of feminist theory, gender issues, and Middle Eastern politics. She devotes chapters to pre-Intifada and post-Intifada Palestinian and Israeli-Jewish women. The Intifada, an uprising of Palestinians from the Occupied Territories, began in December 1987 and was one of the turning points in all these women's lives. Because gender, class, and religious issues complicate the political landscape, Sharoni argues that it is overly simplistic to expect universal bonding based upon gender, no matter how vigorously these two groups of women seek peace. This book would make an excellent textbook for classes dealing with women's issues and/or Middle Eastern politics.

544. Tétreault, Mary Ann, and Una Chapman Cox, eds. *Women and Revolution in Africa, Asia, and the New World.* Columbia: University of South Carolina Press, 1994. 456p. index. ISBN 1570030162; 1570030316pa.

This groundbreaking work received the *Choice* Outstanding Academic Books Award in Political Science for the Years 1992–1997. Tétreault contributes excellent introductory and concluding chapters as well as a chapter on women and revolution in Vietnam and one on women's liberation and reconstruction politics in Kuwait. She provides a theoretical framework for the book's nineteen chapters in her introduction and outlines three issues to be addressed: (1) the structure of the prerevolutionary society with respect to the relative position of women and men, (2) the relationship between family and society in prerevolutionary times, and (3) rhetorical and symbolic (postrevolutionary) bases of legitimacy for victorious governments/regimes. Tétreault has broadened her concept of revolution to include rebellions and nationalistic movements. Chapters address women in various countries of Africa, Asia, the Mediterranean and Islamic world, and the New World (Cuba, Chile, Mexico, and Bolivia). The last chapter, a summary of "lessons learned," warns that "symbolically, women's entitlements disappear through gender-selective forgetting of revolutionary experience" (p. 434).

Another well-received book is *Women and Politics in the Third World* (Routledge, 1996), edited by Haleh Afshar. It contains eleven chapters covering countries in Africa, the Middle East, and Asia. An important chapter by Georgina Waylen warns against a tendency to characterize Third World women as "backwards" in relation to "progressive" Western women.

545. United Nations. *The United Nations and the Advancement of Women, 1945–1996.* New York: Department of Public Information, United Nations, 1996. 845p. (United Nations Blue Books, v. 6). bibliog. index. ISBN 9211006031.

This book provides a comprehensive history of the women's rights initiatives of the United Nations, as well as the text of 139 United Nations documents in their entirety or in significant excerpts. The first 100 pages summarize the documents and situate them historically, geographically, and in terms of their worldwide impact (or lack thereof). Several subject indexes enhance accessibility to this comprehensive collection of primary resources. This source divides the documents into four periods, the last of which includes the 1995 Fourth World Conference on Women held in Beijing, which drew 47,000 attendees.

For an uncompromising and horrifying look at specific human rights violations perpetrated against women in various geographical regions, including Kenya, Pakistan, Kuwait, and Bosnia-Herzegovina, consult *The Human Rights Watch: Global Report on Women's Human Rights* (Human Rights Watch, 1995). Also refer to *Women's Rights, Human Rights: International Feminist Perspectives* (Routledge, 1995), edited by Julie Peters and Andrea Wolper. This collection of thirty-six essays composed by lawyers, activists, scholars, and urban and rural women from twenty-one nations consists of chapters that Peters and Wolper cluster into areas such as "Gendered Law, 'Public' and 'Private,' " "Cultural Difference," "Violence and Health," and "The Persecuted, the Voiceless." These three books illustrate the magnitude of human rights violations faced daily by a number of women worldwide.

546. Young, Elise G. *Keepers of the History: Women and the Israeli-Palestinian Conflict.* New York: Teachers College Press, 1992. 223p. (Athene Series). bibliog. index. ISBN 0807762628; 080776261Xpa.

In 1985 Young received a research grant from the University of Massachusetts at Amherst that enabled her to travel to Israel and the West Bank. During her stay at Bir Zeit University,

Young engaged in several discussions with Palestinian men and women and visited the Kalendia Refugee Camp. These firsthand accounts add poignancy to the scholarly narrative, in which is embedded thorough historical analysis. Young, who takes an unabashedly feminist approach to the topic of women and the Israeli-Palestinian Conflict, contends that although women frequently hold together the fabric of society, their political opinions and needs are ignored. She calls on scholars to revise political discourse and historiography on the Israeli-Palestinian War. Young paves the way for future research through proposing possible solutions to the many problems she explores in this valuable work.

Women in Europe

547. Davis, Rebecca H. *Women and Power in Parliamentary Democracies: Cabinet Appointments in Western Europe, 1968–1992.* Lincoln: University of Nebraska Press, 1997. 137p. (Women and Politics). bibliog. index. ISBN 0803217072.

Davis studies the gendered dynamics of parliamentary politics through her statistical and analytical examination of fifteen Western parliamentary-type governments from 1968 through 1992. The author collected and organized mountains of data from widely disparate literatures to form generalizations about her topic, rather than crafting specialized, local descriptions. She effectively creates a methodology from a woman's perspective, one that might benefit the future collection and interpretation of data in a traditionally male discipline. This study deserves a place in all college-level women's political studies collections. For an in-depth analysis of a particular country, *Women in Electoral Politics: Lessons from Norway* (Praeger, 1995) by Jill Bystydzienski would be an excellent choice. The Scandinavian countries, especially Norway, have consistently posted the highest percentages of women elected to political office. However, despite the high numbers of women in office (often between 30 and 40 percent), the gendered nature of politics and the patriarchal infrastructure remain firmly entrenched in this country. Bystydzienski thus scrutinizes the gains that women truly have made and considers how to implement structural changes to their and other political systems.

548. Einhorn, Barbara. *Cinderella Goes to Market: Citizenship, Gender, and Women's Movements in East Central Europe.* New York: Verso, 1993. 280p. index. (OP)

Despite both the paperback and hardcover editions being out of print, this title should be considered for all college-level women's studies and political science collections. The study raises the question whether the women of East Central Europe (most specifically the former Czechoslovakia, Poland, Hungary, and the German Democratic Republic [GDR]) are better off under their new governmental regimes. Einhorn asks, "Did state socialism in East Central Europe 'emancipate' women? If not, then are democracy and the market likely to do so?" (p. 1). This intriguing book begins with a thorough historical analysis of women's place in these countries during the past century, particularly after 1917. Einhorn enhances her research with interviews of women who are trying to reconcile the "triple burden" many of them experienced under socialism—their roles as mothers, as workers in the labor force, and as active political party members—with the new political regimes. Those in power in these new regimes fired up to 80 percent of women managers from government jobs. These women may never work again at professional jobs since they are now considered "excess" by governments responding to capitalistic market factors by asking women, "for the good of the nation," to go back to hearth, home, and baby raising. This important topic is presented in very readable form.

549. García-Ramon, Maria Dolors, and Janice Monk, eds. *Women of the European Union: The Politics of Work and Daily Life.* New York: Routledge, 1996. 288p. (International Studies of Women and Place). bibliog. index. ISBN 0415118794; 0415118808pa.

Two self-pronounced "feminist geographers" edited this excellent collection of essays emphasizing the less studied countries of southern Europe, Spain, Italy, Greece, and Portugal, as well as the northern countries in the European Union (EU). The editors are mindful that prevailing political analysis tends toward gender blindness and that politics is studied in terms of the economic and legal impact, usually carried out in a public forum. A feminist perspective requires recognition of both the "public" and "private" aspects of politics, which the editors believe can be accommodated by "scales of analysis." García-Ramon and Monk include chapters on comparative multinational politics as well as national case studies and in-depth regional and local studies, all aimed at determining the impact of multistate agreements, such as the EU, and their effect upon the women of these countries. All but two of the fourteen contributors teach in European universities and do not typically write for English-speaking audiences. The editors and contributing authors have created a unique work that all political studies collections should feature.

550. Githens, Marianne, Pippa Norris, and Joni Lovenduski, eds. *Different Roles, Different Voices: Women in Politics in the United States and Europe.* New York: HarperCollins College, 1994. 277p. bibliog. ISBN (OP); 0065013069pa.

This compendium of essays focusing on the European and American political arenas examines many facets of women's political involvement. It begins with two essays questioning whether feminist methodology can be applied to political science research and the study of women. Several excellent political science and feminist scholars, including Vicky Randall, Jean Bethke Elshtain, and Sandra Harding, contributed essays to this work. Each of the nine chapters is preceded by an introduction and followed by a brief bibliography. The work's focus on issues that scholars can treat comparatively to advance our knowledge of women's politics beyond well-defined geographic boundaries makes it an important contribution to the literature. The contributors' treatment of political situations in various countries represents the quest for new methodologies and even new definitions of politics and its relation to women's lives. This easy-to-read work would make an excellent textbook for advanced women's studies and general political science classes.

551. Rule, Wilma, and Norma C. Noonan, eds. *Russian Women in Politics and Society.* Westport, CT: Greenwood Press, 1996. 188p. (Contributions in Women's Studies). bibliog. index. ISBN 0313293635.

In 1991 a group of women affiliated with the Center for Gender Studies in Moscow wrote an article that became the nucleus for this volume. Twelve essays chronicle the political history of Russian women from the founding of the Bolshevik socialist state in 1917 to a few years following the breakup of the Union of Soviet Socialist Republics (USSR) in December 1991. Coeditor Norma C. Noonan characterizes twentieth-century political attitudes toward women as "eight decades of propaganda against feminism" (p. 78). Since the fall of socialism in 1991, new governments' attempts to force a rapid transition to capitalism have been devastating for women. Cutbacks in programs cost almost 80 percent of women managers their jobs. Partially in response to such economic crises, women began to organize politically and were able to elect a number of women to political office in 1993.

A recommended companion volume is Marilyn Rueschemeyer's *Women in the Politics of Postcommunist Eastern Europe* (M.E. Sharpe, 1994), which provides in-depth country-by-country analysis. Her book, which was widely and favorably reviewed, includes chapters on Poland, East and West Germany, Albania, Bulgaria, Croatia, and Slovenia. An additional title is *Gender Politics and Post-Communism: Reflections from Eastern Europe and the Former Soviet Union* (Routledge, 1993) by Nanette Funk and Magda Mueller, which takes a somewhat more philosophical stance than the previous title yet also provides country-by-country analysis.

552. Sales, Rosemary. *Women Divided: Gender, Religion, and Politics in Northern Ireland.* New York: Routledge, 1997. 236p. (International Studies of Women and Place). bibliog. index. ISBN 0415137659; 0415137667pa.

Sales euphemistically refers to the ongoing conflict in Northern Ireland, which all too often erupts into violence and bloodshed, as "the troubles." Although many observers tend to characterize Northern Ireland's instability as simply religious in nature, a result of Protestant versus Catholic, in reality, its highly complicated problems are deeply rooted in Ireland's history. Sales explicates the political, historical, cultural, and religious history of the area in several chapters. She concentrates especially on the view of the male-dominated governments that women's rights are largely irrelevant in light of the continuing conflict in Northern Ireland. The divide between Catholic and Protestant women further complicates the situation, as do both churches, which have taken a hard line on "traditional values," wherein men dominate the families. Despite these many seemingly insurmountable obstacles, several women of Northern Ireland have attempted various peacemaking efforts, yet these efforts have been virtually ignored at the highest policy-making levels. Sales analyzes both formal and informal government reports and interweaves interviews conducted with several Catholic and Protestant women during a four-year period to examine this phenomenon. She effectively summarizes the plight of women in Northern Ireland, including their efforts to organize as feminists despite terrible odds. Begona Aretxaga's excellent ethnographic study *Shattering Silence* (Princeton University Press, 1997) describes what she observed during her fifteen-month stay in West Belfast, where she interviewed women and conducted research.

Women in North America

553. Bashevkin, Sylvia. *Women on the Defensive: Living through Conservative Times.* Chicago: University of Chicago Press, 1998. 318p. bibliog. index. ISBN 0226038831; 0226038858pa.

During the 1960s and 1970s, women in Great Britain, the United States, and Canada made great progress in their feminist agendas. However, with the elections of Margaret Thatcher of Great Britain, Ronald Reagan of the United States, and Brian Mulroney of Canada, these countries established new, more conservative regimes. As a result, a "feminist backlash" occurred in each country between 1979 and 1992 that seriously threatened the gains that the women's liberation and feminist movements had made during the preceding two decades. Sylvia Bashevkin, professor of political science at the University of Toronto, interviewed more than 100 women and consulted a variety of secondary sources, including court cases and policy documents, to write this excellent work. She argues that despite politically conservative governments, the withdrawal of funding for various "women's issues," and the portrayal of feminists as extremists and whiners, women maintained most of their gains. According to Bashevkin, "Although activists clearly desired far more than they achieved, perhaps surviving was equivalent to political success in the dark days" (p. 245). She provides a series of charts that feature relevant court cases and policy decisions in each country during different time periods in "Appendix A." This well-researched work would make a fine addition to any political science collection or a textbook in comparative politics.

554. Boxer, Barbara. *Strangers in the Senate: Politics and the New Revolution of Women in America*. Washington, DC: National Press Books, 1993. 256p. index. ISBN 1882605063; 1882605160pa.

This work by Congresswoman and Senator Barbara Boxer chronicles the liberal senator's career in national politics. Hillary Rodham Clinton wrote the foreword, a five-page overview of women in national politics, and the author's daughter Nicole collaborated with her mother. Boxer served in the House of Representatives from 1982 to 1992, was elected to the U.S. Senate in 1992, and was reelected in 1998. Her decision to run for political office had its roots in the assassinations of Martin Luther King Jr. and Robert Kennedy in 1968 and the sense of outrage she felt. Boxer has remained a liberal throughout her career, even though she has received much criticism for her style and political agendas, including her domestic and environmental concerns.

Pat Schroeder, another experienced female politician, writes with equal candor about her trials and triumphs in *24 Years of Housework . . . and the Place Is Still a Mess* (Andrews McMeel Publishers, 1998). Both works illustrate the hostilities and indignities endured by courageous women who are paving the way for future female politicians.

555. Burrell, Barbara C. *A Woman's Place Is in the House: Campaigning for Congress in the Feminist Era*. Ann Arbor: University of Michigan Press, 1996. 211p. bibliog. index. ISBN (OP); 0472083848pa.

Barbara Burrell's painstaking research has resulted in this compendium of statistical and anecdotal information regarding women in the U.S. House of Representatives. The author collected and analyzed information on all major party nominees and open-seat primary election contenders from 1968 to 1992. Data are summarized in numerous tables and charts. Chapters address popular assumptions that do not bear up under Burrell's twenty-four years' worth of statistical evidence, including the belief that female candidates poorly finance their own campaigns, or that they cannot win elections. Variables measured include votes obtained, win ratios, age, political experience, occupation, and district characteristics. Culminating chapters address legislative initiatives supported by elected women officials, including "women's issues" such as the Family and Medical Leave Act, and suggest ways to support the election of more women in the future.

For a statistical study of elections at the local, regional, state, and national levels, consider *Sex as a Political Variable: Women as Candidates and Voters in U.S. Elections* (Lynne Rienner, 1997) by Richard A. Seltzer, Jody Newman, and Melissa Voorhees Leighton. This work includes research conducted for the National Women's Political Caucus, a bipartisan nonprofit organization dedicated to increasing the number of elected and appointed women in office at all levels. In *The Political Consequences of Being a Woman: How Stereotypes Influence the Conduct and Consequences of Political Campaigns* (Columbia University Press, 1996), Kim Fridkin Kahn conducts content analysis studies of television and newspaper coverage to determine stereotypical behavior toward women candidates and officeholders. Any of these titles would be good as texts or supplementary reading for undergraduate classes in American government, political science, and women's studies.

556. Cantor, Dorothy W., and Toni Bernay, with Jean Stoess. *Women in Power: The Secrets of Leadership*. Boston: Houghton Mifflin, 1992. 316p. bibliog. index. ISBN 039553755X; 0395618606pa.

Although statistics indicate that women who run for elective offices do about as well as men, few women have opted to run for political office in the past. The number of women willing to invest time in local and regional political activities to gain experience as viable candidates has been small. Moreover, a dearth of female role models and mentors has exacerbated this seeming lack of interest. Psychologists Dorothy Cantor and Toni Bernay collaborated with Jean Stoess to interview politically successful women to determine their self-perceived strengths in running for and getting elected to office. The authors focused on both psychological and social characteristics, as opposed to strictly political parameters, gleaning valuable information from their interviewees. Chapters consist of questionnaires and interviews with twenty-five pioneer women politicians. These women held offices in the U.S. House of Representatives, such as Barbara Boxer of California, and Patricia Schroeder of Colorado, and in the U.S. Senate, including Barbara Mikulski of Maryland, and served as secretaries of state, governors, mayors, and state treasurers.

557. Conway, M. Margaret, Gertrude A. Steuernagel, and David W. Ahern. *Women and Political Participation: Cultural Change in the Political Arena.* Washington, DC: CQ Press, 1997. 162p. index. ISBN 0871879220pa.

Professors in search of a good, easily readable, well-researched book to serve as an introductory text for U.S. political science and women's studies classes should consider this work. It provides a broad, historical overview of women's political involvement in the United States, as well as prevailing cultural images of women. Throughout much of history, society looked upon women as unfit to hold political office. This book traces women's historical inroads into the political arena, along with the inevitable backlashes accompanying major cultural change. The authors point to 1992, the supposed "year of the woman," juxtaposed against that year's anorexic fashion models conveying an image of women as frail and helpless. Chapters introduce opposing viewpoints on political issues such as affirmative action. Graphs, tables, and opinion polls capture snapshots of men's and women's perceptions over time about hot topics such as abortion. As stated in the preface, "American women have always been politically involved, even when political scientists ignored them" (p. xii).

Women, Politics, and American Society (Prentice Hall, 1998) by Nancy McGlen and Karen O'Connor examines both "private" and "public" spheres. Since only an examination of both spheres will appropriately accommodate women's role in politics, these two books are a step in the right direction.

558. Darcy, Robert, Susan Welch, and Janet Clark. *Women, Elections, and Representation.* White Plains, NY: Longman Publishing Group, 1987. 181p. (Women and Politics). (OP)

Darcy, Welch, and Clark frame their research with a thorough intellectual and historical overview of women in public office, as well as women's theoretical placement in the democracy of the United States, beginning in the 1500s. The authors present empirical studies, some of which they designed, to support anecdotal evidence often used to explain women's relative scarcity in politics. Nonetheless, Darcy, Welch, and Clark reach two surprising conclusions in this study. First, there does not seem to be overt discrimination against women candidates for elective political offices; and second, female candidates generally do as well as or better than male candidates. The final chapter offers practical suggestions, for example, that women run for "open seats" based upon the authors' statistically supported assertion that candidates win more often when not running against an incumbent. A lengthy bibliography concludes this examination of women's political involvement at the local, state, and national levels. An updated edition of *Women, Elections, and Representation* (University of Nebraska Press, 1994), still in print at the time of this publication, expands the book to 276 pages to accommodate subsequent research. Susan Carroll's complementary work *Women as Candidates in American Politics* (2nd ed., Indiana University Press, 1994) updates the voluminous data that she collected in the first edition, published in 1976, about women candidates running for local, state, and national office. Her studies are the first systematic collections of data on women candidates. Carroll also examines inherent structural barriers in American political systems that work against women seeking office. These two books not only belong in every political science collection, but also in the personal collections of politicians.

559. Ferraro, Geraldine. *Changing History: Women, Power, and Politics.* Wakefield, RI: Moyer Bell; distributed by Publishers Group West, 1993. 193p. (OP)

Given the predominance of men in national elective offices, it goes without saying that women elected to such offices tend to be strong, talented, and articulate individuals. To date, the only woman to run for vice president of the United States on a major national ticket is Geraldine Ferraro, who began her political career in the U.S. House of Representatives. In this collection of speeches from the early 1990s, Ferraro discusses education, the economy, and the overt discrimination and "dirty tricks" she faced as a female candidate in the 1984 campaign. Ferraro, a devout Catholic, was renounced by the church because of her pro-choice stand on abortion and was also rebuffed by the Italian American community, usually so quick to protect "its own." Ferraro edited her speeches so that redundancies, including her "Dan Quayle joke," were minimized.

The Other Elites: Women, Politics, and Power in the Executive Branch (Lynne Rienner, 1997), edited by Mary Anne Borrelli and Janet M. Martin, is a recommended companion volume that deals with women in the federal executive branch of government. Although no women have yet been elected to the highest offices of government in the United States, there have been a few high-level appointments such as U.S. Secretary of State Madeleine Albright and two Supreme Court justices, Sandra Day O'Connor and Ruth Bader Ginsburg. The scholarship in this volume sets the groundwork for future examination of the modern U.S. presidency from a perspective that includes women. A chapter by Barbara Burrell examines the often trivialized office of the First Lady in terms of its potential impact upon national policy.

560. Gill, LaVerne McCain. *African-American Women in Congress: Forming and Transforming History.* New Brunswick, NJ: Rutgers University Press, 1997. 272p. bibliog. index. ISBN 0813523524; 0813523532pa.

This is a straightforward, well-written biographical introduction to African American women who have served in Congress. Gill provides in-depth discussions of the first African American women elected to the House of Representatives, Shirley Chisholm in 1968, and the Senate, Carol Moseley Braun in 1992. Profiles of fifteen additional women who served in Congress between 1969 and 1996 provide "glimpses into the story of a nation" (p. 5). Each chapter covers a politician's political career and features a photograph, a quotation, and a résumé. Gill discusses the politician's early life and influences, her foray into politics, her years in Congress, and her accomplishments both inside and outside of office. The richly contextual chapters touch upon issues of sexism, racism, and classism, which these women often faced.

561. Jeffreys-Jones, Rhodri. *Changing Differences: Women and the Shaping of American Foreign Policy, 1917–1994.* New Brunswick, NJ: Rutgers University Press, 1995. 275p. bibliog. index. ISBN 0813521661; 0813524490pa.

Jeffreys-Jones writes that "because little has been written about women and foreign policy, the historiography of the field is immature" (p. 4). This extensively researched book presents an emerging field reexamining U.S. foreign policy in terms of women's involvement and influence. It covers the period from 1917 through 1994, the second year of the Clinton presidency. The authors conducted research at presidential libraries and surveyed several manuscript collections, including the papers of Bella Abzug and Margaret Chase Smith. Jeffreys-Jones brings to light the sexual slurs and denigrating comments about almost all the early women who aspired to or attained political power. This mind-set underscores the courage of pioneering women such as the first woman member of the U.S. House of Representatives, Jeannette Rankin of Montana, who waged formal protests against World War I, World War II, and the Vietnam War. This book should be required reading for undergraduate courses in American foreign policy and political science, and certainly for women's studies courses.

562. Melich, Tanya. *The Republican War against Women: An Insider's Report from behind the Lines*. New York: Bantam Books, 1996. 356p. bibliog. index. ISBN (OP); 0553378163pa.

Tanya Melich, a lifelong, active member of the Republican Party at the national level, presents a bird's-eye view of how certain religious and ideological factions of the Republican Party effectively jockeyed for power in this behind-the-scenes study of political maneuvering and "dirty tricks." She concentrates on 1980 to 1992, a time when Melich and like-minded Republicans fought for pro-choice and women's issues while the GOP gradually moved in an anti-choice, right-wing direction spurred by the Moral Majority and the Religious Right, led by Phyllis Schlafly, Pat Robertson, Newt Gingrich, and others. During the candidacies of Ronald Reagan and George H.W. Bush, centrist or "Old Guard" Republicans were summarily cut off during convention floor debates. Party leaders repeatedly used the "big tent" metaphor by which all Republicans could, theoretically, agree to disagree (and in which "women's issues" were sub-sumed under "more important issues," especially those that came to be known by the politically charged term "family values"). A tactic of GOP strategists was to recruit moderate Republican women and attempt to co-opt them as spokeswomen for antifeminist causes. In the early 1990s, after years of trying to work within the party, Melich finally decided, "The national GOP had . . . become a fundamentalist party, condemning those who didn't agree with its religious and moral values" (p. 281). This is a must-read reconnaissance manual for women considering a run for state or national office. In an updated edition (Bantam Books, 1998) that covers the 1992 and 1996 presidential election politics, Melich ponders the possibility of a third party that would combine the best of both the traditional Republican ("the party of Lincoln") and Democratic Parties.

563. Pal, Leslie A. *Interests of State: The Politics of Language, Multiculturalism, and Feminism in Canada*. Buffalo, NY: McGill–Queen's University Press, 1993. 330p. bibliog. index. ISBN 0773509747; 0773513272pa.

Leslie A. Pal provides a theoretical and practical analysis of Canadian feminism in this work, exploring Canadian citizenship policy since the 1960s in connection with three fields: official languages, multiculturalism, and feminism. The Canadian government, particularly the Citizenship Branch of the Secretary of State's Office, has heavily subsidized programs for these policy areas. Pal analyzes the reciprocal aspects of the government/special-interest-group rela-tionships in terms of political influence. This richly analytical, theoretical work reveals the give-and-take dynamics between citizens organized around special interests and the government that supports their very creation and existence. According to the author, "How one analyzes govern-ment funding for groups depends in part on how one understands the nature of interest groups, collective action in politics, and the state" (p. 11). *Interests of State* is an excellent introduction to the birth and resurgence of second-wave feminism in Canada, providing important ideas for comparing and contrasting women's involvement in the politics of other nations.

564. Thomas, Sue, and Clyde Wilcox, eds. *Women and Elective Office: Past, Present, and Future*. New York: Oxford University Press, 1998. 241p. bibliog. index. ISBN 019511230X; 0195112318pa.

Editors Thomas and Wilcox have assembled a group of essays discussing women candidates and officeholders in the United States. Important writers on women's politics such as Barbara Burrell, Janet Clark, Georgia Duerst-Lahti, and others have contributed chapters, most of which report on original research. Tables, charts, graphs, and maps illustrate and encapsulate survey data. Chapters address such topics as the portrayal of women candidates by mass media, the dynamics and management techniques of women committee chairpersons in state legislatures, and African American women in state elective offices in the South. This work suggests that political science is beginning to include and make legitimate the experiences of women, which is very encouraging.

In *How Women Legislate* (Oxford University Press, 1994), Thomas incorporates original survey instruments to quantify women's views of their efficiency and performance in their jobs as legislators. Women have developed enough of a presence in political office that data can now be collected to validate previously untested hypotheses and unfounded generalizations about them. Both Thomas and Wilcox are pioneers of this "new" political science, which is creating a methodology based upon a woman-centered mode of inquiry. Both titles should be essential reading for women's studies and political science undergraduates.

565. Vickers, Jill, Pauline Rankin, and Christine Appelle. *Politics As If Women Mattered: A Political Analysis of the National Action Committee on the Status of Women*. Toronto: University of Toronto Press, 1993. 347p. bibliog. index. ISBN 0802058507; 0802067573pa.

Vickers, Rankin, and Appelle have written an excellent critique of women's politics in twentieth-century Canada. The authors examine how women's organizations such as the National Action Committee (NAC), which was founded in 1972, have given women a voice in Canada's political arena. By 1988, the NAC had become an umbrella organization to more than 600 women-related political and special-interest groups, which the authors describe as a "parliament of women." The authors observe that Canadian party platforms have never seriously focused on women's issues, since those in power generally have looked upon these issues as peripheral to the "real" issues of male-dominated politics. As a result, Canadian women have mobilized to create a de facto parallel system designed to address their concerns. According to the authors, women have been unable to infiltrate traditional political systems because "conventional political institutions and ideologies were created by men in an era of strict demarcation between the political and domestic spheres" (p. xi). By working within the federal system and with the help of governmental subsidies, Canadian feminists envision a way for NAC to serve succeeding generations of women. This intriguing study of women's politics in Canada reveals how their strategies developed differently from the more studied women's political systems in the United States. This analysis of how Canadian women work within and alongside their country's traditional political systems provides valuable ideas for women of other countries who struggle for a political voice.

566. Witt, Linda, Karen M. Paget, and Glenna Matthews. *Running as a Woman: Gender and Power in American Politics*. New York: Free Press, 1993. 330p. index. ISBN 0029203155; 0028740696pa.

When veteran congresswoman Patricia Schroeder of Colorado considered running for president in 1987, the press asked her whether she would run as a woman. Her reply: "Do I have an option?" In *Running as a Woman*, three authors—a historian, a journalist, and a political scientist—examine the campaigns of prominent female politicians, exploring the barriers that women have faced. Often, women who ran for office were told to act like men (i.e., be tough and aggressive), but not to be "too male," an often difficult strategy to interpret. Interpretations of appropriate behavior in politics changed with the 1991 Anita Hill/Clarence Thomas debacle. When Hill charged Supreme Court nominee Clarence Thomas with sexual harassment, an all-male Senate panel subjected her to a humiliating inquisition. Outraged women nationwide accused these men of "just not getting it." The following year, more women were elected, at least partly for their "outsider" status as women, to both the House and Senate. Yet despite the 1992 nomenclature as "year of the woman" (women comprised 7 percent of U.S. senators in 1992, up from the previous high of 2 percent), these women did not obtain parity with men.

For a companion text focusing on the year 1992, consult *The Year of the Woman: Myths and Realities*, edited by Elizabeth Adell Cook, Sue Thomas, and Clyde Wilcox (Westview Press, 1994). These essays provide particularly strong analysis on individual races, including those of Dianne Feinstein and Barbara Boxer in California. Other compelling chapters include Leonard Williams's discussion of political advertising in the Year of the Woman and Candace J. Nelson's essay focusing on women's political action committees (PACs). These two books would make a good companion set for women aspiring to political office, as well as excellent textbooks for political science classes.

1999 CORE TITLES

Bacchi, Carol Lee. *Women, Policy, and Politics: The Construction of Policy Problems.* Thousand Oaks, CA: Sage, 1999. 242p. bibliog. index. ISBN 0761956743; 0761956751pa.

Botman, Selma. *Engendering Citizenship in Egypt.* New York: Columbia University Press, 1999. 141p. (History and Society of the Modern Middle East). bibliog. index. ISBN 023111298X; 0231112998pa.

Craske, Nikki. *Women and Politics in Latin America.* New Brunswick, NJ: Rutgers University Press, 1999. 242p. bibliog. index. ISBN 0813526922; 0813526930pa.

Herzog, Hanna. *Gendering Politics: Women in Israel.* Ann Arbor: University of Michigan Press, 1999. 292p. (Interests, Identities, and Institutions in Comparative Politics). bibliog. index. ISBN 0472109456.

Honey, Maureen. *Bitter Fruit: African American Women in World War II.* Columbia: University of Missouri Press, 1999. 424p. bibliog. index. ISBN (OP); 0826212654pa.

Howland, Courtney W., ed. *Religious Fundamentalisms and the Human Rights of Women.* New York: St. Martin's Press, 1999. 326p. bibliog. index. ISBN (OP); 0312293062pa.

Maloof, Judy, ed. *Voices of Resistance: Testimonies of Cuban and Chilean Women*. Lexington: University Press of Kentucky, 1999. 255p. bibliog. index. ISBN 0813120799pa.

Meyer, Mary K., and Elisabeth Prügl, eds. *Gender Politics in Global Governance*. Lanham, MD: Rowman & Littlefield, 1999. 315p. bibliog. index. ISBN 0847691608; 0847691616pa.

Sandilands, Catriona. *Good-Natured Feminist: Ecofeminism and the Quest for Democracy*. Minneapolis: University of Minnesota Press, 1999. 244p. bibliog. index. ISBN 0816630968; 0816630976pa.

Schenken, Suzanne O'Dea. *From Suffrage to the Senate: An Encyclopedia of American Women in Politics*. Santa Barbara, CA: ABC-CLIO, 1999. 922p. bibliog. index. ISBN 0874369606.

Werbner, Pnina, and Nira Yuval-Davis. *Women, Citizenship, and Difference*. New York: Zed Books; distributed in the United States by St. Martin's Press, 1999. 271p. (Postcolonial Encounters). bibliog. index. ISBN 1856496457; 1856496465pa.

Woods, Harriett. *Stepping Up to Power: The Political Journey of American Women*. Boulder, CO: Westview Press, 1999. 252p. bibliog. index. ISBN (OP); 0813398185pa.

WORLD WIDE WEB/INTERNET SITES

567. Eagleton Institute of Politics, Rutgers, the State University of New Jersey. *Center for American Women and Politics (CAWP)*. http://www.rci.rutgers.edu/~cawp/.

This site addresses several aspects of the political life of American women. Coverage ranges from biographical information about women elected to office over the years and demographic studies to the National Education for Women's (NEW) Leadership Program, which informs and encourages young women to run for public office. The CAWP site features links to numerous national and international women's political Web sites, as well as descriptions of print publications available for purchase. A "Women in Congress" link provides information about women elected to the U.S. House of Representatives, beginning with Jeannette Rankin in 1917. Links to other sites provide state-by-state fact sheets on topics such as "Women of Color in Elective Office," general voter information, and "the gender gap and voting behavior" as well as lists of women's political action committees (PACs) and donor lists. These links connect the user to current information (voting records for politicians) as well as historical information (where to find primary research materials on women politicians). This large, evolving, well-organized site is one of the premier Web sites about women in politics.

568. *International Women's Democracy Center (IWDC) Resources Page*. http://www .iwdc.org/links.htm.

The site for the Institute for Women's Policy Research (IWPR), a public policy research organization dedicated to public policy issues of critical importance to women and their families, covers many topics, including poverty and welfare, employment and earnings, work and family issues, violence, and women's civic and political participation. The site features hypertext links to numerous international sites, as well as links to EMILY's List ("Early Money Is Like Yeast," a U.S. political action committee that raises money for women candidates); *Mapping the World of Women's Information Services*, a database of women's information centers and libraries that are open to the public; and the WISH List, the largest fundraising group for pro-choice Republican women candidates at all levels of government. This Web site also includes a page called "The Resources," which contains more than eighty topically arranged links, including "Women's Global Political Participation," "Women and Politics—United States," and "Democracy/Elections." In addition, the site provides sections on continents, such as "Resources—Middle East," and time-lines for women in politics and women's suffrage. This comprehensive, educational site provides worthwhile training information to help women worldwide run for political office.

569. Katz, Nikki. *Women's Issues*. http://womensissues.about.com/mlibrary.htm.

The about.com site is a directory of more than 700 general topics, each hosted by a subject expert ("guide"). Nikki Katz frequently updates the *Women's Issues* site and distributes a free, weekly electronic newsletter to subscribers. The site includes links to such topics as Afghan women, CEDAW, global issues, military women, the Third World, and much more. Topical links feature well-written annotations to the sites they reference. Although *about.com* is a commercial site, Katz treats the subjects she researches with attention to detail and enthusiasm, making this Web site an excellent supplement to academic research sites.

570. *Women in Politics*. http://www.ipu.org/iss-e/women.htm.

This Web site reflects one of the main areas of activity of the Inter-Parliamentary Union, the international organization of parliaments of sovereign states, which was established in 1889. The site contains very useful information such as current statistics on the number of women in parliaments, a world chronology of women's suffrage, instruments of international law relating to women, and information on initiatives by the IPU and other international agencies related to women's political and legal issues. It also provides links to directories and Internet resources, and databases including the Women in Politics Bibliographic Database, which is a free database citing books and articles dealing with women in politics. Most useful are the links to internationally based Web pages and sites in Africa, the Americas, Asia and the Pacific, and Europe.

8 Psychology

Mila C. Su

Feminist thought and the growth of women's studies have influenced psychology in three significant ways: the documentation of women's contributions to the profession, evolving subfields within psychology and psychotherapy concerned with women and gender issues, and biobehavioral components of gender and gender difference. Women contributed to the field of psychology in the nineteenth century; however, women's interests were not reflected in established divisions in the professional psychological associations until 1973 in the United States and 1987 in Great Britain. Not everything written in these areas of study is written from a feminist perspective: do not assume that if a book is about women, it is feminist. The quality of published monographic work varies, and evaluation is complicated by the infusion of popular works and contributions from nonacademics including journalists, freelancers, and other nonpsychologists whose work is incorporated into this field.

Many challenges face the field of psychology today. In addition to a variety of groups, classifications, and approaches that focus on diverse issues within psychology and psychotherapy, some authors question and challenge the overall structure of the discipline. Psychology has become interdisciplinary, incorporating theories and methodologies from fields such as literature, philosophy, sociology, physiology, biology, feminism, and women's studies.

The psychology of women investigates many issues and topics, from women's history in the profession to their contributions to the field and from how physiological and biological influences contribute to women's psychological health to how they are treated by professionals, researchers, and society. Additional areas of focus include teaching feminist psychology and psychotherapy, women's interpersonal relationships, and how women come to create a sense of identity and find their voice. Research on marginalized groups, including women from various ethnic, racial, and socioeconomic categories as well as women of different sexual orientations, continues to expand.

The study and practice of psychology and the psychology of women have also grown as various theories of feminism have influenced, have been integrated, and have infiltrated into areas in psychology, psychoanalysis, and psychotherapy. Perspectives from liberal feminists, psychoanalytic feminists, radical feminists, existential feminists, Marxist feminists, black feminists, social feminists, and postmodern feminists have contributed to the construction, reconstruction, and deconstruction of the many theories, myths, and suppositions in the psychology of women. Each of these theories has specific foci. For example, radical and social feminists view primary conflicts and issues in terms of power and oppression from society and patriarchal influences. Marxists focus on economic and political constructs as the major struggle. Furthermore, differences in philosophy and structure are evident in European and international perspectives, where the focus tends to be more theoretical and often incorporates Marxist and postmodern concepts, compared to American psychology, where greater emphasis is placed on clinical and applied research and conventional methods of experimental psychology.

As evidenced in the titles described in this chapter, the psychology of women is a dynamic field with a range of perspectives. The field will undoubtedly continue to grow and evolve in years to come.

REFERENCE SOURCES

571. O'Connell, Agnes N., and Nancy F. Russo, eds. *Women in Psychology: A Bio-Bibliographic Sourcebook*. New York: Greenwood Press, 1990. 441p. bibliog. index. ISBN 0313260915.

O'Connell and Russo "document, evaluate, preserve, and make visible the diversity and excellence of women's contributions to psychology and society" (p. 4). In section 1, O'Connell and Russo explore the history of the field along with women's contributions as the discipline emerged. The next and largest section contains biobibliographic information about thirty-six distinguished women in psychology. Part 3 lists awards, along with the names of women recognized by such organizations as the American Psychological Association and American Psychological Fellows. Part 4 consists of a bibliography of significant books and other sources of information on female contributors to psychology, as well as autobiographical and biographical information on 185 women. All college and university libraries should carry this book.

572. Schuker, Eleanor, and Nadine A. Levinson, eds. *Female Psychology: An Annotated Psychoanalytic Bibliography*. Hillsdale, NJ: Analytic Press, 1991. 678p. indexes. ISBN 088163087X.

Schuker, of Columbia University, and Levinson, of the San Diego Psychoanalytic Society and Institute, created this now somewhat dated bibliography to assist curriculum development scholars who organize and/or conduct workshops at psychoanalytic institutes and psychiatric residences and for scholars in psychology and women's studies programs. Providing a psychoanalytic perspective on female psychology, the bibliography contains entries written by faculty and practitioners in psychology and psychiatry. In the introduction of each chapter, the editors review the chapter's contents, address trends in the development of important ideas, and indicate areas of psychoanalytic thought that have potential for growth. Schuker and Levinson chronologically arrange the annotations into four major sections focusing on historical, developmental, sexual, and individual development and clinical issues and include journal articles, books, and chapters from books. A fifth section features reading lists. Readers can use this valuable bibliography not only to explore the various types of research that scholars conducted until 1990, but also to note the changes in research since that time.

573. Wright, Elizabeth, ed. *Feminism and Psychoanalysis: A Critical Dictionary*. Cambridge, MA: Blackwell, 1992. 485p. bibliog. index. ISBN 0631173129; 0631183477pa.

Wright incorporates feminist concepts and theories that scholars have applied to women's studies as well as psychoanalytic theory and practice into this fine compendium. Alphabetically arranged with cross-references and a bibliography, each detailed entry features a brief history that contextualizes the application of the concept in question. Major psychoanalytical concepts that continually appear in contemporary feminist studies are discussed, and some context is provided. Contributors, who represent an eclectic group of fields reflecting the interdisciplinary nature of the book, focus on three major aspects within psychoanalysis and feminism in the entries: the historical dimension, the implications of applying feminist theory to Freudian and Lacanian influences in psychology, and how the political perspective of psychoanalytic theory and practice influences social change in society. Contributors address how feminism both challenges and reassesses North American, British, and French theoretical concepts in psychology. All women's studies collections should carry this resource, which provides a valuable overview of basic concepts.

MONOGRAPHS

574. Anderson, Peter B., and Cindy Struckman-Johnson, eds. *Sexually Aggressive Women: Current Perspectives and Controversies*. New York: Guilford Press, 1998. bibliog. index. ISBN 1572301651.

Scholars in psychology, sociology, and human sexuality contribute eleven essays on sexually aggressive women "to challenge prevailing assumptions about the nature of sexual relations between adult heterosexual women and men" (p. 1). In four sections, contributors discuss research and conceptual issues regarding the motives and behavior of sexually aggressive women, compare male and female experiences in sexual coercion, consider prevention of female sexual aggression, and look at treatment and recovery. A brief essay at the beginning of each section outlines research issues and controversies in connection with the study of sexually aggressive women and proposes new directions in research, prevention, and therapy. Contributors illuminate the various types of female sexual aggressors, analyze reactions to these types of women, compare male and female experiences of sexual victimization, and consider feminist research perspectives in this area. This title should interest practitioners, researchers, and students who study human development, psychology, violence, sexual abuse, women's studies, and counseling.

Michele Elliott, a child psychologist and founder and director of the children's protection agency Kidscape (www.kidscape.org.uk), edited *Female Sexual Abuse of Children* (Guilford Press, 1994) (originally published in the United Kingdom in 1993 with subtitle *The Ultimate Taboo*), which contains fifteen essays by clinicians and survivors of sexual abuse. The anthology, which includes survey information from the United States, Canada, and England, features current research, guidelines for therapy, personal accounts, and additional resources. Myths associated with abuse and abusers are explored, particularly noting the excuses of mental illness or coercion and considering problems that arise from using certain methods and therapies.

Examining the patterns and effects of abuse, Jacqui Saradjian considers the psychological and physical welfare of the aggressors and their victims in *Women Who Sexually Abuse Children: From Research to Clinical Practice* (John Wiley, 1996), part of the Wiley Series in Child Care and Protection. Saradjian employs more than fifty interviews, questionnaires, and case studies to profile these women in hope of shedding light upon their reasons for abuse. The author groups the women into four distinct categories and includes an overview of why women abuse children and society's perceptions of and response to these women. The work includes a bibliography, index, and appendices comprised of tables listing abusers and type of abuse experienced as a child. This work should interest practitioners who work in the fields of psychology, sociology, welfare, and legal policy.

575. Appignanesi, Lisa, and John Forrester. *Freud's Women*. London: Weidenfeld & Nicolson, 1992. 563p. bibliog. index. (OP)

In this work, arranged into four parts, the authors examine Freud's personal life in conjunction with his relationship with his patients, women, and the development of his theories on femininity and women. Appignanesi, a novelist, and Forrester, a Freud scholar at Cambridge, include personal stories of women who were influential in Freud's life, including family members, clients, friends, and colleagues. These women were selected based on having a direct and personal contact with Freud: "In the following pages we explore the lives, the work and ideas of the women who, through their contact with Freud, played a part in the invention and history of psychoanalysis" (p. 7). This is an important work for anyone interested in Freudian theories. A related title is Hannah Lerman's *A Mote in Freud's Eye: From Psychoanalysis to the Psychology of Women* (Springer, 1986). Lerman explores some of Freud's life, especially how his personal viewpoints and convictions influenced his understanding and perceptions of women and his patients. She discusses the impact of Freud's theories on psychology, women's role in society, and male dominance.

Related titles about others influenced by Freudian theories include Elizabeth Grosz's *Jacques Lacan: A Feminist Introduction* (Routledge, 1990). Grosz provides an outline of Lacan's framework of psychoanalysis with a feminist construct. She assumes the reader to be familiar with Freud, Lacan, and feminist theory and does not provide supplemental commentary. This title is for advanced researchers and students in psychology or philosophy. Toril Moi, editor of *The Kristeva Reader* (Columbia University Press, 1986), has selected and arranged this overview and introduction to Kristeva's work. The essays encompass all phases of Kristeva's career, represent semiotics, psychoanalysis, and politics, and have different translators. The introduction provides background information and an overview of Kristeva's theories. This book serves well for anyone who wants to gain insight into Kristeva's basic theories. Luce Irigaray and translator Gillian C. Gill in *Sexes and Genealogies* (Columbia University Press, 1993) have compiled a collection of lectures that Irigaray addressed to audiences in Europe and Canada, including some of her classic writings. The topics include religion, gender, and related issues in gender and sexual differences.

576. Baron-Faust, Rita. *Mental Wellness for Women.* New York: William Morrow, 1996. 354p. index. ISBN 0688120725; 0688161138pa.

Baron-Faust, with the assistance of physicians of the New York University Medical Center Women's Health Service and the NYU Department of Psychiatry, integrates descriptions of major mental illnesses with biological, physiological, and psychological perspectives. The essays, written in a clear style, present current research, case studies, and possible treatment methods, including medications. Topics include mood disorders, addiction, anxiety and panic, and the female life cycle. The contributors acknowledge that there is mistreatment and inadequate diagnosis for women and minorities and hope that this book assists in reinforcing that there is no one cure, but rather the necessity to understand that there may be multiple contributing factors to any given "illness." This title would be useful as a supplemental resource for classes in therapy, psychopharmacology, or psychobiology.

Women's Mental Health Services: A Public Health Perspective (Sage, 1998), edited by Bruce L. Levin, Andrea K. Blanch, and Ann Jennings, focuses on public health policy issues and how these policies impact women's mental health services. Their intent in this book is "to bring attention to behavioral health issues (including mental health and substance abuse) of particular concern to women; identify and highlight the unique ways in which women are making important contributions to the organization, management, and delivery of mental health services; and to provide a discussion of these critical services delivery issues within a multidisciplinary public health framework" (p. xv). This work is arranged into two sections: an introduction to "the major organization, financing, and delivery issues in women's mental health services" (p. xvi) and an examination of issues and topics faced by women in this at-risk group.

A related title is *Women and Health Psychology: Mental Health Issues* (Lawrence Erlbaum, 1988) by Cheryl B. Travis. The author evaluates several aspects of mental health issues that affect women. In each of the ten chapters, she outlines the background, discusses various interpretations and theories, and then presents a summary and conclusion of the information. Topics include feminist psychoanalysis, psychotropic drugs, alcoholism, eating disorders, and issues surrounding therapy. This book would provide a good introduction for undergraduate students to issues of politics, feminist theory, and mental health issues faced by women.

577. Belenky, Mary F., Blithe M. Clinchy, Nancy R. Goldberger, and Jill M. Tarule. *Women's Ways of Knowing: The Development of Self, Voice, and Mind.* New York: Basic Books, 1986. 256p. bibliog. index. ISBN 0465092128; 0465092136pa.

This classic earned the Distinguished Publication Award in 1987 from the American Psychological Association. In the quest to validate women's experience, this book investigates women's stages of development, starting with their college experiences. The authors' academic backgrounds are in psychology, social work, and education. Using the framework established by William Perry's research on the developmental stages of college men, the authors conducted 135 interviews of college women to capture what these women said in their own voice. Women interviewed were either current students or recent alumnae from ten different types of institutions of higher education such as community colleges, Ivy League schools, or single-sex schools, "as well as in what we came to call 'invisible colleges'—human service agencies supporting women in parenting their children" (pp. 11–12). By broadening the selection of subjects, the authors achieved some diversity regarding age, economic background, social class, and race. The project began in the late 1970s and took five years. From this study, the authors were able to identify and group "perspectives into five categories: silence, received knowledge, subjective knowledge, procedural knowledge, and constructed knowledge" (p. 15). These categories are developed and explained in the first part of the book. In part 2, the authors explore the roles and relationship of family and school to these women's experiences. Appendices contain the research methods used in this study. This book is valuable because it was one of the first to explore the learning process for women and to demonstrate how various ways of communicating, finding, and using one's voice and intellectual pursuit can all contribute to women's self-esteem. Written in a clear and understandable manner, this book is highly recommended, especially for undergraduates in psychology, sociology, human development, education, and women's studies. In the tenth-anniversary edition, the preface provides a retrospective discussion from the authors on the experience of the project.

Several additional titles address issues of learning, knowledge, and cognition. Elizabeth Wilson's *Neural Geographies: Feminism and the Microstructure of Cognition* (Routledge, 1998) compares and contrasts theories and models of cognition, including those of Freud and Derrida, within the context of psychotherapy. This critical work explores the theory and construction of connectionism and the incorporation of many fields, such as neurology and psychology, into the area of cognition as well as incorporating "the politics of feminist-critical interventions in contemporary scientific psychology" (p. 5). *Gender and Thought: Psychological Perspectives* (Springer, 1989), edited by Mary Crawford and Margaret Gentry, presents essays discussing aspects of cognition from various perspectives and methodologies used by feminist psychologists. Topics include problems with test scores in math, sex bias in language, and the role of self-concept. *Gender Differences in Human Cognition* (Oxford University Press, 1997), edited by John T.E. Richardson, Paula Caplan, Janet S. Hyde, and Mary Crawford, presents a review of research that has been conducted in the area of cognition functioning and gender differences. The first chapter is an introduction and historical/literature review with a concise overview of various theoretical studies that rationalize gender differences. The remaining chapters serve as overviews to specific research methods used in gender differences, such as meta-analysis, cognition, and issues of differences.

578. Benjamin, Jessica. *Shadow of the Other: Intersubjectivity and Gender in Psychoanalysis*. Florence, KS: Taylor & Francis, 1998. 129p. bibliog. index. ISBN 0415912369; 0415912377pa.

In this slim volume, Benjamin contemplates the discourse of identity. She concentrates on intersubjectivity, that is, relationships with oneself and others, as her main focal point in exploring the intersections of psychoanalysis and feminist theory as well as delving into the relationship of subjectivity between analyst and client. "My intention is to push beyond this reversal by contemplating the difficulty of creating or discovering the space in which it is possible for either subject to recognizing the difference of the other" (p. xii). Examining where theories overlap, interact, and flow allows for a different perspective and level of understanding. Graduate students in psychology, gender, and women's studies will find these discussions relevant.

A related title is Jane Flax's *Thinking Fragments: Psychoanalysis, Feminism, and Postmodernism in the Contemporary West* (University of California Press, 1990) (see entry 81). Flax undertakes a critical analysis of psychoanalysis, feminism, and postmodernism focusing on some of the major theorists, including Freud, Lacan, Irigaray, and Chodorow. Patricia Elliot's *From Mastery to Analysis: Theories of Gender in Psychoanalytic Feminism* (Cornell University Press, 1991) employs Lacan's model of four fundamental discourses "of mastery, of bureaucracy, of hysteria, and of analysis" (p. xi) to explore and evaluate theories of gender as developed by Juliet Mitchell, Jacqueline Rose, Dorothy Dinnerstein, Nancy Chodorow, Luce Irigaray, and Julia Kristeva. She discusses the contradictions and paradoxes that exist in gender theory. This title will be useful for students in psychology, gender, or women's studies.

579. Bernstein, Anne E., and Sharyn A. Lenhart. *The Psychodynamic Treatment of Women*. Washington, DC: American Psychiatric Press, 1993. 670p. bibliog. index. ISBN 0880483687.

Bernstein and Lenhart provide a critical and important work on the concepts and structure of psychodynamic treatment of women. Using various case studies revealing a range of diagnosis and functionality of mental illness from those who are high-functioning to those who have been institutionalized, "We differentiate between psychoanalysis and psychodynamic psychotherapy" (p. xiii). The authors review and evaluate clients and treatment options in the hope that others in this field will want to conduct further research. Chapter 1 includes an overview of the development of female psychology. Topics covered in other chapters include adolescence, problems of self-esteem, careers, motherhood, disorders linked to reproductive functioning, and the abuse of women. Aside from the overview chapter, each chapter begins with an introduction to the issues and then provides theoretical discussion mixed with case studies. Twenty-two appendices cover a range of topics that affect women, such as theories of battering, neurochemistry of panic disorder, and preparation for widowhood. This superb, insightful work is important for students and researchers in psychology, biobehavioral health, women's studies, and mental health issues.

In *Practicing Feminisms, Reconstructing Psychology: Notes on a Liminal Science* (University of Michigan Press, 1994), Jill Morawski, professor of psychology at Wesleyan University in Connecticut, strives to clarify the relationship between feminism and psychology using objectivity, subjectivity, and validity as the three critical points to frame a discussion of psychology in feminist terms. It is in this manner that liminality becomes a powerful technique as well as a scientific method to present positive ways to reconstruct other theories in a feminist slant.

580. Bifulco, Antonia, and Patricia Moran. *Wednesday's Child: Research into Women's Experience of Neglect and Abuse in Childhood and Adult Depression.* New York: Routledge, 1998. 224p. bibliog. index. ISBN 0415165261; 041516527Xpa.

Bifulco, a research fellow at the Royal Holloway University of London and director of the Lifespan research group, has conducted research on family issues of neglect and depression. Moran is a member of the Lifespan Research Group. The authors intend to "enhance understanding of child neglect and abuse, and to investigate its long-term effects with particular emphasis of adult depression, one of the most common emotional disorders in women" (p. 2). This book is based on information collected from four projects conducted between 1977 and the 1990s, each of which lasted from three to five years. The projects included Loss of Mother (1977), in which 100 women who had lost a mother in childhood were interviewed; Representative London Women (1980), in which 300 women who were either from the working class or single women were interviewed; Sister Study (1990), which included 100 women who had been neglected or abused and had a sister; and Adult Risk (1990), in which more than 800 women were interviewed in the context of negative adult experience as a correlation to depression. The first two of three sections address six selected negative childhood experiences related to depression, and the third section focuses on issues of neglect and abuse.

Insight on African American women's family interactions is provided by Sharon H. Smith's *African American Daughters and Elderly Mothers: Examining Experiences of Grief, Loss, and Bereavement* (Garland, 1998). Smith, an assistant professor at Rutgers University School of Social Work, Camden Campus, surveys the role of death and loss within the African American culture through interviews with thirty African American women. The experiences of how the mother's death has affected these women within the context of the African American family structure provide an interesting insight. Smith focuses on the influences of family and community on middle-aged women when their mothers died. She explores the connection, idealization, support, and community loss of the woman's mother as experienced by all. She advocates further exploration in this area of study for different populations and ethnicities. This work will be of interest for those in social work and psychology.

581. Björkqvist, Kaj, and Pirkko Niemelä, eds. *Of Mice and Women: Aspects of Female Aggression.* San Diego: Academic Press, 1992. 414p. bibliog. index. ISBN 012102590X.

This collection of essays written by scholars from around the world features studies comparing the patterns, similarities, and differences between animal and human aggression, specifically, female aggression. Editors Björkqvist and Niemelä arrange the thirty-four essays into six chapters where contributors analyze several topics, including myths of female aggression; contributing factors to female aggression, such as social settings; and comparison of female aggression across cultures. This work stresses the need to look at biological and physiological components in conjunction with psychological and sociological perspectives to better understand the nature of aggression. This unique resource should prove useful to researchers in physiology, psychology, and anthropology.

Canadian journalist Patricia Pearson won the Canadian Arthur Ellis Award in 1998 for her well-researched investigation of the behavior of violent women in *When She Was Bad . . . : Violent Women and the Myth of Innocence* (Viking Penguin, 1997). Moving beyond the myths of the nonviolent woman, Pearson cites various incidents in which women have abused, attacked, killed, or tortured others. In addition to interviewing women within the criminal justice system, who have had firsthand experience with violent women, Pearson includes commentaries from American and Canadian researchers in criminology, sociology, and psychology that depict the types of violent acts committed by women. The author argues that the stereotype of the peaceful, nurturing woman constitutes the largest obstacle in acknowledging women's capacity for violence.

Rene Denfeld explores the images of women and violence through her experience of learning to box in *Kill the Body, the Head Will Fall: A Closer Look at Women, Violence, and Aggression* (Warner Books, 1997). Observations reveal not only how often scholars have overlooked the topics of women as sexual offenders and criminals, but also the relationship between aggression and race in women. Arguing that both men and women experience aggression, she asserts that many people find difficulty in viewing women as aggressors in violent activities such as the military and certain sports.

582. Boston Lesbian Psychologies Collective, ed. *Lesbian Psychologies: Explorations and Challenges*. Urbana: University of Illinois Press, 1987. 375p. bibliog. index. ISBN 0252014030; 0252014049pa.

This excellent collection of essays emerged primarily from a 1984 conference on lesbian psychologies. The authors are mostly clinical practitioners and academicians who work in a variety of settings. The essays vary in length, are well written, and clearly describe and discuss issues central to lesbian identity: "There is no single lesbian identity, nor is there a single lesbian identity development" (p. 4). With such a wide definition, the authors explore many areas that had previously not received attention, including issues of politics, sexuality, identity, relationships, family dynamics, and other topics. The essays are arranged into five categories: identity, relationships, family, therapies, and communities. Some of the essays touch on issues of diversity. Many essays include discussion of common issues experienced by lesbians and therapists, such as intimacy, conflicts with others and within themselves, tensions and pressures, self-worth, and self-image, as well as suggestions and considerations for therapists. This classic book contains essential readings and is a must for all collections. Two similar titles are *Femininity and Shame: Women, Men, and Giving Voice to the Feminine* (University Press of America, 1997) by Barbara L. Eurich-Rascoe and Hendrika Vande Kemp, and Sandra L. Bartky's *Femininity and Domination: Studies in the Phenomenology of Oppression* (Routledge, 1990). The first title explores issues of voice, power, and expression. Focusing on the conflicts that arise out of gender and social expectations and norms, the authors note that shame is used to punish as well as to enforce certain types of behaviors to maintain gendered expectations. Bartky undertakes a philosophical inquiry of the "oppression" of psychology. Reflecting on Marxist philosophy as a tool to raise consciousness, this title challenges politics, social norms, and various feminist theories.

583. Brown, Laura S. and Mary Ballou, eds. *Personality and Psychopathology: Feminist Reappraisals*. New York: Guilford Press, 1992. 272p. bibliog. index. ISBN 0898627745; 0898625009pa.

Contributors to this volume explore the possibilities of transforming traditional theories of personality analysis to be more inclusive of women rather than perpetuating the status quo. The editors intend for the essays to be used to analyze personality theories along with the use of the term "pathology." The editors conclude that there is no perfect theory that can be applied: "Women have different routes by which these disorders are manifested and almost all involve the lack of relative and perceived power in their lives. Socialization experiences that include oppression because of gender, class, race, educational status, and racial, ethnic, and cultural minority group membership are most common in women who develop these mental disorders" (p. ix). The chapters are divided into two parts. Part 1 investigates and critiques feminist perspectives on personality theories, considers traditional theories, and explores new paradigms and theories to better identify and address human nature. Essays in part 2 address the incorporation of the feminist perspective into traditional psychopathology within a historical and research context. The articles are well organized, and while each chapter varies in its structure, usually there is an overview or historical background, a description of critical influences and controversies that contributed to the theory, and an examination of the contributions of the theory to the field of psychotherapy.

A related title is *Feminist Theories and Feminist Psychotherapies: Origins, Themes, and Variations* (Haworth Press, 1997) by Carolyn Z. Enns. In this work, arranged into eight chapters, Enns begins with a quiz assessing the reader's awareness of the topic in the first three chapters as she reviews the values and practices of feminist therapy, focusing particularly on liberal, radical, socialist, and cultural feminism. She also discusses the assessment tools that are used, examines the constraints of women of color on feminist therapy, and concludes with a brief chapter that compares the main characteristics of the major feminist therapies and identifies possible theories that could be combined.

584. Brown, Lyn Mikel, and Carol Gilligan. *Meeting at the Crossroads: Women's Psychology and Girls' Development.* Cambridge, MA: Harvard University Press, 1992. 258p. bibliog. index. ISBN 0674564642.

This work, one of many studies conducted by Gilligan and the Harvard Project on Women's Psychology and Girls' Development, is based on the authors' observations and interviews of girls in a private school from 1986 to 1990. Tracing the evolution, challenges, and responses of a girl's voice to her perception of self and relationships, the authors attempt to determine when and how girls modify their behavior and lose their "voice." Although the interviewees' experiences may not represent those of all girls, the study still sheds light upon the unique experience of girls. Because girls base their behavior on various processes, decisions, and influences, the authors identify this age as a critical time for decision making, relationship building, and self-awareness.

Joan J. Brumberg, a faculty member at Cornell University in history, human development, and women's studies, describes the major social, physiological, and psychological factors that have affected adolescent females during the past century in *The Body Project: An Intimate History of American Girls* (Random House, 1997). Brumberg uses the phrase "body project" to compare issues and pressures faced by young girls throughout the late nineteenth and most of the twentieth century, and to illustrate the social and psychological repercussions of girls' growing focus on their body as a lifelong project. She relies on diaries and other resources to clearly assess the many dangers that today's youth face in conjunction with their relationships with their parents, peers, and society. This work should interest both undergraduates and researchers of adolescence.

585. Buhle, Mari Jo. *Feminism and Its Discontents: A Century of Struggle with Psychoanalysis.* Cambridge, MA: Harvard University Press, 1998. 418p. bibliog. index. ISBN 0674298683; 0674004035pa.

Buhle, a historian at Brown University, begins her review of the development of psychology in the United States with Freud's series of lectures in 1909 at Clark University in Massachusetts. Using this event as the base, she frames the construction of the book to show the relationship between feminism and psychoanalysis and their evolution in the United States. Simultaneously, she also provides "a historical context for the shift from feminist thought to theory, precisely at the nexus between feminism and psychoanalysis" (p. 21). Buhle applies a social, cultural-historical approach as she links various events that influenced and were influenced by psychology's development. Through this construct, she is able to clearly present various theories, discuss splits and shifts, and provide examples of experiences from the patients' and practitioners' viewpoints. Buhle also includes other influences, including Hollywood movies, the impact of the Neo-Freudians, European psychology, and feminists' contributions to the profession. This book is an essential resource. *Living with the Sphinx: Papers from the Women's Therapy Centre* (Women's Press, 1987), edited by Sheila Ernst and Marie Maguire, draws on the experiences of staff of the Women's Therapy Centre in the United Kingdom. Essays examine many issues and dichotomies concerning women, therapy, psychotherapy, and feminism. Personal, pragmatic, and theoretical, the authors challenge themselves and the theories they work with to better understand some of the contention and conflict that face female therapists.

586. Burke, Nancy. *Gender and Envy*. New York: Routledge, 1998. 329p. bibliog. index. ISBN 0415916275; 0415916283pa.

Burke has selected essays, both reprints and originals, to explore gender issues that are both resisted and serve as a barrier to deconstructing envy, in particular, penis envy. The book is arranged into five sections. The first serves as the introduction to the debate, the second identifies various layers and components of the debate, and the third interweaves issues of gender with perceptions of envy. Section 4 studies the intersecting areas between human development and psychoanalysis, and the final section considers how influences in psychology, sociology, and culture contribute to the understanding of envy and gender issues. Students, researchers, or practitioners interested in the historical obsession of penis envy should read this title.

Making a Difference: Psychology and the Construction of Gender (Yale University Press, 1990), edited by Rachel T. Hare-Mustin and Jeanne Marecek, includes six essays that critique how women have been affected by psychological theories of gender. Focusing on the perspective that gender differences are behavioral expectations that have been constructed by social norms, discussions include how gender is interpreted, psychological contributions to understanding gender, what "difference" means, and how politics influences gender roles. Sandra L. Bem's *The Lenses of Gender: Transforming the Debate on Sexual Inequality* (Yale University Press, 1993) earned Best Book in Psychology in 1993 and Women's Distinguished Publication Award by the Association of Women in Psychology in 1994. Bem expands current psychological theory by focusing on three gender lenses that are "embedded in the culture: gender polarization, androcentrism, and biological essentialism. These three gender lenses provide the foundation for a theory of how biology, culture, and the individual psyche all interact in historical context to systemically reproduce power" (p. viii).

587. Burman, Erica, ed. *Deconstructing Feminist Psychology*. Thousand Oaks, CA: Sage Publications, 1997. 211p. (Gender and Psychology, v. 10). ISBN 0803976399; 0803976402pa.

Burman begins this work by summarizing feminist and deconstructionist theories and exploring how deconstruction can serve as a method of feminist critique. The contributors represent an international perspective, with five essays discussing issues of deconstruction within feminist psychology and four essays investigating new directions in feminist psychology by using deconstruction as a method of analysis. *Deconstructing Feminist Psychology* is recommended for students and researchers interested in broadening their theoretical framework in psychoanalysis, sociology, politics, and cultural studies.

Additional methods that could be used by therapists and educators are discussed in Judith Jordan's *Women's Growth in Connection: Writings from the Stone Center* (Guilford Press, 1991) and the subsequent *Women's Growth in Diversity: More Writings from the Stone Center* (Guilford Press, 1997). The Stone Center, based at Wellesley College, serves to provide methods and strategies to prevent psychological problems, understand human development, and develop alternative theoretical and psychological models relating to the development of women. The authors site the key to health and growth in mutual relationships. These two titles evolved out of studies and interviews conducted by the staff and others. Aside from covering various topics, the primary difference between the two titles is that *Women's Growth in Connection* concerns the experiences of the average white woman, while *Women's Growth in Diversity* includes experiences from black and lesbian women. The editor clearly states that there is a lack of representation from Asian and Native American women as well as class experiences from other groups of women. Many of the essays are previous colloquiums that were presented at the Stone Center and include some of the group discussions. Each essay includes a useful bibliography.

588. Burstow, Bonnie. *Radical Feminist Therapy: Working in the Context of Violence.* Newbury Park, CA: Sage Publications, 1992. 302p. bibliog. index. ISBN 0803947879; 0803947887pa.

Using a radical perspective and voice in addressing issues of women as victims in a violent hegemonic world, Burstow identifies feminist therapy as a method separate from the patriarchal structure of psychoanalysis to better "reflect feminist values and female ways of relating" (p. x). She includes personal comments on issues of power, oppression, patriarchy, ethnocentrism, and problems within the profession of psychiatry. In working with women of different racial, ethnic, and economic backgrounds, Burstow intends for this book to "radicalize feminist therapy further and to offer detailed and grounded guidance" (p. xiv). The first two chapters provide an overview of the radical feminist framework of psychiatry. Remaining chapters explore alternative methods for therapists to use in integrating radical feminist practice. At the end of each chapter, Burstow includes selected reading lists, and the appendix includes various client handouts. Students and practitioners who work with women in mental health, social work, or social policy will find this a useful resource to better understand the contributions and inclusions of radical feminist philosophy within the therapeutic setting.

Jean B. Miller and Irene P. Stiver examine women's relationships and how they connect and disconnect with one another in *The Healing Connection: How Women Form Relationships in Therapy and in Life* (Beacon Press, 1997). Using their work at the Stone Center at Wellesley College, the authors incorporate their experiences as clinicians to discuss how people from different backgrounds and experiences interact with one another. *The Healing Connection* explores the importance of relationships, repercussions in relationships, responsibilities of the therapist, and how the community provides empowerment. In *Subversive Dialogues: Theory in Feminist Therapy* (Basic Books, 1994), Laura S. Brown, a practicing therapist in Seattle, believes that successful feminist therapy liberates women from the negative results of other therapies. In a work that is part personal journey, part history, and part inquiry, Brown reviews theories and discusses the roles of feminism and diversity in feminist therapy, including issues of subversiveness, power, and resiliency.

589. Canetto, Silvia S., and David Lester, eds. *Women and Suicidal Behavior.* New York: Springer, 1995. 287p. (Springer Series: Focus on Women). bibliog. index. ISBN 0826186300.

The majority of research on suicide has focused on men. This title is a collection of essays on suicidal behaviors of women. "Two perspectives inform our approach to suicidal behavior in women. First, we examine the experiences and behavior of suicidal women *qua* women. . . . Second, we include consideration of social and cultural factors, such as social class, financial resources, education, employment, social support, gender socialization, and cultural norms, again in contrast to much of the previous literature on suicidal women, which has tended to emphasize individual psychological determinants" (p. 3). The book is arranged in five sections. The first section reviews the theories on suicide, women, and attempted suicide. Section 2 provides a history of women and suicidal studies, including information on Western and non-Western cultures. The third section discusses the danger in generalizing and devaluing women's suicidal attempts. The fourth section presents data concerning experiences of suicidal women from various populations, including Latinas, Asian Americans, African Americans, adolescents, and older women. The final section explores issues of prevention, intervention, and postintervention and suggests further research in these areas to help expand the methods and actions that could be used by different parties. This book provides a clear and easily comprehensible introduction to an important area of research.

An additional title related to suicide and suicidal behaviors is *Why Women Kill Themselves* (Thomas, 1988), edited by David Lester. This is a collection of essays by faculty from various fields of study such as anthropology, psychobiology, and sociology. Several of the brief chapters include statistical data, although various methodologies and cultural dimensions of suicidal behavior are presented. The final two chapters evaluate Virginia Woolf and Dorothy Parker as case studies.

590. Comas-Diaz, Lillian, and Beverly Greene, eds. *Women of Color: Integrating Ethnic and Gender Identities in Psychotherapy.* New York: Guilford Press, 1994. 518p. index. ISBN 0898623715.

This outstanding resource addresses issues of ethnicity, race, and culture within the context of psychotherapy. It explores marginalized women from mostly neglected ethnic and racial groups to provide strategies and insights for therapists to be more inclusive in working with clients of different backgrounds. There are some groups not represented, but the authors address this. The book is divided into three sections; each section has an introduction written by the coeditors that provides a solid overview of the issues explored in that section. The research is impeccable and establishes paradigms for understanding and working within cultural contexts. Appropriately, the editors point out that "there is no monolithic concept of women of color" (p. 7). Section 1 grounds the rest of the work by presenting information on minority women from six ethnic groups. Various chapters explore the differences in how women from different groups may react and interact in therapy and how cultural conscience can affect them in this process. The second section examines various therapies and approaches that could be applied to cross-cultural, feminist, and diversity perspectives. Various case studies illustrate different issues within each framework. The third section addresses special minority populations, including lesbian women of color, who are often overlooked. This is a seminal work that should be read by everyone who is interested in psychotherapy.

591. DeChant, Betsy, ed. *Women and Group Psychotherapy: Theory and Practice.* New York: Guilford Press, 1996. 523p. bibliog. index. ISBN 1572300981.

Therapy takes on different complications and challenges in a group setting. Issues such as group dynamics, leadership, and gender relationships are just a few of the factors that contribute to the need for awareness in a group setting. DeChant, a therapist in private practice, has selected essays that address a variety of issues related to women, authority, group relations, and power.

She arranges the essays into three main sections: an overview of the main principles and philosophies of group practice, a theory of group treatment for women from the feminist perspective, and guidelines for the therapist "from the vantage points of research, ethical issues, and finally, gender- and culture-sensitive supervision, training, and leadership" (p. 9). Group experience has a different meaning for women, and the essays in this book provide new paradigms of theory and practice using a "multifaceted lens" in exploring levels of these experiences. This title will be of interest to practitioners and students who are in training to be therapists and want a better understanding of group dynamics.

Another title focusing on group therapy is *Feminist Groupwork* (Sage Publications, 1991) by Sandra Butler and Claire Wintram. Group dynamics with women provides its own set of challenges and rewards, and according to the authors it is an effective tool for many women. Discussions include how women are marginalized in society, how they can feel marginalized in groups, and group dynamics. The authors write, "Fear, isolation and loneliness lay at the root of the experiences of many of the women with whom we were involved over the years" (p. 2). Several chapters focus on the importance of structuring the group environment, along with discussions of various types of programs and activities. In *Women's Therapy Groups: Paradigms of Feminist Treatment* (Springer, 1987), part of the Springer Series: Focus on Women, Clare M. Brody edited a collection of seventeen essays, some of which are reprints, others, original research, all focusing on various components of women's therapy groups. This title concentrates on how group work, with the variety of experiences and influence each participant brings, can provide a positive change and growth for women.

592. Dinsmore, Christine. *From Surviving to Thriving: Incest, Feminism, and Recovery.* Albany: State University of New York Press, 1991. 208p. (The Psychology of Women). bibliog. index. ISBN (OP); 0791406296pa.

Christine Dinsmore evaluates the process of "recovery" for people affected by incest and sexual abuse through stories that she culled from interviews with various women. She discusses feminist therapy and issues germane to incest survivors, especially trauma; steps in the healing process; and collective denial of incest by family members, friends, and professionals. Emphasizing the status of survivor as opposed to victim, Dinsmore explores how victims talk about the trauma, memories and emotions that can arise during the recovery process, issues that lesbians face, ways in which therapists can more effectively work with survivors, and changes in relationships between family and partners as survivors experience the process. This work will be of interest to therapists, those in therapy, and graduate students.

A related title by Ellen Bass and Laura Davis is *Courage to Heal: A Guide for Women Survivors of Child Sexual Abuse* (Harper & Row, 1988), which looks at the healing process of the survivors.

In *Secret Survivors: Uncovering Incest and Its Aftereffects in Women* (Wiley, 1990), author E. Sue Blume uncovers patterns of emotional and behavioral consequences indicating that incest poses more complex and far-reaching repercussions than previously recognized. She features the tool she created to trace "Post-Incest Syndrome," called the "Incest Survivors' Aftereffects Checklist." Blume considers how incest affects women's relationships and influences social rules and gender expectations, and she examines how abuse contributes to problems such as depression, sexual and eating disorders, compulsive obsession disorder, panic disorders, and drug and alcohol abuse.

Janet L. Jacobs bases *Victimized Daughters: Incest and the Development of the Female Self* (Routledge, 1994) on a study she initiated at a shelter for adolescent girls and then expanded to include a broader range of women from diverse settings and backgrounds. Although the sample population ranged in age from fifteen to forty-two and was mostly white, Jacobs also included African Americans, Latinas, and women representing mixed races or ethnicities. The author implemented the study in three stages: a written questionnaire, an initial interview with survivors, and finally, in-depth interviews. She discusses how incest affects family relationships, particularly the mother-daughter bond; how victims idealize their perpetrators; and how sexual violence emotionally affects victims.

593. Dutton, Donald G. *The Domestic Assault of Women: Psychological and Criminal Justice Perspectives*. Boston: Allyn & Bacon, 1988. 220p. bibliog. index. ISBN 0205113230pa.

Using theoretical and research studies, Dutton, a professor of psychology at the University of British Columbia, considers the domestic assault of women from a social psychological perspective. Dutton focuses on the psychological perspectives of assailants and victims, reviews the relationship between domestic assault and criminal justice policies, considers how abuse affects victims and the treatment they receive, and examines the response of the criminal justice system. The expanded second edition (University of Washington Press, 1994) features new chapters, such as "History and Incidence of Wife Abuse," "The Abusive Personality," and "Traumatic Bonding." He greatly expands the chapter on wife assault in the second edition. Both students and teachers focusing on issues of abuse will find this resource highly valuable.

Valerie N. Chang interviews sixteen women who suffered psychological abuse in *I Just Lost Myself: Psychological Abuse of Women in Marriage* (Praeger, 1996). Arguing that power and domination play key roles in the continuation of abuse, Chang explores how women explain, rationalize, become aware of, and respond to their understanding of abuse in relationships. Chang analyzes factors that contribute to expectations in relationships and considers the roles that susceptibility and shame play in the development of abusive relationships. Social workers, psychologists, and clinicians, among others, should consult this important resource. Mary S. Miller identifies a wide range of nonphysical types of abuse, including verbal, emotional, psychological, social, and economic, in *No Visible Wounds: Identifying Nonphysical Abuse of Women by Their Men* (Fawcett, 1996). Miller describes how women can empower themselves and lists many types of available assistance.

594. Falco, Kristine L. *Psychotherapy with Lesbian Clients: Theory into Practice*. Philadelphia: Brunner/Mazel Publishers, 1991. 208p. bibliog. index. ISBN 0876306229.

This book was inspired by Falco's research for her dissertation, "Psychotherapy with Lesbian Clients: A Manual for the Psychotherapist," which was awarded the Best Unpublished Manuscript Award in Lesbian Psychologies from the Association for Women in Psychology. The chapters are arranged into two sections. In the first section, Falco presents a comprehensive introduction and overview of the challenge of homosexuality for therapists, clients, and feminists. She defines terminology and concepts that lesbian and gay clients and therapists face. Falco examines psychological theories that have contributed negatively and positively to the study of therapy for lesbians, including social and biological stigmas and homophobia. The final chapter in this section is devoted to the therapist and ways to empower those who want to work with lesbian clients. Section 2 explores issues related to therapy, such as homophobia and the association of psychotic disorders with lesbians. Falco also reviews issues of identity and relationship issues. Additional topics include lesbian mothers, lesbians of color, issues of sexuality, addictions, youth and aging, and AIDS. The final chapter provides a hopeful view of future toward the consideration and evolution of psychology of lesbians. Appendices include exercises, an annotated bibliography, and additional resources for assistance.

Part of the series Between Men—Between Women, *Other Women: Lesbian/Bisexual Experience and Psychoanalytic Theory of Women* (Columbia University Press, 1997) by Beverly Burch collects essays incorporating various sources from scholarly (feminist and psychoanalytic) to personal in order to present a selection of explorations of the lesbian experience. These essays serve to connect "feminist thinking, psychoanalytic theory, social constructivist views, and clinical experience" (p. xi). The essays are divided into two sections: the first section focuses on identity issues for individuals, while the second section explores the diverse relationships and family structures lesbians create for themselves.

Lesbian Lives: Psychoanalytic Narratives Old and New (Analytic Press, 1997) by Maggie Magee and Diana C. Miller is part history, part literature review. The authors begin with a review of biological models that were incorporated into psychoanalytic theories to condemn and disregard female homosexuality. They then use a range of materials from clinical reports to biography to literature to "provide psychoanalytic readers heightened appreciation of the 'many-lived forms' of women who love women" (p. xix). The authors discuss such issues as the refusal of the profession to train homosexual therapists as well as concerns of self-identification.

595. Fallon, Patricia, Melanie A. Katzman, and Susan C. Wooley, eds. *Feminist Perspectives on Eating Disorders*. New York: Guilford Press, 1994. 465p. bibliog. index. ISBN 0898621801; 1572301821pa.

This collection of twenty-two essays explores the range of behaviors and influences associated with eating disorders. The essays are grouped into five sections centering on history, space and body, reanalysis of treatment, reconstructing females, and future possibilities in treating the disease. Contributors provide a multitude of perspectives on such diverse topics as appearance, power, therapy, medication, education, and multiculturalism. Each essay incorporates feminist ideas into the discussion, and all the essays provide useful and lengthy bibliographies. Students, educators, and clinicians in psychology and other health fields will find this resource highly valuable. Editor Catrina Brown presents alternative opinions and suggestions regarding fixation on weight in *Consuming Passions: Feminist Approaches to Eating Disorders and Weight Preoccupations* (Second Story Press, 1993). Brown argues that eating disorders reflect economic and cultural role shifts, and that women spend more time worrying about their weight than challenging the cultural structure. The final section focuses on political aspects of eating disorders in light of issues that permeate the larger social structure, exploring necessary changes, addressing the ways in which individuals and organizations lobby for such change, and briefly noting race, class, and sexual orientation issues.

Bridget Dolan and Inez Gitzinger's *Why Women? Gender Issues and Eating Disorders* (Athlone, 1994) took root during a European Council meeting on eating disorders held in the early 1990s. Although the book's fourteen essays primarily focus on European perspectives of females, there are essays that discuss male eating disorders. The authors consider sociological and cultural affluence, therapy, and sexual issues, making this work suitable for students and researchers alike. Joan J. Brumberg considers the psychological context of self-starvation, sacrifice, and martyrdom from a historical viewpoint in *Fasting Girls: The Emergence of Anorexia Nervosa as a Modern Disease* (Harvard University Press, 1988). Brumberg examines the fasting behavior of women throughout history to determine the prevalence of anorexia in light of its psychological, sociological, cultural, and historical origins. She explores the nature of the disease and how it has changed over time, differentiating between the fasting behavior of the medieval period, with its religious and moral overtones, and the modern disease, which was first identified during the 1870s. Although she discusses medical treatments and perceptions in several chapters and features extensive footnotes, Brumberg does not include a bibliography. Finally, Walter Vandereycken and Ron van Deth document the history and role of anorexia in the lives of women from the medieval period to the present, exploring the psychology behind denial and self-sacrifice, in *From Fasting Saints to Anorexic Girls: The History of Self-Starvation* (New York University Press, 1994).

596. Figert, Anne. *Women and the Ownership of PMS: The Structuring of a Psychiatric Disorder.* Hawthorne, NY: Aldine de Gruyter, 1996. 191p. bibliog. index. ISBN 0202305503; 0202305511pa.

Figert explores the history and development of premenstrual syndrome (PMS) from medical and psychological perspectives to its controversial definition and inclusion in the DSM-III-R as a mental illness. She includes outside factors and contributions of politics, pharmaceuticals and medical investments, and other "players" who struggle to "control" PMS. The book is arranged into three sections. The first section looks at the evolution and controversies involved with the description and designation of late luteal phase dysphoric disorder (LLPDD), premenstrual dysphoric disorder (PDD), and periluteal phase dysphoric disorder (PPDD) in the DSM-III-R and IV. The second section discusses a number of perspectives and identifies three domains within the conflict: health and mental health, who defines "woman," and science. The author also looks at the debate on PMS in various fields such as mental health, medicine, and science, as well as incorporating perspectives from economic and political viewpoints. The last section, "Settling the Conflict," discusses the results of PMS as defined in the DSM-III-R and DSM-IV and how this impacted women, science, and medicine. The complex intermingling of politics, medicine, and other fields involved with the diagnosis of this syndrome are clearly developed. This book is a reminder that many medical and psychological developments have been made through outside influences.

Two additional titles that investigate issues of menstruation and psychoanalysis include Mary J. Lupton's *Menstruation and Psychoanalysis* (University of Illinois Press, 1993) and Anne E. Walker's *Menstrual Cycle* (Routledge, 1998). Lupton writes that her title evolved out of her previous contribution in *The Curse: A Cultural History of Menstruation* (Dutton, 1976). In 1988, a revised edition of *The Curse* appeared. The primary focus of *Menstruation and Psychoanalysis* is that "menstrual blood is *gendered* blood—blood that separates and defines women, that has made them the subject of taboo, of exclusion, of difference" (p. 3). The book is divided into three parts: Freud, male analysts, and women analysts. The first part focuses on Freud and Freudian theories and commentaries on menstruation, including the limited approaches of the Freud/Fliess theory. The second part "examines the works of a number of Freudian theorists who incorporated menstruation into their considerations of castration anxiety, circumcision, the Oedipus complex, and other concepts central to the foundations of female sexuality" (p. 9). Part 3 focuses on female analysts' theories, perceptions, and commentaries on menstruation. A significant contribution of this book is the literature review of cultural, psychological, biological, and anthropological aspects of menstruation and the menstrual cycle. Walker examines various methods, models, and findings in menstrual cycle research from cultural and historical perspectives in order to better understand the relationship between psychology, menstruation, the menstrual cycle, and women's status. The first two chapters look at the many myths and perceptions about menstruation, the various contributions made by male researchers to validate these myths, and the eventual acceptance of the myths as scientific fact. Three chapters investigate the relationship between research and understanding of the menstrual cycle and cognition, moods, emotional well-being, and the development and evolution of PMS. An extensive bibliography and notes contribute to this resource.

597. Geller, Jeffrey L., and Maxine Harris, eds. *Women of the Asylum: Voices from behind the Walls, 1840–1945.* New York: Anchor Books, 1994. 349p. bibliog. ISBN 0385474229; 0385474237pa.

This title contains two centuries of narratives of women who were in asylums. Written in the days when women of all classes were institutionalized for reasons of legitimate nature as well as for more illicit rationales, these twenty-six personal chronicles provide a window into their experiences in the asylums. The twenty-six women published these narratives after their liberation from the institutions. The reasons these women chose to publish these stories are as different as the reasons they were institutionalized. For many, it was a way to give voice to what happened "behind the walls." The stories are grouped into four time periods: 1840–1865, 1866–1890, 1891–1920, and 1921–1945. At the beginning of each section a historical overview of women's social expectations integrated with mental health issues is presented. The authors used primary sources from various archives and libraries to identify these accounts and then constructed and reconstructed the stories. This book is recommended reading to all interested in issues related to social history and mental illness.

Yannick Ripa's *Women and Madness: The Incarceration of Women in Nineteenth-Century France*, translated by Catherine du Peloux Menagé (University of Minnesota Press, 1990), begins in 1830 with the creation of the asylum and focuses on the historical development of asylums and the types of treatment established during the following thirty years. She points out that during this time madness was not perceived as an illness, but rather a "danger to be contained and neutralized" (p. 12). The book includes two sections: the conditions and situations of women that led to their commitment to an asylum, and life in the asylum. Ripa has selected a representative collection of stories from the asylum archives, including the interactions between the psychologists (at the turn of the century they were called alienists) and their patients. This is a useful resource that links historical events to the social and psychological developments of society.

598. Gergen, Mary M., and Sara N. Davis, eds. *Toward a New Psychology of Gender: A Reader.* New York: Routledge, 1997. 626p. bibliog. index. ISBN 0415913071; 041591308Xpa.

Gergen and Davis have selected a range of essays that address critical issues within feminist scholarship while concurrently challenging traditional psychology in an effort to create alternatives. The essays are arranged into ten sections that include a critical assessment of the overlapping areas of gender studies and psychology, an examination of research possibilities within social construction, an exploration of gender differences, how reality can be constructed by various interpretations, and the challenge of social roles and interpersonal relations. Other topics include power, sex roles, self-image/perception, therapy, and a dialogue on the postmodern future. These essays would work well as a textbook for feminist psychology courses or as supplemental readings for upper-level undergraduates and graduate students.

The Gender and Psychology Reader (New York University Press, 1998), edited by Blythe M. Clinchy and Julie K. Norem, includes forty-one reprinted essays from some of the key scholars in feminist and gender psychology, arranged in seven sections with an introductory essay. A range of topics on gender are discussed, including research bias, biological determinism, philosophy of gender, social influences of gender, and what relationships mean to women. The editors write that "the book is intended for use alone or as a supplementary text for upper-level undergraduate and graduate courses in gender" (p. 1). In *Women and Gender: A Feminist Psychology* (Temple University Press, 1992), Rhoda Unger and Mary Crawford use four broad themes to analyze and construct the major theories and concepts relevant to gender, including considerations from feminist, sociological, and cross-cultural perspectives. The authors also explore characteristics of language and power, diversity of women, life-span issues, and how social change has affected research. *The Psychology of Gender* (Guilford Press, 1993), edited by Anne E. Beall and Robert J. Sternberg, includes essays employing a variety of theoretical perspectives to explore social and cultural issues relating to the psychology of gender. The topics include thought, behavior, social construction, an overview of gender theories, and life-span and cross-cultural contributions. The book concludes with a summary of the directions and issues within the theories in the psychology of gender.

599. Glassgold, Judith M., and Suzanne Iasenza, eds. *Lesbians and Psychoanalysis: Revolutions in Theory and Practice.* New York: Free Press, 1995. 325p. bibliog. index. ISBN 0028740068.

Contributors to this collection are psychologists and psychoanalysts in private practice or affiliated with academic institutions who critique, analyze, and comment on the status and relationship between homosexuality and psychological themes. The eighteen chapters are arranged into three sections. In the first section, the authors challenge and analyze the construction, definition, and pathology of homosexuality and lesbians. The historical background of various therapies and controversies is presented in relationship to homosexuality and psychology, thus providing insight into the cultural influences and complexities that form the construction of gender identity. The essays in the second section explore issues of sexuality, relationships, family, shame, and identity in the context of professional training and client-therapist relationships. The possibility of a therapist being homophobic is also discussed. The concluding section considers alternate frameworks toward understanding, creating, or transforming lesbian psychology. Working within the framework of lesbian feminist theory provides a number of challenges: "Our hope is that lesbian feminist psychoanalytically informed therapy can begin to hold these apparent tensions and paradoxes. . . . Our experiences of transforming our own 'deficits' into authority and diversity have offered us potential space for expansion of our empathic vantage points and sensitivity to the often hidden injuries of marginalization. . . . we can embody the possibility of clients reauthoring their own experience" (p. 262). This critical work will be of interest to graduate students, teachers, therapists, and other practitioners.

600. Goodman, W. Charisse. *The Invisible Woman: Confronting Weight Prejudice in America.* Carlsbad, CA: Gurze Books, 1995. 207p. bibliog. index. ISBN 0936077107pa.

Goodman seeks to put into perspective social and psychological prejudices and stereotypes related to weight. The author examines forms of "negative visibility" which she defines as society perceiving fat people as shameful, and thus ignoring or condemning them. Concentrating on women and weight, chapters focus on weight control as a business, the representation of overweight women in the media, as well as issues of prejudice, sexism, and discrimination. Lastly, Goodman discusses the political and cultural impact of weight issues in society, and links these issues with personal perspectives of overweight women.

Several other texts contribute varying perspectives concerning eating disorders. In *No Fat Chicks: How Big Business Profits by Making Women Hate Their Bodies—How to Fight Back* (Carol Publishing, 1997), Terry Poulton explores the effects of advertising and marketing by major corporations that exploit social pressures to be thin. Poulton challenges the high value placed on being thin and the cultural assumptions held by many people in our society. For philosophical discussions of weight, see Susan Bordo's *Unbearable Weight: Feminism, Western Culture, and the Body* (University of California Press, 1993) and *The Bodies of Women: Ethics, Embodiment, and Sexual Difference* (Routledge, 1994) by Roslyn Diprose. Bordo reconstructs issues of weight and eating disorders through a collection of her previously published articles on the social representation of bodies. The author emphasizes the necessity of integrating feminist theory into studies of gender and the body. Diprose incorporates feminist theory and philosophy into her analysis of the biomedical, feminist, and nonfeminist research theories on the female body. Using philosophical perspectives from Hegel, Foucault, and Nietzsche as well as psychological criticisms of Luce Irigaray, Drucilla Cornell, and Iris Young, the author reconstructs sexual differences to form new ethics and formulas to identify discrimination and ways to address it. In *The Beauty Myth: How Images of Beauty Are Used against Women* (Morrow, 1996), Naomi Wolf critiques media images of women and the continual use of physical representation of women's body as a form of control that constrains and restrains their self-image, self-worth, and behavior. Other aspects of beauty such as cultural differences, barter, and power are also discussed.

601. Gouldner, Helen, and Mary S. Strong. *Speaking of Friendship: Middle-Class Women and Their Friends.* New York: Greenwood Press, 1987. 189p. (Contributions to Women's Studies, no. 80). bibliog. index. ISBN 0313250682.

Friendship has a broad definition in America, for women define a range of meanings for the different types of friends they have. The authors interviewed seventy-five women from middle- to upper-middle-class backgrounds, mostly from the East Coast, who ranged in age from thirty to sixty-five. The group represents women who worked both in and out of the home, married, divorced, widowed, and single women, and women who were single heads of families. In the introduction the authors state, "Rather than defining 'friendship' to the respondents, we listened to them talk about their friends, be they kin or non-kin, with the intention of learning what the reality of friendship was for them" (p. 12). The survey also examined friendships at various points in the life cycle of an individual. Gouldner and Strong claim that friendships are established and redefined by criteria set by each individual woman, not only for seeking out friendships, but also maintaining and ending them. For most women, evaluation of the relationship includes factoring in constraints such as time and personal situations in what the authors call the "budget of friendship": "Most of the women used complex hierarchies for ranking their friends, and they used intricately defined cut-off points between degrees of closeness to these people" (p. 43). Chapters are organized as steps in the process of creating friendships and the variety of friendships women have with each other. The authors explore the rarely discussed topic of friendships that ended.

In *Between Women: Love, Envy, and Competition in Women's Friendships* (Penguin, 1989), authors Luise Eichenbaum and Susie Orbach explore various components of friendship and how friendship shifts among women. The authors delve into aspects of friendship often not discussed, including fear of abandonment, envy, competition, anger, and speaking up. Writing in a casual tone, the authors use various personal and clinical accounts from the United Kingdom and the United States. While this work does not include discussions of race, class, and sexual orientation, the discussion of the multitude of emotions integral to friendships lends it great value. Janice G. Raymond also explores what friendships represent to women in *A Passion for Friends: Toward a Philosophy of Female Affection* (Beacon Press, 1986). The author writes, "This book aims to restore power and depth to the word and reality of friendship . . . [and] is also concerned with returning friendship to a primary place as a basis of feminist purpose, passion and politics" (p. 9). Raymond incorporates philosophy and history to show how the power of friendship can contribute to strengths and conflicts within women's lives. In *Best Friends: The Pleasures and Perils of*

Girls' and Women's Friendships (Crown, 1998), authors Terri Apter and Ruthellen Josselson conducted a survey on the importance of friendship in the lives of women and girls. The authors examined various patterns in relationships between women, girls, and their mothers to investigate how many females replicated the same patterns developed in early childhood friendships into adulthood. The authors' intention is to show the impact of many of these behaviors on friendships at various ages.

602. Heilbrun, Alfred B., Jr. *Stress and the Risk of Psychobiological Disorder in College Women*. Lanham, MD: University Press of America, 1998. 313p. bibliog. index. ISBN 0761808469; 0761808450pa.

Heilbrun, professor emeritus of psychology at Emory University, investigates three stress-related disorders in college women, anorexia nervosa, menstrual dysfunction, and type A personality characteristics, in relationship to health issues, particularly stress and cardiovascular diseases. Heilbrun conducted three separate studies during the 1980s and the 1990s and discusses the challenges of his various methodologies in an entire chapter. The rest of the chapters focus on the relationship of stress to the previously mentioned disorders as well as the relationship between stress and the risk of cardiovascular diseases and include tables from questionnaires and other methods that were used in the studies. This title is recommended for mental health professionals, developmental psychologists, psychobiologists, and graduate students in these fields.

A different perspective on stress-related behavior is discussed in *The Center of the Web: Women and Solitude* (State University of New York Press, 1993), edited by Delese Wear. This collection of essays defines the personal meaning of solitude to women in relationship to their careers and personal lives. The basic premise of solitude, as stated by the editor, comprises a space to think, reflect, and create away from others. The majority of the nineteen contributors, primarily from academic institutions, explore the meaning and roles of solitude in their lives from a personal perspective. The essays are loosely grouped into three categories: solitude and identity, solitude and culture, and solitude and work. James H. Humphrey's *Stress among Women in Modern Society* (Charles C. Thomas, 1992) presents a general overview of women's stress experiences that will be of interest to undergraduates in psychology. He outlines the changing status of women in the 1980s and how changing roles and expectations contribute to stress, identifies various issues that more commonly affect women, and includes various strategies to cope with managing stress.

603. Henwood, Karen, Christine Griffin, and Ann Phoenix, eds. *Standpoints and Differences: Essays in the Practice of Feminist Psychology*. London: Sage, 1998. 240p. (Gender and Psychology). bibliog. index. ISBN 0761954430; 0761954449pa.

The editors have selected essays that debate and deconstruct psychology using feminism and poststructuralism in order to further establish theories and practices. Many of the contributors are British, in various fields within psychology. Many of the essays touch on one of three critical themes: diverse ways of engaging in feminist politics; issues of power regarding experience, voice, engagement, and authority; and generating new research strategies. The essays are arranged into three sections: modes of arguing/theoretical positions, diverse positions, and reflections on theory and practice. This book is geared to students and researchers in feminist and social psychology, sociology, women and gender studies, and epistemology.

Ilene J. Philipson's *On the Shoulders of Women: The Feminization of Psychotherapy* (Guilford Press, 1993) explores the feminization of the profession, specifically focusing on the field of psychotherapy. Philipson uses this book, which is partly a personal exploration and partly a historical reconstruction, as an "effort to understand the reasons for and the consequences of the feminization of psychotherapy" (p. 9) in the context of social evolution. Combining both theoretical and practical concepts, she integrates sociology, clinical psychology, and feminism while surveying the historical progression of psychotherapy. In *Powerful Wisdom: Voices of Distinguished Women Psychotherapists* (Jossey-Bass, 1993), authors Lourene A. Nevels and Judith Coche developed a questionnaire to identify career developments experienced by 192 female psychotherapists. Of interest to practitioners, clinicians, historians, and students, "*Powerful Wisdom* progresses from a general and theoretical examination of the crucial issues for female adult development, through direct responses from the women represented in our questionnaire, and examination of future issues and directions" (p. xvii). Janis Bohan's *Seldom Seen, Rarely Heard: Women's Place in Psychology* (Westview Press, 1992), a volume in the series Psychology and Gender Therapy, provides a collection of essays in the format of a textbook highlighting women's scholarly contributions to the profession as well as addressing the "neglect of women and women's concerns in psychological theory, research, and practice" (p. 2). This is a good resource for undergraduates and graduate students on the exclusion and marginalization of women in psychology. A related resource by Bohan is *Re-placing Women in Psychology: Readings toward a More Inclusive History* (Kendall/Hunt, 1995).

Michele A. Paludi's *Exploring/Teaching the Psychology of Women: A Manual of Resources* (State University of New York Press, 1990) provides a list of resources and suggestions for outlines, syllabi, discussions, and activities. Categories include foundations, life-span development issues, women's health, achievements and work, the victimization of women, and interpersonal relationships. In the second edition (State University of New York Press, 1996), Paludi presents key components to incorporate into a psychology course. Paludi divides the information into three areas that she considers essential in teaching a course: critical thinking, integration of knowledge, and multiculturalism. Each section provides an introduction on how teachers can incorporate concepts into the class and then includes various techniques and resources that can be used to present different pieces of the issue.

Shaping the Future of Feminist Psychology: Education, Research, and Practice (American Psychological Association, 1997), edited by Judith Worell and Norine G. Johnson, presents essays from a conference on "Education and Training in Feminist Practice." Chapters explore a variety of principles to enhance development in areas of psychology such as assessment, voice, curriculum development, and diversity.

604. Howard, Judith A., and Jocelyn Hollander. *Gendered Situations, Gendered Selves: A Gender Lens on Social Psychology.* Thousand Oaks, CA: Sage. 1997. 208p. (Gender Lens). bibliog. index. ISBN 083956037; 083956045pa.

Howard and Hollander examine three major theories in social psychology through "a gender lens": social exchange, social cognition, and symbolic interaction. The first two chapters frame the discussion of social psychology, including how gender, race, and class have simultaneously contributed to, influenced, and been overlooked in the field. The next three chapters discuss the major points, issues, and concerns within social exchange theory, including behaviorism and social learning; social cognition, including the relationship of knowledge acquisition to social forces as well as individual process in contributing to change; and symbolic interaction, where key concepts of association with symbols, society, and individual interpretations of matters are highlighted. The authors examine connections and common themes between altruism and aggression in another chapter, finally concluding with a review of "key themes of a gendered lens on social psychology

. . . to explain patterns of social interaction" (p. 149). This resource reflects the evolution of gender debates within social psychology and will be of interest to advanced undergraduates and graduate students.

Additional titles explore gender and social psychology. In *The Compulsion to Create: A Psychoanalytic Study of Women Artists* (Routledge, 1993) by Susan Kavaler-Adler, the author conducts psychobiographies of selected women writers—Sylvia Plath, Anaïs Nin, Charlotte and Emily Brontë, Emily Dickinson, and Edith Sitwell—using object relations theory. Some of the common themes Kavaler-Adler notes about these writers are the compulsion to create, how the creative process is revealed in their work, and the relationship these women had with their fathers. This title will be of interest to those in object relations theory.

A related title by Barbara A. Kerr is *Smart Girls Two: A New Psychology of Girls, Women, and Giftedness* (Great Potential Press, 1994). (The first edition appeared in 1985.) Kerr revisits barriers faced by a group of bright women to see what changes have occurred since her first study twenty years ago. Eighty-three pages have been added to tell this story of the experiences of the women in this group and the changes in perceptions of giftedness. As educational and social changes have developed to include talented and gifted females, new research has evolved to address career, self-actualizing, and issues in achievement. The most recent edition, *Smart Girls: A New Psychology of Girls, Women and Giftedness* (Great Potential Press, 1997), includes minimal revisions since *Smart Girls Two*. This is an excellent resource for those in education, psychology, women's studies, and sociology.

605. Jack, Dana C. *Silencing the Self: Women and Depression.* Cambridge, MA: Harvard University Press, 1991. 256p. ISBN (OP); 006097527Xpa.

Jack investigates a small group of women with regard to the complexities of depression, which she conceives as a multicomplex disorder, usually a combination of physical, biological, and psychological obstacles of listening. Jack states, "In order to hear the message of these depressed women, we need to take into account their social context, which includes the lived reality of women's subordinate status as well as cultural history that has demeaned women's orientations" (p. 27). Redefining the concept of depression, Jack begins to explore common experiences shared between these women regarding their relationships with men, their loss of self, and thus the loss of any sense of control or power. The limited study reflects the need for further study of women's depression on many levels. This title is appropriate for students of sociology, developmental psychology, and women's studies and those researching interpersonal relationships.

Women and Depression: Risk Factors and Treatment Issues, edited by Ellen McGrath, Gwendolyn P. Keita, Bonnie R. Strickland, and Nancy F. Russo (American Psychological Association, 1990), is the final report of the American Psychological Association's National Task Force on Women and Depression. The task force reviewed the literature on depression, focusing on factors that contribute to women's depression. The work is divided into four sections. Section 1 focuses on risk factors and research issues related to women and depression. The second section explores various factors that can create depression in women, such as biology and social and economic status. Section 3 reviews various types of treatments. The final section discusses issues relating to specific populations, such as adolescents, the elderly, lesbians, poor women, and those suffering physical abuse.

In *Sex Differences in Depression* (Stanford University Press, 1990), Susan Nolen-Hoeksema, a consultant to the previously mentioned task force, reviews various studies that have been conducted on differences between the sexes in depression. In addition, she comments on various theories that have been developed and adapted to evaluate depression, such as the links and relationships made with biological and social influences, and even some cross-cultural comparisons. Angela Mitchell and Kennise Herring examine depression in black women in *What the Blues Is All About: Black Women Overcoming Stress and Depression* (Perigee Books, 1998). Using case studies of seven women, the authors provide an overview of what depression means for black women. One chapter focuses on stereotypes and role expectations placed upon black women and how these can contribute to depression.

606. Josselson, Ruthellen. *Revising Herself: The Story of Women's Identity from College to Midlife*. New York: Oxford University Press, 1996. 298p. bibliog. index. ISBN 0195108396.

Winner of the Delta Kappa Gamma International Educators Award, Josselson follows a diverse group of thirty women from college to midlife in this longitudinal study. The author wished to discover how women alter their lives between late adolescence and mature adulthood, and also how cultural ideas regarding women during the late 1960s and early 1970s affected women coming of age during this time. Josselson places the thirty women into four groups based on their identity or chosen path in part 1; reviews their experiences during a twenty-year period in part 2; and reassembles the women to analyze changes made after the twenty-year period in part 3. The author discusses a variety of topics and issues that women face, including career and personal decisions, self-assessment, and changing identity. Students in adult development, women's studies, and sociology should consider this informative work.

Clinical psychologist and psychoanalyst Joan Offerman-Zuckerberg edited *Critical Psychophysical Passages in the Life of a Woman: A Psychodynamic Perspective* (Plenum Publishers, 1988), which includes contributions from scholars representing the fields of psychology, education, and health. Essays in part 1 assess early developmental issues, including body image, mother-daughter relationships, and the theories of female development. Parts 2 and 3 explore issues relating to pregnancy, such as the impact of both biochemical and psychological changes during pregnancy and their relationship to a woman's psyche, as well as how childbirth and mothering contribute to changes in the concept of self. In the final sections, contributors explore a range of topics from menopause to cosmetic surgery to eating disorders to infertility. Terri E. Apter identifies midlife (forties and fifties) as a time when women come of age, when they simultaneously begin to trust themselves as well as question their accomplishments, in *Secret Paths: Women in the New Midlife* (Norton, 1995). Apter arranges her interviews with eighty mostly white American women into four lifestyle groups: traditional (conventional feminine framework), innovative (women who deliberately take nontraditional jobs), expansive (women who continue to grow and do not limit themselves), and protesting (resistance). She explores the changes, conflicting desires, and expectations that create complex dilemmas for these women, noting commonly shared experiences. Students in psychology, human development, and women's studies classes will find this title of interest.

607. Laidlaw, Toni A., and Cheryl Malmo, eds. *Healing Voices: Feminist Approaches to Therapy with Women*. San Francisco: Jossey-Bass, 1990. 334p. (Jossey-Bass Social and Behavioral Series). index. ISBN 155542225X.

The editors have chosen thirteen essays that discuss a variety of healing techniques that can be used in therapy. The majority of contributors are Canadian and include information on "dream work, guided and nondirective imagery, body work, imagery, drawings, photos, stories, metaphors, ceremonies, rituals, writing, chair work, ego state therapy, hypnosis, workshops and group work" (p. 320). The book is arranged in four parts. The first looks at different ways women overcome many barriers, the second at how reality and unconscious mind contribute to therapy, the third at the role of memory and feeling in traumatic events, and the fourth at how to integrate various techniques to assist in the healing process of therapy. Each chapter has an overview of the technique and how it worked with one client or participant.

The following two titles focus on healing from a Latina perspective. In *Latina Realities: Essays on Healing, Migration, and Sexuality* (Westview Press, 1997), Oliva M. Espin presents a personal collection of previously published essays from 1984 to 1996 in which she takes on several voices as psychologist, storyteller, and healer. *Latina Realities* incorporates practical advice, reflections on teaching, and theory to better understand issues affecting Latina immigrants. In *Women as Healers, Women as Patients: Mental Health Care and Traditional Healing in Puerto Rico* (Westview Press, 1992), Joan Koss-Chioino discusses how alternative options for women's mental health can be integrated with cultural considerations in Puerto Rico. Data are derived from the Therapist-Spiritualist Training Project, a program the author designed to "create a bridge between conventional biomedical health cares—mental health care in particular—and the popular healing system, *Espiritismo*" (p. 7). Beginning with an introduction to Puerto Rican culture, Koss-Chioino highlights major activities and events from her project, which she then combines with ethnographic analysis and personal interpretations.

608. Landrine, Hope, ed. *Bringing Cultural Diversity to Feminist Psychology: Theory, Research, and Practice*. Washington, DC: American Psychological Association, 1995. 463p. bibliog. index. ISBN 1557982929.

Twenty-nine contributors representing African, Asian, European, Native, and Latina Americans collaborate in seventeen chapters on various issues concerning the inclusion of diversity in feminist psychology. The authors, including professionals, practitioners, and academics (including students), use a variety of methods and approaches to present an understanding of feminist psychology and explore the best models and methods to use for all women. The structure and topics differ for each chapter, as Landrine allowed authors to address issues they considered most relevant and to make their own observations and conclusions about the issues. The essays are grouped into four categories and include an introduction for each section. Essays in part 1 discuss cultural diversity in theory and methodology for feminist psychology. Part 2 covers cultural diversity in feminist practice in psychology, and chapters in part 3 focus on the psychology of women within four ethnic groups. Part 4 considers ethnicity and selected research topics in feminist psychology. This is an essential resource for investigating issues of diversity in feminist psychology.

Another title discussing issues of ethnicity is *Women's Ethnicities: Journeys through Psychology* (Westview Press, 1996). Editors Karen F. Wyche and Faye J. Crosby compiled seventeen essays from American women psychologists who address issues of diversity and ethnicity. Primarily focusing on the dilemmas gender and ethnicity present to academics and practitioners in psychology, these essays investigate how ethnicity affects the experiences of women differently. *Jewish Women Speak Out: Expanding the Boundaries of Psychology* (Canopy Press, 1995), edited by Kayla Weiner and Arinna Moon, includes papers from an international conference on Judaism, feminism, and psychology in 1992. Several of the contributors have an affiliation with one of the Jewish religions, thus providing a voice toward the interrelation of religion, identity, and related issues in psychology, including approaches to working with Jewish women in therapy.

609. Leadbeater, Bonnie J. Ross, and Niobe Way, eds. *Urban Girls: Resisting Stereo-types, Creating Identities*. New York: New York University Press, 1996. 409p. bibliog. index. ISBN 0814751075; 0814751083pa.

Leadbeater and Way have selected contributors who incorporate a variety of quantitative and qualitative research methods into this excellent critical work to show how urban, poor, and working-class adolescent girls define their goals and perceive their identities. The essays explore how girls deal with various obstacles; resist failure; experience racism, sexism, and stereotypes; cultivate their sexuality; and view themselves as women. Insights into the girls' relationships with their families, friends, and their own children further the discussion. The contributors, academics in the fields of psychology, sociology, ethnography, and demography, employ different method-ologies, including questionnaires, survey data, focus groups, and interviews. Leadbeater and Way organize this source into the following categories: identity development, family relationships, peer relationships, mentoring relationships, health risks, and career development. The editors introduce each section with a short overview essay that discusses common themes and issues for that section. This work is best suited for undergraduate and graduate courses in psychology, sociology, eco-nomics, and women's studies, as well as scholars of policy analysis seeking new approaches to prevent poverty.

Women, Girls, and Achievement (Captus University Publications, 1994), edited by Joanne Gallivan, Sharon D. Crozier, and Vivian M. Lalande, resulted from a one-day workshop of the Canadian Psychological Association's Section on Women and Psychology in 1991. Through per-sonal reflection, statistical calculations, in-depth interviews, and large-scale questionnaires, con-tributors address achievement from a broad array of experiences. Essays cover a variety of topics, including minorities, adolescents, self-esteem, careers, and leadership. Maggie Mulqueen examines sex-role socialization for women in the United States, focusing on the conflict between a woman's desire to express both her competence and femininity, in *On Our Own Terms: Redefining Com-petence and Femininity* (State University of New York Press, 1992). This work is best suited for graduate students in women's studies.

610. Lerman, Hannah, and Natalie Porter, eds. *Feminist Ethics in Psychotherapy*. New York: Springer, 1990. 267p. bibliog. index. ISBN 0826162908.

This seminal work focuses on ethical issues in feminist therapy that evolved from the work of the Feminist Therapy Institute (FTI). The members of FTI were the founders of the Code of Ethics, a document to address concerns of ethical behavior and therapy that was approved by the group in 1987. The chapters in each section explore many of the basic issues of professional responsibilities, personal dynamics, accountability, and the use and abuse of power. Arranged into six sections, the issues focus on how feminism provides an ethical construct in therapy, ethics regarding power and therapists (when relationships overlap from professional to personal), per-sonal accountability of the therapist, issues of ethics and oppression, and the therapist and society. After the publication of this book, FTI updated and revised the code in 1999 (see http://www .feministtherapyinstitute.org/ethics.htm). This is an important work for graduate students, practi-tioners, and others working with clients in a counseling/therapeutic setting.

Ethical Decision Making in Therapy: Feminist Perspectives (Guilford Press, 1995), edited by Elizabeth J. Rave and Carolyn C. Larson (who also contributed to the previous title), explores issues of ethics and the work of the FTI. The contributors are primarily academics from the United States, and the chapters discuss issues of labeling, finance and cost of treatment, overlapping relationships such as mentoring or client-patient, violence against women, issues of reproduction, problems with the medical model, when conflicts arise on care decisions, how therapists care for themselves, and considerations for the future. *Representing the Other: A Feminism and Psychology Reader* (Sage, 1996), edited by Sue Wilkinson and Celia Kitzinger, provides a British perspective. This title includes mostly reprinted essays and seeks to address the conflicts and perceived ethical dilemmas that are faced when one is "representing" another group. The perspective of privilege confounding or misrepresenting the experience of "others" when addressing issues of ethnicity, gender, sexual orientation, or disability has been a topic of concern for many feminists and researchers.

611. Malson, Helen. *The Thin Woman: Feminism, Post-structuralism, and the Social Psychology of Anorexia Nervosa.* London: Routledge, 1998. 234p. (Women and Psychology). bibliog. index. ISBN 0415163323; 0415163331pa.

Malson provides a multileveled analysis of anorexia nervosa, questions the concept of anorexia as an "individual pathology," and urges scholars to develop new frameworks to better assess the multitude of issues associated with the disorder, as well as analyze the limitations of the current understanding of anorexia. The work is arranged into three sections. The author includes selections of interviews with women anorexics and discusses the theoretical concepts and constructs of anorexia based on Lacan, Foucault, and feminist psychoanalytic theory in part 1. Considering the institutional pathology of thinness, which she refers to as "a genealogy," from medical, social, psychological, and cultural perspectives, Malson discusses how cultural acceptance of female characteristics contributes to this pathology in part 2. In the final section, the author considers the customary perceptions of thinness and the implications of the body in its relationship to anorexia in light of gender and cultural expectations, eating, self-image, and self-destruction. Appendices include interview questions.

Marta Robertson explores new ways of understanding anorexia nervosa, incorporating ideas from Foucault, Lacan, and several psychoanalysts into her analysis, in *Starving in the Silences: An Exploration of Anorexia Nervosa* (New York University Press, 1992). Robertson questions whether anorexia constitutes a psychiatric illness or another example of women's oppression, arguing not only that the label restricts recovery, but also that various alternative methods are necessary to aid recovery. A lengthy bibliography is included.

612. Mens-Verhulst, Janneke van, Karlein Schreurs, and Liesbeth Woertman, eds. *Daughtering and Mothering: Female Subjectivity Reanalyzed.* New York: Routledge, 1993. 170p. bibliog. index. ISBN 0415086493; 0415086507pa.

Twenty contributors from six different countries provide international perspectives on daughters and mothering. The research presents theoretical and cultural viewpoints, from Freud to fairy tales, and examines the roles of mothers and daughters and how this interaction affects other female relationships: "This book provides analysis of many aspects of mother-daughter relationships that were hitherto neglected or ignored" (p. xiv). Using multidisciplinary approaches, the essays explore relationship issues that arise in family therapy practice. The collection is arranged into three sections, with an introductory essay to each section. The frameworks in many of the essays provide new insights to understanding and appreciating the complexity of the relationship of mothers and daughters. This book will be of use for researchers in women's studies, psychology, family studies, social work, and sociology.

Several additional titles cover the topic of motherhood and mother-daughter relationships. Sue L. Villani and Jane Ryan, in *Motherhood at the Crossroads: Meeting the Challenge of a Changing Role* (Plenum Press, 1997), consider the many psychological and sociological myths assigned to mothers and motherhood. Along with discussing these myths, the authors surveyed approximately 200 women and interviewed more than 50 to determine women's attitudes about motherhood. Kim Chernin uses stories and experiences from her clients to support her analysis of the seven stages that women go through with their mothers in *The Woman Who Gave Birth to Her Mother: Seven Stages of Change in Women's Lives* (Viking, 1998). The seven stages identified by Chernin include idealizing, revision, blaming, forgiving, identifying, letting go, and giving birth. The author argues that through this process, women often recognize both the psychological and emotional influences of their mother as well as the daughters who reconnect with their mothers and teach the mother how to become a mother. Elizabeth Debold, Marie Wilson, and Idelisse Malavé explore the changing relationship between mothers and daughters in *Mother Daughter Revolution: From Betrayal to Power* (Addison-Wesley, 1993). The authors discuss various issues, including the impact of myths on relationships, expectations between mothers and daughters, and many of the silent societal messages that contribute to mother-daughter relationships. This title was slightly revised the following year under the title *Mother and Daughter Revolution: From Good Girls to Great Women*.

A variation of the exploration of the mother-daughter relationship is *The Mother-Daughter Relationship: Echoes through Time* (Jason Aronson, 1997), edited by Gerd H. Fenchel. Seventeen essays discuss various aspects of the mother-daughter relationship at different stages of development. Using clinical examples of various developmental themes, such as envy, identification, and competition, the essays show how psychotherapy can contribute positively to these relationships.

613. Miner, Valerie, and Helen Longino, eds. *Competition: A Feminist Taboo?* New York: Feminist Press at the City University of New York, 1987. 260p. bibliog. ISBN 0935312757; 0935312749pa.

This collection of essays challenges the reader regarding the nature of competition in women's lives: "The first step toward understanding is to acknowledge the existence of competition in our family lives and in our public spheres" (p. 1). Measuring success takes on a different dimension when considering women and self-esteem and women as threats and rivals. The essays explore issues surrounding competition beyond the realm of sport as relationships between women as sisters, mothers, daughters, friends, and colleagues are critiqued; various settings (work, home, academia, and society) provide opportunities for commentaries, and viewpoints from economic, social, and personal perspectives allow various levels and types of competition to be scrutinized. Part 1 is a reprinted article that comments on how women are subtly and not so subtly socialized to compete and how they can interpret and react to competitive situations in everyday life. The second part looks at the structure of competition in society and within families through personal stories. Essays in the final part investigate the role competition plays in women's lives within the family, friendships, and work to home. Trivializing the impact of competition in women's experience or reducing the focus of competition only to physical appearance contributes to the silence about issues of competition between women.

Several other titles examine competition in women's lives. In *The Secret between Us: Women and Competition* (Little, Brown, 1991), Laura Tracy explores various techniques women use to compete, including a subculture of personal rewards and punishments, along with various dilemmas and role playing that support a subtle denial of competition. Competition plays a role in relationships between mothers, daughters, sisters, friends, and partners, resulting in behaviors such as polite acquiescence and deferral and affecting issues such as trust, power, and honesty among these associations.

Kate Fillion unmasks the myth of women's superiority in nurturing relationships in *Lip Service: The Truth about Women's Darker Side in Love, Sex, and Friendship* (HarperCollins, 1996). Relying on interviews that she conducted with both women and men (it is implied that more women than men were interviewed), Fillion explores the contradictions, restrictions, biases, and stereotypes that contribute positively and negatively to women's relationships. Fillion observes that women have adaptive behaviors that can often contribute to passive-aggressive behaviors, including the tendency to portray oneself as a victim or martyr, all of which are negative contributions to friendships. Harriet G. Lerner, a well-known psychologist and author of several self-help books, explores female behavior expectations and the variety of deceptions that occur in relationships in *The Dance of Deception: Pretending and Truth-Telling in Women's Lives* (HarperCollins, 1993). Lerner comments on various ways individuals deceive themselves and in relationships with others. This book is a good overview for students and others interested in some basics of interpersonal relations.

614. Mirkin, Marsha P., ed. *Women in Context: Toward a Feminist Reconstruction of Psychotherapy*. New York: Guilford Press, 1994. 502p. bibliog. index. ISBN 0898620953.

The essays in this book, which address women's experiences in therapy, are arranged in four parts. Part 1 serves as a foundation for presenting a variety of "contexts" that are integral parts of women's experience. This includes a discussion on the conflicts in access and delivery of services in therapy: who has the power (men) to control the access to the services versus who has the needs (women) to use or direct others to the services. Further deliberations in this part incorporate considerations of gender, race, class, and sexual orientation within family relationships as well as the influences of misogyny and homophobia as constructs to maintain women in inferior positions. The second part examines sociopolitical influences on various stages in the life cycle; chapters discuss adolescents and women on the margin (lesbians, the aged, bisexuals, stepmothers, and single women). Part 3 covers major concerns in health such as breast cancer, AIDS, abortion, reproduction, technology/politics, and menopause. The bulk of the essays in the final section examine various issues from the sociopolitical context that influence therapy. Discussion includes factors that affect race/family therapy; violence; poor homeless women; and economic issues. This critical resource is suitable for educators, practitioners, and researchers in mental health, social work, psychotherapy, policy, and women's studies.

A related title is *Feminism and Psychotherapy: Reflections on Contemporary Theories and Practices* (Sage, 1998), edited by I. Bruna Seu and M. Colleen Heenan. The majority of the contributors are practitioners from Great Britain whose essays serve as critical investigations and philosophical inquiries into how feminist psychotherapy contributes to the dynamics of well-being, the conflict with traditional therapy and society, and issues of inequality.

615. O'Connell, Agnes N., and Nancy F. Russo, eds. *Models of Achievement: Reflections of Eminent Women in Psychology*. Hillsdale, NJ: Lawrence Erlbaum Associates, 1983–2001. 023053134pa (v. 1); ISBN 0805800832; 080580322Xpa (v. 2, 1988); ISBN 0805835563; 0805803271pa (v. 3, 2001).

This three-volume set provides a wealth of information on fifty-three preeminent women, mostly from the United States, and their contributions to psychology. The first volume of the set, published in 1983, did not appear in *Women's Studies: A Recommended Core Bibliography: 1980–1985* (Libraries Unlimited, 1986) and thus is covered here. In the first volume, the editors include a history of psychology along with the contributions of women to the profession. Biographical sketches of seventeen prominent female psychologists who contributed to the field at the turn of the twentieth century are presented, many compiled by the women in the sketches. The final section contains a table comparing the women in their achievements, education, and professional and family lives, with commentary and analysis. Volume 2 discusses the careers of seventeen women who entered the field of psychology in the early/middle part of the twentieth century. The editors provide a chapter on the historical/cultural background of the times, and each woman created her personal story highlighting "how historical events such as the Great Depression, World War II, and the women's movement have affected lives, opportunities, and achievements" (p. xii). Representing a range of backgrounds, experiences, and disciplines, the women selected for this volume have achieved an impressive research record and contributed to the profession as leaders and experts under some very challenging situations. As in volume 1, there is a section comparing the educational and professional experiences of these women. The final volume, organized like the previous volumes, includes autobiographies of nineteen women from the middle to the later part of the twentieth century. These women, coming from a wide range of backgrounds, have also accomplished remarkable achievements. As in the two previous volumes, there are tables comparing the educational and personal achievements of the women.

In *Essential Papers on the Psychology of Women* (New York University Press, 1990), Claudia Zanardi presents twenty-three previously published papers on feminism, psychoanalytic theory, and sexuality, representing both classical and current theories. The book is arranged into two sections, of which the first focuses on psychoanalytic views of female sexuality. Section 2, on feminism and psychoanalysis, is further divided geographically to include European and American theories. Zanardi's introduction provides a solid background to some of the basic developments in this area. Joan Raphael-Leff edited *Female Experience: Three Generations of British Women: Psychoanalysts on Work with Women* (Routledge, 1997), which includes essays providing a brief overview of the historical trends of the British Psychoanalytic Society. This title focuses on the analysis of physical and biological issues.

616. O'Connor, Noreen, and Joanna Ryan. *Wild Desires and Mistaken Identities: Lesbianism and Psychoanalysis.* New York: Columbia University Press, 1994. 315p. (Between Men—Between Women: Lesbian and Gay Studies). bibliog. index. ISBN 0231100221; 023110023Xpa.

O'Connor and Ryan, both psychotherapists, critically address questions of sexuality and gender identity, focusing on both practice and theory. Using a variety of approaches, the authors challenge psychology's designation of homosexuality as a form of pathology: "There should be theoretical and conceptual space in psychoanalytic theory for non-pathological possibilities in relation to homosexuality" (p. 10). They then proceed to evaluate various texts, including ones from Freud, Derrida, and Foucault, as well as theorists in object relations, gender identity, and sexuality, to understand the construct of lesbians in relationship to psychoanalysis and social context. Surveying a wide range of historical, sociological, and psychological literature for psychoanalytic ideas about lesbians and sexuality, O'Connor and Ryan address tensions within the profession regarding homosexuality: "Our aim in writing this book, therefore, is to initiate a dialogue about psychoanalytic theories of female homosexuality, and to identify the fundamental issues that have to be addressed by anyone who wishes to work or think within a psychoanalytic framework, but does not subscribe to the universal pathology of homosexuality" (p. 12). *Wild Desires* is a critical resource for clinicians and therapists.

Adria E. Schwartz provides a review of clinical concepts affecting the psychiatric experience of lesbians in *Sexual Subjects: Lesbians, Gender, and Psychoanalysis* (Routledge, 1998). She acknowledges, "There is a tension inherent in writing about lesbians that pervades *Sexual Subjects*. There is the acknowledgment of the ongoing struggle of lesbians to affirm their subjectivities and their sexual/romantic practice within a psychoanalytic and surrounding culture in which they have been largely invisible" (p. xii). Schwartz interweaves discussions of queer theory and postmodernism and their relationship to sexuality in her analysis.

617. O'Connor, Pat. *Friendships between Women: A Critical Review*. New York: Guilford Press, 1992. 224p. (Guilford Series on Personal Relationships). ISBN 0898629764; 0898629810pa.

O'Connor's work provides a partial literature review concerning women's relationships and friendships. Having first presented an overview of previous research that has been conducted on friendship, O'Connor probes topics such as the costs and benefits of establishing and maintaining friendships and why research on women's friendships is both important and valuable. This book is meant to "explore the social and cultural conditions which facilitate and/or inhibit the emergence of particular types of friendship relationships" (p. 7). O'Connor explores the possibility of developing a theory of friendship and examines the role of friendship in the lives of married, elderly, and single women. She further analyzes the importance of friendship versus family and other relationships. Undergraduates, graduates, and researchers in women's studies, family studies, and interpersonal relationships will find this title useful. *Black and White Women as Friends: Building Cross-Race Friendships* (Hampton Press, 1998) by Mary McCullough explores friendships between African American and white women. The first two chapters investigate various types of friendships represented in historical and comparative literature. The third chapter reviews the author's methodology. Following these chapters, the author explores various themes and issues in friendship between races and offers insight to understand some of the underlying tensions that occur.

618. Pipher, Mary B. *Reviving Ophelia: Saving the Selves of Adolescent Girls*. New York: Putnam, 1994. 304p. bibliog. index. ISBN (OP); 0345392825pa.

Pipher explores the multitude of changes and experiences that affect adolescent girls in today's society and examines three main factors contributing to this susceptible time, physical development, cultural pressures, and parental distancing. Using personal and clinical experiences, Pipher provides disturbing examples of cultural reinforcements of the expectations of males and females. She reviews various aspects that influence girls' lives and development, including families, mothers, fathers, depression, body image, drugs, alcohol, and sex. She also raises many other relevant issues, such as the need for the American Psychological Association and other organizations in the fields of psychology and psychiatry to establish guidelines and methods to work with adolescent girls. This book is considered a classic work and should be read by all students, especially those in psychology, education, sociology, and women's studies. In *Adios, Barbie: Young Women Write about Body Image and Identity* (Seal Press, 1998), editor Ophira Edut, founder and editor of *Hear Us Emerging Sister* magazine, provides twenty-eight essays mostly written by freelance writers in their twenties who explore their impressions on weight, sexuality, body image, race, ethnicity, and power as they consider interpretations of body and women's relationship to their bodies.

619. Polster, Miriam F. *Eve's Daughters: The Forbidden Heroism of Women*. San Francisco: Jossey-Bass, 1992. 209p. bibliog. index. ISBN 1555424643.

Drawing upon the character of Eve and other women in mythology, Polster explores new interpretations of female heroes. From a female perspective, the author identifies three components of female heroism: the evolution and concept of a female hero; the intellectual, social, and physical expectations of the female hero; and the patterns of women's heroism, based on exclusion and inclusion. Polster provides characteristics of heroic behavior: "Women have been heroic in all ages; they would have had to be. This book may serve to remind us of their particular heroism, based on different values and expressed in a different manner" (p. 13). Kathleen Noble in *The Sound of a Silver Horn: Reclaiming the Heroism in Contemporary Women's Lives* (Fawcett Book

Group, 1995) provides additional insight into female heroes. Noble identifies four characteristics that exemplify the female hero and includes results from a small survey of women asked about these characteristics. Additionally, the author provides examples of female heroic stories.

620. Russell, Denise. *Women, Madness, and Medicine*. Cambridge, MA: Polity Press, 1995. 195p. bibliog. index. ISBN 0745612601; 074561261Xpa.

Focusing on a medical perspective, this concise title uses epistemological inquiry to review and explore the history and status of biological psychiatry and how the treatment affects women. The author identifies biological psychiatry (also known as medical psychiatry) as a "grouping of theories and practices postulating a distinction between madness, mental illness or disorder on the one side, and sanity or normality on the other" (p. 1). The medical and social beliefs on the relationship of mind to body that were developed in the nineteenth century continue to contribute to problems that exist in psychiatry today, specifically for women. Russell connects the medical profession's use of concepts within mental illness with changes in society as a means to keep women restrained by essence of their reproductive nature. She analyzes how the third revised edition of the *Diagnostic and Statistical Manual of Mental Disorders* (DSM-III-R) was constructed, revealing how descriptions and diagnoses contribute to women's treatment for mental illness. Russell also discusses the restricted focus of the DSM, including why such conditions as depression and PMS are treated within psychiatry, not gynecology. To further explore the context of biological psychology, Russell compares the philosophy of madness as constructed by Phyllis Chesler and Luce Irigaray and briefly examines creativity and the literary construct of women and madness. This title is recommended for upper-level undergraduates and graduate students.

In *Women's Health: Psychological and Social Perspectives* (Sage, 1998), Christina Lee approaches the topic of women's health from a broad social-psychological perspective. Lee argues that four issues—hormones, motherhood, women's work, and women as objects—erroneously reflect aspects of women's social position. The list of references and a variety of case studies from all over the world make this title useful for upper-level undergraduates, graduate students, and researchers.

621. Sang, Barbara, Joyce Warshow, and Adrienne J. Smith, eds. *Lesbians at Midlife: The Creative Transition*. San Francisco: Spinsters Book Co., 1991. 268p. ISBN 0933216777.

This work features a diverse range of materials, including poems, personal narratives, essays, and research studies, representing the many voices of lesbians between the ages of forty and sixty. The selected materials celebrate growing older, being lesbian, and embarking on a life transformation. The editors, all psychotherapists, arrange the contributions according to common themes, such as relating as daughters, relating as mothers, changing bodies, rediscovering creativity and spirituality, and preparing for the future, which explores lesbians' physical, financial, and legal concerns in later life. Therapists and others working with a lesbian clientele will find this resource of interest. Monika Kehoe discusses information gathered from a questionnaire featuring eighty-seven questions focusing on issues of sexual preference, self-determination, the use of free time, and the needs of lesbian women in *Lesbians over 60 Speak for Themselves* (Haworth Press, 1989).

622. Stanton, Annette L, and Sheryle J. Gallant, eds. *The Psychology of Women's Health: Progress and Challenges in Research and Application*. Washington, DC: American Psychological Association, 1995. 649p. bibliog. index. ISBN 1557982961.

Stanton and Gallant include fifteen essays surveying the current status of women's psychological health and directions for future research. Contributors are primarily academics from the United States. Many of the essays are quite lengthy, incorporating biopsychological, psychosociological, and cultural contributions, along with extensive discussions concerning the methodological limitations of previous research in the area of women's health. The essays are arranged into five parts: an overview, common diseases of women, gynecological and reproductive issues, health and habits, and future topics such as aging and health care policy. Each section includes a literature review identifying research that has been conducted, issues relevant to the topic, and how women are included, treated, or represented. In the introduction, the editors state the importance of mental health research on women: "Specifically, it is important to understand the criticisms that have been leveled against the prevailing body of thought regarding women's health, as well as to be aware of the exciting initiatives designed to redress some of the deficiencies in earlier models and policies" (p. 4). Earlier research reflected the opinion "that scientific and professional treatments of women's health have served a) to perpetuate the view of male as normative . . . [and] b) focus on female productive function to the exclusion of other aspects of health" (p. 6). Many of the contributors incorporate various theoretical analyses, thus providing new outlooks on understanding women's health. Tables and graphs provide a wealth of data. Graduate students, practitioners, and researchers in psychology and related behavioral and social sciences, as well as health policy administrators, will find this resource very stimulating.

Psychopharmacology and Women: Sex, Gender, and Hormones (American Psychiatric Press, 1996), edited by Margaret E. Jensvold, Uriel Halbreich, and Jean A. Hamilton, provides nineteen essays varying in length and coverage, arranged into four sections. Section 1 focuses on gender differences in the effects of medications on mental and physiological functions. Section 2 looks at how drugs affect various parts of women's reproductive cycles. Essays in section 3 discuss issues of medicating women with depression, anxiety disorders, schizophrenia, and substance use disorders. The essays in the final section critique and discuss research methodologies that are used in various types of drug testing. *Psychological Perspectives on Women's Health* (Taylor & Francis, 1994), edited by Vincent J. Adesso, Diane M. Reddy, and Raymond Fleming, addresses issues in health and aging, stress and related diseases, drug use and body image, menstruation/pain, sexuality, and future directions in women's health.

623. Tavris, Carol. *The Mismeasure of Women: Why Women Are Not the Better Sex, the Inferior Sex, or the Opposite Sex.* New York: Simon & Schuster, 1993. 398p. bibliog. index. ISBN 0671797492pa.

Tavris, a social psychologist, challenges and deconstructs the concept of women in a social, psychological, and cultural context. Women are measured against men, thus creating a series of misconceptions from the start. The three generalizations most often expressed are the following "Men are normal; women, being 'opposite,' are deficient. . . . Men are normal; women are opposite from men, but superior to them. . . . Men are normal, and women are or should be like them" (p. 20). Tavris insists that by focusing on the "nature" of the sexes, more harm is done to women. It is critical to look at social and political power and their effect on the psychosocial imbalance of gender roles. The author wants to expose the "hidden assumptions" and popular myths surrounding women and men in order to surpass the reliance on the "natural/biological" order and make the changes that need to be made in society for the benefit of both sexes: "The confusion between equality and sameness must be untangled, because it has now become abundantly clear that in many domains the assumption of sameness has led to unfair and unequal results" (p. 95). There are eight chapters, and each one focuses on a specific generalization, such as women's bodies being considered diseased or women being labeled mentally ill as opposed to men merely having problems; several discuss how women are identified as different from men. Tavris reminds the reader that sometimes parts of the stories are missing, which in turn reflects a part of the silence that contributes to the perpetuation of men and women misreading and misunderstanding each other: "But we will not accomplish this in the movement toward particularization, in which each gender, race, or ethnicity seeks only its own validation, celebrates only itself, and rewrites its history and character in false praise of its own superiority" (p. 330). Winner of the Distinguished Media Contribution Award from the American Association for Preventative Psychology, *The Mismeasure of Women* is a thoughtful, insightful, and articulate book that provides a refreshing look at the psychosocial inequities and constraints affecting both genders. It is recommended for all types of libraries.

A complementary title is Shawn M. Burn's *The Social Psychology of Gender* (McGraw-Hill, 1996). Burn presents a solidly integrated resource that discusses such topics as the influences of biology on gender and sex-role expectations. Some chapters include cross-cultural information.

624. Taylor, Jill McLean, Carol Gilligan, and Amy M. Sullivan. *Between Voice and Silence: Women and Girls, Race and Relationship.* Cambridge, MA: Harvard University Press, 1995. 272p. bibliog. index. ISBN 0674068793; 0674068807pa.

This study focuses on the at-risk adolescent girl, in this case, twenty-six girls of African American, Hispanic, white, and Portuguese backgrounds from urban public schools. The authors followed this group for three years and recorded their experiences and insights through a series of interviews. Researchers and study participants discussed the findings at six retreats. Taylor and her colleagues discovered that class issues contributed to perception of voice: "The girls in our study were not living under similar constraints. They could speak, but for the most part felt that few cared or listened to what they had to say. Having a 'big mouth' often got them into trouble, but silence . . . was also devastating" (p. 3). With this realization, the authors restructured the study so the girls' voices would be articulated and heard. The sample was small and selective, but this study reveals the need for additional research on female adolescents' sense of self in relation to others, their relationship with their mothers, and the difficulties of growing up.

In *The Company She Keeps: An Ethnography of Girls' Friendships* (Open University Press, 1997), Valerie Hey interviewed girls from two schools in London during the 1980s. She provides a detailed literature review that includes discussions on the topic of girls' friendships, issues of marginalization, class, and race.

Vivienne Griffiths takes a slightly more personal tone in *Adolescent Girls and Their Friends* (Avebury, 1995), for which she interviewed twenty-six white girls from a coed, mixed-race, working-class school. Griffiths writes, "This book examines the nature of girls' friendships, and aims to show how important these are in providing them with positive self-identity and self-esteem" (p. 3). The author's primary focus is on "who is listening" as well as "who is speaking." What evolved out of these observations is as much about debates that arise between adult women over class, "race," and privilege as it is about young women's lives.

625. Thomas, Sandra P., ed. *Women and Anger.* New York: Springer, 1993. 332p. (Focus on Women, v. 15). bibliog. index. ISBN 0826191007.

One of the few books based on empirical data about women's anger, this collection explores physiological, biological, cultural, and psychological aspects in relationship to women and anger. The editor writes: "This is a book about women's anger, written by women, for women . . . more than 500 women, who told us about the power and pain of their anger. This book addresses the anger experience of all types of women" (p. 1). The introduction sets the stage with discussions about the lack of research on anger. Analysis is based on a three-year study of women's anger, with two stages of data collection and an expanded test battery included in the second phase.

Women came from various backgrounds, environments, and occupations. A portion of the study focuses on how culture contributes to differences in how anger is expressed and accepted. The studies are arranged into chapters discussing various issues, such as an overview of how emotions develop, the relationship of anger to women's self-esteem, and various ways anger is expressed. The authors of the essays explore how anger contributes to other areas in a woman's life, and various ways therapists can work with female clients to address anger issues. This important book only begins to deal with a topic where more research needs to be conducted. Appendices provide data from the survey.

To discover some of the issues young female adolescents face, read Lyn M. Brown's *Raising Their Voices in Anger* (Harvard University Press, 1998). This is a case study that compares small groups of teenage girls from two communities in Maine. Both group and individual interviews are used to better understand verbalization and "girls' active resistance to the often imperceptible forces that threaten to move them out of touch with their experiences" (pp. viii–ix). Brown incorporates social, educational, cultural, and class issues to provide various insights into these girls' experiences.

626. Turner, Barbara F., and Lillian E. Troll, eds. *Women Growing Older: Psychological Perspectives.* Thousand Oaks, CA: Sage Publications, 1994. 282p. bibliog. index. ISBN 0803939868; 0803939876pa.

Women Growing Older incorporates a wide range of psychological theories, concepts, and methods for scholars to use when conducting research on older women. Instead of focusing on biological perspectives, the contributors apply psychological concepts and models from their own research along with empirical data. The introduction provides background information on adult development, gerontology of women, feminist theory, and issues facing nonwhite aging women. The essays employ various methodologies, including longitudinal studies, and range in subject matter from diversity of personal choices regarding work and family to identity issues to research theory in social cognition and cognitive development. Some contributors use models based on adult developmental research, while others apply theories and concepts developed in other areas of psychology. This important resource is best suited for upper-level undergraduates and graduate students in gerontology.

Ruth R. Thone examines the assumptions, perceptions, stigmas, and cultural repercussions associated with aging women in *Women and Aging: Celebrating Ourselves* (Haworth Press, 1992). Thone encourages people to seek empowerment and to embrace aging as a positive experience. *Faces of Women and Aging* (Haworth Press, 1993), edited by Nancy D. Davis, Esther D. Rothblum, and Ellen Cole, features personal narratives, case studies, and research based on surveys and covers a wide range of topics, including body image, ageism, and menopause.

627. Unger, Rhoda K. *Resisting Gender: Twenty-five Years of Feminist Psychology.* Thousand Oaks, CA: Sage, 1998. 239p. (Gender and Psychology). bibliog. index. ISBN 0803978243; 0803978261pa.

Employing various techniques, *Resisting Gender* is part history of psychology, part memoir, and part analysis of the theories and paradigm shifts that have occurred over time. Unger considers methodologies that contribute to feminism and empiricism in psychology, power and status, ideology, epistemology, and other covert agendas: "The psychology of women did not develop as a result of the work of any one 'great woman', but from the work of a critical mass of women who shared both an intellectual tradition and the constraints of being marginalized within that tradition" (p. 1). The author analyzes sexist biases in traditional psychological methodology and examines the question of sex differences. Unger provides an overview of past contributions to the field of feminist psychology, thus showing how paradigm shifts occurred. The author discusses both personal and theoretical biases in the field, along with a variety of continuing problematic issues, such as the relationship between feminist and mainstream psychology, sex differences, and issues affected by science and politics.

A similar title is Nancy Chodorow's *Feminism and Psychoanalytic Theory* (Yale University Press, 1989), a collection of essays the authors highlighting the various theories that influenced her development and theories of "gender consciousness." See also *Disruptive Voices: The Possibilities of Feminist Research* (University of Michigan Press, 1992) by Michelle Fine. The majority of the chapters have been previously published, but several were revised. Challenging the reader to consider other dimensions and contributions to women's loss of voice/power and pushing for activism, Fine establishes a framework of "feminist psychology as a social change strategy" (p. viii). Three major themes emerge: the subjection of women's bodies, the repression and silencing of women's life experiences, and the role of talk. Students in psychology, sociology, and women's studies will find the discussions to be stimulating.

628. Ussher, Jane M. *Women's Madness: Misogyny or Mental Illness?* Amherst: University of Massachusetts Press, 1992. 341p. bibliog. index. ISBN 0870237861; 087023787Xpa.

Ussher provides a historical and cultural analysis of women's experience with mental health issues. She explores the term "madness" and what it represents for women, society, and mental health discourse. The author begins with a discussion of various issues related to the concept of women's madness, including the use of madness as a method to control women as "outsiders" while simultaneously acknowledging that women do suffer from mental health disorders. By incorporating issues of misogyny and control as well as psychological trends in her analysis of madness and how women are represented in mental health, she provides insights into the multiple levels that are entrenched in views of women's mental capabilities and stability. In section 2, Ussher uses Foucauldian methods to trace the evolution of madness through historical events such as witchcraft and the Victorian era. Section 3 analyzes the parameters of the professional stance in terms of diagnosing madness, the development of therapy and treatment, and criticisms of these structures. In the final section, the author comments on the current status of therapy and suggests different approaches that could be used to destigmatize and reconstruct women's madness. A very impressive bibliography enhances this resource.

The following titles incorporate commentary on the construction of madness. In *Crazy for You: The Making of Women's Madness* (Oxford University Press, 1997), Jill Astbury challenges how madness has been assigned to women, beginning with theories of early psychologists and continuing to modern psychobiological beliefs and current pathologies. Astbury analyzes research conducted in medicine and the social sciences that supposes that women are predisposed to madness because of a connection between biology and psychology. This analysis includes a critique of Freud, his development of the female psyche, and his patient, Dora.

Dana Becker in *Through the Looking Glass: Women and Borderline Personality Disorder* (Westview Press, 1997) explores various perspectives concerning borderline personality disorder (BPD) and how both the disorder and the diagnosis affect women. Becker reviews the development of madness, the effect of labeling psychiatric "disorders," and problems brought about by gender bias in the DSM (Diagnostic and Statistical Manual of Mental Disorders).

For nearly two years (October 1930 to May 1932), Karl Menninger hosted an advice column, "Mental Hygiene in the Home," in *Ladies Home Journal*. In *Dear Dr. Menninger: Women's*

Voices from the Thirties (University of Missouri Press, 1997), editors Howard J. Faulkner and Virginia D. Pruitt have selected more than eighty letters to Menninger along with his replies. The letters are arranged chronologically into categories, such as sexual conflicts; depression and anxiety; narcissism and infantilism; philandering, abusive, and disappointing husbands; frigid wives; interfering in-laws; problem parents; problem children; and nonmarital relationships. This snapshot into the social attitude of the times and women's experiences may be of interest to counselors, students in undergraduate and graduate programs, historians, psychologists, and sociologists.

629. Van Den Bergh, Nan, ed. *Feminist Perspectives on Addictions.* New York: Springer, 1991. 222p. index. (OP)

Contributors from a variety of disciplines, including academics and clinicians in psychology, social work, and pharmacology, examine women's addictions from a feminist perspective. The book is arranged in three sections. Section 1 provides an introduction to the feminist perspective of addiction and the various factors that contribute to a culture of addiction. The second section reviews "ingestive" addictions, including alcoholism, drugs, and eating disorders. Discussion includes at-risk groups for these addictions, such as the elderly and lesbians. The last section focuses on "process" addictions such as gambling, codependence, and workaholism. Each essay highlights the current research, important concepts, and possible effects of and cures for each addiction. Several essays comment on how the relationship between addictions and addictive behaviors has contributed to the self-help movement.

Several titles discuss the women's self-help movement. In *The Culture of Recovery: Making Sense of the Self-Help Movement in Women's Lives* (Beacon Press, 1995), Elaine Rapping, a media analyst and critic, investigates various aspects of the self-help and recovery movement. The book combines cultural history with personal commentary. The author investigates twelve-step programs, talk shows, docudramas, and the continuing publication of self-help materials geared toward women.

Sisters of the Yam: Black Women and Self-Recovery (South End Press, 1993) by bell hooks explores psychological strategies, political and social realities, and various examples of pain and suffering expressed in black literature and personal experience. Using the yam as a symbol of endurance and "a life-sustaining symbol of black kinship and community . . . it is a symbol of our diasporic connections" (p. 13), hooks describes her personal experience in creating a support group with other African American women as they worked through issues of esteem, addictions, and healing. She states: "Black females' self recovery, like all black self recovery, is an expression of a libratory political practice" (p. 14).

Challenging Codependence: Feminist Critiques (University of Toronto Press, 1995), edited by Marguerite Babcock and Christine McKay, includes chapters, many of them reprints, from a variety of perspectives, including psychology, counseling, social work, education, and other related fields. The four sections of the book provide a historical overview of codependency, examine the connection between victim blaming and codependency, present various treatments explored in codependency theory, and investigate various political and medical perspectives to show the relationship between female oppression and codependency.

A final title that should be mentioned is *Women and Self-Help Culture: Reading between the Lines* (Rutgers University Press, 1992) by Wendy Simonds, who investigates the reasons why women are the predominant readers of self-help books. The author interviewed publishers, analyzed the publishing industry, and also interviewed thirty predominantly white women, from various religious backgrounds, between the ages of twenty-three and fifty-nine. Simonds notes that the interest in self-help resources likely reflects cultural changes and the challenges of changing role expectations in American society.

630. Waites, Elizabeth A. *Trauma and Survival: Post-Traumatic and Disassociative Disorders in Women.* New York: Norton, 1992. 266p. bibliog. index. ISBN 0393701506.

Waites, a psychotherapist, begins her work by providing an overview of sexual abuse and violence against women, including the subsequent reactions these women experience and the treatments they receive. In the first part, Waites reviews psychobiological reactions that female victims often experience, including traumas such as memory loss, personality changes, and post-traumatic stress disorder. Working with post-traumatic pathologies, the author analyzes various problems in dealing with abuse survivors, such as blaming the victim, overmedicating, and failing to address the victim's psychological needs. The author examines behaviors that can result from abuse such as depression, anxiety, and phobic disorders. In part 2, Waites reviews various diagnoses and treatments of trauma-related disorders, and the final part focuses on special topics, such as revictimization, self-injury, and enactment. Waites strives to empower therapists to assist women in recovery from various traumas and the social stigmas and associations that are applied.

Several titles consider mental health issues among female immigrants and refugees. *Refugee Women and Their Mental Health: Shattered Societies, Shattered Lives* (Haworth Press, 1992), edited by Ellen Cole, presents brief essays covering a range of topics, including understanding refugees, the challenges and rewards of working with refugees, the healing process, and diagnostic studies across cultures. The cultural representation is broad, from Afghanistan to Vietnam to Guatemala. In *The Blue Room: Trauma and Testimony among Refugee Women: Psychosocial Exploration* (Zed Books, 1994) by Inger Agger, translated by Mary Bille, Agger interviewed several refugee women who had experienced a variety of traumas, including rape and torture. The "blue room" refers to both the physical location and the symbolic "safe" space where the interviews were held. Incorporating a variety of methodologies from sociology, anthropology, and psychology, *The Blue Room* provides an interdisciplinary perspective concerning the issues of trauma for refugee women.

631. Weinstock, Jacqueline S., and Esther D. Rothblum, eds. *Lesbian Friendships: For Ourselves and Each Other.* New York: New York University Press, 1996. 309p. (Cutting Edge Series: Lesbian Life and Literature). 309p. bibliog. index. ISBN 0814774725; 0814774733pa.

Weinstock and Rothblum hope "to focus greater attention on the functions and meanings of friendships among lesbians. This includes the role of friendships in the personal lives of lesbians as well as in our theoretical and political discourse" (p. 6). The essays are grouped into five parts: the meaning of friendship for lesbians, changing relationships as friends and lovers, friendships between different types of women, personal and political dimensions of friendship, and the characteristics of lesbian friendship. Many of the essays were solicited through lesbian and feminist newsletters, as well as through academic, social, and political contacts. Personal narratives are integrated with more scholarly essays. Contributors come from backgrounds in psychology and women's or lesbian studies. The editors state their reluctance to "define" friendships because of the diversity and dimensions of the friendships they identified for this volume. They view this book as a way for lesbians to express and define their own version of friendship or lover.

In *On Intimate Terms: The Psychology of Difference in Lesbian Relationships* (University of Illinois Press, 1993), Beverly Burch explores reasons for attraction and bonding between lesbians. The author identifies two types of lesbians in relationships: those who were married, might have children, and think of themselves as bisexual, and those who were never interested in men.

Within this framework, *On Intimate Terms* explores various perspectives regarding the concept of relationships.

632. Weitz, Rose, ed. *Politics of Women's Bodies: Sexuality, Appearance, and Behavior.* New York: Oxford University Press, 1998. 287p. bibliog. ISBN 0195109945; 0195109953pa.

Weitz has compiled an interdisciplinary resource on the construction, representation, and image of women's bodies in relationship to social, political, medical, and psychological influences. The author discusses how the sociopolitical system seeks to control women's bodies and sexuality, as well as various methods females use to resist such constraints. This title could be used as a supplemental text for courses in women's and gender studies, sociology, and cultural studies. A similar title is *Men, Women, Passion, and Power: Gender Issues in Psychotherapy* (Routledge, 1995) by Marie Maguire. Maguire incorporates case studies to explore issues of sexuality from a feminist perspective. Chapters are arranged into two parts: theories of female and male sexuality and contemporary debates in clinical practice.

633. Wilkinson, Sue, and Celia Kitzinger, eds. *Feminism and Discourse: Psychological Perspectives.* Thousand Oaks, CA: Sage, 1995. 193p. (Gender and Psychology). bibliog. index. ISBN 0803978014; 0803978022pa.

Wilkinson and Kitzinger demonstrate how discourse analysis provides insight into significant feminist psychological issues, including adolescence, menstruation, sexual harassment, and language. Essays in part 1 provide a framework for understanding the role of feminist theory in psychology. Essays in part 2 explore traditional and alternative frameworks of discourse analysis. The editors write, "It is difficult to identify foundational premises or techniques which are specific to discourse analysis, not only because of the breadth and conceptual/methodological 'fuzziness' of the term, but also because of the common ground it shares with other critical approaches in social science" (p. 7). This book should be read by all who are engaged in feminist psychological research and discourse analysis.

Wilkinson edited *Feminist Social Psychology: Developing Theory and Practice* (Open University Press, 1986), which includes clear, concise essays on feminist social psychology from the British perspective. This title was updated and revised by *Feminist Social Psychologies: International Perspectives* (Open University Press, 1996). The contributors, all major scholars in the field of feminist social psychology from the United Kingdom, Europe, North America, Australia, and Asia, explore various theories in feminist social psychology. A complementary title on discourse analysis is *Psychology Discourse Practice: From Regulation to Resistance* (Taylor & Francis, 1996), edited by Erica Burman and others. Relying on discourse analysis, contributors link debates concerning the employment of psychological theories to constrain and discredit. Topics include how therapists can challenge traditional expectations and institutional subjectivity; how legal, psychiatric, and research practices contribute to further stigmatization of various groups; and interventions to address the practical and everyday events in women's lives. An earlier title with many of the same contributors is *Challenging Women: Psychology's Exclusions, Feminist Possibilities* (Open University Press, 1995), edited by Burman. This title also incorporates feminist discourse analysis to explore and challenge various psychological theories.

634. Wilkinson, Sue, and Celia Kitzinger, eds. *Heterosexuality: A Feminism and Psychology Reader.* London: Sage, 1993. 282p. bibliog. index. ISBN 0803988222; 0803988230pa.

This book provides a forum for discussion on the relationship between lesbianism, heterosexuality as an institution, and feminist theories. Essays ranging in length and perspective by forty-three contributors were selected on the premise that the "publication of them could advance the development of feminist theory on heterosexuality" (p. 4). Contributors challenge the notion of heterosexuality and debate the role sexual and social norms play in society. This book could be used for supplemental readings in courses on sexuality, women's studies, and psychology.

There are several other titles that deal with this topic. In *Femininities, Masculinities, Sexualities: Freud and Beyond* (University Press of Kentucky, 1994), Nancy J. Chodorow focuses on issues of sexuality, Freud, psychoanalysis, and the interplay of feminist theory and criticism. Gerda Siann's *Gender, Sex, and Sexuality: Contemporary Psychological Perspectives* (Taylor & Francis, 1994) explores the relationship between the psychology of gender, sexuality, and the inequalities experienced between men and women. Gail E. Wyatt in *Stolen Women: Reclaiming Our Sexuality, Taking Back Our Lives* (John Wiley, 1998) employs case studies and interviews to share African American women's experiences with sexuality. Sections explore the historical image of the black woman as slave and sexual servant, current research, sexual development, and sex education. *Women's Sexuality after Childhood Incest* (Norton, 1992) by Elaine Westerlund investigates the sexual attitudes and practices of ten women who experienced childhood incest.

635. Worell, Judith, and Pam Remer. *Feminist Perspectives in Therapy: An Empowerment Model for Women.* New York: Wiley, 1992. 380p. (Wiley Series on Psychotherapy and Counselling). bibliog. index. ISBN 0471918601; 0471931691pa.

Worell and Remer provide an excellent resource that challenges the reader and provides guidelines toward incorporating feminist theories into therapy. Arranging their work in three parts—the foundations, life-span issues, and becoming a feminist therapist—the authors present several important considerations for therapists to keep in mind. To further the challenge, at the beginning of every chapter there is a self-assessment quiz on the topic, followed by self-awareness activities and additional readings. Part 1 provides an empowerment model for counseling and therapy, incorporating discussions on traditional assessments and various models of feminist therapy and psychological interventions. Part 2 considers some of the major internal and external issues women bring to counseling, and part 3 explores challenges faced by those who want to become therapists.

636. Zerbe, Kathryn. *Body Betrayed: Women, Eating Disorders, and Treatment.* Washington, DC: American Psychiatric Press, 1993. 447p. bibliog. index. ISBN 0880485221.

Kathryn Zerbe combines clinical stories with a discussion of the treatment process for a comprehensive eating disorders program. She examines psychotherapy and eating disorders in light of the influences of opposing theories, considers DSM-III criteria on eating disorders and the definition of feminity, and investigates correlations between the two. Zerbe clearly articulates the complex relationships between eating disorders and the patient's self-perception. The author discusses other studies on eating disorders; briefly addresses the relationship between eating disorders and minorities, children, athletes, and older women; provides nutrition and dietary information; and includes appendices on the DSM-III criteria of eating disorders as well as tables on food and vitamins.

Eating Problems: A Feminist Psychoanalytic Treatment Model (Basic Books, 1994), edited by Carol Bloom and others, presents analyses of eating disorders and introduces an alternative treatment model. The authors, all faculty of the Women's Therapy Centre Institute in New York

City, integrate multiple techniques and clinical experiences to address the social, medical, cultural, and psychological influences on a woman's body image.

Becky W. Thompson argues that eating problems, including bulimia, anorexia, and compulsive eating, have an established history of bias in terms of sexuality, race, and class in *A Hunger So Wide and So Deep: American Women Speak Out on Eating Problems* (University of Minnesota Press, 1996). She interviews eighteen women from various ethnic backgrounds (Latina, African American, and white) and sexual orientations to demonstrate how eating problems have been used as a means of self-preservation by women from different backgrounds and age ranges. Thompson's argument effectively expands the narrow studies that scholars previously have conducted on white teenagers.

1999 CORE TITLES

André, Serge. *What Does a Woman Want?* Translated by Susan Fairfield. New York: Other Press, 1999. 350p. (The Lacanian Clinical Field). bibliog. index. ISBN 189274628Xpa.

Arthurs, Jane, and Jean Grimshaw, eds. *Women's Bodies: Discipline and Transgression.* New York: Cassell, 1999. 236p. bibliog. index. ISBN 0304339628; 0304339636pa.

Chodorow, Nancy J. *The Power of Feelings: Personal Meaning in Psychoanalysis, Gender, and Culture.* New Haven, CT: Yale University Press, 1999. 328p. bibliog. index. ISBN 0300079591; 0300089090pa.

Cox, Deborah L., Sally D. Stabb, and Karin H. Bruckner. *Women's Anger: Clinical and Developmental Perspectives.* Philadelphia: Brunner/Mazel, 1999. 254p. bibliog. index. ISBN 0876309457; 0876309465pa.

Espin, Oliva M. *Women Crossing Boundaries: A Psychology of Immigration and Transformations of Sexuality.* New York: Routledge, 1999. 194p. bibliog. ISBN 0415916992; 041591700Xpa.

Fisher, Helen E. *The First Sex: The Natural Talents of Women and How They Are Changing the World.* New York: Random House, 1999. 378p. bibliog. index. ISBN 0679449094.

Forden, Carie, Anne E. Hunter, and Beverly Birns, eds. *Readings in the Psychology of Women: Dimensions of the Female Experience.* Boston: Allyn & Bacon, 1999. 383p. bibliog. ISBN 0205265103.

Gannon, Linda. *Women and Aging: Transcending the Myths.* New York: Routledge, 1999. 228p. ISBN 0415169097; 0415169100pa.

Hughes, Judith M. *Freudian Analysts/Feminist Issues.* New Haven, CT: Yale University Press, 1999. 222p. bibliog. index. ISBN 0300075243.

Jack, Dana C. *Behind the Mask: Destruction and Creativity in Women's Aggression.* Cambridge, MA: Harvard University Press, 1999. 321p. bibliog. index. ISBN 0674064852; 0674005376pa.

Johnson, Norine G., Michael C. Roberts, and Judith Worell, eds. *Beyond Appearance: A New Look at Adolescent Girls.* Washington, DC: American Psychological Association, 1999. 464p. bibliog. index. ISBN 1557985820; 1557986851pa.

Kimmel, Ellen B., and Mary Crawford, eds. *Innovations in Feminist Psychological Research.* New York: Cambridge University Press, 1999. 457p. bibliog. index. ISBN 0521786401.

Lamb, Sharon. *New Versions of Victims: Feminists Struggle with the Concept.* New York: New York University Press, 1999. 217p. bibliog. index. ISBN 0814751520; 0814751539pa.

Lawrence, Marilyn, Marie Maguire, and Jo Campling, eds. *Psychotherapy with Women: Feminist Perspectives.* New York: Routledge, 1999. 229p. bibliog. index. ISBN 0415922658pa.

Lesser, Ronnie C., and Erica Schoenberg, eds. *That Obscure Subject of Desire: Freud's Female Homosexual Revisited.* New York: Routledge, 1999. 365p. ISBN 0415916704; 0415916712pa.

Nadien, Margot B., and Florence L. Denmark, eds. *Females and Autonomy: A Life-Span Perspective.* Boston: Allyn & Bacon, 1999. 176p. bibliog. index. ISBN 0205198562.

Person, Ethel S. *The Sexual Century.* New Haven, CT: Yale University Press, 1999. 387p. bibliog. index. ISBN 0300076045.

Rosenzweig, Linda W. *Another Self: Middle-Class American Women and Their Friends in the Twentieth Century.* New York: New York University Press, 1999. 225p. (The History Of Emotions Series, 6). bibliog. index. ISBN 0814774865.

Roszak, Theodore. *The Gendered Atom: Reflections on the Sexual Psychology of Science.* Berkeley, CA: Conari Press, 1999. 174p. bibliog. ISBN 1573241717.

Segal, Lynne. *Why Feminism? Gender, Psychology, Politics.* New York: Columbia University Press, 1999. 286p. (Gender and Culture). bibliog. index. ISBN 023111964X; 0231119658pa.

Shandler, Sara. *Ophelia Speaks: Adolescent Girls Write about Their Search for Self.* New York: HarperPerennial, 1999. 285p. ISBN 0613161742; 0060952970pa.

Smith, Gerrilyn, Dee Cox, and Jacqui Saradjian. *Women and Self-Harm: Understanding, Coping, and Healing from Self-Mutilation*. New York: Routledge, 1999. 166p. bibliog. index. ISBN 0415924103; 0415924111pa.

Yoder, Janice D. *Women and Gender: Transforming Psychology*. Upper Saddle River, NJ: Prentice Hall, 1999. 450p. bibliog. index. ISBN 0136446000pa.

WORLD WIDE WEB/INTERNET SITES

637. *Association for Gay, Lesbian and Bisexual Issues in Counseling.* http://www .aglbic.org.

This association serves to "educate mental health service providers about issues confronting gay, lesbian, bisexual and transgender (GLBT) individuals." It also serves as a voice in advocating rights for GLBT families and the need to include GLBT issues in counseling, diversity training, and curricula. Users may access the group's online journal and newsletter from this Web site. Links to resources such as a bibliography, resource list, competencies for professionals, and information on mentoring are also included.

638. *Association for Women in Psychology.* http://www.awpsych.org/about.html.

The Association for Women in Psychology (AWP) is a not-for-profit organization that addresses scientific and educational issues from a feminist standpoint. Operating outside the parameters of the American Psychological Association, AWP includes people outside of psychology. This site provides access to conference information, newsletters, and links.

639. *Society for the Psychological Study of Lesbian, Gay, and Bisexual Issues.* http:// www.apa.org/divisions/div44/.

The Society for the Psychological Study of Lesbian, Gay, and Bisexual Issues, a division of the American Psychological Association, serves to educate and inform psychologists and the general public, as well as provide the latest research, educational, and service activities conducted by the division. Additional information contained on this site includes an orientation manual, continuing education workshops, guidelines for psychologists, and links for related organizations and interest groups.

640. *Society for the Psychology of Women.* http://www.apa.org/divisions/div35/.

The Society for the Psychology of Women is another division of the American Psychological Association. The Web site promotes issues for all who teach, conduct research, or practice in any area within the psychology of women. Dedicated to feminist scholarship and practice, this division also is active in advocating public policy changes for equality and social justice. The Web site provides links for information on multicultural issues and to related organizations and discussion groups.

641. *Women's Intellectual Contributions to the Study of Mind and Society.* http://www .webster.edu/~woolflm/womenlist.html.

Hosted by Dr. Linda M. Wolfe at Webster University, this site contains biographical information about women in psychology and psychoanalysis. The site is maintained by students in her seminar of the same name and includes a bibliography.

642. *Women's Mental Health Consortium.* http://www.nimh.nih.gov/wmhc/index.cfm.

The Women's Mental Health Consortium promotes research reflecting gender differences in addressing mental health issues of girls and women from scientific, biobehavioral, pharmacological, and other research standpoints. The site provides access to funding opportunities, conferences and workshops and links to related federal organizations.

Sociology, Social Lives, and Social Issues

Debbi Schaubman

The books and World Wide Web sites described in this chapter share a focus on the differing circumstances and experiences of women's everyday lives. From our daily experiences to the ways we research and learn about those experiences, these titles engage the heterogeneous material realities of women's lives. They are steps toward curing what Shulamith Reinharz has named "gynopia," the "inability to perceive women."

The multiplicity of women's identities is explored in many of these works. From collections of essays, poems, stories, and personal narratives to ethnographic studies of marginalized women, these volumes consider the meaning of identities that are fluid, sometimes contradictory, and often overlapping. African American women, Asian American women, Latina women, Jewish women, white women, biracial and multiracial women, immigrant women, disabled women, women (and girls) who mother and those who have chosen not to do so, prostitutes and other sex workers, homeless women, women receiving welfare, women in prison, lesbians, bisexual women, heterosexual women, older women, teenage girls, poor women, working-class women, middle-class women, and women and girls who fit in several or none of these categories—it is their lives, our lives, that are reflected in these words. Theory is present in these works, sometimes offered explicitly, sometimes as seeds sown for later harvesting.

Many of these works address contemporary social issues. Highly divergent analyses of prostitution/sex work and pornography are in this chapter, as are works on the myriad forms of violence against women. Abortion, homelessness, poverty, single and teenage motherhood, crime, drug use, and other "social problems" are discussed in the titles that follow. A caveat is necessary, however. Social issues and problems are, by definition, embedded in a particular social, cultural, and historical context. The selection of social issues to be addressed in this chapter reflects a U.S.-based perspective. This does not mean that the materials are all focused on the United States; indeed, an attempt was made to include works that explored these issues from the perspectives of women living in different geographic locations. Nonetheless, it is important to note that this chapter will not inform you about what women in Chile, for example, see as the compelling social issues of the day.

Other kinds of works can also be found here. Quantitative studies, historical analyses, and the occasional biographical work are included. Critiques of, and new developments in, social theory and research methods and methodology are a vital component of this chapter. How researchers choose the subjects of their work, how that work is conceptualized and operationalized, how the results of the work are expressed and distributed, and the position of the researcher vis-à-vis the subject of study are all explored in the books described in this chapter. The monographs section consists of three parts—Sociology: Issues, Methods, and Diversities; Social Work, Welfare, and Poverty; Criminal Justice and Crimes Against Women.

REFERENCE SOURCES

643. Bataille, Gretchen M., and Kathleen M. Sands. *American Indian Women: A Guide to Research*. New York: Garland Publishing, 1991. 423p. (Women's History and Culture; Garland Reference Library of Social Science). index. (OP)

This bibliography of materials relevant to the study of Native American women in the United States and Canada contains citations of more than 1,500 works published prior to 1990. The volume is arranged by broad topic area to facilitate browsing. The subjects covered include reference works, ethnography and cultural history, politics, law, health, education, employment, visual and performing arts, literature and criticism, and biography and autobiography. A cross-subject list of films, filmstrips, and videos is also provided. Very brief annotations attempt to place the cited material in an appropriate context; this is especially important because works were not excluded from consideration on the basis of ethnocentricity or offensiveness. Indeed, although the authors do not describe their selection process in detail, it is apparent that a wide variety of sources were consulted. Cited materials include popular magazines and newspapers (e.g., *Time, USA Today*), magazines and newsletters produced by Native American organizations and nations (e.g., *Indian's Friend, Akwesasne Notes*), scholarly monographs, fiction and poetry by Native American women, U.S. government documents, and small press publications. Purposefully excluded from this bibliography are dissertations, most popular fiction, unpublished conference proceedings, non-English-language materials, and works that the authors were unable to locate for annotation. The index provides access by author, subject, broad time period, and Native nation/tribe.

Bataille, with Laurie Lisa, also edited *Native American Women: A Biographical Dictionary* (Garland, 1993), which provides information about historical and contemporary Indian women often accompanied by photographs. Entries focus on careers and accomplishments and the volume contains indexes by endeavor, decade, place of birth, and tribal affiliation. Bataille and Lisa prepared a second edition, which Garland published in 2001.

644. Bullough, Vern L., and Lilli Sentz, eds. *Prostitution: A Guide to Sources, 1960–1990*. New York: Garland Publishing, 1992. 369p. (Garland Reference Library of Social Science). bibliog. index. (OP)

Used in conjunction with earlier volumes (1976, 1977) edited by Bullough and others, this annotated bibliography provides a solid base for scholarship exploring the many aspects of prostitution. Works in European languages are included, along with non-European-language works if an English-language abstract was available for review. A broad range of subject areas are covered, including general bibliographies, studies on feminism and on violence and crime, area studies (arranged by country), biographies, economics, history, psychology and psychiatry, religion, sociology, and representations in literature, art, and music. Both print and microformat materials are listed; journal literature predominates, but monographs, dissertations, and government documents are well represented. An index of personal names and one of subjects provide additional points of access to the almost 2,000 entries. The annotations are brief and usually not evaluative; indeed, a few of the annotations are somewhat misleading (see, for example, the annotation for Linda Lovelace's *Ordeal*). Nonetheless, the scope of this work serves to overcome some of its idiosyncrasies.

645. Castillo-Speed, Lillian, ed. *Chicana Studies Index: Twenty Years of Gender Research, 1971–1991*. Berkeley: Chicano Studies Library Publications Unit, University of California at Berkeley, 1992. 427p. index. ISBN 0918520215.

This index to the Chicana studies literature filled a considerable gap at the time of its original publication. Still useful for those without access to the ongoing *Chicano Database* or with limited access to other journal databases, this volume indexes more than 1,100 English- and Spanish-language journal articles, books, chapters in books, reports, and dissertations on the lives of women of Mexican descent. The indexed periodicals include mainstream journals, government-produced journals, and more specialized research and movement-based materials. A broad range of disciplines are represented: the arts, social sciences, literary criticism, and medicine are particularly well covered. Creative writing has been purposefully excluded. Entries are arranged by the subject headings used in the *Chicano Thesaurus* and, within these groupings, alphabetically by author. The entries are rather sparse: basic bibliographic information is provided, along with a list of index terms. Separate author and title indexes are also provided. Researchers interested in locating more recent material are advised to use the previously mentioned *Chicano Database*, the various women's studies databases, and/or other discipline-specific resources. Additional materials may be identified through several well-established Web sites. Amongst the best known and most stable is the University of California's *CLNet* ("Building Chicana/o Latina/o Communities through Networking"). This Web site contains a Chicana studies Web page (http://clnet.ucr.edu/women/womenHP.html) with links to a variety of resources, including bibliographies.

646. Deegan, Mary Jo, ed. *Women in Sociology: A Bio-bibliographical Sourcebook*. New York: Greenwood Press, 1991. 468p. bibliog. index. ISBN 0313260850.

The lives and work of the "founding sisters" of sociology are explored in this reference work that seeks to document women's contributions to the development and growth of the field. Ranging from the well known to the relatively obscure, the fifty-one women share several traits: they were all born before 1927 and active between 1840 and 1990, and most were U.S. citizens. (All but fourteen were born in the United States, and of those fourteen, six later became citizens.) Most of the entries consist of a brief biographical sketch, an exploration of the thinker's major themes, an overview of writings about her work, and selected bibliographies listing material by and about the subject. Name and subject indexes conclude the volume.

647. Dixon, Penelope. *Mothers and Mothering: An Annotated Feminist Bibliography*. New York: Garland Publishing, 1991. 219p. (Women's History and Culture). index. (OP)

This annotated, selective bibliography provides access to monographic and journal literature; dissertations and theses, historical works, and cross-cultural studies were purposefully excluded. As Dixon herself acknowledges, the collection has a definite white, heterosexual, middle-class, U.S. feminist bias. Despite casting a rather narrow net, the thoroughness and conciseness of the entries does result in a useful reference work. The volume is arranged thematically; subjects include general literature on mothers and mothering, mothers and daughters, mothers and sons, single mothers, working mothers, lesbian and black mothers, mothering and the family, feminism as a framework for mothering, psychoanalysis as a feminist tool, and reproductive issues and technologies relevant to the study of mothering. Each chapter is prefaced by a brief review essay. An author index is provided. Researchers attempting to identify key titles in the study of mothering (within the important constraints noted earlier) would find this volume helpful.

648. Fitzsimmons, Richard, and Joan P. Diana, eds. *Pro-choice/Pro-life Issues in the 1990s: An Annotated, Selected Bibliography*. New York: Greenwood Press, 1996. 284p. (Bibliographies and Indexes in Sociology). index. ISBN 0313293554.

This follow-up to Fitzsimmons and Diana's earlier volume, *Pro-choice/Pro-life: An Annotated, Selected Bibliography (1972–1989)* (Greenwood Press, 1991), covers a broad range of publications issued in the United States from 1990 to 1994. Rather than limiting themselves to texts specifically addressing abortion, the compilers have chosen to include works on birth control, contraception, and family planning. Interestingly, other reproductive choice–related issues (e.g., forced sterilization) have been omitted from coverage. Monographs, legal decisions, congressional hearings, and periodical articles are included. Entries are briefly annotated and, in a rather counterproductive fashion, arranged alphabetically by main entry. A detailed subject index is provided. Materials are presented regardless of political slant; indeed, a special effort appears to have been made to include materials representing the breadth of U.S. discourse on the topic.

Dallas A. Blanchard's *The Anti-abortion Movement: References and Resources* (G. K. Hall, 1996) affords a more detailed look at materials specifically addressing that movement. Books, dissertations, scholarly articles, conference presentations, films, videos, and television broadcasts are included in this annotated bibliography. Relatively little scholarly work is included; although Blanchard asserts that this is the result of a dearth of such writing, the universe of materials he examined is rather limited. Nonetheless, the inclusion of a substantial number of movement publications and nonprint sources makes this a useful source for researchers. The volume is thematically organized and includes author and subject indexes. An appendix lists major antiabortion organizations and their publications.

649. Friedl, Vicki L., comp. *Women in the United States Military, 1901–1995: A Research Guide and Annotated Bibliography*. Westport, CT: Greenwood Press, 1996. 251p. (Research Guides in Military Studies). index. ISBN 0313029657X.

This annotated bibliography fills a considerable gap in the English-language reference literature surrounding U.S. women and the military. A broad range of information sources is covered, including books, journal literature, government documents and publications, technical reports, archival materials, theses and dissertations, conference papers, and research reports. Friedl did not intend the volume to be a comprehensive bibliography; rather, it comprehensively compiles personal narratives and official histories while selectively including other materials. The criteria used to select works are clearly explained. Following a brief introductory chapter on conducting bibliographic research, chapters are subject focused. Early chapters are focused on the services themselves (Navy and Coast Guard, Marine Corps, Army, Women Airforce Service Pilots, Air Force, service academies), whereas later chapters focus on general areas of concern (family and pregnancy, sex, women in combat, veterans). Each chapter is preceded by a brief sociohistorical overview. Appendices provide information on archival resources, women's military associations, a chronology of women's service, and a selection of relevant Web sites. Author, title, and subject indexes are provided.

650. Maggiore, Dolores J. *Lesbianism: An Annotated Bibliography and Guide to the Literature, 1976–1991*. Metuchen, NJ: Scarecrow Press, 1992. 264p. bibliog. index. (OP)

This work is a useful contribution to the literature of lesbian studies. Despite the broad implications of its title, Maggiore's focus is on material likely to be of interest to social workers. Selected monographs, articles, and dissertations are included; purposefully excluded are "foreign and cross-cultural studies, literature on religion and spirituality and highly technical and/or narrowly specialized psychological, medical and legal writings" (p. 1). Maggiore also excludes works that are negative toward lesbians or that focus on gay men and merely include lesbians as an afterthought or generalized extension of the main text. As a result, she has created a focused and practical annotated bibliography for social work practice. The volume begins with an "Introduction to the 1992 Edition" that serves to update the review of the literature that was published in the original 1988 edition of the work. This lengthy review identifies trends in five general topics: the individual lesbian (e.g., identity, self-concept), minorities within a minority (e.g., lesbians of color, rural lesbians, disabled lesbians), lesbian families (i.e., families of origin and of choice), oppression, and special health issues. The volume would have been strengthened considerably had the two introductions been synthesized; nonetheless, read together, they provide a useful overview of the literature. An author and title index provides additional access points to the subject-organized entries.

Linda Garber's *Lesbian Sources: A Bibliography of Periodical Articles, 1970–1990* (Garland, 1993) covers a broader range of subjects than Maggiore's volume. This unannotated bibliography lists articles by and/or about lesbians appearing in nationally and internationally distributed periodicals. Entries are arranged alphabetically by subject; extensive cross-references are provided. A list of periodicals comprehensively indexed (nonfiction only) is included; other periodicals were selectively indexed. A list of special issues of journals is also included. Readers interested in updating the information in these two works are encouraged to use *Gay and Lesbian Abstracts*, a National Information Services Corporation (NISC) index to more than 600 sources, as well as the standard women's studies indexing and abstracting sources.

651. Nordquist, Joan. *Violence against Women: International Aspects: A Bibliography.* Santa Cruz, CA: Reference and Research Services, 1998. 64p. (Contemporary Social Issues). ISBN 0937855960pa.

This unannotated bibliography lists more than 600 entries related to violence against women around the world. As with the other titles in the Contemporary Social Issues series, Nordquist has searched a respected group of reference tools to compile this list. Of particular use to those without access to *Contemporary Women's Issues* or *GenderWatch* is the inclusion of material from these two full-text online sources. The volume is arranged in a combination of geographic and conceptual chapters. Selected chapters include a country index. Other titles by Nordquist in the Contemporary Social Issues series include *Violence against Women: A Bibliography* (1992), *The African-American Woman: Social and Economic Conditions: A Bibliography* (1993), *Women and Aging: A Bibliography* (1994), *Latinas in the United States: Social, Economic, and Political Aspects: A Bibliography* (1995), and *The Asian American Woman: Social, Economic, and Political Conditions: A Bibliography* (1997).

652. Sherrow, Victoria. *Women and the Military: An Encyclopedia.* Santa Barbara, CA: ABC-CLIO, 1996. 381p. bibliog. index. ISBN 097436812X.

This single-volume encyclopedia provides concise articles on a wide range of topics related to women in the military. Sherrow has interpreted "women and the military" quite broadly; there are entries, for example, on victory gardens and Rosie the Riveter. Just as important, Sherrow has not limited the encyclopedia to topics that are specifically related to women; along with the expected entries on such subjects as the Women's Army Corps (WAC), there are entries on, for example, sea duty and officer candidate school. These are not generic entries: each is clearly and specifically related to women. In addition to the numerous biographical sketches, Sherrow has included information on every twentieth-century conflict in which the United States has officially participated. The inclusion of references after most entries somewhat alleviates the disappointment created by their brevity. Supplementing the frequent cross-references is a moderately detailed subject index. A bibliography is also included. Sherrow's introductory essay provides a very brief summary of the history of women in the U.S. military.

653. Wheeler, Helen Rippier. *Women and Aging: A Guide to the Literature.* Boulder, CO: Lynne Rienner Publishers, 1997. 259p. index. ISBN 1555876617.

Wheeler, one of the founders of the National Women's Studies Association's Aging and

Ageism Caucus, has compiled a selective, heavily cross-referenced bibliography focusing on women age thirty-five and up. It includes more than 2,200 entries for English-language materials published from 1980 to 1992. Although there are a few hundred entries for fiction and poetry, the emphasis is clearly on nonfiction materials in the social sciences and humanities. There are entries for books, periodical articles, dissertations, ERIC documents, and U.S. government documents, but only the book entries are annotated. The final chapter, "Women's Studies and the Aging of Females: Locating Additional Resources," includes references to other bibliographic (and other reference) tools, including selected review articles. Also included is a list of relevant periodical special issues.

MONOGRAPHS

Sociology: Issues, Methods, and Diversities

654. Abel, Emily K. *Who Cares for the Elderly? Public Policy and the Experiences of Adult Daughters*. Philadelphia: Temple University Press, 1991. 220p. (Women in the Political Economy). bibliog. index. ISBN 0877228140; 0877229503pa.

Noting that women are disproportionately responsible for the care of disabled elderly parents (representing 77 percent of caregiving children), Abel explores the day-to-day experiences of adult caregiving daughters, as well as the social and historical contexts in which they perform this work. Changes in public policy have resulted in a marked decrease in the services available to low-income disabled elderly people; as a result, responsibility for long-term care has shifted from home- and community-based, government-funded services onto (usually female) family members. Emphasizing the importance of understanding women's lived experience of caregiving, Abel interviewed fifty-one (predominantly white, middle-class) women caregivers. Using analytic concepts that have been used to study the similarly care-intensive experience of mothering, Abel considers the issues of choice, ambivalence, isolation, social devaluation, and the impact of caregiving responsibilities on labor market participation. Abel explicitly rejects the narrow agenda of (then) recent research on caregiving that is task oriented and focuses on the stresses produced by the additional labor. She argues for the central importance of the emotional experiences of caregiving. Chapters explore the conflicts that arise from the competing time demands of caregiving, work, and leisure; relationships between mothers (the majority of the disabled elderly) and caregiving daughters; shifts in middle-class caregiving behavior toward an increase in mediating between formal and informal service providers and elderly family members; and networks of social support. Abel discusses the structural variables that affect who has access to private caregiving services and who (in terms of race and class identifiers) performs these services. Suggestions for creating positive change in the provision of care conclude the volume: giving caregivers financial compensation, increasing the availability of supportive services, and increasing the availability of counseling and educational services and support groups. Noting that these suggestions do not address larger societal issues, Abel further argues for a large-scale social change, including the eradication of the gendered division of domestic work, reorganization of the work world to better accommodate caregivers, nursing-home reform, and an increase in the recognition accorded caring work.

655. Allen, Paula Gunn. *The Sacred Hoop: Recovering the Feminine in American Indian Traditions*. Boston: Beacon Press, 1992. 311p. bibliog. index. ISBN 0807046175pa.

This multidisciplinary collection of essays explores a broad range of Native American historical and contemporary experience. Emphasizing the importance of Woman (as spiritual entity and as social actor) throughout the volume, Allen sheds new light on the hegemonic interpretations of Native American culture and history. Underpinning much of the book is Allen's contention that "the physical and cultural genocide of American Indian tribes is and was mostly about patriarchal fear of gynocracy" (p. 3). Part 1, "The Ways of Our Grandmothers," explores the gynocratic basis of many tribal cultures, rituals, and history and the patriarchalization that followed European contact and colonization. Part 2, "The Word Warriors," contains eight chapters devoted to contemporary and traditional Native American literature. The importance of the oral tradition, the unity and integration of spirituality, and myth making are particularly stressed. The final part, "Pushing up the Sky," explores the lives of contemporary Native American women. These wide-ranging essays address such topics as the impact of colonization on women, lesbians, and gay men; the effects and importance of a "feminist-tribal" interpretation of Native American stories; and the interconnections between the social status of Native American women and the development of the U.S. women's movement. Originally published in 1986, this classic work is frequently (and deservedly) required reading in introductory women's studies courses, as well as in courses specifically exploring racial and ethnic diversity in the United States.

656. Andersen, Margaret L., and Patricia Hill Collins, eds. *Race, Class, and Gender: An Anthology*. 3rd ed. Belmont, CA: Wadsworth, 1998. 562p. bibliog. ISBN 0534528791pa.

Designed as an undergraduate reader, this anthology brings together sixty-one essays that address the ways in which race, class, and gender (along with age, sexual orientation, ethnicity, and religion) interact to create the social realities of people's lives in the United States and, more broadly, worldwide. The editorial perspective is readily summarizable: "Race, class, and gender [are] interlocking categories of experience that affect all aspects of human life; thus, they simultaneously structure the experiences of all people in this society. At any moment, race, class, or gender may feel more salient or meaningful in a given person's life, but they are overlapping and cumulative in their effect on people's experience" (p. 3). The effects of this "matrix of domination" are felt at all levels of experience. The political agenda of this collection is explicitly stated: not content with acknowledging "diversity" as merely the recognition of social and cultural differences, the editors argue for the importance of a careful analysis of differences in power and privilege and the structures that generate them. The volume is divided into five parts, each beginning with an essay that serves to contextualize and organize the succeeding essays. Part 1, "Shifting the Center and Reconstructing Knowledge," presents personal accounts from the perspectives of those frequently excluded. Part 2 analyzes the fundamental concepts of race, class, and gender and explores the interconnections between them. Later parts specifically address institutions (work and economics, family, education, and the state and state policy), social issues (the creation of "American" identity, sexuality, violence, and social control) and the possibilities for creating social change. This is a brilliantly crafted anthology that would be well suited for a wide range of undergraduate sociology and women's or gender studies courses.

657. Antler, Joyce. *The Journey Home: Jewish Women and the American Century*. New York: Free Press, 1997. 410p. bibliog. index. ISBN 0684834448.

Antler interweaves biography and social history in a volume that explores the lives and contributions of more than fifty Jewish women. Jewish identity was an unquestioned fact of life for many of these women; others came to identify as Jewish through a more conscious process of choice and self-discovery. Antler grounds the biographical sketches in an understanding of the relevant social, cultural, and political context of the times. The paths taken to "come home" to Jewish identity and the ways in which this identification affected the women's lives, choices, and work are considered. The volume is split into chronological segments; the biographical sketches are grouped thematically within them. *Talking Back: Images of Jewish Women in American Popular Culture* (Brandeis University Press, 1997), edited by Antler, explores the tensions between representations of Jewish women and their lived realities. Originating in a 1993 conference, "Developing Images: Representation of Jewish Women in American Culture," the chapters discuss a broad range of time periods and cultural texts. Several essays specifically address the images created by Jewish feminists themselves.

658. Armstrong, Louise. *Rocking the Cradle of Sexual Politics: What Happened When Women Said Incest.* Reading, MA: Addison-Wesley, 1994. 305p. bibliog. index. (OP)

Armstrong, the author of *Kiss Daddy Goodnight* (1978), explores the backlash that has come on the heels of feminist organizing around child sexual abuse. She examines the depoliticizing effects of contemporary discourse in this work written for the general public. Asserting that the current media cacophony (from series television, fiction, newspaper accounts, seminars, and so on) drowns out women's and children's voices as effectively as the total silence of twenty-five years ago, Armstrong explores the transformation of incest from a feminist political issue (i.e., the legitimized abuse of power within the family) to an individualized medical issue (e.g., survivors "in recovery" and offenders suffering from a treatable pathology). While arguing that the dominant therapeutic discourse about incest infantilizes and disempowers women ("It is an emphasis on pacification, on deflecting attention from all larger social meaning"), Armstrong nonetheless acknowledges the important role that therapy can play in the lives of individual women and children (p. 266). Stressing that the backlash has taken many forms, Armstrong demonstrates that the explosion of claims of satanic/ritual abuse coupled with the equally loud assertion of the prevalence of false memory syndrome has served to lessen the emphasis placed on "routine paternal child-rape" (p. 259) while, at the same time, countless mothers have been imprisoned for hiding their children (to protect them) or for failing to protect children from their fathers. Although somewhat prone to sarcasm, Armstrong has written a forceful indictment of the mental health, legal, and child welfare establishments and the role each has played in perpetuating male violence against children and in the silencing of children and women.

659. Bacchi, Carol Lee. *Same Difference: Feminism and Sexual Difference.* Boston: Allen & Unwin, 1990. 330p. bibliog. index. ISBN 0044421524pa.

Bacchi, a historian by training, argues that framing feminist discussions in the theoretically opposed concepts of female difference or sameness (from men) obscures both historical specificity and the range of possibilities that exist for the organization of social life. Tracing the debate from the nineteenth century through the interwar years to the second wave of feminist activism, Bacchi challenges the notion that feminists have always been split into these theoretical factions. She contends that these disputes are about a broader issue, that of "conflicting political visions about how best to organize social relations" (p. xiv). She further maintains that there are limitations and strengths to both philosophical approaches. This assertion is illustrated through a series of case studies examining specific social issues: maternity leave, protective legislation in the workplace, affirmative action, child custody, and sexuality-related concerns (e.g., pornography, abortion). To illustrate the issues raised in these case studies, as well as those raised in a chapter devoted to the debates about the very concept of "women," Bacchi blends secondary source material with a rich collection of primary source material gathered in interviews with feminist academics, policy makers, and activists from the United States, Australia, and Great Britain. Bacchi concludes that a new model of social arrangements, one not modeled on a masculine norm, is needed to create a social and political agenda that attends to the needs of women and men.

660. Barry, Kathleen. *The Prostitution of Sexuality.* New York: New York University Press, 1995. 381p. bibliog. index. ISBN 0814712177; 0814712770pa.

In this update to and rethinking of her earlier *Female Sexual Slavery* (1979), Kathleen Barry, one of the founders of the Coalition against Trafficking in Women, argues that "prostitution, with or without a woman's consent, is the institutional, economic and sexual model for women's oppression" (p. 24). Barry explicitly rejects the notion that sexual consent exists under patriarchy, therefore rendering meaningless the differentiation other activists and theorists make between forced and voluntary participation in prostitution. This rejection of the forced/voluntary distinction is a marked change from her earlier work and results in a different approach to organizing and strategy. Noting the "normalization" of prostitution in "nonprostitute sexual exchanges," Barry seeks to explore the ways in which prostitution affects all women: hence "the prostitution of sexuality." Asserting the existence of women as a class under patriarchy (regardless of differences of race, culture, nationality, and economic class), Barry elaborates a human rights approach to international organizing against prostitution based on the notions of decolonization and the right to self-determination. In addition to providing examples of grassroots groups and projects devoted to eradicating the practice of prostitution and/or assisting former prostitutes, Barry details the political history of the Convention against Sexual Exploitation (the text of which is included in the appendix), a proposed international human rights instrument that defines exploitation in terms of "gain, which can be as specific as sexual gratification or as concretely material as financial profit" (p. 305). Ending on a call for change at the deepest personal levels, as well as in the political and material realities of women's lives, Barry tries to envision a "human experience of sex, in which interaction is passionate *with integrity*" (p. 319). An important critique of Barry's work and that of the Coalition against Trafficking in Women appears in Wendy Chapkis's *Live Sex Acts: Women Performing Erotic Labor* (annotated later in this section).

661. Bernard, Jessie. *The Female World from a Global Perspective*. Bloomington: Indiana University Press, 1987. 287p. bibliog. index. (OP)

Rejecting the notion that the specificity of women's experiences in different parts of the world renders meaningless any talk of a "global female world," Bernard attempts to elucidate areas of shared concern without understating the importance of women's diversity. From the opening chapter's overview of demographic variables and the female life course to the three appendices, Bernard links microsociological and macrosociological perspectives through the use of numerous examples. These examples, drawn from both personal contacts and research and from secondary source materials, provide a glimpse into the lives of women of varying classes, races, and nationalities. Much of the book's exploration of the "female world" is devoted to exploring the issues that arise from the notion of "equitable integration" (p. 37) as well as from the separation of women and women's concerns from male (i.e., mainstream) concerns. Chapters address the role of women in international development projects, women's struggles within and concurrent with revolutionary and anticolonialist movements, and issues of parochialism and colonialism within the "Feminist Enlightenment." The final chapters address women's efforts to communicate globally through regional and international meetings, informal networks, and communication media. Special attention is paid to the United Nations–sponsored women's conferences held in Mexico City, Copenhagen, and Nairobi. This classic work is an excellent example of the power that can be derived from a synthesis of primary and secondary source materials.

662. Bornstein, Kate. *Gender Outlaw: On Men, Women, and the Rest of Us*. New York: Routledge, 1994. 245p. bibliog. ISBN 0415908973.

Questions regarding the fluidity of identity are at the heart of Bornstein's gender- and genre-blending text. A "transsexual lesbian whose female lover is becoming a man" (p. 3), Bornstein forces readers to confront innumerable questions of gender assignment, attribution, and identity, as well as deeply held ideas regarding the origins, manifestations, and possibilities for relinquishing male privilege. Poetry, autobiography, social criticism, photographs, interviews, and a play are combined in a collage-like approach that reveals the breadth of societal dichotomization, its conflation of sex and gender, and its construction of (permissible) desire based on these not-so-variable variables. Issues of silence and truth telling (about one's past), of power and play, permeate the text. This extraordinary work of synthesis and creation will be a challenging addition to courses in the sociology of gender and the sociology of sexuality.

663. Carlip, Hillary. *Girl Power: Young Women Speak Out.* New York: Warner Books, 1995. 353p. ISBN 0446670219pa.

Tough, angry, joyous, proud, a multitude of girls' voices are captured in this exciting work. Carlip brings together the writings of a diverse group of girls in a powerful volume that illustrates both the similarities and differences of their lives. While Carlip explicitly acknowledges that the experiences of many of the writers cut across social categories, the book is organized into four main parts: "Outlaws and Outcasts," including homegirls, riot girls, teen mothers, and "queer and bi girls"; "Outskirts," focusing on cowgirls, Native American girls, and "farm chicks"; "Outsiders," with chapters on "rappers and sistas," "surfers and sk8rs," and jocks; and "Insiders," presenting the voices of sorority girls, homemakers, and teen queens. Despite this labeling (or, more accurately, in reclaiming these words), many of the excerpts explode the stereotypes one might expect to find reflected under such headings. Interspersed with the girls' voices are Carlip's own brief notes, which provide a context for much of the writing. Photographs by Nicola Goode appear throughout the work.

A Girl's Guide to Taking over the World: Writings from the Girl Zine Revolution (St. Martin's Griffin, 1997), edited by Karen Green and Tristan Taormino, is an amazing collection of writings and drawings from a broad selection of zines. Issues of race, class, and sexuality are raised throughout this thematically organized volume. Rebecca Carroll's *Sugar in the Raw: Voices of Young Black Girls in America* (Crown Trade Paperbacks, 1997) contains fifteen first-person narratives of girls aged eleven through twenty. Drawn from fifty interviews done across the country, these powerful stories reflect a variety of class and regional backgrounds. Ntozake Shange wrote the foreword.

664. Castillo-Speed, Lillian, ed. *Latina: Women's Voices from the Borderlands.* New York: Simon & Schuster, 1995. 284p. (OP)

Castillo-Speed, director of the Chicano Studies Library at the University of California at Berkeley, has brought together stories and essays that provide a glimpse of the diversity of Latina experience and creativity. Words and languages flow together: "It is more than just a combination of English and Spanish: it reflects the reality of women who live in two worlds. Latinas are American and yet not American at the same time" (pp. 17–18). The collection opens with stories of family and home, stories that speak to "The Past We Bring with Us." The "here and now" is explored in the stories in "Our Land, Our Lives." Politics and language form the core of the third section, "Nuestra Politica." Resistance to assimilation echoes throughout the volume; as Cherríe Moraga states, "An art that subscribes to integration into mainstream America is not Chicano art" (p. 218). Among the better-known contributors are Ana Castillo, Cherríe Moraga, Sandra Cisneros, Achy Obejas, and Gloria Anzaldúa. This exciting and sometimes challenging anthology would be a welcome addition to courses on women's writing; it is also well suited to courses exploring Latina life and political stances.

665. Chafetz, Janet Saltzman. *Gender Equity: An Integrated Theory of Stability and Change.* Newbury Park, CA: Sage Publications, 1990. 256p. bibliog. index. ISBN 0803934017; 0803934025pa.

Chafetz has developed an empirically testable theory of the mechanisms and conditions required for change in the gender-stratification system. She considers two critical questions: How is the gender system maintained and reproduced? and How can it be changed? Defining "gender stratification" as "the extent to which males and females who are otherwise social equals (e.g., in terms of age, social class, race/ethnicity, and religion) are equal in their access to the scarce and valued resources [e.g., goods, services, leisure] of their society" (p. 29), Chafetz posits a recursive relationship between gender and various structures and processes at the macro, meso, and micro levels. The system reproduces itself at all levels of analysis and through all societal institutions (e.g., family, religion, economics, politics, and education). Unintentional and intentional change is possible, however; she identifies the gender division of labor as the critical "change target." Unintentional change is generated through technological advancements and economic expansion. She argues that these same factors are implicated in the rise of women's movements; she further contends that *Women's movements should, therefore, be viewed as primarily reflecting and expediting a process already in motion rather than as a fundamental cause of increasing gender equality*" (p. 187; Chafetz's emphasis). Intentional change must be instituted by institutional elites. The role of change movements is to change public opinion and behavior to a level at which elites must respond. Increasing the number of women in elite groups and the incorporation of "traditional feminine values into elite policy formation" (p. 228) are key. Chafetz's emphasis on a "societal level" theory glosses over differences based on class and race; she includes "A Digression on Class and Minority Stratification" to begin to account for these critical factors. Her earlier work *Feminist Sociology: An Overview of Contemporary Theories* (F.E. Peacock, 1988) explores other theorists' approaches to the same issues: causes of gender inequality, maintenance and reproduction of gender systems, social consequences of gender stratification, and change creation.

666. Chapkis, Wendy. *Live Sex Acts: Women Performing Erotic Labor.* New York: Routledge, 1996. 248p. bibliog. index. ISBN 0415912873; 0415912881pa.

Through interviews and careful reading of secondary source materials, Chapkis reveals the contradictions and multiplicities of meaning attached to the practice of prostitution. The voices of sex workers and activists are interspersed throughout the volume, underlining and elaborating Chapkis's analysis. Framing her text with an analysis of the opposing political stances of radical feminists and sex radicals, Chapkis explores the meaning of sex, both private and commercial, in the United States and the Netherlands. In a chapter addressing sexual slavery, forced prostitution, and trafficking, the conflicts between abolitionist-focused approaches (e.g., the work of the U.S.-based Coalition against Trafficking in Women) and those that recognize a distinction between "consensual labor and slavery" are explored. Building on sociological theories that posit that emotions are not "an unmediated communication from the soul to the socialized self but . . . [are themselves] a product of socialization" (p. 73), Chapkis rejects the claim that sex work alienates women from their emotions and their "true selves." Arguing instead that prostitutes are "emotion laborers," with issues similar to those of other such laborers (e.g., flight attendants), she asserts that any negative feelings experienced by prostitutes are derived from working conditions that are less than optimal. Chapkis acknowledges the importance of the social location (class, race, independence from pimps/managers) of sex workers in determining their experiences. Another section explores strategic responses to prostitution: prohibition and informal tolerance; legalization, regulation, and licensing; and sex worker self-advocacy. Chapkis concludes the main text with a call for a prostitution politics with a "hybrid perspective" that acknowledges the need to incorporate aspects of the sex radical and radical feminist analyses and recognizes the right of prostitutes to work in a safe environment. These and related issues are explored from a historical perspective in Barbara Meil Hobson's *Uneasy Virtue: The Politics of Prostitution and the Amer-*

ican Reform Tradition (Basic Books, 1987). Hobson highlights three moments in U.S. history when prostitution reform efforts were especially active: the 1840s, the Progressive Era, and the 1970s.

667. Connell, Robert W. *Gender and Power: Society, the Person, and Sexual Politics.* Stanford: Stanford University Press, 1987. 334p. bibliog. index. ISBN 0804714290; 0804714304pa.

In this challenging and wide-ranging book, Connell argues that neither a macrolevel nor a microlevel conceptualization of gender is adequate to describe the numerous ways in which gender is constructed and employed in everyday life. Instead, he posits a multilevel theory that accounts for gender both as social structure and as "personality." "Personality," in Connell's usage, is not an essence or something one "has"; instead, it is a "way of living certain relationships" (p. 179). Linking these two levels is practice. Gender is defined as a field of social relations (i.e., a structure) with "component structures" (including labor, power, and cathexis) that are implicated in the production of gender in different ways and at different times (p. 103). The "crisis tendencies" (p. 158) produced by the tensions between these structures provide strategic sites for political mobilization. Change, in turn, is possible due to the recursive relationship between practice and structure. Connell's work is deeply rooted in a commitment to the theoretical centrality of historicity and materiality; as a result, concepts often accepted at face value are closely interrogated in his analysis. For example, Connell asserts that not only the social body, but also the physical body is socially constructed. In "Concluding Notes on the World to Which a Social Theory of Gender Might Lead," Connell explores the challenges and opportunities possible in a world without gender. Aware, however, that gender is not the only organizing structure for hierarchical social relations, Connell concludes that gender-focused social and political activism must be part of a larger movement to eradicate all forms of oppression. A key work in feminist social theory, *Gender and Power* is highly recommended for advanced courses concerned with these issues.

Connell further explores these ideas in his later work *Masculinities* (University of California Press, 1995). Positing that masculinities are "configurations of practice structured by gender relations" (p. 44), Connell uses data drawn from life history interviews conducted with four groups of Australian men to investigate the construction of "hegemonic and complicit" and "subordinated and marginalized" masculinities and the political implications of these constructions.

668. Córdova, Teresa, Norma Cantú, Gilberto Cardenas, Juan García, and Christine M. Sierra, eds. *Chicana Voices: Intersections of Class, Race, and Gender.* Albuquerque: University of New Mexico Press, 1993. 223p. ISBN 082631404X.

This collection contains selected proceedings from the 1984 annual conference of the National Association for Chicano Studies. Dedicated to the theme "Voces de la Mujer," the conference was a watershed event in the history of Chicana studies. The plenary session focused on higher education and the place of Chicanas, feminism, and Chicana studies within the university; the texts stress that the "integration of women into Chicano studies rests on the continued development of a systematic analysis of the structures of racism, capitalism, and patriarchy" (p. 25). The remainder of the volume focuses on three areas: labor and politics, research references and resources, and language, literature, and theater. Contributions explore a wide range of topics, including the invisibility of Mexican women's labor in the informal sector, Chicana workers and the structural implications of "triple oppression," struggle and resistance in the maquiladoras, the contradictions of class and gender and their effects on political mobilization, the use of primary documents in an analysis of women's position in colonial New Mexico, Mexican archival resources, and women in the Teatro Campesino. In the "Foreward to the Third Printing," Cordova discusses the continued growth of Chicana presence within the association.

669. Davis, Angela. *Women, Culture, and Politics*. New York: Random House, 1989. 238p. ISBN (OP); 0679724877pa.

Although this collection does not break new theoretical ground, it does present a welcome opportunity for experiencing (albeit a few steps removed) the power of Angela Davis's oratory. Her long-standing commitment to the global struggles against racism, capitalism, sexism, and imperialism is well represented in this collection of speeches and previously published essays. Despite the lack of additional explanatory material that could serve to contextualize the pieces, the specificity of the texts themselves clearly roots them in a particular time and place. Davis's sweeping vision and perceptive analysis can be seen through the breadth of the topics she addresses and connections she draws between them: essays address the need for activists to work together against "our common foe," the politics of black women's health, connections between sexism and militarism, violence against women, the black family and capitalism, women in Egypt, apartheid in South Africa, the critical role played by cultural workers, the connections between national liberation, education, and ethnic studies, and the silenced history of black photographic artists.

670. DeVault, Marjorie L. *Feeding the Family: The Social Organization of Caring as Gendered Work*. Chicago: University of Chicago Press, 1991. 270p. (Women in Culture and Society). bibliog. index. ISBN 0226143597; 0226143600pa.

DeVault's detailed analysis of the organization of "feeding work" stresses both the material and emotional labor involved in the repertoire of tasks associated with meals (planning, shopping, cooking, cleaning up). Not simply presenting another discussion of the uneven division of household labor, DeVault focuses on feeding the family as a prime example of "caring work." This "caring work" is a critical aspect of "family work," the work that is needed for the social reproduction of the family. Using extensive quotations from interviews conducted in thirty households, DeVault examines the everyday activity involved in feeding the family, as well as the discourses about that activity. Although the diversity of the sample of households (white, Latino, African American, Asian American; poor, working class, middle class; single mothers, dual earners, mothers at home) provides a glimpse at the similarities and differences that exist between and among racial and ethnic groups, DeVault acknowledges that relatively little analytic emphasis is placed here. She does, however, place considerable emphasis on the ways in which class differences produce both material (availability of certain types of foods, range of choices) and discursive (the meaning of "care") differences. DeVault's discussion of conflict, deference, choice, and the ways in which feeding work becomes an arena for playing out gendered power relations within the family is particularly fascinating. This book would be a useful addition to graduate-level courses on sociology of the family, as well as those focusing on the sociology of emotions.

671. Dickerson, Bette J., ed. *African American Single Mothers: Understanding Their Lives and Families*. Thousand Oaks, CA: Sage Publications, 1995. 200p. (Sage Series on Race and Ethnic Relations). bibliog. index. ISBN 0803949111; 080394912Xpa.

Arguing that traditional, mainstream approaches to the study of African American single motherhood have silenced and pathologized rather than informed and empowered, the contributors to this important anthology explore the lives of such women using a synthesis of feminist and Afrocentric frameworks. Based on the principle "that the culture, history, and current experiences of African Americans are unique because the descendants of African people have retained elements of African culture and melded them with American culture" (pp. xviii–xix), Afrocentrism asserts a sense of continuity between many historical African values and the current experience of African American family life. The importance of praxis and empowerment, epistemological standpoint, subjectivity, and particularity is stressed throughout the volume. Essays address a variety of institutions and practices (including religion, media, and law), the intersection of race/class/gender/culture, the creation of social meanings, survival strategies and support systems, and suggestions for creating social change.

Some of these issues are explored from a different perspective in Elaine Bell Kaplan's *Not Our Kind of Girl: Unraveling the Myths of Teenage Black Motherhood* (University of California Press, 1997). This ethnographic study of seventeen teenaged mothers and fifteen women who were teenaged mothers explores the feelings, meanings, and motivations the women attached to their experience. Kaplan's analysis stresses the importance of the quality of the women's relationships with their mothers, fathers, schools, and the fathers of their children.

672. Dixon-Mueller, Ruth. *Population Policy and Women's Rights: Transforming Reproductive Choice.* Westport, CT: Praeger, 1993. 287p. bibliog. index. ISBN 0275945049; 0275946118pa.

Arguing that "the exercise of women's reproductive rights depends in fundamental ways on the exercise of women's rights in other spheres" (p. xii), Dixon-Mueller proposes a policy agenda that addresses the broad issues of gender equality. Central to this agenda is a reformulation of the "population problem" from a population-control framework to a framework centered on self-determination and the right to reproductive health. Recognizing that the details of a program based on this framework will vary as needs vary around the world, Dixon-Mueller identifies broad areas of emphasis rather than suggesting specific strategies. She maintains that programs should be based on women's lived experiences, empower women, provide a variety of reproductive health services through a process that is based on informed consent and appropriate follow-up care, include educational components, have linkages with the community and other care providers, and receive appropriate governmental and nongovernmental funding. Dixon-Mueller's argument builds on shifts in international understandings of women's rights (as evidenced by United Nations debate and action) and incorporates an analysis of the ideological underpinnings of the population-control and feminist birth-control movements, as well as data drawn from surveys and ethnographic studies conducted in countries of the South.

Many of these issues are also explored in Betsy Hartmann's *Reproductive Rights and Wrongs: The Global Politics of Population Control and Contraceptive Choice* (Harper & Row, 1987). The degree to which the ideas presented in these volumes have been institutionalized can be seen by examining the final documents of the International Conference on Population and Development and the Fourth World Conference on Women; these and other relevant materials can be found in *The United Nations and the Advancement of Women, 1945–1996* (Department of Public Information, United Nations, 1996) (see entry 545).

673. Driedger, Diane, and Susan Gray, eds. *Imprinting Our Image: An International Anthology by Women with Disabilities.* Charlottetown, Prince Edward Island: Gynergy Books, 1992. 224p. bibliog. index. ISBN 0921881223pa.

Driedger and Gray's groundbreaking anthology brings together the voices of more than thirty disabled women from seventeen countries. Striking a balance between voices from the developed and the developing world, this book includes the writings of women who may have little in common other than the label "disabled" and the strength and courage to work through and around the barriers placed before them. The last chapter, "Dealing with the World," focuses on the growth of disabled people's organizations around the world. *Across Borders: Women with Disabilities Working Together* (Gynergy Books, 1996) can be considered an extension of that chapter. Driedger, with Irene Feika and Eileen Girón Batres, have combined a selection of poetry with essays exploring the growth of disabled women's self-help groups. Brief interviews conducted during the United Nations Fourth World Conference on Women are also included. Driedger's opening essay provides a historical overview of this phenomenon, drawing welcome connections between events and organizations. Either of these volumes would be well suited to undergraduate courses exploring global feminism or feminist activism.

674. Duggan, Lisa, and Nan D. Hunter. *Sex Wars: Sexual Dissent and Political Culture.* New York: Routledge, 1995. 310p. bibliog. index. ISBN (OP); 0415910374pa.

This collection of previously published essays serves as a political and theoretical counterpoint to radical feminist discussions of pornography, sexual practices, and the law. It is premised on a notion of *"sexual dissent*, a concept that invokes a unity of speech, politics, and practices, and forges a connection among sexual expressions, oppositional politics, and claims to public space. Because sexual representations construct identities (they do not merely reflect preexisting ones), restriction and regulation of sexual expression is a form of political repression aimed at sexual minorities and gender nonconformists" (p. 5). Arguing against political strategies based on the right to privacy or an end to discrimination, the authors maintain that public sexual dissent is critical. They focus on three areas: sexual representation, the law, and activism and the academy. The opening essays, written in opposition to the antipornography legislation proposed by Andrea Dworkin and Catharine MacKinnon in the mid-1980s, argue against an interpretation of pornography as simply patriarchal and misogynistic. In contrast, Duggan states that pornography is "full of multiple, contradictory, layered and highly contextual meanings" (p. 7), some of which can be educational, validating, or empowering. Claiming that the use of anticensorship rhetoric to fight the legislation was a strategic choice aimed at political mobilization and was not an uncritical acceptance of a civil libertarian stance, the authors begin to develop a "specifically feminist argument in defense of sexually explicit expression" (p. 8). This analysis is used in a later essay examining public funding of controversial feminist and gay male art. The essays in part 2, "Sexual Dissent and the Law," address the limitations of litigation and definitions of "family" and "marriage." Part 3, "Sexual Dissent, Activism, and the Academy," is devoted to an examination of the "professionalization and institutionalization" of lesbian and gay studies and queer studies.

675. Dunne, Gillian A. *Lesbian Lifestyles: Women's Work and the Politics of Sexuality.* Toronto: University of Toronto Press, 1997. 258p. bibliog. index. ISBN 0802041043; 0802079512pa.

Dunne uses data drawn from life history interviews with sixty women living "lesbian lifestyles" to analyze the "ways that interpretations of sexuality deeply shape the conditions of women's work, both in the home and in the workplace" (p. 2). A cogent overview of the concept of "institutionalized heterosexuality" grounds the discussion. Defining "lesbian lifestyle" as one in which women were "organizing and approaching their lives on the assumption that they would form primary, loving relationships with women" (p. 26) and would not be emotionally or economically dependent on a man, Dunne goes on to explore two themes: given that sexuality is socially constructed, what conditions facilitate a heterosexual outcome and what conditions "facilitate the evaluation, challenging and questioning of the inevitability of this particular outcome?" and given that institutionalized heterosexuality is implicated in men's subordination of women, how does "moving beyond the constraints of heterosexuality" (pp. 21–22) empower women? In considering these themes, Dunne explores such questions as the following: How are alternative scripts for gender and sexual identity devised? Does an increase in employment opportunities lead to a more critical stance regarding heterosexuality and marriage? How does the timing of one's recognition of sexual preference or questioning of "traditional gender paths" affect schooling and employment choices? How do women in lesbian relationships balance work and home life?

676. Featherston, Elena, ed. *Skin Deep: Women Writing on Color, Culture, and Identity.* Freedom, CA: Crossing Press, 1994. 247p. bibliog. (OP)

Opening with a quote from Alice Walker's *In Search of Our Mother's Gardens*, this anthology explores the innumerable ways racism and colorism, defined as the "prejudicial or preferential treatment of same-race people based solely on their color" (p. i), have affected women of color in the United States. A blend of poetry and essays, the forty-eight short pieces reflect the experiences of specific women of color in ways that shed important light on critical questions confronting contemporary U.S. culture(s). The opening part emphasizes the contradictions and pain that come from living in a racist and colorist world; part 2 focuses on ways of healing. Featherston's efforts to include writings from a diverse group of women have resulted in a rewarding volume in which the voices of women from a wide range of cultures and colors (African, Asian, Latina, Sephardic Jew, Native American, Native Hawaiian, Middle Eastern, and mixed heritage) are represented.

677. Feinberg, Leslie. *Trans Liberation: Beyond Pink or Blue.* Boston: Beacon Press, 1998. 147p. ISBN 0807079502; 0807079510pa.

Defining "trans liberation" as "a movement of masculine females and feminine males, cross-dressers, transsexual men and women, intersexuals born on the anatomical sweep between female and male, gender-blenders, many other sex and gender-variant people, and our significant others" (p. 5), Feinberg forcefully and poignantly argues for the importance of unity among all social/political movements devoted to the rights of gender-oppressed communities. A self-identified "masculine, lesbian, female-to-male cross-dresser and transgenderist" (p. 19), Feinberg is a frequent speaker at events focused on issues of gender and/or sexuality; this volume contains revised versions of speeches s/he delivered in 1997. Interspersed among these texts are autobiographical "portraits" of other transgendered or intersexed people and those who love them. Feinberg's *Transgender Warriors: Making History from Joan of Arc to Dennis Rodman* (Beacon Press, 1996) takes a historical look at sex, gender, and the interweaving of class, race, sexuality, ethnicity, and nationality. Feinberg explores numerous issues, including whether female/male and feminine/masculine have always been perceived as exhaustive and exclusive categories and how different societies have treated people who crossed these boundaries. Profusely illustrated, this book details "hir" personal discovery of the long history of transgendered people and their experiences of exalted status, simple acceptance, and fierce struggle.

678. Fine, Michelle, and Adrienne Asch, eds. *Women with Disabilities: Essays in Psychology, Culture, and Politics.* Philadelphia: Temple University Press, 1988. 347p. (Health, Society, and Policy). bibliog. index. ISBN (OP); 0877226695pa.

The essays in this important anthology address a wide range of issues affecting the lives of disabled women. In their outstanding introduction, Fine and Asch integrate a review of feminist and disability scholarship with pertinent U.S. census data in an effort toward developing a more inclusive framework for both traditions. Acknowledging the irony "that the very category that integrates this text, 'disabled girls and women,' exists wholly as a social contruct" (p. 6), the editors briefly explore the various institutions that "turn characteristics into handicaps" (p. 7). Divided into three sections (bodies and body image, relationships, and politics and policy), the subsequent articles draw on a variety of disciplines and perspectives in their explorations of work, family, reproduction, parenting, sexuality, friendship, and politics. Although there have been considerable legal developments since this book was compiled (the Americans with Disabilities Act was passed two years after its publication), its age in no way diminishes its importance or its contribution to furthering our understanding of the social and political issues it raises.

Of some interest may be *Women with Disabilities: Found Voices*, edited by Mary E. Willmuth and Lillian Holcomb (Haworth Press, 1993). Reprinted from an issue of the journal *Women and Therapy*, it contains first-person, empirical, and theoretical accounts of the intersections of disability, gender, and race. Intended for therapists and other mental health professionals, many of the essays provide concrete suggestions for improving services for disabled clients. Several essays also explore issues that arise when the mental health professional is herself disabled.

679. Frankenberg, Ruth. *White Women, Race Matters: The Social Construction of Whiteness*. Minneapolis: University of Minnesota Press, 1993. 289p. bibliog. index. ISBN (OP); 0816622582pa.

Recognizing that "any system of differentiation shapes those on whom it bestows privilege as well as those it oppresses" (p. 1), Frankenberg examines how contemporary white women's lives have been shaped by the racial structure and the ways in which their lives are sites for both reproducing and challenging racism. Stemming from a commitment to feminist theory and practice and a deep concern with the inadequacy of white feminist response to charges of racism in the women's movement, Frankenberg's research explores the meanings and lived realities of whiteness and the possibilities for white feminist antiracist practice. Underlying her analysis is the theoretical claim that "whiteness" is comprised of three linked dimensions: it is a "location of structural advantage," a standpoint (in the epistemological sense), and a "set of cultural practices that are usually unmarked and unnamed" (p. 1). Basing her work on thirty life history interviews conducted in the mid-1980s with white women varying in age, religion, class, sexuality, family status, and political viewpoint, Frankenberg develops a framework for analyzing how positioning in the racial order is produced through the intersections and contradictions between the material relations of racism and discourses on race. Conceptualizing racial discourse as three "discursive repertoires" ("essentialist racism," "color- and power-evasiveness" rather than "color-blindness," and "race cognizant"), Frankenberg explores the historical moments that gave rise to each as well as the ways in which the discourses are deployed by her subjects. Opportunities for social change occur at the points of contradiction, where lived material reality intersects with discourse. Chapters explore childhood memories of racial awareness and racism, interracial intimate relationships, interracial parenting, "thinking through race," and whiteness as cultural practice. This challenging theoretical work is made quite accessible through Frankenberg's clear writing and the words of her subjects themselves. It was the winner of the American Sociological Association Jessie Bernard Award in 1995.

680. Fried, Marlene Gerber, ed. *From Abortion to Reproductive Freedom: Transforming a Movement*. Boston: South End Press, 1990. 317p. bibliog. index. ISBN 0896083888; 089608387Xpa.

Published in the wake of the Supreme Court decision in *Webster v. Reproductive Health Services*, the essays in this anthology seek to broaden the mainstream feminist understanding of reproductive rights issues to include more than simply the right to have an abortion. A wide variety of topics are covered, including sterilization abuse, economic barriers to reproductive freedom, women taking control of both birth control and abortion, the importance of reproductive counseling, the conflicts between "fetal protection" policies and women's rights, and organized attacks on abortion clinics. The strength of this volume is in its diversity of voices and its emphasis on inclusion and coalition building. Three key vision statements are reprinted: the "Reproductive Rights Position Paper" authored by the National Black Women's Health Project, the Religious Coalition for Abortion Rights' Women of Color Partnership Program vision statement, and "Statement of Asian-Pacific Women on Reproductive Health." This volume would serve as a good source of readings for courses on women's health and on health politics and policy.

681. Gabaccia, Donna, ed. *Seeking Common Ground: Multidisciplinary Studies of Immigrant Women in the United States.* Westport, CT: Greenwood Press, 1992. 237p. (Contributions in Women's Studies). bibliog. index. ISBN 0313274835; 0275943879pa.

Gabaccia, a specialist in U.S. immigration history, has compiled this multidisciplinary collection with the stated goal of encouraging cross-disciplinary communication and the development of research questions that emphasize comparative analysis and synthesis. With scholarship drawn from a broad range of disciplines (history, sociology, demography, American studies, women's studies, ethnic studies, and social work), the collection illustrates the commonalities and differences that exist in terminology and methodology. The volume is structured in three parts. Part 1 provides an overview of the treatment of immigrant women in the disciplines of history, sociology, and anthropology. Part 2 focuses on nineteenth-century immigration; included are a case study of German immigrants in light of the international marriage market, a discussion of the migration of Catholic nuns, an analysis of immigrant women's autobiographies, and an examination of the life histories of Japanese, Okinawan, and Korean picture brides. Part 3 considers more recent immigration to the United States. Chapters examine the "variability in the sex composition of U.S. immigrants by national origin" and the experience of postpartum depression among Asian immigrants. Of particular note are the two chapters that explore immigrant women's varying levels of participation in what one author terms "cultural coalescence . . . [in which they] selected, retained, borrowed, and created their own cultural forms" (p. 151). These chapters, an examination of Mexican American chaperonage and an analysis of the shifting perceptions of gender among Cuban women immigrants, provide insights into the development of social change in these communities.

Gabaccia's later work *From the Other Side: Women, Gender, and Immigrant Life in the U.S., 1820–1990* (Indiana University Press, 1994) is a book-length study of immigration that synthesizes material on class, ethnicity, the interrelationships between immigrant women, native-born women, and immigrant men, and the development of ethnic organizations. The shifting meanings attached to such notions as "American," "race," and "womanhood" are also examined. Gabaccia also compiled *Immigrant Women in the United States: A Selectively Annotated Multidisciplinary Bibliography* (Greenwood Press, 1989).

682. Ginsburg, Faye D. *Contested Lives: The Abortion Debate in an American Community.* Updated ed. Berkeley: University of California Press, 1998. 315p. bibliog. index. ISBN 0520217357pa.

Originally published in 1989, *Contested Lives* examines the views and experiences of female grassroots activists on both the pro-life and pro-choice sides of the abortion debate. The study focuses on the conflict that arose in Fargo, North Dakota, following the 1981 opening of the Fargo Women's Health Organization, the first publicly known, freestanding abortion clinic in

North Dakota. Ginsburg takes particular care to situate the Fargo debate in a broad historical and social context; early chapters provide an overview of the criminalization of abortion at the end of the nineteenth century and the concomitant redefinition of abortion as "the Evil of the Age," the growth of the abortion rights movement, and the rise of the right-to-life movement. Drawing on data collected in twelve months of fieldwork conducted in 1982 and 1983 (with a brief return in 1986), Ginsburg creates a vivid picture of the activists, their strategies, and, most significantly, the ways in which the struggle over abortion is part of a much larger struggle for social reform. A series of "procreation stories" (p. 13), narratives drawn from responses to the question "How did they see their own lives in relation to their current activism on the abortion issue?" (p. 133), sheds important light on the construction of self, of gender, and of life history. Ginsburg argues that the abortion debate is part of a larger, ongoing struggle over gender meanings: "Abortion persists as a contested domain in which the struggle over the place and meaning of procreation in women's lives, and its relation to the place of women in reproducing the culture, are being reorganized in oppositional terms" (p. 220). Ginsburg makes clear that this opposition need not lead to ongoing conflict; the formation of Pro-Dialogue, a group that brought pro-choice and pro-life Fargo activists together on issues of shared concern, is discussed in the epilogue. A brief appendix explores the history of female moral reform movements, enabling the reader to draw connections with previous atttempts by female activists to redraw or reaffirm gender definitions. The "Introduction to the Updated Edition" briefly details the recent history of abortion-related activism in Fargo and on the national level.

683. Glenn, Evelyn Nakano, Grace Chang, and Linda Rennie Forcey, eds. *Mothering: Ideology, Experience, and Agency*. New York: Routledge, 1994. 387p. (Perspectives on Gender). bibliog. index. ISBN (OP); 0415907764pa.

Beginning from the premise that "motherhood" as a universal set of practices and meanings is a fiction, the essays in this interdisciplinary collection analyze the myriad forms "mothering" has taken in specific sociocultural contexts existing in the United States in the nineteenth and twentieth centuries. Evelyn Nakano Glenn's introductory essay, "Social Constructions of Mothering: A Thematic Overview," frames the major theoretical issues and provides a useful context for the other contributions. The volume is organized around four themes: diversity in mothering, ideological constructions of motherhood, tensions and coherencies in constructions of motherhood, and women's agency and strategies for resistance. Essays use a variety of theoretical approaches and address a wide range of specific historical and cultural contexts; although ideological constructions of motherhood are discussed in detail, most essays are firmly grounded in an awareness of the material realities of women's lives.

These issues are addressed from a different perspective in *Representations of Motherhood*, edited by Donna Bassin, Margaret Honey, and Meryle Mahrer Kaplan (Yale University Press, 1994), which emphasizes psychoanalytic, film, and literary analysis more than sociological or historical approaches. Patricia Hill Collins's "Shifting the Center: Race, Class, and Feminist Theorizing about Motherhood" appears in both volumes. A less academic tone is taken in *Mother Journeys: Feminists Write about Mothering* (Spinsters Ink, 1994), edited by Maureen T. Reddy, Martha Roth, and Amy Sheldon. This collection of essays, poems, stories, and artwork explores the many facets of mothering from different perspectives and life experiences. The voices of Latina, African American, Asian American, Native American, and European American women are present, as are the voices of lesbian and heterosexual mothers, married and single mothers, birth mothers and adoptive mothers, young and older mothers, and those who have chosen not to mother. The authors describe a range of emotions; joy, pain, sadness, ambivalence, surprise, pride, and anger are all reflected within.

684. Goetting, Ann, and Sarah Fenstermaker, eds. *Individual Voices, Collective Visions: Fifty Years of Women in Sociology*. Philadelphia: Temple University Press, 1995. 362p. (Women in the Political Economy). bibliog. ISBN (OP); 1566392519pa.

The voices of eighteen "senior" American women sociologists are brought together in this collection of autobiographical essays. Although these accounts can be read as independent narratives of academic success or distilled into their similarities and overlapping categories of experience, the editors propose a more ambitious interpretive agenda focused on the importance of biography as a sociological method that is "valued as direct and raw access to the interaction process between individual experience and social structure, which shapes both" (p. 6). This reflexivity of "individual agency and social structure, individual choice, constraint and institutional change" (p. 345) underlies many of the narratives. Divided into five sections, the essays consider the impact of full-time motherhood and marriage on careers, academic mobility (or the lack thereof), isolation, marginality, and community. Four of the essays specifically speak to the experiences of foreign-born/American-educated sociologists. Throughout the book, stories of marginalization overlap with those of the joy of intellectual discovery; the dearth of female, let alone feminist, mentors is eventually mitigated by the creation and discovery of a community of likeminded women. The contributors are Dartha Clapper Brack, Beth B. Hess, Hannah Schiller Wartenberg, Jane E. Prather, Janet Lever, Judy Long, Britta Fischer, Suzanne Keller, Martha E. Gimenez, Helena Znaniecka Lopata, Elaine J. Hall, Diane Rothbard Margolis, Helen Mayer Hacker, Lynda Lytle Holmstrom, Coramae Richey Mann, Shulamit Reinharz, Gaye Tuchman, and Pamela Ann Roby.

685. Golden, Marita, and Susan Richards Shreve, eds. *Skin Deep: Black Women and White Women Write about Race*. New York: Nan A. Talese, 1995. 309p. ISBN (OP); 0385474105pa.

Essays, poems, and stories about race by black, white, and biracial women are brought together in this anthology coedited by a black woman and a white woman. Never simplistic in tone, these pieces "attest as much to our desire for communication and conversation as to the unmitigated legacy of mythology and history that trips us up" (p. 3). As Gayle Pemberton states in "Hello, Stranger," "When black and white women meet as strangers we carry with us parcel and sum of all that our families and this society have made of us" (p. 285). Spanning the life course and a range of emotions, these pieces confront notions of difference, beauty, agency, friendship, resistance, responsibility, solidarity, family, community, and love. The editors have included a range of perspectives and of writing forms. The voices of relatively new writers and those well known (Alice Walker, bell hooks, Eudora Welty, Toni Morrison, Joyce Carol Oates, Naomi Wolf, Mary Morris, and Jewelle Gomez) are included. All but three of the contributions are previously unpublished. This is a very accessible collection that is certain to evoke animated conversation.

686. Harding, Sandra, ed. *Feminism and Methodology: Social Science Issues*. Bloomington: Indiana University Press, 1987. 193p. bibliog. index. ISBN 025332243X; 0253204445pa.

Harding has compiled this collection of classic essays in support of her claim that while feminist social science does have characteristics distinguishing it from traditional social science approaches, a distinctive feminist research method does not exist. In her oft-cited introductory essay, Harding argues that scholars have confused and conflated the concepts of research method (ways of collecting data), methodology ("theory and analysis of how research does or should proceed") (p. 3), and epistemology (the theory of knowledge). Feminist social science is created from particular methodological and epistemological stances; Harding describes three characteristics upon which such work is built. Feminist social analysis "generates its problematics from the perspective of women's experiences" (p. 7) and tests hypotheses against these experiences. It is research "for" women that "insists that the inquirer her/himself be placed in the same critical plane as the overt subject matter, thereby recovering the entire research process for scrutiny in the results of research" (p. 9). In a brief epilogue, Harding describes the two transitional epistemologies that dominate feminist research: feminist empiricism and feminist standpoint. She views the tensions between and within these "justificatory strategies" as a positive force working against the development of a hegemonic feminist stance. Harding introduces each of the ten contributions, posing questions and drawing important connections with the other contributions. A broad range of disciplines and theoretical approaches are reflected; moreover, the essays were selected with an eye toward their interest and comprehensibility to undergraduate students. The contributors include Joan Kelly-Gadol, Marcia Millman and Rosabeth Moss Kantor, Carolyn Wood Sherif, Carol Gilligan, Joyce A. Ladner, Dorothy E. Smith, Bonnie Thornton Dill, Heidi I. Hartmann, Catharine A. MacKinnon, and Nancy C.M. Hartsock. This anthology is essential reading for those interested in the nature of feminist scholarly inquiry and the creation of feminist knowledge.

687. Herbert, Melissa S. *Camouflage Isn't Only for Combat: Gender, Sexuality, and Women in the Military.* New York: New York University Press, 1998. 205p. bibliog. index. ISBN 0814735479; 0814735487pa.

Framed by an understanding of gender shaped by the theoretical work of Candace West and Don H. Zimmerman's essay "Doing Gender," published in the journal *Gender & Society* (vol. 1, no. 2 [June, 1987]: 126–151); Herbert's revised dissertation examines the ways in which "gender and sexuality interact to shape how women manage life in the military" (p. 5). Using data drawn from 285 surveys and fourteen interviews, Herbert focuses on four research questions: In an environment in which masculinity is prized and rewarded, how do women balance the display of femininity (read as incompetence) and masculinity (read as sexually suspect)? What sanctions are used when one violates the "appropriate" balance? Do heterosexual women, lesbians, and bisexual women negotiate these tensions differently? What gender and sexual strategies do women use to survive (let alone succeed) in this environment? This interesting study provides insights that will no doubt be pursued in further research.

688. Hess, Beth B., and Myra Marx Ferree, eds. *Analyzing Gender: A Handbook of Social Science Research.* Newbury Park, CA: Sage Publications, 1987. 580p. bibliog. index. ISBN 0803927193.

Although published more than fifteen years ago, the essays in this now-classic collection continue to provide relevant insights into feminist social science research. In a concise and clear introduction, the editors present the historical/theoretical context for the essays in which they reject both the "sex differences" perspective and the sex-role socialization model in favor of an understanding of gender as constantly "renegotiated and reconstituted" (p. 17), relational, and structural. This conception of gender provides a consistent theoretical basis for the anthology. The volume is divided into five sections. The first contains articles exploring the "meaning of gender and the ways in which gender ideology has been used as an organizing principle for social systems, for knowledge, and for perception itself" (p. 17). Subsequent sections address the social control of female sexuality, economic relations and gender stratification, women's position and experiences in specific areas of civil society (work, family, religion, and health care), and the relationship of gender to the state. Contributors include Christine Ward Gailey, Janet Sayers, Kay Deaux and Mary E. Kite, Barbara Katz Rothman, Beth E. Schneider and Meredith Gould, Christine E. Bose,

Paula England and Lori McCreary, Myra Marx Ferree, Evelyn Nakano Glenn, Helena Z. Lopata, Martha Ackelsberg and Irene Diamond, and Cynthia H. Enloe. Serious students of feminist social science research would be remiss if they have not read these essays; the volume should be considered required reading for graduate students seeking to understand the development of feminist sociological thought.

689. Hillyer, Barbara. *Feminism and Disability*. Norman: University of Oklahoma Press, 1993. 302p. bibliog. index. ISBN (OP); 0806129794pa.

This challenging work by the mother of a physically and mentally disabled daughter explores the contradictions between feminist and disability movement politics as well as those between lived experience and professional literature. Hillyer contends that feminist analysis must be broadened to account for the specific ways in which disabled women may be different from the temporarily able bodied: "To the extent that feminist theory relies on women's ability to understand their situation, it fails to touch the situation of the woman with mental disabilities. When we argue against female dependency in marriage or elsewhere, we should not ignore the existence of individual women who may be unable to avoid dependency" (p. 8). Following an analysis of the "language of disability," Hillyer offers an analysis of reciprocity and interdependence between disabled women and those who care for them that makes a significant contribution to the ongoing feminist discussion of the ethics of care. Noting that recovery programs (i.e., twelve-step programs) were growing in number at the same time as the disability rights movement was gaining momentum in the 1980s, Hillyer examines the practices employed by AA (and its brethren) and its members with an eye toward determining which, if any, might well be incorporated into feminist and disability group practice.

690. hooks, bell. *Outlaw Culture: Resisting Representations*. New York: Routledge, 1994. 260p. bibliog. index. ISBN (OP); 0415908116pa.

This collection of essays by hooks, one of the most influential feminist cultural critics, is far-reaching and challenging and defies ready summarizing. Opening with an introduction that explores the political necessity and context of cultural studies, hooks explains its intellectual appeal: "eclectic, interdisciplinary, inspired by revolutionary political visions.... [A] site where I could freely transgress boundaries" (p. 3). Built around an interplay of theory and practice evidenced throughout the volume, hooks's essays address "cultural practices and cultural icons who are defined as on the edge, as pushing the limits, disturbing the conventional, acceptable politics of representation" (pp. 4–5). Her critiques span the visual imagery produced of and by the formerly transgressive Madonna; the written works of Camille Paglia, Naomi Wolf, and Katie Roiphe; and the films *The Crying Game, The Bodyguard*, and *Malcolm X*. Other essays explore censorship, gangsta culture, the legacy of Columbus, internalized racism, and the shifts in Malcolm X's understanding of gender and sexism. The volume closes with "Love as the Practice of Freedom," a meditation on the transformative and liberatory power of love of self and community. In her earlier collection *Yearning: Race, Gender, and Cultural Politics* (South End Press, 1990), hooks turns her critical eye on a wide range of cultural practices and symbols, including black masculinity, Wim Wenders's *Wings of Desire*, Spike Lee's *Do the Right Thing*, Zora Neale Hurston, the meaning of homeplace, and black writers/scholars and the politics of feminist solidarity.

691. Hurtado, Aída. *The Color of Privilege: Three Blasphemies on Race and Feminism*. Ann Arbor: University of Michigan Press, 1996. 203p. (Critical Perspectives on Women and Gender). bibliog. index. ISBN 0472095315; 0472065319pa.

Defining "blasphemy" as the practice of "questioning what in many ways we have been required not to question" (p. xi) while still being dedicated to betterment of the same community that has set the boundaries on permissible speech, Hurtado explores several key issues involving the interplay of race and gender. Beginning from an analysis of subordination processes as relational, Hurtado outlines key aspects of an inclusive, multicultural feminism. The importance of "border crossing" as a key to the development of a liberatory theory and practice becomes apparent as Hurtado explores the relationship between Chicanas and African American women, their respective communities, and ethnic/racial liberation movements. The final chapter, "On a Reflexive Feminist Theory of Gender Subordination," posits that without an analysis of privilege from the standpoint of the oppressor, existing analyses of subordination are incomplete: "we have yet to chronicle how those who oppress make sense of their power *in relationship* to those they have injured" (p. 124). Hurtado contends that an understanding of this dynamic will strengthen feminists' ability to dismantle the power structures and create a world free of hierarchies based on gender, race, sexual orientation, and class.

692. Jarrett-Macauley, Delia, ed. *Reconstructing Womanhood, Reconstructing Feminism: Writings on Black Women.* New York: Routledge, 1996. 206p. bibliog. index. ISBN 0415116481; 041511649Xpa.

As the first British anthology devoted to readings of "womanhood" and "feminism" through the lens of race and ethnicity, this brief collection provides a glimpse into the varied experiences and perspectives of British women of African and African Caribbean descent. The first five essays are concerned with exploring the lived experiences of black British women, both historical and contemporary: immigration policy and practice, the impacts of black and white churches, images of black female sexuality, and silencing and identity. Part 2 of the collection focuses on cultural politics and representation. Bringing together essays on representation in film, the experiences of black women in British art schools, literature and colonialism, and a reading of Nella Larsen's 1929 novella *Passing*, Jarrett-Macauley seeks to suggest the outline of a cultural politics developed in opposition to sexist, racist, and colonialist discourses. Although issues of "naming" and its relationship to colonialism are most obviously confronted in Felly Nkweto Simmonds's "Naming and Identity," they are of critical importance throughout the volume.

693. Johnson, Janis Tyler. *Mothers of Incest Survivors: Another Side of the Story.* Bloomington: Indiana University Press, 1992. 162p. index. bibliog. ISBN 0253330963; 0253207371pa.

In this ethnographic study based on her dissertation, Johnson explores the experiences of six women whose husbands sexually abused their daughters. She quotes the women extensively, enabling readers to learn how they experienced the "incest event" and what meanings they have since attached to it. Following an introduction in which she analyzes the dominant theoretical views of the role of the mother in the incest family (collusive, powerless, or protective), Johnson briefly introduces each of the women. Their stories are shared in thematically focused chapters with contextual and analytical support from Johnson. This approach serves to bring out both the commonalities and differences in the women's experiences and in the meanings they have attached to them. A chapter devoted to reexamining the theoretical models in light of these women's stories concludes the main text. An epilogue, written six years after the initial interviews, briefly explores the changes in the women's lives and the effect that study participation may have had on them.

Tracy Orr covers similar territory in *No Right Way: The Voices of Mothers of Incest Survivors* (Scarlet Press, 1995). The experiences of four Canadian women are explored with an eye toward exploding the stereotypes surrounding mothers of incest survivors. Rather than interweaving the women's voices around specific subjects, Orr presents each woman in turn. This approach, while maintaining the narrative structure of each woman's life, sometimes makes it difficult to draw the connections between them. Orr supplies some context and interpretations but, for the most part, allows the women to speak for themselves.

694. Kandal, Terry R. *The Woman Question in Classical Sociological Theory*. Miami: Florida International University Press, 1988. 341p. bibliog. index. ISBN 0813007968pa.

This survey of the treatment of women in classical sociological theory provides a solid understanding of the debates that have long surrounded discussions of women's unequal status in Western societies. Kandal places a strong emphasis on context: the writings of each theorist are carefully, albeit briefly, situated in a specific historical and biographical frame. The structure of the book underscores the importance of geographically based sociological traditions; each chapter is focused on the key theorists from a given country (England: John Stuart Mill, Herbert Spencer; France: Alexis de Tocqueville, Auguste Comte, Émile Durkheim; Germany: Max Weber, Georg Simmel, Ferdinand Tönnies, Karl Mannheim; Italy: Vilfredo Pareto, Robert Michels; United States: Talcott Parsons, C. Wright Mills). Kandal quotes extensively from key texts to provide insights into the theorists' views of women's position in society and of the social movements dedicated to improving that position. A concluding chapter evaluates the explanatory power of the texts and provides a brief overview of Marxist and Freudian theories regarding women's position. In a brief final section, Kandal suggests that the key to a "sociological science of women and men" (p. 245) is through historically based cross-cultural studies. This book should be on the reading list in sociology of women courses that attempt to incorporate a historical perspective. Similarly, it would be a strong addition to courses on the history of sociological theory.

695. Kaye/Kantrowitz, Melanie, and Irena Klepfisz, eds. *The Tribe of Dina: A Jewish Women's Anthology*. Rev. and expanded ed. Boston: Beacon Press, 1989. 360p. bibliog. ISBN 0807036056pa.

Bringing together essays, poems, artwork, stories, photographs, consciousness-raising exercises, and interviews, this anthology seeks "to express the wide range of Jewish experience and culture, and to develop more empathy and *support* for Jewish identities which we do not share" (p. 8). A broad range of Jewish women's experience is reflected in the contributions: secular, religious, Sephardic, Ashkenazi, working class, middle class, Zionist, anti-Zionist, lesbian, U.S. based, Israeli, Soviet, Arab, writers of English and of Yiddish, and survivors of the Holocaust. Serving as a testament against assimilation, against "the blurring or erasure of identity and culture" (p. 309), the collection speaks to the ways in which acknowledging Jewish history and culture brings added strength to women's lives and political work. Much of the anthology was originally published in 1986 as a special double issue of *Sinister Wisdom* (29/30); the additional contributions in this expanded edition bring greater depth and currency to the anthology. Well suited for undergraduate use, this collection will be useful in a wide range of women's studies and Jewish studies courses.

696. Kempadoo, Kamala, and Jo Doezema, eds. *Global Sex Workers: Rights, Resistance, and Redefinition*. New York: Routledge, 1998. 294p. bibliog. index. ISBN 0415918286; 0415918294pa.

Building from a framework that clearly sees prostitution and related activities as "sexual labor," this groundbreaking collection of essays explores the experiences of sex workers around the world and the strategies they have used to better their lives and working conditions. Arguing against theoretical models that posit sex work as inherently exploitative, the contributions to this volume recognize the importance of individual subjectivity and agency while not disregarding the importance of "structural constraints and dominant relations of power in the global sex industry" (pp. 8–9). Several essays examine the explanatory power and implications of the forced versus voluntary prostitution dichotomy; others directly challenge readers to forgo morality-based responses to child prostitution and instead examine "the meanings children give to their own activities and identities" (p. 102). Stressing that the concept of "trafficking" is not limited to situations involving coercion, contributors reaffirm the importance of recognizing the rights of sex workers as migrant laborers. Part 3, "Sex Workers' Organizations," includes contributions from Ecuador, Japan, the United States, South Africa, Mexico, India, Malaysia, and Suriname. Part 4 focuses on AIDS-prevention projects that have been designed to empower sex workers in Brazil, Senegal, the European Union, and the Dominican Republic.

697. Kim, Elaine H., Lilia V. Villanueva, and Asian Women United of California, eds. *Making More Waves: New Writing by Asian American Women*. Boston: Beacon Press, 1997. 309p. bibliog. ISBN 0807059137pa.

Combining poetry and prose, fiction and nonfiction, *Making More Waves* crosses boundaries of genre and subject, emphasizing the multiple identities and subjectivities of Asian American women's lives. Created through an open call for submissions and a subsequent editorial process that winnowed nearly 1,000 submissions down to almost 50, the anthology brings together voices established and new. The contributions are presented in five sections ("Memory," "Implosion," "Reflection," "Contestation," and "Movement") without any introductory contextualizing remarks, thereby allowing readers more freedom to interpret and draw their own connections. The range of topics covered includes media representations, living with HIV/AIDS, labor organizing, "comfort women," racialized sexual harassment, sexuality, visual artists, the meaning of family, female gangs, and domestic violence.

The original *Making Waves: An Anthology of Writings by and about Asian American Women* (Beacon Press, 1989), edited by Asian Women United of California, is also comprised of poetry and prose, autobiography and explicit political analysis. The collection is organized thematically, with sections on immigration, war, work, generations, identity, injustice, and activism. *The Forbidden Stitch: An Asian American Women's Anthology* (Calyx Books, 1989), edited by Shirley Geok-lin Lim and Mayumi Tsutakawa, reprints material originally issued in *Calyx: A Journal of Art and Literature by Women* (vol. 11, no. 2/3, Fall 1988). This collection includes poetry, prose, art, and reviews. Stressing the importance of recognizing cultural differences while acknowledging shared experiences of racism and imperialism, the volume "celebrates our plural singularity" (p. 12).

698. Kitzinger, Celia. *The Social Construction of Lesbianism*. Newbury Park, CA: Sage Publications, 1987. 230p. (Inquiries in Social Construction Series). bibliog. index. ISBN 0803981163; 0803981171pa.

This bold radical feminist critique of liberal humanistic ideology (and its corresponding "gay-affirmative," lifestyle-oriented research) focuses on the depoliticization inherent in its framing of the social world. Denying the possibility of objective language, "terminological purity," or "linguistic hygiene" (p. 29), Kitzinger explores the rhetorical techniques underlying scientific writing and the ways in which these techniques have been employed in scientific discourse surrounding lesbianism and male homosexuality. Kitzinger asserts that both the "pathological" and the "individual, lifestyle choice" constructions of lesbianism function as forms of social control, one coercive and abnormal, the other normalizing. Moreover, "gay-affirmative" research is directly implicated in the efforts of "a liberal patriarchal order to contain and control the political challenge of lesbianism" (p. 178). Kitzinger argues that a more liberatory social science will require a thorough deconstruction of normative reality. To this end, she explores in depth the construction of lesbian subjectivities using data collected via interviews and Q methodology factor analysis of a data matrix by rows rather than columns. Separate chapters address lesbian identity, "the set of meanings ascribed by a woman to whatever social, emotional, sexual, political or personal configuration she intends when she describes herself as a 'lesbian' " (p. 90), and lesbian politics, the "ideological or political frameworks which underlie and sustain" lesbian identities (p. 123). Kitzinger argues that the "invention of homophobia" is designed to "construct subjectivities about lesbianism in accordance with liberal humanistic ideology" (p. 154). This issue is further explored in a chapter devoted to heterosexual attitudes toward lesbians.

699. Krieger, Susan. *Social Science and the Self: Personal Essays on an Art Form.* New Brunswick, NJ: Rutgers University Press, 1991. 273p. bibliog. ISBN 0813517141; 081351715Xpa.

Krieger brilliantly balances form and purpose in this treatise on the place of the self in social science. Maintaining that social scientists cannot help but insert themselves into their texts, Krieger argues for greater authenticity through explicit acknowledgment and use of the authorial "I": "The social science disciplines tend to view the self of the social scientific observer as a contaminant. The self—the unique inner life of the observer—is treated as something to be separated out, neutralized, minimized, standardized and controlled. At the same time, the observer is expected to use the self to the end of understanding the world. . . . [T]he contaminant view of the self is something we ought to alter. I think we ought to develop our different individual perspectives more fully in social science, and we ought to acknowledge . . . the extent to which our studies are reflections of our inner lives" (p. 1). Seamlessly integrating autobiography and feminist methodology and epistemology, Krieger explores the ways knowledge is constructed and transmitted in academic settings and writings. In describing her struggle with traditional academic expression and self-presentation, Krieger also sheds light on issues of difference and gatekeeping in the academy. Although emphasizing the practice of writing social science, Krieger also examines the issues involved in translating her epistemological stance into pedagogical practice. Numerous themes recur throughout the text: self-disclosure and vulnerability, individuality and conformity, authority and authorial perspective, and the interconnections of "self, truth and form" (p. 67).

700. Laslett, Barbara, and Barrie Thorne, eds. *Feminist Sociology: Life Histories of a Movement.* New Brunswick, NJ: Rutgers University Press, 1997. 286p. bibliog. index. ISBN 0813524288; 0813524296pa.

Taken together, this collection of twelve essays by a veritable who's who of feminist sociology provides a wealth of insight into the development of "feminist sociology" as a discipline and as a theoretical approach to the core questions of the sociological enterprise. Arguing that a life history approach is a useful addition to the array of techniques used in "doing social theory," Laslett and Thorne state: "Life histories of intellectuals can provide insights into the social processes through which knowledge is created, transmitted, and changed. . . . [They] can demonstrate intersections of social structure and human agency in ways that are more empirically rich and theoretically nuanced than other techniques more commonly used by sociologists" (p. 6). Though the essays vary in tone and emphasis, they share a focus on exploring the set of historical, cultural, institutional, and personal conditions and processes through which the authors have experienced and contributed to the growth of feminist sociology. The essayists are Laslett and Thorne, Joan Acker, Evelyn Nakano Glenn, Judith Stacey, R. W. Connell, Desley Deacon, Susan Krieger, Sarah Fenstermaker, Lynn Weber, Elizabeth Higginbotham, Bonnie Thornton Dill, and Marjorie L. DeVault.

A similar project is undertaken in *Gender and the Academic Experience: Berkeley Women Sociologists* (University of Nebraska Press, 1994), edited by Kathryn P. Meadow Orlans and Ruth A. Wallace. This collection features autobiographical sketches by sixteen women who received Ph.D.'s from the University of California at Berkeley between 1952 and 1972. Contributors include Orlans and Wallace, as well as Arlene Kaplan Daniels, Dorothy E. Smith, Arlie Russell Hochschild, Ruth Dixon-Mueller, and Lillian B. Rubin.

701. Leidholdt, Dorchen, and Janice G. Raymond, eds. *Sexual Liberals and the Attack on Feminism.* New York: Pergamon Press, 1990. 244p. (The Athene Series). bibliog. index. ISBN 0080374581; 0080374573pa.

Arguing that there is a long history of "sexual liberals" opposing feminist efforts to improve the social and economic condition of women, the contributors to this volume analyze past and present "sexual liberal" theory and practice regarding a range of sex-related issues. Most of the contributions are derived from presentations given at the 1987 "Sexual Liberals and the Attack on Feminism" conference. As such, many sacrifice documentation in favor of rhetorical power. Despite this (or, perhaps, because of this stylistic choice), the collection brilliantly conveys the emphatic point of view of one particular branch of late-twentieth-century U.S. feminism. (An alternative perspective on many of these issues can be found in the volume by Duggan and Hunter annotated earlier in this section.) Leidholt's introduction states that sexual liberalism is "a set of political beliefs and practices rooted in the assumption that sexual expression is inherently liberating and must be permitted to flourish unchecked, even when it entails the exploitation or brutalization of others" (p. ix). Issues of women's agency and the nature of consent, as well as the difference (or the lack thereof) between ideology, imagery, and material reality, are explored in interwoven analyses of pornography, prostitution, surrogacy, new reproductive technologies, sexuality, and incest. Although the contributors likely agree on many aspects of these issues, the juxtaposition of two articles on sexual expression ("Sex Resistence in Heterosexual Arrangements" and "Toward a Feminist Praxis of Sexuality") reveals the ways in which some of these issues are still being contested within a radical feminist framework. Contributors include Andrea Dworkin, Catharine MacKinnon, Louise Armstrong, Sonia Johnson, Ann Jones, Gena Corea, Phyllis Chesler, Pauline B. Bart, Sheila Jeffreys, Florence Rush, Wendy Stock, John Stoltenberg, and Mary Daly.

702. Lopata, Helena Znaniecka. *Circles and Settings: Role Changes of American Women.* Albany: State University of New York Press, 1994. 325p. (SUNY Series in Gender and Society). bibliog. index. ISBN 0791417670; 0791417689pa.

Employing a feminist symbolic interactionist perspective, Lopata synthesizes existing theory and research to explore changes in American women's role involvements. Her approach is not to be confused with "sex-role" theory (which she explicitly rejects). Lopata defines a social role as "a set of patterned, mutually interdependent social relations between a social person and a social circle, involving tasks and relational duties and personal rights" (p. 4). Recognizing that social roles change over the life course and that women can lay claim to several social roles simultaneously, Lopata uses the concept of the "role cluster" to identify the constellation of social roles active at a particular time in a woman's life. Arguing that the process of social development/ modernization affects the choice, content, and institutional location (e.g., family, work) of social roles, Lopata posits three ideal-typical periods (traditional, transitional, and modern), each with its own set of opportunities and constraints. Using this framework, Lopata analyzes a subset of the multiple roles historically afforded women: wife, mother, kin (daughter, sister, grandmother), homemaker, employed woman, student, friend, and neighbor. Particular attention is paid to how these social roles change over the life course. Role strain and role conflict are discussed, as are the strategies women use to negotiate these tensions.

703. Lorber, Judith, and Susan A. Farrell, eds. *The Social Construction of Gender*. Newbury Park, CA: Sage Publications, 1991. 374p. bibliog. ISBN 0803939566; 0803939574pa.

With all but two articles drawn from the first four years of *Gender and Society*, the flagship publication of Sociologists for Women in Society, this anthology provides a fascinating snapshot of the issues concerning feminist sociologists in the late 1980s. The eighteen essays are presented in six sections: "Principles of Gender Construction," "Gender Construction in Family Life," "Gender Construction in the Workplace," "Feminist Research Strategies," "Racial Ethnic Identity and Feminist Politics," and "Deconstructing Gender." Each section is preceded by a brief review of the literature that clearly situates the essays in recent research and practice. Although feminist sociological theory has moved beyond the theoretical stances taken in some of the contributions, this volume remains essential reading for anyone interested in the development of feminist sociology. Several classic essays are included: Candace West and Don H. Zimmerman's "Doing Gender," Deniz Kandiyoti's "Bargaining with Patriarchy," Maxine Baca Zinn's "Family, Feminism, and Race in America," and Joan Acker's "Hierarchies, Jobs, Bodies: A Theory of Gendered Organizations."

704. Luker, Kristin. *Dubious Conceptions: The Politics of Teenage Pregnancy*. Cambridge, MA: Harvard University Press, 1996. 283p. bibliog. index. ISBN 0674217020; 0674217039pa.

Examining the social construction of "parental fitness" and "adolescence" and the social implications of age, Luker explores the worldview of teenagers who choose to parent and the effects that decision has on their lives. She examines the meanings of teenage pregnancy, noting that despite its presence throughout U.S. history, teen pregnancy was not deemed a social problem until the mid-1970s. Shifts in the meanings attached to sexuality, marriage, parenthood, and work are explored. A historical overview of reproductive social policy provides an important context for her arguments. Luker refutes numerous earlier studies that drew a causal link between teen pregnancy and subsequent poverty and instead contends that a more methodologically sound analysis demonstrates that the relatively high incidence of poverty among teenage mothers can be explained by other, preexisting conditions. This work raises a broad range of other critical questions, including, why are young mothers likely to be single? why do some young women feel that they are ready for parenting but not for marriage? and what can U.S. society do for teenage parents and their children? This study has important ramifications for the development of more effective and appropriate social policies and services.

705. Maglin, Nan Bauer, and Donna Perry, eds. *"Bad Girls"/"Good Girls": Women, Sex, and Power in the Nineties*. New Brunswick, NJ: Rutgers University Press, 1996. 303p. bibliog. index. ISBN 0813522501; 081352251Xpa.

Gathered to improve the vision of those who see American feminism only as reflected through the eyes of Katie Roiphe, Naomi Wolf, and/or Camille Paglia, the essays in this noteworthy volume "seek to reconnect sexuality to a political analysis, to underscore the pro-sex wing of the women's movement, and to move feminism beyond the simplistic namecalling and dichotomies characteristic of the current debate" (p. xvi). The essays vary greatly in tone and texture: the shifting voices include those of the editorial page, the academic text, and the survivor's narrative. Writers both new and established (e.g., Katha Pollitt, Ellen Willis, bell hooks, and Anna Quindlen) are represented. Each of the book's five parts addresses aspects of the current debates surrounding sexuality and agency/victimization. Part 1, "The Feminist Narrative: The 1970s and the 1990s," explores the ways in which feminist thinking (and media portrayals of that thinking) has changed in the last two decades from a political recognition of the many manifestations of oppression to a focus on the personal and the victimized. The contributions to part 2, " 'Victim' and 'Power' Feminism: Several Takes," directly confront the work of Roiphe, Wolf, and Paglia. In a particularly intriguing essay, Jodi Dean uses an examination of alien abduction narratives to argue against dismissing the work of these popular feminist writers. Later parts focus on political understandings of violence against women and on sexual practices and identities. The last part, on media representations of women, includes two pieces written by visual artists that are especially noteworthy: photographer Matuschka explores the beauty and acceptability of women's bodies through postmastectomy self-portraits; Emma Amos's brief essay (and the accompanying reproductions of her paintings) confronts the ways in which the art establishment has tried to circumscribe the art of African American women. This book would be a useful counterpoint for classes using the Roiphe or Wolf books.

706. Malson, Micheline R., Elisabeth Mudimbe-Boyi, Jean F. O'Barr, and Mary Wyer, eds. *Black Women in America: Social Science Perspectives.* Chicago: University of Chicago Press, 1990. 340p. bibliog. index. ISBN 0226502953; 0226502961pa.

Designed for classroom use, this interdisciplinary collection of articles originally published in *Signs: Journal of Women in Culture and Society* between 1977 and 1989 brings together classic and lesser-known articles in a dialogue that strives to generate new questions and new insights. A brief and brilliantly constructed introductory essay identifies key themes, points of theoretical agreement and disagreement, and the ways in which the authors build on and spin off from each other's work. Among the classic essays included are Diane K. Lewis's "A Response to Inequality: Black Women, Racism, and Sexism," Bonnie Thornton Dill's "The Dialectics of Black Womanhood," and Patricia Hill Collins's "The Social Construction of Black Feminist Thought." Other contributors are Elsa Barkley Brown, Patricia J. Williams, Walter R. Allen, Mary Corcoran, Greg J. Duncan, Martha S. Hill, James A. Geschwender, Rita Carroll-Seguin, Susan A. Mann, Sharon Harley, Dianne F. Sadoff, Cheryl Townsend Gilkes, Maxine Baca Zinn, and Deborah K. King. This volume would be a welcome text for undergraduate courses on African American women and on feminist epistemology and methodology.

Some of the readings in Kim Vaz's collection *Black Women in America* (Sage Publications, 1995) provide an interesting supplement to the theoretical work just mentioned. This interdisciplinary collection of eighteen previously unpublished essays focuses on four themes: African American women's social activism; literary, media, and political representations of African American women; rhetoric and performance; and contemporary psychosocial issues. Of particular interest are the contributions that provide original research on African American women's political organizing.

707. Morell, Carolyn M. *Unwomanly Conduct: The Challenges of Intentional Childlessness.* New York: Routledge, 1994. 204p. bibliog. index. ISBN (OP); 0415906784pa.

In this exploration of the maternalistic imperative and the meaning(s) attached to "motherhood" and "not-motherhood," Morell employs a feminist poststructuralist framework to decipher the social practices and discourses that limit reproductive diversity. Not limiting her analysis to mainstream texts, Morell offers a strong critique of recent feminist writings on motherhood and maternalism. Quoting at length from interviews conducted with thirty-four married, intentionally childless women, she explores the concept of "choice," as well as social relationships and self-definition in an unsupportive culture. From her analysis of the frequency with which "not mothers" must perform "explanatory work" (p. 54) to her description of the phenomenon of "friendship wedges" (p. 127), Morell's work helps to give voice to women who have long been ignored.

In *Without Child: Challenging the Stigma of Childlessness* (Ballantine Books, 1996), Laurie Lisle blends autobiography, history, psychology, and literary and social criticism in an exploration of the multiple meanings attached to childlessness. The influence of, and impact on, love, relationships, work life, friendships, and relationships with (others') children are considered through Lisle's multidisciplinary lens. *Childless by Choice: A Feminist Anthology*, edited by Irene Reti (HerBooks, 1992), presents poetry and essays by a diverse group of feminist women who have chosen to be childless. Elaine Tyler May's *Barren in the Promised Land: Childless Americans and the Pursuit of Happiness* (Basic Books, 1995) discusses voluntary and involuntary childlessness in a study that combines historical discussion and analysis of contemporary qualitative data.

708. Nebraska Sociological Feminist Collective, ed. *A Feminist Ethic for Social Science Research*. Lewiston, NY: Edwin Mellen Press, 1988. 247p. (Women's Studies). bibliog. index. ISBN 0889461201.

Based on a special issue of *Humanity and Society* edited by the collective in 1983, this anthology contains fourteen essays examining social science ethics and methodologies. The contributions focus on four key areas: the ways in which social science methodologies objectify "wimmin," the development of feminist methodologies, the role of language in perpetuating oppressive systems and structures, and the gatekeeping process. Many of the essays begin with a "reflexive statement" by the author. Although some of these statements simply provide abstracts or biographical information, several explicitly turn on its head the traditional social science claim of "objectivity" and "authority" by grounding the essays in first-person statements of the authors' intellectual and political stances. That many of the insights contained within the pages of this collection seem familiar and uncontroversial is testimony to the success of volumes such as this in permeating the consciousness of feminist social scientists. Contributors include the Nebraska Sociological Feminist Collective (Beth Hartung, Jane C. Ollenburger, Helen A. Moore, and Mary Jo Deegan), Dorothy E. Smith, Carol Smart, Pauline Bart, Julia Penelope, Judith A. Cook, and Mary Margaret Fonow.

709. Oakley, Ann. *Social Support and Motherhood: The Natural History of a Research Project*. Cambridge, MA: Blackwell Publishers, 1992. 404p. bibliog. index. (OP)

In this multilayered work, Oakley, a British-based sociologist, details the background, conceptualization, and execution of the Social Support and Pregnancy Outcome study, a research project designed to explore the question "Can social support in pregnancy improve the health of women and their babies?" (p. 17). Throughout the work, issues of epistemology, appropriate research design, and the standpoints of researchers and participants are paramount as Oakley confronts one of the fundamental questions facing feminist social scientists: "how to attempt to advance knowledge at the same time as being critical about the process and model of knowledge-construction itself" (p. 18). Although this work is focused on a discussion of the research process rather than on disseminating the research results, several important insights into the connections between health and social support are discussed. The meaning and content of "health" and its relationship to social factors in people's lives are analyzed as Oakley interrogates the "dominant ideology of our times—that health is, first and foremost, a medical product" (p. 11). The construction of seemingly "objective" indicators (e.g., "low birthweight" and "social class") is also examined. To assist readers interested in further pursuing the outcomes of the research project, a bibliography of publications based on the study is provided in an appendix. Courses exploring feminist research methods, as well as those on the sociology of health, would benefit from this work. It is also highly recommended for those struggling with (or about to embark on) a major research proposal or project.

710. Ollenburger, Jane C., and Helen A. Moore. *A Sociology of Women: The Intersection of Patriarchy, Capitalism, and Colonization.* 2nd ed. Upper Saddle River, NJ: Prentice Hall, 1998. 251p. bibliog. index. ISBN 0136716377pa.

Asserting that feminist and sociological theory have failed to adequately address the diversity of women's experience, Ollenburger and Moore outline a sociology of, for, and about women that emphasizes three separate, yet intersecting, systems of oppression: patriarchy, capitalism, and colonization. Incorporating the concepts of use value ("the subjective meaning of social action") and exchange value ("the empirical relations of exchange in the market"), the authors posit a theory that provides analytical tools for examining women's oppression across historical, cultural, economic, and racial boundaries (p. 41). Ollenburger and Moore test their theoretical construction in three chapters, each devoted to a specific area of social organization: work, education, and law. In the penultimate chapter, the authors explore the experiences of elderly women as the "culmination of discrimination in the workplace, devalued education, and structural limitations" (p. 194). Stressing that work based on a feminist theoretical framework must employ feminist methodologies and feminist ethics, Ollenburger and Moore provide an all-too-brief overview of the rich literature in these areas. The authors also argue that feminist sociology is necessarily practice oriented and, therefore, activist. Ollenburger and Moore suggest some very useful avenues for further research and theoretical development; however, the succinctness of some of their arguments will make this a very challenging reading experience for those not already well versed in traditional and feminist theoretical models.

711. Omolade, Barbara. *The Rising Song of African American Women.* New York: Routledge, 1994. 272p. bibliog. index. ISBN 0415907608; 0415907616pa.

Omolade combines "historical voices, spiritual consciousness, and liberation politics" (p. xvii) in this collection of original and previously published essays. The articles and speeches that comprise the first part of the book are centered on the ways in which historical experiences of family, work, and sexuality shape contemporary experiences. The importance of a historical perspective is also evident in part 2, "Invisible to the Naked Eye: Black Women and the Academy." Essays explore the relationship of black women to institutional power and knowledge and knowledge production, the development of a black feminist intelligentsia, and the development of a black feminist pedagogy. The final part addresses the potential and limitations of a black feminist praxis through an autobiographical examination of the legacy of civil rights movement leader Ella Baker and articles analyzing militarism, ethnic warfare, public discourse, globalization, and the need for concrete strategies engendering local political and social change. In two essays explicitly interrogating relatively recent events that galvanized public attention, the rapes of Tawana Brawley and "the Central Park jogger," Omolade analyzes how the intersection of history, racism, and violence against women distorts and silences the experiences of African American women.

712. Pearsall, Marilyn, ed. *The Other within Us: Feminist Explorations of Women and Aging.* Boulder, CO: Westview Press, 1997. 280p. bibliog. ISBN 061427690X; 0614276896pa.

With a title drawn from Simone de Beauvoir's *Coming of Age*, this collection of previously published essays explores the relationship between sexism and ageism in contemporary U.S. society. The contributions are organized around four central themes: situating, problematizing, representing, and privileging. "Situating" focuses on the "lived experiences" of older women and the "positionality of older women in society" (p. 4); articles address differences in women's and men's experiences of aging, issues of class and race, and urbanization. "Problematizing" scrutinizes the discourses of gerontology and medicine, adult daughters as caregivers, the social construction of older women within lesbian communities, and intersections of race, class, and gender. "Representing" analyzes representations of older women in specific works of film, art, and literature. The narratives in "Privileging" use varying approaches to explore the self-alienation that is perceived as "the other within us." With its inclusion of several older, classic pieces and more recent works that challenge those assumptions and conclusions, Pearsall has fashioned a volume that both demonstrates the continued growth of feminist theorizing and research and contributes to the development of new ways of conceptualizing the questions in this critical area.

713. Penelope, Julia, ed. *Out of the Class Closet: Lesbians Speak.* Freedom, CA: Crossing Press, 1994. 481p. (OP)

This collection of thirty-five essays is devoted to exploring the myriad ways in which class has been defined and experienced in lesbians' (and, more broadly, women's) lives. With contributions from writers from a variety of class, ethnic, racial, and religious backgrounds, this anthology avoids the trap of equating "class" with race or that of associating "class awareness" only with poor and working-class women. Issues of invisibility, the myth of the classlessness of U.S. society, the lack of a meaningful vocabulary with which to discuss class, and the geography of class are discussed. Several essays critique theoretical constructions that derive women's class status from that of the men who may be present in their lives (as husbands or fathers). Others attempt to construct new ways of developing an understanding of class: "lesbians and other women must begin with ourselves, with our lives, with our understandings, with our attempts to grasp the significance of our experiences" (p. 32). In keeping with this method of theory development, many of the essays blend the experiential and the theoretical, interweaving personal history and analysis; others are more explicitly and exclusively theoretical. Regardless of orientation, however, it is clear that class is seen as a complex and dynamic phenomenon: "Class, then, is more than economic status; it is also about the social boundaries we keep" (p. 396). These boundaries shape and are shaped by the various components and outward manifestations of class (including money, privilege, choices, access to resources and skills, food, manners, language, intelligence, and education). The importance of class as an issue within and for the women's movement and women's communities is addressed in several contributions.

714. Pollack, Sandra, and Jeanne Vaughn, eds. *Politics of the Heart: A Lesbian Parenting Anthology.* Ithaca, NY: Firebrand Books, 1987. 358p. bibliog. ISBN 0932379362; 0932379354pa.

This classic anthology gives voice to a variety of lesbian parenting experiences and includes works by new and established authors. The diversity of lesbian parents (and those who choose not to parent) is presented in autobiographical prose, in poetry, and in essays. From coming out to oneself to coming out to one's child, from raising a sister's child to fighting for custody of one's own, from choosing to coparent to choosing to not parent, the voices in this volume raise a multiplicity of issues from a multiplicity of viewpoints. This essential anthology is well suited for use in lesbian studies courses, as well as courses on the family and on mothering and motherhood.

Katherine Arnup's *Lesbian Parenting: Living with Pride and Prejudice* (Gynergy Books, 1995) covers similar ground, but with something of a Canadian twist. Primarily featuring lesser-known authors, this anthology is a welcome supplement to that of Pollack and Vaughn. In *Waiting in the Wings: Portrait of a Queer Motherhood* (Firebrand Books, 1997), Cherríe Moraga writes of her pregnancy, the premature birth of her son, and the fears and joys of motherhood and family.

715. Ragoné, Helena. *Surrogate Motherhood: Conception in the Heart.* Boulder, CO: Westview Press, 1994. 215p. (Institutional Structures of Feeling). bibliog. index. ISBN (OP); 081331979Xpa.

In this ethnographic study of surrogate motherhood and its relationship to traditional models of kinship relations, Ragoné analyzes the meanings, motivations, and feelings attached to the experience by its participants. In the opening overview of surrogacy programs and practices, Ragoné explores the differences between open and closed programs, the application of program guidelines, and the effectiveness of advertising. The importance of creating acceptable terms of discourse based on notions of traditional reproductive strategies is also emphasized. Through interviews conducted with twenty-eight surrogates, Ragoné investigates the reasons women choose to become surrogate mothers: "to be socially rewarded for having made a valuable contribution, made to feel special, and, at least for a short time, made the center of attention for having accomplished something that they consider to be of tremendous value and importance, giving birth to a child" (p. 86). The motivations of fathers and adoptive mothers are explored through interviews conducted with seventeen members of "commissioning couples." Ragoné introduces the concept of the "fertility continuum" to build a theoretical framework for exploring couples' choices regarding the use of nontraditional reproductive strategies. In her concluding chapter, Ragoné explores the many issues surrounding kinship ties that arise from the practice of surrogate motherhood. Special attention is paid to the emotional construction of the relationships between the surrogate mother and each member of the commissioning couple. The fluidity of meanings and symbols is clearly illustrated in Ragoné's analysis of the tension potentially created by a couple's desire for a child that is biogenetically linked to (at least one of) them coupled with the devaluing of the biogenetic relatedness that must occur for the adoptive mother to be affirmed. This fascinating study would be a welcome addition to sociology and anthropology courses focused on kinship and family, as well as to courses examining contemporary American motherhood.

716. Reinharz, Shulamit. *Feminist Methods in Social Research.* New York: Oxford University Press, 1992. 413p. bibliog. index. ISBN (OP); 019507386Xpa.

This classic work surveys and synthesizes a vast assortment of materials in an effort to "collect, categorize and examine the multitude of feminist research voices" (p. 4). Avoiding the politically loaded issues involved in defining "feminist research," Reinharz uses an empirical approach to examining the question "What is feminist research?" As such, materials fall within the scope of this study if one or more of the following conditions are met: the author self-identifies as feminist; the material was published in journals or books that are clearly identified as feminist; or the research "received awards from organizations that give awards to people who do feminist research" (p. 6). The multiplicity of research methods employed in feminist work, as well as the variations within them, is clearly demonstrated. Most chapters are devoted to a particular research method (interviews, ethnography, surveys, experimental research, cross-cultural research, oral history, content analysis, case studies, action research); additional chapters address "multiple methods" research and "original feminist research methods" (including subject self-interviews, network tracing, and the use of drama). Following an overview of each method and its historical roots, Reinharz summarizes and contextualizes research that has employed the method. The inclusion of substantial quotations from the original scholarship greatly enhances understanding of the subtle differences that exist within a given research method. A discussion of methodological issues and areas of dissensus concludes each chapter. Although this interdisciplinary review of the literature emphasizes sociological research, it is heavily informed by writings in anthropology, political science, psychology, and economics, as well as those in history, literature, and the life and health sciences. Detailed source notes and a bibliography comprise almost one-third of the volume. This is an invaluable text for students and researchers seeking to become more familiar with both the breadth of feminist social science research and its methods.

717. Ribbens, Jane, and Rosalind Edwards, eds. *Feminist Dilemmas in Qualitative Research: Public Knowledge and Private Lives.* Thousand Oaks, CA: Sage, 1998. 213p. bibliog. index. (OP)

Asking "who our research is for," the essays in this challenging volume explore the contradictions and synergies that result when feminist researchers conduct qualitative research. The contributors, all past or present members of the British-based Women's Workshop on Qualitative Family/Household Research, focus their work on private/domestic themes often drawn from their own personal experiences. This acknowledged tie to their own lives is the crux of some of the dilemmas they explore. Issues of power and legitimacy resonate through the essays as the authors explore balancing their positions as purveyors of academic discourse deemed distant and authoritative with that of the self-reflexive participant/translator who seeks to provide access to long-ignored voices without placing herself at the center of the narrative. Essays explore the various aspects of the qualitative research enterprise (research design, identifying participants, gathering data, and conceptualizing and writing the analysis) with an ear attentive to the ways methodology and theory affect how voices are heard and subsequently reconstructed. This slim volume would be well suited to graduate courses on research methodology.

718. Risen, James, and Judy L. Thomas. *Wrath of Angels: The American Abortion War.* New York: Basic Books, 1998. 402p. bibliog. index. ISBN 0465092721; 046509273Xpa.

Journalists Risen and Thomas have written a highly readable account of the history of the antiabortion movement in the United States. Opening with an overview of the state of abortion law and practice prior to the 1973 *Roe v. Wade* decision and a brief explication of the legal reasoning behind that decision, the authors detail the rise of an antiabortion backlash they contend was inevitable. Using information gathered in interviews and from secondary sources, as well as from movement publications, Risen and Thomas report on the birth of the rescue movement and its focus on nonviolent civil disobedience, the outbreak of arson and bombings that grew to epidemic proportions, the rise of Operation Rescue, and the violence directed at doctors who perform abortions. Told primarily through tracing the personal, activist biographies of its key figures, this movement history also discusses the role played by intramovement conflicts and politics.

Cynthia Gorney's *Articles of Faith: A Frontline History of the Abortion Wars* (Simon & Schuster, 1998) is also a journalistic account of the history of the abortion conflict, albeit with a different focus. Culminating in the 1989 Supreme Court decision in the Missouri case *Webster v. Reproductive Health Services*, the narrative revolves around twenty years of abortion law, practice, and politics in that state. The broader legal, social, and political context of the abortion debate is successfully woven in throughout the text. *Articles of Faith* briefly mentions the Chicago-based activities of "Jane," an abortion service operating at the end of the pre-*Roe* years. The history of this group, more formally known as the Abortion Counseling Service of Women's Liberation, is detailed in Laura Kaplan's "collective memoir" *The Story of Jane: The Legendary Underground Feminist Abortion Service* (Pantheon Books, 1995). Kaplan, a former member of Jane, tells the group's story from its founding as an abortion counseling service to its transition to abortion provider and its closure following the *Roe* decision.

719. Risman, Barbara J. *Gender Vertigo: American Families in Transition.* New Haven, CT: Yale University Press, 1998. 189p. bibliog. index. ISBN 0300072155; 0300080832pa.

Arguing that existing theories are inadequate to explain the persistence of gendered behaviors and institutions, Risman posits a multilevel structural theory of gender that incorporates institutional, individual, and interactional elements. Particularly interested in why and how women and men make particular choices regarding relationships and parenting, Risman examines how "gender as a social structure affects our everyday interactions." Risman's argument regarding the nature of gender and the possibility of change is based on a review of the literature and several studies conducted by her and her colleagues. In a study of 220 families (55 single fathers, 55 single mothers, 55 dual earners, 55 mothers at home), Risman determines that men can indeed "mother," thereby supporting her claim that interactional context is more important than sex-role socialization in determining behavior. An analysis of previously collected longitudinal data on women's career and domestic choices further supports this contention. A study of fifteen "fair families" who have consciously split the economic and domestic duties of the family illustrates the importance of effecting change on all levels of the gender structure. In her concluding chapter, Risman looks to the possibility of a future in which gender no longer exists. Not single-minded in extolling the virtues of a "post-gender" society, Risman acknowledges the disorienting effect (the "vertigo" of her title) that would result from abolishing the gender structure: "Gender, as we do it, is not only about subordination, inequality, and stratification but also about who we are and how we experience our selves and our relationships" (p. 158). Although limited by its exclusively heterosexual focus, this book will be a valuable addition to sociology of the family, sociology of gender, and feminist theory courses.

720. Roberts, Dorothy. *Killing the Black Body: Race, Reproduction, and the Meaning of Liberty.* New York: Pantheon Books, 1997. 373p. bibliog. index. ISBN 067944226X; 0679758690pa.

Arguing that "regulating Black women's reproductive decisions has been a central aspect of racial oppression in America" and that "the control of Black women's reproduction has shaped the meaning of reproductive liberty in America" (p. 6), Roberts examines the interplay between reproductive liberty and racial oppression in this broad account of reproductive social policy in the United States. Drawing on historical and contemporary examples, she demonstrates that African American women's reproduction has been exploited, suppressed, degraded, and criminalized. The discourses and practices surrounding birth control, sterilization, abortion, and new reproductive technologies are examined. In her concluding chapter, "The Meaning of Liberty," Roberts argues that the reproductive rights movement in the United States, with its traditionally liberal view of liberty as "freedom from government intervention," has ignored the issues and needs of African American women. A new definition of liberty is needed, one that is based on an "affirmative duty of government to protect the individual's personhood from degradation and to facilitate the processes of choice and self-determination" (p. 309). Roberts contends that such a definition, linked to a notion of equality, would have a profound effect on social policy and programs.

721. Rose, Sharon, and Chris Stevens, eds. *Bisexual Horizons: Politics, Histories, and Lives*. London: Lawrence & Wishart, 1996. 324p. bibliog. ISBN 0853158312pa.

Combining theoretical analysis with personal narratives, this collection explores a broad range of concerns; recurrent themes include the instability of sexual categories, the development of a bisexual politic, invisibility, media representations of bisexuals, the impact of HIV/AIDS, coalition building, and lesbian/gay marginalization of bisexuals and bisexuality. Feminist perspectives are present through much of the volume, although not always explicitly acknowledged. Several contributors see important linkages between bisexuality and multiracial identity; in "A New Politics of Sexuality," June Jordan states: "I do believe that the analogy is interracial or multiracial identity. I do believe that the analogy for bisexuality is a multi-cultural, multi-ethnic, multi-racial world view. Bisexuality follows from such a perspective and leads to it, as well. . . . Bisexuality invalidates either/or formulation, either/or analysis" (p. 14). The editors present a wide variety of bisexual experience; contributors identify across a broad range of gender, racial, and ethnic identities. Most contributors to the volume are British; others are from the United States, Australia, Aotearoa/New Zealand, Germany, Tunisia, Belgium, Ireland, and the Netherlands.

This work was preceded by the groundbreaking *Bi Any Other Name: Bisexual People Speak Out* (Alyson Publications, 1991), edited by Loraine Hutchins and Lani Kaahumanu. Also built around a blend of life stories and theoretical work, the anthology is arranged in four parts (Psychology: "Facing Ourselves"; Spirituality: "Healing the Splits"; The Bisexual Community: "Are We Visible Yet?" and Politics: "A Queer among Queers").

722. Russell, Diana E.H. *The Secret Trauma: Incest in the Lives of Girls and Women*. New York: Basic Books, 1986. 426p. bibliog. index. ISBN (OP); 0465075967pa.

This classic work details the findings from the first large-scale probability sample on incest. It provides a wealth of data on the prevalence of incest and the ways in which "victims" (Russell's chosen word) understand their experience and are affected by it. The study is predicated on an important distinction between abusive and nonabusive incest. Defining abusive incest as "any kind of exploitative sexual contact or attempted contact that occurred between relatives, no matter how distant the relationship, before the victim turned eighteen years old" (p. 41), Russell is able to explore the experiences of women who were abused by relatives other than their fathers. As much prior research focused on father-daughter incest, the broader focus of this study sheds a crucial light in areas previously unexplored. Clearly defining her terms and the methods used to code the data, Russell's study effectively challenges earlier research, which claimed a much lower prevalence rate and that incestuous abuse does not have significant emotional effects. The inclusion of lengthy quotations from the interviews allows the reader to gain a fuller understanding of the women's (i.e., children's) experiences and feelings, as well as of their understandings of the ways the incest experience(s) shaped their lives. Russell does not, however, rely entirely on the adult women's recollections and interpretations; when appropriate, she identifies conflicts between the words women used to describe the incest event(s) and the words used to describe their feelings and/or the effect they believe the abuse had on their lives. A detailed methodology chapter describes the San Francisco–based sample of 930 women, the decision to use face-to-face interviews, the design of the interview schedule, and the training of the interviewers.

723. Rust, Paula C. *Bisexuality and the Challenge to Lesbian Politics: Sex, Loyalty, and Revolution*. New York: New York University Press, 1995. 367p. (The Cutting Edge). bibliog. index. ISBN 081477444X; 0814774458pa.

In this challenging work, Rust explores the varied constructions of bisexual identity and the political ramifications and possibilities stemming from these constructions. The opening chapter raises the book's central issues through a reading of articles and follow-up letters in four major lesbian and gay magazines. The differences in how these magazines represent and problematize bisexuality, if they do so at all, leads to the heart of the study: how do lesbians and bisexual women define bisexuality and view bisexual women? Combining quantitative and qualitative data drawn from more than 400 questionnaires filled out by "women who consider themselves to be lesbian or bisexual, or who choose not to label their sexual orientation, or who are not sure what their sexual orientation is" (pp. 40–41), Rust delves into the political stances underlying and resulting from the respondents' expressed attitudes. Acknowledging the antipathy that lesbians expressed toward bisexual women, Rust argues that the conflict is not about bisexuality per se, but rather stems from unresolved issues surrounding the politicization of lesbian identity in the 1970s and the continuing desire to sketch the boundaries of that identity. In the concluding chapter, Rust outlines the development of bisexuality as a political identity unto itself, the challenge this presents to lesbian politics, and the potential the bisexual movement has for furthering sexual self-determination.

724. Shah, Sonia, ed. *Dragon Ladies: Asian American Feminists Breathe Fire*. Boston: South End Press, 1997. 241p. bibliog. index. ISBN 0896085767; 0896085759pa.

With its focus on the ways "the forces of racism, patriarchy, and imperialism specifically affect Asian American women" (p. xiii) and the strategies they use to resist, *Dragon Ladies* employs an explicitly feminist political analysis to examine many of the issues confronting Asian American women today. The anthology is divided into four somewhat overlapping sections: "Strategies and Visions," "An Agenda for Change," "Global Perspectives," and "Awakening to Power." Chapters address such topics as organizing against domestic violence, the conceptualization of "home" and its implications for political organizing, environmental justice movements, sexuality, globalization and the trade in workers, media representations of Asian American women, the myth of the model minority, organizing around women's health, the cultural rootedness of social change organizations, spirituality and religion, and attempts to work through European American women's and leftist organizations.

Shah is also one of the contributors to Shamita Das Dasgupta's *A Patchwork Shawl: Chronicles of South Asian Women in America* (Rutgers University Press, 1998), a collection of essays that examines the construction of identities, community, and family, as well as the importance of the cultural contextualization of activism. Issues addressed include the "language of identity," sexuality and its control, female intergenerational relationships, domestic violence and marital rape, work, and strategies for change.

725. Smith, Dorothy E. *The Everyday World as Problematic: A Feminist Sociology*. Boston: Northeastern University Press, 1987. 244p. (Northeastern Series in Feminist Theory). bibliog. index. ISBN (OP); 1555530362pa.

One of the most frequently cited works in feminist sociology, this volume consists of minimally revised papers written between 1977 and 1986. Taken together, they build, revise, and rework an approach to feminist sociology that laid open new ways of apprehending and conceptualizing the questions that sociology should examine. The book is divided into four parts; the heart of the book is the two essays contained in part 2, "A Sociology for Women" and "The Everyday World as Problematic: A Feminist Methodology." In these chapters, Smith explores the ways in which sociological thought has been part of the "patriarchal relations of ruling" and develops an alternative approach that positions women as subjects and uses women's experiences as the standpoint from which to examine social relations. Asserting the "everyday world as problematic" (i.e., seeing the day-to-day experiences of actual people as the location from which questions originate), Smith's work is devoted to "the project of creating a way of seeing, from where we actually live, into the powers, processes, and relations that organize and determine the everyday context of that seeing." (p. 9) Not content to simply theorize an alternative approach to conducting sociological work, Smith describes a practical research strategy that does not subvert the intentions of the theoretical work.

Smith further develops her ideas in *The Conceptual Practices of Power: A Feminist Sociology of Knowledge* (Northeastern University Press, 1990). Again exploring the ways in which traditional sociological theory and research "alienates and occludes the standpoint of experience," Smith discusses the ways in which sociological writing is ideological and a part of the discourses of ruling. The second half of the book analyzes the institution of psychiatry in terms of its ideological practices. *Knowledge, Experience, and Ruling Relations: Studies in the Social Organization of Knowledge* (University of Toronto Press, 1995), edited by Marie Campbell and Ann Manicom, anthologizes research that builds on and was inspired by Smith's conceptual and methodological work. Smith, recipient of the American Sociological Association's Career of Distinguished Scholarship Award (1999) and Jessie Bernard Award (1993), is one of the key figures in contemporary feminist thought. Her work should be well represented in courses on feminist sociology, sociology of knowledge, and research methodology.

726. Stanley, Liz, ed. *Feminist Praxis: Research, Theory and Epistemology in Feminist Sociology*. New York: Routledge, 1990. 282p. bibliog. index.

This complex collection explores the ways in which feminist knowledge is created, distributed, consumed, and transformed. Stanley's introduction, "Feminist Praxis and the Academic Mode of Production," explores the conditions and relations under which academic knowledge is created. It is her contention that "academic feminist unalienated knowledge" requires that "written accounts of feminist research should locate the feminist researcher firmly within the activities of her research as an essential feature of what is 'feminist' about it" (p. 12). This concern with opening up the processes of knowledge production is crucial to the research enterprise as discussed in each of the contributions). Although the sixteen essays grouped under "Feminist Research Processes" use a variety of theoretical frameworks, each consistently stresses a self-consciousness about the research process and the role of the researcher. The volume is further enhanced by Stanley and Sue Wise's review (with detailed bibliography) of the feminist epistemology literature.

Similar issues are explored by the contributors to Mary Maynard and June Purvis' *Researching Women's Lives from a Feminist Perspective* (Taylor & Francis, 1994). Four themes are central to the essays in this volume: the use of multiple research methods within a given project, the impact of the research on the participants, the validity of the knowledge gained from the research enterprise ("interpretation is a political, contested, and unstable activity"), and the relationship between academe and politics (p. 7). Another compelling collection *Beyond Methodology: Feminist Scholarship as Lived Research* (Indiana University Press, 1991), edited by Mary Margaret Fonow and Judith A. Cook, gathers key essays that review debates about feminist research methodologies during the 1980s. What distinguishes this highly regarded collection is its exploration of the affective component of research and its appreciation of the diversities, ambiguities, and tensions produced by "lived research." These collections are well-suited to graduate courses on feminist epistemology or methods and are essential reading for feminists about to embark on a research project.

727. Strossen, Nadine. *Defending Pornography: Free Speech, Sex, and the Fight for Women's Rights.* New York: Scribner, 1995. 320p. bibliog. index. ISBN (OP); 0814781497pa.

Strossen, president of the American Civil Liberties Union, has written a women's rights–centered critique of the antipornography arguments of Andrea Dworkin and Catharine MacKinnon. Claiming that the "MacDworkinites" are a greater danger to women's rights than is the pornography they seek to outlaw, Strossen opposes restrictions on sexual speech and images "not only because it would violate our cherished First Amendment freedoms . . . but also because it would undermine our equality, our status, our dignity, and our autonomy" (p. 14). Following a brief survey of the history of First Amendment law, Strossen argues that the procensorship/antipornography movement rejects all expression of female sexuality as intrinsically exploitative and submissive. She further argues that even if we could outlaw pornography in a manner that did not censor other forms of protected speech, there would be no lessening of violence against women or of practices that discriminate against women.

Wendy McElroy, in her *XXX: A Woman's Right to Pornography* (St. Martin's Press, 1995), offers a different approach to defending pornography. Stating, "Pornography benefits women, both personally and politically," McElroy explicitly rejects Strossen's approach as being "*against* censorship rather than *for* pornography" (p. vii). McElroy's argument is centered on what she calls "individualist feminism," a feminism rooted in the notion of women's complete agency and "the personal is personal" (p. 125). McElroy's arguments, while not always convincing, do raise some important questions about the nature of consent. Particularly interesting are the concluding chapters that include interviews with women working in the pornography business and a report on a meeting of COYOTE (Call Off Your Old Tired Ethics). A survey of sex workers provides useful background for McElroy's concrete suggestions for improvements in the working conditions of the industry.

728. Thorne, Barrie, and Marilyn Yalom, eds. *Rethinking the Family: Some Feminist Questions.* Rev. ed. Boston: Northeastern University Press, 1992. 316p. bibliog. index. ISBN 155553144X; 1555531458pa.

This revised edition of the classic 1982 anthology of the same name brings together fourteen essays addressing many of the major issues in feminist approaches to the study of "the family." Six of the contributions were included in the earlier edition (although two have been revised for inclusion in the current work); the remaining essays are reprinted from other sources. The editors have organized the volume along five themes: a critique of the ahistorical and acultural ideology of "the monolithic family," the importance of gender and other structures in understanding the dynamics of family formation and change, the varied experiences, both positive and negative, of women in families, the intersection of public institutions and private life, and the "tension between individualism and community [that] is basic to the politics of family change" (p. 5). Well suited for use in classes in sociology of the family, this reader includes essays drawn from the disciplines of anthropology, history, sociology, psychology, and philosophy. It is important to note, however, that despite this breadth of disciplinary coverage, all but one of the essays focus on the United States.

729. Trujillo, Carla, ed. *Chicana Lesbians: The Girls Our Mothers Warned Us About.* Berkeley: Third Woman Press, 1991. 202p. bibliog. ISBN 094321906Xpa.

The poetry and prose of twenty-three writers are brought together in this winner of the 1991 Lambda Literary Award for Lesbian Anthologies. Creating new forms from old, the contributors to this volume transform their families, spirituality, and language to forge an authentic self-definition: "Learning a new language: Lesbian / Some speak in feminism, / some speak in "Het": double standards / Yet all 'out' in the mainstream together. / Speaking in Lesbian / Speaking in English / Speaking in Spanish / Speaking in Spanglish" (Gina Montoya, "Baby Dykes"). The collection is organized to reflect four key aspects of Chicana lesbian lives: "The Life" focuses on identity and the "complexity of our commonality"; "The Desire" considers passion, love, sex, loss, and merging; "The Color" addresses the way skin color affects all relationships; and "The Struggle" is that for Chicana lesbian self-definition, economic survival, and the importance of support and community. The inspiration to create *Chicana Lesbians* came from Trujillo's experience of reading the words of other Chicana lesbians in *Compañeras: Latina Lesbians: An Anthology*, edited by Juanita Ramos (Latina Lesbian History Project, 1987). Containing poetry, oral histories, short fiction, essays, and artwork from forty-seven lesbians born in ten different countries, this earlier collection speaks of experiences of coming out, family connections, relationships with lovers and friends, and political struggle.

730. Van Gelder, Lindsy, and Pamela Robin Brandt. *The Girls Next Door: Into the Heart of Lesbian America*. New York: Simon & Schuster, 1996. 314p. ISBN (OP); 0684839571pa.

Journalists Van Gelder and Brandt take readers inside the world of 1990s lesbian culture and community by way of mass "tribal events": the 1993 and 1994 Michigan Womyn's Music Festivals, the 1994 LPGA Nabisco Dinah Shore Golf Tournament party circuit, and the 1994 Lesbian Avengers cross-country ride. This fun and funny book also considers some serious concerns: the fluidity of sexuality and identity, labeling and the power of naming oneself "lesbian," the nature of desire and sexual attraction, gender identity, sexual practices, political action, expanding definitions of "family," employment benefits, and the definition of "lesbian issues" are all explored in this Lambda Literary Award nominee. Van Gelder and Brandt spoke with more than 100 women in the course of their research; they share stories and quote liberally from these conversations in a text that illustrates the diversity of lesbian lives and experiences. This very accessible book would be an interesting addition to survey courses on women in the contemporary United States.

731. Young, Gay, and Bette J. Dickerson, eds. *Color, Class, and Country: Experiences of Gender*. Atlantic Highlands, NJ: Zed Books, 1994. 252p. bibliog. index. (OP)

This collection of essays is drawn from the proceedings of American University's 1991 conference "Experiences of Gender: Color, Class, and Country." In their introductory essay, the editors briefly discuss the central themes of the volume: gender is relational and historically situated; research and practice should be drawn from women's lived experience; and gender, race/ ethnicity, social class, and national location are "multiple systems of oppression [that] intersect to locate women differently in the matrix of domination" (p. 5). Focusing on the interconnectedness of gender, race, class, and nation, the contributors explore the varied ways in which these hierarchies are both constructed and challenged. Although many of the essays focus on work issues, a number of other topics are also addressed, including upward mobility and the construction of aspirations, the views of leaders of African American women's voluntary organizations on feminism and ethnic identity, U.S. welfare policy, the role of international norms in domestic policy regarding women, and the impact of structural adjustment policies. The final section includes three essays explicitly addressing the need to challenge Western, white, middle-class conceptualizations of women, feminism, and social change. Readings from this volume would be worthwhile additions to courses on women and work, women organizing for change, and sociology of work.

732. Zinn, Maxine Baca, and Bonnie Thornton Dill, eds. *Women of Color in U.S. Society*. Philadelphia: Temple University Press, 1994. 339p. (Women in the Political Economy). bibliog. index. ISBN 1566391059; 1566391067pa.

Well suited for undergraduate classes, this collection of essays contributes to the development of a "multiracial feminism," a theory and practice predicated on the conceptual insight that "racial ancestry, ethnic heritage, and economic status are as important as gender for analyzing the social construction of women and men" (p. 11). Acknowledging that the phrase "women of color" is in itself falsely universalizing, the contributors to this work stress a particularity that refuses to simply replace white men with white women as the "new normative center" (p. xv). The book is divided into four interrelated sections. Taken together, the two introductory chapters provide the theoretical and demographic background for the chapters that follow. Part 2, "The Constraining Walls of Social Location," addresses the barriers confronting women of color in several spheres, with an emphasis on employment and education. Articles address a variety of experiences: African American schoolchildren and professional women, immigrant workers, and Puerto Rican families. Efforts to resist and overcome these constraints are detailed in part 3. Representations of African American women, a class- and race-sensitive analysis of moral reasoning, and a rethinking of the family close out the volume in part 4, "Rethinking Gender."

733. Zinn, Maxine Baca, Pierrette Hondagneu-Sotelo, and Michael A. Messner, eds. *Through the Prism of Difference: Readings on Sex and Gender*. Boston: Allyn & Bacon, 1997. 562p. bibliog. (OP)

Arguing that it is time to move beyond the "patchwork quilt" approach to studying women and men, the editors of this outstanding collection have gathered fifty-eight essays that, taken together, provide entry into a multiracial, multinational study of gender relations. Rejecting the "add difference and stir" approach as inadequate for a more inclusive study of gender, the editors focus on the relationships that exist between power and difference. To this end, the anthology emphasizes contributions that focus on the juxtaposition of several aspects of the gender/race/class/sexuality/nationality matrix. The volume is organized in six parts; each part is preceded by a brief introduction that summarizes and makes connections between the essays. Part 1 explores the ways in which "difference" has been constructed, theorized, and studied. Subsequent parts focus on particular sites of contestation: the body, sexualities, identities, families, public institutions (work and education), and ideology. The final part examines the emergence of social change in and through the daily practices of social institutions. Drawing from a wide variety of source materials (scholarly journals in women's studies, as well as in other disciplines; other anthologies; and excerpts from monographs), the editors have constructed a volume that will be particularly useful in undergraduate sociology of gender courses or in any course that seeks to explore "how gender is organized and experienced differently when refracted through the prism of sexual, racial/ethnic, social class, physical abilities, age, and national citizenship differences" (p. 1).

Social Work, Welfare, and Poverty

734. Abramovitz, Mimi. *Regulating the Lives of Women: Social Welfare Policy from Colonial Times to the Present*. Boston: South End Press, 1988. 406p. bibliog. index. (OP)

In this classic work, Abramovitz explores the historical shifts in the relationships between the welfare state, the ideology of women's roles (referred to as the "family ethic"), and economic policies and structures. Abramovitz demonstrates the ways in which welfare policy reinforces women's oppression through limiting economic opportunities. In her articulation of the ways in which welfare policies regulate women's lives by "channeling some into the home to devote full time to reproducing and maintaining the labor force and others into the labor market where they also create profits for capital" (p. 35), Abramovitz acknowledges the differential effects of race, class, and marital status. The sociopolitical impact of women's (and men's) resistance to welfare policies is also explored. A revised 1996 edition updates the analysis to include the effects of the Family Support Act of 1988 and subsequent governmental attacks on the welfare state.

In *Under Attack, Fighting Back: Women and Welfare in the United States* (Monthly Review Press, 1996), Abramovitz builds on her earlier work to explore and contextualize the contemporary assault on welfare. Following an analysis of the ways in which poor women and welfare have often been demonized, Abramovitz examines the shifts in academic understandings of welfare, emphasizing the important insights gained from applying a feminist approach. The last section of this brief book addresses the organization and expression of women's economic activism. These books should be considered essential reading for courses on women and social policy.

735. Armstrong, Louise. *Of "Sluts" and "Bastards": A Feminist Decodes the Child Welfare Debate*. Monroe, ME: Common Courage, 1995. 344p. bibliog. ISBN 1567510671; 1567510663pa.

Armstrong's journalistic account of the foster care system draws heavily on interviews and research she conducted in the course of writing *Solomon Says: A Speakout on Foster Care* (Pocket Books, 1989). Building on the realization that the very notions of "abuse" and "neglect" are vaguely defined and socially determined, Armstrong examines the underpinnings of the child welfare/child protection system. Her analysis touches on such issues as the system's differential treatment of mothers and fathers, the appropriate level of state intervention in people's lives, the ways in which class overdetermines involvement in the system, and the effects of strict confidentiality rules. The many stories that form the heart of this book illustrate the contradictions of a system that is commonly portrayed as focused on child protection, but whose reality has often been quite different. The voices of foster children, foster parents, and mothers who lost their children, as well as those of "system workers" (social service workers, researchers, and judges), provide insight into the workings of the system.

736. Gordon, Linda. *Pitied but Not Entitled: Single Mothers and the History of Welfare, 1890–1935*. New York: Free Press, 1994. 433p. bibliog. index. ISBN 0029124859; 0674669827pa.

The gendered roots of the U.S. welfare system are revealed in this outstanding work of social history. Gordon analyzes the values and assumptions that influenced the development of the welfare system, stressing the disjunctures between public discourses and lived realities. This disjuncture is made most apparent by the system's basis in the discourse of the "family wage," a frequently unrealized economic fantasy. Gordon demonstrates the ways in which notions of "appropriate" family life and of the "deserving" versus "undeserving" poor are embedded in the design of public assistance programs. The ways in which the system was and is affected by race and class differences are highlighted. Noting that the design of the welfare system was the result of compromise and choice, Gordon explores the social and political dynamics that gave rise to the contemporary two-tiered system.

Women, the State, and Welfare (University of Wisconsin Press, 1990), edited by Gordon, is an interdisciplinary collection of key scholarship on women and the gendered welfare state. It is well suited for classroom use.

737. Harris, Kathleen Mullan. *Teen Mothers and the Revolving Welfare Door*. Philadelphia: Temple University Press, 1997. 195p. (Women in the Political Economy). bibliog. index. ISBN 1566394996.

Arguing that the welfare reform efforts of the 1990s focusing on getting women into the workforce are misguided and doomed to fail, Harris uses data drawn from a twenty-year longitudinal study of inner-city, African American teenage mothers to explore the wide range of issues surrounding entry into and exit from the welfare system. She examines "the effects of early life decisions, changing social and economic circumstances, and life course trajectories on patterns of welfare receipt" (p. 23). Harris identifies three types of welfare behavior: "early exits" (recipients with only one spell of welfare receipt that lasts for one or two years), "persistent recipients" (only one spell of welfare receipt that lasts for three or more years), and "cyclers" (multiple spells of welfare receipt). Harris argues that her data indicate that successful transitions out of the welfare system are most often due to employment; hence welfare programs that stress job training and education will be more successful in assisting women to exit welfare. Moreover, her data support the claim that welfare recipients are working or seeking work, but that the nature of the compensation (low wages, no benefits) results in women cycling in and out of the system: "Policymakers should *not* be asking why recipients do not work, but rather they should ask why the work that welfare recipients *do* does not lift their families out of welfare" (p. 126). Useful in courses on women and work or on poverty, this volume is also well suited as supplementary reading in those feminist methods courses that include event history analysis.

738. Liebow, Elliot. *Tell Them Who I Am: The Lives of Homeless Women*. New York: Free Press, 1993. 339p. bibliog. index. ISBN 0029190959; 014024137Xpa.

Liebow, the author of the classic *Tally's Corner: A Study of Negro Streetcorner Men* (Little, Brown, 1967), has crafted a volume that quietly explodes numerous social myths that surround homeless women. Using data gathered in a participant-observer study conducted in four shelters serving homeless women in a small city outside Washington, D.C., during the mid- to late 1980s, Liebow illustrates the women's ongoing struggle to survive and maintain their dignity. Noting that the sometimes substantial differences between shelters greatly affect the experiences of those using the facilities, Liebow provides needed background information on the shelters' administrative structures, staffing (paid versus volunteer, level of experience and training), philosophical approaches, degrees of bureaucracy, and elaborateness of rules. Drawing heavily on the women's own words, Liebow explores such day-to-day challenges as getting enough sleep, excessive boredom, finding a safe place for one's possessions, and the lack of love and sex. Special attention is paid to the economic and social meanings attached to work and the difficulties of finding and keeping a job. The dynamics of key relationships (between the women and their families, friends, and religions; between shelter workers and residents; between residents) are also discussed. In an attempt to broaden the analysis, Liebow solicited feedback on the manuscript from two shelter residents and a shelter director. Their commentary (sometimes agreeing and clarifying, sometimes disagreeing) is provided throughout the text. Appendices include brief life histories, a "where are they now" section, and an overview of the research method and writing process. Although lacking a specifically gender-based analysis, this study is a rich source of information on the life experiences of homeless women and would be a welcome addition to courses specifically addressing poverty, community institutions, deviance, or research methods.

739. Polakow, Valerie. *Lives on the Edge: Single Mothers and Their Children in the Other America*. Chicago: University of Chicago Press, 1993. 222p. bibliog. index. ISBN 0226671836; 0226671844pa.

Polakow explores the daily lives of mothers and children in poverty and the construction of "otherness" in this well-argued volume. Combining a historical analysis of the discursive practices and structural processes implicated in the poverty of single mothers and children with a case study approach, Polakow reveals how poverty "has been artfully reconfigured as a social/cultural/psychological pathology, corroborated by a public educational discourse of deficiency and remediation" (p. 3). Using data gathered in observing daily life in selected public schools and preschools, Polakow deconstructs the notion of "at risk." Consistently attentive to the effects of race and class and emphasizing the mothers' resiliency, Polakow portrays women actively strategizing on behalf of themselves and their children. Polakow argues that structural changes are necessary to eradicate poverty: "Redistribution of public and private income, an equitable tax structure, the making of an educational democracy, the restructuring of health care and child care, affordable and subsidized housing, and workplace reforms cannot be made as part of leftover policy for the poor" (p. 177).

A somewhat different approach is taken in Virginia E. Schein's *Working from the Margins: Voices of Mothers in Poverty* (ILR Press, 1995). Quoting heavily from interviews with thirty adult single mothers, Schein agrees that women's poverty will never be reduced through efforts to reform welfare. Her recommendations are more conservative, however. Schein argues that the poverty of single mothers can be alleviated through income opportunities (education and non-traditional job training), social supports (child care, affordable housing, opportunities for resource sharing, sense of community), and counseling. An excerpt from Polakow's work appears in Marsha R. Leslie's *The Single Mother's Companion: Essays and Stories by Women* (Seal Press, 1994) along with other pieces that emphasize the variety of women's economic and social experiences of single motherhood.

740. Saulnier, Christine Flynn. *Feminist Theories and Social Work: Approaches and Applications.* New York: Haworth Press, 1996. 253p. (Haworth Social Work Practice). bibliog. index. ISBN 1560249455.

Although social work practitioners and theorists have been incorporating feminist practices and insights into their work for years, this is the first effort to directly connect various feminist theoretical approaches to specific social work practices. A brief overview is provided for each theory (liberal feminism, radical feminism, socialist feminism, lesbian feminism, cultural feminism, ecofeminism, womanism, postmodern feminism, and global feminism). Despite Saulnier's acknowledged overgeneralizing, the overviews provide useful background information on each theory's historical development, key aspects, limitations, and contributions. The implications of each theoretical perspective for six areas of social work practice (social welfare policy, administration, community organizing, group work, case work, and research) are then explored. The final chapter serves to further contrast the theories by examining four social problems (alcohol problems, battering, employment issues, and sex work) and possible intervention strategies in accordance with selected theoretical perspectives.

741. Sidel, Ruth. *Keeping Women and Children Last: America's War on the Poor.* New York: Penguin Books, 1996. 232p. bibliog. index. ISBN 0140246630pa.

Building on and updating her earlier *Women and Children Last: The Plight of Poor Women in Affluent America* (Viking, 1986), Sidel scrutinizes the nature, causes, and effects of poverty in the United States, as well as the rhetoric that surrounds it. Arguing that there are structural causes for the increase in female-headed households, teenage pregnancies, and the number of families living in poverty, she explicitly rejects the notion that poor women are themselves responsible for the economic and social problems they face. Rather, she maintains that the blatant scapegoating and stigmatizing of poor, single mothers serves a political purpose in the absence of the Cold War: that of creating an "enemy within" against which to mobilize conservative public opinion and reassert existing relations of social dominance. Armed with statistics and illustrated by telling quotations from interviews conducted for this book and its predecessor, Sidel reveals the face of poverty in the United States to be predominantly female, young, and of color. The experience of living on welfare and the effects of the efforts to "end welfare as we know it" are briefly described. The consequences of poverty for children's health and well-being are also discussed. In the concluding chapter, Sidel asserts that the U.S. government can and should provide a basic standard of living to all and suggests the necessity of a "Marshall Plan" to rehabilitate the poorest areas of the country. Revisiting the call for a comprehensive family policy made in her 1986 book, Sidel declares the need for a coherent and comprehensive plan for providing a suite of services that would include paid parental leave at the birth or adoption of a child, affordable child care, equality in education, affordable health care, and appropriate housing. This highly readable text is well suited to undergraduate courses dealing with poverty and social policy.

742. Skocpol, Theda. *Protecting Soldiers and Mothers: The Political Origins of Social Policy in the United States*. Cambridge, MA: Belknap Press of Harvard University Press, 1992. 714p. bibliog. index. ISBN 0674717651; 067471766Xpa.

In this carefully argued history of social policy in the United States, Skocpol documents the growth and subsequent demise of a major government-funded benefits program for Northern Civil War veterans and their dependents, the failure of later efforts to, in essence, continue these programs by instituting broad benefits for workingmen and the elderly, and the development of large-scale social spending for women and children. Skocpol's "polity-centered" analysis focuses on "state formation, political institutions, and political processes (understood in non-economically determinist ways)" (p. 40); attention to gender (construed both as gendered social relations and as socially constructed, historically rooted gender identities) is a key component of her analysis. Skocpol argues that a very specific confluence of factors (including an increase in the educational opportunities afforded some women, the rise of women's voluntary associations, and women's lack of electoral rights) led to the success of the efforts to establish "maternalist" social programs benefiting women, children, and society as a whole. Efforts aimed at establishing broad "paternalist" programs for workingmen failed for numerous reasons, including a lack of class consciousness among industrial workers and societal reaction to prior patronage-based political practices. Skocpol's "comparatively informed historical case study" (p. 61) demonstrates how the U.S. pattern of social provision was at odds with the practices of the increasingly well-established welfare states of Europe. The volume concludes with a brief discussion of the legacies of these early modern social policies.

743. Van Den Bergh, Nan, ed. *Feminist Practice in the 21st Century*. Washington, DC: NASW Press, 1995. 376p. bibliog. index. ISBN 0971012448pa.

Almost a decade after she coedited *Feminist Visions for Social Work* (NASW, 1986) with Lynn B. Cooper, Van Den Bergh edited an anthology that raises the myriad issues confronting the future of feminist social work. The volume is divided into three sections: methods, fields of practice, and special populations. Although Van Den Bergh's introduction is somewhat problematic in its interpretation of recent developments in postmodern and feminist theory, the essays provide useful and concrete examples of feminist approaches to a variety of social work concerns, including organizational administration, homelessness, militarism, mental health, workplace issues, substance abuse, and violence against women. Also looking to the future is *Building on Women's Strengths: A Social Work Agenda for the Twenty-first Century* (Haworth Press,

1994), edited by Liane V. Davis. Geared toward social work practitioners, this volume grew out of papers written in advance of a two-day conference held at the University of Kansas in 1990. Based on the notion that a social work practice for the future must address women's issues from a perspective that builds on women's strengths and acknowledges women's realities, the eleven essays explore a variety of policy areas and offer concrete proposals for improving women's lives. Not surprisingly, economic issues permeate the volume; from discussions of child welfare to the lives of aged women, economic inequities shape women's lives and future possibilities. The material does not focus solely on the economic sphere, however. A second thread, that of the importance of reclaiming and/or revising the narratives of women's lives, runs through many of the essays.

Criminal Justice and Crimes against Women

744. Browne, Angela. *When Battered Women Kill.* New York: Free Press, 1987. 228p. bibliog. index. ISBN (OP); 0029038812pa.

In this often graphic book, Browne draws on extensive interviews with forty-two women charged with the murder or attempted murder of their male partners as she explores the women's self-perceptions and understandings of the circumstances in which the crimes occurred. In an effort to determine what makes these women different (i.e., why they killed), Browne also analyzes data gathered from a comparison group of 205 battered women who did not kill their abusers. Surprisingly, no significant differences were found between the groups of women themselves; rather, the significant differences were found between the abusers and their patterns of behavior: men who were killed had a greater frequency of drug and alcohol use and committed more frequent and injurious assaults, their assaultive behavior was more likely to include sexual assault, and they more frequently abused a child. Asserting that early intervention by the police and the courts is necessary to break the pattern of escalating violence, Browne stresses the importance of recognizing the significance of "even 'mild' abuse" (p. 184).

In *Terrifying Love: Why Battered Women Kill and How Society Responds* (Harper & Row, 1989), Lenore E. Walker combines brief case studies, autobiographical detail, and social critique in her analysis of why some battered women kill. Walker, the author of *The Battered Woman* (Harper & Row, 1979) and *The Battered Woman Syndrome* (1984), also details her personal journey to becoming a recognized expert witness.

745. Chesney-Lind, Meda. *The Female Offender: Girls, Women, and Crime.* Thousand Oaks, CA: Sage Publications, 1997. 219p. (Women and the Criminal Justice System). bibliog. index. ISBN 0803950993; 0803951000pa.

Beginning with the recognition that one out of every four young people arrested in the United States is female, Chesney-Lind analyzes the ways in which girls are rendered invisible by the juvenile justice system, its practitioners, and the academics who study the system. Delinquency theory, Chesney-Lind argues, is modeled entirely on boys' experiences and is unable to explain girls' behavior. In contrast, a feminist theory of delinquency will take into account the life experiences of girls and the ways in which social controls are constituted and exerted: the over-representation of girls incarcerated for status offenses (behaviors that are defined in terms of the violation of parental authority) exemplifies the criminalization of girls' strategies for surviving home-based physical and sexual abuse. Chapters explore the myths and realities of girls' participation in gangs, the experiences of girls once ensnared in the juvenile justice system, trends in women's participation in crime, women's pathways into crime, and sentencing trends. Throughout the volume, attention is paid to the ways in which race, ethnicity, and class differently shape girls' and women's involvement with crime and the criminal justice system. Asserting that the nature of women's nonviolent crime is particularly well suited to preventative measures (drug treatment, job-training programs, battered women's shelters) rather than detention, Chesney-Lind further argues for the development of community-based programs for women offenders and the decarceration of women already imprisoned for nonviolent offenses.

746. Davies, Miranda, ed. *Women and Violence: Realities and Responses Worldwide.* Atlantic Highlands, NJ: Zed Books, 1994. 264p. bibliog. index. ISBN (OP); 1856491463pa.

The twenty-eight contributions that comprise this volume give support to the editor's assertion that "the threat of male violence is a fundamental experience that unites women across barriers of race, culture and class throughout the world" (p. vii). The geographic breadth of the anthology is particularly noteworthy: spanning every populated continent, the chapters frequently focus on topics or countries that have not been well represented in the U.S.-based women's studies literature. Numerous manifestations of violence against women (including battery, rape, child abuse, sexual harassment, sati, dowry murders, forced abortion, and genital mutilation) are discussed, as are the roles of economics, war, and ethnic conflict. Just as important, several chapters focus on strategies for change. Although many of the contributions have been previously published, they have not been easily accessible to most readers due to issues of language (several chapters are translations into English) and the limited distribution of the original source (e.g., organizational literature).

Related issues are explored from a U.S. perspective in *Violence against Women: The Bloody Footprints* (Sage Publications, 1993), edited by Pauline B. Bart and Eileen Gil Moran. This collection of articles, most of which were previously published in the December 1989 issue of *Gender and Society*, features theoretical essays and empirical research on many types of violence against women, the structural supports for that violence, institutional responses, and the research implications of studying violence against women.

747. Dobash, R. Emerson, and Russell P. Dobash. *Women, Violence, and Social Change.* New York: Routledge, 1992. 366p. bibliog. index. ISBN (OP); 0415036100pa.

This analysis of the battered women's movements in the United States and Great Britain focuses on the interplay of movement institutions (e.g., shelters) and institutions of the state (e.g., law and courts). Following a chapter outlining the nature and frequency of violence against women in intimate relationships, the authors provide a historical overview of the development of the battered women's movement in the two countries. Underscoring the movements' devotion not only to providing safe havens for women, but also to changing the cultural and institutional patterns that give rise to male violence against women, Dobash and Dobash stress the importance of situating the movements' goals and strategies in "the wider context of the existing economic, political and social position of women in society, and the established philosophies, priorities and practices of existing institutions and agencies of the state" (p. 14). The state is not viewed as a monolithic entity in opposition to the movement; contradictions and conflicts within and between state institutions provide sites for mobilization and resistance. Arguing forcefully that battering is a political issue, the authors critique the therapeutic treatment model that has gained a foothold in the United States as inherently depoliticizing and antithetical to the radical movement for social change. The final chapter provides an important analysis and critique of research focused on violence against women. This extremely accessible volume would be well suited to courses on violence against women and sociology of the family.

Donileen R. Loseke's *The Battered Woman and Shelters: The Social Construction of Wife Abuse* (State University of New York Press, 1992) takes a very different approach to examining the processes at work in battered women's shelters. Noting that women were being beaten long before the category "battered woman" came into use, Loseke investigates the process through which this representation is created at the societal level. She then explores how its construction at the local (i.e., shelter worker) level affects the services shelters provide and who is provided these services. Domestic abuse issues are also addressed in *Gender and Crime* (University of Wales Press, 1995), edited by Dobash, Dobash, and Lesley Noaks. This collection contains a broad range of recent research, primarily from Commonwealth countries. Chapters address media representations of crime, criminal women and the use of violence, masculinity and crime, victims and gender, and the responses of the criminal justice system to violence against women.

748. Gelsthorpe, Loraine, and Allison Morris, eds. *Feminist Perspectives in Criminology*. Philadelphia: Open University Press, 1990. 214p. (New Directions in Criminology). bibliog. index. (OP)

This volume provides insights into the ways in which feminist thought can and should inform the continuing development of criminology. In part 1, "Rethinking Criminology and the Feminist Critique," a series of essays provide a strong critique of traditional criminological theory and of earlier feminist attempts to reform and reformulate that tradition. Moving beyond critique to offer concrete guidelines for the development of a more inclusive criminological enterprise is Marcia Rice's "Challenging Orthodoxies in Feminist Theory: A Black Feminist Critique." Carol Smart's "Feminist Approaches to Criminology; or, Postmodern Woman Meets Atavistic Man" explores developments in feminist epistemology and their implications for criminological research. Part 2 focuses on explorations of feminist research methods and the development of feminist criminology as a "successor science." Law, legal reform, and a feminist critique of crime prevention are the focus of the final part, "Feminism, Politics, and Action." The accessibility of this volume makes it particularly well suited to undergraduate courses on criminological research methods and those on women and crime.

749. Gordon, Margaret T., and Stephanie Riger. *The Female Fear: The Social Cost of Rape*. Urbana: University of Illinois Press, 1991. 230p. bibliog. index. ISBN (OP); 0252061691pa.

Although somewhat dated, this work makes an important contribution to understanding the impact of the fear of rape in women's lives. Most of the data were gathered in telephone interviews conducted with more than 5,100 adults living in Philadelphia, Chicago, or San Francisco in 1977; in-person interviews were conducted with 472 people, most of whom had also participated in the telephone survey. The pervasiveness of women's fear of rape is quite well known; nonetheless, the tables contrasting women's and men's sense of personal safety in various situations and the differences in strategies each employ to increase safety and/or decrease fear are startling. Although the authors state that female fear "is not an idiosyncratic, private emotion, but a social fact with considerable impact on our society and the quality of life in our cities" (p. 47), this insight is not explored in depth. It is, however, one of the starting points for Esther Madriz's *Nothing Bad Happens to Good Girls: Fear of Crime in Women's Lives* (University of California Press, 1997). Arguing that the fear of crime (including, but not limited to, sexual assault) is "one of the most significant mechanisms in the control of women's lives" (p. 35), Madriz explores the varied manifestations of this fear and the ways it constrains women's choices in accordance with a notion of how "good" women behave. Drawing heavily on the words of the women she talked with in focus groups and in-depth interviews, Madriz explores the ways in which social hierarchies (e.g., gender, race, class, and English-language ability) reinforce and are reinforced by women's fear of crime.

750. Maher, Lisa. *Sexed Work: Gender, Race, and Resistance in a Brooklyn Drug Market.* New York: Oxford University Press, 1997. 279p. (Clarendon Studies in Criminology). bibliog. index. ISBN 019826495X; 0198299311pa.

Inspired to research by the prevalence of media-created "moral narratives" that demonized women crack users, Maher focuses her ethnographic study on the experiences of forty-five women and their participation in the street-level drug economy in one of the poorest areas of Brooklyn, New York. Noting that they are neither passive victims nor independent, emancipated actors, Maher explores the issues of women's agency and its relationship to structural constraints and opportunities: "While their narratives contain many of the predictable tropes of poverty, racism, sexism, and violence, these women emerge from their potential victimhood as creative and resiliant actors struggling to confront, challenge, and continually re-make the structures which constrain them" (p. 19). Maher presents the women's stories in their own (albeit mediated) words and employs them in developing an understanding of the interplay between gendered and raced cultural narratives and the structure of illegal work. Maher explicitly addresses three claims that have been made about women crack users; she challenges the sexualized image of female crack users and the confluent idea that they are willing to do anything to acquire more crack, the idea that the drug economy is an equal opportunity employer, and the notion that crack has produced an unprecedented wave of violent female criminals. Maher asserts that her research has implications for several interrelated theoretical issues: women's agency and its relationship to structural constraints and opportunities, the intersectionality of race/ethnicity/gender, and understanding the processes and practices of cultural reproduction.

751. Rafter, Nicole Hahn, and Frances Heidensohn, eds. *International Feminist Perspectives in Criminology: Engendering a Discipline.* Philadelphia: Open University Press, 1995. 244p. bibliog. index. ISBN 0335193897; 0335193889pa.

Purporting to be the first international and multicultural examination of the impact of feminist thought on the discipline of criminology, the essays in this volume are based on papers presented at the 1993 British Criminology Conference and the 1994 American Society of Criminology meetings. Together they examine three key questions involving the theory and practice of criminology and its effects on law and social control policies and practices. These questions bear on the historical bases of criminological research and look to whether the discipline can be reshaped to be both more inclusive and less of a rationale for policies that "contribute to and reinforce structures of power and hegemony" (p. 11). Although the geographic representation is not as broad as the editors had intended (South Africa, Australia, seven European nations, the United States, and Canada), the essays successfully demonstrate the marked differences that exist in criminological theory, research, and practice.

Issues of social control are paramount in the second edition of Rafter's *Partial Justice: Women, Prisons, and Social Control* (Transaction Publishers, 1990). This historical overview of women's prisons stresses the interplay of race, class, and gender. The new edition has been expanded to discuss additional years (1935–1988) and analyze the parity movement, an effort to ameliorate the gender-based injustices and imbalances of the prison system.

752. Renzetti, Claire M. *Violent Betrayal: Partner Abuse in Lesbian Relationships.* Newbury Park, CA: Sage Publications, 1992. 202p. bibliog. index. ISBN 0803938888; 0803938896pa.

This exploratory study of lesbian battering by the current editor of the journal *Violence Against Women* provides useful insights into the factors that may contribute to abusive relationships. Synthesizing data drawn from 100 questionnaires and forty interviews, Renzetti claims that overdependency is a major contributor, albeit insufficient unto itself, to lesbian battering. The relationships between dependency, jealousy, balance of power, substance abuse, and intergenerational violence are explored. Attention is also paid to the places and ways in which battered lesbians seek and receive support; the role of friends, family, battered women's shelters, and the criminal justice system are examined. The survey instrument and interview schedule are included in an appendix.

Naming the Violence: Speaking Out about Lesbian Battering (Seal Press, 1986), edited by Kerry Lobel for the National Coalition against Domestic Violence Lesbian Task Force, is a deeply moving anthology that offers a more personal counterpoint to Renzetti's volume. Chapters alternate between the voices of lesbian survivors and essays on community organizing and strategies for empowerment.

753. Rierden, Andi. *The Farm: Life inside a Women's Prison*. Amherst: University of Massachusetts Press, 1997. 193p. bibliog. ISBN (OP); 1558490809pa.

This journalistic account of life inside the Niantic Correctional Institution, opened in 1918 as one of the first "reformatories" for women, provides a useful corrective to stereotypical depictions of incarcerated women. Although much of the book is devoted to telling the stories of individual inmates, the complex web of social relations that exists among the inmates, correctional officers, and counselors is slowly revealed. Using information drawn from eighteen months of observing and interviewing inmates and their friends and families, as well as the wardens and correctional officers, the narratives speak to the impact of sexual abuse, prostitution, substance abuse, and economic deprivation in some women's lives. Interwoven with and underlying these stories is a historical account of public policy changes and their effects on the prison and its correctional philosophy. Although Rierden does include a brief mention of the sexual abuse of inmates, her account of life in a women's prison bears little resemblance to the horrendous circumstances detailed in the Human Rights Watch Women's Rights Project's *All Too Familiar: Sexual Abuse of Women in U.S. State Prisons* (Human Rights Watch, 1996). This heavily documented report is the result of a lengthy research project involving interviews with current and former inmates, correctional officers, attorneys, and government officials. Relevant historical and legal background is followed by case studies of prisons in selected states (California, Georgia, Illinois, Michigan, and New York) and the District of Columbia. For each jurisdiction, information on its legal and regulatory framework and custodial environment is followed by sections documenting abuses, the system's response, and recommendations. A detailed set of recommendations to the federal government and issues for consideration by state governments are also included.

754. Russell, Diana E.H. *Dangerous Relationships: Pornography, Misogyny, and Rape*. Thousand Oaks, CA: Sage Publications, 1998. 206p. bibliog. index. ISBN 0761905243; 0761905251pa.

Russell, a founding member of Women against Violence in Pornography and Media, uses evidence drawn from earlier studies and her own content analysis to argue that there is a causal link between pornography and rape. Defining pornography as "material that combines sex and/or the exposure of genitals with abuse or degradation in a manner that appears to endorse, condone, or encourage such behavior" (p. 3), Russell claims that "pornography (a) predisposes some males to want to rape women and intensifies the predisposition in other males already so predisposed; (b) undermines some males' internal inhibitions against acting out their desire to rape; and (c) undermines some males' social inhibitions against acting out their desire to rape" (p. 120). Following a review of earlier content analyses of pornography, Russell describes and analyzes 110 pornographic images gleaned from both "mainstream" and underground sources. For legal reasons, the actual images are not included in this volume; they are, however, available in the self-published *Against Pornography: The Evidence of Harm* (Russell Publications, 1993).

An earlier version of the theoretical arguments in *Dangerous Relationships* is included in Russell's *Making Violence Sexy: Feminist Views on Pornography* (Teachers College Press, 1993). This anthology includes testimonies of "survivors of pornography," theoretical analyses and research, and examples of antipornography strategies. Although many of the contributions were previously published, the inclusion of testimonies before various governmental committees and commissions provides access to a wealth of information not widely available. *Femicide: The Politics of Woman Killing* (Twayne Publishers, 1992), edited by Jill Radford and Russell, draws connections between pornography and the misogynous killing of women. Other articles analyze historical accounts of femicide, femicide and racism, the role of the criminal justice system, and feminist resistance to femicide. This collection of previously published materials focuses on the United States, the United Kingdom, and India.

755. Sanday, Peggy Reeves. *A Woman Scorned: Acquaintance Rape on Trial*. Berkeley: University of California Press, 1996. 338p. bibliog. index. ISBN (OP); 0520210921pa.

The relationship between law and common attitudes toward sex is explored in this wide-ranging discussion of acquaintance rape. Arguing that there is an American "sexual culture that victimizes women and seduces males with its addictive power" (p. 18), Sanday draws on early theorists of sexuality (Krafft-Ebing, Ellis, and Freud) as well as on contemporary pornography to show the embeddedness of the assumption of "natural" male sexual aggressiveness and sublimated female desire. Using historical and contemporary examples, Sanday examines how this discourse shapes the social relations that underpin legal responses to acquaintance rape. In a chapter titled "The Crusade against Anti-Rape Activism," Sanday responds to Camille Paglia's and Katie Roiphe's highly publicized criticisms of anti–acquaintance rape activism and research. Sanday's earlier work in the area of acquaintance rape, *Fraternity Gang Rape: Sex, Brotherhood, and Privilege on Campus* (New York University Press, 1990), is an anthropological case study of a particular manifestation of acquaintance rape. Emphasizing "ideology, discourse, and practice" (p. 16), Sanday explores gang rape as a male bonding ritual in which social privilege is reinforced. Sanday's analysis can serve as a powerful tool to understand the events detailed in Bernard Lefkowitz's *Our Guys: The Glen Ridge Rape and the Secret Life of the Perfect Suburb* (University of California Press, 1997), a powerful journalistic account of the rape of a developmentally disabled woman and the trial of the high-school athletes who assaulted her.

756. Schwartz, Martin D., ed. *Researching Sexual Violence against Women: Methodological and Personal Perspectives*. Thousand Oaks, CA: Sage Publications, 1997. 222p. bibliog. index. ISBN 0803973691; 0803973705pa.

The thirteen essays in this volume constitute a significant contribution to the examination of the numerous methodological, epistemological, and ethical questions that arise in the study of sexual violence against women. Part 1, "Introduction: Research on Sexual Assault on College Campuses," gathers material aimed at countering the 1990s backlash against feminist studies of acquaintance rape. A review of the literature, authored by Mary P. Koss (whose earlier work is discussed in Robin Warshaw's *I Never Called It Rape*, annotated later in this section) and Hobart H. Cleveland, provides a thorough understanding of current research. Subsequent chapters summarize several recent U.S. and Canadian studies of campus sexual violence. Part 2, "Emotion in Researching Violence," explores the often ignored issue of researchers' emotional responses to their work. Although each of these essays addresses important concerns and suggests valuable strategies, particularly striking is Elizabeth A. Stanko's claim that these emotional responses can themselves be used as research resources. The final part, "Doing Research on Violence against Women," addresses several key questions for feminist research: How does the researcher affect the research? Who can legitimately conduct research on sexual violence? Do the race and ethnicity of the researcher affect the legitimacy of research conducted in communities other than her own? This collection would be a wise addition to most courses on research methods, as well as to any course that requires reading Katie Roiphe's *The Morning After: Sex, Fear, and Feminism on Campus* (see entry 421).

757. Stiglmayer, Alexandra, ed. *Mass Rape: The War against Women in Bosnia-Herzegovina.* Lincoln: University of Nebraska Press, 1994. 232p. bibliog. ISBN 0803242395; 0803292295pa.

This anthology, comprised of analytical, descriptive, and historical essays, furthers our understanding of the uses of rape in war. Historical and ethnopsychoanalytical overviews of the war in the former Yugoslavia provide a necessary context for the subsequent descriptions and analyses. As numerous authors note, genocidal rape did not come into being with the war in the Balkans, nor is it the first time that media attention has been focused upon the issue; Cynthia Enloe describes how the confluence of several historical, political, and sociocultural variables has served to focus attention and garner action on this specific epidemic of mass rape. The "meaning of rape in and after wars" is explored in Ruth Seifert's "War and Rape: A Preliminary Analysis." Stiglmayer's "The Rapes in Bosnia-Herzegovina" employs extensive survivor testimonies to document the atrocities. Contributions by Catharine A. MacKinnon and by Rhonda Copelon focus on the ability of existing international human rights law to include or account for gender-based violence.

Also of note is Beverly Allen's *Rape Warfare: The Hidden Genocide in Bosnia-Herzegovina and Croatia* (University of Minnesota Press, 1996), which combines analytical insight and first-hand information gathering in a text organized around six themes: identity, representation, facts, analysis, remedies, and implications. *Sexual Violence and Armed Conflict: United Nations Response* (http://www.un.org/womenwatch/daw/public/cover.htm), the April 1998 issue of the United Nations Division for the Advancement of Women's *Women2000*, provides a historical overview of the international response to such violence.

758. Warshaw, Robin. *I Never Called It Rape: The "Ms." Report on Recognizing, Fighting, and Surviving Date and Acquaintance Rape.* New York: Harper & Row, 1988. 229p. index. ISBN (OP); 0060925728pa.

This important volume was the first major book published on the topic of acquaintance rape and was written at a time when the notion of "acquaintance rape" had not yet become a part of popular discourse. The beginning of the book is devoted to establishing that acquaintance rape is real and much too common. Warshaw uses case histories and quantitative data to illustrate the broad range of women's experiences of acquaintance rape; data on men's experiences as rapists are also provided. The statistical information was derived from the *Ms. Magazine* Campus Project on Sexual Assault, the largest (at that time) national study of acquaintance rape ever conducted. This study had five goals: to determine the prevalence of acquaintance rape on college campuses, to describe "typical incidents," to be able to predict sexual aggression, to determine risk factors for rape, and to compare the effects of stranger rape to those of acquaintance rape. The words of survivors are present throughout the book; their voices provide an important grounding for the mass of statistics presented.

759. Zimmerman, Jean. *Tailspin: Women at War in the Wake of Tailhook.* New York: Doubleday, 1995. 336p. bibliog. index. (OP)

Zimmerman's chronicle of the 1991 Tailhook Convention and its aftermath draws on a wealth of primary source material. Using information gathered from government reports, congressional debate, and hundreds of interviews, she constructs a fairly detailed account of the harassment and assaults that occurred that Labor Day weekend. A description of the U.S. Navy and Department of Defense investigations and subsequent prosecutions is also provided. Zimmerman argues that the legal exclusion of women from combat duty had a direct, negative effect on attitudes toward women in the military. The exclusion was, therefore, indirectly responsible for the behavior exhibited at Tailhook.

Sexual harassment, limitations on assignments, and the gendered nature of the military are also major focuses of the essays contained in Laurie Weinstein and Christie C. White's anthology *Wives and Warriors: Women and the Military in the United States and Canada* (Bergin & Garvey, 1997). Contributors also address the social networks and labor of military wives, masculinity and the Virginia Military Institute, women in combat, and the effects of the "don't ask, don't tell" policy on gays and lesbians in the military.

1999 CORE TITLES

Blum, Linda M. *At the Breast: Ideologies of Breastfeeding and Motherhood in the Contemporary United States.* Boston: Beacon Press, 1999. 282p. bibliog. index. ISBN 0807021407.

Chafetz, Janet Saltzman. *Handbook of the Sociology of Gender.* New York: Kluwer Academic/Plenum Publishers, 1999. (Handbooks of Sociology and Social Research). 630p. bibliog. index. ISBN 0306459787.

Clausen, Jan. *Apples and Oranges: My Journey through Sexual Identity.* Boston: Houghton Mifflin, 1999. 253p. ISBN 0395827523.

DeVault, Marjorie. *Liberating Method: Feminism and Social Research.* Philadelphia: Temple University Press, 1999. 275p. bibliog. index. ISBN 1566396972; 1566396980pa.

Ferree, Myra Marx, Judith Lorber, and Beth B. Hess, eds. *Revisioning Gender.* Thousand Oaks, CA: Sage Publications, 1999. (The Gender Lens). 500p. bibliog. index. ISBN 0761906169; 0761906177pa.

Greer, Germaine. *The Whole Woman.* New York: Knopf, 1999. 373p. bibliog. index. ISBN 0375407472.

Romero, Mary, and Abigail J. Stewart, eds. *Women's Untold Stories: Breaking Silence, Talking Back, Voicing Complexity.* New York: Routledge, 1999. 282p. bibliog. index. ISBN 0415922062; 0415922070pa.

Smith, Dorothy E. *Writing the Social: Critique, Theory, and Investigations*. Toronto: University of Toronto Press, 1999. 307p. bibliog. index. ISBN 0802043070; 0802081355pa.

WORLD WIDE WEB/INTERNET SITES

760. *The Alan Guttmacher Institute*. http://www.agi-usa.org.
Founded in 1968 as the Center for Family Planning Program Development, the Alan Guttmacher Institute is dedicated to protecting the reproductive rights of women and men around the world. The site is organized in overlapping topic areas: abortion, law and public policy, pregnancy and birth, prevention and contraception, sexual behavior, sexually transmitted diseases, and youth. Recent statistics, policy papers, and the texts of selected AGI publications are provided. Current issues of AGI periodicals (*International Family Planning Perspectives*, *The Guttmacher Report on Public Policy*, and *Family Planning Perspectives*) are also available. A "custom table maker" enables users to generate their own tables; more than 200 measures are available for more than 100 countries and the states of the United States. Of special interest may be "The Status of Major Abortion Related Laws in the [United] States" and "Sharing Responsibility: Women, Society, and Abortion Worldwide," which provides an overview of abortion practices, laws, and statistics.

761. Association of College and Research Libraries. Women's Studies Section. *Lesbian, Bisexual, and Transgendered Collection Development Resources*. http://carbon.cudenver .edu/public/library/libq/LBT.html.
This clearinghouse site is a bibliographer's dream. The site features a selective list of links to organizations, collections of bibliographies, search engines, publisher directories, book distributors, out-of-print dealers, and book review sources. Information on relevant electronic discussion lists is also provided.

762. *gURL.com*. http://www.gURL.com.
This award-winning site was originally designed in 1996 as a project for a media course in the Interactive Telecommunications Program at New York University. It has since become one of the key Web sites devoted to the interests and concerns of teenage girls. This e-zine contains poems, stories, comics, games, advice columns, and information about issues that are often on girls' minds: body image, sexuality, music, parents, role models, news, sports, movies, friends, and health. Although the site is available for viewing without first registering, access to the interactive portions (e.g., chat rooms and message boards) requires free registration.

763. *National Abortion Rights Action League*. http://www.naral.org.
Many of the features available on this site are designed to increase citizen activism. Voting records, online alerts, and automated e-mail to members of Congress are all available. Fact sheets and news releases are provided on a range of reproductive choice issues, including clinic violence, access to abortion, contraception, minors' issues, RU 486/mifepristone, and sex education. State-level information on abortion law and policy is provided; a separate database provides access to summaries of current state legislation (and brief legislative histories).

764. *Sociologists for Women in Society*. http://newmedia.colorado.edu/~socwomen/.
Although this Web site is not very developed, it does provide basic information on the key professional organization working to "improve the position of women within sociology and within

society in general." SWS is probably best known as the sponsor of the journal *Gender and Society*. A small number of sample syllabi and bibliographies are provided.

765. *Violence against Women Online Resources.* http://www.vaw.umn.edu.
    Cooperatively produced by the U.S. Department of Justice Violence against Women Office and the Minnesota Center against Violence and Abuse (MINCAVA), this clearinghouse site provides the full text of informational documents on domestic violence, sexual assault, stalking, the criminal justice system, child abuse, research and evaluation, model programs, welfare reform, batterer intervention programs, and model legislation. A very selective, annotated list of related links is also provided.

766. *Welfare Information Network.* http://www.welfareinfo.org.
    This clearinghouse of welfare information includes fact sheets, external links, research reports, and statistics on more than forty welfare-related topics, including Temporary Assistance for Needy Families (TANF) work requirements, education and training opportunities, food stamps, and child care. Information on state-specific programs is provided in selected topic areas. Federal and state legislation and state TANF plans are also available. A "Hot Topics" page provides well-organized access to recent high-interest material.

10   Sports

Mila C. Su

Since 1985, monographs on all aspects of women and sport have steadily increased and expanded through a variety of formats, including anthologies, chapters within books, and specific monographs. The authors of these publications are mostly sport journalists and academic sport researchers who provide a wide range of perspectives. Although the contributions are useful, researchers must continue to publish information by and about women and their experiences, influences, and history in sport. One could argue that insights gleaned from exploring different "cultures" could teach women how to adapt and continue to challenge the remaining boundaries in sport. Sport is an interdisciplinary subject, yielding a wide range of titles from different fields that relate the experiences, issues, and histories of women in sport. Academics and nonacademics alike have written these titles, which include many telling cultural issues, among others. The contributors have included some international viewpoints as well.

The study of sport and women involves more than just exercise and fitness, statistics, and Title IX. The framework for the study of sport has several paradigms and covers a wide range of interdisciplinary perspectives, including feminist, feminist separatist, Marxist, and other theoretical structures. Yet not only do integration and acceptance of sport in women's studies continue to exist, but the exclusion of feminist theory in sport studies is present as well. More recent issues included in the periodical literature are gender equity, leadership, equipment, the athletic triad (amenorrhea, osteoporosis, and eating disorders), the media, marketing, and careers in sport. Today, many women compete in sports that have existed since the turn of the twentieth century. Researchers have yet to explore the wealth of additional areas of research about women. Scholars need to address the following topics: the histories and experiences of disabled athletes, the Para Olympics, and events such as the Commonwealth and Pan American Games.

REFERENCE SOURCES

767. Madden, W.C. *The Women of the All-American Girls Professional Baseball League: A Biographical Dictionary.* Jefferson, NC: McFarland, 1997. 288p. ISBN 0786403047.

This work includes more than 600 biographical entries, arranged in alphabetical order, of players from the All-American Girls Professional Baseball League (AAGPBL). Most entries contain a minimum of personal statistics from date of birth to date of death (if applicable), height, weight, position, and team names. The biographical and career information ranges from a few sentences to several paragraphs. The author interviewed 190 former AAGPBL players, managers, and other officials, integrating their postprofessional life stories into the biographies. Madden includes career statistics for players who participated in more than ten games, as well as pictures of various players. Unfortunately, the author failed to document when and where the interviews were conducted. He also does not include a bibliography, which would have enhanced the work. Nonetheless, this reference work should be included in most libraries' collections.

768. Oglesby, Carole A., ed. *Encyclopedia of Women and Sport in America*. Phoenix: Oryx Press, 1998. 360p. bibliog. ISBN 0897749936.

Oglesby, professor of kinesiology at Temple University, is internationally renowned for her research in women and sport. This encyclopedia introduces many important concepts relevant to women in sport, including career information, fundraising, and Latinas in sport. Expanded entries on the history of specific sports and sport organizations also contribute to the value of this encyclopedia. Biographical information on women who have influenced their sport is also provided. Oglesby alphabetically arranges the topics, which include disabled women, lesbian identity, and skill in movement. The author integrates these topics with profiles of coaches, administrators, athletes, commentators, journalists, and other women who work in sport. A useful but selected bibliography is included.

A related work is *American Women in Sport, 1887–1987: A 100-Year Chronology*, edited by Ruth M. Sparhawk and Mary E. Leslie (Scarecrow Press, 1989). This chronology highlights some of the important breakthroughs and successes of American women in all areas of sport.

769. Remley, Mary L. *Women in Sport: An Annotated Bibliography and Resource Guide, 1900–1990*. New York: Macmillan, 1991. 210p. index. ISBN 0816189773.

Mary Remley, professor of kinesiology and women's studies at Indiana University at Bloomington, is one of the pioneers in publishing bibliographies on women in sport. In this source, the first four chapters list books by the following chronological arrangement: 1900–1930, 1931–1960, 1961–1975, and 1976–1990. At the beginning of each chapter, the author presents an overview of events occurring at the time, which provides an evolutionary history concerning the interest in research on women in sport. Annotations run from a few sentences to a paragraph. The majority of the citations cover titles published in the United States, although some titles from Canada and the United Kingdom are also listed. Chapter 5 lists periodicals, sports organizations, and halls of fame, providing addresses and brief descriptions.

Women in Sports: A Select Bibliography by Michelle Shoebridge (Mansell, 1987) includes sources covering a variety of topics, such as the disabled, ethnicity, and sports medicine. The bibliography also covers individual sports and athletes. Within these topical areas, Shoebridge arranges North American, British, and a few European publications under the following categories: monographs, conference proceedings and parts of monographs, articles, and theses. Helen Lenskyj's *Women, Sport, and Physical Activity: Research and Bibliography* (Ottawa, Ontario: Minister of Supply and Services, 1988; rev. ed., 1991) is another useful title for researchers. The author, a renowned Canadian sport researcher, created this resource to generate discussion and further research. The author introduces selected research themes with specific subcategories, followed by a very selective bibliography, in both editions. The author included resources based on the following criteria: sources should be nonsexist and free of bias; sources should not perpetuate negative stereotypes of women; and sources should be neither patronizing nor prescriptive. The third edition of *Women, Sport, and Physical Activity: Selected Research Themes*, also by Lensky, (Gloucester, Ontario: Sport Information Resource Centre for Sport Canada, 1994) includes reviews of research on the sociology of sport, recreation, discrimination, and leadership issues.

770. Woolum, Janet. *Outstanding Women Athletes: Who They Are and How They Influenced Sports in America*. Phoenix: Oryx Press, 1992. 279p. bibliog. index. (OP)

Lauded by the Women's Sports Foundation, *Outstanding Women Athletes* provides a combination of history and biography. The author presents a historical overview of the development of women's sports in the United States in the first chapter. The second chapter includes a chronological history of women's participation and interaction in the Olympics. Biographies of various important women athletes comprise the main part of the book. Each entry has names, dates, career highlights, and an indication of how the individual contributed to or influenced her sport. The appendices include listings of Summer and Winter Olympics winners and listings of awards and championships of other sports. The second edition published in 1998 reorganizes and expands much of the information and includes listings of sporting organizations, major milestones in women's sports history, and descriptions of important teams. This is a very useful resource for all libraries.

Other related titles include Wendy Long's *Celebrating Excellence: Canadian Women Athletes* (Polestar Book Publishers, 1995). Long provides useful biographical information on elite Canadian athletes representing snow skiing, ice skating, water sports, track and field, and gymnastics. She also includes information on disabled athletes and other "trailblazers." *The Women's Sports Encyclopedia*, edited by Robert Markel (Henry Holt, 1997), serves as a guide to selected sports, with brief histories, short profiles of important players, and a variety of sidebars that include records, terminology, and discussions of controversies. Anne J. Johnson's *Great Women in Sports* (Visible Ink Press, 1996) includes some of the sports that Markel covers, but provides more extensive information. Finally, Victoria Sherrow's *Encyclopedia of Women and Sports* (ABC-CLIO, 1996) covers the history of women's sports at the international and national levels. Sherrow includes a lengthy introduction, a selected chronology highlighting various key events in the world of sports, biographies of many female athletes, and histories of specific sports.

MONOGRAPHS

771. Avery, Joanna, and Julie Stevens. *Too Many Men on the Ice: Women's Hockey in North America*. Victoria, British Columbia: Polestar Book Publishers, 1997. 286p. bibliog. index. ISBN 189609533X.

Women have played ice hockey in North America since the late 1800s. Avery and Stevens, a sport journalist and an academic, respectively, trace the development of women's ice hockey in Canada and the United States from its inception. Beginning with the 1994 World Championship, the authors recount the sport's history in Canada and the United States to frame the organizational issues and various events that influenced the development of women's ice hockey in each country. The authors outline how the contributions of grassroots organizations and elite developmental programs in both countries critically influenced the growth of national and regional organizations. The authors describe the factors and controversies involved with body checking and playing with men. Other important discussions include Title IX, scholarships, and the fight for varsity status.

Elizabeth Etue and Megan K. Williams's *On the Edge: Women Making Hockey History* (Second Story Press, 1996) and Brian McFarlane's *Proud Past, Bright Future: One Hundred Years of Canadian Women's Hockey* (Stoddart, 1994) are similar worthwhile titles. *On the Edge* describes the first world championship, held in Ottawa, Canada. The authors then examine the politics, challenges, and developments in women's hockey throughout the Canadian provinces. They discuss organizational politics, equity issues, discrimination, and the development of hockey at an international level. *Proud Past, Bright Future* uses a mix of unfortunately uncited primary source materials and interviews to document the history of women's hockey in Canada.

772. Birrell, Susan, and Cheryl L. Cole, eds. *Women, Sport, and Culture*. Champaign, IL: Human Kinetics, 1994. 408p. bibliog. index. ISBN 087322650X.

The essays in this work, some previously published, explore various theories regarding politics, organization, and representations of women in sport. Some contributors approach their analyses from nonsport or non-American backgrounds; however, the information collectively provides insights and potential topics of research in the evolving study of women in sport. Each of the work's five sections focuses on an aspect of feminist study as applied to women in sport. The first section explores ideological issues within sport, including how male role models have influenced women and sport. The next section examines gender issues around leadership, Title IX, and collegiate experiences. Section 3 deals with various issues related to women's participation in sport and their perceived intrusion into the male domain. The fourth section highlights different issues involving the media and images of women, and section 5 identifies issues related to the politics of sexuality. This would be a useful title for researchers, students, and teachers to expand their understanding regarding the issues within the study of women and sport.

Two other titles that deal with gender roles in sports are *Sport, Men, and the Gender Order: Critical Feminist Perspectives*, edited by Michael A. Messner (Human Kinetics, 1992), and Jim McKay's *Managing Gender: Affirmative Action and Organizational Power in Australian, Canadian, and New Zealand Sport* (State University of New York Press, 1997). Messner's collection of essays focuses on three areas: theoretical and historical foundations, contemporary research and challenges, and possible future alternatives for women in sport. The contributors, well known in the field of feminist and gender studies in sport, provide a cohesive overview of how sport affects both women and men. McKay, a well-known Australian sport researcher, explores how sports programs influenced one another in Australia, Canada, and New Zealand. He examines these countries' differences and similarities through interviews with senior and middle managers of national sporting organizations. However, by focusing on management alone, this title unfortunately excludes other issues that women must face.

773. Cahn, Susan K. *Coming on Strong: Gender and Sexuality in Twentieth-Century Women's Sport*. New York: Free Press, 1994. 358p. bibliog. index. ISBN 0029050758.

Cahn, associate professor of history at the State University of New York at Buffalo and recipient of the North American Society for Sports History Book Award, skillfully details the evolution of women's sports in the United States. The first three chapters examine the activities and images of athletic women in society and academia. Cahn incorporates a historical perspective into these chapters, thus providing an accurate picture of the state of women in sports prior to Title IX. The next three chapters focus on basketball, black women in track and field, and the All-American Girls Professional Baseball League. In each of these chapters, Cahn focuses on some of the critical issues that affected each sport, discusses how the sport evolved, and outlines some of the obstacles and criticisms women faced as a result of their participation in these sports. The author examines issues pertaining to lesbians, the lesbian image, and homophobia in the next two chapters. In the final chapter, covering the 1960s to the present, the author reflects upon the changes in women's sports while also noting that much is still status quo, especially in her analysis of how society continues to demean women. This book provides a highly satisfactory overview of the history of women's sport in America.

Doris Pieroth's *Their Day in the Sun: Women of the 1932 Olympics* (University of Washington Press, 1996) chronicles the experiences of the thirty-seven female athletes who participated in the 1932 Olympics. Despite many challenges, American women competing in these games achieved unprecedented success, claiming medals in several events in swimming and diving and track and field. Pieroth argues that the success of these women and the press coverage of their victories assured the continuation of women's sporting events at the Olympics. Both titles should be included in collections on women's sports and Olympic history.

774. Chambers, Marcia. *The Unplayable Lie: The Untold Story of Women and Discrimination in American Golf.* New York: Simon & Schuster, 1996. 358p. ISBN 0671501550pa.

Chambers investigates women's experiences in the worlds of private golf and country clubs. The author discusses political and social issues, including bias toward female players, minority participation, and low financial rewards for professional women. In the first section, Chambers outlines discriminatory practices faced by women in golf. Beginning with a historical overview of women's golf from the 1880s to the 1990s, the author then reviews the evolution of the all-male clubs and concludes with an analysis of how women gained entry into these clubs. Chambers comments on selected obstacles and challenges that women have faced at different courses and describes how club members reacted to these incidents. In the final section, Chambers discusses the changes needed to encourage more participation by women in American golf. The author consulted court and legislative documents and player records as well as conducting interviews with key individuals involved in managerial or policy decisions. Chambers also incorporates interviews with women who have challenged the "patriarchal" club structure and who struggle to find ways to change policies.

775. Cohen, Greta L., ed. *Women in Sport: Issues and Controversies.* Thousand Oaks, CA: Sage, 1993. 338p. bibliog. index. ISBN 0803949790; 0803949804pa.

Cohen, professor of physical education and women's studies at the University of Rhode Island, has produced an excellent resource that could serve as a textbook for the study of women and sport. Essays written by experts in various fields discuss topics such as role expectations, the historical contributions of individuals and organizations, government and equity policies, the conventions and practices within women's sports, psychological concerns, and economic issues. A list of key words, discussion questions, and footnotes follow each essay. Cohen deliberately structured this book for use as a textbook; instructors could select individual essays from the work for class discussions as well.

Related titles include *Women on Ice: Feminist Essays on the Tonya Harding/Nancy Kerrigan Spectacle*, edited by Cynthia Baughman (Routledge, 1995), and Joan Ryan's *Little Girls in Pretty Boxes: The Making and Breaking of Elite Gymnasts and Figure Skaters* (Doubleday, 1995). Baughman selected an eclectic range of essays and musings from academics and journalists on different aspects of the Harding/Kerrigan incident. Some of the essays are thought-provoking, while others are more erratic and reactionary. Ryan, a sport journalist, examines various issues and trends in figure skating and gymnastics. She raises the important concern of certification for coaches, which all sports should require.

776. Costa, D. Margaret, and Sharon R. Guthrie, eds. *Women and Sport: Interdisciplinary Perspectives.* Champaign, IL: Human Kinetics, 1994. 399p. bibliog. index. ISBN 0873226860.

Costa is a faculty member in physical education and women's studies, and Guthrie is a faculty member in physical education, both at California State University at Long Beach. Their work *Women and Sport: Interdisciplinary Perspectives* contains essays arranged under three general categories: history and culture, biomedicine and physiology, and psychological and sociological frameworks. A general overview precedes each section. Many of the essays include theoretical discussions, a basic overview, and a description of major issues within each topic, and contributors include a lengthy list of references at the end of each essay. The editors provide some sidebars and photographs as well. This is an excellent resource that could be used as a textbook or by researchers interested in different perspectives on women's sports. Chapters by Susan Birrell and

Nancy Theberge concerning the paradigm shift in women's involvement in sport are highly informative.

Another title presenting various approaches to the study of women and sport is *Researching Women and Sport*, edited by Gill Clarke and Barbara Humbestone (MacMillan UK, 1997). This brief work covers different approaches available to scholars wishing to research women and sport. Topics include leadership, elite wheelchair athletes, lesbians, physical educators, and cross-cultural issues. The contributors use various methodologies, including oral history and surveys, not only to incorporate feminist constructs, but also to deconstruct many of the described issues.

777. Creedon, Pamela J., ed. *Women, Media, and Sport: Challenging Gender Values.* Thousand Oaks, CA: Sage, 1994. 358p. bibliog. index. ISBN 0803952333; 0803952341pa.

Personal memories of sport, coupled with her experiences as a feminist, inspired Creedon to generate this collection of essays to "link women, sports, and the mass media with feminist perspectives from history, psychology, women's studies, sociology, kinesiology and mass communication" (pp. ix–x). Contributors explore various viewpoints of the media's relationship to sport in their essays, which Creedon arranges into three parts. The seven essays in part 1 examine the relationship between women, sport, and the media in terms of how the media construct and present female athletes, as well as presenting the experiences of women working in the profession as nonathletes. In an essay evocatively titled "Women in Toyland," Creedon highlights the history (from the 1800s until the present) of female sports participants as well as those who worked in the media profession and the challenges they faced. Essays in part 2 focus on gender values within social and cultural structures and discuss sexuality, the sporting experiences of women, and women as spectators. The final part suggests alternative paradigms in the presentation and conception of women in sport. Extensive bibliographies appear at the end of each chapter. This work could serve as a textbook for upper-division undergraduate and graduate courses in sports studies, communications, women's studies, and sociology.

778. Festle, Mary J. *Playing Nice: Politics and Apologies in Women's Sports.* New York: Columbia University Press, 1996. 379p. bibliog. index. ISBN 0231101627.

Festle takes an alternative approach to the history of women's sports. She separates the evolution of women in sports into four main periods: the early 1950s, 1955 to 1967, 1968 to 1979, and 1980 to 1990. The author analyzes the many sociopolitical influences on women's lives, Americans' general expectations of women's roles in society, and the advancement of women's competitive sports. Focusing on three sports—golf, basketball, and tennis—to frame her study, Festle examines a number of issues previously neglected by scholars of sports history, such as the "apologetic in sport," lesbians, the feminine ideal, and the conflict of competition. The author also comments on the Gay Games and the Senior Olympics, describes the role of the Amateur Athletic Union in women's sports, and traces the philosophical shift concerning women's participation that came about in the 1950s. *Playing Nice* brings to light the many challenges women have faced and continue to face as they struggle for equal participation in the world of sports.

779. Griffin, Pat. *Strong Women, Deep Closets: Lesbians and Homophobia in Sport.* Champaign, IL: Human Kinetics, 1998. 245p. bibliog. index. ISBN (OP); 088011729Xpa.

Griffin brings many issues regarding lesbians and homophobia in the sports world to the forefront in this outstanding work. She integrates her personal experiences as an athlete, teacher, workshop leader on homophobia and heterosexism, and researcher with forty-eight interviews she conducted with lesbian athletes, coaches, and administrators. Most of the individuals she interviewed represent collegiate sports. Combining theoretical concepts with a personal touch, Griffin tackles several critical topics, including the domination of sports by male and heterosexist ideals, the alienation and stereotypes of lesbians, lesbians who choose to remain private, and lesbians who choose to "come out." This preeminent book challenges readers to reconsider the traditional, intimidating tactics that people use to paralyze women who participate in sport.

780. Guttmann, Allen. *Women's Sports: A History*. New York: Columbia University Press, 1991. 339p. bibliog. index. ISBN 0231069561; 023106957Xpa.

Before the publication of Guttmann's groundbreaking work, very few works existed on the history of women's sports incorporating a broad, international scope. Guttmann effectively revived the dialogue on women and sport and received the North American Society for Sports History Book Award for *Women's Sports: A History*. The author reviews the games, recreational activities, and sports that women have participated in from antiquity to the twentieth century. Section 1 outlines the history of women in sports, beginning with chapters discussing sports and recreational activities of the Egyptians, Greeks, and Romans and into the Middle Ages. Later chapters in this section examine the development of sports for females during the Victorian era, specifically focusing on the United Kingdom, and also look at sports programs for women in the Communist countries during the 1920s and 1930s. The chapters in section 2 explore contemporary topics, including how the women's movement affected women's sports, unequal access to funding at the collegiate level, and the controversy over drug testing. This compact volume provides a good, general overview and introduction to the subject matter.

781. Hall, M. Ann. *Feminism and Sporting Bodies: Essays on Theory and Practice*. Champaign, IL: Human Kinetics, 1996. 135p. bibliog. index. ISBN (OP); 087322969Xpa.

Hall, an emeritus professor at the University of Alberta who has published in the fields of sports studies and women's studies, addresses the often ignored separation between sports and feminist theory: "My purpose in *Feminism and Sporting Bodies* is to 'speak feminism' to physical educators, sport studies students and scholars, and sportswomen" (p. v). Recounting her own personal experience with the integration of feminist theory into sports research, the author identifies continuing areas of concern that contribute to the divide between feminism and sports studies. Hall focuses on feminist theory within the fields of sociology, history, and cultural studies that can contribute to new understandings of women in sport. Specific essays cover topics such as biological determinism, class issues, the importance of the body, and masculinity. One chapter provides an excellent overview of the practice of feminist research and would serve as an excellent introduction for beginning students. In her final essay, Hall calls for a more radical and politicized approach to the study of women in sport. The author argues that women involved in physical education and sports and women engaged in feminist theory must come together to create a meaningful dialogue. The combination of personal reflection and academic investigation in this book makes it required reading for all involved with women's studies or women's sports.

782. Hargreaves, Jennifer. *Sporting Females: Critical Issues in the History and Sociology of Women's Sports*. New York: Routledge, 1994. 331p. bibliog. index. ISBN (OP); 0415070287pa.

Hargreaves provides an excellent critique of important issues in women's sports through her use of both historical and sociological methodologies. The first two chapters deal with theories of sport that exclude gender, as well as feminist sports theories that include gender. The author then explores the influences of Victorian and Edwardian societies on the development of women's sports, the evolution of women's sports, and the history and control of women's participation in the Olympics. Hargreaves ends by examining "other" issues, such as separatism, racism, ethnocentrism, lesbians, the elderly, and the disabled, and explores how such diversity may actually help empower women and others to participate in sports. Hargreaves's research is thought-provoking. This title won the North American Sport Sociology Book Award.

783. Henderson, Karla A., M. Deborah Bialeschki, Susan M. Shaw, and Valerie J. Frey-singer. *Both Gains and Gaps: Feminist Perspectives on Women's Leisure.* State College, PA: Venture Publishing, 1996. 337p. bibliog. index. ISBN 0910251797.

The authors state that this work updates their title *A Leisure of One's Own: A Feminist Perspective on Women's Leisure* published in 1989 (Venture). Incorporating historical, psychological, and sociological theories, *Both Gains and Gaps* analyzes the role leisure plays in women's lives. Early chapters explore how feminist research has influenced the study of leisure. The authors discuss the meaning of leisure in society and explore various constraints and challenges women face as they incorporate leisure into their lives. These constraints include gaps between men and women, gaps between women of different classes, and gaps between balancing work and leisure activities. While *Both Gains and Gaps* focuses on the study of leisure in North America among white women, the authors have included some perspectives from women from other countries and races. This work presents a clear introduction to the study of leisure and would prove useful for the novice researcher.

Nicole Samuel's *Women, Leisure, and the Family in Contemporary Society: A Multinational Perspective* (CAB International, 1996) also addresses leisure. Although researchers often categorize the study of leisure within sociology, this collection of essays presents sociological, economic, and global viewpoints regarding the role of leisure in women's lives. Essays address a wide range of topics, including the history of women's leisure, leisure and the family structure, and various viewpoints of the concept of leisure within different regions of the world. Tables, charts, and other statistical data enhance this work.

784. Hult, Joan S., and Marianna Trekell, eds. *A Century of Women's Basketball: From Frailty to Final Four.* Reston, VA: American Alliance for Health, Physical Education, Recreation, and Dance, 1991. 430p. bibliog. index. ISBN (OP); 0883144905pa.

This is the first definitive history of women's basketball. In two parts, one covering the 1890s to the 1930s and the other covering the 1940s to the 1980s, the author presents a detailed, fascinating history of the game. Part 1 describes the early history and varieties of basketball that developed at the interscholastic, collegiate, and competitive levels. Part 2 then goes on to examine the development of women's basketball on the collegiate scene and includes chapters on coaching, championships, and team experiences. Hult also discusses the development of various competitive venues, explores the history of women's wheelchair basketball, and provides a brief overview of various national associations and their relationship to women's and girls' basketball. The final chapter discusses the effect of Title IX on women's basketball and considers the future of the sport.

Women's Basketball: A Bibliography of the Guides Published for the National Association for Girls and Women in Sport and Its Predecessors, 1901–1985 (American Alliance for Health, Physical Education, Recreation, and Dance, 1990) by Nancy C. Dosch provides a historical record of the changes in the game of women's basketball. Working in the archives of the American Alliance for Health, Physical Education, Recreation, and Dance (AAHPERD) and the Basketball Hall of Fame, Dosch indexed all of the information in the guides. Sara Gogol's *Playing in a New*

League: Women's Professional Basketball in the U.S. (Masters Press, 1998) captures the history of the now-defunct American Basketball League (ABL). This is an excellent resource that includes interviews and biographical information on players, coaches, staff, and many others who were involved in establishing and supporting the ABL's existence. Two titles focusing on women's collegiate basketball include *Raise the Roof: The Inspiring Inside Story of the Tennessee Lady Vols' Undefeated 1997–98 Season* by Pat Head Summit (Broadway Books, 1998) and Jan Beran's *From Six-on-Six to Full Court Press: A Century of Iowa Girls' Basketball* (Iowa State University Press, 1993), which traces the unique history of Iowa girls' basketball. Finally, Madeleine Blais's *In These Girls, Hope Is a Muscle* (Atlantic Monthly Press, 1995) focuses on a high-school girls' team in Amherst, Massachusetts.

785. Johnson, Susan E. *When Women Played Hardball: Professional Lives and Personal Stories from the All-American Girls Professional Baseball League, 1943–1954.* Seattle: Seal Press, 1994. bibliog. index. ISBN 1878067435 pa.

When Women Played Hardball chronicles the history of the AAGPBL from its beginnings in 1943 to its final season in 1954. Johnson also details the 1950 championship playoffs between the Rockford Peaches and the Fort Wayne Daisies through chapters dedicated to each game in the series. The author incorporates a variety of sources, including interviews with former players, newspaper articles, and archival collections, to document these women's experiences. This well-written title provides a solid overview of the AAGPBL and should be in all collections.

For additional information on the AAGPBL, consider Lois Browne's *Girls of Summer: The Real Story of the All-American Girls Professional Baseball League* (DIANE Publishing, 1992). Browne, a freelance writer from Toronto, provides an entertaining and informative story through her interviews with former players in the league.

In *Women in Baseball: The Forgotten History* (Praeger, 1994), Gai I. Berlage traces the overlooked contributions of women to baseball. A number of women played on men's teams at the turn of the twentieth century, and this book tells their stories. Researchers will find the bibliography useful. James Overmyer's *Effa Manley and the Newark Eagles* (Scarecrow Press, 1993) pays tribute to Effa Manley, who owned and managed an outstanding team in the Negro Leagues. Manley fought for reform and equality on the baseball field, as well as in society at large. The bibliography provides useful descriptions of primary sources. This book was republished as *Queen of the Negro Leagues: Effa Manley and the Newark Eagles* (Scarecrow Press, 1998). For a photo history, see Barbara Gregorich's *Women at Play: The Story of Women in Baseball* (Harcourt Brace, 1993). Gregorich traces baseball from 1869 to the 1990s and incorporates individual biographies, photographs, and the histories of various stellar teams into her work.

786. Kahn, Liz. *The L.P.G.A., the Unauthorized Version: A History of the Ladies Professional Golf Association.* Menlo Park, CA: Group Fore Productions, 1996. 308p. index. ISBN 088197126X.

Kahn presents the history of women's professional golf from its inception in the late 1800s to the 1990s. During the course of twenty years, Kahn spent hours with professionals on tour, as well as with retired golfers. In chronological groupings by decade, the author artfully integrates individual biographies, interviews of female golfers, and commentary from friends and colleagues. This work begins with a history of women's involvement with golf at the beginning of the twentieth century. Kahn also discusses the creation of the Women's Professional Golfers Association in the early 1940s. Although this organization lasted only five years, the establishment of the WPGA was an important political move for women golfers. Kahn concludes her work with an analysis of the LPGA, including commentary on the increase of international players, competitive tournaments, and earnings. Throughout the work, Kahn addresses controversial topics, such as sexuality, lesbians, racism, religious intolerance, and the media's effect on the sport. She also discusses issues of practical concern to players, including child care and maternity leave. Photographs of the players both on and off the greens, as well as relevant statistics, lend additional perspective to this insightful book.

Jim Burnett's *Tee Times* (Simon & Schuster, 1997) nicely complements Kahn's work. Burnett spent the 1996 season on the LGPA tour interviewing and observing the women athletes. He comments on factors and events affecting women on tour and also gleaned information about how these players interact with each other. Elinor Nickerson's *Golf: A Women's History* (McFarland, 1987) briefly describes women's participation in golf, from ancient to modern times. The author cites many resources that document this history on an international level; however, she mainly focuses on the development of professional golf in the United States. Nickerson includes biographical descriptions of the sport's significant players, as well as information on halls of fame, awards, and trophies.

787. Littlewood, Mary L. *Women's Fastpitch Softball: The Path to the Gold: An Historical Look at Women's Fastpitch in the United States.* Columbia, MO: National Fastpitch Coaches Association, 1998. 274p. bibliog. index. ISBN 0966431006.

This book chronicles the history of women's softball in the industrial, professional, collegiate, and international leagues in the United States from 1887 to the late 1990s. Littlewood provides histories of various teams from different regions and comments on the contributions these teams made to the sport. The author also discusses organizational structures and conflicts, interactions between and among players and managers, and the ways in which teams dealt with racial issues during the various eras. Additional chapters focus on pitching styles and the Amateur Softball Associate rules. Littlewood includes photographs of players, teams, and memorabilia that complement the text and reflect the evolution of softball within American culture. Appendices include a timeline and statistical rankings of various leagues and associations.

788. Lowe, Marie R. *Women of Steel: Female Bodybuilders and the Struggle for Self-Definition.* New York: New York University Press, 1998. 206p. bibliog. index. ISBN 0814750931; 081475094Xpa.

Lowe uses a combination of techniques to provide a construction of women's experiences in the competitive circuit. She interviewed thirty-seven competitors, judges, officials, and journalists and combined the results with "ethnographic observation" to present her findings. Although her writing is somewhat stilted and repetitive, the author properly articulates issues familiar in women's sports and creates a good picture of the competitive experience.

In *Bodymakers: A Cultural Anatomy of Women's Body Building* (Rutgers University Press, 1998), Leslie Heywood, a faculty member in English at the State University of New York at Binghamton, looks at bodybuilding through the lenses of literary and popular culture to evaluate the images and perceptions attached to the sport. Martha McCaughey's *Real Knockouts: The Physical Feminism of Women's Self-Defense* (New York University Press, 1997) explores the conflict between "violence and feminism." McCaughey, a women's studies instructor at Virginia Tech who took a self-defense class, analyzes the tensions among contemporary feminist theories, femininity, and aggression. McCaughey calls her experience "physical feminism," wherein a woman uses her experience in self-defense to gain knowledge about her body's strengths.

789. Mazel, David, ed. *Mountaineering Women: Stories by Early Climbers.* College Station: Texas A&M University Press, 1994. 184p. ISBN 0890966168; 0890966176pa.

This collection of original writings by female climbers and guides from the 1880s to the 1950s provides a vivid picture of the experiences of these women. In the introduction, Mazel discusses the social and patriarchal beliefs that female climbers fought against. Mazel writes, "When women climb well, and when they do so unaccompanied by men, they challenge not just individual male egos but the whole constellation of assumptions about gender in our society" (p. 14). The author chose the writings, which are arranged chronologically and focus on women climbers from Europe, to present a varied perspective of experiences. Thus the writings include stories by ordinary women, and many are not triumphant accounts of reaching the summit. The lengthy bibliography will be useful for readers interested in additional titles on this topic. *Mountaineering Women* presents a unique history of courageous women who not only risked physical injury, but also defied social norms.

Another important title on women climbers is *Women Climbing: 200 Years of Achievement* by Bill Birkett and Bill Peascod (Mountaineers, 1989). This alphabetically arranged work presents a veritable who's who in climbing. The authors provide biographical information on thirteen groundbreaking women who dared to climb. Cyndi Smith's *Off the Beaten Track: Women Adventurers and Mountaineers in Western Canada* (Coyote Books, 1989) introduces the stories of fourteen outstanding women, including female explorers, artists, writers, mountaineers, and guides from the Rockies in Alberta to the coast of British Columbia. The work covers the period from 1885 through World War II. Finally, *The Magnificent Mountain Women: Adventures in the Colorado Rockies* by Janet Robertson (University of Nebraska Press, 1990) "chronicles the exploits of several dozen women—historical and contemporary—who have sought out experiences in some of the most rugged county in America—the mountains of Colorado" (p. xi). In telling the history of these female "pioneers," Robertson includes excerpts from these women's journals and diaries, maps, and photographs. Libraries should consider this book not only for sport collections, but also for collections on the American West and the outdoors.

790. McCrone, Kathleen E. *Playing the Game: Sport and the Physical Emancipation of English Women, 1870–1914*. Lexington: University Press of Kentucky, 1988. 310p. bibliog. index. ISBN 0813116414.

In the preface to this impressive sociological history, McCrone writes of her work: "Its aim is not to establish or submit to review what is known or thought to be known about the Victorian world-view and women's place within it, but rather to investigate reactions against this view and the emergence of a counter-view through sport and exercise" (Preface, p. 1). Using a broad definition of sport that includes both organized, competitive games and various individual recreational activities, the author traces the evolution of middle-class British women's participation in sport during the Victorian era. The excellent introduction discusses the history of games and sport in England from the Middle Ages to the beginning of the twentieth century. McCrone also analyzes the lack of scholarship on the history of women in sport: "Sport is a complex phenomenon which acts as an important agent of both social change and social control and modifies and defines female roles in society at large" (p. 1). Chapters in this work discuss the rise of sports in public schools, the role of sports for college women, and the history of team sports, including hockey, lacrosse, and cricket, as well as individual sports, including lawn tennis, golf, and cycling. Two fascinating chapters discuss the medical and scientific debate concerning women's sports and the role sports played in defining women's fashions.

From "Fair Sex" to Feminism: Sport and the Socialization of Women in the Industrial and Post-industrial Eras, edited by J.A. Mangan and Roberta J. Park (Frank Cass, 1986), provides a similar perspective to that of the previous title. The editors arrange this work into four sections of excellent essays on the medical and physical history of women's sporting experience in North

America, Australia, and England. The following works provide an examination of women and equestrian sports. Jackie C. Burke's *Equal to the Challenge: Pioneering Women of Horse Sports* (Howell Books, 1997) combines biography and the history of women riders in various equestrian events. Burke mainly explores equestrian sports in the United Kingdom and the United States. The author includes a useful bibliography and telling photographs. Mary Mountier's *Racing Women of New Zealand* (Daphne Brasell Associates Press, 1993) chronicles the history of New Zealand women riders, owners, and others engaged in horse racing.

791. Nelson, Mariah B. *Embracing Victory: How Women Can Compete Joyously, Compassionately, and Successfully in the Workplace and on the Playing Field*. New York: William Morrow, 1998. 337p. bibliog. index. ISBN 068814649X.

Embracing Victory represents the culmination of a survey that Nelson, a well-published journalist and popular lecturer (http://mariahburtonnelson.com/tubh.htm), conducted regarding the attitudes of women and girls toward competition, especially within the world of sports. Nelson suggests that even after the gains women have made during the last three decades in sports, women still seem to resist competing against one another, especially for pay at the professional level. Nelson also explores the cultural implications of how coaches and other professionals condition girls differently from boys. However, the real value of this work lies in Nelson's analysis of how competition rules many aspects of women's lives and her bold suggestion that women embrace competition. In one section, Nelson defines and discusses the five aspects of competition, as a relationship, process, opportunity, risk, and a feminist issue. She then goes on to debate the complex issues surrounding women and competition within our society. Nelson concludes by providing examples of how the experiences of losing, winning, and competing empower women, and how women can incorporate these strategies into their lives.

Nelson's *Are We Winning Yet? How Women Are Changing Sports and Sports Are Changing Women* (Random House, 1991) deals with the progression of women's sports from the 1960s until the present. She tells the stories of girls and women who challenged, persevered, and broke barriers in order to gain entry into sport. The author clearly and thoughtfully analyzes critical issues, such as rape, lesbianism, leadership, and coeducational sports. This work, which received the Amateur Athletic Foundation Book Award, would serve as an excellent text for classes in women's sociology.

792. Nelson, Mariah B. *The Stronger Women Get, the More Men Love Football: Sexism and the American Culture of Sport*. San Diego: Harcourt Brace, 1994. 304p. bibliog. index. ISBN 0151813930.

In this groundbreaking book, Nelson argues that football represents one of the last exclusive male domains in society, and that society subtly condones the necessity of preserving this domain. Nelson deconstructs the symbolic relationship between what football represents and how this representation shapes the value and perception of women and sports. The author critically analyzes assumptions regarding the acceptance of sports as a male prerogative and critiques the subtle messages girls and boys learn growing up. Nelson writes, "Sport is a women's issue because on playing fields, male athletes learn to talk about and think about women and women's bodies with contempt" (p. 9). The author scrutinizes athletic privilege, especially behaviors such as aggression and violence, behaviors often condoned as part of the male athletic territory. Providing many examples of acts of rape, sexual assault, and other sexual misconduct in the sports arena, Nelson argues that complex power relations and contradictory values within the world of sports allow such behavior to occur. Sports, after all, feeds on the idea of masculinity based on domination.

Nelson ends with a discussion of expected behavior among female athletes, including not being too aggressive or competitive. *The Stronger Women Get* presents a powerful message concerning the inherently sexist nature of male privilege and domination not only in sports, but also in society as a whole. Useful for classes in women's studies or American studies, this work should generate much class discussion and raise questions about how society still promotes an unacceptable tolerance of male sports behavior.

793. Pink, Sarah. *Women and Bullfighting: Gender, Sex, and the Consumption of Tradition*. Oxford, England: Berg, 1997. 233p. bibliog. index. ISBN 1859739563; 185973961Xpa.

Pink explores the world of women bullfighters in Andalusia, Spain, in *Women and Bullfighting*. She incorporates anthropological, ethnological, feminist, sociological, media, and cultural theories into her research to provide varying interpretations regarding women's role in bullfighting and to learn the meaning of bullfighting in Spanish culture. Relying on her own experience as a female bullfighter and interviews conducted with other female bullfighters, Pink presents the challenges faced by women who participate in this sport. The author analyzes the cultural view of women as weaker than men and the ways in which many women bullfighters have negotiated their survival and success in the sport. Pink concludes with a discussion of how these female bullfighters negotiate outside the arena of sports and the meanings this has for feminism, popular culture, and communicating ideas about gender. Photographs and an appendix of terms enhance this interesting work.

794. Powe-Allred, Alexandra, and Michelle Powe. *The Quiet Storm: A Celebration of Women in Sports*. Indianapolis: Maters Press, 1998. 264p. bibliog. ISBN 1570281866pa.

Powe-Allred and Powe, two Olympic bobsledders who are also sisters, examine the multifaceted experiences of women athletes. The authors interviewed several female athletes to gain an understanding of how these women have overcome the many challenges they have faced by participating in sports. Athletes from a variety of sports, including basketball, long-distance running, and bodybuilding, share their stories of great expectations and grim disappointments and reveal their need for female role models. At the same time, these women acknowledge awareness that they are also role models for young women and girls. One inspirational chapter describes how women athletes triumphed over adversity and discrimination as a result of positive attitudes and determination. While not an academic title, *The Quiet Storm* nonetheless presents a firsthand account of women's experiences in sports.

Lissa Smith's *Nike Is a Goddess: The History of Women in Sports* (Grove/Atlantic, 1998) is an anthology combining history, biography, and stories of women's experiences in sports in the United States. The author covers the history of team and individual sports in a variety of venues, including track and field, basketball, ice hockey, golf, canoeing and other boating events, skiing, figure skating, equestrian events, and gymnastics. She examines events and individuals representing the evolution of each sport. Journalists and sports writers wrote most of the essays, thus providing a different perspective on the growing literature on women and sport history.

795. Rapoport, Ron, ed. *A Kind of Grace: A Treasury of Sportswriting by Women*. Oakland, CA: Zenobia Press, 1994. 385p. ISBN 157143013Xpa.

Rapoport, a sportswriter for the *Chicago Tribune*, collects stories and articles from some of the top female sportswriters in America in *A Kind of Grace*. The author claims that women writers bring an alternative perspective to their stories, one that he firmly believes society should value. The articles included in this work provide a glimpse at the different perceptions that women writers have contributed to the world of sport. The writings reveal the many challenges that women sportswriters have experienced, as well as the challenges faced by female athletes in such sports as tennis and golf. Although female sportswriters have advanced in their profession, Rapoport cautions that these women still have a way to go before achieving equity with their male counterparts. Mary Garber's exceptional essay "Women and Children Are Not Admitted to the Press Box" is a must-read. This work is highly recommended for classes in media, communications, and women's studies.

Uncommon Waters: Women Write about Fishing, edited by Holly Morris (Seal Press, 1991), is the first anthology of writings by women about fishing. This work includes nonfiction, fiction, and poems that represent several countries and covers the period from the 1400s to the early 1990s.

796. Rogers, Susan F., ed. *Sportsdykes: Stories from on and off the Field*. New York: St. Martin's Press, 1995. 385p. ISBN 0312131879.

This collection of interviews, personal narratives, essays, and fiction focuses on the lesbian sport experience. The inclusion of a wide range of authors, including academics and journalists, provides different, yet insightful styles and approaches. Some of the stories were previously published in gay literature. Rogers, a freelance writer, groups the works into topics such as the early lesbian experience, changes in the sport environment since 1979, Martina Navratilova as a lesbian sport icon, and sexuality and sexual issues. The essays and stories in this collection are engaging and range from amusing and satirical to poignant.

797. Salter, David F. *Crashing the Old Boys' Network: The Tragedies and Triumphs of Girls and Women in Sports*. Westport, CT: Greenwood Press, 1996. 163p. bibliog. index. ISBN 0275955125.

Despite the many advances female athletes have made, the author believes that several obstacles remain for women who participate in sports: "It is unbelievable that in 1996 girls and women's sports remain challenged by antiquated beliefs and by an athletics system that is reluctant to change and continues to subdue equitable advances. Enlightenment is not universal" (p. xiii). In this work, Salter shares a variety of stories about women's experiences in sport, including their many struggles and challenges. The author addresses the fact that many institutions have yet to comply with Title IX. Moreover, he discusses how several people continue to resist the idea of women's involvement in any area of sport. Salter examines several issues, such as the socialization of young children toward sports, how college football skews the formula for gender equity, unequal pay for professional coaches, and the role of the media. The underlying theme of this work concerns the power struggles that many female athletes and those who support them must face. Relying primarily on newspaper articles and reports from the National Collegiate Athletic Association, *Crashing the Old Boys' Network* provides a strong case for how far women still have to go in the sports world.

798. Sandoz, Joli, ed. *A Whole Other Ball Game: Women's Literature on Women's Sport*. New York: Noonday Press, 1997. 323p. ISBN 0374525218pa.

Scholars have neglected the literature of sport, both created by and about women, for a long time. In this wonderful anthology, women express their own observations of their involvement in sport. Sandoz, an instructor of women's sport literature at Evergreen State University, includes poems, stories, and excerpts from novels and nonfiction works from the turn of the twentieth century to the present. Contributors include Marge Piercy, Nancy Boutilier, Maxine Kumin, and Pat Griffin. Through these writings, women express their fears and excitements, disappointments and joys. As Sandoz writes, "Here, at last, we can tell the truth: women play, we play hard and well, and we love it—the struggle, the skill, and the game" (p. 17).

Diamonds Are a Girl's Best Friend: Women Writers on Baseball, edited by Elinor Nauen (Faber & Faber, 1994), is a fine collection of essays, stories, and poems that women wrote about their participation in baseball. Nauen arranges her work into three sections: sports journalists, literary writers, and poets.

799. Shangold, Mona M., and Gabe Mirkin, eds. *Women and Exercise: Physiology and Sports Medicine*. Philadelphia: F.A. Davis Co., 1988. 279p. bibliog. index. ISBN 0803678169.

This book consists of articles from scientists presenting various approaches to fitness and exercise, female phases of physical development, training issues, and other conditions affecting women athletes. Each essay includes information on exercise-induced conditions, a list of concepts within the article, and an extensive list of references. Shangold and Minkin index the subcategories in the table of contents and include charts and tables. The second edition, published in 1994, updates and expands some of the information.

A related title on the physiology of female athletes, edited by Shangold and Michelle P. Warren, is *Sports Gynecology: Problems and Care of the Athletic Female* (Blackwell Science, 1997), which deals with performance-enhancing drugs. Two other titles that focus on physiology and active women are *Medical and Orthopedic Issues of Active and Athletic Women*, edited by Rosemary Agostin (Hanley & Belfus, 1994), and *The Athletic Female*, edited by Arthur Pearl (Human Kinetics, 1993). The first title emphasizes sociological, historical, medical, and physiological issues. The second title, drawn from papers presented at the American Orthopedic Society for Sports Medicine, addresses current physiological and medical topics and provides suggestions for future research.

800. Simons, Minot, II. *Women's Gymnastics: A History*. Volume I, *1966–1974*. Carmel, CA: Welwyn, 1995. 403p. bibliog. ISBN 0964606208.

Simons documents the history of gymnastics from 1966 to 1974 through an analysis of the individuals and events that influenced and subsequently changed the sport. The author extensively describes each rotation at both the World Championships and Olympics and includes a general overview of the European Championships. Simons also provides brief biographies of medal winners, such as Olga Korbut, Tamara Lazakovich, Cathy (Rigby) McCoy, and Ludmilla Turischeva, including highlights of their careers and current status of these former athletes. Numerous photographs and diagrams of routines and elements, as well as a glossary, enhance this work. Three forthcoming volumes will cover the following time periods: 1975 to 1980, 1981 to 1988, and 1989 to 1996.

801. Stell, Marion. *Half the Race: A History of Australian Women in Sport*. North Ryde, NSW, Australia: Collins/Angus & Robertson, 1991. 288p. bibliog. index. ISBN 0207169713.

Stell documents the progress of women's sports in Australia from the late 1700s to 1990. In this work, which is arranged semichronologically, the author deals with a variety of topics. Early chapters discuss women's sports in colonial Australia, the experiences of female athletes in universities, and the establishment of professional sports associations for women in the early

1900s. Stell also includes extensive discussion of women's experiences in competitive venues, including the Olympics and the Empire and Commonwealth Games. Several chapters explore more provocative topics, including controversies over women's sportswear, medical and social hurdles women have had to overcome, and how advertising and the media influence women's sports. The author also reflects on racial discrimination, especially the added pressures faced by Aboriginal sportswomen, and gender inequality. Photographs and reproductions of posters and advertisements provide visual evidence of the issues discussed. *South Australian Women in Sport* (published for the Estate of Tanya Tarnogursky by Executor Trustee Australia, 1992) by Tanya Tarnogursky documents the history of sporting achievements of women from southern Australia. Alphabetically arranged, this title discusses specific sports, from aerobatics to water skiing; provides biographical profiles of athletes; and traces important historical developments.

Finally, *Wicket Women: Cricket and Women in Australia* by Richard Cashman and Amanda Weaver (New South Wales University Press, 1991) presents a comprehensive history of women's participation in cricket in Australia. The authors also "explore the prejudice against women playing cricket, and sport in general" (p. vii). In chronological order, the authors trace the development and challenges faced by women as they established cricket clubs in different states in Australia.

802. Todd, Jan. *Physical Culture and the Body Beautiful: An Examination of the Role of Purposive Exercise in the Lives of American Women, 1800–1870*. Macon, GA: Mercer University Press, 1998. 369p. bibliog. index. ISBN 0865545618.

In this important study, Todd argues that many women in antebellum America did not subscribe to the idea of "True Womanhood," the belief that women should remain at home and be submissive. Instead, the author claims that another ideal actually prevailed, which she terms "Majestic Womanhood." Majestic Womanhood, whose adherents included Mary Wollstonecraft, the physician Elizabeth Blackwell, and exercise entrepreneur Dio Lewis, "subscribed to the basic tenets of Real Womanhood but then took the model even further by arguing that women should try to become the physical and intellectual equals of men" (p. 5). Todd discovers that a diverse spectrum of exercise programs for women existed during this time, and that this "purposive exercise" mattered to American women. This study addresses the development of specific calisthenics and gymnastics programs, the evolution of physical education as a profession, the influences of "proexercise" pioneers such as Dio Lewis and Dudley Sargent, and how contemporary scientific theories, such as phrenology, influenced beliefs concerning females and exercise. Todd relies upon a variety of primary sources, including contemporary medical and scientific literature, correspondence, diaries, and scrapbooks, as well as a wealth of secondary sources in her study. *Physical Culture and the Body Beautiful* should generate future interest in this topic and will be of interest to students and researchers in women's studies, history, sociology, and anthropology.

The Eternally Wounded Woman: Women, Exercise, and Doctors in the Late Nineteenth Century by Patricia Vertinsky (University of Illinois Press, 1994) "is about the historical influence of late nineteenth-century medical beliefs and values on the perceived benefits of physical activity for women across their life span" (p. 1). Vertinsky, a professor of human kinetics at the University of British Columbia, organizes her study into three parts. Part 1 reviews contemporary medical notions of the time, especially the prevailing belief held by male physicians of women's inherent weakness and frailty. In part 2, the author analyzes the struggles faced by female physicians as they strove for a voice in the male-dominated field of medicine. The final part offers two radical viewpoints, one by G. Stanley Hall and one by Charlotte Perkins Gilman, which both argued against the prevailing ideals. A third title, *The Rise and Fall of the Sportswoman: Women's Health, Fitness, and Athletics, 1860–1940* (Peter Lang, 1996) by Gregory K. Stanley, provides a short overview of many of the same topics and themes explored in the other two titles.

803. Tricard, Louise M. *American Women's Track and Field: A History, 1895 through 1980*. Jefferson, NC: McFarland, 1996. 746p. bibliog. index. ISBN 0786402199.

This exceptional book traces the evolution of women's track and field from the mid-1800s to 1980. In 1875, Vassar introduced the sport, and in 1895, women at Vassar organized the first field day for women in the United States. Tricard chronologically arranges her work, covering all venues where the sport is practiced, including high schools, colleges, private athletic clubs, recreational/company clubs, and the professional level. The author integrates biographies of some of the top competitors in the sport, as well as individuals who impacted the sport off the field, into each chapter. Appendices list halls of fame, Olympic gold medalists, awards, and marathon winners. This resource provides a multidimensional history of women's experiences in track and field, including the struggles and controversies women have faced. Tricard consulted several primary resources in writing this work, and she includes a listing of archives that contain collections on women's sports. Librarians must include this work in their sport and women's studies collections.

Michael D. Davis's *Black American Women in Olympic Track and Field: A Complete Illustrated Reference* (McFarland, 1992) provides biographical entries that range in length from one sentence to several pages. An "Olympic Checklist" lists the events, times, and place for black female athletes from the 1932 through the 1988 Olympics.

1999 CORE TITLES

Bandy, Susan J., and Anne S. Darden, eds. *Crossing Boundaries: An International Anthology of Women's Experiences in Sport*. Champaign, IL: Human Kinetics, 1999. 311p. bibliog. ISBN 0736000887pa.

Davidson, Scooter Toby, and Valerie Anthony, eds. *Great Women in the Sport of Kings: America's Top Women Jockeys Tell Their Stories*. Syracuse, NY: Syracuse University Press, 1999. 132p. bibliog. ISBN 081560565X.

Epperson, David Canning. *A Woman's Touch: What Today's Women Can Teach Us about Sport and Life*. South Bend, IN: Diamond Communications, 1999. 178p. bibliog. ISBN 1888698284pa.

Hall, M. Ann, and Gertrud Pfister. *Honoring the Legacy: Fifty Years of the International Association of Physical Education and Sport for Girls and Women*. Northampton, MA: International Association of Physical Education and Sport for Girls and Women, 1999. bibliog. ISBN 1894428013.

Macy, Sue, and Jane Gottesman, eds. *Play like a Girl: A Celebration of Women in Sports*. New York: Henry Holt, 1999. 32p. ISBN 0805060715.

Sandoz, Joli, and Joby Winans, eds. *Whatever It Takes: Women on Women's Sport*. New York: Farrar, Straus and Giroux, 1999. 323p. bibliog. ISBN 0374525978pa.

Thompson, Shona M. *Mother's Taxi: Sport and Women's Labor*. Albany: State University of New York Press, 1999. 317p. bibliog. index. ISBN 0791440591; 0791440605pa.

Turco, Mary. *Crashing the Net: The U.S. Women's Olympic Ice Hockey Team and the Road to Gold*. New York: HarperCollins, 1999. 242p. index. ISBN (OP); 0060929812pa.

Welch, Paula D., Lynn P. Whittaker, and Daniel H. Rosenthal, eds. *Silver Era, Golden Moments: A Celebration of Ivy League Women's Athletics: Brown, Columbia, Cornell, Dartmouth, Harvard, Pennsylvania, Princeton, Yale*. Lanham, MD: Madison Books, 1999. 187p. bibliog. index. ISBN 1568331282pa.

White, Philip, and Kevin Young, eds. *Sport and Gender in Canada*. New York: Oxford University Press, 1999. 324p. bibliog. index. ISBN 0195413172pa.

Williams, Jackie. *Playing from the Rough: Women of the LPGA Hall of Fame*. Las Vegas: Women of Diversity Productions, 1999. 268p. bibliog. ISBN 1884724159pa.

Zimmerman, Jean. *Raising Our Athletic Daughters: How Sports Can Build Self-Esteem and Save Girls' Lives*. New York: Doubleday, 1999. 256p. bibliog. ISBN 0385489609pa.

WORLD WIDE WEB/INTERNET SITES

804. *Amy Lewis's Sport Pages*. http://fiat.gslis.utexas.edu/~lewisa/womsprt.html.
     Amy Lewis, an athlete, coach, and fan of women's sports, created this site to promote and increase the visibility of women in sport. The site features an exhaustive, alphabetically arranged list of links to individual sports, which in turn feature links to several relevant Web sites that provide information about issues of interest to female athletes. Lewis includes other informative links on her home page, such as "Athletes," "General Women's and Girls' Sport Pages," "Issues in Women's and Girls' Sports," "Organizations and Associations," and "Publishing and Broadcast Media." These links lead users to many germane and informative Internet sites.

805. *Amy Love's Real Sports Magazine*. http://www.real-sports.com/.
     Amy Love created *Real Sports Magazine* for female athletes, women's sports, and fans of these sports. Through the magazine, Love attempts to challenge the norm and increase coverage of girls' and women's sports. The Web site, although somewhat cluttered, provides practical information about current events and news with links such as "Follow Your Team," "Get in the Game," and "Press Room." "The Magazine" link connects users to specific issues of *Real Sports Magazine* and includes full-text articles.

806. *Canadian Association for the Advancement of Women and Sport and Physical Activity*. http://www.caaws.ca/.
     Members of the Canadian Association for the Advancement of Women and Sport and Physical Activity (CAAWS) encourage women and girls to participate in a wide range of sports. Their Web site features information about women, sports, and health, including links to numerous topics such as leadership, harassment, health, gender equity, the Olympics, and girls and activity. Each link features lengthy articles and reports, some written by scholars. Many articles highlight individual women athletes as well as women's teams. "Hot Links" features information about women's sports organizations of various countries and provinces, related organizations concerning

women and sport, coaching information, popular magazines, specific sports, and other pertinent issues.

807. *Gender Equity in Sports.* http://bailiwick.lib.uiowa.edu/ge/.

Mary C. Curtis and Christine H.B. Grant of the University of Iowa maintain *Gender Equity in Sports*, a Web site devoted to the investigation of issues pertaining to interscholastic and intercollegiate sports. This simply designed, text-heavy site features reports gathered from newspaper articles, the Women's Sports Foundation, and personal references regarding women, equity, and sport. The site provides information about Title IX and the law, complaints and lawsuits, and resources. Although project affiliates claim that they frequently update the site, no one has added any new information to the site since October 2000.

808. *Melpomene Institute.* http://www.melpomene.org/.

The Melpomene Institute, founded in 1982, was named for a Greek woman who ran the first Olympic marathon in 1896. The site serves as a research and resource center for women of varying ages and athletic levels who are engaged or interested in physical activity and features links to relevant issues and news stories. The following links make up the core of the site: "Melpomene," "Research," "Resources," "Girls," "Events," and "Outreach." The resources link features a list of topics, with links to detailed information about these particular topics from the institute's research library. Topics include girls and self-esteem, body image, eating disorders, menstruation, menopause, osteoporosis, pregnancy, nutrition, and women of color. The Web site includes a keyword search engine.

809. *SIRC's Sport Quest.* http://www.sportquest.com/resources/index.html.

SIRC is a bibliographic database that provides information about sport, fitness, and sports medicine information. *SIRC's Sport Quest* is a general sports Web site that features an exhaustive list of sports with links to Web sites about various teams, organizations, news, and directories. The Web site also features several links to relevant Web sites organized under "General Information," "Sports Science," and "Special Interest." A link called "Women" under the last category includes links to sites that contain much information about various women's and girls' sports and news.

HUMANITIES

Art, Architecture, Music, and Dance

Susan Wyngaard

Until the early to mid-1980s monographs on individual artists and performers dominated the literature of women in the visual and performing arts. These monographs continue to be very important in cultivating recognition of forgotten, ignored, or underappreciated women artists and performers, as well as filling in gaping lacunae and fostering new research in these disciplines. In the last fifteen to twenty years, however, a new generation of feminist scholars has given attention to issues of women in artistic disciplines. This shift in scholarly focus from a woman to women has had a far-reaching impact and has opened up new areas of investigation. Feminist historians are rewriting the history of the arts and uncovering primary source materials to support new perspectives. Feminist critical theory has reshaped the way we examine, value, and position artists and their creations. Feminist educators are deconstructing gendered traditions in arts, music, and dance classrooms and studios. Feminist anthropologists and ethnographers are positioning themselves outside the male, Eurocentric box when they study women's artistic contributions. Women performers previously not valued enough to be subjects of serious scholarship, such as country singers, rock stars, and showgirls, are revealed to reflect the political, social, and economic tenor of their time when they are analyzed by feminist scholars. Feminist theories and critical perspectives have changed the ways in which we think about gender, sexuality, and creativity and the ways in which we examine, view, teach, and preserve the artistic contributions of women.

Reflecting this trend in scholarly inquiry and publishing, this chapter includes titles concerning women as creators of art and popular culture and excludes monographs on individual artists and performers. Of all the disciplines reviewed, dance has the fewest new publications utilizing these perspectives and remains a field ripe for deeper feminist investigation. Titles that place special emphasis on women of color and a range of ethnicities were given preference when possible. The "Monographs" section is divided into two subject areas: "Visual Arts, Design, and Architecture" and "Music, Dance, and Performance." Please see chapter 13, "Communications, Mass Media, and Language," for titles covering film and chapter 15, "Literature," for titles covering theater.

REFERENCE SOURCES

810. Anderson, Janet A. *Women in the Fine Arts: A Bibliography and Illustration Guide.* Jefferson, NC: McFarland, 1991. 362p. index. ISBN 0899505414.

This compilation of general reference sources, periodical literature, exhibition catalogs, and newspaper articles about women artists resulted from a quest for text and picture resources to support a college course on women artists. It represents the culmination of ten years of research, numerous grants, and assistance from additional researchers. Anderson created the bibliography, which features literary references to women artists, which historians continue to omit from standard art history texts, as well as citations to illustrations of the artists' work, for scholars, teachers, and students. The author selected individuals who "qualify as fine artists" in painting, sculpture, and architecture, as well as photographers, videographers, performance artists, and women who work with crafts in "a substantially creative way." The bibliography covers the Renaissance to 1990 and is international in scope. Anderson annotates especially important resources and cites obscure sources on particular artists. She supplements the work with an artists' name index. This seminal reference resource is a starting point for research on lesser-known women artists from the Renaissance to 1990.

811. Chiarmonte, Paula L., ed. *Women Artists in the United States: A Selective Bibliography and Resource Guide on the Fine and Decorative Arts, 1750–1986*. Boston: G. K. Hall, 1990. 997p. bibliog. indexes. ISBN 081618917Xpa.

A major reference resource for the history of women artists in the United States, this annotated bibliography represents the combined efforts of several art librarians and art historians to foster critical analysis of the modes of production in which women have excelled. Chiarmonte lists primary and secondary sources on fine arts, decorative and applied arts, contemporary crafts, folk art, and performance art. Primary sources include personal papers and manuscripts from archival repositories and special collections; secondary sources consist of bibliographies, directories, biographical dictionaries, monographs, catalogues raisonnés, dissertations, theses, exhibition catalogs, and periodicals. The editor's organization of citations is somewhat confusing, for she subdivides information from part 1, "Critics, Organizations, and Resources," and part 2, "Literature of the Field," into two sections, "Documents on Women's Art" and "Documents on Women Artists." She arranges indexes according to artist's name, author's name, and title of work cited. A supplemental chart features statistics on the number of male and female artists reviewed in four major art magazines between 1976 and 1979.

The second edition of Sherry Piland's *Women Artists: An Historical, Contemporary, and Feminist Bibliography* (Scarecrow Press, 1994), which Scarecrow Press originally published in 1978, is a basic bibliography for the study of women artists. Piland cites general works (books, periodicals, and catalogs) in the first section of the bibliography. Section 2 contains the names of individual artists, which the author chronologically arranges from about the fifteenth to the twentieth century. Each artist entry contains a brief biographical sketch, citations to written documentation about the artist, and a list of collections that feature the artist's work. Section 3 consists of a brief but inclusive bibliography on needlework.

812. Claghorn, Charles Eugene. *Women Composers and Songwriters: A Concise Biographical Dictionary*. Lanham, MD: Scarecrow Press, 1996. 247p. ISBN 0810831309.

Whereas Claghorn's earlier *Women Composers and Hymnists* (Scarecrow Press, 1986) contains biographical documentation on women who composed hymns and church music, the 1996 edition features composers of both secular and sacred music. The dictionary contains composers of symphonies, instrumental and choral works, chamber music, blues, jazz, heavy metal, rock and roll, hard rock, soul, and country and western. Since he based his work on the membership list of the American Society of Composers, Authors, and Publishers (ASCAP), Claghorn mostly includes American artists who were active during the twentieth century. The concise biographical citations contain birth and death dates, education and training, and titles of compositions. Virginia L. Gratten's *American Women Songwriters: A Biographical Dictionary* (Greenwood Press, 1993) acknowledges the contribution of nearly 200 writers of American popular song. She arranges the succinct biographies according to the type of music that the songwriters composed: blues, gospel, folk, or country. Gratten introduces each section with a brief historical essay on one of the four types of music and supplements individual biographies with a bibliography of additional sources.

She profiles nineteenth-century songwriters in a section called "Early Women Songwriters." Gratten supplements the text with a nine-page bibliography, a list of newspaper obituaries for some women, and a useful song index. This book is suitable for public and school libraries.

Editors Anne Sadie and Rhian Samuel attempt to remedy the modest attention paid to women composers in *The New Grove Dictionary of Music and Musicians* (Grove's Dictionaries of Music, 1980) and *The New Grove Dictionary of American Music* (Grove's Dictionaries of Music, 1986) with the publication of *The Norton/Grove Dictionary of Women Composers* (Norton, 1994). The editors, who use Grove procedures to gather information from notable scholars and critics, feature accomplished women who were born before 1956 in the dictionary. The preface provides an engaging history of lexicographical bibliography of women composers, as well as a twentieth-century perspective on the history of women composers. Dictionary entries contain standard biographical data, such as birth and death dates, training and education, honors and recognitions received, bibliographies, and lists of compositions. The editors include black-and-white illustrations.

813. Cohen, Aaron I. *International Encyclopedia of Women Composers.* New York: Books and Music USA, 1987. 2v. 1151p. bibliog. ISBN 0961748524 set.

The first edition of this work (Bowker, 1981) was the culmination of eight years of dedicated research that yielded the identification of 6,000 women composers from seventy countries. At approximately the same time, the Arts/Letters/Music Committee of the International Council on Women attempted to identify every woman composer, either living or dead, in its seventy-four member countries. After participants of these two projects became aware of the other's work, they decided to merge files, which resulted in this revised and enlarged second edition. Several unique features make the second edition more valuable than the earlier effort: the author lists 643 women composers who lived in countries that formerly had remained "behind the iron curtain"; he presents the work of nine centuries of Arabian songstress-composers and includes an additional 500 women composers referred to "unknowns" in the first edition. Each entry cites additional sources of information and includes a current discography. This valuable reference work is highly recommended for academic libraries.

814. College Art Association of America and Gay and Lesbian Caucus. *Bibliography of Gay and Lesbian Art.* New York: Gay and Lesbian Caucus, 1994. 112p. index. (OP)

Compiled during the 1994 College Art Association conference in New York City to commemorate the twenty-fifth anniversary of the Stonewall riot, *Bibliography of Gay and Lesbian Art*, which features 1,200 citations, covers all periods of Western and non-Western art, from antiquity to the present, in the major Western European languages. Contributors focus on painting, sculpture, architecture, graphic arts, and photography, include few monographs on individual artists, omit unpublished materials, and examine specialized topics in chapters called "Commercial Arts and Advertising" and "Theory and Criticism." The editors organize the chapters according to chronological periods. Although most of the cited works refer to male homosexuals, the bibliography is a fundamental reference resource for all collections of material on women artists, for it provides a major starting point for locating information about lesbian artists.

Editor Whitney Davis's *Gay and Lesbian Studies in Art History* (Haworth Press, 1994) features further readings on lesbians in the history of art. This collection serves multiple purposes: it introduces unfamiliar historical and cultural materials, provides examples of diverse scholarly and interpretive perspectives, and stimulates new ways of thinking and seeing. Although only three out of twelve chapters specifically address lesbianism in art and art history, contributors introduce key topics that explore all facets of homosexuality in art history in other chapters.

815. Ericson, Margaret D. *Women and Music: A Selective Annotated Bibliography on Women and Gender Issues in Music, 1987–1992*. New York: G. K. Hall, 1996. 400p. index. ISBN 0816105804.

Ericson compiled a series of annual bibliographies between 1987 and 1990 on the topic of women and music that resulted in this indexed and annotated guide of more than 1,800 publications about issues related to women, gender, and music. Ericson indexes domestic and international books, essays, periodical articles, theses, conference papers, newspaper articles, sound recording anthologies, score anthologies, media, and online sources. She includes scholarly, alternative, and popular presses and devotes sections of this resource to reference resources, professional organizations, Western music, non-Western music, score anthologies, sound recording anthologies, and other related topics. Ericson provides an especially useful section on publishers, record labels, and distributors of materials about women in music. A name index and a subject index feature additional access to citations.

816. Gaze, Delia, ed. *Dictionary of Women Artists*. Chicago: Fitzroy Dearborn, 1997. 2v. 1512p. ISBN 1884964214 set.

This dictionary provides information on 550 women who have worked and/or continue to work in Western art traditions, with an emphasis on historical artists from the Middle Ages to the present. Each artist entry contains a biography, an exhibition history when possible, primary and secondary bibliographic references, an illustration of the artist's work, and a signed, critical contextual essay about the artist. A series of introductory essays about women artists' education and working conditions prefaces the dictionary.

817. Heller, Jules, and Nancy G. Heller, eds. *North American Women Artists of the Twentieth Century: A Biographical Dictionary*. New York: Garland Publishing, 1995. 612p. (Garland Reference Library of the Humanities). bibliog. index. ISBN (OP); 0815325843pa.

Jules Heller and Nancy G. Heller created this dictionary because of the lack of basic information available about women artists. More than 100 scholars contributed to this resource, which features more than 100 black-and-white illustrations. Each dictionary entry provides biographical and chronological data, location of the artist's works, and a bibliography of additional resources pertaining to the artist. A twelve-page topical index supplements the alphabetical arrangement of the text. Penny Dunford's *A Biographical Dictionary of Women Artists in Europe and America since 1850* (Harvester Wheatsheaf, 1990) is a good reference work geared toward general readers, students of women's studies, artists, and art students. Dunford includes artists who reflect a balanced array of media, nationalities, and time periods. She includes artists who helped improve educational opportunities or exhibiting facilities available to women artists. She unfortunately omits photographers and film/video makers and includes few textile artists. Citations provide biographical information, indicate memberships in societies, address artists' prizes, awards, and publications, note locations of known artworks, and cite literature about the artist. Some color and black-and-white illustrations accompany the text.

818. Hixon, Donald L., and Don A. Hennessee. *Women in Music: An Encyclopedic Biobibliography*. Metuchen, NJ: Scarecrow Press, 1993. 2v. 1824p. index. ISBN 0810827697 set.

The first edition of this work, published in 1975, contains 347 pages of citations to biographies featured in forty-eight standard music encyclopedias and dictionaries. The tremendous surge in interest in women's music during the intervening years created the need for this vastly enlarged and improved second edition. Like the first edition, *Women in Music* indexes biographies of women musicians from selected music dictionaries and encyclopedias, but it also includes references to biographies found in the *Dictionary of National Biography*, the *Dictionary of American Biography*, and other general sources. The editors both geographically and chronologically subdivide major categories, including genre classifications of musical specializations, into categories such as sixteenth-century English lutenists and twentieth-century American electronic music composers. Biographies present basic facts and list reference sources that contain additional information. Jane Weiner LePage's *Women Composers, Conductors, and Musicians of the Twentieth Century: Selected Biographies* (Scarecrow Press, 1980–1988) consists of three volumes, published in 1980, 1983, and 1988, which include the author's research on women musicians of the twentieth century. Each volume features approximately seventeen women, and each entry provides a substantial biography of the artist and, when appropriate, reviews of performances, lists of published works, or discographies. Subject indexes and black-and-white photos supplement the text.

819. Johnson, Rose-Marie, comp. *Violin Music by Women Composers: A Bio-Bibliographic Guide*. New York: Greenwood Press, 1989. 280p. (Music Reference Collection). bibliog. ISBN 0313266522.

Johnson addresses women composers of violin music in this guide, beginning with a historical overview of the uniquely Italian seventeenth-century development of women composers, which features humorous descriptions of the conventions of convents and musical institutions, and continues into the twentieth century, when women began to earn formal recognition for their compositions. Johnson divides the text into three sections, biographies, music, and discography, and provides an alphabetic listing of all composers' names, dates, and nationalities. She organizes the biographies, which include date of composition, publisher, and/or source, into five eras, alphabetically listing composers within each section. The author cites library sources for manuscripts and out-of-print music and concludes the text with a lengthy bibliography.

Other equally useful and thorough volumes in Greenwood Press's Music Reference Collection include *Flute Music by Women Composers: An Annotated Catalog*, compiled by Heidi M. Boenke (Greenwood Press, 1988), *Organ and Harpsichord Music by Women Composers*, compiled by Adel Heinrich (Greenwood Press, 1991), and Janna MacAuslan's *Guitar Music by Women Composers: An Annotated Catalog* (Greenwood Press, 1997). Each volume in the series presents a wealth of detailed information on its respective topic.

820. Kovinick, Phil, and Marian Yoshiki-Kovinick. *An Encyclopedia of Women Artists of the American West*. Austin: University of Texas Press, 1998. 405p. (American Studies). bibliog. index. ISBN 0292790635.

Kovinick's exhibition catalog *The Woman Artist in the American West, 1860–1960* (Muckenthaler Cultural Center, 1976) was the first serious attempt to study the scope and impact of American women artists of the West. This more recent work reflects more than twenty years of further research in obscure archives, studying obituaries, newspaper files, diaries, letters, and other primary source documents, resulting in an encyclopedia that contains biographies of more than 1,000 mostly unknown women painters, sculptors, and graphic artists. The main section of the encyclopedia provides biographies between two to four paragraphs that are alphabetically arranged. Each entry includes the artist's birth and death dates, residence, key occupation, Western themes, selected lists of exhibitions, and current locations of work, along with bibliographic references for further research. Section two contains additional concise biographies of only five to six lines, including similar information on each artist. Black-and-white illustrations, a lengthy bibliography, and an index of artists' names accompany this highly recommended text, which would complement all art and American history reference collections.

Independent Spirits: Women Painters of the American West, 1890–1945 (University of California Press, 1995), edited by Patricia Trenton, marks the first comprehensive, scholarly study of this topic. Eleven scholars and curators retrieve lost artists and explore the economic, social, and political forces shaping the work of women painters in the American West in essays that feature color illustrations of paintings, black-and-white photos of artists at work, and lengthy bibliographic notes. This work highly contributes to the literature of women's studies, American art history, and cultural history of the American West.

821. McCracken, Penny. *Women Artists and Designers in Europe since 1800: An Annotated Bibliography*. New York: G. K. Hall, 1998. 2v. 1059p. index. ISBN 0816105960 (v. 1); 0783800878 (v. 2).

McCracken claims that this work is the first bibliography on women artists to bring together publications in multiple European languages and practitioners in several media. Volume 1, which she opens with a 215-item bibliography of general references on women artists, covers the fields of ceramics, glass, textiles, design (interior design, wallpaper design, and metalwork), fashion, bookbinding, and garden design. Volume 2 includes photography, painting, performance art, and mixed media. She subdivides the entries according to categories such as "Main Sources," "Exhibitions," and "Other Sources" when possible. This work makes a major contribution to the reference resources on European women artists.

The Supon Design Group's helpful companion volume *International Women in Design* (Madison Square Press; distributed by Van Nostrand Reinhold, 1993) includes a history of twentieth-century designers and a catalog of their work. Cheryl Buckley applies feminist perspectives to the history and practice of ceramic art in *Potters and Paintresses: Women Designers in the Pottery Industry, 1870–1955* (Women's Press, 1990). Buckley addresses women's roles in and substantial contributions to the British pottery industry during the stated time period. The text contains a useful glossary of technical terms and a select bibliography.

822. Palmquist, Peter E. *Shadowcatchers: A Directory of Women in California Photography before 1901*. Arcata, CA: P.E. Palmquist, 1990. 272p. bibliog. (OP)

In 1971, Palmquist, a recognized authority on the topic of women in California photography, started gathering information for this volume, which begins with a 230-page directory of women photographers. Palmquist alphabetically arranges the detailed entries, which precede a helpful index that he arranges by California city or region. Black-and-white illustrations accompany the text.

One year later the prolific author published *Shadowcatchers II: A Directory of Women in California Photography, 1900–1920* (P.E. Palmquist, 1991), in which Palmquist not only continues the directory of photographers by geographical index format, but also includes original essays about some of the artists and an appendix to the first volume. Palmquist supplements both volumes with *A Bibliography of Writings by and about Women in Photography, 1850–1950* (P.E. Palmquist, 1994), which was originally published as part of his *Camera Fiends and Kodak Girls: 50 Selections by and about Women in Photography, 1840–1930* (Midmarch Art Press, 1989).

823. Puerto, Cecilia. *Latin American Women Artists, Kahlo and Look Who Else: A Selective, Annotated Bibliography*. Westport, CT: Greenwood Press, 1996. 237p. (Art Reference Collection). index. ISBN 0313289344.

Puerto compiled this annotated bibliography to raise awareness of twentieth-century Latin American women artists' diverse contributions to the art world. Puerto's geographic definition of

Latin America includes Mexico, Central and South America, and the Caribbean, including the West Indies. She includes artists who paint, draw, sculpt, photograph, and work in printmaking, installation, and performance art. Although the majority of selected artists were born in the twentieth century, Puerto includes entries on a few artists who were born during the nineteenth century as long as they carried out their major work during the first quarter of the twentieth century. The year 1994 marks the cutoff date for publications featured in the bibliography. Puerto arranges the citations to the several hundred included artists into two sections: "General Works" and a section organized by name of individual artist. Puerto records monographs, exhibition catalogs, videos, critical reviews, periodical articles, and dissertations and theses; provides annotations for periodical article citations; and includes appendices that list citations by country and major collective exhibitions.

Puerto refers researchers to Annick Sanjurjo's *Contemporary Latin American Artists: Exhibitions at the Organization of American States, 1965–1985* (Scarecrow Press, 1993), which provides information on nearly 1,000 artists, 300 of whom are women. Volume 2 of the same title covers 1941 to 1964 (Scarecrow Press, 1997).

824. Puniello, Françoise S., and Halina R. Rusak. *Abstract Expressionist Women Painters: An Annotated Bibliography: Elaine de Kooning, Helen Frankenthaler, Grace Hartigan, Lee Krasner, Joan Mitchell, Ethel Schwabacher.* Lanham, MD: Scarecrow Press, 1996. 361p. ISBN 0810829983.

Puniello and Rusak critically examine the works of first- and second-generation abstract expressionists who contributed to American art history in this comprehensive and systematic annotated bibliography, which they created to fill a gaping hole in the bibliographic literature. Puniello and Rusak contend that women played a crucial role in the stylistic development of abstract expressionism, the first art movement to establish the United States as a world leader in art. They thoroughly cull together materials from cataloged and noncataloged archives, books, catalogs, and journal articles through 1991, but they omit newspaper articles. They arrange the text by artist and organize citations within each section in reverse chronological order. Robert Henkes provides valuable historical documentation about American women artists who immediately preceded the abstract expressionists in *American Women Painters of the 1930s and 1940s: The Lives and Works of Ten Artists* (McFarland, 1991).

825. Tufts, Eleanor. *American Women Artists, Past and Present: A Selected Bibliographic Guide.* Volume 2. New York: Garland Publishing, 1989. 491p. (Garland Reference Library of the Humanities). ISBN 0824015118.

This second volume supplements and expands on the earlier, highly regarded 1984 publication in several important ways. Whereas volume 1 covered approximately 500 artists, volume 2 features 1,200 artists, along with nearly all 500 artists who appeared in volume 1, even if new information is minimal. Many consider this bibliography a basic building block for any collection of books on women artists.

Tufts's groundbreaking exhibition catalog *American Women Artists, 1830–1930* (National Museum of Women in the Arts, 1987) is another essential, basic work focusing on 100 years of women's painting and sculpture. The catalog accompanied the inaugural exhibition at the first museum in the world devoted solely to women artists, as well as the first major traveling exhibition of American women artists. Tufts arranges the artwork into five categories: landscape, portraiture, still life, genre and history, and sculpture. She supplements the catalog of works exhibited with essays by Gail Levin, Alessandra Comini, and Wanda Corn. The catalog contains an index of artists, a bibliography that highlights additional sources for study, and fine-quality, large-format, color illustrations of work in the exhibition.

826. Walker-Hill, Helen. *Music by Black Women Composers: A Bibliography of Available Scores*. Chicago: Columbia College Center for Black Music Research, 1995. 110p. (CBMR Monographs). index. ISBN 0929911040pa.

Walker-Hill expands on *Piano Music by Black Women Composers: A Catalog of Solo and Ensemble Works* (Greenwood Press, 1992) in this bibliography in response to several requests for a work on music by black women composers who use a variety of instruments. While conducting research for the piano music catalog, she discovered and noted other music, thus forming the nucleus of this more comprehensive list. The author specifically chose the term "black women composers" as opposed to "African American composers" because she features the work of a few women of other nationalities in this resource. Walker-Hill admits that the noncomprehensive bibliography that only contains notated, readily available music limits the representation of black women's musical creativity. She omits several seminal composers, especially in the areas of gospel and religious music, folk, blues, rock, and jazz, because their scores are either unavailable or out of print and acknowledges that the lack of biographical information might frustrate readers. She organizes works cited by performance medium (violin, band, vocal, and so on) and alphabetically lists composers within each category. She provides complete information for each composition, including date, name of transcriber or arranger, publication data, contents, information on performances and recordings, libraries that contain the work, and sources that make the music available. The work includes a separate listing of addresses and telephone and fax numbers for various libraries and other sources.

MONOGRAPHS

Visual Arts, Design, and Architecture

827. Agosin, Marjorie, ed. *A Woman's Gaze: Latin American Women Artists*. Fredonia, NY: White Pine Press, 1998. 272p. bibliog. ISBN 1877727857pa.

Agosin compiles an anthology of essays by respected art historians and art critics about well-known artists, such as Lenora Carrington, Frida Kahlo, and Remedios Varo, as well as artists who have roots in popular culture yet remain unrecognized today. She features women artists who work in all media and represent diverse regions of Latin America. Although no illustrations of the artists' work accompany the essays, an eight-page bibliography refers readers to a rich array of additional resources.

Latin American Women Artists, 1915–1995: Artistas Latinoamericanas (Milwaukee Art Museum, 1995), curated by Geraldine Biller, marks one of the first, if not the first, major exhibitions that document women artists' contributions to the development of twentieth-century Latin American art. The curator reproduces more than thirty works in high-quality color illustrations, which she accompanies with five thoughtful, instructive essays about the role of women artists in Latin American art. Complete listings of works exhibited, short essays on each artist, bibliographies of additional resources on each individual artist, and a general bibliography on the broader topic make this a landmark catalog. Amy Conger's *Compañeras de México: Women Photograph Women* (University Art Gallery, University of California, Riverside, 1990), a catalog published in conjunction with an exhibit of the same name at the University of California at Riverside, and *Desires and Disguises: Five Latin American Women Photographers*, by Amanda Hopkinson (Serpent's Tail, 1992), complement these works.

828. Apostolos-Cappadona, Diana, and Lucinda Ebersole, eds. *Women, Creativity, and the Arts: Critical and Autobiographical Perspectives*. New York: Continuum, 1995. 226p. bibliog. index. ISBN 0826408311.

The editors note that people have idealized and modeled the concept of "artist" on man since the origins of Western culture, and that Sigmund Freud's work, built upon centuries of patriarchal attitudes and cultural restrictions on women, formed twentieth-century Western culture's definition of "woman" and her relationship to creativity. Apostolos-Cappadona and Ebersole include artists who have struggled against cultural restrictions and whose passion to create drives them in this compilation of readings, which encourages and supports the study of women and creativity. The editors present nine essays by psychologists, art historians, art critics, and others who have examined the roles of creative women and raise questions about the creative process, the definition of genius, and cultural categorizations of "women" in part 1. Part 2 contains a collection of autobiographical writings by visual artists, dancers, writers, and others about being female and creative in the twentieth century. The editors identify time as the greatest enemy of women artists and attribute the dearth of women artists' autobiographical writings to lack of time to reflect on the meaning of one's experience and expression of creativity. A series of useful topical bibliographies on women and the creative process concludes the volume.

829. Bentivoglio, Mirella, and Franca Zoccoli. *The Women Artists of Italian Futurism: Almost Lost to History*. New York: Midmarch Arts Press, 1997. 208p. bibliog. index. ISBN 1877675261; 1877675180pa.

Scholars have advanced the idea that the emphatically macho character of futurism excluded women; yet women participated in all areas of futurism, including painting, poetry, visualized poetry, dance, and literature. The authors scoured private and public archives, libraries, and collections to expose an active and productive group of artists whom historians previously have marginalized. They divide the book into two sections: the first focuses on artists who worked with mixed modes of expression, such as word and image, word and dance, and word and object; the second covers women painters of Italian futurism. Both sections provide much detail on artists' lives and work, which the authors supplement with numerous footnotes and information gleaned from primary sources. A glossary of futurist terminology, a selected bibliography, and illustrations of the artists and their work in both color and black and white complete the text.

830. Berkeley, Ellen Perry, ed. *Architecture: A Place for Women*. Washington, DC: Smithsonian Institution Press, 1989. 277p. bibliog. index. ISBN 0874742315pa.

Various authors contribute to this compilation of essays, which focuses on the marginality and complex history of women in architecture from 1848, when a woman wrote the first architectural history published in the United States, to the election of the first woman to the American Institute of Architects in 1888, and through to the future of women in architecture. Part 1 features biographical and critical articles on important early American architects. Contributors examine the history of women architects' education and the response of members of the American Institute of Architects in part 2. Berkeley presents essays on the visible identity and recognition of women architects who have succeeded despite discrimination in part 3 and includes discussions of the future of women in the architectural profession in part 4. An index and a few black-and-white illustrations provide additional topical access to the text.

831. Blair, Karen J. *The Torchbearers: Women and Their Amateur Arts Associations in America, 1890–1930*. Bloomington: Indiana University Press, 1994. 259p. bibliog. index. ISBN 0253311926.

Blair's exploration of women's role in amateur arts organizations in the late nineteenth and early twentieth centuries provides a fascinating portrait of how women enriched their lives and promoted artistic endeavors through women's musical, theatrical, and visual arts societies. Club-women often lent support to women artists and musicians, launching many into professional careers. Although most women who participated in arts associations did not consider themselves feminists, club life provided opportunities for them to gain organizational experience, become involved in their communities, and obtain personal satisfaction. These activities not only provided a respectable escape from traditional domesticity, but also helped shape and foster American sensibilities. Blair's examination of these amateur societies provides a new avenue for studying women, reform, and the Progressive Era.

832. Boffin, Tessa, and Jean Fraser, eds. *Stolen Glances: Lesbians Take Photographs*. London: Pandora Press, 1991. 252p. bibliog. index. ISBN 0044407076pa.

Boffin and Fraser feature constructed, staged, or manipulated imagery that mirrors "the socially constructed nature of sexuality" in this collection of images of lesbians by lesbian photographers. They omit images that present lesbianism as a natural state since she opposes the concept of natural sexuality. The editors introduce thematic chapters, including "Developing Identities," "Lesbian Family Album," and "Dream Girls," with essays and photographic images. Biographical notes on contributors and a bibliography citing additional resources for study of lesbian self-representation complete the volume.

Editors Peter Horne and Reina Lewis investigate the many ways in which lesbian and gay artists have contributed to the visual world in *Outlooks: Lesbian and Gay Sexualities and Visual Cultures* (Routledge, 1996). Critical essays by art historians, cultural theorists, and lesbian and gay activists address homosexual art and artists. The editors supplement the text with lesbian and gay artists' statements, along with more than forty illustrations of artwork. Two related texts include Cherry Smyth's *Damn Fine Art by New Lesbian Artists* (Cassell, 1996) and Shelly Tremain's *Pushing the Limits: Disabled Dykes Produce Culture* (Women's Press, 1996).

833. Borzello, Frances. *Seeing Ourselves: Women's Self-Portraits*. New York: Abrams, 1998. 224p. bibliog. index. ISBN 0810941880.

This beautifully illustrated and thoroughly researched examination of women's self-portraiture from the sixteenth to the twentieth century is the first lengthy historical study on this topic. Borzello, a specialist in the social history of art, argues that women's self-portraits differ from those of men and are more engaging than the traditional history of deprived training and lukewarm support for women might suggest. The author discusses the vocabulary of pose, gesture, facial expression, and accessories as painted autobiography.

Two earlier examinations of the subject, Midori Wakakuwa and Michiko Kasahara's *Exploring the Unknown Self: Self-Portraits of Contemporary Women* (Tokyo Metropolitan Culture Foundation, 1991) and Marsha Meskimmon's *The Art of Reflection: Women Artists' Self-Portraiture in the Twentieth Century* (Columbia University Press, 1996) focus on self-portraits of contemporary artists. While *Exploring the Unknown Self* includes an essay on the history of women's self-portraiture, the featured artists are exclusively contemporary. A wealth of illustrations, brief artists' biographies, and a list of all works in the exhibition accompany the text, written in both Japanese and English. Meskimmon delves into the jarring encounter between women artists engaging in self-representation and the tradition of male artists who have exercised economic, social, and representational or aesthetic control over women in *The Art of Reflection*. Meskimmon compares her reading of women's self-portraiture to the discussion in feminist theory of women's voice in male language. Instead of attempting to create an encyclopedia of artists, a chronological study, or a historical overview, Meskimmon encourages new ways of looking at the works of twentieth-century women artists who deal with self-representation within the stance of poststructuralist theory.

834. Broude, Norma, and Mary D. Garrard, eds. *The Expanding Discourse: Feminism and Art History*. Boulder, CO: Westview Press, 1992. 518p. bibliog. index. ISBN (OP); 0064302075pa.

Presenting the best feminist art historical writing of the 1980s, Broude and Garrard reprint twenty-nine essays from various sources. Broude's *Feminism and Art History: Questioning the Litany* (Westview Press, 1982), the first collection of feminist art historical essays to appear in the United States, collected articles published for the most part in the 1970s. Contributors to this later work include highly respected art historians, such as Linda Nochlin and Abigail Solomon-Godeau, who take a feminist and non-gender-conscious approach to art and art history, covering the Renaissance to the present. As opposed to concentrating on women artists, as in Broude's earlier work, contributors confront the distortion of Western art history caused by sexual bias. The editors feature essays that demonstrate how feminist inquiry affected the values and structure of art history, and how feminist art historical practice both challenged and extended postmodernism, resulting in a shift away from formalist concerns toward a study of the sociopolitical conditions under which artists create. Essays include bibliographic footnotes, and the volume's subject index provides additional access to the contents of the essays.

Broude's *Impressionism: A Feminist Reading: The Gendering of Art, Science, and Nature in the Nineteenth Century* (Westview Press, 1997) explores how scholars have applied insights in feminist theory to produce a new reading of impressionism. Broude discusses how gender distinctions shaped the interpretations of impressionist painting instead of focusing on the roles women played in impressionism.

835. Broude, Norma, and Mary D. Garrard, eds. *The Power of Feminist Art: The American Movement of the 1970s, History and Impact*. New York: Abrams, 1996. 318p. bibliog. index. ISBN (OP); 0810926598pa.

This compilation of essays by eighteen well-respected artists, critics, and art historians in the field of women's art who participated in the events of the 1970s celebrates the twentieth anniversary of the Corcoran Conference on Women in the Visual Arts, the first national conference of women in visual arts professions. Beginning in the early 1970s, the feminist art movement not only challenged mainstream American modernism but also caused sweeping changes. Contributors credit feminism with recognizing female values and experience as a legitimate basis of "high" art, challenging hegemony in modernism, appreciating diversity, and returning to political and personal content in art. The editors contend that these revolutionary lessons became so firmly integrated into contemporary art by the 1990s that people might forget the movement, organizations, and publications that spawned the changes. Part 1 documents early feminist art education; part 2 traces the development of the movement through its publications, organizations, and exhibit spaces; part 3 examines forms of feminist art; and the final part explores the impact of 1970s feminist art on the next generation and the backlash of the 1980s. Editors supplement the essays with ample color and black-and-white illustrations, bibliographic footnotes, a lengthy bibliography, and a foldout chronology of feminism from 1949 to 1995.

In *More Than Minimal: Feminism and Abstraction in the 70's* (Rose Art Museum, Brandeis University, 1996), the catalog of a 1996 exhibition held at the Rose Art Museum of Brandeis University that curator Susan Stoops edited, American artists of the 1970s raise questions about the feminist movement. Contributors analyze relationships between politics and culture, gender and subjectivity, and authority and language in the work of eleven artists. Elsa Honig Fine's *American Women Artists: The Twentieth Century* (Knoxville Museum of Art, 1989) is the catalog of an exhibition celebrating artists published in the first ten years of *Women's Art Journal*. Fine chronologically arranges the material and provides a comprehensive if somewhat idiosyncratic overview of the twentieth century. Catalog entries include reproductions, critical essays, and references to original articles about artists in *Women's Art Journal*.

836. Brunsman, Laura, and Ruth Askey, eds. *Modernism and Beyond: Women Artists of the Pacific Northwest*. New York: Midmarch Arts Press, 1993. 190p. bibliog. index. ISBN 187767513X.

Modernism and Beyond is one volume in a series that Midmarch Art Press publishes to celebrate women artists of regions who host meetings of the College Art Association and the Women's Caucus for Arts. Other volumes in this series include *Pilgrims and Pioneers: New England Women in the Arts*, edited by Sylvia Moore and Alicia C. Faxon (Midmarch Arts Press, 1987); *No Bluebonnets, No Yellow Roses: Essays on Texas Women Artists*, edited by Sylvia Moore (Midmarch Arts Press, 1988); and *Yesterday and Tomorrow: California Women Artists*, edited by Sylvia Moore (Midmarch Arts Press, 1989). The works focus on regional artistic developments and feature essays that rewrite and correct persistent patriarchal myths that define an area's art history. A limited number of illustrations accompany the texts.

837. Burkhauser, Jude, ed. *Glasgow Girls: Women in Art and Design, 1880–1920*. Cape May, NJ: Red Ochre, 1993. 263p. bibliog. index. ISBN 0963698508.

This exhibition catalog provides a comprehensive overview of the contributions of the women artists called "Glasgow Girls," a term that Burkhauser uses to allude to the better-known group of Scottish male artists, the "Glasgow Boys," at a time when Glasgow became a melting pot of cultural forces and a key international center of art and design. Well-researched essays on both painters and designers feature high-quality color illustrations of their work. Archival photographs of the artists and the interiors that they designed allow a glimpse into the social, political, and cultural environment in which these women worked. Burkhauser cites archival and other primary sources in bibliographic notes that provide additional sources on the period.

Women Designing: Redefining Design in Britain between the Wars, edited by Jill Seddon and Suzette Worden (University of Brighton Press, 1994) is a collection of essays, interviews, and reminiscences depicting women designers' experiences after World War I and during the Great Depression, a contradictory period when society pressured women to maintain their "rightful place" as homemakers and primary child care providers while simultaneously urging them to become designers of domestic appliances and experts on consumerism. Contributors examine careers in architecture, advertising, and textile, graphic, and industrial design in essays that feature interviews with designers of that period. Black-and-white photos of the designers and their work accompany this highly recommended text for women's studies and art history collections.

838. Chadwick, Whitney, ed. *Mirror Images: Women, Surrealism, and Self-Representation*. Cambridge, MA: MIT Press, 1998. 193p. bibliog. index. ISBN 0262531577pa.

In this catalog, which accompanied a traveling exhibition curated by Whitney Chadwick, Helaine Posner, and Katy Kline, Chadwick argues that women artists affiliated with the surrealist movement of the 1930s and 1940s heavily influenced contemporary women artists who explore issues of self-representation. Surrealists produced a unique body of self-portraits focusing on sexuality, gender, and culture through the artistic devices of displacement, fragmentation, and fetishizing body parts. Chadwick, well known for her earlier work on women and surrealism, and other noted art and cultural historians compare the contributions of women surrealist artists to those of contemporary artists, including Cindy Sherman, Ana Mendieta, and Kiki Smith. Chadwick supplements seven essays with numerous illustrations and a lengthy bibliography in this work, which would benefit general readers and academic collections.

Editor Penelope Rosemont highlights the quality and diversity of women involved in the international surrealist movement in *Surrealist Women: An International Anthology* (University of Texas Press, 1998). Rosemont argues that until recently, critics and scholars either ignored or overlooked women artists who formed an active, thoroughly integrated component of the movement. She presents a rich, complete compilation of women surrealists' writings consisting of automatic texts, declarations, theoretical articles, and poems, which she organizes into large chronological groupings, from 1924 to the present, making this an excellent reference source. In *Magnifying Mirrors: Women, Surrealism, and Partnership* (University of Nebraska Press, 1994), Renée Riese Hubert examines the mostly heterosexual, collaborative artistic couples of the surrealist movement, whom she became aware of while researching surrealist illustrated books (*Surrealism and the Book*, University of California Press, 1988). Hubert claims that in order to function creatively, women surrealist artists needed to belong to close-knit groups. She analyzes collaborative couples such as Leonora Carrington and Max Ernst, Lee Miller and Man Ray, Valentine and Roland Penrose, Sophie Taeuber and Hans Arp, and Frida Kahlo and Diego Rivera. Stressing the liberation and accomplishment of women surrealists rather than victimization and suppression, Hubert considers how women's artistic creativity evolved before, during, and after partnership, and how many surrealist women artists, who emerged from a patriarchal art education and background, changed the course of modern art. Hubert addresses lesbianism and matriarchy in surrealism, subversion, creativity, and clandestine collaborations. Many color and black-and-white reproductions of artworks reveal exaggerated closeness, distance, or disproportion and subvert the idea of the peaceful bourgeois couple.

839. Chadwick, Whitney. *Women, Art, and Society.* New York: Thames and Hudson, 1997. 448p. bibliog. index. ISBN 0500202931.

Originally published in 1990, this significant work provides students and scholars who previously depended on traditional texts that eliminate women from the study of art history with a well-rounded, inclusive source. Chadwick calls for a new critical analysis of women's art in her introductory essay and then presents her chronological study of women artists from the Middle Ages to the present. Chadwick includes several color and black-and-white reproductions, a seventeen-page bibliography of additional sources arranged by artists' names and specialized topics, such as "Feminist Critique of Art History," and an index that provides access to specific artists and subjects within the texts.

Wendy Slatkin's *Women Artists in History: From Antiquity to the Twentieth Century*, originally published in 1985 (Prentice Hall, 1985) and released in its third edition in 1997 (Prentice Hall, 1997), is another important survey of women artists. Slatkin examines the work of specific Western women artists from prehistory to the present with brief overview essays that outline historical or stylistic periods. The text features black-and-white illustrations and a helpful, albeit brief, bibliography of additional readings. Betty Ann Brown and Arlene Raven survey fifty contemporary artists in insightful, critical essays featuring color photographs of artists and their work in *Exposures: Women and Their Art* (NewSage, 1989). Black-and-white illustrations, a twenty-page chronological bibliography of monographs, articles, and exhibit catalogs, and a name index accompany the text. *Crossing Over: Feminism and Art of Social Concern* (UMI Research Press, 1988) features sixteen critical writings that feminist art pioneer Arlene Raven previously published (except for one). Raven examines major social issues such as aging, poverty, and foreign policy decisions in her strongly feminist interpretations of women's socially committed art. Fair-quality black-and-white reproductions and bibliographic notes accompany the essays.

840. Chalmers, F. Graeme. *Women in the Nineteenth-Century Art World: Schools of Art and Design for Women in London and Philadelphia*. Westport, CT: Greenwood Press, 1998. 144p. (Contributions to the Study of Art and Architecture). bibliog. index. ISBN 0313306044.

Chalmers presents case histories of the Philadelphia School of Design for Women (1848–1932) and London's Female School of Design (1842–1852), which was subsequently renamed the Metropolitan School of Ornament for Females (1852–1862) and the Royal Female School of Art (1862–1908). Chalmers documents the gendered approach to art and design education, discusses its impact in two societies, and looks closely at histories and factual institutions. He supports the text with numerous bibliographic footnotes that lead to primary sources, along with a substantial general bibliography on women artists of the nineteenth century. This book would highly benefit social and educational historians, art historians, art educators, and scholars engaged in women's and gender studies.

Tamar Garb's reworking of her dissertation, *Sisters of the Brush: Women's Artistic Culture in Late Nineteenth-Century Paris* (Yale University Press, 1994), tells the story of the first all-woman exhibiting society in France, the Union des Femmes Peintures et Sculptures. Garb argues that the struggles and debates that this nineteenth-century group experienced are relevant to women artists and critics who still deal with issues of separatism, selectivity, elitism, coercion, and collusion in contemporary feminist art practice. Garb includes a lengthy section of bibliographic footnotes and a bibliography of archival, primary, and secondary sources. Numerous black-and-white illustrations supplement the text.

841. Cherry, Deborah. *Painting Women: Victorian Women Artists*. New York: Routledge, 1993. 275p. bibliog. index. ISBN (OP); 0415060532pa.

Upon viewing an exhibit of women's artwork created between 1840 and 1900, the author was struck by the different ways in which society has perceived, treated, and placed women's work in the history of art. Thus she examines the lives of women painters from the second half of the nineteenth century, including the pictures of women that they created, in this study. Cherry discusses social definitions of women artists as daughters, wives, and spinsters; art education for women; and professional identities in the first part of the book. She investigates the woman artist's gaze on domesticity, workingwomen, and cultural institutions in the second part. Two appendices feature reprints of artists' family trees and the women's petition to the Royal Academy of the Arts of 1859. The text includes black-and-white illustrations as well as bibliographical footnotes and a bibliography indicating additional sources on women artists of the period.

Concentrating on approximately the same time period, Alison Thomas looks at women who trained at the Slade School of Art in London in *Portraits of Women: Gwen John and Her Forgotten Contemporaries* (Polity Press, 1994). Although instructors at Slade considered the artistic talent of women students as superior to that of male students, instructors lent male students a more prominent role in the history of British painting. Thomas thus examines women deemed to have promising artistic careers. Extensive notes document primary sources that Thomas uncovered during her research. *Women in the Victorian Art World* (Manchester University Press; distributed by St. Martin's Press, 1995), edited by Clarissa Campbell Orr, features nine essays published in conjunction with a symposium on women in the Victorian art world. To uncover more about the experience of women artists in the latter half of the nineteenth century, participants explore social and economic backgrounds of women artists, opportunities for professional training, the representation of the woman artist in both art and fiction, and constraints that mores of the period imposed. Although the essays contain several bibliographic notes, Orr incorporates few black-and-white illustrations.

842. Collins, Georgia, and Renee Sandell, eds. *Gender Issues in Art Education: Content, Contexts, and Strategies.* Reston, VA: National Art Education Association, 1996. 164p. bibliog. ISBN 0937652857pa.

This anthology of sixteen essays continues the editors' earlier work published in *Women, Art, and Education* (National Art Education Association, 1984). In the more recent volume Collins and Sandell have culled and presented current research concerning gender in art education. The work is presented in three sections: what is taught, setting and persons involved in the educational process, and methods or techniques for teaching. As a whole, the essays point out that gender bias is not limited to the often studied issue of whose art is deemed historically significant. Gender bias extends into the traditional structure of education: the kind of knowledge valued in schools and museums, styles of interacting with students of art, and teaching aesthetics, art, art history, and art criticism. Practical suggestions for teaching are offered by authors informed by hands-on experience as well as research. This book is recommended for all libraries concerned with education, feminist cultural studies, and art.

843. Courtney-Clarke, Margaret. *African Canvas: The Art of West African Women.* New York: Rizzoli, 1990. 204p. bibliog. ISBN 0847811662.

Courtney-Clarke, a photojournalist drawn to art and design, presents a stunning photo essay on the mural art of West African women reminiscent of her earlier book *Ndebele: The Art of an African Tribe* (Rizzoli, 1986). These photographic records of women's work not only chronicle the inherent impermanence of art forms that rely on mud walls, clay canvases, and indigenous pigments, but also reveal how the rapid industrialization in these countries is destroying many existing structures. Courtney-Clarke is the first author to draw serious attention to traditional rural lifeways expressed through African women's art. The beautiful color photos, rather than the minimal text and short bibliographies, lend value to both books. Courtney-Clarke photographically records North African women's artistic tradition of painting murals, weaving, and ceramics in her most recent volume, *Imazighen: The Vanishing Traditions of Berber Women* (C. Potter, 1996). She provides a short bibliography and glossary.

Labelle Prussin examines nomadic structures, including the tents, houses, and domestic furnishings that women traditionally have constructed as modes of creative expression, in *African Nomadic Architecture: Space, Place, and Gender* (Smithsonian Institution Press, 1995). Prussin supplements the scholarly text of this volume, which evolved from fieldwork and several years of research, with black-and-white and color photographs, numerous site plans and drawings, and a lengthy bibliography.

844. Davidov, Judith Fryer. *Women's Camera Work: Self/Body/Other in American Visual Culture.* Durham, NC: Duke University Press, 1998. 494p. (New Americanists). bibliog. index. ISBN 0822320541; 0822320673pa.

Davidov chronicles the photographic work of women photographers, examining the role that women's photographs have played in the construction of our cultural, political, and social histories. She not only evaluates how women photographers, distributors, and readers of photographic images create histories, but also weighs the cultural importance of photographs. Davidov explores women's photographic networks from the first half of the twentieth century, specifically focusing on photographers such as Gertrude Kasebier, Imogen Cunningham, and Dorothea Lange. She argues that Laura Gilpin, Frances Benjamin Johnson, and other women photographers display a gendered response to their photographic subjects. The author supplements the text with nearly 100 pages of bibliographic footnotes, a subject index, and black-and-white photographic reproductions.

In the anthology of readings edited by Diane Neumaier, *Reframings: New American Feminist Photographies* (Temple University Press, 1996), contributors examine the diverse lives, works, and philosophies of contemporary women photographers, exploring how domesticity, gendered space, female identity, postcolonial legacies, and body imagery thread their work. The book features color and black-and-white reproductions and biographical notes about artists and critics. Both books would complement libraries that emphasize women's studies and/or photography.

845. Deepwell, Katy, ed. *New Feminist Art Criticism: Critical Strategies*. Manchester, England: Manchester University Press, distributed by St. Martin's Press, 1995. 201p. bibliog. index. ISBN (OP); 0719042585pa.

Critics, curators, academics, and artists argue that feminist art criticism is a broad umbrella term that represents diverse positions and strategies of women producing, distributing, and consuming art. Deepwell includes essays that emphasize diversity of critical forms and feminist art practices in this book, which she divides into five areas of criticism and art practice: theory and practice, curatorship, censorship, psychoanalysis, and textile art. She supplements the essays with black-and-white illustrations and a subject index. This book is recommended for academic libraries.

A related text, *New Feminist Criticism: Art, Identity, Action* (IconEditions, 1994), edited by Joanna Frueh, Cassandra Langer, and Arlene Raven, supplements articles featured in the summer 1991 *Art Journal*, edited by Frueh and Raven. The essays represent a variety of critical and methodological perspectives. Fourteen authors, including Harmony Hammond, Laura Cottingham, and Mira Schor, discuss themes of culture, language, identity, and ethics in feminist art criticism. The editors provide biographical notes on all contributors as well as a subject index. Cassandra Langer's *Feminist Art Criticism: An Annotated Bibliography* (G. K. Hall, 1993) is the first major critical bibliography in the field. Langer organizes citations to English-language publications in contemporary art and criticism by format, with author and subject indexes. Formats include reference tools, books (including diaries, letters, autobiographies, and biographies), dissertations, exhibition catalogs, articles in journals, and chapters in books. Citations to articles in feminist art magazines of the 1960s and 1970s that are not indexed elsewhere are particularly valuable. Each citation features an annotation explaining its relevance to feminist culture, art theory, and criticism, as well as an evaluation of its place in the history of feminist art theory and criticism. Frueh and Langer's earlier work *Feminist Art Criticism: An Anthology* (UMI Research Press, 1988) provides insightful historical perspectives for these readings.

846. Deepwell, Katy, ed. *Women Artists and Modernism*. New York: Manchester University Press, 1998. 206p. bibliog. index. ISBN 0719050812; 0719050820pa.

This anthology demonstrates how scholars use different methodologies and approaches to examine women artists of the twentieth century. In her introductory essay, Deepwell questions why society continues to marginalize women artists even though their numbers have increased and professional arts organizations admit more women. She also points out that in current examinations of modernism, the work of women artists rarely receives more than 20 percent coverage in modern art books, exhibitions, and installations in permanent collections. Contributors working in Great Britain, Ireland, Canada, and the United States address the work of artists who primarily work in these countries. They examine works from library archives and museum collections, manuscripts, workbooks, and letters, provide case studies, and question ideas about modernism in ten different essays. A ten-page bibliography provides a list of resources on case studies of women artists, general books on feminism and modernism in the twentieth century, theories of gender, feminist studies of women artists, theories of representation, contemporary feminist art practice, dictionaries, and other reference resources about women in art.

847. Dysart, Dinah, and Hannah Fink, eds. *Asian Women Artists*. Roseville East, New South Wales, Australia: Craftsman House Press, 1996. 143p. bibliog. ISBN (OP); 9766410771pa.

This examination of women who experiment with new materials and technology shatters the Western preconception that ancient traditions constrain the art made in Asian countries. Fourteen contributors profile several artists, many for the first time, representing various Asian cultures, whose exploration of feminism has produced vastly different types of artwork. The contributors, who hail from a variety of nationalities and cultures, bring different perspectives to their critical and descriptive reviews of the artwork of Asian women. The text includes color illustrations of stereotype-breaking artwork.

Editor Lucy Lim selects artists who have made important contributions to contemporary Chinese painting in *Six Contemporary Chinese Women Artists* (Chinese Culture Foundation of San Francisco, 1991). Although four of the artists profiled are from the People's Republic of China and two live in Hong Kong, all six originally studied traditional Chinese ink and brush painting. These artists work in a wide variety of styles, subject matters, and media because of a shared search for artistic self-identity and independence. Lim supplements the text with ample color illustrations, biographies of each artist, and a selected bibliography.

848. Field, Richard S., and Ruth E. Fine. *A Graphic Muse: Prints by Contemporary American Women*. New York: Hudson Hills Press, 1987. 163p. bibliog. index. (OP)

This exhibition catalog, which features critical and biographical essys about twenty-four artists along with color illustrations of their work, highlights work housed in the Mount Holyoke College Art Museum. Field provides a brief but informative overview of women in printmaking in the United States, emphasizing four women active since World War II in his introduction. In a review essay on printmaking since 1960, Field pays homage to the importance of women artists, printers, administrators, and curators in the history of printmaking while insisting that the artists included, as a reflection of women artists in general, do not consciously make feminist statements.

Victoria Hansen and Eleanor Heartney's exhibition catalog *Presswork: The Art of Women Printmakers* (Lang Communications, 1991) offers a sampling of prints that American women made in the 1980s. The authors include a brief review essay on women and contemporary art as well as a discussion of printmaking processes and projects of the 1980s. They also provide color and black-and-white illustrations of the artworks in the exhibition. The artists highlighted in these two catalogs, which together acquaint readers with a spectrum of women practicing printmaking at approximately the same time in history, rarely overlap. Patricia Jaffe focuses on women pioneers of wood engraving in *Women Engravers* (Virago, 1988). She presents a fascinating history of an often overlooked medium in which many women both worked and excelled. Although limits of size, space, and black-and-white reproductions forced Jaffe to omit many fine contemporary women engravers, her elegantly designed book includes many high-quality reproductions of wood engravings as well as a two-page bibliography highlighting other works useful in the study of the history of women engravers, a field in need of additional examination. The book's lack of a table of contents and index prohibits quick reference and easy access.

849. Glaser, Jane R., and Artemis A. Zenetou, eds. *Gender Perspectives: Essays on Women in Museums.* Washington, DC: Smithsonian Institution Press, 1994. 161p. bibliog. ISBN 1560983256pa.

Contributing authors, mostly museum administrators and educators, share their experiences, examine women's historical role in museums, and discuss the scholarly and educational impact of women in museums in twenty-three essays originally delivered as papers at the national seminar "Gender Perspectives: The Impact of Women in Museums." Although the contributors represent different political camps with opposing viewpoints, they all agree that those in control of American museums have ignored the feminist movement. Despite the fact that women have played major roles, from founding and leading museums to influencing directions in scholarship and education, collections, exhibitions, and publications, women generally do not hold positions of power in museums. Twenty-three essays address these and other issues, and a five-page selected bibliography supplements the text.

850. Goldfrank, Janice, ed. *Making Ourselves at Home: Women Builders and Designers.* Watsonville, CA: Papier-Mache Press, 1995. 223p. bibliog. index. ISBN 0918949262pa.

Goldfrank, a general contractor who traveled the United States interviewing women house builders, observed that most women builders who construct houses, communes, apartment buildings, and other structures all over the country have no formal training, improvise, and tend to work in isolation from other female builders. Goldfrank's project evolved into a study of the significant role that the building and design process plays in women's lives. The author describes buildings that women designed, analyzes women's attitudes toward the design process, and includes several black-and-white photographs, a glossary of terms, and a selected bibliography in the text.

Alice T. Friedman describes how strong-willed women clients' goals and expectations, shaped by feminist reform movements, influenced the most renowned architects of the twentieth century, including Frank Lloyd Wright, Mies van der Rohe, and Le Corbusier, in *Women and the Making of the Modern House: A Social and Architectural History* (Abrams, 1998). Arguing that women clients became catalysts for change in twentieth-century domestic architecture, Friedman features designs that demonstrate a shift in definitions of domesticity. The text includes color and black-and-white illustrations. Leslie Kanes Weisman contends that because space is socially constructed, spatial relations reflect and reinforce gender, race, and class relations in society in *Discrimination by Design: A Feminist Critique of the Man-Made Environment* (University of Illinois Press, 1994). Weisman proposes a feminist housing agenda and outlines women's roles in designing a society that honors feminist values. Marion Roberts examines the relationship of gender to housing design with a historical approach in *Living in a Man-Made World* (Routledge, 1991). Roberts looks at how the gender assumptions of architects have determined not only our built environment, but our society as well. The text includes a lengthy bibliography. Papers delivered at the 1990 Princeton University symposium *Sexuality and Space*, edited by Beatriz Colomina (Princeton Architectural Press, 1992), address the close relationships between sexuality and space and the absence of sexuality in critical discourses in architecture.

851. Guerrilla Girls. *The Guerrilla Girls Bedside Companion to the History of Western Art.* New York: Penguin Books, 1998. 95p. bibliog. ISBN 014025997Xpa.

The Guerrilla Girls, an anonymous yet famous collective of women artists and art professionals, use gorilla masks and satiric posters to bring attention to discrimination against women and bigotry in the art world. Their corrected version of art history celebrates women artists through the ages while questioning and poking fun at the who, what, when, where, and why of traditional art history. The group introduces "Mistresspieces" that male critics and historians have overlooked from classical Greece to the present. The authors weave a chronology of important dates in women's cultural history, quotes by and about women artists, and art reproductions that the Guerrilla Girls have "enhanced" for revenge into a fact-filled text. This graphically exciting production packs a great deal of information into a small volume.

852. Heller, Nancy. *Women Artists: An Illustrated History.* New York: Abbeville Press, 1997. 280p. bibliog. index. ISBN 0789203456pa.

Now in its third edition, this beautifully illustrated, well-written survey of women artists, for nonspecialist, originally published in 1987, provides an overview of the range of styles, subjects, and techniques of women painters and sculptors from the Renaissance to the present. This much-needed work supplements standard, male-dominated art historical surveys. A six-page bibliography lists further readings on women artists in general as well as monographs on individual artists.

Olga Opfell provides an overview of North American and European women artists from the Renaissance to the twentieth century for general readers in *Special Visions: Profiles of Fifteen Women Artists from the Renaissance to the Present Day* (McFarland, 1991). Opfell devotes each chapter to a single artist, outlining the main biographical and cultural events that influenced her artistic output. Although Opfell includes only a few poor-quality black-and-white illustrations, Heller provides photos of these artists' works in her survey.

853. Jacobs, Fredrika Herman. *Defining the Renaissance Virtuosa: Women Artists and the Language of Art History and Criticism.* New York: Cambridge University Press, 1997. 243p. bibliog. index. ISBN 0521572703.

Jacobs recognizes that whereas Leonardo, Raphael, and Michelangelo are common names often associated with creative genius and masterpieces of art, the names of Sonfonisba Anguissola, Lavinia Fontana, and Irene de Spilimbergo are unfamiliar, with their works remaining unknown. Jacobs considers the language of art in relation to gender differences by examining art criticism written between 1550 and 1800 about approximately forty women artists who were active in Renaissance Italy. She argues that scholars defined women artists by linking artistic creation with biological procreation and connecting gender and artistic style, and explores how the biases of early critics have affected modern scholarship. Jacobs provides a roster of sixteenth-century Italian women artists and reprints some primary source writings on artists and art in appendices. She also includes a bibliography and black-and-white illustrations.

A related volume, *Picturing Women in Renaissance and Baroque Italy* (Cambridge University Press, 1997), edited by Geraldine Johnson and Sara F. Matthews Grieco, considers women as the subjects, creators, patrons, and viewers of art. The editors broadly define art in order to include popular prints and domestic objects in addition to painting, sculpture, and architecture. Contributors, who view women's experiences and needs as important determinants in the creation and consumption of visual culture, analyze the art histories of women in Italy from the fourteenth to the seventeenth century in nine essays that include black-and-white illustrations and copious bibliographic footnotes. *Creative Women in Medieval and Early Modern Italy: A Religious and Artistic Renaissance* (University of Pennsylvania Press, 1994), edited by E. Ann Matter and John Coakley, is a collection of essays originally presented as papers at the 1991 conference "Creative Women in Medieval and Early Modern Italy," which was held at the University of Pennsylvania. Scholars from a variety of disciplines address artistic life from the thirteenth through the seventeenth century in Italy. Case studies of musicians, theatrical performers, and visual artists demonstrate that the religious life allowed women the creative freedom not found in other aspects of society.

854. Kelly, Mary. *Imaging Desire*. Cambridge, MA: MIT Press, 1996. 253p. bibliog. index. ISBN 0262112140.

Kelly reproduces parts of her exhibit *Post-Partum Document*, which shocked the London art world in 1976, along with exhibition reviews, responses of viewers, and verbatim reprints of conversations between Kelly and other artists and theorists about feminist art. Kelly's examination of *Post-Partum Document* launches a broad, in-depth discussion of conceptual art and feminism during the 1970s and 1980s. Black-and-white illustrations and bibliographic footnotes accompany the text.

Editors Rozsika Parker and Griselda Pollock present texts that document the historical development of feminism through the experiences and expressions of feminist artists, art critics, and art historians in *Framing Feminism: Art and the Women's Movement, 1970–85* (Pandora Press, 1987). Parker and Pollock cover a wide range of subjects and reproduce diverse voices that reflect major developments in women's cultural politics between 1970 and 1985. The editors open the anthology with two review essays about the strategies and practices of feminist art during the stated time period. Black-and-white illustrations, reproductions of exhibition reviews, letters to publications, and other primary source documents supplement the text. Catriona Moore similarly reviews the formative years and historical development of feminist art in *Dissonance: Feminism and the Arts, 1970–1990* (Allen & Unwin, 1994).

855. King-Hammond, Leslie, ed. *Gumbo Ya Ya: Anthology of Contemporary African-American Women Artists*. New York: Midmarch Arts Press, 1995. 350p. (Midmarch Art Books). ISBN 1877675075pa.

This collection of biobibliographic entries by and about nearly 150 contemporary women of African descent in the United States features a unique insight into the black female visual artist's struggle to establish a voice in the contemporary art world. Entries include a critical review of the artist's work, a biography, the artist's statement about her work, a photo of the artist, and black-and-white illustrations of her artwork. A broad range of artists represent a great diversity of medium, content, and style. In the introduction, King-Hammond reviews contributions beginning with the first generation of women artists of African descent, who produced mostly stitched and woven work, and continuing with the painters who became more common in the 1930s and 1940s. Artists today most frequently work in photography, mixed media, installation, and performance. Phoebe Farris-Dufrene's *Voices of Color: Art and Society in the Americas* (Prometheus Books, 1997) serves as a valuable companion volume.

856. LaDuke, Betty. *Africa: Through the Eyes of Women Artists*. Trenton, NJ: Africa World Press, 1991. 148p. bibliog. ISBN 086543199Xpa.

Artist Betty LaDuke traveled for four consecutive years through Africa to discover, interview, and research women artists, twelve of whom she includes in this work, which features women artists of the diaspora as well as African artists. Through a combination of essays, black-and-white illustrations, and interviews, the author demonstrates that African art forms are not limited to the infamous masks that inspired the development of cubism, thus providing a greater understanding of the variety of multifaceted themes that women create in contemporary African art.

LaDuke extends the work of her first book in *Africa: Women's Art, Women's Lives* (Africa World Press, 1997), which she based on her travels and research in Burkina Faso, Mali, Togo, Cameroon, Zimbabwe, and Eritrea. LaDuke interviewed and studied artists who work in all media and represent current and future trends in African art. Several black-and-white photos of artists and their work and bibliographic footnotes accompany the text. *Gendered Visions: The Art of Contemporary Africana Women Artists* (Africa World Press, 1997), edited by Salah M. Hassan, accompanies Cornell University's 1997 exhibit of the same name. Hassan features essays about contemporary women artists of African descent now living and working in Western centers of modernist and postmodernist artistic production. The artists look at gender representation as a way of defining one's self, affirming the diasporic experience, and breaking away from a male-controlled "gaze" in nine essays focusing on the work of six Africana artists. Artist and teacher Marion I. Arnold presents essays about women and art in South Africa in *Women and Art in South Africa* (St. Martin's Press, 1996) to inform South African women artists about their past and the lives and creativity of other women in order to combat the insidious effects of patriarchy within visual culture. Arnold notes that although feminism has made a great impact on Western theory during the past twenty-five years, it has made few strides in Africa. Arnold thus attempts to uncover the histories of South African women. Nine essays explore portraits of servitude, sculpting the body, contemplating self, and other topics. Although the author mostly addresses the lives and works of white artists, they also include some black artists.

857. LaDuke, Betty. *Women Artists: Multi-cultural Visions.* Trenton, NJ: Red Sea Press, 1992. 170p. ISBN 0932415776; 0932415784pa.

This book results from the author's extensive world travel exploring the richness of women's art from Asia, Latin America, Eastern Europe, and the United States. Although the artists included in this study hail from distant corners of the world and represent diverse cultural heritages, all work with the feminine form as a significant theme in their weavings, paintings, sculpture, and mixed-media works. Part 1 examines particular art forms by women of Borneo, India, and Mexico. Part 2 focuses on individual women artists of color from the United States, and part 3 examines the work of two Yugoslavian women whose work dwells on survival in Eastern Europe after World War II. LaDuke makes cross-cultural comparisons through issues such as ecofeminism, the role of the goddess, indigenous self-determination, and racism as experienced by women artists.

LaDuke builds on her earlier book *Compañeras: Women, Art, and Social Change in Latin America* (City Lights Books, 1985), which similarly resulted from years of travel and was motivated by the lack of teaching material about women artists of non-European descent. In all of her books LaDuke writes not as an anthropologist or art historian, but rather as a working artist and art teacher.

858. Leroux, Odette, Marion E. Jackson, and Minnie Aodla Freeman, eds. *Inuit Women Artists: Voices from Cape Dorset.* Seattle: University of Washington Press, 1994. 253p. bibliog. ISBN 0295973897.

The editors begin their study with three essays that address the seldom-recognized artistic expression of Inuit women, and then devote one chapter to each of the nine highlighted Inuit women artists. They translate the artists' statements about their art in Inuktitut into English. Color and black-and-white illustrations and a four-page bibliography featuring both published and primary sources that provide access to additional research enrich the text. These artists share memories, experiences, and successes in maintaining Inuit culture while accommodating and adapting to other ways. Their stories result in a moving and revealing text that sheds new light upon an integral and significant aspect of Inuit culture. The editors discuss traditional and contemporary roles of Inuit women in the final chapter.

859. Lorenz, Clare. *Women in Architecture: A Contemporary Perspective*. New York: Rizzoli, 1990. 144p. bibliog. (OP)

Lorenz highlights the work of contemporary women architects from twenty nations who are highly respected in their home country and have acted as sole designers or lead architects in a design team. She features architectural achievements, special interests, and design solutions that these women created in color and black-and-white illustrations. Lorenz matches her critical commentary with the architects' statements about their work and includes statistical data that allow readers to make comparative analyses by country. The author divides the architects into three groups: those age fifty or older at the time of the book's publication, those who trained in the early 1970s when the feminist movement proved most vocal, and young architects with ten years of experience or less. She compares the experiences of these groups and addresses specific issues of the profession that have posed challenges to each group.

860. McCarthy, Kathleen D. *Women's Culture: American Philanthropy and Art, 1830–1930*. Chicago: University of Chicago Press, 1991. 324p. bibliog. index. ISBN 0226555836; 0226555844pa.

McCarthy deconstructs the enduring American myth that women are and always have been our nation's cultural custodians through an examination of historical records, which reveal that men operated America's first art museums, art unions, and galleries. Women played an extremely limited role. Yet philanthropic endeavors became the primary means through which middle- and upper-class women defined their public roles before winning the vote in 1920. McCarthy thus considers women's impact on cultural institutions in the United States, the ways in which women employed philanthropy for feminist gains, and how women's philanthropic initiatives differed from those of men, emphasizing developments since the Civil War. She discusses Isabella Stewart Gardner, Gertrude Vanderbilt Whitney, and many lesser-known philanthropists in detail and provides a twenty-five-plus-page bibliography that lists primary, unpublished, and secondary sources.

Mona Mender describes how her experience as a fundraiser for a symphony orchestra heightened her awareness of the many women who support music in *Extraordinary Women in Support of Music* (Scarecrow Press, 1997). Mender looks at women in the Western world who have furthered music and helped musicians in innumerable ways in a series of short, biographical sketches. Thematically organized sections range from "Ladies of the Great Salons," including Isabella d'Este and Coco Chanel, to "Creative Administrators," such as Beverly Sills. Mender provides a historical overview of women's patronage and devotes the final chapter to the contributions of choreographers. A seven-page bibliography and name index supplement the text.

861. McQuiston, Liz. *Women in Design: A Contemporary View*. London: Trefoil, 1988. 144p. (Trefoil Design Library). bibliog. (OP)

This book provides the first inventory of the work of contemporary women designers, featuring forty-three women from various countries who work as graphic, product, and interior designers, as well as architects, filmmakers, and design critics. Color and black-and-white reproductions of each woman's work accompany short biographical essays that raise questions about who benefits from design, what the profession demands of women, and how women designers have found a niche in a male-dominated field.

Judy Attfield and Pat Kirkham edited *A View from the Interior: Feminism, Women, and Design* (Women's Press, 1989) because of their frustration with authors of books about women in design who simply insert women's names into orthodox design history as opposed to examining design history from a feminist perspective. In fifteen essays, contributors discuss the application of feminist analysis to design and the examination of "differences" and explore fields of design where women have gained recognition, such as textile and ceramic design. They also consider how the dichotomy of the arts and crafts movement confined women to conventional divisions of labor while it simultaneously created openings for professional women designers. Bibliographic footnotes and black-and-white illustrations accompany the essays. The publisher issued a second edition of this book in 1995, *A view from the Interior: Women and Design*, which reprints the original edition and adds new material.

Design and Feminism: Re-visioning Spaces, Places, and Everyday Things (Rutgers University Press, 1999), edited by Joan Rothschild, resulted from the 1995 CUNY conference "Re-visioning Design and Technology." Chapters present the ideas of a cross section of architects, planners, designers, teachers, and students who have explored and critiqued designed environments from a feminist perspective. An introductory essay provides a literature review of work published in English since 1970 concerning architecture, urban planning, product design, and graphic design. Essays introduce views on urban and suburban space, housing and neighborhood, product design, and process or modes of design. Promoting inclusionary practices to challenge predominant ideologies in architecture, design, and urban planning and the idea that design should not exclude, deny access, nor benefit the privileged few thread the essays together. Noted architectural authorities Susana Torre and Dolores Hayden contribute to this work, and bibliographic notes supplement the text.

862. Moutoussamy-Ashe, Jeanne. *Viewfinders: Black Women Photographers*. New York: Dodd, Mead, 1986. 201p. bibliog. index. (OP)

This valuable work provides data on black women who were previously completely lost to history. Moutoussamy-Ashe presents broad historical overviews with information on specific women photographers in chronologically arranged chapters. The text reprint is well illustrated with reproductions of the artists' works. Brief biographies, a geographical index, and a bibliography supplement the text.

863. Nochlin, Linda. *Women, Art, and Power: And Other Essays*. New York: Harper & Row, 1988. 181p. bibliog. index. (OP)

Feminist art historian Linda Nochlin provides an overview of the development of feminist art criticism in this anthology, which features essays penned from 1968 to 1988. Nochlin arranges the essays in reverse chronological order, presenting the most recent first, encouraging readers to begin with her later concerns and then work back to her early, groundbreaking essay "Why Have There Been No Great Women Artists?" Dominant themes and perspectives and a persistently critical attitude toward mainstream art history thread all of the essays together, providing unity despite the wide range of subjects that the author addresses. Nochlin describes the title essay as an ongoing and open-ended project that she expects to revisit and rehash over time. Bibliographic footnotes, black-and-white illustrations, and an index of artists accompany this important text, which forms an essential component to any collection concerning art and/or women studies. HarperCollins reprinted the anthology in 1998.

864. Pollock, Griselda, ed. *Generations and Geographies in the Visual Arts: Feminist Readings.* New York: Routledge, 1996. 300p. bibliog. index. ISBN 0415141273; 0415141281pa.

Pollock, a well-respected feminist art historian and art critic and the second woman to join the esteemed list of Walter Neurath lecturers, features an international selection of writers who represent diverse cultural and social experiences and explore art made by twentieth-century women in this anthology. While "generations" refers to each artist's treatment of time and historical and political circumstance, "geographies" refers to the significance of place, location, and cultural diversity. The text includes theoretical debates by Pollock and others about art, focusing on the themes of mother, body, land, and history/memory.

Pollock presented *Avant-Garde Gambits, 1888–1893: Gender and the Colour of Art History* (Thames & Hudson, 1993) as the twenty-fourth annual Walter Neurath Memorial Lecture, a series sponsored each spring by the University of London to present lectures in the fields of art, art history, architecture, and philosophy. Pollock addresses the gendering of modern art and ideas of artistic vocation in the nineteenth century in this lecture. Pollock's other notable publications include *Framing Feminism: Art and the Women's Movement, 1970–85*, edited with Rozsika Parker (Pandora Press, (see entry 854), and *Vision and Difference: Femininity, Feminism, and Histories* (Routledge, 1988).

865. Robinson, Hilary, ed. *Visibly Female: Feminism and Art: An Anthology.* London: Camden, 1987. 317p. bibliog. ISBN 0948491310pa.

Robinson targets students who are new to research and/or have no access to academic or feminist libraries in this anthology, which features reprinted articles from various feminist and art magazines that illustrate the diversity of the politics and practices of the feminist art world during the 1980s. She points out that in England and Scotland, although women compose more than half of the art students' population, men mostly serve on the teaching staff. Contributors attribute the oppression of women in the art world to differing causes. The anthology features artists' personal statements, interviews with the artists, reviews of work by women artists, and theoretical essays written by important feminist artists and art historians. The readings note that despite what the media or educational systems frequently attempt to instill, no single "feminist art" exists since feminist artists use a wide array of media and incorporate varying concerns and approaches into their work.

Jo Anna Isaak harangues the idea of a specific female way of creating art and deflates the notion of feminist art practices in *Feminism and Contemporary Art: The Revolutionary Power of Women's Laughter* (Routledge, 1996). Isaak contends that under the influence of feminism, contemporary art provides the basis to critique our key assumptions about art, art history, and the artist's role. The author examines the work of several women artists from the United States, the United Kingdom, Canada, and the former Soviet Union. She presents an original study of contemporary Soviet women's art in the insightful chapter "Reflections of Resistance." Black-and-white illustrations accompany the text.

866. Robinson, Jontyle Theresa and Maya Angelou. *Bearing Witness: Contemporary Works by African American Artists.* New York: Spelman College and Rizzoli Publications, 1996. 176p. bibliog. index. ISBN 0847819620; 0847819639pa.

This catalog, which accompanied an exhibition originally held at Spelman College, features sixty artworks of twenty-five artists. Six essays encourage readers to use African beliefs as a reference point when viewing the works of contemporary African American women, emphasize the presupposition that "art" is not separate from life, and introduce important artists whom mainstream publications continue to exclude. Several high-quality black-and-white and color reproductions accompany the artists' biographies, and the authors include a particularly useful chronology of African American women artists at the back of the book. The catalog is a key contribution to scholarship in American art, African American art, and women's art.

Robert Henkes promotes an awareness and deeper understanding of the underappreciated contributions of African American women in *The Art of Black American Women: Works of Twenty-Four Artists of the Twentieth Century* (McFarland, 1993). Henkes minimizes life stories and focuses on black women's artwork, believing that their work best expresses their voice, integrity, and vision. According to the preface, some artists declined inclusion, preferring universal recognition of their artwork to having it represent a product of ethnic sensibilities. Color and black-and-white illustrations provide a visual repertoire of artwork unlike that produced in other art historical survey texts. Chapters on artists conclude with brief biographies, exhibition histories, and bibliographies.

In his earlier book *American Women Painters of the 1930s and 1940s* (McFarland, 1991), Henkes selects ten depression-era artists who chose to exhibit a "zest for life" in their works as opposed to depicting the tragedies of the times. He supplements the text with black-and-white illustrations and artists' bibliographies.

867. Rosenblum, Naomi. *A History of Women Photographers*. New York: Abbeville Press, 1994. 356p. bibliog. index. ISBN 1558597611.

Although women have actively engaged in photography since its inception in 1839, scholars did not publish major historical surveys of women's work until the 1990s. Rosenblum fills in the gaps through her examination of the connection between women's photography and the underlying economic, social, and cultural conditions of the times; the interaction among women photographers; and the diversity of professional women photographers. The text's chronological arrangement highlights the major periods and developments of the art form, and the author provides several high-quality color and black-and-white reproductions. Peter Palmquist's detailed bibliography of additional resources and informative biographies of featured photographers enhance the text.

Women Photographers (Abrams, 1990), edited by Constance Sullivan with an essay by Eugenia Parry Janis, presents a visual survey of women photographers that features numerous large, high-quality color and black-and-white chronologically arranged photographs. *A Second Look: Women Photographers of the Gernsheim Collection* (Deutsche Fototage, 1993), edited by Andrea Inselmann, features detailed analyses of the work of twelve historically significant artists. The exhibition and catalog *Defining Eye: Women Photographers of the Twentieth Century* (Saint Louis Art Museum, 1997), curated by Olivia Lahs-Gonzales and Lucy Lippard, showcases photos from the Helen Kornblum Collection, which includes the works of an international array of twentieth-century artists who have made significant contributions to the history of photography. The exhibition illustrates how women photographers confront social issues through their work with a distinctive perspective on the human condition. The text includes catalog entries with complete data on each work, several black-and-white and color illustrations, and bibliographies for each artist.

Illuminations: Women Writing on Photography from the 1850s to the Present (Duke University Press, 1996), edited by Liz Heron and Val Williams, demonstrates how women's responses to art widely vary through writings by critics, women historians, biographers, teachers, journalists, and photographers during the course of 150 years. Essays range from nineteenth-century critical commentary by Lady Eastlake and Dorothea Lange's essay on working in photography to analyses of contemporary feminist theory's impact on the art form.

868. Rubinstein, Charlotte Streifer. *American Women Sculptors: A History of Women Working in Three Dimensions*. Boston: G. K. Hall, 1990. 638p. bibliog. index. ISBN 0816187320.

Rubinstein's *American Women Sculptors*, which serves as a companion volume to her earlier work *American Women Artists from Early Indian Times to the Present* (Avon, 1982), is the first publication to address the major accomplishments of women sculptors, despite the fact that they have participated in every significant art movement. Rubinstein contends that even though women sculptors became more visible as a result of the 1970s feminist movement, the general public remains unaware of their long record of achievement. The author includes the creation of three-dimensional forms, such as ceramics, woven forms, and performance, that scholars tend to over-look and eliminates distinctions between art and craft and high and low art, which scholars historically have used to denigrate women's artwork. Rubinstein's chronological survey features the work of African, Asian, Hispanic, and Native Americans and includes an artists' name index.

Virginia Watson-Jones's *Contemporary American Women Sculptors* (Oryx Press, 1986) is a dictionary of American women sculptors of varying ages and backgrounds who have developed distinguished records of production and exhibition. Watson-Jones gathered data from question-naires completed by artists in addition to previously published questionnaires. Entries feature the artist's statement, contact address, education and training information, a list of selected individual and group exhibits, public and private collections of the artist's work, a selected bibliography of additional resources about the artist, and a black-and-white photo of one of her sculptural pieces.

869. Schor, Mira. *Wet: On Painting, Feminism, and Art Culture*. Durham, NC: Duke University Press, 1997. 261p. bibliog. index. ISBN 0822319101; 0822319152pa.

Schor, a former member of the Cal-Arts Feminist Art Program, addresses issues in feminist art criticism and theory in nineteen previously published essays, many of which originally ap-peared in *M/E/A/N/I/N/G*, a journal that she founded. She organizes essays according to themes such as femininity and feminism, teaching, and painting. A twelve-page bibliography supplements the readings.

A special issue of the *Journal of Aesthetics and Art Criticism* resulted in *Feminism and Tradition in Aesthetics* (Pennsylvania State University Press, 1995), edited by Peggy Zeglin Brand and Carolyn Korsmeyer. The book includes a foreword by Arthur Danto and twenty essays by notable authors such as Adrian Piper, Mary Garrard, and bell hooks. Most of the contributors have an academic background in philosophy and discuss issues including "Feminism and the Interpretation of Artworks" and "Feminist Art and the Refusal of Aesthetic Value." Korsmeyer, with Hilde Hein, also edited *Aesthetics in Feminist Perspective* (Indiana University Press, 1993), which explores tensions between essentialism and constructivism as well as other traditional phil-osophical binary pairs. The volume contains essays on the nature of art, music, literature, inter-pretation, and "philosophical and critical legacies" (p. 167).

870. Sinha, Gayatri, ed. *Expressions and Evocations: Contemporary Women Artists of India*. Bombay: Marga Publications, 1996. 172p. bibliog. index. ISBN 8185026343.

Although Sinha covers the last six decades of artistic production in India, the majority of artists featured in this volume have created their most significant works since the 1970s, the decade that marked the turning point for feminism in both India and the West. Most of the featured artists, who hail from diverse backgrounds, do not create consciously feminist artwork, and their work represents disparate themes and concerns. Sinha provides a helpful historical overview of women artists in India, exploring the significant issues, challenges, and successes that these women have experienced. Contributors examine the artwork of fifteen artists whose work spans the earliest signs of modernity to postmodern debate, providing biographical information, critical analyses, and several large-format color illustrations of their work.

Mary-Ann Milford-Lutzker also looks at the achievements of fifteen artists who were active in the fifty years after independence from British colonial rule in *Women Artists of India: A Celebration of Independence* (Mills College Art Gallery, 1997). Milford-Lutzker discusses women's role in Indian art history, the existence of feminist art in India, and the role of political and social commentary in the art of Indian women. She provides concise, factual biographies for each artist included in the exhibition along with color illustrations of their work. Sinha unfortunately profiles approximately half of the artists who appear in Milford-Lutzker's text. Salima Hashmi and Nima Poovaya-Smith's *An Intelligent Rebellion: Women Artists of Pakistan* (City of Bradford Metropolitan Council Arts, Museums, and Libraries Division, 1994), which accompanied an exhibition of the same name, might be of related interest.

871. Slatkin, Wendy. *The Voices of Women Artists*. Englewood Cliffs, NJ: Prentice Hall, 1993. 340p. bibliog. index. ISBN 0139514279pa.

While only two artists, Artemisia Gentileschi and Rosalba Carriera, represent women from 1600 to 1800 and fifteen artists from France, England, America, and Germany cover the years 1800 to 1914, most of the women artists included in Slatkin's edited and excerpted selections of women artists' autobiographical texts represent the years from 1914 to 1985. Slatkin primarily selects the writings of artists whose works significantly contributed to the development of art history, directly relates them to the history of visual arts, and provides insight into the artists' major works. She includes well-known artists such as Georgia O'Keeffe, Frida Kahlo, Louise Nevelson, Judy Chicago, and Faith Ringgold. Slatkin highlights artists' attitudes toward marriage, motherhood, the culturally defined identity of "woman," and artistic creation. The author introduces the readings with short essays on the cultural/social construction of woman and instructs readers on how to read texts that women wrote, such as women's autobiographies. Although few black-and-white illustrations supplement the writings, bibliographic footnotes point to further readings.

Jody Hoy features the autobiographical writings and self-reflections of women in *The Power to Dream: Interviews with Women in the Creative Arts* (Global City, 1995). Hoy spent more than twenty years interviewing women about how they satisfy the demands of their creative will while simultaneously maintaining an intimate life. She begins with a series of in-depth interviews with Anaïs Nin and then gradually moves on to Maxine Hong Kingston, Judy Chicago, Lucy Lippard, Judy Dater, and many others. Brief introductions precede each interview.

872. Spain, Daphne. *Gendered Spaces*. Chapel Hill: University of North Carolina Press, 1992. 294p. bibliog. index. ISBN (OP); 0807843571pa.

Spain approaches her investigation of the relationship among gender, status, and space with the underlying thesis that spatial segregation not only creates a physical distance, but also affects the distribution of knowledge that women use to change their position in society. Spain engages several disciplines, including anthropology, architectural history, labor history, and gender politics, to support her arguments. In her conclusion she proposes possible ways of bringing change to the current structure, especially advocating for spatial integration to redress the distribution of knowledge and balance of power. A lengthy bibliography and appendix explaining the data and methods follow the text.

873. Sterling, Susan Fisher, and National Museum of Women in the Arts (United States). *Women Artists: The National Museum of Women in the Arts.* New York: Abbeville Press, 1995. 319p. index. (OP)

The mission of the National Museum of Women in the Arts is to highlight the work of women artists in all media and educate the public about their achievements. *Women Artists*, the museum's first collection catalog, discusses and features illustrations of 239 out of approximately 500 artworks from the museum's collection (as of 1995). Prints, paintings, photographs, ceramics, and sculptures offer tangible proof of women's artistic accomplishments from the Renaissance to the present. The catalog begins with Alessandra Comini's provocative essay explaining why a separate art museum for women should exist. Contributors chronologically arrange the artists from the seventeenth through the twentieth century, devote a one-page essay to each artist, and include at least one if not several large-format, high-quality color illustrations. Some high-quality black-and-white reproductions accompany the text. A select bibliography and an index of artists' names complete the work, which forms a core publication in any collection about women artists. Abbeville Press reissued the catalog in 1997.

Philippa Glanville identifies and studies women who marked silver and whose works are in the Museum of Women in the Arts in *Women Silversmiths, 1685–1845: Works from the Collection of the National Museum of Women in the Arts* (National Museum of Women in the Arts, 1990). Glanville features many high-quality color and black-and-white illustrations in this exquisite book, which focuses on women smiths of the United Kingdom. A biographical appendix lists more than 300 women silversmiths working between the seventeenth and nineteenth centuries; a collection checklist, a glossary of terms, and a subject index complete the volume.

Susan Waller's anthology *Women Artists in the Modern Era: A Documentary History* (Scarecrow Press, 1991) features more than sixty documents that chronicle the historical experiences of women artists. Selections, which range from the mid-eighteenth-century Enlightenment to the close of the industrial age in the twentieth century, demonstrate how women's gender affected their educational training, opportunities to exhibit, choices of subject and media, and critical reviews. Documents include letters, journals, artists' memoirs, reviews of critics, and minutes and reports of the artists' societies and schools. Waller mostly secured her sources from France, England, and the United States, although she also includes a few sources from Germany and Austria. She thematically and chronologically arranges the writings and supplements the text with a complete bibliography and an index of artists' names.

874. Tucker, Marcia, and New Museum of Contemporary Art. *Bad Girls.* Cambridge, MA: MIT Press, 1994. 144p. bibliog. ISBN 0262700530pa.

This catalog documents a two-part exhibition held at the New Museum of Contemporary Art in New York that featured artists dealing with feminist issues in new and refreshing ways. Tucker uses "bad girl" to describe women artists who defy conventions and proprieties of traditional feminism and challenge audiences to view women as they have existed in the past, live today, and want to be in the future. Tucker focuses her discussion of the artists featured in the exhibit on three concerns: the importance of self-representation in effecting change in status, women's use of humor, and the role of popular culture and mass media in shaping contemporary feminist activity. She supplements lengthy essays that explore these issues with photographs of the artists' works, an exhibition checklist, a list of exhibitions organized around feminist issues from 1990 to 1994, and a lengthy bibliography.

875. Weidner, Marsha, ed. *Flowering in the Shadows: Women in the History of Chinese and Japanese Painting*. Honolulu: University of Hawaii Press, 1990. 315p. bibliog. index. ISBN 0824811496.

The publication of this volume closes the era of the general exclusion of women artists from the histories of Chinese and Japanese art. In this compilation, which is composed of six original and two translated essays from earlier Asian sources, Weidner illuminates many women who were active throughout Japanese and Chinese history as artists as well as influential patrons and collectors. Bibliographic notes, glossaries, and numerous color and black-and-white illustrations accompany the text.

Patricia Fister's catalog *Japanese Women Artists, 1600–1900* (Spencer Museum of Art, 1988) provides an excellent historical survey and discussion of political, social, and economic conditions that shaped the work of Japanese women artists. She analyzes the many contributions of Japanese women artists and explores the concept of "women's style" in Japanese art. The text includes good-quality color and black-and-white illustrations as well as a lengthy bibliography.

A second catalog, *Views from Jade Terrace: Chinese Women Artists, 1300 to 1912* (Indianapolis Museum of Art, 1988), which features essays by Marsha Weidner and others, accompanied the first exhibition devoted to paintings by Chinese women. Unlike the situation in Japan, collectors' catalogs and scholarly texts published before 1900 document the history of women artists in China. Although China has silenced women's art during the twentieth century, this volume introduces nearly fifty artists and their works and features several high-quality color illustrations. This important resource includes essays that provide a historical overview of 600 years of art by women, an index of extant and reproduced paintings by women, a chronology, a glossary of Chinese and Japanese terms, and a selected bibliography of additional readings.

876. Weltge-Wortmann, Sigrid. *Women's Work: Textile Art from the Bauhaus*. San Francisco: Chronicle Books, 1993. 208p. bibliog. index. (OP)

As the study of the Bauhaus has proven, textiles and women have held lowly positions in the hierarchy of art history. Instead of fully integrating them into the Bauhaus, men segregated women, giving them their own workshop called the Weaving Workshop. Although scholars generally recognize the Bauhaus as the foremost design phenomenon of the twentieth century, they have devoted little attention to the Weaving Workshop, the longest-standing and most successful Bauhaus workshop. Weltge-Wortmann addresses this oversight in her text, which contains several high-quality color and black-and-white reproductions, biographical notes, a lengthy bibliography, and a detailed chronology of the Weaving Workshop.

Editor Amanda Wadsley's valuable companion volume *Domesticity and Dissent: The Role of Women Artists in Germany, 1918–1938* (Leicestershire Museums, 1992) explores German women artists of the same period of history, yet focuses on how the contemporary ideal of the "New Woman" affected women's contributions to the art world. Marsha Meskimmon's title essay follows a discussion that provides a general background on Weimar culture. Artists' biographies, catalogs of their work, and illustrations follow the essays.

877. Witzling, Mara R., ed. *Voicing Today's Visions: Writings by Contemporary Women Artists*. London: Women's Press, 1995. 342p. index. (OP)

Witzling reprints previously inaccessible letters, diaries, poems, and essays of twenty women artists of the nineteenth and twentieth centuries in her earlier work, *Voicing Our Visions: Writings by Women Artists* (Women's Press, 1992). She introduces each artist with a black-and-white reproduction of one of her works, includes a brief biography that assesses her achievement, and identifies major artistic themes. A seven-page index cross-references the original documents. In *Voicing Today's Visions*, the author follows the same format, reprinting artists' writings as self-expression. While emphasizing that writings of both genders represent important primary sources, Witzling argues that women artists use their writings to articulate deep sentiments from an isolated and marginalized perspective. She selects readings that address questions of social change, canon reconstruction, the gendered subject, and gender and genre as subjects of women. Witzling introduces each of the fourteen women artists, who were born in the twentieth century, with a black-and-white illustration of her work and then provides a critical biography that places the artist in contemporary art history. Bibliographic notes accompany primary source documents, including letters, poems, diaries, and essays, and a seven-page index cross-references the artists' writings.

Editors Judith Collins and Elsbeth Lindner focus on women writers who discuss women artists in *Writing on the Wall: Women Writers on Women Artists* (Weidenfeld & Nicolson, 1993), which is linked with an exhibit of the same name that invited viewers to create their own literary responses to artworks. The editors asked twenty well-known British women writers to write about their favorite woman artist's work featured in the Tate Gallery. They asked participants to write about 2,000 words, resulting in stories, poems, essays, and reveries.

878. Zegher, M. Catherine de, ed. *Inside the Visible: An Elliptical Traverse of 20th Century Art in, of, and from the Feminine.* Cambridge, MA: MIT Press, 1996. 495p. bibliog. (OP)

This catalog accompanied an exhibition of the works of women artists who explore sexual and racial "otherness." The idea for the exhibition resulted from a study of "women's work" that was executed at a medieval secular convent in Belgium. Curator M. Catherine de Zegher selects the work of thirty-seven artists to reflect the breadth of concerns, diversity of media, and intensity of vision characteristic of twentieth-century women's art. She highlights three distinct periods, the 1930s to the 1940s, the 1960s to the 1970s, and the 1990s, as politically and socially intense times to which women artists responded with great imagination. In more than forty essays, contributors explore the connection between women artists' work and how women develop language outside of patriarchal culture, which, according to Zegher, marks the starting point for understanding women's artwork in the twentieth century. The catalog includes biographical and bibliographic information on the artists, an exhibition checklist, and numerous black-and-white and color illustrations.

Sexual Politics: Judy Chicago's Dinner Party in Feminist Art History (UCLA at the Armand Hammer Museum of Art and Cultural Center in association with University of California Press, 1996), edited by Amelia Jones, is a substantial scholarly catalog that accompanied an exhibition of the same name at the UCLA Art Museum in 1996. Although contributors focus on *The Dinner Party*, Chicago's work represents merely one component of an exhibition composed of more than 100 works by fifty-five artists covering the years 1960 to 1996. The exhibition places *The Dinner Party* within the context of past and current feminist art practice and theory. Copiously illustrated with reproductions of the works of contemporary artists, the catalog includes a very useful feminist chronology spanning from 1945 to 1995, compiled by Laura Meyer.

Music, Dance, and Performance

879. Banes, Sally. *Dancing Women: Female Bodies on Stage*. New York: Routledge, 1998. 279p. bibliog. index. ISBN 0415096715.

This revolutionary and oft-cited study by a prominent dance scholar rewrites traditional nineteenth- and twentieth-century dance history from a feminist perspective. Publication of this text opens new doors of inquiry and invites other dance historians to follow. Banes synthesizes ten years of feminist critical studies covering the Western dance canon: French and Danish romantic ballet, Russian ballet, forerunners of American modern dance and historical modern dance, early modern ballet, and contemporary ballet. Chapters examine topics such as representations of women in dance, choreography as a reflection of cultural attitudes about female identity, and the dance stage as symbolic of attitudes toward women's bodies. Rejecting the concept of "the male gaze," Banes analyzes several dances from a woman-centered perspective in each chapter. This important contribution is recommended for all library collections addressing feminism, theory, and dance and is also available as an e-book through NetLibrary.

Christy Adair's *Women and Dance: Sylphs and Sirens* (New York University Press, 1992) introduces a history of dance from the point of view of gender and positions dance in the center of gender and culture studies. Adair agrees with scholars who insist that feminist cultural studies start with the body and discusses the power of the moving and dancing body as well as cultural repressions of it. Within this framework she looks at the cultural and social elements of women's dance training, representations of women in dance, and achievements of women dancers and choreographers. Numerous black-and-white photos of historical and contemporary dancers and performances accompany essays. This book is recommended for all academic dance and women's studies collections.

880. Bourgeois, Anna Stong. *Blueswomen: Profiles of 37 Early Performers, with an Anthology of Lyrics, 1920–1945*. Jefferson, NC: McFarland, 1996. 176p. bibliog. index. ISBN 0899509630.

Bourgeois profiles important women blues singers from the stated period, known as the flowering of the blues, with concise biographies and a selection of their complete lyrics in this first anthology of women's blues lyrics. These songs were either never copyrighted or lapsed into the public domain. The increasing popularity of women's blues, as evidenced by the release of several recent boxed sets and complete collections, make this a timely study. Appendices include a discography for each featured artist, an index of first lines of songs, and an index of themes.

881. Bufwack, Mary A. *Finding Her Voice: The Saga of Women in Country Music*. New York: Crown Publishers, 1993. 594p. bibliog. index. (OP)

Bufwack weaves fifteen years of research, travel, and interviews into her examination of country music, the art form created by persons whom Tillie Olsen calls "our silenced people." The author traces the roots of country music beyond Nashville and male superstars, exposing early origins of the music of the disenfranchised, overlooked, and ignored. She presents multifarious heroines, voices, stories, and points of view in her discussion of country songs as documents of women's lives, as well as significant sources of information about women's economic, social, and political conditions. She thematically presents copious findings concerning folk music, World War II, rockabilly, protest, working-class pride, and other genres in eighteen chapters. Sidebar graphics with factual details accompany several black-and-white photos. This well-documented, fact-filled, highly accessible, and entertaining text concludes with a thorough and lengthy bibliography in which Bufwack cites both publications and recordings.

882. Buonaventura, Wendy. *Serpent of the Nile: Women and Dance in the Arab World.* New York: Interlink Books, 1990. 207p. bibliog. index. (OP)

The author, a teacher and performer of dance, has written a fascinating history of the art form in the Middle East. She explains that dance was originally connected with religious worship at a time when religion was an integral part of Arabic life. Eventually dance developed into a form of secular entertainment, and professional performers emerged. In the patriarchal Arab world the acceptance of dance was interwoven with the role of women in society and what was forbidden them. The text surveys Arabic dance as a social custom, the history of dance performed by Arabic women for other women, and dance in different social and economic strata of Arabic society. A discussion of costume is supplemented with several illustrations. The book is heavily illustrated with beautiful color reproductions of paintings, etchings, old postcards, and early photographs and includes a very helpful glossary of Arabic terms. The final chapter addresses new directions in Arabic women's dance. This book is appropriate for all dance, women's studies, and international studies collections.

In a useful companion study, *A Trade like Any Other: Female Singers and Dancers in Egypt* (University of Texas Press, 1995), Karin van Nieuwkerk shares many years of historical and ethnographic research. Nieuwkerk hopes to "de-exoticise" the women's entertainment trade in Egypt, in contrast to previous studies of Middle Eastern dance that largely focus on belly dancing and use that single genre as the epitome of the "sensual East." Nieuwkerk focuses her study on a single group: female singers and dancers from lower- and lower-middle-class backgrounds. By doing so, she highlights the contrast in the way female singers and dancers in different social classes are perceived. She investigates concepts of honor, shame, gender, and marginality as reflected in social class and the entertainment trade. In her text female singers and dancers openly discuss their lives and struggles, always under the protection of pseudonyms. Nieuwkerk exposes the plight of Egyptian women who wonder why their art forms cannot be considered "a trade like any other" and draws sympathy to their situation. This highly welcome addition to the literature of women in dance contributes greatly to our understanding of performance, dance, music, gender, and class in Middle Eastern culture. It is highly recommended for libraries collecting in these fields.

883. Champagne, Lenora, ed. *Out from Under: Texts by Women Performance Artists.* New York: Theatre Communications Group, 1990. 185p. ISBN 1559360097pa.

This work features women performance artists or theatrical soloists who write their own material, such as Holly Hughes, Diamanda Galas, Laurie Anderson, Rachel Rosenthal, and Karen Finley. A brief introduction deals with women's special role in performance art and its subversive origins, while the body of the work contains reprinted works of performance art. The postscript chronicles how five artists discussed in the text were recommended to the National Endowment for the Arts for funding; however, the NEA denied support to two of them because of the nature and content of their art.

Contributors examine women performance artists who consistently and effectively criticize social and political conditions in *Angry Women* (RE/Search Publications, 1991), edited by Andrea Juro and V. Vale. The work includes interviews with fifteen women performance artists, many photographs of works, bibliographies, discographies, and videographies.

Peggy Phelan, an instructor in the Department of Performance Studies, Tisch School of the Arts, New York University, includes seven essays with a strongly feminist point of view in *Unmarked: The Politics of Performance* (Routledge, 1993). Although Phelan deals with perform-ance art by both men and women, she focuses on the political aspects of women in performance art. Phelan's scholarly footnotes and extensive bibliography alone could serve as a useful reference tool.

Rebecca Schneider's *The Explicit Body in Performance* (Routledge, 1997) reflects thirty years of research on feminist explicit body performance art. Schneider identifies several recurrent themes: the historical drama of gender and race, women as objects who should be seen and not do the seeing, exposure of desire and commodity capitalism, and a fascination with the sexual body. She examines the individual performance pieces of contemporary women artists, including Carolee Schneemann, Annie Sprinkle, and Linda Montano, to illustrate the complexity of these themes.

884. Davis, Angela Y. *Blues Legacies and Black Feminism: Gertrude "Ma" Rainey, Bessie Smith, and Billie Holiday.* New York: Pantheon Books, 1998. 427p. bibliog. index. ISBN 067945005X.

Although Davis focuses on only three individuals in this study, she documents the many ways in which their large remaining bodies of work represent unacknowledged traditions of black feminist consciousness. Davis juxtaposes the historical developments of the 1920s, 1930s, and 1940s with the recorded performances of Gertrude "Ma" Rainey, Bessie Smith, and Billie Holiday, examining what they reveal about present social consciousness. She notes that because black feminist historical traditions exclude the ideas of poor and working-class women, especially women without means to publish texts, many of these women created a rich cultural legacy through their music. Unfortunately, the majority of literature on blues and jazz women that Davis encountered consists of biographies and technical studies. Davis argues that intellectuals of the Harlem Renaissance overlooked African American women's musical contributions because they embodied sexualities associated with working-class black life, which some Renaissance figures saw as the antithesis of their cultural movement. Davis thus documents how the music of these three women addressed urgent social issues and shaped black consciousness. She organizes the chapters according to themes, such as the politics of blues protests, blues and the black aesthetic, and social implications of love songs. "Ma" Rainey and Bessie Smith's recorded song lyrics, extensive bibliographic notes, and black-and-white photos of Rainey, Smith, and Holiday accompany the text. This work is appropriate for both scholars and fans.

885. Dickerson, James. *Women on Top: The Quiet Revolution That's Rocking the Music Industry.* New York: Billboard Books, 1998. 256p. bibliog. index. ISBN 0823084892.

Starting from the premise that women are transmuting popular music and taking it to a new level, Dickerson discusses genre trends during the last five decades of the twentieth century. He proposes that social and cultural forces made change inevitable in the male-driven music industry. Dickerson analyzes the trajectory of the careers of various women artists from 1954 into the 1990s. The text features statistical charts that provide documented support for Dickerson's thesis, as well as a lengthy bibliography of books and magazine articles.

Dickerson argues that the changes occurring in rock and roll reflect the growth of contemporary feminism in *Angry Women in Rock*, volume 1 (Juno Books, 1996). He discusses a new generation of musicians that includes women and gays, reflects multicultural influences in the larger society, and represents a plurality of social issues, varied forms of artistic expression, and a range of political positions. He structures chapters devoted to individual musicians such as Joan Jett, Chrissie Hynde, and Phranc as informal interviews with Andrea Juno and supplements the text with numerous black-and-white photos, discographies, and equipment lists. The breadth and depth of information of this study make it an important addition to women's studies and music collections.

886. Friedler, Sharon E., and Susan B. Glazer, eds. *Dancing Female: Lives and Issues of Women in Contemporary Dance*. Amsterdam: Harwood Academic Publishers, 1997. 318p. (Choreography and Dance Studies). bibliog. index. ISBN 9057020254; 9057020262pa.

This particular volume of Choreography and Dance Studies focuses on the richness and complexity of women's contributions to dance. The editors present numerous essays that explore the diverse worlds in which women create, teach, perform, and direct dance and that reflect a variety of forms, including African American tap, Andalusian flamenco, and ballet. In the first section, authors utilize background research and interviews to examine lives of women in dance and the ways in which they transmit their art form to the next generation. Authors in the second section address common issues that women in dance face throughout their careers: the female dancer's physicality, the impact of dance on her psychological and spiritual being, and the cultural context in which she works. The text, well illustrated with black-and-white photos of female dancers in performance, is highly recommended for libraries concerned with dance and/or feminist studies.

Lili Cockerille Livingston's *American Indian Ballerinas* (University of Oklahoma Press, 1997) examines the careers of four specific women, Maria Tallchief, Rosella Hightower, Marjorie Tallchief, and Yvonne Chouteau, to demonstrate changes in American ballet during a period of twenty-five years. Each dancer recounts her youth and years on the stage, presenting her version of her greatest achievements and her contributions to the future of dance. Many historical photos of the ballerinas and their performances, as well as a chronology of events in each woman's life, accompany the text. Livingston's study somewhat disappoints because the author does not address the social implications of these four women achieving fame at a time when racial discrimination was tolerated in the United States. This book is recommended for both public and academic library collections.

887. Gaar, Gillian G. *She's a Rebel: The History of Women in Rock and Roll*. Seattle: Seal Press, 1992. 467p. bibliog. index. ISBN 1878067087pa.

Gaar tells the story of the women who shaped rock and pop music, covering the early rhythm and blues singers of the 1950s to the women rappers of the 1990s. She examines girl groups, Motown, folk rock, and punk through a historical review, interviews, and biographies. Gaar not only exposes the frequently accepted premise that female rock performers created a new "trend" in the 1980s as false, but also delineates the broad contributions that women have made to rock history. She supplements the text with a lengthy bibliography of books, articles, and videos; song and album title indexes; and black-and-white photos.

Editor Barbara O'Dair contends that the women's liberation and pro-sex movements set historical precedents for the women's movement in rock in *Trouble Girls: The Rolling Stone Book of Women in Rock* (Random House, 1997). She chronologically arranges the essays, focusing on about 150 individual artists from early rock pioneers moving through the 1950s, 1960s, and 1970s until the present. Discographies, rankings from *Billboard*'s pop charts, photographs, and extensive bibliographies of biographies, autobiographies, and books on music genres, movements, and histories support the discussions.

Simon Reynold and Joe Press's *The Sex Revolts: Gender, Rebellion, and Rock 'n' Roll* (Harvard University Press, 1995) began as a critique of misogyny in rock music, gradually evolved into a survey of images of femininity in rock, and finally emerged as an analysis of male and female rebellions in rock. The authors examine gender and rock in three thematic sections: the male rebel poised against the "feminine," idealized images of women and femininity in rock, and an exploration of the ways in which women rock artists have struggled to create a specifically and uniquely female rebellion within the genre.

888. Garafola, Lynn, ed. *Rethinking the Sylph: New Perspectives on the Romantic Ballet.* Hanover, NH: University Press of New England, 1997. 287p. (Studies in Dance History). bibliog. index. ISBN (OP); 0819563269pa.

During the romantic era of the 1830s and 1840s, ballet was reinvented and became an international movement spanning New York to South America, Europe, and Russia. During this era the ballerina emerged as an icon of femininity: graceful, teasing, mysterious, and the embodiment of female beauty. In this volume recognized dance scholars examine the increasingly central role of female dancers in ballet from a feminist viewpoint. The "feminization" of ballet, demonstrated by the development of strictly female practice, the transfer of the adagio focal point from the male to the female dancer, and the evolution of females playing males' roles changed the way dance was perceived. The text is well illustrated with period engravings and is recommended for academic dance collections.

Elizabeth Aldrich offers another examination of the changing role of women in nineteenth-century dance in *From the Ballroom to Hell: Grace and Folly in Nineteenth-Century Dance* (Northwestern University Press, 1991). In this volume Aldrich presents historical documentation supporting the work of earlier feminist scholars who examined dance as a reflection of sexual politics. She shares primary sources, including reprints from nineteenth-century journals, books, dance manuals, and etiquette manuals that described women's social role and position in terms of dance. This fascinating compilation of materials will contribute to several areas of women's studies and is recommended for all academic libraries.

889. Gourse, Leslie. *Madame Jazz: Contemporary Women Instrumentalists.* New York: Oxford University Press, 1996. 273p. bibliog. index. ISBN 0195106474pa.

Gourse profiles more than twenty-five active contemporary women jazz instrumentalists who are primarily located in New York City, providing biographical information, overviews of the musicians' professional careers, and analyses of their artistic influences. She emphasizes particular obstacles and prejudicial attitudes that have impeded women in jazz and notes the individuals, clubs, and venues that have provided support, encouragement, and opportunity. Reminiscences by female jazz pioneers permit firsthand accounts of the experiences and frustrations endured during the early years of jazz. Successful contemporary jazz artists discuss sources of inspiration and share important lessons. Gourse unfortunately litters the text with highly judgmental and unsupported statements, thereby weakening the value and veracity of the information presented. She supplements the text with black-and-white photos and an appendix of women instrumentalists who were active during the 1980s and 1990s.

890. Groh, Jan Bell. *Evening the Score: Women in Music and the Legacy of Frédérique Petrides.* Fayetteville: University of Arkansas Press, 1991. 138p. bibliog. index. (OP)

This study features reprints of the groundbreaking newsletter *Women in Music*, which Frédérique Petrides edited and published from 1935 to 1945, along with explanatory textual annotations, many black-and-white photos of women musicians, and a biography of Petrides. *Women in Music* played a key role in expanding the participation of women in the professional music world. Mid-nineteenth-century European and American society saw the harp and piano as the only "ladylike" instruments, making women violinists rare; however, by the turn of the century, society deemed the violin and viola acceptable instruments for women. Segregated musical ensembles were the norm until World War II, when society permitted women to fill positions vacated by men who left for military service. Petrides, a conductor, tirelessly lectured, frequently appeared on radio talk shows, and wrote several letters to expose prejudice against women in music. In 1935 she began her *Women in Music* newsletter, the first and only publication in the history of music journalism to examine the little-known history of women conductors, instrumentalists, and orchestras. Groh provides an appendix that reprints Petrides' 1935 article "Outline of Prejudice" as well as a helpful subject index to the newsletter.

891. Halstead, Jill. *The Woman Composer: Creativity and the Gendered Politics of Musical Composition.* Brookfield, VT: Ashgate, 1997. 286p. bibliog. index. ISBN 1859281834.

Halstead argues that scholars must study women's contributions to musical composition in terms of women's wider position in a society, wherein they lack tradition, value, authority, and power. Rather than using the traditional methodology of studying artists' lives and works, the author examines the psychological and cultural theories, social and musical systems, and traditions that have created the woman composer's current status. Halstead divides the work into three sections: psychology, education and social history, and the gendered politics of music. She examines historical arguments against female creativity and musical ability through a cross-disciplinary review of biological, neurological, psychological, and anthropological research in part 1. In part 2 she focuses on the social and educational factors that continue to affect women composers in the twentieth century, concentrating on the lives, education, and experiences of a highly diverse group of nine British women composers. Halstead analyzes the basic polarity of gender upon which society is constructed in part 3. She supplements the text with a twenty-two-page bibliography that features unpublished material, personal correspondence, taped interviews, and scholarly texts. This work would prove valuable to undergraduate and graduate students and music professionals.

892. Herndon, Marcia, and Suzanne Ziegler, eds. *Music, Gender, and Culture.* New York: F. Noetzel, 1990. 307p. (Intercultural Music Studies). bibliog. index. ISBN 3795905931.

The first publication by the Music and Gender Study Group of the International Council for Traditional Music, this collection of fifteen essays represents an eclectic mix of disciplines, such as ethnomusicology, popular music studies, and music technology. Short introductions accompany four thematic sections: implications of gender on change, construction of self through life stories, the performative nature of gender, and gendering of music technology. The unifying subtext of this anthology is the clarification of each author's positions on gender and music vis-à-vis her own work as it changed and developed over time.

In *Cecilia Reclaimed: Feminist Perspectives on Gender and Music* (University of Illinois Press, 1994), editors Susan C. Cook and Judy S. Tsou present an anthology of essays by music scholars who reposition gender as the central focus in their particular areas of study. Contributors claiming that gender influences all aspects of music history, reexamine questions considered long resolved and reject restrictive definitions such as Western and non-Western or high and popular culture. Topics include images of women in rap music, women's performance traditions, gender in balladry, and women in the history of English, Venetian, and French music. Lengthy bibliographic footnotes and biographical material about the authors accompany each essay.

Musicologist Susan McClary, in *Feminine Endings: Music, Gender, and Sexuality* (University of Minnesota Press, 1991), employs feminist critical theory to pursue new questions about music. Her essays focus on five issues usually neglected in traditional studies: musical constructions of gender and sexuality, gendered aspects of traditional music theory, gender and sexuality in musical narrative, music as a gendered discourse, and discursive strategies of women musicians. All of these titles belong in any academic music or women's studies collection.

893. Jezic, Diane. *Women Composers: The Lost Tradition Found.* New York: Feminist Press at the City University of New York, 1988. 250p. (OP)

In the preface of this work Jezic declares her dismay at discovering that as late as 1985 the three leading music appreciation textbooks excluded women composers. Rapid growth in feminist scholarship between 1988 and 1994 required publication of a second edition (Feminist Press at the City University of New York, 1994) of *Women Composers,* in which Jezic updates publication, recording, and biographical information for a third of the composers. She includes a new appendix of publishers specializing in women's music and corrects typographical and factual errors as well. The author discusses twenty-five composers in chronological order, ranging from Hildegard of Bingen (1098–1179) to Judith Lang Zaimont (b. 1945), situating the lives and works of women composers in the communities within which they worked while emphasizing the reconsideration of periodicity. Jezic provides biographical and historical documentation to encourage teachers to inquire into women composers from a broader, feminist stance. Six valuable indexes accompany the text's biographical and historical information. The first index features a listing of music appreciation textbooks ranked in order of the number of women composers mentioned. Finally, Jezic includes lists of record companies featuring women composers, selected publishers featuring women composers, and selected twentieth-century women conductors. Two sound cassettes with musical recordings were issued in 1988 for readers to use in conjunction with the text.

894. O'Brien, Lucy. *She Bop: The Definitive History of Women in Rock, Pop, and Soul.* New York: Penguin Books, 1996. 464p. bibliog. index. ISBN 0140251553pa.

O'Brien recognizes that women historically have played a significant role in the construction of modern-day pop, from blues to rock and roll. She argues that women always have positioned themselves at the center of popular music cults and mass marketing, from blues women whose artistry appealed to vaudeville audiences to female singers who sold big-band music to mass followings. O'Brien also examines how women have created pop in their own image. During a ten-year period the author conducted more than 200 interviews in the United States and Great Britain and consulted countless secondary sources. She organizes the material according to themes, trends, and genres, analyzing topics such as areas of power for women in pop, the singer/songwriter genre, female world-music artists, women who have directed political protests through music, women in the music industry, and women as consumers of rock, pop, and soul.

Editor Lee Fleming's *Hot Licks: Lesbian Musicians of Note* (Gynergy Books, 1996) is the first anthology devoted entirely to lesbian musicians. Twenty-three profiles featuring photos, lyrics, brief biographical data, and discographies document contemporary lesbian solo and group performers in folk, blues, salsa, rock, pop, and country. Written in an easily accessible format, *Hot Licks* supplements other works about women in contemporary popular music with emphasis on lesbians. Editor Sarah Cooper assembles twelve essays of uneven depth and value written by journalists, fans, academics, and women in the music industry about women in pop, rock, jazz, classical music, and opera in *Girls! Girls! Girls! Essays on Women and Music* (New York University Press, 1996).

895. Pendle, Karin, ed. *Women and Music: A History*. Bloomington: Indiana University Press, 1991. 358p. bibliog. index. ISBN 0253343216; 025321422Xpa.

This historical survey of women's participation in music performance, composition, teaching, and patronage from ancient Greece through the 1980s is designed as a supplementary text to titles traditionally used in undergraduate music history courses, especially *Historical Anthology of Music by Women* (Indiana University Press, 1987), edited by James R. Briscoe, and its accompanying set of three audiocassettes (1991). Through fifteen well-referenced essays Pendle exposes students to scholarship by noted authorities about women from all historical periods in Western music since notation came into use. A general bibliography of books and articles about the history of women in music follows the essays, and a printed list of recordings cites music provided on Briscoe's cassettes.

In *Rediscovering the Muses: Women's Musical Traditions* (Northeastern University Press, 1993), edited by Kimberly Marshall, eleven essays address the fact that standard musical histories have excluded women, at least in part because of scholarly bias toward notated music. These essays favor musical cultures, such as Australian Aboriginals, ancient Egypt and Israel, classical Greece, and the Byzantine Empire, that have left little notated music. By reconstructing the active role played by women, the essays uncover rich musical traditions in diverse cultures.

In the revised edition of *Women in Music: An Anthology of Source Readings from the Middle Ages to the Present* (Northeastern University Press, 1996), editor Carol Neuls-Bates presents contemporary accounts of women musicians and training opportunities available to them, as well as prescriptive literature that dictated to women their proper roles in music. Introductions place readings in their historical and cultural contexts. *Women and Music in Cross-Cultural Perspective* (Greenwood Press, 1987), edited by Ellen Kosskoff, supplements all of these readings with an emphasis on the history and criticism of women in folk music.

896. Post, Laura. *Backstage Pass: Interviews with Women in Music*. Norwich, VT: New Victoria Publishers, 1997. 222p. ISBN 0934678847pa.

Post defines the boundaries of "women's music" through performance at women's festivals, presence in women's music markets, artists' self-definition, or audience definitions in this collection of interviews with forty active artists or groups in contemporary women's music. Post's training as a psychiatrist brings insight, honesty, and directness to her brief yet informative and entertaining interviews. Selected artists range from "mothers" of women's music, including Ronnie Gilbert and Alix Dobkin, to rocker Marianne Faithfull and new-wave singer Ani DiFranco. Each interview concludes with a discography of the artist's works.

Bonnie J. Morris chronicles the origins of women's festival culture based on her attendance at women's music festivals during a seventeen-year period in *Eden Built by Eves: The Culture of Women's Music Festivals* (Alyson Publications, 1999). Morris relied on her collection of photographs, tape recordings, documents, and notebooks to craft this book, which features interviews with prominent festival organizers. She examines matriarchal structure, questions why people fear matriarchal communities, and discusses political and social controversies and generational shifts in relation to women's music. Interviews with festival performers and excerpts of feminist comedians' stage routines re-create the experience of women's music festivals. She provides a list of U.S. festivals with their founding year, contact addresses for current and ongoing festivals, and names and addresses of women's music distributors. A bibliography of books pertaining to festivals, women's cultures, and women's music scores, a lexicon of festival slang and terminology, and selected first-person responses to a survey of more than 800 festival attendees conducted during a ten-year period conclude the text. Morris's articles on this topic have appeared in *Hot Wire: The Journal of Women's Music and Culture.*

897. Roberts, Robin. *Ladies First: Women in Music Videos.* Jackson: University Press of Mississippi, 1996. 218p. bibliog. index. ISBN 0878059334; 0878059342pa.

Roberts posits that record companies primarily produce music videos because of the creation of a marketable self. She argues that feminist videos demonstrate how one can transform advertising, which society traditionally has used for misogynist and sexist purposes, into a feminist tool by promoting a strong female image. Roberts quotes studies indicating that music videos have become a particularly strong social construction for both women and minorities. She describes how music videos communicate with their audience on three levels: music, images, and music and image combined. Roberts arranges her discussion of music videos by genre and theme and supplements the text with a twenty-five-minute video recording of the same title. Extensive bibliographic footnotes, an eleven-page bibliography of additional source material, a short videography, and a subject index accompany the text. E. Ann Kaplan's *Rocking around the Clock: Music Television, Postmodernism, and Consumer Culture* (Methuen, 1987) and Lisa A. Lewis's *Gender Politics and MTV: Voicing the Difference* (Temple University Press, 1990) also address music videos.

898. Shapiro, Sherry B., ed. *Dance, Power, and Difference: Critical and Feminist Perspectives on Dance Education.* Champaign, IL: Human Kinetics, 1998. 194p. bibliog. index. ISBN 0880117478pa.

Shapiro, an educator, dancer, and choreographer, proposes that cultural and aesthetic assumptions determine how we think about dance, and how dance is taught, researched, and critiqued. She further asserts that these assumptions, being Eurocentric, patriarchal, racist, and classist, are misleading and detrimental and should no longer be a part of educational systems. To this purpose, dance educators from around the world borrow social, cultural, and critical theories from other disciplines to deconstruct the educational traditions of dance. The text is divided into three sections: questions concerning curriculum, pedagogy, research, power, gender, and identity; personal, autobiographical accounts exploring broader issues of interdisciplinary, multicultural dance education; and the role of dance in social politics and as a tool of empowerment for disenfranchised populations. This book would be a useful addition to academic libraries concerned with philosophy of education, feminist theory, feminist cultural studies, and dance.

Of related interest is Lucy Green's *Music, Gender, Education* (Cambridge University Press, 1997), the first book to focus on education in relation to gender and music. Through ethnographic methodology the author examines interactions of boys, girls, and their teachers to a wide range of musical styles, from classical to jazz to popular music. Believing that the school music classroom serves as a microcosm of society, Green concludes that music education is a continuation of gendered musical practices, and she proposes specific interventions in the music curriculum.

899. Story, Rosalyn M. *And So I Sing: African-American Divas of Opera and Concert.* New York: Warner Books, 1990. 236p. bibliog. ISBN 0446710164.

Story rescues the lost legacies of nineteenth- and twentieth-century black divas from obscurity to tell the stories of the greatest black women in opera. Determined to write the first book on this topic, Story invested many years interviewing vocal artists and composers in addition to scouring research libraries, opera archives, newspaper files, and special collections. The author did not intend for the resulting book to serve as a comprehensive encyclopedia: she deliberately narrowed her coverage to those women who emerged from the American social system to achieve greatness, especially those who played a pivotal role in the struggle for civil rights. Story chronicles black women singers beginning with those who shed the chains of slavery, because according to the author, the history of the black diva begins well before Marian Anderson broke the color barrier at the Metropolitan Opera in the mid-1950s. Story devotes less attention to younger stars in the final chapter, "Voices of a New Generation."

900. Stuart, Andrea. *Showgirls*. London: J. Cape, 1996. 242p. bibliog. index. ISBN 0224036157.

Until the publication of this book, the showgirl, one of the most recognized female icons of the modern era, was neglected in critical study. In this very informative study Stuart decodes the contexts in which the showgirl flourished, charts her development, and restores the icon to her place in cultural studies. A meticulous social history of the icon is presented through biographies of six famous showgirls, including Josephine Baker, Mae West, and Marlene Dietrich. Each chapter, devoted to a different showgirl, presents the particular showgirl as a social, political, and economic barometer of her time. Stuart closes with an examination of the fate of the showgirl after World War II, when a shift from femme fatale to docile victim reflected the need of returning soldiers to reassert their role in the workforce and in the family. The text is supplemented with thirty-two black-and-white photographic plates of the most famous showgirls. This book is highly recommended for library collections concerned with feminist history, dance, music, and entertainment.

901. Thomas, Helen, ed. *Dance, Gender, and Culture*. New York: St. Martin's Press, 1993. 219p. bibliog. index. ISBN (OP); 0312124856pa.

Thomas gathers diverse points of view in exploring how dance and gender intersect in cultural contexts and presents original chapters representing many areas of study. More than half of the chapters concentrate on women in dance, some employing feminist theory as a tool of analysis. The anthology is divided into three broad sections: cultural studies, ethnography, and theory and criticism. Bibliographic notes and references accompany each essay, and black-and-white photos illustrate the text. This book is recommended for all academic humanities, social sciences, and fine arts collections.

Gender in Performance: The Presentation of Difference in the Performing Arts, edited by Laurence Senelick (University Press of New England, 1992), is similar in purpose. This anthology of essays by notable writers resulted from the 1988 Salzburg Seminar on Gender in the Humanities. Although the text as a whole is not exclusively about women or feminist theory and dance, a large section of the book, "Revising Women," provides a new look at the roles and contributions of women in dance and performance. The wide range of periods discussed makes the book a useful reader for courses in theater, women's studies, and dance.

Judith Lynn Hanna's *Dance, Sex, and Gender: Signs of Identity, Dominance, Defiance, and Desire* (University of Chicago Press, 1988) also is not exclusively about women in dance. Hanna questions if men and women produce and perform dance differently because of anatomy and physiology or because of culture and cognition. An interesting appendix of coding variables for gender patterns in dance concludes the text. Hanna draws on psychological, anthropological, and semiotic theory to create a text highly recommended for dance and women's studies collections.

In a fascinating first book, *Gestures of Genius: Women, Dance, and the Body* (Mercury, 1994), dancer Rachel Vigier discusses how the presence of sex-role definitions in dance and the evolution of dance as a muscular activity have caused women to be "terrorized out of our bodies." Vigier examines the contributions of Isadora Duncan, Leonora Carrington, Zelda Fitzgerald, and the poet H.D. to take the reader on a journey that casts women's bodies and movement in a new light. Interviews with ten women dancers and members of a women's dance collective conclude the book. The text is supplemented with a black-and-white photo essay of diverse women in acts of dance. This book is highly recommended for all dance, physical education, and women's studies collections.

1999 CORE TITLES

Barkin, Elaine, and Lydia Hamessley, eds. *Audible Traces: Gender, Identity, and Music*. Los Angeles: Carciofoli, 1999. 358p. plus one sound disc. bibliog. index. ISBN 3905323001; 390532301Xpa.

Barlow, Margaret. *Women Artists*. New York: Hugh Lauter Levin Associates, 1999. 328p. index. (OP)

Bloom, Lisa. *With Other Eyes: Looking at Race and Gender in Visual Culture*. Minneapolis: University of Minnesota Press, 1999. 268p. bibliog. index. ISBN 0816632227; 0816632235pa.

Chicago, Judy, and Edward Lucie-Smith. *Women and Art: Contested Territory*. New York: Watson-Guptill Publications, 1999. 192p. index. ISBN 0823058522.

Farris-Dufrene, Phoebe, ed. *Women Artists of Color: A Bio-Critical Sourcebook to Twentieth-Century Artists in the Americas*. Westport, CT: Greenwood Press, 1999. 496p. bibliog. index. ISBN 0313303746.

Henkes, Robert. *Latin American Women Artists of the United States: The Works of 33 Twentieth-Century Women*. Jefferson, NC: McFarland, 1999. 245p. bibliog. index. ISBN 0786405198.

Hillstrom, Laurie Collier, and Kevin Hillstrom, eds. *Contemporary Women Artists*. Detroit: St. James Press, 1999. 760p. bibliog. index. ISBN 1558623728.

Kerr, Joan and Jo Holder, eds. *Past Present: The National Women's Art Anthology*. Sydney, Australia: Craftsman House, 1999. bibliog. index. ISBN 9057041413.

Kintanar, Thelma B., and Sylvia Mendez Ventura. *Self-Portraits: Twelve Filipina Artists Speak*. Quezon City, Philippines: Ateneo de Manila University Press, 1999. 220p. bibliog. index. ISBN 9715503225.

Kreisel, Martha. *American Women Photographers: A Selected and Annotated Bibliography*. Westport, CT: Greenwood Press, 1999. 368p. (Art Reference Collection, no. 18). index. ISBN 0313304785.

Lloyd, Fran, ed. *Contemporary Arab Women's Art: Dialogues of the Present.* London: Women's Art Library, 1999. 259p. bibliog. index. ISBN 1902770005.

Newman, Marilyn Stephanie Mercedes. *The Comprehensive Catalogue of Duet Literature for Female Voices: Vocal Chamber Duets with Keyboard Accompaniment Composed between 1820–1995.* Lanham, MD: Scarecrow Press, 1999. 572p. bibliog. index. ISBN 0810836475.

Pollock, Griselda. *Differencing the Canon: Feminist Desire and the Writing of Art's Histories.* New York: Routledge, 1999. 345p. bibliog. index. ISBN 0415066999; 0415067006pa.

Sullivan, Mairéid. *Celtic Women in Music: A Celebration of Beauty and Sovereignty.* Kingston, Ontario: Quarry Press, 1999. 255p. bibliog. ISBN 1550822462pa.

WORLD WIDE WEB/INTERNET SITES

902. *National Museum of Women in the Arts (NMWA).* http://www.nmwa.org.
     The National Museum of Women in the Arts recognizes the achievements of women artists of all periods and nationalities and acquires, exhibits, and fosters research on art made by women. The collection includes more than 650 artists. The Web site provides a virtual tour of the museum collection, information on special events, and access to the museum's library and research center.

903. *University of Texas Center for Women's Studies: Dance, Performance Studies, and Theater.* http://www.utexas.edu/depts/wstudies/publications/wslist/dance.html.
     The University of Texas Center for Women's Studies has compiled and made available a comprehensive yet selected reading and resource list of materials concerning women in dance, performance studies, and theater.

904. *Women Artists Archive.* http://libweb.sonoma.edu/special/waa.
     The Women Artists Archive, which is located in the University Library at Sonoma State University, contains information about more than 1,400 women artists from the Middle Ages to the present. The Web site accesses a gallery of images, links to other Web sites, and the *Women Artists Archive* database, which browsers can search by name, century, ethnicity, movement, and/ or medium.

905. *Women Artists: Curriculum and Web Resources.* http://www.getty/artsednet/ resources/Women/index.html.
     A wonderfully rich site maintained by ArtsEdNet of the J. Paul Getty Trust, this resource consists of two parts. The first section, "Curriculum Resources on ArtsEdNet," provides links to existing lesson plans and curriculum ideas about women artists. The second part, "Web Resources," contains links to other Web sites about women artists and their work.

906. *Women Composers and Women's Music.* http://www.music.indiana.edu/music _resources/women/html.

The William and Gayle Cook Music Library of the Indiana University School of Music maintains this valuable site, which provides several links to important resources such as "Women in Music: Reference Tools," "Women Composers: A Bibliography of Internet Resources," and more.

12 Autobiography, Biography, Diaries, Memoirs, and Letters

Linda A. Krikos

Scholars in women's studies have challenged assumptions of traditional biography, which they characterize as focusing on lives of "great" men of exceptional achievement. They question the private/public divide by including details about subjects such as sexuality that reveal the relevance of the personal to biography studies, thereby contradicting the idea that only public matters make someone a worthy subject for a biography. In contrast to the belief in the biographer's impartiality, women's studies biographers acknowledge that their own background and research process influence the perspective(s) of their particular work.

Introductions in many of the biographies in this chapter provide instructive overviews of various theories of biography. With regard to autobiography, diaries, letters, and other personal writings, feminist scholars recognize that each writer is situated within a specific time and social context, tempered by her race, class, ethnicity, religion, and geographic location. They consider personal accounts important primary sources that provide access to real women's thoughts, feelings, and knowledge. Women's studies research in biography and autobiography has produced insightful, critical examinations of subjectivity, self-representation, agency, identity formation, and the authority of women's voices.

The titles in this chapter discuss various forms of personal writing and reflect the diversity and range of women's lived experiences and voices. Please see chapter 15, "Literature," for titles that examine biography and autobiography as genres.

REFERENCE SOURCES

907. Adamson, Lynda G. *Notable Women in World History: A Guide to Recommended Biographies and Autobiographies.* Westport, CT: Greenwood Press, 1998. 401p. bibliog. index. ISBN 0313298181.

In compiling this informative bibliography, Adamson features women who met the following criteria: birth outside the United States, noteworthy achievement, and full-length biography (or autobiography, letters, or diaries) published in English since 1970 that is listed in the Library of Congress catalog. Entries for 500 women include name(s), dates, country of birth, and field of endeavor followed by brief biographical information focusing on family background, education, career, and achievements or awards. Each entry concludes with a list of no more than five biographical sources, which Adamson briefly describes. Appendices list the women chronologically, by country of birth, and by field. Since Adamson arranges entries alphabetically by name, the name index seems redundant but allows users to find all references to specific entrants. The source works as both a biographical dictionary and a guide to biographical titles and should be helpful for basic research.

908. Cline, Cheryl. *Women's Diaries, Journals, and Letters: An Annotated Bibliography.* New York: Garland, 1989. 716p. (Garland Reference Library of the Humanities, v. 780). indexes. ISBN 0824066375.

Cline compiles entries for nearly 3,000 personal writings, focusing on titles published in English, with selected writings in French, German, Polish, Spanish, and other languages. Though not stated, dates of coverage appear to be the early 1800s through 1985. Cline provides a lengthy introduction discussing different forms of personal writings, women's contributions to life writing, and life writing as a literary form. She arranges entries alphabetically by author, includes full citation information, and briefly describes the contents of the works. The book contains several indexes that list authors by profession, subject, location (country), and title and enhance access to the writings. Researchers should find the profession and subject indexes particularly helpful. The location index, however, dumps hundreds of entries under the United States, England, and France without subdivisions. Nevertheless, this is an important and time-saving bibliography.

For an emphasis on American women, see *The Published Diaries and Letters of American Women: An Annotated Bibliography* (G. K. Hall, 1987), compiled by Joyce D. Goodfriend, which begins coverage in 1669 and continues to 1985. *Personal Writings by Women to 1900: A Bibliography of American and British Writers* (Mansell, 1989), compiled by Gwenn Davis and Beverly A. Joyce, lists autobiographies, letters, diaries, and travel commentaries included in the Library of Congress and the British Library catalogs, supplemented by the OCLC database and standard biographies, bibliographies, and other sources. The three titles overlap somewhat, but each provides coverage that the other two do not.

909. *International Who's Who of Women: A Biographical Reference Guide to the Most Eminent and Distinguished Women in the World.* London: Europa, 1992. 553p. index. (OP)

In an attempt to address the dearth of women in other who's who publications, this volume presents biographical and career information for nearly 5,000 women from around the world representing a variety of fields. It contains standard information typical of these publications, including surname, first name and title(s), honors, degrees earned, nationality, profession, place and date of birth, personal history (marriages, children, and so on), education, career history, titles of major works or accomplishments, and contact information (often for a publisher or agent). Unlike many other who's who publications, this title includes a career index that lists the women, along with their nationalities and specific occupations, by seventeen broad categories, including academics, art, broadcasting and journalism, diplomacy, economics, fashion, law, science, sports, and religion. An index listing the women by nationality would have further enhanced the volume. The dictionary lives up to its subtitle by providing information on women deserving recognition, unlike some questionable works that include anyone willing to answer a questionnaire and buy a copy of the book. This source could be useful as a starting point for research. Europa published a second edition in 1997.

910. Ireland, Norma Olin. *Index to Women of the World from Ancient to Modern Times: A Supplement.* Metuchen, NJ: Scarecrow Press, 1988. 774p. bibliog. ISBN 0810820927.

A companion volume to Ireland's *Index to Women of the World from Ancient to Modern Times: Biographies and Portraits* (Faxon, 1970), this title includes new biographies as well as new sources for the biographies in the original publication. Arranged alphabetically, each entry provides name(s), dates, nationality, and occupation followed by symbol(s) representing the 380 collective biographies used to compile the index. As in the first edition, Ireland covers all periods of history all over the world. Since inclusion in the index is based on "accomplishment alone" (p. ix), she mentions blind and/or deaf women but chooses not to identify women by race/ethnicity. Though both of Ireland's indexes emphasize popular books, they provide broader coverage than most other titles.

Katharine Phenix in her book *Subject Guide to Women in the World* (Scarecrow Press, 1996) lists the more than 24,000 women from Ireland's volumes by occupation or subject, supplemented by a geographic index that lists the women by country and, occasionally, city. This guide adds significant access to Ireland's indexes and is essential for collections owning either of these publications.

911. Sweeney, Patricia F. *Biographies of American Women: An Annotated Bibliography.* Santa Barbara, CA: ABC-CLIO, 1990. 290p. index. (OP)

This bibliography lists and describes 1,391 English-language biographies of 700 American women, representing a variety of eras and fields of endeavor. It includes books, memoirs, and portraits written by family members and friends, evaluative books on careers or work, and doctoral dissertations that date from the early 1800s through 1990. Arranged alphabetically by the name of the subject, entries provide dates and full bibliographic information for the biographies. Brief but useful annotations describe each book's scope, special features, methodology, and strengths or weaknesses. Sweeney also provides cross-references to name variations and pseudonyms, colleagues, relatives, and other people associated with the subject. An appendix lists the women under fifty fields from abolitionists to war heroines and patriots. It includes an entry for Native American women but unfortunately does not include entries for African American, Asian, or Hispanic women. An index of authors and titles completes the volume.

Sweeney also compiled *Biographies of British Women: An Annotated Bibliography* (Garland, 1994), which lists 2,014 biographies about 700 women who lived from the 1600s through 1992. This title mirrors the arrangement and features of the American volume.

912. Uglow, Jennifer S., and Frances Hinton, eds. *The Continuum Dictionary of Women's Biography.* New expanded ed. New York: Continuum, 1989. 621p. bibliog. index. (OP)

A revision of the award-winning title *The International Dictionary of Women's Biography* (Continuum, 1982), this edition adds 250 entries covering more than 1,700 women from all time periods and cultures and revises and expands entries that appeared in the 1982 edition. As in the first edition, alphabetically arranged entries provide name(s), dates, nationality, and brief descriptions about contributions. Rather than provide sources with each entry, Uglow provides an extensive list of general, national, and women-specific sources. She also includes a subject index listing the women by four broad fields of accomplishment, each with several subdivisions.

Lesser-Known Women: A Biographical Dictionary (Lynne Rienner, 1992), compiled by Beverly E. Golemba, concentrates on the unrecognized achievements of women beginning in the year 1600. Golemba uses a chronological arrangement but provides indexes for names, countries, and professions and a bibliography listing almost 800 sources. Both of these titles provide badly needed broad historical coverage on women and their accomplishments.

MONOGRAPHS

913. Adams, Jerome R. *Notable Latin American Women: Twenty-Nine Leaders, Rebels, Poets, Battlers, and Spies, 1500–1900.* Jefferson, NC: McFarland, 1995. 191p. bibliog. index. ISBN 0786400226.

Adams scoured many histories, articles, and bibliographies written in Spanish, Portuguese, and English to find accounts of individual women in the history of Latin America. The resulting stories begin during the period of conquest and continue through the wars for independence. The book includes Indian women as well as women from Peru, Mexico, Brazil, Chile, and other countries and stresses the importance of women leaders and fighters. The biographies are presented in chronological order, and each is approximately six pages long. Adams usually attempts to provide some political, social, cultural, and historical context and includes translations from many of the women's letters, poetry, or other writings, which add depth to the narratives.

Bobette Gugliotta in her book *Women of Mexico: The Consecrated and the Commoners, 1519–1900* (Floricanto, 1989) presents short biographies of businesswomen, nuns, translators, transvestites, and ordinary women who were catapulted by extraordinary circumstances to become leaders in Mexico's history. Gugliotta provides historical context for each biography, including quite useful descriptions of costumes and artistic renderings. Like Adams, Gugliotta uses many primary and secondary sources in Spanish but mars some of her accounts with imagined dialogue and thoughts. The books overlap somewhat, but both provide badly needed historical accounts in English of the lives of historical Latin American women.

914. Adler, Kathleen, and Tamar Garb. *Berthe Morisot*. Ithaca, NY: Cornell University Press, 1987. 128p. bibliog. index. (OP)

One of the first English-language studies of artist Berthe Morisot, this book corrects inaccuracies about the artist's life and work. It especially debunks the belief that Morisot's painting style was "natural" for a woman. Adler and Garb, both established feminist art historians, focus on obstacles Morisot, as an upper-middle-class woman, faced to become an artist, the motivations behind her desire to paint, and how she "reconciled" her public and private lives. They examine how gender affected the subject matter of Morisot's paintings, the critical reception of the artist's work, and connections to other artists, especially the impressionists.

Anne Higonnet's critical biography *Berthe Morisot* (Harper & Row, 1990) also examines contradictions between Morisot's gender and profession within the context of the French Third Republic. Higonnet believes that the freedom of impressionist painting provided room for Morisot to paint from a feminine point of view, develop her own style, and compete on her own terms. *Berthe Morisot: Impressionist* (Hudson Hills Press; distributed by Rizzoli, 1987) by Charles F. Stuckey, William P. Scott, and Suzanne G. Lindsay provides a comprehensive biography of Morisot and her role in the impressionist movement. It includes an appendix that discusses the artist's technical procedures and 123 excellent color plates and 116 black-and-white illustrations, including all of Morisot's exhibition pieces.

915. Alexander, Meena. *Fault Lines: A Memoir*. New York: Feminist Press, 1993. 226p. (Cross-Cultural Memoir Series). ISBN 1558610588; 1558610596pa.

Alexander uses the term "fault lines" to represent the crack of dislocation and shifts between present and past. Born in India to a Syrian Christian family, the author, during the course of her life, also lived in the Sudan, England, and Manhattan, uprooted so many times that she felt connected to nothing. Alexander shares childhood stories about the fear of being born female, discusses the anguish of being torn between the intellectual achievement prized by her father and the traditional feminine life advocated by her mother, and describes the essential role poetry has played in her quest to create and sustain herself and live as a woman. This beautifully written memoir provides insight into connections between postcolonial life and ethnicity in America. In another title in the series, *I Dwell in Possibility: A Memoir* (Feminist Press, 1991), author Toni McNaron talks about growing up white in segregated Alabama. Although she describes the spiritual strength she received from her mother, her attempts to live up to ideals of southern femininity, alcoholism, coming out as a lesbian, and her passion for teaching and literature, she frames her story around her growing awareness of race and racism. She was an eyewitness to brutal suppressions of attempts to integrate the University of Alabama and public parks in Birmingham. The book sheds light on the many ways in which culture shapes an individual and the myriad obstacles an individual faces when attempting to make changes. The Cross-Cultural Memoir Series publishes works by women of various racial and ethnic backgrounds living in America.

916. Angelou, Maya. *All God's Children Need Traveling Shoes*. New York: Random House, 1986. 210p. (OP)

In this installment of Angelou's serial autobiography, the author talks about the years she spent living in Ghana during the early 1960s. Whether writing about her son's car accident and his growing maturity, people she meets, experiences she has, or visitors such as Malcolm X, Angelou writes honestly and poetically. Most poignant is her account of a visit to a village where the inhabitants' facial features and voice tone match her own. While she does not elaborate on the emotional impact of these experiences as fully as in her previous autobiographies, Angelou aptly conveys her longing for freedom and "home" and the immense dignity of African people who still mourn those lost generations ago. Random House issued a reprinted volume in 1997.

917. Bair, Deirdre. *Simone de Beauvoir: A Biography*. New York: Summit Books/Simon & Schuster, 1990. 718p. bibliog. index. ISBN (OP); 0671741802pa.

Bair, a National Book Award winner for her biography of Samuel Beckett, bases this work on a series of interviews with Simone de Beauvoir that took place between 1980 and 1986. As she discusses Beauvoir's life, Bair provides historical, political, and social contexts, since she believes that these are critical to truly understanding Beauvoir's intellectual development and evolution. Particularly interesting are discussions of the circumstances surrounding Beauvoir when she wrote such major works as *The Mandarins* and *The Second Sex*. Jean-Paul Sartre, who played a huge role in Beauvoir's life and work (and she in his), is necessarily very present in the book, but as a supporting, albeit major, character. This well-organized, meticulous biography includes extensive and informative notes as well as a thorough index and contributes greatly to the understanding of Beauvoir and her ideas.

Toril Moi also interweaves Beauvoir's life, education, art, work, and philosophy with the realities of her times in *Simone de Beauvoir: The Making of an Intellectual Woman* (Blackwell, 1994). *Letters to Sartre* (Arcade, 1991), edited and translated by Quentin Hoare, consists of English translations of two-thirds of the letters contained in the controversial 1990 French publication *Lettres à Sartre*, edited by Beauvoir's adopted daughter, Sylvie Le Bon de Beauvoir. The letters cover only the periods during which Beauvoir and Sartre were separated, but they provide new insight into their relationship and the times in which they lived.

918. Barry, Kathleen. *Susan B. Anthony: A Biography of a Singular Feminist*. New York: New York University Press, 1988. 426p. bibliog. index. (OP)

Barry, a feminist sociologist, prepared for writing this biography by reading all of Anthony's papers, correspondence, and diaries and even books from her personal library in an attempt to portray her as an "acting subject" (p. 362) rather than as an object of study from the perspective of traditional sex roles. Though Barry discusses a new theory of writing women's biography in an appendix, she stays with the conventional chronological format. She begins with Anthony's childhood in a Quaker family and covers her exhausting years as a teacher, her commitment to the temperance and abolitionist causes, and the sexism of the leaders of these causes that finally ignited her involvement in the fight for women's rights. Barry then traces Anthony's career from the early vilification to the reverence of later years and examines her extraordinary relationship with Elizabeth Cady Stanton. Throughout the book, Barry effectively incorporates numerous, often pithy, Anthony quotes and skillfully places Anthony's personal actions within the social, political, cultural, and economic context of nineteenth-century America. Although Barry could have taken a more critical view of her subject, she has written a thoroughly researched, extremely readable biography.

Lynn Sherr's *Failure Is Impossible: Susan B. Anthony in Her Own Words* (Times Books, 1995) collects a wide selection of Anthony's quotes from letters, speeches, and other writings. Sherr supplements quotes with contemporary newspaper accounts, photos, and illustrations and connects everything with descriptive narrative. This title is more suitable for undergraduates but provides a solid introduction to Anthony and the issues of the period.

919. Bell-Scott, Patricia, ed. *Life Notes: Personal Writings by Contemporary Black Women.* New York: Norton, 1994. 429p. ISBN 039303593X.

In this collection, Bell-Scott, who coedited the classic *All the Women Are White, All the Men Are Black, but Some of Us Are Brave: Black Women's Studies* (Feminist Press, 1982), presents journal entries written by fifty black women from Europe, North America, Africa, and the Caribbean. Some writers, like bell hooks, Rita Dove, and Alice Walker, are well known, while others have never published. All the writers except Audre Lorde were alive at the time of publication and varied in age (eight to sixty-four), life situations, and economic statuses. Bell-Scott arranges the writings into eight categories: girlhood, self-identity, work, love, abuse, resistance, life transitions, and travel/politics. Each begins with a series of excerpts that set the tone for the section. Each author prefaces her selection with a brief paragraph describing the circumstances that motivated it. The selections themselves reflect a variety of heartfelt emotions from anger and despair to great joy and love. This collection, the first of its kind, is appropriate for high-school and college classes in a variety of subjects. Bell-Scott, with several others, also edited the award-winning *Double Stitch: Black Women Write about Mothers and Daughters* (Beacon Press, 1991) and *Flat-Footed Truths: Telling Black Women's Lives* (Henry Holt, 1998), in which various writers discuss their own creative lives or the lives of historical women through essays, poetry, interviews, and photography.

920. Black, Allida M. *Casting Her Own Shadow: Eleanor Roosevelt and the Shaping of Postwar Liberalism.* New York: Columbia University Press, 1996. 298p. bibliog. index. ISBN 0231104049.

Black, a historian, combed through many primary sources, including Roosevelt's letters and syndicated columns, to analyze her as a political agent and leader in her own right. Although the author discusses Roosevelt as First Lady, she concentrates on Roosevelt's activities concerning domestic issues, especially civil rights and civil liberties, and her influence on the Truman presidency and the election and early presidency of John F. Kennedy. This intriguing political biography also serves as a history of mid-twentieth-century American liberalism and political events and highlights the consistency of Roosevelt's beliefs and efforts to keep New Deal ideology alive in the Democratic Party and the minds of the public.

In *Eleanor Roosevelt: First Lady of American Liberalism* (Twayne, 1987), author Lois Scharf takes a broader view than Brown does of Roosevelt's activism by considering her work in the United Nations and her tireless efforts to further principles of international cooperation. The author also frankly discusses Roosevelt's personal life: her difficulties with her husband and children and the sustenance she received from her group of female friends. This concise and engaging biography successfully synthesizes the most important aspects of previous accounts of Roosevelt's life.

Blanche Wiesen Cook's *Eleanor Roosevelt, Volume 1, 1933–1938* (Viking, 1999), continues what promises to be the most complete version of Roosevelt's life. The author provides a staggering amount of detail about the Roosevelt marriage, her tenacious efforts on behalf of minorities, the poor, and women, her involvement with the development of the New Deal, and her romantic friendship with journalist Lorena Hickok. Although Cook manages to untangle some of Roosevelt's contradictions, she also frankly points out her subject's shortcomings, both personal and political, such as her inexplicable failure to speak out about the German persecution of the Jews. These titles provide fresh perspectives on the life of one of the twentieth century's most admired women and her times.

921. Blackburn, Julia. *Daisy Bates in the Desert.* New York: Pantheon Books, 1994. 232p. bibliog. (OP)

In this unconventional biography Blackburn discusses the role of imagination in writing biography. She examined Bates's papers and letters and interviewed those who knew her. Since Bates, who went to live in the Australian desert at age fifty-three in 1913 to study Aborigine culture, left contradictory accounts of her childhood and early adulthood, Blackburn presents all the information she could find rather than try to discern the "truth," which she believes differs from what is remembered. In the second part of the book, the author speaks in Bates's voice about her years living and working in the desert. Blackburn's use of powerful and evocative language allows readers to glimpse Bates's world and feel her sympathy for the people and environment in which she lived.

Katherine Frank examines the life of another famous traveler from a feminist perspective in *Voyager Out: The Life of Mary Kingsley* (Houghton Mifflin, 1986). At the age of thirty, Kingsley transformed herself from a spinster dutiful to family needs to an independent and influential woman when she made two trips to West Africa to collect fish specimens and study indigenous religious traditions. Frank uses new or previously underutilized sources to create a clear sense of Kingsley's life as well as the African peoples and environment where she worked.

Women into the Unknown: A Sourcebook on Women Explorers and Travelers (Greenwood Press, 1989) by Marion Tinling includes accounts of Bates and Kingsley along with forty other women who traveled to relatively unexplored areas (for whites) around the world. Each entry consists of an introductory overview outlining the subject's travels and activities, a four- to six-page biographical sketch focusing on the subject's accomplishments, often integrating quotes from the subject's writings, and lists of works by and about the subject. Several entries also provide location information for subjects' papers and manuscripts. This informative and entertaining title introduces readers to women who flouted convention by refusing to stay home and creating full, useful lives for themselves.

922. Blanchard, Paula. *Sarah Orne Jewett: Her World and Her Work.* Reading, MA: Addison-Wesley, 1994. 397p. (Radcliffe Biography Series). bibliog. index. (OP)

Based on letters and diaries of Jewett and her associates, this book explores the relationship between Jewett's life and fiction. Blanchard portrays Jewett's life as a full one with many friendships with such luminaries as John Greenleaf Whittier, Henry James, and Oliver Wendell Holmes. She talks frankly about Jewett's health problems and depressions and their effect on her writing and presents a convincing argument that author Theophilus Parsons and his Swedenborgian teachings significantly affected Jewett's literary style. Blanchard's sensitive exploration of Jewett's intense "romantic friendships" with women, especially Anne Fields, widow of *Atlantic* publisher

James Fields, adds depth to the complexities of both women and their relationship. Interspersed with the chronological biographical account are chapters that summarize and analyze Jewett's fiction, most notably *Deephaven* and *The Country of the Pointed Firs*. Blanchard concludes with a chapter that provides insight into Jewett's mentorship of Willa Cather.

Drawing on literary, psychoanalytical, anthropological, feminist, and other theories, Sarah Way Sherman critically examines Jewett's fiction within the context of Victorian America in *Sarah Orne Jewett, an American Persephone* (University Press of New England, 1989). The author examines Jewett's often ignored relationship with her mother, which she believes was the source of Jewett's strong, independent female characters, as a stepping-stone for tracing the Demeter-Persephone mother-daughter bond in the pivotal fiction, including "A White Heron," *Deephaven*, and *The Country of the Pointed Firs*. Although some scholars criticize Sherman's framework as too narrow, several others credit her with original and insightful readings of Jewett's fiction and for her exploration of the female pastoral and Jewett's role in it.

923. Boyd, Melba Joyce. *Discarded Legacy: Politics and Poetics in the Life of Frances E.W. Harper, 1825–1911*. Detroit: Wayne State University Press, 1994. 260p. (African American Life Series). bibliog. index. ISBN 0814324886. (OP).

With this insightful book, Boyd resurrects the legacy of Frances Ellen Watkins Harper, poet, speaker, and antislavery and women's rights advocate. Arguing that past critics have misread Harper's works by ignoring their historical and literary contexts, Boyd organizes the book around the publication of the works themselves, thereby reflecting the evolution of Harper's writing, political ideas, and life. She includes many of Harper's poems and long passages from letters and speeches and discusses each work thematically and structurally against a biographical framework. This is a carefully researched and readable book about an important, neglected writer.

Libraries should also consider *The Complete Poems of Frances E.W. Harper* (Oxford University Press, 1988), part of the Schomburg Library of Nineteenth-Century Black Women Writers series, and *A Brighter Coming Day: A Frances Ellen Watkins Harper Reader* (Feminist Press, 1990), edited by Frances Foster. Foster's introduction considers Harper's life, work, and reputation, and the selections include letters, essays, and speeches as well as fiction and poetry. The editor also provides an appendix listing the contents of all of Harper's books and an index to the first lines of Harper's poems.

924. Brave Bird [Crow Dog], Mary, and Richard Erdoes. *Lakota Woman.* New York: HarperPerennial, 1991. 263p. ISBN 0060973897pa.

In telling the story of her life, Mary Brave Bird also reveals the brutal racism, poverty, and cruelty inflicted on native peoples in the United States. She spent her early life on the Rosebud Indian Reservation in South Dakota, where drinking, violence, unemployment, forced sterilization, and hopelessness were the norm and children were sent away to mission schools as a matter of course. After rebelling and spending a few years roaming around the country, Crow Dog discovered the American Indian Movement (AIM) and joined the fight for Indian civil rights. Her account of the seventy-one-day siege at Wounded Knee in 1973, when she gave birth to her first child during a shootout, is absolutely chilling. Since Crow Dog's husband was a Sioux medicine man and peyote priest, she provides many details about traditional spiritual beliefs and explains their purposes and effects. Crow Dog tells her story in a straightforward, unassuming, and very effective manner that makes for compelling reading. This book won an American Book Award in 1991 and is suitable as a text in courses in women's biography and women in social movements.

In *Ohitika Woman* (Grove, 1993), the author, with Erdoes, discusses the tensions of being a mother, a woman, and a Sioux feminist. She talks frankly about contradictions between her husband's family, who were traditional Sioux, and her family, who were Christianized, that contributed to the breakup of her marriage. While this title is not as engaging as *Lakota Woman*, it provides insight into twentieth-century Native American life.

925. Brightman, Carol, ed. *Between Friends: The Correspondence of Hannah Arendt and Mary McCarthy, 1949–1975.* New York: Harcourt Brace, 1995. 412p. bibliog. index. ISBN 015100112X.

Brightman charts the somewhat unlikely friendship between political philosopher and German Jewish émigré Arendt and Catholic, American author McCarthy from 1949 until Arendt's death in 1975. The editor worked with McCarthy before her death in 1989 to determine the protocols for editing the letters. She cuts only unimportant references, repetitions, and material injurious to people still living at the time of publication and does not correct Arendt's spelling or idiosyncratic English. Brightman does briefly identify people, events, and places and provides bibliographic information for references to books, articles, and other publications. She arranges the letters in segments that mark turning points in Arendt and McCarthy's lives, introducing each with biographical and contextual information. The friendship grew in part because both women thought alike and because each was attracted to the other by cultural differences. The women sustained each other when critics attacked them (McCarthy for *The Group* and Arendt for *Eichmann in Jerusalem*). While the letters include gossip and details of daily life, they also cover a wide range of topics such as student revolts, crime, economics, other writers, political issues, and each author's work. They certainly reveal the importance to both Arendt and McCarthy of engaging in critical thought that connected mundane occurrences with the contemplation of them.

926. Brown, Elaine. *A Taste of Power: A Black Woman's Story.* New York: Pantheon Books, 1992. 452p. ISBN 0679419446.

Brown devotes the first few chapters of the book to her childhood and adolescence in North Philadelphia, her flight to Los Angeles, and the development of her political consciousness. She focuses, however, on her ten-year involvement, beginning in 1968, with the Black Panther Party as both member and leader. She provides an inside account of the power struggles, events, and personalities of other members, particularly Huey Newton. She also describes the growth of her feminist awareness, which influenced her to elevate women to key roles in the party, but does not discuss her friendships or working relationships with other women at any length. Brown deals quite frankly with her sexual involvements and recurring mental problems as well as the violence and anger rampant among Panther members.

Assata Shakur (Joanne Chesimard) alternates chapters depicting her childhood, adolescence, and activist awakening with chapters discussing her trials, fugitive life, and imprisonment during the early 1970s in *Assata: An Autobiography* (L. Hill, 1987). Shakur's forceful account reveals the organized efforts of the Federal Bureau of Investigation (FBI) and other law enforcement agencies to infiltrate and undermine black movements and the personal harassment tactics they used against her. Shakur escaped prison to Cuba, which granted her political asylum. Neither Brown nor Shakur provide much analysis, but both tell their stories in a powerful and compelling manner and present extraordinary personal perspectives of a tumultuous period in American history.

927. Capper, Charles. *Margaret Fuller: An American Romantic Life: The Private Years.* New York: Oxford University Press, 1992. 423p. bibliog. index. ISBN 0195045793 (v. 1).

The 1990s produced a miniexplosion of books about Margaret Fuller and her work. Capper's book, however, the first of two volumes, won the Bancroft Prize for American History, and many consider it one of the best biographies on Fuller ever published. Since Capper wrote his biography partially as a "historical recovery" (p. x) of Fuller, he based it on her letters and journals as well as the extensive papers of her family, friends, and colleagues, something few previous biographers have done. This volume covers Fuller's life from childhood through 1840, when she was about to become the editor of the transcendentalist journal the *Dial*. Capper focuses on the intellectual influences of antebellum America and clearly explains the concepts of transcendentalism, romanticism, Unitarianism, and republicanism and their importance to Fuller's thought and work. The second volume, tentatively subtitled *The Public Years*, will examine Fuller's transition to internationally known journalist, literary critic, and leader of women's culture until her untimely death in a shipwreck near Fire Island in 1850.

In *Minerva and the Muse: A Life of Margaret Fuller* (University of Massachusetts Press, 1994), author Joan Van Mehren focuses on Fuller herself: the development of her character, her search for intimacy and expression, and the relationship between her private life and her political beliefs and actions. Informed by Carolyn Heilbrun and other feminist literary theorists, Donna Dickerson's *Margaret Fuller: Writing a Woman's Life* (St. Martin's Press, 1993) compares details of Fuller's life with the extremely negative myth as constructed by Ralph Waldo Emerson, Nathaniel Hawthorne, and others after her death in order to highlight Fuller's intellectual and literary significance.

928. Cayleff, Susan E. *Babe: The Life and Legend of Babe Didrikson Zaharias*. Urbana: University of Illinois Press, 1995. 327p. (Women in American History; Sport and Society). bibliog. index. ISBN 0252017935.

Cayleff presents a groundbreaking, in-depth account of Zaharias, often called the greatest female athlete of the twentieth century. She covers Zaharias's childhood in a Norwegian immigrant, working-class family in Texas and her prowess at the 1932 Amateur Athletic Union National Track and Field Championships and Los Angeles Olympics, which made her a household name. The author also discusses Zaharias's role in establishing the Ladies Professional Golf Association (LPGA) and her tireless efforts in the fight against cancer. Most compelling is Cayleff's examination of the ambivalence of the media and public toward Zaharias due to her androgynous appearance and unfeminine physicality. The author suggests that the relentless speculation about Zaharias's sexuality sparked her transition from defiant tomboy to feminine role model, which culminated with the athlete's marriage to wrestler George Zaharias in 1938. Also intriguing is Cayleff's treatment of Zaharias's relationship with golfer Betty Dodd, who postponed her career to nurse Zaharias through her bouts with cancer until her death at age forty-five in 1956. This is a fascinating account of a physically gifted woman who tried to make it in a male profession during a period of gender-role conformity.

929. Chesler, Ellen. *Woman of Valor: Margaret Sanger and the Birth Control Movement in America*. New York: Simon & Schuster, 1992. 639p. bibliog. index. (OP)

Chesler spent more than twenty years researching and writing this biography of Margaret Sanger, using many more primary sources, including many of Sanger's papers, correspondence, and journals, than previous biographers. As a result, the author provides a richly detailed background to the religious, social, political, and medical influences on both the public and private Sanger. Born into a large but poor family in Corning, New York, Sanger grew up at a time when many Americans believed in the vast potential of human progress. Her work as a nurse in the immigrant slums of New York City, however, influenced Sanger to argue that birth control "would be a tool for redistributing power fundamentally, in the bedroom, the home, and the larger community" (p. 14). She went to jail in 1917 for distributing contraceptives in one of her clinics and spent the 1920s and 1930s tirelessly writing, lecturing, and traveling in support of birth control. Though the Great Depression and World War II precipitated a backlash against contraception, Sanger lived long enough to see the Supreme Court decide that the right to contraception was constitutionally protected (*Griswold v. Connecticut*, 1965).

Constance Chen wrote the first full-length biography of Mary Ware Dennett, Sanger's rarely mentioned colleague and rival, titled, *"The Sex Side of Life": Mary Ware Dennett's Pioneering Battle for Birth Control and Sex Education* (New Press, 1996). The biography's title is taken from Dennett's 1915 pamphlet *The Sex Side of Life: An Explanation for Young People*, which became the subject of a landmark censorship/obscenity court case (*United States v. Dennett*) in 1929.

930. Chicago, Judy. *Beyond the Flower: The Autobiography of a Feminist Artist*. New York: Viking, 1996. 282p. index. (OP)

This sequel to *Through the Flower: My Struggle as a Woman Artist* (Doubleday, 1975) by feminist artist Judy Chicago describes twenty years of making art and struggling with political aspects of the art world since the publication of the 1975 title. As with the first autobiography, Chicago wrote *Beyond the Flower* to help resolve conflicts about her life in art. In particular, she reflects on circumstances that caused her to seriously consider giving up art despite international attention and strong, albeit not always positive, public reaction to her work. As she chronicles setbacks, critical condemnation, and frustration that her work spent most of its time in storage, Chicago also describes establishing the corporation Through the Flower, relives the opening of and controversy surrounding *The Dinner Party*, and discusses the development of *The Birth Project* and *The Holocaust Project*. The book's title, *Beyond the Flower*, refers to Chicago's efforts to expand her personal and artistic perspectives beyond gender while still using feminism as her cornerstone. Those who have followed Chicago's career or read the books *The Birth Project* (Doubleday, 1985) and *The Holocaust Project: From Darkness into Light* (Penguin, 1993) might not find much new here, but the candid and provocative *Beyond the Flower* is well worth reading.

931. Clifford, Deborah Pickman. *Crusader for Freedom: A Life of Lydia Maria Child*. Boston: Beacon Press, 1992. 367p. bibliog. index. (OP)

During the mid-1800s, most people knew the name Lydia Maria Child, but in the late twentieth century most people know her for editing Harriet Jacobs's *Incidents in the Life of a Slave Girl* (1861). Child first built a reputation as a writer of domestic advice, novels, and children's books, but when she embraced the unpopular antislavery cause in the 1830s, her reputation waned. For the rest of her life, Child continued to write in support of abolition as well as women's rights, justice for American Indians, religious tolerance, and other social causes, though championing them resulted in the loss of her livelihood. Clifford examined many unpublished as well as published sources, including Child's papers and letters, to provide the first scholarly full-length biography to be published about Child in decades. The author successfully presents a well-documented, highly readable account of the literary career and difficult life of this complex, contradictory, often feisty, and very important writer.

The First Woman in the Republic: A Cultural Biography of Lydia Maria Child (Duke University Press, 1994) by Carolyn L. Karcher complements Clifford's book by providing more cultural analysis with her discussions of Child's life and literary work. The book is thoroughly documented, but quite detailed and of more interest to advanced researchers.

932. Conway, Jill. *The Road from Coorain*. New York: Knopf, 1990. 238p. ISBN (OP); 0679724362pa.

Conway's memoir focuses on her tumultuous childhood and adolescence growing up on a ranch in the isolated Australian outback where the family suffered through drought and the deprivations of World War II. When she was ten, her father died suddenly, and she moved with her mother and brothers to Sydney. The death of her oldest brother a few years later marked the beginning of her mother's depression and emotional dependency. Conway attended the University of Sydney but returned periodically to Coorain and ran the ranch. Always considered highly intelligent, Conway found in her studies a new awareness of class, colonialism, race, and, more personally, the manipulations of her mother. She earned a master's degree in history and taught for a few years at the university. The memoir ends with her acceptance into Harvard's Ph.D. program. Conway easily conveys her great love for the Australian land, and her depiction of herself as an uncomfortable adolescent will remind many readers of their own teenage discomfort. Readers might also identify with Conway's emotional struggle with her mother, a once strong woman shattered from too many blows.

In *True North* (Knopf, 1994), Conway continues her story, covering her cultural adjustments while at Harvard and the University of Toronto, her intellectual development, which coincided with the establishment and growth of women's studies and the turmoil of the late 1960s and 1970s, her marriage and personal life, and her acceptance of the presidency of Smith College in 1975. The author writes intelligently and honestly about the difficulties facing women who wanted an academic career and the effects of a suffocating family and colonial mentality on her life.

933. Conway, Jill, ed. *Written by Herself: Autobiographies of American Women: An Anthology*. New York: Vintage Books, 1993. 672p. bibliog. ISBN 0679736336pa.

Conway includes excerpts from autobiographies of twenty-five women, some better known than others, written between the 1840s and the 1970s. She uses literary quality as the only criterion for selection in order to "present the most powerful female voices commenting on the American experience" (p. xii). She organizes the anthology into four sections: "My Story Ends in Freedom," consisting of African American autobiographies, "Research Is a Passion with Me: Women Scientists and Physicians," "Arts and Letters," and "Pioneers and Reformers." Conway introduces each section with an essay that briefly examines the historical context of the writers as a group and outlines both similar and unique themes in the writings. Each excerpt, arranged chronologically within each section, begins with a biographical sketch of the author and reveals a wide range of perspectives, experiences, hopes, dreams, and challenges. Conway very sensibly provides longer excerpts from writings available only as manuscripts or out-of-print books. Her succinct and instructive introduction discusses the history of women's autobiography and the diverse approaches women chose to present their stories.

In 1996, Conway edited a second volume, *Written by Herself: Women's Memoirs from Britain, Africa, Asia, and the United States* (Vintage Books), which presents excerpts from writings of fourteen twentieth-century women. The format of this volume follows that of the first, but in this case the four sections are "Imperial England," "Colonial Africa," "Indian Nationalism," and "Postcolonial America."

934. Corey, Elizabeth. *Bachelor Bess: The Homesteading Letters of Elizabeth Corey, 1909–1919*. Edited by Philip L. Gerber. Iowa City: University of Iowa Press, 1990. 462p. (American Land and Life Series). index. ISBN 0877453020; 0877453039pa.

Lured by the promise of free land and the chance to escape her crowded home in Iowa, Bess Corey (1888–1954) set out at the age of twenty-one to stake a claim in South Dakota in 1909. With an outgoing personality and a family that expected to be entertained, Corey filled her letters with detailed accounts of homesteading as well as local entertainment, personalities, gossip, and tall tales. Her land, not suitable for conventional farming and too small for ranching, forced Corey to work as a schoolteacher or cook while she held down her claim. Since she changed schools almost annually and spent part of each year as a boarder in various homes, Corey discusses a large number of characters and changing circumstances in her life, reducing repetition in the letters. Gerber provides a lengthy, detailed introduction that discusses Corey's background and various themes of the letters and includes a brief history of the area where Corey homesteaded. He presents the letters with minimal editing and provides explanatory information in notes at the end of the book. An epilogue contains thirty-four years of letters Corey wrote after leaving her homestead in 1920, and an afterword, written by Wayne Franklin, provides a history of home-steading in the United States.

The Adventures of the Woman Homesteader: The Life and Letters of Elinore Pruitt Stewart (University of Nebraska Press, 1992), edited by Suzanne K. George, depicts life in Wyoming between the years 1909 and 1933. Stewart's *Letters of a Woman Homesteader* (1914), which became a feminist classic when Houghton Mifflin reprinted it in 1982, and *Letters of an Elk Hunt* (1915) have engaged and delighted readers since their publication. Editor George collects Stew-art's previously unpublished and little-known writings and skillfully integrates them into her own extensive contextual research to produce the fullest portrait to date of Stewart (known as "the Woman Homesteader"). The editor also describes her editorial process and considers fictional aspects of Stewart's writing and her development as an author. The result is an informative and entertaining title. Both *Bachelor Bess* and *The Adventures of the Woman Homesteader* contribute to our knowledge about women's roles in homesteading and settling the American West and would make suitable texts for women's history or literature courses.

935. Daly, Mary. *Outercourse: The Be-dazzling Voyage: Containing Recollections from My Logbook of a Radical Feminist Philosopher (Be-ing an Account of My Time/Space Travels and Ideas—Then, Again, How, and Now)*. San Francisco: HarperSanFrancisco, 1992. 477p. index. (OP)

One of the most creative, inventive, and challenging contemporary radical feminists, Mary Daly sets her story into four intersecting "spiral galaxies" (p. 2) that blend the "Crone-logical" (p. 1) with her philosophical and theoretical voyages. The first section covers her life from pre-existence to her radical awakening (OH! through 1970); the second details her explorations of philosophies and religions beyond Christianity (1971–1974); the third section focuses on her fascination with language (1975–1987); and the final section examines the process of writing about her life ("Acts of Momentous Re-Membering"). The book also serves as a fine introduction to the ideas espoused in her previous, sometimes difficult books since Daly discusses life events and intellectual processes that lead to their creation. This is a unique approach to autobiography from an important and provocative feminist thinker.

936. Daniels, Doris G. *Always a Sister: The Feminism of Lillian D. Wald*. New York: Feminist Press, 1989. 207p. bibliog. index. (OP)

In *Always a Sister*, Daniels asserts that Wald, a nurse, social reformer, and founder/director of the Visiting Nurse Service and Henry Street Settlement in New York City, committed herself to improving the lives of women out of her belief in sexual equality. To support her argument, the author tells her story thematically rather than chronologically, examining Wald's feminist early work as a nurse, her introduction to reform work, her political influence and social philos-ophy, her suffrage work, and efforts on behalf of working women. While the book is more synthesis than critical analysis, it contributes to our knowledge of women in the reform movement and our awareness of Wald as a dynamic agent within this movement.

Editor Clare Coss presents some of Wald's letters and speeches to give an idea of the range of her ideas and principles in *Lillian D. Wald, Progressive Activist* (Feminist Press, 1989). Coss also includes biographical information on Wald, some political and social context for the times in which she lived, and a short one-character play. The book serves as an excellent introduction to Wald and her achievements.

937. Davis, Thadious M. *Nella Larsen, Novelist of the Harlem Renaissance: A Woman's Life Unveiled.* Baton Rouge: Louisiana State University Press, 1994. 492p. bibliog. index. ISBN (OP); 0807120707pa.

Davis spent five years combing city directories, telephone books, vital statistics in four states, employment records, school transcripts, and other official documents and interviewing friends and neighbors in order to trace the life of the "mystery woman of the Harlem Renaissance" (p. xvi), Nella Larsen. Larsen rose from comparative obscurity to become one of only three African Americans to have two novels published by major New York firms by the end of the 1920s. This established her importance in the development of the novel as a creative form for African American writers and in attracting attention to women writers. The novels, *Quicksand* (Knopf, 1928) and *Passing* (Knopf, 1929), won Larsen meteoric popularity, awards, and a Guggenheim Fellowship. Though she continued to write throughout the 1930s, nothing substantial was published, and she quietly disappeared. Davis claims that Larsen herself limited what is known about her and often provided contradictory information about her life. The author does an admirable job of presenting historical context, particularly concerning race and culture, throughout Larsen's life, thereby providing insight into Chicago history during the early 1900s, Harlem in the 1920s, job opportunities open to African American women, color and class consciousness among African Americans, and gender constraints. Davis also offers insightful analysis of the novels and concludes that Larsen was a complex woman, full of contradictions, who, like the protagonists in her novels, sought "to fully express her racial, social, and sexual identities."

938. Deacon, Desley. *Elsie Clews Parsons: Inventing Modern Life.* Chicago: University of Chicago Press, 1997. 520p. (Women in Culture and Society). bibliog. index. ISBN 0226139077.

Based on extensive primary and other sources, this impressive and intelligently written biography of sociologist and anthropologist Elsie Clews Parsons examines her efforts to free herself "from the prison house of classification" (p. 130), prominent during the nineteenth century, in both her life and work. After earning a doctorate from Columbia University in 1899 and marrying (which she considered experimental), Parsons taught at Barnard College through two pregnancies and produced a large number of articles examining sex roles, sexual morality, and the family. Her use of ethnography, however, led her to cultural anthropology and the work of Franz Boas and to extensive fieldwork in the American Southwest (with Pueblo Indians), Mexico, and the Caribbean. Using these data, she argued for flexible morality, inclusive social relationships, tolerance, cultural diversity and mobility, and freedom for all individuals regardless of gender, race, ethnicity, or geographic location. Deacon provides a selected bibliography of Parsons's writings, including unpublished papers, and extensive notes. This title made the shortlist for a Pulitzer Prize and was awarded a Hamilton Prize from the University of Texas.

Margaret M. Caffrey examines the life of an anthropologist influenced by Parsons and Boas in *Ruth Benedict: Stranger in This Land* (University of Texas Press, 1989). Benedict, author of the major work *Patterns of Culture* (1934), attended Vassar College and spent most of her professional life at Columbia University, where she made considerable accomplishments in her field and American intellectual life. Caffrey identifies Benedict as a cultural feminist because she focused on culture's values and beliefs, as well as internal attitudes about individuality, self, and independence. The author also examines Benedict's role in the development of the Culture and Personality movement in anthropology, her impact on social policies during the 1940s, particularly regarding race and the postwar reconstruction of Japan, and her poetry. Both of these excellent titles provide insight into the life and work of two fascinating and important anthropologists, the history and development of modernity as well as anthropology, and social history during the first half of the twentieth century.

939. Delany, Sarah Louise, and A. Elizabeth Delany, with Amy Hill Hearth. *Having Our Say: The Delany Sisters' First 100 Years.* New York: Kodansha America, 1993. 210p. ISBN 156836010X.

The result of thousands of recollections told to Hearth during an eighteen-month period, this book presents the life stories of Sarah (Sadie) and Elizabeth (Bessie) Delany, who were 103 and 101 years old at the time. They were born and raised in Raleigh, North Carolina, where their father, a former slave, served as vice principal at St. Augustine's School and their mixed-race mother ran the school's day-to-day operations. Both sisters taught in the rural South and lived under the shadow of Jim Crow before moving to Harlem in 1916. Bessie earned a degree in dentistry from Columbia University in 1923 and became the second black woman licensed to practice in New York City. Sadie earned a master's degree in education and became the first black home economics teacher in New York City's high schools. Hearth arranges the reminiscences chronologically, using the words of the sisters themselves, and provides footnotes that briefly identify people or events. Some chapters contain both sisters' voices; other chapters chronicle events from either Bessie's or Sadie's point of view. The sisters forthrightly share their opinions about such topics as the movie *Gone with the Wind*, the civil rights movement, and the assassinations during the 1960s and talk about meeting entertainers such as Cab Calloway, Lena Horn, and Paul Robeson. The sisters tell their stories to pass their knowledge and experience to the next generation and to live up to the family motto, "Your job is to help somebody" (p. 4). Bessie Delany died in 1995 at the age of 104; Sadie Delany died in 1999 at the age of 109. This would be an excellent text in women's autobiography, African American women writers, and history courses.

940. Farnsworth, Martha. *Plains Woman: The Diary of Martha Farnsworth, 1882–1922.* Edited by Marlene Springer and Haskell Springer. Bloomington: Indiana University Press, 1986. 322p. index. ISBN (OP); 0253204801pa.

Martha Farnsworth (1867–1924) began keeping a journal at the age of fourteen. As years passed, the journal became more detailed, leaving a wonderfully full record of Farnsworth's life and times. She lived most of her life in Kansas and was, at different times, teacher, photographer, housewife, and suffragist. She also lived during a period of tremendous change and mentions railroad expansion, the telephone, electricity, indoor plumbing, automobiles, and other technological advances. The diary reveals that Farnsworth was an intelligent, though uneducated, independent woman who was more interested in politics and public events than her contemporaries. Farnsworth wrote quite frankly about her marriage to an unsympathetic first husband, her miscarriages, the deaths of her daughter and sister, widowhood, remarriage, and personal life. The Springers judiciously condense the diaries by omitting repetitious entries and uneventful years. They also provide useful explanatory notes and occasional narrative within the diary, as well as a detailed introduction that summarizes Farnsworth's life and discusses various aspects of her personality, making this a very interesting and readable book.

941. Flanagan, Sabina. *Hildegard of Bingen, 1098–1179: A Visionary Life*. New York: Routledge, 1989. 230p. bibliog. index. (OP)

One of the most remarkable women of her time, Hildegard of Bingen founded convents, corresponded with secular and church leaders, preached, and produced an impressive array of writings, extraordinary achievements for a woman living in medieval Germany. Her writings covered medicine, theology, and music, and Flanagan devotes four chapters to describing the contents and interrelations of her major works. Other chapters describe Hildegard's birth and death, her family, cloister life, her pastoral activities, and her conflicts with ecclesiastical superiors. The final chapter examines the intriguing possibility that Hildegard's visions were related to migraine headaches. Flanagan acknowledges that she does not include in-depth context for twelfth-century ideas of the world or compare Hildegard's works with those of contemporaries. Nevertheless, she succeeds in providing a "comprehensive introduction" (p. xiii) to Hildegard and her work.

Research collections will also want to obtain *The Letters of Hildegard of Bingen* (Oxford University Press, 1994–), a projected four-volume set consisting of almost 400 letters, translated by Joseph L. Baird and Radd K. Ehrman. Volume 1 includes 90 of Hildegard's letters along with their responses. Baird and Ehrman provide explanatory notes with the letters, an informative discussion of medieval letters as a genre, and an examination of Hildegard's life and significance. Volume 2 (Oxford University Press, 1998) contains 176 letters and is notable for the correspondence between Hildegard and Guibert of Gembloux, who persistently asked detailed questions about the saint's life and visions.

942. Freydberg, Elizabeth Amelia Hadley. *Bessie Coleman: The Brownskin Lady Bird*. New York: Garland, 1994. 156p. (Studies in African American History and Culture). bibliog. index. ISBN 0815314612.

Freydberg profiles the life of Bessie Coleman, the first African American woman pilot and the first American to earn an international aviator's license. Born and raised in the cotton fields of Texas, Coleman eventually went to Chicago and became a manicurist, but always yearned to make something of herself. After being denied admission to aviation schools in the United States because of her race and sex, she attended school in France in 1920, where she earned her international pilot's license. Unable to find a job in commercial aviation in the United States, she returned to France to learn stunt flying and parachuting. In 1921, she came back to America and became a highly popular and successful barnstormer. She performed in air shows all over the country and lectured at schools and churches, encouraging other African Americans to become involved in aviation, until she was killed in a plane accident in 1926. The value of Freydberg's book lies in its attention to the political, cultural, and social contexts of Coleman's life, which included the Jim Crow era, the antilynching campaign of Ida B. Wells, and the Harlem Renaissance. Freydberg portrays Coleman as a shrewd, determined woman who realized that entertainment was one of the few areas where African Americans could succeed and that Jim Crow laws did not exist in aviation. She bases her account on African American newspapers, interviews with relatives and friends, and other sources. In *Queen Bess: Daredevil Aviator* (Smithsonian Institution Press, 1993), author Doris Rich also depends on interviews and African American newspapers for her account. Both titles help recover Coleman's legacy.

943. Gomez, Jewelle. *Forty-Three Septembers: Essays*. Ithaca, NY: Firebrand Books, 1993. 196p. (OP)

In a series of short chapters Gomez talks about the people and events that shaped her life. She discusses various members of her family, especially her father and the great-grandmother who raised her, with warmth, love, and appreciation for the sustenance and strength they provided. Her analysis of the Catholic Church, portrayals of African Americans in advertisements, motivations behind her highly praised vampire novel *The Gilda Stories* (Firebrand Books, 1991), humor as survival tactic, or the Black Power and feminist movements are written from the perspective of an African/Native American lesbian woman. These examinations are astute and compelling and reflect how homophobia, racism, and sexism permeate all aspects of life. Firebrand Books, now defunct, in publishing the life of Gomez and the authors discussed in the Pratt annotation later in this chapter, celebrated the infinite diversity of lesbian lives and realities.

944. Graham, Elspeth, Hilary Hinds, Elaine Hobby, and Helen Wilcox, eds. *Her Own Life: Autobiographical Writings by Seventeenth Century Englishwomen*. New York: Routledge, 1989. 250p. bibliog. index. ISBN 0415016991; 0415017009pa.

The editors arrange selections chronologically in order to reflect the changes in women's personal narratives against the social and political context of the period. The twelve selections represent a cross section of women from disparate economic and political circumstances who used a variety of forms (diaries, letters, verse, narratives) to convey their thoughts and feelings about their lives. Many were written with publication in mind since conversion narratives, accounts of journeys, trials, and imprisonment, and appeals against oppression were commonly published as pamphlets. Brief but informative introductions to each woman provide background information and discuss the writing(s) that follow. Notes that explain people, events, biblical allusions, and the like accompany each selection. A quite useful and informative introduction briefly describes gender roles of the period, the importance of class, and the fundamental connection between politics and religion that led to civil war. Also helpful is the chronology of seventeenth-century England that lists historical/political events and important written texts. This title provides female perspectives about an important period of English history using hard-to-find primary sources.

Natalie Zemon Davis's *Women on the Margins: Three Seventeenth-Century Lives* (Harvard University Press, 1995) examines the lives of Glikl bas Judah Leib (Glikl of Hamlen), a Jewish merchant, Marie Guyart (Marie de l'Incarnation), a French Catholic mystic and cofounder of the first Ursuline girls' school in America, and Maria Merian, a German Protestant artist, naturalist, and author. The author used the women's writings as the basis to compare both public and private elements of their lives, especially the role of religion. This compelling book succeeds in portraying the rich diversity of early modern European women's lives despite gender constraints and contributes to our knowledge of commerce, art, family life, work, imperialism, and spirituality of the period.

945. Graham, Martha. *Blood Memory: An Autobiography*. New York: Doubleday, 1991. 279p. (OP)

Dancer and choreographer Graham dictated this book in the months before her death at age ninety-six in 1991. She discusses her childhood in Pittsburgh and Santa Barbara, her years as a dance student at Denishawn, the school established by Ruth St. Denis and Ted Shawn, her many friends and lovers, her infamous temper, her passion for dancer Erick Hawkins, establishing her own dance company, and her creation of various dances and the symbolic meanings behind them. Readers who followed her career might not find much new here, and Graham does not reveal much about herself to any depth. The book contains numerous black-and-white photographs of Graham's family and friends as well as the dancer throughout her career, some of which are not reproduced very well. The studies by Imogen Cunningham and Soichi Sunami, however, are stunning.

Agnes de Mille, friend and younger contemporary of Graham, began *Martha: The Life and*

Work of Martha Graham (Random House, 1991) in the 1960s. De Mille tells her own version of events, lovers, and colleagues, which does not always correspond with Graham's version. The author is at her best when discussing Graham's technique, creative process, physical attributes, style of movement, and specific dances. She also talks frankly about Graham's creative decline, alcoholism, and rages. Reviewers found several errors concerning dates and names, but this does not diminish a fascinating read. De Mille includes an intriguing section of black-and-white photographs of Graham, other dancers, performances, and associates as well as appendices that list Graham's awards and dances, discuss the basics of Kundalini yoga, and provide brief biographical and career information about dancers in Graham's company.

946. Hause, Steven C. *Hubertine Auclert: The French Suffragette.* New Haven, CT: Yale University Press, 1987. 268p. bibliog. index. ISBN 0300038453.

Hause compares the efforts of Hubertine Auclert (1848–1914) toward women's suffrage in France to those of Susan B. Anthony and Elizabeth Cady Stanton in the United States and Millicent Fenwick and the Pankhursts in Great Britain, yet notes that she is not well known even in her own country. He traces Auclert's life and career, beginning with her childhood in a prosperous but politically active family and continuing through her commitment to feminism, alliances with socialist groups, her activities in support of education for Arab girls in Algiers, and her various campaigns for suffrage. Since Auclert founded two newspapers and these and other papers were preserved, Hause bases much of his research on her own words. He portrays Auclert as a "great propagandist, agitator, and activist" (p. 128) rather than a theorist, but emphasizes the political seriousness of her writing and her dedication to "integral feminism" (p. 128), equality for women in all aspects of their lives. Hause recognizes the importance of providing background for the social and political realities of nineteenth-century France, but assumes that readers know and understand the context and importance of such terms as the Commune of 1871, Jacobinism, and republicanism. Two useful appendices list Auclert's newspaper articles and published platforms, and several tables within the text list her petitions. The bibliography includes primary, contemporary, government, and secondary sources. This book serves as a fine introduction to this self-proclaimed martyr and to militant French feminism.

Felicia Gordon in *The Integral Feminist: Madeleine Pelletier, 1874–1939: Feminism, Socialism, and Medicine* (Polity Press, 1990) examines the career of one of the next generation's militant feminists whose life and work overlapped with Auclert's and, at the same time, provides a history of French feminism and society into the twentieth century. In *The Feminism of Flora Tristan* (Berg, 1992), Máire Cross and Tim Gray critically analyze Tristan's various feminisms as reflected in her novels and her writings concerning women and the working class. Although many scholars identify Tristan as a socialist, Cross and Gray suggest that liberalism also played a large role in the development of her ideology. This intriguing book also sheds light on French feminism during the first half of the nineteenth century.

947. Hayslip, Le Ly, with Jay Wurts. *When Heaven and Earth Changed Places: A Vietnamese Woman's Journey from War to Peace.* New York: Plume, 1989. 368p. (OP)

Born in 1949 in central Vietnam to a peasant farmer family, Le Ly Haslip tells the harrowing story of a simple life torn apart by unending war. Initially Hayslip supported the Vietcong (VC) and the North Vietnamese Communists since they wanted an independent Vietnam under one government. She served as a courier and lookout for the VC until they accused her of treason, then raped, beat, and expelled her. She fared no better with the South Vietnamese or American armies, and she spent her teens traveling between Danang and Saigon, surviving by becoming a servant, black marketer, drug dealer, and bar girl. Eventually she worked for Americans and finally met and married an older man and moved to California in 1970. Throughout the book, Hayslip intersperses diary entries written during a return trip to Vietnam in 1986 to find out what became of her family, village, and friends. She concludes the book with a plea to end the "chain of vengeance" (p. 366) still evident in both countries. This harrowing personal account details the destruction of a family, culture, and country and provides insight into the hard compromises people must make to survive war.

Hayslip, with her son James Hayslip, continues her story with *Child of War, Woman of Peace* (Doubleday, 1993), which begins in 1970 when she came to the United States as the bride of an American civilian engineer. She discusses the difficulties of life as a stranger who lives with "the enemy" in a confusing culture, struggling to come to terms with a horrific past and move on to a better, more hopeful and safe future for herself and her children. Although not as powerful as her first title, *Child of War* gives voice to struggles and issues facing dispossessed people. Film director Oliver Stone adapted these titles as part of his Vietnam trilogy. Both titles are suitable for women's biography, immigrant women, and women and war courses.

948. Head, Bessie. *A Woman Alone: Autobiographical Writings*. Selected and edited by Craig MacKenzie. Portsmouth, NH: Heinemann, 1990. (African Writers Series). 107p. ISBN 0435905783pa.

MacKenzie collects a selection of sketches, essays, and autobiographical writings representing various periods in the creative life of Bessie Head (1937–1986), the renowned South African author of such novels as *When Rain Clouds Gather* (1969), *Maru* (1971), and *A Question of Power* (1974). He arranges the pieces into three roughly chronological sections, early life in South Africa, exile in Botswana, and as a Botswana citizen, with the intention of letting Head tell her own story. Each section begins with an excerpt from one of Head's autobiographical pieces that sets the tone of the period to come, followed by letters, stories, essays, notes, social commentaries, and forewords to books such as Ellen Kuzwayo's compelling autobiography *Call Me Woman* (Women's Press, 1985). MacKenzie believes that Head's writing details the realities of life for "coloured" women in South Africa, who suffered under the brutal discriminatory practices of the government. Head died of hepatitis at the age of forty-nine.

The first full-length biography, *Bessie Head: Thunder behind Her Ears: Her Life and Writing* (Heinemann, 1995) by Gillian Stead Eilersen, is based on Head's voluminous letters, her papers, and interviews with family, colleagues, and friends. Eilersen provides detailed summaries of Head's major works along with insightful commentaries and excerpts from reviews as she tells the story of Head's chaotic life, which included exile, mental illnesses, and many difficulties. These titles should help Head receive the critical attention she deserves.

949. Hedrick, Joan D. *Harriet Beecher Stowe: A Life*. New York: Oxford University Press, 1994. 507p. bibliog. index. (OP)

As the first biography of Harriet Beecher Stowe (1811–1896) to be published in more than fifty years, this book succeeds admirably in its examination of Stowe's life on several levels. It is meticulously researched and extremely well written and does not ignore Stowe's race and class biases as it highlights her many achievements. Indeed, the book's strength lies in its detailed portrayal of the cultural, political, religious, social, and literary circumstances of nineteenth-century America. By providing a comprehensive background of the times, Hedrick helps readers understand how Stowe, in *Uncle Tom's Cabin*, could dramatize the plight of slaves on one hand while appropriating their stories and perpetuating stereotypes on the other. She also presents a new analysis of American literary history by tracing its transition from "parlor literature" (p. viii) in the hands of amateurs (mostly women) to "professionalized literature" (p. viii) in the hands of men. However, the book covers Stowe's life beyond her literary influence and provides a complete picture of the contradictory woman so difficult for many feminists to reclaim. Hedrick uses many primary sources, including many letters discovered since the publication of previous biographies, and provides extensive notes and a selective but very useful bibliography.

A title that serves as a fine complement to Hedrick's biography is *The Limits of Sisterhood: The Beecher Sisters on Women's Rights and Woman's Sphere* (University of North Carolina Press, 1988) by Jeanne Boydston, Mary Kelley, and Anne Margolis. In this book, each author examines the life, work, ideology, and vision of one of the three activist Beecher sisters: Harriet, Catherine Beecher, who championed expanded educational and professional opportunities for women (but not the vote), and Isabella Beecher Hooker, who became a leader in the most militant wing of the women's rights movement. The authors provide excellent discussions of each sister's interpretation of the cult of domesticity, supplemented by excerpts from their diaries, letters, and published works.

950. Heilbrun, Carolyn G. *The Education of a Woman: The Life of Gloria Steinem*. New York: Dial Press, 1995. 451p. bibliog. index. (OP)

This is the first book-length biography of possibly the most famous second-wave feminist in the world. It is a straightforward account based on interviews and Steinem's writings and papers. Heilbrun provides details concerning Steinem's childhood in a working-class neighborhood in Toledo, Ohio, her education at Smith College, her years as a journalist and political columnist, the founding of *Ms.*, and the years of celebrity. The book reflects Steinem's compassion, devotion to feminism and women's issues, commitment to *Ms.*, sense of fairness, and identification with the underdog. It also reports conflicts and hostilities within the feminist movement and in the production of the magazine and records Steinem's many celebrity liaisons. Despite the reputation of Heilbrun, author of the classic *Writing a Woman's Life*, the biography comes across as flat. Heilbrun describes but does not analyze Steinem's relationship to the women's liberation movement or the distrust Steinem garnered from the radical component of the movement as someone who worked within the system, nor does she probe Steinem's complications or contradictions. The stature of both the author and the subject, however, makes the title important to women's studies collections.

951. hooks, bell. *Bone Black: Memories of Girlhood*. New York: Henry Holt, 1996. 183p. ISBN 0805041451.

In more than sixty vignettes, hooks tells stories of her rebellion and struggle to create her own identity and sense of self within African American southern culture and a family that sometimes sustained her and sometimes abused her, and as she grappled with race and class realities. Believing that emotional responses are more important than events themselves, the author focuses on the dreams, fantasies, and experiences of her youth that continue to influence her life and work instead of presenting a traditional chronological story. Hooks writes about ideas, perceptions, and intuitive knowledge of a child, but presents some experiences in the third person to conceptualize herself as an observer rather than subject.

A sequel titled *Wounds of Passion: A Writing Life* (Henry Holt, 1998) connects sex, love, and writing to oppression and intersperses stories of her childhood with her life with literary mentor and lover Nathaniel Mackey. The author states that she wanted to provide an alternative to the stereotypical portrayal of African American man-woman relationships. These powerful and poetic memoirs attempt to reveal a fuller awareness of her inner life and consciousness.

952. Horowitz, Daniel. *Betty Friedan and the Making of "The Feminine Mystique": The American Left, the Cold War, and Modern Feminism*. Amherst: University of Mas-

sachusetts Press, 1998. 354p. (Culture, Politics, and the Cold War). bibliog. index. ISBN 1558491686.

In this unauthorized biography of the acknowledged founder of the modern feminist movement, Horowitz situates his subject within the broader political, social, and historical context of her times. The author makes an intriguing suggestion: Friedan's feminism developed as an outgrowth of her extensive involvement in labor politics, including women's issues, throughout the 1940s and 1950s. This directly contradicts Friedan's own story of her feminist awakening, which she attributes to a questionnaire she sent out for a Smith College reunion in 1957. Horowitz examined Friedan's papers, undergraduate papers, and editorials she wrote for the campus newspaper to support his case, finding that Friedan often wrote about the rights of women workers. He further speculates that McCarthyism and red-baiting made Friedan feel vulnerable to attack and caused her to present herself as a naïve and discontented housewife in *The Feminine Mystique* (Norton, 1963). Horowitz takes Friedan and her ideas seriously in this fascinating book, which also provides insight into America during the early Cold War and raises questions about representation and self-representation.

953. Jones, Hettie. *How I Became Hettie Jones*. New York: Dutton, 1990. 239p. (OP)

Hettie Cohen Jones claims that she started to leave home, where security and upward mobility was the expected goal, when she was six years old. This memoir examines how Jones finally did leave home to find herself and become the woman writing it. At the age of seventeen, Jones left Queens to attend school in Virginia, but returned to New York after graduation to attend Columbia University. While working for the magazine *Record Changer*, Cohen met LeRoi Jones (later Imamu Amiri Baraka), whom she married. Most of the book describes their life during late 1950s and early 1960s lower Manhatten where the new jazz, poetry, and politics of the Beat movement flourished. Though LeRoi Jones and his work feature prominently in the book, it focuses on Hettie's search for her own expression, made more difficult after the birth of two daughters. Jones's story provides some insight into the predicaments faced by white women in the 1950s who aspired to become more than June Cleaver. The book succeeds very well in conveying the bohemian atmosphere and describing personalities of the period. Jones, like many wives of artists and writers, put her own ambitions aside, yet gives the impression that the years of her marriage were among her happiest, even though she "became Hettie Jones," successful author of poetry and children's books, after it ended. Brenda Knight in her book *Women of the Beat Generation: The Writers, Artists, and Muses at the Heart of a Revolution* (Conari, 1996) provides brief biographical information about thirty-five women, both well known and not, accompanied by excerpts of writings and bibliographies of their published and unpublished works.

954. Kahlo, Frida. *The Diary of Frida Kahlo: An Intimate Self-Portrait*. New York: Abrams, 1995. 295p. bibliog. index. ISBN 0810932210.

Although not a diary in the conventional sense, this title reproduces the actual diary Kahlo kept during the last ten years of her life, 1944–1954, complete with illustrations, and contains a translation of the entries and informative commentary by Sarah M. Lowe and an introduction by Carlos Fuentes. The diary is filled with Kahlo's feelings for her husband, artist Diego Rivera, and her preoccupation with the pain and torment from injuries she sustained in a streetcar accident at the age of eighteen, which shaped both her life and art.

Frida Kahlo: An Open Life (University of New Mexico Press, 1993) by Argentinean art critic and historian Raquel Tibol is an English translation of the first monograph devoted to Kahlo published in 1977. It collects articles covering the artist's childhood and family, her years as a teacher, her husband, the contemporary art world, and her home. In *Frida Kahlo: Pain and*

Passion (Benedikt Taschen, 1992), author Andrea Kettenmann presents a brief but thorough and clearly written account that covers key events in Kahlo's life and art, including her chronic ill health, ambiguous feelings toward her husband, her disconnectedness from herself and others, the conflicts she faced as an artist, and intriguing interpretations of Kahlo's paintings. The book is a fine introduction to Kahlo's creative process and life. *The Letters of Frida Kahlo: Cartas Apasionadas* (Chronicle Books, 1995) by Martha Zamora consists of translations of eighty letters Kahlo wrote between 1924 and the early 1950s to her first boyfriend, her doctor, and her friends and lovers. The letters give readers an idea of Kahlo's daily life and thoughts about her own painting as well as Rivera's work. All of these titles add greatly to our knowledge of this important Mexican artist, but do not take the place of the definitive biography by Hayden Herrera, *Frida: A Biography of Frida Kahlo* (Harper & Row, 1983).

955. Keller, Rosemary Skinner. *Patriotism and the Female Sex: Abigail Adams and the American Revolution.* Brooklyn: Carlson, 1994. 239p. (Scholarship in Women's History, v. 8). bibliog. index. ISBN 0926019694.

Based on Keller's dissertation, this book is one of the first to examine Abigail Adams (1744–1818) as an intellectual and serious agent in history. The author focuses on the American Revolutionary War period (1774–1784), when Adams was in her thirties and "doubled in wedlock" (p. xix), almost totally responsible for the care of children, home, farm, and family finances. The first two chapters provide historical context and discuss the personalities of the Adams, Quincy, and Smith families. In the remaining chapters, Keller argues that Abigail Adams appropriated justifications for American independence and used them as a basis for arguments to expand the rights of women. Keller cites a number of primary sources, quoting liberally from Adams's wonderful letters. Like Keller, Edith B. Gelles examines Adams's intellectual contributions and agency in *Portia: The World of Abigail Adams* (Indiana University Press, 1992). Gelles believes that the chronological arrangement of most biographies of Abigail Adams forces an emphasis on historic events and husband John Adams. The author therefore organizes her biography topically, with each chapter designed to analyze one facet of Adams's life and stand on its own. This creative approach succeeds only partially since different chapters repeat certain quotes and details. Gelles continues her examination of Adams in *"First Thoughts": Life and Letters of Abigail Adams* (Twayne, 1998). This second biography, like *Portia*, consists of episodic, freestanding chapters, but focuses on Adams's letters and her contributions as a writer. Phyllis Lee Levin spent sixteen years researching and writing *Abigail Adams: A Biography* (St. Martin's Press, 1987), using a vast array of primary and contemporary sources. The result is an in-depth, detailed account of the woman, the period, and the historical events and personalities. All of these titles contribute significantly to our information about women's lives in eighteenth-century America.

956. Kerr, Andrea Moore. *Lucy Stone: Speaking Out for Equality.* New Brunswick, NJ: Rutgers University Press, 1992. 301p. bibliog. index. ISBN 0813518598; 0813518601pa.

Despite the importance of Lucy Stone (1818–1893) to the struggle for U.S. women's suffrage, she has been ignored compared to Susan B. Anthony and Elizabeth Cady Stanton. This biography helps remedy her undeserved obscurity. Stone, a compelling speaker and brilliant organizer, split with Anthony and Stanton over their opposition to the Fourteenth and Fifteenth Amendments, which extended citizenship and the right to vote to black males. As a result, Anthony and Stanton greatly diminished Stone's role in their massive *History of Woman Suffrage*. This book presents Stone's side of the disagreement along with a discussion of her entire women's rights career, including her role in establishing the *Woman's Journal*, the newspaper produced by the American Woman Suffrage Association. It also includes a frank account of her unorthodox and difficult marriage to Henry Blackwell. Kerr could have provided more coverage of Stone's antislavery activities and more analysis of her career. Nevertheless, the author bases her account on an impressive number of primary, contemporary, and secondary sources and treats Stone with the respect she deserves.

Friends and Sisters: Letters between Lucy Stone and Antoinette Brown Blackwell, 1846–93 (University of Illinois Press, 1987), edited by Carol Lasser and Marlene Deahl Merrill, traces the relationship and work of the two women, which began during their years at Oberlin Collegiate Institute. They later became sisters-in-law when they each married into the Blackwell family. While Stone concentrated on suffrage and abolition, Brown Blackwell became the first ordained woman in the Protestant Congregational ministry. These titles complement each other quite well and help provide a clearer picture of Stone and life for nineteenth-century American women.

957. Lane, Ann J. *To Herland and Beyond: The Life and Work of Charlotte Perkins Gilman*. New York: Pantheon Books, 1990. 413p. bibliog. index. (OP)

As indicated in the title, Lane focuses on Gilman's creation of her life and the significance of her work since both are essential to understanding Gilman herself. Gilman, author of the feminist classic "The Yellow Wallpaper," became an internationally known social critic but often struggled with conflicting demands between her role as a wife and mother and her desire to write and lecture. Structuring the book around Gilman's core relationships, including each parent, two husbands, intimate friends, her neurologist, and her daughter, enables Lane to examine Gilman's inner life as well as outside events and to revisit themes from different perspectives as Gilman's life progresses. Based on Gilman's letters, diaries, personal writing, and published and unpublished essays, Lane's book illuminates the complexities of this passionate author and theorist who wrote through the lens of her experience as a woman. Emily Toth focuses on Kate Chopin, author of another feminist classic, *The Awakening* (1899) in *Kate Chopin* (Morrow, 1990). Twenty years in the making, this meticulously researched biography is based on an impressive number of sources, including Chopin's personal writings, interviews with descendants, and genealogies and histories of the three cities where Chopin lived, St. Louis, New Orleans, and Cloutierville, Louisiana. Hence Toth includes extensive information about Chopin's family, career, friends, and the cultures in which she lived. She also provides insightful biographical readings of Chopin's fiction, often finding real-life models for fictional characters, including Edna's lover in *The Awakening*. Many scholars consider Toth's biography essential to Chopin studies.

958. Lear, Linda J. *Rachel Carson: Witness for Nature*. New York: Henry Holt, 1997. 634p. bibliog. index. ISBN 0805034277.

Lear meticulously traces the life of Rachel Carson, credited with galvanizing the modern environmental movement through her poetic book *Silent Spring* (Houghton Mifflin, 1962), which alerted the world to the danger of the indiscriminant use of pesticides to all living things. As the author reconstructs Carson's early life, education, and career in the U.S. Fish and Wildlife Service, she discusses the difficulties facing women scientists, the constraints placed on Carson by family responsibilities, the influence of female mentors, and her indefinable relationship with a married woman. Dorothy Freeman. Lear also examines Carson's successes, efforts to discredit her after the publication of *Silent Spring*, and her final illness, which she battled while writing her landmark work. This very readable title provides insight into the evolution of American environmental policy as well as the life, times, and achievements of an eminent scientist.

Always, Rachel: The Letters of Rachel Carson and Dorothy Freeman, 1952–1964 (Beacon Press, 1995), edited by Martha Freeman, collects more than 700 letters between the two women over the period of their deep and loving relationship, which ended with Carson's death in 1964. The letters contain many new and wonderful descriptions of plants, animals, and birds and provide insight into Carson's writing process. H. Patricia Hynes contributes a feminist reading of *Silent Spring* and discusses negative reactions to the book by the chemical and agribusiness industries in *The Recurring Silent Spring* (Pergamon Press, 1989). The author also provides detailed examples of research conducted since 1962 that supports Carson's conclusions and evaluates the effectiveness of the Environmental Protection Agency and its mission. Using Carson's principles of environmental protection, Hynes suggests policies for regulating reproductive technologies and workplace protection for women, and the revitalization of the EPA. This book contributes to knowledge about Carson and her work and to feminist analysis of the (male) domination of nature and women's bodies.

959. Lee, Hermione. *Virginia Woolf.* New York: Knopf, 1997. 893p. bibliog. index. ISBN 0679447075. (OP)

In this impressively researched biography, Lee conducts an open and critical examination of Woolf's life that recognizes the writer's complexities and contradictions. The author immersed herself in biographies, letters, memoirs, and scholarly materials in addition to Woolf's own life writing and her fiction and nonfiction. She begins by discussing Woolf's preoccupation with biography, representation, and self-representation and her contributions to modernism and feminism. Lee also addresses previous biographical treatments of Woolf, crediting the authors for asking important questions and illuminating aspects of Woolf's life even when she disagrees with their conclusions. The author also provides richly detailed context for the world(s) in which Woolf lived and wrote.

The culmination of fifteen years of studies on Woolf, *Virginia Woolf: The Impact of Childhood Sexual Abuse on Her Life and Work* (Beacon Press, 1989) by Louise DeSalvo thoroughly investigates sexual assaults on Woolf by her half brothers. DeSalvo examines Woolf's often ignored juvenilia, her representations of child characters and their interpretations of the world, and Woolf's own childhood and family, as well as Victorian childrearing practices and 1980s studies on child sexual abuse. Some scholars dismissed the book as reductive and faulted DeSalvo's interpretation of some of the evidence. Nevertheless, this controversial title contributes to debates on biography, sexual abuse and its consequences, and the authority of women and children's voices.

960. Lee, Mary Paik. *Quiet Odyssey: A Pioneer Korean Woman in America.* Edited with an introduction by Sucheng Chan. Seattle: University of Washington Press, 1990. 201p. bibliog. (OP)

In this commendable collaboration between Lee, a Korean immigrant, and Chan, a historian of Asian immigrants to the United States, Lee tells the story of her well-to-do family who fled the Japanese occupation of Korea in 1905. Family members were forced to take a series of subsistence-level jobs in farming and mining, first in Hawaii and then in California, where they faced constant individual and institutionalized racism. Lee highlights the major presence of the Christian church both in Korea, where it taught about democracy and fed nationalist sentiments, and in the United States, where it served as a community center to immigrants. She also provides details about family marriages and careers and contrasts opportunities available to first- versus fourth-generation Korean Americans. Chan, the editor, contributes an introduction that examines the social and political context of Lee's story and an invaluable bibliographic essay of materials in English about Korean history and Korean American immigrant experiences, as well as appendices that describe the editorial and research process and Korean American farming in California.

Bound Feet and Western Dress (Doubleday, 1996) by Pang-Mei Natasha Chang is really a dual memoir about the author and her quiet, unsophisticated, slightly masculine great-aunt, Chang Yu-I. While she was a student in Chinese studies, Pang-Mei, a first-generation Chinese American, found her great-aunt's name in a history book. She discovered that Yu-I had been married to China's most notable modern poet, had run the Shanghai Women's Savings Bank in the 1930s, and had obtained China's first divorce. The book tells the wonderfully detailed story of a woman who constantly rebelled against expectations of her well-to-do family and others of her class, her first rebellion being her refusal to bind her feet. In accounts interspersed within Yu-I's story, Pang-Mei describes her mixed feelings about her Chinese heritage, her search for her own identity, and facing constant struggle between her family's and her own expectations about living her life. Both of these fascinating memoirs could be supplementary texts in courses on women's biography or immigrant women.

961. Leslie, Kent Anderson. *Woman of Color, Daughter of Privilege: Amanda America Dickson, 1849–1893.* Athens: University of Georgia Press, 1995. 225p. bibliog. index. ISBN 0820316881; 082031871Xpa.

Born to a thirteen-year-old slave and her white master, Dickson was raised on the plantation of her prestigious father but was considered a slave until the Emancipation. When her father died in 1885, he left the bulk of his considerable estate to his only child, who was thirty-five at the time. White relatives challenged the will and took the case all the way to the Georgia Supreme Court. The court found the will valid, making Dickson the richest African American woman in the South. Leslie bases his account of Dickson's life on court transcripts as well as the white Dickson family papers, African American Dickson oral history, and other contemporary documents, since Amanda Dickson left no letters or memoirs. He shows that Amanda Dickson's personal identity was influenced by "her sense of class solidarity with her father, . . . her gender role as a lady, and her racial definition as a person to whom racial categories did not apply" (p. 2). The result is a highly interesting and creative examination of the legal rights of women and African Americans in nineteenth-century Georgia.

962. Levy, Marion Fennelley. *Each in Her Own Way: Five Women Leaders of the Developing World.* Boulder, CO: Lynne Rienner, 1988. 181p. bibliog. ISBN 1555870945pa.

Inspired by the United Nations Decade for Women (1975–1985) and her involvement with United Nations agencies, Levy examines the lives of five women who made significant contributions to emerging countries and whose work highlights primary issues of concern for rural women all over the world. Hasina Khan developed a nonformal education program of self-awareness for women in Bangladesh that enabled them to articulate their needs in community development programs. Elvina Mutua used her degree from business school to train farm women in Kenya in small business enterprise and marketing. Reyna de Miralda formed a grassroots organization of peasant women in Honduras that lobbies the government for change. Elizabeth O'Kelly provided technology appropriate to women's work in Cameroon and helped form the effective Corn Mill Societies. Aziza Hussein pioneered the family-planning and women's rights movements in Egypt. Levy provides the social context for women in the countries under study and bases her stories on interviews with the women themselves as well as with colleagues and friends and, in some cases, on letters and writings. She uses the same series of questions for all of the women, enabling them to talk about their childhoods, families, educations, and societies in their own words. This method provides coherence to the book and highlights both similarities and differences between the women and their work. Levy also provides useful lists of references and supplementary readings at the end of each chapter. Sue Ellen M. Charlton provides a fine introduction that examines tensions between tradition and change, changes caused by war, decolonization, and civil conflicts, the role of the government in supporting, hindering, or manipulating women's causes, and the role of women's organizations and leadership in emerging nations.

963. Lister, Anne. *I Know My Own Heart: The Diaries of Anne Lister, 1791–1840.* Edited by Helena Whitbread. London: Virago, 1988. 370p. ISBN 0860688402pa.

The dates provided in the title mislead a bit since they represent the life span of Anne Lister rather than the dates of the diaries themselves (1817 to 1824). Though the diaries provide details of upper-class, provincial life in early-nineteenth-century England, their real value lies in their contribution to lesbian history. Lister, a not particularly likeable snob, supplies quite frank descriptions, written in a secret code, about her love for women. Luckily for Whitbread, one of Lister's descendants and his friends had cracked the code, so the key to it was available with the diaries. In the preface, the editor describes how she came to write about Lister, briefly discusses her decision to focus on Lister's long-term love affair with Marianna Lawton, and provides very basic background information about Lister and where she lived.

Whitbread continues her research of Lister in *No Priest but Love: Excerpts from the Diaries of Anne Lister, 1824–1826* (New York University Press, 1992), which covers Lister's two-year trip to Paris, where a new love interest, Maria Barlow, caused her to question the nature of her sexual identity. In recording her struggle, Lister, through Whitbread's translation, provides unique insight into the expectations placed on women's lives and sexuality during the time period and leaves a rare primary account of lesbian life. In contrast, Jill Liddington's *Female Fortune: Land, Gender, and Authority: The Anne Lister Diaries and Other Writings* (New York University Press, 1998) focuses on Lister's writings during the 1830s to examine social relations, the rights of women landowners, urbanization, gender, class, politics, and economics.

964. Logan, Onnie Lee, with Katherine Clark. *Motherwit: An Alabama Midwife's Story.* New York: Dutton, 1989. 177p. (OP)

This oral history of African American Onnie Lee Logan tells the story of a woman who practiced midwifery in Alabama from 1931 to 1984. Although she worked as a maid for a prominent family, Logan considered midwifery her true vocation and attributed her motherwit (common sense or wisdom) to God. She lived during the period when government agencies began regulating midwifery and trained and licensed midwives. Logan talks about more than midwifery, however. She bears witness to the brutal poverty, racism, and backbreaking work of African American life in the rural South, as well as the sense of community and spiritual strength that sustained her during difficult times and situations. Clark contributes a short introduction that provides context to Logan's life. *Listen to Me Good: The Life Story of an Alabama Midwife* (Ohio State University Press, 1996), coauthored by Margaret Charles Smith and Linda Janet Holmes, recounts Smith's life, particularly her experiences as a midwife in a rural area of the state. Each chapter begins with brief historical context, provided by Holmes, discussing subjects such as medicine in Alabama during the late 1800s, tenant farming, midwifery regulation, medicinal plants, and the civil rights movement. The remainder of each chapter consists of Smith's recollections of birth practices, segregation, poverty, and hard work. Both titles affirm the important roles of African American women to both black and white communities and preserve the wisdom of a vanishing way of life.

965. Mairs, Nancy. *Waist-High in the World: A Life among the Nondisabled.* Boston: Beacon Press, 1996. 212p. bibliog. ISBN (OP); 0807070874pa.

Mairs, diagnosed with multiple sclerosis (MS) many years ago and now using a wheelchair, writes about the myriad ways in which disability shapes a person's life, both inward adjustments and relationships with the outer world. As in most of her previous titles on the subject, she examines her own experiences to dispel negative myths about disability and to offer a path for others facing unexpected, life-changing events. She believes that "a life commonly held to be insufferable can be full and funny" (p. 11).

Carnal Acts: Essays (Harper & Row, 1990) consists of pieces written to help Mairs make sense of her MS so her life would be bearable. She concentrates on ways to live a deliberate and responsible life without becoming emotionally hardened or hopeless and to welcome ambivalent feelings about experiences that are simultaneously good and bad. Mairs wrote *Plain Text: Essays* (University of Arizona Press, 1986) after a suicide attempt that made her realize that she was responsible for her own life. Her essays deal frankly with rape, madness, motherhood, agoraphobia, and MS as well as suicide. Mairs's sensitive, powerful, and witty titles have been used in women and disability courses or components.

966. Mathews, Nancy Mowll. *Mary Cassatt: A Life*. New York: Villard Books, 1994. 383p. bibliog. index. (OP)

Cassatt scholar Mathews provides one of the most complete examinations of the artist's life and career in this readable and well-researched account. She discusses Cassatt's family background and early life, travels in Europe, her education, friendships, trips to Spain and Italy to broaden her art education, the influences of the impressionists, especially Edgar Degas and Berthe Morisot, and the changing critical response to her work. Mathews suggests that Cassatt's many sketches of her nieces and nephews helped form her interest in mother-and-child paintings, which were also popular and the source of several commissions. This detailed account of one of the most successful female painters contains discussions of specific paintings but could have included more critical interpretations of them and explored their relationships to other artists' work.

Mathews, with Barbara Stern Shapiro, explores Cassatt's influence as a printmaker in *Mary Cassatt: The Color Prints* (Abrams, 1989), which includes many illustrations in color. Griselda Pollock's *Mary Cassatt: Painter of Modern Women* (Thames & Hudson, 1998) serves as a fine overview of Cassatt's life and career to 1893 and a synthesis of previous Cassatt scholarship. Nancy Hale's important and readable *Mary Cassatt* (Addison-Wesley, 1987) traces the phases of Cassatt's development as an artist and the barriers she faced as a woman in a male profession.

967. Mernissi, Fatima. *Dreams of Trespass: Tales of a Harem Girlhood*. Reading, MA: Addison-Wesley, 1994. 242p. ISBN 0201626497.

Feminist sociologist Mernissi has written a passionate, analytical memoir about her privileged childhood in French Morocco during the 1940s, a period of rapid social and political change. She focuses on daily life in the family harem, which confines women to the home, and its highly regulated, communal aspects. For the most part she talks about her mother and other older female relatives obsessed with "dreams of trespass," life beyond the gate that constrains them. While writing through her child's eyes about small rebellions (listening to the forbidden radio), contrasts between harem life in the city versus the country, nationalist politics, or early Arab feminists, Mernissi interweaves information about Islam and Arab culture and history. It is her evocation of the many ways in which the women sustain and entertain each other that stands out. The book is suitable for courses on Arab women, women's autobiography, and international women.

Mernissi cites opposition to Benazir Bhutto's rule of Pakistan on religious grounds as a springboard to search Islamic history for women rulers in *The Forgotten Queens of Islam* (University of Minnesota Press, 1993). Drawing on traditional Islamic and other sources, she examines the lives of several women, forgotten or ignored by historians, who did in fact rule Muslim empires. The author particularly analyzes the circumstances of their rise to power and what this might imply about both past and present gender relations in Islamic countries.

In *Women in Islamic Biographical Collections from Ibn Sa'd to Who's Who* (Lynne Rienner, 1994), Ruth Roded supplies a statistical analysis of the number of women included in biographical compendia from the ninth century to 1987. The author also offers brief biographies of women representing a variety of endeavors, including music, literature, scholarship, and politics. Roded and Mernissi both suggest that male interpretations of Islam, not the teachings of the Prophet Muhammad, have been responsible for women's lesser status. They also challenge Western interpretations of a monolithic Islamic history and open avenues for further research.

968. Millett, Kate. *The Loony Bin Trip*. New York: Simon & Schuster, 1990. 316p. (OP)

Diagnosed with manic depression (now termed bipolar disorder) in 1973, Millett, author of the feminist classic *Sexual Politics*, recounts her battle with the disease in this harrowing memoir. In 1980, the author made the decision to stop taking lithium, a drug with serious side effects, while trying to build a women's community on a farm in Poughkeepsie. She describes her abandonment by lover, friends, and family and memories of forced confinements in mental institutions. Millett heroically provides a chilling account of mental illness from the patient's perspective, revealing the brutality and politics of the Western mental health paradigm, the harm of stereotypes and misconceptions about mentally ill people, and the havoc caused by the terror and stigma of madness.

969. Mills, Kay. *This Little Light of Mine: The Life of Fannie Lou Hamer*. New York: Dutton, 1993. 390p. bibliog. index. ISBN (OP); 0452270529pa.

Born to a family of poor sharecroppers in the Mississippi Delta, Fannie Lou Hamer (1917–1977) endured years of poverty, hard work, and racism. In 1962, at the age of forty-four, she risked her life when she attempted to register to vote. This experience galvanized her, and she dedicated the rest of her life to the civil rights movement. Despite her lack of formal education, Hamer became a highly respected speaker and passionate singer who traveled widely to support civil rights efforts around the country. She took part in freedom marches, worked with the Student Non-Violent Coordinating Committee (SNCC), suffered through a vicious police beating, ran for public office, challenged the national Democratic Party and the president, and was a founding member of the National Women's Political Caucus and Freedom Farm Cooperative. Mills successfully and briefly describes the brutal atmosphere of intimidation, hatred, reprisal, and racism in 1960s Mississippi and provides a factual, but very readable, account of Hamer's life and work. Some might question whether Mills, a white journalist, does justice to Hamer's story. Aware of this point, Mills depends on quotes by and about Hamer from family, friends, and other activists and does not attempt to analyze the importance of Hamer's work. Chana Kai Lee's *For Freedom's Sake: The Life of Fannie Lou Hamer* (University of Illinois Press, 1999) examines Hamer's life and work through a lens of "moral pragmatism" and is notable for its discussion of the class bias Hamer experienced, not only from whites, but also from African American professionals in national civil rights leadership.

970. Morgan, Sally. *My Place*. New York: Seaver Books, 1988. 1st American edition. 360p. (OP)

The author, born in Perth, Australia, grew up thinking that her ancestors came from India, only to learn in her midteens that her grandmother was really Aborigine. Her grandmother and mother denied their heritage for years due to racism and refused to tell Morgan and her siblings anything about it. After finishing school, getting married, and starting a family, Morgan decided to write a family history, but the only cooperative person was her great-uncle. Morgan traveled to the area where her mother and grandmother had grown up and received a warm welcome from relatives and friends who remembered them. Eventually both her mother and grandmother told Morgan their life stories, and the last third of the book consists of transcriptions of these stories along with her great-uncle's. Their lives reveal the servitude, assimilation, and racist policies forced on Australian Aborigines. Morgan effectively describes her childhood and the prejudices she faced for having dark skin. The search for her heritage and the life histories of her family are also quite compelling. However, the depiction of her college years and life before marriage bogs down the narrative. Nevertheless, the book provides one of the few first-person accounts from an Australian Aborigine point of view and effectively describes working-class life during the 1950s and 1960s.

971. Murray, Pauli. *Song in a Weary Throat: An American Pilgrimage*. New York: Harper & Row, 1987. 451p. index. (OP)

Although Murray was born in Baltimore in 1910, she grew up with an aunt in the Jim Crow South, specifically, Durham, North Carolina. Whether discussing family members, some of whom passed for white, or incidents in their lives or her own, she powerfully and eloquently conveys what it was like to be African American and female in the United States during segregation, the depression, World War II, and the civil rights era. The author credits the love and pride that her extended family instilled in her as a source of personal strength that helped her overcome the many limitations she faced as an African American woman who strove for achievement. Refusing to attend a segregated college, Murray attended Hunter College and was the only African American in the school. The University of North Carolina denied her application for graduate studies because of her race, and Harvard Law School denied her application because of her sex. Despite these and many other setbacks, Murray succeeded in becoming a poet, writer, activist, teacher, lawyer, Episcopalian priest, and a founder of the National Organization for Women (NOW). This moving book is suitable for courses on African American women or autobiography.

972. Nestle, Joan. *A Restricted Country*. Ithaca, NY: Firebrand Books, 1987. 189p. bibliog. ISBN (OP); 0932379370pa.

Nestle, cofounder of the Lesbian Herstory Archives in New York City (now located in Brooklyn), challenges previous conceptions of autobiography, believing that "my body made my history" (p. 10). In these twenty-seven pieces she often connects erotic life to history and traces events in her childhood that radicalized her and helped shape the political adult. Nestle grew up in the 1950s in a Jewish working-class neighborhood in the lower east side of New York, daughter of a woman widowed five months before she was born. Whether writing about her mother, passing women, or her involvement in the activist 1960s, Nestle includes sexuality, her own and that of others, as part of life. Winner of the American Library Association's 1988 Gay/Lesbian Book Award, this title conveys the warmth, compassion, and humanity of its writer.

In *A Fragile Union: New and Selected Writings* (Cleis, 1998), Nestle again uses sexuality as the underlying theme in her discussions of people who in some way touched her, transgenderism, the arrogance of Reagan's America, and her battle with colon cancer, diagnosed in 1995. She also edited an important anthology, *The Persistent Desire: A Butch/Femme Reader* (Alyson Publications, 1992), a collection of poems, stories, personal accounts, and essays by lesbians from diverse backgrounds, ethnicities, races, and geographic locations honoring butch/femme relationships, past and present, in all their variety. This collection is credited with revitalizing dialogue about these often misunderstood, complex, even subversive erotic identities. Nestle's titles are suitable for courses on lesbianism or sexuality.

973. Ortiz Cofer, Judith. *Silent Dancing: A Partial Remembrance of a Puerto Rican Childhood*. Houston: Arte Publico, 1990. 158p. ISBN 1558850155pa.

Since Ortiz Cofer's father was in the navy, she spent her childhood traveling between the small island town in Puerto Rico where she was born and a small apartment in New Jersey. Using Virginia Woolf as her "literary mentor" (p. 13), Ortiz Cofer identifies the events, people, and "moments of being" (p. 11) that helped shape her personality. She also explores the effects of the constant adjustment between languages and cultures. Rather than chronologically relaying dates, marriages, deaths, and other details like conventional autobiographies, Ortiz Cofer in both prose and poetry celebrates the stories mothers, aunts, grandmothers, and other women used to enlighten girls about the realities they would face as Puerto Rican women. These stories vividly contrast with the "shades of gray" (p. 87) that dominate her memories of New Jersey. Ultimately, Ortiz Cofer argues that storytelling helps women, particularly those with "double" lives, develop their sense of place in the world.

In *When I Was Puerto Rican* (Addison-Wesley, 1993), Esmeralda Santiago provides a sharply detailed account of her childhood in rural Puerto Rico and the culture shock she and her family faced when they moved to New York City. The author continues her story in *Almost a Woman* (Perseus, 1998), which depicts her teen and young adult life. She writes with passion, humor, and depth about the challenges of learning a new language, helping her younger siblings and other family members negotiate the confusing, sometimes contradictory and hostile mixture of cultures in New York City, and coping with puberty. These titles are suitable as texts in women's biography and literature courses.

974. Painter, Nell Irvin. *Sojourner Truth: A Life, a Symbol*. New York: Norton, 1996. 370p. bibliog. index. ISBN 0393027392.

Painter, an award-winning historian, is concerned with tensions between self-representations and representations by historians, novelists, and biographers. She uses the *Narrative of Sojourner Truth*, various contemporary accounts, and visual images of Sojourner Truth (Isabella Van Wagenen) in her attempt to discover Truth the person and to examine the myths associated with her. Most notable are Painter's extensive discussions of the importance of religious influences in Truth's life and development and her analysis of photographic images of Truth, which she believes Truth mediated herself. This meticulously researched title sparked debates about research methodologies, contextual agendas that influence them, and the place of biography within the field of women's history. Earlene Stetson and Linda David employ a black feminist framework to analyze the words of Sojourner Truth and the context in which she spoke (or dictated) them in *Glorying in Tribulation: The Lifework of Sojourner Truth* (Michigan State University Press, 1994). They suggest that Truth's political consciousness developed from listening to people read the Bible and abolitionist newspapers and attribute part of her power as a speaker to her appropriation and reversal of biblical truths to make her point. This powerful and distinctive book contains appendices that present the text of some of Truth's lectures, songs, and letters, and an impressive bibliography.

Another scholarly, more conventional biography, *Sojourner Truth: Slave, Prophet, Legend* (New York University Press, 1995) by Carleton Mabee and Susan Mabee Newhouse, also uses original, contemporary sources to carefully reconstruct Truth's words, activities, and influence. All three titles examine the contexts of Truth's life, debunk Frances Dana Gage's version of

Truth, especially her rendition of the famous "Ar'n't I a Woman?" speech, and present more complex, richer portraits of Truth's life.

975. Parks, Rosa, with James Haskins. *Rosa Parks: My Story*. New York: Dial Press, 1992. 192p. index. ISBN 0803706731.

Parks, best known for refusing to give up her seat to a white person on a bus and igniting the Montgomery Bus Boycott, played an active role in the civil rights movement well before and after this incident. She began her career in 1943 by trying to register to vote and refusing to board a bus using the rear door. By 1949 she had became an advisor to the National Association for the Advancement of Colored People (NAACP) Youth Council and for many years was one of only two women activists in the Montgomery NAACP. Her arrest on December 1, 1955, and the boycott that followed it ultimately resulted in the U.S. Supreme Court declaring bus segregation laws unconstitutional in *Browder v. Gayle*. Parks remained active, participating in marches, speaking at conventions, working for Congressman John Conyers of Detroit, and founding the Rosa and Raymond Parks Institute for Self-Development. The book presents Parks's moving story in a first-person conversational style appropriate for undergraduates. A chronology completes the book. *Ready from Within: Septima Clark and the Civil Rights Movement*, edited by Cynthia Stokes Brown (Wild Tree Press, 1986), provides a similar treatment of Clark, who established citizenship schools throughout the southeastern United States, championed pay equalization for African American teachers, and dedicated herself to civil rights and political reform.

976. Peters, Margot. *May Sarton: A Biography*. New York: Knopf, 1997. 474p. bibliog. index. ISBN 0679415211.

The first biography of lesbian feminist poet, novelist, and journal writer May Sarton, this book provides an in-depth chronological account of the life, character, and personality of this inspirational writer. Peters bases her account on interviews with Sarton conducted in the years before her death in 1995 at age eighty-three. Sarton also granted Peters access to her voluminous papers, letters, journals, and photographs. In contrast to Sarton's version of her life as depicted in *Plant Dreaming Deep* (Norton, 1968) and *Journal of a Solitude* (Norton, 1973), Peters finds that Sarton could not bear to be alone and spent her life in relentless pursuit of women to serve as the muse necessary for her creative efforts. She contends that *Mrs. Stevens Hears the Mermaids Singing* (Norton, 1965), Sarton's coming-out novel written during her forties, served as a watershed in the writer's life and career, crediting it with popularizing Sarton's work in the budding lesbian feminist movement. Peters unflinchingly describes Sarton as a domineering, needy, willful, and egotistical woman who placed responsibility to her work above responsibility to other people. While many Sarton fans will not like this biography, it nevertheless provides a fair account of the writer's turbulent and passionate life that fully appreciates the woman, the writer, and the work.

977. Peters, Sarah Whitaker. *Becoming O'Keeffe: The Early Years*. New York: Abbeville Press, 1991. 397p. bibliog. index. (OP)

Peters chooses to focus on the period between 1915 and 1930, the years when O'Keeffe developed the style that defined her work. The author's meticulous research allows her to provide a full analysis of the artist's development within the larger artistic context, including a discussion of art nouveau and symbolist theory, as well as a fine exposition of O'Keeffe's influence on husband and photographer Alfred Stieglitz and his circle. Peters supports her points with 162 excellent illustrations, 46 of them in color, informative notes, and an extensive bibliography. Originally written during the 1950s with O'Keeffe's cooperation, *A Woman on Paper: Georgia*

O'Keeffe (Simon & Schuster, 1988) by her longtime friend Anita Pollitzer was not published earlier because O'Keeffe considered it too sentimental and romantic. The book is more successful as an affectionate memoir than as a critical biography. Pollitzer includes many examples of letters between the two women that provide insight into their world and early aspirations. Though short on analysis, the book discloses many new biographical details about O'Keeffe. The first author to have the cooperation of O'Keeffe's family, Roxana Robinson in *Georgia O'Keeffe: A Life* (Harper & Row, 1989) presents a well-documented, detailed account of the artist's entire life: her childhood in the Midwest during the 1890s, avant-garde New York after World War I, and New Mexico during later life. Using excerpts from letters, the author emphasizes O'Keeffe's struggle to balance love and work and the problems women faced as artists. *O'Keeffe: The Life of an American Legend* (Bantam Books, 1992) by Jeffrey Hogrefe is notable for its account of several sexual relationships between O'Keeffe and other women. The author also conducted several interviews with Juan Hamilton, O'Keeffe's last companion.

978. Pratt, Minnie Bruce. *S/he*. Ithaca, NY: Firebrand Books, 1995. 189p. ISBN 1563410605; 1563410591pa.

Poet and essayist Pratt calls on incidents from her life to explore daily choices, such as wearing a skirt, that help construct gender identity, and how sex and desire can give new meanings to gender beyond the polarized "masculine" and "feminine." She revisits lesbian feminist ideas about love, sex, and gender during the 1970s and 1980s, writing movingly about the pain and confusion she felt when other lesbian feminist women rejected her femme lesbian identity and erotic desires.

Another lesbian who self-identifies as femme, Dorothy Allison, addresses some of the same issues in *Skin: Talking about Sex, Class, and Literature* (Firebrand Books, 1994). The author, whose autobiographical novel *Bastard out of Carolina* (Dutton, 1992) made the shortlist for the National Book Award, also talks about the contempt heaped on those raised in poor, working-class families as she was, and how class permeates and shapes all aspects of her life. Like Pratt, Allison turned to activism within the lesbian community, only to find that she did not fit any of the "rules" about what a lesbian was and what lesbians were supposed to do in bed. Both authors write explicitly and frankly about their erotic desires, their struggle to come to terms with their expressions of gender/sexuality, and the high cost to self-concept and identity that toeing the lesbian feminist line caused them.

979. Prince, Mary. *The History of Mary Prince, a West Indian Slave, Related by Herself.* Edited by Moira Ferguson. London: Pandora Press, 1987. 124p. bibliog. (OP)

Originally published in 1831, this is the only known testimony in English of a West Indian slave woman. Editor Ferguson's introduction provides a concise contextual history, explains characteristics of British slave narrative structure, and discusses the politics, sexual and otherwise, of slavery. Born in 1788 in Bermuda, Mary Prince details the brutal physical, mental, and sexual conditions endured by slaves, particularly women. She was sold away from her mother and siblings to a series of vicious families who refused to allow her to buy her freedom. It took Prince twenty years of hard work, failing health, and psychological resistance to finally win her freedom. The book includes the revealing footnotes, introduction, and commentary of Thomas Pringle, the narrative's original editor and secretary of the Anti-Slavery Society, the narrative's original publisher. This important title provides a rare perspective of British slavery and contributes to the knowledge of the legal, economic, and social history of the Caribbean. The University of Michigan Press published a reprint of this book in 1993 and a revised and expanded edition in 1996.

980. Rittner, Carol, and John K. Roth, eds. *Different Voices: Women and the Holocaust*. New York: Paragon House, 1993. 435p. bibliog. index. ISBN (OP); 155778504Xpa.

The first anthology of its kind in English, this title adds an important component to Holocaust studies. The first section, titled "Voices of Experience," consists of eyewitness accounts of torture, medical experiments, hunger, and other aspects of life in Auschwitz. The second section, titled "Voices of Interpretation," consists of analyses written by historians, sociologists, and other scholars who examine such subjects as Nazi racism and sexism, daily lives of German Jewish women before the war, women in the resistance, and the complicity of Nazi wives in carrying out the "final solution." The third section, titled "Voices of Reflection," consists of literary reactions to the Holocaust. Brief biographical and contextual information precedes each piece, and maps, a chronology, statistics, and suggestions for further reading enhance the text. This poignant, moving, and powerful collection opens new avenues for research in Holocaust studies and serves as a fine tribute to the Jewish women who suffered one of the more horrific experiences of the twentieth century.

981. Romero, Patricia W., ed. *Life Histories of African Women*. Atlantic Highlands, NJ: Ashfield, 1988. 200p. index. (OP)

The contributors to this book include folklorists, linguists, historians, and anthropologists who employed different methodologies to record the life stories of seven African women from South Africa, Nigeria, Ethiopia, Ghana, and Kenya. One woman represents Hausa royalty, but most of the other women lead ordinary lives and came to the attention of the contributors during fieldwork. Contributors provide introductions for each woman's story, though the contents vary. Some provide historical and political contexts, while others focus on cultural traditions such as oral history or genealogies. The life of a Xhosa woman from South Africa is presented in one long transcribed narrative, but most stories include long quotes from the women connected by explanatory narrative. Notes and at least one map accompany each life story, and three stories include genealogies. Though some readers may prefer uniform methodologies and introductory information, this book quite ably illustrates different approaches to writing biography and helps undermine the monolithic category "African women."

982. Romney, Catharine Cottam. *Letters of Catharine Cottam Romney, Plural Wife*. Edited by Jennifer Hansen. Urbana: University of Illinois Press, 1992. 317p. bibliog. index. ISBN 0252018680.

The 170 letters collected in this book begin in 1873, shortly before Catharine Cottam's marriage to Miles Romney, and continue until a few months before her death in 1918. Hansen, Romney's great-granddaughter, arranges the letters in chronological order and divides them into four sections according to the places Romney lived: Utah, Arizona, Mexico, and back in the United States. Romney wrote most of the letters to her parents, and she provides details of an often difficult life as a pioneer, exacerbated by the prejudice against and illegality of polygamy. For most of her marriage, she shared her husband harmoniously with two other women and bore ten children. Even after Miles Romney's death, the women continued to live and work together until they were forced to flee Mexico in 1912 as a result of the revolution. Romney, sustained by a strong religious faith and sense of duty and sacrifice, provides a valuable account of daily frontier and Mormon life. For another, less harmonious account of a Mormon wife (and acquaintance of Romney) during the same time period, see *Mormon Odyssey: The Story of Ida Hunt Udall, Plural Wife* (University of Illinois Press, 1992), edited by Maria S. Ellsworth.

983. Rose, Phyllis, ed. *The Norton Book of Women's Lives*. New York: Norton, 1993. 826p. index. ISBN 0393035328.

Rose presents excerpts from twentieth-century memoirs, journals, letters, autobiographies, and oral histories available in English of more than sixty women. She selects the writings of many well-known women such as Maya Angelou, Billie Holiday, Beryl Markham, Helen Keller, and Gertrude Stein, as well as "ordinary" women such as Alabama midwife Onnie Lee Logan. The collection contains many excerpts representative of white American and European writers, but also includes writings of women from Africa, China, Vietnam, Brazil, and Puerto Rico. The selections depict a variety of experiences and methods, from the poetry of Angelou to the oral history of African tribe member Nisa. Rose arranges the women alphabetically and provides biographical background for each author along with useful suggestions for other writings included in the book (and some that are not) with common aspects, for instance, writings from the same time period, geographical area, and ethnic background or those with the same theme or form. Subject entries in the index or an appendix listing the books by these interests would have improved access to them. As it stands, the index consists of name and title entries. Rose's lengthy but informative introduction traces her lifelong interest in autobiography and discusses her selection process.

984. Sklar, Kathryn Kish. *Florence Kelley and the Nation's Work: The Rise of Women's Political Culture, 1830–1900.* New Haven, CT: Yale University Press, 1995. 436p. bibliog. index. ISBN 0300059124 (v. 1).

In this first of two volumes, Sklar does much more than provide information about the first forty years of Florence Kelley's life. She also traces the history of the cultural, economic, and social climate that enabled women to develop political cultures in nineteenth-century America. The author covers Kelley's early life, education (she was among the first generation of women who could attend college), her exposure to European socialism, and her brief marriage to a sometimes violent Russian expatriate. After leaving her husband, Kelley found her way to Jane Addams's Hull House, which provided a supportive environment and resources for her to find practical applications for her intelligence, her desire to live a meaningful life, and her commitment to social justice through labor activism. The volume ends with Kelley's appointment as general secretary of the National Consumers League, one of the subjects to be covered in the forthcoming second volume. Sklar provides extensive notes and bibliography in this excellent analysis of women's organizations, radical politics, industrialization, and labor developments through the lens of one extraordinary woman's life.

Eleanor J. Stebner's *Women of Hull House: A Study in Spirituality, Vocation, and Friendship* (State University of New York Press, 1997) contributes to our knowledge of Addams and Hull House through biographical sketches of eight key women, including Addams and Kelley. The author especially examines the personal and spiritual traits that motivated the women to live useful lives and dedicate themselves to helping their community reflect their ideals of Christian justice.

985. Tula, Maria Teresa. *Hear My Testimony: Maria Teresa Tula, Human Rights Activist of El Salvador.* Translated and edited by Lynn Stephen. Boston: South End Press, 1994. 240p. bibliog. ISBN 089608485X; 0896084841pa.

Tula, born in poverty and with little formal education or experience in politics, briefly discusses her childhood and difficult life as a working-class housewife. She spends most of the book examining her activism, which resulted from her husband's imprisonment for taking part in a workers' strike. In 1978 she joined the Committee of Mothers and Relatives of Political Prisoners, Disappeared, and Assassinated of El Salvador (CO-MADRES) and traveled to other countries to publicize the work of the organization and expose the brutality of the junta government. She tells an absolutely blood-chilling story of unmarked mass graves, assassinations, massacres of civilians, imprisonment, torture, and rape. Tula finally escaped to the United States in 1987 after her husband and other leaders were killed. Kelley Ready provides a succinct chapter examining women's roles in El Salvador's economy. Two other chapters discuss the history of women's grassroots organizing and the importance and purpose of testimonial literature. Only these supplementary chapters provide references, although editor Lynn Stephen supplies useful explanatory notes of customs, definitions, and other information throughout the book.

In *Crossing Borders* (Verso, 1998), Rigoberta Menchú revisits many of the themes of *I, Rigoberta Menchú: An Indian Woman in Guatemala* (Verso, 1984) and examines new topics in a series of lyrical essays that address winning the Nobel Peace Prize in 1992, her activism for the rights of indigenous peoples, her family and community, Guatemalan politics, a village massacre, and the sustaining cultural legacy of the Mayas. Both of Menchú's titles sparked controversy. Menchú has been accused of taking credit for others' work, ignoring conflicts of interest, and omitting important information about her activities, family, and other details. Tula and Menchú contribute riveting and forceful perspectives about corrupt and cruel governments that could serve as texts in courses in women's biography, women in social movements, and women and violence.

986. Ulrich, Laurel Thatcher. *A Midwife's Tale: The Life of Martha Ballard, Based on Her Diary, 1785–1812*. New York: Knopf, 1990. 444p. ISBN 0394568443.

In an epilogue, Ulrich tells the remarkable story of how the diary of Martha Ballard, aunt of Clara Barton, was passed down through generations of descendants until she learned of its existence in the Maine State Library. Though Ulrich begins each chapter with a series of transcribed entries, most of the book consists of her own interpretation, based on wills, deeds, court records, minutes from town meetings, county files, archives, contemporary histories, and other documents, of what the diary reveals about eighteenth- and early-nineteenth-century life. Tables and graphs, interspersed throughout the book, provide intriguing information about maternal mortality rates, stillbirth rates, and paternity and fornication court cases. The diary not only records the births of many of the 814 babies Ballard delivered but provides valuable insight into the female economy and attitudes toward debt, sexuality, death, and the nature of aging. Ulrich also provides a useful introduction that examines the history of Ballard's family and Hallowell, Maine, where most of the diary was written, as well as a fascinating appendix listing all herbs mentioned in the diary with their applications. Ulrich's writing and storytelling skills result in a highly readable and informative book.

987. Underhill, Lois Beachy. *The Woman Who Ran for President: The Many Lives of Victoria Woodhull*. Bridgehampton, NY: Bridge Works, 1995. 347p. bibliog. index. ISBN 1882593103.

Depicted as "Mrs. Satan" by Thomas Nast due to her controversial beliefs, Victoria Woodhull led a scandal-filled life that eventually alienated most of her supporters. This advocate of woman suffrage, spiritualism, socialism, and free love was the first woman to address Congress, the first woman to run for president (with Frederick Douglass as running mate), the first woman to originate and run her own weekly newspaper (*Woodhull and Claflin's Weekly*), and the first woman to establish and run her own brokerage firm. After publishing an article that accused preacher Henry Ward Beecher of having a mistress, Woodhull was imprisoned and lost everything she had. She and her family fled to England in 1877, where she reinvented her past, married for financial security, and totally denied her previous beliefs, claiming that others had published the controversial articles under her name. Underhill used a variety of primary and secondary sources, including various archives and Woodhull's papers, and has produced a well-researched factual account. While she provides historical, political, and social context for Woodhull's life and work, she does not provide much analysis on Woodhull's influence. However, this book is an overdue assessment of a fascinating personality.

Mary Gabriel, a journalist, uses contemporary newspaper accounts to present Woodhull's public life in *Notorious Victoria: The Life of Victoria Woodhull, Uncensored* (Algonquin Books, 1998). This clear account is most useful for its analysis of the brokerage firm Woodhull, Claflin and Co. and *Woodhull and Claflin's Weekly*. Many scholars, however, criticized the title for its lack of analysis, simplification of characters and events, and faulty knowledge of nineteenth-century America.

988. Van Voris, Jacqueline. *Carrie Chapman Catt: A Public Life*. New York: Feminist Press, 1987. 307p. (Women and Peace Series). bibliog. index. (OP)

Susan B. Anthony handpicked Carrie Chapman Catt (1859–1947) to succeed her as president of the National American Woman Suffrage Association (NAWSA) when she stepped down in 1900. Though Catt initially held the office only a few years, she was elected again in 1915 and led the successful campaign for Congress to pass the Nineteenth Amendment in 1919, which extended the right to vote to women. Between her stints as president of NAWSA, Catt founded the International Woman Suffrage Alliance (IWSA) in 1904 and traveled extensively throughout the world, and herein lies the value of Van Voris's account. Using many primary sources, including Catt's letters, travel diary, and published articles, Van Voris examines Catt's entire career rather than focusing solely on her contributions to American women's suffrage. Catt remained active in the fight for international women's suffrage and world peace long after women won the vote in the United States. In contrast, *Carrie Catt: Feminist Politician* (Northeastern University Press, 1986) by Robert Booth Fowler focuses on Catt as political strategist, leader, and visionary in the American women's suffrage campaign. Neither Van Voris nor Fowler found enough personal material to produce a full-fledged biography (Catt destroyed most of her personal papers), but both books are well researched and provide valuable insight into Catt's public life and work.

989. Victor, Barbara. *The Lady: Aung San Suu Kyi, Nobel Laureate and Burma's Prisoner*. Boston: Faber & Faber, 1998. 226p. ISBN 0571199445.

Although the government of Burma (also called Myanmar) placed limits on the author's movements and forbade her to meet Aung San Suu Kyi, winner of the Nobel Peace Prize in 1991, Victor valiantly attempts to present a fair account of her subject's life. Aung San Suu Kyi had lived in other countries for twenty years when she returned to Burma in 1988 to nurse her sick mother and became caught up in the democratic movement taking place there. She helped found the National League for Democracy (NLD), a group dedicated to nonviolence and human rights. Victor discusses events that influenced Daw Suu Kyi, her life and education in India, Japan, and Britain, the difficult choices she made between her family and her country, and her belief in her moral obligation to bring democracy to her country. The author is much more successful in providing historical, political, and cultural background on Burma and in conveying the climate of fear caused by government spies, censorship, forced labor, and relocation, the huge disparity between rich and poor, and the brutality of the State Law and Order Restoration Council (SLORC). Daw Suu Kyi's father, a national hero who negotiated independence from Britain in 1947, plays a large role in the country's political history and as a legacy in his daughter's life. (He was assassinated in 1948 when Daw Suu Kyi was two years old). This is a poignant, biting, and revealing account of the costs of dictatorship to a country, its people, and an individual woman. It would make a suitable text in women and politics, international women, and women's biography courses.

990. Wade-Gayles, Gloria Jean. *Pushed Back to Strength: A Black Woman's Journey Home*. Boston: Beacon Press, 1993. 276p. ISBN 0807009229.

Gloria Wade-Gayles, poet and professor at Spelman College, aptly calls these autobiographical pieces "rememberings" (p. xi) since they represent returns to her past. Some chapters deal with growing up in the housing projects in Jim Crow Memphis, Tennessee, in a loving extended family, while others tell more recent stories. Whether Wade-Gayles recalls the early civil rights movement, sending a daughter to college, or a disastrous haircut, she returns to the powerful lessons she learned from her family, particularly her mother, grandmother, and aunts. Wade-Gayles writes very effectively and movingly about being a southern black female who constantly faces racism and sexism, and while many of her stories are chilling, they are ultimately inspirational. Wade-Gayles also authored a collection of personal essays, *Rooted Against the Wind: Personal Essays* (Beacon Press, 1996).

991. Ware, Susan. *Partner and I: Molly Dewson, Feminism, and New Deal Politics*. New Haven, CT: Yale University Press, 1987. 327p. bibliog. index. ISBN 0300038208.

Continuing an argument introduced in *Beyond Suffrage* (Harvard University Press, 1981) that feminism did not die after 1920, Ware uses the career of Dewson to reveal the vitality and influence of women in the political arena. She covers Dewson's education and early career in women's voluntary associations, where she championed labor policies affecting working women, her work as director of the Democratic National Committee's Women's Division during the 1930s, her mentors (including Florence Kelley and Eleanor Roosevelt), and her efforts to help other women, notably Frances Perkins, obtain positions in various government agencies. Ware also provides sensitive treatment of Dewson's fifty-year relationship with Mary (Polly) Porter, the "partner" of the title. In fact, she believes that Dewson's woman-centered life affected career decisions and helped develop a feminism based on networking with other reform women. This intelligently written book provides details of the daily activities in reform circles and insightfully explores connections between women social workers and working women.

Elisabeth Israels Perry examines the life and influence of one of Dewson's largely forgotten colleagues in the meticulously documented *Belle Moskowitz: Feminine Politics and the Exercise of Power in the Age of Alfred E. Smith* (Oxford University Press, 1987). Moskowitz officially served as publicist for Smith (governor of New York) and campaign manager for his 1928 presidential bid, but in reality she researched and wrote much of the progressive legislation he introduced during his tenure. She was also considered one of the most powerful women in the country.

992. Wells-Barnett, Ida B. *The Memphis Diary of Ida B. Wells*. Edited by Miriam DeCosta-Willis. Boston: Beacon Press, 1995. 214p. (Black Women Writers Series). bibliog. index. ISBN 0807070645.

One of the few diaries written by an African American woman to be published, this book provides insight into the personality of journalist Ida B. Wells during three different, highly significant periods of her life. The first and longest diary was written in Memphis between 1885 and 1887, during the post-Reconstruction period when many gains for African Americans eroded and acceptable roles for middle-class African American women were limited to the domestic sphere. Wells taught school but felt restless and called to do more. Her diary reveals the intelligence, uncertainty, vanity, ambition, self-determination, and high standards that would become the hallmark of the mature public activist. She consciously used her diary as a "literary apprenticeship" (p. 11), and many of the structures and strategies of her later writings are in evidence. The second and briefest diary, her 1893 travel journal, records an account of the beginning of a trip to England and Scotland to obtain international support for her antilynching campaign. The third diary, written in Chicago in 1930, covers Wells-Barnett's unsuccessful campaign for a seat in the Illinois State Senate the year before her death. Selected articles written by Wells between 1885 and 1888 and an afterword consisting of excerpts from an interview of Alfreda Barnett Duster, Wells-Barnett's youngest daughter and editor of her autobiography, complete the book. DeCosta-Willis provides an instructive introduction, prefaces for each diary, and commentaries between entries.

Also using the diaries and other archival material, Linda O. McMurry attempts to uncover the reasons for Wells-Barnett's achievements, influence, and ultimate exclusion from power in *To Keep the Waters Troubled: The Life of Ida B. Wells* (Oxford University Press, 1998). This title is especially noteworthy for its examination of gender tensions and conflicts with the African American community. Scholars criticized it, however, for placing race above gender and ignoring previous African American feminist research on Wells. Nevertheless, this book, as well as DeCosta-Willis's volume, opens new avenues for research about Wells's life.

993. Wexler, Alice. *Emma Goldman in Exile: From the Russian Revolution to the Spanish Civil War.* Boston: Beacon Press, 1989. 301p. bibliog. index. ISBN 0807070041; 0807070475pa.

In this continuation of Wexler's *Emma Goldman in America* (Beacon Press, 1984), the author concentrates on the last twenty years of Goldman's life, the period after the United States deported her to Russia in 1919 when she was fifty years old. Wexler begins with an account of the two years Goldman spent in the Soviet Union and her disillusionment with the revolution after the Bolsheviks brutally took control. The author contends that Goldman's conflation of political persecution with Bolshevism ironically helped create the virulent anti-Communist mind-set that dominated Cold War politics. She further believes that this simplified stance eroded her support within socialist and other leftist groups. The second section covers Goldman's restless travel to England, Canada, Sweden, and other countries searching for an outlet for her work, while the final section examines Goldman's involvement in the Spanish civil war and other antifascist work until her death in 1940. Goldman's voluminous letters after her exile enrich Wexler's project. The correspondence connects Goldman's inner feelings with events taking place in the world and produces a juxtaposition between her private and public selves. Wexler creates a sensitive portrait of a cruelly disappointed, depressed, and isolated woman who was determined to live according to anarchist ethical principles. While some scholars faulted the book for its strong psychological orientation, its greatly detailed account provides insight into Goldman as well as world politics in the late nineteenth and twentieth centuries.

994. Willard, Frances Elizabeth. *Writing Out My Heart: Selections from the Journal of Frances E. Willard, 1855–96.* Edited by Carolyn De Swarte Gifford. Urbana: University of Illinois Press, 1995. 474p. (Women in American History). bibliog. index. ISBN 0252021398.

The journals of Frances Willard (1839–1898), lost for years, were rediscovered in 1982. This book provides, for the first time, selections from these forty-nine journal volumes, written during Willard's teens, twenties, and fifties. Best known for her work in the Woman's Christian Temperance Union (WCTU), Willard also actively supported voting rights for women, public kindergartens, separate prisons for women, and other social reforms. Gifford carefully describes her selection process and editorial method and includes an informative introduction that summarizes Willard's life, work, and influence. Her useful annotations identify people as well as biblical, literary, and historical allusions mentioned in the entries. Gifford's judicious journal selections focus on the young Willard's intellectual, spiritual, and moral development and the world-famous older Willard's involvement in WCTU controversies and building a reform network with counterparts in Great Britain.

Ruth Bordin's *Frances Willard: A Biography* (University of North Carolina Press, 1986) was the first biography written after the discovery of Willard's journals. In it, Bordin argues that the WCTU was the first mass women's organization in America and that Willard brilliantly used it as a stepping-stone to women's involvement in other reform issues. Both books complement each other quite well and supply fuller accounts of, for instance, Willard's love for other women and her ambiguous stand on lynching. Richard W. Leeman in his book, *"Do Everything" Reform: The Oratory of Frances E. Willard* (Greenwood Press, 1992) critically analyzes the rhetoric of Willard's best speeches, which are reprinted in the book.

995. Winslow, Barbara. *Sylvia Pankhurst: Sexual Politics and Political Activism.* New York: St. Martin's Press, 1996. 236p. bibliog. index. (OP)

In this political biography, Winslow focuses on Pankhurst's significance both within and beyond the British suffrage movement. To this end, she concentrates on Pankhurst's life and work between the years 1912 and 1924. Winslow follows Pankhurst's struggle to combine feminism and socialism, covering Pankhurst's years living in London's East End, where she learned about class oppression, her pacifism during World War I, when she switched to activism within class-based organizations, and her involvement in international Communism. The author also addresses Pankhurst's stands against capitalism, colonialism, and fascism. While Winslow presents a straightforward account of Pankhurst's life and work, she does not provide enough context to create the complex, multifaceted analysis her subject deserves, nor does she incorporate 1990s scholarship on Pankhurst's better-known and more militant mother, Emmeline, and sister, Christabel.

Sylvia Pankhurst: From Artist to Anti-Fascist (St. Martin's Press, 1992), edited by Ian Bullock and Pankhurst's son Richard, collects essays that discuss Pankhurst's art and her work on behalf of Ethiopia in addition to her suffrage, socialist, Communist, and antifascist activism. Most compelling is the analysis of Pankhurst's designs for the Women's Social and Political Union (WSPU), the organization founded by her mother, sister, and others. The definitive biography of this compelling and still relevant activist has yet to be written.

996. Woodress, James Leslie. *Willa Cather: A Literary Life.* Lincoln: University of Nebraska Press, 1987. 583p. bibliog. index. ISBN (OP); 0803297084pa.

In this revised and very much expanded edition of the author's 1970 publication, Woodress, a Cather scholar for more than twenty years, adds more than 300 pages of detailed information. He excels at providing thorough and accurate descriptions of the places in which Cather lived, worked, and traveled and in his readings of Cather's fiction. The author chooses not to speculate on Cather's sexuality and criticizes those who label her lesbian. Although Woodress paraphrases from previously unavailable letters (Cather forbade direct quotes from her personal papers), he has written a book best viewed as a resource for scholars rather than as an interpretation of Cather's life.

Sharon O'Brien uses feminist and psychoanalytic theories to examine Cather's early life and work up to the publication of *O Pioneers!*, her second novel, in *Willa Cather: The Emerging Voice* (Oxford University Press, 1987). The author focuses on the development of Cather's fictional voice and the role her gender played in it. O'Brien also believes that Cather faced deep gender conflict because the youthful author signed her name "William" and dressed as a boy and associated writing with masculinity. She credits a letter from author Sarah Orne Jewett for giving

Cather the encouragement she needed to write as a woman. O'Brien's approach leads to insightful new readings of Cather's early fiction.

Hermione Lee's *Willa Cather: Double Lives* (Vintage Books, 1991) explores the theme of duality in Cather's life and fiction. Lee considers Cather lesbian since all of her major attachments were to women but acknowledges that Cather never used the term. She cautions, however, against using this as a key to the fiction. Lee's title is notable for its examination of the ways in which Cather's inner and outer experiences helped shape her writing, and its analysis of language and voice in the novels and later fiction. The book was published as *Willa Cather: A Life Saved Up* (Virago, 1989) in Great Britain.

1999 CORE TITLES

Ahmed, Leila. *A Border Passage: From Cairo to America—A Woman's Journey*. New York: Farrar, Straus and Giroux, 1999. 307p. ISBN 0374115184.

Blair, Emily Newell. *Bridging Two Eras: The Autobiography of Emily Newell Blair, 1877–1951*. Edited by Virginia Jeans Laas. Columbia: University of Missouri Press, 1999. 382p. bibliog. index. ISBN 0826212549.

Brownmiller, Susan. *In Our Time: Memoir of a Revolution*. New York: Dial Press, 1999. 360p. bibliog. index. ISBN 0385314868.

Edelman, Marian Wright. *Lanterns: A Memoir of Mentors*. Boston: Beacon Press, 1999. 180p. bibliog. ISBN 0807072141.

Geniesse, Jane Fletcher. *Passionate Nomad: The Life of Freya Stark*. New York: Random House, 1999. 402p. index. ISBN 0394583965.

Jay, Karla. *Tales of the Lavender Menace: A Memoir of Liberation*. New York: Basic Books, 1999. index. ISBN 0465083641.

Pasachoff, Naomi E. *Frances Perkins: Champion of the New Deal*. New York: Oxford University Press, 1999. 157p. (Oxford Portraits). bibliog. index. ISBN 0195122224.

Rife, Patricia. *Lise Meitner and the Dawn of the Nuclear Age*. Boston: Springer, 1999. 432p. bibliog. index. ISBN 081763732X.

Saadawi, Nawal. *A Daughter of Isis: The Autobiography of Nawal El Saadawi*. New York: Zed Books, 1999. 294p. ISBN 1856496791; 1856496805pa.

Thurman, Judith. *Secrets of the Flesh: A Life of Colette*. New York: Knopf, 1999. 592p. bibliog. index. ISBN 039458872X.

Uglow, Jennifers, and Maggie Hendry, eds. *The Northeastern Dictionary of Women's Biography*. 3rd. ed. Boston: Northeastern University Press, 1999. 622p. bibliog. index. ISBN 155553421X.

Wallace, Christine. *Germaine Greer: Untamed Shrew*. New York: Faber & Faber, 1999. 1st American edition. 333p. bibliog. index. ISBN 0571199348.

WORLD WIDE WEB/INTERNET SITES

997. *Distinguished Women of Past and Present*. http://www.distinguishedwomen.com/.
Maintained by Danuta Bois, this extensive site includes biographical information about historical and contemporary women, representing a variety of endeavors and geographic locations, who made significant contributions to culture. Users can search by subject or name or browse by category (Black History Month, books about women, and recent additions). The site contains numerous links to related sites, many of which focus on women in various race and ethnic groups, specific occupations, or geographic locations. Bois plans to add biographies and links as they become available.

998. *FemBio*. http://www.fembio.org.
This site consists of a subset of 600 biographies from the *Notable Women International Database* developed by Luise F. Pusch. Each record contains name, dates and places of birth and death, nationality, information about the subject's life and work (if available), and a list of sources for further research. The site provides flexible full-text searching in English or German and can be used to find women in the same occupation, from the same time period, or from the same country. Pusch adds new entries to the database daily and hopes to find funding to move the more than 30,000 biographies from the database to the Web.

999. *Women's Biography Sites*. http://home.earthlink.net/~sharynh/womensbiography .htm.
Created by Sharon Hushka, this site links to more than 250 biography Web sites. Users can consult an alphabetical list of sites or browse subdivisions under nine broad categories. Women represent various time periods (ancient, medieval), occupations, and races and ethnicities. Some of the more intriguing subdivisions include deaf women, witches, and Crusades.

13 Communications, Mass Media, and Language

Ellen Broidy

Since the beginning of the second wave of the women's movement and the rise of women's studies as an academic discipline, scholars both within the academy and outside have debated the significance of representation. One of the earliest rallying cries of the movement and most especially its academic wing was for women to have a "voice," to be empowered to tell their own stories and narrate their own lives in language that embraced fully this experience and these lives. This desire to speak (and be heard) was severely constrained by language systems that assumed the universal male. Feminist students of language analyzed the gendered basis and bias of the written and spoken word and marshaled a dazzling array of theoretical arguments in their efforts to understand (and explain) the invidious nature of commonly accepted discursive practices. At the same time, other scholars began the arduous task of deconstructing visual media, most specifically, cinema and television, and showing us how complicated and multifaceted even the most readily accepted aspects of popular culture really were. Still others took to task the news media, exposing the stereotypes and biases that passed for neutrality in the pages of the daily newspapers, between the covers of glossy magazines, and over the airwaves.

This hard work of overturning long-accepted cultural norms and conventions has borne fruit, particularly in the last decade. The works in this chapter cover three distinct yet interrelated facets of "representation": communications (language), film and television, and mass media. The titles selected range from autobiographical/biographical works depicting the lives of women who had enormous impact on mass culture to analyses of soap operas and other entertainment aimed at female audiences. Some of the titles, such as Deborah Tannen's *Talking from 9 to 5* and *You Just Don't Understand*, have themselves become part of the lexicon of gendered communication, while others focus more specifically on academic debates on how language constructs reality and tend to have a more limited audience. Taken as a whole, the works in this chapter reflect a decade's worth of sophisticated and complex thinking about many of the things we take most for granted— how we communicate, what we read, and the ways we see ourselves and others.

REFERENCE SOURCES

1000. Galerstein, Carolyn L. *Working Women on the Hollywood Screen: A Filmography.* New York: Garland, 1989. 470p. indexes. (Garland Reference Library of the Humanities, v. 469). (OP)

Published posthumously, Galerstein's book provides a listing, organized by occupation or job category, of the portrayal of working women in Hollywood cinema. Within each occupational category (ranging from "Advertising" to "Writer"), the contents (names of films in which women portray advertising executives, airline stewardesses, writers, and so on) are further subdivided by date of the film's release. Each occupational category begins with a brief analysis of the dominant themes of the films portraying women in these jobs. For example, the introductory text to the occupational category "Athlete" explains, "Generally women athletes are more entertainers than athletes in the movies, as exemplified by the aqua shows graced by Esther Williams" (p. 19). While the information provided on the majority of films listed does not go beyond title, date, studio, director, and actress portraying the profession, some do contain descriptive annotations of the films. The book has some illustrations, and access is enhanced by indexes to films and actresses.

1001. Kuhn, Annette, ed., with Susan Radstone. *The Women's Companion to International Film.* Berkeley: University of California Press, 1994. 464p. index. (OP)

Originally published by Virago (London) in 1990, this truly international guide presents an A-to-Z listing of short encyclopedia-like articles on people, places, and events critical to an understanding of women and film. This is the place to go for a clear and concise explanation of feminist film theory or for a discussion of a particular film genre. Noted filmmakers and academics contributed the brief essays. Scattered throughout the volume are "trivia questions," for example, "What species of bird is Hara-Mari?" (p. 58). The answers appear in a special section near the back of the book. The final section contains an index of films directed, written, or produced by women with page references to entries where the fuller discussions appear.

1002. Lent, John A., comp. *Women and Mass Communications: An International Annotated Bibliography.* New York: Greenwood Press, 1991. 481p. (Bibliographies and Indexes in Women's Studies, no. 11). bibliog. index. ISBN 0313265798.

This is a selectively annotated look at books, journal articles, and serial publications on the broad topic of women and mass communications. A careful reading of the preface is critical to appreciation of what Lent is attempting to do. In the preface, he lays out everything from the history of the representation of women in media-focused literature to the details of his computer search strategies and the rationale for the organization of the book. The first part, "Women and Mass Communications: Global and Comparative Perspectives," "cuts across geographical boundaries" (p. xii) to provide these comparative perspectives. The section is further divided into six subsections: "General Studies," "Historical Studies," "Images of Women," "Women as Audience," "Women Practitioners," and "Women's Media." The remainder of the bibliography is organized geographically, beginning with Africa and the Middle East and ending with the longest and most substantive section, North America. The geographically focused sections have subdivisions mirroring the organization of the initial chapter. Not everything is annotated, and most of the annotations are quite cursory. The author and subject indexes provide useful points of access to the contents. Lent updated the bibliography for the 1990s in 1999. (Sup.)

1003. Maggio, Rosalie. *The Nonsexist Word Finder: A Dictionary of Gender-Free Usage.* Phoenix: Oryx Press, 1987. 210p. bibliog. (OP)

While acknowledging the challenges inherent in determining whether a word is, in and of itself, sexist, Maggio's handy dictionary offers a wide variety of alternatives to words and phrases we often take for granted. The problem word or phrase appears in boldface type, listed alphabetically and followed by either an explanation of why the term or phrase is neutral rather than sexist or, more frequently, a group of italicized nonsexist options. The terms listed in boldface range from the everyday such as "manhandle" (p. 87), where Maggio offers "mistreat," "maltreat," "mishandle," and others as replacements for the offending term, to less common words and phrases such as "vizier" (a position always held by a man and therefore not a sexist term). In addition to the dictionary of alternative terms, the book also contains an appendix of "Writing Guidelines." Found here are definitions of concepts central to the debate over nonsexist language, including a short analysis of the important distinction between "sex" and "gender." The appendix also includes a section of "General Rules" (p. 168) for nonsexist writing and speaking. Appendix A concludes with brief discussions of "Special Problems" in writing, including "sex role words," "feminine endings," and "name calling." Appendix B is devoted to a series of very short essays on the significance and use of nonsexist language.

A prolific author, Maggio also compiled *The Dictionary of Bias-Free Usage: A Guide to Nondiscriminatory Language* (Oryx Press, 1991). In 1997, Maggio expanded upon both these earlier works in a volume titled *Talking about People: A Guide to Fair and Accurate Usage* (Oryx Press, 1997). This later guide also contains a section on "Writing Guidelines," but this time it has pride of place, appearing before the dictionary of terms. While covering much the same ground as the 1987 work, Maggio goes even farther, picking up on her 1991 book's inclusion of biased terms connoting race and physical ability in addition to sex. The essays in the 1997 volume are also more substantive, including one in which she refutes the arguments of so-called guardians of the language (William Safire, for example) who ridicule efforts to free written and spoken language from the chains of bias. The terms in the dictionary are likewise expanded to include alternatives to derogatory terms for a wide variety of people, places, objects, and conditions. Another useful title along the same lines is Marilyn Schwartz's *Guidelines for Bias-Free Writing* (Indiana University Press, 1995), a project of the Task Force on Bias-Free Language of the American Association of University Presses. Similar to Maggio's 1997 publication, this one covers bias in writing about gender, race, ethnicity, and nationality.

1004. Murray, Raymond. *Images in the Dark: An Encyclopedia of Gay and Lesbian Film and Video.* Philadelphia: TLA Publications, 1994. 573p. bibliog. index. ISBN 1880707012.

Using a running time of sixty minutes or longer as a criterion for inclusion, Murray has compiled a very personal encyclopedia of gay and lesbian images in cinema and video. Organized into nine parts, including "Favorite Directors," "Favorite Stars," "The Arts" (writers, directors, composers, dancers), and a chapter each dedicated to queer, lesbian, gay male, and transgender "interest," the entries cover the corpus of work of individuals, starting with a brief biographical essay, and annotations of major films with lesbian and/or gay content. Although slanted somewhat toward a gay male perspective, it contains sufficient focus on lesbian material to warrant inclusion in this chapter. Two other reference titles, less encyclopedic in scope, are also important to the study of lesbians and gay men in film: Jenni Olson's *Ultimate Guide to Lesbian and Gay Film and Video* (Serpent's Tail, 1994) and James Robert Parish's *Gays and Lesbians in Mainstream Cinema: Plots, Critiques, Casts, and Credits for 272 Theatrical and Made-for-Television Hollywood Releases* (McFarland, 1993).

1005. Segrave, Kerry, and Linda Martin. *The Post-feminist Hollywood Actress: Biographies and Filmographies of Stars Born after 1939.* Jefferson, NC: McFarland, 1990. 313p. bibliog. index. (OP)

In an effort to support their contention that in spite of the fact that "the period 1964 to the middle of the 1980s . . . coincided with a period of strong feminist sentiment" (p. vii), the visibility of women both in front of and behind the camera lagged far behind the women's movement's other successes, the authors focus on the lives and careers of women performing during this period. The fact- and opinion-filled introduction provides a historical overview of women in cinema and traces the reactions in the film community to changes in the nature and scope of acting roles for women from the 1960s onward. The picture Segrave and Martin paint is quite bleak, whether they are focusing on a comparison of salaries of male and female "stars," the types and quality of roles available to women, or the percentage of women in positions of authority and leadership in the film industry. The biographical sketches themselves, the bulk of the book, are presented in four sections: "Superstars," "Leading Ladies," "New Screen Stars," and "Up and Coming Actresses." A brief explanatory note describing what each category represents precedes the entries. Each short portrait contains biographical data, critical commentary on the actress and her roles, and a filmography. An appendix, "Gender Differences in Film," provides statistical data that compare, for example, the percentage of male and female characters in Oscar-winning films and the percentage, by gender, of the first five billed characters in films from 1936 to 1985.

1006. Signorielli, Nancy, ed. *Women in Communication: A Biographical Sourcebook.* Westport, CT: Greenwood Press, 1996. 501p. bibliog. index. ISBN 0313291640.

A compilation of short biographical sketches of women communication professionals, this volume covers both historical figures and women still active today. Signorielli's introductory essay traces the history of mass communications, especially newspapers, and identifies the point at which women began to be a force in journalism. The introduction also outlines the structure and organization of the essays that follow and make up the bulk of the book. All of them present information in the same fashion: family background, education, career development, major contributions and achievements, critical evaluation of contributions and achievements, integration of personal and professional life, and selected bibliography. The entries themselves are presented in alphabetical order from Mary Clemmer Ames (1831–1884) to Ida B. Wells-Barnett (1862–1931). Following the group of more substantive essays on the best-known women in the field, there is an appendix containing capsule biographies of "Notable Women in Communications," the vast majority of whom are academics.

1007. Unterberger, Amy L., ed. *Women Filmmakers and Their Films.* With introductory essays by Gwendolyn Audrey Foster and Katrien Jacobs. Detroit: St. James Press, 1998. 573p. bibliog. index. ISBN 1558623574.

A truly monumental undertaking, this encyclopedia offers signed articles on women filmmakers from the early days of cinema up to the present time. Two very informative introductory essays, one by Gwendolyn Audrey Foster, the other by Katrien Jacobs, provide excellent historical and theoretical contexts for an understanding of women behind the camera, directors, producers, editors, writers, and so on. Organized alphabetically, the entries provide brief biographical sketches, lists of films and other creative endeavors, and a bibliography of books and articles about the filmmaker. Following this introductory section, there is a short critical essay on the filmmaker's work. Although the vast majority of entries focus on an individual filmmaker, there are also some entries devoted to noteworthy and/or pathbreaking films (e.g., *Born in Flames, Deutschland, bleiche Mutter*). Indexes include "Nationality," "Occupation," "Awards," and "Film Titles." There is also a selected list of distributors of films by women filmmakers. A good companion piece, although more limited in its occupational scope, is Gwendolyn Audrey Foster's *Women Film Directors: An International Bio-critical Dictionary* (Greenwood Press, 1995).

MONOGRAPHS

General Communications

1008. Allen, Donna, Ramona Rush, and Susan J. Kaufman, eds. *Women Transforming Communications: Global Intersections.* Thousand Oaks, CA: Sage, 1996. 377p. bibliog. index. ISBN 0803972660; 0803972679pa.

The essays of this collection, which focus on communications and "networking," introduce new arguments and expand upon previous ideas about networking in essays that Rush and Allen gathered in *Communications at the Crossroads: The Gender Gap Connection* (Ablex, 1989). In *Women Transforming Communications*, the editors discuss networking using feminist communications theory and practice with an eye on diversity and inclusiveness. They organize the work into three interrelated parts: "Communications Visions," "Communications Chasms," and "Transformative Communications." Contributors explore ways in which women have used and transformed communications media and technologies to subvert the dominant order and connect with one another. A clarion call to free communications from gender, class, racial, and cultural bias, this collection bridges the often artificial disciplinary and professional divide between communications and mass-media studies, demonstrating how one informs and often changes the other.

Women and Language in Transition (State University of New York Press, 1987) by editor Joyce Penfield represents an earlier attempt to cover much of the same ground. Yet whereas Allen and colleagues incorporate race throughout their work, Penfield's volume follows a slightly older identity politics model and isolates the three articles on women of color into a single section.

1009. Bate, Barbara, and Judy Bowker. *Communication and the Sexes*. 2nd ed. Prospect Heights, IL: Waveland Press, 1997. ISBN 0881339334.

A combination textbook and guide for improving communications between women and men, *Communication and the Sexes* takes a proactive approach to the problem of understanding and being understood. Careful to distinguish between sex and gender, Bate and Bowker argue that individuals create and re-create gender in communication. The authors theoretically frame their work with this idea, which they explain in detail in the first chapter. They outline major arguments in the field of communications and compare basic approaches to the study of communication and the sexes in chapters 2 through 4. In the remaining six chapters, Bate and Bowker discuss communication in specific contexts, including stages of relationship development; children's efforts to interpret interpersonal messages among family members, whether or not such messages meet children's expectations for appropriate masculine or feminine behavior; public communication between teachers and students; communication at the workplace; mass media; and the impact of the women's and men's movements on changing personal communications styles. Each essay begins with a chapter overview and includes a conclusion, discussion questions, and cases for analysis. Barbara Bate and Anita Taylor edited *Women Communicating: Studies of Women's Talk* (Ablex, 1988), a collection of essays that examine diverse topics, such as Judy Chicago's *Dinner Party*, implementing feminist principles at the National Film Board of Canada, and the politics of weight loss and women's identity.

1010. Cameron, Deborah. *Feminism and Linguistic Theory*. 2nd ed. New York: St. Martin's Press, 1992. 247p. bibliog. index. ISBN 0312083769.

Cameron first published her overview of feminist theories of language in 1985. In less than a decade, significant changes occurred within the scholarly work of feminism and language, as well as feminist political theory, that warranted a second edition. In both editions, Cameron elucidates highly intricate arguments about linguistics without diluting their complexity or power. She organizes the work into eight substantive chapters, along with an introduction, "Language and Feminism," and a conclusion, "Problems and Practices." The author tackles issues such as sexist language and devotes two chapters to delineating the various theoretical and empirical approaches to sex differences in language. Although Cameron again devotes considerable space to Dale Spender's arguments about language and gender, she provides a compelling theoretical alternative to these arguments in the 1992 edition. In her second chapter on feminist models of language, she introduces postmodernism and the "debate on the gendered subject," clearly one of the most significant and contentious theoretical debates within feminism. In addition to footnotes and a bibliography, Cameron includes a glossary of terms critical to an understanding of modern linguistic theory.

In 1998, Cameron published a second edition of *The Feminist Critique of Language: A Reader* (Routledge, 1998). She retains many selections from the earlier edition, but broadens the scope of her argument to include diversified feminist debates on language, as well as discussions that expand beyond the realm of literature. Cameron and Jennifer Coates edited the influential *Women in Their Speech Communities* (Longman, 1989). Coates followed up her significant 1986 work *Women, Men, and Language: A Sociolinguistic Account of Gender Differences in Language* with a second edition (Longman, 1993).

1011. Crawford, Mary. *Talking Difference: On Gender and Language.* Thousand Oaks, CA: Sage, 1995. 207p. (Gender and Psychology). ISBN 0803988273; 0803988281pa.

Crawford approaches the ongoing debates about the relationship between language and gender through an analysis of conversation. The author focuses on talk, or "language as social action" (p. xii). Crawford criticizes essentialist arguments that posit a difference based on gender in terms of how men and women use and relate to language; these theorists frequently conclude that women's talk is limited and ineffectual. The author begins her analysis with a critical overview of some of the dominant theories of sex difference and language, criticizing the tendency of proponents of certain theoretical schools who treat "women as a global category" (p. 7), which, she posits, fails to account for other key differences, such as class, (dis)ability, race, and age. She critiques some of the most visible and frequently cited authorities on men, women, and language, including Deborah Tannen, Robin Lakoff, and Cheris Kramarae. Crawford argues that her social constructionist view of language potentially could dispel the view of sex-difference theorists that speech features are static in meaning (p. 17). Crawford concludes with an appeal to feminists to subvert the sex-difference argument through the use of her research to create new strategies for imaging alternative approaches to studying the interaction between language and lives.

1012. Glenn, Cheryl. *Rhetoric Retold: Regendering the Tradition from Antiquity through the Renaissance.* Carbondale: Southern Illinois University Press, 1997. 235p. bibliog. index. ISBN 0809319292; 0809321378pa.

Glenn approaches rhetoric and language from a uniquely historical perspective. She begins with an overview of language and rhetoric in a chapter titled "Mapping the Silences, or Remapping Rhetorical Terrain." She discusses her goal of regendering the rhetorical tradition through the identification, location, and analysis of women writers' works from antiquity through the Renaissance, historical epochs not widely known for women's voices. This work introduces women writers who have appeared as little more than footnotes in most discussions of the rhetorical traditions of their period. Glenn discusses both well-known and obscure women writers from antiquity. Instead of focusing on the object of Sappho's poetry, often interpreted as lesbian, Glenn argues that Sappho's use of language altered traditional forms, describing women as active agents. Glenn also introduces Aspasia and Diotima, hardly household names in the study of rhetoric. In subsequent chapters on medieval and Renaissance culture, she analyzes women's writing that appeared "inscribed in the margins" (p. 118). Glenn provides both a historical and theoretical context for her argument, examining women's words in terms of historical and rhetorical tradition.

1013. Graddol, David, and Joan Swann. *Gender Voices.* Oxford: Basil Blackwell, 1989. 214p. bibliog. index. (OP)

Graddol and Swann review the complex theories on gender and language that predominated during the 1980s. The authors divide the work into the following seven sections: "The Study of Language and Gender," "The Voice of Authority," "Accents of Femininity," "Conversation: The Sexual Division of Labor," "Is Language Sexist?" "Language, Communication, and Consciousness," and "Linguistic Intervention." In section 1, "The Study of Language and Gender," Graddol and Swann describe clearly some of the most significant and complex theories about the study of language and linguistics, as well as important aspects of the relationship between language and gender. They assert that linguistic and social practices are "mutually supportive" (p. 10). In the remainder of the book, the authors diverge from purely linguistic or language-based arguments, focusing instead on social theories that explain the role of language in gender relations. In the final section, "Linguistic Intervention," the authors use case studies to examine what they call "practical interventions": linguistic strategies used to disrupt language-based social and gender inequities. Much early and continuing work on language and gender is based in British universities, which creates a form of linguistic inequality for U.S. students as they sometimes encounter difficulties when negotiating the unfamiliar terrain of the "other" English. Graddol and Swann use clear prose and demystify difficult concepts with ease, making this work accessible to students unfamiliar with British English.

1014. Hall, Kira, and Mary Bucholtz, eds. *Gender Articulated: Language and the Socially Constructed Self.* New York: Routledge, 1995. 512p. bibliog. ISBN 0415913985; 0415913993pa.

In 1975, Robin Lakoff published *Language and Women's Place* (Harper & Row), marking one of the first attempts to examine the gendered nature of language, in conjunction with its academic counterpart, linguistics. Lakoff's work unleashed a firestorm of criticism while simultaneously opening up an entire field of academic inquiry. Hall and Bucholtz rely upon Lakoff's organizing principle for this collection of essays. The editors bring together feminist scholars who attempt neither to refute nor embrace Lakoff's work. Hall and Bucholtz divide the work into three parts: "Mechanisms of Hegemony and Control," "Agency through Appropriation," and "Contingent Practices and Emergent Selves." Each title reflects an important theoretical stance in feminist scholarship on language. In part 1, contributors examine how people perpetuate cultural norms through language. Part 2 features contributions by Robin Lakoff, as well as an essay by Susan Herring, Deborah A. Johnson, and Tamra DiBenedetto about tensions surrounding women's demands for equality in Internet chat rooms. Contributors analyze how women have subverted dominant or hegemonic linguistic practices in "Agency through Appropriation," while articles in the third part, "Contingent Practices and Emergent Selves," deal with the way individuals use language to construct identity and community. Although not an easy read, *Gender Articulated* introduces critical concepts and important debates in communications and linguistic theory.

Alette Olin Hill's *Mother Tongue, Father Time: A Decade of Linguistic Revolt* (Indiana University Press, 1986) also relies upon Robin Lakoff's pioneering work. Hill even refers to the period in which she began her initial explorations of gender and language as "B.L. (Before Lakoff . . .)" (p. xiv). This work represents Hill's contributions to scholarship tracing gender-related changes in American English between 1976 and 1986.

1015. Kalbfleisch, Pamela J., and Michael J. Cody, eds. *Gender, Power, and Communication in Human Relationships.* Hillsdale, NJ: Lawrence Erlbaum Associates, 1995. 366p. bibliog. index. ISBN 0805814035; 0805814043pa.

This book of essays, all written during the 1990s, provides theoretical viewpoints and review chapters that examine various aspects of power in female/male relationships. The editors arrange the volume into four sections. In the first section, an introduction and overview, Cody and Ka-lbfleisch connect the collection to current events, ranging from the "two for the price of one" presidency of Bill Clinton to snippets from articles in the daily newspaper. They also explain how the work represents an interdisciplinary conversation between psychology and communications. After the introduction, the editors provide a highly useful table of synopses of all of the essays contained therein. Each summary or précis includes a short paragraph that outlines how the author deals with "History of Research," "Equality: The Good and the Bad," and "Female and Male Relationships." The editors divide the bulk of the volume into three parts: "Gender-Based Expectations and Beliefs," "Women and Men Together," and "Women and Men in Society." In "Gender-Based Expectations and Beliefs," essayists analyze how stereotyping and typecasting women and men affect their view of behaviors toward gender. Contributors to "Women and Men Together," the longest part in the book, concentrate on communications and power within intimate interpersonal relationships, focusing on dating, negotiating safe sex, and managing both anger and money. Essays of the last part examine relationships between women and men on a macro level, focusing on social bellwethers such as television, shopping, and other family activities. This volume contains a subject index and a very useful author index.

1016. Kotthoff, Helga, and Ruth Wodak, eds. *Communicating Gender in Context*. Philadelphia: John Benjamin, 1997. 424p. (Pragmatics Beyond; New Series42) bibliog. index. ISBN 1556198043.

European scholars contribute to this collection of essays, which focuses on scholarship, language, and gender from a non-U.S. perspective. According to the editors, gender markers are far more apparent in Germanic, Slavic, and Romance languages than in English. Thus Kotthoff and Wodak give European scholars a platform to describe their social and cultural norms, as well as "to contextualize statements about gender and arrangements between the sexes within a cultural, situational, or institutional framework" (p. vii). Contributors examine instances that illustrate how gender is produced and reproduced through "context-specific gendered activities" (p. ix). Readers should read the book's preface, in which the editors define their philosophical and theoretical orientation and constructively criticize other theoretical positions, especially, deconstruction. The preface also includes an article-by-article overview of the volume's contents. Although somewhat complex, *Communicating Gender in Context* is one of only a few works that incorporate a feminist analysis of language and communication that is not completely Anglocentric. However, all of the articles are in English.

1017. Livia, Anna, and Kira Hall, eds. *Queerly Phrased: Language, Gender, and Sexuality*. New York: Oxford University Press, 1997. 460p. (Oxford Studies in Sociolinguistics). bibliog. ISBN 0195104706; 0195104714pa.

In this collection, which marks one of the first efforts to fold queer and linguistic theories into an analysis of sexual orientation and language, contributors examine the intersections of queer, feminist, and traditional linguistic theory. The notable absence of nonheterosexual perspectives on linguistics inspired Livia and Hall to include the work of scholars who realize how the linked categories of gender and sexuality both differ and converge. In the introduction, the editors define the tenets of queer theory that are most pertinent to linguistics. They arrange the articles into three sections: "Liminal Lexicality," "Queerspeak," and "Linguistic Gender-Bending." The editors include essays that address a wide variety of marginal national, historic, and linguistic practices. "Liminal Lexicality" contains essays about signing practices among deaf gays, lesbians, and bisexuals; queer male representation in Jewish American speech; and word meaning during the early sixteenth century. The final two sections examine equally diverse topics, including lesbian coming-out stories, e-mail, and the gendered and sexualized use of language in French, Hausa, and Japanese.

1018. Mills, Sara, ed. *Language and Gender: Interdisciplinary Perspectives*. New York: Longman, 1995. 282p. bibliog. index. (OP)

Contributors to this volume initially presented their work in 1992 at the Language and Gender Conference at Loughborough University. Revised and updated to reflect more current research, which indicates how swiftly ideas change in this field, the collection offers a cross section of theories on the complex interrelationship of language and gender. Mills contextualizes the essays and provides a theoretical framework for the problems inherent in examining gender and language as separate terms in her introduction. She organizes the essays according to their arrangement at the 1992 Loughborough conference. The first section, "Position Papers: Difference or Dominance," which features essays by Deborah Cameron and Jennifer Coates, delineates the theoretical terms of the debate. Coates discusses the difference perspective, a theoretical approach that looks at how men and women use language, attributing the distinctions to the notion that women and men are raised in gendered subcultures. Cameron argues that the difference theory does not account sufficiently for issues of power and dominance. Drawing on a wide range of both disciplinary and interdisciplinary perspectives, the remaining contributions cover diverse topics, such as lesbian poetics, including essays on Djuna Barnes and Sappho; gender and genre, including an examination of cyborgs and cyberpunk; and the intersections of feminist linguistic theory and gender with visual and media studies. Two sections contain essays on language, gender and children; one focuses specifically on education issues. The collection concludes with Mills indicating new directions for feminist work on language and gender and includes an excellent bibliography. Mills uses feminist and linguistic theory to analyze sexism in texts, as well as the ways in which point of view, agency, metaphor, and transitivity closely relate to gender in *Feminist Stylistics* (Routledge, 1995).

1019. Perry, Linda A.M., Lynn H. Turner, and Helen M. Sterk, eds. *Constructing and Reconstructing Gender: The Links among Communication, Language, and Gender*. Albany: State University of New York Press, 1992. 310p. (SUNY Series in Feminist Criticism and Theory). bibliog. index. ISBN 0791410099; 0791410102pa.

This volume consists of twenty-five essays that originated as papers delivered at the Tenth and Eleventh Annual Meetings of the Organization for the Study of Communication, Language, and Gender (OSCLG). The editors arrange the work into two broad sections: "Constructing Gender" and "Reconstructing Gender." Both sections contain several subcategories, or units, that introduce the essays. Extremely broad in scope, the volume includes an essay that posits that *Women on the Edge of Time* is a "liberating narrative," as well as a comparison of gender differences in perceptions of organizational stress by Brazilian and American managers. Other chapters deal with pedagogy, the mechanics of language, uses of women's bodies in advertising in the 1920s, tests of gender scales, and assertiveness in negotiation. Each unit begins with a brief introduction that both contextualizes and ties together the disparate contributions. Editors conclude each chapter with a list of references and include an index for the entire work.

1020. Rakow, Lana F., ed. *Women Making Meaning: New Feminist Directions in Communications*. New York: Routledge, 1992. 302p. bibliog. index. (OP)

According to Rakow, her emphasis on feminist work in the field of communications distinguishes her work from others on feminism and communication. She divides the collection into three parts. Part 1, "Women Making Meaning," features four essays that "take up some of the most significant political questions that feminist scholars in the field of communications face" (p. viii), including Rakow's analysis of the struggles of feminist scholars to change the field. Part 2, "Beyond the Field's Boundaries," explores communications scholarship on pornography, women's alternative media, and sexual harassment. The first essay in part 2, Elspeth Probyn's "Theorizing through the Body," represents one of the most exciting and challenging directions in which feminists have taken the study of communications. The essays in part 3, "Case Studies in Making Meaning," cross a wide range of disciplinary boundaries and examine various different methodological approaches. Case studies range from an analysis of women's narratives in a Puerto Rican community in New York City to a discussion of the race, class, and gender dynamics of the short-lived television sitcom *Frank's Place*. Rakow introduces each section with a short paragraph that contextualizes the essays.

1021. Talbot, Mary M. *Language and Gender: An Introduction*. Malden, MA: Blackwell Publishers, 1998. 257p. bibliog. index. ISBN 0745616798; 0745616801pa.

Talbot wants her work to make readers more aware of gender as a social category, the divisions made on this basis, and the role that language plays in both establishing and sustaining such divisions. In this introductory textbook, Talbot takes great pains not only to make this complicated material intellectually accessible, but also to give her readers the ability to apply what they learn to a variety of communications problems. She divides the work into three major parts: "Preliminaries: Airing Stereotypes and Early Models," "Interaction among Men and Women," and "Discourse and the Construction of Gender." Each section contains three or four chapters that detail major arguments and trends in linguistic theory. The author's exceedingly helpful short introductions to each chapter set the tone and context for the discussions that follow, making her work accessible to a wide range of readers.

1022. Tannen, Deborah. *Gender and Discourse*. New York: Oxford University Press, 1994. 203p. bibliog. index. ISBN 0195089758.

Tannen calls her work "discourse analysis," separating her field of study from that of other linguists. She approaches the study of communication as "connected language 'beyond the sentence' " (p. 5). A prolific author who writes books for disparate audiences, Tannen crafted *Gender and Discourse* for an academic audience. She begins with an overview of recent linguistic theory and then situates her own theoretical approach to the study of gender and language within significant currents in the field. In addition, Tannen addresses how her ideas about the nature of dominance differ from those of leading feminist critics. Each chapter consists of an individual essay that begins with an italicized preface that serves both to introduce the major theme of the chapter and, where appropriate, to tie it to the preceding one. Essays cover a range of topics, such as "Ethnic Style in Male-Female Conversation," an analysis of conversational strategy in Ingmar Bergman's *Scenes from a Marriage*, and a study of physical alignment and proximity in conversations between four pairs each of male and female best friends.

Tannen also edited *Gender and Conversational Interaction* (Oxford University Press, 1993), a volume in the series Oxford Studies on Sociolinguistics. She also has published *You Just Don't Understand: Women and Men in Conversation* (Ballantine Books, 1991) and *Talking from 9 to 5: How Women's and Men's Conversational Styles Affect Who Gets Heard, Who Gets Credit, and What Work Gets Done* (William Morrow, 1994). These two works are far more accessible than *Gender and Discourse* or Tannen's chapters in *Gender and Conversational Interaction*.

1023. Wodak, Ruth, ed. *Gender and Discourse*. Thousand Oaks, CA: Sage, 1997. 303p. (Sage Studies in Discourse). bibliog. index. ISBN 0761950982; 0761950990pa.

Presented in part as an introductory set of readings on the gendered nature of communications, this collection brings together scholarly work from a wide range of theoretical perspectives. In her highly informative introduction, "Issues in Gender and Discourse," Wodak presents an overview of the critical arguments and major theoretical positions in the field. Although Wodak clearly favors certain theoretical positions over others, she carefully defines each concept and provides an in-depth list of references for readers who wish to delve further into a particular argument.

1024. Wood, Julia T. *Gendered Lives: Communication, Gender, and Culture*. 2nd ed. Belmont, CA: Wadsworth, 1997. 471p. bibliog. index. ISBN 0534507700pa.

Novices frequently encounter difficulty grasping the highly theoretical and seemingly inaccessible field of gender and communications. Wood directly addresses this problem in *Gendered Lives*, a textbook that includes discussion questions and suggestions for further reading. Wood slowly unravels arcane concepts embedded in language and communications theory in this work. Rather than immediately launching into the topic, she situates herself in the conversation by declaring her feminist stance, defining the various "feminisms," and describing herself as a "European-American, heterosexual, middle-class woman." She discusses how her race and class privilege her, although her sex places her at a disadvantage. Wood looks at standpoint analysis and considers how her particular positioning influences who she is and what she can do. She divides the book into three main parts: "Conceptual Foundations," "Creating Gendered Identities," and "Gendered Communication in Practice." The chapters of each part introduce a particular problem, theory, concept, or methodology, including analyses of the study of communication, gender and culture, and how particular social institutions are gendered. Wood clearly introduces major themes in feminist approaches to language and communications in *Gendered Lives*, which she wrote for a nonacademic and potentially hostile audience.

Film and Television

1025. Brunsdon, Charlotte. *Screen Tastes: Soap Opera to Satellite Dishes*. New York: Routledge, 1997. 236p. bibliog. index. ISBN 041512154X; 0415121558pa.

In *Screen Tastes*, Brunsdon, an influential feminist cultural critic, analyzes British soap operas, crime dramas created to attract a female audience, and 1970s "independent woman" and "postfeminist" Hollywood films of the last two decades. Written during the previous twenty years, the essays foreground Brunsdon's interest in women's experience with popular or mass culture. She introduces each section with a contextualization of the essays that follow, as well as some new insights. In part 1, "The Defense of Soap Opera," Brunsdon looks at popular British productions, particularly the show *Crossroads*, which became a veritable laboratory for critical media studies. In chapters 3 and 4, she explores the significance of soap operas in relation to the development of critical feminist television studies. In the final three parts of the book, Brunsdon considers the changes in feminism and feminist media theory since 1970. The essays in part 2, "Career Girls," address feminist ideas that individuals have appropriated and re-presented in mainstream, mostly Hollywood, film. In part 3, "Questions of Quality," Brunsdon looks at the institutionalization of television studies in the Anglophone academy and the end of European public service broadcasting. She describes the use of satellite dishes to illuminate both the public and private aspects of the "taste wars" that raged in Britain upon the introduction of satellite television in the essay "Satellite Dishes and the Landscapes of Taste." In the final part, "Feminist Identities," the author explores several of the most significant arguments in the development of feminist film and television studies to demonstrate how they relate to the changing definitions of feminism.

1026. Brunsdon, Charlotte, Julie D'Acci, and Lynn Spigel, eds. *Feminist Television Criticism: A Reader*. Oxford: Clarendon Press, 1997. 386p. (Oxford Television Studies). bibliog. index. ISBN 0198711522; 0198711530pa.

Feminist Television Criticism, edited by three highly regarded feminist media scholars, consists of twenty-three essays that include a variety of feminist theoretical approaches to television/media studies regarding the multiple ways in which television represents women. Pioneers of feminist media studies contribute to this work, which spans twenty years of feminist theorizing about television. Essays range from Tania Modleski's 1979 essay about soap operas "The Search for Tomorrow in Today's Soap Operas: Notes on a Narrative Form" to Julie D'Acci's article "Leading up to *Roe v. Wade*: Television Documentaries in the Abortion Debate" (forthcoming during publication of this collection). Although the essayists mainly focus on British and American work, they also tackle some international issues. The editors include essays on programming in India, as well as the importation and reception of American television in other parts of the world. They also include Suvendrini Perera's essay about a dispute between Australia and Malaysia over the construction of representation as a subject for diplomatic consideration in the Australian series *Embassy*. *Feminist Television Criticism* contains important essays on African Americans and the media and on lesbian representation on the small screen. The editors organize the essays according to three broad headings: "Housewives, Heroines, Feminists," "Audiences and Reception Contexts," and "Private Bodies, Public Figures." Each section begins with an editor's introduction that both contextualizes and ties the essays together. The collection concludes with a very complete bibliography.

1027. Carson, Diane, Linda Dittmar, and Janice R. Welsch, eds. *Multiple Voices in Feminist Film Criticism*. Minneapolis: University of Minnesota Press, 1994. 547p. bibliog. index. ISBN (OP); 0816622736pa.

Carson, Dittmar, and Welsch's *Multiple Voices in Feminist Film* deals with many of the same issues and theoretical orientations that Patricia Erens covered in *Issues in Feminist Film Criticism* (Indiana University Press, 1990) (see entry 1039); however, the editors reprint only one of the essays that appeared in Erens's work. Part 1, "Perspectives," includes essays that range from overviews of feminist film studies published between 1980 and 1990 to discussions of specific forms of feminist film criticism, most notably those influenced by semiotics, psychoanalysis, and Marxism. The second part, "Practice," consists of articles that focus on specific films or groups of films. The essays in this part explicitly resist "both canon formation and a feminist counter-canon" (p. 11), highlight the multiple ways in which gender intersects with other identities and experiences, and demonstrate how women are portrayed in film through gender and identity. The last part, "Course Files," presents excellent models for teaching feminist film studies using design, cinema, and monographic resources, as well as other related curricular materials.

Feminisms in the Cinema (Indiana University Press, 1995), edited by Laura Pietropaolo and Ada Testaferri, brings together papers presented at a conference at York University in Canada in conjunction with other chapters solicited especially for this collection. Several leading scholars in feminist film studies contributed to this work, which the editors divide into four parts: "Modes of Identification and Representation," "The Role of Fantasy in Lesbian Representation and Spectatorship," "Inscribing Women in Socio-Historical Context," and "Feminist Film Readings: Personal Politics/Social Politics." Both volumes focus on the voices and experiences of minority and lesbian women and include perspectives beyond the Anglophone world of film criticism.

1028. Cowie, Barbara. *Representing the Woman: Cinema and Psychoanalysis*. Minneapolis: University of Minnesota Press, 1997. 397p. bibliog. index. ISBN (OP); 0816629137pa.

Cowie deconstructs psychoanalytic and feminist film theories through discussions of central topics, including spectatorship, the masculine gaze, and image and identity. She painstakingly dissects and clarifies several relevant theories in her first chapter, titled "Feminist Arguments." Cowie relies heavily upon Lacan, yet simultaneously engages in Freudian theory. Although the author intellectualizes various theoretical positions, she makes her work accessible via illustrating her arguments with stills of the various films that she examines.

Additional works that explore the intersections of feminism and psychoanalytic film theory include Kaja Silverman's *The Acoustic Mirror: The Female Voice in Psychoanalysis and Cinema* (Indiana University Press, 1988); Barbara Creed's *The Monstrous-Feminine: Film, Feminism, Psychoanalysis* (Routledge, 1993), a contribution to psychoanalytical and feminist work on the horror film; and Laura Mulvey's *Visual and Other Pleasures* (Indiana University Press, 1989). *Female Spectators: Looking at Film and Television*, edited by E. Deidre Pribram, (Verso, 1988), features nine essays by academic film theorists and filmmakers. The authors apply, critique, and expand upon psychoanalytic and semiotics approaches in their analyses of topics that range from E. Ann Kaplan's essay on MTV to Jacqueline Bobo's examination of "*The Color Purple*: Black Women as Cultural Readers." Pribram is one of the first scholars to bring together theoretical work on film and television. In *Looking for the Other: Feminism, Film, and the Imperial Gaze* (Routledge 1997), by E. Ann Kaplan, one of the pioneers of feminist film theory, the author employs psychoanalytical and postcolonial theories to explore links between intergender and interracial relations in travel films, as well as the inseparability of the male and imperial gaze in Western patriarchal culture.

1029. Dow, Bonnie. *Prime-Time Feminism: Television, Media Culture, and the Women's Movement since 1970*. Philadelphia: University of Pennsylvania Press, 1996. 240p. (Feminist Cultural Studies, the Media, and Political Culture). bibliog. index. ISBN 0812233158; 0812215540pa.

Through a close examination of five popular television programs, four situation comedies and a prime-time drama series, Bonnie Dow discusses the relationship between feminism and popular culture, specifically television, during the past two decades. Dow examines the impact of feminism on the media and the portrayal of gender in mass-appeal programming in the sit-coms *The Mary Tyler Moore Show, Designing Women, One Day at a Time*, and *Murphy Brown* and the drama series *Dr. Quinn, Medicine Woman*. Dow describes television as an interpreter of social change and manager of cultural beliefs, a function that she sees as related to the role that public oration played in the nineteenth and early twentieth centuries. She also makes a compelling case for examining television on its own terms rather than using "television texts to illustrate some larger theoretical or conceptual argument" (p. xiii). Dow devotes an entire chapter to each of the five programs, concentrating on various aspects of television's message about and address to women. The chapter titled "1970s Lifestyle Feminism and the Single Woman" analyzes *The Mary Tyler Moore Show*, and "The Other Side of Postfeminism: Maternal Feminism" explores *Dr. Quinn, Medicine Woman*. In her introduction and afterword, titled "Feminist Image, Feminist Politics," Dow brings together the major points of her argument about television, feminism, and postmodern cultural criticism.

Margaret J. Heide's *Television Culture and Women's Lives: Thirtysomething and the Contradictions of Gender* (University of Pennsylvania Press, 1995), an earlier volume in the University of Pennsylvania Press's Feminist Cultural Studies, the Media, and Political Culture series, approaches her subject matter in a similar fashion to Dow's. Heide concentrates on one show, *Thirtysomething*, analyzing the representation of complex gender and generational issues. Heide focuses on women's responses to the fictive representation of their lives in *Thirtysomething*, which helps scholars understand television's role in the cultural construction of gender. Julie D'Acci analyzes character development, cast changes, and narrative streams in the show *Cagney and Lacey* in *Defining Women: Television and the Case of Cagney and Lacey* (University of North Carolina Press, 1994).

1030. Gledhill, Christine, and Gillian Swanson, eds. *Nationalising Femininity: Culture, Sexuality, and the British Cinema in the Second World War.* Manchester: Manchester University Press, 1996; distributed in the United States by St. Martin's Press. 307p. bibliog. index. ISBN 0719042593.

Although this work does not deal solely with cinematic representations, the editors use film as a capstone to their analysis of the "refashioning of femininity for a wartime homefront" (p. 1). Gledhill and Swanson make cinema a site of cultural meaning by dividing the book into three distinct but interrelated sections: "Mobile Women: Change and Regulation," "Fashioning the National Self: Cultural Practices and Representations," and "Nationalising Femininity: The Case of British Cinema." The structure reinforces the importance of connecting film to other cultural practices. The essays in sections 1 and 2 contribute to an understanding of the sociopolitical and cultural significance of the war at home and detail how cinema functioned in the British consciousness during the war. The seven essays in section 3 explore "the concentrated intersection of government, culture and personal life" (p. 8) in the highly visible arena of cinematic representation. Antonia Lant's *Blackout: Reinventing Women for Wartime British Cinema* (Princeton University Press, 1991) and Pam Cook's *Fashioning the Nation: Costume and Identity in British Cinema* (British Film Institute, 1996) also explore gender and British cinema.

1031. Grant, Barry Keith, ed. *The Dread of Difference: Gender and the Horror Film.* Austin: University of Texas Press, 1996. 456p. bibliog. index. ISBN 0292727933; 0292727941pa.

Horror films especially fascinate feminist film theorists. Scholars have published several noteworthy monographs, including Rhona Berenstein's *Attack of the Leading Ladies: Gender, Sexuality, and Spectatorship in Classic Horror Cinema* (Columbia University Press, 1996) and Carol Clover's groundbreaking *Men, Women, and Chainsaws: Gender in the Modern Horror Film* (Princeton University Press, 1992). The twenty-one articles featured in *The Dread of Difference* bring together nearly twenty years of academic writing on the centrality of gender to horror films, from the beginning of cinema to the present. According to Grant, although some films feature genderless monsters, such as blobs, parasites, and gremlins, gender-specific monsters predominate. Grant divides the collection into three sections. Section 1 contains three "classics" of film theory that build on Laura Mulvey's pioneering work on psychoanalytic film theory. Linda Williams's 1983 article "When the Woman Looks," Barbara Creed's "Horror and the Monstrous-Feminine: An Imaginary Abjection," and Carol Clover's "Her Body, Himself: Gender in the Slasher Film," which also appears in Clover's *Men, Women, and Chainsaws*, introduce an important theoretical perspective on horror in the second section. The articles contextualize horror-film production and provide analyses of the work of individual directors who were closely associated with the genre. The final section features ten chapters that offer gendered readings of films ranging from *King Kong* to *Fatal Attraction*.

1032. Haskell, Molly. *Holding My Own in No Man's Land: Women and Men, Film and Feminists.* New York: Oxford University Press, 1997. 207p. (OP)

Film theorists and academic feminists frequently have accused film critic and teacher Molly Haskell of oversimplifying the complexities of cinema. Haskell's first book, *From Reverence to Rape: The Treatment of Women in the Movies* (2nd ed., University of Chicago Press, 1987), a historical account of the stereotypical images of women in film from the 1920s through the 1960s, essentially opened the field for feminist film criticism. *Holding My Own in No Man's Land* is a collection of "thought pieces," essays, articles, and interviews on various aspects of cinema that originally appeared in publications such as *Ms.* and *Vogue*. Haskell focuses on four main themes: "Dames," "Guys," "Literary Heroines," and "The Nineties: Where Do We Go from Here?" "Dames" consists of essays about individual film and television personalities ranging from Gloria Swanson to Lena Wertmuller. "Guys" deals with personalities, including John Wayne, and features a well-known 1976 essay titled "Rape: The Two Thousand Year Old Misunderstanding," which originally appeared in *Ms.* The final two sections, "Literary Heroines" and "The Nineties," tackle subjects such as Henry James's *The Bostonians*, Colette, and female comedians. Haskell's engaging and accessible collection contains little "high theory" since she wrote her work for the popular press. The author even dismisses theory and feminist academics' overly cerebral analysis and dissection of film in the introduction.

1033. Hershfield, Joanne. *Mexican Cinema/Mexican Woman, 1940–1950*. Tucson: University of Arizona Press, 1996. 159p. (Latin American Communication and Popular Culture). bibliog. index. ISBN 0816516367.

Hershfield's work, which is one of only a few books that explicitly deal with gender issues in Mexican cinema from a feminist standpoint, focuses on the decade of the "aesthetic and economic height of the Golden Age of Mexican cinema" (p. 7). Hershfield examines this period not only because of the changes and tensions that permeated postrevolutionary Mexico, but also because of the quality and quantity of the cinema produced. She analyzes six different films, situating the discourse about gender relations in the larger conversation about nation and identity. The author organizes her work into five broad areas or chapters, using specific films to illustrate major points. In chapter 1 she discusses two important figures in Mexican history and mythology, La Malinche and the Virgin of Guadalupe, Mexico's version of the Madonna/whore polarity. Hershfield explores the development of a Mexican national cinema in an effort to elucidate the "cinematic conventions and narrative structures that defined the films of the 1940s" (p. 10) in chapter 2. In the remaining three chapters, the author analyzes six films, two per chapter, considering how they portray women, gender, family, economic and social relations, and questions of identity and national character. Many critics have lambasted Hershfield for basing her critique on a very narrow body of work, a criticism made sharper by considering that three of the six films she discusses are the work of a single director.

1034. Joyrich, Lynn. *Re-viewing Reception: Television, Gender, and Postmodern Culture*. Bloomington: Indiana University Press, 1996. 244p. (Theories of Contemporary Culture). bibliog. index. ISBN 0253330769; 025321078Xpa.

Theorist, cultural critic, and scholar of film and television Lynn Joyrich is also a self-described "avid" television viewer. In *Re-viewing Reception*, Joyrich threads facets together in an analysis of the gendered nature of television. She persuasively argues that "gender affects the reception, not simply of particular programs, but of TV as a whole" (p. 10). She investigates how the close connection between television and commodity consumption has created a strong relationship to the feminine, making television an especially rich field for gender/feminist scholarship. The work begins with an overview and analysis of critical television studies and its place in the larger arena of cultural studies, affirming some cultural critics' degree of scorn and derision for television. Joyrich explicitly disagrees with their dismissal and lobbies for the importance of postmodernist interventions in the critique of this pervasive cultural form. However, she does warn feminists to look at television through a critical lens. Joyrich then examines melodrama (i.e., soap operas), easily the most frequently studied television genre. Chapters 4 and 5 focus on specific shows, including *Moonlighting, Max Headroom*, and *Pee-Wee's Playhouse*. While many readers may find Joyrich's sophisticated and often dense use of theory difficult to follow, others may encounter problems with the historical specificity of her argument. Joyrich concludes with a discussion about how feminism and postmodernism could prove fruitful in understanding and interpreting both gender and television as postmodern phenomena.

1035. Mayne, Judith. *The Woman at the Keyhole: Feminism and Women's Cinema.* Bloomington: Indiana University Press, 1990. 260p. (Theories of Representation and Difference). bibliog. index. ISBN (OP); 0253206065pa.

The term "women's cinema" has a dual meaning. In a conventional sense, it refers to cinema specifically created to appeal to women: those movies frequently called "women's films." The second, more complex meaning encompasses films directed or produced by women, ranging from directors of big-budget Hollywood films to independent documentaries with a decidedly feminist orientation. Judith Mayne tackles both meanings, which frequently overlap, creating ambiguity, in her analysis of films that not only underscore the tensions between "woman" and "women," but also reveal eclectic ways of looking at and understanding cinematic pleasure and female desire. She divides the book into three major sections: "Spectacle and Narrative," "Female Authorship," and "Early Cinema and Women's Films." She subdivides each section into two chapters: the first sets a theoretical context, and the second examines specific films in relation to that context or construct. The author scrutinizes full-length feature films, shorter productions, independent films, Hollywood movies, well-known directors, and obscure directors. Mayne elaborates on the terms "ambiguity" and "ambivalence," which form critical components in her analysis, in the afterword. *The Woman at the Keyhole* breaks new ground in film studies as one of the first major works to examine the connection between lesbianism and female "authorship," a concept that Mayne expands upon in her important book *Directed by Dorothy Arzner* (Indiana University Press, 1994).

1036. Mellencamp, Patricia. *A Fine Romance: Five Ages of Film Feminism.* Philadelphia: Temple University Press, 1995. 330p. (Culture and the Moving Image). bibliog. index. ISBN 1566394007; 1566394115pa.

Patricia Mellencamp appropriated the title for her work, which chronicles a tempestuous twenty-five-year relationship between feminist theory and cinema, from a sarcastic song that Ginger Rogers sang to Fred Astaire in the 1936 film *Swingtime*. Writing in a highly personalized style, the author divides feminist film criticism into five ages of feminism: intellectual, irascible, experimental, empirical, and economical. In her introduction, "What Cinderella and Snow White Forgot to Tell Thelma and Louise," Mellencamp identifies the ages as historical, encompassing the 1970s through the 1990s; personal, representing the time period of her professional life; and descriptive, revealing a taxonomy derived from feminist film critics' tactics. The author organizes the book into five ages that directly correspond to how she categorizes feminist film theory. The films discussed in each age cover a range of time periods and cinematic styles. In the first age, "Intellectual Feminism," Mellencamp discusses the influential role that psychoanalytic theory has played in feminist film studies. In the second age, "Irascible Feminism," she examines the significance of specific cinematic representations of women in films that feature a "cryptofeminist" female protagonist, such as *Silence of the Lambs, Basic Instinct*, and *Thelma and Louise*, as well as films with strong women characters. The appearance of women directors and films in which women tell stories about other women marks the third age, "Experimental Feminism." Mellencamp discusses the work of filmmakers such as Jane Campion, Sally Potter, and Yvonne Rainer, considering how race, class, age, and sexuality affect these works, instead of purely relying on psychoanalytic theory. The author deals with economic and social contradictions in light of sexuality in the fourth age, "Empirical Feminism." Finally, Mellenchamp analyzes how sexual and money economies converge in Sally Potter's film adaptation of Virginia Woolf's *Orlando* in "Economic Feminism."

1037. Modleski, Tania. *Feminism without Women: Culture and Criticism in a "Postfeminist" Age.* New York: Routledge, 1991. 188p. bibliog. index. ISBN (OP); 041590417Xpa.

Modleski's book sparked controversy since it appeared not only when women's studies evolved into gender studies, but also during the emergence of new developments in critical theory. Concerned with the potential and occasionally actual erasure of the category "woman" from theoretical discourse, Modleski questions what might befall women and feminism as these new scholarly directions take hold. She divides her work into three parts: "Theory and Methodology," "Masculinity and Male Feminism," and "Race, Gender, and Sexuality." The author painstakingly chips away at theories that either overtly or covertly posit that feminism has achieved its goals. She focuses on literature and literary theory in the first part of the book and concentrates on film in parts 2 and 3. Modleski examines the misogynistic tones that lie just beneath the surface in diverse films, including *Full Metal Jacket* and *Three Men and a Baby*. Modleski carefully sets up the historical and social context of each film that she analyzes, which serves as a core strength of the book. The final chapter, "Lethal Bodies: Thoughts on Sex, Gender, and Representation from the Main Stream to the Margins," provides a good overview of the anti-, the anti-anti-, and the anti-anti-anti-pornography debates that occupied much feminist and postfeminist theory of the early 1990s. Modleski's earlier book *The Women Who Knew Too Much: Hitchcock and Feminist Theory* (Methuen, 1988) has become a standard text in courses on feminist film criticism/theory and in the increasing number of courses that view Hitchcock through the lens of feminism.

1038. Mumford, Laura Stempel. *Love and Ideology in the Afternoon: Soap Opera, Women, and Television Genre.* Bloomington: Indiana University Press, 1995. 165p. (Arts and Politics of the Everyday). bibliog. index. ISBN 0253328799; 025320965Xpa.

Mumford, an independent scholar and self-confessed "soap opera viewer," both defines the genre and examines its audience. She raises significant questions about how to define the genre and challenges persistent and facile approaches, including the argument that soap operas and hour-long, prime-time melodramatic shows belong in the same category. Mumford contends that the link between soap operas and an "interest in a fictional community" constitutes a unique feature of the genre. She examines the genre's narrative, framing her discussion on the political "agendas" played out for the audience. In a chapter titled "Public Exposure," the author explores the elision of the private and public spheres that marks the soap opera narrative as an entrée for viewers into the transparent life of a fictive community. She also examines narrative structure in the chapter "How Things End," bringing fresh insights to the debates about how the dearth of plot/character closure affects the appeal of soap operas. Mumford subsequently tackles the gendered nature of soap operas, persuasively championing the significance of theorizing about the genre. Moreover, the author underscores the implicit and explicit political agenda that soap operas promote and delves into the "naturalizing" of patriarchal, classist, racist, and heterosexist assumptions embedded in the ongoing narrative.

Mary Ellen Brown takes a slightly different approach in *Soap Opera and Women's Talk:*

The Pleasure of Resistance (Sage, 1994). Rather than specifically focusing on narrative structure or plot line, Brown examines soap operas as a form of resistance found in the pleasure derived from viewing and talking about them. According to Brown, the genre provides its largely female audience a way to engage with and perhaps counter hegemonic male notions about femininity.

1039. Penley, Constance, ed. *Feminism and Film Theory*. New York: Routledge, 1988. 271p. bibliog. (OP)

Feminist study of film and television has become an exceptionally active field: between 1986 and 1998, several major compilations of articles and essays were published. In *Feminism and Film Theory*, Penley brings together fifteen essays by several groundbreaking feminist film scholars, including Claire Johnston, Laura Mulvey, and Mary Ann Doane, that foreground semiotics, psychoanalytic theory, and textual analysis. Penley theoretically and historically contextualizes the essays in her excellent introduction. Patricia Erens broadly approaches feminist film theory in her collection of twenty-nine essays, *Issues in Feminist Film Criticism* (Indiana University Press, 1990). Erens adheres to multiple views of feminist film criticism in her work. Each of the four sections, "Critical Methodology: Women and Representation," "Rereading Hollywood Films," "Critical Methodology: Feminist Filmmaking," and "Assessing Films Directed by Women," begins with a brief introductory essay that defines the section's focus, contextualizes the essays, and connects the selections. Erens's collection provides a fine introduction to the varied perspectives that constitute feminist film criticism.

1040. Penley, Constance, Elisabeth Lyon, Lynn Spigel, and Janet Bergstrom, eds. *Close Encounters: Film, Feminism, and Science Fiction*. Minneapolis: University of Minnesota Press, 1991. 298p. (A Camera Obscura Book). bibliog. index. ISBN (OP); 0816619123pa.

The nine essays that constitute *Close Encounters* update and expand upon a special issue of *Camera Obscura* published in 1986. Both the issue and this collection examine the categories, construction, and displacement of difference in science fiction films. In traditional science fiction, difference connotes the human/nonhuman divide portrayed in many films. Recently, however, "pressures from feminism, the politics of race and sexual orientation, and dramatic changes in the structure of the family . . . seem to have intensified the symptomatic wish to pose and re-pose the question of difference" (p. vi). The first four essays examine how recent science fiction films, such as *Blade Runner, Terminator*, and *Alien*, have dealt with questions of masculinity and femininity, maternity and paternity. The following three essays investigate the relationship between technology and fantasy and its connection to gender. The final two essays address science fiction audience and television, focusing on topics including the growth of "fanzines" and the construction of the hybrid of science fiction fantasy and domestic comedy, aimed at the 1960s suburban family. The collection concludes with the complete script of the 1987 film *Friendship's Death*, which features a "cyborg feminist" (p. xi). Although focusing less on the genre than on its audience, Camille Bacon-Smith's ethnographic study of women's art, literature, and community grounded in popular television programs, titled *Enterprising Women: Television Fandom and the Creation of Popular Myth* (University of Pennsylvania Press, 1992), offers a fascinating analysis of a complex phenomenon.

1041. Press, Andrea L. *Women Watching Television: Gender, Class, and Generation in the American Television Experience*. Philadelphia: University of Pennsylvania Press, 1991. 238p. bibliog. index. ISBN 0812281691, 081221286Xpa.

Combining feminist theory, class analysis, and empirical research, Andrea Press enters into a debate in television studies between scholars who see television as a preeminent exemplar of the tightening of hegemonic controls and those who see a modicum of resistance to hegemony among female viewers. Press analyzes interview responses to learn where and how television "reinforces patriarchal values in our culture" and to examine the idea that women use television to undermine this dominance. The author examines how mass-media images, especially televised images, affect women's construction of their gender identities. Press also explores how different television programs, composed of eclectic characters, resonate across generational and class boundaries. Press sampled twenty working-class and twenty-one middle-class women, ranging from seventeen to seventy-eight years old. The author became a participant-observer while also acknowledging her own exposure to television, asserting that "television, more than any other medium, has been a pervasive presence in my inner life" (p. 9). Press outlines her theoretical framework in the first section, then analyzes three stages of the televised representations of women: prefeminist, feminist, and postfeminist. Section 2, "Women Interpreting Television," is comprised of portions of Press's interviews, as well as the analysis of her findings, including a generational comparison of attitudes toward television that cuts across class lines. Press delineates her finding in the final section, "Conclusion: Television Reception as a Window on Culture." She articulates how class-specific differences and hegemony determine how television operates in American culture. The appendix contains useful information on methodology and sampling techniques.

1042. Redding, Judith M., and Victoria A. Brownworth. *Film Fatales: Independent Women Directors*. Seattle: Seal Press, 1997. 293p. bibliog. ISBN 1878067974pa.

Redding and Brownworth define filmmaking as intensely political, arguing that directors affect every facet of a film, from production to audience reception. Contributors profile twenty-eight women directors who have created a wide range of films, from short, 8-mm experimental films to full-length feature films. Regardless of preferred format or distribution method, all of these filmmakers work outside of the Hollywood studio system. They also each bring a distinct female perspective or "female lens" to cinema. The editors and contributors profile diverse directors, including Susan Seidelman (*Desperately Seeking Susan*), Michelle Parkinson (*A Litany for Survival: The Life and Work of Audre Lord*), and Jan Oxenberg (*Comedy in Six Unnatural Acts*). The editors organize the international biofilmographies into three film categories: documentary, experimental, and narrative. A fourth category, "Beyond the Director's Chair," introduces four women who remain instrumental in the promotion and distribution of independent film: Debra Zimmerman of Women Make Movies, producer Christine Vachon (*Safe, Swoon*), Ada Gay Griffin, executive director of Third World Newsreel, and Naiad Press's Barbara Grier. Although this work excludes some notable women directors, the editors bring many important voices of cinema to the forefront.

Gwendolyn Audrey Foster's *Women Filmmakers of the African and Asian Diaspora: Decolonizing the Gaze, Locating Subjectivity* (Southern Illinois University Press, 1997) is another critical contribution to works on women filmmakers. Although Foster focuses on six directors, Zeinabu Irene Davis, Ngozi Onwurah, Julie Dash, Pratibha Parmar, Trinh T. Minh-Ha, and Mira Nair, covered in Redding and Brownworth's volume, she presents a far more analytical and theoretical discussion of the themes, both political and cinematic, of their work. *With Eyes Wide Open: Women and African Cinema* (Rodopi, 1997), a special issue of the journal *Matatu*, edited by Kenneth W. Harrow, covers some of the same ground. The collection features critical essays and bibliographies on African women filmmakers, such as Trinh T. Minh-Ha, who portray Africa in their work, and the portrayal of African women in the works of male directors. University of Wisconsin at Madison librarian Emilie Ngo-Nguidjol's annotated bibliography on women in African cinema in the Harrow volume is highly informative.

1043. Rich, B. Ruby. *Chick Flicks: Theories and Memories of the Feminist Film Movement*. Durham, NC: Duke University Press, 1998. 419p. bibliog. index. ISBN 0822321068; 0822321211pa.

Independent scholar and theorist B. Ruby Rich has written about film, feminism, mass media, popular culture, and, more recently, information technologies since the 1970s. *Chick Flicks* combines critical works previously published elsewhere between the early 1970s and 1991 that feature highly personal ruminations on feminism, film criticism, academic film studies, and Rich's own life. In the preface to the collection, "Jews without Books," a play on Mike Gold's seminal work *Jews without Money*, Rich situates herself as the child of working-class Jews for whom books were a luxury, not a necessity. Rich bemoans the fact that academic film studies has replaced the excitement of the early days of "cinefeminism," arguing that "the operative noun is theory, not criticism, not history, not women's studies" (p. 83). She does, however, see academic film studies moving in an extremely positive direction with the explosion of queer studies. Rich uses her personal reflections, called "Prologues," to introduce and contextualize her essays on specific films, genres, directors, and actors. Her effort to move between the personal and the academic/political underscores her approach to feminist film criticism, vividly exemplifying her clarion call to return to the grass roots of the enterprise.

1044. Robertson, Pamela. *Guilty Pleasures: Feminist Camp from Mae West to Madonna*. Durham, NC: Duke University Press, 1996. 195p. bibliog. index. ISBN 0822317516; 0822317486pa.

Robertson, a film studies lecturer at the University of Newcastle, Australia, combines scholarship and political activism in her examination of the rehabilitation of a distinctly female variety of camp. Recognizing the extent to which people have defined and limited camp to the cultural production of a specific urban gay male sensibility, Robertson challenges two dominant positions about camp. First, she challenges the notion that camp must remain in the domain of men because of its exaggerated portrayal of women. Second, Robertson lobbies for a distinctly feminist camp. She asserts that camp can serve as a "model for critiques of gender and sex roles" (p. 6). The author looks at camp through a historical lens, examining four case studies: Mae West, *Gold Diggers of 1933*, Joan Crawford's performance in *Johnny Guitar*, and Madonna. While acknowledging the points of intersection between gay male and feminist camp, Robertson clearly identifies decidedly antifeminist aspects of camp. She also demonstrates how feminist and antifeminist aspects of camp occasionally clash, as in the case of Joan Crawford.

1045. Shattuc, Jane. *The Talking Cure: TV Talk Shows and Women*. New York: Routledge, 1997. 242p. bibliog. index. ISBN 0415910870; 0415910889pa.

Daytime talk shows have emerged as one of the most influential entertainment genres of the past two decades. Whether these shows are hosted by men or women, producers target them for a decidedly female audience. Accordingly, producers tend to highlight personal tragedies and triumphs that they think will attract women viewers. Shattuc, an academic and self-professed Oprah fan, compellingly accounts for the popularity of the genre through an examination of its historical antecedents and its appeal in an age of identity politics. Shattuc defines five attributes of daytime talk shows that distinguish them from other seemingly similar media: they are issue oriented, involve active audience participation, present the host as moral authority, target a female audience, and are productions of nonnetwork production companies. Shattuc applies these definitions to a broader analysis of how historical and sociopolitical contexts influence the "conventions of an industrial entertainment form" (p. 3). This work is both theoretical and empirical, ranging from critical engagement with Foucault to viewing more than twenty-four hours of daytime television talk shows. The author concludes that although daytime television talk shows are not feminist, "they do represent popular TV at its most feminist. . . . They give a voice to normally voiceless women" (p. 136).

1046. Smith, Valerie. *Not Just Race, Not Just Gender: Black Feminist Readings*. New York: Routledge, 1998. 166p. bibliog. index. ISBN 0415903254; 0415903262pa.

This collection features five essays by UCLA professor Valerie Smith that cover the Central Park jogger case, racial crossing, class mobility, experimental documentary films by black film-makers, and the challenges of reading and teaching complex material in the context of real-life events. Although she analyzes a diverse range of topics, Smith adheres to the unifying theme of "cultural convergences," of race and gender ideologies. This work also highlights Smith's interest in "intersectionality," that is, how race, gender, class, and sexuality operate as interrelated ideologies that produce relationships of both domination and subordination. However, according to Smith, they can also function as sites of social change. Although the first chapter, "Split Affinities: Representing Interracial Rape," does not address cinematic representations, Smith's trenchant analysis of a sensationalized and racialized news account and an Alice Walker short story sets a vivid context for the film-related chapters that follow.

1047. Stacey, Jackie. *Star Gazing: Hollywood Cinema and Female Spectatorship*. New York: Routledge, 1994. 282p. bibliog. index. ISBN (OP); 0415091799pa.

Stacey breaks new ground in her study of the relationship between the spectator and the image on the silver screen. Rather than follow the more common pattern in feminist film theory of "reading" the cinematic text to discern either the image of women or women as images, Stacey focuses on spectators' experience as they view films. The emerging field of cultural studies informs her analysis, which centers on a very specific subset of female moviegoers who understood and interpreted femininity as embodied in female images that the male-dominated studio industry produced for presumably male spectators. Stacey argues that spectators are not passive, making a compelling case for the active spectator who negotiates a relationship of sorts with the cinematic image. The author lobbies for a particularized and localized study of spectatorship, stressing the importance of setting a historical context for the interplay between spectator and star. She uses a questionnaire to elicit the reactions of British women who watched American films in the 1940s and 1950s. Stacey had these women answer demographic questions pertaining to the 1940s, the 1950s, and the time period of her study. She also inquired about their interest in and relationship to American and British female film stars. While this work is heavily theoretical, the questionnaire, coupled with the interspersion of respondents' voices throughout the text, considerably enlivens it. The author also uses still shots to both illustrate her points and clarify her argument. Judith Mayne's *Cinema and Spectatorship* (Routledge, 1993) and Miriam Hansen's *Babel and Babylon: Spectatorship in American Silent Film* (Harvard University Press, 1991) constitute two equally valuable works on film and spectatorship.

1048. Staiger, Janet. *Bad Women: Regulating Sexuality in Early American Cinema*. Minneapolis: University of Minnesota Press, 1995. 226p. bibliog. index. ISBN (OP); 0816626251pa.

The first generation of American cinema reflected technological advancement and significant change in how Americans viewed themselves, one another, and society. Staiger's theoretical and historical examination of the sociopolitical context and narrative structure of early American films provides an excellent window into a formative moment in American cultural history. The first chapter addresses economic, cultural, and social transformations that provide the backdrop for cinematic representation. An additional chapter focuses entirely on the image of the "new woman" and the frequently conflicting messages that it conveys about proper behavior. The author also analyzes how the U.S. film industry responded to and perhaps created social change, along with the degree of latitude or self-imposed regulation that it enforced. Staiger concludes with an examination of three feature-length films: *Traffic in Souls* (1913), *A Fool There Was* (1914), and *The Cheat* (1915). Although these films portray the "new woman" as "Bad Woman," they also reveal a "new, independent, intelligent, and aggressive woman, even a desiring woman" (p. xvi). Staiger includes a filmography and bibliography.

Amy Lawrence considers the intersection of cinema history and theory in *Echo and Narcissus: Women's Voices in Classical Hollywood Cinema* (University of California Press, 1991). Lawrence uses the myth of Echo and Narcissus to introduce the conflict between sound and image in mythology and cinema and to analyze whether classical Hollywood film silenced women's voices.

1049. Straayer, Chris. *Deviant Eyes, Deviant Bodies: Sexual Re-orientations in Film and Video.* New York: Columbia University Press, 1996. 349p. (Film and Culture; Between Men—Between Women). bibliog. index. ISBN 0231079788; 0231079796pa.

In a volume in the influential Columbia University series Between Men—Between Women, Straayer examines the role of gender in both mainstream and independent film in *Deviant Eyes, Deviant Bodies.* The author analyzes specific films and film genres, illustrating how self-conscious cinematic constructions lead audiences to read the narrative in particular ways. Straayer focuses on transgressive images, especially representations of transvestitism, that discomfort viewers who had felt secure in their reading of sex and gender prior to seeing the film. Throughout the book, Straayer confronts readers with images that challenge set notions of male and female and presents new ways of interpreting sexual acts and sexual pleasure. She uses film and film theory to argue for the dismantling of a system of sexual difference. In chapter 5, she confronts the differences between feminist theory and queer theory, criticizing most feminist film theorists for failing to develop the idea of "lesbian perspective as a potentially disruptive force" (p. 5) in a field that often fails to challenge heterosexual assumptions. This work is a difficult read: the author uses dense and complex language and depends upon semiotics to bolster her argument. However, Straayer's work still holds considerable value. She succinctly analyzes several films and frequently introduces obscure, independent productions. The book also features an excellent film/videography.

Lynda Hart traces the historical "invention and circulation of 'lesbians' as a haunting secret" (p. viii), a necessary facet in the construction of a hetero/homo binary, in *Fatal Women: Lesbian Sexuality and the Mark of Aggression* (Princeton University Press, 1994). Although she covers material that lies outside the realm of film theory, Hart fleshes out her central thesis in chapters on the films *Single White Female* and *Basic Instinct.*

1050. Thornham, Sue. *Passionate Detachments: An Introduction to Feminist Film Theory.* London: Arnold, 1997; distributed in the United States by St. Martin's Press. 204p. bibliog. index. ISBN 0340652268; 034065225Xpa.

Influenced by Laura Mulvey's 1973 pathbreaking essay "Visual Pleasure and Narrative Cinema," Thornham attempts to encapsulate twenty-five years of passionate debate about cinematic representations of women in *Passionate Detachments.* Thornham provides a brief, chronological overview of major themes in second-wave feminism and then ties them to the emergence of 1970s feminist critiques of film in the United States. She examines parallel developments in feminist film theory in England in the second chapter. The author devotes chapter 3 to spectatorship and the scholarly debates regarding if and how women derive pleasure from patriarchal cinematic representations. Thornham also analyzes the nature of melodrama, the quintessential "woman's film," in chapter 3. She examines the influence of British cultural studies on audience/reception studies and feminist film theory in chapter 4. She addresses feminist work on fantasy, horror, and the body in chapter 5. In the following chapters, "Rereading Difference(s) 1: Conceiving Lesbian Desire" and "Rereading Difference(s) 2: Race, Representation, and Feminist Theory," Thornham describes how lesbians and women of color rightfully criticized early feminist film theory for its homogenizing view of femininity as white, middle class, and heterosexual and considers how people who occupy marginalized positions relate to both dominant and other marginalized positions. She also discusses feminist film theory and postmodernism. Thornham's analysis of this exciting, volatile field is highly complex and sophisticated.

Maggie Humm's *Feminism and Film* (Indiana University Press, 1997) is more introductory and explanatory material. Lucy Fischer's *Shot/Countershot: Film Tradition and Women's Cinema* (Princeton University Press, 1989) offers an "intertextual approach to the issue of women and cinema" (p. xi). Fischer examines films that both men and women produced about similar topics, demonstrating "how the latter works critique, 'rewrite,' and even exorcise the former" (p. 12). Annette Kuhn's *Women's Pictures: Feminism and Cinema* (Verso, 1994) provides a pioneering and useful introduction to feminist film theory.

1051. Willis, Sharon. *High Contrast: Race and Gender in Contemporary Hollywood Film.* Durham, NC: Duke University Press, 1997. 266p. bibliog. index. ISBN 0822320290; 082232041Xpa.

Willis analyzes how racial and sexual difference intersect in contemporary popular film. She divides the work into "The Battle of the Sexes" and "Ethnographies of the 'White' Gaze." Part 1 is comprised of three thematic chapters that feature discussions about two or more films. Willis considers how heterosexual negotiations and debates influence big-money Hollywood films. In chapter 3, "Combative Femininity," Willis explores the cinematic and social contexts of films such as *Thelma and Louise* and *Terminator 2*, which "display and manipulate images and stories of feminine rage" (p. 98). The second part of the book focuses on the work of three auteur filmmakers, David Lynch, Spike Lee, and Quentin Tarantino, who bridge the divide between big-budget Hollywood film and independent cinema. Willis examines representations of race in both character and language and devotes an entire chapter to each director.

Unlike Willis's work, Lisa M. Anderson's *Mammies No More: The Changing Image of Black Women on Stage and Screen* (Rowman & Littlefield, 1997) concentrates exclusively on women. Moving between theatrical and cinematic representations, Anderson uncovers the extent to which icons and images, and not lived experience, came to signify black women (see entry 1295).

1052. Wilton, Tamsin, ed. *Immortal, Invisible: Lesbians and the Moving Image.* New York: Routledge, 1995. 235p. bibliog. index. ISBN 0415107245; 0415107253pa.

Tamsin Wilton, a senior lecturer in health and social policy at the University of the West of England in Bristol, includes twelve essays that cover a wide range of subjects on the theme of cinematic and televised representations of lesbians in *Immortal, Invisible*. In her introduction, "On Invisibility and Immortality," Wilton explains how she partly derived the collection's title from U.S. lesbian filmmaker Barbara Hammer's 1970 declaration that lesbian cinema exists on an invisible screen. The other half of the title stems from recognizing the power of film to confer an immortality that is not granted to lesbians. Although contributors to this collection discuss the concepts of the invisible and immortal, they mostly explore how best to define "lesbian," whether as spectator, star, character, or auteur. In her contribution titled "What's a Nice Lesbian like You Doing in a Film like This?" American cultural critic Cindy Patton examines the structural and narrative roles that lesbian characters have played in mainstream films, citing the 1988 film *Internal Affairs*, featuring Richard Gere, to illustrate her argument. Julia Knight examines the controversial career of German filmmaker Monika Treut, whose 1988 film *Virgin Machine* became an instant classic. Knight ponders if, when, and under what conditions one should label a filmmaker a "lesbian filmmaker." Other essays deal with topics such as k.d. lang's performance in *Salmonberries*, the making of *Desert Hearts*, and what this film reveals about the possibilities for cinematic representation of lesbian love. Wilton also contributes to the volume with "On Not Being Lady Macbeth: Some (Troubled) Thoughts on Lesbian Spectatorship." The collection concludes with an interview with filmmakers Greta Schiller (*Before Stonewall: The Making of a Gay and Lesbian Community*) and historian, critic, and filmmaker Andrea Weiss, who wrote *Vampires and Violets: Lesbians in Film* (Penguin, 1993). Wilton includes a filmography of every film mentioned in the essays.

Media and Journalism

1053. Alpern, Sara. *Freda Kirchwey: A Woman of The Nation.* Cambridge, MA: Harvard University Press, 1987. 319p. bibliog. index. ISBN 0674318285.

From article "clipper" in 1918 to owner, publisher, and editor in 1937, Freda Kirchwey's story and the history of *The Nation* are intimately entwined. A daughter of privilege, Kirchwey moved in a circle of educated men and women who espoused a form of equality for women that, even in the heady days of World War I and its immediate aftermath, was quite radical. In this detailed and well-crafted biography, Alpern chronicles Kirchwey's life, both as a public intellectual and a woman struggling, often with remarkable success, to combine motherhood and career. With chronology as its organizing principle, Alpern uses her biography of Kirchwey to tell the far larger story of a nation and *The Nation* during some of the most turbulent years of the twentieth century. From her earliest days as a journalist writing about the struggle for woman's suffrage through the travails of World War II and the rightward shift of the McCarthy era, Kirchwey interacted with and wrote about the major figures of the day. Committed to women's rights, internationalism, and democracy, Kirchwey endured the death of a child to tuberculosis in 1932, attacks on *The Nation* for being soft on Communism, and ultimately, her letting go of the reins of the magazine as it struggled with attacks on its politics and an increasingly difficult financial situation. While Kirchwey is rarely included in the pantheon of twentieth-century feminist visionaries (and role models), Alpern's biography certainly makes a compelling case for renewed attention to her as a powerful and notable figure in U.S. women's history.

Katharine Graham, whose father told her that, as a woman, she would never amount to much in the newspaper business, took over as publisher of the *Washington Post* upon the death of her husband and certainly proved her father wrong. Her autobiography, *Personal History* (Knopf, 1997), provides yet another example of a forceful woman whose intelligence, foresight, and perseverance changed the face of newspaper publishing. Her story stands as an interesting companion piece to Alpern's portrait of Freda Kirchwey.

Along the same lines of pioneering voices in the media, Wilda M. Smith and Eleanor Bogart tell the story of Peggy Hull, a woman who breached a seemingly impenetrable journalistic wall. *The Wars of Peggy Hull: The Life and Times of the First Accredited Woman Correspondent* (Texas Western Press, 1991) relates another story of indomitable courage and conviction in the face of seemingly impossible odds. Peggy Hull appears in another book, this one by veteran foreign correspondent Lisa Edwards. In her volume *Women of the World: The Great Foreign Correspondents* (Houghton Mifflin, 1988), Edwards tells the story of women who, often against odds made even more difficult by the sexist attitudes of their newspapers and the overt bias of the military, ventured into perilous terrain and came out with the story.

1054. Alwood, Edward. *Straight News: Gays, Lesbians, and the News Media*. New York: Columbia University Press, 1996. 386p. (Between Men—Between Women: Lesbian and Gay Studies). bibliog. index. ISBN 0231084366; 0231084374pa.

A volume in Columbia University Press's groundbreaking series Between Men—Between Women: Lesbian and Gay Studies, Alwood's book is an examination of the historical trajectory of news coverage of lesbian and gay issues from World War II to the mid-1990s. Approaching the topic chronologically, Alwood begins his examination in 1943 in a section titled "The News Media Discover Homosexuality: World War II to Stonewall, 1943–1969." The subsequent sections cover the decade immediately following Stonewall, which he calls "Progress and Backlash, 1970–1980," and "Requiem for the Media, 1981–1994," in which he discusses the reporting on the AIDS epidemic and the consequences of outing in the media. Alwood uses the example of the *New York Times* as a bellwether of change. Within three decades, the *Times* went from an outright (if unwritten) policy of exclusion of any positive mention of lesbians and gay men to far more balanced and inclusive coverage of gay issues. In addition to providing an eminently readable history of the often stormy relationship between lesbians, gay men, and the popular press, Alwood raises significant questions about the role of the media in reflecting and creating public opinion. In the epilogue to the book, he challenges reporters to act truly as neutral observers and recorders of events. He demands a level of accuracy and fairness that this book proves is elusive at best, in spite of journalists' statements to the contrary. Alwood sums up his study thusly: "By looking at the coverage of gays and lesbians from the 1940s to today, it is striking how often the double standard has been defended by the media, most often under the guise of protecting the sensibilities of their audiences" (p. 328). "Protecting sensibilities" is all too often a code for treatment of homosexuals, either to "render . . . invisible or paint them as a menace" (p. 329).

1055. Benedict, Helen. *Virgin or Vamp: How the Press Covers Sex Crimes*. New York: Oxford University Press, 1992. 309p. bibliog. index. ISBN (OP); 0195086651pa.

As a newspaper reporter who had written extensively on sex crimes and as a trained rape crisis counselor, Benedict came to her subject from the vantage point of someone well acquainted with the gritty reality of these crimes. As an academic, she combines that knowledge with a critical understanding of how biases, stereotypes, and preconceived notions of women and sexuality pervade even the most seemingly neutral reporting on rape. She bases her examination of press attitudes on four highly publicized cases and uses each to illustrate "a critical factor in public opinion about gender roles" (p. 4). Through analysis of the language used in the reports on each case and interviews with reporters and editors, Benedict delves into the ways in which the press both reflects and shapes popular opinion. The introduction contains a very useful outline of some social and commercial components that affect the way stories are reported, beginning with "competition," "deadlines," "reporters' ambitions," and "what sells" and moving on to more socially charged concepts such as "racism," "sexism," and "class prejudice." Three of her four case studies involve these issues. Benedict is also quite forthright in stating her ultimate goal of her research and this book, which is "to show reporters and editors how to cover sex crimes without further harming the victims" (p. 11). Organized into six chapters and a conclusion, the book begins with two general chapters covering rape myths, the portrayal of women in the media, and a brief history of the coverage of sex crimes in the press. She devotes the bulk of the work to analysis of press coverage of the Greta and John Rideout marital rape case (1978–1979), the gang rape at Big Dan's Bar in New Bedford, Massachusetts (1983–1984), the rape and murder of Jennifer Levin (1986), and the Central Park jogger beating (1989–1990).

1056. Bonner, Elizabeth, Lizbeth Goodman, Richard Allen, Linda Janes, and Catherine King, eds. *Imagining Women: Cultural Representations and Gender.* Cambridge: Polity Press, in association with Blackwell Publishers and the Open University, 1992. 361p. bibliog. index. (OP)

This collection, which complements the course "U207: Issues in Women's Studies" offered by the Open University in England, examines how both men and women present images of women. Although the editors clearly designed this work as an introductory overview, contributors include highly sophisticated arguments, examining the production, distribution, and consumption of texts from feminist perspectives. The editors organize the book according to overarching themes of cultural representation in relation to the field of cultural studies, providing analysis of literary representation in the following sections: "Self as Subject," visual images or fine arts, film and television, and "Comic Subversions," which deals with gender and humor. The editors also include a section on pornography that features discussions about the possibility of pornography for women, feminists as censors, and the exploitation of black women's bodies. Each section begins with a terse preface by an editor that introduces, contextualizes, and brings the chapters into dialogue with one another. Since representation is both visual and textual, the collection contains approximately fifty black-and-white and color images. Contributors include Elaine Showalter, Alicia Ostriker, Michelle Cliff, and Patricia Hill Collins. This work is well organized and highly accessible.

1057. Braden, Maria. *She Said What? Interviews with Women Newspaper Columnists.* Lexington: University Press of Kentucky, 1993. 208p. bibliog. ISBN 0813118190.

Writing a column is arguably the most independent job on any newspaper staff. For most of the nineteenth and well into the twentieth century, men held the vast majority of these coveted positions. While women did write columns, they tended to be relegated to the "woman's page" or the features section. Prior to the mid-1970s, they were hardly ever found in the hard-news or op-ed portions of the paper. In her excellent introduction, Braden discusses the groundbreaking work of Dorothy Thompson in the 1930s and 1940s and traces the change to the influence of the women's movement when a number of newspapers revamped their women's pages, turning them into less gender-bound lifestyles sections. The majority of the book consists of brief profiles of thirteen women who were especially successful in getting their voices heard and opinions noticed, ranging across the political spectrum from Mona Charen on the right to Molly Ivins and Ellen Goodman, representing far more progressive views. Braden supplements her snapshot of each woman with three columns particularly representative of each woman's unique style and perspective. In addition to spanning the political horizon, Braden also presents quite an array of journalistic styles and topics, covering important women columnists from Erma Bombeck to Anna Quindlen. Photos of each of the women profiled add a wonderful visual touch to their stories. Braden is also the author of *Women Politicians and the Media* (University Press of Kentucky, 1996), which analyzes the coverage of women politicians in the news media. Employing a basically chronological approach, Braden covers female "politicians" from Susan B. Anthony to Christine Whitman, with stops in between for discussions of press coverage of such notable women in politics as Helen Gahagan Douglas, Barbara Jordan, Dianne Feinstein, and Shirley Chisholm.

1058. Cuklanz, Lisa M. *Rape on Trial: How the Mass Media Construct Legal Reform and Social Change.* Philadelphia: University of Pennsylvania Press, 1996. 135p.

(Feminist Cultural Studies, the Media, and Political Culture). bibliog. index. ISBN 0812233212; 0812215591pa.

A volume in the University of Pennsylvania Press's admirable series Feminist Cultural Studies, the Media, and Political Culture, Cuklanz's work examines the struggle to change attitudes toward victims of rape, in this instance women, and the role the news media play in both perpetuating and destroying stereotypes. (Focusing on high-profile cases in the media involving such celebrity defendants as Mike Tyson and far less well known individuals, Cuklanz also details how feminist legal and social activism worked to overturn ingrained attitudes toward rape.) An important part of her argument centers on the significance (or lack thereof) of "public trials" in high-profile cases and whether the attention the media gave to these trials actually served to foster a reconsideration of the image of the victim. She is particularly attentive to the impact, over time, that public trials have on women's capacity to speak for themselves and to define their own experiences. As she states in her conclusion, "Public discussion of these trials is about the power to define, to articulate, to speak, and to be heard" (p. 120). The mass media are clearly the format through which this speaking and defining is translated to the general public.

1059. Fineman, Martha A., and Martha T. McClusky, eds. *Feminism, Media, and the Law*. New York: Oxford University Press, 1997. 319p. bibliog. (OP)

This book is the fourth volume to come out of Columbia University School of Law's Feminism and Legal Theory Project. While both of the editors are legal scholars, the contributors to this volume represent a number of different disciplines, including law, journalism, cinema studies, and women's studies. Divided into four sections, each containing an introductory, context-setting essay, *Feminism, Media, and the Law* covers multiple aspects of the media ranging from hate radio to press coverage of welfare "reform." A significant proportion of the essays, some thirteen out of a total of twenty-three, deal with the treatment of women in the news, focusing on recent events. Section 1, "Portrayals of Feminism in the Media," contains essays that analyze Rush Limbaugh and Howard Stern (Patricia J. Williams's contribution "Hate Radio: Why We Need to Tune into Limbaugh and Stern" is particularly enlightening) as well as critical commentary on Anita Hill and an analysis of media reporting on campus feminism. The second section, "Feminism, Law, and Popular Culture," focuses on film and television, dissecting such issues as the representation of woman lawyers in Hollywood stories. The essays in "Essentializing Gender," the third section, tackle the difficult issues of "the power of language to control and create reality" (p. 171). Finally, the contributions in section 4, "Media Images of Violence," clearly illustrate the gendered nature (and bias) of reporting on crimes against women. The authors writing here deal with the intersections of race and sex and how these are constructed in (and by) the media. The volume contains an excellent twenty-seven-page bibliography (called "References") as well as a brief table of cases cited.

1060. Joseph, Ammu, and Kalpana Sharma, eds. *Whose News? The Media and Women's Issues*. Thousand Oaks, CA: Sage, 1994. 335p. index. (OP)

Joseph and Sharma draw together a collection of articles analyzing the portrayal of women's concerns in the print media in India. Divided into two major parts, the English-language press and the Indian-language press (with one essay on television), the essays discuss press coverage of five issues critical to women: dowry deaths, rape, sex-determination tests, sati (widow burning), and the religious and political controversy over support payments to a divorced Muslim woman. What makes India such a fascinating and important case study is that the print media wield such power and prestige in a country with a large illiterate population. The power of the press rests less in the number of actual readers than in the fact that these readers make up the educated elite in the country. This means that the "written word carries weight which is out of proportion to its outreach" (p. 15). What journalists report on, analyze, and critique has immediate bearing on the status and role of women, which, by obvious extension, has an impact on society as a whole.

1061. Keller, Kathryn. *Mothers and Work in Popular American Magazines*. Westport, CT: Greenwood Press, 1994. 194p. (Contributions in Women's Studies, no. 130). bibliog. index. ISBN 031328864Xpa.

Keller critically examines how women's magazines, particularly *Ladies Home Journal, McCall's, Parents*, and *Good Housekeeping*, reflect women's changing roles in modern society. Keller posits that these magazines do more than simply mirror popular notions about women's place; they serve as vehicles to either transmit or challenge dominant ideologies. She argues that the publication of eclectic items such as recipes, letters to the editor, and articles by pediatricians, psychologists, religious leaders, and other "specialists" both determined and reinforced social norms. Reviewing forty years' worth of magazines and 450 articles, Keller selected magazines to analyze based on longevity, circulation, and availability of citations in *Reader's Guide to Periodical Literature*. Yet, according to the author, this method led to a homogenous view of American womanhood, foregrounding the lives of white, middle-class women while almost completely silencing the voices of women of color. However, Keller's acknowledgment of the limitations of her selection process highlights the types of images that the publications printed. Keller divides each section by decade, beginning with the 1950s. She subtitles the chapter on the 1950s "Hairline Cracks in the Traditional Mold" to indicate the first tentative stirrings of a new awareness among women of the possibility of change. By contrast, she subtitles the chapter on the 1980s "Ideological Retreat to the 1950s versus Facing Economic Realities." Keller concludes the work with a section on how women's magazines have reflected and somewhat contributed to the creation of changing family structures.

Keller continues her examination of women's representation in popular magazines in her 1998 work *Women's Magazines, 1940–1960: Gender Roles and the Popular Press* (Bedford/St. Martin's Press, 1998). Covering the two decades immediately preceding the second wave of feminism, Keller examines a period marked by both fluidity and rigidity.

1062. Lacey, Kate. *Feminine Frequencies: Gender, German Radio, and the Public Sphere, 1923–1945*. Ann Arbor: University of Michigan Press, 1996. 299p. (Social History, Popular Culture, and Politics in Germany). bibliog. index. ISBN 0472096168; 0472066161pa.

Lacey uses the medium of radio to explore critical moments in German history, both in terms of changes in the nation state and with respect to women's place in society. She focuses on a period that began a few years after the end of World War I and concluded with the end of World War II. These were particularly crucial years in Germany as the country struggled to recover after the devastation of World War I, experienced a deep economic depression, witnessed the fall of the Weimar Republic and the rise of National Socialism, and ultimately faced defeat in yet another worldwide conflagration. Radio was a potent force during this period. Among its other significant attributes, radio was the medium that most clearly breached the public/private divide, bringing the male public world into the feminine private sphere. Lacey takes a chronological and thematic approach to her topic, describing first the role of radio in the Weimar Republic, where the goal was to keep the medium free from politics and thus preserve the home as depoliticized and private. In the next section, titled "Feminine Frequencies," she traces the development of programs specifically aimed at women. The history of women's programming continues into the National Socialist era. The Nazis used radio and women's programs in particular as both a potent propaganda tool and a way of "bridging the (gendered) divide between the home front and the front line" (p. 13). The final part of the book, "Experts on Air," continues Lacey's in-depth analysis of women's programming, comparing and contrasting this programming during the Weimar and National Socialist periods. In the concluding chapter, "Gender, German Radio, and the Public Sphere," Lacey returns to one of the main themes of her thesis and "problematizes the concept of the public-private divide" (p. 14). She effectively uses radio as an example of a medium that both "mediated and recuperated challenges to the delineation of the separate spheres while in itself constituting a radical extension of the public sphere and a redefinition of the private" (p. 15).

1063. Lont, Cynthia M., ed. *Women and Media: Content, Careers, and Criticism.* Belmont, CA: Wadsworth, 1995. 415p. bibliog. index. (OP)

This collection of twenty-two essays addresses women's roles in seven different media and communications fields, including journalism, women's magazines, advertising, prime-time television, television news, film, and popular music. Contributors cover each of the fields in separate sections, which begin with a short overview of the topic that includes important historical events, trends in the portrayal of women, an assessment of the employment outlook, a list of references, and a listing of pioneering women as well as those currently active in the field. Lont cleverly juxtaposes information on ways in which the media represent women with data on women in the media, or women who are "doing" the representing. This work is primarily an introductory text, designed for use in a classroom setting. Although the work is more textbook than scholarly treatise, Lont provides ready access to critical and insightful readings on the complex and changing relationship between women and media.

Pamela Creedon's *Women in Mass Communication* (2nd ed., Sage, 1993) covers much of the same territory; however, the essays in Creedon's collection focus on the status of women in mass communications, the representation of women in the mass-communications classroom, and the impact of mass communications on both culture and the academy. Contributors examine diverse issues, such as the effects of a perceived "glass ceiling" on mass-communications students, women of color in academia, and representations of gender in journalism textbooks.

1064. Norris, Pippa, ed. *Women, Media, and Politics.* New York: Oxford University Press, 1997. 269p. bibliog. index. ISBN (OP); 0195105672pa.

Norris's collection represents a truly interdisciplinary conversation that began at a conference held at the Joan Shorenstein Center on the Press, Politics, and Public Policy at Harvard's Kennedy School of Government. *Women, Media, and Politics* features political science scholarship dealing with the obstacles that women face when running for elected office, women's voting patterns, and the emerging role of women journalists and media commentators. Contributors include academics in journalism, communications, and political science who attempt to determine whether "media coverage of women in America reinforces rather than challenges the dominant culture, and thereby contributes towards women's marginalization in public life" (p. 1). Although the essays cover some familiar ground, their placement in dialogue proves enlightening. For instance, in a section on campaign coverage, one contributor examines the gender gap in conjunction with stereotypes of how women candidates run for office and how the media frame their candidacy, giving the gender gap concept a larger, more critical meaning. This section builds on the idea of "gendered frames," which, according to Norris, is a device journalists use "to simplify, prioritize, and structure the narrative flow of events" (p. 6). The collection also tackles the particularly thorny issue of the representation of feminism and the women's movement in popular media. The chapters in the final section, "Framing the Women's Movement, Feminism, and Public Policy," move beyond the issue of electoral politics to embrace debates about media coverage of the women's movement. A somewhat more lighthearted (although at its core, intensely serious) analysis of women and media, Susan J. Douglas's *Where the Girls Are: Growing Up Female with the Mass Media* (Random House, 1994) offers a provocative and readable account of, among other things, girl groups, television, and the news media's handling of the women's liberation movement.

1065. Okker, Patricia. *Our Sister Editors: Sarah J. Hale and the Tradition of Nineteenth-Century American Women Editors.* Athens: University of Georgia Press, 1995. 264p. bibliog. index. (OP)

A remarkable woman, Sarah Hale has left her mark on generations of women (and men) magazine editors and, probably without their explicit knowledge, on thousands of students searching the Web for primary source materials. Editor of *Godey's Lady's Book* for forty years, from 1837 until 1877, two years before her death at the age of ninety, Hale passed judgment on most of what occupied the pages of the journal. In addition to her editorial responsibilities, Hale contributed reviews and wrote literature and poetry for *Godey's*. In what is more than simply a biography of Hale, Okker places her subject in the larger context of nineteenth-century women editors of periodicals (of whom she has identified more than 600, whom she lists in the appendix). More significantly, perhaps, Okker uses Hale's life and work as a lens through which to examine both nineteenth-century literary culture and the importance of gender and sexual difference in post–Civil War America.

Another remarkable woman who left her mark on the American media consciousness, although in perhaps a somewhat less elevated fashion than Sarah Hale, was Elizabeth Jane Cochran, better known as Nelly Bly, who was arguably the most famous "girl reporter" in the nation. Brooke Kroeger's *Nelly Bly: Daredevil, Reporter, Feminist* (Random House, 1994) offers an extremely readable account of a reporter whose contributions to journalism may turn out to have greater significance than her many exploits and media stunts. According to Sherilyn Cox Bennion, Sarah Hale and Nelly Bly are relatively well known because of an accident of geography. Women editors in the western part of the United States were pretty much ignored. Bennion strives to undo that neglect in her *Equal to the Occasion: Women Editors of the Nineteenth-Century West* (University of Nevada Press, 1990). She introduces almost 300 women who held editorial positions in western states from 1854 to 1899 and details the lives and careers of thirty-five of them.

1066. Robertson, Nan. *The Girls in the Balcony: Women, Men, and the New York Times.* New York: Random House, 1992. 274p. bibliog. index. (OP)

The *New York Times* comes as close to being a national newspaper as any published in the United States. In this engaging and very personal work, Nan Robertson, who describes herself as having arrived "when I was twenty-eight years old and left after my hair had gone white" (author's note), chronicles the changes that took place during the newspaper's turbulent history. It was very much the product of a "dynasty," a family-run operation for a significant portion of its life as a major force in news media. Robertson traces the first phase of women's power at the *Times* to Iphigene Ochs Sulzberger, the daughter of the founder of the dynasty, Adolph Ochs. However strong she was, Iphigene was, in Robertson's estimation, "the power behind the throne" (p. 55). Iphigene's rise to prominence at her father's death in 1935 did, however, signal the slow beginning of the end of "the Dark Ages for women" (p. 59) at the *Times*. The appointment of Kathleen McLaughlin, the first woman hired under Och's successor (and Iphigene's husband) Arthur Hayes Sulzberger, was a major turning point, although change at the paper proceeded at a snail's pace. While other newspapers rushed to replace men lost to the draft during World War II, the *Times* successfully resisted this trend. Finally, a successful lawsuit against the paper, settled out of court in 1978, turned the tide. A Pulitzer Prize–winning journalist, Robertson presents an intensely personal story of women at the *Times*. She relates her own experiences and those of women such as Ada Louise Huxtable, the first full-time architecture critic on an American newspaper, Anna Quindlen, renowned op-ed page columnist, and other women who, through sheer dedication and perseverance, changed the *Times* from a bastion of male privilege to a newspaper far more representative of the people about whom it reported.

A century earlier, Ida Tarbell broke new ground as a crusading "muckraking" reporter who covered the major stories of her time. Robert C. Kochersberger Jr. has brought together a collection of Tarbell's articles, book chapters, speeches, and unpublished work in *More Than a Muckraker: Ida Minerva Tarbell's Life in Journalism* (University of Tennessee Press, 1995). This makes for a nice companion piece to Robertson's work. Maurine Beasley and Sheila Gibbons also contribute to the emerging picture of women and/in the media. Their 1993 work *Taking Their Place: A Documentary History of Women and Journalism* (American University Press, 1993), provides an important historical frame into which to situate and better understand the experiences of women at the *New York Times*.

1067. Sanders, Marlene, and Marcia Rock. *Waiting for Primetime: The Women of Television News*. Urbana: University of Illinois Press, 1988. 214p. bibliog. index. (OP)

In television journalism, as in print media, much of the most valuable insight and critical analysis of women in the profession has come from insiders. *Waiting for Primetime* is no exception. Marlene Sanders toiled for years at both ABC and CBS as a reporter, correspondent, anchorwoman, and manager. She relates the story of women in broadcasting largely through her own experience, although her extensive network of colleagues gave her access to others in the industry. Among other issues Sanders and Rock cover is the question of whether aging has a greater impact on women newscasters than on their male counterparts. Based on the comments recorded in *Waiting for Primetime*, the jury is still out. Other critical points raised in the book concern the challenges of combining motherhood and career, women in management, and the differences and distinctions between feature reporting and hard-news reporting. *Waiting for Primetime* offers a clearly gendered analysis of all of these issues.

A less personal but equally valuable perspective is David Hosley and Gayle Yamada's 1987 book *Hard News: Women in Broadcast Journalism* (Greenwood Press, 1987). Hosley and Yamada take a chronological approach to the subject, starting at the very earliest moments in commercial broadcasting. In a particularly significant chapter, they examine the case of Christine Craft, who sued Metromedia for sex discrimination in the early 1980s. Craft's lawsuit makes for an interesting comparison with Sanders's respondents who thought that age had little to do with a woman's success in broadcasting. Christine Craft tells her own story of her struggle with the network in her bitterly titled and biting work *Too Old, Too Ugly, and Not Deferential to Men* (Prima Publishing, 1988).

1068. Thom, Mary. *Inside Ms.: 25 Years of the Magazine and the Feminist Movement*. New York: Henry Holt, 1997. 244p. index. ISBN 0805058451pa.

Thom's engaging work provides a much-needed corrective for anyone who simply considers *Ms. Magazine* a glossy, mildly political, middle-of-the-road publication of little historical interest. Relying largely upon oral history, Thom begins her narrative with a description of a rally in New York City in August 1970. Several of the women who eventually would create the new women's magazine attended the rally, which marked the fiftieth anniversary of women's suffrage in the United States. Thom then discusses the production of the first issue, an insert in *New York Magazine*. Thom chronicles *Ms.*'s complicated and tempestuous history, detailing the commercial and political upheavals associated with the publication from its inception. Thom implicitly distinguishes between an independent publication and one that is alternative, grassroots, or underground. The author explores issues that *Ms.*'s creators dealt with, including paid advertising and a conservative backlash that reached its peak during the Reagan years. Thom outlines editorial and business strategies taken to sustain the magazine, as well as the litany of financial and political crises that marked the publication's first twenty-five years. The book ends with an epilogue titled "Rebirth" that chronicles the change of ownership and introduces some of the new voices that followed Gloria Steinem and the original *Ms.* cohort.

A somewhat more academic (and less personal) view of *Ms. Magazine*, Amy Farrell's *Yours in Sisterhood: Ms. Magazine and the Promise of Popular Feminism* (University of North Carolina Press, 1998) presents a cogent discussion of the role the magazine played in constructing the popular view of second-wave feminism. For a far less positive analysis of *Ms. Magazine*, see Ellen McCracken's *Decoding Women's Magazines: From Mademoiselle to Ms.* (St. Martin's Press, 1993). McCracken places *Ms.* squarely in the genre of glossy women's magazines with one major purpose: the advancement of consumerism and capitalism.

1069. Valdivia, Angharad N., ed. *Feminism, Multiculturalism, and the Media: Global Diversities*. Thousand Oaks, CA: Sage, 1995. 332p. bibliog. index. ISBN (OP); 0803957750pa.

This collection focuses on how feminism and multiculturalism interact and frequently conflict with media analysis. In an important contribution to the growing body of work on global feminism, contributors vehemently lobby for multiple voices in feminist analysis. Yet the essays also reveal the tendency in both mainstream academic feminism and mainstream media to marginalize or silence people who exist outside of the cultural mainstream. Valdivia arranges the volume into three broad sections: "The Production of Interventions," "(Con)Textual Analysis," and "Combining Methodologies and Narratives," revealing a more global view of media. Part 1 focuses on the individual who produces media and whose race, class, and gender inform that production, as well as the organizations whose established practices determine the media produced. The essays in this part range from general, introductory pieces, such as "Feminist Media Studies in a Global Setting," to discussions of specific topics, including an analysis of films and videos by Asian American and Canadian women. "(Con)Textual Analysis" delves into how "social and cultural influences and outcomes" (p. 123) inform and complicate particular aspects of media representation. These essays uncover the tensions and intersections embedded in the politics of gender, race, and sexual orientation/identity. The contributors thus engage in socially grounded, culturally mediated (con)textual analysis. Contributors also examine "lesbian chic," how Hollywood portrays and/or silences working-class women, and how feminist analysis of a rape case empowered women while simultaneously targeting a minority community. The final part of the book consists of three essays "that use a combination of methodologies to study feminist multicultural issues" (p. 217).

1999 CORE TITLES

Bucholtz, Mary, A.C. Liang, and Laurel A. Sutton, eds. *Reinventing Identities: The Gendered Self in Discourse*. New York: Oxford University Press, 1999. 431p. (Studies in Language and Gender). bibliog. index. ISBN 0195126297; 0195126300pa.

Gibbon, Margaret. *Feminist Perspectives on Language*. New York: Longman, 1999. 186p. (Feminist Perspectives Series). bibliog. index. ISBN 0582356369.

Holborow, Marnie. *The Politics of English: A Marxist View of Language.* Thousand Oaks, CA: Sage, 1999. 216p. bibliog. index. ISBN 0761960171; 076196018Xpa.

Isaacs, Susan. *Brave Dames and Wimpettes: What Women Really Are Doing on Page and Screen.* New York: Ballantine Books, 1999. 159p. (The Library of Contemporary Thought). index. ISBN 0345422813pa.

Lent, John A. *Women and Mass Communications in the 1990's: An International, Annotated Bibliography.* Westport, CT: Greenwood Press, 1999. 510p. (Bibliographies and Indexes in Women's Studies, no. 29). bibliog. index. ISBN 031330209X; 0313265798pa.

Lowe, Denise. *Women and American Television: An Encyclopedia.* Santa Barbara, CA: ABC-CLIO, 1999. 513p. bibliog. index. (OP)

McHugh, Kathleen. *American Domesticity: From How-To Manual to Hollywood Melodrama.* New York: Oxford University Press, 1999. 235p. bibliog. index. ISBN 0195122615.

Robin, Diana, and Ira Jaffe, eds. *Redirecting the Gaze: Gender Theory and Cinema in the Third World.* Albany: State University of New York Press, 1999. 377p. (SUNY Series: Cultural Studies in Cinema/Video). bibliog. index. ISBN 0791439933; 0791439941pa.

Romaine, Suzanne. *Communicating Gender.* Mahwah, NJ: Lawrence Erlbaum Associates, 1999. 406p. bibliog. index. ISBN 0805829253; 0805829261pa.

Sochen, June. *From Mae to Madonna: Women Entertainers in Twentieth-Century America.* Lexington: University Press of Kentucky, 1999. 240p. bibliog. index. ISBN 0813121124.

Sutherland, Christine Mason, and Rebecca Sutcliffe, eds. *The Changing Tradition: Women in the History of Rhetoric.* Calgary: University of Calgary Press, 1999. 279p. ISBN 1552380084.

Wood, Julia T. *Gendered Lives: Communication, Gender, and Culture.* 3rd ed. Belmont, CA: Wadsworth, 1999. 448p. bibliog. index. ISBN 0534562590pa.

WORLD WIDE WEB/INTERNET SITES

1070. *BRUBYRICH.* http://www.brubyrich.com/ruby.html.
This is the Web site of film critic and social/cultural theorist B. Ruby Rich, author of *Chick Flicks: Theories and Memories of the Feminist Film Movement.* Rich includes a "Discourse & Dish" link on the page. She describes this as "an ongoing experiment in creating community." Two discussion groups are available, one dealing with feminism and film, the other with upcoming events.

1071. *MCS: The Media and Communication Studies Site*. http://www.aber.ac.uk/media/index.html.

Although not specifically geared to issues of women and communications and mass media, this site has an excellent link to topics on gender and ethnicity.

1072. *Women in Cinema: A Reference Guide*. http://www.people.virginia.edu/~pm9k/libsci/womFilm.html.

This site is a particularly good example of a university library-based Web site. Organized into ten parts, including an introductory essay and a bibliography, it includes a separate part devoted to electronic sources.

1073. *Women Make Movies*. http://www.wmm.com/.

This site includes links to WMM's own excellent film and video catalog, news and events, and an extremely useful set of "links and resources."

1074. *Women's Studies Database—Women's Film Reviews*. http://www.mith.2.umd.edu/EdRes/Topics/WomensStudies/FilmReviews/.

Part of the superior *Women's Studies* site at the University of Maryland, this site provides an alphabetical listing of feminist reviews of films, including feature films and documentaries.

14 History

Cindy Ingold

History was one of the first academic disciplines to embrace the study of women. Although for years the teaching and study of "patriarchal" history was the norm, women's history is now an accepted field of study. Many large research universities have specializations in women's history, and smaller universities and colleges can often boast of a faculty member who specializes in some aspect of the study of women in different historical eras. High-school and elementary-school teachers are even incorporating the teaching of women's history into the curriculum. In the more than three decades that have passed since Gerda Lerner, one of the founders of women's history, wrote her dissertation on the Grimké sisters in 1966 and the first Berkshire Conference on Women's History was held in 1973, women's history has evolved into an established field of study.

The monographs in this chapter present a wide variety of methodologies, periods, and subjects. While the study of women in the United States and Western Europe and the period from the mid-nineteenth to the twentieth centuries still predominates, many titles now exist on the history of women from other parts of the world and from other time periods. For this reason, this chapter has been subdivided by geographic regions and time periods as follows: "General Theory and Historiography," "Ancient, Medieval, and Renaissance History," "Africa and the Middle East," "Asia and Oceania (Including Australia)," "Central America, South America, and the Caribbean," "Europe," and "North America."

Historians of women's history are writing about a wide variety of topics: the religious experiences of women, women in the founding of nations, how ethnicity and race have shaped women's experiences, the intellectual history of women, and lesbian women. Topics such as suffrage, women in the so-called 'private sphere', or the evolution of women's organizations still remain popular, yet the monographs cited here reflect a more mature, complex analysis of the roles women have played in the historical arena. While this chapter does include titles on women in other parts of the world, more attention needs to be paid to women in developing parts of the world. Historical studies of other disciplines will be found in appropriate subject chapters.

REFERENCE SOURCES

1075. Claghorn, Charles Eugene. *Women Patriots of the American Revolution: A Biographical Dictionary*. Metuchen, NJ: Scarecrow Press, 1991. 499p. bibliog. ISBN 0810824213.

Women Patriots of the American Revolution includes short biographies of "six hundred women who performed patriotic acts during the war" (p. 1). Arranging his work into three parts, Claghorn briefly discusses the history of the American Revolution, especially highlighting activities of women, in part 1. Part 2 includes brief biographies of individual women. Each biography provides the place of residence, date of birth, date of marriage, number of children, and date of death when known and outlines what the woman did during the Revolution. *See* references are included for some entries but not for all of them. Part 3 lists more than 5,000 women who performed some type of service during the Revolution, with a one-sentence mention of what the women did. *Women Patriots of the American Revolution* is recommended for libraries with comprehensive reference collections only.

1076. Cosner, Shaaron, and Victoria Cosner. *Women under the Third Reich: A Biographical Dictionary.* Westport, CT: Greenwood Press, 1998. 203p. bibliog. index. ISBN 0313303150.

Women under the Third Reich contains biographical portraits of approximately 100 women whose lives were affected by the Nazi regime. Individuals were included based primarily on the availability of English-language material about them, and priority was given to those individuals who had published biographies or autobiographies. Women from all walks of life will be found here, including writers, artists, filmmakers and film stars, musicians, and scientists. The authors have attempted "to include at least one woman from every part of the intricate web that made up the occupied territories of the Third Reich" (p. xi), which represents a range of ages, occupations, nationalities, and political affiliations. Entries run from one paragraph to two pages and provide the years of birth and death, occupations, and activities. Photographs accompany several entries, and all list a short bibliography of sources. This source has two appendices: one listing roles/occupations, the other listing country of origin. *Women under the Third Reich* will be a valuable reference source for research libraries.

1077. Cullen-DuPont, Kathryn. *The Encyclopedia of Women's History in America.* New York: Facts on File, 1996. 339p. bibliog. index. ISBN 0816026254.

This encyclopedia brings together short entries "about the organizations founded, the books and newspapers published, the speeches given, the documents signed, the demonstrations and conventions held, the legislative actions proposed and enacted, the task forces and committees convened, and the legal rulings rendered—all in the course of 'Women's History in America'" (p. ix). The encyclopedia also includes individual women who were chosen based on the following criteria: women who have affected the general course of American history, women important in the struggle for equal rights, barrier-breaking women, visionary women, and women who have made especially important contributions to the cultural and intellectual life of America. The short entries appear in alphabetical order and cover everything from Pocahontas to the Year of the Woman. Each entry provides a short bibliography. One appendix includes important documents from the Constitution to the Married Woman's Property Act, New York, 1848, and the National Organization for Women's Bill of Rights. One index is included with cross-references. *Handbook of American Women's History*, edited by Angela Howard Zophy (Garland, 1990), is another excellent one-volume reference tool on events, organizations, concepts, and individuals. Designed as a source for individuals new to the field of American women's history, the *Handbook* includes short articles (from one page to several) by contributors including faculty, graduate students, editors of women's journals, docents of museums, and freelance authors, among others. Entries include a basic bibliography of primary sources, if available, and secondary sources.

A final source that should be mentioned is *The Reader's Companion to U.S. Women's History* (Houghton Mifflin, 1998), edited by Wilma Mankiller, Gloria Steinem, and others. More than 300 contributors, including such notables as Rita Mae Brown, Cynthia Enloe, Patricia Ireland, Vivien W. Ng, and Rosemary Radford Ruether, provide 400 short articles on a variety of alphabetically arranged topics, such as ethnic women, gambling, legal studies, prostitution, and women's studies. Some but not all entries include bibliographic references, and no criteria are listed for inclusion of topics.

1078. Echols, Anne, and Marty Williams. *An Annotated Index of Medieval Women*. New York: M. Wiener Publishing, 1992. 635p. bibliog. indexes. ISBN 0910129274.

Compiled to remedy the dearth of reference tools that include adequate information about medieval women, this index contains entries for 1,500 women from nearly thirty countries and covers the years 800 to 1500 A.D. In their attempt to present a cross section of women's participation in medieval life, the editors include ordinary women, for example, a mole catcher from Paris, in addition to famous women like Joan of Arc. Arranged alphabetically by first name, each entry consists of name variations, dates, country of origin, brief biographical information, category designations (abbess, builder, merchant, spy, and the like), and short bibliographic references. The editors provide the full citations to the references in a separate, fairly extensive bibliography. They also include lists cross-referencing the women by date, country, category, last names, titles, regions, and cities. Though the editors do not claim comprehensive coverage, they have produced one of the first reference works on the subject.

1079. Fischer, Gayle, comp. *Journal of Women's History Guide to Periodical Literature*. Bloomington: Indiana University Press, 1992. 501p. bibliog. ISBN 0253322197; 0253207207pa.

With more than 5,500 entries compiled from periodicals published between 1980 and 1990, this guide is arranged into forty subjects, many of them with subdivisions. Subjects include countries and regions of the world, along with topics such as agriculture, art, economics, friendship, material and popular culture, politics, sexuality, theory, and women on the U.S. western frontier. In the introduction, historian Joan Hoff notes that 14 percent of the entries deal with work, including economics and professions; 8 percent deal with religion; and 23 percent concern the history of women in countries other than the United States. The preface by Christie Farnham provides a succinct overview of the status of women in the history profession. The guide is extensively cross-referenced, but it lacks an index, forcing the researcher to rely on the forty-subject table of contents to find relevant information. The volume includes the list of serials cited in the back.

1080. Hine, Darlene Clark, ed. *Facts on File Encyclopedia of Black Women in America*. New York: Facts on File, 1997. 11v. ISBN 0816034249 set.

This eleven-volume encyclopedia presents brief essays on black women in America from a variety of professions. Each volume has a similar format, which includes a table of contents, a very brief description of the contents, an introduction to the women and organizations in that volume, and then the entries. Each volume has a chronology of events and an index for that volume. A bibliography listing general titles and works on black women is repeated in all eleven volumes; additional titles specific to black women in the disciplines or areas covered are included in the bibliography for that specific volume. Finally, every volume lists "Contents of the Set Organized by Volume" and "Contents of the Set Listed Alphabetically by Entry." Volume 1 includes entries on individuals and organizations whose achievements occurred primarily before the twentieth century. The contents of the remaining ten volumes are as follows: volume 2, women in literature; volume 3, women in dance, sports, and visual arts; volume 4, women in business and professions; volume 5, women in music; volume 6, women in education; volume 7, women in religion and community; volume 8, women in law and government; volume 9, women in theater arts and entertainment; volume 10, women in social activism; and volume 11, women in science, health, and medicine. The encyclopedia includes photos and other illustrations. This easy-to-use, well-organized encyclopedia is most appropriate for high-school and undergraduate students.

Black Women in America: An Historical Encyclopedia, edited by Hine in two volumes

(Carlson, 1993), includes contributed entries: 641 biographies of black women and 163 entries on general topics and organizations. Hine indicates that black women were included in this encyclopedia if they made a difference on the national scene; she also notes that women were included who cannot be found in other reference sources. The entries run from a few paragraphs to lengthy articles, such as the one on slavery, which runs to more than twenty-five pages. Each entry provides a list of sources for additional reading or sources the contributor used in creating the entry. Several biographical entries include photographs. Volume 2 contains a classified list of women by profession, a chronology of black women in the United States, and a lengthy bibliography. There is also a substantial index.

Other noteworthy titles that provide biographical information about historical and contemporary African American women are *African American Women: A Biographical Dictionary* (Garland, 1993), edited by Dorothy C. Salem, and *Notable Black American Women* (Gale, 1992), edited by Jessie Carney Smith. Salem's volume is part of Garland's excellent Biographical Dictionaries of Minority Women series. Smith's volume is a title in Gale's "unofficial" Notable Women series, which also includes two editions of *Notable Hispanic American Women* (1993, 1998). Gale published *Notable Black American Women: Book II* in 1996.

1081. Hyman, Paula E., and Deborah Dash Moore, eds. *Jewish Women in America: An Historical Encyclopedia*. New York: Routledge, 1997. 2v. 1770p. bibliog. index. ISBN 0415919363.

This outstanding two-volume encyclopedia "aims to recover the rich history of American Jewish women and to make visible their diverse accomplishments" (p. xvi). This source provides 800 biographical entries and 110 entries on other topics, contributed by hundreds of scholars. For the biographies, preference was given to women no longer living, but living women aged sixty or above are also included. The editors complement entries of well-known and influential women by being "sensitive to regional and professional diversity as well as contribution to Jewish communal life and American civic activity as volunteers" (p. xxii). Individual biographies include vital statistics, such as dates of birth and death, but the essays focus on each woman's contributions and activities. Topical entries provide overviews of a variety of subjects, events, or organizations, such as immigration, Yiddish literature, higher education, or television. Other topical entries provide interpretive essays on women's role in Jewish and American culture or the several denominations of Judaism. Volume 1 includes a complete alphabetical list of all the entries. Volume 2 contains notes on contributors, a comprehensive index, and a classified list of the biographical entries arranged by occupation. An "Annotated Bibliography and Guide to Archival Resources on the History of Jewish Women in America" by Phyllis Holman Weisbard is also included in volume 2.

1082. Opfell, Olga S. *Queens, Empresses, Grand Duchesses, and Regents: Women Rulers of Europe, A.D. 1328–1989*. Jefferson, NC: McFarland, 1989. 282p. bibliog. ISBN 0899503853.

Opfell compiles information on thirty-nine female rulers from the fourteenth through the twentieth centuries, hoping to show the achievements and failures of these women, along with their impact. All of the kingdoms and empires represented are European. Native spellings have been followed except in cases where the anglicized version is more familiar; titles have all been anglicized. Opfell relied on a variety of sources to compile her information, including encyclopedias, travel books, general histories, embassy information, and *Burke's Royal Families of the World*. Additional sources are listed in a bibliography under the name of each ruler. Guida M. Jackson's *Women Who Ruled* (ABC-CLIO, 1990) has a much broader scope, including "all women rulers, de facto rulers, and constitutional monarchs, living or deceased, of the world's kingdoms, islands, empires, nations, and tribes since the beginning of time" (p. xi). The introduction provides a survey of women rulers by region of the world. The alphabetical entries are brief, including birth and death years and a description of the woman's impact. Several entries do include photographs.

1083. Scanlon, Jennifer, and Shaaron Cosner. *American Women Historians, 1700s–1990s: A Biographical Dictionary*. Westport, CT: Greenwood Press, 1996. 269p. bibliog. index. ISBN 0313296642.

This dictionary records the lives and work of approximately 200 women who have practiced the craft of history in the United States, from the 1700s to the 1990s. The women are all American by birth or citizenship. It contains deceased and living women from all fields of history, including public history, academia, archival work, art history, and writers of popular history. The authors include women based primarily on their publications, but other criteria include "participation in defining a field of study, influence on other historians or related scholars, cross-disciplinary achievements, and contributions to the work of others" (p. ix). Several of the names are familiar, including Natalie Zemon Davis, Laurel Thatcher Ulrich, Barbara Tuchman, Mary Ritter Beard, and Gerda Lerner. The entries, which run from a paragraph to two to three pages, include basic biographical information and significant achievements. Entries also may include a bibliography of sources by the woman. All entries include sources for additional biographical information. A short section of selected photographs can be found at the end of the source.

1084. Sherr, Lynn, and Jurate Kazickas. *Susan B. Anthony Slept Here: A Guide to American Women's Landmarks*. New York: Times Books, a division of Random House, 1994. 579p. bibliog. index. (OP)

Susan B. Anthony Slept Here includes information on more than 2,000 places in America where women made history, organized alphabetically by state and then by city. The authors include museums and "public" sites along with private homes, monuments, courthouses, hospitals, graves, and even trails. In preparing this source, an update to *The American Woman's Gazetteer*, published in 1976, also by Sherr and Kazickas, the authors discovered regional and topographic trends that shaped many of these women's lives. The authors note that all of the women chosen as subjects had died as of January 1993. The term *site of* within an annotation indicates that the landmark is no longer preserved, and the term *private* indicates that a site is occupied and not accessible to the public. Several of the entries include photos. The authors include a lengthy bibliography of the books, articles, and pamphlets consulted during the project as well as one alphabetical index.

A similar source is *Women Remembered: A Guide to Landmarks of Women's History in the United States* (Greenwood Press, 1986) by Marion Tinling. Tinling arranges her work by regions—New England, the South, the Mid-Atlantic, the Midwest, and the West—then alphabetically by state, city, and named women. The source includes women, no longer living, who were "memorable for contributions to society, for acts of heroism, or as participants in some historical event" (p. xii); it does not include women who were known chiefly in relation to men. All of the sites noted in *Women Remembered* are public sites, including statues, markers, homes, institutions, schools, towns, parks, and grave markers in special cases. The entries include a woman's first name, maiden name, and married name (if relevant), as well as pen names or nicknames such as Calamity Jane. The entries note if a biography of the woman can be found in *Notable American Women, 1607–1950* or *Notable American Women: The Modern Period*. Tinling gives sources of information and quotations along with suggestions for further reading in notes at the end of each state's entry. Tinling's work is also well indexed and includes a list of women by category (educators, performers, politicians, pioneers, and so on). Each source has unique items, and both would be welcome additions to public and academic libraries.

MONOGRAPHS

General Theory and Historiography

1085. DePauw, Linda Grant. *Battle Cries and Lullabies: Women in War from Prehistory to the Present*. Norman: University of Oklahoma Press, 1998. 395p. bibliog. index. (OP)

DePauw presents a clear chronological narrative of women's roles in war, beginning with prehistory and ending with a chapter called "Third World Wars." In between, the author examines women's roles in war in the ancient world, medieval Europe, the age of imperialism, both world wars, and the Cold War. In the preface, DePauw writes, "No one has attempted to write a book like this one before, for I wished to place women, in all their diversity, in the context of the history of war" (p. xiii). Defining war "as a disciplined and socially sanctioned use of deadly force by one group of people against another" (p. 9), DePauw provides an excellent overview of the issues and controversies surrounding women's roles in war and the military in her introduction. She groups women's military roles into four categories: classic women's roles, including victim or instigator of conflict; combat support roles or "camp followers"; virago roles, such as war leaders, covert operatives, or amazons; and finally, androgynous warriors, or women who fought, often disguised as men, alongside males in battle. DePauw's clear narrative provides an excellent introduction to women's roles in war and paves the way for future analysis of women in war. This book is highly recommended for all libraries.

Behind the Lines: Gender and the Two World Wars, edited by Margaret Randolph and others (Yale University Press, 1997), includes essays by various scholars "that analyze the gender implications of wartime discourses" (p. 4) for women in the United States, France, Great Britain, and Germany. Arguing that "war must be understood as a gendering activity, one that ritually marks the gender of all members of society, whether or not they are combatants" (p. 4), these essays discuss female literary reactions to war, women's activism during wartime, women and unionism during World War II, and postwar experiences and memories of women.

1086. Duberman, Martin Bauml, Martha Vicinus, and George Chauncey Jr., eds. *Hidden from History: Reclaiming the Gay and Lesbian Past*. New York: New American Library, 1989. 579p. bibliog. (OP)

The editors write that this volume on gay and lesbian history "is intended to summarize the research done in the 'first phase' of historical reclamation during the last decades and to point to some of the questions the next generation of historical scholarship must address" (p. 2). As such, *Hidden from History* contains new and revised essays by some of the most noteworthy names in the field, including John Boswell, Paula Gunn Allen, Shari Benstock, Allan Bérubé, and Leila Rupp. The essays are divided into five sections, including the ancient world; preindustrial societies, which looks at medieval Europe, imperial China, and American Indian cultures; the nineteenth century; the early twentieth century, with essays on the lesbian and gay subculture of Harlem, lesbianism in Paris in the early part of the century, and homosexuality in Nazi Germany; and World War II and the modern era. As the editors write, "We have deliberately assembled essays crossing national and temporal boundaries, as well as those of race and gender, in order to encourage the varying histories to speak to one another" (p. 8). The introduction provides an excellent overview of the slow growth of gay and lesbian history during the latter half of the twentieth century, with the editors concluding that gay and lesbian history has finally come into its own. This collection of essays is essential reading and belongs in the collections of all large public, college, and research libraries.

1087. Gluck, Sherna Berger, and Daphne Patai, eds. *Women's Words: The Feminist Practice of Oral History*. New York, Routledge, 1991. 234p. bibliog. index. ISBN (OP); 0415903726pa.

This collection of thirteen essays, resulting from the first meeting of the National Women's Studies Association in 1977, examines the practice and pitfalls of oral history as a method for feminist research: "The essays in this volume highlight the ways in which feminist oral history, in interrogating other discourses as well as its own assumptions, has produced a spiraling effect" (p. 221). The contributors come from a variety of academic disciplines, including history, cultural studies, anthropology, folklore, literature, speech communications, and women's studies. The four parts cover the techniques of interviewing, problems in the interpretation and analysis of women's words, the dilemmas scholars face in terms of their own biases and training, and finally, essays discussing actual projects the contributors engaged in. The essays reveal the problems many of these scholars faced in trying to reinvent traditional methods of oral history practice in terms of new feminist methodologies; many of the authors admit failures. However, collectively the essays raise important new questions about the practice of women's oral history and reveal "that there is not merely one appropriate methodology, nor one type of research project, that all scholars should rush to duplicate" (p. 222).

1088. Hunt, Lynn, ed. *The Invention of Pornography: Obscenity and the Origins of Modernity, 1500–1800*. New York: Zone Books, distributed by MIT Press, 1993. 411p. bibliog. index. ISBN 094229968X; 0942299698pa.

This collection of essays from a conference held at the University of Pennsylvania in 1991 presents the evolution of pornography as an idea. Hunt traces many of the developments leading to pornography as a distinct category of understanding in the introduction. She argues that pornography became such a category between the Renaissance and the French Revolution, largely because of the growth of print culture. The lines between the modern pornographic tradition and its censorship can be traced back to sixteenth-century Italy and seventeenth- and eighteenth-century France and England. The essays in this volume focus on this time period and these places. Hunt asserts that over time pornography came to be defined by the conflicts "between writers, artists, and engravers on the one side and spies, policemen, clergymen and state officials on the other" (p. 11). It is linked to characteristics of modern culture, including freethinking, scientific inquiry, protests against political authority, and growing ideas about gender differences; thus, Hunt argues, understanding the history of pornography is essential to understanding current debates. The essays, divided into three categories, trace the early political and cultural meanings of pornography, discuss philosophical issues, and finally, focus on the emergence of pornography as a literary and visual culture in the eighteenth century. This book is highly recommended for all libraries.

1089. Laqueur, Thomas. *Making Sex: Body and Gender from the Greeks to Freud*. Cambridge, MA: Harvard University Press, 1990. 313p. bibliog. index. ISBN 0674543491.

In this dense yet stimulating book, Thomas Laqueur hopes to "show how a biology of hierarchy in which there is only one sex, a biology of incommensurability between two sexes, and the claim that there is not publicly relevant sexual difference at all, or no sex, have constrained the interpretation of bodies and the strategies of sexual politics for some two thousand years" (p. 23). *Making Sex* is not a history of sex or a history of the body; instead, it is a theoretical analysis of the social, political, and epistemological changes in beliefs about maleness and femaleness over 2,000 years. Examining a variety of texts from Aristotle, Galen, and Origen to William Harvey, Jean-Jacques Rousseau, and Sigmund Freud, Laqueur claims that a one-sex belief of the "sexual body" existed up to the Enlightenment. This one-sex model postulated that men and women were essentially the same and saw women's genitals as internal counterparts to male genitals.

Laqueur believes that the change to the two-sex model, or the belief that men's and women's bodies are totally different, occurred because of two broad historical developments, one episte-mological and the other political. By the eighteenth century "the body was no longer regarded as a microcosm of some larger order. . . . Science no longer generated the hierarchies of analogies" (p. 10). Furthermore, historical events such as the industrial revolution and the rise of the class system, as well as emerging social and political beliefs about marriage and views of public spaces, helped further the idea of two separate sexes. Laqueur further claims that by the Enlightenment, the view that female orgasm was necessary for conception died out and that the "purported independence of generation from pleasure created the space in which women's sexual nature could be redefined, debated, denied, or qualified" (p. 3). This sexual difference between men and women became solidly grounded in nature and was used as a means to argue that women were less than men, that they deserved fewer rights than men. Laqueur claims that "sex is contextual" (p. 16) and that he "wants to show on the basis of historical evidence that almost everything one has to *say* about sex—however sex is understood—already has in it a claim about gender" (p. 11). Drawing on literary theory, Foucault, structuralism, and historical evidence, *Making Sex* is an important though difficult text because of what it relates to modern readers about the current nature of sexual relations. This book is recommended for graduate students and faculty.

1090. Lerner, Gerda. *The Creation of Patriarchy*. New York: Oxford University Press, 1986. 318p. (Women and History, v. 1). bibliog. index. (OP)

Gerda Lerner is one of the founding mothers of women's history, and *The Creation of Patriarchy* is a seminal work. In the opening words to her book, Lerner exclaims, "Women's history is indispensable and essential to the emancipation of women" (p. 3). Thus the American historian spent eight years studying the history of ancient Mesopotamia and the Hebrew world to understand why women have been left out of the making of history: "The tension between women's actual historical experience and their exclusion from interpreting that experience I have called the 'dialectic of women's history'. This dialectic has moved women forward in the historical process" (p. 5). The author believes that the "establishment of patriarchy" was a "process developing over a period of nearly 2,500 years, from app. 3100 to 600 B.C." (p. 8). In this work she traces "by means of historical evidence, the development of the leading ideas, symbols and metaphors by which patriarchal gender relations were incorporated into Western civilization" (p. 10).

Lerner outlines several propositions in her introduction that she develops in the course of the book. First, "The appropriation by men of women's sexual and reproductive capacity occurred *prior* to the formation of private property and class society" (p. 8). The subordination of women's sexual rights was institutionalized in the earliest law codes. Another important proposition is that "Class for men was and is based on their relationship to the means of production. . . . For women, class is mediated through their sexual ties to a man, who then gives them access to material resources" (p. 9). Women continued to play important roles as priestesses, seers, and healers; but gradually, dominant male gods began to overthrow the goddess religion with the establishment of kingship, and the monotheistic God of the Hebrews completely obliterated the goddess religion. Women's access to the divine was then relegated to their function as mothers. Finally, Lerner writes, "This symbolic devaluing of women in relation to the divine becomes one of the founding metaphors of Western civilization. The other founding metaphor is supplied by Aristotelian philosophy, which assumes as a given that women are incomplete and damaged human beings of an entirely different order than men" (p. 10). This ambitious, important work belongs in every library.

In another work, *The Creation of Feminist Consciousness, from the Middle Ages to Eighteen-Seventy* (Oxford University Press, 1993; volume 2 of Women and History), Lerner attempts to "trace the creation of feminist consciousness in Western Europe and the United States from approximately the 7th century A.D. to 1870" (p. 13). She ends with 1870 because she feels that the mid-nineteenth century marked a point when significant numbers of women gained feminist consciousness and began organized movements for women's rights. Lerner defines feminist consciousness as the awareness of women that they belong to a subordinate group, that they have suffered wrongs as a group, and that this subordination is not natural—along with the belief that they "can provide an alternate vision of societal organization in which women as well as men will enjoy autonomy and self-determination" (p. 14). Using the extant surviving written words of women, Lerner documents the long history of women's struggle for full access to education, economic independence, and a political voice.

Why History Matters (Oxford University Press, 1997) presents essays written by Lerner between 1980 and 1996. The essays encompass the growth of Lerner as a scholar and her coming to consciousness as a Jewish woman. For the author, history matters profoundly because it teaches us about injustice, it reminds us of who has won and who has lost, and with the growth of the history of women and other minority groups, it can provide a voice for those whose story might have been lost. This is a challenging, thoughtful, provocative book that all graduate students studying history should read.

1091. Offen, Karen, Ruth Roach Pierson, and Jane Rendall, eds. *Writing Women's History: International Perspectives*. Bloomington: Indiana University Press, 1991. 552p. bibliog. index. (OP)

How has women's history developed in other countries? What are the connections between the contemporary women's movement and the emergence of women's history as a discipline? What do scholars of women's history from different countries have to learn from each other? These are among the questions that *Writing Women's History* seeks to answer. The lengthy introduction provides an overview of the development of women's history as a discipline worldwide. The editors comment that the field of women's history is expanding because of the continuing evolution of women's movements in many countries, and because of the growth of women's studies as an academic discipline. Nonetheless, several challenges remain in providing international perspectives on women's history. The status of women's history in the United States may be overshadowing research on women from other parts of the world. Many scholars from other countries also continue to write from a national perspective. Finally, the acceptance of women's history in the academy is still marginal, even in Western Europe. This volume of essays by scholars from twenty-two countries provides an excellent introduction to the state of women's history from around the world. Essays in part 1 explore various conceptual and methodological issues, including deconstructing long-standing methods of viewing women in history and pointing the way to future explorations. Essays in part 2 provide perspectives on the state of women's history from various countries, mostly in Western Europe. This volume provides an excellent introduction to international women's history and paves the way for continued scholarship in this area.

Another source providing an international perspective on the study of women's history is *Expanding the Boundaries of Women's History: Essays on Women in the Third World* (published for the *Journal of Women's History* by Indiana University Press, 1992), edited by Cheryl Johnson-Odim and Margaret Strobel. This collection focuses on the history of women from Africa, Asia, Latin America, the Caribbean, and the Middle East during the nineteenth and twentieth centuries. The essays are grouped by major themes, including cross-cultural contact and the discourse used to study women in Western and Third World cultures, women as activists engaged in sociopolitical movements, and women as workers. While the contributions range widely in subject, the focus of this volume reminds readers of the different themes and methodologies historians may need to explore when studying women from the Third World. This work also illuminates the common issues that women face globally, such as injustice, family rights, and political disenfranchisement.

1092. Scott, Joan Wallach. *Gender and the Politics of History*. New York: Columbia University Press, 1988. 242p. (Gender and Culture). bibliog. index. (OP)

This classic text presents essays by historian Scott as she grapples with the interconnected and elusive meanings of gender, politics, and history: "Gender, in these essays, means knowledge about sexual difference," she states (p. 2). But Scott's view of knowledge, borrowed from Foucault, is not absolute; it is simply a way of ordering the world. Additionally, gender itself is not a fixed category. How then should history respond? In Scott's approach, history figures in "as a participant in the production of knowledge about sexual difference. I assume that history's representations of the past help construct gender for the present" (p. 2). Scott also cites the inadequacies in historical analysis when doing feminist history. She explores poststructuralism and deconstruction as ways to provide new "intellectual directions." Poststructuralists insist that meanings are not fixed in culture, but are always dynamic. To Scott this implies focusing on the "conflictual processes that establish meanings . . . to the play of force involved in any society's construction and implementation of meanings: to politics" (p. 5). Within this framework, politics becomes "the process by which plays of power and knowledge constitute identities and experience" (p. 5), and feminist politics and academics need not be oppositional. They can be "part of the same political project: a collective attempt to confront and change existing distributions of power" (p. 6). Scott's ambitious rethinking of the power of gender in the study of history and as a force that can reshape the world is groundbreaking and visionary. This book is highly recommended for all large public libraries and all academic and research libraries, and it should be required reading for graduate seminars in historical theory.

In *Only Paradoxes to Offer: French Feminists and the Rights of Man* (Harvard University Press, 1996), Scott discusses the French feminists Olympe de Gouges, Jeanne Deroin, Hubertine Auclert, and Madeleine Pelletier, who challenged the "practice of excluding women from citizenship" (p. x). In France, citizens were defined as men from the time of the Revolution in 1789 until 1944. Paradoxically, in arguing for women's rights, these activists acted on behalf of all women "and so invoked the very difference they sought to deny" (p. x). Scott argues, however, that these paradoxical dilemmas actually helped the feminists' arguments.

Feminism and History, edited by Scott (Oxford University Press, 1996), offers classic essays by such scholars as Denise Riley, Evelyn Brooks Higginbotham, Gisela Bock, Lyndal Roper, and Scott herself along with new pieces. Discussing the tensions between feminist activists and feminist scholars around questions of "sameness" and "difference" and around "essentializing" or "historicizing" approaches, Scott argues that the chapters in this anthology "make the case for the usefulness to feminism of historicizing categories of social differentiation" (p. 10). The essays rely on a multitude of theoretical approaches, including Marxism, cultural anthropology, psychoanalysis, literary criticism, and deconstruction. Scott's works are essential for any collection.

Ancient, Medieval, and Renaissance History

1093. Brooten, Bernadette J. *Love between Women: Early Christian Responses to Female Homoeroticism*. Chicago: University of Chicago Press, 1996. 412p. bibliog. index. ISBN 0226075915.

Amassing evidence from a wealth of sources, including medical texts, astrological hand-books, pastoral letters, ancient romances, vase paintings, satires, dream handbooks, and scriptural commentaries from a geographic region stretching from the cities of Rome, Ephesos, and Alexandria to smaller cities in North Africa and rural villages in Egypt, Bernadette Brooten presents solid evidence for the existence of erotic love between women in the early centuries of the Christian era. She grounds her research within the context of ancient history, women's history, and gay lesbian history, citing previous scholarship within her introduction. Focusing not so much on female homoeroticism as on male response to it, the author wants to uncover why "erotic contact between women elicited such vociferous responses in the early church and its environment" (p. 10). In part 1, the author examines four categories of sources for female homoeroticism from the late Roman/early Christian period, including love spells by women to attract other women, astrological texts, medical texts, and dream-classification texts. In part 2, Brooten analyzes responses to love between women by male writers, including Paul, Tertullian, Clement of Alexandria, and Hippolytos. Brooten clearly demonstrates why males reacted so vociferously to the idea of female homoeroticim: it would destablize the "natural" patriarchal hierarchy of the ancient world. Expertly researched and clearly written, *Love between Women* is a foundational contribution to women's history.

1094. Bynum, Caroline Walker. *Holy Feast and Holy Fast: The Religious Significance of Food to Medieval Women.* Berkeley: University of California Press, 1987. 444p. bibliog. index. ISBN (OP); 0520063295pa.

Bynum traces the food-related practices and food images in the piety of medieval European women from the thirteenth and fourteenth centuries. She argues that food was a more significant religious motif for medieval religious women than poverty and chastity. For women, food was a way to control the self, but also a way to commune with God. Bynum rejects current definitions about food obsession, claiming that medieval ideas about food were more diverse: "To religious women food was a way of controlling as well as renouncing both self and environment. But it was more. Food was flesh, and flesh was suffering and fertility. In renouncing food and directing their being toward the good that is Christ, women moved to God not merely by abandoning their flawed physicality but also by becoming the suffering and feeding humanity of the body on the cross, the food on the altar" (p. 5).

Bynum intended this work for both scholars and general readers; thus, in her first three chapters, she provides background information on the religious options available to medieval women, the religious food practices of medieval Christians, and the nature of her sources, which include chronicles, law codes, sermons, and the writings of contemporary male figures about food practice. In chapters 4 and 5, the author presents the stories about women and the writings on which the stories are based. The heart of the book demonstrates "how women were able to use food practices to shape their experience and their place in both family and community, and, second, what food-related behavior and symbols actually meant to medieval women" (p. 6).

Refuting standard interpretations of asceticism as a rejection of the world, and the characterization of medieval women as "constrained on every side by a misogyny that they internalized as self-hatred or masochism," Bynum views these practices as a means to see all the variance or possibilities of fleshliness. Conceding that most of the holy women she discusses, including Mary of Origines, Catherine of Siena, Elizabeth of Hungary, and Catherine of Genoa, are exceptional, the author asserts that the lives of these women provided a lens that the rest of society found valuable. This important book belongs in all college, large public, and academic libraries.

Fragmentation and Redemption: Essays on Gender and the Human Body in Medieval Religion (MIT Press, 1991), also by Caroline Walker Bynum, brings together seven of the author's previously published essays written between 1982 and 1989. The essays speak most importantly about the body, the relationship of parts to the whole, and discuss how sex roles were conceptualized in medieval society.

1095. Cohn, Samuel Kline. *Women in the Streets: Essays on Sex and Power in Renaissance Italy.* Baltimore: Johns Hopkins University Press, 1996. 250p. bibliog. index. ISBN (OP); 0801853095pa.

Providing a new analysis of women's status in Renaissance Italy, Cohn writes that his seven essays "bespeak the darker side of the Renaissance and, in particular, the decline in Italian women's status from the late fourteenth century until the Counter Reformation visitations of the 1570s" (p. 1). The author's sociological and quantitative study, along with case studies, provides ample evidence that women's status did decline during the Renaissance: their means to address grievances both on the streets and in court, their rights to inherit property, and their clout in shaping wills were all weakened during the period from the late fourteenth century until the late 1500s. Cohn compares women from all walks of life—artisans, laborers, peasants, and patrician ladies—from both rural and urban areas, focusing on the means many women used to counter their declining standing: "these essays chart societal changes in law, the structure and accessibility of the criminal courts to women, and the customs and mentalities that shaped women's lot, from infanticide to the control of sexual mores in the territorial state" (p. 15).

1096. Elliott, Dyan. *Spiritual Marriage: Sexual Abstinence in Medieval Wedlock.* Princeton, NJ: Princeton University Press, 1993. 375p. bibliog. index. (OP)

Elliott traces the tradition of spiritual marriage in the West from the time of Christ up to 1500. Calling it neither celibacy nor chastity, the author carefully defines what she means by spiritual marriage: a man and a woman living together without having sexual relations for any given period of time. Arguing that spiritual marriage was a more important religious practice for medieval women than has previously been acknowledged, Elliott believes that women used spiritual marriage as one means to rebel against society's expectations; thus it posed a threat to patriarchal authority. The author relies on a variety of sources, including Scripture, theology, and canon law, all of which provided theoretical concepts concerning the study of spiritual marriage; expressions of this theory to the laity through such modes as legends, confessors' manuals, sermons, and popular folktales; and the actual lives, or hagiography, of saints, as well as chronicles and other documents that mention the practice of spiritual marriage among the common people.

Elliott grounds her study within the context of larger issues, including the Gregorian reform and developments in theology and in the canon law of marriage, to show how the practice of spiritual marriage was shaped by the ideologies of the time. The church fathers possessed an ambivalent view toward spiritual marriage: "one might say that they [church fathers] tended to see women for their sexual potential, sex for its procreative potential, and marriage as the institution for housing these two most essential, but rather dangerous components of society. But the patristic ambivalence toward carnal relations was ultimately destabilizing to this convenient view of marriage. In their elevation of virginity, the church fathers also, wittingly or unwittingly, opened the door to a spiritual definition of marriage that allowed the institution to exist independent of sex" (p. 5). Ultimately, Elliott claims, the idea of spiritual marriage was used against women.

In *The Body and Society: Men, Women, and Sexual Renunciation in Early Christianity* (Columbia University Press, 1988), Peter Brown studies "the practice of sexual renunciation—continence, celibacy, life-long virginity as opposed to observance of temporary periods of sexual abstinence—that developed among men and women in Christian circles in the period from a little before the missionary journeys of Saint Paul, in the 40s and 50s A.D., to a little after the death of St. Augustine" (p. xiii). Brown examines how these practices affected society, the development of the newly emerging religion, Christianity, and relations between men and women.

1097. Goldberg, P.J.P. *Women, Work, and Life Cycle in a Medieval Economy: Women in York and Yorkshire, c. 1300–1520.* New York: Oxford University Press, 1992. 406p. bibliog. index. (OP)

Goldberg examines women's work during a time period that historians have not frequently examined. The author's key question is "How far was marriage an economic necessity for medieval women?" (p. 1). Goldberg focuses on the city of York and the outlying area of Yorkshire during the late medieval period and compares these areas to other regions in England and Tuscany of the same time period. The author argues that the way in which local economies responded to the effects of the Black Death, as well as opportunities available to women in the workforce, varied according to region. The book's seven chapters detail women's varied roles within the medieval economy of York and examine various social norms of the time period, such as marriage rituals, servanthood, and the lack of geographic mobility for many workers. Goldberg does note that women who married after entering the workforce often had a stronger role in the marriage. In the conclusion, Goldberg speculates on the implications that women's role in the medieval economy had for future generations and calls for further research. The author consulted a wealth of sources, including wills, poll tax returns, deposition records, manor and city rolls, and borough ordinances. He provides a thorough description of these source types in the introduction, as well as in three appendices. Maps and tables further enhance this study.

Opera Muliebria: Women and Work in Medieval Europe by David Herlihy (McGraw-Hill, 1990) is a more general work that examines similar issues. Herlihy analyzes women's work from ancient times to the 1500s, concentrating on four countries: England, Iberia, France, and Italy. He concludes that women's work had become less valued and less visible by the Middle Ages. Herlihy explores why this occurred; however, he primarily relies on secondary sources to make his argument. Nonetheless, his work provides a good introduction to a topic that many scholars continue to overlook.

1098. Leyser, Henrietta. *Medieval Women: A Social History of Women in England, 450–1500.* New York: St. Martin's Press, 1995. 337p. bibliog. index. (OP)

This work succeeds in unlocking the world of medieval women's lives for the student and the general reader alike. Beginning in part 1 with the Anglo-Saxon period, Leyser discusses the strengths and weaknesses of the historical evidence—from archaeology to literature—and uncovers some of the hidden women of this period. In the three remaining parts, the author looks at women in the eleventh century and the High and later Middle Ages, family roles, and culture and spirituality. Leyser explores many aspects of women's lives, such as marriage, motherhood, and raising children; women in the working world, including different classes of women; widowhood; and the roles women played in religion and the arts. Several illustrations enhance the text. A useful appendix with excerpts from primary sources in English provides readers a glimpse at these otherwise inaccessible sources.

In *Of Good and Ill Repute: Gender and Social Control in Medieval England* (Oxford University Press, 1998), Barbara Hanawalt examines medieval sermons, advice books, popular poetry, legal treatises and court records, and city and guild ordinances to explore the lines between good and bad behavior in medieval English society. She argues that gender, class, social status, connections, wealth, and community all played a vital role in determining a person's reputation.

1099. Petroff, Elizabeth Alvilda. *Body and Soul: Essays on Medieval Women and Mysticism.* New York: Oxford University Press, 1994. 225p. bibliog. index. ISBN (OP); 0195084551pa.

Body and Soul presents eleven of the author's essays, which discuss the lives and writings of sixteen holy women from England, France, the Low Countries, and Italy. Petroff provides both literary and historical analyses of the women's own writing, including autobiographical texts, sermons, meditations, and lyric poems. The author also examines writings about these women, especially hagiographic writings, in order to determine how contemporaries viewed them. The essays are grouped into three sections. Section 1 presents chapters providing an introduction to these women and the idea of mysticism in the medieval world. Essays in section 2 are concerned with the relationship between tradition and these holy women. Last, chapters in section 3 explore the "issues of female authority from various angles" (p. viii). Petroff's close readings of these texts provide a fine analysis of how these women were able to transgress the limits of their misogynistic society to express their most profound thoughts and feelings.

Forgetful of Their Sex: Female Sanctity and Society, ca. 500–1100 (University of Chicago Press, 1998) by Jane Tibbetts Schulenburg presents a narrative history of female saints over a period of several hundred years during which women's economic and political powers gradually eroded as the church and government attempted to keep women out of public life. Schulenburg relied on previous studies of 2,200 saints as well as examining primary sources, including chronicles, legislation, correspondence, liturgical collections, and art, architecture, and archaeology.

1100. Pomeroy, Sarah B., ed. *Women's History and Ancient History.* Chapel Hill: University of North Carolina Press, 1991. 317p. bibliog. index. ISBN (OP); 0807843105pa.

This collection of twelve essays seeks to show the relationship between the "public and private in the lives of women in antiquity" (p. xi). For women, the private domain preceded the public, yet many of the essays portray how women exercised their political power as wives, daughters, or mothers. The essays cover the period from early Greece of the third century B.C. to late antiquity of the third century A.D. and span a wide geographic area, including Greece, Rome, and the expanding Hellenistic world. The focus is on upper-class women not only because more sources exist depicting these women's lives, but also, Pomeroy argues, because these upper-class women served as role models for women of other classes. Subjects include the lyrics of Sappho, marriage in Athenian law, the construct of the female body in classical Greek science, women in the Spartan revolutions, and the history of menstrual taboos in early Judaism and Christianity. Because of the wide array of subjects covered and the variety of methodologies used, *Women's History and Ancient History* provides an excellent overview of the lives of ancient women.

1101. Watt, Diane, ed. *Medieval Women in Their Communities.* Toronto: University of Toronto Press, 1997. 250p. bibliog. index. ISBN 0802042899; 0802081223pa.

Although Watt does not provide a general overview of women during the Middle Ages (500–1500) in this collection of essays, she does offer "detailed small-scale studies of women as members of a whole range of communities" (p. 9). She thus succeeds in providing a sort of overview of women's roles during this time period. Watt opens the work with an explanation of the problems that scholars encounter when attempting to define community in the medieval world. She then cautions readers not to apply current ideas of feminism and feminist communities to the medieval world. The essays in this work explore women from a wide geographical region, including countries such as England, Wales, France, Italy, and Germany. Contributors also write about medieval women from many social and cultural perspectives, including Christian and Jew, rich and poor, religious and secular, and noblewoman and commoner. Most essays focus on the time period 1200–1500. Contributors include historians and literary scholars (mostly from England

and Wales); therefore, the essays cover an eclectic group of topics, including women in convents, mysticism, gender and poverty, and the portrayal of women in various literary texts, such as Chaucer and mystery plays. Each essay includes notes and a short bibliography.

Africa and the Middle East

1102. Badran, Margot. *Feminists, Islam, and Nation: Gender and the Making of Modern Egypt*. Princeton, NJ: Princeton University Press, 1995. 352p. bibliog. index. ISBN 069103706X; 069102605Xpa.

From the perspective of Egyptian feminists, Badran recounts the story of the Egyptian feminist movement from the latter decades of the nineteenth century to the early part of the twentieth century. She has drawn from oral history and print materials, such as correspondence, essays, speeches, newspaper articles, poetry, fiction, bylaws of women's organizations, and the most important records for Egyptian women, those of the Egyptian Feminist Union (EFU).

The insightful and informative introduction provides historical background regarding the many changes in Egyptian society and the Egyptian economy that have made the rise of Egyptian feminism possible. Part 1 covers the rise of women's consciousness in the latter half of the nineteenth century, focusing on two significant early leaders, Huda Sha'rawi and Nabawiyah Musa, and the establishment of the EFU. Part 2, the core of the book, details the rise of the political feminist movement and its interaction with the pragmatic movement. Badran also chronicles the attempts that women have made to improve their education, employment, politics, and daily life. The final part of the book, which covers the late 1930s through the 1940s, details how members of the EFU brought Egyptian and other Arab women together to defend the Palestinian national cause.

The Women's Awakening in Egypt: Culture, Society, and the Press by Beth Baron (Yale University Press, 1994) also deals with the history of Egyptian women. Covering the period from 1892 to 1919, Baron explores the rise of a female literary culture in Egypt through the production of periodicals by, for, and about women.

1103. Coles, Catherine M., and Beverly Mack, eds. *Hausa Women in the Twentieth Century*. Madison: University of Wisconsin Press, 1991. 297p. bibliog. index. (OP)

According to the editors of this volume, the Hausa people "constitute one of the largest and most influential ethnic groups in Africa" (p. 4), yet scholarship on women in Hausa society has focused only on women as subordinates, ignoring the interrelationships between men and women and changing gender roles within Hausa society. Coles and Mack hope to prompt a wider discussion of women in Hausa society through this group of essays from scholars of history, literature, anthropology, political science, economics, and linguistics. Chapter 1 provides an overview of the four sections of this book: Hausa women in Islam, women and power, women and the economy, and women's voices in ritual, the arts, and the media. Each section includes specific case studies or theoretical discussions of issues such as Islamic leadership positions, women and law, urban economies and women's work, and women's roles in the contemporary Hausa theater. The editors admit that some aspects of Hausa women's lives are not represented, especially women in relation to agriculture; however, they hope that this volume marks the beginning of future research on Hausa women.

1104. Coquery-Vidrovitch, Catherine. *African Women: A Modern History*. Translated by Beth Gillian Raps. Boulder, CO: Westview Press, 1997. 308p. bibliog. index. ISBN (OP); 0813323614pa.

According to Coquery-Vidrovitch, most images of African women appear through the lens of male observers, especially Western males. Thus in *African Women: A Modern History*, Coquery-Vidrovitch attempts "to understand why African women have lacked the leisure and often even the right to observe themselves" (p. 1), as well as to explain African society from the viewpoint of women. Rightly observing that scholars cannot look upon all African women as one collective whole, the author includes collective and individual stories in this work that emphasize the following themes: economic activity; work and labor migration; marriage; divorce and sexuality; politics; and artistic creativity. Drawing on a variety of sources, including oral histories, public records, and private documents, the work covers the colonial period of the early nineteenth century to the present, albeit not chronologically.

Coquery-Vidrovitch discusses the evolution of African women's struggles with colonial oppression; forced economic changes, which frequently have resulted in women turning to prostitution to earn a living; migration to urban areas; and political upheavals. Arguing that African women are beginning to find their voice, especially through artistic expression, she claims that women represent the best hope for the future of Africa. Because of its breadth and period coverage, this title would serve as a good text for courses on the history of women in Africa.

Women and Gender in Southern Africa to 1945, edited by Cherryl Walker (James Curry, 1990), covers roughly the same time period. Walker states that she mainly is concerned with two overriding and dominant patriarchal systems: the indigenous system and the settler-sex or colonizer system. Essays are arranged in the following categories: transition from the precolonial era, colonial patriarchy, Christianity and education for domesticity, migrant labor, and women's roles as heroines, deviants, or suffragists in the early part of the twentieth century. One could use several of these essays for women's history courses.

In a related work, *The Comforts of Home: Prostitution in Colonial Nairobi* (University of Chicago Press, 1990), Luise White details the history of prostitution in Nairobi, the capital of Kenya, from the late 1800s to around 1930. Basing her book on interviews with seventy prostitutes, White deals mainly with the economic aspect of prostitution: "I am concerned with studying the labor processes of prostitution in a way that reveals the two sides of prostitution, what prostitutes do with their customers and what they do with their earnings" (p. 12). *The Comforts of Home* adds a different, much-needed perspective to the history of prostitution.

1105. Keddie, Nikki R., and Beth Baron, eds. *Women in Middle Eastern History: Shifting Boundaries in Sex and Gender*. New Haven, CT: Yale University Press, 1991. 343p. bibliog. index. ISBN 0300050054; 0300056974pa.

Women in Middle Eastern History is a collection of seventeen essays focusing on different aspects of women's lives in the Middle East, as well as the changing nature of male and female boundaries in that particular part of the world. Keddie opens the volume with an analysis of some of the major questions in Middle Eastern women's history. She also contemplates what future research might entail. The editors divide the remainder of the book into four time periods: women in the first centuries of Islam, women in the Mamluk period in Egypt from 1250 to 1517, women in modern Turkey and Iran, and women in the modern Arab world. The essays in the first two parts of the book deal with an array of topics, including Muhammad's favorite wife A'isha, women and Islamic education in medieval Egypt, and an examination of prescriptive moral texts for women. Several essays cover the modern period, in which contributors focus on women's spheres of action in rural Iran, as well as marriage customs and traditions in modern Egypt. Each essay includes notes.

In *Gendering the Middle East: Emerging Perspectives* (Syracuse University Press, 1996), a small volume about women's roles in the Middle East, editor Deniz Kandiyoti includes eight essays about topics such as feminism and Islam in Iran, property rights in Palestine, and women's writing in Egypt. These essays support Kandiyoti's claim that a growing awareness of gender analysis exists in Middle Eastern studies. According to the author, "What these contributions suggest, is that we have already traversed some of the considerable distance separating an initial preoccupation with 'women's condition' in the Middle East to developing gendered perspectives on diverse aspects of culture and society" (p. ix–x).

1106. Peirce, Leslie P. *The Imperial Harem: Women and Sovereignty in the Ottoman Empire*. New York: Oxford University Press, 1993. 374p. (Studies in Middle Eastern History). bibliog. index. ISBN (OP); 0195086775pa.

Peirce explores the complex relationships involving women and power in the Ottoman Empire during the sixteenth and seventeenth centuries, a time of relative stability when much of the governance rested within the harem, the sultan's inner circle. According to the author, Western notions of the public/private dichotomy do not work in this analysis, because during this time period, Ottoman society was characterized "by distinctions between the privileged and the common, the sacred and the profane—distinctions that cut across the dichotomy of gender" (p. 8). Indeed, women of the harem, especially elder women and the mother of the sultan, enjoyed great power during this time, which they expressed in many ways. First, elder women exercised power over junior members of the harem, both male and female, making sure that they obeyed proper sexual and social codes. Second, the sultan placated members of the ruling elites, who potentially could overthrow him, through marriage into the royal family, an area where women had great say. Finally, women exercised power through the role of dynastic image making, since imperial women donated money to the beautification of the city, building projects, and other civic events. Peirce relies on a great deal of primary and secondary research.

1107. Schmidt, Elizabeth. *Peasants, Traders, and Wives: Shona Women in the History of Zimbabwe, 1870–1939*. Portsmouth, NH: Heinemann, 1992. 289p. (Social History of Africa). bibliog. index. ISBN (OP); 0435080660pa.

In an in-depth analysis of the complex ways in which African and European patriarchs constrained Shona women prior to and during the colonization of Zimbabwe, Schmidt demonstrates how these women coped with and often resisted the many restraints forced upon them. Emphasizing the diversity among Shona women, Schmidt details the roles that they played within the household and community and considers the intricate class and relationship structures that shaped Shona women's lives.

In the first two chapters of this book, Schmidt chronicles the history of Shona women's economic and domestic lives prior to colonization. Throughout the remainder of the work, the author explores how various actions and reactions of colonizers—from colonial officials to missionaries and wives of colonists—affected the lives of these women in complex and often destructive ways. Although Schmidt counsels new studies about women's roles in the history of Zimbabwe, she also encourages future studies of women in other colonized areas.

Belinda Bozzoli's *Women of Phokeng: Consciousness, Life Strategy, and Migrancy in South Africa, 1900–1983* (Heinemann, 1991) and *Marriage in Maradi: Gender and Culture in a Hausa Society in Niger, 1900–1989* (Heinemann, 1997) are two additional works in this series. In *Women of Phokeng*, Bozzoli presents the life stories of seventeen women, born around the turn of the century, who discuss their childhood, adolescence, marriage, careers, and retirement. As much a sociological study as a historical one, *Women of Phokeng*, like *Peasants, Traders, and Wives*, offers a more complete view of African history since it includes the lives of the once invisible: women. In *Marriage in Maradi*, Bozzoli focuses on marriage to explore the complex sociopolitical and economic changes that have taken place in Niger during the twentieth century. These works include photographs, maps, and charts and together provide an emerging picture of African women's agency in shaping their own lives.

Asia and Oceania (Including Australia)

1108. Bray, Francesca. *Technology and Gender: Fabrics of Power in Late Imperial China*. Berkeley: University of California Press, 1997. 419p. bibliog. index. ISBN (OP); 0520208617pa.

How do technologies shape the social and political values of a culture? This is only one of the major questions that Francesca Bray attempts to answer in this fascinating and complex study of imperial China, covering the years 1000 to 1800. Bray focuses on a set of technologies "that one might call . . . gynotechnics: a technical system that produces ideas about women, and therefore about a gender system and about hierarchical relations in general" (p. 4).

The author examines the social and cultural meanings of these sets of technologies and how the technologies evolved during the time period. In part 1, she explores the process of house building, arguing that domestic space composed a microcosm of the larger social or cosmic space of Chinese society. Part 2 explores women's work in China, focusing on the historical changes in the production of cloth and the marginalizing effect of commercialization on lower-class women. In the final part, Bray considers the complex issues of "technologies" surrounding reproduction. She claims that although Chinese women regarded their roles as mothers highly, their roles as wives were even more significant. All women could be mothers, even slaves and concubines, yet not all women were wives.

The introduction provides an overview of the history of technology and discusses how technology has been used as a "central element in the discourse of Western superiority" (p. 7). For Bray, a central question is "To what extent can we use material technologies as a guide to how people think about nature, about society, about meanings?" (p. 16). She examines a wide variety of sources, including legal and philosophical texts, technological treatises, works on craft making, history, economic writings, paintings, novels, poetry, and even artifacts. *Technology and Gender* is an essential work that belongs in every academic and large public library.

1109. Damousi, Joy. *Depraved and Disorderly: Female Convicts, Sexuality, and Gender in Colonial Australia*. New York: Cambridge University Press, 1997. 221p. bibliog. index. ISBN (OP); 0521587239pa.

From 1788 to 1868, about 160,000 convicts were transported from Britain to Australia; 25,000 of these convicts were female. Damousi focuses on the transportation of convicts from Britain to New South Wales during the period from the 1820s to the 1840s, when transportation of convicts reached its peak. During these two decades, shifts in prison reform, the movement of convict women out of the prison system to work as domestic servants, the development of orphan schools, and the rise of free immigrants to New South Wales all coalesced to create disturbances in the social order.

Damousi's aim "is to ask different questions of Australia's convict period by focusing on the ways in which cultural meaning is shaped, and on the nature of relationships. In doing this, a central purpose is to make gender and sexual difference the basis of cultural analysis, rather than simply 'adding' women to the mix" (p. 3). She explores the meanings and relationships of cultural symbols of the nineteenth century, including masculinity, femininity, sexuality, fatherhood, motherhood, cleanliness, order, identity, race, resistance, and space, within the context of the colonial society of Australia. Damousi articulates several significant themes, including the contrasting notions of purity and pollution, the meanings of punishment, the views of abandonment and displacement, especially regarding mothers abandoning children, and concepts of transgression within and outside of boundaries. *Depraved and Disorderly* clearly illustrates how anxiety about gender and sexuality shaped ideologies of colonial Australian culture.

In *Convict Maids: The Forced Migration of Women to Australia* (Cambridge University Press, 1996), Deborah Oxley presents a reassessment of the occupational skills convict women brought to Australia, and how these women helped shape the newly forming economy and society. In her sociological study, Oxley includes several charts and graphs to substantiate her arguments. Finally, in *Barmaids: A History of Women's Work in Pubs* (Cambridge University Press, 1997), Diane Kirby surveys Australian women's work behind the bar over the course of two centuries, focusing on cultural meanings attached to such work, sexual difference and sexuality in the workplace, and the "creation of a gendered and racialised natural cultural identity" (p. 2).

1110. Ebrey, Patricia Buckley. *The Inner Quarters: Marriage and the Lives of Chinese Women in the Sung Period*. Berkeley: University of California Press, 1993. 332p. bibliog. index. ISBN (OP); 0520081587pa.

Focusing on the Sung period (960–1279), a time of rapid social, economic, and political change, Ebrey attempts to uncover how "women come to fashion their lives" (p. 8) within the context of marriage in *The Inner Quarters*. Although Chinese women served primarily as wives and mothers during this time period, the author claims that women faced many ambiguous changes. For example, the practice of binding feet burgeoned during the Sung period; however, Chinese women simultaneously could claim more property rights than ever before. Ebrey relies on a wide variety of sources, including government records, legal treatises, advice books, narratives about individuals, funerary biographies, poems, paintings, and philosophical writings, to explore the complexities and struggles that women faced within marriage and the family. She analyzes how women from different classes approached and reacted to various topics such as divorce, claiming property rights, concubines' roles within the household, the status of elite women, and the importance of the parent-child relationship in all families. Since men created most of the sources, Ebrey argues that one can never really know what Chinese women felt. However, *The Inner Quarters* provides a vivid picture of Chinese women's lives during an important period in that country's history.

In *Marriage and Inequality in Chinese Society* (University of California Press, 1991), editors Ebrey and Rubie S. Watson include several essays that explore the relationship between marriage and three forms of inequality: the political power of rulers, social and economic differences among families, and inequalities between men and women. Covering 700 B.C. to the present, contributors examine a variety of topics, including imperial marriages, concubines' and maids' roles within the family during the early part of the twentieth century, and women's property rights in the People's Republic of China.

1111. Forbes, Geraldine Hancock. *Women in Modern India*. New York: Cambridge University Press, 1996. 290p. (The New Cambridge History of India, v. 4, pt. 2). bibliog. index. ISBN 0521268125; 0521653770pa.

This short history covers women in India from the nineteenth century up through the 1980s. Focusing primarily on "elite" women, Forbes begins with the British reform movements of the late 1800s, which included the education of women. Arguing that women's education helped them define their own problems, the author details how the early Indian women's rights movements sprang up in the 1920s and 1930s. Indian women also took part in the movement for independence, but Forbes believes that Indian women were already politically active before Gandhi, writing that "Gandhi gave them a blueprint for action" (p. 7). Forbes examines women's work and the growth and divergence of women's activism in two chapters. She ends with a discussion of issues relating to women in independent India, including political activism, economics, and the current state of the women's movement. Relying on oral histories, letters and diaries, songs, pamphlets, literature, and photographs, *Women in Modern India* provides a good introduction to the history of Indian women in modern times.

1112. Hershatter, Gail. *Dangerous Pleasures: Prostitution and Modernity in Twentieth-Century Shanghai.* Berkeley: University of California Press, 1997. 591p. bibliog. index. ISBN (OP); 0520204395pa.

Hershatter focuses on prostitution in Shanghai from the late nineteenth century to the early 1990s in *Dangerous Pleasures*. She explores the multiple and continually shifting meanings that different classes associated with prostitution over time: "Prostitution was not only a changing site of work for women but also a metaphor, a medium of articulation in which the city's changing elites and emerging middle classes discussed their problems, fears, agendas, and visions" (p. 4). Hershatter argues that prostitution in Shanghai began as a site of pleasure and an almost romanticized story of courtesans; however, as social mores changed, prostitution moved to a site of danger featuring degenerate streetwalkers. The need for regulation became apparent beginning in the 1920s and 1930s.

Hershatter's story, which the author divides into five parts, begins with an important discussion about the recovery of voices from the past, especially the voices of subalterns. In parts 2 and 3, the author considers prostitution in its various manifestations in historical memory, first as a site of pleasure and then as a site of danger. In part 4, she examines the attempts that early- to mid-twentieth-century reformers made to regulate prostitution in the city and includes medical and social contextualization. Hershatter looks at the reemergence of prostitution in the 1980s and 1990s and presents the heated public debate over this issue in the final part. The author relies upon a variety of sources, including guidebooks that men wrote about courtesans, collections of courtesans' poetry and stories, gossip columns from tabloid newspapers, police and legal reports, municipal regulations, doctors' and social workers' medical surveys, and records from relief agencies on kidnapping and trafficking of women.

1113. Ko, Dorothy. *Teachers of the Inner Chambers: Women and Culture in Seventeenth-Century China.* Stanford, CA: Stanford University Press, 1994. 395p. bibliog. index. ISBN 0804723583; 0804723591pa.

Dorothy Ko studies an elite group of women in seventeenth-century China to help create a broader understanding of women in Chinese history. Seeking to portray women as neither victims nor total agents of their own destinies, Ko broadens the term "teachers of the inner chambers" from simply meaning a class of itinerant female teachers to include all wives, daughters, and widows who "taught each other about the vicissitudes of life through their writings. . . . Although the lives, thoughts, and circumstances of these poets, teachers, artists, writers, and readers may not have been shared by the majority of the population, they are most instructive to us for the way they highlight the possibilities for fulfillment and a meaningful existence even within the confines the Confucian system imposed upon women" (p. 4). Arguing that seventeenth-century China was the best and worst time for women, the author presents a tripartite model of the lives of these women: the ideal or theoretical, the practical, and their own self-perceptions. *Teachers of the Inner Chambers* studies women in urbanized area of Jiangnan, a wealthy, highly urbanized, densely populated region, where many women experienced a rich intellectual and social world. Ko argues that even in this strict patriarchal culture, the boundaries of gender relations were continuously being negotiated and renegotiated.

Susan Mann's *Precious Records: Women in China's Long Eighteenth Century* (Stanford University Press, 1997) offers writing from elite women of the eighteenth century from a small area of China in the lower Yangzi. The writing, including poetry and some biography, is presented "to correct distortions inherent in the male gaze and to see how women themselves articulate value and meaning in a society dominated by Confucian norms" (p. 4). Together, both *Teachers of the Inner Chambers* and *Precious Records* provide a valuable depiction of the history of Chinese women.

Central America, South America, and the Caribbean

1114. Bouvard, Marguerite Guzman. *Revolutionizing Motherhood: The Mothers of the Plaza de Mayo*. Wilmington, DE: Scholarly Resources, 1994. 278p. bibliog. index. ISBN 0842024867; 0842024875pa.

The mothers of the Plaza de Mayo first appeared on the world stage in 1977 after the coup by the military junta in Argentina, protesting against the disappearance of their children. By 1983, when a constitutional government had replaced the junta, the mothers had transformed their activism into a powerful, pacifistic organization championing human rights worldwide. *Revolutionizing Motherhood* tells the extraordinary story of these housewives, teachers, and salesclerks who defied a patriarchal, militaristic society. Early chapters describe the rise of the junta, its fall, and the origins of the mothers' resistance. Later chapters detail the model the mothers developed for human rights struggles and explore feminism in Latin America. Bouvard contends that the mothers created a new political space, defying both the societal patriarchal ideologies and the closed hierarchical political system of Latin America. They used their anger, spoke the truth, and took their fight to the streets, eventually turning their protests to transform the democratic government of Argentina.

In *The Hour of the Poor, the Hour of Women: Salvadoran Women Speak* (Crossroad, 1991), Renny Golden presents the personal testimonies and life histories of Salvadoran women working to make lives for themselves and their families in a war-torn country. In this powerful work, Golden imparts the importance of the Christian faith "as an initial and sustaining source of commitment to the liberation process" (p. 18) for these women. The author also persuasively argues for the importance of including women's voices in the historical story. This book is recommended for all libraries.

1115. Bush, Barbara. *Slave Women in Caribbean Society, 1650–1832*. Bloomington: Indiana University Press, 1990. 190p. (Columbus Series of Caribbean Studies). bibliog. index. ISBN (OP); 0253212510pa.

Barbara Bush attempts to recast the image of the female slave in Caribbean society by revealing individualities. She focuses on slave societies in the British Caribbean, drawing a good deal of evidence from Jamaica. Explaining that the common image of the black female slave "is a compound of the scarlet woman, the domineering matriarch, and the passive workhorse" (p. 5), Bush emphasizes three areas of slave society that contribute to an expanded view of the woman slave.

First, the author makes a clear distinction between the public and private lives of slaves, arguing that much of what is known about the domestic lives of slaves comes from biased sources and inaccurate assumptions. In the realm of work, the female slave was seen primarily as an important economic commodity. In the domestic realm, the role of the black woman slave differed greatly from that of men. She was primarily wife and mother, and she worked hard at resisting the laws and rules of the white masters.

Resistance is a second theme running throughout this work, and the author discusses the female slaves' role in the many uprisings in Caribbean slaveholding societies. A third theme for Bush is culture: "As the transposed African cultural patterns of the slaves heavily influenced their response to enslavement, any study of the woman slave would be inadequate if it ignored her cultural heritage" (p. 7). Indeed, the slave woman's fight to hold onto her cultural heritage in terms of religion, marriage values, and kinship patterns existed across most West African slave societies. This book attempts to recast the stereotype of the slave woman, to show her as an individual who "exhibited a strength and independence with which she has not been previously credited" (p. 8).

In *Engendering History: Caribbean Women in Historical Perspective*, edited by Verene Shepherd, Bridget Brereton, and Barbara Bailey (St. Martin's Press, 1995), contributors present various perspectives on African and African Caribbean women, spanning the period from the 1770s to the 1900s. Six sections, arranged chronologically, cover such topics as slavery, land revolt, migration, education, and political protest. The first two sections provide an overview of theoretical perspectives and the various sources and methodologies used to uncover Caribbean women's history.

1116. Fowler-Salamini, Heather, and Mary Kay Vaughan, eds. *Women of the Mexican Countryside, 1850–1990: Creating Spaces, Shaping Transitions*. Tucson: University of Arizona Press, 1994. 253p. bibliog. index. ISBN 0816514151; 0816514313pa.

The essays in this collection "make women of the countryside visible as they trek through the tumultuous transition from fledgling agrarian republic to industrialized nation-state, from the middle of the nineteenth century to the present" (pp. xi, xiii). The editors note that this work contributes to the need to "modify assumptions and explore new perspectives" (p. xvi) in several areas, including the impact of capitalism on women's incorporation into the workforce, the changing nature of the rural household, and how revolution and sociopolitical movements intersect with gender identity.

Drawing from a variety of sources (archives, travelers' accounts, war records, census data, governmental records, judicial hearings, and statistics, as well as observation and oral history), contributors examine "the ways rural women shape transitions and carve spaces for themselves within the context of patriarchal gender ideology and macrostructural constraints" (p. xvi) at four levels: women as individuals, women within the context of rural households, women within their communities, and women within regions. The essays fall into three chronological sections: those that focus on women during the process of state formation from 1850 to 1910, those that explore the sociopolitical effects of revolution and war during 1910 to 1917 and state construction from 1917 to 1940, and those that focus on the effects of rapid urbanization and industrialization on rural women since 1940. *Women of the Mexican Countryside* provides new and valuable insights into the ways in which rural women have negotiated their lives during the course of revolution and war, economic change, and cultural evolution.

In *Soldaderas in the Mexican Military: Myth and History* (University of Texas Press, 1990), Elizabeth Salas presents a fascinating account of Mexican women who participated in war from preconquest times to the 1930s. After an exploration of "women's roles in ritual and ancient warfare, as mother/war goddess, as intermediary and sexual companion to warriors" (p. xii), Salas discusses the various duties Mexican women have performed in warfare, including camp follower, worker, and sexual companion. She also reflects on the lingering cultural impact of these women in film, art, and literature for both contemporary Mexicans and Chicanas who have immigrated to the United States.

Indian Women of Early Mexico, edited by Susan Schroeder, Stephanie Wood, and Robert Haskett (University of Oklahoma Press, 1997), brings together essays by fourteen contributors who "seek to reveal native women in the context of their societies, by focusing on life experiences in an evolving cultural continuum representative of several regions of Mexico" (p. 3). The essays cover the period from the mid-1500s to the present and explore several topics, including Aztec wives, Indian-Spanish marriages, women and crime in colonial Oaxaca, Mayan women and rebellion in colonial Mexico, and Indian women in Jesuit missions. Maps, figures, and tables enhance this work.

1117. Nazzari, Muriel. *Disappearance of the Dowry: Women, Families, and Social Change in São Paulo, Brazil (1600–1900)*. Stanford, CA: Stanford University Press, 1991. 245p. bibliog. index. ISBN 0804719284.

Investigating the disappearance of the dowry as a means to uncover the changing social, economic, and cultural values within Brazil, Nazzari states, "My hypothesis at a general level is that the institution of dowry was among the many fetters to the development of capitalism, such as entail, monopolies, and the privileges of the nobility, of churchmen, and of army officers, that disappeared as the influence of industrial capital spread worldwide" (p. xix). The author examined inventários, the records of the Brazilian judicial process for the settlement of estates, which provide a detailed amount of information including the inventory of an estate, a will of the deceased, lists of debts owed the estate, demands of creditors, receipts of payments, and the final distribution of the estate among heirs. Information taken from these documents during three centuries provided an analysis of change over time. The author limited the study to São Paulo and the surrounding area and studied only the inventários from the middle two decades of each century. She concludes that between the seventeenth and nineteenth centuries, a new concept of property developed, one in which the family became the locus of consumption rather than the locus of production and consumption. The power of a hierarchal, family-based society gradually developed to a "more individualistic society in which contract and the market increasingly reigned" (p. xix). *Disappearance of the Dowry* is a fascinating study focusing on the interconnections between family practices, market values, and larger social change.

In *Emancipating the Female Sex: The Struggle for Women's Rights in Brazil, 1850–1940* (Duke University Press, 1990), June Edith Hahner outlines the struggle for women's rights in Brazil. Hahner begins with the movement by upper- and middle-class women in the mid-nineteenth century who advocated for expanded educational opportunities for females and ends with the granting of female suffrage in 1932. In between, the author details the struggles of the movement to include working-class women, details the growth of early feminist organizations, and analyzes the dormancy of feminist activism from the 1940s to the 1960s.

Europe

1118. Allen, Ann Taylor. *Feminism and Motherhood in Germany, 1800–1914*. New Brunswick, NJ: Rutgers University Press, 1991. 299p. bibliog. index. ISBN 0813516862.

Beginning with the writings of Mary Wollstonecraft, Allen explores how a maternalistic ideology evolved over the course of 100 years, moving from the private or purely domestic realm to a notion of "public motherhood." The author claims that nineteenth-century German feminists applied this growing theory of maternal feminism to argue that a female ethic could be applied to society as a whole; thus women should be given stronger roles in social and political arenas.

German feminists, unlike their counterparts in Great Britain or the United States, believed that equal rights were earned, not an inherent birth right. They argued for an expanded role in a society that represented a large family, a "family" that required maternal nurturing. As the focus on motherhood shifted to the biological and medical, these feminists took on issues including childrearing and child health, reproductive rights, and family structure and began to argue for practical reforms in these areas. In her conclusion and epilogue, Allen explores the role that German feminism played in the rise of ideas appropriated by the National Socialists. However, Allen does not blame nineteenth-century German feminists; rather, she places them in their historical context as women who had a goal of a more nurturing and compassionate society.

Mothers in the Fatherland: Women, the Family, and Nazi Politics by Claudia Koonz (St. Martin's Press, 1987) examines the roles of women in German society from 1919 to the end of World War II. Arguing, as many historians have, that the failing economy and weak political system of the Weimar era factored into the rise of National Socialism, Koonz also suggests that German women retreated back to more traditional gender roles because they felt safe and normal. While disturbing, *Mothers in the Fatherland* nonetheless provides readers with an inside view of women's role in Nazi Germany.

1119. Anderson, Bonnie S., and Judith Zinsser. *A History of Their Own: Women in Europe from Prehistory to the Present.* New York: Harper & Row, 1988. 2v. bibliog. indexes. (OP)

A History of Their Own is one of the best general surveys of women in European history, covering the period from the ninth century to the present. In the introduction the authors state, "The central thesis of this book is that gender has been the most important factor in shaping the lives of European women" (p. xv). As they continued to conceptualize the book, Anderson and Zinsser realized that the traditional periodization of history, Middle Ages, Renaissance, and so on, would not work for women. Instead, the authors used the concepts of "place" and "function" to understand history as if it were seen through the eyes of women. Sections include women of the fields, women of the churches, women of the castles and manors, and women of the walled towns. The first section explores ideas about women from the Greek, Roman, Hebrew, Celtic, Germanic, and Christian traditions and demonstrates how these early ideologies shaped the lives of women for the next 1,500 years. Bringing the reader to the modern period, the authors end with a history of feminism. Illustrations and numerous notes greatly enhance the work. A new edition of this work appeared in 2000.

The Prospect before Her: A History of Women in Western Europe by Olwen Hufton (Knopf, 1996) surveys the lives of women from several countries and varying economic classes in Western Europe from 1500 to 1800. Even as the reigning patriarchal institutions, such as the church, or the rising professions of law and medicine portrayed women as lustful temptresses, unworthy, or inferior, Hufton demonstrates that women played an active role in many economic and social arenas. Women farmed, were midwives, ran cottage industries and schools, and took part in various social movements. Relying on a variety of sources, including women's diaries and letters, legal documents, medical and theological treatises, and advice manuals, this volume provides a balanced overview of the role women played in the development of modern Europe.

1120. Breitenbach, Esther, and Eleanor Gordon, eds. *Out of Bounds: Women in Scottish Society, 1800–1945.* Edinburgh: Edinburgh University Press, 1992. 228p. (Edinburgh Education and Society Series). bibliog. index. ISBN 0748603727.

While the editors acknowledge that this title presents a limited exploration of women in Scotland, essays in *Out of Bounds* nonetheless cover a variety of topics. Two major themes intertwine the essays: the conflict of interest between classes and the extensive involvement of Scottish women in public life. The first theme emerges in essays concerning the education of Scottish women, the punishment of women in nineteenth-century Scotland, and working-class women's political activity during World War I. Reflecting on the second theme, the editors note that Scottish women's role in politics has been quite extensive, yet it has never been fully acknowledged. Essays covering this theme discuss the Scottish women's suffrage movement and Scottish women in Parliament in the first half of the twentieth century.

A second volume in the same series is *The World Is Ill Divided: Women's Work in Scotland in the Nineteenth and Early Twentieth Centuries* (distributed in North America by Columbia University Press, 1990), also edited by Breitenbach and Gordon. This volume focuses on three major areas of women's work in Scotland: agricultural work, domestic service, and work in the textiles industry. There are case histories, including one focusing on textile workers in a small Scottish village, as well as essays touching on broader discussions such as the public regulation of prostitution. Most of the essays reveal one underlying theme: the economic and social effects on workingwomen of the sexual division of labor. These two volumes present a valuable picture of life for Scottish women in the nineteenth and twentieth centuries.

1121. Burton, Antoinette M. *Burdens of History: British Feminists, Indian Women, and Imperial Culture, 1865–1915*. Chapel Hill: University of North Carolina Press, 1994. 301p. bibliog. index. ISBN 0807821616; 0807844713pa.

Burton explores British feminists' views of imperialism, especially their ideas about colonized women: "Relocating British feminist ideologies in their imperial context and problematizing Western feminists' historical relationships to imperial culture at home and abroad are, therefore, the chief concerns of this book" (p. 2). Beginning in the middle of the nineteenth century and ending with World War I, the author reexamines feminist writings of the period to demonstrate how these women helped propagate colonial ideology. Arguing that many feminists agreed with the ideologies behind imperialism, even the belief in the racial and cultural superiority of the British, Burton shows how these women employed the idea of saving the colonized woman as a means to advance their own agenda for full political participation in the governance of the empire.

After a thoughtful discussion concerning the evolution of feminist and racial ideologies in British culture, Burton outlines how these ideologies helped frame feminists' views of female emancipation, notions of the "Other," and images created of the "Other," particularly that of Indian women. While providing an important addition to the history of British imperialism, the author also presents new insights into the history of Western feminism: "This study is intended as an intervention in the historiography of the Western European feminist past in order to begin to account for the impact of imperial culture on historically feminist movements and to suggest its significance for feminist history and feminist politics in the present" (p. 22).

Another work seeking to problematize ideas of imperialism and gender is *The White Woman's Other Burden: Western Women and South Asia during British Colonial Rule* (Routledge, 1995) by Kumari Jayawardena. The author examines various roles and beliefs of Western women whom the colonized might see as "devils" or "goddesses." Members of the first category included missionaries and social reformers who brought Christianity and Western ideas to the colonies and wanted to civilize the colonized peoples. Members of the second category were theosophists, Orientalists, and Holy Mothers who "perceived Asia as the model of an alternative society that was also the site of their ideal of womanhood. Asia had, in their eyes, achieved a degree of wisdom and spirituality far superior to the materialist development of the West" (p. 5). In presenting these contrasting and complex views, Jayawardena provides important insights on the intersection of race, gender, and imperialism.

1122. Clark, Anna. *The Struggle for the Breeches: Gender and the Making of the British Working Class*. Berkeley: University of California Press, 1995. 416p. (Studies on the History of Society and Culture, 23). bibliog. index. (OP)

The Struggle for the Breeches details the rise of the working class in Britain from 1780 to 1850. Clark's study contrasts artisan workers in London with textile workers in Lancashire and Glasgow to demonstrate the various ways working men and women coped with the economic hardships brought on by the industrial revolution. Clark argues that such hardships eroded already troubled marital relationships in low-wage-earning families. Radical labor organizers, who hoped to mobilize the working class to gain stronger economic benefits, faced the dilemma of trying to infuse a unified political consciousness among a group fractured by "heavy drinking, sexual antagonism, and divisions between trades" (p. 8). Clark contends that only in the latter half of the nineteenth century did a true working-class consciousness finally emerge, and that this consciousness was heavily imbued with misogynistic and patriarchal overtones. Clark relies on primary sources, including much of the popular culture of the day, such as ballads, melodramas, newspapers, and caricatures, as well as secondary sources to ground her study.

1123. Clark, Stuart. *Thinking with Demons: The Idea of Witchcraft in Early Modern Europe*. Oxford: Clarendon Press, 1997. 827p. bibliog. index. (OP)

Stuart Clark's substantial work presents an intellectual history of witchcraft. After surveying texts from the fifteenth through the eighteenth centuries, Clark recounts what these writers said and the reasons why. He argues that beliefs in witchcraft survived for so many years because they were "sustained by a whole range of intellectual commitments" (p. vii). Clark suggests that these writers often used the idea of witchcraft to think through other ideas: "In effect demonology was a composite subject consisting of discussions about the workings of nature, the processes of history, the maintenance of religious purity, and the nature of political authority and order" (p. viii).

Discussions are grouped in four areas: science, history, religion, and politics. Each section begins with an overview of the ideas that are formulated within the section. This is followed by an analysis of the texts that places them within a larger context of intellectual debate. Clark draws upon an impressive amount of source material, much of it from continental Europe. *Thinking with Demons* is highly recommended for university and research libraries.

Lyndal Roper's *Oedipus and the Devil: Witchcraft, Sexuality, and Religion in Early Modern Europe* (Routledge, 1994) investigates the "importance of the irrational and the unconscious in history" (p. 4), the importance of the body, and the relation of the two to sexual difference. Focusing specifically on Augsburg, Germany, individual essays delve into relations between the sexes, gender norms and assumptions during the period, and finally, how magic and witchcraft were connected to gender relations and individual subjectivities.

Witches and Neighbors: The Social and Cultural Context of European Witchcraft by Robin Briggs (Viking, 1996) presents a wide-ranging social, cultural, and psychological history of the European witch-hunts. Covering a broad geographic area, including England, Scotland, the Low Countries, Scandinavia, France, and parts of Germany, Briggs wants to show how the belief in witchcraft "related to reality and how far it pervaded the mental and social worlds of our ancestors" (p. 10).

Last, James Sharpe's *Instruments of Darkness: Witchcraft in Early Modern England* (University of Pennsylvania Press, 1997) is a scholarly history of witchcraft beliefs in England from the mid-sixteenth to the mid-eighteenth century. Sharpe studies the belief systems, looks at witchcraft on a variety of social levels, and discusses the eventual decline in belief in witchcraft and why this occurred.

1124. Clements, Barbara Evans. *Bolshevik Women*. Cambridge: Cambridge University Press, 1997. 338p. bibliog. index. ISBN 0521454034; 0521599202pa.

Clements, a leading scholar of Russian women's history, crafts a fascinating, detailed study of the Bolshevichki, or female Bolsheviks. Her work covers the personal lives and political careers of two generations of women who joined the Russian Socialist Democratic Party, women who joined the party before the revolution of 1917 and women who joined during the Civil War, from 1917 through 1921. Using statistics of party members, personal memoirs of these women, newspaper and periodical articles, and official party documents, Clements attempts to uncover the sociological and psychological motivations of these women, along with the intellectual and political factors that shaped their lives. Two main questions shape Clements's inquiry: why did these women accept the dictatorial form of government that emerged as the Socialist Democrats took control of Russia, and why did they abandon feminism? She concludes that the Bolshevichki adhered to the collective identity of the party because their goal involved the eventual transformation of society to a truly egalitarian system.

Clements, Barbara Alpern Engel, and Christine D. Worobec edited *Russia's Women: Accommodation, Resistance, Transformation* (University of California Press, 1991), a collection of essays encompassing women's roles in Russian history from the eleventh to the twentieth century. Framing their work around the premise that Russian women lived under a rigid patriarchal system, scholars attempt to understand how women survived and fought against this system of oppression. Divided into two broad time categories, chapters cover everything from childrearing and marriage in section 1 to essays on reproductive rights and female factory workers in section 2.

1125. Corbin, Alain. *Women for Hire: Prostitution and Sexuality in France after 1850*. Translated by Alan Sheridan. Cambridge, MA: Harvard University Press, 1990. 478p. bibliog. index. ISBN 0674955439.

Corbin crafts a detailed sociological study of prostitution in France from the early nineteenth century through the 1960s. While prostitution was never legal in France, it was tolerated. Corbin organizes his work into three periods. The strict first period, which lasted until the late 1850s, was concerned with the strict confinement and regulation of prostitution. Alexandre Parent-Duchâtelet, a doctor and expert on public hygiene, championed this "legalized" form of prostitution and took it as his task to enforce laws of weekly inspections of prostitutes. The second period, characterized by a relaxation of the strict regulation of prostitution, emerged during the Second Empire and the Third Republic. Nonetheless, French authorities still kept surveillance over prostitutes. The final period in Corbin's work, which emerged after World War I, concentrated on medical supervision of prostitutes, but French prostitutes were forced to carry medical certificates until the mid-twentieth century. Corbin provides a wealth of details in his study through graphs and charts. Concerned not so much with redeeming the prostitute, Corbin wants more to understand what prostitution represented in French society: "This book is not an exploration of a thesis but an attempt to discern the coherence between sexual need on the one hand and, on the other, the structural, behavioral, discursive, and political aspects of prostitution" (p. xvii).

1126. De Grazia, Victoria. *How Fascism Ruled Women: Italy, 1922–1945*. Berkeley: University of California Press, 1992. 350p. bibliog. index. ISBN 0520074564; 0520074572pa.

How Fascism Ruled Women is a broad sociological study of Italian women between the two world wars. De Grazia considers the complex, often paradoxical conditions that Italian women lived in during Mussolini's regime: "From the start, then, this book tells of the deep conflict within the fascist state between the demands of modernity and the desire to reimpose traditional authority" (p. 2). The author situates her story within the broader context of European ideologies, including concerns over population stability, economic growth, and growing democratic ideals: "A restructuring of gender relations thus went hand in hand with the recasting of economic and political institutions to secure conservative interests in the face of economic uncertainty and the democratization of public life" (p. 3). De Grazia argues that fascism believed that men and women were different, so "the government politicized this difference to the advantage of males and made it the cornerstone of an especially repressive, comprehensive new system for defining female citizenship, for governing women's sexuality, wage labor, and social participation" (p. 7). De Grazia illustrates how women lived under and reacted to this regime, which pulled women in two directions: toward modernity and state building while strongly encouraging traditional, submissive roles for women. The author also presents an interesting account of how popular culture, especially fashions and urban lifestyles portrayed in foreign films and magazines, fascinated young Italian women and girls.

Perry Willson's *The Clockwork Factory: Women and Work in Fascist Italy* (Clarendon Press, 1993) looks specifically at women's roles in the workforce in Fascist Italy. According to the author, this study of a group of northern working-class women employed at a then-modern company is one of the first studies "to look at the complex history of an Italian firm from a feminist point of view" (p. 13).

1127. Duby, Georges, and Michelle Perrot, general eds. *A History of Women in the West.* Cambridge, MA: Belknap Press of Harvard University Press, 1992–1994. 5v. bibliog. index. Translation of *Storia delle donne in Occidente.* ISBN 0674403703 (v. 1); 0674403711 (v. 2); 067440372X (v. 3); 0674403738 (v. 4); 0674403746 (v. 5).

This five-volume series is perhaps one of the most significant pieces of historical scholarship to emerge in the last fifteen years. According to Natalie Zemon Davis and Joan Wallach Scott, who wrote an introductory two-page essay to the series, "Women are seen as both the objects of discourse and as active subjects. The distance between what women say about themselves and what men say about them is one of the most intense landscapes mapped in the five volumes" (p. viii). In exploring this distance, the editors focus mainly on women in Europe, as well as women in North America. While the series is organized in what the editors note is "the customary periodization of European history" (p. xviii), from the ancient world to the Renaissance up to the twentieth century, each volume editor employed his or her own organization and style. Titles within the series include *From Ancient Goddesses to Christian Saints* (v. 1); *The Silences of the Middle Ages* (v. 2); *Renaissance and Enlightenment Paradoxes* (v. 3); *Emerging Feminism from Revolution to World War* (v. 4); and *Toward a Cultural Identity in the Twentieth Century* (v. 5). While the series deals with a variety of themes, a few general themes thread all of the volumes together. First, the editors and contributors analyze how society has represented women throughout history. The editors and contributors also examine how women's role in society has gradually changed over time. Essays explore how and when women began to establish their own voice. Finally, the contributors ask important questions regarding how men have controlled and governed women. According to the editors, "The series is intended to be not so much a history of women as a history of the relation between the sexes" (p. xix). More than seventy historians from several countries contributed to this work, which every academic and large public library should own.

1128. Engel, Barbara Alpern. *Between the Fields and the City: Women, Work, and Family in Russia, 1861–1914*. New York: Cambridge University Press, 1994. 254p. bibliog. index. ISBN 0521442362.

Between the Fields and the City places peasant women, a neglected group in the field of history, in the forefront of Russian history and women's studies. Focusing on the period from 1861 to the beginning of World War I, Engel looks at women who migrated from rural areas to work in cities. Although peasant women comprised only a small minority of those migrating to cities, Engel encompasses the varied experiences women faced. Engel offers that for a small percentage of these women, leaving their villages was emancipating. For most women, however, the decision to move to the city was an economic necessity. Unfortunately, many women bore illegitimate children, turned to prostitution, or were forced to cohabit with other families. Drawing on archival sources, including court records, official petitions to authorities, divorce testimonies, and case studies, Engel surveys the evolving social and economic factors that forced changes in these women's lives as well as the overarching pervasiveness of patriarchy within Russian society.

1129. Goldman, Wendy Z. *Women, the State, and Revolution: Soviet Family Policy and Social Life, 1917–1936*. New York: Cambridge University Press, 1993. 351p. (Cambridge Russian, Soviet, and Post-Soviet Studies, 90). bibliog. index. ISBN 0521374049; 0521458161pa.

How did the Russian Revolution affect women and families? To answer this question, Goldman analyzes shifting ideologies and policy changes concerning divorce, child care, abortion, and women's employment during the two decades after the Bolsheviks came to power. The introduction provides a historical overview of Bolshevism and outlines the ideological beliefs inherent in the four components of the Marxist vision as "free union, women's liberation through waged labor, the socialization of housework, and the withering away of the family" (p. 57). Unfortunately, this vision was turned on its head when ideology encountered the harsh realities of Russian life. In describing the problems of homeless children, women left destitute by "freer" divorce laws, and restrictive abortion politics, Goldman effectively demonstrates how the ideals of Marxism eroded during just twenty years. The author concludes that these new ideas clashed with age-old traditions, so that by the mid-1930s, the state had regressed to a more traditional view of the family.

Women in Russia: A New Era in Russian Feminism (Verso, 1994), edited by Anastasia Posadskaya and translated by Kate Clark, is a collection of twelve essays by Russian female scholars, many affiliated with the Centre for Gender Studies in Moscow. The essays critique the status of women in post-Soviet Russia. Chapters explore many topics, including women in the labor market, women in politics, images of women presented by the media, lesbianism in Russia, and the emergence of a women's movement. Sadly, the essays reveal that despite the rhetoric Russian policy makers have produced under the guise of various "gender programmes," women in contemporary Russia suffer in a number of areas.

1130. Hall, Catherine. *White, Male, and Middle-Class: Explorations in Feminism and History*. New York: Routledge, 1992. 307p. bibliog. index. ISBN (OP); 0415906636pa.

This collection of previously published essays reflects Hall's growth as a historian and her attempt to come to terms with the complex intersection of race, class, and gender. The essays raise key questions concerning the development of masculine and feminine identities within the middle class. Topics include the formation of a Victorian domestic ideology, the family during the industrial revolution, women and employment in nineteenth-century England, and the role of gender in defining politics. Closely related in its attempt to understand the intersection of race, class, and gender is *Beyond the Pale: White Women, Racism, and History* by Vron Ware (Verso, 1992), which is part history, part personal autobiography, and part sociological study. The themes of this book include "first, the need to perceive white femininity as a historically constructed concept, and second, the urgency of understanding how feminism has developed as a political movement in a racist society" (p. xiii). Topics in *Beyond the Pale* include the politics of anti-slavery, British women's role in reform movements in India, and the connection between anti-lynching and anti-imperialism movements in Britain.

1131. Holton, Sandra Stanley. *Feminism and Democracy: Women's Suffrage and Reform Politics in Britain, 1900–1918*. New York: Cambridge University Press, 1986. 201p. bibliog. index. (OP)

Holton examines the relationship between the British suffrage campaign and the party politics of the day, challenging conventional descriptions of female suffragists as militant, constitutionalists, or radicals. Focusing instead on the work of "democratic suffragists," a term coined to describe suffragists who worked for an alliance between votes for women and a fully independent Labour Party in the House of Commons, the author argues, "It was the successful realization of democratic-suffragist strategy in feminist-labour alliances . . . which ensured the eventual granting of the vote to women, not militancy as the leaders of the Women's Social and Political Union were afterwards to claim" (p. 6). The democratic suffragists succeeded largely because of their belief that the disenfranchisement of women was tied to larger social inequities. Because of this stance, women from all social classes became involved in the fight to grant women the right to vote.

In *Suffrage Days: Stories from the Women's Suffrage Movement* (Routledge, 1996), Holton outlines the lives and work of seven lesser-known British suffragists, all of whom were active from 1865 to 1918. Here Holton concentrates on the personal and public connections between these individuals.

Another work, *The Spectacle of Women: Imagery of the Suffrage Campaign, 1907–14* (University of Chicago Press, 1988), explores how suffrage imagery, including banners, political cartoons, posters, theatrics, and advertisements, worked both politically and as propaganda to secure the right to vote. Author Lisa Tickner argues that by filling the streets with beautiful banners, signs, and posters, these women used the doctrine of separate spheres to their advantage, essentially creating a "woman's space" in public.

Finally, *The Women's Suffrage Movement: New Feminist Perspectives* (Manchester University Press, distributed by St. Martin's Press, 1998), edited by Maroula Joannou and June Purvis, presents fourteen essays on the British suffrage movement covering a variety of topics, including regional studies and literary representations of the movement. An appendix lists British repositories that include suffrage material.

1132. Hull, Isabel V. *Sexuality, State, and Civil Society in Germany, 1700–1815*. Ithaca, NY: Cornell University Press, 1996. 467p. bibliog. index. ISBN 0801431263; 0801482534pa.

During the transition from absolutism to the beginnings of a modern civil society, Hull traces "the history of the changing public interest in sexual behavior at the moment of fundamental transformation toward the modern" (p. 6) in German-speaking Central Europe. Hull argues that this transformation cannot be fully understood until one looks at it through the lens of sex and gender. Examining legal documents on poverty, paternity, and child support and sources detailing relations of the church to the state, the author expertly depicts the shifting and complex move from a society where the state gradually relinquished its power as moral regulator to one where the individual citizen chose his own moral path. As this social shift evolved, the citizen was viewed as a male, married heterosexual who derived his rights from his private familial status. Hull concludes that by the nineteenth century "moral content" was reintroduced into positive law, thus creating a stricter enforcement of sexual behavior and increasing the dichotomy of gender roles.

Gender Relations in German History: Power, Agency, and Experience from the Sixteenth to the Twentieth Century (Duke University Press, 1997), edited by Lynn Abrams and Elizabeth Harvey, presents essays covering a wide array of topics, including abortion, marriage in early modern Germany, nursing during World War I, and National Socialist policies toward lesbians. While the essays cover a variety of subjects, they all depict the construction and enforcement of gender roles in Germany, detailing how in times of chaos, these categories often shifted and became unstable.

Women in German History: From Bourgeois Emancipation to Sexual Liberation by Ute Frevert, translated by Stuart McKinnon-Evans (Berg, 1989), looks at women in Germany from the late 1700s up to 1988. Frevert's central question is "how bourgeois society, while claiming to be a society of free and 'emancipated' individuals, has treated women and how women in Germany have come to grips with the 'conditions and restrictions' they have experienced" (p. 6).

1133. Kaplan, Marion A. *The Making of the Jewish Middle Class: Women, Family, and Identity in Imperial Germany.* New York: Oxford University Press, 1991. 351p. bibliog. index. ISBN (OP); 0195093968pa.

Kaplan has crafted a significant book expertly interweaving the overlapping areas of German history, Jewish history, and women's history. Covering the period from 1871 to 1918, Kaplan argues that the roles Jewish women claimed inside the home as well as certain arenas outside the home helped to shape emerging ideas about the bourgeoisie, women's roles within society, and redefinitions of gender. Organizing the book into two sections, women in the home and women outside the home, Kaplan stresses that her "underlying theme is the interconnections and tensions between these realms of life" (p. 20). Chapters in the first section of the book cover running the household, raising children, marriage, leisure, and women's role in Judaism. Chapters in part 2 deal with women in academia, women's employment, women's organizations, and social movements. Kaplan consulted a range of sources, including census documents, memoirs, newspaper articles, literary texts, and secondary sources, to frame her arguments.

Paula E. Hyman's *Gender and Assimilation in Modern Jewish History: The Roles and Representations of Women* (University of Washington Press, 1995) provides a comparative study of the assimilation of women in Jewish history: "I have attempted to accomplish two linked tasks in this book: to reclaim the experience of Jewish women as they accommodated to the socioeconomic and ideological challenges of modernity in western and central Europe, eastern Europe, and the United States, particularly in the latter part of the nineteenth century and the beginning of the twentieth; and to explore the role of ideas about gender in the construction of Jewish identity in the modern period" (p. 5). This is a groundbreaking work that belongs in all libraries.

1134. Langland, Elizabeth. *Nobody's Angels: Middle-Class Women and Domestic Ideology in Victorian Culture.* Ithaca, NY: Cornell University Press, 1995. 268p. bibliog. index. ISBN (OP); 0801482208pa.

Langland writes that her book "focuses on the intersection of class and gender ideologies in a Victorian icon: the Angel in the House" (p. 8). The author challenges prevailing critiques of the Victorian middle-class woman as powerless and idle, claiming instead that the Victorian housewife performed an important social function of managing class power: "To say that beginning in the 1830s and 1840s middle-class women controlled significant discursive practices is to argue that they helped to ensure a middle-class hegemony in mid-Victorian England" (p. 9). Langland blurs concepts of Victorian middle-class women and domestic servants and reveals "women's critical role in consolidating the genteel middle class" (p. 11). The author rereads domestic novels of Charles Dickens, George Eliot, Jane Austen, and Elizabeth Gaskell along with works of nonfiction, including domestic tracts, etiquette guides, household management manuals, ladies' magazines, and cookbooks, to argue that while many of these texts reinforced prevailing ideology, they also presented contradictory ideas of women controlling the social or cultural currency of Victorian society: "Thus, this analysis reads narrative form both for its reproduction of ideology and for its revelations of the paradoxes and contradictions in representations of the Victorian Angel" (p. 12). This complicated work, which explores the intersection between patriarchy and class status, offers nuanced readings of classic novels and enriches our view of women's role in Victorian society. *Nobody's Angel* will be of interest to literary scholars, historians, and sociologists.

1135. Lewis, Jane. *Women and Social Action in Victorian and Edwardian England.* Stanford, CA: Stanford University Press, 1991. 338p. bibliog. index. ISBN 0804719055.

In this in-depth study of five female social reformers, Beatrice Webb, Helen Bosanquet, Octavia Hill, Mary Ward, and Violet Markha, Jane Lewis attempts to show "how their ideas about the proper relationships between individual, family and the state were forged in relation both to their gendered (and often contested) concepts of duty and citizenship, and to their social conviction that on the commitment to social action depended social progress" (p. 1). Lewis explores the often contradictory beliefs that seemed to be inherent in middle-class Victorian society, such as beliefs about the proper role for women in society, about the boundaries between the public and private spheres, and about solutions to poverty. Using letters, diaries, and secondary sources, the author paints a portrait of five individuals who often held similar beliefs, yet who also had unique ideas and concerns, especially concerning suffrage: "The image of the upright Victorian figure, confidently directing the business of her own home and extending her rule to the homes of the poor, whether through the pursuit of scientific charity or a science of society, dissolves into a more complicated series of problems and contradictions" (p. 5). Lewis wants to "make clear their own priorities, concepts and frameworks of analysis, which have tended to be obscured by historians whose main concern had been to locate their work in relation to a much larger canvas" (p. 5). *Women and Social Action in Victorian and Edwardian England* adds to the literature on the history of social activism and presents a more extensive picture of Victorian middle-class women than may have previously been shown.

1136. Mangini-Gonzalez, Shirley. *Memories of Resistance: Women's Voices from the Spanish Civil War.* New Haven, CT: Yale University Press, 1995. 226p. bibliog. index. ISBN 0300058160.

Mangini-Gonzalez offers tribute to the forgotten women of Spain who played a role in forging the Second Spanish Republic (1931–1936), the Spanish civil war (1936–1939), and the leftist resistance from 1939 to 1975. After presenting an overview of Spanish women's history from the nineteenth century to 1931, part 1 reveals how the seeds of rebellion grew among Spanish women beginning in the 1800s. Parts 2 through 4 provide the heart of the book, or the "memories of resistance," as the title implies, for here the author includes war writings, prison memoirs, and the literature of exile. Illustrations amplify the words of the women. Mangini-Gonzalez discusses the historian's difficulty in assessing the truth when using memoirs and autobiographical texts, yet the author reveals that the purpose of her book is simply "to analyze above all how women told their stories of war and repression, prison and exile, and what they told, in order to understand what was of utmost importance to them within the context of the trauma and devastation that the Spanish civil war caused" (p. 59). Cutting across the disciplines of history, women's studies, autobiography, and cultural studies, *Memories of Resistance* documents the courage, political determination, and strength of these women.

Mary Nash's *Defying Male Civilization: Women in the Spanish Civil War* (Arden Press, 1995) provides a broader view of women's experiences during the civil war than the previous work. Nash attempts to explore the change and continuity of women's roles during the war and to give a collective view of women. She considers women directly involved in revolutionary organizations and fighting, but also looks at women on the home front. The work provides a chronology and a glossary of terms.

1137. Mason, Michael. *The Making of Victorian Sexuality.* New York: Oxford University Press, 1994. 338p. bibliog. index. (OP)

The two-pronged question Mason raises in this provocative and richly detailed work is whether sexual liberation or sexual excess is truly liberating or rather a detriment to progress. In studying the sexual beliefs and practices of the Victorians, Mason hopes to provide some insight and perhaps even lessons for modern readers. While the term "Victorian" has often denoted sexual prudishness, Mason concludes that a wide array of sexual beliefs and practices existed during the nineteenth century. The author incorporates the beliefs of radical thinkers of the time, including Havelock Ellis, along with the ideas of contemporary feminist writers and the Chartists to reveal the social and political milieu of the day. Mason argues that many of these theorists believed that unrestrained sexual behavior was a detriment to progress. Belief, however, does not predict behavior, and the author provides a thorough decade-by-decade account of various sexual practices among England's different social classes, covering such topics as prostitution, masturbation, birth control, bachelordom, premarital sex, courtship, and female sexuality. *The Making of Victorian Sexual Attitudes* (Oxford University Press, 1994), also by Mason, examines the religious, political, and moral beliefs preceding and during the Victorian era to better understand "the place of sexuality within some of the period's major ideological schemes" (preface). Together, both volumes provide significant and fascinating insights into the politics and social and sexual beliefs of the Victorians.

1138. McClintock, Anne. *Imperial Leather: Race, Gender, and Sexuality in the Colonial Contest.* New York: Routledge, 1995. 449p. bibliog. index. ISBN 0415908892; 0415908906pa.

Imperial Leather explores the intersecting dynamics between race, gender, class, and imperialism. McClintock writes that her work "sets out to explore this dangerous and contradictory liaison—between imperial and anti-imperial power; money and sexuality; violence and desire; labor and resistance" (p. 4). The introduction outlines McClintock's major themes as well as providing an excellent overview of concepts about imperialism, postcolonialism, gender, and race. The book is divided into three parts. Part 1 explores ideas concerning the cult of domesticity, the commodity of racism, and the rejection of women's work. McClintock also offers a fascinating chapter exploring how the newly emerging technology of photography provided a means to exhibit imperialism at home by presenting photographs of indigenous peoples from Britain's many colonies, and a chapter on cross-dressing and gender ambiguity. Part 2 looks at the colonies, those in Africa in particular, as the "theater for exhibiting the cult of domesticity and the reinvention of patriarchy" (p. 16). The final section takes the case of South Africa from the 1940s onward as an example of the attempts to resist imperialism. McClintock employs an impressive variety of sources, including diaries, photographs, ethnographies, advertisements, novels, and oral histories. Underlying this work are McClintock's complex definitions of power, class, race, and gender and how these meanings must continue to be reworked and intertwined in historical discourse.

1139. Melman, Billie. *Women's Orients: English Women and the Middle East, 1718–1918: Sexuality, Religion, and Work.* Ann Arbor: University of Michigan Press, 1992. 417p. bibliog. index. (OP)

In *Women's Orients*, Melman argues that Europe's view of the Orient was neither unified nor linear, and that middle-class female travelers of the eighteenth and nineteenth centuries experienced a very different view of the British colonies than their male counterparts. The geographic scope of this work includes the territories under Ottoman rule in Europe, Asia Minor, modern Iraq, Syria, Palestine, and Egypt. Melman examined various writings by women, including travelogues, letters and memoirs, papers published at scientific meetings, harem literature, religious discourse written by evangelicals and missionaries, and accounts by women interested in the evolving sciences of geography, Egyptology, and anthropology. Melman emphasizes that female travelers constructed independent ideas about colonization outside the traditional male centers of power, and that women's writings reflect a unique view of colonization and imperialism. This in turn allows readers to reconsider the complex notions of imperialism as well as the changing views of gender roles, the debate between public and private spheres, and the growing political awareness of women within the British Empire.

In *Imperial Eyes: Travel Writing and Transculturation* (Routledge, 1992), Mary Louise Pratt provides a provocative reading of travel writing about Africa and South America produced between 1750 and 1980. Her main question is "How has travel and exploration writing *produced* 'the rest of the world' for European readerships at particular points in Europe's expansionist trajectory?" (p. 5). Pratt defines transculturation as a "phenomenon of the contact zone" (p. 6) suggesting a more complicated relationship between the traveler and native. Pratt analyzes travel writing up through the 1960s and 1970s, showing that the complicated interrelationship between the traveler, often the privileged in terms of wealth and status, and the native still exists today.

1140. Owings, Alison. *Frauen: German Women Recall the Third Reich.* New Brunswick, NJ: Rutgers University Press, 1993. 494p. bibliog. index. ISBN 0813519926.

Owings, an American journalist fluent in German, interviewed fifty German women who spent their formative years during the thirteen-year reign of the Third Reich. The author's intent was to fill a gap and to discover what these women had to say about living in Germany during Hitler's reign. The women came from all social, economic, political, and geographical backgrounds. The women interviewed included Communists and anti-Communists, countesses, farmers, housewives, a former member of the Nazi Party, and even a concentration camp guard. Owings discovered early on that these women had quite different stories to tell and that most were more than willing to talk to her. Owings concludes with a heartfelt discussion of the enduring impact these stories had on her and adds that she hopes that the stories will affect readers the same way.

1141. Ross, Ellen. *Love and Toil: Motherhood in Outcast London, 1870–1918.* Oxford and New York: Oxford University Press, 1993. 308p. bibliog. index. ISBN (OP); 0195083210pa.

Believing that the institution of motherhood is acutely embedded in "social and cultural practices," Ross writes, "The act of examining the way that another era defined and arranged the pieces of 'motherhood' permits us to be sharper observers of the fissures and fantasies in our contemporary versions" (p. 4). Specifically, *Love and Toil* examines motherhood as experienced by working-class Londoners between the years 1870 and 1918. Ross argues that these were crucial years in the evolution of family life in Britain as middle- and upper-class reformers attempted to transform the practice and ideology of motherhood. Intertwining various methodologies from history, sociology, anthropology, and literary studies, Ross details the daily experiences of working-class women as they attempted to negotiate the complex relationships and practices of marriage, feeding a family, and caring for and educating children. Early chapters introduce readers to the life of poverty in London and place "the mother in household, local, national, and international economies (food) and in systems of relationships with both women and men (marriage)" (p. 4). Remaining chapters cover childbirth, childrearing, caring for sick children, and the ways in which motherhood was transformed as it was discovered by social workers and other reformers in the early decades of the twentieth century. Ross consulted a vast array of sources to write this book, including court records, oral histories, published biographies and autobiographies, newspapers and periodicals, hospital records, and legal documents. This is an exceptional work outlining how the complex, interweaving ideologies of motherhood and childrearing have evolved in domestic, social, and political spheres.

Another work nicely complementing *Love and Toil* is *Model Mothers: Jewish Maternity Provision in East London, 1870–1939* by Lara V. Marks (Oxford University Press, 1994). Covering a similar time period and geography to those of Ross, Marks focuses on the experiences of motherhood and childrearing for Jewish families.

1142. Summerfield, Penny. *Reconstructing Women's Wartime Lives: Discourse and Subjectivity in Oral Histories of the Second World War*. New York: Manchester University Press, 1998; distributed in the United States by St. Martin's Press. 338p. bibliog. index. ISBN 071904460X.

Summerfield interviewed forty-two women who had experienced various types of wartime work to discover "whether wartime training made a difference to women's labour market position during and after the war" (p. 7). While a great deal of research has been done on women's work during World War II, this book is the first to explore women's subjective views of their experiences during the war. In the introduction and first chapter, Summerfield considers several debates that form the theoretical framework for the book, including various notions of women, war, and social change; if personal testimony can provide a valid account of history; how memory is produced; and whether memory is gendered. Interweaving personal recollections along with discussion of contemporary social and political events, Summerfield looks at a variety of topics, such as the construction of female identity during the 1930s and 1940s, ideas of work as gendered, cultural representations of men and war, the myth of national support for the war, and finally, the demobilization of female workers after the war ended.

Angela Woollacott explores similar themes in *On Her Their Lives Depend: Munitions Workers in the Great War* (University of California Press, 1994). One million women from diverse socioeconomic classes (although most were working class), ages, and backgrounds worked in a variety of capacities at munitions factories all over England during the war. Like Summerfield, Woollacott discusses the limited interpretations of masculinity and femininity re-created during the war. She argues that British society mythologized female munitions workers on the home front as counterparts to the mythologized views of male soldiers or Tommies on the front lines. Although Woollacott concludes that wartime work positively influenced many of these women, their experiences of this work were varied and complex. In *Out of the Cage: Women's Experiences in Two World Wars* (Pandora Press, 1987), authors Gail Braybon and Penny Summerfield contend that neither of the world wars had a lasting impact on changing society's views of men's and women's roles: "The belief that men and women naturally occupy separate spheres within which they pursue quite different tasks was not shaken during either war" (p. 2). All of these works present a complex depiction of British women's work experiences during the two world wars.

1143. Valiulis, Maryann Gialanella, and Mary O'Dowd, eds. *Women and Irish History: Essays in Honour of Margaret MacCurtain*. Niwot, CO: Irish American Book Company, 1997. 351p. bibliog. index. (OP)

The essays in this collection demonstrate the ways in which Irish women have negotiated and even altered their relationship with the state, the role of Irish women in political activities, and Irish women's ideas regarding wartime activities, peace, pacifism, and violence. Contributors come from America and Great Britain. The introductory essay discusses the work of female historians in Ireland from the 1790s to the 1990s. Further essays examine such subjects as women and politics in nineteenth-century Ireland, women and pacifism in Ireland, and rural women and access to clean water. The collection ends with a bibliography of the works of Margaret Mac-Curtain, a renowned scholar of women's history. This work provides a valuable introduction to women in Irish history.

Gender Perspectives in Nineteenth-Century Ireland: Public and Private Spheres, edited by Margaret Kelleher and James H. Murphy (Irish Academic Press, 1997), includes essays on women in Irish history from historical, sociological, literary, and theological perspectives. Themes in the book include new perspectives of Irish women's history, women and literature, women's travel writing, and women in social and religious institutions. A final title worth mentioning is *Husbandry to Housewifery: Women, Economic Change, and Housework in Ireland, 1890–1914* by Joanna Bourke (Oxford University Press, 1993). This work investigates the economic, social, and demographic factors that led many Irish women to work at domestic unpaid labor in the early part of the twentieth century.

1144. Walkowitz, Judith R. *City of Dreadful Delight: Narratives of Sexual Danger in Late-Victorian London*. Chicago: University of Chicago Press, 1992. 353p. bibliog. index. ISBN (OP); 0226871460pa.

This fascinating cultural history explores the often contradictory beliefs about sexuality that emerged in London in the late Victorian era. Framing her work in the 1880s, Walkowitz analyzes various discourses of the time to demonstrate how Victorian beliefs were manifested in both the public and private spheres. She begins by arguing that London culture evolved from a predominantly male sphere with specific social, class, and gender boundaries to one where boundaries began to break down, both physically and metaphorically. As these boundaries disappeared, an atmosphere ripe for the creation of narratives of sexual danger emerged.

Walkowitz focuses on two sensationalist accounts of sexual danger: an exposé of child prostitution and the media coverage of Jack the Ripper. She examines discourses that often contradicted the notions set forth in the newspapers. In particular, Walkowitz describes an institution called the Men and Women's Club, where intellectuals of both sexes met to debate the meanings of sexuality, heterosexism, and gender, and she demonstrates how these discourses, and the ideas embodied in them, began to permeate every aspect of Victorian life, including work, reproduction, fashion, and male-female relationships. In the epilogue, the author analyzes the media coverage of the Yorkshire Ripper in the early 1980s and comments on recent feminist campaigns against pornography and the representation of violence. With somber conviction, Walkowitz notes that media coverage of female violence has not moved far beyond the sensationalism of the 1880s, and that the campaigns against violence toward women still have far to go.

While Walkowitz examines discourses of sexuality in Victorian England, Lucy Bland's *Ban-*

ishing the Beast: Sexuality and the Early Feminists (New Press, 1995) explores the attempts of early English feminists to dismantle contemporary ideology contrasting men as lustful creatures unable to control their "inner beasts" with women who were expected to show sexual restraint. After a discussion of contemporary definitions of femininity, sex, and morality that early British feminists used to frame their discussions and campaigns, the author moves to the various arenas where these beliefs were played out, including marriage, prostitution, contraception, and eugenics.

1145. Yalom, Marilyn. *Blood Sisters: The French Revolution in Women's Memory*. New York: Basic Books, 1993. 308p. bibliog. index. (OP)

Blood Sisters presents accounts of the French Revolution from eighty female memoirists. Comprising a distinctive array of personalities and lifestyles, the eighty women of this study include aristocrats, bourgeois women from the upper and middle classes, peasants and servants, actresses, writers, a painter, and a few nuns. While the quality and style of the memoirs vary, the women were all part of one "generation," "a cohort of individuals marked by the same dominant political and social events" (p. 4). Yalom clearly understands the problems inherent in trusting words written several years after events occurred. Nonetheless, these memoirs provide a vivid portrait of how women viewed the French Revolution and what it meant to them. Often interweaving personal experiences of the memoirists with the social and political events of the day, Yalom writes that these women "wrote to give meaning and order to uncustomary chaos, to create out of disaster an art of survival and transcendence. As a literary corpus, their personal narratives form a collective expression of women's memory—one that reconstitutes, humanizes, feminizes, and ultimately mythologizes a great national event" (p. 7). *Blood Sisters* provides a unique and important perspective on the French Revolution.

Rebel Daughters: Women and the French Revolution, edited by Sara E. Melzer and Leslie W. Rabine (Oxford University Press, 1992), includes essays by historians and literary scholars that question the many contradictions of women fighting for a revolution where they would gain few rights. Nonetheless, the editors note that women's active participation in the French Revolution was crucial in order for it to succeed. Essays discuss the formation of the revolutionary ideology through the use of the allegory of the female body, women as active militants, the cultural heritage of the revolution in art and literature, and finally, how the Revolution helped give birth to modern feminism.

North America

1146. Bernhard, Virginia, Betty Brandon, Elizabeth Fox-Genovese, and Theda Perdue, eds. *Southern Women: Histories and Identities*. Columbia: University of Missouri Press, 1992. 203p. bibliog. index. (OP)

This book, the first of several to result from the Southern Conference on Women's History, includes nine essays that present a complex, evolving story of how gender conventions, so closely tied to class and race, changed for southern women during the course of two centuries. Covering the period from the colonial era to the twentieth century, the essays tell the stories of individual women and distinct classes of women, or, as the editor notes, "distinct dimensions of southern women's identities" (p. 1). Topics covered include everything from women's roles in Bacon's Rebellion and the image of the Mammy to southern women's involvement in the struggle to gain suffrage. The final essay, by Darlene Clark Hine, explores black women's need to dissemble their inner feelings in response to rape as protection from a harsh and judgmental outer world. Other works produced as a result of the Southern Conference on Women, all published by the University of Missouri Press, include *Hidden Histories of Women in the New South* (1994) edited by Virginia Bernhard, Betty Brandon, Elizabeth Fox-Genovese, Theda Perdue, and Elizabeth H. Turner; *Taking Off the White Gloves: Southern Women and Their Histories* (1998) edited by Michele Gillespie and Catherine Gillespie; and *Beyond Image and Convention: Explorations in Southern Women's History* (1998) edited by Janet L. Caryell, Martha H. Swain: Sandra G. Treadway; and Elizabeth H Turner. *Hidden Histories of Women in the New South*, spanning the years from the 1870s to the 1960s, describes the lives of "hidden women," including those in prisons, in mental institutions, or from rural areas. The second book, which includes new and previously published writings, presents stories of women's lives from the fifteenth through the twentieth century. Topical essays on suffrage and labor are presented along with tributes to female historians who have opened the field of southern women's history for future scholars. The essays from the last title explore the lives of unconventional women, including those who stood up against religious, political, or sexual conventions in their worlds.

1147. Blee, Kathleen M. *Women of the Klan: Racism and Gender in the 1920s.* Berkeley: University of California Press, 1992. 228p. bibliog. index. ISBN 0520078764pa.

In this powerful, often disturbing text, Kathleen Blee examines the Women's Ku Klux Klan (WKKK) during the 1920s. Blee notes that as many as half a million women joined the KKK in the 1920s, and in many states, females constituted nearly half of Klan membership. Focusing on her home state of Indiana, the author interviewed eighteen former WKKK members. To her surprise, Blee found that many of these women did not regret their time in the Klan. Speculating on how these women failed to comprehend the devastating effects the Klan wrought on people's lives, Blee argues that many of these women felt a sense of entitlement and privilege as white females, and they saw Jews, immigrants, blacks, and Catholics as the "other." While not on the front lines, female KKK members did their part for the cause, including spreading malicious rumors or organizing boycotts of shops and businesses owned by Jews, Catholics, or African Americans. Blee contends that these actions complemented those of male KKK members, and that they could often be much more destructive because these activities were so intertwined into the daily lives of most women. This powerful book belongs in academic and public libraries.

Blee also edited *No Middle Ground: Women and Radical Protest* (New York University Press, 1998), which offers essays that examine women's radicalism in the United States during the second half of the twentieth century. The essays, including first-person accounts and scholarly research, attempt to answer several questions, including what role women play in militant and radical politics, what prompts women to organize on behalf of unpopular causes, and how women are changed by these activities. Blee argues that the exclusion of the study of female radicals in historical scholarship has many causes, including the narrow definition of radicalism and where scholars look for evidence. This work should generate further research and study of women in radical and militant movements.

1148. Bleser, Carol, ed. *In Joy and in Sorrow: Women, Family, and Marriage in the Victorian South, 1830–1900.* New York: Oxford University Press, 1991. 330p. bibliog. (OP)

A volume of papers stemming from a conference, *In Joy and in Sorrow* presents a detailed picture of marriage and family life in the Victorian South. Two themes run throughout the essays. The first theme is tension, "tensions between family loyalties, between ideals and realities, between conflicting family roles, and between racial and class pursuits of common family ideals" (p. xxii). Second, and more disturbing, *In Joy and in Sorrow* depicts how slavery crippled both individuals and families before and after the Civil War. As Bleser writes, "This theme of the impact of the legacy of slavery on the family, on marriage, and especially on private individuals is of extreme importance" (p. xii). Essays depict marriages and family life of persons from all walks of life, including those of wealthy plantation owners, sharecroppers, and free black slaveholders. Topics such as incest, insanity, and miscegenation are openly discussed. A similar title is Joan E. Cashin's *A Family Venture: Men and Women on the Southern Frontier* (Johns Hopkins University Press, 1991), which explores the migration of planter families from the southern seaboard to the frontiers of the South (territories west of the Alabama-Georgia state line, as well as areas of Florida, Tennessee, and Kentucky) during the years 1810 to 1860. Cashin argues that migration differed greatly among the sexes: men experienced a sense of independence and freedom, while women often experienced a loss of kinship and grew even more dependent on spouses in their new homes. Cashin further argues that the patriarchal, racist values of these southern slaveholders were only heightened in the new frontier.

1149. Breines, Wini. *Young, White, and Miserable: Growing Up Female in the Fifties.* Boston: Beacon Press, 1992. 261p. bibliog. index. (OP)

This cultural history asks, "How did young women who had grown up in the narrowly defined gender environment of the 1950s become feminists?" (p. ix). Using sociological data, autobiographies, letters, fiction, and interviews, Breines hopes to uncover the "cultural discontent and resistance" (p. xi) she believes was just under the surface of many young women's consciousness. The introduction provides a good overview of the various contradictions and paradoxes that existed in postwar America. A time of significant change, America in the 1950s had more wealth and seeming stability than ever before. Breines argues, however, that for young people, especially young women, the opportunities were restricted by a conservative political and cultural landscape. Providing an interesting analogy to the containment of Communism, the author writes: "I want to suggest that postwar culture was a culture of containment with women and black people as its objects. In this perspective, American politics and culture were structured by a defense of masculinity and whiteness; the changes that accompanied the formation of an advanced capitalist society were perceived and experienced as threats from those outside American borders and from those who had been excluded within those borders, women and blacks and homosexuals" (p. 10). Breines covers a variety of topics, including contemporary social scientists' views of gender, family life during the period, sexual and romantic ambiguities, and rebellious girls. Her conclusion discusses how "the shape of the feminist movement in the late 1960s and 1970s owes much to these contradictions" (p. 24).

1150. Clinton, Catherine, ed. *Half Sisters of History: Southern Women and the American Past.* Durham, NC: Duke University Press, 1994. 239p. bibliog. ISBN 0822314835; 0822314967pa.

Clinton's stated aim is to "bring together powerful and provocative pieces which symbolize some of the best work of the past quarter century" (p. 5). These ten pieces, written between 1974 and 1992, represent scholarship by some of the finest historians of southern women's history. Authors of the essays raise several pertinent questions, including the following: What were the experiences of elite southern women, and how did they differ from those of women in urban areas? What impact did industrialization have on the lives of these women? How clearly does the image of the southern lady reflect reality? What role did class dynamics play? How have those in control marginalized slave women and other outside groups? The introduction surveys the field of southern women's history, stating that by examining issues of race, class, and specific geographic areas, one gains a broader and clearer picture of southern history as a whole. The essays cover a variety of topics, from the status of slave women during the American Revolution and

Appalachian women's involvement in the labor movement to the deconstruction of Scarlett O'Hara as a cultural icon. Because of the range of topics covered, this resource would serve as an excellent text for upper-division and graduate classes in women's history.

Another title that would serve as a key text for women's history classes is *Daughters of Canaan: A Saga of Southern Women* by Margaret Ripley Wolfe (University Press of Kentucky, 1995). The first attempt by a historian to write a comprehensive history of southern women from colonial times to the present, *Daughters of Canaan* presents the real lives of southern women, black, white, and Native American. Wolfe draws on scholarship from the past twenty-five years, and her notes provide an excellent bibliography of previously published scholarship in this field. Illustrations also enhance the text.

Sally McMillen explores privileged southern women's experiences with childbirth and childrearing in *Motherhood in the Old South: Pregnancy, Childbirth, and Infant Rearing* (Louisiana State University Press, 1990). McMillen reveals the importance of motherhood for southern women by drawing on their personal letters and journals. Concentrating on the health and medical concerns of these women, the author also examines the "shifting role of the antebellum medical profession in obstetrics and infant care" (p. 3).

1151. Clinton, Catherine, and Nina Silber, eds. *Divided Houses: Gender and the Civil War*. New York: Oxford University Press, 1992. 418p. bibliog. index. ISBN (OP); 0195080343pa.

The eighteen essays in *Divided Houses*, arranged in six sections, explore varying ways in which the Civil War evoked a crisis of gender. Topics include everything from how men in battle redefined and reinterpreted their masculinity to how women fought to retain independence after the war ended. One of the more fascinating sections includes essays on women's personal experiences of the war, including nurses, spies, and women living with the terror of guerilla warfare. Two sections compare and contrast women's roles on the home front in both the North and the South, noting how women of the North often took on increased responsibilities in the labor force and how women of the South often took on more responsibilities for keeping farms or plantations running. The final section of essays explores how gender politics and the politics of Reconstruction became entwined, noting for example, the victimization of women, especially Southern women, by harsh divorce laws or discrimination by men unwilling to yield any power.

Two other titles that should be mentioned are *Civil Wars: Women and the Crisis of Southern Nationalism* by George Rable (University of Illinois Press, 1989) and *Yankee Women: Gender Battles in the Civil War* by Elizabeth Leonard (Norton, 1994). In *Civil Wars*, Rable "examines the role and status of white women in a society based on racial, class, and sexual hierarchy" (p. ix). Rable, explaining that our view of Southern women is inadequate, contends that by the end of the war, Southern women might no longer have believed in the South's causes, but these same women did not question the traditional racial or patriarchal doctrines of their culture. For Rable, this becomes a crisis for Southern nationalism. *Yankee Women* focuses on the stories of three Northern women and attempts to answer several questions, including how the war affected gender roles. The women—one a nurse, one a volunteer for a philanthropic organization, and one a physician—often challenged the assumptions and beliefs about women's place in society.

1152. Cott, Nancy F., ed. *A Woman Making History: Mary Ritter Beard through Her Letters*. New Haven, CT: Yale University Press, 1991. 378p. bibliog. index. ISBN 0300048254.

Nancy Cott writes, "This book is an attempt to restore Mary Ritter Beard's place in history by bringing to light her private letters, against her own wishes" (p. ix). Ironically, Beard was devoted to finding and preserving women's documents of all kinds, yet she wanted only her published work to stand for her accomplishments.

A renowned historian and intellectual, Beard collaborated on several textbooks with her husband Charles Beard, the most influential historian in the United States in the first half of the twentieth century, as well as authoring her own works, including *On Understanding Women* (1931), *America through Women's Eyes* (editor, 1933), and the influential *Woman as Force in History* (1948). Cott explains that Beard "insisted that history was not whole without women's story. She persevered in seeing women both as cooperators with men and as makers, themselves, of *civilization* (a word she imbued with particular meaning)" (p. 1).

Because Beard destroyed most of her correspondence before her death in 1958, Cott searched for her letters in the correspondence of other women. She was able to locate several hundred letters written between 1910 and the 1950s. Cott organizes the letters by topic, such as the suffrage years, the activist intellectual emerges, or the postwar years, and she provides commentary in between to weave the letters together. From these letters, Mary Ritter Beard emerges as a woman with strong convictions, a weighty intellect, and a passion for assuring that women's voices throughout history were not lost.

In *The Grounding of Modern Feminism* (Yale University Press, 1987), Nancy Cott looks at the emergence of the word "feminism" in the United States: "The appearance of Feminism in the 1910s signaled a new phase in the debate and agitation about women's rights and freedoms that flared for hundreds of years" (p. 3). Feminism, both the word and the idea, took hold because the woman movement (Cott deliberately uses the singular "woman") of the nineteenth century was too limiting, asserting that all women shared the same beliefs and goals for equality. During this period, Cott purports that considerations about women's identity and consciousness became paramount. Modern feminism evolved from the belief that it encouraged "sexual equality that includes sexual difference" (p. xx). *The Grounding of Modern Feminism* provides the historical antecedents for the development of ideas about feminism, ideas still being debated to this day.

1153. Devens, Carol. *Countering Colonization: Native American Women and Great Lakes Missions, 1630–1900*. Berkeley: University of California Press, 1992. 185p. bibliog. index. (OP)

Countering Colonization, a fascinating and significant work, addresses the central roles of Native American women in the history of the United States and as actors within their own cultures. Devens concentrates on missionaries' interactions with three groups of Native American peoples in the Great Lakes area for two reasons: one, the missionaries had interactions with Native Americans in this region over nearly three centuries, and two, they often left detailed records of their impressions of these people, including the women. The author identifies three patterns of response to colonization by the Native Americans over time. Initially, the Indians presented a united front to expel the missionaries, but gradually, the Indians reluctantly began to accept conversion to Christianity, mostly because of dire economic conditions. Finally, Devens contends that responses to colonization split along gender lines, which is the most compelling and tragic piece of this history. The author writes, "When evangelicals preached their combined gospel of assimilation and female domesticity, the outcome was either general accommodation or a course of action that divided women and men" (p. 4). Native American men often wanted to culturally assimilate with Anglo-Americans, mostly as a way of survival, while Native American women clung to traditional ways. Thus the colonizers not only helped to destroy the way of life known to the Native peoples of America, but they also created a bitter friction between men and women and accelerated a loss of autonomy for the Native women within their own communities.

Another work on Native American women is *Negotiators of Change: Historical Perspectives on Native American Women*, edited by Nancy Shoemaker (Routledge, 1995), which offers ten original research articles spanning nearly 400 years. The essays explore many different aspects of Native American women's roles and cover everything from responses to colonization to economic roles of women within their own communities to ideas of marriage and divorce.

Cherokee Women: Gender and Cultural Change, 1700–1835 (University of Nebraska Press, 1998) presents a broad history of Cherokee women, focusing on gender relations among the Cherokees and the effects of colonialism on these people. Theda Perdue treads the line between historian and anthropologist, giving an account of the belief systems as well as the rites and rituals of the Cherokee people, but from a female perspective.

1154. DuBois, Ellen Carol. *Harriot Stanton Blatch and the Winning of Woman Suffrage.* New Haven, CT: Yale University Press, 1997. 353p. bibliog. index. (OP)

In this biography of one of the foremost leaders of the women's suffrage movement in America, Ellen Carol DuBois asserts that Harriot Stanton Blatch, the daughter of Elizabeth Cady Stanton, understood, more than any other suffrage leader, precisely what the movement needed in order to succeed: "She believed that the key to winning suffrage in the twentieth century lay with the masses of women wage-earners, who were transforming what it meant to be a woman in the modern age" (p. 3). Blatch understood the importance of working women because of their numbers, and because "they made it clear that autonomy for women was fundamentally an economic issue" (p. 3). Blatch also understood that all classes of women needed to be united to win the fight for suffrage, and she effectively recruited wealthy and educated women, emphasizing their duty in the cause. More than her ability to unite women across class lines, DuBois argues that Blatch's greatest skill was her political acuity. Blatch believed that "political equality must be won politically; to secure it, women would have to learn how to wield legislative, partisan, and electoral tools" (p. 4).

Woman Suffrage and Women's Rights (New York University Press, 1998) presents essays written by DuBois between 1975 and 1997. The essays trace the suffrage story along evolving social views regarding politics, sexuality, race, religion, and class.

In *Rampant Women: Suffragists and the Right of Assembly* (University of Tennessee Press, 1997), Linda J. Lumsden analyzes "the role the First Amendment right to assemble peaceably played in the twentieth-century suffrage campaign and the reciprocal, little known role the suffrage protests played in the development of twentieth-century conceptions of the rights to assemble" (p. xiv). *Century of Struggle: The Woman's Rights Movement in the United States* (enlarged ed., Harvard University Press, 1996) by Eleanor Flexner and Ellen Fitzpatrick tells the story of the struggle for suffrage for women over a 100-year period, from 1820 to 1920. Part 1 discusses women's position in American life up to 1800 and the beginnings of the movement, including the Seneca Falls convention of 1848. Part 2 covers the Civil War and the growth of women's organizations and political struggle after the war. Part 3, covering 1900 to 1920, presents the dramatic story of the passage of the Nineteenth Amendment. Appearing in two prior editions (1959, 1975), *Century of Struggle* in this enlarged edition includes an afterword by Ellen Fitzpatrick surveying the state of women's rights up to the mid-1990s.

1155. DuBois, Ellen Carol, and Vicki L. Ruiz, eds. *Unequal Sisters: A Multicultural Reader in U.S. Women's History.* New York: Routledge, 1990. 473p. bibliog. index. (OP)

Such distinguished names as Paula Baker, Linda Gordon, Christine Stansell, and Alice Kessler-Harris are among the thirty contributors in this work, a multicultural approach to the study of women's history. The editors argue that a uniracial or even biracial formula for the study of women's history does not work and instead write that through the multicultural approach, they "seek to focus on the interplay of many races and cultures" (p. xii). This formula presents a more complex, often disquieting notion of women's history because it brings into focus the power relations not only among men and women, but also between women. Centering around the themes of family, work, politics, sexuality, and women's relationships, the essays cover such topics as the image of Native American women in American culture, Mexican cannery workers in southern California, and Japanese American women in domestic service. Four selected bibliographies on African American women, Asian American women, Latinas, and Native American women add to the richness of this work.

A second edition of *Unequal Sisters* appeared in 1994. It includes thirty-six articles, twenty-four covering women of color. The editors write that while the dynamics of race and gender are the "pivotal point of this collection," the collection also provides expanded views of indigenous women, Asian American women, and class, generational, and sexual orientation issues. A concise, insightful discussion on the debate over multicultural history appears in the introduction.

In *From out of the Shadows: Mexican Women in Twentieth-Century America* (Oxford University Press, 1998), Ruiz presents the history of Mexican American women in the twentieth century who lived in the Southwest. Basing her work on oral histories, Ruiz is interested in the ways these women fought for some control over their lives at home, at work, and in their communities. She moves from the early twentieth century, when many women migrated from Mexico to borderlands in the United States, up to the Chicana feminist movements of the 1980s and 1990s.

A Shining Thread of Hope: The History of Black Women in America by Darlene Clark Hine and Kathleen Thompson (Broadway Books, 1998) covers the history of African American women in the United States. Twelve chapters trace the history of black women from the earliest years of this country to the 1980s. Drawing on a variety of sources, including slave narratives, letters, oral histories, and novels, the authors explore issues of community, educational equity, and the importance of self-worth and dignity for black women.

Finally, Hupina Ling's *Surviving the Gold Mountain: A History of Chinese American Women and Their Lives* (State University of New York Press, 1998) offers a broad-based history of Chinese American women in the United States. Dividing her work into three parts, Ling discusses the history of Chinese American women immigrants from the 1840s to 1943, Chinese American women in postwar America, and contemporary Chinese American women. The women in this book come from large urban regions as well as rural areas and from all walks of life, including servant girls, prostitutes, wives of merchants, laborers, farmers, students, and intellectuals.

1156. Edwards, Laura F. *Gendered Strife and Confusion: The Political Culture of Reconstruction*. Urbana: University of Illinois Press, 1997. 378p. (Women in American History). bibliog. index. ISBN 0252022971; 0252066006pa.

Gendered Strife and Confusion investigates the interaction of race, class, and gender issues in the South after the Civil War. The study centers on Greenville County, North Carolina. Edwards wants to show how social and political history overlap by focusing on the complex ways in which the public and private worlds of men and women, whites and blacks, became conflated as the social and political world of the Confederacy collapsed. Edwards reveals the importance of the household within southern society, especially before the Civil War, and how the identities of individuals and the households they belonged to "provided the framework that structured social and political relations in the South as a whole" (p. 6). The author believes, however, that gender, race, and class "dimensions of private and public power converged" (p. 7) in the decades before the Civil War, and that after the war, the household became a contested area as gender roles, especially for freed blacks and poor whites, were unclear. Chapter 1 discusses marriage and households that "provided the institutional recognition of family life and the basis for claiming civil and political rights" (p. 19). From there, Edwards discusses labor issues, gender roles in elite white households, gender roles in poor black and white households, civil and political rights, and how the Democratic Party excluded African Americans and poor whites from the political process. This essential resource accurately demonstrates the complex political and social issues during Reconstruction as white conservatives angled to hold onto power.

Nancy Isenberg's *Sex and Citizenship in Antebellum America* (University of North Carolina Press, 1998) offers a broad overview of the "many ways women's rights advocates encountered antebellum political culture" (p. xiii). Isenberg questions how women's rights advocates framed "their understanding of rights within antebellum theories of representation" and how this struggle over rights incorporated "several distinct but overlapping legal and political debates that characterized the antebellum period" (p. xiv). *To 'Joy My Freedom: Southern Black Women's Lives and Labors after the Civil War* (Harvard University Press, 1997) by Tera M. Hunter offers a history of black working-class women from the final days of slavery during the Civil War through the Great Migration during World War I. Hunter's geographical focus is Atlanta, yet she presents a comprehensive history of working women—cooks, maids, child-nurses, laundresses—looking at their lives as mothers, lovers, consumers, religious devotees, and activists. Hunter relied on a vast array of sources, including diaries, household account books, newspapers, census data, municipal records, personal correspondence, oral interviews, government reports, and business and organization records to provide this rare account of African American working-class women.

1157. Faderman, Lillian. *Odd Girls and Twilight Lovers: A History of Lesbian Life in Twentieth-Century America.* New York: Columbia University Press, 1991. 373p. bibliog. index. ISBN 0231074883.

Faderman traces the evolution of lesbianism in twentieth-century America, proposing that while "romantic friendships" between women were quite common in the nineteenth century, they were not seen as deviant, and that the idea of sexual relationships between such women was never considered. Only in the twentieth century, with the advent of psychoanalysis and theories espoused by sexologists, did the term "lesbian" emerge, along with the identification of women as lesbians.

In tracing this history, Faderman examines the development of lesbian subcultures, particularly in large cities; the effects of class on these subcultures; the effects of all female institutions such as women's colleges and bars on the development of lesbianism; and how the feminist and gay liberation movements have changed views of women loving women. Faderman drew from archival and secondary sources for much of the historical discussion within *Odd Girls*. She also conducted 186 interviews with lesbians of various ethnic, racial, and economic backgrounds, ranging in age from seventeen to eighty-six, who came from the following states: New York, Texas, Massachusetts, Pennsylvania, Nebraska, Missouri, and California. Several photographs enhance the text.

In *Boots of Leather, Slippers of Gold: The History of a Lesbian Community* (Routledge, 1993), Elizabeth Lapovsky Kennedy and Madeline D. Davis provide a comprehensive history of the lesbian community in Buffalo, New York, from the 1930s to the 1970s. The authors' primary sources include oral histories that were conducted with older working-class lesbians who were part of the community prior to 1970.

Similarly, *Cherry Grove, Fire Island: Sixty Years in America's First Gay and Lesbian Town* (Beacon Press, 1993) by Esther Newton provides a cultural history of Cherry Grove, a resort community on Fire Island about forty-five miles east of New York City. Newton conducted interviews with 100 people, both gay and straight men and women, to produce her story of this community from the 1930s to the 1980s. All three titles present an extensive history of lesbian and gay communities in the United States and should be included in all large public libraries and in academic libraries.

1158. Fox-Genovese, Elizabeth. *Within the Plantation Household: Black and White Women of the Old South*. Chapel Hill: University of North Carolina Press, 1988. 544p. (Gender and American Culture). bibliog. index. ISBN 0807818089; 080784232Xpa.

Fox-Genovese exposes the complicated relationships among various members of plantation households during the years 1820 to 1861. Defining household as "a basic social unit in which people, whether voluntarily or under compulsion, pool their income and resources" (p. 31), Fox-Genovese explores the various ways gender relations influenced this system. The plantation household, based on the social system of slavery and dominated by one male authority figure, comprised different meanings for the women within the system. For slaveholding women, the domination by a male, be he husband, father, or brother, was legitimate and even natural. For slave women of the household, the author contends that the relationship to the master was distorted: "It superceded their relations as daughters, wives, and mothers with the men and women of their slave community" (p. 30). The majority of the book explores various relationships within plantation households, most notably, the relationship between white and black women. Fox-Genovese speculates that this relationship was the most antagonistic, and that many slaveholding women were more crudely racist than their male counterparts. Relying on private letters, diaries, and journals of a small number of elite slaveholding women and on narratives depicting the lives of slave women, *Within the Plantation Household* presents valuable insight into the lives of plantation women in antebellum America.

In *Tara Revisited: Women, War, and the Plantation Legend* (Abbeville Press, 1995), Catherine Clinton writes: "This book is not an attempt to *find* Tara but to relocate the legend in a complex interweaving of myths and memories, particularly in relation to the lives of Southern women" (p. 15). Clinton investigates the actual impact of the war on southern women, especially the impact of the war on gender relations, not only between the sexes but also between white and black women.

1159. Gaspar, David Barry, and Darlene Clark Hine, eds. *More Than Chattel: Black Women and Slavery in the Americas*. Bloomington: Indiana University Press, 1996. 341p. (Blacks in the Diaspora). bibliog. index. ISBN 0253330173; 0253210437.

The editors of this volume begin with this question: what are the connections between slavery and women's history? Interested in conceptual frameworks, they write, "The contributors to this volume . . . explore diverse dimensions of slavery and the related forces that shaped slave society to show that one of the most decisive of these forces was gender" (p. ix). Gender serves as an important lens through which to examine slavery because slave women experienced their bondage quite differently than men. Because black slave women struggled to nurture children and keep families together, their forms of resistance were not as overt as men's. Nonetheless, Gaspar and Hine contend that these women still resisted their captivity and fought for survival and for a measure of dignity because they did see "themselves as more than chattel, as more than the personal property of another" (p. x).

The book is divided into three parts. Part 1 presents a thought-provoking essay examining the sexual divisions of labor and family life and looks at what "must be taken into account about African society and culture, in order to interpret" (p. x) the experiences of slave women in the Americas. Part 2 focuses on the daily lives of slave women and includes essays on health and healing, childbearing and rearing, domestic work, commercial employment, and the importance of the black family. The final part explores various ways in which slave women rebelled against their bondage and also looks at the lives of free black women.

Discovering the Women in Slavery: Emancipating Perspectives on the American Past, edited by Patricia Morton (University of Georgia Press, 1996), also a volume of contributed essays, presents case studies on individual slave women as well as antislavery activists. Part 2 of this volume explores group systems, including black Methodist women, slave women in Connecticut and New Orleans, and slaveholding women. Morton also wrote *Disfigured Images: The Historical Assault on Afro-American Women* (Greenwood Press, 1991), which analyzes the portrayal of black women in historical studies from the late nineteenth to the late twentieth century.

Darlene Clark Hine is also the series editor for *Black Women in United States History* (Carlson, 1990), a set of sixteen volumes. The set includes subsets of smaller series of one to four volumes that include articles by various contributors. These subsets include *Black Women in American History: From Colonial Times through The Nineteenth Century* (volumes 1–4); *Black Women in American History: The Twentieth Century* (volumes 5–8); *Black Women's History: Theory and Practice* (volumes 9–10); and *Women in the Civil Rights Movement: Trailblazers and Torchbearers, 1941–1965* (volume 16). The five remaining volumes are monographs. Volume 16 includes a comprehensive guide to the entire series; each title includes a separate index. This series is recommended for all types of libraries.

1160. Gilmore, Glenda Elizabeth. *Gender and Jim Crow: Women and the Politics of White Supremacy in North Carolina, 1896–1920*. Chapel Hill: University of North Carolina Press, 1996. (Gender and American Culture). 384p. bibliog. index. ISBN 0807822876; 0807845965pa.

The story of southern politics at the turn of the twentieth century is recounted from the vantage point of middle-class African American women in North Carolina. One such woman who figures prominently in this story is Sarah Dudley Pettey, who wrote a 'woman's column' for the African American newspaper the *Star of Zion*. In her first column, written in 1896, Pettey decreed racial injustice within the United States, the eagle. Pettey wrote that the American eagle protected "beneath his mighty wings all of his white children: while with his talons he ruthlessly claws all who are poor and especially those who trace their lineage to ebony hued parentage" (p. xv). Pettey represents the essence of what these well-educated black women believed: they saw themselves as ambassadors for the less fortunate. Even though they could not vote, these women took their roles as citizens very seriously, feeling it their duty to fight oppression.

Early chapters trace the roots of racial oppression in the South, focusing on the roles white supremacists played in the disenfranchisement of black men and the reaction by the black community to these events. Later chapters focus on the activities of black women in the political arena from 1900 up to the winning of female suffrage in 1920. Gilmore argues that the disenfranchisement of black men in 1900 created an opportunity for African American women to become more politically engaged: "Ironically, as black men were forced from the political, the political underwent a redefinition, opening new space for black women" (p. xxi). Gilmore uncovered a variety of unknown archival sources relating to these women, including school histories, church meeting minutes, correspondence, and other personal papers, which she interprets along with "new readings" of white texts. Through her research, the author expertly crafts a new version of southern political history.

Another important work focusing on African American women's political clout is *Righteous Discontent: The Women's Movement in the Black Baptist Church, 1880–1920* (Harvard University Press, 1993) by Evelyn Brooke Higginbotham. Here the author argues "that women were crucial to broadening the public arm of the church and making it the most powerful institution of racial self-help in the African-American community" (p. 1). During the years covered by this study, the black church served as a rallying point to encourage black men and women to fight against racial oppression. Together, these works provide a stunning portrait of the tremendous courage and determination of black women and men in the fight for equality and justice.

1161. Goossen, Rachel Waltner. *Women against the Good War: Conscientious Objection and Gender on the American Home Front, 1941–1947*. Chapel Hill: University of North Carolina Press, 1997. 180p. (Gender and American Culture). bibliog. index. ISBN 080782366X; 0807846724.

Women against the Good War focuses on those women who defined themselves as conscientious objectors (COs) during World War II. Most of these women were affiliated with the Civilian Public Service (CPS) program, a government-sponsored group designed to accommodate conscientious objectors by providing them work with conservation, forestry, or social service fields. Often, the women were wives, sisters, or daughters of CPS workers, but sometimes they worked in CPS camps, especially as nurses or dieticians. Additionally, a majority of the female COs had been raised in religious traditions emphasizing peace and pacifism, such as the Mennonites, Brethren, and Friends, thus instilling in them at an early age nonconformist views that allowed them to go against the overwhelming tide of support for the war as adults. In the opening chapters, Goossen sets the historic and cultural stage, presenting an overview of the government's conscription policies and a description of the Civilian Public Service. She then covers the lives of women who were camp followers of men in the CPS, women who actively worked at these camps, and college women who identified themselves as COs.

Two other titles focusing on women's roles in peacemaking during times of war are *The Women and the Warriors: The U.S. Section of the Women's International League for Peace and Freedom, 1915–1946* by Carrie A. Foster (Syracuse University Press, 1995) and *Reconstructing Women's Thoughts: The Women's International League for Peace and Freedom before World War II* by Linda K. Schott (Stanford University Press, 1997). Both works explore the WILPF, which was founded in 1915 as the Women's Peace Party by Jane Addams, yet each asks different questions. Foster provides an in-depth historical account of the evolution and growth of the WILPF, asking ultimately why the group failed. The author argues that the women of the WILPF needed to be more revolutionary, rather than reformist, and that by working within an ultimately patriarchal, plutocratic governmental system, they were bound to fail. Schott, on the other hand, is concerned with the intellectual history of the leaders of the WILPF and examines "the ideas that brought the leaders of the WILPF into the organization and that shaped WILPF policy throughout the period between World War I and World War II" (p. 4). She argues that women's intellectual history has been ignored, and that it must be examined more diligently by scholars to provide a more inclusive understanding of our nation's intellectual heritage.

1162. Graham, Sara Hunter. *Woman Suffrage and the New Democracy*. New Haven, CT: Yale University Press, 1996. 234p. bibliog. index. ISBN 0300063466.

Graham's fascinating study places the women's suffrage movement within the context of pressure-group politics. Focusing on the National American Woman Suffrage Association (NAWSA), Graham argues that this group evolved into one of the first and most successful pressure groups in American history: "Why and how the NAWSA suffragists accomplished this feat, and what their experiences tell us about pressure politics, women's rights, and American democracy, are the subjects of this book" (p. xi).

When NAWSA was created in 1890, the women's suffrage movement had stalled. NAWSA leaders, including its vocal spokeswoman Carrie Chapman Catt, quickly learned to employ not only indirect influence or outsider strategies, borrowed from many women's groups of the nineteenth century, but also direct power techniques to achieve their goals. According to Graham, it was this move to direct power, including adopting insider strategies such as staging political demonstrations, creating propaganda, and organizing at the local level, that revitalized the suffrage movement and eventually led to the passage of the Nineteenth Amendment.

In *Woman Suffrage and the Origins of Liberal Feminism in the United States, 1820–1920* (Harvard University Press, 1996), author Suzanne Marilley explores the evolving nineteenth-century "feminist" political arguments that women's rights activists employed to achieve their goals. The feminism of equal rights argument (1820 to the 1870s) insisted that women's natural rights be recognized as no less sacred than men's. The feminism of fear argument, prevalent in the late 1800s, claimed that granting suffrage to women would allow them to be moral leaders who could vote on issues important to women's safety and protection. Finally, the argument of personal development (early 1900s) maintained that "because individuals generate ideas and achieve goals, no government . . . should prohibit the exercise of personal freedom" (p. 8).

Lee Ann Banaszak's *Why Movements Succeed or Fail: Opportunity, Culture, and the Struggle for Woman Suffrage* (Princeton University Press, 1996), a comparative analysis of suffrage movements in two countries, ponders why women were granted suffrage in the United States by 1920, yet not until 1971 in Switzerland. Banaszak maintains that U.S. suffragists succeeded primarily because they organized across state lines, they lobbied state and national legislative bodies, and they were not afraid of confrontation, all things Swiss suffragists failed to do. All three works provide important insights into the history of women's struggle for suffrage.

1163. Gutiérrez, Ramón A. *When Jesus Came, the Corn Mothers Went Away: Marriage, Sexuality, and Power in New Mexico, 1500–1846.* Stanford, CA: Stanford University Press, 1991. 424p. bibliog. index. ISBN (OP); 0804718326pa.

Gutiérrez presents a social history of the Spanish colony of New Mexico over three centuries: "Using marriage as a window into intimate social relations, this study examines the Spanish conquest of America and its impact on one group of indigenous peoples, the Pueblo Indians" (p. xvii). The author hopes to provide a voice to the conquered, as well as to analyze the complex historical interactions between the conquered and the conquerors.

Each of the three parts explores a different century. Part 1 investigates the marriage customs of the Pueblos during the sixteenth century, looking at such issues as polygamy and how gift giving and marriage reinforced basic inequalities in the society. Part 2 traces the history of the Spanish conquest, beginning in 1540. Here Gutiérrez explores the complex, often competing views of marriage among the three primary cultures in the region: the Franciscans, the Pueblo Indians, and the Spanish soldiers. By examining the contrasting views of this institution, Gutiérrez sheds light on larger tensions and conflicts among the various social groups. The final part deals with marriage formation and social control in the eighteenth-century colony formed after reconquest, looking specifically at various groups in Spanish towns and villages: the nobility, the landed and landless peasantry, and the Indian slaves. Relying on a wealth of sources, including explorers' narratives, chronicles of conquest, church and state records, reports by friars, ethnographies, and archaeological site surveys, Gutiérrez weaves a fascinating tale of power and control, with marriage offering the "window into the social, political, and economic arrangement of a society" (p. xviii). This title is recommended for all libraries.

In *A Contest of Faiths: Missionary Women and Pluralism in the American Southwest* (Cornell University Press, 1991), Susan M. Yohn explores another type of conquest: "This book examines the process by which Anglo-Protestant missionaries attempted to introduce a particular set of religious and cultural values to the Hispano-Catholic population of the area that is now northern New Mexico and southern Colorado in hopes of 'Americanizing' these people" (p. 1). The principal actors of this conquest were Presbyterian missionary women working during the latter part of the nineteenth century. Like Gutiérrez, Yohn explores the complex interactions among the Hispanic people and the missionaries: "Their efforts to subdue elements they saw as 'foreign,' that is the Indian, Spanish and Catholic heritage, and to remake the territory in their own image were only partially successful. Instead of a monument to the hegemony of Protestant ideals, this conquest was marked by a series of ongoing contests that called into question commonly held stereotypes and forced the missionaries and their supporters to reconsider and reassess their goals" (p. 2).

1164. Iacovetta Franca, and Mariana Valverde, eds. *Gender Conflicts: New Essays in Women's History.* Buffalo: University of Toronto Press, 1992. 303p. bibliog. ISBN 0802027342; 0802067735pa.

Gender Conflicts provides eight essays representing the diversity of Canadian women. The editors discuss several themes central to this collection in the introduction, including the complex power relationships that exist within society and how Canadian women fought against patriarchal views. Using women's history to provide analytical tools for exploring social relations as a whole is a second major theme. Finally, the editors believe that women's history, which should not be relegated to a subdiscipline of "mainstream history," can help us see history in a new and vital way. Contributors cover a gamut of fields, including law, politics, business, labor, and crime, and employ a variety of methodologies. Individual essays discuss such topics as heterosexual relations among rural youth, bourgeois women and the rise of the department store, immigrant women's experiences of violence, and the social politics of Canadian feminists. While the geographic scope of the collection is limited to Ontario, *Gender Conflicts* provides a good overview of a variety of topics in the history of Canadian women.

Peggy Bristow's *We're Rooted Here and They Can't Pull Us Up: Essays in African Canadian Women's History* (University of Toronto Press, 1994) includes essays on black women in Canada's history. The essays cover the history of black women from seventeenth-century Nova Scotia to after World War II. The editors claim that writing black history is very different in the United States and Canada; that black history is not a legitimate field of study in Canada. This collection hopes to challenge the Eurocentric view prevalent in the Canadian intellectual community and provide new avenues for research.

1165. Jameson, Elizabeth, and Susan Armitage, eds. *Writing the Range: Race, Class, and Culture in the Women's West.* Norman: University of Oklahoma Press, 1997. 656p. bibliog. index. ISBN 0806129298; 0806129522pa.

This lengthy work includes twenty-nine essays by scholars of history, anthropology, and sociology, among other fields, who try to uncover the various complexities of writing about women of different races, classes, and ethnicities in the American West. The book is organized into seven parts, each of which begins with a short introduction outlining the case studies in that part. Each part explores a different theme, such as women living on colonial frontiers, women resisting conquest, or women who went west to seek independence and a measure of empowerment. Essays represent women from different classes and of varying ethnicities, including African American women, Native American women, Japanese women, Chinese women, and Irish women.

1166. Jeffrey, Julie Roy. *The Great Silent Army of Abolitionism: Ordinary Women in the Antislavery Movement.* Chapel Hill: University of North Carolina Press, 1998. 311p. bibliog. index. (OP)

Tracing women's role in the abolitionist movement from the 1830s through the Civil War, Jeffrey strives to provide a picture of the many women, mostly from rural areas and small towns, who played a role in abolitionism. The author argues that these women provided the backbone for the movement with their many activities, including raising money, distributing propaganda, circulating and signing petitions, and lobbying legislators. Using correspondence, diaries, articles from the abolitionist press, and organizational records, Jeffrey clearly reveals that the movement could not have survived without the work of these women. Several women who took part in this movement are discussed in this work, but certain individuals stand out. These include Mary White, a farmer's wife from Massachusetts; Abigail Goodwin, a Quaker from New Jersey, who collected money and signatures for the cause and was active for thirty years; and Mary Still, an African American woman from Philadelphia who worked for abolitionism but also founded schools to educate black children. *The Great Silent Army of Abolitionism* brings to the forefront the work of ordinary women for abolition.

Several other titles on this topic should be mentioned. The first is *Ahead of Her Time: Abby Kelley and the Politics of Anti-slavery* by Dorothy Sterling (Norton, 1991). Sterling, the author of several books, including a biography of Harriet Tubman, traces the life and career of a quiet Quaker woman who became one of the most radical, outspoken, and politically influential abolitionists of the mid-nineteenth century.

Neither Ballots nor Bullets: Women Abolitionists and the Civil War by Wendy Hamand Venet (University Press of Virginia, 1991) focuses on the work of women abolitionists during the Civil War. Venet depicts the work of women from all walks of life who became abolitionists, including the authors Harriet Beecher Stowe and Julia Ward Howe, as well as actress Fanny Kemble.

1167. Juster, Susan. *Disorderly Women: Sexual Politics and Evangelicalism in Revolutionary New England*. Ithaca, NY: Cornell University Press, 1994. 224p. bibliog. index. ISBN 0801427320.

Juster demonstrates how the transformation of the evangelical Baptist Church in New England between the 1730s and the 1780s mirrored the erosion of women's power within the broader community. Juster claims that after the Great Awakening of the 1730s, Baptist women shared with Baptist men or Brethren much of the formal authority within the power structure of the church. Juster effectively argues that this was possible because evangelical religion was seen as "feminine." The Baptists believed that only grace could bind true believers together.

The "feminine" qualities of humility and that the state of one's heart mattered more than wealth before God served the evangelicals well as long as they remained a marginalized sect within Puritan New England. However, the Baptist faith gradually transformed itself from a sect to a denomination, from a "community of saints into a society of churchgoers" (p. 6), as Baptists grew in numbers and strove to gain legitimacy among the Congregationalists. Furthermore, the evangelical leadership became more politically involved during the Revolution.

As congregations and involvement in the political world grew, the "feminine" qualities of piety, seen as humility, and equality of all souls before God became problematic. The Baptists, Juster argues, began to acquire a more masculine image by using patriarchal language and metaphors of the church as a family with a ruling "father" figure and by adopting a bureaucratic form of governance, including the creation of committees of men to make decisions. Most important, however, feminine qualities gradually came to be seen as sinful. Juster provides a fascinating analysis of the politics of power, illustrated within a spiritual community, that shows how the American Revolution was quite inhospitable to the idea of female citizenship: "Women's slide into marginality within the evangelical church prefigured the success of the American Revolution in aligning political and patriarchal authority in the form of the manly citizen" (p. 11).

In *Female Piety in Puritan New England: The Emergence of Religious Humanism* (Oxford University Press, 1992), Amanda Porterfield details how the Puritans used female imagery to depict their relationship to God. Within the domestic sphere, marriage also was seen as a trope of grace with God: Porterfield asserts that the Puritan idea of grace can be seen as a growing belief in religious humanism and that this "religious humanism played an important role in the process of social change and modernization that Puritanism facilitated" (p. 5). The author, however, points out that women's status did not increase because of these beliefs. Both of these books provide excellent insights into the nature of female piety in early America.

1168. Keetley, Dawn, and John Pettegrew, eds. *Public Women, Public Words: A Documentary History of American Feminism.* Madison, WI: Madison House Publishers, 1997. 3v. bibliog. index. ISBN 0945612443; 0945612451pa. (vol. 1); 0742522245 (vol. 2); 0742522350 (vol. 3).

This collection of primary documents "traces the development of feminist thoughts from Colonial North America through United States political and popular culture of the late-twentieth century" (p. xi). The purpose of the collection, according to the editors, is to provide sources for the conceptual study of women along with showing how women have used ideas practically to gain power. The primary goals of the collection are to show the confluence between thought and action in the history of American feminism, to represent the diversity of American feminism, and to represent the various views of feminism through a variety of texts, including speeches and manifestos, fiction and poetry, articles in radical and popular magazines, articles from underground newspapers, articles from academic and professional journals, courtroom transcripts, and records of other professional proceedings.

Volume 1, covering the period from early colonial days to 1900, includes poems by Anne Bradstreet, various writings by first-wave feminists and women reformers, including Lucy Stone, Angelina Grimké, Susan B. Anthony, and Lucretia Mott, and several post–Civil War writings reflecting the struggle for political and social equality by women such as Victoria Woodhull, Harriot Stanton Blatch, Myra Blackwell, and Charlotte Perkins Gilman. It also contains an introduction to the concepts and definitions the editors employed in choosing the documents in the collection, as well as a concise overview of the competing definitions of feminism found throughout its history.

Volume 2, covering the period from 1900 to 1960, includes writings by Emma Goldman, Jane Addams, Margaret Sanger, Mary Beard, Pearl S. Buck, Eleanor Roosevelt, and Bella Abzug. The last volume covers 1960 to the present. It includes writings by Betty Friedan, Robin Morgan, Rita Mae Brown, Angela Y. Davis, Paula Gunn Allen, and bell hooks, as well as writings from various groups such as the National Organization for Women (NOW) and the United Nations Fourth World Conference on Women. This three-volume set is an essential source for all libraries.

Second to None: A Documentary History of American Women (University of Nebraska Press, 1995), edited by Ruth Barnes Moynihan, Cynthia Russet, and Laurie Crumpacker, offers a history of American women through primary documents. This is an eclectic, diverse collection of sources written by both men and women. The editors sought to represent the experiences of a variety of women. They also wanted to show how women have been treated throughout the history of the United States; thus they include a variety of writings by men, such as letters, religious tracts, pieces from advice manuals, and the like. The documents are arranged chronologically, and each document includes a headnote with background information about the document and what it illustrates. Within each chronological division, the editors group documents by theme. Volume 1, comprising material from the sixteenth century to the Civil War, includes such items as passenger lists to Massachusetts, ads for wet nurses in the eighteenth century, poems by Anne Bradstreet and Phillis Wheatley, descriptions of plantation life, and a variety of letters. Volume 2 covers 1865 to the present and includes documents such as one on scientific housework by Ellen Richards, an African American woman of 1912 describing her condition, Betty Crocker Kitchen's low-budget menu for families during the depression, a description of the birth of NOW, and the debate from the *Congressional Record* over the Family Medical Leave Act.

1169. Kerber, Linda K., Alice Kessler-Harris, and Kathryn Kish Sklar, eds. *U.S. History as Women's History: New Feminist Essays*. Chapel Hill: University of North Carolina Press, 1995. 477p. (Gender and American Culture). bibliog. index. ISBN 0807821853; 0807844950pa.

In the introduction to this volume, dedicated to Gerda Lerner, the editors write, "The essays in this book reflect the continuing dialogue over what we are as a field as well as how we influence the process of historical understanding" (p. 7). Indeed, as noted in the introduction, women's history has come a long way since Lerner began her dissertation on the Grimké sisters in 1963. Women's history has evolved through various stages: biographical analysis, acknowledging women's roles in history, and finally, the current stage, one where women are central to historical scholarship. Three overarching concepts frame this work: state formation, the uses of power, and the creation of knowledge, areas where women's voice and presence have been neglected in previous historical scholarship. Essays in part 1 focus upon state formation and cover topics such as women and the obligations of citizenship, welfare and child reform, and how marriage is often shaped by state policy. Essays in part 2 discuss females in prison, public health issues related to women, and women and slavery. Essays in the final part, centering around the idea of knowledge creation, explore a range of issues, from how different groups of readers have interpreted the novel *Little Women* to the origins of contemporary American feminism. The contributors, a stellar cast of historians, including Linda Gordon, Nancy F. Cott, and Darlene Clark Hine, have placed women in the center and have shown in this volume that U.S. history truly is women's history.

Linda Kerber's *Toward an Intellectual History of Women: New Feminist Essays* (University of North Carolina Press, 1997) includes writings composed between 1973 and 1993. The essays address the role of women in early American history and place them more broadly in cultural and intellectual history. Kerber hopes that these essays will spur new work on uncovering women's intellectual history, and that they will "have contributed to the next generation of revision in which we will understand that both men and women think seriously about large matters." (p. 19).

1170. Ladd-Taylor, Molly. *Mother-Work: Women, Child Welfare, and the State, 1890–1930*. Urbana: University of Illinois Press, 1994. 211p. bibliog. index. ISBN 0252020448.

In this impressive work, Ladd-Taylor traces the roots of the welfare system by focusing on the intersection of the two components of what she calls "mother-work": women's roles as mothers in the home and the growth of the concept of social maternalism. This ideology espoused the views that care and nurturing were uniquely feminine qualities, that mothers perform a service to the state by raising good citizens and soldiers, and that women are united across class, race, and nationality by motherhood. Various groups of female reformers took advantage of these beliefs to lobby for legislation to improve conditions for women and children. Ladd-Taylor expertly interweaves the arguments, debates, and conflicts of three distinct reform groups: the sentimental maternalists, associated with the National Congress of Mothers, which eventually became the Parent-Teacher Association (PTA); progressive maternalists, affiliated with Hull House and the National Children's Bureau; and early feminists, many who felt that the public debates surrounding women could support other causes such as the fight for female suffrage. While the philosophies and tactics of these groups varied, the concerns these groups raised did not go unheard. During the first two decades of the twentieth century, several pieces of significant legislation related to working conditions, health care for children, and pension benefits for women were passed.

Regina Kunzel's *Fallen Women, Problem Girls: Unmarried Mothers and the Professionalization of Social Work, 1890–1945* (Yale University Press, 1993) traces the growth of social work as a "scientific" profession in the first half of the twentieth century, arguing for an inclusion of gender in this analysis. Kunzel begins her study with the work of evangelical reform women, who founded homes for unwed mothers in the early years of the twentieth century and saw unwed mothers as "fallen sisters" who needed guidance and benevolent care. Then tracing the "professionalization of social work," Kunzel depicts the intense struggles between evangelical women and social workers, not only for control over the fate of unwed mothers, but more important, for control of the definition of female sexuality: "The competition between evangelical women and social workers for authorship of popular understandings of out-of-wedlock pregnancy, for recognition as legitimate authorities, and for control of maternity homes raised larger questions of how female sexuality would and could be represented and understood" (p. 5).

Finally, *Delinquent Daughters: Protecting and Policing Female Sexuality in the United States, 1885–1920* (University of North Carolina Press, 1995) by Mary Odem explores the struggle to control female sexuality in the early years of the twentieth century, a time when moral reformers began to demand state intervention to control this "problem." The author explores the concerns and positions of all groups involved in the campaign for the regulation of female sexuality: moral reformers; state officials; working-class teenage girls, the principal targets for regulation; and working-class parents. Odem argues for two distinct stages in moral reform activities. The first stage, occurring from the mid-1880s to the early 1900s, placed the blame for female sexual delinquency on men; the second stage, occurring from the early 1900s to the 1920s, acknowledged a woman's role in her own sexuality and thus began to place the blame on the environment within working-class families. Together, these three outstanding books provide an important historical account of the development of ideologies concerning welfare, single mothers, and women's sexuality, ideologies that still continue to condemn and blame women even today.

1171. Marshall, Susan E. *Splintered Sisterhood: Gender and Class in the Campaign against Woman Suffrage*. Madison: University of Wisconsin Press, 1997. 347p. bibliog. index. ISBN 0299154602; 0299154645pa.

Splintered Sisterhood explores the roles and motives of female antisuffragists in a superb study covering the period from the end of the Civil War to 1920. Marshall believes that female antisuffragists, while hiding behind a cloak of traditionalism and the ideal of female domesticity, sought to protect a privileged way of life: "antisuffrage women engaged in the protection of gendered class interest. . . . The women who led the antisuffrage campaign were not a group of secluded homemakers, but a privileged urban elite of extraordinary wealth, social position, and political power" (p. 5). Shedding light on the motives and political strategies employed by the antisuffragists, the author contemplates several key questions: Why did certain women protest against women's rights? How did class and gender affect suffrage opposition? How did the male and female antisuffragists differ and how were they alike? How did the movement progress and who were its leaders? Marshall examines a wide variety of sources, including the organizational records of the Massachusetts Association Opposed to the Further Extension of Suffrage to Women, genealogies, club records, newspapers, census data, and a variety of secondary sources, to seek answers to these questions. The final chapter draws parallels between the female antisuffragists of the 1890s and modern antifeminist groups such as the Eagle Forum and Concerned Women for America, reminding us of the "ongoing political interaction between both sides of the women's rights movement" (p. 235) and the need for continued research on right-wing women.

1172. Meyer, Leisa D. *Creating GI Jane: Sexuality and Power in the Women's Army Corps during World War II*. New York: Columbia University Press, 1996. 260p. bibliog. index. ISBN 0231101457pa.

In *Creating GI Jane*, Leisa Meyer explores the development of the Women's Army Corps (WAC) to help readers understand the continuing debates concerning the proper role of women and gays in the military: "Understanding the process by which women were accepted into this 'masculine' institution, and a new category of 'female soldier' was constructed, helps us to evaluate better the challenges to gender and sexual hierarchies mounted during the war and the consequence of these challenges for twentieth-century American culture" (p. 2). Given the contemporary acceptable social roles for men and women, the army saw the WAC, which was established in May 1942, as an expedient means to handle the multitude of menial tasks created by the onset of the war. Some civilians hailed the entrance of women into the army as an opportunity to expand women's rights, while others saw the entrance of women into this male institution as a threat. Meyer writes that in the 1940s "sexual respectability was a fluctuating category for women" (p. 8), so that women's entrance into the military had to be tightly controlled and appropriately represented. Nonetheless, the author addresses the role of minority women and lesbians in the Women's Army Corps, as well as prostitution: "The entire construction of the WAC by Corps' leaders was organized to limit public fears that the state was advocating changes in sexual, gender, race or class hierarchies" (p. 8). Using archival records, contemporary popular media coverage, and oral histories, *Creating GI Jane* provides a fascinating history concerning the rights of women and gays to serve in the military, an issue still being heavily debated today.

Brenda L. Moore provides a detailed history of the 6888th Central Postal Directory Battalion, the only group of African American women to serve in the WAC during World War II, in *To Serve My Country, to Serve My Race: The Story of the Only African American WACs Stationed Overseas during World War II* (New York University Press, 1996). An estimated 855 African American WACs served with this division. Relying primarily on interviews with survivors, Moore attempts to discern who these women were, why they joined the army, and how it affected their lives. *Coming Out under Fire: The History of Gay Men and Women in World War Two* (Free Press, 1990) is a powerful, compelling text, detailing the stories of the thousands of gay men and women who served in the armed forces during World War II. Allan Bérubé, an independent historian, incorporates governmental archives, personal papers, medical records, and oral histories to present a vivid social history.

1173. Norton, Mary Beth. *Founding Mothers and Fathers: Gendered Power and the Forming of American Society*. New York: Knopf, 1996. 496p. bibliog. index. (OP)

This densely written treatise combines political theory with gender analysis to critique the power relationships in colonial America circa 1620–1670. Norton compares and contrasts the social and political worldviews of the colonists in New England with those of the colonists in the Chesapeake valley, showing that women in colonial America often exercised an amazing amount of power within their families and communities. Because the males who settled in New England mostly came with families, Norton contends that New Englanders had a primarily Filmerian worldview (named after Sir Robert Filmer, an English theorist) that was quite paternalistic and "assumed the necessity of hierarchy in family, polity and society at large" (p. 4). The settlers of the Chesapeake region, on the other hand, were often single males who may or may not have started families after settlement. Norton argues that these inhabitants possessed a more Lockean view of society: that the world is divided "into an all-male realm (politics and society) and a realm of heterosexual relationships (family), thereby breaking down the unified worldview that characterized familial theory" (p. 11). Using court records from each area, Norton examines the gendered power relationships in the family, the community, and the state.

In *Good Wives, Nasty Wenches, and Anxious Patriarchs: Gender, Race, and Power in Colonial Virginia* (University of North Carolina Press, 1996), Kathleen Brown demonstrates how the unquestioned belief in the superiority of men over women in colonial Virginia helped create the view of Anglos' superiority over Africans. The English who settled the colonies had little exposure to Africans or to the moral implications of race; thus, Brown writes, "Discourses of gender, the division of labor by sex, and the regulations of white women's sexuality were integral to the process of defining race and contributed significantly to the establishment of slavery and political stability in Virginia" (p. 1).

A final title focusing on women in early America is *First Generations: Women in Colonial America* (Hill and Wang, 1996) by Carol Berkin. Less theoretical than the previous titles, *First Generations* presents vivid portraits of women from various regions, occupations, classes, and ethnicities. Whether she is telling the story of Eliza Lucas Pinckney, a rice and indigo planter from South Carolina, Margaret Hardenbroeck Philipsen, a Dutch immigrant and tradeswoman, or Watemo, a woman of the Wampanoag peoples, Berkin's life stories allow readers to contrast the struggles and achievements of a variety of women from various ethnicities and classes in early America.

1174. Passet, Joanne Ellen. *Cultural Crusaders: Women Librarians in the American West, 1900–1917.* Albuquerque: University of New Mexico Press, 1994. 208p. bibliog. index. (OP)

The development of libraries in the rural West in the early years of the twentieth century coincided with the growth of newly trained professional librarians from prestigious library schools in the East and Midwest. Joanne Ellen Passet discusses the life and work of more than 300 professionally trained female librarians who "sought to share their cherished Anglo-American canon with a diverse western readership that included rural and urban residents, children and adults, working and middle class men and women, immigrants, Native Americans, and African Americans" (p. xiii). Passet wants to put women at the center of the history of library development, as well as illustrate how these independent women constructed meaning in their lives and helped shape the communities in which they lived. Relying on a variety of primary source materials, including personal letters and papers, archives, correspondence of prominent library educators and state officials, annual reports, local histories, newspapers, and photographs, the author details the lives and work of female librarians from eleven western states, including Arizona, California, Colorado, Idaho, Montana, Nevada, New Mexico, Oregon, Utah, Washington, and Wyoming. The author argues that female librarians transformed the profession and transformed libraries into "dynamic cultural and educational institutions" (p. xvi).

Reclaiming the American Library Past: Writing the Women In (Ablex, 1996), edited by Suzanne Hildenbrand, brings together essays focusing on early women pioneers of librarianship. Contributors raise questions about the linkages between librarianship and other female-intensive professions, revealing how these linkages have contributed to writing these women out of the history of the profession. In *Daring to Find Our Name: The Search for Lesbigay Library History* (Greenwood Press, 1998), editor James V. Carmichael assembles essays reflecting on the past, present, and future of gays, lesbians, and bisexuals in the library profession. Part 1 explores theoretical issues and problems that can arise when doing research in this area. Essays in part 2 cover some of the pioneering groups in lesbigay library history, including the Gay, Lesbian, and Bisexual Taskforce of the American Library Association. Part 3 discusses various archival and library collections relating to gays, lesbians, and bisexuals. Recent graduates within the library profession tell their personal stories in part 4.

1175. Peavy, Linda S., and Ursula Smith. *Women in Waiting in the Westward Movement: Life on the Home Frontier.* Norman: University of Oklahoma Press, 1994. 381p. bibliog. index. ISBN 0806126167; 0806126191pa.

Peavy and Smith argue that women played a significant role in the settlement of the West, even as they were left in waiting. As men went off to seek fortunes or better opportunities for themselves and their families, women at home were left with paying mortgages, keeping farms and businesses running, and raising children. The opening chapter explores the many reasons why men went west and provides insight, through excerpts from letters and diaries, into some of the frustrations, loneliness, and unease felt by many women. The remainder of *Women in Waiting* depicts the lives of six couples in great detail. The authors chose the couples because of the availability of primary sources, including letters from both spouses; letters to other family members, friends, and business associates; diaries and journals; and business records. Photographs and family genealogies help complete stories. Through these stories, the fears and frustrations, but ultimately the courage and persistence of these women become clear.

Another work exploring the lives of frontier women is *The Female Frontier: A Comparative View of Women on the Prairie and the Plains* by Glenda Riley (University of Kansas Press, 1988). Like Peavy and Smith, Riley argues that women's role in the settlement of the West has been overlooked, sentimentalized, or stereotyped. Riley compares in detail various aspects—home and hearth, employment, and community participation—of the lives of the female settlers on the prairie and the plains, recounted mostly from diaries, daybooks, journals, letters, and some interviews. Riley divides the plains and the prairie based mainly on the terrain of each area, but she also notes that each area had unique cultural differences. Nonetheless, Riley contends that the women of both regions shared more commonalities than differences, and that "these shared experiences and responses of frontierswomen constituted a 'female frontier' " (p. 2).

Covered Wagon Women: Diaries and Letters from the Western Trails, 1840–1890 by Kenneth L. Holmes (A. H. Clark Co., 1983–1993) is an eleven-volume compilation of women's letters and diaries as they traveled west. The letter writers were teenage girls, housewives, mothers, and grandmothers. Holmes sought out unpublished manuscripts in libraries, historical societies, and private family collections throughout the United States. The final volume includes a gazetteer, bibliography, and index. This collection belongs in all academic and large public libraries.

1176. Pleck, Elizabeth Hafkin. *Domestic Tyranny: The Making of Social Policy against Family Violence from Colonial Times to the Present.* New York: Oxford University Press, 1987. 273p. bibliog. index. (OP)

Domestic Tyranny surveys various efforts to combat family violence in America from 1641 to the 1970s. Pleck argues that family violence became a matter of public interest in American society during three distinct periods. The first period, 1640 to 1680, saw the Puritans enacting laws to combat violence because they felt that it would "disrupt their divinely sanctioned settlement" (p. 5). A second period of public interest occurred during the last thirty years of the nineteenth century as various reform movements swept the country. Finally, family violence again came into focus in the mid-1960s, at the same time the civil rights and women's rights movements brought issues of individual rights and equal treatment to the nation's attention. Asking the question "Why did family violence become a matter of public policy in these three periods of American history?" (p. 4), Pleck contends that reform efforts against violence have often occurred in the United States during times of social or political upheaval. Examining these three periods along with events leading up to them, Pleck explores such issues as the ideology of motherhood, how feminists in the 1850s viewed the problem, the role the courts and the legal profession have played, and what the psychiatric profession had to say. Pleck argues that "the single most consistent barrier to reform against domestic violence has been the Family Ideal" (p. 7), an ideal that places privacy, the rights of parents, and the ideal of family stability above larger societal concerns. *Domestic Tyranny* is recommended for all libraries.

A more focused study can be found in *Improper Advances: Rape and Heterosexual Conflict in Ontario, 1880–1929* (University of Chicago Press, 1993) by Karen Dubinsky. The author examines sexual crimes in twenty-five rural southern and northern Ontario counties during a fifty-year period. Investigating everything from rape, attempted rape, and indecent assault to abortion, incest, infanticide, and sex-related murder charges, Dubinsky attempts to "discover the historical roots of the association of gender, sexuality, and conquest" (p. 2). Both of these works offer significant scholarship concerning the nature of sexual violence and the abuse of power in a patriarchal society.

1177. Reis, Elizabeth. *Damned Women: Sinners and Witches in Puritan New England.* Ithaca, NY: Cornell University Press, 1997. 212p. bibliog. index. (OP)

In *Damned Women*, Elizabeth Reis investigates witchcraft in Puritan New England through the lens of religion. Focusing on the Salem witch trials of 1692, Reis considers how these events happened rather than why. Her intent is to shed light on "how Puritanism functioned as lived religion and how gender was constructed socially" (p. 3). Examining the confessions of the accused, Reis suggests "that some Puritans enjoyed greater flexibility in performing their identities than others" (p. 3), as men could better show their true "natures" through their deeds, while women were seen as inherently sinful. Women's souls were thought to be weaker than men's and thus more easily tempted by Satan. Reis also argues that the concept of predestination, the belief that God preordained salvation or damnation, caused many Puritans to despair over their eternal fate, especially women, whom Reis believes often internalized the clergy's negative messages about their sinful nature. Reis acknowledges that complex social and economic factors could have played a part in the witchcraft episodes of 1692; however, for her, religion also condemned the accused.

Spellbound: Women and Witchcraft in America (Scholarly Resources, 1998), which Reis edited, is a fascinating collection linking the Salem witchcraft trials with the continued persecution of practitioners of modern-day Wicca. The collection presents a diversity of essays that cover such topics as gender and the meanings of confession in early New England, the economic basis of witchcraft, African American women and spirituality in churches in New Orleans, witchcraft as goddess religion, and misogynist ideas in the construction of goddess and women. This text is ideal for public and high-school libraries, but would also be a good addition for academic libraries.

In *A Delusion of Satan: The Full Story of the Salem Witch Trials* (Doubleday, 1995), novelist and journalist Francis Hill provides a detailed analytical study of the trials. Hill contends that Puritanism's strict notions of good and evil created a daily atmosphere of terror, guilt, and suspicion that were fueled by economic and political strife within the community.

1178. Ryan, Mary. *Women in Public: Between Banners and Ballots, 1825–1880.* Baltimore: Johns Hopkins University Press, 1990. 202p. bibliog. index. (OP)

Mary Ryan writes, "To search for women in the public is to subvert a longstanding tenet of the modern Western gender system, the presumption that social space is divided between the public and the private and that men claim the former while women are confined to the latter" (p. 4). Ryan's task is to find the women in public, "to retain the concept of public but shun its gender correlate" (p. 4).

In discussing the controversial and slippery meanings of the word *public* from Aristotle to Hannah Arendt to Jürgen Habermas, Ryan acknowledges that all of them defined *public* in a way that privileged men. Ryan situates her search for women in public by examining three American cities, New York, New Orleans, and San Francisco, during the years 1825 to 1880. She chose these cities because they had a vigorous public culture: New York had robust politics; New Orleans had exciting public festivals; and San Francisco had a unique cosmopolitan culture. In four essays, she explores and analyzes the public life of these cities in four urban institutions. The first institution encompasses the grand civic ceremony at times designated as holidays, where public meaning was created and displayed. Chapter 2 deals with everyday space—the streets, squares, and parks—spaces open to women, yet where women "were channeled into selective sectors of public space, where their movements were charted by both gender prescriptions and class distinctions" (p. 16). Chapter 3 addresses the most commonly defined public sphere, the political arena. Here Ryan explores issues of power and the growing discontent of women at being excluded from political life. In the last chapter, public discourse is examined, specifically in the form of city newspapers, where women "appear irregularly and surrounded with the most distortion" (p. 17). *Women in Public* is highly recommended for all libraries and would be an excellent text for classes in gender and political science.

1179. Schneider, Dorothy, and Carl J. Schneider. *Into the Breach: American Women Overseas in World War I.* New York: Viking, 1991. 368p. bibliog. index. (OP)

Into the Breach tells the story of the 25,000 American women who volunteered for service during World War I. These women, ranging in age from early twenties to sixties, came from mostly middle- and upper-class backgrounds. Many were well educated and often had professional careers in the United States. The vast majority of women served as nurses, either with the armed services or the Red Cross, but they also served as canteen workers, physicians, correspondents and journalists, librarians, telephone operators, accountants, dieticians, interpreters and translators, and entertainers. These women traveled to England, France, Belgium, Italy, and Germany, but also to the Balkans, Russia, and the Near East. Upon their arrival overseas, the women worked for British and French relief and medical agencies, for private charities founded by wealthy individuals, for well-established organizations such as the YMCA, YWCA, Red Cross, and Salvation Army, or for newspapers and magazines. Most of the women felt a patriotic and humanitarian duty to volunteer, although some went for the adventure or to escape lives of boredom at home. Using diaries, letters, memoirs, and organizational records, the Schneiders allow these women to tell their own stories.

American Women in World War I: They Also Served by Lettie Gavin (University Press of Colorado, 1997) focuses on women's war work during 1917 to 1918 only. Gavin concentrates on the women who served in the various branches of the armed services, including navy yeomen, female marines, army nurses, AEF Signal Corps telephone operators, and Army Medical Department civilian aides. These titles make known the work of these courageous, adventurous women, whose stories have been ignored.

1180. Scott, Anne Firor. *Natural Allies: Women's Associations in American History.* Urbana: University of Illinois Press, 1991. 242p. (Women in American History). bibliog. index. ISBN (OP); 0252063201pa.

Scott provides a fascinating history of women's associations from the end of the eighteenth century through the 1930s. The author's main thesis is that voluntary organizations became a place for women "to exercise the public influence otherwise denied them" (p. 177). These associations, including the Woman's Christian Temperance Union, the Young Women's Christian Association, and the National Association of Colored Women's Clubs, occupied themselves with a variety of social ills such as poverty, alcohol abuse, prostitution, child labor, and occupational safety, and they often helped influence societal beliefs and even encourage legislation in ways individual women could not. Communities also benefited from the work of these groups in the founding of orphanages, homes for the elderly, juvenile courts, and libraries. Part 1 reviews three phases in the early evolution of women's associations prior to the Civil War: benevolent societies, organizations dedicated to reform such as temperance and antislavery groups, and aid societies for soldiers both during and immediately after the war. In part 2, Scott organizes the histories of women's groups into three categories: religious, self-improvement, and community and social improvement organizations.

In *Women and the Work of Benevolence: Morality, Politics, and Class in the Nineteenth-Century United States* (Yale University Press, 1990), Lori D. Ginzberg writes that her book "reevaluates changes in the ideology and practice of a specifically female benevolent activism in light of the essentially class nature of benevolence" (p. 7). Ginzberg argues that class and gender activities interacted to shape benevolent activity during the nineteenth century. Both a social and intellectual history, *Women and the Work of Benevolence* provides new insights into how the changing nature of women's benevolent work not only altered gender and class ideologies, but also helped shape American political life in the late nineteenth century and beyond.

1181. Terborg-Penn, Rosalyn. *African American Women in the Struggle for the Vote, 1850–1920.* Bloomington: Indiana University Press, 1998. 192p. (Blacks in the Diaspora). bibliog. index. ISBN 0253333784; 025321176Xpa.

This book tells the story of three generations of black female suffragists, beginning with the antebellum years and moving through the Progressive Era. Simultaneously fighting racism and sexism, African American women nonetheless worked for universal suffrage as early as the 1860s. African American suffragists began by joining established suffrage organizations, such as the American Woman Suffrage Association. Finding such organizations to be racist, however, black suffragists established separate organizations and worked within their local communities to secure universal suffrage. This struggle is told through the lives of several important black activists, including Sarah Parker Redmond, Angelina Weld Grimké, Mary Ann Shadd Cary, and other lesser-known women. The final chapter explores the disillusionment felt by many African American women after passage of the Nineteenth Amendment because many black women continued to be disenfranchised for many years after 1920. Nonetheless, Terborg-Penn argues that African American women learned valuable lessons in their fight for suffrage, lessons that would help them as they struggled to gain political and social equality after 1920.

Another title devoted to this topic is *African American Women and the Vote, 1837–1965*, edited by Ann D. Gordon and others (University of Massachusetts Press, 1997). The ten essays cover the period from 1837, the date of the first Anti-Slavery Convention of American Women, to 1965, the year of the passage of the Voting Rights Act. Essays provide case studies of individual women and also investigate larger themes such as clubwomen and electoral politics in the 1920s. *How Long? How Long? African American Women in the Struggle for Civil Rights* by Belinda Robnett (Oxford University Press, 1997) presents a gendered analysis of the struggle for civil rights. Employing interviews, archival materials, and secondary sources, Robnett focuses on women's roles as leaders in the movement.

1999 CORE TITLES

Berger, Iris, and E. Francis White. *Women in Sub-Saharan Africa: Restoring Women to History.* Bloomington: Indiana University Press, 1999. 169p. (Restoring Women to History). bibliog. index. ISBN 0253334764; 0253213096pa.

Boris, Eileen, and Nupir Chaudhuri, eds. *Voices of Women Historians: The Personal, the Political, the Professional*. Bloomington: Indiana University Press, 1999. 259p. bibliog. index. ISBN 0253334942; 0253212758pa.

Burton, Antoinette, ed. *Gender, Sexuality, and Colonial Modernities*. New York: Routledge, 1999. 232p. (Routledge Research in Gender and History, 2). bibliog. index. ISBN 0415200687.

Commire, Anne, ed. *Women in World History: A Biographical Encyclopedia*. Waterford, CT: Yorkin Publications, 1999. 16v. bibliog. index. ISBN 078763736X set.

Faderman, Lillian. *To Believe in Women: What Lesbians Have Done for America—A History*. Boston: Houghton Mifflin, 1999. 434p. bibliog. index. ISBN 039585010X; 0618056971.

Finnegan, Margaret Mary. *Selling Suffrage: Consumer Culture and Votes for Women*. New York: Columbia University Press, 1999. 222p. (Popular Culture, Everyday Lives). bibliog. index. ISBN 0231107382; 0231107390pa.

Leonard, Elizabeth D. *All the Daring of the Soldier: Women of the Civil War Armies*. New York: Norton, 1999. 368p. bibliog. index. ISBN 0393047121 (OP); 0140298584pa.

Nashat, Guity, and Judith E. Tucker. *Women in the Middle East and North Africa: Restoring Women to History*. Bloomington: Indiana University Press, 1999. 160p. (Restoring Women to History). bibliog. index. ISBN 0253334780; 0253212642pa.

Navarro, Marysa, and Virginia Sanchez, with Kecia Ali. *Women in Latin America and the Caribbean: Restoring Women to History*. Bloomington: Indiana University Press, 1999. 128p. (Restoring Women to History). bibliog. index. ISBN 0253334799; 025321307Xpa.

Pez, Emma. *The Decolonial Imaginary: Writing Chicanas into History*. Bloomington: Indiana University Press, 1999. 181p. (Theories of Representation and Difference). bibliog. index. ISBN 0253335043; 0253212839pa.

Prell, Riv-Ellen. *Fighting to Become Americans: Jews, Gender, and the Anxiety of Assimilation*. Boston: Beacon Press, 1999. 319p. bibliog. index. ISBN 0807036323; 0807036331pa.

Ramusack, Barbara N., and Sharon Sievers. *Women in Asia: Restoring Women to History*. Bloomington: Indiana University Press, 1999. 266p. (Restoring Women to History). bibliog. index. ISBN 0253334810; 0253212677pa.

Rupp, Leila. *A Desired Past: A Short History of Same-Sex Love in America*. Chicago: University of Chicago Press, 1999. 232p. bibliog. index. ISBN 0226731553; 0226731561pa.

Scott, Joan Wallach. *Gender and the Politics of History*. Rev. ed. New York: Columbia University Press, 1999. 267p. (Gender and Culture). bibliog. index. ISBN 0231118570.

Sinha, Mrinalini, Donna Guy, and Angela Woollacott, eds. *Feminisms and Internationalism*. Oxford: Blackwell, 1999. 264p. bibliog. index. ISBN 0631209190.

Thompson, Kathleen, and Hilary MacAustin, eds. *The Face of Our Past: Images of Black Women from Colonial America to the Present*. Bloomington: Indiana University Press, 1999. 258p. bibliog. index. ISBN 025333635X.

Vivante, Bella, ed. *Women's Roles in Ancient Civilizations: A Reference Guide*. Westport, CT: Greenwood Press, 1999. 389p. bibliog. index. ISBN 0313301271.

WORLD WIDE WEB/INTERNET SITES

1182. *American Women's History: A Research Guide*. http://www.mtsu.edu/~kmiddlet/history/women.html.

This Web site provides citations to more than 2,000 print and Internet sources and more than 400 links to digitized collections. Ken Middleton, a reference librarian at Middle Tennessee State University, maintains the site. Middleton also has a master's degree in history. This well-organized site includes five broad categories: general reference and biographical sources; a subject index to research sources, which provides eighty specific topics; state and regional history sources; a guide to finding books, articles, and theses; and a guide to finding primary sources. Each of these five categories is appropriately organized according to the subject, format, or material on that page. For example, the page listing general reference sources is divided into different types of reference resources such as statistical sources, encyclopedias, or bibliographies. Each of the eighty topics on the subject page includes reference sources for that topic, but also links to primary collections if they exist. A bonus feature of this page is a section called "Talking about Women's History" that leads the researcher to online interviews dealing with that topic. While Middleton says that the audience for this site is serious researchers, it will be valuable for undergraduates and even high-school students.

1183. *Diotíma: Materials for the Study of Women and Gender in the Ancient World*. http://www.stoa.org/diotima/.

According to the welcome message, *Diotíma* "serves as an interdisciplinary resource for anyone interested in patterns of gender around the ancient Mediterranean and as a forum for collaboration among instructors who teach courses about women and gender in the ancient world." The site includes course materials, a searchable bibliography, and links to many online resources, including articles, book reviews, databases, and images. One page called "Anthology" provides access to several translated materials, including scholarly works and translated primary sources. Another page provides access to a variety of Internet sources on biblical studies. The images button offers links to several sources of images, including the *Perseus Art Databases* with more than 30,000 images, as well as links to several museums. The searchable bibliography allows users to search by keyword or to find resources under specific topics. *Diotíma* is a part of the STOA Consortium, an organization for electronic publishing in the humanities.

1184. *A Geographic Guide to Uncovering Women's History in Archival Collections.*
http://www.lib.utsa.edu/Archives/WomenGender/links.html.

This site serves as a guide to Web pages of libraries, archives, and other repositories that have primary source collections by or about women. A project of the Archives for Research on Women and Gender Project at the University of Texas at San Antonio, the guide represents those libraries and repositories that have Web pages with information about women's collections. The index is arranged alphabetically by state. Each listing provides a brief annotation of the collection with a link to the site. There is also a listing for institutions outside the United States. While this guide is not comprehensive, it is nonetheless an excellent access point for scholars and librarians to "uncover" resources relating to women's history.

1185. *H-Women.* http://www2.h-net.msu.edu/~women/.

H-Women is a subset of HNet, an international interdisciplinary organization maintained at Michigan State University "dedicated to developing the enormous educational potential of the Internet and the World Wide Web." *H-Women* serves as an electronic discussion group to provide a forum for college and university historians to discuss women's history. Subscription is free, and subscribers automatically receive messages in their computer mailboxes. Additional resources on *H-Women* include reviews of new books; syllabi and other teaching materials, including outlines and handouts; bibliographies; finding aids for manuscript collections and links to organizations with significant manuscript collections; and reports on new software, datasets, and CD-ROMs. *H-Women* also posts announcements of conferences, fellowships, and jobs. This is an excellent source for faculty and scholars interested in women's history.

1186. *Lesbian History Project.* http://isd.usc.edu/~retter/main.html.

The Lesbian History Project has several goals: to increase visibility of lesbians; to provide an online record of lesbian history; to aid lesbian archives and collections in providing links to their holdings; to aid scholars in finding materials; to promote research about lesbian and LGBT history; to encourage individuals and groups to donate original papers, documents, and memorabilia to archives; to assist individuals and projects in doing oral histories on lesbians; to use the Web site as an educational and training tool; and to network with other institutions doing similar work. Maintained by Yolanda Retter, a librarian at the University of Southern California, the site includes notable lesbians, archives and collections, bibliographies and syllabi, a list of dissertations and theses on lesbian history from 1968 to 1998, articles and interviews, and links to lesbian history in other countries and sites relating to lesbian history. There is no indication of how often *Lesbian History Project* is updated. However, Retter has done an amazing job of pulling together information on lesbian history.

1187. *Medieval Feminist Index or Feminae: Medieval Women and Gender Index.* http://www.haverford.edu/library/reference/mschaus/mfi/whatis.html.

This Web-based index to journal articles, book reviews, and essays in books about women, sexuality, and gender during the Middle Ages was started by librarians and scholars in 1996. Margaret Schaus, librarian at Haverford College, currently serves as the coordinator. *Feminae* indexes articles from more than 400 women's journals and collections of essays. Indexing goes back to 1994, but the editors note that the index is far from complete. For example, indexing for the year 1995 is 95 percent complete, but for 2001 only 38 percent of the indexing is finished. *Medieval Feminist Index* covers the time period from 450 C.E. to 1500 C.E., with Russia extending to 1613, the beginning of the Romanov dynasty. The geographic scope is Europe, North Africa, and the Middle East as well as areas in which Europeans traveled. Since 1996, publications in

English, French, German, and Spanish have been indexed, and in 2001, materials in Italian began to be included in the database.

1188. *National Women's History Project.* http://www.nwhp.org/.

The mission of this exceptional site is to "recognize and celebrate the diverse and historic accomplishments of women by providing information and educational materials and programs." Founded in 1980, the NWHP was the lead body in lobbying Congress to designate March as National Women's History Month. The attractive, well-organized Web site includes links across the top of the front page to news and events, frequently asked questions, a catalog of publications, information on Women's History Month, and a section called "The Learning Place," designed to provide information and materials about women's history. "The Learning Place" has a biography center, links to museums and organizations by states, a teacher's lounge, a student center, and a parents' corner. This site will be especially valuable to K–12 teachers and public librarians, but many others will benefit from the wealth of information available. The *National Collaboration for Women's History Sites* (http://ncwhs.oah.org) was created in 2001 by members from twenty organizations who wanted to promote the preservation of historic sites where women have made history. NCWHS provides links to the twenty sites, which include historic sites such as the Women's Rights Historic Park in Seneca Falls, libraries such as the First Ladies Library, museums, organizations, and individuals and institutions who work with the project.

1189. *WWW Virtual Library: Women's History.* http://www.iisg.nl/~womhist/vivalink .html.

Maintained by the International Institute of Social History, this site is one of the few women's history Internet sources with an international focus. The top page, which is well organized and quite attractive, includes several general headings such as reference, conferences and calls for papers, and Web resources organized chronologically, geographically, and by special topic. Each general heading has subheadings listed underneath. A search box on the top page allows users to easily locate a resource by keyword. This site also hosts *ViVa*, a current international bibliography of articles published in English, French, German, Dutch, Danish, Norwegian, and Swedish, selected from 160 European, American, Canadian, Asian, Australian, and New Zealand journals. The database includes records for more than 7,000 articles published from 1975 to 2003 in historical and women's studies journals. *WWW Virtual Library: Women's History* is an excellent resource for serious scholars.

15   Literature

Rebecca S. Albitz, Vicki Litzinger, Dorothy Mays

Women and literature is an expansive topic that produces a great deal of original thought and overlaps with many other subject areas. During the latter half of the twentieth century, the focus of much of the scholarship in the area incorporated feminist literary criticism in order to frame discussions of genre, the canon, and the place of women's literature within the academy. Through these examinations, the image of the woman as the "other" predominates. Whether it be through the depiction of women as aliens, women as the inferior gender, or women's experiences as unusual or abnormal, feminist literary criticism has focused on and explored this phenomenon.

This chapter focuses on works that explore women's writings in all genres and from all parts of the world. Titles have been organized in the following categories: "General Theory and Criticism," "Biography and Autobiography," "Europe," "Great Britain," "North America," "Women's Literature from Other Countries," and "Theater."

To be included in this chapter, titles had to be well reviewed and determined to have made a contribution to the field. However, there are a few exceptions that we decided to include that were not widely reviewed, but addressed an area of women's literary studies that had not been studied previously. One of the primary hurdles facing this chapter's authors was the lack of reviews for publications in this last area. Outside of those journals that focus on women's literary studies (*Tulsa Studies in Women's Literature*) and some more general literary journals (*American Literature*), few publications consistently reviewed new publications in women's literature. For example, many titles were found in the genre of African women's literature, but most titles had three or fewer reviews, and even fewer yet were in literature or women's studies publications. Further, these titles were purchased only by a handful of libraries, and many of these libraries did not freely lend these titles through interlibrary loan services.

Even though there is a lack of review sources, there was a profusion of titles published in this field during the period covered by this bibliography. Because of the volume of titles and space restrictions within this reference publication, the authors chose to include only reference works, Web sites, close readings of texts, and theoretical discussions about texts and women's literature in general. Actual literary works were not included, and anthologies were included only if the introduction or other original observations were considered important to this area's scholarly dialogue.

Despite our best efforts, we wonder what significant titles have been missed in this process and certainly question the overall review process of new titles. We also realize that many critical works on specific genres, such as mysteries or romance, may have been missed because they are not yet part of the canon. We cannot help but ask, "What literature remains hidden, what voices remain silenced, and what insights are lost in this process?"

Dorothy Mays wrote the Theater section. The books presented in this section document women's participation in theater from antiquity through the 1990s. Most selections examine women's contributions in the areas of acting, playwriting, directing, and history; however, this chapter also features explorations of women's use of theater as an avenue for social protest and commentary. Several titles reflect the philosophical implications of feminism within the evolving discipline of theater studies. With the exception of Shakespeare, this work does not include feminist interpretations and critiques of works by male playwrights. Since scholars have published several critical studies about significant women, this chapter delves into broader movements, genres, and historical eras. This chapter does not cover individual plays, collections of plays by the same author, or, with a few exceptions, anthologies of plays by various authors. The featured anthologies provide supplementary representation to the scant number of definitive studies that exist for specific time periods or groups of playwrights. For readers interested in research on individual women of the theater, the theater reference titles will provide excellent points of entry.

REFERENCE SOURCES

1190. Beach, Cecilia. *French Women Playwrights before the Twentieth Century: A Checklist*. Westport, CT: Greenwood Press, 1994. 251p. bibliog. index. ISBN 0313291748. *French Women Playwrights of the Twentieth Century: A Checklist*. Westport, CT: Greenwood Press, 1996. 515p. bibliog. index. ISBN 0313291756.

Beach addresses the long-neglected topic of French women playwrights in this two-volume reference set, compiling the most comprehensive listing on the subject at the time of publication. The first volume lists active playwrights from the sixteenth through the nineteenth centuries. Each entry includes the playwright's place and date of birth, date of death, other professions and activities that the playwright engaged in, the titles of her plays, and coded references to the Parisian libraries that house the plays. The second volume covers twentieth-century playwrights and mirrors the first volume in both arrangement and featured information. Due to the size of this project, Beach limits inclusion to playwrights who actually lived in France, as opposed to expanding the scope of the work to include writers living in other French-speaking areas of Europe, Africa, and the Americas. However, the excellent anthology *Plays by Women: An International Anthology* (Ubu Repertory Theater, volume 1, 1988; volume 2, 1994; volume 3, 1996), edited by Françoise Kourilsky and Catherine Temerson, features the plays of these and other French-speaking women playwrights. Katherine Kelly's anthology *Modern Drama by Women, 1880s–1930s: An International Anthology* (Routledge, 1996) includes rare works by twelve women playwrights from other geographical locations, including Japan, Russia, Argentina, the United States, and various European countries.

1191. Berney, K.A. *Contemporary Women Dramatists*. Detroit: St. James Press, 1994. 335p. bibliog. index. ISBN 1558622128.

Focusing on women playwrights from the United States, the United Kingdom, and Canada, this reference work provides biographical information on both well-known and emerging writers. Each of the eighty-four entries begins with a listing of the writer's birthplace, degrees, marital status, occupational history, and awards, followed by a complete list of published plays, screenplays, radio plays, and critical studies, followed by an essay that outlines the major themes, influences, and accomplishments of the playwright and sometimes includes her comments. For information about playwrights working in Great Britain, see *British and Irish Women Dramatists since 1958* (Open University Press, 1993), edited by Trevor Griffiths and Margaret Llewellyn-Jones. This important work analyzes various theater trends, records women's achievements, and examines each playwright's approach to themes, including sexuality, oppression, and the body. More appropriate titles for the circulating collection that provide rare insight into diverse aesthetics, methods, and issues facing women playwrights who work in countries such as China, Japan, and Indonesia include *Interviews with Contemporary Women Playwrights* (Beech Tree,

1987), edited by Kathleen Betsko and Rachel Koenig, and *Performing Women, Performing Feminisms: Interviews with International Women Playwrights* (Australian Drama Studies Association Academic Publications, 1997), which emerged from the Third International Women Playwrights Conference in 1995, edited by Joanne Tompkins and Julie Holledge. Susan Bassnett documents the ongoing Magdalena Project, established in 1986 in Cardiff, which provides research opportunities for women in all aspects of theater practice, in *Magdalena: International Women's Experimental Theatre* (Berg, 1989). She examines the workshops, performances, participants (thirty-eight women from fifteen countries), and theoretical debates that took place during the First International Festival of Women in Contemporary Theatre, held in Cardiff, Wales, August 1986.

1192. Blain, Virginia, Patricia Clements, and Isobel Grundy, eds. *Feminist Companion to Literature in English: Women Writers from the Middle Ages to the Present.* New Haven, CT: Yale University Press, 1990. 1231p. bibliog. index. (OP)

Feminist Companion to Literature in English is a biographical resource that spans six centuries (1400 through the mid-1980s), focusing on women writers from around the world who write in English. Although the majority of the entries document women from Great Britain, the United States, and Canada, the editors also include women writers from Asia, Africa, the Caribbean, and the South Pacific, allowing a glimpse at a variety of cultures and regions. The editors include diarists, pamphleteers, and genre writers, further broadening the scope of this work. The editors alphabetically organize the brief entries according to the author's most commonly known name, provide information about birth names and pseudonyms within the entries, and also include ample cross-references to other biographical entries and to a limited number of subject and genre entries. A separate subject listing, as well as an index of writers arranged chronologically by birth date, is provided at the end of the work.

Maureen Bell, George Parfill, and Simon Shepherd's *A Biographical Dictionary of English Women Writers, 1580–1720* (Wheatsheaf, 1990) deals with a variety of women writers who worked between 1580 and 1720. The dictionary section contains more than 550 entries, which the authors organize according to the most commonly used name for the writer, although they include cross-references to pseudonyms. Entries also include places of birth, residence, occupation, religion, husband's name and occupation, and a bibliography of the author's writings. A series of appendices provide more focused information, including lists of anonymous works that scholars have attributed to women writers, as well as critical discussions of issues that arose during the creation of the dictionary. While other reference works may cover the same period, this dictionary is valuable for its breadth of coverage and discussion of process.

1193. Boos, Florence, ed., with Lynn Miller. *Bibliography of Women and Literature: Articles and Books by and about Women from 600 to 1975.* New York: Holmes & Meier, 1989. 2v. 781p. ISBN 0841906939.

This ambitious work represents a compilation of three major annual bibliographies that the *Journal of Women and Literature* issued between 1976 and 1978. An appendix augments this bibliography with entries from *PMLA: The Journal of the Modern Language Association* and *Modern Language Research* bibliographies from 1979 to 1981. This work includes well over 10,000 entries that Boos compiled from more than 300 different journals. *Bibliography of Women and Literature* includes chapters for Great Britain, America, Canada, Australia, New Zealand, and other English-speaking countries. It includes works in non-English languages, as well as chronological subdivisions for Great Britain and America. Boos subdivides each chapter by genre and alphabetically arranges the articles according to the particular author discussed in the article. The editor divides the three indexes that provide access to this substantial work according to authors discussed in the articles, authors of the articles, and genre.

1194. Buck, Claire, ed. *The Bloomsbury Guide to Women's Literature.* New York: Prentice Hall, 1992. 1171p. (OP)

Buck has compiled a one-volume reference work that focuses on women's writings, covering every geographic region and time period. This work includes all types of literature, such as fiction, diaries, and letters. Forty scholars contributed to this work. The guide, which Buck alphabetically arranges and cross-references, contains more than 5,000 entries regarding writers, seminal works, traditions, movements, and philosophies. Although the entries provide a large amount of rich information, a series of essays that explore the history of women's writing represents the unique strength of this work. Organized both chronologically and geographically, these essays place the entries that follow in their appropriate historical and sociological contexts. Numerous cross-references that link the essays to the guide entries direct readers to more detailed information about the person or concept under discussion. The international scope, detailed entries, and the contextualization of these essays make this a truly useful reference source.

1195. Davidson, Cathy N., and Linda Wagner-Martin, editors in chief. *The Oxford Companion to Women's Writing in the United States.* New York: Oxford University Press, 1995. 1021p. bibliog. index. ISBN 0195066081.

Although the editors limit this work's geographic scope to the United States, this single volume contains an immense amount of valuable information. This source includes women who, although born in other countries, lived in the United States. *The Oxford Companion to Women's Writing in the United States* represents writers of all genres, such as literature, the sciences, and the social sciences. The editors include historic and literary movements, literary theories, and a variety of additional topics in 400 alphabetically arranged entries. Cross-references within entries refer readers to more in-depth entries on related topics. The index provides lists of subtopics that this work covers under broader subject headings. Two parallel timelines provided at the end of this work include highlights of social history and everyday life in the United States, as well as a history of women's writing. These timelines create a visual tool that offers readers an efficient means to compare major historical events with specific events in the literary world. *The Oxford Companion to Women's Writing in the United States* is one of the most complete resources for those conducting research on women writers in the United States.

1196. Fister, Barbara. *Third World Women's Literature: A Dictionary and Guide to Materials in English.* Westport, CT: Greenwood Press, 1995. 390p. index. ISBN 0313289883.

Only a few reference works concentrate exclusively on women writers from the Third World. Fister's work, a useful addition to this body of literature, focuses on women born in Western-defined regions within the Third World, in addition to women who spent a substantial portion of their lives in such regions. Fister includes the following regions in her work: the Caribbean, Central and Latin America, Africa, the Middle East, South Asia, and Asia (excluding Japan, Australia, and New Zealand). Entries consist of a brief biography of each writer and a list of selected works and criticism, available in English or English translation. Entries focusing on individual works consist of brief summaries and commentaries on the style and significance of the work. Thematic entries introduce issues and ideas relevant to Third World women's literature. According to Fister, she subjectively selected writers based on availability of the works. Substantial appendices include lists of writers organized by geographic affiliation and chronology, as well as bibliographies and general criticism. Although this work is not exhaustive, it provides a useful overview of literature from areas that are becoming of great interest in the field of women's literature.

1197. Furtado, Ken, and Nancy Hellner. *Gay and Lesbian American Plays: An Annotated Bibliography*. Metuchen, NJ: Scarecrow Press, 1993. 217p. bibliog. indexes. ISBN 0810826895.

Furtado and Hellner update Terry Helbing's groundbreaking work *The Gay Theatre Alliance Directory of Plays* (JH Press, 1980) in this much-needed bibliography. Furtado and Hellner organize the nearly 700 plays according to playwright, mostly well-known and regional American authors. The authors present the following information about each play: publication information (if applicable); type of play (farce, dramatic monologue, or comedy); a brief synopsis; the number of acts, sets, and characters; date and location of initial production (if applicable); and original holder of performance rights. The authors also include a short bibliography of books on gay and lesbian theater history and criticism, an appendix listing plays with incomplete information, and a generous number of indexes, arranged according to agent, playwright, theater, and title. The title index features up to three codes per play and covers categories such as gay primary theme and lesbian or transgender major characters. Furtado and Hellner exclude performance pieces, camp, drag, and other alternative genres. Nevertheless, this work successfully fills in several gaps in the literature.

1198. Kester-Shelton, Pamela. *Feminist Writers*. Detroit: St. James Press, 1996. 641p. bibliog. indexes. ISBN 1558622179.

In the traditional style of other St. James Press reference titles, Kester-Shelton compiles nearly 300 entries that center on novelists, authors of other fictional genres, and writers of non-fiction with a feminist stance. The author selected writers according to the following criteria: feminist content in the author's work, the degree to which scholars have studied the author, and the availability of English-language versions of the works. Kester-Shelton relied on several well-known scholars in the field of feminist writing to help her generate a list of writers. International in scope, this work concentrates primarily on twentieth-century female writers, although the author does include earlier writers' works that scholars consider seminal. Each author entry provides biographical data, a complete list of published works arranged by genre, and a list of works focusing on the author, including biographies, critical essays, and interviews. Entries present critical essays that place the authors within the feminist movement while simultaneously revealing the impact of their writing on the movement. Kester-Shelton provides indexes for authors, titles, and subjects, as well as bibliographies that refer to special collections, feminist periodicals, and online resources. The number of writers that this work deals with is limited since each entry is so detailed. Nonetheless, this excellent source is a valuable introduction to specific feminist writers in that it provides an overall perspective of the feminist writing movement.

1199. Nordquist, Joan. *Feminist Literary Theory*. Santa Cruz, CA: Reference and Research Services, 1998. 64p. (Social Theory: A Bibliographic Series, 52). ISBN 1892068036pa.

This bibliography contains citations for recent and key core books, pamphlets, papers, dissertations and theses, and articles that appear both in books and periodicals concerning feminist literary theory. Focusing on social, philosophical, literary, and feminist literature, Nordquist includes publications not only from mainstream or well-known publishers, but also from alternative publishers, small presses, and activist organizations. The author organizes *Feminist Literary The-*

ory according to broad topics or geographic locations and includes works by women from several ethnicities and regions of the world, including Latina, African American, Native American, Asian American, and other women of color. Nordquist also includes lesbian literary theory. Nordquist alphabetically arranges each entry by author or corporate author within each section. Although she does not clearly indicate the inclusion dates of the titles, her coverage of these critical writings makes this work an excellent starting point for anyone conducting research in the field.

1200. Peterson, Jane T., and Suzanne Bennett. *Women Playwrights of Diversity: A Bio-bibliographical Sourcebook*. Westport, CT: Greenwood Press, 1997. 399p. bibliog. index. ISBN 0313291799.

Since mainstream theaters rarely produce the work of minority women playwrights, Peterson and Bennett highlight the careers and work of such women to expose them to a wider audience. The volume begins with four short essays that chronicle the history and achievements of Asian American, African American, Latina, and lesbian women playwrights. The majority of this work, however, consists of entries devoted to individual playwrights. Each entry contains a biographical sketch, a description of the plays, a selected production history for each work, notes on play availability, a list of awards, and a brief bibliography of criticism and reviews. This resource should prove beneficial for both professional practitioners and academic researchers who wish to expand their knowledge on the number and variety of plays that minority women playwrights have crafted. Excellent anthologies that contain works of some of the women covered in the sourcebook include *Shattering the Myth: Plays by Hispanic Women* (Arte Publico, 1992), selected by Denise Chavez and edited by Linda Feyder; *The Politics of Life: Four Plays by Asian American Women* (Temple University Press, 1993), edited by Velina Hasu Houston; and *Unbroken Thread: An Anthology of Plays by Asian American Women* (University of Massachusetts Press, 1993), edited by Roberta Uno, who provides a useful appendix that contains production histories for almost 268 plays by approximately seventy playwrights. Uno and Kathy A. Perkins edited *Contemporary Plays by Women of Color: An Anthology* (Routledge, 1996), a collection that represents a variety of voices and styles of Latina, African American, Asian American, and Native American playwrights.

1201. Pollack, Sandra, and Denise D. Knight, eds. *Contemporary Lesbian Writers of the United States: A Bio-bibliographical Critical Sourcebook*. Westport, CT: Greenwood Press, 1993. 640p. bibliog. indexes. ISBN 0313282153.

Along with other titles in the Greenwood Press Bio-bibliographical Sourcebook series, *Contemporary Lesbian Writers* provides useful information about major writers who identified themselves as lesbians sometime between 1970 and 1992. Pollack and Knight opted not to include authors who publicly have not come out as lesbians; they contacted writers whose status was unknown and followed the author's wishes. Each entry includes five key components: the writer's biography, a discussion of the author's major works and themes, an overview of critical studies, a bibliography of the writer's works, and a bibliography of critical works. As a result of the dearth of critical writings in mainstream literature, two bibliographies list citations from both traditional publishing resources and more ephemeral ones, such as newsletters and pamphlets. The scholarly quality of the signed essays, the vast amount of information contained within each entry, and the quality of research evident make this an important reference tool. Other titles in this series include *Women Writers in German-Speaking Countries: A Bio-bibliographical Critical Sourcebook*, edited by Elke P. Frederiksen and Elizabeth G. Ametsbichler, 1998; *Nineteenth-Century American Women Writers: A Bio-bibliographical Critical Sourcebook*, edited by Denise D. Knight, 1997; *Spanish Women Writers: A Bio-bibliographical Source Book*, edited by Linda Gould Levine, Ellen

Engelson Marson, and Gloria Feiman Waldman, 1993; *Spanish American Women Writers: A Bio-bibliographical Source Book*, edited by Diane E. Marting, 1990; *Italian Women Writers: A Bio-bibliographical Sourcebook*, edited by Rinaldina Russell, 1994; *French Women Writers: A Bio-bibliographical Source Book*, edited by Eva Martin Sartori and Dorothy Wynne Zimmerman, 1991; and *Jewish American Women Writers: A Bio-bibliographical and Critical Sourcebook*, editor in chief Ann R. Shapiro, 1994. These reference sources provide researchers with an excellent starting point for uncovering brief biographical information about women writers. With some variation from title to title, editors generally employ the following format: a biographical sketch, an essay discussing the context of the author's work, a discussion of themes evident throughout the writer's works, a bibliography of the author's works, and a bibliography of critical writings. The editors determined the scope of each work and outlined the criteria that they used to include authors in each sourcebook.

1202. Robinson, Alice M., Vera Mowry Roberts, and Milly S. Barranger, eds. *Notable Women in the American Theatre: A Biographical Dictionary*. New York: Greenwood Press, 1989. 1008p. bibliog. index. ISBN 0313272174.

Although scholars have produced several reference resources about famous actresses and playwrights, the value of this dictionary lies in its coverage of the less glamorous theatrical professionals: choreographers, theater critics, producers, directors, educators, designers, and agents. Focusing on American theater history from colonial times through the 1980s, the editors profile an astonishing number of prominent women in a wide array of theatrical professions. Each entry is three to five pages in length, explores the entrant's family life, education, and professional career, and concludes with an extensive bibliography. With more than 450 entries, this work provides a comprehensive resource for identifying and gathering hard-to-find biographical information on women who became successful in a male-dominated field.

Jane Kathleen Curry's *Nineteenth-Century American Women Stage Managers* (Greenwood Press, 1994) examines the various obstacles, including legal restrictions and societal beliefs about acceptable gender roles, that women who wanted to manage theaters had to contend with. Curry covers more than fifty managers (all of them white) from various regions of the country and includes a useful bibliography.

1203. Schierbeck, Sachiko. *Japanese Women Novelists in the 20th Century: 104 Biographies, 1900–1993*. Copenhagen: Museum Tusculanum Press, 1994. 378p. bibliog. ISBN 8772892684pa.

This work, one of the few in-depth resources that address Japanese women novelists, is an invaluable biographical source for advanced researchers and novices. The introduction provides not only a historical overview of writing in Japan, but also a discussion of women's place within this universe. The introduction specifically places the featured writers within their historic and social contexts. The chronologically arranged entries provide brief biographical sketches, synopses of the writer's most significant works, and a bibliography of works published in Japanese. Entries also include titles that scholars have translated into English, as well as other Western European languages. Schierbeck selected the women featured in this work according to whether they had received one of a number of Japan's major literary prizes.

Schierbeck's *Postwar Japanese Women Writers: An Up-to-Date Bibliography* (East Asian Institute, University of Copenhagen, 1989) follows the same organizational format, but focuses on women who won prestigious literary prizes for the novel between 1947 and 1989. The author addresses how the American occupation and postwar conditions in Japan affected the social and political climate of the country, creating a boom period for women writers. Although many of the authors discussed in these two resources overlap, *Postwar Japanese Women Writers* provides a more focused approach and would prove useful to individuals interested in the postwar era. Chieko Mulhen's *Japanese Women Writers: A Bio-critical Sourcebook* (Greenwood Press, 1994) is another source that deals with Japanese women authors. It follows the same format as other titles in this series.

1204. Shattock, Joanne. *The Oxford Guide to British Women Writers*. New York: Oxford University Press, 1993. 492p. bibliog. (OP)

The *Oxford Guide to British Women Writers* provides a broad, biographical overview of British women writers from the medieval period until the early 1990s. In this work, Shattock attempts to make known the works of more than 400 women writers whose works cover a broad range of genres. She includes scholarly and critical works, particularly those written during the past twenty years, about these writers. Shattock selected women for inclusion in this resource based upon either birth or residence in the United Kingdom during the years the women actively engaged in writing. Shattock also included writers whom scholars have studied, as well as women writers who potentially could gain the interest of current scholars. Each entry includes a brief biography, a list of the writer's major publications, and significant features of her work. The author includes suggestions for further reading at the end of each entry. Although most entries focus on writers, Shattock also provides subject entries.

British Women Writers: A Critical Reference, edited by Janet Todd (Continuum, 1989), also presents the lives of women working in mainstream literature, such as the novel. This title includes women whose works represent such genres traditionally classified "female" as children's literature and the public letter of advice. Each entry includes a list of the author's publications, as well as critical writings about the author's works. This source provides an index of terms and people mentioned within the essays. *An Encyclopedia of British Women Writers* by Paul Schlueter and June Schlueter (Rutgers University Press, 1998) is a similar, more recent encyclopedia that includes biographies of women living in Great Britain, as well as women who immigrated to Great Britain from Commonwealth countries. Entries include biographical information and citations to literary criticism in periodical literature. These three reference sources nicely complement each other.

1205. Steadman, Susan M. *Dramatic Re-visions: An Annotated Bibliography of Feminism and Theatre, 1972–1988*. Chicago: American Library Association, 1991. 367p. index. ISBN 0838905773.

Although Steadman devotes several chapters to feminist theory and performance issues in this work, other chapters cover pioneering and contemporary playwrights, as well as feminist reassessments of men's playwriting. This comprehensive bibliography includes citations for both books and journal articles, with brief descriptive annotations. Appendices list special issues of journals that feature women's topics, as well as resources for women in theater. Name, title, era, and subject indexes make this work a definitive resource for locating information on feminist theater during the 1970s and 1980s. Christy Gavin assesses key titles in feminist theater criticism, includes an annotated list of book chapters, journal articles, and special issues of journals covering theater and playwrights, and examines individual playwrights in conjunction with critical responses to their work in *American Women Playwrights, 1964–1989: A Research Guide and Annotated Bibliography* (Garland, 1993).

1206. Wilson, Katharina M. *Encyclopedia of Continental Women Writers*. New York: Garland, 1991. 2v. 1389p. ISBN 0824085477.

The focus and depth of the *Encyclopedia of Continental Women Writers* make this work of unique interest to researchers. Concentrating on 1,800 women writers who write fiction and non-fiction, this encyclopedia includes writers who are central in women's literature, as well as writers better known for their work in other fields, such as art and film. Spanning 1,500 years and organized alphabetically, this source provides brief (approximately one-half- to one-page) yet informative essays about the featured writers. Signed entries include dates and locations of birth, languages and genres of each writer, and lists of works. Some entries also contain brief bibliographies.

MONOGRAPHS

General Theory and Criticism

1207. Barr, Marleen S. *Feminist Fabulation: Space/Postmodern Fiction.* Iowa City: University of Iowa Press, 1992. 312p. bibliog. index. ISBN (OP); 0877453772pa.

In the introduction to this thought-provoking work, Marleen Barr writes, "*Feminist Fabulation: Space/Postmodern Fiction* is written to argue for respecting marginalized feminist fiction which attempts to correct patriarchy's problematic depictions of humanity" (p. xii). Barr argues that postmodern fiction must recognize a new "supergenre" of women's writing, which she terms "feminist fabulation." Whether she is dealing with mainstream women's writing, science fiction, fantasy, the supernatural, the utopian, or writings of feminist male authors, Barr wants to move this contemporary feminist or marginalized fiction into the space of the postmodern canon. In three sections, Barr expertly uses feminist texts to argue for reclaiming canonical space, redefining gendered space, and reconceiving narrative space. Juxtaposed within these chapters are artworks that "illuminate my intersection between the empowered and the marginalized" (p. xxi).

Barr's *Lost in Space: Probing Feminist Science Fiction and Beyond* (University of North Carolina Press, 1993) is a collection of essays the author wrote before and after her creation of the phrase "feminist fabulation." The essays in part 1 deal with feminist science fiction. The essays in part 2 focus on criticism of feminist fabulation, discussing writers such as Octavia Butler, Saul Bellow, Margaret Atwood, and Salman Rushdie. Jenny Wolmark's *Aliens and Others: Science Fiction, Feminism, and Postmodernism* (University of Iowa Press, 1994) is a critical examination of women's science fiction and postmodernism. Wolmark compares feminist science fiction writers, such as Octavia Butler and Gwyneth Jones, to examine the differences and similarities between writings that use utopian, dystopian, gender, and cultural themes. Wolmark also investigates the intersections among science fiction and postmodernism, feminism and postmodernism, and feminism and science fiction. All of these telling works would complement women's literature studies, science fiction studies, or feminist studies.

1208. DeKoven, Marianne. *Rich and Strange: Gender, History, Modernism.* Princeton, NJ: Princeton University Press, 1991. 248p. bibliog. index. ISBN (OP); 0691014965pa.

DeKoven, a prominent feminist critic, says of modernism that she finds "an unresolved contradiction or unsynthesized dialectic . . . that enacts in the realm of form an alternative to culture's hegemonic hierarchical dualisms, roots of those structures that socialism and feminism proposed to eradicate" (p. 4). In chapter 1, the author confronts this contradiction and explores the connection between literary modernism and political radicalism, especially the politics of race, gender, and class conflicts. She further explores the change in modernism during the early twentieth century, when modernist form became hidden or obscured in unresolved contradictory states.

In the remaining chapters, DeKoven pairs male- and female-signed texts to trace the evolution of modernism from its inception to its disintegration into postmodernism. DeKoven's brilliant re-readings of such texts as "The Yellow Wallpaper" and *The Turn of the Screw, The Awakening,* and *Lord Jim* and works by Adrienne Rich and John Barth bolster her view that "Male modernists generally feared the loss of hegemony the change they desired might entail, while female modernists feared punishment for desiring that utter change" (p. 4). *Rich and Strange*, an intelligent, albeit complicated, critical study, would serve as an excellent supplementary text for graduate-level courses in modern fiction.

The following works also analyze modernism and/or postmodernism: *The Pink Guitar: Writing as Feminist Practice* (Routledge, 1990) by Rachel Blau DuPlessis and *Feminine Fictions: Revisiting the Postmodern* (Routledge, 1989) by Patricia Waugh. In *The Pink Guitar*, DuPlessis, a well-respected poet and critic, updates and revises previously published essays. Essay topics include gender ideologies of male modernists and avant-garde writers, as well as modernist and postmodernist women writers' rhetorical strategies. Waugh examines the relationship between male postmodernism and female writers in *Feminist Fictions*. She considers "postmodern" a predominantly masculine and negative term. She thus explores postmodern male self-destruction and female construction, concluding that women writers "have not felt comfortable with an aesthetics of impersonality as it appears in many modernist and postmodernist manifestos" (p. 20).

1209. Donawerth, Jane. *Frankenstein's Daughters: Women Writing Science Fiction.* Syracuse, NY: Syracuse University Press, 1997. 213p. bibliog. index. ISBN 081562686X; 0815603959pa.

In *Frankenstein's Daughters*, Donawerth's topic is "women writers' responses to the defining constraints within the genre of science fiction" (p. xvii). The author argues that the pervasiveness of these constraints—science as a masculine preserve, the image of woman as alien, and the use of a male narrator—forces female science fiction writers to co-opt or circumvent these strategies just to get published. Employing historical and cultural studies methodologies as well as psychoanalytic theory in her arguments, Donawerth surveys various responses to these constraints in three thematic chapters. Chapter 1 discusses the creation of feminist utopias and quasi-utopias in various works and explores ways in which female science fiction writers use science to counter Western "masculinist" culture. Donawerth juxtaposes depictions of women and racial minorities with aliens or the "other" in chapter 2. In the final chapter, "Cross-Dressing as a Male Narrator," Donawerth depicts the various ways women have subverted the use of the male narrator in science fiction, including parodying the narrator with a female voice, punishing the narrator, or providing multiple voices for the narration. Clearly well read in women's science fiction, the author competently crafts a thoughtful and useful resource that instructors could use in courses on feminist psychology, science theory, literary theory, and gender and cultural studies.

Utopian and Science Fiction by Women: Worlds of Difference (Syracuse University Press, 1994), edited by Donawerth and Carol Kolmerten, and *Feminism, Utopia, and Narrative* (University of Tennessee Press, 1990), edited by Libby Falk Jones and Sarah Webster Goodwin, are also insightful works. *Utopian and Science Fiction by Women* contains eleven chapters in which contributors analyze and establish a history of women's texts written between 1666 and 1989. The fourteen essays in *Feminism, Utopia, and Narrative* cover a wide range of philosophical and literary topics, including the intersections between and theories of the three title words, as well as sexual politics depicted in American and British utopias.

1210. Felski, Rita. *Beyond Feminist Aesthetics: Feminist Literature and Social Change.* Cambridge, MA: Harvard University Press, 1989. 223p. bibliog. index. ISBN (OP); 0674068955pa.

Felski argues "that there exist no legitimate grounds for classifying any particular style of writing as uniquely or specifically feminine, and that it is therefore not possible to justify the classification of literary forms along gender lines or the study of women's writing as an autonomous and self-contained aesthetic body" (p. 19). Early chapters explore feminist aesthetics and subjectivity as the author discusses a variety of topics, including how one defines a feminine text, the nature of subversive writing, phallocentric language, and essentialism and apoliticism. Felski then moves on to address specific types of writing such as autobiography, narratives of emancipation and self-discovery, and romance. The author closes with a discussion of politics, aesthetics, and the feminist public sphere. Felski draws upon American and French feminist literary theory, English Marxism, and German social and aesthetic theory to argue that "there is a need for feminism to develop further interdisciplinary approaches" (p. 18). This is a difficult book that will appeal to graduate students and scholars who have been exposed to feminist literary theory.

Kate Fullbrook's *Free Women: Ethics and Aesthetics in Twentieth-Century Women's Fiction* (Temple University Press, 1990) presents close, powerful readings of texts by several female writers, including Willa Cather, Zora Neale Hurston, Dorothy Richardson, Djuna Barnes, Christina Stead, Margaret Atwood, and Toni Morrison. Fullbrook charts "the ways in which women have directed the aesthetic course of the novel in the twentieth century and the ways in which these changes are related to the ethical debates regarding women which their fiction so urgently addresses" (p. 9). Shari Benstock's *Textualizing the Feminine: On the Limits of Genre* (University of Oklahoma Press, 1991) addresses the "bricks and mortar," the everyday, the details, or the unseen in texts. Relying on a literary methodology that she refers to as "psychogrammanalysis," defined as the intersection of psychoanalysis and grammatology (punctuation, marginalia, rhetorical modes, and letters), the author closely reads James Joyce's *Finnegan's Wake* and *Ulysses*, Jacques Derrida's *The Post Card*, Virginia Woolf's *Three Guineas*, and H.D.'s *Helen in Egypt*. Benstock argues that it "is not that there is anything inherently 'feminine' in the forms of rhetoric, grammar, and punctuation I discuss but rather that apostrophes, ellipses, footnotes, and certain epistolary forms, orthographical conventions, and alphabetic signifiers occupy a textual space of loss or oversight" (p. xvii).

1211. Ferrante, Joan M. *To the Glory of Her Sex: Women's Roles in the Composition of Medieval Texts*. Bloomington: Indiana University Press, 1997. 295p. (Women of Letters). bibliog. index. ISBN 0253332540; 0253211085pa.

Ferrante analyzes letters written by or to women, as well as histories, religious texts, and courtly writings that women either commissioned or wrote themselves under the guise of a male voice. The work encompasses French, German, English, Anglo-Saxon, and Italian texts primarily from the late eleventh century to the early thirteenth century, although the author does include some material from the late classical period. Through these works, Ferrante illustrates that many women achieved the authority to determine the outcome of their lives despite the misogyny and patriarchy of the time. According to the author, "What is particularly striking in the letters and in texts commissioned by women is how much women, even those playing male roles in secular government or rising above sex in their religious lives, are aware of themselves as women and identify with powerful or effective, not oppressed, women in history" (p. 7). In section 1, Ferrante uses women's correspondence to illustrate the degree to which women were involved in all aspects of society. Section 2 demonstrates the influence women had on the writing of religious texts, history, and courtly literature. Ferrante argues that even though men authored most of these texts, the texts often emphasize women's achievements in public life. The final chapters reveal how much these writers, "religious or secular, are aware of themselves as women and speak to women in their audience, though none of them writes exclusively for women" (p. 9). *To the Glory of Her Sex* would make an excellent choice for an introductory survey on the topic.

1212. Foster, Shirley, and Judy Simons. *What Katy Read: Feminist Re-readings of "Classic" Stories for Girls.* Iowa City: University of Iowa Press, 1995. 223p. bibliog. index. ISBN 0877454930.

In *What Katy Read*, the authors examine a number of children's classics, especially girls' fiction, to explore the cultural and theoretical similarities and differences between girls' childhoods in Britain and America. Foster and Simons study girls' fiction written in America and Britain from 1850 to 1920 to demonstrate how these works influenced the lives of young girls at the time. This work explores several popular works, including *The Wide, Wide World; The Daisy Chain; Little Women; What Katy Did; The Railway Children; Anne of Green Gables; The Secret Garden; The Madcap of the School.* The authors demonstrate that while most of these works supported the status quo, several of them, such as *The Wide, Wide World* and *The Daisy Chain*, also questioned standard notions of femininity.

Linda K. Christian-Smith takes an alternative approach to the study of girls' literature in *Becoming a Woman through Romance* (Routledge, 1990). Christian-Smith blends historical and theoretical frameworks to argue that romance novels negatively affect developing young women. The author focuses on girls' literature written between 1942 and 1982 and includes interviews, questionnaires, and a sampling of thirty-four novels to demonstrate how girls can become socialized through romance. This work provides impressive research on a popular genre.

1213. Friedman, Ellen G., and Miriam Fuchs, eds. *Breaking the Sequence: Women's Experimental Fiction.* Princeton, NJ: Princeton University Press, 1989. 325p. bibliog. index. (OP)

Claiming that women's experimental fiction is overlooked and that male writers dominate the genre, editors Friedman and Fuchs bring together eighteen essays "to introduce and explore the rich tradition of women's experimental fiction in this century" (p. xi). The essayists present a wide variety of viewpoints and methodologies while focusing on both well-known and lesser-known female writers. The opening chapter by Friedman and Fuchs provides an overview of women's experimental fiction in English and sets the stage for the remaining essays, which are divided into sections covering three generations of writers. Section 1 covers the first generation, women who wrote before 1930, and includes an exemplary piece by Rachel Blau DuPlessis providing an intertextual reading of Virginia Woolf through the ideas of Gertrude Stein. Section 2 covers women writers from 1930 to 1960; here essayists analyze Jean Rhys's *Wide Sargasso Sea*, Djuna Barnes's *Nightwood*, various works of H.D., and a wealth of Anaïs Nin's writing. The 1960s represented a turning point for both women's studies and experimental fiction. In section 3, contributors discuss Christine Brook-Rose's *Amalgamemnon*, Marguerite Young's *Miss MacIntosh, My Darling*, and Joyce Carol Oates's *Bellefleur*. Larry McCaffrey's study of punk aesthetics in Kathy Acker is one of the most compelling essays in this volume. *Breaking the Sequence* is a solid and valuable work on women's experimental fiction.

1214. Gilbert, Sandra M., and Susan Gubar. *No Man's Land: The Place of the Woman Writer in the Twentieth Century.* New Haven, CT: Yale University Press, 1988–1994. 3v. 1252p. bibliog. index. ISBN (OP) (v. 1); (OP) (v. 2); 0300056311 (v. 3).

This three-volume work is a sequel to the now-classic *The Madwoman in the Attic*, a study of women writers in the nineteenth century. In *No Man's Land* Gilbert and Gubar intend to show how modernism developed, how it has affected both male and female writers, and, most important, how writers respond to "no man's land," the social and literary-historical spaces, both literal and figurative, with which men and women continuously struggle. The authors write, "Taken together, all three books will, we hope, help illuminate the radical transformations of culture that we must all continue to face, transformations that have made not just the territory of literature but the institutions of marriage and the family, of education and the professions into a no man's land— a vexed terrain—in which scattered armies of men and women all too often clash by day and by night" (v. 1, p. xiii). Volume 1, *The War of the Words*, explores the growth of modernism and the growing rivalry between the sexes that began to be played out in a number of arenas, including literature: "Indeed, we will argue here that, especially in the twentieth century, both women and men engendered words and works which continually sought to come to terms with, and find terms for, an ongoing battle of the sexes that was set in motion by the late nineteenth century rise of feminism and the fall of Victorian concepts of 'femininity' " (v. 1, p. xii). In volume 2, *Sexchanges*, the authors address the evolving literary and feminist climates beginning at the turn of the century through World War I and into the 1920s and 1930s. The authors' primary focus in this volume is the "changing definitions of sex and sex roles as they evolve through three phases: the repudiation or revision of the Victorian ideology of femininity . . . the antiutopian skepticism that characterized the thought of such writers as Edith Wharton and Willa Cather . . . the virtually apocalyptic engendering of the new for both literary men and literary women" (v. 2, p. xii). *Letters from the Front*, volume 3, explores the ways in which women writers, "far from being behind the lines, . . . found themselves situated on an embattled and often confusing cultural front" (v. 3, p. xi), and how these writers reshaped social and literary rules and behaviors to create a feminist modernism. Gilbert and Gubar discuss writers such as Virginia Woolf, Edna St. Vincent Millay, H.D., Zora Neale Hurston, and Sylvia Plath. Gilbert and Gubar have crafted a significant work of enormous scope for anyone interested in modernist or feminist literary studies.

Carolyn Heilbrun's *Writing a Woman's Life* (Norton, 1988) complements *No Man's Land*, particularly volume 2, *Sexchanges*. This work is neither literary criticism nor commentary on social or literary history. Instead, Heilbrun sets out "to examine how women's lives have been contrived, and how they may be written to make clear, evident, out in the open, those events, decisions, and relationships that have been invisible outside of women's fictions, where literary critics have revealed" (p. 18). Seeking to present women's own stories, Heilbrun explores events and relationships that society has made invisible outside of women's fictions. The author examines the quest theme in Dorothy Sayers's work and life, as well as the overt anger in the works of poets such as Denise Levertov, Carolyn Kizer, Maxine Kumin, Anne Sexton, Adrienne Rich, and Sylvia Plath. This is a small, provocative, very readable book.

1215. Greene, Gayle, and Coppelia Kahn, eds. *Changing Subjects: The Making of Feminist Literary Criticism.* New York: Routledge, 1993. 283p. bibliog. index. (OP)

In this collection of essays, twenty female academics, including Rachel Blau DuPlessis, Barbara Christian, and Nancy K. Miller, offer insightful and personal discussions about their role in the creation of a feminist literary movement. The editors hope to provide an engaging discussion on the value of going personal to "articulate the vital connection feminism makes between lived experience and theory" (p. 1). These autobiographical essays present collective histories of the women who fought for a voice and a place within the literary canon. This collection provides an excellent overview and extensive range of views on various critical theories, the role of feminism in the development of academic scholarship, and the value of autobiography. This work will be of value to faculty and students in literature, women's studies, and history.

Gayle Greene's *Changing the Story: Feminist Fiction and the Tradition* (Indiana University Press, 1991) integrates a variety of discourses, including Marxism, deconstruction, and psychoanalysis. Greene compares the self-conscious fiction, or metafiction, of Doris Lessing, Margaret

Drabble, Margaret Atwood, and Margaret Laurence to writings from the traditional literary canon. *Listening to Silences: New Essays in Feminist Criticism* (Oxford University Press, 1994), edited by Elaine Hedges and Shelley Fisher, also examines how people write and read literature to effect social change. This work reflects upon the groundbreaking work *Silences* written by Tilly Olsen in 1978, which demonstrated how the effects of family and social pressures silenced the female voice. Relying on new feminist literary theories, the essays in *Listening to Silences* explore the ways in which women's literary voices continue to be silenced and illustrate the continuing connection between personal expression and public voice.

1216. Griffin, Gabriele. *Heavenly Love? Lesbian Images in Twentieth-Century Women's Writing*. New York: St. Martin's Press, 1993. 202p. bibliog. index. ISBN (OP); 0719028817pa.

This short study examines lesbian writing from a variety of genres. The introduction provides a discussion of what constitutes lesbian writing; Griffin herself "made a decision to focus exclusively on *writing by women*, for the most part known lesbian writers, rather than discussing . . . male writing on lesbians as well" (p. 8). Griffin examines well-known works such as Radclyffe Hall's *The Well of Loneliness* along with the works of more marginalized writers from a wide range of genres, including fiction, poetry, biography, history, and essays. Moving in a chronological fashion, the author discusses lesbian writing from the 1950s and 1960s, lesbian texts from the 1970s and 1980s, the celebration of friendship, representations of lesbian sexuality in women's writing, and images of older lesbians. While highly selective, *Heavenly Love?* provides a good introduction to a variety of works that explore the various images of lesbians in twentieth-century literature.

Griffin also edited *Outwrite: Lesbianism and Popular Culture* (Pluto Press, 1993), a collection of essays examining various forms of lesbian cultural production, including popular production, while focusing on lesbians as consumers of lesbian and mainstream popular culture. Contributors survey an eclectic array of topics, including lesbian sex and romance, lesbian "herstories," various genres of literature, including thrillers and science fiction, and popular culture such as cinema and music. *Professions of Desire: Lesbian and Gay Studies in Literature* (Modern Language Association of America, 1995), edited by George E. Haggerty and Bonnie Zimmerman, is a useful resource for undergraduate courses in lesbian and gay literary studies or queer studies. Although only six out of the eighteen essays specifically focus on lesbian studies, contributors ground the work in pedagogy, with twelve essays that concentrate on teaching. Many essays illustrate the differences between gay and lesbian studies, while some contributors attempt to identify a coherent group of literature that serves both gays and lesbians.

Bonnie Zimmerman's *The Safe Sea of Women: Lesbian Fiction, 1969–1989* (Beacon Press, 1990) critically surveys contemporary lesbian fiction. This well-organized and comprehensive work is among the first to recognize lesbian literature as a unique genre. Her study contains a brief history of lesbian literature, an analysis of how lesbian feminists established a sense of community and cultural identity, and an examination of the relationship between myth and reality in lesbian feminist fiction.

1217. Hanley, Lynne. *Writing War: Fiction, Gender, and Memory*. Amherst: University of Massachusetts Press, 1991. 151p. bibliog. ISBN 0870237381; 0870237489pa.

In *Writing War*, Hanley compares men's bellicosity and memorialization of war with opposing feminist perspectives, specifically the disillusionment and abhorrence of war and its relation to domestic violence. Hanley challenges the views espoused in *The Great War and Modern Memory* by Paul Fussell, arguing that society excludes others' experiences during war as a result of concentrating on the experiences of white American and European soldiers. In another essay, Hanley analyzes the works of female authors written in response to various wars, including World Wars I and II, as well as wars in Vietnam and El Salvador. In examining works such as Virginia Woolf's *A Room of One's Own*, Joan Didion's *Salvador*, Doris Lessing's *Prisons We Choose to Live Inside*, and Jean Rhys's *After Leaving Mr. Mackenzie*, Hanley effectively portrays women's varied responses to war and its meaning in their lives. *Writing War* is a well-crafted and significant contribution to the feminist literary criticism of war and militarism.

Women's Fiction and the Great War (Clarendon Press, 1997), edited by Suzanne Raitt and Trudi Tate, and Gill Plain's *Women's Fiction of the Second World War: Gender, Power, and Resistance* (St. Martin's Press, 1996) are both insightful additions to the literature on women's responses to war. Raitt and Tate present a collection of essays that deal with diverse literary forms, from Edwardians to modernists and antimodernists. The examined texts include romances, journals, propaganda, letters, short fiction, and novels. In *Women's Fiction of the Second World War*, Plain's analysis of "gendered responses to the Second World War begins . . . not from a belief in the essential pacifism of women writers, but rather from an observation of the complex and contradictory frameworks within which women's wartime identities and roles are constructed" (p. ix). Both works further the discussion on women's voices and literature of war.

1218. Meese, Elizabeth A. *(Ex)Tensions: Re-figuring Feminist Criticism*. Urbana: University of Illinois Press, 1990. 206p. bibliog. ISBN 0252016823; 0252061055pa.

In *(Ex)Tensions*, Meese continues her examination of the state of feminist criticism that she began in *Crossing the Double-Cross: The Practice of Feminist Criticism* (University of North Carolina Press, 1986). The author writes that the specific focus of this work "is the ways in which women's writing helps us to figure the relationship between the consolidation of identity (individual or personal and collective/feminist) and the politics of inclusion which threatens the notion of singular identity but appears to be politically necessary for a socially effective and responsible feminism" (p. ix). Concerned with the conflict between the theoretical and the political practice of committed feminism, Meese strives to address key conflicts between established "pioneering feminist literary critics" and feminist deconstructive theorists, such as herself. She sees the "establishment" or the dominant view of Western thought as hostile to the multiplicity of voices that exist within feminist literary criticism, yet hopes to develop a field wherein mutual respect is possible. In eight chapters, Meese focuses on critical issues in the field through reading a variety of texts, including *I, Rigoberta Menchú*, Sherley Anne Williams's *Dessa Rose*, Leslie Silko's *Ceremony*, Nadine Gordimer's *Burger's Daughter*, Marguerite Duras's *The Lover*, and works by Adrienne Rich. These essays explore issues inherent in the canon, conflicts between African American and white feminists, and the value of theory. The author has crafted an excellent work that would benefit upper-level undergraduates and scholars alike.

In *The Writing or the Sex? Or Why You Don't Have to Read Women's Writing to Know It's No Good* (Pergamon Press, 1989), Dale Spender presents what she calls a simple theme: "It is that men have been in charge of according value to literature, and that they have found the contributions of their own sex immeasurably superior" (p. 1). Arguing for a change, chapters in part 1 address the inherent sexism in every stage of literary creation from language to publishing to reviewing. Part 2 offers responses from women, including women critiquing male literary theorists, and how female writers and feminist literary critics are working together to enact change.

1219. Miller, Jane. *Seductions: Studies in Reading and Culture*. Cambridge, MA: Harvard University Press, 1990. 194p. (Convergences). bibliog. index. ISBN 0674796799.

Miller defines seductions to mean "all those ways in which women learn who they are in cultures which simultaneously include and exclude them, take their presence for granted while denying it, and entice them finally into narratives which may reduce them by exalting them" (p. 2). In chapter 1, Miller outlines her themes by drawing together three disparate ideas: her evolution as a feminist, her definition of seduction in relation to Antonio Gramsci's use of "hegemony," and her rereading of two novels, *Clarissa* and *Sense and Sensibility*, in which female characters are seduced by powerful male characters. Miller explores the writings of prominent male critics and theorists such as Raymond Williams, Edward Said, and Frantz Fanon who dismiss women from their writings. She also investigates women's relations to imperialism, slavery, and racism. The final chapters cross genres and juxtapose the writings of Said and Fanon against Toni Morrison's *Beloved*, and the Soviet critic Mikhail Bakhtin against Margaret Atwood's *Cat's Eye*. Both literary critique and political polemic, this work powerfully suggests how women can resist and answer back to the slippery seductions of male power.

1220. Munt, Sally, ed. *New Lesbian Criticism: Literary and Cultural Readings*. New York: Columbia University Press, 1992. 207p. (Between Men—Between Women). bibliog. ISBN 0231080182; 0231080190pa.

According to Munt, lesbian theory must be defended because lesbian studies has been marginalized in the academy. Through an intersection with critical theory, however, lesbian studies has become more acceptable within the academy. Essays in *New Lesbian Criticism* demonstrate the interrelationship between lesbian studies and literary theory, and the influences of poststructuralist and postmodern theories. Scholars such as Bonnie Zimmerman, Reina Lewis, Anna Wilson, and Gillian Spraggs write on everything from the state of lesbian criticism in the 1990s to the evolution of lesbian popular culture. Individual essays also examine specific genres, including lesbian utopian fiction and lesbian pornography; critique individual authors such as Audre Lorde; or analyze specific texts, including *We Too Are Drifting*, *The Price of Salt*, and *Desert of the Heart*. *New Lesbian Criticism* provides a valuable overview and introduction to lesbian literary criticism.

Patricia Juliana Smith's *Lesbian Panic: Homoeroticism in Modern British Women's Fiction* (Columbia University Press, 1997) examines "the function of lesbianism—or, more specifically, a socially and culturally ingrained *fear* of lesbianism and the stigma pertaining thereunto—in specific narrative texts" (p. xii). Smith explores the texts of Virginia Woolf, Elizabeth Bowen, Muriel Spark, Fay Weldon, Brigid Brophy, and Jeanette Winterson.

1221. Paglia, Camille. *Sexual Personae: Art and Decadence from Nefertiti to Emily Dickinson*. New Haven, CT: Yale University Press, 1990. 718p. bibliog. index. ISBN 0300043961.

"I see sex and nature as brutal pagan forces" (p. xiii). So begins this massive, provocative, engaging work by one of the most controversial social and literary critics of the 1990s. By combining a range of disciplines including art history, literature, religion, and psychology, Paglia argues that Western culture still flourishes and always has: "The book accepts the canonical western tradition and rejects the modernist idea that culture has collapsed into meaningless fragments" (p. xiii). Arguing that sex is biologically predetermined, Paglia contends that woman and nature are at war with man and art. Beginning with antiquity and moving to the *fin de siècle*, Paglia critiques everything from Egyptian art and Greek mythology to a range of Western writers, including Shakespeare, Spencer, Rousseau, the English romantic poets, and Oscar Wilde, as well as several American writers, such as Poe, Hawthorne, Melville, and Emily Dickinson. More of a personal treatise than an academic text, *Sexual Personae*, which became a best-seller, is straightforward, witty, and thought-provoking, with extensive commentary on specific literary texts that privilege white Western male tradition. Whether one agrees or disagrees with Paglia, this work cannot be ignored for its audacious view of Western culture.

Sex, Art, and American Culture (Vintage Books, 1992), also by Paglia, collects previously published pieces addressing popular culture. Discussing a range of topics from Madonna to rape to the crisis in academe, Paglia writes that she wants to "rethink American cultural history in order to clarify the heritage of my generation of the Sixties, which heroically broke through Fifties conformism but which failed in many ways to harness or sustain its own energies" (p. vii). In *Vamps and Tramps* (Vintage Books, 1994), a collection of new essays, Paglia's central theme is "wanderlust, the erotic, appetitive mind in free movement" (p. xiii). Claiming as her highest ideals free thought and free speech, Paglia once again chastises higher education, feminism, and so-called liberals for clamping down on free speech and for not providing arenas for free thought to flourish.

1222. Russ, Joanna. *To Write like a Woman: Essays in Feminism and Science Fiction.* Bloomington: Indiana University Press, 1995. 181p. bibliog. index. ISBN 0253329140; 0253209838pa.

Sarah Lefanu introduces this collection of imaginative and provocative essays, saying about Russ, "She is interested in the economic, sexual, and social position of those who write and of those who read, she is interested in cultural traditions and how they are passed on, or refused, or transformed, or assimilated by those who write and by those who read" (pp. viii–ix). These essays, gathered in one place for the first time and spanning more than twenty years, present some of Russ's finest criticism on women's writing and science fiction. An introduction to each essay places the work within a historical context; Russ also explains the work's relevance to today's audience. Topics covered range from science and technology to politics and popular culture to female writers and sexuality. The six essays in part 1 focus on "masculinist" traditions in science fiction. In part 2, Russ explores the lives and works of individual female writers and the cultural constraints under which they wrote. The author explains that an underlying theme of her work is "what Adrienne Rich once called 're-vision,' i.e. the re-perceiving of experience . . . because so much of what's presented to us . . . is so obviously untrue that a great deal of social energy must be mobilized to hide that gross and ghastly fact" (p. xv). Russ searches for the hidden meaning and/or the hidden experience in women's lives. Russ's work is a valuable resource for scholars and nonacademics interested in literary criticism, science fiction, and/or feminism.

Where No Man Has Gone Before: Women and Science Fiction (Routledge, 1991), edited by Lucie Armitt, gathers thirteen essays by scholars and science fiction writers from Great Britain and Europe. Several essays address individual authors who have had a unique and powerful impact on science fiction during the twentieth century, including Charlotte Haldane, Katherine Burdekin, C. L. Moore, Ursula K. Le Guin, and Doris Lessing. Sections 2 and 3 look at the sense of "otherness" often found in the work of female science fiction writers, the blurring of boundaries between science fiction and other genres, and the inherent sexism in publishing and marketing science fiction.

1223. Snyder, Jane McIntosh. *The Woman and the Lyre: Women Writers in Classical Greece and Rome.* Carbondale: Southern Illinois University Press, 1989. 199p. (Ad Feminam: Women and Literature). bibliog. index. ISBN 080931455X; 0809317060pa.

This book is the first modern survey, translated into English, of Greek and Roman women authors. Snyder includes a variety of poetry and prose writings from pagan and Christian traditions. The author begins with an analysis of the life and writings of Sappho of Lesbos, perhaps the best-known female writer from classical times. Snyder then discusses the works of other, "unknown" female poets from fifth-century and Hellenistic Greece, including Myrtis, Praxilla,

Nossis, and Erinna. Snyder also examines female philosophers' writings, concentrating on the philosophical schools of the Epicureans (Leontion), the Cynics (Hipparchia), and the Pythagoreans (Hypatia), as well as discussing women writers in Rome. Through her analysis of this literature, Snyder argues that these female writers focused on themes of importance to them as women: love, friendship, relationships, spiritual matters, and concerns of daily life. *The Woman and the Lyre* effectively restores the silenced voices of Greek and Roman female writers.

1224. Trinh, T. Minh-Ha. *Woman, Native, Other: Writing Postcoloniality and Feminism.* Bloomington: Indiana University Press, 1989. 173p. bibliog. index. ISBN 0253366038; 0253205034pa.

Trinh T. Minh-Ha, a writer, filmmaker, and composer, presents an innovative and imaginative work through her examination of the intersections among feminist practice, women's studies, anthropology, cultural studies, and literary criticism. The author not only questions the "male-is-norm" literary and theoretical establishment, but also refutes linearity, the rational, and the knowable through a deconstruction of conventional patterns of organized criticism. The first three parts of this book deal with each of the key words in the title: woman, native, and other. In part 1, Trinh traces the falsehoods regarding the way instructors both teach and recognize writing and the ways in which authority structures reinforce writing. In part 2, the author argues against the theories of the "Great Masters," Bronislaw Malinowski and Claude Lévi-Strauss, and the privileging of the white mainstream anthropological position claiming that writers of anthropology must "maintain a critical language" and a "critique of (their) language" (p. 71). In part 3, the author explores the differences between "native" and "Third World" to demonstrate the importance of creating without mirroring existing forms and languages. Trinh T. Minh-Ha illustrates the work with stills from her own films and poems and epigraphs from writings of other women, many of whom are racial minorities. This intelligent work provides much depth and insight.

1225. Warhol, Robyn R., and Diane Price Herndl, eds. *Feminisms: An Anthology of Literary Theory and Criticism.* New Brunswick, NJ: Rutgers University Press, 1991. 1118p. bibliog. index. ISBN 0813517311; 081351732Xpa.

Bringing together a wide range of writings from current feminist critics, this work is intended to show "what is going on in feminist literary studies in the United States today" (p. 2). Gathering previously published essays and book chapters crafted by a variety of critics and theorists, the editors acknowledge that the diversity of opinions and approaches in these works can at times present conflicts. Organizing the writings under several broad categories or concepts, such as canon, body, desire, men, ethnicity, history, and class, Warhol and Herndl provide very brief introductions to each section in an attempt to bring the various pieces together. This anthology contains writings by the best scholars in the field of feminist literary theory, including Annette Kolondy, Nina Baym, Elaine Showalter, Barbara Smith, Paula Gunn Allen, and Amy Ling, among others. The revised edition, published in 1997, includes many new essays, a reorganization of the sections, and an increased focus on women of color and lesbian voices. The breadth of this impressive collection makes it a useful resource for beginning students as well as advanced scholars.

Biography and Autobiography

1226. Benstock, Shari, ed. *The Private Self: Theory and Practice of Women's Autobiographical Writings.* Chapel Hill: University of North Carolina Press, 1988. 319p. bibliog. index. ISBN 0807817910; 0807842184pa.

Two overarching themes appear in *The Private Self*. The first is the challenge of discussing "self" and levels of self-consciousness when reading autobiographical writings. This question interacts with the definition of "private"; privacy functions as a link to understanding the definition of self in the production of autobiography. The second theme, reflected in the subtitle of this work, is the dichotomy between theory and practice. According to Benstock, the application of traditionally European male-dominated theory to women's writings may lend legitimacy to women's texts, but the result may be the subversion of the works themselves. *The Private Self* examines writers and their works from the eighteenth through the twentieth century and explores complex questions of self, as well as the challenges of reading autobiography within the traditional theoretical constructs established by the academy. The conclusions reached sometimes conflict, yet this is an appropriate reflection of the challenges facing those working with women's autobiographical writings.

1227. Blodgett, Harriet. *Centuries of Female Days: Englishwomen's Private Diaries.* New Brunswick, NJ: Rutgers University Press, 1988. 331p. bibliog. index. ISBN 0813513146.

Centuries of Female Days is the first critical study of Englishwomen's diaries. Blodgett examines the private, eclectic diaries of sixty-nine women, spanning the period from the late sixteenth century to just before World War II. The author covers additional diaries in the afterword. The selected diaries represent the lives of women from a variety of social, economic, and political backgrounds and provide a rare glimpse into the lives of these women, including their perceptions of contemporary events. Blodgett notes that none of the diarists constructed their works for publication, nor did they revise them, although the diaries currently are published in some form. This reduces the potential for self-censorship when conveying personal thoughts and events. This work argues for the study of diaries as a legitimate literary form and illustrates the subordinate nature of women throughout the centuries, enabling readers to observe the traditional status of women and their growing self-awareness as expressed through personal writings.

1228. Broughton, Trev Lynn, and Linda Anderson, eds. *Women's Lives/Women's Times: New Essays on Auto/Biography.* Albany: State University of New York Press, 1997. 291p. bibliog. index. ISBN 0791433978; 0791433986pa.

This collection of essays, compiled from a series of conference papers, focuses on "the complex interrelation between the personal, the theoretical, and the political offered by women's autobiographical writing which thus seems to defy or exceed both generic and disciplinary boundaries" (p. xi). Essayists from the disciplines of sociology, anthropology, education, and literature address the literary aspects of these writings, as well as their social and political contexts. The diversity of topics covered in each of the four parts of this work illustrates the varied theoretical and disciplinary approaches employed in the study of autobiography. Part 1 explores the diverse ways women use autobiography, such as to create "communities of support." Part 2 addresses the complex construction of the "self" or "I" and the "other" and how these two concepts play into the reading of women's autobiography. Women view themselves as "I," yet often see themselves as the "other" within varied personal contexts. Part 3 asks the following questions: "Whose story, whose subjectivity, is at stake; how must the story be changed if the woman is to become its subject; from where can she say I?" (p. 176). In the last section, "Lives in Practice," the writers reflect on their role in creating meaning. This work is appropriate for upper-division undergraduates and graduate students in a variety of disciplines.

1229. Bunkers, Susan L., and Cynthia A. Huff, eds. *Inscribing the Daily: Critical Essays on Women's Diaries.* Amherst: University of Massachusetts Press, 1996. 296p. bibliog. index. ISBN 1558490108; 1558490116pa.

The editors of this collection of essays raise a number of questions about the placement of diaries in literary, historical, and feminist theoretical contexts. In three sections, contributors explore issues pertaining to diary writing, such as public versus private, men's diary writing versus women's writing, and the placement of diaries in the canon. Essayists examine the theoretical frameworks available for reading women's diaries in section 1 and place the diaries within their social and cultural contexts in section 2. In the third section, contributors examine diary writing as a literary form, discuss strategies women employ to lend form to their writings, and explore how fiction influences the selected forms. Contributors extensively quote diaries of famous and lesser-known women in each of these sections. The introduction and bibliography provide useful overviews and key sources of seminal writings in women's autobiographical and diary studies.

Alexandra Johnson's *The Hidden Writer: Diaries and the Creative Life* (Doubleday, 1997) is a nice companion piece to Bunkers and Huff's work. Johnson presents excerpts from diaries of women ranging in age from a six-year-old girl to May Sarton, who began keeping a diary at sixty. Johnson explores the relationship between the development of the public writer and private diary writings. This work provides an insightful introduction to this area of literary studies.

1230. Culley, Margo, ed. *American Women's Autobiography: Fea(s)ts of Memory.* Madison: University of Wisconsin Press, 1992. 329p. (Wisconsin Studies in American Autobiography). bibliog. index. ISBN (OP); 0299132943pa.

Culley delineates the evolution of autobiographical writings in America in this collection of essays, which not only represents the use of varied critical approaches to women's autobiography, but also celebrates women's lives. While all autobiography is self-reflexive, Culley suggests that self-reflection grows more deliberate as women become more empowered to present their lives in their own voices and for their own purposes. The first set of essays examines conversion narratives, which Puritans required before allowing anyone to join a congregation. Culley suggests that through these tales of one's spiritual life, American women initially began to translate their own life experiences into the written word. Other essays address the writings of frontier women, Gertrude Stein, and black and white civil rights workers. Each of these essays illustrates the development of the author's awareness of self, as well as the tension between truth and construct inherent in autobiography. The final essays, written by non-Anglo-American women, relay the uniqueness of their experiences. These essays force the reader to question the definition of "Americanness" and how it shapes one's story.

1231. Gilmore, Leigh. *Autobiographics: A Feminist Theory of Women's Self-Representation.* Ithaca, NY: Cornell University Press, 1994. 255p. (Reading Women Writing). bibliog. index. ISBN (OP); 0801480612pa.

In this important examination of women writing autobiography, Gilmore theorizes about the politics and possibilities found when women attempt self-representation through their writings. This work does not simply provide a theoretical study of writing autobiography; rather, it offers an application of feminist theory to autobiographical production. The selected texts for this study represent a variety of genres outside the narrow definition of autobiography, such as literature and biography. Gilmore calls this broadened theoretical approach to women's self-representation "autobiographics," which she defines as "the changing elements of the contradictory discourses and practices of truth and identity which represent the subject of autobiography" (p. 13). This approach raises the issue of truth versus lying, since many critics view fiction and other "creative" writing as false, but look upon autobiography as truth. This expanded study of autobiographical writings includes writings by women from a variety of ethnic, social, and historical backgrounds. Gilmore believes that such diversity greatly expands and enhances feminist literary studies. *Autobiographics* will challenge those interested in women's autobiography.

1232. Miller, Nancy K. *Getting Personal: Feminist Occasions and Other Autobiographical Acts*. New York: Routledge, 1991. 164p. bibliog. index. ISBN (OP); 0415903246pa.

Scholarship dealing with autobiographical works became common during the 1980s. But what is the role of autobiography in the creation and explication of this scholarship? How are one's own experiences transferred to scholarly endeavors? Miller asks these questions through a series of essays—papers originally presented at conferences or academic meetings—that focus on issues of feminism. The essays address a variety of subjects, including teaching, feminist pedagogy, and autobiography. Although the academy has traditionally undervalued narrative criticism, Miller encourages the personalization of critical writings and argues that this approach to feminist scholarship not only broadens one's thinking about a particular field, but also provides opportunities to expand beyond established academic parameters. These essays give readers a broad and engaging view of Miller's development as a leading feminist scholar.

1233. Smith, Sidonie. *Subjectivity, Identity, and the Body: Women's Autobiographical Practices in the Twentieth Century*. Bloomington: Indiana University Press, 1993. 226p. bibliog. index. ISBN (OP); 060805044Xpa.

How does the woman autobiographer construct her own life? How do context, history, culture, and gender influence her? How does she define "I"? Smith explores these questions in *Subjectivity, Identity, and the Body*. Smith's fascination with "complex ways in which histories of the subject, discourses of identity, cultural inscriptions of the body, and laws of genre coalesce in the autobiographical 'I' " is a driving force behind this work (p. 4). She examines several women's autobiographies written during the last half of the nineteenth century and throughout the twentieth century. This work is not a historical survey of autobiographical writings, but an exploration of individuals and their autobiographical practices. The bulk of this work consists of essays that explore the writings of Elizabeth Cady Stanton, Harriet Jacobs, Gertrude Stein, Virginia Woolf, and Zora Neale Hurston. The final two chapters define autobiography in much broader terms, incorporating diverse approaches to the body as representative of gender (the breast) and race (skin). Smith also addresses the use of photography—defined as a method of scrutinizing oneself and resisting the oppressor in order to make one's own power visible—as a form of autobiography. This densely written work explores both traditional and nontraditional autobiography as a means for women to construct their own lives, tell their own stories, and create their own "I."

1234. Smith, Sidonie, and Julia Watson, eds. *De/Colonizing the Subject: The Politics of Gender in Women's Autobiography*. Minneapolis: University of Minnesota Press, 1992. 484p. bibliog. index. (OP)

As Liz Stanley suggests in her work *The Auto/Biographical I*, annotated later in this section, people in power—white middle- or upper-class men—tend to form the focal point of biographical writings. What happens, however, when those who are not in power seek to have their voices heard? Smith and Watson ask this question in *De/Colonizing the Subject*. Although this collection incorporates women's writings from areas of geographical colonization (Indochina/Vietnam, India, and Kenya), the editors broadly define colonization. According to Chandra Talpade Mohanty, "Colonization almost invariably implies a relation of structural domination, and a suppression—often violent—of the heterogeneity of the subjects in question" (p. xvii). In these essays, women in colonial, postcolonial, or transitional situations explore autobiography as a means not only to overthrow the suppression of cultural domination, but also to express an alternate viewpoint in order to change the political climate. These women ultimately question the dominance of Western literary theory and its application to non-Western writings, alternatively suggesting that writings from non-Western cultures require the modification, if not the total refashioning, of literary theory to appropriately address divergent critical issues.

Smith takes a broader, more historical approach to the same issues in her earlier work *A Poetics of Women's Autobiography: Marginality and Fictions of Self-Representation* (Indiana University Press, 1987). Attempting to reclaim women's autobiographical writing, Smith argues that traditional theoretical approaches privilege the patriarchal position because the masculine approach to autobiography, which emphasizes the subject's differences and autonomy, diverges from the feminine approach. Smith examines the autobiographies of Margery Kempe, Margaret Cavendish, Charlotte Clarke, Harriet Martineau, and Maxine Hong Kingston to explore the inherent conflict between the genre of autobiography as a public expression of self and the dominant patriarchal expectation that women remain silent.

1235. Smith, Sidonie, and Julia Watson, eds. *Women, Autobiography, Theory: A Reader.* Madison: University of Wisconsin Press, 1998. 526p. (Wisconsin Studies in American Autobiography). bibliog. index. ISBN 0299158403; 0299158446pa.

This text serves as a guide to key writings of women's autobiography. In the introduction, Smith and Watson outline the following goals: locating the theoretical parameters of women's autobiography, ordering the field through a survey of the stages of critical activity, identifying significant theoretical moments that have reframed discussion, reflecting on the history of the field as illustrated in the selected essays, and proposing future areas of inquiry (p. 4). Essays are organized under the following broad categories: experience and agency, subjectivities, modes and genres, histories, voice and memory, bodies and sexuality, and politics and pedagogy. These sections address critical issues within the study of women's autobiography. The introduction provides a history of the study of autobiography, focusing on key issues or events that changed the field. According to the introduction, readers should use the work "as a set of tools—or building blocks, guides, recipes—for enabling your own entry into the activity (and the self-reflexivity) of theorizing women's autobiography" (p. 4).

1236. Stanley, Liz. *The Auto/Biographical I: The Theory and Practice of Feminist Auto/Biography.* New York: Manchester University Press, 1992. 289p. bibliog. index. ISBN 0719046491.

Can a biographer ever produce a truly objective work without imparting some of himself or herself in the final product? In this discussion of biography, autobiography, and social feminist theory, Liz Stanley suggests that the conventional separation between biography and autobiography is contrived and false. Since most biographers traditionally craft biographies to illuminate the "great lives," those of white middle- or upper-class men, the boundaries of the canon are very narrow. Stanley, a feminist social scientist, argues that recounting the lives of a privileged few is incomplete since it commonly ignores a large number of unprivileged, yet extraordinary, subjects. The typical biography also overlooks the social and cultural influences that shape the lives of all people. Stanley reflects on a broad variety of enterprises, including a discussion of her own approach to editing the diaries of Hannah Cullwick, a domestic servant who married her employer. Through this exercise, Stanley demonstrates how her strong sense of connection with Hannah, whose life parallels the author's, influenced how she constructed Hannah's life. This text provides one of the first feminist, social science approaches to biography and autobiography, offering much insight into what has become a topic of great interest among literary feminists.

1237. Swindell, Julia. *The Uses of Autobiography*. London: Taylor & Francis, 1995. 227p. (Feminist Perspectives on the Past and Present). bibliog. index. ISBN 0748403655; 0748403663pa.

This collection of papers originally presented at a conference held in 1994 at Homerton College, Cambridge, provides a sweeping approach to autobiographical studies because it addresses works from different eras, written by men and women from diverse social and political backgrounds. Since autobiography is a means of self-expression, Swindell stresses that she included papers from writers who work both within and outside of the traditional academic power structure. Thus this work presents a variety of definitions and critical approaches to autobiography, with authors employing feminist theory, cultural studies, and historical approaches to examine a wide range of texts. The texts include two versions of Frederick Douglass's autobiography, letters women wrote during World War II, the diaries of Elizabeth Barrett and George Sand, and the use of autobiographical writings to examine experiences of education. Although this work is not groundbreaking, it provides a broad overview of autobiography and its applications to other fields and makes an excellent starting point for studies in this area.

Europe

1238. Atack, Margaret, and Phil Powrie, eds. *Contemporary French Fiction by Women: Feminist Perspectives*. New York: Manchester University Press, 1990. 207p. bibliog. index. ISBN 0719030846.

With this collection of essays, Atack and Powrie "attempt to correct what we see as an imbalance in the attention devoted to French feminist literary theory at the expense of fiction" (p. 1). These scholars, who hail primarily from Great Britain, examine the works of twentieth-century French women novelists, incorporating feminist literary theory from France but also from North America. The essays are divided into two sections. Section 1 investigates fiction by such authors as Simone de Beauvoir, Annie Ernaux, and Djanet Lachment and focuses on the socio-political discourse found in the works of these women. Section 2 concerns language, "in particular women writers' attempts to relate language and women's experience, textually rather than narratively. The accent here is on signifying difference" (p. 9). These essays include discussions of well-known writers such as Geneviève Serreau and Hélène Cixous, as well as newer writers such as Chantel Chawaf. The contributors provide broad discussions of women's writing of this century, as well as the application of a variety of theoretical approaches to literature. *Contemporary French Fiction by Women* is a solid introduction to French women's writing within a theoretical context.

Jennifer Waelti-Walter's *Feminist Novelists of the Belle Epoque: Love as a Lifestyle* (Indiana University Press, 1990) is a study of novels that women wrote and published between 1900 and 1914. Waelti-Walters examines the plot of texts written by well-known as well as obscure authors to illustrate challenges women have faced. The author includes extensive plot summaries of the novels because of the obscurity of many of these works. This work would serve as a useful introduction to a very focused group of texts.

1239. Charnon-Deutsch, Lou. *Narratives of Desire: Nineteenth-Century Spanish Fiction by Women*. University Park: Pennsylvania State University Press, 1994. 223p. bibliog. index. ISBN 027101007X.

In *Narratives of Desire*, Charnon-Deutsch explores "what gender may have to do with writing practices that are commonly marginalized to the periphery of dominant realist discourses" (p. 7). Relying on the theories of Michel Foucault and Jacques Lacan, feminist psychoanalysis, and comparisons with male-authored texts, the author explores the ways in which female novelists depict ideas about gender and women's place within nineteenth-century Spanish society. Charnon-Deutsch analyzes several authors not normally considered a part of Spain's literary canon, including Rosalía de Castro, Concepción Gimeno de Flaquer, and Faustina Sáez de Melgar. Charnon-Deutsch admits that the female writers she examined often portray gender ideology in ways similar to those of male writers; nonetheless, she hopes that her book "attempts a reading of women's texts as a staging area for conflicts of gender, as they are reflected in its domestic ideology" (p. 11). To further her argument for the gendered ways women were portrayed in this culture, the author includes illustrations from popular periodicals of the time.

Charnon-Deutsch's 1990 book *Gender and Representation: Women in Spanish Realist Fiction* (John Benjamin's Publishing Co., 1990) takes a slightly different approach to the same topic. She examines the portrayal of women in Spanish fiction by focusing on male-authored texts. The canonical works that Charnon-Deutsch examines "reflect the private fantasies and expiatory necessities of the men who created them" (p. 18). Both of these works assume knowledge of the language and, in *Gender and Representation*, the literary works discussed, thus making them more appropriate for the advanced scholar or someone who has a solid grasp of the Spanish language.

1240. Chester, Pamela, and Siblelan Forrester. *Engendering Slavic Literatures*. Bloomington: Indiana University Press, 1996. 249p. bibliog. index. ISBN 0253330165; 0253210429pa.

The essays in this volume examine issues raised by scholars of gender studies and literary studies from five different Slavic literary traditions, Poland, Ukraine, Serbia, Croatia, and Russia. The editors explore inherent similarities among writings from diverse regions and different authors, including women, as well as men writing about women, during the nineteenth and twentieth centuries. Contributors examine known literary figures, such as Leo Tolstoy and Ivan Turgenev, alongside little-known female authors, including Maria Kuncewicz and Natasha Kolchevska. Although an awareness of Western literary theory and feminist theory guides much of the discussion, the authors consider the difficulties inherent in imposing one region's theoretical model on another. Because gender studies and feminist literary studies are more pervasive in Europe and the United States than in Slavic countries, this work provides a unique perspective on both well-known and unknown Slavic works.

1241. DeJean, Joan. *Tender Geographies: Women and the Origins of the Novel in France*. New York: Columbia University Press, 1991. 297p. bibliog. index. ISBN 0231062303.

Many scholars consider that French women writing during the seventeenth and eighteenth centuries created the novel. In this study, DeJean reevaluates the origins of this genre, placing the creation of the novel within the social and political context of the time. The title *Tender Geographies* refers to the constant association between the public and the private found in these works. Women played major roles in France's history during the seventeenth and eighteenth centuries, a period of great political and social upheaval, and women's writings during this period reflect such activism. Although many contemporaries considered these writings frivolous and overly romantic, these women rarely addressed the romantic without connecting it to the social and political events of the day. DeJean also discusses the political motivations behind the elimination of all women authors from the literary canon, despite the fact that they had played a key role in the creation of the novel. This critical work is useful for its reassessment of women's role in the history of the novel in France and their place in literary history in general.

Focusing on a more specific genre, Faith Beasley looks at the memoir and its interaction with fiction in *Revising Memory: Women's Fiction and Memoirs in Seventeenth-Century France* (Rutgers University Press, 1990). Each genre allowed the author not only to record historic events, but also to place them within their contemporary contexts. Beasley's book complements DeJean's in its specificity.

1242. DeJean, Joan, and Nancy K. Miller, eds. *Displacements: Women, Tradition, Literatures in French*. Baltimore: Johns Hopkins University Press, 1991. 336p. bibliog. ISBN 0801840708.

DeJean and Miller address the ongoing debate within women's studies regarding the construction of the literary canon by focusing on French literature. Authors speculate about why certain French female writers, from France as well as other French-speaking regions of the world, are included or excluded from the academic literary canon, particularly in the United States. Contributors cite the following reasons: the unavailability of women's writings in translation, the high cost of translations, and the perpetuation of this problem by those who compile anthologies. The chapter containing interviews with a number of contemporary French female authors reveals much about this problem. These women challenge the importance of discussing the canon within the context of feminist literary criticism and explain that French women within the academy often do not question the status quo, a key strategy in feminist literary criticism. This work provides a telling discussion about the historic status of women authors.

1243. Garton, Janet. *Norwegian Women's Writing, 1850–1990*. Atlantic Highlands, NJ: Athlone, 1993. 306p. (Women in Context). bibliog. index. ISBN 0485910012; 0485920018pa.

Garton addresses the gap in the availability of criticism about Norwegian women writers, primarily assigning the problem to the dearth of English translations. The book is organized chronologically, and each section begins with a historical outline of the period in question. Because these works are not well known, the author provides substantial background information in order to place each title in its proper context. Each entry contains some biographical information; however, Garton focuses on critical analysis of the writings. Two criteria determined the inclusion of works in this title: the availability of translations and the author's relative historic and literary importance in Norway. Garton's work is the first in a monographic series, Women in Context, that Athlone produced. The series provides a survey, country by country, of women's writing from "the beginning of the major struggle for emancipation until the present day" (frontpiece). It deals with literature, yet includes discussions of the sociopolitical and cultural contexts in which each woman wrote and the current theoretical atmosphere in that country as well. Other titles in this series include *French Women's Writing, 1848–1994* by Diana Holmes (1996), *Italian Women's Writing, 1860–1994* by Sharon Wood (1995), *Spanish Women's Writing, 1849–1996* by Catherine Davies (1998), and *Swedish Women's Writing, 1850–1995* by Helena Foras-Scott (1997).

1244. Herrman, Claudine. *The Tongue Snatchers*. Translated and with an introduction and notes by Nancy Kline. Lincoln: University of Nebraska Press, 1989. 145p. bibliog. index. ISBN (OP); 0803272529pa.

For the first time in its entirety, the complete English translation of the classic feminist work *Les Voleuses de langue* (1976) is available for research and study. Herrman emphasizes close textual readings through an exploration of feminist criticism, as opposed to feminist literary theory, to expresses her argument that "woman lives in a colonized ('virile') culture and speaks a colonized ('virile') language" (p. xxii). If women can succeed in stealing this male language, they must hide this achievement through writing and communicating in a code that men cannot identify as virile. Unlike scholars who work within French feminist literary theory, Herrman does not propose that women completely separate themselves from the existing language; instead, she encourages women to live within that world, appropriating and complementing the current language. Kline's introduction to the text provides a telling examination of how two of Herrman's earlier writings foreshadow *The Tongue Snatchers*. Kline also examines the sociopolitical, literary, and historical contexts within which Herrman created this book. These insights by Kline lend an understanding to the significance of *The Tongue Snatchers* and its continuing importance today. Herrman's work is essential to any women's studies collection, and this is the only translation of this historically important writing within the arena of French feminist criticism.

1245. Lazzaro-Weis, Carol. *From Margins to Mainstream: Feminism and Fictional Modes in Italian Women's Writing, 1968–1990.* Philadelphia: University of Pennsylvania Press, 1993. 223p. bibliog. index. ISBN 0812231953; 0812214382pa.

In *From Margins to Mainstream*, Lazzaro-Weis examines the shift within women's writing that has occurred in Italy during the past forty years. The avant-garde style employed during the 1970s alienated many readers, thus creating a movement during the 1980s to return to more traditional literary styles. Lazzaro-Weis does not view these transitions as an abandonment of a feminist literary style or feminist tradition, but as an opportunity for these traditions to meld. In comparing these differing literary approaches, Lazzaro-Weis establishes a framework to differentiate between contemporary Italian women writers and the effects of their writings on Italian literary tradition. She explores the relationships among feminism, feminist theory, and Italian women's contemporary narrative prose. Lazzaro-Weis also examines the development of various literary genres, including the romance and the historical novel, and demonstrates how Italian feminism has affected these genres over the course of time. Finally, the author discusses how scholars in Italy have adapted the theories of American and French feminist literary critics, especially their discussions of genre and cultural studies.

1246. Martin, Elaine, ed. *Gender, Patriarchy, and Fascism in the Third Reich: The Response of Women Writers.* Detroit: Wayne State University Press, 1993. 309p. bibliog. index. ISBN (OP); 0608105562pa.

Scholars have documented how World War II affected women, both those in military service and those on the home front. Martin, however, collects essays addressing works written by women during the 1970s and 1980s that reflect on their involvement in the Third Reich. According to the editor, these works compose an obscure body of literature that focuses on women's descriptions and interpretations of their experiences during World War II. Three major themes—the link between fascism and patriarchy, National Socialism as part of a historical continuum, and Nazism as a contemporary phenomenon and continuing threat—thread together the essays in this text. Martin chronologically organizes this work based on the author's birth date. She includes only non-Jewish writers from East and West Germany and Austria. These women writers present a rare viewpoint about the Third Reich, making the work particularly important to literary and history scholars studying this era.

1247. Sellers, Susan. *Language and Sexual Difference: Feminist Writing in France*. New York: St. Martin's Press, 1991. 196p. bibliog. index. ISBN 0312061617; 0312061625pa.

In this well-organized and well-written work, Sellers successfully accomplishes her primary goal, to introduce French feminist theory to non-French speakers by examining the works of key writers in the field. As opposed to Anglo-American feminist theorists, who often employ socio-logical analysis in their readings, French feminist theorists employ a philosophical approach. Sellers suggests that for women to move forward within literary studies, they must question the system rather than try to gain equality with men. To illustrate this point, Sellers examines the works of three major French feminist theorists: Hélène Cixous, Luce Irigaray, and Julia Kristeva. The author carefully places their writings within the appropriate theoretical context via incorpo-rating the critique of male theorists who focus on language and meaning, including Barthes, Lévi-Strauss, Foucault, and Saussure. Sellers also examines contemporary writings of French female authors to trace how they reflect elements of French feminist theory. Sellers provides a clear, understandable presentation of a potentially unwieldy and complex topic by illustrating connec-tions among the three major French feminist theorists within the broader arena of literary theory.

Sellers investigates the relationship between theory and practice in more detail in *Hélène Cixous: Authorship, Autobiography, and Love* (Blackwell, 1996). Focusing on Cixous's creative output, Sellers illuminates the cohesion between the literary and critical and also describes the contradictions. Finally, Sellers served as translator and editor of *The Hélène Cixous Reader* (Rou-tledge, 1994), making her one of the leading experts on both the literary and critical works of one of the twentieth century's most important French feminist critics.

Great Britain

1248. Bohls, Elizabeth A. *Women Travel Writers and the Language of Aesthetics, 1716–1818*. New York: Cambridge University Press, 1995. 309p. (Cambridge Studies in Ro-manticism, 13). bibliog. index. ISBN 0521474582.

Bohls explores eighteenth-century aesthetic theory and practice to expose "the unabashed elitism of eighteenth-century aesthetics" (p. 8). She define aesthetics "as a discourse, or a closely related set of discourses. . . . Aesthetic discourse deals with concepts of art, beauty, sublimity, taste, and judgment, and more broadly with the pleasure experienced from sensuous surfaces or spectacles" (p. 5). Bohls analyzes the work of seven white middle- and upper-class women to show how these women challenged three of aesthetics' founding assumptions: the generic per-ceiver, the idea of impartial contemplation, and the belief that aesthetics has nothing to do with political or moral concerns. Bohls examines everything from the letters of Mary Wortley Mo-ntague to the political writing of Mary Wollstonecraft and the fiction of Ann Radcliffe and Mary Shelley to show how these "women writers attack the very foundations of modern aesthetics" (p. 10). Bohls does point out that these writers often present a diversity of opinions and concerns; they were entitled by their class to be observers, but were excluded to the category of the "other," along with many of the races observed in their travels, by their gender. Bohls argues that we need to relearn to reread these "ambivalent" texts, for these women "initiated a counter-tradition of aesthetic thought especially valuable to those of us concerned to challenge the present-day legacy of this powerful discourse" (p. 22).

Whereas Bohls's work covers the mid-eighteenth century to the early nineteenth century, Sara Mills's *Discourses of Difference: An Analysis of Women's Travel Writing and Colonialism* (Routledge, 1992) analyzes women's travel writing of the mid-nineteenth to the early twentieth century. Integrating colonial discourse, feminist theories, and the theories of Michel Foucault,

Mills concentrates on women writers who traveled to colonized countries under British rule. Unlike other critics of the genre, Mills does not compare the subordination of women in colonizing societies to that of colonized peoples. Contributors to *Women's Writing in Exile* (University of North Carolina Press, 1989), edited by Mary Lynn Broe and Angela Ingram, focus exclusively on "exilic texts" by twentieth-century women. They examine displacements from the "mother" country, as well as displacements according to literary criteria. This work provides a thoughtful study of alienation themes.

1249. Ezell, Margaret J.M. *Writing Women's Literary History*. Baltimore: Johns Hopkins University Press, 1996. 205p. bibliog. index. ISBN 080185508X.

Drawing on new historicism and French feminist theory, the aim of this study "is to suggest that feminist literary history has reached the level of critical development and self-confidence necessary to examine its own hidden assumptions as carefully as it has done those of the orthodox critics" (p. 6). Ezell argues for scholars to rethink the direction of feminist literary history and consider whether the same critical framework used to study women's writing from the nineteenth and twentieth centuries can be used to study women's texts written before 1700. Ezell begins her work by considering the current state of women's literary history and examines assumptions about genre, authorship, and history itself. Subsequent chapters explore the establishment of the women's literary canon during the eighteenth, nineteenth, and twentieth centuries. Through an examination of anthologies of women's verse and writings from each of these centuries, Ezell hopes to show how the women's literary canon developed, based on notions of what constitutes a female tradition. Throughout these chapters, the author presents two striking images of the female author. The first, Judith Shakespeare, a creation of Virginia Woolf, attempts and fails to earn her living as a commercial writer; the second, Clarissa, a character by novelist Samuel Richardson, must hide her tremendous talent as a writer until her death. The final chapter applies Ezell's feminist revisionist theories to the lost works of Quaker women between 1650 and 1672, thereby challenging assumptions about literary production and historiography. Ezell even discusses new modes of literary production that will continue to develop, and how writers can use such technology to make women's literary past available in the twenty-first century. Ezell's work is worthwhile for scholars of feminist literary history, as well as for an introductory class on literary studies.

1250. Fraiman, Susan. *Unbecoming Women: British Women Writers and the Novel of Development*. New York: Columbia University Press, 1993. 189p. (Gender and Culture). bibliog. index. ISBN (OP); 0231080018pa.

In this work, Fraiman asks the following question: "Is there a female *Bildungsroman*?" Her priority does not lie in answering the question, but in providing a model for deconstructing the phrase "female *Bildungsroman*." The "unbecoming" of the title "is intended to push back against conventional assumptions about becoming and stories of becoming, and this pressure is obtained in large part by focusing on *women*" (p. i). In the male *Bildungsroman* men mature in a linear process; however, because of the "burdens" of femininity, including finding a sense of worth through home and love, society restricts the development of women. Fraiman argues that "these narratives do not simply proceed toward the destination of adulthood but go on themselves to constitute the adult self, which is always fluid and emergent" (p. xiii). The author studies the narratives of Frances Burney, Jane Austen, Charlotte Brontë, George Eliot, and several conduct-book authors to explore variations of growing up female. In the opening chapter, Fraiman considers whether a female *Bildungsroman* really exists. Remaining chapters compare such texts as *Pride and Prejudice* and *The Mill on the Floss* with male "novels of development," including

David Copperfield and *Wilhelm Meister*. Although at times her work is densely argued, Fraiman presents a fine model for reading the female *Bildungsroman*.

1251. Froula, Christine. *Modernism's Body: Sex, Culture, and Joyce*. New York: Columbia University Press, 1996. 316p. bibliog. index. ISBN 0231104421; 023110443Xpa.

Intersecting the theories of Sigmund Freud, Jacques Lacan, and Jacques Derrida with feminist theory, Froula creates a bold and persuasive new reading of Joyce in *Modernism's Body*. The author examines Joyce's autobiographical writing and his inherited assumptions about masculine and feminine identity. According to Froula, Joyce takes his analysis of masculinity further than either Freud or Lacan by creating a law of gender. In Joyce, Froula sees "a distinction between the oedipal Law of the Father, which subsumes identificatory desire within sexual desire, and what I call the law of gender: the social and cultural taboo against the son's identificatory desire for his mother, the maternal body, and those attributes his culture categorizes as 'feminine' " (p. 12). The author relies extensively on *Exiles, Dubliners*, and Joyce's letters and manuscript materials to conduct her study. Throughout, Froula traces Joyce's "vivisecting" of his masculinist assumptions, which do not pertain to phallic loss, but to the loss of identification with the maternal and feminine. *Modernism's Body* is a welcome addition to the canon on Joyce.

1252. Grewal, Inderpal. *Home and Harem: Nation, Gender, Empire, and the Cultures of Travel*. Durham, NC: Duke University Press, 1996. 286p. (Post-contemporary Interventions). bibliog. index. ISBN 0822317311; 0822317400pa.

In this fascinating study, Grewal traces "the impact of the nineteenth-century European culture of travel on social divisions in England and India in order to show the cultural basis and effects of imperialism" (p. 1). The author uses the discourse of travel and mobility as a lens for examining nation formation, imperialism, colonial modernity, and feminism in nineteenth-century India and Britain. Grewal departs from similar studies of travel and imperialism because she examines the impact of imperialism on all social classes and races. Part 1 explores domestic space, viewed as "home" or "in England," wherein society formed class, gender, and a national identity. In one telling chapter, Grewal analyzes how British museum guidebooks served to persuade the working and middle classes of the ideology of empire. In part 2, the author surveys the writings of Indian men and women and the impact of travel and colonization on these "harem" spaces: "My concern is with the formation of colonial modernity through the discourse of Euroimperial travel as it becomes incorporated into the lives of colonized people" (p. 15).

Readers unfamiliar with Victorian women's travel writing may also want to read *A Wider Range: Travel Writing by Women in Victorian England* (Fairleigh Dickinson University Press, 1994) by Maria H. Frawley. Frawley surveys the writing of five women well known within their fields of art history, art criticism, social science, journalism, and social reform. The author argues that their professions not only gave these women an identity, but also cultural legitimacy and subject authority to write. *A Wider Range* adds to the discourse on Victorian literary history and Victorian women's travel writing through a combination of travel and disciplinary professional writing.

1253. Hall, Kim F. *Things of Darkness: Economies of Race and Gender in Early Modern England*. Ithaca, NY: Cornell University Press, 1995. 319p. bibliog. index. ISBN (OP); 0801482496pa.

Things of Darkness is a thoroughly researched and thoughtfully argued piece of work wherein Hall analyzes economies of race and gender in early modern England. Appropriating a phrase from Shakespeare's *The Tempest* for her title, Hall relies on "canonical" texts to investigate blackness, colonialism, race, and femininity. She integrates black feminist criticism with postcolonial studies to illustrate how society constructed "self" and "other," black and white, or dark and light in early modern English literature and material culture. Hall divides her work into five chapters: travel narratives and early histories of Africa; the dark/fair dichotomies produced in Elizabethan sonnets, such as Sidney's *Astrophel and Stella*; drama as discussed through Jonson's *Masque of Blackness* and Shakespeare's *Antony and Cleopatra* and *The Tempest*; race and English women writers, including Wroth's *Urania*; and material culture and representations of blackness and gender. Hall also provides excellent illustrations, an epilogue calling for more study, and an appendix with *Poems of Blackness*.

Moira Ferguson's *Subject to Others: British Women Writers and Colonial Slavery, 1670–1834* (Routledge, 1992) describes the constructions of race and gender in British literature through the voice of white female writers. With a clear feminist agenda, Ferguson includes useful analysis of women's writing about slavery and examines the intersections of women's experiences with slavery and colonialism. Although Ferguson thoroughly researched and clearly crafted *Subject to Others*, the work may prove too scholarly for most undergraduates. Overall, however, students, teachers, and scholars should encounter multiple levels of inquiry in these excellent works.

1254. Hansen, Elaine Tuttle. *Chaucer and the Fictions of Gender*. Berkeley: University of California Press, 1992. 301p. bibliog. index. ISBN 0520071336; 0520074998pa.

Discussing several of Chaucer's works, including *The Legend of Good Women*, "The Wife of Bath's Tale," *The Book of the Duchess, The Parliament of Fowls*, "The Clerk's Tale," and "The Merchant's Tale," Hansen reads Chaucer with a strong feminist eye, yet her approach differs from other feminist critics. The author focuses on the misogynistic anxiety of Chaucer's male characters and male narrators, and not on the construction of women through the male voice: "I have stressed, then, that in the very real continuity of concern throughout Chaucerian fiction, with the representation of women, I hear not a swelling chorus of female voices entering the text and speaking for and about themselves, but something of a monotone making known both feminine absence and masculine anxiety" (p. 12). Hansen argues that Chaucer was writing during a time of great uncertainty and instability about gender identity. Thus the real problem in Chaucerian fiction is "the gendered identity of male characters, male narrators, and (?male) readers. The problem is always represented in large part as a problem of the feminization of men" (p. 12). Hansen provides a fascinating and complex examination of Chaucerian fiction.

Jill Mann's *Geoffrey Chaucer* (Harvester Wheatsheaf, 1991), a title in the Feminist Readings series, contains several of the same themes as Hansen's book. Mann analyzes stories from the *Canterbury Tales* and *Troilus and Criseyde*. Yet the authors' points of view diverge regarding the subject of the hero. Both works are valuable to academic audiences.

1255. Jordan, Constance. *Renaissance Feminism: Literary Texts and Political Models*. Ithaca, NY: Cornell University Press, 1990. bibliog. index. ISBN 0801421632; 0801497329pa.

Jordan reads a wide range of works, including marriage manuals, prose romances, government treatises, political pamphlets, and letters, as well as the writings of Aristotle, Erasmus, Agrippa von Nettesheim, Giovanni Boccaccio, Philip Sidney, and others, to uncover the varying beliefs about women during the Renaissance. The author argues that while these works may not qualify as true feminist texts, many do present a "prowoman" argument. These writings reflect upon the subjugation of women and issues of power: "Throughout all these works—and it has been perhaps the only feature they consistently share—is a pervasive concern with questions of authority and subordination, that is, with the origins of the control of man over woman and its expression in postlapsarian history, and with the rights of the woman who is subject to a male superior" (p. 3). Jordan argues that feminist Renaissance texts often fell into three categories: straightforward defenses of women; moralistic writing, claiming women as the more virtuous sex; and misogynistic discourse, which "by portraying the sturdy reliance of their objects of scorn often transform blame into a kind of grudging or implied praise" (p. 2).

On a similar theme, Pamela Joseph Benson's *The Invention of the Renaissance Woman: The Challenge of Female Independence in the Literature and Thought of Italy and England* (Pennsylvania State University Press, 1992) must also be considered. Benson demonstrates the contradictory ways in which early Italian and English men discussed the "woman question." She rereads a selection of canonical texts from Boccaccio's *De mulieribus claris*, Spenser's *The Fairie Queene*, Vives, Castiglione, Thomas More, and Sir Thomas Eliot. Extensively researched and thoughtfully argued, *Renaissance Feminism* will appeal to upper-level undergraduates, graduate students, and scholars in history, women's studies, or feminist criticism. *The Invention of the Renaissance Woman* is an easier read, making it a more appropriate choice for undergraduate students.

1256. Krontiris, Tina. *Oppositional Voices: Women as Writers and Translators of Literature in the English Renaissance.* New York: Routledge, 1992. 182p. bibliog. index. ISBN 0415063299; 0415162637pa.

Relying on cultural materialist and feminist methodologies, Krontiris examines six female writers and their secular works, published in England between 1500 and 1640. Three central chapters discuss the lives of these women and the context in which they wrote. Within each chapter, Krontiris provides a useful and thoughtful comparison of Isabella Whitney with Margaret Tyler, former domestic servants; Mary Sidney Herbert, countess of Pembroke, with Elizabeth Cary, Lady Falkland; and Aemilia Lanyer with Mary Wroth, both with ties to the Jacobean court. These chapters and pairings permit a strong discussion of social class, culture and gender relations, and political and economic contexts with an emphasis on the lives of each author. The first and last chapters provide a theoretical yet thoughtful introduction and conclusion to this fine work.

There are two other titles worth mentioning that complement Krontiris's work, *Tudor and Stuart Women* (Indiana University Press, 1994) and *The Renaissance Englishwoman in Print: Counterbalancing the Canon* (University of Massachusetts Press, 1990). *Tudor and Stuart Women* by Louise Schleiner focuses on the same writers mentioned in the preceding paragraph and draws on the works of the Cooke sisters, Elizabeth Weston, John Donne, and Anne Southwell. Examining similar themes, Schleiner's aim is to illustrate how English women writers, from the 1560s to the 1630s, moved their writing into the male-dominated public or semipublic realms and away from the boundaries of their personal lives. *The Renaissance Englishwoman in Print*, edited by Anne M. Haselkorn and Betty S. Travitsky, includes eighteen essays by respected literary critics that examine the literary texts of the Tudor and Stuart periods, with particular focus on the correlation between the canonized male texts and the marginalized female texts. While *Tudor and Stuart Women* is a thought-provoking feminist literary history with comprehensive appendices helpful for anyone wishing to do further research, *The Renaissance Englishwoman in Print* will be useful mostly to scholars.

1257. Leighton, Angela. *Victorian Women Poets: Writing against the Heart.* Charlottesville: University Press of Virginia, 1992. 321p. (Victorian Literature and Culture Series). bibliog. index. ISBN (OP); 0813914272pa.

Literary critics, while favoring a few female poets of the nineteenth century, generally have given little attention to women's poetry as a distinct genre. Hoping to correct this omission, Leighton examines the lives and works of eight mostly forgotten female poets: Felicia Hemans,

Letitia Elizabeth Landon, Augusta Webster, Michael Field, Alice Meynell, and Charlotte Mew, with Elizabeth Barrett Browning and Christina Rossetti being the exceptions. The author recognizes the originality of these poets, yet Leighton also claims that a discussion of their work "opens up into a continuous and connecting discussion of the nature of the nineteenth-century female imagination" and the "struggle with and against a highly moralized celebration of women's sensibility" (p. 3). Leighton analyzes the strategies these women used to create poetry that was "against the heart," poetry unconnected to prescribed female emotions. Leighton discusses contemporaneous ideas regarding sensibility and the ideal of creative, yet suffering, femininity and argues that these women could not escape the ideologies of their time. Leighton grounds her arguments in biographical-historical materials and formalist-aesthetic interpretations of the poetry, which highlight the tension that these poets experienced. Leighton constructs a very readable and valuable study via placing the poetry of women into the context of a tradition of women's poetry, as opposed to a typical historical context.

1258. Mellor, Anne K. *Romanticism and Gender.* New York: Routledge, 1993. 275p. bibliog. index. ISBN (OP); 0415906644pa.

Anne K. Mellor, a well-known author within the field of feminist literary criticism who has contributed numerous books, including *Romanticism and Feminism* (1988, 1997) and *British Literature, 1780–1832* (1996), with Richard Matlak, provides another important study of women's literature. Focusing on the romantic period in British literature, Mellor begins by discussing the exclusion of several hundred female writers—poets, novelists, playwrights, essayists, and journalists—from critical study. Instead, scholars have based the current canon of British romanticism on the work of six men, William Wordsworth, Samuel Taylor Coleridge, William Blake, George Gordon, Lord Byron, Percy Bysshe Shelley, and John Keats. Mellor illustrates a paradigm shift in this canon by examining the works of women writers of the same period, including Ann Radcliffe, Mary Wollstonecraft, Maria Edgeworth, Jane Austen, Felicia Hemans, Letitia Landon, Charlotte Smith, Jane Taylor, and Emily Brontë. The author argues that the works of the male writers relied heavily on the use of polarity, or a binary model, of ego versus non-ego and thesis versus antithesis to create a threatening "other." However, Mellor writes that female romanticism "was based on a subjectivity constructed in relation to other subjectivities, hence a self that is fluid, absorptive, responsive, with permeable ego boundaries" (p. 209). Mellor links men with "masculine Romanticism" and women with a "feminine Romanticism," which expresses an inherent polarity of thinking. The romantic period is therefore more complex than scholars of the current canon believe. *Romanticism and Gender*, an ambitious project, is a fine addition to the study of British romanticism and an excellent introduction to this growing field.

1259. Mermin, Dorothy. *Godiva's Ride: Women of Letters in England, 1830–1880.* Bloomington: Indiana University Press, 1993. 181p. (Women of Letters). bibliog. index. ISBN (OP); 0253208246pa; 0585001022 (e-book).

The legend of Lady Godiva clearly illustrates Mermin's thesis: "She represents to the highest degree, and in a singularly enabling form, the multifarious contradictions that encompassed women writers in early and mid-Victorian England" (p. xvi). Lady Godiva, whose self-exposure revealed both vulnerability and strength, inspired many of the writers Mermin examines in her work. In parts 1 and 2, Mermin discusses the work of several Victorian writers, including Elizabeth Barrett Browning, Elizabeth Gaskell, Charlotte Brontë, George Eliot, Christina Rossetti, Jean Ingelow, Augusta Weber, and Anna Jameson. The author argues for the inclusion of all of these women in the literary canon. Mellor considers women's nonfiction writing, especially works that deal with religion and science, in part 3. Throughout, Mellor focuses on the paradoxical pressures that

Victorian women writers faced, whether they wrote fiction, poetry, or nonfiction. This fine work encompasses and synthesizes a broad range of genres of Victorian women's writing.

Rediscovering Forgotten Radicals: British Women Writers, 1889–1939 (University of North Carolina Press, 1993), edited by Angela Ingram and Daphne Patai, includes essays on a group of women active in suffrage, socialism, free love, and peace movements who also wrote fiction. The thirteen essays in this volume examine how these women's political lives shaped their literary work. *Rediscovering Forgotten Radicals* provides an important critique on the literature produced by these unknown women, but unfortunately, all of the works themselves are out of print.

1260. Michie, Elsie B. *Outside the Pale: Cultural Exclusion, Gender Difference, and the Victorian Woman Writer.* Ithaca, NY: Cornell University Press, 1993. 190p. (Reading Women Writing). bibliog. index. ISBN (OP); 080148085Xpa.

Michie provides a model for literary criticism by focusing on gender differences across social economies in this well-researched and clearly written work. Covering the period from 1818 to 1870, the author examines novels by Mary Shelley, Charlotte and Emily Brontë, Elizabeth Gaskell, and George Eliot and analyzes the authors' relationships with male mentors in the publishing world. Michie attempts to illustrate how society defined or constructed femininity, often referred to as the "other" or the "inferior race," not only in relation to the author's specific historical moment, but also in relation to how the authors captured that construction in their novels. Michie's goal is not simply "to identify the historical concerns that motivated a particular definition of femininity, but to analyze *how* discourses having to do with gender work together with discourses having to do with politics, economics, colonial thinking, or class relations" (p. 7). Mitchie clearly outlines how these female authors responded to the changing social and economic concerns of their times, both in their personal lives and through their writings. While Victorian ideology may have felt repressive to these women as writers, Michie argues that they responded with varying strategies of resistance in their writing.

The following works from the series Reading Women Writing contribute to this topic as well. In *Imperialism at Home: Race and Victorian Women's Fiction* (Cornell University Press, 1996), Susan Meyer addresses selected works of Charlotte and Emily Brontë and George Eliot to explore race as a metaphor for gender and to demonstrate how these authors' works questioned racial hierarchies.

Karen R. Lawrence includes feminist texts written from 1656 to 1969 in *Penelope Voyages: Women and Travel in the British Literary Tradition* (Cornell University Press, 1994). Lawrence considers the work of several feminist literary critics, including Hélène Cixous, as well as poststructuralist, postcolonial, and psychoanalytic work, to analyze women's "exilic wandering," in which women reinvent their lives and social constructions.

In *Borderwork: Feminist Engagements with Comparative Literature* (Cornell University Press, 1994), edited by Margaret R. Higonnet, contributors examine the similarities between comparative literature and feminist criticism and argue for a redefinition of the inherent boundaries between the two fields. Each author displays a thorough knowledge of theory and criticism, as well as a firm grasp of the complex issues relevant to her topic. These complex works would complement courses for upper-level undergraduates, graduates, and scholars who study literature, women's studies, history and culture, or feminist theory. The series Reading Women Writing, edited by Shari Benstock and Celeste Schenck, includes works that spark debate on feminist theory and practice, emphasizing culture, histories, and experiences.

1261. Showalter, Elaine. *Sexual Anarchy: Gender and Culture at the Fin de Siècle.* New York: Viking Press, 1990. 242p. index. (OP)

According to Showalter, a noted feminist scholar, this book "is about the myths, metaphors, and images of sexual crises and apocalypse that marked both the late nineteenth century and our own *fin de siècle*, and its representations in English and American literature, art, and film" (p. 3). The author intelligently explores parallel social issues that occurred at the end of the nineteenth and twentieth centuries, including sexual scandal, rampant disease, family crises, and race and class relations. Critics and historians agree that the *fin de siècle* is noted for a battle of the sexes and the antagonism over women's rights. Showalter argues that a battle between the sexes actually occurred because of changing gender identities and roles. The author analyzes *The Strange Case of Dr. Jekyll and Mr. Hyde* and *Dracula*, as well as the works of such authors as George Eliot, Rudyard Kipling, Oscar Wilde, Joseph Conrad, and Olive Schreiner. Showalter also explores issues relating to lesbianism and homosexuality. Several excellent illustrations enhance this text.

1262. Wilson, Carol Shiner, and Joel Hafner, eds. *Re-visioning Romanticism: British Women Writers, 1776–1837*. Philadelphia: University of Pennsylvania Press, 1994. 329p. bibliog. index. ISBN 0812232313; 0812214218pa.

In this thought-provoking work, Wilson and Hafner address four major issues dominating romantic studies: new narratives of critical histories and the canon, new constructions of aesthetics, new strategies of reading, and contextualization. Essayists discuss works by familiar and unfamiliar writers, including Mary Robinson, Felicia Hemans, Phillis Wheatley, Hannah More, Anna Barbauld, Ann Griffiths, Charlotte Smith, and Joanna Bailie. Contributors consider the role of power, authority, and female authorship in contextualizing specific literary pieces in the first part. In part 2, contributors deal with "women writers' responses to culturally defined expectations of female sentiments and behavior" (p. 10). In part 3, essayists question various concepts of genre, communal space, genius, and the commonplace and leave the door open for a discussion of gay and lesbian drama theory. Despite some overlap, each essay furthers discourse on how these women contributed to re-visioning British romanticism.

Cheryl Turner surveys women's involvement in the early book trade in *Living by the Pen: Women Writers in the Eighteenth Century* (Routledge, 1992). She uses a historical approach to discuss various issues, including women's survival in the field of writing, publishers' responses to women authors, the social and economic background of the writers, and attitudes about writing as a female occupation. Even though Turner focuses on fiction, she also examines other genres of writing that women practiced, such as poetry, drama, religious prose, journalism, and children's books. This work includes two appendices: a catalog of women's fiction published in book form between 1696 and 1796 and a chronological list of women authors between these same dates.

Dale Spender's *Mothers of the Novel: 100 Great Women Writers before Jane Austen* (Pandora Press, 1986) provides a fine and easily readable introduction to women fiction writers from the sixteenth to the eighteenth century. Spender challenges the established canon of male writers through critique and contextualization of the women's works and lives, respectively. Spender includes a biography of each writer and a summary of each writer's best works.

North America

1263. Ammons, Elizabeth. *Conflicting Stories: American Women Writers at the Turn of the Twentieth Century*. New York: Oxford University Press, 1991. 234p. bibliog. index. ISBN (OP); 0195080386pa.

During the turn of the century, women authors, many of whom produced works that conformed to expected generic structures such as the sentimental novel, experienced prolific times.

Elizabeth Ammons suggests that many of these authors refused to approach writing as a profession and instead viewed themselves as literary artists, thus defying conventional expectations. These women, including Willa Cather, Kate Chopin, Gertrude Stein, and Edith Wharton, form a countercanon of authors whose works are connected through their "gender, historical context and self-definition" (p. 4). Ammons insightfully argues that although these women hailed from diverse ethnic, social, and economic backgrounds, their divergence from traditional literary forms and their interest in similar themes of power, exploitation, and violence linked them together. Through a comparison of such different authors' works, Ammons raises questions about race, racism, literary form, and the reception of these issues.

1264. Braxton, Joanne M., and Andrée Nicola McLaughlin, eds. *Wild Women in the Whirlwind: Afra-American Culture and the Contemporary Literary Renaissance*. New Brunswick, NJ: Rutgers University Press, 1990. 441p. bibliog. index. ISBN 081351441X; 0813514428pa.

In *Wild Women and the Whirlwind*, the editors celebrate the boom in Afra-American literature as it relates to the "intercontinental boom in literature by Black women" (p. xiii). This anthology, however, is highly inclusive: the editors juxtapose essays that fall under the broader umbrella of cultural studies (the arts, music, and history) with essays that deal exclusively with works of literature. Contributors examine "foremothers" in the first group of essays: leaders, workers, and nurturers of Afra-American women's cultural traditions, including blues singer Ma Rainey, activist Sojourner Truth, and diarist Charlotte Forten. In the second group of essays, contributors deal with the outer boundaries of this renaissance in conjunction with experiences faced by African American women. Topics include challenges that African American lesbian writers face, the backlash of African American men against African American feminist writings, and the slow growth of African American women's history in the academy. In the final section, essayists attempt to create a future for black female writers by addressing the past through literature and other cultural expressions. The impressive breadth of topics included in this anthology and the intermingling of literary criticism with social and cultural issues create an impressively broad portrait of the Afra-American cultural renaissance.

In *Black Women Writing Autobiography: A Tradition within a Tradition* (Temple University Press, 1989), Braxton focuses on African American women and their autobiographical writings. She traces the development of black women's autobiographical writings from slave narratives, such as Harriet Jacobs's *Incidents in the Life of a Slave Girl*, and writings by fugitive slaves to Maya Angelou's *I Know Why the Caged Bird Sings*. The author includes diaries, journals, letters, and other forms that literary scholars previously have ignored.

1265. Burstein, Janet Handler. *Writing Mothers, Writing Daughters: Tracing the Maternal in Stories by American Jewish Women*. Urbana: University of Illinois Press, 1996. 205p. bibliog. index. ISBN 0252022521.

Burstein examines the works of Jewish American women and their portrayal of the mother-daughter relationship in an attempt to address the author's own confusion about the inherent contradictions that she often observed in her mother's behavior as a strong woman, yet a secondary participant in religious practices. Burstein's study, which begins with the immigrant experience and culminates in a discussion of feminism and tradition, deals with unique issues pertaining to the relationships between Jewish mothers and daughters, as expressed through their writings. The author examines forty different pieces that both well-known and obscure writers crafted about the mother-daughter dynamic. The authors trace the psychological, social, political, and literary development of Jewish women's interpersonal interactions, which places their works into historical, cultural, and literary contexts. Burstein, who considers both literary and autobiographical writings, argues that although history may provide facts, only literature is truly faithful to both the facts and the feelings inherent in interpersonal relationships. She incorporates Jewish feminist and psychoanalytic theories into her work to dispel the negative stereotypes associated with Jewish mothers and daughters.

1266. Coultrap-McQuin, Susan. *Doing Literary Business: American Women Writers in the Nineteenth Century.* Chapel Hill: University of North Carolina Press, 1990. 253p. bibliog. index. ISBN 080781914X; 0807842842pa.

Coultrap-McQuin analyzes the publishing industry from the 1840s to the early 1900s, when publishers treated clients more like family members than business associates. Indeed, the publisher played the role of a patriarch. According to Coultrap-McQuin, women authors flourished in this atmosphere because they could maintain a sense of "True Womanhood" and compete on a level playing field with male writers. The author illustrates the paradox of the submissive female versus the savvy writer and businesswoman through the literary lives of five writers: E.D.E.N. Southworth, Harriet Beecher Stowe, Mary Abigail Dodge (also known as Gail Hamilton), Helen Hunt Jackson (also known as H.H. and Saxe Holm), and Elizabeth Stuart Phelps (also known as Elizabeth Stuart Phelps Ward). The author reveals a world in which women dominated the publishing industry in both volume of production and sales. As the publishing world evolved into a more impersonal, business-like industry, however, production of sentimental literature decreased, while scientific and rational works became more acceptable. Since women writers apparently did not create scientific literature, a decline in women's authorship occurred. This study is engaging not only because of the description of the five authors' business lives, but also because the author provides a historical context in which these women and others produced a vast volume of literature.

1267. Donovan, Kathleen M. *Feminist Readings of Native American Literature: Coming to Voice.* Tucson: University of Arizona Press, 1998. 181p. bibliog. index. ISBN 0816516324; 0816516332pa.

Donovan explores the connections between Native American women's literature and feminisms. Invoking bell hooks's writing, Donovan's central theme is women finding their voice: "Who can speak? and how? and under what circumstances? What can be said? And after the ideas find voice, what action can be taken?" (pp. 7–8). The author agrees with hooks's belief that women's search for a voice is both an act of resistance and an act of self-transformation. Donovan considers several themes in Native American women's writing, including the "agency of women of color interacting with the dominant culture; . . . the feminist reader encountering misogyny in a 'canonical' Native American text; [and] . . . intertextuality among women's texts from different cultures" (p. 9). Six chapters cover Metis women writers; Havasupai women's songs; female characters in the novels of M. Scott Momaday; the relationship between Mourning Dove, one of the first Native American female authors to write a novel, and her editor; connections between the works of Paula Gunn Allen and Toni Morrison; and "the complex link between the darkness and femaleness" (p. 13) in the works of Hélène Cixous and Joy Harjo. This book is recommended for all research libraries.

Writing as Witness: Essay and Talk (Women's Press, 1994) presents a collection by the Mohawk writer and lesbian activist Beth Brant. Brant delves into everything from the evolution of Native American women's writing to the life of Pocahontas to the homophobia she encounters as a lesbian writer. In *Native American Women Writers* (Chelsea House Publishers, 1998), editor Harold Bloom brings together brief critical extracts on eleven Native American women writers, including Maria Campbell, Louise Erdrich, Linda Hogan, Wendy Rose, and Leslie Marmon Silko. With brief biographical information and a short bibliography on each writer, this book would be an excellent text for undergraduate courses in American women's literature. *Reinventing the Enemy's Language: Contemporary Native Women's Writing of North America* (Norton, 1987), edited by Joy Harjo and Gloria Bird, brings together poetry, fiction, prayers, and memoirs from more than eighty writers representing fifty nations. This collection is recommended for both public and academic libraries.

1268. Dubey, Madhu. *Black Women Novelists and the National Aesthetic*. Bloomington: Indiana University Press, 1994. 195p. bibliog. index. ISBN 0253318416; 0253208556pa.

An African American movement called the National Aesthetic occurred during the 1970s. This movement, which hinged on racial issues, discouraged discussion of "gender and other differences that might complicate a unitary conception of the Black experience" (p. 1). The unitary experience theoretically represented the African American community as a whole; however, the movement focused more on issues affecting black men. Within this context, Dubey provides close textual readings of six novels written during the 1970s by three major African American female novelists, Alice Walker, Toni Morrison, and Gayl Jones. While the authors' works greatly differ, they all challenge the National Aesthetic's tendency to marginalize writers, especially women writers, who do not privilege community over the individual. Employing black feminist literary criticism to analyze these texts, Dubey concentrates on two principles: the conflict created by the use of stereotypes versus realistic characters, and the employment of oral folk culture, a source of uniquely black feminist literary authority. The author readily applies these two principles to the texts and challenges the representation of black femininity apparent in the discourse of the National Aesthetic.

1269. Foster, Frances Smith. *Written by Herself: Literary Production by African American Women, 1746–1892*. Bloomington: Indiana University Press, 1993. 206p. bibliog. index. ISBN (OP); 025320786Xpa.

Scholars consider 1892 a watershed year for African American women writers, especially with the publication of Anna Julia Cooper's *A Voice from the South by a Black Woman of the South*. However, the literary production of African American women has a long history, dating back to the eighteenth century. Foster traces the development of several of these writers who created numerous works despite the obstacles they faced as a result of their gender and ethnic background. The author examines the texts alongside the literary writings of other "subcultures," including African American men and white women, to more fully reveal the contemporary social and political contexts of the era. *Written by Herself* provides a literary legacy to writers that many people generally have forgotten. Hazel V. Carby examines African American women's writings where Foster ends her analysis in *Reconstructing Womanhoods: The Emergence of the Afro-American Woman Novelist* (Oxford University Press, 1987).

1270. Halio, Jay L., and Ben Siegel, eds. *Daughters of Valor: Contemporary Jewish American Women Writers*. Newark: University of Delaware Press, 1997. 286p. bibliog. index. ISBN 0874136113.

In this collection of essays that focus on accomplished women writers within a broad variety of genres, contributors address women as double outsiders, outsiders within their own patriarchal religion as well as in society as a whole. The essayists also examine other themes, including the Holocaust, the formation of Israel, and the Six-Day War, addressing how these authors' "Jewishness" has shaped their work. Essayists analyze the work of writers such as Erica Jong, Cynthia

Ozick, Norma Rose, and Pauline Kael, defining them as identifiably Jewish authors who focus on many of the same themes. Although the editors acknowledge the tremendous visibility and recognition of Jewish American women writers during the past thirty years, scholars rarely have studied them as a group prior to the growth of feminist literary study. The essays convey the belief that scholars and students should not focus on gender when studying these works because the intellectual quality of these writers and the themes expressed in their works are of greater importance.

Diane Lichtenstein also locates thematic similarities in the writings of Jewish women, but she concentrates on women writing during the nineteenth century in *Writing Their Nations: The Tradition of Nineteenth-Century American Jewish Women Writers* (Indiana University Press, 1992). Lichtenstein argues that Jewish women with similar cultural values, experiences, and heritage created a "tradition," or a group of writings, that expressed similar concerns. Many of these themes reoccur in contemporary Jewish women's literature, which makes *Writing Their Nations* an important work for the continuing study of Jewish women's works.

1271. Holloway, Karla F.C. *Moorings and Metaphors: Figures of Culture and Gender in Black Women's Literature*. New Brunswick, NJ: Rutgers University Press, 1992. 218p. bibliog. index. ISBN 0813517451; 081351746Xpa.

In *Moorings and Metaphors*, Karla Holloway argues that despite the vast geographical distance separating the United States from West Africa, similarities exist between the literatures produced by female writers from both regions. "Moorings" refer to a center where "behavior, art, philosophy, and language unite as a cultural expression within an African-American literary tradition" (p. 1). Holloway claims that black women's writings reflect their community through these cultural expressions, especially literature, whether the writing emerges from the United States or West Africa. "Metaphor" references the unifying themes that thread the writings of black women together. Holloway is particularly drawn to the construct of the goddess/ancestor, since it reflects a commonality among these writers. In part 1, she explores various theories and their applications to culture and gender, including the politics of literary theory. In part 2, the author applies this theoretical discussion to U.S. and West African authors' texts and continues to explore the unifying theme of the goddess/ancestor. Holloway's theoretical discussions employ jargon-laden language that detracts from her argument, and she focuses mostly on theory rather than application. Only graduate students and faculty members can likely decipher this otherwise important work.

1272. Horno-Delgado, Asunción, Eliana Ortega, Nina M. Scott, and Nancy Saporta Sternbach, eds. *Breaking Boundaries: Latina Writings and Critical Readings*. Amherst: University of Massachusetts Press, 1989. 263p. bibliog. ISBN (OP); 0870236369pa.

In *Breaking Boundaries*, the editors present a variety of rich literary works crafted by women of Latin American origin living in the United States. The work is chronologically organized according to when a particular Latin American ethnic group established a literary tradition in the United States. The editors include women's writings from the following ethnic groups: Chicana, Puerto Rican, and Cuban, as well as Latin American women writers who identify with other groups. Each subsection consists of a Latina writer's testimonial, coupled with essays that incorporate a variety of critical approaches. An extensive bibliography lists the works of Latina writers, as well as Latina literature published in both English and Spanish. The bibliography also provides a list of journals that publish writings of or critical discussions about Latinas, anthologies, and critical essays.

Although *Breaking Boundaries* presents a fine starting point for research in Latina literature, Marie Herrera-Sobek and Helena Maria Viramontes's *Chicana Creativity and Criticism: Charting*

New Frontiers in American Literature (Arte Publico Press, 1988), reissued with an updated introduction in 1996, offers a more focused approach to Chicana writers' works. The authors critique primary texts, including poetry, prose, and reproductions of Chicanas' artworks, to examine how traditional literary criticism affects a marginalized group of writings and other works.

1273. Kafka, Phillipa. *(Un)Doing the Missionary Position: Gender Asymmetry in Contemporary Asian American Women's Writing.* Westport, CT: Greenwood Press, 1997. 189p. (Contributions in Women's Studies). bibliog. index. ISBN 0313301611.

Kafka analyzes selected texts of five contemporary Chinese and Japanese American women writers to explore how these writers confront gender asymmetry, that is, the continuing suppression of women in the white patriarchal structure. Kafka brings the works of these feminist and postfeminist authors to the forefront to address the lack of attention paid to Asian American female authors in mainstream feminist criticism. Hoping to create "a transcultural or transglobal feminism" (p. xviii) within literary theory, Kafka seeks dialogue between the differing positions of feminist literary theorists; she believes that the problem of gender asymmetry is a global problem requiring a global perspective. The author analyzes the work of Amy Tan, Fae Myenne Ng, Gish Jen, R.A. Sasaki, and Cynthia Kadohata, paying particular attention to how these writers confront gender asymmetry. Kafka notes several common characteristics among these writers, including how the major female characters react to power, how the characters are often unreliable narrators, the importance of extended families in these characters' lives, and the techniques of subterfuge used by the characters "as a dodge against gender asymmetry" (p. 7). Framing her work within the thinking of postmodern, deconstructionist, and postcolonial theorists, Kafka presents a valuable interpretation of the work of contemporary Asian American female writers.

In *Images of Asian American Women by Asian American Women Writers* (Peter Lang, 1995), Esther Mikyung Ghymn studies the images of Asian American women in the works of twelve prominent Asian American female authors, including Amy Tan, Maxine Hong Kingston, Monica Sone, Mary Paik, and Yoshiko Uchida, among others. Ghymn examines nine novels, four autobiographies, two short stories, and one poem that portray varying images of Asian American women as mothers and daughters, wives, madwomen, prostitutes, and pariahs. In *Asian American Women Writers* (Chelsea House Publishers, 1997), editor Harold Bloom brings together brief critical extracts on eleven Asian American female authors, including Diana Chang, Joy Kogawa, Bharati Mukherjee, Jade Snow Wong, and Hisaye Yamamoto. With biographical information and a short bibliography on each writer, this book would be an excellent text for undergraduate courses in American women's literature. Finally, Amy Ling critically examines the work of more than thirty female authors in *Between Worlds: Women Writers of Chinese Ancestry* (Pergamon Press, 1990). Arranging her work chronologically, Ling begins with Sui Sin Far in the late nineteenth century and ends with Amy Tan. Ling writes that among the books "written in English by ethnic Chinese and Chinese Eurasians and published in the United States, the women not only outnumber the men but the women's books are more authentic, more numerous, quite simply—better" (p. xii). *Between Worlds* brings to light the literary creations of several previously ignored yet important female writers.

1274. McDowell, Deborah E. *"The Changing Same": Black Women's Literature, Criticism, and Theory.* Bloomington: Indiana University Press, 1995. 222p. bibliog. index. ISBN 0253336295; 0253209269pa.

This outstanding collection of essays illuminates the evolving approaches to literary criticism, especially within the realm of black feminist criticism. These essays address black women's writing from three major eras: the "Women's Era" of the 1890s, the Harlem Renaissance of the

1920s and 1930s, and the 1970s and 1980s, when black women authors' works became commercially viable and widely discussed. McDowell wrote many of these essays during the 1980s, and she has done little editing. By maintaining the original text of the essays, McDowell not only provides a critique of African American women's writing, but also presents a history of the changing critical and theoretical approaches to these works. McDowell discusses many works by African American women, including those by Alice Walker, Nella Larsen, and Toni Morrison. *"The Changing Same"* presents an important review of literary theory and its place within the arena of black feminist criticism.

1275. Morris, Linda A., ed. *American Women Humorists: Critical Essays.* New York: Garland Publishing, 1994. 441p. (Garland Studies in Humor). bibliog. index. ISBN 0815306229.

Considering the explosion in women's comedy occurring in all forms today, this title provides a useful tool for the beginning scholar interested in women's humor and humorists. Focusing primarily on humor writers, Morris compiled this collection of classic essays and a few new writings in order to stimulate critical discourse in an area that scholars largely have ignored. Morris organizes the collection into three general categories. First, contributors provide a historical overview of critical thought via introductory essays from anthologies on women's humor. The second section presents essays focusing on subgenres within women's humor along with broader critical essays. Finally, the essayists address the works of individual humorists. Encompassing women humorists from Dorothy Parker to stage performer Kate Clinton, this collection provides a useful overview of the critical study of women's humor.

Nancy Walker attempts to prove that women reveal their sense of humor through the written word in *A Very Serious Thing: Women's Humor and American Culture* (University of Minnesota Press, 1988). Through illustrations of personal realities, women poke fun at their subordinate positions in society in an attempt to reverse stereotypes. Walker's fine bibliography directs readers to a large number of primary texts that would supplement both of these titles.

1276. Ostriker, Alicia Suskin. *Stealing the Language: The Emergence of Women's Poetry in America.* Boston: Beacon Press, 1986. 315p. bibliog. index. ISBN (OP); 0807063037pa.

In 1650, a collection of poetry by Anne Bradstreet was published in the United States. Since then, women have both produced and published their poetry as a means of self-expression. In this insightful examination of women's contemporary poetry, Ostriker argues that the nature of women's poetry changed dramatically in the 1960s. The 1960s saw the publication of a number of highly influential collections, including Anne Sexton's *To Bedlam and Part Way Back*, Syvia Plath's *Ariel*, and H.D.'s *Helen in Egypt*. These and other poetry collections rejected the submissive posturing and genteel nature common in women's poetry prior to this period; instead, these poets embraced concepts explicitly defined as female. Ostriker illustrates this evolution by organizing her work by themes rather than by poet and includes chapters on the history of women's poetry until 1960, the quest in this poetry for self-definition, a feminine aesthetic grounded in the physical body, female anger and violence, and the feminine erotic. Although the author discusses many poets, she does not analyze individual texts or poets in great detail.

Betsy Erikkila focuses on the lives and poems of five poets, Emily Dickinson, Marianne Moore, Elizabeth Bishop, Adrienne Rich, and Gwendolyn Brooks, in *The Wicked Sisters: Women Poets, Literary History, and Discord* (Oxford University Press, 1992). She addresses two issues: the first involves the influence of other women on the lives and literary production of these five writers. Although many believe that these relationships are always supportive, Erikkila proposes that in fact they often pose problems. The second issue involves the influence of French feminist theorists and the illusion that common experiences "reduce all women writers to an economy of the same" (p. 3). Erikkila suggests that women's literature, as revealed through the poetry she examines, is really a site for conflict and dissension.

1277. Showalter, Elaine. *Sister's Choice: Tradition and Change in American Women's Writing*. Oxford: Clarendon Press, 1991. 198p. bibliog. index. ISBN 0198123833; (OP)

Elaine Showalter, author of the groundbreaking *A Literature of Their Own: British Women Novelists from Brontë to Lessing* (Princeton University Press, 1977) employs the metaphor of the quilt in an attempt to trace the development of women's writing throughout American history in *Sister's Choice*. Showalter discusses the inherent diversity and contradiction of American women's writings, which are comprised of many subcultures, from the 1650s to the 1990s. Although these subcultures are marginalized, the language of the dominant patriarchy continues to influence them. The author examines this conflict in chapter 2, called "Miranda's Story," in which Showalter draws a parallel between Shakespeare's Miranda, who learns her language from her father Prospero, and American women writers' reliance on male language and literary convention. The title's concluding chapter, using the quilt as metaphor, expertly describes the challenges faced by women authors. Showalter explicitly compares the collection of scraps, piecing, and communal sewing of a quilt to American female literary history. She defines quilting as "an art of making do and eking out, an art of ingenuity, and conservation. It reflects the fragmentation of women's time, the scrappiness and uncertainty of women's creative or solitary moments" (p. 149). The same can be said of women's literary history in America.

1278. Thurston, Carol. *The Romance Revolution: Erotic Novels for Women and the Quest for a New Sexual Identity*. Urbana: University of Illinois Press, 1987. 259p. bibliog. index. ISBN 025201247X.

The romance novel, which critics have ignored and treated as a waste of time, has enjoyed a rise in popularity among loyal fans, as well as scholars. Carol Thurston's sociological approach to the study of the "erotic" romance novel juxtaposes the genre's growth in popularity to changes in culture and society. Thurston relied on four different methodologies to gather data to support her arguments: a systematic content analysis of 100 texts, a survey employing a semantic differential scale to gather data about hero/heroine personality traits as assessed by readers, two separate mail surveys sent to 600 romance readers requesting information about their reading habits, and personal interviews with authors, editors, and publishers. Thurston's findings suggest a complex interplay between entertainment, society, and the audience. Moreover, they indicate that women who read "erotic" romances often identify with heroines who reflect their own interest in self-reliance. Thurston's work demonstrates how quantitative studies can be applied to a discipline that primarily relies upon qualitative analysis. It provides an important scholarly analysis of a literary genre that can no longer be ignored.

1279. Wall, Cheryl. *Women of the Harlem Renaissance*. Bloomington: Indiana University Press, 1995. 246p. bibliog. index. ISBN 0253329086; 0253209803pa.

In *Women of the Harlem Renaissance*, Cheryl Wall attempts to "chart the journeys of the women of the Harlem Renaissance" through their works and their lives (p. xv). She also strives to place the writings of three key women, Jessie Redmon Fauset, Nella Larsen, and Zora Neale Hurston, into their cultural and historic contexts through an examination of what the Harlem Renaissance meant to the women who wrote during that period. In chapter 1, Wall describes a Harlem Renaissance remembered through its male artists and writers. The Harlem Renaissance, however, represents something altogether different when perceived through the eyes of women. These women viewed the Harlem Renaissance as an outlet for the young, a perception that played a major role in these three women's lives and the lives of others during this era. The remaining three chapters address the lives and works of the three women by tracing their careers and suggesting that their works took each of them on a similar journey, both literally and figuratively.

In her previously published collection *Changing Our Own Words: Essays on Criticism, Theory, and Writing by Black Women* (Rutgers University Press, 1989), Wall approaches African American women's writings as a whole, rather than focusing on a specific historical period. Compiled from papers given at a symposium held at Rutgers University in 1987, these writings address issues of gender, class, and race in literature. Scholars apply a variety of literary theories and critical approaches to the works of Toni Morrison, Alice Walker, June Jordan, and Zora Neale Hurston.

Women's Literature from Other Countries

1280. Almeida, Irène Assiba d'. *Francophone African Women Writers: Destroying the Emptiness of Silence*. Gainesville: University Press of Florida, 1994. 222p. bibliog. index. ISBN 081301302X.

In this groundbreaking work on African women who write in French, Almeida discusses well-known and emerging writers from Cameroon, the Central African Republic, Ivory Coast, Gabon, and Senegal. This study begins with women's writing from the late 1970s because the author argues that women were silenced before this time. Almeida divides the study into three parts, which she argues parallel the development of women's literary production. Part 1 concerns self and analyzes autobiography, beginning with discussion of *A Dakar Childhood* by Nafissatou Diallo, the first Francophone African woman to write about her life. This part also includes a discussion of Andrée Blouin's *My Country, Africa* as a perfect example of "how the definition of autobiography as concerned with the self can expand to encompass historical, social, and political issues" (p. 25). The second part concentrates on family and analyzes novels representing a woman's role within the family. Almeida discusses Calixthe Beyala's *Your Name Will Be Tanga*, Angèle Rawiri's *Cries and Fury of Women* (both published only in French at the time of this book), and Mariama Bâ's *Scarlet Song*. The final part, paralleling the last stage of women's literary development, "discusses how female novelists link problems that affect women's lives to those affecting society at large" (p. 26). Here Almeida examines the following French authors: Werewere Liking, Aminata Sow Fall, and Véronique Tadjo. Reading the texts within the context of their time and with a sensitivity of not imposing Western literary critical interpretations, Almeida provides perceptive and at times unprecedented translations of these works.

1281. Castillo, Debra A. *Talking Back: Toward a Latin American Feminist Literary Criticism*. Ithaca, NY: Cornell University Press, 1992. 344p. (Reading Women Writing). bibliog. index. ISBN 0801426081; 0801499127pa.

Opening with the idea of recipe sharing as a form of reciprocity and intimacy among women, Castillo discusses the development of a feminist literary criticism that specifically will address Latin American women. In the process of creating this new methodology, Castillo questions both the uncritical application of Anglo-European approaches and the current state of Latin American feminist criticism, which tend to idealize and marginalize women's voices. Castillo instead proposes an amalgam of diverging critical approaches that scholars can apply to these writings, thereby highlighting the distinctive nature of Latin American women's writing. The author applies her narrative tactics to a variety of different writers and works, including Luisa Valenzuela, Rosario Ferre, Clarice Lispector, María Loisa Puga, and Maxine Hong Kingston. This results in an empowering of Latin American women writers, as well as the evolution of a new, critical approach to their work.

In *Easy Women: Sex and Gender in Modern Mexican Fiction* (University of Minnesota Press, 1998), Castillo studies the maneuvering room available to women as writers, characters, and readers in Mexican fiction. She discusses the following authors: Federico Gamboa, Antonia Mora, María Luisa Mendoza, Irma Serrano, Eduardo Muñuzuri, and Elena Garro. This work represents a much-needed resource on the study of Mexican women's literature.

1282. Chancy, Myriam J.A. *Searching for Safe Spaces: Afro-Caribbean Women Writers in Exile*. Philadelphia: Temple University Press, 1997. 246p. bibliog. index. ISBN 1566395399; 1566395402pa.

Chancy, a Haitian exile, examines the work of both Anglophone and Francophone women writers in *Searching for Safe Spaces*. Chancy discusses how women have used writing to resist dominant and oppressive social structures, as well as explore meaning concerning the loss of homeland. In women's writing about their exilic experiences, Chancy observes a process that encompasses alienation, self-definition, recuperation, and return. Through the writings of Joan Riley, Beryl Gilroy, M. Nourbese Philip, Dionne Brand, Makeda Silvera, Audre Lord, Rosa Guy, Michelle Cliff, and Marie Chauvet, Chancy explores various themes, including race, sex, class, sexuality, age, and nationality. Chancy's primary goal is to "uncover the suppressed history of Afro-Caribbean women and to connect that history to the experiences of Afro-Caribbean women surviving exile under multiple forms of oppression as expressed through their literature" (pp. xxii–xxiii). In her *Framing Silence: Revolutionary Novels by Haitian Women* (Rutgers University Press, 1997), Chancy analyzes the literature of Haitian women. Chancy weaves together storytelling, personal biography, historiography, radical feminist theories, and literary criticism to study the effects of oppression and violence against women, as seen in the literary gaps and textual silences in Haitian women's writing.

1283. Cudjoe, Selwyn R., ed. *Caribbean Women Writers: Essays from the First International Conference*. Wellesley, MA: Calaloux Publications, 1990. 382p. bibliog. ISBN 0870237314; 0870237322pa.

This work grew out of a conference sponsored in 1988 by the Black Studies Department of Wellesley College. More than fifty women writers and critics from the United States, Europe, Trinidad, Grenada, Jamaica, Belize, Barbados, and Guyana convened to share their common experiences of identity, patriarchy, slavery, colonialism, and neocolonialism. In the introduction, editor Selwyn R. Cudjoe writes, "This volume records their testimonies as they give voice to their experiences and join in the attempt of women throughout the world, particularly in the African diaspora, to define their being without the interference of any other agents" (p. 5). The long introduction provides an excellent overview of the history of writing in the Caribbean and of women's contributions to this endeavor. Section 1 provides the theoretical, social, and historical context for the rest of the volume, presenting essays dealing with "the problems inherent in unearthing the female condition in Caribbean history" (p. 43). In section 2, female Caribbean writers discuss their works alongside critiques of their writing. Writers represented in this section include Jean Rhys, Phyllis Shand Allfrey, Sybil Seaforth, Erna Brodber, Toni Cade Bambara, and Jamaica Kincaid, to name just a few. The final section provides a broad overview of writings in the Dutch, French, and Spanish languages from the Caribbean area. The title includes a selected bibliography, but an author and title index would have proven helpful for the novice reader. A timely and important work, *Caribbean Women Writers* reveals the diversity of writing from this area and provides an important voice to the works of a few known, but many other lesser-known female Caribbean writers.

1284. Ferguson, Moira. *Colonialism and Gender Relations from Mary Wollstonecraft to Jamaica Kincaid: East Caribbean Connections.* New York: Columbia University Press, 1993. 175p. bibliog. index. (OP)

In this complex work, Ferguson reads texts of British and eastern Caribbean women writers spanning 150 years in an attempt to find new subtexts in their common experiences with colonialism. Focusing on the writings of Mary Wollstonecraft, Anne Hart Gilbert, Elizabeth Hart Thwaites, Jane Austen, Jean Rhys, and Jamaica Kincaid, the author argues that these women created a complex, evolving discourse concerning women, slavery, and nationalism: "Using the historical backdrop of slavery and colonialism, the text investigates how white and African-Caribbean women writers configure feminist, abolitionist, and post-emancipationist agendas" (p. 2). Two points of departure mark this study. The first concerns Antigua as a critical site "of textual and historical contestation where opposition to white male control . . . plays itself out," while the second concerns the "complex textual embedding of imposed sexuality as a sign of domination" (p. 2). Ferguson begins her study by arguing how the writings of Wollstonecraft imply that slavery represents a human construct with multilayered meanings, including both colonial and sexual slavery. Ferguson then moves on to discuss the writings of Anne Hart Gilbert and Elizabeth Hart Thwaites and Jane Austen's *Mansfield Park.* The Hart sisters, who lived in Antigua, address slavery in their writings, yet they do so from the status of racial and religious privilege; Austen, on the other hand, "writes from the 'mother country' about a restless colony" (p. 4). Finally, Ferguson analyzes the multiple intertextual layers of race, class, and gender in Jean Rhys's *Wide Sargasso Sea* and Jamaica Kincaid's views of gender relations and sexual identity in her works *Annie John* and *A Small Place.* Arguing that this complex discourse is always changing and evolving, Ferguson concludes, "In their discussions of the ways in which representations of black and white women are both different and similar, these six writers reveal the crucial role played by place, time, sexuality, and cultural positionality in fostering critical intersections of race, class, and gender" (p. 7).

1285. Jones, Anny Brooksbank, and Catherine Davies, eds. *Latin American Women's Writing: Feminist Readings in Theory and Crisis.* New York: Clarendon Press, 1996. 250p. (Oxford Hispanic Studies). bibliog. index. ISBN 0198715129; 0198715137pa.

In *Latin American Women's Writing*, Jones and Davies have assembled an impressive collection of essays of theoretical sophistication and diversity. The editors consider Latin American feminist discourse in cultural, social, and political movements and address the role of theory as an index and precipitator of social and cultural change. The thirteen essays incorporate a variety of theoretical approaches from theorists such as Mikhail Bakhtin, Gayatri Chakravorty Spivak, Julia Kristeva, Jacques Derrida, and Homi Bhabha, to name a few. Each essay discusses the writings of a different author such as Griselda Gambaro, Isabel Allende, or Alejandra Pizarnik. Anny Jones provides an overview essay on the state of Latin American feminist criticism.

Several other works complement this title. Myriam Yvonne Jehenson's *Latin-American Women Writers: Class, Race, and Gender* (State University of New York Press, 1995) provides an overview of the sociohistorical contexts that have shaped the lives and works of several recently canonized writers. She discusses Latin American women's fiction from a number of countries, races, and classes. Magdalena García Pinto's *Women Writers of Latin America: Intimate Histories* (University of Texas Press, 1991), translated by Trudy Balch and the author, originally published in 1988 as *Historias intimas*, consists of interviews with Latin American women writers. Many of these writers call themselves feminists and no longer see themselves as exceptions, thus affirming the connection between the personal and the intellectual. Susan Bassnett has edited an eclectic group of essays in *Knives and Angels: Women Writers in Latin America* (Zed Books, 1990). Despite the subtitle, several essays discuss women not known primarily as writers, such as Victoria Ocampo, a woman of letters and cultural patron, and María Luisa Bemberg, an Argentinean filmmaker. The essays vary in approach, providing historical overviews, insight into women's lives, and thoughtful examinations of literary works.

1286. Malti-Douglas, Fedwa. *Woman's Body, Woman's Word: Gender and Discourse in Arabo-Islamic Writing*. Princeton, NJ: Princeton University Press, 1991. 206p. bibliog. index. ISBN (OP); 0608095729pa.

Studying Arabic-language literary discourse, Malti-Douglas creates an excellent work that considers the intersections of woman's sexuality, woman's body, and woman's voice in the Arabo-Islamic cultural sphere. The author applies perspectives of contemporary gender studies to selected texts of Arabic prose, focusing on literary figures such as Shahrazâd, female characters from the *adab* tradition of medieval Arabic literature, and modern authors, including Nawal El Saadawi and Fadwâ Tûqân, to demonstrate the dialectic between mental structures involving women and sexuality from the classical period to the contemporary era. In addition to her analysis of contemporary women's literature, Malti-Douglas uses feminist discourse to read traditional male texts from across several centuries. Throughout this work, the author provides most translations from the Arabic originals while also noting English and other European translations. Malti-Douglas finds that "[c]lassical or modern, woman's voice in Arabo-Islamic discourse is indissolubly tied to sexuality and the body. Whether a woman must speak through the body (as in the classical) or in reaction to it (as in the modern), the conclusion remains the same. For woman, the word remains anchored to the body" (p. 10). *Woman's Body, Woman's Word* is an easily readable and welcome addition to the field.

1287. Milani, Farzaneh. *Veils and Words: The Emerging Voices of Iranian Women Writers*. Syracuse, NY: Syracuse University Press, 1992. 295p. (Contemporary Issues in the Middle East). bibliog. index. ISBN 081562557X; 0815602669pa.

In this fascinating book, Milani equates the silencing of Iranian women writers with the practice of veiling. The veil expresses multilayered values in Iranian society: moral, sexual, political, economic, and aesthetic. The author argues that veiling/unveiling could also serve as yet another representation, like public versus private or rational versus emotional, depicting polarized conceptions of masculine and feminine. Milani believes that a connection exists among women's voices, their literary self-revelation, and unveiling, or their bodily self-revelation: "[T]he norms and values that regulated women's physical concealment applied equally to their literary expression . . . a woman's physical invisibility was completed by her silence, her public nonexistence" (p. 46). Milani divides her study into four sections. Section 1 discusses the significance of the veil and how it has affected the literary expression of women. Sections 2 and 3 discuss women's poetry and fiction. In the last section, Milani reviews women's writing in postrevolutionary Iran and discusses the work of Simin Behbahani, a contemporary female poet. Milani incorporates a variety of theories into her analysis, including the work of Elaine Showalter, Sandra Gilbert, Julia Kristeva, Luce Irigaray, and Hélène Cixous.

1288. Nasta, Susheila, ed. *Motherlands: Black Women's Writing from Africa, the Caribbean, and South Asia*. New Brunswick, NJ: Rutgers University Press, 1992. 366p. bibliog. index. ISBN 0813517818; 0813517826pa.

This anthology presents sixteen essays exploring a selection of texts by women writers from Africa, the Caribbean, and South Asia. The essays compare and contrast how living in patriarchal and colonial societies affects these women's lives. Nasta arranges this work into three sections, each exploring a specific motif. In the first section, contributors examine the idea of " 'mother-nations,' and 'motherlands,' as encoded in patriarchal and western symbolic systems" (p. xx) from a variety of perspectives. Essays explore the themes of motherhood, power, rebellion, and voice as reflected in the fiction of African women writers. Contributors in section 2 investigate the powerful use of traditional and metaphorical mother figures in women's writing. Particular essays address whether ideas such as universal feminism and global sisterhood can be used to speak of women from a variety of cultural and ethnic backgrounds. Additional essays analyze the metaphorical use of mother-daughter relationships to critique ideas of empire/colony. In the final section, the essays provide a cross-cultural and comparative approach to writers who have experienced migration or exile from their homelands. Nasta has compiled a useful resource for anyone interested in an introduction to women's literary production in English from diverse cultural contexts of Africa, the Caribbean, and South Asia. *Motherlands* provides insightful analysis of geographical, political, and social connections in black women's writing from a global and feminist perspective.

Another editor, Obioma Nnaemeka, has created a bold work, *The Politics of (M)Othering: Womanhood, Identity, and Resistance in African Literature* (New York: Routledge, 1997), that emphasizes the mother/"other" as a locus of knowledge, power, and agency. This volume "engages feminist theory itself by showing how issues in feminism—voice, victimhood, agency, subjectivity, sisterhood, etc.—are recast in different, complex and interesting ways in African literature, in general, and works by African women writers, in particular" (p. 1). *The Politics of (M)Othering* is also issued within Routledge's Opening Out: Feminism for Today series. This is an excellent resource about the relationship between African literature and feminist discourse.

1289. Schalow, Paul Gordon, and Janet A. Walker, eds. *The Woman's Hand: Gender and Theory in Japanese Women's Writing*. Stanford, CA: Stanford University Press, 1996. 511p. bibliog. index. ISBN 0804727228; 0804727236pa.

Schalow and Walker have produced a fine collection of fifteen essays, many originally presented at the Rutgers Conference on Japanese Women Writers in April 1993, which considered a variety of Japanese women's writing traditions. Primarily focusing on women's postwar contemporary fiction, the editors chose to divide the book into four parts. Part 1 surveys the important work of women writers within Japan's literary history, dating back to the Heian period (794–1185). The essays in part 2 focus on writers of the 1960s and 1970s, "who broke the silence and claimed the right to self-formulation by 'writing the body' " (p. 7). In part 3, authors identify the safe and historically sanctioned places for female authors within Japanese literary tradition. In the final part, contributors situate women writers within various cultural contexts, focusing on writing produced immediately after World War II and into the 1990s. The essays cover a variety of topics, including ritual recitation, the problematic categorization of Japanese women writers, the female "novel of development," how the female body is imagined in fantasy, and war and the atomic bomb. *The Woman's Hand* represents a passionate, perceptive, and articulate breakthrough in Japanese literary studies that scholars and instructors should welcome in courses on Asian studies, women's studies, and comparative literature.

Sally Taylor Lieberman's *The Mother and Narrative Politics in Modern China* (Charlottesville: University Press of Virginia, 1998) draws on feminist critical theory, postmodernism, psychoanalysis, and the "alien argument" to address Chinese studies. She examines representations of motherhood within various classes in romantic, realist, canonical, noncanonical, and male- and female-authored works. Although Lieberman mostly considers fiction, she also covers other genres.

1290. Stratton, Florence. *Contemporary African Literature and the Politics of Gender.* New York: Routledge, 1994. 200p. bibliog. index. ISBN (OP); 0415097711pa.

In this original work, Stratton contrasts African women writers' works against one another, as well as against male-authored texts. She creates this dialogue to examine the discussion on nationalism and gender in African literature. "This book is about the place of African women writers in African literature. . . . The aim is to provide a more comprehensive definition of the contemporary African literary tradition" (p. 1). In the first section, Stratton examines the male literary tradition in African literature and challenges the authority of some canonical texts, including Chinua Achebe's *Things Fall Apart* (1958). She also deconstructs familiar tropes of women, such as Mother Africa and prostitutes. In the second section, Stratton studies how women writers have subverted male-initiated sexual allegories through her reading of works by the following authors: Grace Ogot, Flora Nwapa, Buchi Emecheta (all Anglophones), and Mariama Bâ (Francophone). In the final section, Stratton explores how male writers respond to female writing and consequently advocates an intertextual reading of male and female writers. Scholars and general readers alike will find *Contemporary African Literature and the Politics of Gender* both insightful and engaging.

In Their Own Voices: African Women Writers Talk (Heinemann, 1990), edited by Adeola James, presents interviews with fifteen African women writers, all of whom write or translate their works into English except for the Tanzanian playwright Penina Muhando. The women discuss several issues, including how the publishing world often intimidates and exploits and the difficulties that they face as both writers and mothers (writing is a secondary activity for most).

Theater

1291. Anderson, Lisa M. *Mammies No More: The Changing Image of Black Women on Stage and Screen.* Lanham, MD: Rowman & Littlefield, 1997. 147p. bibliog. index. ISBN 0847684199.

Anderson examines the various cultural representations of black women on television, the stage, and the media in this work. According to the author, black women typically portray three roles: the Mammy, a large, boisterous, and domineering woman; the tragic mulatta, who has a more refined demeanor, but whose tragic flaw ultimately leads to her downfall; and the jezebel, a sexually voracious woman who corrupts the men around her. Anderson persuasively argues that these stereotypes deny the true diversity and meaning of the black experience in America. She explores the evolution of these stereotypes, which both black and white writers created, and highlights positive deviations from the norm.

Susanna A. Bosch's *"Sturdy Black Bridges" on the American Stage: The Portrayal of Black Motherhood in Selected Plays by Contemporary African-American Playwrights* (Peter Lang, 1996) compares stereotypes of black motherhood to black mothers' lived realities both on and off the stage. The author examines portrayals of motherhood in the work of Ntozake Shange and five lesser-known playwrights, supplementing analysis with performance photos, excerpts of dialogue, and playwrights' quotes.

1292. Brater, Enoch, ed. *Feminine Focus: The New Women Playwrights.* New York: Oxford University Press, 1989. 283p. bibliog. index. (OP)

Noting that women playwrights authored a minority of plays presented during the 1980s, editor Enoch Brater compiles essays that call attention to the fresh, new voices of women from Great Britain, France, and the United States in late-twentieth-century theater. He also points out, however, that a surge of influential and critically acclaimed playwrights, such as Tina Howe, Beth Henley, Caryl Churchill, Marsha Norman, and Wendy Wasserstein, enrich the stage with their interpretations of the female experience. The essays address a variety of issues, including highly theoretical explorations and practical matters of dramatic style, performance, and perception. Some of the essays emphasize the work of a particular playwright, while others focus on generalized topics such as images of women or sexuality on stage.

1293. Brown, Janet. *Taking Center Stage: Feminism in Contemporary U.S. Drama.* Metuchen, NJ: Scarecrow Press, 1991. 171p. bibliog. index. ISBN 0810824485.

Brown builds and expands on her previous title *Feminist Drama: Definition and Critical Analysis* (Scarecrow Press, 1979) in *Taking Center Stage*, which addresses major issues that authors such as Karen Malpede, Elizabeth Natalle, and Jill Dolan discuss in their works, published in the 1970s and 1980s, about feminist theater and drama. She also delineates the ideas of feminist theorists, including Nancy Chodorow, Carol Gilligan, Jean Elshtain, and Annette Kolodny, who enjoyed prominence during the same time period. Brown uses their theories as the organizing principles for her examination of eleven well-known texts that both men, such as David Rabe, and women, including Ntozake Shange, Caryl Churchill, Lily Tomlin, and Jane Wagner, crafted to uncover "evidence of both a distinctively female narrative structure and a distinctively feminist rhetorical intention" (p. 3). Brown argues that feminist plays rely upon different forms, venues, and styles to address diverse issues, yet share a commitment to foregrounding women's central role in the human experience. Brown's work is a succinct, clearly written introduction to feminist theory. Other titles that address feminism and theater in the United States during the 1970s and 1980s include Charlotte Canning's *Feminist Theaters in the U.S.A.: Staging Women's Experience* (Routledge, 1996), which documents specific feminist grassroots theaters, and the revised, expanded edition of the seminal work *Women in American Theatre* (Theatre Communications Group, 1987), edited by Helen Krich Chinoy and Linda Walsh Jenkins.

1294. Brown-Guillory, Elizabeth. *Their Place on the Stage: Black Women Playwrights in America.* New York: Greenwood Press, 1988. 163p. bibliog. index. ISBN 0313259852.

This thoroughly researched, clearly written work serves as an excellent source for background information on twentieth-century African American women playwrights of the United States. Brown-Guillory succinctly discusses the African origins of the black theater tradition and images of African Americans on stage. She devotes the majority of the book to an analysis of the works of three key playwrights: Lorraine Hansberry, Alice Childress, and Ntozake Shange. She explores the tone and structure of the plays as well as the images of the black characters featured in them.

Brown-Guillory also edited *Wines in the Wilderness: Plays by African-American Women from the Harlem Renaissance to the Present* (Greenwood Press, 1990), which features fifteen mostly out-of-print or difficult-to-locate plays penned by nine African American women, including Maria Brown, Eulalie Spence, May Miller, and Sybil Kein. Another excellent historical anthology of African American women's plays, *Black Female Playwrights: An Anthology of Plays before 1950*, (Indiana University Press, 1989) edited by Kathy A. Perkins, reverberates with themes of miscegenation, birth control, racism, and lynching.

1295. Burkman, Katherine H., and Judith Roof, eds. *Staging the Rage: The Web of Misogyny in Modern Drama*. Madison, NJ: Fairleigh Dickinson University Press, 1998. 272p. bibliog. index. ISBN 0838637639.

This diverse collection of essays treats issues of misogyny in plays, exploring how female characters respond to inherently discriminatory societal structures. The editors arrange the essays into four sections. Section one deals with various manifestations of misogyny represented in plays by several contemporary playwrights. Section two explores how female characters in drama have often exhibited one particular response to misogyny, a response "though often self-destructive, is a self-destruction that paradoxically tends to be an assertion of their female autonomy" (p. 17). Section three looks at other responses to misogyny by female characters, while the final section discusses "the fluidity of gender structures . . . in dramas that explore or in some cases unconsciously depict the fear of women that is central to the rage that informs misogyny" (p. 17). Some of the essayists discuss specific playwrights, such as David Mamet, Sam Shepard, and Amiri Baraka, who have written plays that many feminist critics believe evince varying degrees of hostility toward women. Other contributors examine gender fluidity, the rage of specific female characters, and nineteenth-century misogyny. The destructive nature of misogyny for both men and women threads these essays together. Froma Zeitlin examines the relationship between several Greek Athenian dramas and the society that helped shape them in her engaging historical treatment of gender issues, including misogyny, in *Playing the Other: Gender and Society in Classical Greek Literature* (University of Chicago Press, 1996). This work also provides a fine literature review of feminist criticism of ancient Greek literature.

1296. Case, Sue-Ellen. *Feminism and Theatre*. London: Macmillan, 1988. 147p. bibliog. index. ISBN 0416015018pa.

Drawing on history, stage practice, and feminist theory, Case provides an analytical overview that examines the relationship between women and theater. She deconstructs the classics of ancient Greek and Elizabethan drama, questioning what male playwrights' and actors' portrayals of women reveal about practical assumptions of women's cultural positions in theater and society. Case also discusses early women pioneers in theater and analyzes radical and materialist feminists' contributions to theater studies. Since women enjoy limited roles as directors and producers in traditional theater, Case explores alternative productions, such as feminist witch rituals and performance art. This work provides a daring and exciting introduction to the history of feminism in theater.

Case also edited *Performing Feminisms: Feminist Critical Theory and Theatre* (Johns Hopkins University Press, 1990), a collection of articles originally published in *Theatre Journal* between 1984 and 1989 covering topics such as race, ethnicity, and meanings of gender, representing various strands of 1980s feminist theater criticism. Scholars of the well-chosen articles in *Feminist Theatre and Theory* (St. Martin's Press, 1996), edited by Helen Keyssar, debate about realism, psychoanalysis, and the antagonism that some practitioners harbor toward theory or the examination of textual and theatrical aspects of specific plays and productions, including audience reactions. Keyssar includes chapters that describe the state of Chicana and contemporary French theaters and images of women in Chinese historical plays. Elaine Aston presents a fine, clearly written overview of the complex, evolving relationship between feminism and the theater in *Introduction to Feminism and Theatre* (Routledge, 1995), which explores a range of theories, methods, and practices reflecting the diversity and intricacies of feminist theater studies.

1297. Case, Sue-Ellen, ed. *Split Britches: Lesbian Practice/Feminist Performance*. London: Routledge, 1996. 276p. bibliog. index. ISBN 0415127653.

As one of the most influential forces in late-twentieth-century feminist and lesbian theater, the troupe known as Split Britches has become an icon for collaborative and innovative performance techniques. In 1980, Peggy Shaw, Lois Weaver, and Deb Margolin founded the troupe, whose members write, direct, and perform their own work. Mixing genres and performance styles, this three-woman team also creates innovative interpretations of classics, including *Little Women*, *A Streetcar Named Desire*, and the *Beauty and the Beast* fable. Case's collection features seven of the troupe's best-known plays: *Split Britches, Beauty and the Beast, Upwardly Mobile Home, Little Women, Belle Reprieve, Lesbians Who Kill,* and *Lust and Comfort.* Case surveys the history, critical reception, and influence of the troupe, along with brief commentary on each play, in the introduction. Several performance photos and a list of books, academic articles, and play reviews complete this informative volume. Another notable lesbian play anthology, Rosemary Keefe Curb's *Amazon All Stars* (Applause, 1996), features works that analyze varied themes by thirteen playwrights. The editor includes commentary on and introductions to each play, brief biographies of the playwrights, and a bibliography. Both collections provide insight into the complexities and realities of diverse lesbian lives.

1298. Cerasano, S.P., and Marion Wynne-Davies, eds. *Renaissance Drama by Women: Texts and Documents.* London: Routledge, 1996. 237p. bibliog. index. ISBN 0415098068; 0415098076pa.

Although Shakespeare, Marlowe, and other giants have long overshadowed women's contribution to Renaissance drama, this work provides a fascinating window into the lives of a number of aristocratic women who privately indulged in writing valuable and insightful plays. The editors assemble four plays, one fragment, and one masque, accompanying each with a lengthy introduction that explores the history of both author and text. The second half of the book features writings that examine women's participation in the theater as spectators, performers, writers, patrons, and theater owners. This section also explores society's perceptions of women in theater. The editors modernize spellings within the texts and provide extensive notes, which makes this book an excellent contribution to the study of Renaissance drama.

Karen Newman explores how economic growth and rapid social change affected women both on and off the stage during the English Renaissance in *Fashioning Femininity and English Renaissance Drama* (University of Chicago Press, 1991). She generally accepts the traditional view that English women did not greatly benefit during this period, but notes the curious attention that issues of "female rebellion" aroused in the contemporary record. She explores this theme in the era's popular plays, mostly penned by men, and reveals how the stage both fashioned and represented women's roles as they evolved during the sixteenth and seventeenth centuries. Newman creatively incorporates documents such as domestic handbooks, sermons, court cases, and medical texts contemporary to the plays to support her thesis, providing a richly textured analysis of women's experiences during one of England's most fascinating eras.

1299. Cohen, Sarah Blacher, ed. *Making a Scene: The Contemporary Drama of Jewish-American Women.* Syracuse, NY: Syracuse University Press, 1997. 370p. bibliog. index. ISBN 0815627130; 0815604041pa.

Although many play anthologies devoted to a particular ethnic group highlight the works of underrepresented or underappreciated writers, Sarah Blacher Cohen acknowledges that Jewish playwrights have celebrated enormous success, attracting both critical and popular acclaim. Yet male authors often do not provide realistic portrayals of Jewish women characters, while female authors frequently do not write specifically about the Jewish experience. Cohen thus features plays that reflect the unique perspectives, cultural traditions, and experiences of Jewish American women. Playwrights in this volume include Wendy Wasserstein, Barbara Lebow, Sarah Blacher Cohen, Lois Roisman, Barbara Kahn, Hindi Brooks, and Merle Feld.

1300. Davis, Tracy C. *Actresses as Working Women: Their Social Identity in Victorian Culture*. London: Routledge, 1991. 200p. bibliog. index. ISBN 0415056527; 0415063531pa.

A disproportionate amount of research on Victorian actresses concentrates on a few prominent women, which skews the history of the profession. Davis thus researched the lives of more typical women in the theater: chorus girls, dancers, and stock players. Using playbills, census records, court cases, and newspaper accounts, Davis paints a portrait of women struggling on the edges of respectability in a world constantly rife with threats of unemployment and sexual harassment. The author divides the book into five chapters that explore subjects such as the socioeconomic organization of the theater, social demography, respectability, actresses, and pornography. Davis's clear writing style and commitment to exploring the lives of the ordinary workingwoman in the Victorian theater make her work a fresh and welcome contribution to literature on theater history.

Kerry Powell interprets Victorian women as actresses and playwrights from a feminist perspective in *Women and Victorian Theatre* (Cambridge University Press, 1997). Powell argues that rhetorical strategies in plays reinforced repressive gender codes and reflected contradictory attitudes toward actresses, other women in the theater, and women in general. Catherine Schuler examines the unique experiences and conditions facing actresses in Russia in *Women in Russian Theatre: The Actress in the Silver Age* (Routledge, 1996).

1301. Diamond, Elin. *Unmaking Mimesis: Essays on Feminism and Theater*. London: Routledge, 1997. 226p. bibliog. index. ISBN 0415012287; 0415012295pa.

Many scholars have credited Elin Diamond with reviving the study of mimesis, the imitation of aspects of the sensible world in literature and performance. In *Unmaking Mimesis*, Diamond uses this concept to survey the relationship between feminist theories of sexuality and their physical representation on the stage. She argues that gestures, voices, props, and the use of space play crucial roles in the interpretation of text. Moreover, she claims that the complex relationship between mimesis and text can shift over time. Asserting the importance of Freudian theory and postmodernism to the evolution of mimesis studies, Diamond examines the work of diverse playwrights, such as Henrik Ibsen, Aphra Behn, and Caryl Churchill. Her ambitious work applies contemporary feminist theory to a wide range of both classic and cutting-edge theatrical performances. Serena Anderlini-D'Onofrio's *The "Weak" Subject: On Modernity, Eros, and Women's Playwriting* (Fairleigh Dickinson University Press, 1998) is another important work on mimesis. The author applies labial, as opposed to phallocentric, mimesis to her examination of plays by European and North American authors, such as Lillian Hellman, Doris Lessing, Natalia Ginzburg, and Marguerite Duras. This thought-provoking work contributes to debates on female self-representation, eroticism, and gender and performance.

1302. Dolan, Jill. *The Feminist Spectator as Critic*. Ann Arbor: University of Michigan Press, 1988. 154p. (Theater and Dramatic Studies, no. 52). bibliog. index. ISBN 0835718743.

Dolan, cofounder of *Women and Performance: A Journal of Feminist Theory* (Women and Performance Project at New York University, Tisch School of the Arts, Department of Performance Studies, 1983–), established a reputation as a bold, challenging, and insightful feminist performance theorist with the publication of *The Feminist Spectator as Critic*. This key text helped diversify theatrical discourse beyond textual analysis through its discussions of topics such as the ideal spectator (white, middle-class, and heterosexual male), representation, canon building, sexuality and gender in performance, and pornography. She thoroughly analyzes the texts, ideologies, structures, intentions, direction, lighting, costumes, casting decisions, set designs, and character interpretations of the plays. Dolan cogently reviews cultural, liberal, and materialist feminisms as she develops her own ideological and methodological stance. Dolan presents ten essays published after 1988 in *Presence and Desire: Essays on Gender, Sexuality, Performance* (University of Michigan Press, 1993) that provide more extensive context for the development of the feminist materialist stance outlined in *The Feminist Spectator as Critic*. She examines subjects such as censorship, realism, cultural feminism, and theater's aversion to theory and describes her subversive interpretations and direction of three productions at the University of Wisconsin at Madison.

1303. Donkin, Ellen, and Susan Clement, eds. *Upstaging Big Daddy: Directing Theater As If Gender and Race Matter.* Ann Arbor: University of Michigan Press, 1993. 344p. bibliog. index. ISBN 047209503X; 0472065033pa.

Beginning with the premise that white men have written and directed most theater, Donkin and Clement claim that women's roles are underrepresented and distorted in the theater. Nineteen essays trace the impact of race and gender on the decisions that the director makes throughout the production of a play, including selection, preproduction, rehearsal, performance, and analysis. Most contributors either recount experiences of specific productions at American colleges and universities or address issues such as cross-casting along racial, gender, and generational lines, lesbian theater, political discourse, and audience reception. The most engaging essays include rare, highly instructive insight into the experiences of directors who innovatively approached productions that subsequently ended in failure. The bold, imaginative essays in this work should prove useful to directors who want to stretch the traditional limits of race and gender on the stage. Other informative works regarding how gender issues affect the directing process include Rebecca Daniels's *Women Stage Directors Speak: Exploring the Influence of Gender on Their Work* (McFarland, 1996), a collection of interviews with thirty-five American directors that features a telling section on collaboration, and Helen Manfull and others' *In Other Words: Women Directors Speak* (Smith & Kraus, 1997), a collection of viewpoints from directors working in Great Britain.

1304. Dudden, Faye E. *Women in the American Theatre: Actresses and Audiences, 1790–1870.* New Haven, CT: Yale University Press, 1994. 260p. bibliog. index. ISBN 0300056362; 0300070586pa.

Dudden thoughtfully examines white women's roles in the polarization of nineteenth-century American theater. Although women enjoyed opportunities to develop honest careers built on performances in traditional melodramas and tragedies in respectable theater, other actresses performed in cheap burlesque shows that attracted large audiences, which ultimately objectified, sexualized, and exploited them. Most chapters focus on particular women's careers, such as those of Fanny Kemble, Laura Keene, and Charlotte Cushman. Other chapters address thematic topics, including the segmentation of theaters and the rise of the burlesque show. Extensive notes enrich this clearly written and engaging survey of women's roles in nineteenth-century American theater.

Jo Tanner's *Dusky Maidens: The Odyssey of the Early Black Dramatic Actress* (Greenwood Press, 1992) documents the untold story of the evolution of African American women actresses from their early roles as reciters, singers, and dancers in black theatricals to later major roles as dramatic actresses. Tanner chronologically organizes the material according to key figures such as Elizabeth Taylor-Greenfield, who opened doors on the stage, within the context of black theater from the 1800s through the 1920s.

1305. Gay, Penny, ed. *As She Likes It: Shakespeare's Unruly Women.* London: Routledge, 1994. 208p. bibliog. index. ISBN 0415096952.

Rather than attempting yet another analysis of Shakespeare's subtext and its implications for women characters, Gay focuses on how directors and actors of the Royal Shakespeare Company (RSC) interpreted Shakespeare's most controversial "women plays" between 1946 and 1990. The RSC, the most prominent and influential Shakespearean company in the world, serves as an excellent microcosm for Gay to explore the evolving treatment of women during a period in which gender roles underwent unprecedented changes. Using contemporary reviews, promptbooks, and interviews with actors and directors, Gay examines specific productions, concluding that the RSC generally failed to grant Shakespeare's comic heroines the authority and legitimacy they deserve.

Carol Chillington Rutter also analyzes the RSC and gender in *Clamorous Voices: Shakespeare's Women Today* (Routledge, 1989). She interviewed five of the company's most versatile leading actresses, focusing on tensions that resulted from working in a male-dominated company. Irene G. Dash persuasively argues that persistent gender stereotypes repeatedly have influenced directors' decisions, especially staging and dialogue cuts or rewrites, in her fascinating study *Women's World in Shakespeare's Plays* (University of Delaware Press, 1997).

1306. Goodman, Lizbeth. *Contemporary Feminist Theatres: To Each Her Own.* London: Routledge, 1993. 313p. bibliog. index. ISBN 0415073065.

Goodman focuses on the development and perceptions of feminist theater in Great Britain from 1968 through the early 1990s. The author explores feminist theater in relation to its cultural context, examines differences within the feminist movement, and considers how theatrical performance reflects these differences. Rather than couching her study in highly theoretical textual analysis, she discusses practical issues, such as funding structures and working practices. She also interviews practitioners, scrutinizes audience composition, and considers membership in cultural associations. Goodman allows practitioners to speak for themselves by focusing on these concrete manifestations of feminist theater. She thus creates an intriguing portrait of the highly diverse, rapidly evolving field of feminist theater studies.

Goodman continues to document British practitioners in *Feminist Stages: Interviews with Women in Contemporary British Theatre* (Harwood Academic, 1996). Goodman and Jane de Gay edited *The Routledge Reader in Gender and Performance* (Routledge, 1998), a collection of fifty essays featuring historical, theoretical, and descriptive analyses of women in the theater and of theater as institution.

1307. Hart, Lynda, and Peggy Phelan, eds. *Acting Out: Feminist Performances.* Ann Arbor: University of Michigan Press, 1993. 406p. bibliog. index. ISBN 0272094793.

In recognition of the disproportionate amount of feminist theater research devoted to text-based studies, Hart and Phelan have assembled a collection of nineteen essays that focus on the performance aspects of feminist theater. They arrange the essays under three general headings: "The Politics of Identity," "Performing Histories," and "The Reproduction of Visibility." Most contributors heavily emphasize issues of race and sexuality in their examinations of traditional theater, stand-up comedy, performance art, and musicals. Hart and Phelan intended this work to function as a sequel to Hart's highly regarded *Making a Spectacle: Feminist Essays on Contemporary Women's Theatre* (University of Michigan Press, 1989), in which leading feminist theater theorists discuss the work of several, women playwrights, mostly American, focusing on their creation of powerful, multifaceted, even subversive female characters.

1308. Howard, Jean E., and Phyllis Rackin. *Engendering a Nation: A Feminist Account of Shakespeare's English Histories*. New York: Routledge, 1997. 248p. (Feminist Readings of Shakespeare). bibliog. index. ISBN 041504748X; 0415047498pa.

Routledge created this series to make feminist trends and debates in Shakespearean studies accessible to undergraduate students and general readers. Howard and Rackin, highly regarded scholars, attempt to remedy the relative neglect of other feminist scholars' research on Shakespeare's history plays. They argue that the plays in the first tetralogy, as well as *King John*, contain strong, independent, powerful women characters; however, the plays in the second tetralogy contain objectified, domestic, peripheral women characters. Howard and Rackin also claim that the evolution of characterizations of women reflects England's complex political, social, economic, and ideological transformation from feudal state to early modern nation. This intriguing work makes a strong case for incorporating analysis of the history plays into feminist Shakespearean studies, theatrical history, and early modern literature. Coppelia Kahn examines ideas of masculinity in Shakespeare's plays, but focuses on the Roman histories, another group of plays that feminist scholars have neglected, in *Roman Shakespeare: Warriors, Wounds, and Women* (Routledge, 1997). Kahn argues that "Romanness is virtually identical with an ideology of masculinity" (p. 2) during the Renaissance and insightfully interprets some of the best-known plays, including *Julius Caesar*. These skillfully written works not only fill gaps in the literature, but also open up new areas of research in Shakespearean studies and related fields.

1309. Howe, Elizabeth. *The First English Actresses: Women and Drama, 1660–1700*. Cambridge: Cambridge University Press, 1992. 224p. bibliog. index. ISBN 0521422108pa.

A renewed interest in the early history of women in the acting profession has created a proliferation of studies on the topic. In *The First English Actresses*, Howe provides excellent research on the formative years of the Restoration period, when definitions of women's roles as performers began to emerge. She asks two primary questions: what happened as a result of women portraying roles that directors traditionally assigned to men? and did exceptionally prominent actresses, such as Elizabeth Barry, individually influence characterizations? Howe also examines how the first English actresses to portray female characters both affected and challenged traditional, patriarchal attitudes. Though this work is written for an academic audience, Howe's lucid writing style makes it accessible to nonspecialists.

Sandra Richards concentrates on actresses known for innovative role interpretation in *The Rise of the English Actress* (St. Martin's Press, 1993), which covers the seventeenth century through the mid-1980s. In *Curtain Calls: British and American Women and the Theater, 1660–1680* (Ohio University Press, 1991), edited by Mary Ann Schofield and Cecilia Macheski, contributors examine accomplishments of both well-known and neglected female actresses, playwrights, producers, and critics in theater, usually providing social and political context. This fine collection presents a more complete theater history for the time period than many standard theater histories.

1310. Larson, Catherine, and Margarita Vargas, eds. *Latin American Women Dramatists: Theater, Texts, and Theories*. Bloomington: Indiana University Press, 1998. 320p. bibliog. index. ISBN 0253212405pa; 0253334616.

Contributors to Larson and Vargas's work examine several Brazilian, Argentinean, Chilean, Mexican, and Puerto Rican playwrights who were active during the second half of the twentieth century. The editors arrange the work into four categories: theatrical self-consciousness, politics, history, and feminist positions. The essays feature an introduction that provides the writer's background information and concludes with notes and references. An in-depth analysis of at least one characteristic text constitutes the heart of each essay. Many contributors concentrate on the playwright's treatment of themes, such as censorship, social injustice, and repression. Other contributors examine staging, ideological positions, and use of space. This work helps recover ignored or forgotten dramatists and provides critical insight into a neglected literary heritage.

Ann Witte's *Guiding the Plot: Politics and Feminism in the Work of Women Playwrights from Spain and Argentina, 1960–1990* (Peter Lang, 1996) covers the same general time period. Witte looks at two playwrights from each country, particularly considering adjustments in their work as governments changed and opportunities for women increased.

1311. Quinsey, Katherine M., ed. *Broken Boundaries: Women and Feminism in Restoration Drama.* Lexington: University Press of Kentucky, 1996. 244p. bibliog. index. ISBN 0813119456; 0813108713pa.

Contributors to *Broken Boundaries* focus on how female participation, including playwrights, actresses, patrons, and spectators, in the theater affected issues of gender, sexuality, and power in eighteenth-century Europe. Jacqueline Pearson provides a particularly insightful and rare look at women who rewrote men's plays, discussing what this act might imply about the development of race and gender stereotypes. Three essays focus on the most famous female Restoration playwright, Aphra Behn, with many contributors concentrating on the nature and development of her feminism. Other essays assess male-authored plays that reveal contradictory expectations facing eighteenth-century women as captivating object of sexual desire while simultaneously remaining chaste and maternal. Contributors analyze the burgeoning of gender-centered themes in Restoration drama in the final section.

David and Susan Mann's *Women Playwrights in England, Ireland, and Scotland, 1660–1823* (Indiana University Press, 1996) provides extensive plot synopses of plays and features biographical information about the women who wrote them. Margarete Rubik's *Early Women Dramatists, 1550–1800* (St. Martin's Press, 1998), written for both students and general audiences, explores women's contributions to the theater within the context of their times. Ellen Donkin's *Getting into the Act: Women Playwrights in London, 1776–1829* (Routledge, 1995) examines reasons why a significant number of women had their plays produced on the stages of London. Donkin largely credits actor/manager David Garrick, who took pride in assisting the professional playwriting careers of several women. An introductory chapter outlines the history of British women playwrights from 1660 to 1800. The remaining chapters focus on the careers of seven playwrights, such as Hannah Cowley, Elizabeth Inchbald, and Frances Burney. Donkin explores each woman's professional success and briefly discusses why the number of British women playwrights declined after 1829.

1312. Soufas, Teresa Scott. *Dramas of Distinction: A Study of Plays by Golden Age Women.* Lexington: University Press of Kentucky, 1997. 200p. bibliog. index. ISBN 0813120101.

Soufas provides a rare English-language analysis of female playwrights who were active during the Golden Age of Spain, roughly between 1500 and 1700, a period of substantial growth in Spanish culture, literature, and drama. Soufas frames her analysis using gender to understand how societal and political pressures of the day influenced the content of plays that women wrote. The author largely examines the work of five playwrights: Angela Azevedo, Ana Caro Mallen de Soto, Leonor de la Cueva y Silva, Feliciana Enriquez de Guzman, and María de Zayas y Sotomayor. Soufas thematically arranges the chapters, including women in the upper-class marriage market, women's relationship to the monarchy, and cross-gendered characters. The portrayal of women in the *comedia* of this period is examined in *The Perception of Women in Spanish Theater of the Golden Age* (Bucknell University Press, 1991), edited by Anita K. Stoll and Dawn L. Smith, which features the essays of highly regarded American Hispanists who employ Marxist and structuralist theories, feminist criticism, semiotics, and Shakespearean studies. Both men and women essayists shed light upon perceptions of society's views of women in Spain during the sixteenth and seventeenth centuries. Other contributors explore the implications of twentieth-century critical appraisals of historical perceptions and views.

1313. Stowell, Sheila. *A Stage of Their Own: Feminist Playwrights of the Suffrage Era.* Ann Arbor: University of Michigan Press, 1992. 170p. bibliog. index. ISBN 0472103342.

Theater was just one of many fronts that early feminists appropriated to wage their battle for suffrage. Stowell selects four landmark plays, crafted by Elizabeth Robins, Cicely Hamilton, Elizabeth Baker, and Githa Sowerby and produced between 1907 and 1912, that represent the various social and political objectives of English suffragists and compares them with mainstream theater of the time to explore contemporary responses to feminist theater within the suffrage movement and in society in general. Stowell devotes a chapter to a highly informative overview of suffrage drama in England.

Editors Vivien Gardner and Susan Rutherford cover the English suffrage movement on the stage in *The New Woman and Her Sisters: Feminism and Theatre, 1850–1914* (University of Michigan Press, 1992), which features studies of feminist activities in music halls, straight theater, theater management, and even the circus that challenged the dominant male view of acceptable roles for women. Editor Bettina Friedle provides excellent insight into suffrage and theater in the United States in her anthology *On to Victory: Propaganda Plays of the Woman Suffrage Movement* (Northeastern University Press, 1987). Friedle collects plays that authors such as William B. Fowle, Alice E. Ives, Alice C. Thompson, Mary Shaw, and Emily Sargent Lewis wrote between 1856 and 1917, which they intended for private parlor theatricals or for amateur performances in homes, town halls, and hotels. Beyond mere agitation for the vote, these plays address issues including child support, food safety, the dangers of alcohol, and other social evils.

1999 CORE TITLES
1999 Core Literature Titles

Bassard, Katherine Clay. *Spiritual Interrogations: Culture, Gender, and Community in Early African Women's Writing.* Princeton, NJ: Princeton University Press, 1999. 183p. bibliog. index. ISBN 0691016399; 069101647Xpa.

Beaulieu, Elizabeth Ann. *Black Women Writers and the American Neo-Slave Narrative: Femininity Unfettered.* Westport, CT: Greenwood Press, 1999. 177p. bibliog. index. ISBN 0313308381.

Galvin, Mary E. *Queer Poetics: Five Modernist Women Writers.* Westport, CT: Praeger, 1999. 143p. bibliog. index. ISBN 0313298106.

London, Bette. *Writing Double: Women's Literary Partnerships.* Ithaca, NY: Cornell University Press, 1999. 234p. bibliog. index. ISBN 0801435633; 080148555Xpa.

Peterson, Linda H. *Traditions of Victorian Women's Autobiography: The Poetics and Politics of Life Writing*. Charlottesville: University Press of Virginia, 1999. 256p. bibliog. index. ISBN 0813918839.

Rodriguez, Barbara. *Autobiographical Inscriptions: Form, Personhood, and the American Woman Writer of Color*. New York: Oxford University Press, 1999. 228p. ISBN 0195123417.

Sarra, Edith. *Fictions of Femininity: Literary Inventions of Gender in Japanese Court Women's Memoirs*. Stanford, CA: Stanford University Press, 1999. 328p. bibliog. index. ISBN 0804733783.

Tomei, Christian D., ed. *Russian Women Writers*. New York: Garland, 1999. 2v. 1548p. ISBN 081517972.

Waldron, Mary. *Jane Austen and the Fiction of Her Time*. New York: Cambridge University Press, 1999. 194p. bibliog. index. ISBN 0521651301.

Young, Elizabeth. *Disarming the Nation: Women's Writing and the American Civil War*. Chicago: University of Chicago Press, 1999. 389p. bibliog. index. ISBN 022696080; 0226960889pa.

1999 Core Theater Titles

Arrizon, Alicia. *Latina Performance: Traversing the Stage*. Bloomington: Indiana University Press, 1999. 218p. bibliog. index. ISBN 0253335086; 0253212855pa.

Brewer, Mary F. *Race, Sex, and Gender in Contemporary Women's Theatre: The Construction of "Woman."* Portland, OR: Sussex Academic Press, 1999. 218p. bibliog. index. ISBN 1902210182; 1902210190pa.

Findlay, Alison. *A Feminist Perspective on Renaissance Drama*. Oxford: Blackwell, 1999. 206p. bibliog. index. ISBN 063120508X; 0631205098pa.

Gavin, Christy, ed. *African American Women Playwrights: A Research Guide*. New York: Garland, 1999. 253p. (Critical Studies on Black Life and Culture, 31; Garland Reference Library of the Humanities, 1996). index. ISBN 0815323840.

Marsh-Lockett, Carol P., ed. *Black Women Playwrights: Visions on the American Stage*. New York: Garland, 1999. 227p. (Garland Reference Library of the Humanities, v. 2051; Studies in Modern Drama, v. 1). bibliog. index. ISBN 0815327463.

Murphy, Brenda, ed. *The Cambridge Companion to American Women Playwrights*. New York: Cambridge University Press, 1999. 285p. (Cambridge Companions to Literature). bibliog. index. ISBN 0521571847.

Orgel, Stephen, and Sean Keilen, eds. *Shakespeare and Gender*. New York: Garland, 1999. 338p. bibliog. index. ISBN 0815329628.

WORLD WIDE WEB/INTERNET SITES

1314. Cavanagh, Sheila, director. *Emory Women Writers Resource Project*. http:// chaucer.library.emory.edu/wwrp/index.html.

Designed as a pedagogical tool to teach graduate students and undergraduates how to edit literary texts, the *Emory Women Writer's Project* provides access to a broad variety of both edited and unedited texts that women from the seventeenth to the nineteenth century have written. Records edited for texts contain extensive background about the works. The true value of this site, beyond the texts themselves, is the in-depth discussion about the editorial process. Under the option "Research Guide," users will find instructions related to the curricular role of the site, as well as a bibliography that contains information regarding editing literary texts. Another site dedicated to instruction, *Voices from the Gaps: Women Writers of Color* (http://voices.cla.umn .edu), focuses on undergraduate and high school students. The English and American Studies Programs at the University of Minnesota developed and maintain this site to illuminate the lives and works of North American women writers of color. Available records primarily include biographical summaries of works that the authors wrote, as well as links to other Web sites about the author. High-school and college students created these records, and anyone can contribute records or suggest additional authors to be added to the site. Editors created the site to encourage students studying women's writing to research the authors' lives in order to better understand the works that they read. Editors of this Web site provide suggestions on how to incorporate this site into the classroom. Although the author records are uneven in quality, this site provides a useful teaching and learning tool for instructors and students alike.

1315. Kushingian, Nancy, general editor. *British Women Romantic Poets, 1789–1852*. http://www.lib.ucdavis.edu/English/BWRP/index.htm.

The Kohler Collection, housed in the Shields Library at the University of California at Davis, is the source for this valuable archive, which contains more than 14,000 volumes of poetry published in Great Britain and Ireland between 1789 and 1918. The editors of the site have created a unique electronic collection of unusual and rare texts that is available to all scholars. The advisory board focused on lesser-known writers, whose works are not likely available in electronic format. The editors marked up and made the works available in both SGML and HTML formats and alphabetically organized the information on this site by author. Although the entire collection currently is not searchable by keyword, editors have established a beta site to test keyword searching on a subset of these texts. This site contains a selective list of links to other related Web pages, including those concerning romantic literature and women and English literature, as well as online journals, newsletters, and critical projects.

1316. New York Public Library Digital Library Collection: Digital Schomburg. *African American Women Writers of the 19th Century*. http://digital.nypl.org/schomburg/ writers_aa19/.

In response to a blossoming interest in African American women writers during the 1960s, Henry Louis Gates and staff from the Schomburg Library, a branch of the New York Public Library (NYPL), published a thirty-volume set called *The Schomburg Library of Ninteenth Century Black Women*. Although this multivolume resource is out of print, the Schomburg Library has made fifty-two of the texts included in this collection available through its Web site. Librarians have marked up these works via Standard Generalized Markup Language (SGML), making the whole collection keyword searchable. This allows users to locate words and concepts across all fifty-two texts. Users can also browse the collection by title, author, and genre (fiction, poetry, biography/autobiography, and essays). The records for each work include information about the edition used to create the electronic text, as well as a scanned image of the original title page. This site contains no links to other resources outside the New York Public Library, but does connect to the home page of NYPL and to the complete NYPL digital library collection. This site is critical for anyone conducting research that deals with the writings of nineteenth-century African American women.

1317. Ockerbloom, Mary Mark, ed. *A Celebration of Women Writers.* http://digital .library.upenn.edu/women/.

This site promotes awareness of the variety of women's writing in existence. Site editors built a comprehensive metasite, linking it to other World Wide Web resources maintained at other locations, to accomplish this goal. The site provides biographical and bibliographic sites and links to full-text editions of women's writing made available through major full-text archives, such as Project Gutenberg. Texts created and maintained by site editors are located under the "What's Local" option. Users can access the site by genre and author. They also can browse the links by author, the century during which these authors lived, and the country most commonly associated with a writer. While the site itself is updated frequently, the editors cannot control the reliability of the site's links. Moreover, a local search engine would be of great assistance. Despite these two minor drawbacks, this site is a stable, highly valuable resource for anyone conducting research involving women's writing.

1318. Willett, Perry, general editor. *Victorian Women Writers Project.* http://www .indiana.edu/~letrs/vwwp/.

The editors designed this full-text archive, originally conceived as a supplement to Chadwyck-Healey's *The English Poetry Full-Text Database*, to make accurate transcriptions of works by nineteenth-century British women writers available. More than just poetry, these texts include examples of a variety of genres, such as novels, children's books, and religious tracts. All of these titles primarily are accessible through an author index, from which the user can access a list of available titles by each author. The site editors included 100 of the titles in the archives in a beta test that allows users to perform keyword searches across the collection. A keyword search produces citations for the author, work, date, and a chapter where one can locate the word or concept sought after. Since site editors have marked up all of the titles included in the complete database using SGML, the future availability of keyword searching across the whole collection is highly probable. A list of the advisory board members responsible for selecting titles for inclusion in this archive, a list of potential authors for inclusion, and a list of works currently in preparation for the collection are also available. This is an excellent site for accessing unusual works that are often difficult to locate.

1319. *Women Writers Project.* http://www.wwp.brown.edu/project/index.html.

Otherwise known as the Brown University Women Writers Project, this site is devoted to early modern women's writing, focusing on pre-Victorian women writers. A catalog that lists transcribed documents or documents that scholars are currently transcribing serves as the primary organizing tool for this vast collection. These titles may be available in electronic form, in printed form (which can be ordered and paid for online), or both. The catalog contains a citation for each text, including publication information, details about the source text (length, size, location, and so on) and available bibliographic information. Users can search the catalog via keyword in author, title, publication date, publisher, and publication place fields. Editors organized the texts according to author, although one can also sort the texts by title, date, and format (print or online). One can search each individual text by keyword, allowing users to locate concepts within a single text. The superb organization of the vast number of texts available at this frequently cited site makes it one of the most useful tools for literary scholars.

16   Religion and Philosophy

Don Welsh

This chapter contains books and Web resources that pertain to the traditional branches of philosophy and their relationships to women, gender, and feminism. The chapter "Feminist Theories and Women's Movements" examines titles that deal with feminist theoretical thought. The Pennsylvania State University Press publishes an excellent feminist series on philosophy called Re-reading the Canon that consists of titles such as *Feminist Interpretations of Plato, Feminist Interpretations of Jacques Derrida*, and more than a dozen other relevant works. This series is both informative and engaging. However, with a few exceptions, books pertaining to individual philosophers are generally not included in this chapter.

General academic titles on women and religion, women in the major religions of the world, feminist theologies from around the world, and the roles of women throughout the history of the major religions and religious institutions comprise the materials concerning religion. Books that deal with the history of women in particular denominations (e.g., *History of Women in the Methodist Church*) and popular and "how-to" books on "finding one's spiritual side" are excluded. The "Monographs" section is divided into two areas: "Religion, Theology, Spirituality, and Mythology" and "Philosophy, Philosophers, and Philosophical Subjects."

REFERENCE SOURCES

1320. Ann, Martha, and Dorothy Myers Imel, eds. *Goddesses in World Mythology*. Santa Barbara, CA: ABC-CLIO, 1994. 655p. bibliog. indexes. ISBN 0874367158.

The editors of this highly useful book gather widely scattered information about important female deities in religious traditions from around the world. Arranged geographically, the book notably examines traditions in Africa, the Near East, Southeast Asia and India, the Americas, and Oceania. More than 7,000 brief entries provide each deity's name, including equivalent names and alternate spellings, people, region, attributes, and story with cross-references and citations to titles listed in the book's bibliography. An index of goddesses by name refers readers to the chapter containing a goddess's entry. An index of goddesses by attribute groups goddesses by characteristics such as agriculture and creation. This title provides an excellent starting point for further research.

Women of Classical Mythology (ABC-CLIO, 1991) by Robert E. Bell is one of the first attempts to compile a comprehensive biographical dictionary of women in Greek and Roman myths. It contains approximately 2,600 entries, varying in length from a sentence to several pages, that highlight each subject's importance and her contributions to the myth. An index of better-known males associated with each subject helps place subjects in their mythological contexts.

1321. Barth, Else M. *Women Philosophers: A Bibliography of Books through 1990*. Bowling Green, OH: Philosophy Documentation Center, 1992. 213p. bibliog. index. ISBN 0912632917.

This bibliography, which began as a hobby for the author, attempts to demonstrate how faculty could construct a complete philosophy curriculum using only books by women. The resulting bibliography lists nearly 2,000 books and dissertations; however, Barth does not include descriptions or annotations. Barth also employs very broad criteria for inclusion of titles, including whether the author of cited works holds an academic position in a philosophy department. The bibliography begins with listings of directories, handbooks, guidebooks, and journals established or coedited by women. The core of the book arranges citations by traditional philosophical subfields and historical treatments of subfields. Some readers may experience some trouble when attempting to use the book because Barth arranges the sections according to a rather confusing classification system that scholars in the Netherlands generally employ. Academic libraries should carry this work.

1322. Benowitz, June Melby. *Encyclopedia of American Women and Religion*. Santa Barbara, CA: ABC-CLIO, 1998. 466p. bibliog. index. ISBN 0874368871.

This work explores the role of women in religion throughout the history of America. In more than 300 entries, the author primarily emphasizes Christianity, although she does not include all denominations and groups. Benowitz provides several individual biographies of women, from Hannah Greenebaum Solomon, founder of the National Council of Jewish Women, to Shirley MacLaine, actress and "leading spokesperson for the New Age movement" (p. 201). Many entries list secondary sources, and the book contains a useful twenty-one-page bibliography. The volume also includes a detailed chronology that records the dates for "firsts," including when members of various denominations first elected women to such positions as bishop and rabbi, and when various women's organizations were founded.

Women in American Religious History: An Annotated Bibliography and Guide to Sources (G. K. Hall, 1986), compiled by Dorothy C. Bass and Sandra Hughes Boyd, features more than 500 entries covering colonial times to 1984. The largest section deals with Protestantism, including both general works and denominational histories. The authors also include chapters that deal with Roman Catholicism, Judaism, African American religions, Native American religions, and alternative religious movements. Bass and Boyd provide excellent annotations that contain dozens of references to related works. The authors clearly emphasize historical context; thus readers will find very little dealing with contemporary writers. Scholars and general readers alike should find this important work highly engaging and useful.

1323. Carson, Anne. *Feminist Spirituality and the Feminine Divine: An Annotated Bibliography*. Trumansburg, NY: Crossing Press, 1986. 139p. index. (OP)

Carson's extensive bibliography provides a comprehensive listing of more than 700 books and articles of interest to researchers, instructors, students, and others who would like to know more about feminist spirituality. The work includes material on "the Goddess in her many guises, how women are interacting with Her, feminist theology in particular, and the feminist worldview in general" (p. 6). Most of the titles date to the 1970s and 1980s, but coverage begins with titles published as early as 1833. The author, a librarian at Cornell University, has created a highly resourceful volume that both public and academic libraries could use.

Carson's companion volume, titled *Goddesses and Wise Women: The Literature of Feminist Spirituality, 1980–1992* (Crossing Press, 1992), lists books, articles, periodicals, and audiovisual materials about goddess religions, witchcraft, feminist Wicca, Christianity, and Judaism, as well as fiction and fantasy literature and children's literature. Both volumes include selected, albeit not translated, titles in Spanish, Portuguese, French, Italian, German, Dutch, and Japanese.

1324. Finson, Shelley Davis, comp. *Women and Religion: A Bibliographic Guide to Christian Feminist Liberation Theology*. Toronto: University of Toronto Press, 1991. 207p. index. ISBN 0802058817.

Finson culled citations from databases, including DOBIS of the National Library of Canada, publications of the American Theological Library Association (ATLA), dissertation indexes, and other sources to compile this invaluable bibliography, consisting of books, journal articles, anthologies, special issues of journals, dissertations, newsletters, reports, and other resources published between 1975 and 1988. She especially focuses on works that consciously and critically consider women's experiences of the Christian church and its traditions (including oppressive ones), reconstruct usable traditions, and discuss liberating sources in women's lives. Excluded are hostile works and works about women and Christianity or the church that do not include critical reflection. The source covers the expected topics concerning the Bible, women in church history, language, theology, Mariology, ministry, worship, and pastoral care. It also includes chapters about Christian feminist dialogues with Judaism and liberating aspects of other spirituality movements, such as Wicca. Although Finson does not annotate citations, she briefly describes each chapter's contents and succeeds in documenting a wide range of feminist Christian thought.

1325. Fischer, Clare Benedicks. *Of Spirituality: A Feminist Perspective*. Lanham, MD: American Theological Library Association with Scarecrow Press, 1995. 279p. (ATLA Bibliography Series, no. 35). index. ISBN 081083006X.

Fischer recognizes that spirituality affects every aspect of women's lives and includes a broad range of voices and topics reflecting complexities and tensions in feminist spirituality. Her bibliography consists of books, including classic titles, published in English, for the most part from the 1970s through the early 1990s. She arranges citations, which she does not annotate, into thirteen chapters, covering not only theo/alogy, Scripture analysis, the goddess, ministry, and spiritual practices, but also autobiography, poetry, fiction, plays, visual and musical arts, and literary criticism. A cross-cultural chapter lists titles by Jewish, Christian, African American, Latina, Asian, and Native American women as well as titles concerning Hinduism, Buddhism, Islam, and African and other indigenous traditions. She also provides chapters on psychology, feminist and lesbian theory, the family, health/environment, and global connections. A listing of pertinent journals, publishers, and centers and an author index complete the bibliography.

A title in the Garland Reference Library of Social Science series, *Women and Judaism: A Selected Annotated Bibliography* (Garland, 1988) by Inger Marie Ruud, covers many aspects of Jewish women's lives in religion and society from ancient to modern times. Ruud consulted the holdings of libraries in Oslo, Copenhagen, London, and New York as well as a range of magazines and journals for books, journal articles, book chapters, doctoral dissertations, and essays from anthologies published in English, German, French, and Scandinavian languages. Short, concise, and descriptive annotations accompany complete citations. Coverage includes all countries with significant Jewish populations, but focuses on Israel and the United States. A topographical, author, and subject index completes the source.

1326. Kadel, Andrew. *Matrology: A Bibliography of Writings by Christian Women from the First to the Fifteenth Centuries*. New York: Continuum, 1995. 191p. bibliog. indexes. (OP)

Kadel coined the word "Matrology," which means "words of our mothers," to parallel the usage of the terms "patrologia" or "patrology," which scholars have employed since the nineteenth century. This comprehensive bibliography includes citations to religious and nonreligious writings crafted by 250 Christian women between the first and fifteenth centuries. Entries are arranged chronologically, with each entry including a brief biographical sketch, secondary sources about the author, and lists of English editions of their works, original-language editions, and translations. Alphabetical and chronological indexes are included. This highly useful and accessible work fills gaps in ancient and medieval studies.

1327. Kersey, Ethel M., and Calvin O. Schrag. *Women Philosophers: A Bio-critical Source Book*. New York: Greenwood Press, 1989. 230p. bibliog. index. ISBN 0313257205.

During the 1980s researchers began to ask Kersey, a librarian, for information about pre-twentieth-century women philosophers. Since information was scattered and difficult to find, she compiled this very useful book. With apologies, Kersey stays with the traditional male, Western philosophical fields, such as ethics, logic, and metaphysics, as her framework. She excludes famous writers like Mary Wollstonecraft who discussed the philosophy of women, as well as writers whose work falls more within the definitions of sociology and psychology, since other sources cover them. She also excludes women who wrote exclusively devotional or visionary titles. Though Kersey arranges the philosophers alphabetically by name, she provides an introduction outlining the history of philosophy that places many of the women in chronological context. The 150 entries vary in length according to the amount of available information. At the very least, they provide dates, country, school of philosophy, brief description, and list of sources. Longer entries also include education, honors, and more discussion of life influences and career accomplishments. An appendix in the form of a table lists the philosophers by name, time period, country, and discipline. The table's alphabetical arrangement by name at first appears redundant, but it enhances the reader's ability to find women who share each category. A name index, covering main entries and people mentioned within the text, completes this worthwhile source.

1328. Russell, Letty M., and J. Shannon Clarkson, eds. *Dictionary of Feminist Theologies*. Louisville, KY: Westminster John Knox Press, 1996. 351p. bibliog. ISBN 0664220584.

Aimed at a wide audience, this dictionary is the first of its kind to be published in English. It covers all aspects of Christianity from a variety of viewpoints, including womanist, mujerista, Asian, African, and Latin American, as well as feminist engagements with theologies of other religious traditions. Contributors include important scholars, such as Maria Pilar Aquino, Katie Cannon, Cynthia Eller, Elisabeth Schüssler Fiorenza, Carter Heyward, Judith Plaskow, Emilie Townes, and Rosemary Radford Ruether. Longer entries for introductory areas, such as women's spirituality, biblical studies, feminist theories, contemporary, historical, and feminist theologies, and church histories, provide the basis for many related subjects. Signed entries are well written and accessible to nonspecialists. Most entries contain cross-references to related entries and conclude with a list of brief citations that refer to an excellent and broad bibliography. The information about each contributor lists her subject entries, but this does not make up for the lack of an index. Nevertheless, this important dictionary covers subjects from different contexts, cultures, and disciplines and belongs in most academic reference collections.

1329. Walker, Barbara G. *The Woman's Dictionary of Symbols and Sacred Objects*. San Francisco: HarperSanFrancisco, 1988. 563p. index. bibliog. ISBN (OP); 0062509233pa.

The Woman's Dictionary of Symbols and Sacred Objects is a comprehensive guide, with 753 entries and 636 illustrations, to the history and mythology of woman-related symbols. Walker arranges the various sections according to type of symbol, such as round motifs and multipointed motifs. The author also describes histories of traditional sacred objects and "deity signs," as well as the signs of the zodiac, animal and bird symbols, and plants, fruits, and stones. Entries range from half a page to a full page; most include illustrations. Walker provides histories and various interpretations of symbols with references. This work is a useful resource for students and scholars alike. General readers of all backgrounds will find this work both insightful and entertaining.

MONOGRAPHS

Religion, Theology, Spirituality, and Mythology

1330. Adler, Rachel. *Engendering Judaism: An Inclusive Theology and Ethics*. Philadelphia: Jewish Publication Society, 1998. 269p. bibliog. index. ISBN 0827605846.

This title won Adler, a professor at the University of Southern California and Hebrew Union College, the National Jewish Book Award for Jewish Thought. Some scholars have described this work as pivotal in bringing in the next wave of Jewish feminism. Like other feminist Jewish scholars, Adler seeks to redress the silencing of women in Judaism. She claims, however, that many early Jewish feminist scholars rejected Judaism and did not include both male and female perspectives in their writings. Adler, a scholar descended from five generations of Reform Jews, has lived as an Orthodox Jew for many years. She believes that traditional Judaism provides avenues for women to protest and correct their subordination, and she proposes conceptual changes in the marriage contract. Adler writes with humor and an anecdotal style, making this work accessible to general readers. However, it is also very sophisticated and highly appropriate for scholars. Judith Hauptman also examines the marriage contract as well as other subjects pertaining to women in *Rereading the Rabbis: A Woman's Voice* (Westview Press, 1998). She analyzes rabbinical debates in Jewish legal texts and compares them with the biblical text. She believes that rabbis consistently revised laws to provide more rights and recognitions to women and women's needs. Both Hauptman and Adler urge women to reinterpret and challenge Jewish texts to change unacceptable laws rather than reject traditional Judaism out of hand.

1331. Ahmed, Leila. *Women and Gender in Islam: Historical Roots of a Modern Debate*. New Haven, CT: Yale University Press, 1992. 296p. ISBN (OP); 0300055838pa.

In this important work, Ahmed traces the Islamic discourses on women and gender from the ancient world to the present. Beginning with the Middle East prior to the rise of Islam, the first section examines early concepts of gender and family. In section 2, Ahmed traces the changes that came with the rise of Islam in the Middle East. The third section starts with the turn of the nineteenth century and documents the many changes that the modern world brought to Islam. Ahmed focuses almost entirely on Egypt as the most modern Arab state in the latter part of her work. *Women and Islamization: Contemporary Dimensions of Discourse on Gender Relations* (Berg, 1998), edited by Karin Ask and Marit Tjomsland, illustrates "how Muslim women in various national settings contribute to the Islamization of their societies" (p. 1).

Fatima Mernissi provides an alternative view of this issue in her book *The Veil and the Male Elite: A Feminist Interpretation of Women's Rights in Islam* (Addison-Wesley, 1991). Mernissi claims that Muhammad asserted the equality of women, envisioning an egalitarian society. Moreover, according to the author, discrimination against women does not comprise a fundamental tenet of Islam. All three works would complement the collections of an academic library; however, Mernissi's book would best benefit people unfamiliar with Islamic society.

1332. Bartholomeusz, Tessa J. *Women under the Bo Tree: Buddhist Nuns in Sri Lanka*. New York: Cambridge University Press, 1994. 284p. bibliog. index. ISBN 0521461294.

Bartholomeusz traces the emergence of lay female renunciants beginning with the nineteenth century and continuing into the 1990s. She combines a number of historical sources and interviews from her fieldwork to examine conditions that enabled lay nuns to establish communities supported by lay donors (dayakas), independent from the authority of monks.

In *Lives of the Nuns: Biographies of Chinese Buddhist Nuns from the Fourth to Sixth Centuries: A Translation of the Pi-ch `iu-ni chuan*, compiled by Shih Pao-chang (University of Hawaii Press, 1994), Kathryn Ann Tsai translates the biographies of sixty-five nuns collected by a Buddhist monk around 516 C.E. using both written and oral sources. Even though Buddhism conflicted with Confucianism by promoting monastic celibacy, many women overcame resistance of their families and communities to preach, meditate, chant, convert laity, and train disciples according to Buddhist principles. Tsai contributes historical context to the biographies, which provide rich details of the nun's religious lives.

1333. Bendroth, Margaret Lamberts. *Fundamentalism and Gender, 1875 to the Present.* New Haven, CT: Yale University Press, 1993. 179p. bibliog. index. ISBN (OP); 0300068646pa.

Bendroth's work, which presents a sympathetic portrait of fundamentalists, focuses on the conflicts between doctrine and practice in a movement led by men, but whose constituency was mostly female. The book explores the "antifeminist image" of Christian fundamentalism in the United States, which is "in fact a stereotype, glossing over some deep conflicts within evangelical ranks" (p. 2). Bendroth begins this work by examining ideas of masculinity and antifeminism in early fundamentalism. In chapters 3 and 4, the author analyzes the appearance of gender issues in various groups and institutions during the twentieth century. In chapter 5, Bendroth considers issues of parenthood and gender roles in the fundamentalist family. She provides an epilogue on "The Meaning of Evangelical Feminism." Bendroth, a professor of history at Calvin College, has constructed an informative study that most academic libraries should carry.

Now in its third edition, *All We're Meant to Be: Biblical Feminism for Today* (Abingdon, 1992) by Letha D. Scanzoni and Nancy A. Hardesty continues to examine connections between feminist and evangelical perspectives. Fifteen chapters discuss such topics as same-sex relationships, work and family conflicts, gender roles, sexuality, discrimination, and biblical revelation. An updated "Where Do We Go from Here—Again?" addresses topics that arose during the 1980s and early 1990s: backlash, elder care, divorce, domestic violence, and sexual abuse. A study guide and topically arranged bibliography complete the book.

1334. Brink, Judy, and Joan Mencher, eds. *Mixed Blessings: Gender and Religious Fundamentalism Cross Culturally.* New York: Routledge, 1997. 275p. bibliog. index. ISBN (OP); 0415911869pa.

The editors derived the title of this book from the premise that fundamentalism affects women in different ways according to the culture within which they live. In the first part, contributors discuss how women can benefit from fundamentalism in countries such as Colombia, Sri Lanka, and China. In Colombia, for example, the evangelical movement battles the culture of machismo and works to make men responsible for their families. In the next two sections, contributors present case studies from nine other countries that address women's struggles against fundamentalisms' restrictions and oppression. The inclusion of a variety of experiences insightfully portrays women living within fundamentalist groups from a feminist point of view.

In *Fundamentalism and Gender* (Oxford University Press, 1994), editor John Stratton Hawley provides a substantial introduction in which he discusses the nature of fundamentalism, its meaning in different cultural contexts, and its relationship to gender. He then presents four case studies that examine American fundamentalism and fundamentalist theology's perceptions of women; Islam in India and its conflicts with civil law in divorce cases; the Hindu tradition of sati, wherein a widow is burned on the funeral pyre with her dead husband, and other ideas of gender in Indian culture; and the changing ideas of gender in the new religions of modern Japan. In the two concluding essays, Jay M. Harris attacks the notion that scholars should apply the term "fundamentalism" to movements other than American Protestantism, and Karen McCarthy Brown sees fundamentalism as "the religion of the stressed and disoriented" (p. 175).

Shahin Gerami's *Women and Fundamentalism: Islam and Christianity* (Garland, 1996) is a comparative study of Muslim Iranian and Egyptian women and American women of the new Christian right. The author uses interviews and statistical tables to present a gendered vision of religious fundamentalism. Gerami's book is particularly helpful in understanding issues facing women in the Middle East. Academic libraries would benefit from carrying all these titles.

1335. Cahill, Susan Neunzig, ed. *Wise Women: Over Two Thousand Years of Spiritual Writing by Women*. New York: Norton, 1996. 395p. bibliog. index. ISBN 0393039463; 0393316793pa.

This diverse, thought-provoking anthology of essays, poems, prayers, journals, and stories covers 5,000 years of women's spirituality. The collection includes writers from Sappho and Teresa of Avila to contemporary women such as Dorothy Sayers, Hannah Arendt, and Denise Levertov. Cahill includes writers from many faiths, such as Islamic, Buddhist, and Taoist. Native American writers are presented alongside Christian and Jewish authors. Readers will find this work both engaging and accessible, since the volume includes writings that are not overtly religious in nature. Brief introductions to each piece will help students understand the significance of the work.

An Anthology of Sacred Texts by and about Women (Crossroad, 1993), edited by Serinity Young, includes writings from Judaism, Christianity, Islam, ancient Greek and Roman religions, paganism, Shamanism, Hinduism, Buddhism, Confucianism, Taoism, and "alternative religious movements." This illuminating anthology of short excerpts from a wide variety of works is quite comprehensive. The volume includes a short bibliography, as well as an index of names and subjects. Both small and large libraries would benefit from carrying this title.

1336. Chaves, Mark. *Ordaining Women: Culture and Conflict in Religious Organizations*. Cambridge, MA: Harvard University Press, 1997. 249p. bibliog. index. ISBN 0674641450; 0674641469pa.

This significant study of the 100 largest Christian denominations in the United States includes analysis of the groups as well as a discussion of their official documents. Chaves discovers that the policies enforced frequently differ from the practices employed. Moreover, many sociological factors outside the church influence policy. Chaves examines the theological reasons for resisting ordination, as well as the tendency to resist as a protest against modernism and liberalism. While concentrating on ordination, the author discovers a variety of roles that women fill in the various denominations. All academic libraries should house this work.

Ruth Tucker and Walter Liefeld provide a comprehensive historical survey tracing women's church leadership in *Daughters of the Church: Women and Ministry from New Testament Times to the Present* (Academic Books, 1987). The authors supply fascinating, succinct, and useful discussions of historical, international, and interdenominational arguments pertaining to women's ordination and contributions to Christianity. In *Women Who Would Be Rabbis: A History of Women's Ordination, 1889–1985* (Beacon Press, 1998), Pamela S. Nadell provides a thorough, authoritative, and lucidly written account of Jewish women's quest for ordination in the United

States. Using specific women as examples, she traces the situation in Reform and Conservative Judaism and the beginning of debates within Orthodox Judaism.

1337. Chmielewski, Wendy E., Louis J. Kern, and Marilyn Klee-Hartzell, eds. *Women in Spiritual and Communitarian Societies in the United States.* Syracuse, NY: Syracuse University Press, 1993. 275p. (Utopianism and Communitarianism). bibliog. index. ISBN 0815625685; 0815625693pa.

In this anthology, scholars representing a variety of disciplines seek to recover and interpret women's experiences in intentional communities that include Owenites, Shakers, Mormons, the Texas Woman's Commonwealth, Brook Farm, Lubavitcher, and Catholic sisters. Each essay analyzes the group in terms of how well it lived up to its aspirations. Contributors find that the most successful communities valued women's domestic labor and did not burden women with double shifts. The collection addresses common themes among diverse groups in specific contexts and provides insight into the complex relationship between religious ideologies and social structures, and myriad difficulties in overcoming mainstream gender ideologies.

In *Chaste Liberation: Celibacy and Female Cultural Status* (University of Illinois Press, 1989), winner of the first Illinois NWSA Book Award, Sally L. Kitch is more concerned with sources of female power than with the successes and failures of three groups: the Shakers, the Koreshan Unity, and the Texas Woman's Commonwealth (also called Sanctificationists). She particularly explores connections between religious ideology and gender equality and between celibacy and reconstructions of gender roles and each group's social, economic, and religious practices. Kitch provides many insights into the daily work and lives of Commonwealth members in *This Strange Society of Women: Reading the Letters and Lives of the Woman's Commonwealth* (Ohio State University Press, 1993), based on 2,400 pages of letters and business documents. This title won a Helen Hooven Santmyer Prize from the publisher.

1338. Christ, Carol P. *The Laughter of Aphrodite: Reflections on a Journey to the Goddess.* San Francisco: Harper & Row, 1987. 240p. bibliog. index. (OP)

In this collection of essays on feminist theology from one of the most influential writers on religion today, Carol P. Christ describes her rejection of Judaism and Christianity and her explorations of a women-centered spirituality. Christ's chronicle of this journey creates accessible, yet scholarly essays that analyze the work of other feminist theologians. While there is a great deal of information on the history of feminist spirituality, Christ includes personal experiences, important people in her life, and stories from her own journey to spirituality. This is a good introduction to many of the issues in feminist spirituality.

Christ, with Judith Plaskow, edited *Weaving the Visions: New Patterns in Feminist Spirituality* (HarperSanFrancisco, 1989). This sequel to Christ's and Plaskow's popular *Womenspirit Rising* (Harper & Row, 1979) presents thirty-three essays that examine the diversity of religion in North America. Most collections should carry these important works. Christ also crafted *Rebirth of the Goddess: Finding Meaning in Feminist Spirituality* (Addison-Wesley, 1997), a systematic theology of the Goddess that explores the history of Goddess religion and what it means, and *Odyssey with the Goddess: A Spiritual Quest in Crete* (Continuum, 1995), an autobiographical work that documents Christ's struggle with depression and her relationship to the divine.

1339. Daly, Lois K., ed. *Feminist Theological Ethics: A Reader.* Louisville, KY: Westminster John Knox Press, 1994. 325p. (Library of Theological Ethics). bibliog. ISBN 066425327Xpa.

This work contains twenty-two essays by distinguished feminist scholars who discuss a wide range of issues from a variety of perspectives. The first section includes essays that examine feminist ethics and racial issues, including explorations of womanist and mujerista frameworks. In the second section, essayists attack some of the beliefs within traditional theology, such as the subordination of women and the emphasis on heterosexuality. In the third section, contributors explore personal issues, including procreative choice, altruism, ecofeminism, and women in combat. Although some of the essays are not theological in nature, this collection offers a good introduction to feminist social ethics and would serve as a good reader in the classroom (the editor refers to the work as a "public syllabus").

Many scholars credit Katie G. Cannon with laying the groundwork for an ethics from the viewpoint of African American women. In *Black Womanist Ethics* (Scholars Press, 1988), the author makes important distinctions between dominant, or traditional, ethics, which assumes that self-directing moral agents have the freedom and autonomy to make a wide range of choices, and womanist ethics, which uses the concept of marginalization to explore African American values, duties, and obligations in a nation that institutionalizes oppression based on gender, race, and class. Cannon turns to the life and work of Zora Neale Hurston, the theologies of Martin Luther King Jr. and Howard Thurman, and a historical reconstruction of African American women's moral situation from 1619 to the 1980s to argue for an ethics based on lived experiences rather than theory or "objective" values and norms. This book helped open a rich dialogue of many voices in this interdisciplinary field and belongs in all academic libraries.

1340. Eller, Cynthia Lorraine. *Living in the Lap of the Goddess: The Feminist Spirituality Movement in America.* New York: Crossroad, 1993. 276p. bibliog. index. (OP)

Eller examines wide-ranging forms of feminist spirituality, from individual enlightenment to group rituals, in this objective and informative history of the feminist spirituality movement in the United States. Eller invested ten years in studying this movement, which she describes as "unique in its determination to remain true to the concerns of women, both politically and spiritually" (p. ix). The author provides a well-researched sociological profile of the movement, determining that it is generally affiliated with white, well-educated, and middle-class women in the process of seeking new answers. Eller provides several personal histories about how certain women became involved in the movement as well as information about ancient matriarchies, medieval witchcraft, and the modern political agenda.

Ursula King, author of *Women and Spirituality: Voices of Protest and Promise* (Pennsylvania State University Press, 1989), believes that spirituality is an ontological existential category that permeates all aspects of life. The author examines the place of spirituality in feminism by exploring women's spiritual traditions, including the goddess, mysticism, androgyny, and matriarchy, to find paths that might lead to integrated ideas about lived human experience. King's impressive knowledge of women's spirituality in many cultures and religions makes this important book a fascinating read. The second edition of Carol Ochs's highly regarded *Women and Spirituality* (Rowman & Littlefield, 1997) clarifies various ideas originally presented throughout in the 1983 edition (Rowman & Allenheld) and adds two chapters. One explores women's relationship with time and how this relationship helps in understanding the spiritual quest. The other discusses two new role models from the Bible: Elisheba, wife of Aaron, who serves as an example of authentic mourning, and Miriam the prophet, who exemplifies a new spirituality.

1341. Fabella, Virginia, and Sun Ai Lee Park, eds. *We Dare to Dream: Doing Theology as Asian Women.* Kowloon, Hong Kong: Asian Women's Resource Centre for Culture and Theology; Manila, Philippines: EATWOT Women's Commission in Asia, 1989. 156p. bibliog. (OP)

Prominent Asian feminist theologians contribute the sixteen essays in this introductory collection. The essays are grounded in women's efforts to do theology in ways that reflect their own experiences and life context. Several contributors examine theological themes such as Christology, ecclesiology, and the Holy Spirit. Others explore the exploitation and subordination of women in specific Asian contexts within theological frameworks. Authors of essays in the final section explore theology from Indian, Korean, Filipino, and Chinese perspectives.

Struggle to Be the Sun Again: Introducing Asian Women's Theology (Orbis Books, 1990) by Hyun Kyung Chung also discusses theological challenges of Asian women. Chung provides an overview of the social and historical contexts for Asian women's theology that includes a description of the origins of the Women's Commission of the Ecumenical Association of Third World Theologians (EATWOT). She also examines meanings of Mary and Jesus and diverse manifestations of Asian women's spirituality. The author succeeds in providing a synthesis of new theological insights from women struggling with issues of survival and liberation. Both titles provide clear introductions to Asian feminist theologies and belong in academic collections.

1342. Gimbutas, Marija. *The Language of the Goddess: Unearthing the Hidden Symbols of Western Civilization.* San Francisco: Harper & Row, 1989. 388p. bibliog. index. (OP)

Anthropologist Gimbutas examined hundreds of artifacts of prehistoric Europe and the Near East (7000 to 3500 B.C.E.), especially those created during the Neolithic period, and examined evidence in folklore, linguistics, and comparative mythology as the basis for this thought-provoking and generously illustrated title. The parallel themes in these sources lead Gimbutas to believe that the images, signs, and symbols comprised a "language" of the Great Goddess, used in a widespread culture based on worshipping her. She further asserts that this "language" underpins Western civilization and is essential to our understanding of it.

Gimbutas followed with *The Civilization of the Goddess: The World of Old Europe* (HarperSanFrancisco, 1991), which provides contextual information for the previous work. A number of scholars, including feminists, criticized Gimbutas for universalizing across cultures and time periods, reaching conclusions not necessarily supported by the evidence, and lack of theoretical rigor. Her work, however, made original contributions to the field, generated much debate and research, and influenced the contemporary feminist goddess movement.

Scholars who conduct research along similar lines include Riane Eisler (*The Chalice and the Blade: Our History, Our Future*, HarperSanFrancisco, 1987) (see entry 233), and Elinor Gadon (*The Once and Future Goddess: A Symbol for Our Time*, Harper & Row, 1989). Specialists in the field present chapters addressing some of the theoretical contentions of Gimbutas and others in *Ancient Goddesses: The Myths and the Evidence* (British Museum, 1998), edited by Lucy Goodison and Christine Morris. Contributors use both old and new evidence to reexamine previous research, and the collection's useful introduction traces the history of interest in the goddess beginning with the nineteenth century.

1343. Grant, Jacquelyn. *White Women's Christ and Black Women's Jesus: Feminist Christology and Womanist Response.* Atlanta: Scholars Press, 1989. 264p. (American Academy of Religion Academy Series, no. 64). bibliog. ISBN 1555403026; 1555403034pa.

Grant states that feminist and classical ideas of Christ are white, racist, and therefore inadequate for African American women. She explains that many African American women see Jesus as a divine sufferer who identifies with unjust oppression and persecution by empowering the weak. After reviewing traditional and white feminist theologies and ideas about Christ, Grant proposes a womanist Christ who emerges from an analysis of race, sex, and class oppressions.

She believes that African American women's engagement with both the symptoms and the underlying causes of oppression yields a constructive, liberating Christology that can connect oppressed groups.

In *The Black Christ* (Orbis Books, 1994), Kelly Brown Douglas traces ideas of the Black Christ, connections between these ideas and African American struggles, and the development of theology. She analyzes African American women's commitment to family and community as well as their experiences with multiple oppressions, including sexual orientation, both outside of and within their communities to develop a womanist theology based on multidimensional political and social examinations of wholeness. Both of these important titles challenge traditional and white feminist theologies and create new canons based on African American women's spiritual and political experiences.

1344. Gross, Rita M. *Buddhism after Patriarchy: A Feminist History, Analysis, and Reconstruction of Buddhism.* Albany: State University of New York Press, 1993. 365p. bibliog. index. ISBN (OP); 0791414043pa.

Gross, a professor of religion at the University of Wisconsin at Eau Claire, has created a significant scholarly study about the role women have played in the history of Buddhism. The author reexamines the basic texts of Buddhism, subjecting them to the same kind of feminist analysis employed by scholars studying Christianity and Judaism. Although Gross questions whether Buddhism is an appropriate religion for women, she ultimately believes that the core teachings of Buddhism promote gender equity as opposed to male dominance.

In *Passionate Enlightenment: Women in Tantric Buddhism* (Princeton University Press, 1994), Miranda Shaw analyzes this often misrepresented and misunderstood tradition. She examines relatively obscure texts to argue that women, as well as men, participated in and contributed to the development of Tantric Buddhism even to the point of devising specific practices and theories. Since women represent the goddess, Shaw believes that sexual relations empower both partners, not just males. Despite winning the James Henry Breasted Prize from the American Historical Association, *Passionate Enlightenment* was criticized by some scholars because it radically challenged established interpretations.

One of the earliest scholarly examinations of Buddhism to use gender analysis as a framework, *Buddhism, Sexuality, and Gender* (State University of New York Press, 1992), edited by José Ignacio Cabezón, collects essays exploring the influence of gender in different Buddhist traditions. The title presents textual, social, and historical perspectives, including an examination of Buddhist symbols and a rare discussion of homosexuality, and suggests new aspects about Buddhist attitudes toward women, gender, and sexuality. Academic libraries should house all of these important works.

1345. Heyward, Carter. *Touching Our Strength: The Erotic as Power and the Strength of God.* San Francisco: Harper & Row, 1989. 195p. bibliog. (OP)

In a series of seven meditative essays, Heyward, a lesbian Episcopalian priest and professor of theology, celebrates sex, regardless of sexual orientation, as the "embodied relational response to erotic/sacred power, and *theology* to a critical reflection on the shape of the Sacred in our life" (p. 3). She believes that relationships reveal the presence of God according to the degree of mutuality and enrichment that spark each partner toward full humanity. The author traces what she calls erotophobia to the Council of Elvira (c. 309 C.E.), which she believes undermined one of the original purposes of Christianity, to resist oppressive power relations, and helped lay the groundwork for antisex codes. The author further maintains that the resulting male supremacy and heterosexual theology helped support sexist, racist, heterosexist, and often violent social frameworks and came to define sexuality as evil. Using the Christa (female Christ) as a metaphor, Heyward urges people to develop justice in mutual relationships that can transform the social order. She concludes by articulating various aspects of her Christian and feminist ethics.

1346. Hogan, Linda. *From Women's Experience to Feminist Theology*. Sheffield, England: Sheffield Academic Press, 1995. 192p. bibliog. index. ISBN 1850755205pa.

Hogan, a professor of theology and religious studies at the University of Leeds, explores the origins of the primary categories of women's theology: women's experience and praxis, the practical application and practice of theology. The author examines methodological questions raised by important feminist reformist theologians, such as Elisabeth Schüssler Fiorenza and Rosemary Radford Ruether, explores women's experience as expressed in the womanist writings of Zora Neale Hurston and Alice Walker, and investigates ideas of "post-Christian feminists" such as Carol Christ and Christine Downing, who have "turned to the goddesses as a source of spirituality" (p. 141). This well-written scholarly study could serve as an introduction for those unfamiliar with feminist theology.

Lisa Isherwood and Dorothea McEwan's *Introducing Feminist Theology* (Sheffield Academic Press, 1993) is another accessible introduction to the subject of feminist theology. Isherwood and McEwan edited a companion to this volume titled *An A to Z of Feminist Theology* (Sheffield Academic Press, 1996), an invaluable encyclopedic dictionary that explains key concepts and terms in the field from a variety of feminist perspectives. *Feminist Theology: A Reader* (Westminster John Knox Press, 1990), edited by Ann Loades, collects twenty-two essays, many of which were previously published in various books and journals. It features several leading writers in the field of theology, including Elisabeth Schüssler Fiorenza, Rosemary Radford Ruether, and Ursula King, as well as a number of lesser-known writers. Essayists address topics such as *The Woman's Bible* by Elizabeth Cady Stanton, feminist hermeneutics, the ideas of Paul, Augustine, and Luther, and gender and patriarchy. The last section, "Practical Consequences," contains essays that explore societal influences on theology and reevaluate Christian theological tradition. All of these works would prove useful for anyone new to the field of feminist theology.

1347. Isasi-Diaz, Ada María. *Mujerista Theology: A Theology for the Twenty-First Century*. Maryknoll, NY: Orbis Books, 1996. 210p. bibliog. index. ISBN 1570750815pa.

Isasi-Diaz comprehensively introduces U.S. Hispanic feminist theology in this collection of previously published articles. The first part of the work includes autobiography and describes the author's experience of self-discovery. The essays in the second part "are elaborations of the issues that grassroots Latinas face daily, the themes we discuss when we gather, and the concerns expressed in vocal prayers" (p. 4). In these daily lives, Latinas deal with poverty, powerlessness, and marginalization, sometimes from their own churches. The author attempts to bring together these experiences and theories. Isasi-Diaz also wrote *En la Lucha—In the Struggle: A Hispanic Women's Liberation Theology* (Fortress, 1993), which "is a platform for the voices of Latinas because their lived-experience is the source of mujerista theology" (p. 1). Her book includes interviews as well as Spanish-language summaries of the chapters. Both books are easily readable and should interest anyone drawn to mujerista theology.

In *Our Cry for Life: Feminist Theology from Latin America/Nuestro Clamor por la Vida* (Orbis Books, 1993), author María Pilar Aquino bases her theology on both liberating and oppressive experiences in women's lives. She argues that Latin American feminist theology is distinct from both Western feminist theologies and Latin American liberation theology since it arose from women's daily lives within the context of colonialism, capitalism, and public and private oppressive social and cultural structures. This important title reflects the communal and dialogic aspects of Latin American women's theology.

1348. Johnson, Elizabeth A. *She Who Is: The Mystery of God in Feminist Theological Discourse.* New York: Crossroad, 1992. 316p. bibliog. indexes. ISBN (OP); 0824513762pa.

In this carefully researched and persuasively argued text, Johnson examines Scripture and traditional Christian, Jewish, and feminist theologies for language that frees women and other groups from patriarchal oppression and exclusion. Within these sources, she finds many female images of God and, as a result, reinterprets Sophia (wisdom): Spirit Sophia, an immanent God who renews the world, Jesus Sophia, wisdom incarnate, and Mother Sophia, the divine mystery. This important, elegantly written title was a winner of the 1992 Crossroad Women's Studies Award and serves as a widely used feminist text in theological education. In *Consider Jesus: Waves of Renewal in Christology* (Crossroad, 1990), Johnson thoroughly and succinctly reviews various sources that answer the question "Who was Jesus?" to provide a solid grounding of feminist and other Christologies.

Jesus, Miriam's Child, Sophia's Prophet: Critical Issues in Feminist Christology (Continuum, 1995) by Elisabeth Schüssler Fiorenza grew out of interest in the Jesus movement chapter in the author's *In Memory of Her* (Crossroad, 1983). This new title critically explores feminist and other theoretical frameworks underpinning discourses about Jesus in order to begin articulating a feminist Christology. By naming Jesus as a child of Miriam and prophet of divine Sophia (wisdom), the author creates the rhetorical and hermeneutical space "to decenter hegemonic malestream christological discourses and to reframe them in terms of a critical feminist theology of liberation" (p. 3) that is meaningful to women struggling against "multiplicative forms of oppression" (p. 14).

1349. King, Ursula, ed. *Feminist Theology from the Third World: A Reader.* Maryknoll, NY: Orbis Books, 1994. 434p. bibliog. index. ISBN (OP); 0883449633pa.

This key collection is comprised of thirty-eight writings by theologians, lay theologians, journalists, and activists from several Third World countries. King provides a general introduction that discusses the context and background of the book, as well as brief introductions to the five sections. The first section contains articles written by women in countries in South America, Africa, and Asia, as well as minority women in the United States, exploring various perspectives of theology. Contributors in section 2 concentrate on oppression and violence against women, while those in section 3 explore sources of empowerment in various parts of the Bible. The remaining two sections question traditional thinking and look to possible future roles of theology as a liberating force for women from around the globe.

Another collection, titled *Inheriting Our Mothers' Gardens: Feminist Theology in Third World Perspective* (Westminster Press, 1988), edited by Letty M. Russell and others, also serves as an excellent introduction to the subject and is notable for its very useful annotated bibliography covering feminist theologies, subdivided by geographic region. For an accessible collection of essays reflecting theology from African women's perspectives, see *The Will to Arise: Women, Tradition, and the Church in Africa* (Orbis Books, 1992), edited by Mercy Amba Obduyoye and Musimbi R.A. Kanyoro.

1350. Klein, Anne. *Meeting the Great Bliss Queen: Buddhists, Feminists, and the Art of the Self.* Boston: Beacon Press, 1995. 307p. bibliog. index. ISBN (OP); 0807073075pa.

In this thoughtful title, Klein presents the rich historical past of Indo-Tibetan Buddhism and analyzes its potential relevance to Western feminism. She carefully explains that Buddhists see the self in terms of mutuality and relatedness, while most Westerners see it as psychological and individual. Using three specific Buddhist concepts, mindfulness, compassion, and emptiness, Klein connects feminist and Buddhist ideas about relatedness and mutuality in an attempt to show how both perspectives strive to combine theory with living practice. She believes that feminist engagement with the Great Bliss Queen, who represents enlightenment, can empower women by expanding their understanding of themselves and all varieties of experience.

Editor Marianne Dresser includes approximately thirty critical (in the sense of mindful) essays in *Buddhist Women on the Edge: Contemporary Perspectives from the Western Frontier* (North Atlantic Books, 1996), which offers diverse viewpoints from American women who practice, study, and teach Buddhism. Contributors, including Klein, Sandy Boucher, bell hooks, Miranda Shaw, and Rita Gross, address topics such as Buddhist institutions, monastic and lay practices, teacher-student relationships, cross-cultural adaptation and appropriation, psychological issues and the role of emotions, and spiritual connections to personal relationships and social activism. *Turning the Wheel: American Women Creating the New Buddhism* (Harper & Row, 1987; 2nd ed., Beacon Press, 1993) by Sandy Boucher traces the history and development of North American Buddhism and discusses women leaders from various schools and retreat centers.

1351. Kraemer, Ross Shepard. *Her Share of the Blessings: Women's Religions among Pagans, Jews, and Christians in the Greco-Roman World.* New York: Oxford University Press, 1992. 275p. bibliog. index. ISBN (OP); 0195086708pa.

Kraemer examines women and religion in the Greek, Hellenistic, and Roman worlds, in Jewish communities of the Greco-Roman world, and during the dawning of Christianity. Her study, which spans roughly 400 B.C.E. to 400 C.E., relies upon archaeological evidence and early literary sources, including the Bible. In the first seven chapters, which deal with the ancient pagan world, the author argues that women held a variety of leadership roles, from Vestal Virgins to the high priestess in the worship of Isis. In the next two chapters, which deal with women's lives in the rabbinical world and the Greco-Roman diaspora, Kraemer discovers evidence of strong female leadership in synagogues in both worlds. In the last four chapters, she examines women in the world of early Christianity, discussing Christianity's appeal to women, the roots of gender-role antagonism, and women in heretical movements. Again, she finds much evidence of women's participation in religious offices and leadership. The author adds a gender component to anthropologist Mary Douglas's grid/group analysis to analyze relationships among social experience, religious behavior, and individual freedom and to reveal the extent of women's religious diversity. This title provides contextual information and commentary to Kraemer's earlier title *Maenads, Martyrs, Matrons, Monastics* (Fortress, 1988), an excellent collection of primary sources addressing women's many and varied activities in Greco-Roman religious traditions. Source, personal name, and divine name indexes and the author's discussion of Greek, Latin, and Hebrew abbreviations, symbols, and the like add immensely to the value of the work. Kraemer's titles cover a period in women's history that scholars infrequently discuss.

1352. Larrington, Carolyne, ed. *The Feminist Companion to Mythology.* London: Pandora Press, 1992. 480p. bibliog. indexes. (OP)

Aimed at nonspecialists and scholars in adjacent disciplines, this volume seeks to examine women's roles in myths across cultures and time periods and to explore myths' influences on structures of their societies. It covers myths from the Near East, Asia, Europe, Oceania, and North and South America. Contributors with firsthand knowledge of languages and texts of the cultures use historical, anthropological, narratological, structuralist, and other approaches to develop essays in the most appropriate way for the myth system and culture they discuss. Most authors point out that myths exist within a web of other cultural ideas, that meanings attributed to myths change over time, and that both myths and their meanings can be appropriated and misrepresented. The source contains name and theme indexes. The latter index, which groups myths into broad categories such as origin myths, tricksters, animal goddesses, and the underworld, helps connect parallel themes in different cultures.

1353. Lindley, Susan Hill. *"You Have Stept out of Your Place": A History of Women and Religion in America.* Louisville, KY: Westminster John Knox Press, 1996. 500p. index. ISBN 0664220819.

Lindley, a professor of religion at St. Olaf College, has created a lengthy, one-volume history of women in American religion from colonial times to the present. While the book is primarily focused on Protestantism, it also delves into women's roles in specific religious groups such as Quakers, Puritans, Roman Catholicism, and Judaism. The author also presents contributions that Native American and African American women have made to religious experience. Overall, Lindley successfully incorporates a wide range of materials to demonstrate the diversification of religious experiences of American women throughout history. The author ends with predictions on the future of women and religion in the United States in the twenty-first century. Although Lindley does not provide a bibliography, she includes more than fifty pages of notes that list the wide range of works that she consulted.

1354. McNamara, Jo Ann. *Sisters in Arms: Catholic Nuns through Two Millennia.* Cambridge, MA: Harvard University Press, 1996. 751p. bibliog. index. ISBN 067480984X; 0674809858pa.

This highly detailed scholarly study covers the history of Christian religious women from the time of Christ to the present. McNamara focuses on issues of gender, choosing the title *Sisters in Arms* instead of *Brides of Christ* since the latter title is "a male concept of female sexuality" (p. ix). Presenting more than a straight history of events, McNamara examines the ideas of chastity, gender, identity, and personal relationships between the men and women of the church.

Penelope D. Johnson's *Equal in Monastic Profession: Religious Women in Medieval France* (University of Chicago Press, 1991) analyzes the daily lives of nuns in twenty-six communities in northern France between the eleventh and thirteenth centuries. Sally Thompson's *Women Religious: The Founding of English Nunneries after the Norman Conquest* (Clarendon Press, 1991) is an excellent study of 139 nunneries founded between 1100 and 1250. Sharon Elkins's *Holy Women of Twelfth-Century England* (University of North Carolina Press, 1988) also covers this period. Bruce Venarde's *Women's Monasticism and Medieval Society: Nunneries in France and England, 890–1215* (Cornell University Press, 1996) challenges the view that women's monastic communities were dying out between the tenth and twelfth centuries, arguing instead that they thrived during this period.

1355. Mitter, Sara S. *Dharma's Daughters: Contemporary Indian Women and Hindu Culture.* New Brunswick, NJ: Rutgers University Press, 1991. 198p. bibliog. index. ISBN 0813516773; 0813516781pa.

Mitter constructs a fascinating study about women's experiences in one of the world's largest countries, India, based upon extensive research, interviews, and her own experiences as a visitor and resident of India. Mitter divides her study into three sections. She presents the numerous roles women play in an urban area of a developing country in the first section. The second part deals with Hindu myths and traditions that affect Indian women's lives. Mitter discusses the resistance and mobilization of Indian women since the 1970s in the third section. The author's inclusion of her observations and travels in India makes this work an engaging and informative read not only for beginners, but for scholars as well.

Roles and Rituals for Hindu Women (Fairleigh Dickinson University Press, 1991), edited by Julia Leslie, is yet another excellent work that offers more of a historical perspective. This collection of ten extensive articles covers issues such as "The Ritual Wife," "Power in the Home," ritual dance, and salvation. Both of these scholarly works deserve a place in academic libraries.

1356. Mollenkott, Virginia Ramey. *Godding: Human Responsibility and the Bible.* New York: Crossroad, 1987. 164p. bibliog. (OP)

Evangelical lesbian feminist Mollenkott believes that the highest human responsibility "entails godding [a term coined by Carter Heyward], an embodiment or incarnation of God's love in human flesh, with the goal of co-creating with God a just and loving human society" (p. 2). Not limiting the concept to Christians, the author focuses on biblically grounded ideas about inclusivity, relation, and mutuality in her examination of sexual identity, darkness, peacemaking, and other subjects. Ultimately Mollenkott urges readers to change negative, divisive attitudes and behaviors and move toward wholeness.

In *Sensuous Spirituality: Out from Fundamentalism* (Crossroad, 1992), Mollenkott encourages readers to live out of their sacred and eternal core in order to create a spirituality concerned about conditions of other people, living creatures, even Earth itself. Using metaphysical, literary, psychoanalytic, and religious sources, the author critically examines social and religious ideologies based on inequitable power structures, especially those pertaining to gender and sexual orientation. Again Mollenkott asserts that embracing diversity, justice, and pluralism leads to true spiritual liberation.

1357. Plaskow, Judith. *Standing Again at Sinai: Judaism from a Feminist Perspective.* San Francisco: HarperSanFrancisco, 1990. 281p. bibliog. index. ISBN (OP); 0060666846pa.

Plaskow, a professor of religious studies at Manhattan College, creates a comprehensive study of Judaism that is scholarly, yet highly accessible to a general audience. In the first chapter, the author frames her subject and covers reasons that necessitate the development of a feminist Judaism. Chapter 2 discusses the Torah and its relationship to feminist Judaism. Chapter 3 covers Israel, the issue of community, and the Zionist movement. The various images of God and an examination of feminist spirituality are covered in Chapter 4. Chapter 5 looks at sexuality, Jewish attitudes toward it, and a new theology of sexuality. The last chapter, "Feminist Judaism and the Repair of the World," concerns religion and politics in Judaism and society.

Readers may also wish to consult Tamar Frankiel's *The Voice of Sarah: Feminine Spirituality and Traditional Judaism* (Harper, 1990), a personal devotion written from both an Orthodox and feminist perspective. These important works should appeal to Jewish people, as well as anyone interested in Judaism or religion in general.

1358. Ruether, Rosemary Radford. *Gaia and God: An Ecofeminist Theology of Earth Healing.* San Francisco: HarperSanFrancisco, 1992. 310p. bibliog. index. ISBN (OP); 0060669675pa.

Gaia and God is a theological exploration of ecofeminist assumptions about the world. Ruether examines various creation stories and their implications in part 1. In part 2, the author presents narratives that deal with destruction, the apocalypse, and the nature of human evil. In part 3, Ruether explores the meaning of evil in conjunction with nature; the domination of women and subjugated people; the fall from paradise; and patterns of patriarchal societies. The final section focuses on healing. Reuther traces lines of various biblical and Christian traditions, seeking to reclaim them, imagining an ideal world where a sustainable, Earth-friendly society replaces wasteful systems of production and consumption. Ruether provides an insightful introduction to the major ideas of ecofeminism, incorporating fascinating theological background.

Ruether also edited *Women Healing Earth: Third World Women on Ecology, Feminism, and Religion* (Orbis Books, 1996), a collection of fifteen essays by women in Latin America, Asia, and Africa about ecological subjects with a theological bent. Also including perspectives from women in various countries and religions is *Ecofeminism and the Sacred* (Continuum, 1993), edited by Carol J. Adams, author of the award-winning and thought-provoking title *The Sexual Politics of Meat: A Feminist-Vegetarian Critical Theory* (Continuum, 1991). Contributors to the anthology explore links between the oppression of women and the domination of nature, the potential of ecofeminist spirituality's contributions to ecofeminism, and ecofeminist engagements with specific issues like abortion and nuclear power. One of the first anthologies on the subject, *Healing the Wounds: The Promise of Ecofeminism* edited by Judith Plant (New Society, 1989), advocates transforming social structures according to feminist and ecofeminist principles. Although criticized for essentialism, the collection clearly describes basic ideas of one branch of the movement.

1359. Ruether, Rosemary Radford. *Women and Redemption: A Theological History.* Minneapolis: Fortress, 1998. 366p. bibliog. index. ISBN 0800629477; 0800629450pa.

This telling work focuses on the history of the question "Are women redeemed by Christ?" Ruether examines various paradigms of gender, concluding that paradigm shifts between the sixteenth and nineteenth centuries helped shape twentieth-century feminism. Shifts in thinking began in the sixteenth century with such thinkers as Agrippa von Nettesheim, who "argued that women were created equally in the image of God" (p. 5). Quakers incorporated this belief into their theology in the seventeenth century. Ruether presents informative summaries of leading feminist, womanist, and mujerista theologians of all nationalities for all of the centuries under study. Instructors should require this detailed, scholarly work for anyone interested in women and religion.

Ruether, with Rosemary Keller, edited *In Our Own Voices: Four Centuries of American Women's Religious Writing* (Harper, 1996), which presents ten essays written by theologians and academics of various faiths, including Catholic, Protestant, Jewish, and evangelical, as well as different ethnic groups, such as African American and American Indian. Additional topics include social reform, ordination, communal societies, and pluralism.

1360. Russell, Letty M. *Church in the Round: Feminist Interpretation of the Church.* Louisville, KY: Westminster John Knox Press, 1993. 253p. bibliog. index. ISBN 066425070Xpa.

The title of this book stems from Russell's use of a round table, symbolizing hospitality, dialogue, and equality, as a metaphor for the church. She believes that leadership is "authority in community" (p. 15) and that churches should become communities of faith in the struggle for justice of oppressed groups. Russell argues that members of a church should welcome all people and accordingly criticizes white mainline American churches that do not hold a place at the table for women, people of color, the poor, and gays and lesbians. This theological work includes strong biblical scholarship and historical research while simultaneously providing inspiration.

Russell also wrote *Household of Freedom: Authority in Feminist Theology* (Westminster Press, 1987), in which she explores power and authority from the bottom of the Christian hierarchy. She discusses the function of language in theology, summarizes themes of feminist Christian theology, and advocates a paradigm not of domination and submission, but of partnership and mutuality. Both works are scholarly, yet accessible, and belong in academic collections.

1361. Schüssler Fiorenza, Elisabeth. *But She Said: Feminist Practices of Biblical Interpretation*. Boston: Beacon Press, 1992. 261p. bibliog. index. ISBN (OP); 0807012157pa.

In this book, Schüssler Fiorenza creates a complex scholarly journey into the realm of hermeneutics, the discipline of biblical interpretation. The author believes "that feminists must develop a critical interpretation for liberation not in order to keep women in biblical religions, but because biblical texts affect all women in Western society" (p. 7). She divides the book into three sections: section 1 examines the field of feminist biblical interpretation and demonstrates the practice with a passage from the Book of Luke; section 2 seeks to explore the process by examining types of hermeneutics, historical, political, and theological; and section 3 examines new ways of biblical interpretation in education and reading biblical text. Scholars experienced with such theories of textual analysis will find this a stimulating work; however, the uninitiated may find *But She Said* difficult to unravel.

Schüssler Fiorenza's *Discipleship of Equals: A Critical Feminist Ekklesia-ology of Liberation* (Crossroad, 1994) collects twenty-four of the author's essays, spanning 1962 to 1992. The book's chronological arrangement enables readers to trace the development of the author's thought on topics such as apostolic succession, women's ordination, liberation theology, and essentialist assumptions of "woman." It also introduces readers to her ideas about other religious traditions, race, class, and global concerns.

1362. Schüssler Fiorenza, Elisabeth, ed. *Searching the Scriptures*. New York: Crossroad, 1993. 2v. 1291p. bibliog. index. ISBN (OP); 0824517016pa (v. 1); (OP); 0824517024pa (v. 2).

This landmark work originated in discussions of the Women in the Biblical World section of the Society of Biblical Literature to mark the 1995 centennial celebration of Elizabeth Cady Stanton's *The Woman's Bible*. The first volume, titled *A Feminist Introduction*, provides a comprehensive overview of the diverse locations and voices shaping feminist hermeneutics, theological approaches, and methods of inquiry. It encompasses historical interpretations by women such as Anna Julia Cooper and Sojourner Truth and more contemporary feminist interpretations from Africa, Latin America, and Asia that suggest new ways of reading and teaching the Scriptures. The second volume, *Feminist Commentary*, consists of forty essays (and 900 pages) interpreting specific early Christian, Jewish, and extracanonical texts. Again, the essays represent a variety of theoretical perspectives, interpretive methods, and conceptualizations. A group of impressive international feminist scholars contributed to this sophisticated work.

In *The Women's Bible Commentary* (Westminster John Knox Press, 1992), editors Carol A. Newsom and Sharon H. Ringe strive for biblical interpretation that will resonate with women across age, economic, racial, and cultural boundaries. Despite implications of the title, the collection is not a commentary on Elizabeth Cady Stanton's *The Woman's Bible*, yet the book's spirit honors Stanton's groundbreaking work. Most of the sixty chapters cover a specific book in the Bible. Contributors discuss general critical issues and summarize content, but concentrate on sections relevant to women, such as legal statuses, religious economic principles, female symbols and characters, or marriage and family issues. A short introductory chapter examines the many ways of interpreting the Bible and the importance of language used to talk about God and gender. Other chapters provide useful context about women's roles in New Testament times. This volume is a fine introduction to feminist biblical scholarship. Both academic and seminary collections should house these works.

1363. Shallenberger, David. *Reclaiming the Spirit: Gay Men and Women Come to Terms with Religion*. New Brunswick, NJ: Rutgers University Press, 1998. 281p. bibliog. ISBN 0813524881.

Shallenberger, a professor at DePaul University, interviewed twenty-six gay men and lesbian women. He presents the stories of twelve of the interviewees in *Reclaiming the Spirit*. The participants describe growing up, early spiritual experiences, and how they came to know themselves as they completed their spiritual journey. Most of the men and women whom Shallenberger interviewed have Judeo-Christian backgrounds, including one "gay-affirming" man who considers himself a fundamentalist. However, the author also includes discussions on Wicca and Taoism. This work should interest young people, members of the general public, and academics. Thus most libraries should include it in their holdings.

Is the Homosexual My Neighbor? A Positive Christian Response (rev. and updated ed., HarperSanFrancisco, 1994) by Letha Scanzoni and Virginia Ramey Mollenkott, both evangelical feminists, argues for sexual inclusiveness, revisits themes from the now-classic first edition (1978), subtitled *Another Christian Response*, and updates exegetical and other sources, including the annotated bibliography. This readable book presents a full range of perspectives and is appropriate for academic and public libraries.

1364. Sharma, Arvind, ed. *Women in World Religions*. Albany: State University of New York Press, 1987. 302p. (McGill Studies in the History of Religions). bibliog. index. ISBN (OP); 0887063756pa.

Contributors to this volume provide concise histories of women's religious roles, beliefs, and practices in seven major religious traditions (Hinduism, Buddhism, Confucianism, Taoism, Judaism, Islam, and Christianity) and one tribal religion (Aborigine). The authors do not all examine the same set of issues, nor do they make sweeping generalizations concerning women and the religion being discussed. Instead, each discusses important issues within the historical and social context of the specific tradition. Katherine Young's thought-provoking introduction is a useful examination of feminist theories about religion and culture during the 1980s, and Rita Gross's essay on Aborigines is an intriguing consideration of the two-sex method.

Sharma edited two companion volumes that help correct gaps in *Women in World Religions*. *Today's Woman in World Religions* (State University of New York Press, 1994) continues the discussion of the traditions covered in the first volume into the 1980s. *Religion and Women* (State University of New York Press, 1994) extends discussion to traditions not covered in the other two titles: Native American, African, Shinto, Jainist, Zoroastrian, Sikh, and Baha'i. All these excellent titles are suitable for texts in women and religion courses.

After Patriarchy: Feminist Transformations of the World Religions (Orbis Books, 1991), edited by Paula M. Cooley, William R. Eakin, and Jay B. McDaniel, contains insightful essays written by women from eight spiritual traditions who explore potentially liberating aspects of their respective traditions. The authors of the chapters discussing Hinduim, Islam, womanist, and Apache traditions remain fairly faithful to their traditions; the authors of the chapters on Judaism, Christianity, Buddhism, and free thought, however, advocate revising their traditions to accommodate feminist perspectives.

1365. Stowasser, Barbara Freyer. *Women in the Qur'an: Traditions and Interpretations*. New York: Oxford University Press, 1994. 206p. bibliog. index. ISBN (OP); 0195111486pa.

Stowasser produces a meticulously researched volume (52 of the 206 pages are notes) that includes an examination of the extent to which writers represent women in the writings of Islam. In part 1, the author analyzes women and the sacred history of Islam. In part 2, Stowasser explores the Qur'an, the hadith (the sayings and deeds of Muhammad), and modern Muslim interpretations in connection with women and the history of Islam. Through a thorough exploration of the Sunni tradition in Islam, Stowasser exposes the complicated gender issues at work. The author argues that people must consider much of the Qur'an as "progressive" since the Prophet sought to improve society, which he saw as full of inequities. However, Islam spread to conservative cultures, which resulted in conservative interpretations. Thus male "revolutionary" fundamentalists view the role of women in a very conservative light, while the "reformist" men are more liberal. This landmark scholarly work would complement upper-level courses on Islam.

In *Qur'an and Woman* (Fajar Bakti, 1992), author Amina Wadud presents one of the first interpretations of the Qur'an from the point of view of women. She believes that analyzing the concept "woman" in the text itself, rather than in interpretations written by Islamic scholars, and emphasizing the text's principles of social justice and equality can be used to contest the inequitable treatment of women in Islamic countries. In the U.S. edition, titled *Qur'an and Woman: Rereading the Sacred Text from a Woman's Perspective* (Oxford University Press, 1999), Wadud elaborates on the growing influence of gender analysis in her work in the introduction.

1366. Townes, Emilie M. *In a Blaze of Glory: Womanist Spirituality as Social Witness.* Nashville: Abingdon, 1995. 160p. bibliog. ISBN 0687187575pa.

Townes addresses African American women's struggle to overcome injustices and inequalities and build a world based on justice and love. She begins with a historical overview of the development of African American spirituality that encompasses (West) African cosmologies, slave spirituals, narratives, oral histories, speeches, sermons, and the like. She also considers the influence of nineteenth-century evangelicalism on black women and the ethics reflected in the social reform movement they built. The heart of the book, however, consists of the author's analysis of the novels *Beloved* (Toni Morrison), *The Color Purple* (Alice Walker), and *Praisesong for the Widow* (Paule Marshall) that focuses on their representation of social and ethical issues. Townes concludes this powerful and moving text by exploring ways that womanist spirituality serves as a social witness connecting these issues.

Townes edited *A Troubling in My Soul: Womanist Perspectives on Evil and Suffering* (Orbis Books, 1993), the first anthology of womanist thought. Contributors, including Dolores S. Williams, Jacqueline Grant, and Clarice Martin, represent a number of disciplines and use a variety of approaches and sources to address the subjects. Most authors turn to the lives and writings of both historical and contemporary black women. This impressive and sensitive collection provides a fine introduction to womanist ethical discourse and theology. *Embracing the Spirit: Womanist Perspectives on Hope, Salvation, and Transformation* (Orbis Books, 1997), also edited by Townes, contains essays by many of the same contributors who continue conversations begun in *A Troubling in My Soul.* They consider personal, political, social, and theological aspects of lived experience, critical thought theory, praxis, God language, blues and gospel music, and salvation.

1367. Umansky, Ellen M., and Dianne Ashton, eds. *Four Centuries of Jewish Women's Spirituality: A Sourcebook.* Boston: Beacon Press, 1992. 350p. bibliog. index. ISBN (OP); 0807036137pa.

This anthology includes prayers, poems, sermons, speeches, and other writings by approximately 100 Jewish women, written between 1560 and 1990, with an emphasis on works since the 1960s. In addition, the timelessness of early writings, juxtaposed with contemporary writings, demonstrates the long-held concern for feminism and modern social issues. The authors represent all four of the major religious movements in Judaism as well as different ages and backgrounds. This work could serve as an excellent introduction to writings of Jewish women. Therefore, this notable book belongs in all collections.

Jewish Women in Historical Perspective (Wayne State University Press, 1991; 2nd ed., 1998), edited by Judith R. Baskin, is another excellent resource on the history of Judaism. This collection of essays covers all time periods, from antiquity to the twentieth-century United States.

1368. Williams, Dolores S. *Sisters in the Wilderness: The Challenge of Womanist God-Talk*. Maryknoll, NY: Orbis Books, 1993. 287p. bibliog. index. (OP)

Williams uses the biblical story of the slave Hagar as a paradigm for the suffering and fight for survival in the lives of African American women. She expands black womanist conversations by engaging with Asian, Latin American, and white feminist theologies, black liberation theology, African American denominations, and the egalitarian tradition of the Universal Hagar's Spiritual Church. Most intriguing are her biblical hermeneutics, based on reading from an oppressed perspective, and her idea of atonement that focuses on Jesus' ministry rather than his suffering and sacrifice.

In *My Soul Is a Witness: African American Women's Spirituality* (Beacon Press, 1995), editor Gloria Wade-Gayles collects a wide variety of what she terms "testimonies" in genres including poetry, essays, autobiographical narratives, and chapters from novels written by authors such as Toni Morrison, Alice Walker, and Toni Cade Bambara. Contributors address historical contributions of women to African American spiritual traditions, life-changing spiritual experiences, challenges to traditions, and participation in different faiths. The concluding section contains stories of healing and rituals for performing. Anyone interested in African American womanist theologies and spiritualities will gain many insights from these titles.

Philosophy, Philosophers, and Philosophical Subjects

1369. Antony, Louise M., and Charlotte Witt, eds. *A Mind of One's Own: Feminist Essays on Reason and Objectivity*. Boulder, CO: Westview Press, 1993. 302p. index. ISBN (OP); 0813379385pa.

Thirteen women feminist philosophers contributed essays to this useful collection examining the value of the traditional canon from a feminist point of view. The editors include pieces "that make the case both for and against a feminist philosophy that uses the traditional philosophical tools of reason and objectivity" (p. xvii). Essayists such as Annette Baier, Naomi Scheman, and Charlotte Witt analyze the rational ideal of Aristotle, Cartesian reason, various theories of epistemology, Willard Van Orman Quine, objectivity, the "maleness" of reason, and the legal thought of Catharine MacKinnon from a variety of perspectives. All academic libraries should house this illuminating work, which also would prove quite useful in philosophy courses.

Pamela Sue Anderson also examines the concepts of "objectivity" and "reason" in terms of how male philosophers have defined them in *A Feminist Philosophy of Religion: The Rationality and Myths of Religious Belief* (Blackwell, 1998). Anderson, however, seeks to reconstruct a feminist view of reason in order to develop an alternative feminist philosophy of religion. She is one of the first scholars to attempt to create a comprehensive groundwork for a feminist philosophy of religion. Her complex arguments are intended for philosophers and students of philosophy; nevertheless, most academic libraries should carry this important work.

1370. Bar On, Bat-Ami, ed. *Engendering Origins: Critical Feminist Readings in Plato and Aristotle*. Albany: State University of New York Press, 1994. 247p. bibliog. index. ISBN 0791416437; 0791416445pa.

Bar On, a professor of philosophy and director of Women's Studies at the State University of New York at Binghamton, has collected a wide-ranging group of essays written by well-known feminist philosophers. Although Bar On does not provide a theme for this volume, she includes works by important scholars such as Nancy Tuana and Christine Pierce. Essays on Plato discuss everything from class and gender in the *Republic* and *Politics* to Plato's views of dualism. The essays concerning Aristotle concentrate on his views of women, his science, and his moral philosophy. The editor provides a list of suggested readings. *Feminism and Ancient Philosophy* (Routledge, 1996), edited by Julia K. Ward, collects essays crafted by women philosophers that connect classical studies and the history of philosophy with modern feminism. In the first section, contributors examine the texts of Plato, Aristotle, and the Stoics to uncover what they wrote about "women's nature and capabilities" (p. 1). In the second section, contributors concentrate on the relationship of reason to the emotions in the work of Aristotle. The third section consists of two chapters on the "application of Aristotelian ethics." Ward presents two chapters on "logos and desire" in the last section.

Bar On also edited *Modern Engendering: Critical Feminist Readings in Modern Western Philosophy* (State University of New York Press, 1994), a collection of feminist critiques of several philosophers, including René Descartes, John Locke, David Hume, Jean-Jacques Rousseau, Immanuel Kant, Georg Hegel, Karl Marx, and Friedrich Nietzsche. Bar On created both volumes as a result of her students' encouragement. Both would prove useful as textbooks and should be housed in academic libraries.

1371. Battersby, Christine. *Gender and Genius: Towards a Feminist Aesthetics*. Bloomington: Indiana University Press, 1990. 192p. bibliog. index. ISBN 0253311268; 0253205786pa.

Battersby provides a readable, engaging history of the Western concept of genius. She shows that nineteenth-century romantic definitions of genius specifically exclude women but include traits, such as sensitivity and creative self-expression, usually associated with the feminine. The author believes that this definition devalues femaleness, not the feminine, and that the distinction between the two provides the framework for a feminist aesthetics that can reconstruct history and reclaim genius. This provocative title should appeal to undergraduate students as well as advanced scholars. In *The Phenomenal Woman: Feminist Metaphysics and the Patterns of Identity* (Routledge, 1998), Battersby articulates her belief that the postmodern-modernist debates yield a false homogenous metaphysics based on the concept of "being." She attempts to develop a new metaphysics using the embodied female self (one who can become two through pregnancy), based on the concept of "becoming." The author explores ideas of philosophers, notably Immanuel Kant, Theodor Adorno, Søren Kierkegaard, and Luce Irigaray, to develop a relational ontology that considers natality, unequal basic relationships, entwinement of self and others, embodiment, and singularity. Battersby, a feminist who neither totally embraces nor totally dismisses traditional metaphysics, succeeds in illuminating contributions of other philosophers but is less successful in developing her own undertaking. This book makes some intriguing theoretical arguments and is more suitable for those familiar with the field of metaphysics.

1372. Benhabib, Seyla. *Situating the Self: Gender, Community, and Postmodernism in Contemporary Ethics*. New York: Routledge, 1992. 266p. bibliog. index. ISBN (OP); 0415905478pa.

In this collection of previously published essays, Benhabib seeks to "soften the boundaries which have been drawn around universalist theories and feminist positions, communitarian aspirations and postmodern skepticism" (pp. 3–4). Benhabib attempts to reconcile the ideals of liberal democracy with poststructuralist and feminist theory. Like many feminists, she rejects the Kantian idea of "universal legislative reason." Drawing on ideas of Jürgen Habermas and the Carol Gilligan–Lawrence Kohlberg moral theory debates, Benhabib develops an interactive universalism that gives moral weight to self-other relations. Most libraries should house this ambitious and challenging title.

Benhabib also wrote *The Reluctant Modernism of Hannah Arendt* (Sage Publications, 1996), which examines Arendt's political philosophy, her writings on totalitarianism, and her relationships with Martin Heidegger and Habermas. Benhabib coauthored *Feminist Contentions: A Philosophical Exchange* (Routledge, 1995) with Judith Butler, Drucilla Cornell, and Nancy Fraser. The volume consists of theoretical essays and responses between the philosophers about feminist engagements with postmodernism. They discuss concepts such as utopias and discourse, as well as the ideas of Jacques Lacan, Michel Foucault, Jacques Derrida, and Habermas. Linda Nicholson provides an introduction outlining the major debates that extend throughout the chapters.

1373. Bluestone, Natalie Harris. *Women and the Ideal Society: Plato's Republic and Modern Myths of Gender*. Amherst: University of Massachusetts Press, 1987. 238p. bibliog. index. ISBN 087023580X; 0870235818pa.

In this scholarly discussion of women's role in the ideal state, Bluestone attempts to uncover the biases present in scholarship on Plato. She considers not only the importance of Plato in Western philosophy, but also new feminist interpretations of his work, as well as interpretations of "objective" scholars who merely attempt to "make clear what Plato really meant" (p. 4). Bluestone places contemporary writers into two groups: those who accept Plato as a feminist and those who do not. Section 1 examines writings from 1870 to 1970 and inventories the types of anti-female bias in Plato scholarship. Section 2 examines the new, post-1970 feminist scholarship, with its resurgence of interest in "Philosopher Queens," and considers Plato's assertion in the *Republic* that men and women should rule equally. Section 3 discusses the continuing importance of Plato's questions. This work is available in netLibrary.

In *Feminist Interpretations of Plato* (Pennsylvania State University Press, 1994), editor Nancy Tuana presents twelve essays that also deal with these issues. The first group of essays focuses on Plato's political and social theory, while the second group deals with Plato's assumptions about gender. Readers in academic libraries would benefit from both of these works.

1374. Card, Claudia. *Lesbian Choices*. New York: Columbia University Press, 1995. 310p. (Between Men—Between Women). bibliog. index. ISBN (OP); 0231080093pa.

Card regards the term "lesbian" as a quality rather than an identity, which can meaningfully apply to persons, relationships, or experiences. Using Ludwig Wittgenstein's concept of family resemblance and Friedrich Nietzsche's genealogical method, she asserts that lesbian qualities connect to each other in patterns of resemblance and difference without necessarily sharing an essential characteristic. This broad and provocative idea of the term makes it possible for any woman to have lesbian experiences. Card also calls upon ideas in Sarah Hoagland's *Lesbian Ethics: Toward a New Value* (Institute of Lesbian Studies, 1988), annotated in a separate entry for Hoagland later in this section. Card served as editor for the collection *Adventures in Lesbian Philosophy* (Indiana University Press, 1994), which presents essays by Card and others on a wide range of topics, including creativity, knowledge, community, pornography, sadomasochism, racism, and abuse.

Card also edited *Feminist Ethics* (University Press of Kansas, 1991), a collection of accessible articles written by contributors who include Maria Lugones, Alison Jaggar, Ruth Ginzberg, Sarah Hoagland, and Michele Moody-Adams. The first section provides a history of feminist ethics and sets the context for the other writings. The remaining two sections address questions of survival, the self, and integrity, and women's voices and care, respectively. This collection contains an extensive bibliography and thorough index and offers a wide range of women's moral voices. It would prove informative as an introduction to the subject for undergraduates.

1375. Cole, Eve Browning, and Susan Margaret Coultrap-McQuin, eds. *Explorations in Feminist Ethics: Theory and Practice*. Bloomington: Indiana University Press, 1992. 203p. bibliog. index. ISBN 0253313848; 0253206979pa.

Resulting from a conference held in Duluth, Minnesota, in October 1988, this title includes eighteen short essays that explore issues in feminist ethical thought, especially the idea of care in the work of Carol Gilligan and Nell Noddings. Cole and Coultrap-McQuin chose works by well-known writers, such as Charlotte Bunch, Marilyn Freedman, Sarah Hoagland, and Sara Ruddick, who examine traditional subjects, including altruism and moral agency, to challenge Western moral theories and propose new feminist directions.

Rita C. Manning, in *Speaking from the Heart: A Feminist Perspective on Ethics* (Rowman & Littlefield, 1992), also utilizes the concept of care in the work of Gilligan and Noddings to provide a more personal perspective on the topic. The author advocates an ethics and politics of caring within each profession. Manning's work provides a solid introduction to feminist ethics for those new to the subject. Linda A. Bell, however, rejects the traditional canon as well as the "care ethics" of feminists such as Gilligan and Noddings in *Rethinking Ethics in the Midst of Violence: A Feminist Approach to Freedom* (Rowman & Littlefield, 1993). Using Jean-Paul Sartre's concept of authenticity, Bell argues for a new feminist paradigm of ethics based on freedom, which she believes is necessary to resist violence and oppression in society.

1376. Deutscher, Penelope. *Yielding Gender: Feminism, Deconstruction, and the History of Philosophy*. London: Routledge, 1997. 224p. bibliog. index. ISBN 0415139449; 0415139457pa.

This complex scholarly work will engage anyone interested in modern philosophy. In the introduction, Deutscher explains, "Gender has never been a stable matter," embracing the position that "constitutive instability is simultaneously destabilizing and stabilizing" (p. 1). In the first chapters, the author concentrates on some of the debates regarding Jacques Derrida and deconstruction and deconstructive feminism by examining different feminist interpretations of the history of philosophy as represented by Genevieve Lloyd's *The Man of Reason: "Male" and "Female" in Western Philosophy* (University of Minnesota Press, 1984; 2nd ed., 1993) and Karen Green's *The Woman of Reason* (Continuum, 1995). The book also critically explores the philosophies of Jean-Jacques Rousseau, Michèle Le Doeuff, Luce Irigaray, and Simone de Beauvoir, among others. Deutscher concludes with a discussion of contradictions and instabilities about women and gender in historical philosophical texts. All philosophy collections would benefit from including this work.

1377. Diquinzio, Patrice, and Iris Marion Young, eds. *Feminist Ethics and Social Policy*. Bloomington: Indiana University Press, 1997. 302p. (A Hypatia Book). bibliog. index. ISBN 0253332966; 0253211255pa.

The fourteen essays included in this work apply feminist ethics to a variety of social issues, from family leave and health care to immigrant women. Other topics include pornography, women in the military, mixed-race identity, abortion, AIDS, disabilities, fathers' rights, comparable worth, and self-defense. Nine of the essays previously appeared in *Hypatia: A Journal of Feminist Philosophy*. Contributors represent the fields of philosophy, women's studies, religion, public and international affairs, and philosophy of science. While the authors do not all use the same feminist framework for their projects, they all question traditional concepts of freedom, equality, justice, autonomy, and the like, as well as gender neutrality and moral theories based on principles.

In the preface of *Moral Dilemmas of Feminism: Prostitution, Adultery, and Abortion* (Routledge, 1994), Laurie Shrage details her encounter with a prostitution rights activist who raised some of the same issues feminists rely upon to defend abortion, including privacy and the right to control one's own body. This exchange serves as a starting point to Shrage's provocative examination of moral discussions about sexuality, abortion, prostitution, pornography, and erotica. The author asks her readers to set "ethnocentric ethics" aside, not only to better examine these issues, but also to consider their historical and cultural contexts. Shrage incorporates writings from gay and lesbian studies and critical race theory that challenge the analyses of white feminist academics. Far from suggesting easy answers, this thought-provoking and fascinating study raises several important questions and is appropriate for most libraries.

1378. Held, Virginia. *Feminist Morality: Transforming Culture, Society, and Politics.* Chicago: University of Chicago Press, 1993. 285p. (Women in Culture and Society). bibliog. index. ISBN 0226325911; 0226325938pa.

Held critiques the traditional understanding of morality as a male-centered enterprise based on social contracts between strangers. She builds on the work of Carol Gilligan, whose writings on psychology, women's development, and feminism are well known. Held proposes a more caring and personal morality, stating, "An adequate moral theory should be built on appropriate feelings as well as appropriate reasoning" (p. 30). Held considers the principles of several well-known feminist theorists, including Sara Ruddick, Nancy Hartsock, and Annette Baier, as well as male philosophers, such as Immanuel Kant, Plato, and John Rawls. She then uses feminist moral approaches to examine issues of birth and death, violence, individualism and democracy, and liberty and equality. This exciting work offers a solid introduction to the principles of moral theory and provides a good beginning for those new to the discipline of philosophy.

Held and Gilligan both contributed essays to *Women and Moral Theory* (Rowman & Littlefield, 1987), edited by Eva Feder Kittay and Diana T. Meyers, a collection of sixteen essays resulting from a conference held at Stony Brook in 1985. The essays serve as philosophical responses to Gilligan's *In a Different Voice* (Harvard University Press, 1981) and seek to answer this question: can existing moral theory, based on justice, incorporate care? Gilligan provides a brief review of empirical research pertaining to the two moral perspectives. In the core of the book, several contributors use care as the basis for their own projects, while others incorporate care into liberal moral theory, often using specific issues, such as peace, pornography, and battered women who murder their abusers, to illustrate their positions. This significant title offers many ideas for further development, research, and reflection.

1379. Hoagland, Sarah Lucia. *Lesbian Ethics: Toward New Value.* Palo Alto, CA: Institute of Lesbian Studies, 1988. 349p. bibliog. index. ISBN 0939403034.

In this pioneering work, Hoagland discusses common ethical subjects, such as moral agency, reason, and altruism, but does not use traditional ethics as her framework. Instead, the author turns to the lived experiences of lesbians via her participation in lesbian communities, interviews, and discussions as well as her examination of lesbian and feminist writings and dialogues. Hoagland adds emotions to reason, considers caring and connecting more important than duties and obligations, and believes in a self that is interdependent, one of many, neither autonomous nor controlled. The author's ideas recognize lesbians as moral agents and open paths of resistance for lesbians in an oppressive, "heterosexualist" society. They also can lead to the greater understanding and valuing of differences between women.

Jeffner Allen presents previously published and new essays to propose a radical woman-centered ethics, epistemology, and ontology in *Lesbian Philosophy: Explorations* (Institute for Lesbian Studies, 1986). She rejects "the ideology of heterosexual virtue" (p. 43) as a product of male domination that separates women from themselves and each other, often through violence. She challenges the absence of women in the history of Western philosophy by seeking subjectivity from her own lived experiences, which she transforms into "life-preserving weapons" (p. 9). Allen's passionate and personal arguments should engage readers. Allen also edited *Lesbian Philosophies and Cultures* (State University of New York Press, 1990), an unabashed celebration of lesbian plurality.

1380. Holland, Nancy J. *Is Women's Philosophy Possible?* Savage, MD: Rowman & Littlefield, 1990. 194p. (New Feminist Perspective Series). bibliog. index. ISBN 084767620X.

The author contends that British empiricism, a powerful influence in Anglo-American philosophy and gender ideology, actively excludes women's experiences (if not women themselves) from the very structure of philosophy, thereby making women's philosophy impossible. Applying deconstruction as a tool (as opposed to a theory), Holland provides a detailed feminist analysis of empiricism's master texts, focusing on works by John Locke and David Hume. She explores the phenomenology of Martin Heidegger and Maurice Merleu-Ponty, the existentialism of Jean-Paul Sartre and Simone de Beauvoir, their development by Roland Barthes, Jacques Derrida, Michel Foucault, and Jacques Lacan, and ideas of French feminists Monique Wittig, Hélène Cixous, Luce Irigaray, and Julia Kristeva for ways to reconstruct a philosophy that theorizes women's experiences as they define them.

The Thinking Muse: Feminism and Modern French Philosophy (Indiana University Press, 1989), a collection edited by Jeffner Allen and Iris Marion Young, features essays by feminist philosophers like Judith Butler, Linda Singer, and Jo-Ann Pilardi who present various perspectives about works by most of the same philosophers as Holland. All contributors especially consider ideas about female subjectivity and representations of gender and sexual difference.

1381. Jaggar, Alison M., and Susan R. Bordo, eds. *Gender/Body/Knowledge: Feminist Reconstructions of Being and Knowing.* New Brunswick, NJ: Rutgers University Press, 1989. 376p. bibliog. index. ISBN 0813513782; 0813513790pa.

This collection of seventeen essays addresses a variety of disciplinary, methodological, and ideological issues. All the essays, however, question dominant concepts of knowledge and reality in Western philosophical traditions, especially since the seventeenth century. Contributors of the first group of essays explore philosophical concepts of the body, the self, subjectivity, and sexuality. In the second section, "Feminist Ways of Knowing," contributors examine ethics, care, epistemology, and possible impacts of feminism on the sciences and social sciences. The final group of essays considers feminist revisions of research methods. This landmark collection serves as an excellent introduction to debates, divisions, and commonalities in Western feminism during the 1980s. Like Bordo's later work *Unbearable Weight: Feminism, Western Culture, and the Body* (University of California Press, 1993), this volume is justifiably widely read, cited, and used in women's studies and other courses.

Another anthology, *Women, Knowledge, and Reality: Explorations in Feminist Philosophy*

(Unwin Hyman, 1989; 2nd ed., Routledge, 1996), edited by Ann Garry and Marilyn Pearsall, concentrates on feminist epistemology and its subfields. This work includes twenty essays by Lorraine Code, Ann Ferguson, Elizabeth Spelman, Maria Lugones, and others on the theory of knowledge, methodologies used in the discipline, and metaphysics, as well as essays on the philosophies of science, language, the mind, and religion.

1382. Kourany, Janet A., ed. *Philosophy in a Feminist Voice: Critiques and Reconstructions.* Princeton, NJ: Princeton University Press, 1998. 322p. bibliog. index. ISBN 0691033137; 0691019363pa.

The editor compiled this collection to "offer a clear understanding . . . of what feminist philosophy is about, why it is important, and what it offers to philosophy" (p. ix). The essays provide a feminist critique of most of the major areas of philosophy, featuring chapters on ethics, epistemology, language, aesthetics, and several other topics. All of the authors are academics, many of them well known, such as Susan Bordo, Lorraine Code, Virginia Held, and Andrea Nye. This collection provides a solid base for both beginners and experienced students who want to stay abreast of 1990s trends in the discipline.

1383. Le Doeuff, Michèle. *Hipparchia's Choice: An Essay Concerning Women, Philosophy, etc.* Cambridge, MA: Basil Blackwell, 1991. 364p. bibliog. index. (OP)

French philosopher Le Doeuff examines the history of philosophy for gender biases, using existentialism as an example. Since the author believes that philosophical ideas cannot stand self-contained and separate from the context that produces them, her critical analysis of the work of Jean-Paul Sartre and Simone de Beauvoir considers the relationship between the two as revealed by their diaries and letters. In discussions of other philosophers, their ideas, and their influence on social policies relating to feminist issues, she includes brief autobiographical vignettes reflecting her responses to them as a woman, philosopher, and feminist.

In an earlier title, *The Philosophical Imaginary* (Athlone, 1989), Le Doeuff analyzes the imagery and metaphors used in the work of major philosophers such as René Descartes, Immanuel Kant, Georg Hegel, Thomas More, and Francis Bacon. She argues that philosophers resorted to these devices to conceal discrepancies in their arguments or logic and finds that they often depict women in unequal power relationships.

1384. McAlister, Linda Lopez, ed. *Hypatia's Daughters: Fifteen Hundred Years of Women Philosophers.* Bloomington: Indiana University Press, 1996. 345p. (A Hypatia Book). bibliog. index. ISBN 0253330572; 0253210607pa.

The editor selects eighteen articles written about women philosophers from Hypatia to Angela Davis. Essays reflect a variety of approaches and methods and represent early expository articles, many of which first appeared in the journal *Hypatia: A Journal of Feminist Philosophy.* Several of the essays cover women, such as Sor Juana and Hildegard of Bingen, who have been excluded from traditional histories of philosophy. This rewarding collection recognizes the important role that social, political, and cultural context plays in the interpretation of philosophical texts and ideas and values perspectives outside the mainstream.

Margaret Louise Atherton, editor of the short but useful anthology *Women Philosophers of the Early Modern Period* (Hackett Publishing, 1994), collects excerpts of writings from the seventeenth and eighteenth centuries by Princess Elizabeth of Bohemia, Margaret Cavendish, Anne Viscountess Conway, Damaris Cudworth (Lady Masham), Mary Astell, Catherine Trotter Cockburn, and Lady Mary Shepherd. Atherton highlights works by women regarding philosophical issues during this fertile period of thought. This collection would highly complement the holdings of libraries and would prove useful in modern philosophy courses.

Therese B. Dykeman, editor of *American Women Philosophers, 1650–1930: Six Exemplary Thinkers* (Edwin Mellen Press, 1993), familiarizes readers with the philosophical writings of Anne Bradstreet, Mercy Otis Warren, Judith Sargent Murra, Frances Wright, Ednah Dow Cheney, and Mary Whiton Calkins, women whom scholars have completely ignored or identified as poets, historians, or other categories. Dykeman provides an introduction, excerpts of the women's writings, critical analysis, chronologies, and bibliographies for each philosopher. Although Dykeman could have included other significant philosophers in her work, she provides a solid introduction to six leading women philosophers.

1385. Nye, Andrea. *Philosophia: The Thought of Rosa Luxemburg, Simone Weil, and Hannah Arendt*. New York: Routledge, 1994. 280p. bibliog. index. ISBN (OP); 0415908310pa.

Nye produces an engaging and far-ranging work based upon the formative ideas of three women: Rosa Luxemburg, Simone Weil, and Hannah Arendt. Many scholars did not consider them to be "philosophers" until recently. Moreover, these women have written little about sex and gender and have never defined themselves as feminists. Yet according to Nye, "Leaving aside the critique of masculinity, it may be possible to trace other lines of thought" (p. xviii). Nye thus examines the ideas of these three women, who are all known better for their activism in politics and writings on social issues as opposed to their philosophical ideas. This work provides an informative and interesting introduction to these important thinkers as a result of Nye's fresh approach to the subject matter.

Nye also wrote *Feminist Theory and the Philosophies of Man* (Croom Helm, 1988), which applies feminist theory to nineteenth-century liberalism, Marxism, existentialism, patriarchy, and semantics. Nye puts a new slant on an old subject in *Words of Power: A Feminist Reading of the History of Logic* (Routledge, 1990). She believes that the history of logic reveals many disparate histories based in various historical, social, economic, and political contexts, rather than one unitary history. By critically examining the ideas of major classical, medieval, and twentieth-century figures, from Aristotle to Gottliob Frege, Nye reveals how logic has served as an abstract form of (male) language to construct "truth" that privileges some and oppresses others. The book also serves as a readable and critical introduction to philosophies of logic.

1386. Nye, Andrea. *Philosophy and Feminism at the Border*. New York: Twayne, 1995. 232p. (The Impact of Feminism on the Arts and Sciences). bibliog. index. ISBN 0805797637; 0805797785pa.

Nye succinctly reviews Western feminist philosophy's impact on contemporary mainstream philosophy and its subfields, including logic, ethics, epistemology, languages, and political philosophy, since World War II. She critically examines the work of major feminist theorists in philosophy and other disciplines, emphasizing their responses to and reconfiguration of mainstream ideas. An appendix provides intriguing information about the number of women in the American Philosophical Association, feminist content in philosophy textbooks, women authors in philosophical journals, and the number of women faculty and doctorates within the discipline. Informative notes, a bibliography, and a bibliographic essay of further reading complete the book. This fine work clearly reflects the breadth of feminist philosophies and their relationship to each other.

Eve Browning Cole's *Philosophy and Feminist Criticism: An Introduction* (Paragon House, 1993) reviews feminist criticism of traditional Western thought as well as new philosophical thought introduced by feminist philosophers. The book contains sections on the mind/body (and gender) problem, epistemology, and ethics and provides a good introduction for those new to the field.

1387. Tuana, Nancy. *The Less Noble Sex: Scientific, Religious, and Philosophical Conceptions of Woman's Nature.* Bloomington: Indiana University Press, 1993. 224p. (Race, Gender, and Science). bibliog. index. ISBN (OP); 0253208300pa.

Tuana, who has written widely on the subject of women in philosophy, provides an analysis of man's misguided and prejudicial thinking about women throughout time. From the Book of Genesis and the works of Aristotle through the writings of Darwin and Freud, the "author traces the centuries-old tradition in Western intellectual thought that views woman as inferior to man" (p. ix). After examining various claims regarding woman's status as being less perfect than man's, Tuana addresses specific imperfections that philosophers and scientists have attributed to women and explores various ideas, such as viewing Pandora as a punishment to man and the nineteenth-century view that women posed a grave danger to society. Tuana also examines ways in which women's role in reproduction affected the mentality of male writers and resulted in the branding of women as "the beautiful evil." This scholarly study includes a fine bibliography and extensive notes and is a provocative read that a wide audience should enjoy.

Tuana, with Rosemarie Tong, also edited *Feminism and Philosophy: Essential Readings in Theory, Reinterpretation, and Application* (Westview Press, 1994), a collection of twenty-seven essays about philosophy from various feminist perspectives (radical, Marxist, socialist, phenomenological, and others). Each of the nine sections includes a bibliography of works for further reading, which helps to make this a good basic resource for feminist philosophy. The first essay, titled, "Reading Philosophy as a Woman," of Tuana's *Woman and the History of Philosophy* (Paragon House, 1992) should be required reading for all students new to philosophy. The author examines some of the great canonical philosophers in order to "reveal the complexity of woman's exclusion from their philosophies" (p. 11). Tuana begins with Plato's and Aristotle's views of women and moves to "The Maleness of Reason," which examines the philosophies of René Descartes and Jean-Jacques Rousseau. Sections that follow examine the moral philosophy of Immanuel Kant and David Hume and the political philosophy of John Locke and Georg Hegel. Instructors could put this book to good use as a textbook for introductory philosophy classes.

1388. Waithe, Mary Ellen, ed. *A History of Women Philosophers.* Boston: Kluwer Academic, 1987–1995. 4v. bibliog. index. ISBN 0792331818pa (set); 9024733685pa (v. 1); 9024735726pa (v. 2); (OP) (v. 3); 0792328078; 0792328086pa (v. 4).

This extensive, scholarly history of women in philosophy includes four volumes. Volume 1 is *Ancient Women Philosophers from 600 B.C.–500 A.D.*; volume 2 is *Medieval, Renaissance, and Enlightenment Women Philosophers, 500–1600*; volume 3 is *Modern Women Philosophers, 1600–1900*; and volume 4 is *Contemporary Women Philosophers, 1900–Today.* Each volume contains about 500 pages and includes an extensive bibliography, index, and notes. Waithe arranges the volumes according to the individual philosophers, with the amount of space devoted to each philosopher depending upon her importance. The early volumes contain a great deal of information about many lesser-known female philosophers, such as Aesara of Lucania and Diotima of Mantinea. In volume 4, Waithe devotes single chapters to Ayn Rand, Simone de Beauvoir, and Simone Weil. Waithe provides a few pages on other twentieth-century figures, including Evelyn Underhill and May Sinclair. The valuable work, which would benefit any collection, resulted from several years of painstaking research.

1389. Whitford, Margaret. *Luce Irigaray: Philosophy in the Feminine*. New York: Routledge, 1991. 241p. bibliog. index. ISBN (OP); 0415059690pa.

Over the years, scholars have extensively discussed and often misinterpreted the writings of French feminist Luce Irigaray. Irigaray's writings, which first appeared in the field of linguistics, have branched out into the fields of politics, psychoanalysis, and feminist thought. Whitford seeks to explain Irigaray and establish her as an important philosopher through an examination of the whole of Irigaray's writings, including her works on language and psychoanalysis, as well as some nontranslated works. Whitford's telling introduction to a writer who both confounds and intrigues many makes for an excellent read.

Whitford also edited *The Irigaray Reader* (Basil Blackwell, 1991), which includes a variety of excerpts from Irigaray's groundbreaking works, such as *This Sex Which Is Not One, Speculum of the Other Woman, An Ethics of Sexual Difference, Sexes and Genealogies*, and *Thinking the Difference*, as well as several essays published in English for the first time. Whitford supplies a glossary of terms and succinct discussions of context, themes, and critical responses to each work. Finally, *Engaging with Irigaray* (Columbia University Press, 1994), edited by Whitford, Carolyn Burke, and Naomi Schor, contains critical essays by prominent feminists such as Rosi Braidotti, Judith Butler, and Elisabeth Grosz examining a wide range of Irigaray's thought.

1999 CORE TITLES

Bach, Alice. *Women in the Hebrew Bible: A Reader*. New York: Routledge, 1999. 539p. bibliog. ISBN 0415915600; 0415915619pa.

Bednarowski, Mary Farrell. *The Religious Imagination of American Women*. Bloomington: Indiana University Press, 1999. 240p. (Religion in North America). bibliog. index. ISBN 0253335949; 025321338Xpa.

Berkovic, Sally. *Straight Talk: My Dilemma as a Modern Orthodox Jewish Woman*. Hoboken, NJ: KTAV, 1999. 254p. bibliog. ISBN 0881256617.

Bianchi, Emanuela. *Is Feminist Philosophy Philosophy?* Evanston, IL: Northwestern University Press, 1999. 266p. (Northwestern University Studies in Phenomenology and Existential Philosophy). bibliog. ISBN 0810115948; 0810115956pa.

Buchan, Morag. *Women in Plato's Political Theory*. New York: Routledge, 1999. 189p. bibliog. index. ISBN 041592183x; 0415921848pa.

Collier, Diane M., and Deborah F. Sawyer, eds. *Is There a Future for Feminist Theology?* Sheffield, England: Sheffield Academic Press, 1999. 210p. (Studies in Theology and Sexuality, 4). bibliog. index. ISBN 1850759634; 1850759790pa.

Dykeman, Therese Boos. *The Neglected Canon: Nine Women Philosophers, First to the Twentieth Century*. Norwell, MA: Kluwer Academic, 1999. 366p. bibliog. index. ISBN 0792359569.

Gimbutas, Marija, and Miriam Robbins Dexter. *The Living Goddesses*. Berkeley: University of California Press, 1999. 286p. bibliog. index. ISBN 0520213939; 0520229150pa.

Hendricks, Christina, and Kelly Oliver. *Language and Liberation: Feminism, Philosophy, and Language*. Albany: State University of New York Press, 1999. 402p. (SUNY Series in Contemporary Continental Philosophy). bibliog. index. ISBN 0791440516; 0791440524pa.

Kraemer, Ross Shepard, and Mary Rose D'Angelo, eds. *Women and Christian Origins: A Reader*. New York: Oxford University Press, 1999. 406p. bibliog. indexes. ISBN (OP); 0195103963pa.

Kvam, Kristen E., Linda S. Schearing, and Valerie H. Ziegler, eds. *Eve and Adam: Jewish, Christian, and Muslim Readings on Genesis and Gender*. Bloomington: Indiana University Press, 1999. 515p. bibliog. index. ISBN 025333490X; 0253212715pa.

Manning, Christel J. *God Gave Us the Right: Conservative Catholic, Evangelical Protestant, and Orthodox Jewish Women Grapple with Feminism*. New Brunswick, NJ: Rutgers University Press, 1999. 283p. bibliog. index. ISBN 0813525985; 0813525993pa.

Mir-Hosseini, Ziba. *Islam and Gender: The Religious Debate in Contemporary Iran*. Princeton, NJ: Princeton University Press, 1999. 305p. (Princeton Studies in Muslim Politics). bibliog. index. ISBN 0691058156; 0691010048pa.

Moghissi, Haideh. *Feminism and Islamic Fundamentalism: The Limits of Postmodern Analysis*. New York: Zed Books, distributed by St. Martin's Press, 1999. 166p. bibliog. index. ISBN 1856495892; 1856495906pa.

O'Connor, Frances B., and Becky S. Drury. *The Female Face in Patriarchy: Oppression as Culture*. East Lansing: Michigan State University Press, 1999. 144p. bibliog. index. ISBN 0870134949pa.

Prokhovnik, Raia. *Rational Woman: A Feminist Critique of Dichotomy*. New York: Routledge, 1999. 197p. (Routledge Innovations in Political Theory). bibliog. index. ISBN 0415146186. Also in netLibrary.

Robinson, Catherine A. *Tradition and Liberation: The Hindu Tradition in the Indian Women's Movement*. New York: St. Martin's Press, 1999. 230p. bibliog. index. ISBN 0312227183.

Schüssler Fiorenza, Elisabeth. *Rhetoric and Ethic: The Politics of Biblical Studies*. Minneapolis: Fortress, 1999. 220p. bibliog. ISBN 0800627954pa.

Sharma, Arvind, and Katherine K. Young. *Feminism and World Religions*. Albany: State University of New York Press, 1999. 333p. (McGill Studies in the History of Religions). bibliog. index. ISBN (OP); 0791440249pa. Also in netLibrary.

Simons, Margaret A. *Beauvoir and the Second Sex: Feminism, Race, and the Origins of Existentialism*. Lanham, MD: Rowman & Littlefield, 1999. 263p. bibliog. index. ISBN 0847692566; 0847692574pa.

Tsomo, Karma Lekshe. *Buddhist Women across Cultures: Realizations*. Albany: State University of New York Press, 1999. 326p. (SUNY Series: Feminist Philosophy). bibliog. index. ISBN 0791441377; 0791441385pa.

Walsh, Mary-Paula. *Feminism and Christian Tradition: An Annotated Bibliography and Critical Introduction to the Literature*. Westport, CT: Greenwood Press, 1999. 456p. (Bibliographies and Indexes in Religious Studies, no. 51). bibliog. indexes. ISBN 0313264198.

Washington, Harold C., Susan Lochrie Graham, and Pamela Thimmes, eds. *Escaping Eden: New Feminist Perspectives on the Bible*. New York: New York University Press, 1999. 292p. bibliog. indexes. ISBN 0814793525; 0814793533pa.

Young, Serinity, ed. *Encyclopedia of Women and World Religion*. New York: Macmillan Reference, 1999. 2v. 1152p. bibliog. index. ISBN 0028646088 (set).

WORLD WIDE WEB/INTERNET SITES

1390. Korenman, Joan. *Women-Related Religion/Spirituality Sites*. http://www-unix.umbc.edu/~korenman/wmst/links_rel.html.

This highly selective listing of women-related sites focuses on religion and/or spirituality. The sites "provide especially rich sources of information appropriate for an academic women's studies program." Each site listing includes a brief annotation that describes what the Web site features. Joan Korenman of the University of Maryland maintains the site.

1391. Larson, Christine M. *WSSLINKS: Women and Theology*. http://www.earlham.edu/~libr/acrlwss/wsstheo.html.

This site provides a selective, annotated list of links to "Internet resources on women and religion, feminist theology, or the feminine divine." It is part of WSSLINKS, a project of the Women's Studies Section of the Association of College and Research Libraries. Christine M. Larson, a librarian at Earlham College, who maintains the site, lists nearly 100 sites, arranged in various categories, including general sites on women and religion, Buddhism, Judaism, Christianity, Islam, and "Other Traditions." Each site listing contains a short annotation that details its scope and content.

1392. *Monastic Matrix: A Scholarly Resource for the Study of Women's Religious Communities from 400–1600 C.E.* http://matrix.bc.edu/MatrixWebData/about.html.

Matrix is an "ongoing collaborative effort by an international group of scholars of medieval history; religion; history of art; archaeology; religion; and other disciplines, as well as librarians and experts in computer technology." This site chronicles the lives of Christian women in medieval Europe between 400–1600 C.E. It includes both primary and secondary sources and is "designed for use by scholars, students, and anyone interested in the study of women, medieval Europe, or the history of Christianity."

1393. Porter, G. Margaret. *WSSLINKS: Women and Philosophy Web Sites*. http://www. nd.edu/~colldev/subjects/wss/index.shtml.
    G. Margaret Porter of the Hesburgh Library at the University of Notre Dame created and maintains this resourceful site, which provides a short but useful list. It includes links to directories; "Internet Collections"; bibliographies; an electronic discussion forum; a newsletter; and organizations. This site is a good place to start searching for information on women and philosophy.

SCIENCE AND TECHNOLOGY

17   Medicine and Health

Linda A. Krikos

In 1990, the U.S. General Accounting Office released a report disclosing significant gaps in research on women's public and professional health issues, health care services, and health education, putting women's health at risk. Although the report's conclusions surprised neither activists in the women's health movement nor feminist health researchers, they stunned the health care industry, sparking a national interest in women's health and the Women's Health Initiative. Recent developments in medical technologies have changed the way people think about female bodies, conception, parenthood, families, childbirth, the fetus, and especially motherhood. Visual and imaging technologies in particular have separated the fetus from the mother's body, helping to construct the fetus as an individual "life" with rights of its own. Pregnancy, once a private matter, now has become a public debate. Furthermore, the state of girls' and women's health in Third World countries remains dismal despite studies documenting the importance of female health to the family, community, and region. All of these developments have had significant, far-reaching impacts, both positive and negative, on women, their health, and their lives.

This chapter focuses on works that examine political, sociological, ethical, and historical aspects of medicine, medical research, general health, health policy and activism, specific diseases and conditions, and healers and healing. Several authors recognize the roles that race, ethnicity, class, age, sexual orientation, geographic location, and other social factors play not only in women's health, but also in the care that they receive. This chapter features works that reflect a variety of methodologies, from textual and discourse analysis to ethnography, and includes selected titles written for practitioners and consumers. While several titles aimed at practitioners also consider social and economic aspects of women's health, the authors of consumer titles, with some exceptions, tend to assume a white, middle-class, and heterosexual audience. Works in the "Monographs" section are subdivided into the following categories: "Medicine, Healers, and Health Care Issues, Policies, and Treatments," "Reproductive Issues," and "Self-Help and Consumer Titles." Each contains historical titles as appropriate.

REFERENCE SOURCES

1394. Allison, Kathleen Cahill. *Everywoman's Guide to Prescription and Nonprescription Drugs.* New York: Broadway Books, 1997. 770p. indexes. ISBN 0553069063pa.

Because men and women react to drugs in differing ways, according to studies conducted in the 1990s, Cahill urges women to monitor their bodies' reactions to drugs. She explains how the Food and Drug Administration (FDA) approves drugs and then clearly and thoroughly discusses drugs that women use, including contraceptives and hormone replacements. The author also addresses important drug-related issues, such as bone density reduction and the menstrual cycle's effect on drug absorption and metabolism. Cahill incorporates drug profiles, which she obtained from the U.S. Pharmacopeia (UPA), which the independent, nonprofit organization that sets standards for medicines sold in this country produces, into approximately half of the book, along with a drug identification guide, an extensive drug index, and a general index. Reference lists and suggestions for further reading would have enhanced this work.

The PDR Family Guide to Women's Health and Prescription Drugs (Medical Economics Data, 1994) contains detailed drug profiles that include relevant information for pregnant or breast-feeding women. The guide features a table that outlines and rates the risk of taking specific drugs during pregnancy, lists of sources and support groups, a glossary, an index arranged according to disease/disorder, and a general index. Unfortunately, neither title devotes sufficient attention to homeopathic and other alternative remedies.

1395. Belmonte, Frances R. *Women and Health: An Annotated Bibliography.* Lanham, MD: Scarecrow Press, 1997. 203p. (Magill Bibliographies). bibliog. indexes. ISBN 0810833859.

Belmonte, a substance abuse counselor and feminist theologian who teaches medical humanities courses at Loyola University, incorporates works that examine multiple facets of women's health into this bibliography. She features 300 popular and scholarly books, chapters, and articles, published in English from the 1970s to the mid-1990s, that focus on women's health in the United States and Canada. She arranges entries into five broad topics: historical, social, philosophical, and religious views of women; care of women; care by women; self-help, self-education, and the women's health care movement; and financial aspects. Each entry consists of complete citation information and an annotation that discusses major themes, with particular attention to race and ethnicity, and references to related entries in the book. Although the author topically arranges this bibliography, writings about specific subjects are scattered throughout the book, since many of the works analyze more than one aspect of women's health. Thus the author includes author, title, and subject indexes. Because Belmonte links women's health with other social factors, she compiles a broad-ranging bibliography that reflects her own interests. Some users might argue that her approach obfuscates conventional health titles.

1396. Horton, Jacqueline A., ed. *The Women's Health Data Book: A Profile of Women's Health in the United States.* Washington, DC: Jacobs Institute of Women's Health, Elsevier, 1992; 2nd ed., 1995. 176p. index. ISBN 0444100024.

Horton presents available data about various health concerns facing American women in this work. Major categories include reproduction (abortion, pregnancy, contraception, infertility); infectious diseases (sexually transmitted diseases, HIV/AIDS); chronic diseases (cancer, cardiovascular diseases); mental health (depression, suicide, eating disorders, Alzheimer's disease); violence (rape, battering, homicide); alcohol, drugs, and cigarettes; and access to care. Horton both clarifies and summarizes data that accompany tables, charts, figures, and other graphics; includes lists of references at the end of each chapter; and notes the sources for charts, tables, and the like. The book also features an appendix that describes the limitations of major statistical sources, a glossary of health and statistical terms, and a detailed index. The author provides more information disaggregated by race and ethnicity in the second edition and briefly examines issues affecting lesbians' use of health services.

1397. Rothman, Barbara Katz, ed. *Encyclopedia of Childbearing: Critical Perspectives.* Phoenix: Oryx Press, 1993. 446p. bibliog. index. ISBN 0897746481.

Rothman, a sociologist who studies pregnancy and motherhood, gathers brief (usually about 500 words or less) yet informative articles written by well-known birth or women's health advocates who represent many disciplines. Some of the more unusual topics covered in the book include maternity clothing, birth metaphors in art, and vegetarianism during pregnancy. Rothman incorporates some cross-cultural essays in which authors examine practices that differ from those in North America in geographically diverse countries. Each signed article includes summaries of the topic, cross-references to related entries, and a bibliography. Many contributors supplement the well-written texts with charts, tables, photographs, and other visual aids, making the encyclopedia a fine starting point for research on topics related to childbirth. Rothman also wrote *Recreating Motherhood: Ideology and Technology in a Patriarchal Society* (Norton, 1989), a woman- and class-sensitive exploration of how reproductive technologies affect society's concepts of motherhood, fatherhood, reproduction, and children.

MONOGRAPHS

Medicine, Healers, and Health Care Issues, Policies, and Treatments

1398. Apple, Rima D., ed. *Women, Health, and Medicine in America: A Historical Handbook*. New York: Garland, 1990. 580p. (Garland Reference Library in Social Science, v. 483). bibliog. index. ISBN 0824084470.

Authors of this fine collection of articles examine women's historical agency in health care. Apple divides this work into twenty chapters featuring extensive notes, which she groups into five main sections: definitions of health and disease, orthodox care, alternative care, social and political aspects of health and care, and women providers of health care. Chapter topics include race as a factor in health and health care, surgical gynecology, patent and sectarian medicine, physical education, and pharmacy. The book contains a lengthy bibliography.

Susan E. Cayleff's *Wash and Be Healed: The Water-Cure Movement and Women's Health* (Temple University Press, 1987) and Deborah Kuhn McGregor's *From Midwives to Medicine: The Birth of American Gynecology* (Rutgers University Press, 1998) cover some of the subjects that Apple incorporates into her collection. Cayleff's book describes how hydrology challenged prevailing nineteenth-century beliefs that linked women's bodies with inferiority and disease in her fascinating study. Hydrology also emphasized health and prevention and empowered women by giving them personal control of their own and their families' health. McGregor looks at how doctors experimented on women, usually poor, African American, or slave women, to develop new medical treatments that formed the basis of a new medical specialty. These works greatly add to the literature on American medical history, women's health, and the sociology of medicine.

1399. Batt, Sharon. *Patient No More: The Politics of Breast Cancer*. Charlottetown, Canada: Gynergy, 1994. 417p. bibliog. index. ISBN 0921881304.

Award-winning Canadian journalist Sharon Batt presents a highly critical feminist examination of the political, market, and economic forces surrounding breast cancer research and treatment. She thoroughly discusses controversies, including the use of the drug tamoxifen and the effectiveness of mammograms, and criticizes the medical establishment for emphasizing treatment as opposed to prevention, and research focusing on hereditary and not environmental causes of the disease.

Liane Clorfene-Casten also focuses on environmental causes of breast cancer and compellingly links commonly used toxic contaminants with cancer, exposing various connections between drug companies, cancer research, chemical polluters, and government agencies, in the well-researched *Breast Cancer: Poisons, Profits, and Prevention* (Common Courage, 1996). Medical journalist Roberta Altman provides an excellent overview of the disease, examining factors such as environmental hazards, poverty, heredity, and hormones, thorough discussions of controversies and treatment options, extensive listings of organizations, and informative notes in *Waking Up, Fighting Back: The Politics of Breast Cancer* (Little, Brown, 1996). Journalist Karen Stabiner skillfully interweaves personal stories, profiles, rivalries, alliances of the major players, and developments in research and treatment in the fight against breast cancer in *To Dance with the Devil: The New War on Breast Cancer* (Delacorte, 1997).

1400. Bayne-Smith, Marcia, ed. *Race, Gender, and Health*. Thousand Oaks, CA: Sage Publications, 1996. 210p. (Sage Series on Race and Ethnic Relations, v. 15). bibliog. index. ISBN 0803955049; 0803955057pa.

This volume serves as a fine introduction to health care issues that affect African American, American Indian and Alaska Native, Asian/Pacific Islander American, and Latina women. Following a contextual overview that discusses how poverty, race, class, gender, and the Western medical model affect access to health care, a member of the group in question examines the overall health status for that group, as well as specific diseases and behaviors, such as drug and alcohol use and smoking, within socioeconomic, political, and cultural contexts, in four separate chapters. Each chapter features suggestions for further research and improvements in health care. The final chapter includes an examination of specific reforms and policies, beginning with a redefinition of health, that would vastly improve health care for women of color.

Health Issues for Women of Color: A Cultural Diversity Perspective (Sage, 1995), edited by Diane L. Adams, also examines health issues of these four groups, with the addition of discussions about incarcerated, homeless, and Arab American women. *Wings of Gauze: Women of Color and the Experience of Health and Illness* (Wayne State University Press, 1993), edited by Barbara Bair and Susan E. Cayleff, combines personal, sociological, and literary writings about the importance of traditional medicine, cultural beliefs, connections between physical and mental health, historical access to care, and community action. All of these titles reveal appalling discrimination toward women of color in health care, social, economic, and cultural institutions.

1401. Beck, Christina S., with Sandra L. Ragan and Athena Dupre. *Partnership for Health: Building Relationships between Women and Health Caregivers*. Mahwah, NJ: Lawrence Erlbaum Associates, 1997. 184p. (LEA's Communication Series). bibliog. index. ISBN 0805824448; 0805824456pa.

Utilizing data collected from more than 150 interactions between women patients and their health care providers in three different settings, along with ethnographic field notes from other facilities, Beck and her colleagues consider how provider/patient encounters affect the quality of the health care that women receive. The authors argue that patients and providers bring multiple, sometimes conflicting identities and expectations to medical relationships in a postmodern society, and therefore both must assume responsibility for the construction of these encounters. Beck, Ragan, and Dupre use examples of dialogue that "co-accomplish" this construction, enabling women to fully participate in their health care.

Medical sociologist Sue Fisher conducts a sociolinguistic examination of the power dynamics involved in decisions pertaining to Pap smears and hysterectomies in *In the Patient's Best Interest: Women and the Politics of Medical Decisions* (Rutgers University Press, 1986). Fisher argues that doctors' cultural beliefs about race, class, and gender affect their diagnosis and treatment. Fisher compares communication styles of physicians and nurse practitioners in *Nursing Wounds: Nurse Practitioners, Doctors, Women Patients, and the Negotiation of Meaning* (Rutgers University Press, 1995), determining that nurse practitioners generally use a more conducive style than doctors that results in positive health encounters and successful care. Alexandra Dundas Todd also presents a sociolinguistic analysis of doctor-patient communication concerning birth control in *Intimate Adversaries: Cultural Conflicts between Doctors and Women Patients* (University of Pennsylvania Press, 1989). She suggests that physicians' narrow focus on bodies, orientation toward science and technology, and assumptions about race, sex, and class interfere with their ability to provide appropriate care.

1402. Blechman, Elaine A., and Kelly D. Brownell, eds. *Behavioral Medicine for Women: A Comprehensive Handbook*. 2nd ed. New York: Guilford Press, 1998. 876p. bibliog. indexes. ISBN 1572302186.

Many scholars consider the first edition of this book, *Handbook of Behavioral Medicine for Women* (Pergamon Press, 1988), groundbreaking not only because the editors recognize how environmental and social factors affect women's physical and mental health, but also because they emphasize encouraging behavior skills that increase feelings of competence and control. The second edition provides new and authoritative, albeit contradictory, information in nine sections written by experts in each field that explore topics including substance use and body image, sexuality and reproduction, and physical and mental dysfunctions. Contributors treat some subjects, such as breast cancer, HIV infection, and alcohol use, from different perspectives in more than one section of the book. Although the book is written for consumers, practitioners, scientists, researchers, and students, the list of additional readings at the end of each chapter consists mainly of clinical and medical journal articles.

Contributors to *Women's Health Care: A Comprehensive Handbook* (Sage, 1995), edited by Catherine Ingram Fogel and Nancy Fugate Woods, also support increased personal responsibility for health while persuasively arguing for medicine to expand limited biomedical approaches to women's health and care. This liberally illustrated collection is accessible to informed laypersons.

1403. Bonner, Thomas. *To the Ends of the Earth: Women's Search for Education in Medicine*. Cambridge, MA: Harvard University Press, 1992. 232p. bibliog. illus. index. notes. ISBN 0674893034.

Using an impressive array of published and unpublished primary and secondary sources, Bonner documents women's struggle to obtain medical education comparable to that of men during the period of professionalization, roughly between 1850 and World War I. His study focuses on conditions in Britain, imperial Germany, Russia, and the United States that forced thousands of women to endure many hardships in order to attend medical schools in Zurich and Paris, the only schools that admitted women at the time. Bonner supplements the narrative with capsule biographies, often accompanied by photographs, many of "pioneers," throughout his engaging work. Although short on analysis, Bonner focuses on a pivotal period in medical history when women attempted to obtain acceptable healing roles.

Women Healers and Physicians: Climbing a Long Hill (University Press of Kentucky, 1997), edited by Lillian R. Furst, focuses on women healers in various cultures, mostly Western, during antiquity, the medieval and Renaissance periods, and the nineteenth century. Jeanne Achterberg presents an intriguing, well-referenced, and broad historical account of women healers beginning with ancient shamans in *Woman as Healer* (Shambhala, 1990). Like Bonner and Furst, Achterberg examines the obstacles that women faced whenever and wherever they attempted to heal outside the private realm.

1404. Cadden, Joan. *Meanings of Sex Difference in the Middle Ages: Medicine, Science, and Culture*. Cambridge: Cambridge University Press, 1993. 310p. bibliog. index. ISBN 0521343631.

Cadden mines print medical sources and Latin manuscripts for classical, medieval, and university-based discussions of sex and conception in this book, winner of the 1994 Pfizer Award for Outstanding Book in the History of Science. Her intricate, detailed analysis of these literatures emphasizes the wide diversity of medical, philosophical, and religious opinions on the topics. Cadden also examines changes in anatomy-based definitions of gender and their effect on broader cultural assumptions about male and female roles.

Other insightful works that apply gender analysis to medicine in various historical periods and geographic locations include Lesley Dean-Jones's *Women's Bodies in Classical Greek Science* (Clarendon Press, 1996), an intriguing study of the writings of Aristotle and Hippocratic writers that reveals a range of beliefs about bodies and gender; Renate Blumenfeld-Kosinski's *Not of Woman Born: Representations of Caesarean Birth in Medieval and Renaissance Culture* (Cornell University Press, 1990), a readable, interdisciplinary analysis of the cultural context surrounding birth processes, especially caesarean birth, that asserts that men used their surgical skills to marginalize midwives; Barbara Duden's *The Woman beneath the Skin: A Doctor's Patients in Eighteenth-Century Germany* (Harvard University Press, 1991), an interdisciplinary examination, based on eight volumes of one doctor's notes about diseases in women, about how culture influences and changes ideas about biological and social bodies over time; and Lindsay B. Wilson's *Women and Medicine in the French Enlightenment: The Debate over "Maladies des Femmes"* (Johns Hopkins University Press, 1993), an investigation of three controversies—miraculous healing, the definition of "late birth," and mesmerism—that provide insight into beliefs about women's proper role.

1405. Candib, Lucy M. *Medicine and the Family: A Feminist Perspective*. New York: Basic Books, 1995. 360p. bibliog. index. ISBN 0465023746.

Candib, a physician and feminist, presents what she calls a model of being-in-relationship for family health care in *Medicine and the Family*. Candib contends that white male bias within the medical profession underpins medicine's assumptions about life-span development, sexual abuse, rape, and battering. The author further argues that human development theories, family cycle, and family systems emphasize separation and autonomy, key goals of male development, which can result in poor, even disastrous health care for women and children. Candib provides cogent explanations of each theory, which she accompanies with feminist criticism, informed by the work of Carol Gilligan, Jean Baker Miller, and the Stone Center for Developmental Services and Studies at Wellesley College. In the last half of the book, Candib applies her feminist model, which she believes both empowers patients and promotes healing, to clinical relationships in family practice. Although this is not reflected very well in the book's index, she considers the impact of race, age, and class on obtaining quality care as well. This readable, compassionately narrated work concludes with lengthy, informative notes and an extensive bibliography.

Mary Mahowald also draws on the work of Gilligan and Miller to develop an egalitarian model of care that reveals differences among individuals and groups of women in *Women and Children in Health Care: An Unequal Majority* (Oxford University Press, 1993). After examining white male gender biases and persistent stereotypes in medicine, Mahowald applies her model to a variety of topics, including gender socialization in adolescents, abortion, fertility curtailment and enhancement, moral agency in children, reproductive technologies, disabled newborns, and the feminization of poverty.

1406. Carter, Pam. *Feminism, Breasts, and Breast Feeding*. New York: St. Martin's Press, 1995. 266p. bibliog. indexes. ISBN 033362310X; 0333623118pa.

Carter, a British sociologist, applies a feminist poststructuralist framework to her examination of infant-feeding practices, arguing that many studies accept the maxim "breast is best" while ignoring the lived experiences of women who do or do not breast-feed their infants. Carter skillfully integrates personal stories about infant feeding choices, which she gleaned from interviews with working-class women in England, with her analysis of dominant discourses about femininity, modesty, mothering, race, class, gender relations, and medicine's involvement in childbirth and infant care. The author's analysis of the sexualization of public and private spaces is particularly intriguing. Although Carter's suggestions for change lack depth, she raises important questions that could lead to better research on women's infant-feeding choices.

Naomi Baumslag, a physician, and Dia L. Michels, a science writer, vehemently support breast-feeding under all circumstances in *Milk, Money, and Madness: The Culture and Politics of Breastfeeding* (Bergin & Garvey, 1995). The authors carefully document formula manufacturers' misconduct, explain the nutritional and immunological differences between breast milk and various formulas, articulate the negative public health consequences of bottle feeding, and make practical suggestions for reducing constraints on breast-feeding. Yet they simultaneously reinforce an essentialist concept of "woman" and insensitively dismiss cultural and class differences.

Noteworthy earlier works, such as Gabrielle Palmer's *The Politics of Breastfeeding* (Pandora Press, 1988; 2nd ed., 1993) and Penny Van Esterik's *Beyond the Breast-Bottle Controversy* (Rutgers University Press, 1989), examine the worldwide ecological consequences that result from the production of infant formula. These titles all illuminate the complex politics involved in breast-feeding and provide extensive bibliographies.

1407. Corea, Gina. *The Invisible Epidemic: The Story of Women and AIDS.* New York: HarperCollins, 1992. 356p. bibliog. index. ISBN 0060166487.

Corea gathers information from government reports, newspaper and journal articles, published and unpublished material, and interviews with diverse women affected by HIV/AIDS to document chronologically the epidemic in the United States from 1981 to 1990. The author focuses on exposing sexist, racist, and homophobic beliefs that allowed health officials either to ignore totally the risks facing women or to blame them for spreading the disease. Corea argues that these beliefs established a pattern of neglect and misinformation that resulted in the denial of health services to women with HIV/AIDS. The moving personal stories not only add a strong emotional component to the factual material and sociopolitical context, but also powerfully reveal the major impact of the disease on women.

Other works that discuss racism, sexism, and AIDS include Diane Richardson's *Women and AIDS* (Methuen, 1988), one of the first works to use a feminist framework, which still serves as a fine introduction to examine the AIDS crisis and its impact on women, and the ACT UP/New York Women and AIDS Book Group's *Women, AIDS, and Activism* (South End Press, 1990), which identifies the politics of treatment issues, examines the social constructions of gender and AIDS that silence women's experiences with the disease, and presents strategies for resisting policies that in reality abet the spread of the disease.

1408. Dan, Alice J., ed. *Reframing Women's Health: Multidisciplinary Research and Practice.* Thousand Oaks, CA: Sage, 1994. 410p. bibliog. index. ISBN 0803957734; 0803958609pa.

Dan, founder of the Center for Research on Women and Gender at the University of Illinois at Chicago, features thoroughly documented papers presented at the first conference that specifically focused on the development of a women's health specialty in medicine in *Reframing Women's Health*. Contributors, mostly academics and health care providers, examine topics such as provider/patient relationships, violence, medical school curriculum revision, and sexuality using varying approaches. Most contributors criticize the hierarchical organization of health care institutions, which results in power imbalances and a "blame-the-victim" mentality. They call for a holistic model of health that centers the experiences on women, rather than practitioners, and considers race, class, sexuality, and other social and cultural factors that profoundly affect women's health and health care. This accessible, key text belongs in every women's studies and health collection.

Sue V. Rosser effectively critiques the male model of health care in *Women's Health: Missing from U.S. Medicine* (Indiana University Press, 1994), arguing that excluding women (including women of color and elderly and lesbian women) from clinical studies results in inadequate treatment and underdiagnosis of serious conditions. Rosser explores various feminist methodologies and suggests changes in medical education to address male bias in research, evaluation, teaching methods, and curricula.

1409. Davis, Kathy. *Reshaping the Female Body: The Dilemma of Cosmetic Surgery.* New York: Routledge, 1995. 211p. bibliog. index. notes. ISBN (OP); 0415906326pa.

Based on fieldwork and interviews with surgery recipients, physicians, plastic surgeons, and medical inspectors, Davis attempts to combine feminist analysis of cosmetic surgery and "an equally feminist desire to treat women as agents who negotiate their bodies" (p. 5) in this work. Davis, a clinical psychologist with a background in medical sociology, conducted her studies in the Netherlands—the only country in the world to include cosmetic surgery in its national health insurance plan—focusing her argument on three themes: identity, agency, and morality, or justification. She surprisingly finds that most women have surgery to become more ordinary, as opposed to more beautiful, and to do something for themselves, rather than someone else. The women criticized unrealistic beauty norms and morally legitimized their choice to have surgery. The author concludes that cosmetic surgery can become an empowering act of defiance and resistance, although it simultaneously exploits women. While many feminists roundly criticized this work, Davis's inclusion of women's thoughts, anxieties, and experiences makes it significant. For a more general yet well-documented and readable treatment of cosmetic surgery in America that examines race, ethnicity, economic, social, and psychological issues, see Elizabeth Haiken's *Venus Envy: A History of Cosmetic Surgery* (Johns Hopkins University Press, 1997).

1410. Doyal, Leslie. *What Makes Women Sick? Gender and the Political Economy of Health.* New Brunswick, NJ: Rutgers University Press, 1995. 280p. bibliog. index. ISBN 0813522064; 0813522072pa.

Doyal, a founder of the Women's Health Information Centre in London, deftly argues that the political aspects of health, especially external factors such as poverty and geographic location, affect women's health as much as medical aspects and therefore deserve immediate collective action. Consolidating a variety of feminist viewpoints, she applies her theoretical analysis to a wealth of data, covering topics such as waged and domestic labor, childbirth, reproductive choices, abuse, mental distress, and sexuality, which she supplements with examples of women's health activism from world cultures. Doyal ultimately insists that true understanding of women's health issues requires a multidisciplinary, holistic model of medicine.

Like Doyal, contributors to *Women, Health, Politics, and Power: Essays on Sex/Gender, Medicine, and Public Health* (Baywood Publishing, 1994), edited by Elizabeth Fee and Nancy Krieger, contest the adequacy of the biomedical model to solve women's health problems. The editors present international, interdisciplinary essays and case studies originally published in *International Journal of Health Services*, a journal emphasizing political and social aspects of health.

Many essays link women's health problems to race, ethnicity, and class as well as gender and assert that social contexts help shape women's health.

Jane S. Stein also attests to the inadequacy of traditional biomedical research frameworks in *Empowerment and Women's Health: Theory, Methods, and Practice* (Zed Books, 1997). Using ideas culled from modernity, development, health, and women's studies literatures, she presents empowerment ideologies within a feminist framework to create a comprehensive plan for improving health research, evaluation, and care for women around the world.

1411. Ettorre, Elizabeth, and Elianne Riska. *Gendered Moods: Psychotropics and Society.* New York: Routledge, 1995. 177p. bibliog. indexes. ISBN 0415082137; 0415082145pa.

In *Gendered Moods*, Ettorre, author of the woman-centered *Women and Substance Use* (Macmillan, 1992), and Riska, both medical sociologists, provide one of the first feminist examinations of psychotropics—drugs that affect the central nervous system. The authors begin with a critical survey of the medical and sociological discourses pertaining to psychotropic drug use and then argue that most previous studies either do not articulate underlying theoretical frameworks or use frameworks laden with unrecognized gender assumptions. After more detailed analysis of various social scientific perspectives, Ettorre and Riska construct their own framework that centers on various social actors (individuals, groups, doctors, pharmaceutical companies, and health care systems) and layers (expression, behavior, and cognition) that construct psychotropic drug use. They insightfully apply their framework to analyze drug advertisements, individual user narratives, lay cultural interpretations, and formal health care systems using clear, logical, and accessible language.

Another groundbreaking title, *Psychopharmacology from a Feminist Perspective* (Haworth Press, 1995), edited by Jean A. Hamilton and others, collects a mix of theoretical, practical, and empirical chapters covering a broad range of women's physical conditions, from infertility to hypertension, that all promote gender-sensitive approaches to psychopharmacology. Both works emphasize how people must consider differences in age, race, ethnicity, class, sexual orientation, and (dis)ability to form a multidimensional understanding of the subject.

1412. Farmer, Paul, Margaret Connors, and Janie Simmons, eds. *Women, Poverty, and AIDS: Sex, Drugs, and Structural Violence.* Monroe, ME: Common Courage, 1996. 473p. (Health and Social Justice). bibliog. glossary. index. ISBN 1567510752; 1567510744pa.

The publisher's new series focuses on the effects of poverty and other social inequities on health issues. Contributors argue that poverty and gender inequality represent leading factors in the spread of HIV/AIDS in women worldwide in this inaugural volume, which begins with an overview of AIDS in women and then thoroughly reviews the social science, public health, and clinical medicine literatures to determine to what extent authors of the articles consider issues relevant to poor women. The contributors unfortunately find that the vast majority of the articles do not consider them at all. Other sections consist of profiles of successful health activist groups within and outside the United States, a glossary, informative notes, and an extensive bibliography. The book's overall tone of advocacy and its focus on economic conditions of women with AIDS are very much needed.

Women Resisting AIDS: Feminist Strategies for Empowerment (Temple University Press, 1995), edited by Beth E. Schneider and Nancy E. Stoller, presents chapters written by women involved in AIDS prevention, policy, research, caregiving, and activism that describe successful programs in the United States, Latin America, and Africa. Like the contributors in *Women, Pov-*

erty, and AIDS, the authors believe that economic inequalities and social, cultural, and political factors greatly increase women's vulnerability to the disease.

1413. Friedman, Emily, ed. *An Unfinished Revolution: Women and Health Care in America*. New York: United Hospital Fund, 1994. 285p. bibliog. index. ISBN 1881277178.

Friedman presents chapters written by health professionals, academics, and administrators with impressive credentials that provide a broad overview of the importance of women's roles as patients, practitioners, caregivers, and leaders in health care. Contributors cover noteworthy subjects, such as health laws and patients' rights, the enormous burden of unpaid caregiving, economic and social factors that affect older women's health, and the impact of women as academics, health administrators, and hospital trustees. Two chapters focus on women of color: one explores economic, social, cultural, and historical factors that account for the low health status of women of color; the other articulates the many contributions of these women to the care and healing of others. Editors of the collection interweave factual information with personal experiences and, in several chapters, supplement text with charts that clarify statistical information.

The policy makers, academics, activists, and lawyers who contributed chapters to *Man-Made Medicine: Women's Health, Public Policy, and Reform* (Duke University Press, 1996), edited by Kary L. Moss, explore interactions among legal systems, research and development industries, Congress, the popular media, academia, and health care. The chapters address the persistent and insidious gender, race, and class stereotypes that both underpin inequitable policies and permeate the health care system, affecting the level of care women receive. Not only do contributors support the need for an interdisciplinary approach to both short- and long-term reforms, but several also examine barriers to health care that prisoners, disabled women, and immigrants experience. Others discuss the need to separate tort reform from healthcare reform, media portrayals of women's biology and health issues, and the health system's response to HIV/AIDS in girls and women.

1414. Golden, Janet Lynne. *A Social History of Wet Nursing in America: From Breast to Bottle*. New York: Cambridge University Press, 1996. 215p. (Cambridge History of Medicine). index. notes. ISBN 052149544X.

Golden traces the changing medical, economic, social, and political conditions in America that influenced decisions regarding wet nursing since colonial times, when maternal mortality and illness were widespread. She links the nineteenth-century decline in wet nursing to the rise of the middle class, changing perceptions of motherhood, and the growing tendency of physicians to intervene in child care. Although Golden is limited to sources such as poorhouse ledgers and newspaper advertisements, she incorporates race and class dynamics into her analysis. Golden strongly argues that infant-feeding choices both reflect and help determine cultural meanings of motherhood.

In contrast to Golden, Valerie A. Fildes mines the more abundant sources on the subject in European countries, where wet nursing often fell under religious and state control, in *Wet Nursing: A History from Antiquity to the Present* (Basil Blackwell, 1988). Fildes, who studied both nursing and biology, presents a richly detailed, chronological and factual history of wet nursing based on a variety of primary and secondary sources listed in the book's bibliography. The book contains useful tables, illustrations, notes, and a glossary. Fildes also examines wet nursing in *Breasts, Bottles, and Babies: A History of Infant Feeding* (Edinburgh University Press, 1986). Rima D. Apple analyzes the subject in the United States in *Mothers and Medicine: A Social History of Infant Feeding, 1890–1950* (University of Wisconsin Press, 1987), which nicely complements Golden's title.

1415. Goldstein, Nancy, and Jennifer L. Manlowe, eds. *The Gender Politics of HIV/ AIDS in Women: Perspectives on the Pandemic in the United States*. New York: New York University Press, 1997. 460p. index. notes. ISBN 0814730949; 0814730930pa.

The 1994 Gender Politics of HIV conference at Connecticut College inspired this volume of essays, whose authors argue that the best understanding of HIV/AIDS is rooted not only in gender and biological constructs, but also in cultural, ideological, and social constructs, since class, race, and sexuality play major roles in women's response to the disease. Several contributors examine assumptions regarding women during the development of the biomedical model of HIV/ AIDS. They then discuss how various institutions supported status quo power relations by ignoring and stigmatizing marginalized groups, including sex workers, prisoners, drug users, homosexuals, and women of color. Other contributors analyze how the disease directly affects women and present personal stories of HIV-positive women. Each chapter features extensive notes.

Tamsin Wilton draws on feminist constructional and queer theories to examine how safe sex and health education discourses affect cultural constructions of gender and sexuality in the United States, Scandinavia, the United Kingdom, and English-speaking Commonwealth countries in *Engendering AIDS: Deconstructing Sex, Text, and Epidemic* (Sage, 1997). Cindy Patton, inspired by cultural and social constructional studies, provides a wide-ranging, gendered analysis of women and AIDS in which she suggests how to make HIV/AIDS policies and practices more responsive to women in *Last Served? Gendering the HIV Epidemic* (Taylor & Francis, 1994). Patton, a longtime AIDS activist and scholar, also wrote the first safe sex guide for women with Janis Kelly, called *Making It: A Woman's Guide to Sex in the Age of AIDS* (Firebrand Books, 1987).

1416. Greer, Germaine. *The Change: Women, Aging, and the Menopause*. New York: Knopf, 1991. 422p. bibliog. index. ISBN 0394582691.

Greer provocatively traces social, cultural, psychological, and physical beliefs about menopause and aging over a 200-year period, paying special attention to negative stereotypes and attitudes that blame women for a natural life transition. Greer examines the evolution of treatment beginning with traditional practices, such as purging, bleeding, and herbs, and then considers allopathic and alternative treatments. She urges women to take responsibility for their health, challenge common beliefs, and work toward achieving the power, serenity, and growth that menopause can bring them in this important work, which chipped away at the taboo on discussing menopause.

Sandra Coney boldly examines how the drug industry discovered an untapped market, midlife women, developed products aimed at that audience, and convinced doctors that they needed to provide routine, preventative treatment for menopause using drugs in *The Menopause Industry: How the Medical Establishment Exploits Women* (Hunter House, 1994). Coney examines years of hormone replacement therapy (HRT), mammography, and bone density research and incorporates firsthand accounts of diverse women's experiences with menopause in this work. She explores the negative implications of routine medical intervention in natural processes, arguing that doctors exaggerate connections between menopause and disease while downplaying the negative effects of treatments. Coney also elucidates the pharmaceutical industry's role in creating health information in this book, originally published in New Zealand by Penguin in 1991. Editor Joan C. Callahan collects updated papers on social and cultural aspects of menopause, film portrayals of menopause, historical metaphors and rhetoric connected with menopause, effects of medical theories of menopause on older women's material lives, and various aspects of HRT from a 1989 conference in *Menopause: A Midlife Passage* (Indiana University Press, 1993).

1417. Haseltine, Florence P., and Beverly Greenberg Jacobson, eds. *Women's Health Research: A Medical and Policy Primer*. Washington, DC: Health Press International, 1997. 364p. bibliog. index. ISBN 0880487917.

Several experts from a variety of health-related fields present research and policy agendas for improving women's health in this guidebook, which begins with a succinct historical overview that sets the context for developments during the 1990s, when the Society for the Advancement of Women's Health Research, whose members address gender inequities in research and funding in the United States, was founded. Contributors clearly outline members of the medical community's knowledge (and lack of knowledge) about many specific diseases, identify how the system for funding medical research is flawed, reiterate the importance of including women in clinical trials, recommend changes in medical education that emphasize women's health issues, and call for multidisciplinary research. This work belongs in medical, legal, academic, and other specialized collections.

The two-volume *Women and Health Research: Ethical and Legal Issues of Including Women in Clinical Studies* (National Academy Press, 1994), edited by Anna C. Mastroianni, Ruth Faden, and Daniel Federman, also would complement such collections. The first volume contains a complete report that the Institute of Medicine's Committee on the Ethical and Legal Issues Relating to the Inclusion of Women in Clinical Studies prepared, while the second volume consists of workshop presentations and commissioned chapters that address recruitment, compensation, and liability issues in research. The report *Assessment of the NIH* [National Institutes of Health] *Women's Health Initiative* [WHI] (National Academy Press, 1993) recommends modifications to the initiative to improve the WHI's contribution to U.S. women's health. Beryl Lieff Benderly provides a useful framework for helping women evaluate the daunting amount of health data and frequently conflicting health information in *In Her Own Right: The Institute of Medicine's Guide to Women's Health Issues* (National Academy Press, 1997).

1418. Hine, Darlene Clark. *Black Women in White: Racial Conflict and Cooperation in the Nursing Profession, 1890–1950*. Bloomington: Indiana University Press, 1989. 264p. (Blacks in the Diaspora). bibliog. index. ISBN 0253327733; 0253205298pa.

Hine documents the sexism and racism entrenched in medicine, hospital structures, and nursing, revealing how southern training institutions denied access to black women, while northern institutions accepted black women as nurse trainees, although administrators denied them employment. Hine also explores the establishment of separate black hospitals and colleges to provide nurse training in the late nineteenth and early twentieth centuries and the founding of the National Association of Colored Nurses in 1908 and Chi Eta Phi sorority in 1932. These institutions and groups led the struggle not only to improve health care in black communities, but also to gain access to hospital employment, which proved difficult well into the 1960s. Hine's well-researched work contributes to an understanding of the complexities within nursing history and health care and provides a framework for studying the role of black women in advocacy groups and politics.

Susan Reverby examines sexism within health care, focusing on tensions between caring and power, as exacerbated by class differences, which prevented unity among nurses in their struggle for professional status and control of training, in *Ordered to Care: The Dilemma of American Nursing, 1850–1945* (Cambridge University Press, 1987). She juxtaposes the developments of nursing as a profession with the hospital industry in light of a society that valued concrete, quantifiable outcomes over caring. Both Hine and Reverby explore how women's values and status might have contributed to the nursing profession's subservient position. Both authors use a vast array of primary and secondary sources to provide thoughtful analyses of the important roles that gender, class, and, in Hine's case, race play in labor history and professional identity.

1419. Krotoski, Danuta, Margaret A. Nosek, and Margaret A. Turk, eds. *Women with Physical Disabilities: Achieving and Maintaining Health and Well-Being.* Baltimore: P.H. Brookes, 1996. 482p. bibliog. indexes. ISBN 1557662347.

Most studies on disabilities in medical research generally ignore women; thus Krotoski, Nosek, and Turk organized this compilation of conference papers, aimed at a broad audience, including health care providers and researchers in many disciplines, to illuminate the situation. The first papers explore overriding issues, laying the foundation for specialized sections on sexuality and reproduction, stress and well-being, bladder and bowel management, and physical fitness. Authors of papers included in these sections examine topics such as contraception, pregnancy, sexuality, urinary tract infections, sports, and exercise. Editors incorporate a brief consideration of the added impact of race/ethnicity and lesbianism to disability. Contributors ultimately call for a broader scope in disability research, in addition to a holistic, more sensitive understanding of disabled women and female disability issues. All papers feature useful lists of references and suggestions for future research.

Libraries requiring more practical information should consider *A Woman's Guide to Coping with Disability* (Resources for Rehabilitation, 1994; 2nd ed., 1997; 3rd ed., 1999), which presents basic information about various disabilities and lists of pertinent books, articles, tapes, vendors of assistive devices, and, in the later editions, Web sites and e-mail addresses. The book also provides useful, albeit brief, general information about rehabilitation, travel, housing adaptation, work, and legal resources. Veronica Marris based *Lives Worth Living: Women's Experience of Chronic Illness* (HarperCollins, 1996) on interviews with women suffering from conditions such as arthritis, diabetes, epilepsy, lupus, and multiple sclerosis who discuss their efforts to maintain control over their bodies and lives. Marris explores their experiences with isolation, sex, work, and caregivers.

1420. Lewis, Judith A., and Judith Bernstein, eds. *Women's Health: A Relational Perspective across the Life Cycle.* Sudbury, MA: Jones & Bartlett, 1996. 346p. bibliog. illus. index. ISBN 0867204850.

Nurse practitioners Lewis and Bernstein present chapters that integrate medical aspects of women's health with discussions of women's growth in developmental aspects. Contributors analyze traditional psychological, moral, and personality development models as applied to women, exposing their underlying discriminatory standards, in the first section. They then propose a relational psychology framework, informed by the work of Carol Gilligan, Jean Baker Miller, and psychologists from the Stone Center, that validates and builds on women's strengths. In the next section, contributors apply this framework to health issues that women face during each stage of the life cycle, emphasizing wellness in connection with common health hazards. In the third section, contributors analyze the complexity of individual, familial, and community roles that women must fill, proposing a new holistic model for women's health that recognizes all personal, interpersonal, and environmental aspects of women's lives. Chapters feature reference lists, and most consider the effects of race and class on health. Although the book focuses on women's health in the United States, the editors include a global overview of women's health, along with case studies conducted in Panama and South Africa. The book would complement a text for courses in nursing and related fields. Contributors to *Women's Health across the Lifespan: A Comprehensive Perspective* (Lippincott, 1997), edited by Karen Moses Allen and Janice Mitchell Phillips, consider developmental and medical perspectives of women's health in their discussions of health promotion and prevention, specific illnesses, cultural differences in health statuses and beliefs among women of various races and ethnicities, occupational health, and economic and social factors, such as homelessness, poverty, and incarceration.

1421. Long, Lynellyn D., and E. Maxine Ankrah, eds. *Women's Experiences with HIV/AIDS: An International Perspective*. New York: Columbia University Press, 1996. 426p. bibliog. index. ISBN 0231106041; 023110605X.

Collecting the work of policy makers, educators, health professionals, researchers, and academics from around the world, this volume combines international empirical data with personal experiences of women within diverse socioeconomic and cultural contexts. Contributors cover the following subjects: prostitution, lesbianism, poverty, support systems, ethics, female-controlled vaginal microbicides, breast-feeding, and AIDS education. The book concludes with suggestions for new policies that address the very real risks of women who deal with HIV/AIDS.

An earlier, woman-centered title, *Women and HIV/AIDS: An International Resource Book* (Pandora Press, 1993), edited by Marge Berer with Sunanda Ray, also deftly combines personal accounts with clearly written, factual information about medical, social, and political issues facing HIV-infected and at-risk women. More than fifty women from various countries contributed to this work, in which the editors supplemented many chapters with descriptions of programs, prototype leaflets, guidelines, research summaries, and other useful information. Highly regarded international collections of personal experiences of women with AIDS include *AIDS: The Women* (Cleis, 1988), edited by Ines Rieder and Patricia Ruppelt, and *Positive Women: Voices of Women Living with AIDS* (Second Story Press, 1992), edited by Andrea Rudd and Darien Taylor.

1422. Lorber, Judith. *Gender and the Social Construction of Illness*. Thousand Oaks, CA: Sage, 1997. 148p. (Gender Lens). bibliog. index. ISBN 0803958137; 0803958145pa.

Sage initiated the Gender Lens series to highlight and make accessible to students feminist research across disciplines that use gender as the organizing principle. Lorber, a sociologist, examines the social aspects of health, physical illness, and medical care and critiques the construction of medical knowledge along with the social assumptions embedded in it. She uses the "transformation of the body through gendered social practices" (p. 3) as the framework, to examine epidemiological information on life expectancy, causes of death, disability, and illnesses throughout the life span, and to attribute differences in outcome to gender, race, ethnicity, and economic status. The author also provides an engaging analysis of normal female experiences, such as premenstrual syndrome and menopause, that medicine defines as disorders, as well as the disease AIDS. Lorber's examination of how gender, race, and ethnicity play major roles in a variety of medical encounters is particularly noteworthy. This well-referenced, highly readable work could supplement reading in medical sociology or women and health courses.

1423. McClain, Carol Shepherd, ed. *Women as Healers: Cross-Cultural Perspectives*. New Brunswick, NJ: Rutgers University Press, 1989. 274p. bibliog. index. ISBN 0813513693; 0813513707pa.

Prompted by the growing interest in feminist anthropology and medical sociology, McClain collects several case studies on women healers conducted in various countries to document the importance of cross-cultural gender studies in medicine and healing. After concisely comparing the approaches of feminist anthropologists, medical sociologists, and ethnographers, McClain presents the studies according to the following categories of healing: informal (Ecuadorian Indian family healer, local healer in Sri Lanka, and Mexican peasant healer), metaphorical (Jamaican mothering and balm, American Christian Science, and Serbian conjuring), and ritualistic (Korean shaman, Puerto Rican espiritista, and African diviner-medium). Contributors consider women in traditional healing roles (rural healer in Benin and American lay midwife) within the context of cultural change in the final section.

In *Medicine Women, Curanderas, and Women Doctors* (University of Oklahoma Press,

1989), Bobette Perrone, H. Henrietta Stockel, and Victoria Krueger argue that blending modern and traditional medicine could result in more effective holistic healing through ten stories of women healers that reflect three distinct perspectives: Native American, Southwest Hispanic, and Western scientific. Each healer tells her story in her own way, presenting it within a cultural context. Mark St. Pierre features interviews with Native American, including Lakota, Crow, and Cheyenne, healers and their families that provide insight into women's participation in sacred traditions in *Walking in the Sacred Manner: Healers, Dreamers, and Pipe Carriers—Medicine Women of the Plains Indians* (Simon & Schuster, 1995).

1424. Messing, Karen. *One-Eyed Science: Occupational Health and Women Workers.* Philadelphia: Temple University Press, 1998. 244p. (Labor and Social Change). index. notes. ISBN 1566395976; 1566395984pa.

In an attempt to make studies in occupational health more gender sensitive, Messing examines how the fields of biology, ergonomics, and social relations essentially ignore women's occupational health issues in this book. Messing first describes male/female differences in jobs, health, and basic biology and then examines how science functions as a social institution: how and why research projects get funded and how results become scientific knowledge. She next presents case studies that illustrate scientific treatments of specific issues that are significant to women workers, including stress, reproductive hazards, office work, and muscle and skeletal disease. The author's analysis, which excludes race/ethnicity, reveals that researchers often fail to consider gender differences at all or, in the case of reproductive issues, focus merely on the fetus and not on pregnant women or male reproductive systems. Messing concludes by suggesting that researchers not only need to develop new standards for exposure to various pollutants and physical exertion, but also must include cultural, social, physical, and emotional contexts in future occupational health studies. Lin Nelson, Regina Kenen, and Susan Klitzman's more activist title *Turning Things Around: A Women's Occupational and Environmental Health Resource Guide* (National Women's Health Network, 1990) briefly addresses safe workplaces and restored environments within the context of the struggle for social justice and explains how to use the (U.S.) resources listed both alphabetically and geographically in the appendices.

1425. Moscucci, Ornella. *The Science of Woman: Gynaecology and Gender in England, 1800–1929.* Cambridge: Cambridge University Press, 1990. 278p. (Cambridge History of Medicine). bibliog. index. ISBN 0521327415.

In this engaging social history, Moscucci argues that many practices of gynecology are based on Enlightenment thought, which equated "man" with the brain and "woman" with reproductive organs. Using a wide range of sources, including hospital records, proceedings of medical societies, and novels, the author asserts that the number of ovarian surgeries partly increased because male gynecologists wanted to increase both their professional status and income. She compellingly considers the relationships among the advent of surgery, which helped dispel the mystery of women's bodies, social and political developments in medicine, and medical attitudes about women. Moscucci also discusses the rise of male midwives and the establishment of women's hospitals and medical societies for gynecologists and obstetricians.

Related titles include Adrian Wilson's *The Making of Man Midwifery: Childbirth in England, 1660–1770* (Harvard University Press, 1995), a thoroughly researched, illuminating study that considers social, cultural, and political issues in its analysis of the emergence of male midwives; Ann Dally's *Women under the Knife: A History of Surgery* (Routledge, 1992), a well-documented, lively account of the development of modern gynecological surgery within the framework of power imbalances between doctors and women patients; and Irvine Loudon's *Death in Childbirth:*

An International Study of Maternal Care and Maternal Mortality, 1800–1950 (Clarendon Press, 1992), an imaginative and meticulous interpretation of quantitative data from three continents that provides the framework to study the history of childbirth.

1426. Muller, Charlotte Feldman. *Health Care and Gender.* New York: Russell Sage Foundation, 1990. 258p. bibliog. indexes. ISBN 0871546108.

Muller, a health economist, presents one of the first reviews of health care and gender research, particularly within the United States, in which she effectively argues that existing health indicators do not reflect women's unmet needs, and that a market-driven system only perpetuates gender inequalities. Although not especially feminist in her analysis, the author explores gender differences in utilizing health care services, examines women's increasing need for care as they age, and discusses health insurance coverage and health care finance. Muller provides a wealth of statistical data throughout the book and concludes each chapter with a valuable list of references.

Helen Roberts, a longtime health activist in Great Britain, also deems health statistics and data sets inadequate indicators of women's health needs, yet encourages feminists to reexamine them in hope of discovering new findings, patterns, and variations for further analysis in *Women's Health Counts* (Routledge, 1990). Penny Kane uses available data from countries such as Germany, Finland, Sri Lanka, China, and Great Britain to discern trends in women's health and compare main patterns of illness and death between men and women by stage of life to provide direction for improving women's health in *Women's Health: From Womb to Tomb* (Macmillan, 1991). All of these titles suggest new ways to interpret quantitative data that can lead to more meaningful conclusions pertaining to gender and health.

1427. O'Leary, Ann, and Loretta Sweet Jemmott, eds. *Women at Risk: Issues in the Primary Prevention of AIDS.* New York: Plenum Press, 1995. 278p. (AIDS Prevention and Mental Health). bibliog. index. ISBN 0306450410.

Aimed at practitioners yet accessible to laypersons, this collection features chapters whose authors consider socioeconomic status, gender roles, race, and ethnicity as factors that increase women's risk of contracting AIDS. Some contributors explore prevention strategies and issues pertaining to adolescent girls, Latinas, lesbians, African American women, drug users, and sex workers, while others feature examinations of the relationship between AIDS and other sexually transmitted diseases, as well as child sexual abuse. Unlike many edited volumes, this work provides a cohesive political, proactive, woman-centered agenda arguing for culturally specific interventions that consider language, religion, poverty, race, and ethnicity. Contributors to *Women and AIDS: Coping and Care* (Plenum Press, 1996), also edited by O'Leary and Jemmott, focus on the complex medical, psychological, and social dilemmas unique to HIV-positive women and review research on women's coping, intervention, and access issues.

One of the first books to analyze psychology's role in the HIV/AIDS epidemic, editor Corinne Squier's *Women and AIDS: Psychological Perspectives* (Sage, 1993), asserts that practitioners must challenge the institutionalized racism, sexism, and classism inherent in public health systems, which particularly ignore the needs of poor and minority women with AIDS. Contributors to *Until the Cure: Caring for Women with HIV* (Yale University Press, 1993), edited by Ann Kurth, examine ethical and legal issues, reproductive counseling, gynecological issues, and global epidemiology. They also make specific suggestions for improving programs and policies.

1428. Parrott, Roxanne Louiselle, and Celeste Michelle Condit, eds. *Evaluating Women's Health Care Messages: A Resource Book.* Thousand Oaks, CA: Sage, 1996. 445p. bibliog. index. ISBN 076190056X; 0761900578pa.

Using a broad communication framework, the authors of the chapters featured in this collection comprehensively and systematically review medical, social science, and public health messages about women's health, especially reproduction. More than thirty contributors, employing a variety of perspectives and methodologies, examine topics such as legal abortion, prenatal care, breast cancer, reproductive technologies, menstrual health, AIDS, and smoking, alcohol, and drug consumption during pregnancy. The editors devote two chapters to each topic. The first presents a literature review of medical and social science research on the subject, while the second includes critical analysis of messages about the topic in mass media, such as news magazines, newspapers, and television movies. This thorough approach reveals disparities between research results about women's health and how the media present information about these results. The chapters share these assumptions: health care is contested; the media usually identify health care providers as "right"; and some messages carry more weight than others. Contributors also delineate the influential roles that political and historical agendas play in women's health issues and priorities. This book makes key contributions to public health, communication studies, and women's studies.

1429. Roberts, Joan I., and Thetis M. Group. *Feminism and Nursing: An Historical Perspective on Power, Status, and Political Activism in the Nursing Profession*. Westport, CT: Praeger, 1995. 369p. bibliog. index. ISBN 0275949168; 0275951200pa.

In the first of several interrelated texts analyzing the effects of gender stratification on the nursing profession, Roberts and Group examine the extent of nurses' awareness of and reactions to gender issues within the field over time. The authors analyze the historical writings of nurses and others interested in professional health care from the United States, Canada, Great Britain, and other English-speaking countries. They begin with the perspectives of Florence Nightingale, commonly acknowledged as the founder of modern nursing, and proceed into the 1990s, supplementing analysis with contextual information. The authors consider various topics, such as prejudice and racism within nursing and medicine, the complex issues that affect nursing during war, both positive and negative reactions toward suffrage, political activism and women's rights, and public health reforms initiated by nurses.

Sandra Beth Lewenson also explores the historical interrelations between nursing and women's rights in *Taking Charge: Nursing, Suffrage, and Feminism in America, 1873–1920* (Garland, 1993), solely focusing on the United States. She argues that women's struggle for the ballot played a huge role in nurses' fight for professional autonomy and control of nursing education and practice. She traces the activities of the four national nursing societies, including the National Association of Colored Nurses, that were established between 1893 and 1912 to fight the prevailing paternalistic ideology that prevented nurses from controlling their education, working conditions, and professional standing. This title won the Lavinia L. Dock Award for Historical Scholarship and Research in Nursing from the American Association for the History of Nursing.

1430. Ruzek, Sheryl Burt, Virginia L. Oleson, and Adele E. Clarke. *Women's Health: Complexities and Differences*. Columbus: Ohio State University Press, 1997. 689p. (Women and Health). bibliog. index. ISBN 0814207049; 0814207057pa.

The essays featured in this work use feminist social science frameworks, include empirical information, and share a common theme: social conditions produce women's health and influence health practices. Contributors insist that researchers must consider differences in race, class, gender, ethnicity, language, culture, and religion in order to develop a truly complex, holistic model for women's health care. Several contributors examine disability, age, cultural values, chronic stressors, and power as experienced by lesbians, women of color, and rural women. This cohesive, integrated collection of extensively referenced essays, aimed at a broad audience, would serve as an excellent text.

Ruzek, Olesen, and Clarke edited the groundbreaking titles *Teaching Materials on Women, Health, and Healing* and *Syllabi Set on Women, Health, and Healing: Fourteen Courses*, which the Women, Health, and Healing Program in the Department of Social and Behavioral Sciences at the University of California at San Francisco published in 1986. Olesen and Clarke also organized a conference to create new theories about and celebrate more than twenty years in women's health that resulted in the publication of *Revisioning Women, Health, and Healing: Feminist, Cultural, and Technoscience Perspectives* (Routledge, 1998). Contributors consider ethnicity, race, gender, culture, and class in their examination of topics such as midlife health, HIV/AIDS, and reproductive technologies. The chapters ultimately support the need for new knowledge with a constantly shifting base to enable more complex, nuanced understandings of the myriad factors that affect women's health.

1431. Sargent, Carolyn F., and Caroline B. Bretell, eds. *Gender and Health: An International Perspective*. Upper Saddle River, NJ: Prentice Hall, 1996. 370p. bibliog. ISBN 0130794279.

Sargent and Bretell include interdisciplinary essays that examine how gender roles and ideologies affect health care systems, statuses, and policies in this work. The contributors, mostly anthropologists who conduct cross-cultural studies, all adhere to the premise that broad political, social, and economic forces construct and influence biological health and medicine. They thus examine diverse topics such as ethics, AIDS, political violence, medical/scientific language's role in perpetuating oppressive health care, and the effects of gender, race, ethnicity, and class on health and care.

Another anthropologically based title, *Women and Health: Cross-Cultural Perspectives* (Bergin & Garvey, 1988), edited by Patricia Whelehan and others, presents case studies conducted in various countries, including Vietnam, Turkey, and Ecuador, that reveal women's adaptability and flexibility in resolving health problems, many of which result from a lack of economic resources, high stress levels, and sex-role conflicts. *The Health of Women: A Global Perspective* (Westview Press, 1993), edited by Marge Koblinsky, Judith Timyan, and Jill Gay, includes analyses of widespread poverty, malnutrition, poor-quality care, and discriminatory practices that contribute to women's generally poor care around the world. It features practical, concrete policy suggestions for improvements as well as an arresting section of photographs.

1432. Smith, Susan L. *Sick and Tired of Being Sick and Tired: Black Women's Health Activism in America, 1890–1950*. Philadelphia: University of Pennsylvania Press, 1995. (Studies in Health, Illness, and Caregiving). 247p. bibliog. index. ISBN 0812232372; 0812214498pa.

In the first book-length effort to examine health reforms initiated by African American women, Smith contends that black clubwomen's voluntary efforts formed the basis of the black health movement. She traces the origins of the Tuskegee Institute, established in 1881, and the Office of Negro Health Work, established in 1932 within the U.S. Public Health Service, and analyzes specific programs, such as the infamous Tuskegee syphilis experiment, the work of black midwives in rural Mississippi, and the Alpha Kappa Alpha (Sorority) Mississippi Health Project. This well-documented study, which includes an extensive bibliography and notes, significantly contributes to U.S. health care history, women's history, and African American history.

The more recent health activism of Byllye Avery, founder of the National Black Women's Health Project, inspired editor Linda Villarosa's practical and clearly written *Body and Soul: The*

Black Women's Guide to Physical Health and Emotional Well-Being (HarperCollins, 1994). Contributors sensitively outline specific strategies for dealing with a frequently hostile health care system and encourage women to take charge of and improve their overall health by creating healthy lifestyles for themselves and their families. Pertinent organizations, books, and other useful resources are listed at the end of each chapter. Finally, *¡Salud! A Latina's Guide to Total Health* (HarperCollins, 1997), by Jane L. Delgado and the National Hispanic Women's Health Initiative, similarly addresses physical, emotional, spiritual, and cultural aspects of Latina health and provides lists of pertinent books, hot lines, and organizations.

1433. Stark, Evan, and Anne Flitcraft. *Women at Risk: Domestic Violence and Women's Health*. Thousand Oaks, CA: Sage, 1996. 264p. bibliog. indexes. ISBN 0803970404; 0803970412pa.

Stark and Flitcraft, highly regarded scholars who study violence against women, combine scholarship and advocacy in this important book, which represents the result of twenty years of collaborative research. The authors reveal the extent of the connection between violence and female injury, argue that violence contributes to a range of family and women's health problems (suicide, homicide, child abuse, and rape), contend that medical responses to battering are unwittingly coercive, inappropriate, and part of the problem, and propose interventions that blend a reformulated trauma theory with empowerment strategies in order to greatly improve services for battered women. Stark and Flitcraft explore social factors, education, age, marital status, and race throughout their analysis.

Editor Carolyn M. Sampselle reviews the anthropological, legal, psychological, and nursing literature pertaining to violence against women, identifies themes and agendas for future nursing research, and suggests ways that undergraduate and graduate nursing programs can incorporate the topic into the curriculum in *Violence against Women: Nursing Research, Education, and Practice Issues* (Hemisphere Publishing, 1992). Sampselle notably includes international context and analysis to examine race and ethnicity and makes recommendations for improving and promoting nursing intervention.

1434. Stewart, Mary White. *Silicone Spills: Breast Implants on Trial*. Westport, CT: Praeger, 1998. 223p. bibliog. index. ISBN 0275963594.

Sociologist Mary White Stewart scrutinized court documents, examined legal and medical articles, conducted interviews with jurors and women with implants, analyzed questionnaires, and attended trials in this thorough investigation of the silicone breast implant controversy. She traces the development of implants and the role of the Food and Drug Administration within the context of cultural and social beliefs in the United States, considering the medicalization and objectification of women's bodies, the American obsession with appearance, and stereotypes about women and health. She concludes that based on the company's own research, representatives of Dow Corning knew not only that silicone was an unstable substance that could migrate through the body, but also that implants often ruptured. Yet the company used its economic and political clout to market implants anyway.

Stewart's conclusions starkly contrast with those of physician Marcia Angell, who argues that scientific evidence does not connect implants with later medical problems in *Science on Trial: The Clash of Medical Evidence and the Law in the Breast Implant Case* (Norton, 1996). Although Angell analyzes the interconnections among media coverage, public opinion, law, politics, and scientific research, she mars her account with superficial, simplistic, and even misleading interpretations of feminist and other critiques of science. Works that feature personal perspectives on the subject include John A. Byrne's *Informed Consent: Inside the Silicone Breast Implant Crisis*

(McGraw-Hill, 1996), which presents a clear chronology of the controversy, and medical sociologist Susan M. Zimmerman's *Silicone Survivors: Women's Experience with Breast Implants* (Temple University Press, 1998), which is based on interviews with forty women who discuss their motivations for and reactions to breast implant surgery.

1435. Weisman, Carol S. *Women's Health Care: Activist Traditions and Institutional Change*. Baltimore: Johns Hopkins University Press, 1998. 300p. bibliog. index. ISBN 0801858259; 0801858267pa.

Weisman, a highly regarded sociologist and health services researcher who sees women's health as a national public issue, looks at data from the 1993 Commonwealth Fund Survey of Women's Health, her own research, and research with colleagues to analyze women's experiences with health and health care institutions. First she presents theoretical perspectives and concepts underpinning the project, such as gender as a cause of health and illness, the body and health as social constructions, and the cultural significance of women's health in the United States. Weisman then provides social and historical contexts for what she calls "waves in a women's health megamovement" (p. 2) with a historical overview of five specific policy-making campaigns that took place in the nineteenth and twentieth centuries. She examines women's inequitable access to health care in the 1990s, explores benefits and costs of gender-segregated health care for women, and discusses ways to incorporate women's concerns into health care policy. Weisman buttresses her clearly written, thoughtful analysis of the issues surrounding health services and policy making with informative notes and an extensive bibliography. Looking more closely at race and ethnicity, however, would have strengthened her work.

Health researchers who contributed to *Women's Health: The Commonwealth Fund Survey* (Johns Hopkins University Press, 1996), edited by Marilyn M. Falik and Karen Scott Collins, used a multidisciplinary approach to reexamine the data of the Commonwealth Fund Survey. Contributors clearly explain the use of health care services, midlife and older women, physician-patient communication, Latinas, African American women, poverty, depression, violence, employment, and insurance. The editors include useful charts and figures. These titles, which significantly contribute to the understanding of social aspects of women's health care in the United States, both belong in women's studies and health collections.

1436. White, Jocelyn, and Marissa C. Martinez, eds. *The Lesbian Health Book: Caring for Ourselves*. Seattle: Seal Press, 1997. 397p. bibliog. index. ISBN 1878067311.

Physician Jocelyn White and science writer Marissa C. Martinez combine information, essays, personal stories, guidelines, and resources aimed at empowering lesbians to improve their health and health care. In the first section they review the history of the lesbian health movement within the context of the women's health movement and discuss the rampant homophobia of some providers, which often prevents lesbians from seeking care. The authors then present stories of diverse lesbians of varying ages, races, and economic backgrounds about topics such as breast reduction surgery, HIV/AIDS, pregnancy, chronic pain/illness, menopause, and sexuality. The tragic, angry, and compassionate stories provide valuable insight into dealing with medical systems and health care providers. In the final section the authors discuss the need for better research paradigms, improved access to medical care, coalition building, and other topics. The book concludes with an extensive listing of organizations, hot lines, Web sites, books, newsletters, support groups, and other resources.

Jocelyn White contributed to editor Christy Ponticelli's *Gateways to Improving Lesbian Health and Health Care: Opening Doors* (Haworth Press, 1998), which was simultaneously published as a special issue of *Journal of Lesbian Studies* (vol. 2, no. 1, 1998). This work features authors who delve into the experiences and lives of lesbian participants, particularly lesbians of color, to examine sexual abuse, domestic violence, aging, communication, isolation, and other topics in ten studies. An earlier collection, *Lesbian Health: What Are the Issues?* (Taylor & Francis, 1993), edited by Phyllis Noerager Stern, began as a special issue of the journal *Health Care for Women International* (vol. 13, no. 2, 1992). It became a book after the issue consistently sold out. Contributors, who mostly hail from the United States, address subjects such as prejudice, mistreatment, childbearing, alcohol abuse, and recovery. Finally, the *Lesbian Health Bibliography* (National Center for Lesbian Rights, 1994; 2nd ed., 1995), compiled by Liza Rankow, belongs in all academic libraries. Tamsin Wilton's *Good for You: A Handbook on Lesbian Health* (Cassell, 1997) is similar to the classic *Alive and Well: A Lesbian Health Guide* (Crossing Press, 1988), edited by Cuca Hepburn and Bonnie Gutierrez. Although based in England, Wilton discusses general topics of interest to lesbians and includes resource listings for the United States and Europe as well as Great Britain.

1437. Wolf, Susan M., ed. *Feminism and Bioethics: Beyond Reproduction.* New York: Oxford University Press, 1996. 398p. bibliog. index. ISBN 019508568X; 01905095561.

Contributors to this excellent volume explore the connections among gender, feminist analysis, and bioethics pertaining to topics such as euthanasia, medical research, patient-physician relationships, HIV/AIDS, genetics, and health care allocation. They also examine how these issues affect women of color, particularly African American women, in several chapters. Each chapter concludes with extensive and informative notes.

Another fine title, *Feminist Perspectives in Medical Ethics* (Indiana University Press, 1992), edited by Helen Bequaert Holmes and Laura M. Purdy, features articles originally published in two special issues of *Hypatia: A Journal of Feminist Philosophy*, along with some newly commissioned pieces that delve into various topics, such as caring in health care, women in medical research, HIV/AIDS, disability, surrogacy, and in vitro fertilization (IVF). Rosemarie Tong, a highly regarded feminist philosopher, cogently reviews nonfeminist and feminist theoretical approaches to ethics and bioethics in *Feminist Approaches to Bioethics* (Westview Press, 1997). Tong analyzes familiar reproductive issues that affect both sexes, including contraception, sterilization, abortion, IVF, artificial insemination, surrogacy, and genetic screening. Susan Sherwin documents researchers' propensity to discount and ignore women's interests within the field of bioethics and constructs an excellent bibliography covering these issues in *No Longer Patient: Feminist Ethics and Health Care* (Temple University Press, 1992).

1438. Wolinsky, Ira, and Dorothy Klimis-Tavantzis, eds. *Nutritional Concerns of Women.* Boca Raton, FL: CRC Press, 1996. 335p. (Modern Nutrition). bibliog. index. ISBN 0849385024.

Using a public health perspective, contributors to this edited scholarly volume clearly write about an impressive number of topics, including osteoporosis, eating disorders, premenstrual syndrome, cancer and other diseases, athletes, older women, and pregnant women. Particularly notable subjects include nutrition, oral contraceptives, and the evaluation of weight-control programs. Each chapter contains an introduction, a summary of research, and an extensive list of references. Editors Debra A. Krummel and Penny Kris-Etherton take a life-stage, preventative approach in another fine title aimed at health professionals, *Nutrition in Women's Health* (Aspen, 1996). Although this work covers some of the same issues as the previous title, contributors also address vegetarianism, provide a detailed description of the nutrition component in the National Women's Health Initiative, and include numerous figures and tables.

Consumer-oriented titles include Elizabeth Somer's *Nutrition for Women: The Complete*

Guide (Henry Holt, 1993), which contains accessible, comprehensive information and an excellent glossary and list of references, and Jaime Ruud's *Nutrition and the Female Athlete* (CRC Press, 1996), a well-organized, clearly written work that covers physiological, psychological, and environmental issues, including eating disorders. *A New Agenda for Women's Health and Nutrition* (World Bank, 1994), by Anne Tinker and others, features a rare international assessment that claims that improving women's health affects future generations. This work includes recommendations aimed at international agencies and middle- and lower-income countries to initiate or improve women's health and nutrition programs.

1439. Worchester, Nancy, and Marianne H. Whatley, eds. *Women's Health: Readings on Social, Economic, and Political Issues.* 2nd ed. Dubuque, IA: Kendall/Hunt, 1994. bibliog. ISBN 0840396910.

In this work, compiled as a supplementary textbook for an introductory feminism and health course at the University of Wisconsin at Madison, Worchester and Whatley reprint both classic and recent, popular and scholarly short readings that address how political and social issues, such as racism, heterosexism, and class, affect women's health services. Each section includes an introductory overview of the topic and concludes with worksheets designed to encourage thought, discussion, and analysis. Revisions of the title reflect changing developments in the field and new concerns in women's health care.

Researchers should use this book in conjunction with the Boston Women's Health Book Collective's *The New Our Bodies, Ourselves: A Book by and for Women* (updated and expanded for the 1990s, Simon & Schuster, 1992), which adds resources and information about AIDS, female condoms, and conditions not covered in previous editions; Ethel Sloane's *Biology of Women* (3rd ed., Delmar, 1993), which explores cultural and sociological factors that influence female health throughout life and reviews research concerning AIDS, premenstrual syndrome, hormone therapy, reproductive technologies, and gender differences in brain anatomy; and the groundbreaking *The Black Women's Health Book: Speaking for Ourselves* (Seal, 1990; exp. ed., 1994), edited by Evelyn C. White, which effectively and powerfully combines personal and analytical writings by black women for black women. Libraries should also obtain the Boston Women's Health Book Collective's *Our Bodies, Ourselves for the New Century* newly-revised and updated edition (Simon & Schuster, 1998), which adds information about global women's health issues and health resources for women.

Reproductive Issues

1440. Adams, Alice E. *Reproducing the Womb: Images of Childbirth in Science, Feminist Theory, and Literature.* Ithaca, NY: Cornell University Press, 1994. 267p. bibliog. index. ISBN 0801429455; 0801481619pa.

Drawing on psychoanalytic and literary theory, women's poetry and fiction, medical writings, feminist theories of motherhood, and feminist speculative fiction, Adams delves into an analysis of discursive and visual representations of the American birth process. She explores tensions that occur when a society highly values individualism while simultaneously looking upon individual pregnant women as nonparticipants. Adams asserts that visual birth technologies separate the fetus from the mother's body, giving the fetus subjectivity via medical discourse, and appeals to feminist theory to restore women's subjectivity, despite its complexity.

Barbara Duden uses a wide array of sources to investigate cultural beliefs about the unborn in *Disembodying Women: Perspectives on Pregnancy and the Unborn* (Harvard University Press,

1993). She traces graphic representations of pregnant women's bodies from seventeenth- and eighteenth-century woodcuts and drawings to twentieth-century ultrasounds to demonstrate how people historically have looked upon the human fetus as a manufactured construct of modern society. She argues that visual technology, media reports, and conservative discourse not only constructed the maternal body as dangerous to the fetus, but also gave the fetus "a life" with separate rights. Susan Merrill Squier examines British scientific memoirs, popular science writings, and literature to illuminate the historical interconnections between literature and biology in *Babies in Bottles: Twentieth-Century Visions of Reproductive Technology* (Rutgers University Press, 1994). She argues that advances in visual technology helped make a baby in a bottle the most common image of modern reproduction. Although Squier may incorporate too much theory, she effectively reveals how reproductive images play a large role in shaping political, cultural, and social constructions of pregnancy, childbirth, and motherhood. Adams and Squier provide extensive bibliographies and informative notes in their works.

1441. Borst, Charlotte G. *Catching Babies: The Professionalization of Childbirth, 1870–1920*. Cambridge, MA: Harvard University Press, 1995. 254p. bibliog. index. ISBN 0674102622.

Borst examines the replacement of female midwives and home birth with male physicians and hospital birth in four representative counties in Wisconsin in this fascinating, detailed study. She creatively uses statistical data and information culled from birth certificates, midwife and physician licenses, city directories, and census data to analyze trends in the childbirth practices of midwives and physicians within the context of their specific communities. Like previous scholars, Borst determines that the professionalization of medicine played a major role in the decline of midwifery. Yet she also asserts that gender, class, ethnic, and cultural factors greatly influenced women's childbirth decisions. Informative notes and an appendix that addresses inconsistencies between data sets increase the value of this work.

Anthropologist Gertrude Jacinta Fraser provides an important ethnographic analysis of the decline of midwifery in Green County, Virginia, between 1900 and 1950 in *African American Midwifery in the South* (Harvard University Press, 1998). Fraser uses historical material to trace how public health initiatives, embedded in race and class assumptions, gradually changed birth from a local, personal, and spiritual event that midwives performed to an impersonal, standardized, bureaucratic process that occurs in a hospital. The final section, based on nearly 100 interviews with retired midwives, women who used them, and other members of the community, explores African American interpretations of the changes in birth practices. Fraser's findings parallel Debra Anne Susie's in her earlier study *In the Way of Our Grandmothers: A Cultural View of Twentieth-Century Midwifery in Florida* (University of Georgia Press, 1988), based on interviews with African American midwives, their descendants, and women attended by midwives. In *Granny Midwives and Black Women Writers: Double-Dutched Readings* (Routledge, 1996), Valerie Lee uses double-Dutch jump roping as a metaphor to describe the "dual cultural performances" (p. 3) of historical granny midwives in conjunction with literary depictions of them in the works of Toni Morrison, Gloria Naylor, and other African American women writers.

1442. Brodie, Janet Farrell. *Contraception and Abortion in Nineteenth-Century America*. Ithaca, NY: Cornell University Press, 1994. 373p. bibliog. index. ISBN 0801428491.

Brodie argues that fertility declined during the nineteenth century due to the knowledge of and access to birth control, rather than abstinence. She bases her argument on the wealth of freely available information about methods and commercial products for birth control and abortion—legal if performed before quickening, which encompassed the first trimester—in books, medical literature, pamphlets, druggist catalogs, marriage and advice literature, letters, and diaries. Brodie, who limits her study to the white middle class, finds that by 1870, social purity proponents, upset by changing relationships between races, sexes, and classes, and physicians, anxious to eliminate irregular practitioners, pushed for laws making birth-control and abortion illegal. She provides extensive notes, numerous illustrations, and a selected bibliography of birth-control literature published between 1830 and 1880 in this engaging and thoroughly researched work.

John M. Riddle, a classics scholar, provides a broader historical perspective of abortion and contraception in *Contraception and Abortion from the Ancient World to the Renaissance* (Harvard University Press, 1992), in which he posits that women from a wide variety of cultures, beginning in ancient Egypt, had access to effective recipes for controlling fertility. In *Eve's Herbs: A History of Contraception and Abortion in the West* (Harvard University Press, 1997), Riddle suggests that information about abortifacients became coded and eventually lost due to legal and theological definitions of the fetus as a person and the persecution of witches, who often served as healers. Like Brodie, Riddle uses an impressive range of sources, providing insight into connections between both historical and twentieth-century forces that attempt to keep contraceptives either unavailable and/or illegal.

1443. Callahan, Joan C., ed. *Reproduction, Ethics, and the Law: Feminist Perspectives.* Bloomington: Indiana University Press, 1995. 427p. bibliog. index. ISBN 0253329388; 025320996Xpa.

Contributors of the chapters in this collection examine issues connected with reproductive technologies, such as frozen embryos, gestational maternity contracts, and prenatal health, in terms of the ethics and legalities pertaining to their appropriate use. They provide both scientific and anecdotal information for each topic, discuss key court decisions, explore a variety of feminist stances, and include lengthy notes and references. This thought-provoking collection reveals how reproductive policies and practices produce very different consequences for men and women.

Cheryl L. Meyer reaches the same conclusion in *The Wandering Uterus: Politics and the Reproductive Rights of Women* (New York University Press, 1997). She cogently discusses seemingly divergent reproductive issues, including abortion, infertility, surrogacy, birth, hysterectomies, the status of the fetus, and workplace hazards, and exposes many common elements among the issues by examining their policies and practices from legal, political, medical, and psychoanalytical perspectives, allowing her to point out the sometimes highly different impact of each issue on women compared to men. Both titles are well researched and compelling; however, more race and class analysis would have made them more complete.

1444. Cecil, Roseanne, ed. *The Anthropology of Pregnancy Loss: Comparative Studies in Miscarriage, Stillbirth, and Neo-natal Death.* Washington, DC: Berg, 1996. 226p. bibliog. index. ISBN 1859731201; 1859731252pa.

Cecil provides ethnographic examinations of pregnancy loss in countries such as Jamaica, India, Tanzania, Cameroon, and New Guinea, which she supplements with historical accounts in eighteenth-century England and Ireland in this collection, one of the first to explore pregnancy loss in various cultures. The well-written chapters reveal dramatic differences in beliefs about and definitions of pregnancy and life that shape maternal feelings of attachment and loss. This work ultimately serves as a reminder that grief is a psychosocial process with existential, spiritual, and religious components that vary according to geographic location, time period, and culture.

Claudia Malacrida crafted her excellent, compassionate work *Mourning the Dreams: How Parents Can Create Meaning from Miscarriage, Stillbirth, and Early Infant Death* (Qual Institute, 1998) for men and women in Western societies. She reveals the complex social, psychological, emotional, and physical aspects involved in grieving this kind of loss via gathering qualitative data through participant observation and interviews with parents who experienced perinatal loss, as well as their supporters. Malacrida uses the complicated mourning theoretical framework that Therese Rando developed to conceptualize the interrelated processes and buttress her argument for holistic care. This work, which is very accessible to lay readers, should benefit counselors and other professionals.

1445. Goer, Henci. *Obstetric Myths versus Research Realities: A Guide to Medical Literature.* Westport, CT: Bergin & Garvey, 1995. 385p. bibliog. index. ISBN 0897894278.

Goer, a childbirth educator and doula, or birth partner, examines medical research pertaining to childbirth interventions in hospitals to demonstrate that medical research does not support these widespread technological practices. She summarizes different types of medical studies, defines how to evaluate them, and provides basic statistical concepts in her first, highly informative chapter. She then examines birth technologies, including fetal monitoring, episiotomies, and epidurals, as well as birth alternatives, such as midwifery, home birth, and birthing centers. Goer writes in clear prose, uses the same format for each chapter, succinctly analyzes mainstream beliefs, particularly their misconceptions, highlights important points culled from the research, and lists references. In the conclusion, she presents a theory based on anthropologist Robbie E. Davis-Floyd's *Birth as an American Right of Passage* (University of California Press, 1992), in which she views birth procedures as a series of cultural rituals.

Marsden Wagner, senior advisor for the World Health Organization (WHO), uses a mass of statistics and other information from three WHO-sponsored conferences to provide a rare international assessment of the use of birth technologies in *Pursuing the Birth Machine: The Search for Appropriate Birth Technology* (ACE Graphics, 1994). Not only do Goer and Wagner address many of the same issues, but Wagner's data also reinforce Goer's findings that researchers have not adequately tested birth technologies; doctors often inappropriately use them; and technological interventions dehumanize the birth process. The authors also suggest that midwives should oversee routine births, and that social and psychological support, rather than routine technological intervention, creates optimal conditions for both women and babies.

1446. Hartouni, Valerie. *Cultural Conceptions: On Reproductive Technologies and the Remaking of Life.* Minneapolis: University of Minnesota Press, 1997. 175p. bibliog. index. notes. ISBN 0816626235.

Using public controversies such as the Baby M and Anna Johnson court cases, Hartouni lucidly examines the images and language used in medical, legal, scientific, and popular discourses pertaining to reproductive relationships. In her analysis of abortion, surrogacy, fetal monitoring, Norplant, genetics, and cloning, the author discusses the effects of two disheartening trends: racist public policy and the belief in the fetus as a separate entity. She argues that these technologies not only confuse the meanings of the female body, but reinforce existing patriarchal power structures as well.

Sarah Franklin, an anthropologist based in England, uses a historical overview of the anthropological "virgin birth" controversy to argue that the biological model makes myriad cultural assumptions about concepts such as kinship, parenthood, "truth," and empiricism in *Embodied Progress: A Cultural Account of Assisted Conception* (Routledge, 1997). Franklin, who optimistically asserts that opposing discourse serves an important purpose within the reproductive rights movement, also examines how popular media present reproductive technologies, women in central England who sought out assisted conception technologies, parliamentary debates, and social scientists.

Journalist José Van Dyck uses texts from medicine, journalism, and fiction to analyze public debates about reproductive technologies in *Manufacturing Babies and Public Consent* (New York University Press, 1995). She points out that accounts of seemingly isolated uses of reproductive technology obscure its relationship to other methods of reproductive control. She also persuasively reveals how science, news media, and other cultural sources establish authority by borrowing discursive elements from each other, thereby enabling them to create modified meanings of procreation, sexuality, fertility, and motherhood, which in turn influences the public to accept these technologies.

1447. Leavitt, Judith Walzer. *Brought to Bed: Childbearing in America, 1750 to 1950.* New York: Oxford University Press, 1986. 284p. bibliog. index. ISBN 0195038436; 0195056906pa.

Leavitt, a historian, presents a well-documented study of the transition of childbirth from a social, woman-centered event that took place at home to a medical, male-centered event that occurred in a hospital. She chronologically and contextually examines how cultural beliefs, practices, ideologies, and factors such as geographic mobility, urbanization, professionalization, and views toward science influenced the birth experience. She uses diaries, letters, and other autobiographical writings not only to reveal women's deep fear of pain and possible death, but also to demonstrate their agency in negotiating procedures with physicians. Leavitt shows that by the 1920s, many women saw anesthesia as a means to freedom from pain and preferred the germ-free environments of hospitals.

Editor Pamela S. Eakins thoroughly reviews the evolution of the practice of obstetrics in *The American Way of Birth* (Temple University Press, 1986). Contributors examine a variety of important childbirth issues, including the renewed interest in midwifery, the relationship between women and their doctors, the increasing rate of caesarean births, and the effects of social class, race, and ethnicity on birth experiences. Several contributors discuss the importance of cultural, religious, and political influences reflected in laws and professional codes.

1448. Lublin, Nancy. *Pandora's Box: Feminism Confronts Reproductive Technology.* Lanham, MD: Rowman & Littlefield, 1998. 187p. bibliog. index. ISBN 0847686361; 084768637Xpa.

Lublin, an abortion and reproductive rights activist, urges feminists not only to develop a flexible, comprehensive theoretical framework that they can apply to a broad range of present and future reproductive technologies, but also to promote equitable policies in the political and legal arenas. Lublin carefully and lucidly reviews and critiques the extensive feminist literature on reproductive rights, which reflects a variety of positive, negative, and privacy-based perspectives. She extracts what she considers the strengths from each stance to develop materialist praxis feminism, uniting theory with practice, and addresses the situations of diverse groups of women in the United States. The author concludes each chapter with informative notes and supplies a selective, yet wide-ranging bibliography.

Like Lublin, Robert H. Blank argues for the development of flexible, cohesive policies for "technically mediated reproduction" (p. 11), or TMR, in *Regulating Reproduction* (Columbia University Press, 1990). He believes that unregulated uses of TMR can change concepts about family, motherhood, fatherhood, and reproduction, which could destabilize society. Blank reviews specific TMRs, identifying ethical, biological, social, and political issues of each from a variety of feminist and various other perspectives. Most important, he recognizes that economics affect equity and access, which could lead to unfair and even dangerous practices and policies.

1449. Marsh, Margaret S., and Wanda Ronner. *The Empty Cradle: Infertility in America from Colonial Times to the Present.* Baltimore: Johns Hopkins University Press, 1996. 326p. (Henry E. Sigerist Series in the History of Medicine). bibliog. index. ISBN 0801852285.

Using an impressive array of sources that include memoirs, patient records, medical texts, letters, popular magazines, and scholarly journals, historian Marsh and her sister, gynecologist and obstetrician Ronner, provide a fascinating overview of infertility treatment. By examining changing ideas about family, sex roles, parenthood, and community via blending both historical and medical information, the authors discover that women sometimes very aggressively pursue even the most intrusive medical intervention. Marsh and Ronner debunk common myths, such as the "infertility epidemic" of the 1980s and 1990s (in reality, the infertility rate tottered between 10 to 13 percent for most of the twentieth century). They also discredit the idea that delayed pregnancy causes infertility (twenty- to twenty-four-year-olds are the only age group with an increased rate) and the notion that infertility affects mostly white middle-class women (poor, working-class women represent the highest rate). The authors clearly define medical and technical terms, sympathetically and fairly present controversies, and include extensive, informative notes.

Nurse Margarete Sandelowski looks at historical and twentieth-century beliefs about infertility in *With Child in Mind: Studies of the Personal Encounter with Infertility* (University of Pennsylvania Press, 1993). She applies a feminist framework to statistical and technological research, social contextual analysis, and personal stories of black and white lower- and middle-income women and couples facing infertility. Sandelowski draws from literature to develop a philosophical framework aimed at infertility practitioners; addresses problematic dichotomies, such as caring versus curing and professional versus private; and considers patients' circumstances along with the broader social forces that influence them.

1450. Martin, Emily. *The Woman in the Body: A Cultural Analysis of Reproduction.* Boston: Beacon Press, 1987. 276p. bibliog. index. ISBN 0807046043.

Anthropologist Martin sets out to determine how medical metaphors for menstruation, childbirth, and menopause affected women's attitudes and behaviors about these processes in late-twentieth-century, capitalist America. In the first section, Martin presents a well-documented examination of historical and contemporary medical texts, arguing that the texts portray women's bodies as designed almost solely for producing babies. The machine metaphors that authors use in these texts reflect this belief, which helps to fragment and objectify women's bodies. The author asserts that these metaphors are socially constructed, indicating economic and cultural attitudes about gender, race, and class. Martin explores women's own perceptions of their bodies, based on interviews with 165 women who represent diverse races and classes, in the second section. She discovers that women assign a multiplicity of meanings to their bodies and body processes that both accept and resist medical beliefs and treatment.

Robbie Pfeufer Kahn, a sociologist and contributor to editions of *Our Bodies, Ourselves*, published in the 1980s and 1990s also explores historical and contemporary medical texts for metaphors connected with childbirth in *Bearing Meaning: The Language of Birth* (University of Illinois Press, 1995). She interweaves her textual analysis with examinations of twentieth-century birth practices, counternarratives to medical stories, and her own memories of childbirth. Like Martin, Kahn finds that men have appropriated childbirth and tend to see women as reproductive systems. Yet Kahn believes counternarratives can be used as a basis for reframing childbirth in ways that can improve the experience for all parties, especially women and babies. This book won the Jessie Bernard Award of the American Sociological Association in 1997.

1451. Purdy, Laura. *Reproducing Persons: Issues in Feminist Bioethics.* Ithaca, NY: Cornell University Press, 1996. 257p. bibliog. index. ISBN 080143243X; 0801483220pa.

Purdy, a leading feminist bioethicist and scholar, reviews bioethical views of reproductive technologies, surrogacy, abortion, contract pregnancy, and choices about whether or not to have children. She defines what she considers core feminism: since society does not equally consider women's interests with those of men's, women, as a group, are worse off. Purdy protests that the resulting injustice requires immediate attention. She analyzes various rights-based proponents' arguments, including a classical bioethical theory often articulated by legal scholars such as John Robertson, author of *Children of Choice: Freedom and the New Reproductive Technologies* (Princeton University Press, 1994). Finally, Purdy considers how the marketplace, limited access, and poverty affect the many stages of the reproductive process. Purdy also edited the excellent, wide-ranging *Issues in Reproductive Technology I: An Anthology* (Garland, 1992) with Helen Bequaert Holmes.

Another highly regarded bioethics scholar, Ruth Macklin, creates a couple to explore the ethical dilemmas and difficult choices involved in treating infertility in *Surrogates and Other Mothers: The Debates over Assisted Reproduction* (Temple University Press, 1994). This effective device allows Macklin not only to present opposing views, but also to examine the complex debates on motherhood, sexuality, and power. Christine Overall posits that antifeminist and "neutral" ethical positions on subjects such as sex preselection, infertility technologies, surrogacy, and abortion effectively erase women from the reproductive process in the well-researched *Ethics and Human Reproduction: A Feminist Analysis* (Allen & Unwin, 1987). Overall draws on several feminist perspectives to develop a framework to critically examine the effects of reproductive technologies on women in this key work.

1452. Raymond, Janice G. *Women as Wombs: Reproductive Technologies and the Battle over Women's Freedom.* San Francisco: HarperSanFrancisco, 1993. 254p. bibliog. index. ISBN 0062508989; 0062508997pa.

Raymond, a founder of the Feminist International Network of Resistance to Reproductive and Genetic Engineering (FINRRAGE), presents a radical feminist stance on reproductive technologies, arguing that they "violate the integrity of a woman's body . . . [and] are a form of medical violence against women" (p. viii). In this very political work, the author effectively examines reproductive liberalism, its discussion of language, media, and marketing, and its consideration of contrasting attitudes in the so-called First and Third Worlds. Raymond's analysis of international adoption and trafficking of fetuses, organs, and children, however, proves less persuasive.

Other valuable titles that FINRRAGE members either wrote or edited include Australian feminist and social psychologist Robyn Rowland's *Living Laboratories: Women and Reproductive Technologies* (Indiana University Press, 1992); Renate Klein's *Infertility: Women Speak Out about Their Experiences of Reproductive Medicine* (Pandora Press, 1989), which documents discrepancies between media accounts of assisted conception and real experiences of international women; and editors Patricia Spallone and Deborah Lynn Steinberg's *Made to Order: The Myth of Reproductive and Genetic Progress* (Pergamon Press, 1987). Editor Michelle Stanworth collects chapters whose authors analyze the tensions created from the challenges that reproductive technologies pose for concepts of motherhood, sexuality, and family in *Reproductive Technologies: Gender, Motherhood, and Medicine* (University of Minnesota Press, 1987). Contributors look at social, political, and cultural conditions that enabled technologies to develop and articulate how reproductive technologies produce differing impacts between women and men, as well as among women of various races, ethnicities, and classes.

1453. Richter, Judith. *Vaccination against Pregnancy: Miracle or Menace?* Melbourne, Australia: Spinifex; London: Zed Books, 1996. 182p. bibliog. index. ISBN 1875559574 (Spinifex), 1856492818 (Zed); 1856492826pa.

Richter, a consumer advocate, investigates the risks and benefits of what she refers to as immuno-contraceptives, a birth-control class that advocates often inappropriately call "vaccines." Researchers tout this class of birth control as long lasting, reversible, easy to administer, and relatively inexpensive to produce. Richter critically analyzes the conceptual frameworks and practices of research studies, questions the adequacy of the human drug trials for discerning long-term effects on the health of women and subsequent children, and argues that the potential for abusing poor women of color and Third World women exponentially increases with immuno-contraceptives. She concludes by tracing several international organizations' efforts to convince population-control centers to halt this line of research. Richter includes notes at the end of each chapter, a bibliography, a glossary, and useful appendices.

Richter contributed a chapter on the same topic to *Power and Decision: The Social Control of Reproduction* (Harvard University Press, 1994), edited by Gita Sen and Rachel Snow, in which contributors consider how the social, development, religious, and state policies (often embedded in gender, race, and class biases) in different countries greatly affect women's reproductive options. A companion volume, *Population Policies Reconsidered: Health, Empowerment, and Rights* (Harvard University Press, 1994), edited by Gita Sen, Adrienne Germain, and Lincoln C. Chen, features papers that activists, academics, and program administrators with diverse backgrounds presented at the International Conference on Population and Development in Cairo in 1994. Contributors to this groundbreaking collection view women's empowerment, health, and reproductive rights as the cornerstone of new programs and place population programs within development and human rights frameworks.

1454. Rooks, Judith Pence. *Midwifery and Childbirth in America.* Philadelphia: Temple University Press, 1997. 548p. bibliog. index. ISBN 1566395658.

Rooks, a nurse-midwife, addresses public misconceptions about midwifery in America through a wealth of information in this well-documented, factual study. Although her concise, historical contextualization of midwifery is international in scope, she mostly concentrates on developments that took place in the United States between 1980 and 1994. She sensitively discusses safety, effectiveness, and training issues, examines differences between midwifery and the medical model, and compares the midwifery situation in the United States to those in other "developed" countries. In the final chapter, Rooks analyzes the state of midwifery in the 1990s and summarizes recommendations made by midwifery proponents.

Older but still relevant titles about American midwifery include Deborah A. Sullivan and Rose Weitz's *Labor Pains: Modern Midwives and Home Birth* (Yale University Press, 1988), a balanced, interdisciplinary account of midwifery in the United States during the mid-1980s; Judy Barrett Litoff's *The American Midwife Debate: A Sourcebook on Its Origins* (Greenwood Press, 1986), which features reprints of reports, articles, statistics, and other documents originally published between 1900 and 1930 that pertain to midwifery; and Ann Oakley and Susanna Houd's excellent, comprehensive summary of midwifery in European countries in *Helpers in Childbirth: Midwifery Today* (Hemisphere Publishing, 1990).

1455. Rothman, Barbara Katz. *The Tentative Pregnancy: Prenatal Diagnosis and the Future of Motherhood.* New York: Viking, 1986. 274p. bibliog. ISBN 0670808415.

Rothman provides one of the first feminist assessments of technologies for prenatal testing, based on field observations and interviews with genetic counselors and 120 pregnant women who were deciding whether or not to undergo amniocentesis. The author, who refers to pregnancies as "tentative" because some women choose to terminate their pregnancies if tests like amniocentesis reveal birth defects, argues that these tests alter pregnancy experiences of women and privilege medical "facts" over women's knowledge of their own bodies. She also raises questions about choice, medicine and pregnancy, power, and the "neutrality" of information.

Rothman contributed an essay on the topic to editors Karen H. Rothenberg and Elizabeth J. Thomson's *Women and Prenatal Testing: Facing the Challenges of Genetic Technology* (Ohio State University Press, 1994), a key collection of chapters updated from papers given at a 1991 National Institutes of Health conference that focus on the emotional impact of prenatal testing on women. The contributors, who represent disparate backgrounds, including law, disability rights, philosophy, social work, and public health, examine ethical, social, and psychological implications of the increasingly routine use of prenatal tests. Although a few chapters note access and financial issues for poor women, none feature a broader economic analysis of who benefits from testing. In *Prenatal Testing: A Sociological Perspective* (Bergin & Garvey, 1994), Aliza Kolker and B. Meredith Burke discuss 120 surveys that include thirty-one interviews with women who underwent amniocentesis or chorionic villus sampling (CVS), as well as thirty-six interviews with genetic counselors. The results provide insight into the culture of genetic counseling and societal attitudes toward abortion, disabilities, and motherhood, while the firsthand accounts highlight how prenatal testing emotionally affects women.

1456. Watkins, Elizabeth Siegel. *On the Pill: A Social History of Oral Contraceptives, 1950–1970.* Baltimore: Johns Hopkins University Press, 1998. 183p. bibliog. index. ISBN 0801858763.

Watkins succinctly reviews the historical development of the Pill and birth-control choices during the 1950s and then concentrates on positive and negative reactions to the Pill's wide availability during the 1960s and 1970s. She particularly explores the politics surrounding the Pill, especially the reactions of the government and the Planned Parenthood Association of America to critics, including Barbara Seaman, author of *A Doctor's Case against the Pill* (P.H. Wyden, 1969). Watkins, who acknowledges that the advent of the Pill changed the practice of medicine, persuasively argues that it also helped strengthen the consumer rights movement, altered women's interactions with their doctors, and prepared the way for later feminist critiques of the medical profession. This excellent work contains notes and a ten-page bibliographic essay.

Bernard Aspell provides a fairly detailed, albeit journalistic, account of the history of the Pill in *The Pill: A Biography of the Drug That Changed the World* (Random House, 1995). He features more information about the drug trials in Puerto Rico, Mexico, and Haiti than Watkins and thoroughly reviews the Catholic Church's response to the Pill. The book contains an appendix that reproduces the text of instructions for the trials developed by Gregory Pincus, who played an integral role in the "invention" of the Pill.

Self-Help and Consumer Titles

1457. Barbach, Lonnie. *The Pause: Positive Approaches to Menopause.* New York: Dutton, 1993. 256p. bibliog. index. ISBN 0525937021.

Barbach, a psychologist, concisely discusses physical and emotional aspects of menopause based on interviews with medical researchers and women. She clearly defines menopause, considers all sides of treatment controversies, such as the link between hormone replacement therapy and breast cancer, and examines both alternative and allopathic options for relief of common symptoms.

Gail Sheehy bases *Silent Passage: Menopause* (Pocket Books, 1991; revised and updated, 1995 and 1998) on interviews with medical practitioners as well as more than 100 American women who represent a variety of life circumstances. Although Sheehy considers negative and stressful aspects of menopause, she also emphasizes menopause's great potential to empower women. Susun S. Weed's *Menopausal Years the Wise Woman Way* (Ash Tree, 1992), a mixture of herbal lore, rituals, and practical advice in which she first examines the most gentle noninvasive approaches, and the fourth edition of Sadja Greenwood's classic *Menopause Naturally: Preparing for the Second Half of Life* (Volcano, 1996) consider natural therapies. *Women of the Fourteenth Moon: Writings on Menopause* (Crossing Press, 1991), edited by Dena Taylor and Amber Coverdale Sumrall, features engaging writings about the menopause experiences of several well-known writers, such as Ursula Le Guin, Brooke Medicine Eagle, and Marge Piercy. This work includes perspectives of women of color, lesbians, and working-class women.

1458. Baron-Faust, Rita. *Preventing Heart Disease: What Every Woman Should Know.* New York: Hearst Books, 1995. 280p. bibliog. index. ISBN 0688120709.

Although heart disease affects women and men in different ways, many physicians used a male model to treat women who suffered from the disease until the health initiatives of the 1990s. Baron-Faust, who worked with physicians affiliated with the New York University Medical Center Women's Health Service and Division of Cardiology, provides a practical, clearly written guide focusing on prevention strategies, risk factors (and how they differ from men's), and treatments specifically aimed at women. She supplies information about issues such as food choices and recipes that reflect cultural backgrounds, specifically targeted for African American, Asian, and Latina women. The work contains food tables, a list of useful organizations, support groups, and other resources, and a bibliography with brief annotations.

Other highly regarded titles pertaining to this topic include Marianne Legato and Carol Coleman's *The Female Heart: The Truth about Women and Coronary Artery Disease* (Simon & Schuster, 1991), which features cogent explanations of complicated tests and procedures; Morris Notelovitz and Diana Tonnessen's *The Essential Heart Book for Women* (St. Martin's Press, 1996), which the authors based upon woman-centered heart studies; and Elizabeth Ross's (with Judith Sachs) *Healing the Female Heart: A Holistic Approach to Prevention and Recovery from Heart Disease* (Pocket Books, 1996), which provides excellent advice for obtaining high-quality heart care.

1459. Doress-Worters, Paula B., and Diana Laskin Siegal. *Ourselves, Growing Older: Women Aging with Knowledge and Power.* New York: Simon & Schuster, 1987. 511p. bibliog. index. ISBN (OP); 0671644246pa.

This title, written in cooperation with the Boston Women's Health Book Collective, takes positive and empowering approaches to the physical and emotional health of midlife women. The authors cover a wide spectrum of issues, such as sexuality, birth control, cosmetic surgery, retirement, housing, specific health conditions, and dying and death. Most important, they recognize that socioeconomic inequities and race profoundly affect women's health statuses and quality of health care. The authors thoroughly update information in each chapter in the revised edition *The New Ourselves Growing Older: Women Aging with Knowledge and Power* (Simon & Schuster, 1994). Both editions contain more than sixty pages that list organizations, publications, and audiovisual resources in addition to end-of-chapter notes.

Ruth Bell and coauthors of *Our Bodies, Ourselves* and *Ourselves and Our Children*, along with members of the Teen Book Project, concentrate on puberty and beyond in the expanded third edition of *Changing Bodies, Changing Lives: A Book for Teens on Sex and Relationships* (Times Books/Random House, 1998). Contributors present both useful and reassuring information about love, sex, friendships, school problems, parents, volunteering, violence, and emotional and physical health. They supplement the text with checklists, tips, resources, poetry, cartoons, and other writings by hundreds of teens from a variety of backgrounds. The Boston Women's Health Book Collective titles belong in every academic, public, and school library.

1460. Epps, Roselyn Payne, and Susan Cobb Stewart, medical editors. *The Women's Complete Healthbook.* New York: Delacorte, 1995. 708p. bibliog. index. ISBN 0385313829.

Associated with the American Medical Women's Association (AMWA), the editors emphasize personal responsibility for disease prevention and health maintenance, provide suggestions for coping with health care systems, and feature information about body systems, including discussions about symptoms, diagnosis, and treatment, in this work. Appendices describe diagnostic tests in detail and list associations and organizations specializing in women's health.

The AMWA also supported publication of *The Women's Complete Wellness Book* (Golden Books, 1998), edited by Debra R. Judelson and Diana Dell, who supplement accessibly written text with numerous tips, checklists, symptoms, tables, illustrations, and an extensive list of resources. Another highly regarded title, *American Medical Association Complete Guide to Women's Health* (1996), edited by Kathleen Cahill Allison and Ramona I. Slupik, includes information aimed at specific age groups, from puberty on up, which the editors supplement with charts, illustrations, and a color anatomy atlas. Readers who prefer alphabetical rather than topically arranged data should consider *The Harvard Guide to Women's Health* (Harvard University Press, 1996), edited by Karen Carlson, Stephanie A. Eisenstadt, and Terra Ziporyn, which presents clear information about 300 common diseases and health-related topics, often accompanied by lists of pertinent organizations, books, videos, and Web site addresses, and the third edition of *The New A-to-Z of Women's Health: A Concise Encyclopedia* (Facts on File, 1995), edited by Christine Ammer, which includes entries for various alternative practices, prenatal testing, and gene therapy.

1461. Gladstar, Rosemary. *Herbal Healing for Women: Simple Home Remedies for Women of All Ages.* New York: Simon & Schuster, 1993. 303p. bibliog. index. ISBN 0671767674.

Gladstar, a longtime herbalist, provides a brief background on herbalism, makes practical suggestions for beginners, and devotes several chapters to the preparation of tinctures, liniments, teas, oils, pills, and syrups, which she accompanies with recipes for basic, commonly used treatments, in this primer for women's use of herbs. The next few chapters detail specific herbal remedies for conditions that correspond to three stages of women's lives: adolescence, childbearing years, and menopause. Several appendices list books, sources for herbs, newsletters and other educational sources, abortion references, formulas, and a sample health plan.

Deb Soule contributes a rare feminist, albeit somewhat essentialist, perspective to herbalism in *A Woman's Book of Herbs: The Healing Power of Natural Remedies* (Carol Publishing, 1995). She pairs easy, practical guidelines for growing and gathering herbs with detailed instructions for their proper storage and use. The book contains extensive lists of books, newsletters, organizations, sources for herbs and flower essences, and other resources. Another experienced herbalist, Susun S. Weed, introduces seven key herbs, provides recipes for both food and medicine, and includes detailed instructions for their many uses, reflecting the Wise Woman tradition of sustenance and nourishment, in *Wise Woman Herbal Healing Wise* (Ash Tree, 1989).

1462. Golub, Sharon. *Periods: From Menarche to Menopause.* Newbury Park, CA: Sage, 1992. 282p. bibliog. index. ISBN 0803942052; 0803942060pa.

Golub, a psychologist who sees menstruation as a normal process, presents a solid and systematic assessment of social science, biological, and medical research on menstruation in this thorough, well-conceived book. She not only features practical advice for relieving discomfort in her discussion of physical, emotional, and experiential aspects of periods, but also explores controversial topics, such as premenstrual syndrome and hormone replacement therapy. Golub briefly analyzes cross-cultural and religious traditions, carefully debunking harmful myths and stereotypes that often influence how girls and women feel about themselves, and includes a detailed table of contents and index.

Excellent consumer-oriented works that address specific aspects of menstruation include Susan M. Lark's *PMS Premenstrual Self-Help Book: A Woman's Guide to Feeling Good All Month* (4th ed., Celestial Arts, 1997) and *The Endometriosis Sourcebook* (Contemporary Books, 1995) by Mary Lou Ballweg and the Endometriosis Association. Lark, a physician, uses clinical work, personal experiences, and medical information to encourage women to make simple lifestyle changes that would help minimize discomfort caused by the imbalances in metabolism connected with PMS. She provides detailed guidelines, meal plans, recipes, and exercises that incorporate yoga and acupressure massage. Ballweg presents balanced discussions that address conflicting opinions and controversies surrounding endometriosis and informs women about what to expect in terms of diagnosis and treatment.

1463. Haas, Adelaide, and Susan Puretz. *The Woman's Guide to Hysterectomy.* Berkeley, CA: Celestial Arts, 1995. 294p. bibliog. index. ISBN 0890877432pa.

Haas and Puretz discuss female biology and general gynecological health maintenance, then present straightforward, thorough technical information about symptoms and conditions that often lead doctors to recommend a hysterectomy. The authors also examine tests, diagnoses, treatment options, risks, and complications associated with surgery in this clearly written guide. Considering both emotional and physical concerns, Haas and Puretz provide practical suggestions regarding surgery preparation and recovery for women facing a hysterectomy and include information about hormone replacement therapy, sex, nutrition, and exercise to maintain health. The authors incorporate women's emotional reactions before, during, and after having hysterectomies, based on responses from questionnaires received from 1,278 women, aged twenty-one to eighty-four, in this well-researched, accessible work. Each chapter concludes with medical references, and many chapters provide lists of suggested readings. The authors supplement the text with useful tables, charts, drawings, and questions and include a glossary, a detailed medical history form, and an index.

Haas and Puretz cite *The No-Hysterectomy Option: Your Body, Your Choice* (John Wiley, 1990; rev. and updated ed., 1997) by Herbert Goldfarb, a gynecological surgeon, and Judith Greif, a nurse practitioner, which focuses on empowering women and preserving uterine function. Goldfarb and Greif explain conditions that warrant a hysterectomy and suggest useful strategies to prepare for and recuperate from surgery. The book contains lists of pertinent organizations and diets designed to promote heart and bone health.

1464. Kitzinger, Sheila. *The Complete Book of Pregnancy and Childbirth.* New York: Knopf; distributed by Random House, 1996. 432p. New rev. and expanded ed. bibliog. index. ISBN 0679450289.

An internationally known expert on childbirth and early parenthood, Kitzinger thoroughly updates her classic and comprehensive woman-centered work that covers all aspects of pregnancy, childbirth, and childbirth choices. Kitzinger uses neutral language (birth partner rather than man) and, as in previous editions, supplements the well-written text with numerous diagrams, tables, and 300 photographs in the 1996 edition.

Other woman-centered works include Gail J. Dahl's *Pregnancy and Childbirth Tips* (Innovative, 1998), which features practical advice about technological interventions, their effects, and how to avoid them, and a directory of advocacy resources, and Suzanne Arms's *Immaculate Deception II: A Fresh Look at Childbirth* 2nd Edition (Celestial Arts, 1994), which combines interviews, personal stories, striking photographs, and practical information with annotated lists of sources. Arms adds much more information about the physiological impact of emotion during childbirth and caring for children during the first few years of life in than she did in the first edition, *Immaculate Deception: A New Look at Women and Childbirth in America* (Houghton Mifflin, 1978). Works that combine clearly presented practical material about pregnancy, childbirth, and infant care with cultural information are Dennis Brown and Pamela Toussaint's *Mama's Little Baby: The Black Woman's Guide to Pregnancy, Childbirth, and Baby's First Year* (Dutton, 1997), which explores African, Caribbean, and African American heritages, and rabbi Baruch Finkelstein and midwife and nurse Michal Finkelstein's exploration of Jewish law in *B'sha'ah Tovah: The Jewish Woman's Clinical and Halachic Guide to Pregnancy and Childbirth* (Feldheim, 1993).

1465. Love, Susan M. *Dr. Susan Love's Hormone Book: Making Informed Choices about Menopause.* New York: Random House, 1997. 362p. bibliog. index. ISBN 0679449701.

Love presents thorough, comprehensive information in a clearly written, accessible style in her discussion of the pros and cons of a variety of approaches to relieving menopausal symptoms, including herbal treatments and other alternative methods. Love also questions the widespread use of hormone replacement therapy (HRT) and encourages women to consider short- and long-term lifestyle changes. The book contains a personal survey that Love designed to help women make informed decisions about their care, as well as several useful appendices that list practitioners, remedy sources, books, videos, newsletters, organizations, and other resources.

Gretchen Henkel provides an overview of menopause, concentrating on the effects of estrogen depletion, discusses the benefits and drawbacks to estrogen replacement from multiple perspectives, and includes guidelines to help consumers review, understand, and evaluate medical information in *Making the Estrogen Decision* (Lowell House, 1992), another clearly written, empowering work. Titles with pro-drug stances include Lisa Nachtigall's *Estrogen* (Harper & Row, 1986; 2nd ed., HarperPerennial, 1995), which emphasizes the importance of correctly taking estrogen, and the *American Medical Association Essential Guide to Menopause* (Pocket Books, 1998). Carol Anne Rinzler analyzes links between estrogen and cancer in *Estrogen and Breast Cancer: A Warning to Women* (Macmillan, 1993; 2nd ed., Hunter House, 1996).

1466. Love, Susan M., with Karen Lindsey. *Dr. Susan Love's Breast Book.* Reading, MA: Addison-Wesley, 1990. 445p. bibliog. index. ISBN 020109665X.

Love, a surgeon, and Lindsey present a veritable primer on breast health in which they cogently explain in detail many options beyond "slash, poison, and burn" available to women diagnosed with breast cancer. The authors supplement the text with many illustrations, tables, and resources; discuss topics such as silicone breast implants, hormone therapy, tamoxifen, and mammography; update information about new procedures and discoveries; and add a chapter about the roles that exercise and diet might play in preventing the disease in the second edition (Addison-Wesley, 1995).

Michael DeGregorio and Valerie Wiebe present a well-written, detailed comparison of the drug tamoxifen with other chemotherapies and discuss the risks, benefits, and limitations of each in *Tamoxifen and Breast Cancer: What Everyone Should Know about the Treatment of Breast Cancer* (Yale University Press, 1994). Social workers Julianne S. Oktay and Carolyn A. Walker use a developmental framework to examine how psychological and emotional responses of women with breast cancer vary according to their stage of life in *Breast Cancer in the Life Course: Women's Experiences* (Springer, 1990). Consumer titles that delve into emotional factors while featuring practical information include Renee Royak-Schaler and Beryl Lieff Benderly's *Challenging the Breast Cancer Legacy* (HarperCollins, 1992), which considers general risk factors, prevention techniques, and monitoring programs, and Kathy LaTour's *The Breast Cancer Companion* (Morrow, 1993), which includes extensive, clearly written, and practical information about the myriad medical and emotional issues facing women with breast cancer.

1467. McGinn, Kerry A., and Pamela J. Haylock. *Women's Cancers: How to Prevent Them, How to Treat Them, How to Beat Them*. Alameda, CA: Hunter House, 1992. bibliog. index. 432p. ISBN 0897931033; 0897931025pa.

Oncology nurses and cancer survivors, McGinn and Haylock provide lucid information about cancers that occur most commonly in women. They define cancer, discuss how it acts, and examine various issues surrounding treatment, such as choosing a medical team, local versus systemic treatments, alternative treatments, and dealing with family and friends. The authors specifically examine breast cancer and various gynecological cancers, supplementing their discussions with clear diagrams. McGinn and Haylock conclude with a discussion of life after cancer in which they consider the importance of body image and the effect of treatments on women's sense of femininity. The book also contains resource lists, an organization listing, bibliographies, and a glossary. The authors thoroughly update material in the second edition (Hunter House, 1998), in which they explore new treatments and controversies and add chapters on lung cancer, colorectal cancers, and cancer activism.

Another excellent, comprehensive guide, *Cancer Sourcebook for Women* (Omnigraphics, 1996), edited by Alan R. Cook and Peter D. Dresser, features individual publications that both government and private sources produced in forty-nine chapters, in which contributors accessibly present information about specific cancers, treatments, coping, prevention, and risk factors. Worthwhile titles that focus on the political and personal aspects of cancer in women include *1 in 3: Women with Cancer Confront an Epidemic* (Cleis, 1991), edited by Judith Brady, and *Cancer as a Women's Issue: Scratching the Surface* (Third Side Press, 1991) and *Confronting Cancer, Constructing Change: New Perspectives on Women and Cancer* (Third Side Press, 1993), both edited by Midge Stocker.

1468. Northrup, Christiane. *Women's Bodies, Women's Wisdom: Creating Physical and Emotional Health and Healing*. Des Plaines, IL: Bantam Doubleday Dell, 1994. 753p. bibliog. index. (OP). Completely rev. and updated ed. Bantam Books, 1998. 906p. bibliog. index. ISBN 0553110330; 0553379534pa.

Northrup, a traditionally trained obstetrician and gynecologist, realized after a health crisis that life choices and cultural contexts drastically affect women's health, and that medical training neither acknowledges nor prepares one for this. This book reflects the author's holistic view of women's medicine, which combines conventional, nutritional, and alternative approaches, and her belief that women's intuition, bodies, and life patterns provide clues that help diagnose physical conditions. After examining prevailing cultural beliefs about women's bodies and medicine, Northrup counters with views that incorporate profound connections between the mind, body, and spirit. She describes specific diseases and conditions that affect women and presents information designed to help women create their own healing plan. Copious notes and lists of resources make this an empowering source. The revised edition completely updates practical information and contains an appendix that compares hormone replacement therapies.

Titles focusing on specific alternative approaches to women's health include Marie E. Cargill's *Well Women: Healing the Female Body through Traditional Chinese Medicine* (Bergin & Garvey, 1998) and Barry Rose and Christina Scott-Moncrieff's *Homeopathy for Women: A Comprehensive, Easy-to-Use Guide for Women of All Ages* (Collins & Brown, 1998). Acupuncturist and herbalist Cargill explains the principles underpinning Chinese medicine, exploring how various applications of these principles can relieve symptoms associated with conditions such as menopause, premenstrual syndrome, morning sickness, and chronic fatigue. Rose and Scott-Moncrieff succinctly describe ailments, arranged by body area or system and supplemented with charts listing symptoms and dosages, in the first section of their book. The second section describes common homeopathic medicines and the physical and emotional symptoms that indicate their use.

1469. Teaff, Nancy Lee, and Kim Wright Wiley. *Perimenopause: Preparing for the Change: A Guide to the Early Stages of Menopause and Beyond.* Rocklin, CA: Prima, 1995. 204p. bibliog. index. ISBN 155958579X.

Focusing on the whole person, Teaff, an obstetrician and reproductive endocrinologist, and Wiley, a medical journalist, cover the basics of perimenopause and menopause beyond the medical model. They provide accessible information about copious symptoms and treatment options, emphasize healthy lifestyle changes, briefly discuss natural remedies, and offer tips for finding supportive doctors.

Other worthwhile titles on the subject include Mary Jane Minkin and Carol V. Wright's *What Every Woman Needs to Know about Menopause: The Years Before, During, and After* (Yale University Press, 1996), which uses a conversational question-and-answer format supplemented with charts and figures to provide fairly comprehensive allopathic information about physical and emotional symptoms and concerns, and Ann Louise Gittleman's *Before the Change: Taking Charge of Your Perimenopause* (HarperCollins, 1998), a nutritional approach that includes a diet designed to regulate the three interconnected hormonal systems, ovarian, stress, and blood sugar, along with a self-diagnostic test designed to help women create better dietary habits and find natural alternatives to traditional medicine.

1470. Turiel, Judith Steinberg. *Beyond Second Opinions: Making Choices about Fertility Treatment.* Berkeley: University of California Press, 1998. 393p. bibliog. index. ISBN 0520089456; 0520208544pa.

Turiel wrote this compassionate, highly informative work after she became pregnant using infertility treatments, only to give birth prematurely and lose her baby. To understand how this could happen and determine how to prevent it from happening again, she thoroughly examined the medical literature, which, according to Turiel, is permeated with disagreements and conflicting conclusions. The author also finds that many infertility doctors base their knowledge of specific treatments on information from the pharmaceutical industry, and that the government, sensitive to religious and political fallout, does not provide adequate oversight of infertility treatments. Many people accordingly act as unknowing participants in what essentially equates to experimental procedures. To counter potential misinformation that sometimes results from a profit-driven health care system, Turiel provides sets of questions for women to ask themselves, their surgeons, and their doctors to help women make truly informed choices and develop realistic expectations of treatment outcomes.

Psychologist Susan Lewis Cooper and clinical social worker Ellen Sarasohn Glazer partially update their well-regarded work *Beyond Infertility: The New Paths to Parenthood* (Lexington Books, 1994) in *Choosing Assisted Reproduction: Social, Emotional, and Ethical Considerations*

(Perspectives Press, 1998). They expand their discussion of emotional and ethical considerations and provide a framework designed to help people make the many decisions involved in choosing among the various assisted reproductive technologies (ARTs). The authors discuss the most common ARTs, pregnancy after ART, and pregnancy loss in the first section and examine third-party parenting options, including sperm, ovum, and embryo donation, surrogacy, and gestational care, in the second section. Cooper and Glazer use clear, accessible language throughout the book and include lists of organizations and references. Although the authors do not provide a particularly feminist treatment of the subject, they remain sensitive to the emotional impact of infertility treatments on women.

1471. Winikoff, Beverly, and Suzanne Wymelenberg, eds. *The Whole Truth about Contraception: A Guide to Safe and Effective Choices*. Washington, DC: Joseph Henry, 1998. 274p. bibliog. index. ISBN 030905494X.

Winikoff and Wymelenberg clearly and thoroughly discuss available hormonal, barrier, surgical, and natural birth-control options. The editors provide research findings, effectiveness for preventing pregnancy and sexually transmitted diseases, risks and benefits, instructions for use, and costs for each method. They include material aimed at adolescents, examine how personality traits significantly affect one's choice in birth-control method, provide information about female condoms, and consider abortion as a birth-control choice.

Rebecca Chalker and Carol Downer analyze abortion options based on years of research that health activists in the women's self-help movement conducted in detail in *A Woman's Book of Choices: Abortion, Menstrual Extraction, RU-486* (Four Walls Eight Windows, 1992). The authors effectively explain various procedures and list resources for more information. Janice Raymond, Renate Klein, and Lynette J. Dumble provide detailed information on RU 486 in *RU-486: Misconceptions, Myths, and Morals* (Institute on Women and Technology, 1991). The authors explore scientific studies conducted between 1984 and 1990 on the chemical abortifacient, criticizing the rapid change from animal to human testing, the uncritical promotion of the drug, and the dismissal of women's reports of side effects.

1999 CORE TITLES

Alvord, Lori Arviso, and Elizabeth Cohen Van Pelt. *The Scalpel and the Silver Bear*. New York: Bantam Books, 1999. 204p. bibliog. ISBN 0553100122.

Burfoot, Annette, ed. *Encyclopedia of Reproductive Technologies*. Boulder, CO: Westview Press, 1999. 404p. bibliog. index. ISBN 0813366585.

Denton, Margaret A. *Women's Voices in Health Promotion*. Toronto: Canadian Scholars' Press, 1999. 317p. bibliog. index. ISBN 1551301520.

Donchin, Anne, and Laura Purdy, eds. *Embodying Bioethics: Recent Feminist Advances*. Lanham, MD: Rowman & Littlefield, 1999. 286p. (New Feminist Perspective Series). bibliog. index. ISBN 0847689247; 0847689255pa.

Furth, Charlotte. *A Flourishing Yin: Gender in China's Medical History, 960–1665*. Berkeley: University of California Press, 1999. 355p. bibliog. index. ISBN 0520208285; 0520208293pa.

Goer, Henci. *The Thinking Woman's Guide to a Better Birth*. New York: Berkley, 1999. 367p. bibliog. index. ISBN 0399525173.

Griffith, H. Winter. *Women's Health: A Guide to Symptoms, Illness, Surgery, Medical Tests, and Procedures*. New York: Perigee Books, 1999. 393p. bibliog. index. ISBN 0399525181.

Howell-White, Sandra. *Birth Alternatives: How Women Select Childbirth Care*. Westport, CT: Greenwood Press, 1999. 164p. (Contributions in Sociology, no. 123). bibliog. index. ISBN 0313299528.

Humphries, Drew. *Crack Mothers: Pregnancy, Drugs, and the Media*. Columbus: Ohio State University Press, 1999. 206p. (Women and Health). bibliog. index. ISBN 0814208169.

Kearney, Margaret H. *Understanding Women's Recovery from Illness and Trauma*. Thousand Oaks, CA: Sage, 1999. 186p. (Women's Mental Health and Development, v. 4). bibliog. index. ISBN 0761905588; 0761905596pa.

Kramer, Elizabeth Jane, Susan L. Ivey, and Yu-Wen Ling, eds. *Immigrant Women's Health: Problems and Solutions*. San Francisco: Jossey-Bass, 1999. 438p. bibliog. indexes. ISBN 0787942944.

Leavitt, Judith Walzer, ed. *Women and Health in America: Historical Readings*. 2nd ed. Madison: University of Wisconsin Press, 1999. 692p. bibliog. ISBN 0299159604; 0299159647pa.

Leopold, Ellen. *A Darker Ribbon: Breast Cancer, Women, and Their Doctors in the Twentieth Century*. Boston: Beacon Press, 1999. 334p. bibliog. index. ISBN 0807065129.

More, Ellen Singer. *Restoring the Balance: Women Physicians and the Profession of Medicine, 1850–1995*. Cambridge, MA: Harvard University Press, 1999. 340p. bibliog. index. ISBN 067476661X.

Morgan, Lynn M., and Meredith W. Michaels, eds. *Fetal Subjects, Feminist Positions*. Philadelphia: University of Pennsylvania Press, 1999. 345p. bibliog. index. ISBN 0812234960; 081221689Xpa.

Rapp, Rayna. *Testing Women, Testing the Fetus: The Social Impact of Amniocentesis in America*. New York: Routledge, 1999. 361p. (The Anthropology of Everyday Life). bibliog. index. ISBN 0415916445; 0415916453pa.

Robinson-Walker, Catherine. *Women and Leadership in Health Care: The Journey to Authenticity and Power*. San Francisco: Jossey-Bass, 1999. 227p. bibliog. index. ISBN 0787909335.

Scialli, Anthony, ed. *The National Women's Health Resource Center Book of Women's Health: Your Comprehensive Guide to Health and Well-Being.* New York: Morrow, 1999. 680p. index. ISBN 0688124348.

Solarz, Andrea L., ed. *Lesbian Health: Current Assessment and Directions for the Future.* Washington, DC: National Academy Press, 1999. 234p. bibliog. index. ISBN 0309060931; 0309065674pa.

WORLD WIDE WEB/INTERNET SITES

1472. *Boston Women's Health Book Collective.* http://www.ourbodiesourselves.org.
In addition to information about the collective's origins and publications, this site provides links to information on health issues, including smoking, microbicides, and reproductive health; articles and position papers; and specific illnesses, such as AIDS, chronic fatigue syndrome, and osteoporosis. The collective's Web site also includes links to sites geared toward consumers, including African American women (National Black Women's Health Project, http://www .nationalblackwomenshealthproject.org/), Latinas (National Latina Health Organization, http:// www.latinahealth.org), lesbians and bisexuals (Lesbian Health Fund, http://www.glma.org/ programs/lhf/index.html), Asian women (National Asian Women's Health Organization, http:// www.nawho.org), and Native American women (Native American Women's Health Education Resource Center, http://www.nativeshop.org). The site features links to global women's health and U.S. government sites as well. It also provides information in Spanish.

1473. *International Women's Health Coalition (IWHC).* http://www.iwhc.org.
The IWHC endeavors to generate policies, funding, and programs that support the health and rights of women and girls from around the world, especially in Africa, Asia, Latin America, and postsocialist countries. This site includes links and information about conferences on health issues, publications, and projects. It also hosts an international group of women's health activists called HERA (Health, Empowerment, Rights, and Accountability), who advocate, help construct, and implement strategies that provide sexual and reproductive rights for women. *Face to Face Campaign for Women* (http://www.facetoface.org) is another valuable Web site devoted to the international health and rights of girls and women.

1474. *National Health Information Resources.* http://cpmcnet.columbia.edu/dept/ rosenthal/Women.html.
Hosted by the Rosenthal Center for Complementary and Alternative Medicine, which was established at Columbia University in 1993, this extensive site contains links to general sources, online journals, professional associations, government resources, research and clinical trials, alternative health sites, general health, and specific conditions, illnesses, and diseases.

1475. *National Women's Health Information Center (NWHIC).* http://4women.gov.
A service offered through the Office on Women's Health (http://www.4women.gov/owh/) of the Department of Health and Human Services, *NWHIC* features information for women, women health professionals, and the media. The site contains many links to publications, fact sheets, news, statistics, and sites for girls, older women, and minority women. It also provides links to sites about specific health issues and illnesses, as well as sites for Spanish speakers.

1476. *Women's Health Sites.* http://cc.usu.edu/~fshrode/wss_health.htm.

Maintained and updated by members of the Women's Studies Section of the Association of College and Research Libraries (ACRL) within the American Library Association, this site provides annotated links to a variety of health resources, including Internet subject guides, online publications, subject-oriented sites, and government agencies and organizations.

1477. *Yahoo Directory: Health: Women's Health.* http://dir.yahoo.com/Health/women _s_health/.

This excellent site provides links to research, expert advice, and recipes arranged by categories such as breast cancer, cervical dysplasia, menopause, morning sickness, and female genital mutilation.

Science, Technology, and Mathematics

Linda A. Krikos

Feminist science studies cover a wide range of topics using a variety of tools across many disciplines. Science historians have rescued lost, ignored, and forgotten women scientists and their contributions and critically analyzed the origins of modern science. Other scholars have addressed women's exclusion from technology and science in terms of curricula and pedagogy. Most important, philosophers and sociologists of science have challenged the "objectivity" and "neutrality" of science and the knowledge it produces, biological definitions of sex, gender, race, and other categories, and the use of animal models to explain human behaviors. Feminist scholars have repeatedly revealed that social, cultural, political, historical, economic, and geographic contexts greatly affect subjects chosen or ignored in research, the interpretation of research results, and the production of "knowledge."

The works in this chapter cover feminist critiques of science and technology, curricula and pedagogy, the contributions of women scientists, inventors, naturalists, and the like, and the impact of technologies, including computer and information technologies, on women's lives. The monographs section is divided into two categories, "Science, Nature Studies, and Mathematics" and "Technologies." Please see the "Medicine and Health" chapter for titles covering medical technologies and the "Business, Economics, and Labor" chapter for titles covering workplace technologies.

REFERENCE SOURCES

1478. Bailey, Martha J. *American Women in Science: A Biographical Dictionary*. Santa Barbara, CA: ABC-CLIO, 1994. 463p. index. ISBN 0874367409. *American Women in Science, 1950 to the Present*. ABC-CLIO, 1998. 455p. index. ISBN 0874369215.

Bailey offers biographical information about more than 400 women who made contributions to both the physical and natural sciences during the nineteenth and early twentieth centuries in *American Women in Science: A Biographical Dictionary*. Her broad definition of science includes contributions of some women, such as anthropologist Zora Neale Hurston and home economist Fannie Farmer, not generally found in scientific sources. Each entry, which typically consists of one page or less, provides name, dates, occupation(s), education, employment, a brief summary of achievements, and a short bibliography, often accompanied by a photograph, of the featured scientist. The index features titles of journals and books mentioned in the text and includes names, subjects, and occupations as well.

Although the follow-up title uses the same format as the previous work, *American Women in Science, 1950 to the Present* focuses on women in the social and behavioral sciences; lists the scientists by name and occupation, featuring more than seventy-five ranging from anatomy to zoology; and includes index entries arranged by race and ethnicity. These two dictionaries present accurate information from standard science as well as women's studies biographical sources in an accessible manner. Librarians, students, and other researchers should find them quite useful.

1479. Bindocci, Cynthia Gay, comp. *Women and Technology: An Annotated Bibliography*. New York: Garland, 1993. 229p. (Women's History and Culture, v. 7; Garland Reference Library of Social Sciences, v. 517). indexes. ISBN 0824057899.

Bindocci incorporates books, dissertations, scholarly journal articles, and proceedings published in English between 1979 and 1991 into this work. She provides complete citations with brief yet informative annotations, often listing books' tables of contents. She includes a general sources section that lists reference titles, biographical sources, and works in collections, as well as a categories section, in which Bindocci subdivides the materials into sixteen subjects, such as agriculture/food technologies, communications, energy/ecology, household technologies, industrial technologies, reproductive technologies, and women in development. In addition, this work features an author index and a subject index, which particularly helps one locate titles pertaining to specific countries, continents, and ethnicities. The broad coverage of this fine bibliography facilitates scholars' study of the sociological and cultural aspects of technology.

1480. Grinstein, Louise S., and Paul J. Campbell, eds. *Women of Mathematics: A Biobibliographic Sourcebook*. New York: Greenwood Press, 1987. 292p. indexes. ISBN 0313248494.

One of the first reference titles to focus on women mathematicians, this sourcebook contains information about forty-three women, including Hypatia (c. 370 to 415), who were mainly active from the eighteenth century to the present. The entries, which the editors arrange alphabetically by name, yield concise biographical information; however, attempts to provide understandable discussions of the women's contributions remain only partially successful. Entries include selected bibliographies of works both by and about the various women mathematicians, as well as other sources to supplement the entries. Appendices contain a chronological listing of the mathematicians, a table that lists place of origin, highest education, place of work, and field specialty for each woman, and a list of references in standard biographical dictionaries, indexes, and other sources. Name and subject indexes complete the source.

Charlene Morrow and Teri Perl, editors of *Notable Women in Mathematics: A Biographical Dictionary* (Greenwood Press, 1998), collect biographical information on fifty-nine mostly contemporary mathematicians who hail from multifarious backgrounds and countries. Although this work features information on approximately one-third of the women included in the previous title, the books supplement each other, making both sources must-haves for libraries to provide complete coverage. Claudia Henrion's *Women in Mathematics: The Addition of Difference* (Indiana University Press, 1997), a title appropriate for circulating collections, juxtaposes descriptions of the lives of successful contemporary women mathematicians with discussions of the most common myths and stereotypes about mathematics and mathematicians.

1481. Grinstein, Louise S., Rose K. Rose, and Miriam H. Rafailovich, eds. *Women in Chemistry and Physics: A Biobibliographic Sourcebook*. Westport, CT: Greenwood Press, 1993. 721p. index. ISBN 0313273820.

This title provides biographical information, examinations of work, and bibliographies for seventy-five women from approximately twenty countries who represent the fields of chemistry and physics from antiquity to the early twentieth century. The format and features essentially mirror Grinstein's and Campbell's *Women of Mathematics: A Biobibliographic Sourcebook*; however, Grinstein, Rose, and Rafailovich add appendices that list references to each scientist in standard biographical dictionaries and feature codes for associations/organizations, periodicals, and publishers mentioned in the entries.

Grinstein and Rose, with Carol A. Biermann, also edited *Women in the Biological Sciences:*

A Biobibliographic Sourcebook (Greenwood Press, 1997), which provides information about sixty-five women from various eras and countries, mostly in Europe and North America. The editors use criteria based on achievements in research and publication, teaching, field experience, or policy to choose the women featured in this work, which includes several useful appendices.

1482. Herzenberg, Caroline. *Women Scientists from Antiquity to the Present: An Index: An International Reference Listing and Biographical Directory of Some Notable Women Scientists from Ancient to Modern Times.* West Cornwall, CT: Locust Hill Press, 1986. 200p. bibliog. index. ISBN 0933951019.

Herzenberg compiles biographical and related information for approximately 2,500 women who contributed to science, medicine, technology, and engineering. The entries, which the author alphabetically arranges by name, include dates of birth and activity, major field(s) of endeavor, country of origin, codes to the approximately 130 readily accessible sources of information listed in the book, and other information. Herzenberg provides cross-references to pseudonyms, married names, and variant spellings, as well as a highly useful appendix grouped in approximately 100 detailed categories, including astrophysicists, metallurgists, hydrologists, midwives, and ornithologists, with cross-references to related categories. Chronologically and geographically (by country of origin) arranged appendices would have proven useful features.

Marilyn Bailey Ogilvie's complementary work *Women in Science: Antiquity through the Nineteenth Century: A Biographical Dictionary with Annotated Bibliography* (MIT Press, 1986), an extensive annotated bibliography that provides biographical information for more than 180 women, features chronological subdivisions and an alphabetically arranged table that lists time period, field, and nationality of the scientists. Ogilvie also compiled *Women and Science: An Annotated Bibliography* (Garland, 1996), which lists nearly 2,700 books and articles organized alphabetically by author, with indexes by field, nationality, persons/institutions, time period, form, and theme.

1483. Searing, Susan E., ed., with Rima D. Apple. *The History of Women and Science, Health, and Technology: A Bibliographic Guide to the Professions and the Disciplines.* Madison: University of Wisconsin System, Women's Studies Librarian, 1988. 54p. (OP)

This collaborative effort by members of the Women's Caucus of the History of Science Society and coeditor Searing, the women's studies librarian at the University of Wisconsin between 1982 and 1991, makes widely scattered materials accessible to students, researchers, and teachers. The guide, which focuses on English-language books and journal articles published in women's studies and subject periodicals, consists of four parts: reference sources; science, subdivided by branch, for example, astronomy, physics, and home economics; health, including women health professionals, biological and medical views of women, and health care issues; and technology—all technological sciences and engineering. Although this work does not contain an index, its table of contents lists all subdivisions within the four sections and provides adequate access to the material. Searing's successor, Phyllis Holman Weisbard, edited the second edition (University of Wisconsin System, Women's Studies Librarian, 1993), which elevates home economics/domestic sciences from a subdivision to a bona fide section. Weisbard also incorporates new subdivisions within each section, adds a list of titles appropriate for older children and young adults, and includes an author index. Both editions are excellent sources for building basic collections in these subjects.

1484. Sherer, Benjamin F., and Barbara S. Sherer, eds. *Notable Women in the Physical Sciences: A Biographical Dictionary.* Westport, CT: Greenwood Press, 1997. 479p. bibliog. index. ISBN 0313293031.

Although it consists of only ninety-six entries, *Notable Women in the Physical Sciences* includes women scientists who lived in Europe, Asia, and North America from antiquity onward. Each signed entry features full name(s); date(s); occupation(s); a chronology of important life events, such as family, education, career, and recognitions; a three- to five-page narrative that outlines basic biographical information and highlights career contributions and obstacles faced as a result of gender; notes; and a bibliography of materials both by and about the scientist. The editors conclude the work with appendices that list the scientists by occupation and award name and an index that includes entries by nationality (Chinese, Canadian, American). The Sherers also edited *Notable Women in the Life Sciences: A Biographical Dictionary* (Greenwood Press, 1996), which provides similar coverage for ninety-seven women anatomists, botanists, bacteriologists, geneticists, physicians, zoologists, and the like.

1485. Stanley, Autumn. *Mothers and Daughters of Invention: Notes for a Revised History of Technology*. Metuchen, NJ: Scarecrow Press, 1993. 1116p. bibliog. index. ISBN 0810825864.

Stanley examined U.S. patent records and feminist reassessments of archaeological and anthropological information for ten years to painstakingly document women's technological achievements, making this book the most complete record to date on the subject. She discusses technologies in five major areas: agriculture/food, health/medicine, sex, fertility, and antifertility, machines, and computers. With the exception of computers, Stanley begins her analysis of each area with an examination of developments in prehistory, continuing chronologically to incorporate the stories of specific inventors and devices as they become identifiable, usually by the eighteenth century. Several appendices list women patentees and their inventions in various areas, as well as other pertinent information. The book's detailed name, title, and subject index and extensive bibliography make it an excellent reference source; however, librarians should consider the paperback edition for circulating collections.

Margaret Alic's *Hypatia's Heritage: The History of Women in Science from Antiquity to the Late Nineteenth Century* (Women's Press, 1986), which also features prehistory and covers some of the same ground as Stanley, is a less detailed account of European women's contributions to the physical and natural sciences and mathematics. Although Alic does not examine history through the lens of gender critique, her work filled a gap in the literature at its time of publication and not only would serve as a useful text in history of science or feminism and science courses, but also makes another good candidate for circulating collections.

1486. Welch, Rosanne. *Encyclopedia of Women in Aviation and Space*. Santa Barbara, CA: ABC-CLIO, 1998. 286p. bibliog. index. ISBN 0874369584.

Welch provides more than 250 entries covering individuals, events, and organizations from North American, European, and other countries. Most entries include basic information, cross-references to related entries, and two or three sources. Welch focuses her entries about individuals, which she often accompanies with a photograph, on their accomplishments. Although the encyclopedia includes pilots and astronauts who represent different races and ethnicities, with the exception of African Americans, the index does not reflect this inclusiveness very well.

Titles appropriate for circulating collections include *Women of the Air* (Dodd, Mead, 1987) by Judy Lomax and *Sisters of the Wind: Voices of Early Women Aviators* (Trilogy, 1994) by Elizabeth S. Bell. Lomax traces women's involvement in aviation from the first balloon flight, which took place in France in the 1700s, through the 1930s. She insightfully compares women and men aviators in terms of reactions from the public, the industry, and the press. Bell concentrates on women pilots, for the most part British and American, during the 1920s and 1930s.

Mining the diaries, journals, and published contemporary accounts of both famous and unknown women aviators, she constructs an informative, intriguing, but uncritical account of personalities and events during the period when aviation was new, unregulated, and therefore more open to women.

MONOGRAPHS

Science, Nature Studies, and Mathematics

1487. Birke, Lynda. *Women, Feminism, and Biology: The Feminist Challenge*. New York: Methuen, 1986. 210p. bibliog. index. (OP)

Birke, a highly respected biologist, thoroughly reviews biological ideas about women, which she characterizes as hierarchical, competitive, and reductionist. Birke particularly objects to the concept of scientific objectivity, arguing that attempting to view science through an objective lens causes one to ignore the social, cultural, and political contexts of scientific research. She draws on a variety of feminist ideas, most notably ecofeminism, in which behavior, environment, and biology interact, to introduce a practical research model that could lead to new, dynamic concepts of gender. Despite its early publication date, several scholars cited this work throughout the 1990s.

Sue Rosser provides a cogent explanation of feminist critiques of science, yet focuses on pragmatic rather than theoretical applications of these critiques in *Biology and Feminism: A Dynamic Interaction* (Twayne, 1992). Rosser asserts that a curriculum that identifies and corrects biases in the sciences could lead to a cooperative, symbiotic relationship between feminism and biology. Her accessible writing style and useful bibliography, which covers science studies and biology, make her work an apposite text for feminism and biology or science courses.

1488. Duran, Jane. *Philosophies of Science/Feminist Theories*. Boulder, CO: Westview Press, 1998. 206p. bibliog. index. ISBN 0813332990; 0813333253pa.

Duran coherently and succinctly reviews the philosophy of science and feminist and radical critiques of science for philosophers, feminist theorists, scientists, and students in this work, in which she addresses positivism, the Vienna Circle, and the ideas of Thomas Kuhn on the nature of scientific revolutions, the growth of sociological interest in science, and the advent of feminist critiques of science. Duran argues that most feminist critiques focus on the practice of science rather than science itself and suggests that feminist critiques' insistence on accountability comprises one of their most important contributions. The author provides brief, cogent summaries of the work and ideas of key theorists, including Sandra Harding, Helen Longino, Ruth Hubbard, and Donna Haraway. Since this work is one of the few to interweave feminist theory, philosophical and sociological examinations of science, and general science studies, it clearly belongs in most academic collections.

Scholars already familiar with the subject might find *Feminism, Science, and the Philosophy of Science* (Kluwer Academic, 1996), edited by Lynn Hankinson Nelson and Jack Nelson, informative. Contributors strive to increase awareness in the science community about differing perspectives on the relationships between science and society and the implications of cultural influences in the production of scientific "knowledge" in this work, which features essays that compare feminist and nonfeminist approaches to science.

1489. Hanson, Sandra L. *Lost Talent: Women in the Sciences*. Philadelphia: Temple University Press, 1996. 220p. (Labor and Social Change). bibliog. tables. ISBN 1566394465.

Hanson not only collects information about girls and women's experiences in science, but also attempts to identify possible causes of their experiences by examining how gender interacts with family resources, school resources, and individual resources in four areas: achievement (grades and test scores), access (course taking), attitudes, and activities (use of calculators, computers, and so on). Utilizing large national samples in certain categories enables Hanson to make comparisons based on race and class as well as gender. This carefully constructed, multivariate study reveals many complex trends, making it a worthwhile addition to academic libraries.

The Equity Equation: Fostering the Advancement of Women in the Sciences, Mathematics, and Engineering (Jossey-Bass, 1996), edited by Cinda-Sue Davis and others, also examines race, ethnicity, class, and other categories to recommend future research and policy development. Finally, the National Science Foundation's biennial publication *Women, Minorities, and Persons with Disabilities in Science and Engineering* (National Science Foundation, 1994–) provides statistics that reflect the participation of these groups in science and engineering since elementary school.

1490. Haraway, Donna Jeanne. *Simians, Cyborgs, and Women: The Reinvention of Nature.* New York: Routledge, 1991. 287p. bibliog. index. ISBN 0415903866; 0415903874pa.

Haraway, a biologist and science historian, presents a collection of essays that she originally published between 1978 and 1989, including the classics "Manifesto for Cyborgs: Science, Technology, and Socialist-Feminism in the Late Twentieth Century" and "Situated Knowledges: The Science Question in Feminism and the Privilege of Partial Perspective," that comment on the evolution of bodies, politics, and stories, as well as the invention and reinvention of nature. Haraway asserts that primate studies illuminate gender, power, and knowledge relationships, and that feminist scientists must fight to identify the role of nature and experience. She also explores how various feminist concepts of gender might influence concepts of difference in a postmodern world. Haraway provides copious notes and an excellent, extensive bibliography. The author examines the history of primatology since 1920 from a feminist standpoint, suggesting that only multiple, interlinked, and partial realities exist, as opposed to one linear "true" reality, in *Primate Visions: Gender, Race, and Nature in the World of Modern Science* (Routledge, 1989). She presents a political analysis of computers and cyberspace in *Modest-Witness@Second-Millennium.FemaleMan©-Meets-OncoMouse*™ (Routledge, 1998). Haraway's long, convoluted sentences and plays on language make her works appropriate for upper- and graduate-level courses. The author's solid, innovative contributions to feminist theory make her work essential to academic collections.

1491. Harding, Sandra G. *The Science Question in Feminism.* Ithaca, NY: Cornell University Press, 1986. 271p. bibliog. index. ISBN 0801418801; 0801493633pa.

Harding, a feminist philosopher of science and leading standpoint theorist, surveys several feminist theories and critiques of science, including equity studies, uses and abuses of science, critiques of biology and social sciences, textual critiques of science, and epistemological studies, in *The Science Question in Feminism.* She further develops her ideas, adopting concepts from the peace and ecology movements, the sociology of science, and the Third World, in *Whose Science? Whose Knowledge? Thinking from Women's Lives* (Cornell University Press, 1991) to explore how Western feminists can incorporate the perspectives of non-Western peoples into dominant discourses that direct feminist standpoint theory. In each self-contained chapter Harding discusses how scholars need to acknowledge and truly understand how Western biases within the development of science influence all societies, and that all varieties of feminism simultaneously influence and are influenced by other "liberatory movements" (p. ix). The author examines postcolonial histories of science from the standpoint of cultures in the South, including how these histories are relevant to theories of knowledge, in *Is Science Multicultural? Postcolonialisms, Feminisms, and Epistemologies* (Indiana University Press, 1998). Although those new to theoretical writing might find these books demanding, Harding's significant contributions to feminist theory make her works must-haves for all academic collections.

1492. Hubbard, Ruth. *The Politics of Women's Biology.* New Brunswick, NJ: Rutgers University Press, 1990. 229p. bibliog. index. ISBN 0813514894; 0813514908pa.

Hubbard, a former Harvard biologist, claims that she evolved from "doing science to studying it" (p. 2) after realizing the profoundly political aspects of women's biology. Hubbard discusses feminist issues related to the sociology of science, especially the belief that science is totally objective, arguing that unacknowledged subjectivity in the research of women's biology affects scientific conclusions in specific areas, such as genetics, sex differences, and concepts of human nature. The author's clearly written, influential work features a valuable bibliography, making *The Politics of Women's Biology* an appropriate introductory text for science and feminism courses.

Hubbard and Elijah Wald provide a cogent overview of the social and ethical implications of genetic research for the general public in *Exploding the Gene Myth* (Beacon Press, 1993). They clearly explain the construction and functions of cells, asserting that in addition to biology, human behavior results from complex interactions among social, cultural, and environmental factors. The authors reveal the commercial interests of many geneticists, biotechnologists, and physicians and question the legitimacy of the Human Genome Project. This work would make a fine text for introductory gender and science courses. Hubbard's *Profitable Promises: Essays on Women, Science, and Health* (Common Courage, 1995) features talks and previously published essays that build on the ideas presented in her other two works.

1493. Kass-Simon, G., Patricia Farnes, and Deborah Nash, eds. *Women of Science: Righting the Record.* Bloomington: Indiana University Press, 1990. 398p. indexes. ISBN 0253332648pa.

This volume features historical overviews of the contributions of women scientists in areas such as astronomy, engineering, geology, mathematics, medicine, and crystallography. Most accounts cover achievements in America and Europe, begin with the early nineteenth century, and note the relationship between prevailing social roles for women and the nature and extent of women's involvement in the various fields of science. Contributors not only discuss highly recognizable women, including Rachel Carson and Marie Curie, but also analyze women who made groundbreaking but frequently noncredited discoveries. Chapters conclude with impressive lists of notes, and name and subject indexes provide excellent access to the material.

Editor Marina Benjamin features nine historically specific, interdisciplinary case studies within the context of the increasing professionalization and industrialization of the sciences in *Science and Sensibility: Gender and Scientific Enquiry, 1780–1945* (Blackwell, 1991). Editors Pnina Abir-Am and Darinda Outram include six sociohistorical studies and six biographical studies that examine the premise that (male) scientists' failure to consider contributions that originated in the (female) domestic sphere partially accounts for women's lack of representation in the field in *Uneasy Careers and Intimate Lives: Women in Science, 1789–1979* (Rutgers University Press, 1987). Finally, in *Ladies in the Laboratory? American and British Women in Science, 1800–1900: A Survey of Their Contributions to Research* (Scarecrow Press, 1998), Mary R. S. Creese weaves biographical sketches into a historical survey of science in which she addresses the achievements of women who published articles in the 680 scientific journals listed in the London Royal Society's *Catalogue of Scientific Papers, 1800–1900* (Cambridge University Press, 1867–1925).

1494. Keller, Evelyn Fox. *Secrets of Life, Secrets of Death: Essays on Language, Gender, and Science.* New York: Routledge, 1992. 195p. bibliog. ISBN 0415905249; 0415905257pa.

Keller, a highly regarded feminist historian and philosopher of science who links scientific "objectivity" with male psychological development, includes essays written between 1985 and 1991 that reflect her attempts to place gender and science studies within the more general framework of historical, sociological, and philosophical science studies in this work. These essays also reveal Keller's fascination with technologies of life and death, particularly molecular biology and nuclear physics. Her exploration of language, which she believes "simultaneously reflects and guides the development of scientific models and methods" (p. 6), which enables some discoveries while obscuring others, is especially noteworthy. This dense yet intriguing work provides new insight into the meanings of science and the knowledge it produces.

Body/Politics: Women and the Discourses of Science (Routledge, 1990), which Keller, Mary Jacobus, and Sally Shuttleworth edited, features conference papers by several well-known feminist researchers and theorists who emphasize "the political urgency of the relationship between science and the feminine body" (p. 1). Contributors also identify how social ideologies have framed scientific discourse since 1800.

1495. Kessler, Suzanne J. *Lessons from the Intersexed.* New Brunswick, NJ: Rutgers University Press, 1998. 224p. bibliog. index. ISBN 0813525292; 0813525306pa.

Kessler builds on one of the earliest critiques of the gender and sex distinction, an ethnomethodological study that she conducted with Wendy McKenna in 1978, in *Lessons from the Intersexed.* Kessler used interviews with experts on pediatric intersexuality, people with intersexed conditions, and letters solicited by an intersexed child's mother to analyze the management of intersexed individuals. She argues that understanding how doctors assign sexual categories to intersexed children reveals multiple assumptions about gender, sex, and sexuality. Kessler also believes that doctors exaggerate the importance of genitals, and that they cause needless pain and confusion in their rush to surgically "fix" intersexed children.

Alice Domurat Dreger provides a historical perspective by examining scientific and medical literature from France and England between 1860 and 1915 in *Hermaphrodites and the Medical Invention of Sex* (Harvard University Press, 1998). After examining 200 case studies, she determined that ambiguous genitalia disturbed doctors because they felt that they could lead to unwitting homosexual contact. Dreger argues that this fear, which homosexual and feminist activism fueled, caused many doctors to "correct" genital anomalies according to rigid ideas about sexual dimorphism. Both Kessler and Dreger develop theoretical attacks on the two-gender system, question the surgical "fix," and examine the ideas of the Intersexual Society of North America, which Cheryl Chase established in 1992. Bernice L. Hausman traces the history of the term "gender" to medical research on intersexuality conducted during the 1950s in *Changing Sex: Transsexualism, Technology, and the Idea of Gender* (Duke University Press, 1995), another equally fascinating but less accessibly written title. She calls on feminists to examine the technological aspects of transsexualism in order to achieve a true understanding of Western concepts of gender.

1496. Kirkup, Gill, and Laurie Smith Keller, eds. *Inventing Women: Science, Technology, and Gender.* Cambridge, England: Polity Press, 1992. 342p. bibliog. index. (OP)

The editors designed this anthology, which features highly readable chapters that reflect a variety of experiences presented in alternative forms, including poetry and fiction, to introduce women's studies students to some of the major feminist debates about science and technology. Contributors cover several subjects, including sex differences, prenatal screening for genetic diseases, science education for girls, the connection between technology and power, gender and the military, ecofeminism, computers, and domestic technologies. Unlike many other introductory anthologies, *Inventing Women* contains informative pieces written by and about women from countries in the Third World.

Additional collections that would serve as good texts or sources for supplementary course readings include *Feminism and Science* (Oxford University Press, 1996), edited by Evelyn Fox Keller and Helen Longino, a collection of important, representative articles originally published in a variety of journals over a fifteen-year period; editor Ruth Bleier's *Feminist Approaches to Science* (Pergamon Press, 1988), which features diverse feminist approaches to science studies; *Sex and Scientific Inquiry* (University of Chicago Press, 1987), edited by Sandra Harding and Jean O'Barrs, a collection of key articles originally published in several issues of *Signs: Journal of Women in Culture and Society*; editor Nancy Tuana's *Feminism and Science* (Indiana University Press, 1989), which contains an excellent overview of the field as well as reprinted articles from special issues of the journal *Hypatia*; and editor Maureen McNeil's *Gender and Expertise* (Free Association Book, 1987), which not only surveys feminist debates about female inequality since the late 1700s, but also substantially covers the sciences and technology. The collections edited by Keller and Longino, Bleier, Tuana, and McNeil contain good bibliographies in addition to references or notes at the end of each chapter.

1497. Lykke, Nina, and Rosi Braidotti, eds. *Between Monsters, Goddesses, and Cyborgs: Feminist Confrontations with Science, Medicine, and Cyberspace.* London: Zed Books, 1996. 260p. index. (OP)

The Gender-Nature-Culture international feminist research network and the science cluster of the Network of Interdisciplinary Women's Studies in Europe (NOISE) fomented the creation of this volume, which builds on the monster and cyborg metaphors that Donna Haraway introduced in her works (please see Haraway annotation earlier in this section). Contributors who represent a variety of disciplines, including physics, engineering, biomedicine, philosophy, sociology, and cultural and literary studies, explore the unstable boundaries between the "virtual/artefactual" and "nature" worlds as a place for feminist dialogue with science and technology. Contributors address topics such as the big bang theory, ecofeminism, alternative medicine, reproductive technologies, and menopause. Although the chapters cover a wide range of subjects, they all reflect a belief in the importance of investigating the historical separation between cultural and natural sciences and emphasize the connections between science/technology and power structures that intersect on many levels.

Other works influenced by Haraway's cyborg metaphor include Claudia Springer's *Electronic Eros: Bodies and Desire in the Postindustrial Age* (University of Texas Press, 1996), in which she posits "that popular culture plays out contemporary cultural conflicts over sexuality and gender roles in its representation of cyborgs" (p. 10), and Anne Balsamo's *Technologies of the Gendered Body: Reading Cyborg Women* (Duke University Press, 1996), which applies feminist Foucauldian analysis to bodybuilding, cosmetic surgery, virtual reality, and science fiction narratives to illustrate "the ways in which gendered identities are technologically produced for material bodies" (p. 154).

1498. Nelson, Lynn Hankinson. *Who Knows: From Quine to a Feminist Empiricism.* Philadelphia: Temple University Press, 1990. 401p. bibliog. index. ISBN 0877226474.

Nelson bases her arguments on the work of American philosopher and mathematical logician Willard Van Orman Quine to attempt to resolve feminist standpoint theorists and feminist post-modernists' objections to feminist empiricist theories of science. Since many feminists not only consider empiricism, the accepted standard of modern scientific inquiry, and its claims to objectivity as apolitical, but also even reject empiricism out of hand, Nelson proposes a modified, more flexible feminist empiricism that eliminates the individualism that detractors view as inherent in the tenet. Although she builds on Quine's belief that empiricism represents a theory of evidence that is distinct from empiricist accounts of science, Nelson deviates from Quine in her assertion that theories can and should include political views. The author's lucid writing style, informative chapter notes, and extensive bibliography make this a worthwhile work.

Helen E. Longino also advocates a modified empiricism that she calls contextual empiricism, which treats experience as the basis of knowledge while simultaneously insisting upon the relevance of context to the construction of knowledge, in *Science as Social Knowledge: Values and Objectivity in Scientific Inquiry* (Princeton University Press, 1990). She also claims that feminists who counter arguments supporting biological determinism with arguments asserting the importance of environmental influences inadvertently encourage and perpetuate dualistic thinking. Both books contribute to the ongoing feminist debate in the field, making them useful to researchers already familiar with feminist critiques of science.

1499. Norwood, Vera. *Made from This Earth: American Women and Nature*. Chapel Hill: University of North Carolina Press, 1993. 368p. (Gender and American Culture). bibliog. index. ISBN 0807820628; 0807843962pa.

Norwood explores how women have perceived nature, their place in it, and differences between male and female perceptions through her examination of the work of women naturalists in the United States, beginning in the early nineteenth century. She discusses women whose work fell within the approved gender expectations and covers the origins of women's nature study, nature writing, scientific illustration, and garden/landscape design in the book's early chapters. Remaining chapters not only address the work of women, including Rachel Carson and Dian Fossey, who faced opposition to their efforts to enter fields that did not fit prevailing gender norms, but also explore ecological feminism, or ecofeminism, wildlife, and future roles for women naturalists. Norwood also considers why historians excluded women of color from the history of nature studies and examines different cultural views of land history and animal imagery in her analysis of poetry, fiction, and other writing. This fascinating work features informative notes and an excellent bibliography.

Marcia Myers Bonta profiles twenty-five women botanists, ornithologists, ecologists, and entomologists who carried out field studies of plants and animals, beginning in the mid-eighteenth century, in *Women in the Field: America's Pioneering Women Naturalists* (Texas A&M Press, 1991). Anne B. Shteir turns her attention to another part of the world in *Cultivating Women, Cultivating Science: Flora's Daughters and Botany in England, 1760–1860* (Johns Hopkins University Press, 1996), in which she analyzes the roles and contributions of women in the field, particularly early on. The American Historical Association awarded this title the Joan Kelly Memorial Prize in Women's History for 1996.

1500. Rogers, Pat, and Gabriele Kaiser, eds. *Equity in Mathematics Education: Influences of Feminism and Culture*. London: Falmer Press, 1995. 278p. index. ISBN 0750704004; 0750704012pa.

Rogers and Kaiser attempt to adapt a model that Peggy McIntosh originally developed to make effective changes in the field of mathematics education using feminist, cross-cultural perspectives. The model consists of five phases: mathematics without women, women in mathematics, women seen as problems in mathematics, women become central to mathematics, and the reconstruction of mathematics. In the first part of the book, the editors present an overview of the approaches used during the past decade to increase women's participation in mathematics, focusing on approaches that involve changing the attitudes of female students and teachers. The second section emphasizes the importance of social and cultural attitudes toward mathematics education for girls and features case studies of programs developed in Singapore, France, Papua New Guinea, Malawi, and other countries. In the last section, contributors examine the influences of feminist pedagogy in mathematics education; the epilogue challenges readers to imagine a mathematics that white men do not dominate. Chapters conclude with useful lists of references; however, the editors do not include an overall bibliography.

Mathematics and Gender (Columbia University Press, 1990), edited by Elizabeth Fennema and Gilah C. Leder, features chapters written by established authors in the field who examine cultural factors that can account for differences in women and men's participation in mathematics-related careers. Several contributors evaluate specific programs designed to encourage girls to take more math courses.

1501. Rose, Hilary. *Love, Power, and Knowledge: Towards a Feminist Transformation of the Sciences.* Bloomington: Indiana University Press, 1994. 326p. (Race, Gender, and Science). bibliog. index. ISBN 0253350468; 0253209072pa.

Rose, who was active in the radical science movement during the 1960s, combines personal reflection with a study of gender issues in science (and occasionally technology). She discusses the content and development of feminist critiques of science, particularly standpoint and postmodern theories of epistemology, in light of their historical and geographic contexts in the first few chapters of the book. Rose analyzes institutions of science in conjunction with women's place in them in the next few chapters. She specifically looks at the British Royal Society and the Nobel Science Committees, exposing a long-standing, complex web of sexist attitudes that essentially ignore the contributions of women scientists. Rose then addresses her concerns about what she calls the genetic turn in reproductive technology in connection with the culture of science. She further discusses feminist science fiction as well as possible future developments of science informed by feminism. Rose provides informative chapter notes and a wide-ranging bibliography. Sharon Bertsch McGrayn also considers why so few women have won the Nobel Prize by examining specific obstacles in the careers of fourteen women who either were awarded the prize or made significant contributions to prize-winning projects in *Nobel Women in Science: Their Lives, Struggles, and Momentous Discoveries* (Carol Publishing Group, 1993).

1502. Rosser, Sue V. *Re-engineering Female Friendly Science.* New York: Teachers College Press, Columbia University, 1997. 188p. (Athene Series). bibliog. index. ISBN 0807762873; 0807762865pa.

Rosser, one of the early proponents of integrating feminist teaching methods into science classrooms, assesses the curricular and pedagogical changes, particularly in terms of how they affect women, that have taken place since the publication of her previous works, most notably *Female-Friendly Science: Applying Women's Studies Methods and Theories to Attract Students* (Pergamon Press, 1990). In *Re-engineering Female Friendly Science*, Rosser uses feminist theories of science to critically examine the effects of curriculum integration, the importance of including race and gender in science, lessons that coeducational schools can glean from single-sex schools, and gender equity in school-to-work programs. She also makes practical suggestions regarding how to evaluate programs and summarizes the various feminist critiques of science, as well as their applications. An excellent bibliography of sources mostly published after 1989 concludes the work.

Rosser also edited *Feminism within the Science and Health Care Professions: Overcoming Resistance* (Pergamon Press, 1988) and *Teaching the Majority: Breaking the Gender Barrier in Science, Mathematics, and Engineering* (Teachers College Press, 1995), a collection of chapters written by female educators who not only provide specific examples of gender bias in science curricula, but also suggest ways to implement pedagogical change. Angela Calabrese Barton focuses on what she calls "liberatory education," which recognizes "that teachers and students are agents and actors who actively and collectively shape and reshape their own understandings of the world and themselves from historically and culturally determined standpoints" (p. ix), in *Feminist Science Education* (Teachers College Press, 1998), another title from the Athene Series.

1503. Rossiter, Margaret W. *Women Scientists in America: Before Affirmative Action, 1940–1972.* Baltimore: Johns Hopkins University Press, 1995. 584p. bibliog. index. ISBN 0801848938.

This excellent sequel to Rossiter's *Women Scientists in America: Struggles and Strategies to 1940* (Johns Hopkins University Press, 1982) continues her comprehensive examination of the history of American women scientists, beginning with the "manpower" shortage that World War II caused. Despite the encouragement that the administrations of government, the industry, and colleges aimed at professional women scientists, most of them could find only entry-level positions. As in many other professions, men expected women scientists to step aside after the war to make jobs available for the returning men. Although women earned a record number of degrees in the sciences during this period, few found few employment opportunities, even with traditional employers such as women's colleges. Nevertheless, women made invaluable contributions to the sciences, both during and after the war, and Rossiter skillfully incorporates their stories into her study, which she supplements with statistical tables and photographs. She also provides extensive notes and a bibliographic essay.

1504. Russett, Cynthia Eagle. *Sexual Science: The Victorian Construction of Womanhood.* Cambridge, MA: Harvard University Press, 1989. 245p. bibliog. index. ISBN 067480290X.

Although scientific interest in "woman's nature" has a long history, Russett argues that women's desire to become active outside of the home during the nineteenth century not only galvanized scientific and social interests, particularly in Great Britain and the United States, but also contributed to the development of a new "sexual science." She bases this conclusion on her examination of the scientific literature on sex differences published during the period within its social and cultural context. Russett believes that developments in the natural and social sciences, which Charles Darwin and his evolution hierarchy greatly influenced, allowed sexual scientists to claim that they based their findings on more empirical information than previously possible. She persuasively asserts that the need to maintain differing social roles between the sexes frequently affected the results of research on sex differences, and that scientists based a great deal of theory on a very small amount of reliable data. Ludmilla Jordanova makes excellent use of illustrations in her insightful study of ideas, representations, and images about sex differences as depicted in medical and scientific literature, film, sculpture, painting, and other cultural sources in *Sexual Visions: Images of Gender in Science and Medicine between the Eighteenth and Twentieth Centuries* (University of Wisconsin Press, 1989) which nicely complements Russett's book.

1505. Schiebinger, Londa L. *The Mind Has No Sex? Women in the Origins of Modern Science*. Cambridge, MA: Harvard University Press, 1989. 355p. bibliog. index. ISBN 0674576233.

A constructivist who believes that science is a social product, Schiebinger analyzes the place of gender in the origins and rise of modern science in Europe during the seventeenth and eighteenth centuries. She presents her examinations in four interdependent sections: gender boundaries within institutions (monasteries, universities, salons, academies); the work of specific women who attempted to function within these boundaries, particularly in England, France, and Germany; biological sciences' interpretations of sex and gender in women's bodies; and cultural understandings of "masculinity" and "femininity" and their influence on debates about women's scientific abilities. Schiebinger's meticulous research, clear, well-constructed prose, informative chapter notes, and thorough bibliography make the book an appropriate text for women's studies or history of science courses. In *Nature's Body: Gender in the Making of Modern Science* (Beacon Press, 1993), Schiebinger critically analyzes modern science's classification systems of the natural world and discusses how scientists' cultural assumptions about sex and gender permeated their ideas about nature and natural history.

1506. Sonnert, Gerhard, with Gerald Holton. *Who Succeeds in Science? The Gender Dimension*. New Brunswick, NJ: Rutgers University Press, 1995. 248p. bibliog. ISBN 0813522196; 081352220Xpa.

Based on information gleaned from 699 questionnaires and 200 interviews of men and women who showed early promise for successful careers in science, this study investigates the effects of gender on career outcome, particularly for women. Sonnert and Holton used the difference model (internal outlooks that make women act differently in science) and the deficit model (external structural barriers that treat women differently in science) to examine the variety of obstacles that prevent women from becoming and remaining professional scientists. The authors intersperse excerpts from interviews with their findings, allowing for comparisons between men and women, as well as between women who stayed in science and women who did not. They conclude the work with specific suggestions aimed at policy makers and novice scientists in hope of alleviating some of the problems that hinder successful science careers for women. Sonnert and Holton present a more technical and statistical version of this study targeted for theorists and academics in *Gender Differences in Science Careers: The Project Access Study* (Rutgers University Press, 1994).

1507. Tobach, Ethel, and Betty Rosoff, eds. *Challenging Racism and Sexism: Alternatives to Genetic Explanations*. New York: Feminist Press, 1994. 337p. (Genes and Gender, 7). ISBN 1558610898; 1558610901pa.

The Genes and Gender Collective compiled the chapters that compose this volume in response to the ideas espoused by a proponent of sociobiology, "the dominant theory in all disciplines" (p. viii), to present alternative answers to genetic determinism. The collective consists of a diverse group of activists and scholars who not only advocate responsible research in the natural and social sciences, but challenge studies or theories claiming that genetic processes determine human behaviors as well. Contributors provide evidence of racism and sexism in biological, physiological, and psychological research and discuss how racist and sexist assumptions distort knowledge derived from such research in the first several essays. The second section provides historical and philosophical contexts of racism and sexism as illustrated by the eugenics movement, intelligence quotient (IQ) studies, and the social origins of Nazi genetic ideology. The final section features descriptions of contemporary racism and sexism in research conducted in specific cultures in various countries. The powerful essays included in this clearly written work make it an apposite introductory source for arguments against genetic determinism.

The second edition of Anne Fausto-Sterling's important text *Myths of Gender: Biological Theories about Men and Women* (Basic Books, 1992) also serves as an excellent antidote to biological determinism. It features a chapter on sex differences in brain anatomy and homosexuality, as well as an afterword that discusses information published since the 1985 edition. Finally, Robert Poole takes feminist scientists, especially Fausto-Sterling, to task for their supposed "female" irrationality and prejudice, attributing many sex differences to hormonal levels in the womb, in *Eve's Rib: The Biological Roots of Sex Differences* (Crown, 1994).

1508. Wijngaard, Marianne van den. *Reinventing the Sexes: The Biomedical Construction of Femininity and Masculinity*. Bloomington: Indiana University Press, 1997. 171p. (Race, Gender, and Science). bibliog. index. ISBN 0253332508; 0253210879pa.

Using constructivist and social network frameworks, Wijngaard argues that biomedical studies of transgendered people help construct and maintain dimorphic ideas about sex and gender. She also provides an important critique of the organization theory, which credits hormones in the womb for triggering the development of a distinctly male or female brain and therefore distinctly masculine and feminine behaviors. The author argues that scientists embraced the organization theory because it meshed nicely with prevailing "knowledge" about sex differences and ignored conflicting studies. This significant book contains informative notes and a fine bibliography.

Nellie Oudshoorn also applies a social network perspective to her study of conditions surrounding the "discovery" and subsequent history of sex hormones in *Beyond the Natural Body: An Archeology of Sex Hormones* (Routledge, 1994). She believes that material practices of and interactions between gynecologists, pharmaceutical companies, and laboratory scientists during the 1920s and 1930s led to research that changed the basis of sex differences from anatomy to hormones. She also claims that the mass production of hormones and the development of contraceptive pills helped turn the concept of a hormonal body into "knowledge." Adele Clarke examines the interconnecting "social worlds" of biology, medicine, agriculture, philanthropy, and birth-control advocacy that shaped the development of reproductive science in *Disciplining Reproduction: Modernity, American Life Sciences, and the Problem of Sex* (University of California Press, 1998). Clarke accounts for the political, moral, ethical, and cultural factors that influenced the course of science and the construction of knowledge in the field of reproductive science in this multifaceted, complex analysis, the result of twenty years of research. These titles not only contest the immutability of sex and the "natural" body, but also question distinctions among natural and cultural and the "objectivity" of knowledge production.

Technologies

1509. Appleton, Helen, ed. *Do It Herself: Women and Technical Innovation*. London: Intermediate Technology Publications, 1995. 310p. bibliog. ISBN 1853392871.

In an effort to challenge the common view that women passively respond to technology, the Do It Herself research project, funded by UNIFEM, the Ford Foundation, and other organizations, was conceived to examine women's contributions to technical innovations at a grassroots level. Appleton features twenty-two descriptions of case studies covering technologies such as land reclamation in Bangladesh, pottery technology in Kenya, and banana drying in Bolivia. An informative introduction provides background information, explains the terminology and methodology employed in the study, briefly discusses reasons for women's invisibility in technological development, and identifies common themes that the research yielded. Detailed descriptions of technologies and their impact on their communities follow case studies that feature useful information, including education levels, economic factors, and sociopolitical situations, about each country.

Intermediate Technology also published *Missing Links: Gender Equity in Science and Technology for Development*, a 1995 report by the Gender Working Group of the United Nations Commission on Science and Technology, established in 1993, which features essays that explore how science, technology, and gender affect basic human needs in rural areas. The well-written essays, which cover topics such as energy, food security, indigenous knowledge, and literacy, suggest areas for future research and provide specific policy recommendations. This work also features an extensive bibliography and appendix that reviews previous United Nations recommendations regarding science and technology, making it an excellent introduction to the field. Since few studies focus on the gendered aspects of local technologies in the South, these titles belong in every women's studies collection.

1510. Avakian, Arlene Voski. *Through the Kitchen Window: Women Explore the Intimate Meanings of Food and Cooking*. Boston: Beacon Press, 1997. 315p. ISBN 0807065099.

Avakian features the stories, essays, poetry, favorite recipes, and reminiscences about food and cooking of writers such as Julie Dash, Marge Piercy, Dorothy Allison, and Maya Angelou in this collection. She looks at ethnic and cultural backgrounds to connect food to the preservation of identity and heritage in several engaging pieces. Although Margaret Randall's contribution is the only piece that addresses eating disorders, the collection achieves its goal of celebrating the eclectic, if sometimes sensual, meanings of food, eating, and cooking. This work reflects feminism's evolution from viewing cooking, food, and kitchens as sources of oppression and drudgery to places of creative, even subversive activity.

Contributors also explore the connections among women, ethnicity, and food as a site of resistance in the title *In Memory's Kitchen: A Legacy from the Women of Terezin* (Jason Aronson, 1996), edited by Cara de Silva. The author presents traditional recipes that starving Jewish women interned at the Terezin concentration camp in Theresienstadt, Czechoslovakia, gathered during World War II and briefly discusses how collecting these recipes increased their will to survive. This work, an important Holocaust document, provides English translations of the recipes and conversion guidelines for European measurements.

1511. Cassell, Justine, and Henry Jenkins, eds. *From Barbie to Mortal Kombat: Gender and Computer Games*. Cambridge, MA: MIT Press, 1998. 360p. bibliog. index. ISBN 0262032589.

This work, which a daylong symposium at MIT inspired, may be the first published collection that deals with gender and computer games. The eclectic group of contributors, which consists of game software designers, developmental psychologists, educators, industry representatives, game reviewers, and media, technology, and cultural scholars, encourages the game industry to examine core assumptions about gender and games in order to bridge the digital gender divide. The collection features descriptions of the rise of the girls' games movement, presents interviews with six industry leaders who develop computer games for girls, and supports abandoning the prevailing gender dichotomy in light of the desires and needs that girls express in the design of games. One particularly illuminating chapter features editorials that female gamers wrote in response to various discussions about computer games and girls. Chapters conclude with notes and useful reference lists, which often include Web sites, as well as several fine illustrations.

Roberta Furger's *Does Jane Compute? Preserving Our Daughters' Place in the Cyber Revolution* (Warner Books, 1998) also deals with bridging the digital gender gap, but targets parents, teachers, and counselors. The author not only outlines problems faced by girls who are interested in computers, but also offers strategies and resources, such as Web sites, software, and organizations, as a means to solve them.

1512. Cherny, Lynn, and Elizabeth Reba Weise, eds. *Wired Women: Gender and New Realities in Cyberspace*. Seattle: Seal Press, 1996. 269p. ISBN 1878067737.

Cherny and Weise include sixteen thought-provoking essays that women who are actively engaged in cyberspace crafted, including a software engineer, a computer scientist, and various Internet researchers. Contributors examine the present and possible future "shape" of cyberspace, discuss the wide variety of cultures that exist on the Internet, explore gender issues, such as online harassment and censorship, and analyze text-based role-playing environments, including MUDs (multiuser domains, dimensions, or dungeons), which make gender bending and virtual sex possible, even common occurrences. Although the editors do not reflect on the main points of the essays, they effectively create an intriguing and vital collection about an often confusing and complex subject. Dale Spender provides an enthusiastic newcomer's perspective on the Internet in *Nattering on the Net: Women, Power, and Cyberspace* (Spinifex, 1995). The book's strength lies in the first several chapters, in which the author insightfully compares the print and computer revolutions. Later chapters summarize various feminists' works about the enormous impact of the Internet and highlight discussions about the implications of these changes for women.

1513. Cockburn, Cynthia, and Ruža Fürst-Dilić, eds. *Bringing Technology Home: Gender and Technology in a Changing Europe*. Philadelphia: Open University Press, 1994. 187p. index. ISBN 0335191592; 0335191584pa.

Cockburn, coeditor with Susan Ormrod of *Gender and Technology in the Making* (Sage, 1993), in which she provided a detailed study of the development of the microwave oven, continues her efforts to document and explain how gendered technology affects its design and use in this work. Cockburn and Fürst-Dilić present nine empirical studies that researchers conducted specifically for this project to trace the development of technologies such as centralized vacuum cleaning, computerized banking, and teledata systems from design through manufacture, marketing, sale, purchase, use, and maintenance. Although researchers remain cognizant of how social relations affect each step along the way, they frequently emphasize different steps within the process. Nevertheless, the studies share common reference points, all focusing on the extent to which society considers or ignores women when developing new technologies. This work generally conveys the idea that innovative technology "cannot fulfill its creative promise when it is shaped in relations of dominance, whether of race, class, or gender" (p. 20).

The Gender-Technology Relation: Contemporary Theory and Research (Taylor and Francis, 1995), edited by Keith Grint and Rosalind Gill, presents both empirical research and theoretical articles in order to carve out a theoretical framework for future studies about gender-technology relationships. Both works provide valuable models for future feminist research in the field.

1514. Kramarae, Cheris, ed. *Technology and Women's Voices*. New York: Routledge & Kegan Paul, 1988. 246p. index. (OP)

Arguing that technology interconnects with women's speech, contributors examine how specific technological devices such as microphones, computers, typewriters, and sewing machines affect women's social processes and interactions. Although the collection limits discussion to examples from England, Canada, and the United States, it calls for an extension of this kind of work on an international level. Even though many authors investigate the social impacts of specific technologies on women in several excellent works, such as Virginia Scharff's *Taking the Wheel: Women and the Coming Motor Age* (Free Press, 1991) and Michelle Martin's *"Hello Central?": Gender, Technology, and Culture in the Formation of Telephone Systems* (McGill–Queen's University Press, 1991), *Technology and Women's Voices* is one of the few works to concentrate on technology and women's communication. Kramarae, with H. Jeannie Taylor and Maureen Eben, also edited *Women, Information Technology, and Scholarship* (University of Illinois/Center for Advanced Study, 1993), which contains selected articles and digests that the Women, Information Technology, and Scholarship (WITS) Colloquium presented at the yearlong series of seminars and workshops at the University of Illinois.

1515. MacDonald, Anne L. *Feminine Ingenuity: Women and Invention in America.* New York: Ballantine Books, 1992. 514p. bibliog. index. ISBN 0345358112.

MacDonald presents a historical survey of women patent holders in the United States beginning in 1809, the year the author believes the U.S. Patent Office granted a patent to the first woman, Mary Kies, for her straw-weaving process. MacDonald examined materials from a number of libraries and archives, notably the Library of Congress and the National Archives, as well as many periodicals, pamphlets, books, and other resources that she lists in the book's extensive bibliography. She discovered an impressive array of patents, ranging from domestic devices such as knife sharpeners and self-heating irons to chemical compounds, including Liquid Paper and Kevlar. The author also tells the unfortunately common stories of stolen ideas, patent interference suits filed against women, and brothers, husbands, and other men earning undue credit. An appendix listing patents cited in the text and copious notes conclude the book.

Ethlie Ann Vare and Greg Ptacek briefly discuss a wide variety of women inventors from around the world, particularly those whose work was attributed to men, in *Mothers of Invention: From the Bra to the Bomb: Forgotten Women and Their Unforgettable Inventions* (William Morrow, 1988). Unlike McDonald, Vare and Ptacek claim that Mrs. Samuel Slater was the first woman granted an American patent in 1793 for cotton sewing thread. The historical and geographic coverage of this popular book sheds light upon the existence and achievements of women inventors.

1516. McIlwee, Judith Samsom, and J. Gregg Robinson. *Women in Engineering: Gender, Power, and Workplace Culture.* Albany: State University of New York Press, 1992. 248p. (SUNY Series in Science, Technology, and Society). indexes. ISBN 0791408698; 0791408701pa.

This work, which reflects the authors' interests in gender, career segregation, and the increase in high-tech professions during the 1980s, features the results of a study comparing the career paths of men and women engineers who graduated from two southern California schools between 1976 and 1985. The authors provide background information on women's status in the workforce, including nontraditional occupations; survey theoretical perspectives that scholars use to explain women's status; and discuss professional engineering culture. Throughout several chapters of the book, McIlwee and Robinson compare the men and women engineers' childhood backgrounds, college years, workplace environments, and adult families. The authors argue that women's success varied according to area of specialization and type of work environments they encountered. The authors effectively present theory with data in clear prose, often incorporating excerpts from the eighty-two in-depth interviews they conducted, making this work both accessible and thought-provoking.

1517. Morgall, Janine Marie. *Technology Assessment: A Feminist Perspective*. Philadelphia: Temple University Press, 1993. 249p. (Labor and Social Change). bibliog. index. ISBN 1566390907; 1566390915pa.

A feminist sociologist, Morgall contributes one of the first critical analyses of technology assessment (TA), a field that emerged in the 1960s, whose proponents examine the consequences of a particular technology or technological trend on a societal level. According to Morgall, however, two major shortcomings hamper the study of TA: its lack of a theoretical and methodological base and the fact that TA scholars often do not critically analyze results, especially in light of women and gender. The author critically reviews the evolution of TA and medical technology assessment (MTA), outlines frequently used methodologies and their limitations, and introduces feminist research on technology development and feminist approaches to TA and MTA. She then examines research in clerical work and human reproduction that illustrates gender-specific effects of technology that have informed her development of critical, feminist guidelines for TA and MTA. Informative notes and a lengthy bibliography round out this fine work, which would serve as a good primer for studies on these fields.

1518. Penn, Shana. *The Women's Guide to the Wired World: A User-Friendly Handbook*. New York: Feminist Press, 1997. 307p. index. ISBN 1558611673.

Developed from the experiences of the Network of East-West Women (Europe), this work describes electronic tools, including gopher, file transfer protocol (ftp), and e-mail, complete with clear explanations of their applications. Penn makes suggestions for successfully moderating on-line meetings and includes listings for technical support resources maintained by and for women in her guide, which is international in scope. Much of the book functions as a directory for sites devoted to topics such as health, relationships, and gender studies programs or ones geared toward international groups of women such as lesbians and women of color.

Rye Senji and Jane Guthry also present clear, practical "how-to" information, which they supplement with illustrations and step-by-step instructions, in *The Internet for Women* (Spinifex, 1996). However, Senji and Guthry feature more discussion about the social implications of the Internet, such as pornography, privacy, harassment, and gender identity. A significant portion of this book consists of listings for women-oriented Web sites from around the globe, devoted to a variety of topics.

1519. Stage, Sarah, and Virginia B. Vincenti, eds. *Rethinking Home Economics: Women and the History of a Profession*. Ithaca, NY: Cornell University Press, 1997. 347p. index. ISBN 0801429714; 0801481759pa.

In her introduction, Stage argues that even women historians look down upon home economics because of their tendency to focus on the field's connection to nineteenth-century ideas about domesticity. Stage and Vincenti thus collect chapters written by scholars from a variety of backgrounds that examine the intersection of gender and professionalization that took place within the field, beginning early in the twentieth century. They present studies on an eclectic array of topics, including nutrition, the Black Home Extension Services in South Carolina, and rural electrification, interspersed with reminiscences of home economists. They also include a chronology that starts in 1841 and ends in 1995, as well as a list of suggested readings.

Laura Shapiro, whom Stage accuses of using a negative framework in *Rethinking Home Economics*, asserts that the domestic science movement's attempt to give dignity to women's work in the home and increase respect for housewives ironically reinforced prevailing sex roles, thus buttressing support for separate spheres, in *Perfection Salad: Women and Cooking at the Turn of the Century* (Farrar, Straus and Giroux, 1986). The author's use of multifarious sources, including cookbooks, advice columns, recipes, reports from cooking schools, and publications aimed at women, informs her skillfully written exploration of the social, cultural, historical, and scientific developments in nineteenth-century America that produced the movement. Stage's criticism notwithstanding, Shapiro's work is both well researched and highly engaging.

1520. Stewart Millar, Melanie. *Cracking the Gender Code: Who Rules the Wired World?* Toronto: Second Story Press, 1998 (Women's Issues Publishing Program). 230p. bibliog. index. ISBN 1896764142.

Using *Wired* magazine (Wired USA, 1994 to the present) as a prominent example of digital culture, Stewart Millar applies gender discourse analysis to the magazine's messages regarding online technologies and concludes that these messages perpetuate profoundly sexist and racist belief systems. She places the magazine within its socioeconomic context to reveal the differing material effects on men and women. The author also critiques feminist discourse on cyberspace, examining the ideas of authors such as Lynn Cherny and Dale Spender (please see the Cherny and Weise annotation earlier in this section) and cyberfeminists, including Sadie Plant, author of *Zeros + Ones: Digital Women + the New Technoculture* (Doubleday, 1997), who believes that women's political engagement on the Internet automatically will destabilize masculine dominance. Stewart Millar outlines a "feminist politics of anticipation" (p. 67) to develop viable, proactive strategies to ensure positive outcomes for women and other minorities. Other feminist attempts to theorize about cyberspace and/or computer systems include Zillah Eisenstein's woman-centered, Marxist analysis focusing on power relations that re-create "preexisting racial, sexual, and gender inequalities" (p. 70) in *Global Obscenities: Patriarchy, Capitalism, and the Lure of Cyberfantasy* (New York University Press, 1998), and Alison Adam's examination of the myriad, subtle ways in which concepts of masculinity and femininity and mainstream masculine knowledge, rationality, and reasoning become inscribed in artificial intelligence, computer systems designed to model some aspect of human intelligence, in *Artificial Knowing: Gender and the Thinking Machine* (Routledge, 1998). Feminist standpoint and postmodern epistemologies influence Adam in her suggestions to make epistemologies that apply to cyberculture, virtual reality, and the Internet culturally, socially, and politically aware.

1521. Wajcman, Judy. *Feminism Confronts Technology*. Cambridge, England: Polity Press, 1991. 184p. bibliog. index. ISBN 0745607772; 0745607780pa.

Challenging the widespread belief that technology is gender neutral, Wajcman attempts to provide a coherent, feminist theoretical framework to analyze the social interests that support the structure and applications of any number of technologies. She reviews feminist theories of technology and science and then examines specific sectors, including the technologies of production, reproductive technologies, domestic technology, and the built environment. In each chapter, Wajcman critically surveys feminist and sociological literature, particularly emphasizing what she sees as the male bias in the definition and development of technology within each sector. She then analyzes technology's relationship to masculine culture and the consequent tenuous connection between women and technology. She provides excellent chapter notes and an extensive bibliography, making her work a fine introduction to the field.

Technoculture (University of Minnesota Press, 1991), edited by Constance Penley and Andrew Ross, features a postfeminist, postmodern analysis covering less traditional areas of technology, such as cyberpunk, computer hacking, techno-art, and rap music. The essays included in *Processed Lives: Gender and Technology in Everyday Life* (Routledge, 1997), edited by Jennifer Terry and Melodie Calvert, also examine less traditional technologies, including cyberspace, the virtual female, and body morphing, exploring how technologies affect all aspects of people's lives, thus reflecting and often structuring and creating the hierarchically arranged binary opposition of masculinity and femininity that characterizes the current system of gender.

1999 CORE TITLES

Angier, Natalie. *Woman: An Intimate Geography.* Boston: Houghton Mifflin, 1999. 398p. bibliog. index. ISBN 0395691303.

Bryld, Mette. *Cosmodolphins: Feminist Cultural Studies of Technology, Animals, and the Sacred.* New York: Zed Books; distributed in the United States by St. Martin's Press, 1999. 245p. bibliog. index. ISBN 1856498158; 1856498166pa.

Harcourt, Wendy, ed. *Women@Internet: Creating New Cultures in Cyberspace.* New York: Zed Books, 1999. 240p. bibliog. index. ISBN 185649571X; 1856495728pa.

Hawthorne, Susan, and Renate Klein, eds. *Cyberfeminism: Connectivity, Critique, and Creativity.* North Melbourne, Australia: Spinifex, 1999. 434p. ISBN 187555968X.

Hopkins, Patrick D. *Sex/Machine: Readings in Culture, Gender, and Technology.* Bloomington: Indiana University Press, 1999. 510p. (Indiana Series in the Philosophy of Technology). bibliog. index. ISBN 0253334411; 0253212308pa.

Jordanova, Ludmilla J. *Nature Displayed: Gender, Science, and Medicine, 1760–1820: Essays.* New York: Longman, 1999. 260p. bibliog. index. ISBN 0582301904; 0582301890pa.

Kohlstedt, Sally Gregory, ed. *History of Women in the Sciences: Readings from Isis.* Chicago: University of Chicago Press, 1999. 379p. bibliog. index. ISBN 0226450694; 0226450708pa.

Oldenziel, Ruth. *Making Technology Masculine: Men, Women, and Modern Machines in America, 1870–1945.* Amsterdam: Amsterdam University Press, 1999. 271p. bibliog. index. ISBN 9053563814.

Schiebinger, Londa L. *Has Feminism Changed Science?* Cambridge, MA: Harvard University Press, 1999. 252p. bibliog. index. ISBN 0674005449.

Selby, Cecily Cannan, ed. *Women in Science and Engineering: Choices for Success.* New York: New York Academy of Sciences, 1999. 263p. (Annals of the New York Academy of Sciences, v. 869). bibliog. index. ISBN 1573311669; 1573311677pa.

Warren, Wini. *Black Women Scientists in the United States.* Bloomington: Indiana University Press, 1999. 366p. bibliog. index. ISBN 0253336031.

Yount, Lisa. *A to Z of Women in Science and Math.* New York: Facts on File, 1999. 254p. (Facts on File Library of World History). bibliog. index. ISBN 0816037973.

WORLD WIDE WEB/INTERNET SITES

1522. *The Ada Project.* http/:www.mills.edu/.

The Ada Project (TAP), named in honor of Ada Lovelace, often credited with working on a precursor to the modern computer, is a clearinghouse for information and resources related to women in computing. It contains information about conferences, fellowships, organizations, and publications, as well as an extensive listing of links to related sites, some of them aimed at girls. The site is a project of the Association of Computing Machinery's Committee on the Status of Women in Computing.

1523. *Center for Women and Information Technology.* http://www.umbc.edu/cwit/.

Maintained by the University of Maryland in Baltimore County, this page contains an excellent listing of curricular resources on technology issues, as well as links and resources on issues of interest to women in IT or computing. CWIT strives to enhance people's understanding of the relationship between gender and IT.

1524. *4000 Years of Women in Science.* http://www.astr.ua.edu/4000WS/4000WS.html.

This Web site, which the Astronomy Program at the University of Alabama hosts, features many biographies of women in science listed in alphabetical order, by time period, or by discipline (from agronomy to zoology). It also contains photographs, bibliographies of books, journal articles, and other sources, and links to related sites, including sites appropriate for K–12 students.

1525. *International Gender, Science, and Technology Information Map/Women in Global Science and Technology.* http://www.Wigsat.org/GSTPMap.html.

This site provides extensive links to organizations, programs, networks, policy institutes, and pertinent reports from the United Nations relevant to women, development, and technology. It also features links to books, articles, university programs, and other resources that address wide-ranging issues related to the subject.

1526. *Women and Computer Science.* http://www.mills.edu/ACAD_INFO/MCS/ SPERTUS/Gender/gender.html.

Ellen Spertus at Mills College maintains this site, which contains links to online writings, statistics, syllabi, and other material pertaining to women and computer science as well as women and men in academic computer science.

1527. *Women-Related Web Sites in Science/Technology.* http://www-unix.umbc.edu/ ~korenman/wmst/links_sci.html.

This informative Web site, which Joan Korenman of the University of Maryland in Baltimore County maintains, includes annotated lists of sites focusing on science, mathematics, engineering, computing, and information technology. It also links to e-zines, organizations, and associations (including African American Women in Technology, http://www.aawit.net/), statistics, programs, books, and papers. Korenman updates this site, along with her other ones, on a regular basis.

1528. *WSSLINKS: Women and Gender Studies Science and Technology Web Sites.* http:// libraries.mit.edu/humanities/WomensStudies/Tech2.html.

This fine site contains links to books, articles, professional organizations, academic groups, Internet collections, and directories in areas such as archives, education, film, history, theology, as well as sites for international women's issues and lesbians.

PERIODICALS

19   Periodicals

Linda A. Krikos

An increase in the number of scholarly journals in the field is one indication of a discipline's maturity. Both interdisciplinary titles and titles based in traditional disciplines whose authors use gender, women, or feminism as lenses to investigate their subjects mark the maturity of women's studies. Unlike most well-established disciplines, women's studies explores the vital connections between academics and activism since it developed within the women's liberation movement during the late 1960s. Several journals in the field continue to examine these important and dynamic connections. This chapter examines titles still in existence in March 2004 that reflect these developments, as well as the field's increased emphasis on international issues and coverage.

Sources useful to the compilation of this chapter include Betty Glass's "Women: Feminist and Special Interest" section in the seventh through tenth editions of *Magazines for Libraries* (Bowker, 1969–), edited by Bill Katz and Linda Sternberg Katz; *Feminist Periodicals*, published by the Office of the University of Wisconsin System's Women's Studies Librarian; Patrice McDermott's "The Risks and Responsibilities of Feminist Academic Journals" (*NWSA Journal*, vol. 6, no. 3, Fall 1994, pp. 373–383); McDermott's *Politics and Scholarship: Feminist Academic Journals and the Production of Knowledge* (University of Illinois Press, 1994); and Audrey Eaglen's three-part series "Spreading the Word about Women: Contemporary Women's and Feminist Journals" (*WLW Journal*, vol. 14, no. 4, Summer 1991; vol. 15, no. 1, Spring 1992; and vol. 15, no. 2, Summer 1992). This chapter covers periodicals that began publishing after the last edition of this book was released. Refer to the appendix for a list of special issues of both new and selected older women's studies journals published between 1986 and 1999. Quotes within annotations are derived from the journal's statement of purpose. Citations reflect information from issues of journals as of March 2004 and include the journal or publisher's e-mail and Web page addresses if provided.

1529. *Abafazi: The Simmons College Review of Women of African Descent*, Vol. 1– , No. 1– . Boston: Simmons College, 1991– . http://www.simmons.edu/abafazi/. semiannual. ISSN 1078–1323.

Members of the African American Studies Department of Simmons College established the journal *Abafazi*, which means "women" in Ndebele, to heighten awareness and understanding of women of African descent within the academic field of Africana studies. They welcome contributions from all disciplines, theoretical perspectives, and methodological approaches, especially work that explores interactions between race, gender, class, sexuality, and geographic location. Issues typically include interviews with women such as Paule Marshall and Miriam DeCosta Willis, profiles of women such as bell hooks, Angela Davis, and Buchi Emecheta, and articles on topics such as mysticism in Toni Morrison's work, adolescent girls, and apartheid. The journal also features photo-essays, poetry, brief discussions about the work of artists such as Valerie Maynard, Deborah Willis, and Winnie Owens Hart, and a section that lists conferences, workshops, calls for papers, and grant opportunities. This title partially fills the gap caused by the cessation of *Sage: A Scholarly Journal on Black Women* (Sage Women's Educational Press, 1984–1995).

1530. *Affilia: Journal of Women and Social Work*, Vol. 1– , No. 1– . Thousand Oaks, CA: Sage Publications, 1986– . info@sagepub.com. http://www.sagepub.com. quarterly. ISSN 0886-1099.

Founded to explore the impact of the women's movement on social work, *Affilia* publishes articles that apply feminist values, theories, and knowledge to social work research, education, and practice. The journal's staff is interested especially in works that focus on ending discrimination based on gender, race, class, ethnicity, age, disability, and sexual orientation. Issues contain articles, editorials, research reports, literary pieces, and book reviews written by specialists. The editors also consider manuscripts from other fields that feature analysis of women within a social welfare context.

1531. *Asian Women*. Vol. 1– . Seoul, Korea: Research Center for Asian Women, Sookmyung Women's University Press, 1995– . ISSN 1225-925X.

Established in 1960, the Research Center for Asian Women conducts interdisciplinary research in a variety of subjects, including literature, economics, politics, sociology, and international relations. Scholars affiliated with the center founded this journal not only to encourage communication among researchers of women's issues in Asian and other countries, but also to publish articles representing several perspectives that present challenges in the field of women's studies. Issues include articles, book reviews, conference reports, and resource materials. The interdisciplinary *Asian Journal of Women's Studies* (Asian Center for Women's Studies, Ewha Woman's University [Seoul, Korea], 1995–) is based in Korea as well. Other notable journals from Asian regions and countries include *Lila: Asia Pacific Women's Studies Journal* (Institute of Women's Studies, St. Scholastica's College [Manila, Philippines], 1992–), which produces theme-based issues containing scholarly articles, reviews, and other features; *Pakistan Journal of Women's Studies/Alam-e-Niswan* (Town University of Karachi, 1994–), an interdisciplinary journal that publishes research, reviews, curricula and course outlines, and conference reports; *Indian Journal of Gender Studies* (Sage Publications, 1994–), established to analyze gender categories and present a holistic view of the family, community, and society; and *U.S.-Japan Women's Journal: English Supplement* (Josai Center c/o Extension Center, University of California at Riverside, 1991–), which publishes scholarship about women and gender in Japan, the United States, and other countries.

1532. *Critical Matrix: The Princeton Journal of Women, Gender, and Culture*, Vol. 1– , No. 1– . Princeton, NJ: Program in Women's Studies, Princeton University, 1985– . matrix@princeton.edu. http://www.princeton.edu/~prowom/CM/. semiannual. ISSN 1066-288X.

Originally consisting of working papers presented within Princeton University's Program in Women's Studies and the Graduate Research Colloquium in Women's Studies, *Critical Matrix* strives to open a dialogue among researchers from various disciplines who concentrate on issues and methodologies in women's studies. In 1992, however, the editorial policy broadened to examine the boundaries between academic research and the real world. The graduate students who continued to edit the journal thus began to solicit new visual or written material that combined academic, creative, and political approaches to gender. The Council of Editors of Learned Journals named this journal winner of the Phoenix Award for Significant Editorial Achievement in 1995.

1533. *differences: A Journal of Feminist Cultural Studies*, Vol. 1– , No. 1– . Bloomington: Duke University Press, 1989– . http://www.dukeupress.edu/journals. 3/yr. ISSN 1040-7391.

Affiliated with the Pembroke Center for Teaching and Research on Women at Brown University, *differences* examines cultural politics and discursive practices as informed by feminist criticism. The editors, who model the journal's format and theoretical orientation on poststructuralist rather than feminist journals, use the "dilemma of difference" as a basis for cultural criticism and accordingly have produced some groundbreaking special issues (see the appendix). Editors model the journal *Genders: Presenting Innovative Work in the Arts, Humanities, and Social Theories* (University of Colorado at Boulder, 1988–) on poststructuralist journals as well. *Genders* concentrates on the construction of gender within the arts and humanities and publishes articles that explore theoretical issues pertaining to how sexuality and gender relate to social, political, racial, economic, or stylistic concerns. Originally published three times a year, *Genders* changed format in 1994 by designing each semiannual issue as a stand-alone anthology. However, the journal ended its anthology format with issue 27 (1998), becoming available only on the Internet (http://www.genders.org) at no charge.

1534. *European Journal of Women's Studies*, Vol. 1– , No. 1– . Thousand Oaks, CA: Sage Publications, 1994– . subscriptions@sagepub.co.uk. http://www.sagepub.co.uk. quarterly. ISSN 1350-5068.

Nominated for the United Kingdom Women in Publishing New Venture Award in 1994, the *European Journal of Women's Studies* demonstrates the vitality of feminist research and women's studies in Europe via analyzing how all aspects of human activity reflect gender. Although most articles are written in English, summaries in French and German also are included. Each issue offers book reviews, conference reports, and other features. The Hull Centre for Gender Studies, which is located in Great Britain, connects the academy to the community in the interdisciplinary *Journal of Gender Studies*: An International Forum for the Debate on Gender in All Fields of Study. (Carfax, Taylor & Francis, 1991–), which features accessibly written articles targeted for general but informed readers. The articles contribute to gender debates on several subjects from various feminist, political, and theoretical perspectives. Issues include reviews and lists of conferences, organizations, calls for papers, and networking opportunities as well. Another interdisciplinary title from Europe that concentrates on regional interests is *NORA: Nordic Journal of Women's Studies* (Taylor & Francis, 1993–), which publishes examinations of women's lives in Nordic countries, along with interdisciplinary and theoretical work of general interest to feminist researchers.

1535. *Feminism and Psychology: An International Journal*, Vol. 1– , No. 1– . Thousand Oaks, CA: Sage Publications, 1991– . subscription@sagepub.co.uk. http://www. sagepub.co.uk. quarterly. ISSN 0959-3535.

Contributors to this journal delve into intersections between feminism (as opposed to women, gender, or sex roles) and psychology, primarily focusing on feminism. Although the editors welcome work from other disciplines, most notably sociology, philosophy, anthropology, education, and literary criticism, the work must clearly addresses psychological implications. The editors particularly encourage theoretical and practical articles that explore conjunctions among race, class, disability, age, and other categories. Journal issues feature theoretical and empirical work, as well as research reviews, reports, interviews, book reviews, and debates about a variety of issues. Unabashedly based in British radical feminism, the creators of this journal have set their own agenda for influencing social changes.

1536. *Feminist Economics*, Vol. 1– , No.1– . Philadelphia: Routledge, Taylor & Francis, 1995– . info@tandf.co.uk, http://www.tandf.co.uk/journals/, http://www .feministeconomics.org. 3/yr. ISSN 1354-5071.

The official journal of the International Association for Feminist Economics, *Feminist Economics* opens new areas of economic inquiry and discourse to develop more enlightening theories that can lead to improved living conditions for all men, women, and children. The editors explore the many implications of feminist economic research in related fields and welcome essays that use historical, institutional, cross-disciplinary, or cross-cultural perspectives. Contributors have examined topics such as paid housework, women's agency in classic economic thought, and lesbian, gay, and bisexual perspectives of economics. The Council of Editors of Learned Journals in 1997 voted this title, which is the first international, scholarly journal devoted to feminist analysis of economics and economic issues, "Best New Journal."

1537. *Gender and Development*, Vol. 3– , No. 1– . Cambridge, MA: Taylor & Francis, 1995– . enquiry@tandf.co.uk. http://www.tandf.co.uk/journals. http:www.oxfam .org/publish/jgen. 3/yr. ISSN 1355-2074. Continues *Focus on Gender*, Vol. 1, No. 1– Vol. 2, No. 3, 1993–1994.

A product of Oxfam, a nongovernmental organization in Great Britain, *Gender and Development* specifically focuses on international gender and development issues and initiatives to connect theoretical and practical work in the field. Activists, practitioners, and academics comprise the journal's list of contributors, who provide articles, case studies, conference reports, interviews, and other materials for each theme-based issue (see the appendix). Themes have included urban settlement, women and culture, gender and migration, women's poverty in the North, and gender and technology.

1538. *Gender and Society*, Vol. 1– , No. 1– . Thousand Oaks, CA: Sage Publications, 1987– . order@sagepub.com. http://www.sagepub.com. 6/yr. ISSN 0891-2432.

Gender and Society, the official publication of the Sociologists for Women in Society, seeks to contribute to research and theory on the social aspects of gender, which the society considers "a basic principle of social order and a primary social category." The journal contains articles that examine the institutional and situational processes that construct this category. Contributors who represent various disciplines, including anthropology, history, economics, political science, sociology, and psychology, cover a broad range of subjects, such as racial politics within feminist organizations, migration patterns of Turkish rural women, and micro enterprise. Each issue features perceptive book reviews usually written by specialists in the field.

1539. *Gender, Place, and Culture: A Journal of Feminist Geography*. Vol. 1– , No. 1– . Philadelphia: Carfax, Taylor & Francis, 1994– . enquiry@tandf.co.uk. http:// www.tandf.co.uk/journals. quarterly. ISSN 0966-369X.

Founded to provide a "focal point" for the considerable amount of research produced in feminist geography and related fields since the 1970s, *Gender, Place, and Culture* features material that examines how gender divisions vary according to geographic location. Issues generally include several articles, reactions to articles previously published in the journal, commentaries, short reports, and book reviews. Contributors analyze the cultural constructions and politics of gender, particularly how gender intersects with race, nationality, class, ethnicity, sexuality, age, and other social categories. *Gender and Education* (Carfax, 1989–), another discipline-focused journal by the same publisher, welcomes disparate works that concentrate on gender as a category in education and contribute to feminist knowledge, action, debate, consciousness, and theory. Geographic coverage appears to focus on Great Britain, Commonwealth countries, and developing countries.

1540. *Journal of Feminist Family Therapy: An International Forum*, Vol. 1– , No. 1– . Binghamton, NY: Haworth Press, 1989– . getinfo@haworthpress.com. http://www.haworthpress.com. quarterly. ISSN 0895–2833.

Aimed at both scholars and practitioners, this journal explores the relationship between feminist theory and family therapy practice/theory in terms of education, training, supervision, treatment issues, and institutional practices. Editors publish theoretical articles, empirical research, clinical applications, and interviews covering topics such as family violence, child care responsibilities among dual-career couples, mother/daughter connections, and power dynamics within therapeutic relationships.

1541. *Journal of Feminist Studies in Religion*, Vol. 1– , No. 1– . Williston, VT: Society of Biblical Literature, 1985– . sblorders@aidcvt.com. http://www.sbl-site.org. semiannual. ISSN 8755–4178.

Based in both the academy and the feminist movement, this scholarly journal strives to transform religious studies as a discipline and increase feminist perspectives and ideas within religious and cultural institutions. Articles reflect a wide range of feminist voices that represent diverse religious perspectives. Subjects examined in articles include Pauli Murray's theological development, Jewish spirituality, Buddhist contributions to feminism, prostitution, and female priests in ancient Egypt. Issues include review essays, rather than reviews of individual titles, and reports on conferences, projects, activism, and feminist theological developments from around the world.

1542. *Journal of Lesbian Studies*, Vol.1– , No. 1– . Binghamton, NY: Haworth Press, 1996– . getinfo@haworthpress.com. http://www.haworthpress.com. quarterly. ISSN 1089–4160.

The *Journal of Lesbian Studies* is the only professional journal solely devoted to lesbian experiences, scholarship, and commentary at an international level. Whereas the first two issues reprinted "classic" articles in lesbian studies, later theme-based issues have featured articles on topics that include open relationships, nonmonogamy, and casual sex; sexuality, gender, and performance; work and family life; and lesbian health issues. Issues contain several book reviews as well. Academic libraries also should consider *GLQ: A Journal of Lesbian and Gay Studies* (Gordon & Breach, 1993–1997; Duke University Press, 1998–), which publishes "cutting-edge" theoretical articles and book and film reviews.

1543. *Journal of Women and Aging: The Multidisciplinary Quarterly of Psychosocial Practice, Theory, and Research*. Vol. 1– , No. 1/2/3– . Binghamton, NY: Haworth Press, 1989– . getinfo@haworthpress.com. http://www.haworthpress.com. quarterly. ISSN 0895–2841.

Targeted for students, practitioners, administrators, and educators in a wide variety of disciplines, this journal publishes articles that delve into practical theory and research about specific and diverse issues that affect aging women. The editors indicate that despite the fact that most of the present and future aging population is female, much of the literature focuses on aging men or the aged as a group. Because the editors recognize the "invasive and historical patterns of socioeconomic and gender stratification in society," they provide information to improve policies and treatment of older women. Articles have examined subjects such as spirituality, African American women, cosmetic surgery, retirement, and economic realities of rural women.

1544. *Journal of Women's History*, Vol. 1– , No. 1– . Bloomington: Indiana University Press, 1989– . journals@indiana.edu. http://www.iupjournals.org. quarterly. ISSN 1042–7961.

The first scholarly, refereed title to focus solely on women's history, the *Journal of Women's History* provides an arena for important theoretical and methodological debates in the field regardless of time period or geographic location. Geared toward specialists in women's history and others who want to integrate women and gender issues into courses in related fields, the journal contains English translations of important articles written in other languages, as well as reviews of books, textbooks, films, oral histories, and exhibits. It also includes sections wherein contributors discuss methodologies and research processes and/or report problems and issues facing women in troubled areas of the world. *Women's History Review* (Triangle Journals, 1992–) also deals with women as opposed to gender, examining both commonalities and differences of women's experiences. Each issue features research articles, book reviews, and short pieces often based on the author's life experiences. In contrast to these two titles, *Gender and History* (Blackwell, 1989–) also addresses men and masculinity to explore ways in which power relations between men and women have shaped various societies.

1545. *N. Paradoxa: International Feminist Art Journal*. London: KT Press, 1998– . Semiannual. ISSN 1461-0434. Available quarterly online at http://web.ukonline.co.uk/n.paradoxa/.

Edited by noted feminist scholar Katy Deepwell, *N. Paradoxa* claims to be the "only international feminist art journal exploring feminist theory and contemporary women's art practices." Issues usually contain theoretical and critical articles, interviews with artists, and reviews of exhibits, books, and Web sites, as well as artists' pages. The quarterly publication *Women in the Arts* (National Museum of Women in the Arts, 1991–) regularly features "museum watch," a calendar of exhibitions of works by women artists, a calendar of NMWA events, articles about women artists, and artwork owned by NMWA. High-quality, color illustrations often accompany the text. *Women Artists News Book Review* (Midmarch Associates, 1993–), which continues the numbering of the superseded *Women Artists News* (1978–1992), also contains articles, editorials, and reviews of art by women and is available online via the database *GenderWatch* by subscription.

1546. *NWSA Journal: A Publication of the National Women's Studies Association*, Vol. 1– , No. 1– . Bloomington: Indiana University Press, 1988– . journals@indiana .edu. http://www.iupjournals.org. 3/yr. ISSN 1040–0656.

This scholarly journal publishes research stemming from and supporting the women's movement as it has evolved since the late 1960s. According to Patricinio Schweickart, the editor from 1992 through 1997, the journal's guiding principle is scholarship as social action. Since the NWSA considers itself a major resource for teaching women's studies, the journal reviews textbooks and other curricular materials beginning with kindergarten and announces scholarships, NWSA news, workshops, calls for papers, publications, and other items of interest.

1547. *Phoebe: An Interdisciplinary Journal of Feminist Scholarship, Theory, and Aesthetics*, Vol. 1– , No. 1– . Oneonta, NY: Women's Studies Department, State University of New York at Oneonta, 1989– . semiannual. ISSN 1045–0904.

Phoebe serves as an arena for cross-cultural feminist analysis, original research, debate, and exchange about women's experiences and conditions within their sociopolitical contexts. The editors particularly welcome theoretical work from scholars representing a variety of disciplines who examine race, gender, class, or sexual minorities on topics such as household economics, colonialist discourse, female-to-male transsexuals, and African American studies. Issues usually contain poetry and short fiction as well.

1548. *Race, Gender, and Class: An Interdisciplinary and Multicultural Journal.* Vol. 2, No. 2. New Orleans: Department of Social Sciences, Southern University at New Orleans, 1995– . http://www.suno.edu/sunorgc/. quarterly. ISSN 1082–8354.

Race, Gender, and Class publishes articles, film and book review essays, autobiographies, and other items about any number of interdisciplinary subjects that deal with the intersection of these categories. Articles are written in an accessible language for undergraduate students enrolled in introductory or general education classes across disciplines. Issues have included discussions of environmental justice and injustice, Chicana feminist standpoint epistemologies, biological determinism, postmodernism and indigenous peoples, and multiculturalism in Australia and New Zealand.

1549. *Social Politics: International Studies in Gender, State, and Society*, Vol. 1– , No. 1– . New York: Oxford University Press, 1994– . jnlorders@oup-usa.org. http://www.sp.oupjournals.org. 3/yr. ISSN 1072–4745.

Geared toward scholars, activists, and policy makers, *Social Politics* features articles that examine the profound influence of gender in the development and politics of states. The editors recognize the interactive influences of gender and social policy on gender relationships in the family and society and at work. Issues often contain an "agendas" section that delves into contemporary debates and issues in gender politics in different countries, and sections providing cultural and historical background for various areas and countries. The editors publish review essays of core books in the field as opposed to individual book reviews and solicit articles written in languages other than English.

1550. *Violence against Women: An International and Interdisciplinary Journal*, Vol. 1– , No. 1– . Thousand Oaks, CA: Sage Publications, 1995– . order@sagepub.com. http://www.sagepub.com. 12/yr. ISSN 1077–8012.

Recognizing that violence against women is both a global health and human rights issue, the editors of *Violence against Women* publish empirical studies, historical and cross-cultural analysis, theoretical articles, and articles pertaining to treatment, advocacy, policy, and related issues. Articles have addressed topics such as domestic violence, sexual assault, harassment, female infanticide, female circumcision, and female sexual slavery. Aimed at survivors as well as academics, practitioners, advocates, and activists, the journal also includes the poetry and other creative works of abuse survivors.

1551. *Women: A Cultural Review*, Vol. 1– , No. 1– . Oxford, UK: Taylor & Francis, 1990– . http://www.tandf.co.uk. 3/yr. ISSN 0957–4042.

Developed partially to fill the void caused by the cessation of the noteworthy British titles *m/f* (m/f, 1978–1986) and *Women's Review* (Women's Review, 1985–1987), *Women: A Cultural Review* contributes to debates about sexuality and gender through analysis of the many ways in which the arts and culture represent women, both past and present. The journal's editors broadly define arts and culture to include theater, poetry, fiction, television, history, law, education, dance, film, and anthropology. Two issues per year focus on specific topics (see the appendix). All issues feature long book reviews, which specialists in the field typically compose, and a section announcing conferences, calls for papers, exhibits, books, and other information.

1552. *Women and Criminal Justice*, Vol. 1– , No. 1– . Binghamton, NY: Haworth Press, 1989– . getinfo@haworthpress.com. http://www.haworthpress.com. quarterly. ISSN 0897–4454.

With an international editorial board, *Women and Criminal Justice* uses an interdisciplinary perspective to provide a single, global forum for members of the academy and representatives of governments, private institutions, and agencies to exchange information about the myriad issues associated with women in criminal justice. Articles address topics such as women terrorists, women in criminal justice professions, health care for incarcerated women, and women as victims in literature, television, and film and present cross-national or cross-cultural research, policies, and practices. In 1996, the journal introduced a section that discusses teaching methods in criminal justice classrooms.

1553. *Women and Music: A Journal of Gender and Culture*, Vol. 1– . Washington, DC: International Alliance for Women in Music, 1997– . annual. ISSN 1090–7505.

Women and Music consists of scholarly articles and reviews, written largely by academics, about topics such as music history, contemporary music, various music genres, and gender studies. Extensive bibliographic footnotes and black-and-white illustrations supplement the text. The IAWM also publishes *IAWM Journal/International Alliance for Women in Music* (International Alliance for Women in Music, 1995–), which supersedes *ILWC Journal/International League of Women Composers* (International League of Women Composers, 1989–1995), in February, June, and October. It contains CD, cassette, book, and concert reviews, as well as articles on women in music and sex discrimination in music, and prints reports of professional conferences, award announcements, and broadcast schedules of music by women. It is available online at http://music.acu.edu/www/iawm. Each issue of *Women of Note Quarterly: The Magazine of Historical and Contemporary Women Composers* (Vivace Press, 1993–) contains at least one profile of a woman composer, often written as an interview, as well as scholarly articles, reviews of CDs and albums, news briefs, and notes of awards. Issues are brief, usually between twenty-five and thirty pages, but provide timely and worthwhile information.

1554. *Women in Judaism: A Multidisciplinary Journal*, Vol.1– , No.1– . Toronto: University of Toronto, 1997– . http://www.utoronto.ca/wjudaism/. semiannual. ISSN 1209–9392.

Available only on the Internet, this refereed journal encourages scholarly debates pertaining to gender issues in Judaism. Issues contain articles that discuss topics such as lesbianism in Jewish law, wife beating, and feminist readings of the story of Adam and Eve, along with reviews, essays, and bibliographies. Academic libraries also should consider *Nashim: A Journal of Jewish Women's Studies and Gender Issues* (International Research Institute on Jewish Women/Seminary of Judaic Studies, 1998–), which features scholarly articles from a variety of disciplines, literary and artistic pieces, and reviews.

A more activist title, *Bridges: A Journal for Jewish Feminists and Our Friends* (Bridges Association, 1990–), which explores relationships among the lesbian, feminist, and Jewish renewal movements, provides "a specifically Jewish voice within the multi-ethnic feminist movement." *Bridges* is appropriate for high-school, public, and academic libraries.

1555. *Women in Sport and Physical Activity Journal*, Vol.1– , No. 1– . Las Vegas, NV: Women of Diversity Productions, 1992– . dvrsty@aol.com. http://women ofdiversity.org. semiannual. ISSN 1063–6161.

Made possible by a grant from the Women's Sports Foundation, this journal was created to enhance the visibility of research activities relating to women and girls in sport and physical activity. The journal targets teachers, coaches, researchers, and administrators involved with physical education, intramurals, sport science, kinesiology, women's studies, and fitness, exercise, and health. Editors consider works in a variety of formats, including research articles, review essays, creative writing, or book, film, and instructional resource reviews.

1556. *Yale Journal of Law and Feminism*, Vol.1– , No.1– . New Haven, CT: Yale Law School, 1989– . http://www.yale.edu/lawnfem/law&fem.html. semiannual. ISSN 1043–9366.

The *Yale Journal of Law and Feminism* enhances feminist perspectives in mainstream legal scholarship via concentrating on how the law affects women's lives. Although the editors welcome submissions of artwork, poetry, autobiographical pieces, and other creative writing, most issues consist of case studies, legal briefs, and articles examining topics such as reproductive freedom, welfare reform, pornography, lynching, antidiscrimination, and the absence of young gays and lesbians in legal discourse.

Other notable law journals from the United States include *Columbia Journal of Gender and Law* (Columbia School of Law, 1991–), which publishes legal and interdisciplinary articles on subjects inadequately addressed in mainstream law journals, and *Berkeley Women's Law Journal* (University of California at Berkeley, 1986–), mandated "to publish research, analysis, narrative, theory, and commentary that addresses the lives and struggles of underrepresented women." For a European perspective, see *Feminist Legal Studies* (University of Canterbury, 1993–), which contributes to debates in feminist legal theory and examines how the law applies to women's issues.

1999–2000 CORE TITLES

Feminist Theory, Vol. 1– , No. 1– . Thousand Oaks, CA: Sage Publications, 2000– . subscriptions@sagepub.co.uk. http://www.sagepub.co.uk. 3/yr. ISSN 1464–7001.

International Feminist Journal of Politics, Vol. 1– , No. 1– . Philadelphia: Routledge Journals, Taylor & Francis, 1999– . enquiry@tandf.co.uk. http://www.tandf.co.uk. 3/yr. ISSN 1461–6742.

Journal of the Association for Research on Mothering, Vol. 1– , No. 1– . Toronto: Center for Research on Mothering, York University, 1999– . crm@yorku.ca. http://www.yorku.ca/crm/. semiannual. ISSN 1488–0989.

Meridians: Feminism, Race, Transnationalism, Vol. 1– , No. 1– . Middletown, CT: Wesleyan University, 2000– . http://www.smith.edu/meridians/. semiannual. ISSN 1536–6936.

WORLD WIDE WEB/INTERNET SITES

1557. *Feminist and Women's Journals.* http://www.feminist.org/research/pubjourn.html.
Part of the page maintained by the Feminist Research Center and the Feminist Majority Foundation, this annotated list focuses on scholarly journals in economics, law, feminist theory, medicine, psychology and psychotherapy, and other subjects. The page provides links to publishers' Web sites.

1558. *Magazines and Newsletters on the Web (Women-Focused); Women's Studies/ Women's Magazines E-Journals at UW-Madison.* http://www.library.wisc.edu/libraries/ WomensStudies/.
Both of these lists are maintained by the Office of the Women's Studies Librarian at the University of Wisconsin at Madison. The first site focuses on popular and news titles and connects to free sites or sites that contain sample articles and table of contents information. The second list focuses on more scholarly titles and their availability via databases such as *Contemporary Women's Issues, ProQuest Research Library, Lexis-Nexis/Academic Universe, GenderWatch,* and *Academic Search Elite* for affiliates of the university.

1559. *Women's Studies, Feminist, and Gender Periodicals.* http://www.nau.edu/~wst/ access/periodichome.html.
Maintained by Northern Arizona University, this database lists information for more than 1,000 scholarly journals, newsletters, newspapers, and zines that regularly include feminist research or items of interest pertaining to gender, women, or feminism. Users can access the list by broad subject (Chicana/Latina studies, disability, film, labor studies, lesbian studies, and so on) or alphabetically by title. It also indicates each title's electronic availability via full text (*Contemporary Women's Issues, Catchword, GenderWatch, EBSCO, Project Muse,* and the like), table of contents, and abstract services. The site also provides links to periodicals publishers, other Web listings, and library listings of journals.

1560. *Women's Studies Section Core Journals for Women's Studies* http://libr.org/wss/ projects/serial.html.
This extremely useful site was developed by the Women's Studies Section (WSS) of the Association of College and Research Libraries to assist librarians in building women's studies journal collections that support a foundation for study and research from various feminist perspectives. It includes currently published titles in the social sciences, humanities, sciences, and women's studies suitable for academic libraries. Citation information provides the first year of publication, the publisher, the number of issues per year, and the ISSN. Brief annotations describe the purpose of the journal and the type of articles it publishes. Entries also provide indexing information in women's studies indexes and disciplinary indexes, electronic coverage, and the publisher's URL. WSS intends to review the list annually.

Appendix:
Special Issues of Journals, 1986–1999

Special issues listed here were identified as such on the issue's cover or table of contents page. Thematic sections consisting of at least three articles are also included. Citations are provided for journal titles mentioned in annotations in chapter 19 ("Periodicals") and selected older journals still being published in 2004 and include title, place of publication, publisher, date of initial publication, publisher's e-mail and Web addresses (if provided), frequency, International Standard Serial Number (ISSN), and electronic availability as of March 2004. Citation information is not repeated for main entries in Chapter 19. *Feminist Periodicals* (Office of the Women's Studies Librarian at Large, University of Wisconsin System, 1981–) and publishers' Web sites were consulted for issues missing from Ohio State University Libraries. Issues published in 2000 are included if they complete the volume.

Affilia: Journal of Women and Social Work.

　　A Feminist Look at Women in Families Vol. 7, No. 2 (Summer 1992)

Asian Women.

　　Toward 2000: Gender Equality Vol. 1 (1995)

　　Women and Power Vol. 2 (1996)

　　Gender and the Politics of the College Curriculum Vol. 3 (Winter 1996)

　　Women and the Media in the Asia-Pacific Area Vol. 4 (Spring 1997)

　　Women's Movements in Asia: Social, Historical, and Cultural Perspectives Vol. 5 (Fall 1997)

　　Gender and Body Politics Vol. 6 (June 1998)

　　Gender and Globalization in Asia I: Women's Employment History and Patterns Vol. 7 (1998)

　　Gender and Globalization in Asia II: Representation of Women in Literature and Arts Vol. 8 (June 1999)

　　Women and the Millennium in Asia Vol. 9 (December 1999)

Atlantis, a Women's Studies Journal/Revue d'études sur les Femmes, Vol. 1– , No. 1– . Halifax, Nova Scotia: Institute for the Study of Women, Mount St. Vincent University, 1975– . atlantis@msvu.ca. http://www.msvu.ca/atlantis/. semiannual. ISSN 0702–7818.

　　Part One of Peace Issue Vol. 12, No. 1 (Fall 1986)

　　Part Two of Peace Issue Vol. 12, No. 2 (Spring 1987)

　　Connecting Practices, Doing Theory Vol. 21, No. 1 (Fall 1996)

　　Feminism and the New Right in Canada Vol. 21, No. 2 (Spring 1997)

　　Sexualities and Feminisms Vol. 23, No. 1 (Fall/Winter 1998)

　　Sexual Economics Vol. 23, No. 2 (Spring 1999)

Australian Feminist Studies. No. 1–   . Philadelphia: Carfax, Taylor & Francis, 1985–   . enquiry@tandf.co.uk. http//www.tandf.co.uk. 3/yr. ISSN 0816-4649. elec: EBSCO; IG; ISI; OCLC; RC; Swets.

>   *Feminism and the Body* 5 (Summer 1987)
>
>   *Sex/Gender* 10 (Summer 1989)
>
>   *Writing Lives: Feminist Biography and Autobiography* 16 (Summer 1992)
>
>   *Gender and Ethnicity* 18 (Summer 1993)
>
>   *Women and Citizenship* 19 (Autumn 1994)
>
>   *Third International Playwrights Conference* 21 (Autumn 1995)
>
>   *Sex and the Body Politic* 25 (April 1997)
>
>   *Feminist Science Studies* 29 (April 1999)

Bridges: A Journal for Jewish Feminists and Our Friends. Vol. 1, No. 1–   . Eugene, OR: Bridges Association, 1990–   . ckinberg@pond.net. http://www.pond.net/~ckinberg/bridges. semiannual. ISSN 1046-8358.

>   *Young Jewish Women Ages 13–30* Vol. 6, No. 2 (Spring 1997)
>
>   *Sephardi and Mizrahi Women Write about Their Lives* Vol. 7, No. 1 (Winter 1997–1998)

Camera Obscura Feminism, Culture, and Media Studies. No. 1–   . Durham, NC: Duke University Press, 1976–   . subscriptions@dukeupress.edu. http://www.dukeupress.edu/. 3/yr. ISSN 0270–5346. elec: EBSCO; Gale; GW; IG; ISI; LN; OCLC; PM; RC; Swets.

>   *Science Fiction and Sexual Difference* 15 (Fall 1986)
>
>   *Television and the Female Consumer* 16 (January 1988)
>
>   *Male Trouble* 17 (May 1988)
>
>   *On Contemporary China* 18 (September 1988)
>
>   *The Spectatrix* 20/21 (May/September 1989)
>
>   *Feminism and Film History* 22 (January 1990)
>
>   *Popular Culture and Reception Studies* 23 (May 1990)
>
>   *Unspeakable Images* 24 (September 1990)
>
>   *Imaging Technologies, Inscribing Science* 28 (January 1992)
>
>   *Lifetime: A Cable Network "For Women"* 33/34 (May/September/January 1994/1995)
>
>   *Black Women, Spectatorship, and Visual Culture* 36 (September 1995)
>
>   *Angels Dinosaurs Aliens* 40/41 (May 1997)

Canadian Woman Studies/les cahiers de la femme. Vol. 1, No. 1–   . North York, Ontario: Inanna Publications and Education, York University, 1978–   . cwscf@yorku.ca. http://www.yorku.ca/cwscf. quarterly. ISSN 0713–3235. elec: CWI; Gale; LN; OCLC; Wilson.

>   *Post Nairobi* Vol. 7, No. 1/2 (Spring/Summer 1986)
>
>   *Canadian Women's History* Vol. 7, No. 3 (Fall 1986)
>
>   *Canadian Women's History* Vol. 7, No. 4 (Winter 1986)
>
>   *Women and Media* Vol. 8, No. 1 (Spring 1987)
>
>   *Mediterranean Women* Vol. 8, No. 2 (Summer 1987)
>
>   *Margaret Laurence* Vol. 8, No. 3 (Fall 1987)

Women's Psychology Vol. 8, No. 4 (Winter 1987)

Women Working for Peace Vol. 9, No. 1 (Spring 1988)

Nordic Women Vol. 9, No. 2 (Summer 1988)

Women and Literacy Vol. 9, No. 3/4 (Fall/Winter 1988)

Refugee Women Vol. 10, No. 1 (Spring 1989)

Native Women Vol. 10, No. 2/3 (Summer/Fall 1989)

Soviet Women Vol. 10, No. 4 (Winter 1989)

Feminism and Visual Art Vol. 11, No. 1 (Spring 1990)

Women and Housing Vol. 11, No. 2 (Fall 1990)

A Decade of CWS/CF Vol. 11, No. 3 (Spring 1991)

Violence against Women Vol. 11, No. 4 (Summer 1991)

Violence against Women: Strategies for Change Vol. 12, No. 1 (Fall 1991)

Growing into Age Vol. 12, No. 2 (Winter 1992).

Gender Equity and Institutional Change Vol. 12, No. 3 (Spring 1992)

Women in Poverty Vol. 12, No. 4 (Summer 1992)

South Asian Women: Lives, Histories, Struggles Vol. 13, No. 1 (Fall 1992)

Women in Science and Technology: The Legacy of Margaret Benston Vol. 13, No. 2 (Winter 1993)

Women and the Environment Vol. 13, No. 3 (Spring 1993)

Women and Disability Vol. 13, No. 4 (Summer 1993)

Women Writing Vol. 14, No. 1 (Fall 1993)

Racism and Gender Vol. 14, No. 2 (Spring 1994)

Women and Health Vol. 14, No. 3 (Summer 1994)

Women of the North Vol. 14, No. 4 (Fall 1994)

Women Entrepreneurs Vol. 15, No. 1 (Winter 1994)

Women's Rights Are Human Rights Vol. 15, No. 2/3 (Spring/Summer 1995)

Women and Girls in Sports and Physical Activity Vol. 15, No. 4 (Fall 1995)

Women in Central and Eastern Europe Vol. 16, No. 1 (Winter 1995)

Lesbians and Politics Vol. 16, No. 2 (Spring 1996)

Post-Beijing Vol. 16, No. 3 (Summer 1996)

Jewish Women in Canada Vol. 16, No. 4 (Fall 1996)

Female Spirituality Vol. 17, No. 1 (Winter 1997)

Bridging North and South: Patterns of Transformation Vol. 17, No. 2 (Spring 1997)

Women of Ireland Vol. 17, No. 3 (Summer/Fall 1997)

Women and Education Vol. 17, No. 4 (Winter 1998)

Women and Work Vol. 18, No. 1 (Spring 1998)

Looking Back, Looking Forward: Mothers, Daughters, and Feminism Vol. 18, No. 2/3 (Summer/Fall 1998)

Remembering Mary O'Brien Vol. 18, No. 4 (Winter 1999)

Women and Justice Vol. 19, No. 1/2 (Spring/Summer 1999)

Immigrant and Refugee Women Vol. 19, No. 3 (Fall 1999)

Women in Conflict Zones Vol. 19, No. 4 (Fall 1999)

Critical Matrix: The Princeton Journal of Women, Gender, and Culture.

    Rethinking Female Authorship: Literary Traditions and National Contexts Vol. 2, No. 1/3 (1986)

    Violence, Feminism, and the History of Sexuality: Papers from the 4th Annual Graduate Women's Studies Conference: Feminism and Its Translations Special Issue 1 (Spring 1988)

    Cultural Studies Special Issue Vol. 7, No. 2 (1993)

    Sexualities and Reproduction Vol. 8, No. 2 (1994)

    Feminist Legacies: Agency, Victimhood, and Interpretive Strategies Vol. 9, No. 2 (1995)

    "The Birthday of Myself": Martha Moulsworth, Renaissance Poet Vol. 10 (1996)

    Body Parts Vol. 11, No. 1 (1997)

    Gendered Labor, Labored Gender Vol. 11, No. 2 (1997)

differences: A Journal of Feminist Cultural Studies.

    Life and Death in Sexuality: Reproductive Technologies and AIDS Vol. 1, No. 1 (Winter 1989)

    The Essential Difference: Another Look at Essentialism Vol. 1, No. 2 (Summer 1989)

    Male Subjectivity Vol. 1, No. 3 (Fall 1989)

    Sexuality in Greek and Roman Society Vol. 2, No. 1 (Spring 1990)

    Notes from the Beehive: Feminism and the Institution Vol. 2, No. 3 (Fall 1990)

    Politics/Power/Culture: Postmodernity and Feminist Political Theory Vol. 3, No. 1 (Spring 1991)

    Queer Theory: Lesbian and Gay Sexualities Vol. 3, No. 2 (Summer 1991)

    The Phallus Issue Vol. 4, No. 1 (Spring 1992)

    Trouble in the Archives Vol. 4, No. 3 (Fall 1992)

    On Addiction Vol. 5, No. 1 (Spring 1993)

    The City Vol. 5, No. 3 (Fall 1993)

    More Gender Trouble: Feminism Meets Queer Theory Vol. 6, No. 2/3 (Summer/Fall 1994)

    Universalism Vol. 7, No. 1 (Spring 1995)

    On Violence Vol. 8, No. 2 (Summer 1996)

    Love, Anger, and the Body Vol. 9, No. 1 (Spring 1997)

    Special Section: Parité in France Vol. 9, No. 2 (Summer 1997)

    Eating and Disorder Vol. 10, No. 1 (Spring 1998)

    Writing in the Realm of the Senses Vol. 11, No. 2 (Summer 1999)

    America the Feminine Vol. 11, No. 3 (Fall 1999/2000)

European Journal of Women's Studies.

    Special Issue on Technology Vol. 2, No. 3 (August 1995)

    Special Issue on the Body Vol. 3, No. 3 (August 1996)

    Women, War, and Conflict Vol. 4, No. 3 (August 1997)

    The Idea of Europe Vol. 5, No. 3/4 (November 1998)

Feminism and Psychology: An International Journal.

    Homosexuality Vol. 2, No. 3 (October 1992)

    Shifting Identities, Shifting Racisms Vol. 4, No. 1/2 (February 1994)

    Social Class Vol. 6, No. 3 (August 1996)

Responses to the "False Memory" Debate Vol. 7, No. 1 (February 1997)

Exploring the Interface: Applications of Feminist Theory, Practice, and Research Vol. 7, No. 2 (May 1997)

Postgraduate Work in Progress Vol. 7, No. 3 (August 1997)

"Bias in Psychology": A Reappraisal Vol. 8, No. 1 (February 1998)

Feminist Economics.

A Special Issue in Honor of Margaret Reid Vol. 2, No. 3 (Fall 1996)

Expanding the Methodological Boundaries of Economics Vol. 3, No. 2 (Summer 1997)

Explorations in Lesbian, Gay, and Bisexual Economics Vol. 4, No. 2 (Summer 1998)

Employment and Inequality in the U.S. in Honor of Barbara R. Bergmann Vol. 4, No. 3 (Fall 1998)

Feminist Issues. Vol. 1, No. 1–   Vol. 15, No. 1/2. New Brunswick, NJ: Rutgers University, 1980–1997. ISSN 0270–6679. Continued by *Gender Issues*; Vol. 16– , No. 1–2– . New Brunswick, NJ: Transaction Publishers. 1998– . orders@transactionpub.com. http://www.transactionpub.com. quarterly. ISSN 1098-092X. elec: IG.

Symposium Feminists Targeted for Murder? Montreal 1989 Vol. 11, No. 2 (Fall 1991)

Editorial Board Members Examine Power Imbalances between the Sexes Vol. 16, No. 1/2 (Winter/Spring 1998)

Women in the Military Vol. 16, No. 3 (Summer 1998)

Gender and Immigration, Part I Vol. 16, No. 4 (Fall 1998)

Gender and Immigration, Part II Vol. 17, No. 1 (Winter 1999)

Feminist Review. 1– . New York: Palgrave Macmillan, 1979– . subscriptions@palgrave.com. http://www.feminist-review.com. 3/yr. ISSN 0141–7789. elec: EBSCO; Gale; IG; ISI; RC; Swets.

Socialist-Feminism out of the Blue 23 (Summer 1986)

Family Secrets: Child Sexual Abuse 28 (Spring 1988)

Abortion: The International Agenda 29 (Spring 1988)

The Past before Us: Twenty Years of Feminism 31 (Spring 1989)

Perverse Politics: Lesbian Issues 34 (Spring 1990)

Shifting Territories: Feminism and Europe 39 (Winter 1991)

Women's Health 41 (Summer 1992)

Feminist Fictions 42 (Autumn 1992)

Issues for Feminism 43 (Spring 1993)

Nationalisms and National Identities 44 (Summer 1993)

Thinking Through Ethnicities 45 (Autumn 1993)

Sexualities: Challenge and Change 46 (Spring 1994)

New Politics of Sex and the State 48 (Autumn 1994)

Feminist Politics—Colonial/Postcolonial Worlds 49 (Spring 1995)

The Irish Issue: The British Question 50 (Summer 1995)

The World Upside Down: Feminism in the Antipodes 52 (Spring 1996)

Speaking Out: Researching and Representing Women 53 (Summer 1996)

Contesting Feminist Orthodoxies 54 (Autumn 1996)

Consuming Cultures 55 (Spring 1997)

Debating Discourses, Practising Feminism 56 (Summer 1997)

Citizenship: Pushing the Boundaries 57 (Autumn 1997)

International Voices 58 (Spring 1998)

Rethinking Caribbean Difference 59 (Summer 1998)

Feminist Ethics and the Politics of Love 60 (Autumn 1998)

Snakes and Ladders: Reviewing Feminisms at Century's End 61 (Spring 1999)

Contemporary Women Poets 62 (Summer 1999)

Negotiations and Resistances 63 (Autumn 1999)

Feminist Studies: FS. College Park: University of Maryland, 1972– . femstud@umail.umd.edu. http://www.feministstudies.org. 3/yr. ISSN 0046–3663. elec: CWI; EBSCO; Gale; GW; ISI; OCLC; PQ.

Meanings of Motherhood and Childhood Vol. 13, No. 2 (Summer 1987)

Feminism and Deconstruction Vol. 14, No. 1 (Spring 1988)

Women and Work in the Past and Present Vol. 14, No. 2 (Summer 1988)

On Gender and Representation Vol. 14, No. 3 (Fall 1988)

Women, Family, and Work Vol. 15, No. 1 (Spring 1989)

The Problematics of Heterosexuality Vol. 15, No. 2 (Summer 1989)

Feminist Reinterpretation/Reinterpretations of Feminism Vol. 15, No. 3 (Fall 1989)

Speaking for Others/Speaking for Self: Women of Color Vol. 16, No. 2 (Summer 1990)

Constructing Gender Difference: The French Tradition Vol. 17, No. 2 (Summer 1991)

Women's Bodies and the State Vol. 19, No. 2 (Summer 1993)

Who's East? Whose East? Vol. 19, No. 3 (Fall 1993)

Scenarios of the Maternal Vol. 20, No. 1 (Spring 1994)

Women's Agency: Empowerment and the Limits of Resistance Vol. 20, No. 2 (Summer 1994)

Re-reading Feminist Readings/Re-reading Representation and Difference Vol. 20, No. 3 (Fall 1994)

Bodies Politic/Affairs of States, States of Affairs Vol. 21, No. 3 (Fall 1995)

Women and the State in the Americas Vol. 22, No. 1 (Spring 1996)

Global Feminism after Beijing Vol. 22, No. 3 (Fall 1996)

The Geography of Feminist Disruption/Refashioning the Past Vol. 23, No. 1 (Spring 1997)

Feminists and Fetuses Vol. 23, No. 2 (Summer 1997)

Nation and Race, Sex and Work/Gender and Sexual Identity in the Public Sphere Vol. 23, No. 3 (Fall 1997)

On a Precipice: Women, the Welfare State, and Work/Internationalism and Women's Welfare Vol. 24, No. 1 (Spring 1998)

Disciplining Feminism? The Future of Women's Studies Vol. 24, No. 2 (Summer 1998)

Female Forms of Resistance/Masculinities in Motion Vol. 24, No. 3 (Fall 1998)

Activism within Academy Walls/Rewriting Gender, History, and Labor/Gender and the Politics of the State Vol. 25, No. 1 (Spring 1999)

Privacy Reconsidered: Law, Bodies, Rights/Signifying Identities/Wittgenstein and Feminist Theory Vol. 25, No. 2 (Summer 1999)

Activists as/and Mothers Vol. 25, No. 3 (Fall 1999)

Frontiers: A Journal of Women Studies. Vol. 1, No. 1– . Lincoln: University of Nebraska Press, 1975– . pressmail@unl.edu. http://www.nebraskapress.unl.edu/frontiers.html. 3/yr. ISSN 0160–9009. elec: EBSCO; Gale; OCLC; PM; PQ; Swets.

> *The Women's Studies Movement: A Decade inside the Academy* Vol. 8, No. 3 (1986)
>
> *SEX: Sexuality, Contraception and Abortion, Reproductive Technology* Vol. 9, No. 1 (1986)
>
> *Women in the American South* Vol. 9, No. 3 (1987)
>
> *Women and Worth* Vol. 10, No. 2 (1988)
>
> *Women and Words* Vol. 10, No. 3 (1989)
>
> *Las Chicanas* Vol. 11, No. 1 (1990)
>
> *Spirituality, Values, and Ethics* Vol. 11, No. 2/3 (1990)
>
> *Daughters of the Desert* Vol. 12, No. 3 (1992)
>
> *Feminist Dilemmas: A Fieldwork* Vol. 13, No. 3 (1993)
>
> *Women, Family, Community, and Work* Vol. 14, No. 1 (1993)
>
> *Chicana Identity* Vol. 14, No. 2 (1994)
>
> *Women, Marginality, and Resistance* Vol. 14, No. 3 (1994)
>
> *Women Filmmakers and the Politics of Gender in Third Cinema* Vol. 15, No. 1 (1994)
>
> *Gender, Nations, and Nationalities* Vol. 16, No. 2/3 (1996)
>
> *Lesbian Community* Vol. 17, No. 1 (1996)
>
> *Intersections of Feminisms and Environmentalisms* Vol. 18, No. 2 (1997)
>
> *History and Biography* Vol. 18, No. 3 (1997)
>
> *Identity, the Body, and the Menopause* Vol. 19, No. 1 (1998)
>
> *Varieties of Women's Oral History* Vol. 19, No. 2 (1998)
>
> *Problems and Perplexities in Women's Oral History* Vol. 19, No. 3 (1998)
>
> *Latina/Chicana Leadership* Vol. 20, No. 1 (1999)
>
> *Motherhood and Maternalism* Vol. 20, No. 2 (1999)

Gender and Development.

> *Women and the Environment* Vol. 1, No. 1 (February 1993)
>
> *Focus on Gender: Perspectives on Women and Development* Vol. 1, No. 2 (June 1993)
>
> *Women and Economic Policy* Vol. 1, No. 3 (October 1993)
>
> *Women and Emergencies* Vol. 2, No. 1 (February 1994)
>
> *Population and Reproductive Rights* Vol. 2, No. 2 (June 1994)
>
> *North-South Co-operation* Vol. 2, No. 3 (October 1994)
>
> *Women and Culture* Vol. 3, No. 1 (February 1995)
>
> *Women and Rights* Vol. 3, No. 2 (June 1995)
>
> *Societies in Transition* Vol. 3, No. 3 (October 1995)
>
> *Urban Settlement* Vol. 4, No. 1 (February 1996)
>
> *Women and the Family* Vol. 4, No. 2 (June 1996)
>
> *Employment and Exclusion* Vol. 4, No. 3 (October 1996)
>
> *Organizational Culture* Vol. 5, No. 1 (February 1997)
>
> *Men and Masculinity* Vol. 5, No. 2 (June 1997)
>
> *Poverty in the North* Vol. 5, No. 3 (November 1997)

Gender and Migration Vol. 6, No 1 (March 1998)

Gender, Education, and Training Vol. 6, No. 2 (July 1998)

Violence against Women Vol. 6, No. 3 (November 1998)

Gender, Religion, and Spirituality Vol. 7, No. 1 (March 1999)

Gender and Technology Vol. 7, No. 2 (July 1999)

Women, Land, and Agriculture Vol. 7, No. 3 (November 1999)

Gender and Education. Vol. 1, No. 1– . Philadelphia: Carfax Publishing, Taylor & Francis, 1989– . enquiry@tandf.co.uk. http://www.tandf.co.uk. quarterly. ISSN 0954–0253. elec: EBSCO; IG; OCLC; PQ; RC.

Race, Gender, and Education Vol. 1, No. 3 (1989)

Equal Opportunities in Practice Vol. 2, No. 3 (1990)

Women's Education in Europe Vol. 4, No. 1/2 (1992)

Gender, Education, and Development Vol. 6, No. 2 (1994)

Masculinities in Education Vol. 9, No. 1 (March 1997)

Gender and History. Vol. 1, No. 1–. Oxford: Blackwell, 1989– . jnlinfo@blackwellpublishers .co.uk. http://www.blackwellpublishers.com. 3/year. ISSN 0953-5233. elec: EBSCO; IG; OCLC; RC; Swets.

Auto/Biography Vol. 2, No. 1 (Spring 1990)

Gender and the Right Vol. 3, No. 3 (Autumn 1991)

Motherhood, Race, and the State in the Twentieth Century Vol. 4, No. 3 (Autumn 1992)

Gender, Nationalism, and National Identities Vol. 5, No. 2 (Summer 1993)

Public History Vol. 6, No. 3 (November 1994)

Presentations of the Self in Early Modern England Vol. 7, No. 3 (November 1995)

Gendered Colonialisms in African History Vol. 8, No. 3 (November 1996)

Gender and the Body in Mediterranean Antiquity Vol. 9, No. 3 (November 1997)

Feminisms and Internationalism Vol. 10, No. 3 (November 1998)

Gender and History: Retrospect and Prospect Vol. 11, No. 3 (November 1999)

Gender and Society.

Special Issue in Honor of Jessie Bernard Vol. 2, No. 3 (September 1988)

Violence against Women Vol. 3, No. 4 (December 1989)

Women and Development in the Third World Vol. 4, No. 3 (September 1990)

Marxist Feminist Theory Vol. 5, No. 3 (September 1991)

Race, Class, and Gender Vol. 6, No. 3 (September 1992)

Gender and Social Movements, Part 1 Vol. 12, No. 6 (November 1998)

Gender and Social Movements, Part 2 Vol. 13, No. 1 (February 1999)

Genders. Vol. 1– . Boulder: University of Colorado, 1988– . http://www.genders.org. semi-annual. ISSN 0894–9832. elec: Gale; LN.

Theorizing Nationality, Sexuality, and Race 10 (Spring 1991)

Challenging Abuse and Assault 16 (Spring 1993)

Cyberpunk: Technologies of Cultural Identity 18 (Winter 1993)

Sexual Artifice: Persons, Images, Politics 19 (Spring 1994)

Eroticism and Containment: Notes from the Flood Plain 20 (Winter 1994)

Forming and Reforming Identity 21 (Spring 1995)

Post-Communism and the Body Politic 22 (Winter 1995)

Bodies of Writing, Bodies in Performance 23 (Spring 1996)

On Your Left: The New Historical Materialism 24 (Winter 1996)

Sex Positives? The Cultural Politics of Dissident Sexualities 25 (1997)

The Gay '90s Disciplinary and Interdisciplinary Formations in Queer Studies 26 (1997)

GLQ: A Journal of Lesbian and Gay Studies. Vol. 1, No. 1– . Durham, NC: Duke University Press, 1993– . subscriptions@dukeupress.edu. http://www.dukeupress.edu. quarterly. ISSN 1064–2684. elec: CWI; EBSCO; IG; ISI; OCLC; PM; RC; Swets.

Premodern Sexualities in Europe Vol. 1, No. 4 (1995)

Pink Freud Vol. 2, No. 1/2 (1996)

Inqueery/Intheory/Indeed Vol. 2, No. 4 (1996)

Identity/Space/Power: Lesbian, Gay, Bisexual, and Transgender Politics Vol. 3, No. 4 (1997)

Thinking Sexuality Transnationally Vol. 6, No. 4 (1999)

Health Care for Women International. Vol. 5, No. 1– . Philadelphia: Taylor & Francis, 1979– . enquiry@tandf.co.uk. http://www.tandf.co.uk. 8/yr. ISSN 0739–9332. elec: EBSCO; IG; OCLC; RC; Swets.

Culture, Society, and Menstruation Vol. 7, No. 1/2 (1986)

Sexually Transmitted Diseases Vol. 8, No. 1 (1987)

Women's Work, Families, and Health Vol. 8, No. 2/3 (1987)

Pregnancy and Parenting Vol. 8, No. 5/6 (1987)

Gender, Health, and Illness Vol. 10, No. 2/3 (1989)

Third International Congress on Women's Health Issue Vol. 11, No. 1 (1990)

Women at Midlife and Beyond Vol. 12, No. 1 (January/March 1991)

Fourth International Congress on Women's Health Issue Vol. 12, No. 4 (October/December 1991)

Lesbian Health: What Are the Issues? Vol. 13, No. 2 (April/June 1992)

Fifth International Congress on Women's Health Issue Vol. 14, No. 4 (July/August 1993)

Sixth International Congress on Women's Health Issues Vol. 16, No. 6 (1995)

Gender and Quality of Health Care for Women Vol. 17, No. 5 (1996)

Special Issue on Mental Health Vol. 20, No. 4 (1999)

Special Issue on Native Women and Cancer Vol. 20, No. 5 (1999)

Hecate: An Interdisciplinary Journal of Women's Liberation. Vol. 1– . Brisbane, Queensland: Hecate, 1975– . http://emsah.uq.edu.au/awsr/main.html. semiannual. ISSN 0311–4198. elec: EBSCO; Gale; GW; OCLC; PQ.

Black Women, Racism, Multiculturalism, Black Oppression, and Resistance Vol. 12, No. 1/2 (1986)

Women/Australian Theory Vol. 17, No. 1 (1991)

Special Aotearoa/New Zealand Issue Vol. 20, No. 2 (1994)

Focus on Asia and Australia Vol. 22, No. 2 (1996)

Hypatia: A Journal of Feminist Philosophy. Vol. 1, No. 1– . Bloomington: Indiana University Press, 1986– . journals@indiana.edu. http://iupjournals.org/hypatia/. quarterly. ISSN 0887–1213. elec: Gale; GW; LN; OCLC; PM; PQ; RC; Wilson.

Motherhood and Sexuality Vol. 1, No. 2 (Fall 1986)

Philosophy and Women Symposium Vol. 2, No. 1 (Winter 1987)

Feminism and Science, Part I Vol. 2, No. 3 (Fall 1987)

Feminism and Science, Part II Vol. 3, No. 1 (Spring 1988)

French Feminist Philosophy Vol. 3, No. 3 (Winter 1989)

History of Women in Philosophy Vol. 4, No. 1 (Spring 1989)

Feminist Ethics and Medicine Vol. 4, No. 2 (Summer 1989)

Ethics and Reproduction Vol. 4, No. 3 (Fall 1989)

Feminism and Aesthetics Vol. 5, No. 2 (Summer 1990)

Ecological Feminism Vol. 6, No. 1 (Spring 1991)

Feminism and the Body Vol. 6, No. 3 (Fall 1991)

Philosophy and Language Vol. 7, No. 2 (Spring 1992)

Lesbian Philosophy Vol. 7, No. 4 (Fall 1992)

Feminism and Pragmatism Vol. 8, No. 2 (Spring 1993)

Special Cluster on Eastern European Feminism Vol. 8, No. 3 (Fall 1993)

Special Cluster on Spanish and Latin American Feminist Philosophy Vol. 9, No. 1 (Winter 1994)

Feminism and Peace Vol. 9, No. 2 (Spring 1994)

Feminist Philosophy/Religion Vol. 9, No. 4 (Fall 1994)

Feminist Ethics and Social Policy, Part I Vol. 10, No. 1 (Winter 1995)

Feminist Ethics and Social Policy, Part II Vol. 10, No. 2 (Spring 1995)

Analytic Feminism Vol. 10, No. 3 (Summer 1995)

The Family and Feminist Theory Vol. 11, No. 1 (Winter 1996)

Women and Violence Vol. 11, No. 4 (Fall 1996)

Third Wave Feminisms Vol. 12, No. 3 (Summer 1997)

Citizenship in Feminism: Identity, Action, and Locale Vol. 12, No. 4 (Fall 1997)

Border Crossings: Multicultural and Postcolonial Feminist Challenges to Philosophy, Part 1 Vol. 13, No. 2 (Spring 1998)

Border Crossings: Multicultural and Postcolonial Feminist Challenges to Philosophy, Part II Vol. 13, No. 3 (Summer 1998)

The Philosophy of Simone de Beauvoir Vol. 14, No. 4 (Fall 1999)

Iris: A Journal about Women. No. 1– . Charlottesville: University of Virginia, 1980– . iris@ virginia.edu. http://womenscenter.virginia.edu/iris.htm. semiannual. ISSN 0896–1301. elec: CWI; Gale; GW; LN; OCLC.

Women and Humor No. 20 (Fall/Winter 1988).

Women in the Workplace No. 22 (Fall/Winter 1989).

Virginia Women Artists No. 23 (Spring/Summer 1990).

Women Resist Violence No. 31 (Summer 1994).

The Politics of the Body No. 38 (Winter/Spring 1999)

Women in Peace No. 39 (Fall 1999)

Journal of Feminist Family Therapy: An International Forum.

Feminist Approaches for Men in Family Therapy Vol. 2, No. 3/4 (1990)

Women and Power: Perspectives for Family Therapy Vol. 3, No. 1/2 (1991)

Feminism and Addiction Vol. 3, No. 3/4 (1991)

Expansions of Feminist Family Therapy through Diversity Vol. 5, No. 3/4 (1994)

Ethical Issues in Feminist Family Therapy Vol. 6, No. 3 (1994)

Lesbians and Gays in Families: The Last Invisible Minority Vol. 7, No. 3/4 (1995)

Transformation of Gender and Race: Family and Developmental Perspectives Vol. 10, No. 1 (1998)

Journal of Feminist Studies in Religion.

Special Section on Women and Initiation Vol. 3, No. 1 (Spring 1987)

Special Section on Asian and Asian American Women Vol. 3, No. 2 (Fall 1987)

Special Section on Recent Feminist Foremothers Vol. 4, No. 2 (Fall 1988)

Special Section on Neopaganism Vol. 5, No. 1 (Spring 1989)

Special Section on Feminist Translation of the New Testament Vol. 6, No. 2 (Fall 1990)

Special Section on Feminist Anti-Judaism Vol. 7, No. 2 (Fall 1991)

Special Section: Appropriation and Reciprocity in Womanist/Mujerista/Feminist Work Vol. 8, No. 2 (Fall 1992)

Special Issue in Honor of Beverly Wildung Harrison Vol. 9, No. 1/2 (Spring/Fall 1993)

Rhetorics, Rituals, and Conflicts over Women's Reproductive Power Vol. 11, No. 2 (Fall 1995)

Special Section: The Legacy of the Goddess: The Work of Marija Gimbutas Vol. 12, No. 2 (Fall 1996)

Special Section: New Directions in the Feminist Psychology of Religion Vol. 13, No. 1 (Spring 1997)

Journal of Gender Studies. An International Forum for the Debate on Gender in All Fields of Study. Vol. 1, No. 1– . Philadelphia: Carfax Publishing, Taylor & Francis, 1991– . enquiry@ tandf.co.uk. http://www.tandf.co.uk. 3/year. ISSN 0958–9236. elec: EBSCO; Gale; IG; ISI; LN; PQ; OCLC.

Post-colonial Issues Vol. 5, No. 3 (November 1996)

Transgendering Vol. 7, No. 3 (November 1998)

"Diana" Special Issue Vol. 8, No. 3 (November 1999)

Journal of Lesbian Studies.

Classics in Lesbian Studies, Part One Vol. 1, No. 1 (1997)

Classics in Lesbian Studies, Part Two Vol. 1, No. 2 (1997)

Gateways to Improving Lesbian Health and Health Care: Opening Doors Vol. 2, No. 1 (1998)

Acts of Passion: Sexuality, Gender, and Performance Vol. 2, No. 2/3 (1998)

Living "Difference": Lesbian Perspectives on Work and Family Life Vol. 2, No. 4 (1998)

Lesbian Polyamory Reader: Open Relationships, Non-monogamy, and Casual Sex Vol. 3, No. 1/2 (1999)

Lesbian Sex Scandals: Sexual Practices, Identities, and Politics Vol. 3, No. 3 (1999)

Journal of Women and Aging: The Multidisciplinary Quarterly of Psychosocial Practice Theory and Research.

Women As They Age: Challenge, Opportunity, and Triumph Vol. 1, No. 1/2/3 (1989)

Women Aging and Ageism Vol. 2, No. 2 (1990)

Women in Mid-life: Planning for Tomorrow Vol. 4, No. 4 (1993)

Women and Healthy Aging: Living Well in Spite of It All Vol. 5, No. 3/4 (1993)

Older Women with Chronic Pain Vol. 6, No. 4 (1994)

The Enduring Spirit: Selected Conference Papers Vol. 8, No. 1 (1996)

Relationships between Women in Later Life Vol. 8, No. 3/4 (1996)

Old, Female, and Rural Vol. 10, No. 4 (1998)

Fundamentals of Feminist Gerontology Vol. 11, No. 2/3 (1999)

Journal of Women's History.

Women in Africa, Asia, Latin America, and the Middle East Vol. 1, No. 2 (Fall 1989)

Women in Africa, Asia, Latin America, and the Middle East Vol. 2, No. 1 (Spring 1990)

Central and East European Women Vol. 5, No. 3 (Winter 1994)

Special Double Issue on Irish Women Vol. 6, No. 4/Vol.7, No. 1 (Winter/Spring 1995)

Chinese Women's History Vol. 8, No. 4 (Winter 1997)

Sexing Women's History Vol. 9, No. 4 (Winter 1998)

Women and Twentieth-Century Religious Politics: Beyond Fundamentalism Vol. 10, No. 4 (Winter 1999)

Women's History in the New Millennium: Women, Work, and Family after Two Decades Vol. 11, No. 3 (Autumn 1999)

Marginalizing Economies: Work, Poverty, and Policy Vol. 11, No. 4 (Winter 2000)

Kalliope: A Journal of Women's Literature and Art. Vol. 1, No. 1–   . Jacksonville, FL: F.C.C.J., 1979–   . http://www.fccj.org/kalliope. 3/yr. ISSN 0735–7885.

Special Humor Issue Vol. 8, No. 3 (1986)

Miami Artists Vol. 9, No. 2 (1987)

Women Portray Men Vol. 9, No. 3 (1987)

Men Portray Women Vol. 10, No. 3 (1988)

Theme: The Spiritual Quest Vol. 11, No. 3 (1989)

Special Fiction Issue Vol. 12, No. 3 (1990)

Women's Body Issue Vol. 14, No. 3 (1992)

Women of the Future Vol. 15, No. 3 (1993)

Theme: Families Vol. 16, No. 3 (1994)

Theme: Daring to Love Vol. 17, No. 3 (1995)

Secrets Vol. 19, No. 1 (1997)

Men Speak to Women Vol. 20, No. 1 (1998)

Legacy: A Journal of Women Writers. Vol. 1, No. 1– . Lincoln: University of Nebraska Press, 1984– . pressmail@unl.edu. http://www.nebraskapressunl.edu/legacy.html. semiannual. ISSN 0748–4321. elec: Gale; GW; OCLC; PM; RC; Swets.

> *Emily Dickinson: A Centenary Issue* Vol. 3, No. 1 (Spring 1986)
>
> *Willa Cather Special Issue* Vol. 9, No. 1 (1992)
>
> *19th-Century American Women Writers in the 21st Century* Vol. 15, No. 1 (1998)
>
> *Discourse of Women and Class* Vol. 16, No. 1 (1999)

NWSA Journal.

> *Global Perspectives* Vol. 8, No. 1 (Spring 1996)
>
> *Sexual Harassment* Vol. 9, No. 2 (Summer 1997)
>
> *Women, Ecology, and the Environment* Vol. 9, No. 3 (Fall 1997)
>
> *Affirmative Action Reconsidered* Vol. 10, No. 3 (Fall 1998)
>
> *Woman Created, Woman Transfigured, Woman Consumed* Vol. 11, No. 2 (Summer 1999)
>
> *Appalachia and the South: Place, Gender, Pedagogy* Vol. 11, No. 3 (Fall 1999)

Phoebe: An Interdisciplinary Journal of Feminist Scholarship, Theory, and Aesthetics.

> *Radical Women's Lives* Vol. 1, No. 1 (February 1989)
>
> *Lives of Women of Color* Vol. 1, No. 2 (November 1989)
>
> *Women, Crime, and Justice* Vol. 2, No. 1 (Spring 1990)
>
> *Politics of Pleasure* Vol. 2, No. 2 (Fall 1990)
>
> *Women in Ireland; Women on War* Vol. 3, No. 1 (Spring 1991)
>
> *Women and World Wars I and II* Vol. 3, No. 2 (Fall 1991)
>
> *Women's Relationships* Vol. 5, No. 2 (Fall 1993)
>
> *Women's Relationships* Vol. 6, No. 1 (Spring 1994)
>
> *Women Writing* Vol. 6, No. 2 (Fall 1994)
>
> *Interrogating Intersections: Women's Studies/Ethnic Studies* Vol. 7, No. 1/2 (1995)
>
> *Undergraduate Issue: Memories and Meditation* Vol. 8, No. 1/2 (Spring/Fall 1996)
>
> *Ecofeminism/Ecocriticism, Part One* Vol. 9, No. 1 (Spring 1997)
>
> *Ecofeminism/Ecocriticism, Part Two* Vol. 9, No. 2 (Fall 1997).
>
> *Gendered Journeys: Leaving Home/Making Home* Vol. 10, No. 1 (Spring 1998)
>
> *The Corporate Academy: Voices of Resistance* Vol. 10, No. 2 (Fall 1998)
>
> *Latina Sexuality* Vol. 11, No. 1 (Spring 1999)
>
> *Youth Cultures* Vol. 11, No. 2 (Fall 1999)

Psychology of Women Quarterly. Vol. 1– . New York: Blackwell, 1976– . inlinfo@ blackwellpublishers.co.uk. http://www.blackwellpublishing.co.uk. quarterly. ISSN 0361–6843. elec: EBSCO; Gale; IG; RC; Swets.

> *Hispanic Women and Mental Health: Contemporary Issues in Research and Practice* Vol. 11, No. 4 (December 1987)
>
> *Women's Health: Our Minds, Our Bodies* Vol. 12, No. 4 (December 1988)
>
> *Theory and Method in Feminist Psychology* Vol. 13, No. 4 (December 1989)
>
> *Focus: Violence toward Women* Vol. 14, No. 2 (June 1990)

Women at Midlife and Beyond Vol. 14, No. 4 (December 1990)

Women's Heritage in Psychology: Origins, Development, and Future Directions Vol. 15, No. 4 (December 1991)

Women and Power Vol. 16, No. 4 (December 1992)

Mini-series: Gender and Health Vol. 17, No. 3 (September 1993)

Gender and Culture Vol. 17, No. 4 (December 1993)

Transformations: Reconceptualizing Theory and Research with Women Vol. 18, No. 4 (December 1994)

Special Section: Fathering and Feminism Vol. 20, No. 1 (March 1996)

Measuring Beliefs about Appropriate Roles for Women and Men Vol. 21, No. 1 (March 1997)

Integrating Gender and Ethnicity into Psychology Courses Vol. 22, No. 1 (March 1998)

Special Section: Measuring Diversity in Feminist Attitudes Vol. 22, No. 3 (September 1998)

Innovations in Feminist Research Vol. 23, No. 1 (March 1999)

Innovations in Feminist Research Vol. 23, No. 2 (June 1999)

Race, Gender, and Class.

Race, Gender, and Class Perspectives on Canadian Anti-racism Vol. 2, No. 3 (Spring 1995)

Domination and Resistance of Native Americans Vol. 3, No. 2 (Winter 1996)

Working Class Intellectual Voices Vol. 4, No. 1 (1996)

Race, Gender, and Class: Latina/o American Voices Vol. 4, No. 2 (1997)

Race, Gender, and Class: Asian American Voices Vol. 4, No. 3 (1997)

Environmentalism and Race, Gender, Class Issues Vol. 5, No. 1 (1997)

Race, Gender, and Class Studies in Australia, Canada, and U.S. Vol. 5, No. 2 (1998)

A Race, Gender, and Class Critique of Genetic Determinism Vol. 5, No. 3 (1998)

Environmentalism and Race, Gender, Class Issues, Part II Vol. 6, No. 1 (1998)

Race, Gender, and Class: African-American Perspectives Vol. 6, No. 2 (1999)

Interdisciplinary Issues on Race, Gender, Class Vol. 6, No. 3 (1999)

Race, Gender, and Class: American Jewish Perspectives Vol. 6, No. 4 (1999)

Resources for Feminist Research: RFR/Documentation sur la Recherche Feministe: DRF Vol. 8, No. 1– . Toronto: University of Toronto, 1979– . rfrdr@oise.utoronto.ca. http://www.oise. utoronto.ca/rfr/. quarterly. ISSN 0707–8412. elec: CWI; Gale; LN; OCLC.

Women and the Criminal Justice System/Les femmes et la justice criminelle Vol. 14, No. 4 (December/January 1985/86)

Issue of the Decade: Feminists and State Processes/La Décennie pour la femme: Feministes et pratiques d'état Vol. 15, No. 1 (March 1986)

Women and Sciences/Femmes et sciences Vol. 15, No. 3 (November 1986)

Feminist Practice in Quebec/Les pratiques du féminisme au Québec Vol. 15, No. 4 (December/ January 1986/87)

Immigrant Women/Les femmes immigrées Vol. 16, No. 1 (March 1987)

Women and Philosophy/Femmes et philosophie Vol. 16, No. 2 (September 1987)

New Feminist Research/Nouvelles recherches féministes Vol. 16, No. 3 (December 1987)

New Feminist Research/Nouvelles recherches féministes Vol. 17, No. 2 (June 1988)

Feminist Perspectives on the Canadian State/Perspectives féministes sur l'état canadien Vol. 17, No. 3 (September 1988)

New Feminist Research/Nouvelles recherches féministes Vol. 17, No. 4 (December 1988)

New Feminist Research/Nouvelles recherches féministes Vol. 18, No. 2 (June 1989)

Feminist Theory: The Influence of Mary O'Brien/Theorie féministe: L'Influence de Mary O'Brien Vol. 18, No. 3 (September 1989)

New Feminist Research/Nouvelles recherches féministes Vol. 18, No. 4 (December 1989)

New Feminist Research/Nouvelles recherches féministes Vol. 19, No. 2 (June 1990)

Confronting Heterosexuality/Confronter l'hétérosexualité Vol. 19, No. 3/4 (September/December 1990)

Communications Vol. 20, No. 1/2 (Spring/Summer 1991)

Transforming Knowledge and Politics/Transformer savoir et politique Vol. 20, No. 3/4 (Fall/Winter 1991)

Writing and Literature/Écriture/littérature Vol. 21, No. 3/4 (Fall/Winter 1992)

Gender and Language: An Annotated Bibliography Vol. 22, No. 1/2 (Spring/Summer 1993)

Colonialism, Imperialism, and Gender/Colonialisme, impérialisme, et sexisme Vol. 22, No. 3/4 (Fall/Winter 1993)

New Feminist Research/Nouvelles recherches féministes Vol. 23, No. 1/2 (Spring/Summer 1994)

New Feminist Research/Nouvelles recherches féministes Vol. 23, No. 3 (Fall 1994)

Race, Gender, and Knowledge Production/Race, sexe, et la production du savoir Vol. 23, No. 4 (Winter 1994/95)

New Feminist Research/Nouvelles recherches féministes Vol. 24, No. 1/2 (Spring/Summer 1995)

Equity in Practice/Pratique de l'équité Vol. 24, No. 3/4 (Fall/Winter 1995/96).

Franco-Ontarian Women Writers/Écrivaines de l'Ontario français Vol. 25, No. 1/2 (Spring/Summer 1996)

Passionate Ethics/Une éthique passionée Vol. 25, No. 3/4 (Winter 1997)

New Feminist Research/Nouvelles recherches féministes Vol. 26, No. 1/2 (Spring 1998)

Confronting Violence in Women's Lives/Contrer la violence faite aux femmes Vol. 26, Nos. 3/4 (Fall/Winter 1998)

Women's Studies and the Internet/Les études des femmes et le réseau Internet Vol. 27, No. 1/2 (Spring 1999)

Restructuring and Women's Work/La restructuration et le travail des femmes Vol. 27, No. 3/4 (Fall/Winter 1999)

Sex Roles: A Journal of Research. Vol. 1– . New York: Kluwer Academic, 1975– . http://www.wkap.nl/journal 12/yr. ISSN 0360–0025. elec: EBSCO; Gale; IG; ISI; KO; OCLC; PQ; RC.

Sex, Gender, and Social Change Vol. 14, No. 11/12 (June 1986)

Social Networks and Gender Differences in the Life Space of Opportunity Vol. 17, No. 11/12 (December 1987)

African American Women and Affirmative Action Vol. 21, No. 1/2 (July 1989)

Gender and Ethnicity: Perspectives on Dual Status Vol. 22, No. 7/8 (April 1990)

On Aggression in Women and Girls: Cross Cultural Perspectives Vol. 30, No. 3/4 (February 1994)

Globalization and Local Cultures: Maya Women Negotiate Transformations Vol. 39, No. 7/8 (October 1998)

Signs: Journal of Women in Culture and Society. Vol. 1, No. 1– . Chicago: University of Chicago Press, 1975– . subscriptions@press.uchicago.edu. http://www.journals.uchicago.edu/ Signs/home.html. quarterly. ISSN 0097–9740. elec: EBSCO; Gale; ISI; OCLC; PQ.

> *Reconstructing the Academy* Vol. 12, No. 2 (Winter 1987)
>
> *Within and Without: Women, Gender, and Theory* Vol. 12, No. 4 (Summer 1987)
>
> *Women and the Political Process in the United States* Vol. 13, No. 1 (Autumn 1987)
>
> *Working Together in the Middle Ages: Perspectives on Women's Communities* Vol. 14, No. 2 (Winter 1989)
>
> *Common Grounds and Crossroads: Race, Ethnicity, and Class in Women's Lives* Vol. 14, No. 4 (Summer 1989)
>
> *The Ideology of Mothering: Disruption and Reproduction of Patriarchy* Vol. 15, No. 3 (Summer 1990)
>
> *From Hard Drive to Software: Gender, Computers, and Difference* Vol. 16, No. 1 (Autumn 1990)
>
> *Women, Family, State, and Economy in Africa* Vol. 16, No. 4 (Summer 1991)
>
> *Special Cluster: Simone de Beauvoir* Vol. 18, No. 1 (Autumn 1992)
>
> *Theorizing Lesbian Experience* Vol. 18, No. 4 (Summer 1993)
>
> *Feminism and the Law* Vol. 19, No. 4 (Summer 1994)
>
> *Postcolonial, Emergent, and Indigenous Feminisms* Vol. 20, No. 4 (Summer 1995)
>
> *Feminist Theory and Practice* Vol. 21, No. 4 (Summer 1996)
>
> *Feminisms and Youth Cultures* Vol. 23, No. 3 (Spring 1998)
>
> *Institutions, Regulations, and Social Control* Vol. 24, No. 1 (Summer 1999)

Sinister Wisdom: A Journal for the Lesbian Imagination in the Arts and Politics. No. 1– . Berkeley, CA: Sinister Wisdom, 1976– . sw@alexander.org. http://www.sinisterwisdom.org. quarterly. ISSN 0196–1853.

> *The Tribe of Dina: A Jewish Women's Anthology* 29/30 (1986)
>
> *Special Issue on Wisdom* 33 (Fall 1987)
>
> *Lesbian Visions, Fantasy, Sci Fi* 34 (Spring 1988)
>
> *Passing* 35 (Summer/Fall 1988)
>
> *Surviving Psychiatric Assault and Creating Emotional Well-Being in Our Communities* 36 (Winter 1988/1989)
>
> *With an Emphasis on Lesbian Theory* 37 (Spring 1989)
>
> *With an Emphasis on Lesbian Relationships* 38 (Summer/Fall 1989)
>
> *On Disability* 39 (Winter 1989/1990)
>
> *On Friendship* 40 (Spring 1990)
>
> *Italian Americans Reach Shore* 41 (Summer/Fall 1990)
>
> *Lesbian Voices* 42 (Winter 1990/1991)
>
> *15th Anniversary Retrospective* 43/44 (Summer 1991)
>
> *Lesbians and Class* 45 (Winter 1991/1992)
>
> *Dyke Lives* 46 (Spring 1992)
>
> *Lesbians of Color* 47 (Summer/Fall 1992)
>
> *Lesbian Resistance* 48 (Winter 1992/1993)
>
> *The Lesbian Body* 49 (Spring/Summer 1993)

Not the Ethics Issue 50 (Summer/Fall 1993)

Allies 52 (Spring/Summer 1994)

Old Lesbians/Dykes 53 (Summer/Fall 1994)

Lesbians and Religion 54 (Winter 1994/1995)

On Language 56 (Summer/Fall 1995)

On Healing 57 (Winter/Spring 1996)

Social Politics: International Studies in Gender, State, and Society.

Gender, Transitions to Democracy, and Citizenship Vol. 1, No. 3 (Fall 1994)

Between East and West Vol. 2, No. 1 (Spring 1995)

Citizenship: Intersections of Gender, Race, and Ethics Vol. 2, No. 2 (Summer 1995)

Gender Inequalities in Global Restructuring Vol. 3, No. 1 (Spring 1996)

Gender and Citizenship in Transition Vol. 3, No. 2/3 (Summer/Fall 1996)

Gender and Rationalization in Comparative Historical Perspective—Germany and the U.S. Vol. 4, No. 1 (Spring 1997)

Gender and Welfare Regimes Vol. 4, No. 2 (Summer 1997)

Gender and Care Work in Welfare States Vol. 4, No. 3 (Fall 1997)

Feminism, Comparison, and Historical Social Science Vol. 5, No. 1 (Spring 1998)

Citizenship in Latin America Vol. 5, No. 2 (Summer 1998)

Middle East Politics: Feminist Challenges Vol. 6, No. 3 (Fall 1999)

Tulsa Studies in Women's Literature. Vol. 1, No. 1– . Tulsa, OK: University of Tulsa, 1982– . Linda-frazier@utulsa.edu. http://utulsa.edu/tswl. semiannual. ISSN 0732–7730. elec: Gale; ISI; JSTOR.

Women and Nation Vol. 6, No. 2 (Fall 1987)

Toward a Gendered Modernity Vol. 8, No. 1 (Spring 1989)

Women Writing Autobiography Vol. 9, No. 1 (Spring 1990)

Redefining Marginality Vol. 10, No. 1 (Spring 1991)

South African Women Writing: A Forum Vol. 11, No. 1 (Spring 1992)

Is There an Anglo-American Feminist Criticism? Vol. 12, No. 2 (Fall 1993)

On Collaborations, Part I Vol. 13, No. 2 (Fall 1994)

On Collaborations, Part II Vol. 14, No. 1 (Spring 1995)

After Empire I Vol. 15, No. 1 (Spring 1996)

After Empire II Vol. 15, No. 2 (Fall 1996)

Political Discourse/British Women's Writing, 1640–1867 Vol. 17, No. 2 (Fall 1998)

Violence against Women.

Fraternities, Athletes, and Violence against Women on Campus Vol. 2, No. 2 (June 1996)

Violence against Women in Australia Vol. 2, No. 4 (December 1996)

Intimate Relationship Status Variations in Woman Abuse Vol. 3, No. 6 (December 1997)

Women, Violence, and the Media Vol. 4, No. 1 (February 1998)

Welfare, Work, and Domestic Violence: Current Research and Future Directions for Policy and Practice Vol. 5, No. 4 (April 1999)

Violence against South Asian Women, Part 1 Vol. 5, No. 5 (May 1999)

Violence against South Asian Women, Part 2 Vol. 5, No. 6 (June 1999)

Wife Rape Vol. 5, No. 9 (September 1999)

Collaboration in Research on Violence against Women Vol. 5, No. 10 (October 1999)

Violence against Women in China Vol. 5, No. 12 (December 1999)

Women: A Cultural Review.

Creating the New Europe Vol. 3, No. 3 (Winter 1992)

Gender, Islam, and Orientalism Vol. 6, No. 1 (Summer 1995)

Women Thinkers Vol. 6, No. 2 (Autumn 1995)

Open Forum: The New Woman to Post-feminism Vol. 6, No. 3 (Winter 1995)

Recent British and American Fiction: Horrors, Histories, Bodies, Books Vol. 7, No. 1 (Spring 1996)

Open Forum: Gender, Race, and History Vol. 7, No. 2 (Autumn 1996)

Women and War in the Twentieth Century: World Wars and Civil Wars Vol. 8, No. 1 (Spring 1997)

The Work of Gillian Rose: Rethinking Aesthetics Vol. 9, No. 1 (Spring 1998)

Lives and Letters Vol. 9, No. 2 (Summer 1998)

The Politics of Desire: Film and Fiction Vol. 9, No. 3 (Autumn 1998)

Fin-de-Siècle Modernisms: The New Woman Vol. 10, No. 1 (Spring 1999)

Anglo-American Feminisms: What Future Has Feminism? Vol. 10, No. 2 (Summer 1999)

Open Forum: Feminist Fashioning, Feminine Fictions Vol. 10, No. 3 (1999)

Women and Criminal Justice.

The Criminalization of a Woman's Body, Part 1 Vol. 3, No. 1 (1991)

The Criminalization of a Woman's Body, Part 2 Vol. 3, No. 2 (1992)

Women's Culture and the Criminal Justice System Vol. 7, No. 1 (1995)

Women and Domestic Violence: An Interdisciplinary Approach Vol. 10, No. 2 (1999)

Women and Environments. Toronto: WEED Foundation, 1980–1997. ISSN 0229–480X. Continued by *WE International.* Toronto: No. 42/43–No. 48/49. Institute for Women's Studies and Gender Studies, University of Toronto, 1997–2004. we.mag@utoronto.ca. http://www.weimag. com. quarterly. ISSN 1499–1993. elec: EBSCO; OCLC; Wilson.

Women and Work Vol. 11, No. 1 (Fall 1988)

Urban Safety Vol. 12, No. 1 (Fall 1989/Winter 1990)

Women's Experience of Social Environments Vol. 12, No. 1 (Spring 1990)

Charting a New Environmental Course Vol. 12, No. 3/4 (Winter/Spring 1991)

Communities That Work for Women Vol. 14, No. 2 (Spring 1995)

Farm and Rural Business Women in Canada 38 (Spring 1996)

Women and Habitat, Vancouver-Istanbul 39/40 (Summer 1996)

WomanTech 42/43 (Fall/Winter 1997/98)

Urban Agriculture 44/45 (Spring/Summer 1998)

Community by Design 46/47 (Winter 1999)

Women and Health. Vol. 1– . Binghamton, NY: Haworth Press, 1976– . getinfo@ haworthpressinc.com. http://www.haworthpressinc.com. quarterly. ISSN 0363–0242. elec: Gale; ISI.

Women and Cancer Vol. 11, No. 3/4 (Fall/Winter 1986)

Women, Health, and Poverty Vol. 12, No. 3/4 (1987)

Embryos, Ethics, and Women's Rights: Exploring the New Reproductive Technologies Vol. 13, No. 1/2 (1987)

Government Policy and Women's Health Care: The Swedish Alternative Vol. 13, No. 3/4 (1988)

Women in the Later Years: Health, Social, and Cultural Perspectives Vol. 14, No. 3/4 (1988)

Women, Work, and Health Vol. 25, No. 4 (1997)

Issues in Breast Cancer Vol. 26, No. 1 (1997)

Women, Drug Use, and HIV Infection Vol. 27, No. 1/2 (1998)

Australian Women's Health: Innovations in Social Science and Community Research Vol. 28, No. 1 (1998)

Breast Cancer Vol. 28, No. 4 (1999)

Women and Language. Vol. 1– . Fairfax, VA: George Mason University, 1976– . http:// www.gmu/departments/comm./wandl.html. semiannual. ISSN 8755–4550. elec: EBSCO; Gale; OCLC; PQ; Wilson.

Women Unaligned-Aligned Vol. 11, No. 2 (Winter 1988)

Feminist Cultural Studies Vol. 13, No. 1 (Fall 1990)

Women's Linguistic Innovation Vol. 15, No. 1 (Spring 1992)

Rethinking Gender Vol. 20, No. 1 (Spring 1997)

Women and Performance: A Journal of Feminist Theory. Vol. 1, No. 1– . New York: New York University Tisch School of the Arts, 1983– . editor@womenandperformance.org. http:// www.womenandperformance.org. semiannual. ISSN 0704–770X.

The Body as Discourse Vol. 3, No. 2 (1987/1988)

Feminist Americana Vol. 4, No. 1 (1988/1989)

Celebrating the Women and Theatre Program Vol. 4, No. 2 (1989)

Feminist Ethnography and Performance Vol. 5, No. 1 (1990)

Feminist Ethnography and Performance Vol. 5, No. 2 (1992)

Feminist Pedagogy and Performance Vol. 6, No. 1 (1993)

Feminist Film and Video Vol. 6, No. 2 (1993)

Tenth Anniversary Issue Vol. 7, No. 1 (1994)

New Hybrid Identities Vol. 7, No. 2/Vol. 8, No. 1 (1995)

Queer Acts Vol. 8, No. 2 (1996)

Sexuality and Cyberspace: Performing the Digital Body Vol. 9, No. 1 (1996)

Staging Sound: Feminism and Re/Production Vol. 9, No. 2 (1997)

Performing Autobiography Vol. 10, No. 1/2 (1999)

Bodywork Vol. 11, No. 1 (1999)

Holy Terrors: Latin American Women Perform Vol. 11, No. 2 (2000)

Women and Politics. Vol. 1– . Binghamton, NY: Haworth Press, 1980– . getinfo@ haworthpress.com. http://www.haworthpress.com. quarterly. ISSN 0195–7732.

>   *Symposium on Gender and Socialization to Power and Politics* Vol. 5, No. 4 (Winter 1985/ 1986)
>
>   *Women as Elders: Images, Visions, and Issues* Vol. 6, No. 2 (Summer 1986)
>
>   *The Politics of Professionalism, Opportunity, Employment, and Gender* Vol. 6, No. 3 (Fall 1986)
>
>   *Feminism and Epistemology: Approaches to Research in Women and Politics* Vol. 7, No. 3 (Fall 1987)
>
>   *Women, Politics, and the Constitution* Vol. 10, No. 2 (1990)
>
>   *Women and Public Administration: International Perspectives* Vol. 11, No. 4 (1991)
>
>   *The Politics of Pregnancy: Policy Dilemmas in the Maternal-Fetal Relationship* Vol. 13, No. 3/ 4 (1993)
>
>   *Politics and Feminist Standpoint Theories* Vol. 18, No. 3 (1997)

Women and Therapy. Vol. 1, No. 1– . Binghamton, NY: Haworth Press, 1982– . getinfo@ haworthpress.com. http://www.haworthpress.com. quarterly. ISSN 0270–3149.

>   *A Woman's Recovery from the Trauma of War* Vol. 5, No. 1 (Spring 1986)
>
>   *The Dynamics of Feminist Therapy* Vol. 5, No. 2/3 (Summer/Fall 1986)
>
>   *Women, Power, and Therapy: Issues for Women* Vol. 6, No. 1/2 (Spring/Summer 1987)
>
>   *Treating Women's Fear of Failure* Vol. 6, No. 3 (Fall 1987)
>
>   *The Politics of Race and Gender in Therapy* Vol. 6, No. 4 (Winter 1987)
>
>   *Women and Sex Therapy* Vol. 7, No. 2/3 (1988)
>
>   *Lesbianism: Affirming Nontraditional Roles* Vol. 8, No. 1/2 (1988)
>
>   *Fat Oppression and Psychotherapy: A Feminist Perspective* Vol. 8, No. 3 (1989)
>
>   *Diversity and Complexity in Feminist Therapy, Part 1* Vol. 9, No. 1/2 (1990)
>
>   *Diversity and Complexity in Feminist Therapy, Part 2* Vol. 9, No. 3 (1990)
>
>   *Motherhood: A Feminist Perspective* Vol. 10, No. 1/2 (1990)
>
>   *Women's Mental Health in Africa* Vol. 10, No. 3 (1990)
>
>   *Jewish Women in Therapy: Seen but Not Heard* Vol. 10, No. 4 (1990)
>
>   *Professional Training for Feminist Therapists: Personal Memoirs* Vol. 11, No. 1 (1991)
>
>   *Women, Girls, and Psychotherapy: Reframing Resistance* Vol. 11, No. 3/4 (1991)
>
>   *Finding Voice: Writing by New Authors* Vol. 12, No. 1/2 (1992)
>
>   *Refugee Women and Their Mental Health: Smattered Societies and Shattered Lives, Part 1* Vol. 13, No. 1/2 (1992)
>
>   *Refugee Women and Their Mental Health: Smattered Societies and Shattered Lives, Part 2* Vol. 13, No. 3 (1992)
>
>   *Faces of Women and Aging* Vol. 14, No. 1/2 (1993)
>
>   *Women with Disabilities: Found Voices* Vol. 14, No. 3/4 (1993)
>
>   *Bringing Ethics Alive: Feminist Ethics in Psychotherapy Practice* Vol. 15, No. 1 (1994)
>
>   *Wilderness Therapy for Women: The Power of Adventure* Vol. 15, No. 3/4 (1994)
>
>   *Women's Spirituality, Women's Lives* Vol. 16, No. 2/3 (1995)
>
>   *Feminist Foremothers in Women's Studies, Psychology, and Mental Health, Part 1* Vol. 17, No. 1/2 (1995)

Feminist Foremothers in Women's Studies, Psychology, and Mental Health, Part 2 Vol. 17, No. 3/4 (1995)

Lesbian Therapists and Their Therapy: From Both Sides of the Couch Vol. 18, No. 2 (1996)

Classism and Feminist Therapy: Counting Costs Vol. 18, No. 2/3 (1996)

A Feminist Clinician's Guide to the Memory Debate Vol. 19, No. 1 (1996)

Couples Therapy: Feminist Perspectives Vol. 19, No. 3 (1996)

Sexualities Vol. 19, No. 4 (1996)

More than a Mirror: How Clients Influence Therapists' Lives Vol. 20, No. 1 (1997)

Children's Rights, Therapists' Responsibilities: Feminist Commentary Vol. 20, No. 2 (1997)

Breaking the Rules: Women in Prison and Feminist Theory, Part One Vol. 20, No. 4 (1997)

Breaking the Rules: Women in Prison and Feminist Theory, Part Two Vol. 21, No. 1 (1998)

Feminism and Therapy as a Political Act Vol. 21, No. 2 (1998)

Learning from Our Mistakes: Difficulties and Failures in Feminist Therapy Vol. 21, No. 3 (1998)

Assault on the Soul: Women in the Former Yugoslavia Vol. 22, No. 1 (1999)

Beyond the Rule Book: Moral Issues and Dilemmas in the Practice of Psychotherapy Vol. 22, No. 2 (1999)

For Love or Money: The Fee in Feminist Therapy Vol. 22, No. 3 (1999)

Women in Sport and Physical Activity Journal.

Sexualities, Culture, and Sport Vol. 6, No. 2 (Fall 1997)

Women's History Review. Vol. 1, No. 1–   . Wallingford, Oxfordshire: Triangle Journals, 1992– . journals@triangle.co.uk. http://www.triangle.co.uk. quarterly. ISSN 0961–2025. elec: ISI; Swets.

Women's Sexualities: Contest and Control Vol. 1, No. 3 (1992)

Australian Feminisms Vol. 2, No. 3 (1993)

Women in Central and Eastern Europe Vol. 5, No. 4 (1996)

Irish Women's History Vol. 6, No. 4 (1997)

Between Rationality and Revelation: Women, Faith and Public Roles in the Nineteenth and Twentieth Centuries Vol. 7, No. 2 (1998)

Revisiting Motherhood: New Histories of the Public and Private Vol. 8, No. 2 (1999)

Women's Rights Law Reporter. Vol. 1–   . Newark, NJ: Women's Rights Law Reporter, 1971– . quarterly. ISSN 0085–8269.

Women and the Judiciary Vol. 9, No. 2 (Spring 1986)

Women's Self-Defense Law Vol. 9, No. 3/4 (Fall 1986)

Webster v. Reproductive Health Services Selected Amicus Briefs Vol. 11, No. 3/4 (Fall/Winter 1989)

The Jurisprudence of Justice Sandra Day O'Connor Vol. 13, No. 3/4 (Summer/Fall 1991)

Women's Studies: An Interdisciplinary Journal. Vol. 1–   . New York: Gordon & Breach Science Publishers, 1972– . editlink@gbhap.com. http://www.gbhap.com. 6/yr. ISSN 0049–7878. elec: EBSCO; Gale.

Canadian and American Women Writers Vol. 12, No. 1 (February 1986)

The Female Imagination and the Modernist Aesthetic Vol. 13, No. 1/2 (1986)

As the World Turns: Women, Work, and International Migration Vol. 13, No. 3 (1987)

American Women's Narratives Vol. 14, No. 1 (1987)

Feminism Faces the Fantastic Vol. 14, No. 2 (1987)

From Amateur to Professional: American Women and Careers in the Arts Vol. 14, No. 4 (1988)

Last Laughs: Perspectives on Women and Comedy Vol. 15, No. 1/3 (1988)

Emily Dickinson: A Celebration for Readers Vol. 16, No. 1/2 (1989)

Across Cultures: The Spectrum of Women and Lives Vol. 17, No. 1/2 (1989)

Women in the Renaissance: An Interdisciplinary Forum Vol. 19, No. 2 (1991)

Religion and Anglo-American Women Vol. 19, No. 3/4 (1991)

Women's Autobiographies Vol. 20, No. 1 (1991)

Reading the Letters of Edith Wharton Vol. 20, No. 2 (1991)

Is Multi-culturalism Enough? Vol. 20, No. 3/4 (1992)

Women in the Visual Arts Vol. 22, No. 1 (1992)

Women on Faulkner/Faulkner on Women Vol. 22, No. 4 (1993)

Gender, Literature, and the English Revolution Vol. 24, No. 1/2 (1994)

Issues in Medieval and Renaissance Scholarship Vol. 24, No. 3 (1995)

Studies in Nineteenth-Century British Art and Literature Vol. 24, No. 4 (1995)

Women and Medicine Vol. 24, No. 6 (1995)

Studies in 20th-Century American Literature, Criticism, and Art Vol. 25, No. 1 (1995)

Gender and Film Vol. 25, No. 2 (1996)

International Perspectives on Art Vol. 25, No. 3 (1996)

Women and Nature Vol. 25, No. 5 (1996)

Women and Travel Vol. 26, No. 5 (1997)

"A Whole New Poetry Beginning Here": Adrienne Rich in the Eighties and Nineties Vol. 27, No. 4 (1998)

American Women Poets and the Long Poem Vol. 27, No. 5 (1998)

Early American Women Writers Vol. 28, No. 1 (1998)

Virginia Woolf in Performance Vol. 28, No. 4 (1999)

Women's Studies in Communication. Vol. 9, No. 1– . Fort Collins: Colorado State University, 1977– . semiannual. ISSN 6749–1409.

Help Ourselves: Feminist Analyses of Self-Help Literature Vol. 18, No. 2 (Fall 1995)

Gender and the World of Disney Vol. 19, No. 2 (Summer 1996)

Women's Studies International Forum. Vol. 5, No. 1– . New York: Pergamon, Elsevier Science, 1978– . http://www.elsevier.nl/locate/issn/02775395. 6/yr. ISSN 0277–5395.

Women and the Law Vol. 9, No. 1 (1986)

Women Studies Administrators: Personal and Professional Intersections Vol. 9, No. 2 (1986).

Women and Folklore Vol. 9, No. 3 (1986)

Political Fiction Vol. 9, No. 4 (1986)

Personal Chronicles: Women's Autobiographical Writings Vol. 10, No. 1 (1987)

The Fawcett Library: Britain's Major Research Resource on Women Past and Present Vol. 10, No. 3 (1987)

The Gendering of Sport, Leisure, and Physical Education Vol. 10, No. 4 (1987)

Feminism in Ireland Vol. 11, No. 4 (1987)

"In the Great Company of Women": Nonviolent Direct Action Vol. 12, No. 1 (1989)

Feminism and Science: In Memory of Ruth Bleier Vol. 12, No. 3 (1989)

British Feminist Histories Vol. 13, No. 1/2 (1990)

Western Women and Imperialism Vol. 13, No. 4 (1990)

Reaching for Global Feminism: Approaches to Curriculum Change in the Southwestern United States Vol. 14, No. 4 (1991)

A Continent in Transition: Issues for Women in Europe in the 1990s Vol. 15, No. 1 (1992)

Women's Studies at the University of Utrecht Vol. 16, No. 4 (July/August 1993)

Images from Women in a Changing Europe Vol. 17, No. 2/3 (March/June 1994)

Selected Proceedings of the Women's Studies Conference, Lodz, Poland, May 17/21, 1993 Vol. 18, No. 1 (January/February 1995)

Women in Families and Households: Qualitative Research Vol. 18, No. 3 (May/June 1995)

Links across Differences: Gender, Ethnicity, and Nationalism Vol. 19, No. 1/2 (January/April 1996)

Changing Schools: Some International Feminist Perspectives on Teaching Girls and Boys Vol. 19, No. 4 (July/August 1996)

Gender and Dance Vol. 19, No. 5 (September/October 1996)

Concepts of Home Vol. 20, No. 3 (May/June 1997)

Cultures of Womanhood in Israel Vol. 20, No. 5/6 (September/December 1997)

Women, Imperialism, and Identity Vol. 21, No. 3 (May/June 1998)

Feminism and Globalization Vol. 22, No. 4 (July/August 1999)

Women's Studies Quarterly. Vol. 9, No. 1– . New York: Feminist Press at the City University of New York, 1981– . fempress@gc.cuny.edu. http://www.feministpress.org. semiannual. ISSN 0732–1562. elec: PQ.

Teaching about Women, Race, and Culture Vol. 14, No. 1/2 (Spring/Summer 1986)

Teaching about Women and the Visual Arts Vol. 15, No. 1/2 (Spring/Summer 1987)

Feminist Pedagogy Vol. 15, No. 3/4 (Fall/Winter 1987)

Teaching the New Women's History Vol. 16, No. 1/2 (Spring/Summer 1988)

Women and Aging Vol. 17, No. 1/2 (Spring/Summer 1989)

Women's Non-traditional Literature Vol. 17, No. 3/4 (Fall/Winter 1989)

Curricular and Institutional Change Vol. 18, No. 1/2 (Spring/Summer 1990)

Women's Studies in Economics Vol. 18, No. 3/4 (Fall/Winter 1990)

Women, Girls, and the Culture of Education Vol. 19, No. 1/2 (Spring/Summer 1991)

Literature and History: Reading and Writing That Changes Lives Vol. 19, No. 3/4 (Fall/Winter 1991)

Feminist Psychology: Curriculum and Pedagogy Vol. 20, No. 1/2 (Spring/Summer 1992)

Women's Studies in Europe Vol. 20, No. 3/4 (Fall/Winter 1992)

Spirituality and Religions Vol. 21, No. 1/2 (Spring/Summer 1993)

Feminist Pedagogy: An Update Vol. 21, No. 3/4 (Fall/Winter 1993)

Feminist Teachers Vol. 22, No. 1/2 (Spring/Summer 1994)

Women's Studies: A World View Vol. 22, No. 3/4 (Fall/Winter 1994)

Working-Class Studies Vol. 23, No. 1/2 (Spring/Summer 1995)

Rethinking Women's Peace Studies Vol. 23, No. 3/4 (Fall/Winter 1995)

Beijing and Beyond: Toward the 21st Century of Women Vol. 24, No. 1/2 (Spring/Summer 1996)

Curriculum Transformation in Community Colleges: Focus on Intro Courses Vol. 24, No. 3/4 (Fall/Winter 1996)

Looking Back, Moving Forward: 25 Years of Women's Studies History Vol. 25, No. 1/2 (Spring/Summer 1997)

Teaching African Literature in a Global Literary Economy Vol. 25, No. 3/4 (Fall/Winter 1997)

Working-Class Lives and Culture Vol. 26, No. 1/2 (Spring/Summer 1998)

Internationalizing the Curriculum Vol. 26, No. 3/4 (Fall/Winter 1998)

Teaching about Violence against Women: International Perspectives Vol. 27, No. 1/2 (Spring/Summer 1999)

Expanding the Classroom: Fostering Active Learning and Activism Vol. 27, No. 3/4 (Fall/Winter 1999)

Author Index

Reference is to entry number. **Boldface** type refers to mentioned authors; regular typeface refers to main entries.

Aaron, Jane, 390
AAUW. *See* American Association of University Women Educational Foundation
Abbot, Pamela, 339
Abel, Emily K., 654
Abir-Am, Pnina, 1493
Abramovitz, Mimi, 734
Abrams, Lynn, 1132
Abu-Lughod, Lila, 146
Achterberg, Jeanne, 1403
Acker, Sandra, 431
Acosta-Belen, Edna, 207
Adair, Christy, 879
Adam, Alison, 1520
Adams, Alice E., 1440
Adams, Carol J., 1358
Adams, Diane L., 1440
Adams, Jerome R., 913
Adams, Maurianne, 388
Adamson, Lynda G., 907
Adamson, Nancy, 145, 192
Adesso, Vincent J., 622
Adkins, Lisa, 143
Adler, Kathleen, 914
Adler, Leonore Leob, 1
Adler, Nancy J., 328
Adler, Rachel, 1330
Afkhami, Mahnaz, 541
Afshar, Haleh, 146, 219, **312**, **544**
Agger, Inger, 630
Agosin, Marjorie, 827
Agostin, Rosemary, 799
Ahern, David W., 557
Ahmed, Leila, 1331
Ahmed, Sara, 64
Aisenberg, Nadya, 409
Albelda, Randy Pearl, 308, **346**
Albrecht, Lisa, 147
Aldrich, Elizabeth, 888
Alexander, M. Jacqui, 65
Alexander, Meena, 915
Alic, Margaret, 1485
Allen, Ann Taylor, 1118
Allen, Beverly, 757
Allen, Donna, 1008
Allen, Jeffner, 1379, 1380
Allen, Karen Moses, 1420

Allen, Paula Gunn, 655
Allen, Richard, 1055
Allen, Sheila, 329
Allison, Dorothy, 978
Allison, Kathleen Cahill, 1394, **1460**
Allwood, Gill, 121
Almeida, Irène Assibad, 1280
Alonso, Harriet Hyman, 518
Alpern, Sara, 1053
Altfield, Judy, 861
Altman, Roberta, 1399
Alvarez, Sonia E., 538
Alwood, Edward, 1054
American Association of University Women Educational Foundation, 424
Ames, Kenneth L., 366
Ametsbuchler, Elizabeth G., 1201
Amico, Eleanor, 18
Ammer, Christine, 1460
Ammons, Elizabeth, 1263
Amott, Teresa L., 309, 330
Anderlini-D'Onofrio, Serena, 1301
Andermahr, Sonya, 56, **408**
Andersen, Margaret, 656
Anderson, Bonnie S., 1119
Anderson, Janet A., 810
Anderson, Linda, 1228
Anderson, Lisa M., **1051**, 1291
Anderson, Pamela Sue, 1369
Anderson, Peter B., 574
Angell, Marcia, 1434
Angelou, Maya, 916
Anker, Richard, 364
Ankrah, Maxine, 1421
Ann, Martha, 1320
Anschuetz, Kurt F., 208
Antler, Joyce, 389, 657
Antony, Louise M., 1369
Anzuldúa, Gloria, 194
Apostolos-Cappadona, Diana, 828
Appelle, Christine, 565
Appignanesi, Lisa, 575
Apple, Rima D., 1398, 1414, 1483
Appleton, Helen, 1509
Apter, Terri E., 601, 606
Aquino, María Pilar, 1347
Ardner, Shirley, 314

Aretxaga, Begona, 552
Ariel, Joan, 20
Arjava, Antti, 458
Armitage, Susan, 1165
Armitt, Lucie, 1222
Arms, Suzanne, 1464
Armstrong, Louise, 658, 735
Arnold, Marion I., 856
Asche, Adrienne, 678
Ashcraft, Donna Musialowski, 19
Ashton, Dianne, 1367
Ashworth, Georgina, 179
Asian Women United of California, 697
Ask, Karin, 1331
Askey, Ruth, 836
Aslanbeigu, Nahid, 310
Aspell, Bernard, 1456
Astbury, Jill, 628
Aston, Elaine, 1296
Atack, Margaret, 1238
Atherton, Louise, 1384
Atkinson, Camille, 323
Atkinson, Jane, 259
Attfield, Judy, 861
Augustin, Ebba, 269
Avakian, Arlene Voski, 1510
Avery, Joanna, 771
Aymer, Paula, 311

Babb, Florence E., 317
Babcock, Barbara, 275
Babcock, Marguerite, 629
Baca Zinn, Maxine. *See* Zinn, Maxine Baca
Bacchi, Carol Lee, **358**, 659
Bacon-Smith, Camille, 1040
Bacus, Elisabeth, 208
Badran, Margot, **146**, 1102
Bailey, Barbara, 1115
Bailey, Martha J., 1478
Bair, Barbara, 1400
Bair, Deirdre, 917
Baird, Joseph L., 941
Baker, Alison, 148
Balaghi, Shiva, 238
Ballou, Mary, 583
Ballou, Patricia K., 24

Title Index

Numbers refer to entries unless otherwise noted. Italic typeface refers to titles mentioned within annotations; regular typeface refers to main entries.

Subject Index

Numbers refer to entries.

Abolition movement and abolitionists (U.S.), 1166; African American, 923, 974; biography, 931, 949, 956

Aboriginal women (Australia). *See* Indian women (Americas); Indigenous women (Australia)

Abortion: bibliography, 648; cross cultural aspects, 460, 468. *See also* Birth control; Pregnancy; Reproductive rights

Abortion, United States, 682, 718, 763, 1377; legal aspects, 459, 460, 487; history, 1442; multicultural aspects, 680

Abstract Expressionism, 824

Abused women, 462, 593, 630, 744, 747, 752. *See also* Violence against women

Abusive women, 581

Achievement motivation, 604, 609

Acquaintance rape, 466, 755, 758. *See also* Rape; Sex crimes; Violence against women

Actors, 1005, 1300, 1304

Adams, Abigail, 955

Addams, Jane, 984

Addiction, 629

Adolescent mothers, 737

Adolescents, 476, 762, 1149; delinquency, 745, 1170; friendships, 624; health, 595 pregnancy, 671, 704; psychological aspects, 584, 608, 618, 624

Adult child abuse victims, 580

Adultery, 1377

Advertising and marketing, gender issues, 331, 332

Aesthetics, 869, 1371; in literature, 1210; periodicals, 1547

Affirmative action, 358, 484; sports—cross cultural perspectives, 772

Africa: gender issues, 288, 326; women's movements, 187

African American Congresswomen, 560

African American feminism, 74, 95, 101, 105, 656, 669, 690, 691, 884

African American girls, 663

African American professional women, 371

African American women, 685, 706, 710; biography, 916, 923, 926, 931, 939, 942, 961, 971, 975, 990; culture and society, 1265, 1268, 1269, 1271, 1291, 1291, 1294; diaries, memoirs, letters, 919, 992; dictionaries, 1080; education, 348; employment, 309; employment history, 337, 348, 371; family issues, 671; in film, 1046; health care, 1400, 1432, 1439; history, 1080, 1148, 1155, 1156, 1158, 1159, 1160; in literature, 1046; mental health, 605, 629; periodicals, 1529; psychology, 580, 617; religious experience, 1339, 1343, 1359,1368; Suffrage, 1181. *See also* Women of color

African American women actors, 1304

African American women artists, 855, 866

African American women Baptists, 1160

African American women composers, 826

African American dramatists, 1291, 1294

African American women journalists and editors, 992

African American women lawyers, 470

African American women in literature, 923, 937

African American women midwifery and midwives, 964, 1441

African American women military personnel, 1172

African American women photographers, 862

African American women singers, 884, 899

African American women writers, 1264, 1268, 1269, 1271, 1274, 1279, 1291, 1294, 1314, 1316; biography, 923, 937, 943, 949, 957, 976, 978, 996

African Americans, suffrage, 1160

African Canadian women, 1164

African Diaspora, 124

African women, 919, 948, 981; culture and society, 843, 856, 1271, 1288, 1290; employment, 320; history, 1103, 1104, 1107

Age and aging, 654, 712, 1416; bibliography, 653; feminist perspectives, 1459; periodicals, 1543; psychological aspects, 626

Agency, 84, 89, 115

Aggressiveness (psychology), 574, 581

Agriculture: bibliography, 305; environmental aspects, 264

AIDS (disease): cross cultural perspectives, 1412; feminist perspectives, 1407, 1412, 1415, 1421; multicultural perspectives, 1427

AIM. *See* American Indian Movement

Air pilots. *See* Aviators and astronauts

Algeria, women's movements, 146

Algerian women, 245

All-American Girls Professional Baseball League, 767, 785. *See also* Baseball and softball; Negro Leagues

Allison, Dorothy, 978

Amateur art associations, 831

American Civil Liberties Union, 490

American Indian Movement (AIM), 924

American Indian women. *See* Indian women (Americas)

American Revolution. *See* United States, history: American Revolution

American women: biography, 933; culture and society, 817, 820, 836, 1200,1205,1214,1263; education—history, 348; employment, 309, 330, 349, 375, 376–380; employment history, 330, 335, 340, 348, 354, 365, 366, 374; encyclopedias, 4, 5; handbooks, 15, 16, 32; history, 1151, 1152, 1155, 1164,

About the Editors and Contributors

Rebecca S. Albitz, Electronic Resources and Copyright Librarian
Pennsylvania State University, University Park

Joan Ariel, Research Librarian for History and Women's Studies
University of California, Irvine

Tracy Bicknell-Holmes, Chair, Research and Instructional Services
University of Nebraska, Lincoln

Ellen Broidy, Head, YRL Collection Management Department
Bibliographer for Anglo-American History, History of Science, Women's
    Studies, LGBT Studies
Interim Bibliographer for English and American Literature
University of California, Los Angeles

Linda Friend, Head Libraries Information Technology
Pennsylvania State University, University Park

Cindy Ingold, Women and Gender Resources Librarian
University of Illinois, Urbana-Champaign

Linda A. Krikos, Head, Women's Studies Library
Acting Head, Black Studies Library
Ohio State University, Columbus

Vicki Litzinger, Director of Library Instructional Technology
Lyndon State College, Lyndonville, VT

Dorothy Mays, Reference Librarian
Rollins College, Winter Park, FL

Jill Morstad, Adjunct Professor of Professional and Technical Communications
University of Nebraska, Lincoln

Debbi Schaubman, InMICH Project Coordinator
Michigan State University, East Lansing

Mila C. Su, Associate/Women's Studies Librarian
Pennsylvania State University, Altoona

Linda D. Tietjen, Senior Instructor
Auraria Library, University of Colorado, Denver

Don Welsh, Head of Reference Services
College of William and Mary, Williamsburg, VA

Susan Wyngaard, Head, Fine Arts Library
Ohio State University, Columbus

Hope Yelich, Reference Librarian
The College of William and Mary, Williamsburg, VA

—